POLLARD'S HISTORY OF FIREARMS

POLLARD'S HISTORY OF FIREARMS

General Editor Claude Blair

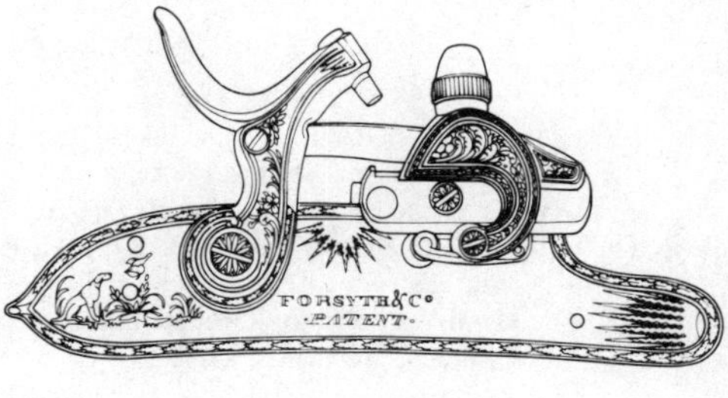

COUNTRY LIFE BOOKS

Half-title:
Illustration of a centaur with a matchlock gun, 1468,
from a Froissart manuscript
in Breslau City Library.

Frontispiece:
Engraving of a musketeer, 1607,
from *The Exercise of Arms* by Jacob de Gheyn.

Title page:
Forsyth's sliding-magazine fulminating-power lock,
*c.*1813. (See p. 163.)

Dedication page:
Illustration of a figure firing a matchlock gun, 1468,
from a Fróissart manuscript
in Breslau City Library.

Published by Country Life Books,
an imprint of Newnes Books,
a Division of the Hamlyn Publishing Group,
84-88 The Centre, Feltham, Middlesex, TW13 4BH, England
and distributed for them by
The Hamlyn Publishing Group Limited
Rushden, Northants, England.

First published 1983

ISBN 0 600 33154 7

Printed in England

To the memory of
Major Hugh Bertie Campbell Pollard
1888-1966

Contents

Contributors

General Editor Claude Blair
Keeper of Metalwork at the Victoria and Albert Museum, and from 1953 to 1978 Honorary Editor of the *Journal of the Arms and Armour Society*. Author of numerous publications on arms and armour, including *European Armour* (1958), *European and American Arms* (1962), *Pistols of the World* (1968), *The James A. de Rothschild Collection at Waddesdon Manor. Arms, Armour and Base Metalwork* (1974).

Howard L. Blackmore
Until recently Deputy Master of the Tower of London Armouries and formerly Honorary President of the Arms and Armour Society. Author of numerous publications on arms, especially firearms, including *Guns and Rifles of the World* (1965), *Hunting Weapons* (1971) and the classic *British Military Firearms* (1st edn 1961).

Dr Irena Grabowska
Curator of arms and armour in the National Museum, Cracow. Specialist in the decorative arts, and author of publications in Polish on arms and armour.

Ian V. Hogg
Authority on modern firearms and author of numerous publications on the subject, including *Military Pistols and Revolvers. The Handguns of the Two World Wars* (1970) and (with John Weekes) *Military Smallarms of the Twentieth Century* (1973). He served for twenty-seven years with the Royal Artillery, attaining the rank of Master Gunner, of whom there were only fourteen in the entire British Army.

Harold L. Peterson
Until his untimely death in 1978, Chief Curator to the United States National Park Service, and the best-known of all American writers on arms and armour. His very numerous publications include *Arms and Armor in Colonial America* (1956) and *The Treasury of the Gun* (1st edn. 1962), subsequently reissued in numerous editions in a variety of languages, some with slightly different titles), while he also edited the *Encyclopedia of Firearms* (1964).

William Reid
Director of the National Army Museum, London, and also President of the International Association of Museums of Arms and Military History. Author of many publications on European, and especially Scottish, arms and armour, including *The Lore of Arms* (1976).

Dr C. H. Roads
Formerly Deputy Director of the Imperial War Museum, London. President of the Historical Breechloading Smallarms Association. Authority on nineteenth- and twentieth-century firearms, and author of various publications on the subject, including *The British Soldier's Firearms, 1850-1864* (1964). He is also a noted rifle-shot.

A. W. F. Taylerson
Formerly Honorary President of the Arms and Armour Society, and an authority on the early history of the revolver. His numerous publications include: *The Revolver, 1818-1865* (with R. A. N. Andrews and J. Frith) (1968); *The Revolver, 1865-1888* (1956); and, *The Revolver, 1889-1914* (1970).

Professor Dr Zdisław Żygulski, Junior
Keeper of the Czartoryski Collection (attached to the National Museum), Cracow, and also President of the International Association of Museums of Arms and Military History, 1975 to 1981. He is an authority on Polish and Eastern arms and armour and his many publications on these subjects include *Bron w Dawnej Polsce* (History of Polish Arms and Armour), (Warsaw, 1975).

* * *

A. R. E. North (Illustrations Research and Referencing)
Research Assistant in the Department of Metalwork at the Victoria and Albert Museum. Author of various publications on arms and armour, including (with Ian Hogg) *The Book of Guns and Gunsmiths* (1978).

Notes

1. *Imperial and Metric Measurements*
As a result of historical and geographical factors and to maintain accuracy, the measurements, have been left as supplied by contributors; therefore, both imperial and metric figures are used. Unless otherwise specified, measurements are in inches.

2. Photographs are cross-referenced by plate numbers in the margins.

3. *International Museums List*
For the convenience of readers, museums mentioned in the text are listed below, in English and in the language of origin, in alphabetical order by city. Some collections have changed locations since the reference was written, and where known, are noted.

AACHEN (West Germany)
Suermondt Museum
Suermondt-Ludwig-Museum
ALTON (Hampshire, England)
Curtis Museum
AMSTERDAM (Netherlands)
National Museum *Rijksmuseum*
ARBOGA (Sweden)
Arboga Museum
BERLIN (West Germany)
Museum of German History
Museum für Deutsche Geschichte
BERN (Switzerland)
Historical Museum
Bernishes Historishes Museum
BIRMINGHAM (England)
City of Birmingham Museum and Art Gallery
BOSTON (U.S.A.)
Museum of Fine Arts
BRUSSELS (Belgium)
Porte de Hal Museum
Musée de la Porte de Hal
BUDAPEST (Hungary)
National Museum
Magyar Nemzeti Múzeum
CHICAGO (U.S.A.)
George F. Harding Museum
(now in) Art Institute of Chicago
COLOMBO (Sri Lanka [Ceylon])
Colombo Museum
National Museum of Sri Lanka
COPENHAGEN (Denmark)
National Museum *Nationalmuseet*
Rosenborg Castle
De Danske kongers kronologiske Samling pa Rosenborg
The Tøjhusmuseum (Royal Arsenal)
Tøjhusmuseet
DRESDEN (East Germany)
Historical Museum *Staatliche Kunstsammlungen–Historisches Museum*
DUNDEE (Scotland)
Albert Institute
City Museum & Art Gallery
EDINBURGH (Scotland)
National Museum of Antiquities of Scotland
Scottish National Portrait Gallery
ENFIELD LOCK (England)
Royal Small Arms Factory (Pattern Room Collection)
FEZ (Morocco)
De Batha Museum
Musée du Dar Batha
GENEVA (Switzerland)
Museum of Art & History
Musée d'Art et d'Histoire
GLASGOW (Scotland)
Glasgow Art Gallery & Museum
HARTFORD (Connecticut, U.S.A.)
Wadsworth Atheneum
HAVANT (Hampshire, England)
Havant Museum & Art Gallery (Vokes Collection)
HELSINKI (Finland)
Finnish National Museum
(National Board of Antiquities & Historical Monuments)
Suomen Kansallismuseo
HONOLULU (Hawaii, U.S.A.)
Art Museum
INNSBRUCK (Austria)
Castle Ambras *Kunsthistorische Sammlungen, Schloss Ambras*
ISTANBUL (Turkey)
Topkapi Palace Museum
Topkapi Sarayi
KRAKOW (Cracow) (Poland)
National Museum
Muzeum Narodowe w Krakowie
Wawel State Art Collection
Panstwowe Zbiory Sztuki na Wawelu
LONDON (England)
Imperial War Museum
The Armouries, H.M. Tower of London
Victoria & Albert Museum
Wallace Collection
MADRID (Spain)
Royal Armoury *Real Armeria*
MILWAUKEE (Wisconsin, U.S.A.)
Milwaukee Public Museum (Nunnemacher Collection)
MOSCOW (U.S.S.R.)
Oruznaya Palace, Kremlin
Oružejnaja palaca Gosudarstvenye muzei Moskovskogo Kremlja
MUNICH (West Germany)
Bavarian National Museum
Bayerisches Nationalmuseum
Ethnographical Museum
Staatliches Museum für Völkerkunde
NEUCHÂTEL (Switzerland)
Historical Museum
Musée d'Art et d'Histoire
NEW YORK (U.S.A.)
Metropolitan Museum of Art
NUREMBERG (West Germany)
Germanic National Museum
Germanisches Nationalmuseum
OXFORD (England)
Pitt-Rivers Museum
PARIS (France)
Army Museum *Musée de l'Armée*
Louvre *Musée du Louvre*
Pauilhac Collection
(now mostly in *Musée de l'Armée*)
PEKING (People's Republic of China)
Historical Museum (Imperial Palace Museum of Chinese History)
National Liberation Army Museum
Museum of the Chinese Revolution
PERTH (Scotland)
Art Gallery & Museum
PETERBOROUGH (Northampton, England)
City Museum & Art Gallery
PILSEN (Czechoslovakia)
Pilsen Museum *Západočeské Muzeum*
PRAGUE (Czechoslovakia)
Army Museum *Vojenské Muzeum*
ROME (Italy)
Castle of St. Angelo *Museo Nazionale di Castel Sant' Angelo*
Odescalchi Collection,
(in) *Museo di Palazzo Venezia*
ST. LOUIS (Missouri, U.S.A.)
The St. Louis Art Museum
SCHWARZBURG (Rudolstadt, East Germany)
Schwarzburg Castle
Schloss Schwarzburg
SKOKLOSTER (Sweden)
Castle *Skokloster slott*
STOCKHOLM (Sweden)
Royal Armoury *Livrustkammaren*
TURIN (Italy)
Artillery Museum *Museo Nazionale Storico d' Artiglieria*
Royal Armoury *Armeria Reale*
VEDELSPANG (Schleswig-Holstein, Germany)
Castle
WARSAW (Poland)
Museum of the Polish Army
Muzeum Wojska Polskiego (P.A.M.)
WARWICK (England)
Warwick Castle
Warwickshire Museum
WASHINGTON, D.C. (U.S.A.)
Smithsonian Institution
WINDSOR (Berkshire, England)
Windsor Castle
WOOLWICH (Kent, England)
The Rotunda Museum

Foreword

A *History of Firearms* by Major H. B. C. Pollard first appeared in 1926, and was the first general and fully comprehensive work on its subject ever to be published in English, and also probably the first general firearms book in any language intended specifically for collectors. It remained–in the revised edition published in 1930–the only work of its kind available until the late 1950s, when large quantities of new books on firearms began to pour off the printing presses of Britain and America (to say nothing of the Continent). So much new material then appeared in so short a space of time that Major Pollard realised that the manuscript of a third edition of his *History* which he had prepared was already hopelessly out of date. I agreed, at his request, to undertake the task of revising it but, having started work, quickly came to the conclusion that mere revision was no longer practicable, and that what was needed was a complete rewrite: it was also obvious to me that, because of the range of new material available, the task of doing this to a consistently high standard throughout was now beyond the scope of any one specialist. Major Pollard had already mentioned to me that his ultimate ambition for the book was that–like *Gray's Anatomy*–its author's name should become part of the title, however much the contents were changed by revision. I suggested to him, therefore, that the task of producing his new edition should be divided between a group of leading authorities on the history of firearms, under my general editorship, and published as *Pollard's History of Firearms*, and to this he readily agreed. Publication has been delayed by various circumstances, but I am now delighted to be able to introduce it to the public. Very little of Major Pollard's original text remains, but the concept is his, and it is right and proper, therefore, that his name should be associated with it. Like his original edition it covers the whole history of firearms all over the world, from medieval to modern times: something that no other book does in such detail or with so much authority.

So many people, apart from the contributors, have assisted in the production of this book that it is impossible to acknowledge them all by name. I must, however, record my grateful thanks to my colleague Mr A. R. E. North for his work in collecting, captioning and keying-in the illustrations and for preparing the bibliography, to Mr D. W. Bailey not only for preparing the Index, but also for making a great many corrections and suggestions about improvements to both text and illustrations; also to Mrs Patricia Pierce, Mr Karel Feuerstein, and Miss Margaret Saunders of Country Life Books for their work on the actual production of the book–including the design of the jacket by the last named, and especially for their constant patience and good humour even in the midst of editorial disputes.

CLAUDE BLAIR

A Memoir of Hugh Pollard

The work of the late Major Hugh B. C. Pollard was undoubtedly one of the more important early twentieth-century contributions to the enormous stockpile of published information on firearms. During the nine years from 1917 to 1926, he published a series of specialized works culminating in his famous *A History of Firearms* which confirmed his reputation as an authority. In addition, during the same years, he published four books on subjects other than firearms, one of which was a thriller written under a pseudonym. It was a period of sustained industry, considering that he was a serving officer in Military Intelligence until 1921 and that he was also engaged for much of this time, as for many years afterwards, in editorial work, other journalistic commitments, and in original research in firearms identification for forensic purposes. Quite early in this, his most productive period, he had clearly established the pattern and the inter-related themes of his whole career.

Most of this is on record; but the man himself, especially the younger man already able and prepared for his years of opportunity, is not so easily discovered. In *The Other Mr. Churchill*, Macdonald Hasting gives an excellent picture of Pollard as the established firearms expert of mature years. But by what roads did he come to be a recognized expert in practice and theory, accepted in forensic cases and in firearms literature, and what originally set him on the road? That is always the interesting question. I never met Major Pollard. To me, familiar only with some of his firearms works, he was that shadowy figure, the author. For the more one takes a work for granted and refers to it for factual content, the less one speculates about the writer. So to me, most likely, shadowy he would have remained; but by some conjunction of time and chance–and the good offices of Mr. Hastings–two years after Major Pollard's death in 1966, his Executors asked me to identify and evaluate what they described as 'a parcel of his papers'.

It was a parcel, I suppose. It weighed about forty pounds. Mixed up with masses of MSS. and typescript, some loose and some secured with bits of bootlace and insulated wire, and with pigeons' tail feathers inserted as markers, it also contained the outline of the working life of this extraordinarily versatile man: not recognizably at first, but in hints and clues in long-forgotten letter drafts, ancient correspondence, scraps of earliest writings, yellowed press cuttings and all the unswept oddments of a writer's life. All that was needed was time and patience to follow the clues. In the end, with luck, the author would be seen more clearly.

The son of an eminent surgeon, Joseph Pollard, M.R.C.S., of St. Marylebone, Hugh Bertie Campbell Pollard was born on 6th January 1888. He was admitted to Westminster School as a day boy in Rigaud's House in September 1897 and left in December 1903. No other information is available from the School records on his attainments or characteristics. Little is known of his early life. For another thing, in later life Pollard became a most reticent, almost secretive, man in some ways and committed few personal details to paper.

In the light of his later achievements, it is not surprising to find that, like so many boys of similar background, he was encouraged to make an early start in shooting. As a young lad, he learned to shoot rabbits at his grandfather's place in Hertfordshire and soon progressed to game shooting proper with his father who was a keen shooting man. As a schoolboy, he was also taught to shoot with a rifle. This remained a life-long interest and he was later well known as a member of the English Twenty Club.

He knew most of the London gunsmiths' shops and, it is said, used to arrange his journeys to and from school so as to pass as many as possible. It seems that he had started collecting in a limited way even then. Old firearms, of course, were ridiculously cheap by today's crazy standards; they were, in fact, often given away as of no account. New weapons were cheap enough and there was little bother about restrictions, not even for a youngster, especially if one came from the right address. Pocket money was still only pocket money, of course, but he came from a well-to-do family. At all events, he was well accustomed to firearms and to using them long before he was accustomed to using a razor. But his youthful interest in guns and shooting seems unremarkable enough now compared with the enormous enthusiasm for all firearms lore today–especially since he himself was destined to be one of those who fathered this same growth of enthusiasm.

Pollard's first employment was with Armstrong Whitworth's from January 1905 to August 1906 at the Elswick Engine Works. In 1906 he was elected as a graduate of the Institution of Mechanical Engineers. Then, for the next two years, he attended the Crystal Palace School of Practical Engineering. At this point, at the age of twenty, his taste for travel and adventure asserted itself and he joined the Redmond-Hardwick Exploration Syndicate for six months as an assistant on a prospecting venture in Morocco. Back in England in 1909, he took the Royal Geographical Society's plane table course and then promptly went abroad again as a surveyor to the Land Company of Chianas, Mexico. Later, he went to Mexico City. During this time, he was able to acquire for his collection various items such as his old 5 mm. Charola y Anitua pistol at give-away prices simply because they were obsolete. Travelling about, he mixed with all sorts of people, learned about Mexican affairs, and learned something of the language. Also, I think, his sympathies with the Spanish stemmed from this period. But squinting through a theodolite must have been a dicey occupation in that troubled country.

Because of the revolutions rending Mexico, Pollard came home again early in 1912, not so much because he minded revolutions as such (far from it) as because of their adverse financial effect on a 'Gringo' trying to pay his way. He was once described to me as an adventurer at heart and, in some ways, an opportunist. But, as an adventurer, he was unusual in that he never adventured beyond his means. As an opportunist, if he was one, he was also unusual: the opportunities he seized were for the sheer hard work of the immediate writing that followed each new experience. Back at home in 1912, capitalizing on his experience in the way that was to become characteristic, he wrote his first book, *A Busy Time in Mexico*, which was published in 1913 by Constable.

Despite finishing his formal education at a comparatively early age, which seems strange in his circumstances, it is evident from his later work that Pollard had kept up his reading. He became a studious, widely read man with considerable literary taste; and, apart from working at subjects such as mathematics and chemistry, he seems somehow to have acquired a useful knowledge of anatomy, probably from his father's books and with his help. It was all grist to the mill.

In May 1912, Pollard was commissioned as a Territorial Army officer in the London Regiment where, amongst other things, he was able to pursue his interest in rifle and revolver shooting. In that same year, he began his journalistic career as an assistant editor of a periodical called *The Cinema*. He then became the Editor of *The Territorial Monthly*, the Technical Editor of *The Autocycle* and a correspondent of *The Daily Express*, all of which he continued until the outbreak of the 1914 war. With this journalism, and with one book in print, Pollard was already committed to a career as a writer–and to arms. He did not have much in the way of paper qualifications but he had what Conrad called 'Ability in the abstract' and, in any case, he was to write his own paper qualifications, in very good measure. Wittingly or not, he was developing abilities in readiness for this busiest time.

In August 1914, Pollard was mobilized as a T.A. officer i/c motor-cycle dispatch riders, Royal Engineers, London. On November 3, he was given a special appointment as a staff Lieutenant seconded to the Intelligence Corps with the British Expeditionary Force. He served in Flanders through the first and second battles of Ypres and had intimate experience not only of *Ypres la morte* but of that whole salient soaked in squandered blood. On leave in February 1915, in the period between the two battles, he married Ruth Marie Gibbons. Then he returned to the salient until November when he was released for five months to manage grenade production for James Gibbons' Engineering Works in Wolverhampton, at that time controlled by Francis James Gibbons, a pre-war shooting friend of Pollard's (and then his father-in-law). Pollard had been blown off his motorbike into a crater and wounded at Ypres, which probably facilitated this arrangement.

During this period of release, he also worked on his book *The Story of Ypres*, a clear account of the battles for the city that was the key of the roads to the coast, and a blazing indictment of the Germans' systematic bombardment and complete destruction of the ancient, gracious city when their attacks failed. It was an extremely moving document, written at white-heat yet with controlled passion and pathos in a graphic style he seems never to have used again. This was published in 1917 by McBride, New York, and translations were later printed in French, German and, I believe, in Swedish.

What spark fired Pollard to produce the first of his series of sound and still-used text-books on firearms will probably never be known. But his first practical work on firearms, *The Book of The Pistol and Revolver*, was also published by McBride in 1917; and he was set upon a certain course. Whether or not the book was part-written or even planned before the war is not known, though it seems most likely. During his active service Pollard had had ample opportunity to increase his knowledge of arms, and to increase his collection–'by right of conquest', as he put it later on. It seems that, with another book to his credit in 1916, and with a favourably impressed publisher, he probably decided on firearms, one of his main interests, as his next subject and put together all his notes to complete *The Book of The Pistol and Revolver* as quickly as possible.

Meanwhile, from April 1916, he had resumed military duties. In 1916, too, he was upgraded to an Associate Member of the Institution of Mechanical Engineers, which strikes an odd note in his war. Promoted to Captain, he was appointed to the staff of the Intelligence Directorate, War Office, until 'disembodied' in January 1919. According to his own records, Pollard was directing the publicity of the Ministry of Labour Appointments Department from 1918 to 1919, but no details are given. He was then attached to the Irish Office as an Intelligence officer until he 'relinquished' his commission (as records put it) in September 1921 but retained the rank of Captain.

Pollard's second firearms work, *Automatic Pistols*, was published by Pitman in 1920. This had been completed in 1918 and was the first book in English solely devoted to the subject. It described practically all known automatics of that time and gave the ballistics of existing cartridges together with general data and formulae. It also sheds some more light on Pollard's early days. He refers to several unusual weapons in his possession. ('The 5 mm Bergmann is rather delightful . . . less noise than a .22 . . . and is splendid to use in a room.') He had some experience of at least two shooting galleries of the day which he recommended: King's Range, Oxenham St., London; and Gastinne Rennette's, 39, Ave. d'Antrin, Paris, where he had hob-nobbed with Walter Winans. (He relates elsewhere that he had once succeeded in shooting Walter Winans in the groin in a mock duel with wax bullets. Winans was hurt more in his vanity than in his pants and, for a while, Paris expected a more serious meeting. But the hatchet was buried and they became good friends again.) The personal experience that informs Pollard's advice on suitable holsters for use on horseback in rough country obviously stems from his time in Mexico. The book also shows that he had known Robert Churchill for some time, for he recommends him as 'a gunsmith who thoroughly understands all types of pistol.'

Then we have another example of Pollard's 'oportunism' in sheer industry and speed of production. In 1922, shortly after the termination of his duties with the Irish Office, his book *The Secret Societies of Ireland* was published by Philip Allan & Co. For some reason, this title was later listed as *The Secret Societies, Their Rise and Progress.*

References to Pollard's 'cloak and dagger' activities are always oblique but, from various unpublished notes, there is reason to believe that he got involved in several affrays where his expertise with the pistol stood him in good stead. In an uncompleted MS. on pistol shooting, written about 1921 judging from his early rounded handwriting, he wrote the following: 'In fighting, nothing ever happens as it does on the range. You are in a hurry, you are excited, short of breath, and I am personally subject to shortness of temper and fits of alarm . . . In range shooting, the target is static; in fighting shooting, it may be incredibly mobile. It may not be front ways on; it may be in profile or–well, in reverse. It may be flapping about in that destracting thing, a loose raincoat. I once missed twice at about ten yards by shooting through the median line of a wind-blown raincoat! The slender rogue was on the windward side (of the raincoat) but I have never forgotten how puzzled I was momentarily at his apparent invulnerability. Then,' Pollard concluded grimly, 'then, I corrected.'

About this time (it was not dated), a thriller called *Outwitted*, which Pollard had written under the pen-name 'Oliver Bland', was published by Odhams. Obviously inspired by his war-time release period, this was a yarn in the early Buchan style about a young Captain who, after getting a shrapnel ball in the shoulder in Flanders, was temporarily released to sort out a munitions problem and who finally pursued saboteurs to a cataclysmic denouement. At a later date, another thriller, *The Adventures of a Modern Occultist*, was written under the same pen-name and was published by Dodd, Mead & Co., New York. How many more such books and stories were written is not known. As an example of Pollard's secretiveness in some matters, his widow Ruth Pollard told me that one of their two daughters Diana and April–Diana, I believe it was–once found one of 'Oliver Bland's' productions in her father's study. Having read it, she asked her amused and close-lipped sire why he couldn't write something like that!

Pollard's third work on firearms, *Shotguns, Their History and Development*, was published by Pitman in 1923. For Pollard, this was an eventful year; and it heralded the busiest time of his whole busy life. He had the restless drive, the energy to write–to keep on writing far into the nights. All his work was written out in his scratchy longhand, page after page at high speed with few erasures–and little punctuation–and it was mostly at night for at that time he was on the staff of *The Daily Express*. Oddly, the *Express* could find no record of this; but two contemporaries, Maurice Cowan and James Wentworth Day, clearly recalled his presence in the early 1920s. The issue would naturally be confused because for long enough before and after this time Pollard was a special correspondent of the paper.

At that time, too, he was much pre-occupied with writing chapters on 'The Revolver' and on 'The Self-Loading Pistol' for the revised 1929 edition of *The Text Book of Small Arms*. It involved an enormous amount of correspondence and re-writing before everyone was satisfied and the final draft was approved. But a certain *cachet* accrued from all this–Pollard had been officially recognised as a firearms expert.

Always a 'revolver man', he was eventually very disappointed by the new ·380 Service revolver which fell far short of the high standard of the ·38 Webley and Scott prototype of which he had written in the draft for the *Text Book*: 'A new type of ·38 cartridge with a 200-grain bullet was found to give results considerably superior to the ·38 Special with the 156-grain bullet and to yield results comparable in efficiency (stopping power) with the Service ·455.'

Years later, in his notes, he wrote: '. . . but the revolver was altered and spoilt, and a compromise cartridge is used. Webley's produced an excellent prototype weapon. . . . Between the wars, progress was shelved. . . . In the 1930s a new revolver was designed by Enfield. In this, the original Webley length of cylinder and frame was shortened, thus saving some fraction of weight. The 200-grain bullet could, it is true, be got into the chamber, *but only if it was flat-nosed.* When the revolver appeared at Bisley in 1937, the attention of the authorities was called to *the fuss* (my italics) made by the Germans when a similarly shaped ·455 revolver bullet was a Service issue in 1914. The ·38 bullet was promptly modified to a conical shape with consequent loss of weight and efficiency. Early in 1939 it was again modified and given an envelope of cupro-nickel, this further reducing its efficiency. During these changes, modifications in powder took place and the respectable 700-odd ft./sec. of the lead bullet gave place not, as one might expect, to higher velocities but to lower ones. It is a very bad cartridge indeed. . . .'

However, in 1923, probably the most important event for Pollard in the long term was that he was consulted by the Hon. C. H. Cahan, K.C., of Montreal, on firearms evidence for the defence in the notorious Abbé Delorme murder trials. This was the first of the many legal cases in which Pollard was to act as a consultant or as an 'expert witness'.

The Abbé J. Adelard Delorme's half-brother Raoul Delorme had been found shot dead in the snow in a Montreal street early in the morning. All the evidence pointed to the priest as a cold-blooded fratricide: amongst other damaging facts, he had heavily insured his half-brother shortly before; he had bought a ·25 Bayard pistol two weeks before; the neighbours had heard shots the night before the body was found. The Abbé's main defence was that he knew nothing about it: the shots he had fired from his *little pocket automatic*, and fouled the barrel, had been fired at a *rabbit* the day before. Not surprisingly, it was considered a thin story. As Pollard drily noted, 'the case was complicated by a good deal of political and sectarian rancour.'

Pollard had become increasingly interested in the comparatively new science of firearms identification and evidence (or 'forensic ballistics', as it was sometimes called) ever since sitting on courts martial in the war and studying evidence on allegedly self-inflicted wounds. He was convinced that scientific medico-legal knowledge of gunshot wounds and weapons was inadequate.

In Britain, Robert Churchill, gunmaker, was *the* specialist on the subject and as such was frequently called upon as a consultant or as an expert witness for the prosecution by the Metropolitan Police. In those days, to identify suspected crime weapons with crime bullets, laborious techniques were employed. Wax or sulphur moulds were cast in the barrel bores and then withdrawn to compare the rifling characteristics with marks on the bullets. Also, marks on test bullets, fired into cotton wool and recovered undeformed, and marks on crime bullets were compared by various complex and indirect methods using photography. Pollard, always interested in new techniques but working on different lines, had set up a laboratory in his home and spent a great deal of time on experimental methods of identifying typical and also individually characteristic weapon markings on bullets and cartridge cases, and on experimental low-power comparison microscopes.

Mr. Cahan, who was in Paris between the Delorme trials for a consultation with French experts, got in touch with Pollard and visited him in September 1923. In his ballistics notes twenty-six years later, Pollard wrote: 'Mr. Cahan had been at the head of a Canadian Intelligence department during the first World War and was satisfied that a serious miscarriage of justice was involved in the first trial of the Abbé. I had served in Intelligence and was suggested as a possible authority. The re-trial was entirely successful as, on my suggestion, the body of the victim was exhumed, X-rayed and more bullets were found. They bore no relation at all to the pistol for which the accused had a permit (a ·25 Bayard automatic, the alleged murder weapon). Some extremely dubious 'evidence' by some American experts was destroyed. I did not appear as a witness but the forensic ballistics side of the Delorme case was worked out in my house in St. John's Wood. . . .'

Perhaps the most important aspect of this case for Pollard was that it drew him into collaboration with Robert Churchill. During Mr. Cahan's visit, Pollard had recommended him to consult Churchill. In the event, the firearms evidence that Pollard and Churchill had worked out was not a salient feature of the final trial. No doubt, if all had hung on the original firearms evidence for the prosecution, it would have been demolished. In his notes all those years later, Pollard seems to think it was. But this may be on account of a letter from Cahan, dated 1st November 1924, and preserved in his early files, which states simply: 'You will be pleased to learn that in the third trial of the Abbé Delorme, which closed last evening, the jury rendered a verdict of acquittal.' How much Pollard was pleased is not on record. He could have had little faith in the Abbé's innocence but neither had he any faith at all in the *firearms* evidence of guilt.

From this time, Pollard and Churchill became close associates and eventually close friends. Pollard was drawn more and more into the forensic aspect of firearms work. His by-line 'Major Hugh B. C. Pollard (Author of *The Book of The Pistol*, etc.)' appeared more frequently in the *Express* above informed reports on the firearms aspects of crimes. In 1924, he took over the editorship of *Discovery*, a scientific monthly, and in two years he worked it up into a highly respected journal. In November 1924, he published his own famous article 'What the Bullet Tells', a concise statement of firearms identification techniques of that time, which attracted a great deal of attention. His description of comparing bullets under compound microscopes 'whose stereoscopic effect is useful' foreshadowed the use of the comparison-microscope in this country by some three years.

A curious feature of Pollard's work in 1924 was that the rank of Major used in his by-line was dropped and not used again for twenty years or more. His earlier by-lines had used the rank of Captain and the use of Major seemed a normal-enough promotion. But, in fact, through no fault of his own, he had been using the rank of Major incorrectly for nearly two years. What had happened was that he had been notified by letter dated 17th July 1922, that he was appointed to the Regular Army Reserve of Officers in the rank of Major. But this was gazetted as Captain. Seeing the Army List of 1924, Pollard wrote to the War Office querying the discrepancy. After investigation, during which he grew increasingly irritated, the War Office sent a letter stating with apologies that the rank of Major given in their letter of 17th July 1922, was due to a clerical error.

This affair rankled, as is shown in some of his papers. Pollard never had, nor sought, any kind of patronage: all his progress, all he had become, was due to his own efforts; to sheer hard work, the unremitting and peculiarly exhausting grind of continual writing on technical subjects. No wonder his humour, often enough sardonic in any case, sometimes became more caustic, especially on matters concerning the military establishment. His ballistics notes contain references to highly placed men 'with some physiological but no mathematical conception of a square root', to the River Wool in the Royal Arsenal at Woolwich being 'so narrow that even a Brigadier could jump it before lunch', and to certain 'long-range planners remote from actual contact with rude saltpetre or its modern successors.'

In addition to his own writing at this time–numerous articles as always, at least two books under way, and one of these his *magnum opus*–Pollard found time to collaborate with Churchill not only in firearms investigations but also in writing Churchill's well-known *How to Shoot* published in 1925. This expounded Churchill's shooting techniques with his 25-inch-barrelled game guns and faithfully presented his ideas and instructions but Pollard did practically all of the writing, just as Macdonald Hastings, who became a great friend of both Churchill and Pollard a decade later, wrote almost every word of Churchill's highly successful book *Game Shooting*.

With the publication of his best-known work, *A History of Firearms*, Hugh Pollard was firmly established. A copy of this book, first published in 1926 by Geoffrey Bles, is now a collector's item. It was a pioneer work: it embodied a great deal of original research long before the present flood of literature on the subject. It was, I believe, the first book in any language, certainly the first in the English language, to deal with the subject with the needs of the firearms collector especially in mind. It was, is now, his monumental achievement.

If Pollard's achievements seem any the less remarkable in the light of the greater and more widespread technical knowledge of today, it must be remembered that he was delving away at data for his first firearms books before the 1914 war, long before the modern craze for firearms lore and the present boom in collecting were even dreamed of. His sources, far fewer than nowadays, were largely foreign works, museums, manufacturers' data records and his own experiments. His work on the Delorme case in 1923 was before the first Forensic Science Laboratory in Britain or the early Bureau of Forensic Ballistics in New York was founded. It was the day of the independent specialist. Like Robert Churchill, he was one of the early back-room boys. But, unlike Churchill, whose practically entire life was devoted to sporting guns, shooting, and firearms identification, Pollard had great versatility and wide-ranging interests.

During his two years as Editor of *Discovery* (1924–26), Pollard had himself written many articles on a surprising diversity of subjects including microscopy, photography, early wireless techniques, speculations on wireless control of unmanned bombers and missiles, and–of all things–a study of why

By the early 1920s Hugh Pollard had established himself as a firearms expert – one of the first – through his wartime experience, as the author of several of the first text-books on guns, and by conducting his own experiments in the comparatively new science of 'forensic ballistics'. In 1923 he was first consulted on firearms evidence in a notorious murder trial. Many such cases followed. (*Above, left*) Taking a cast of the inside of a pistol barrel.

Above, right Using a skull for comparison purposes, he calculates the angle at which a shot was fired into the head of a man.

Left In middle age. By then he was well-established and enjoying the fruits of success. *A History of Firearms* had been published in 1926. Book followed book on a fascinating diversity of subjects.

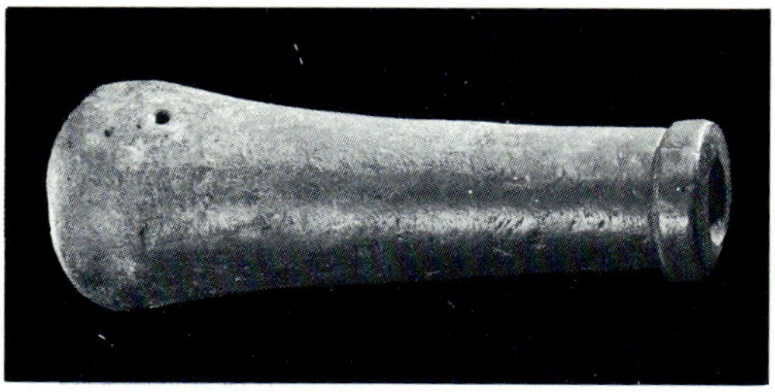

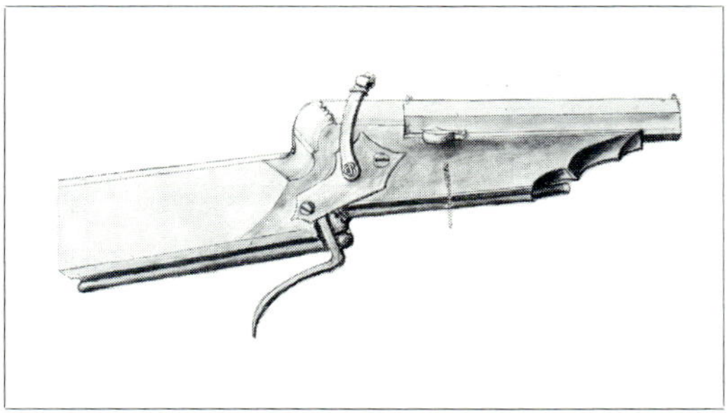

1 *Top, left* Bronze gun from Loshult, Sweden. Early fourteenth century.

2 *Top, right* Bronze hand cannon with recoil stop from the sea near Mörkö, Sweden. German, late-14th century. Statens Historiska Museum, Stockholm (1 and 2).

3 *Middle, left* Man firing gun with earliest serpentine. Ger. MS. 1411. Nationalbibliothek, Vienna.

4 *Middle, right (top)* Matchlock from the *Fireworks Book* of Martin Merz. German, dated 1475. Staatsbibliothek, Munich (4 and 5).

5 *Middle, right, (bottom)* Soldier with a matchlock gun, the *Fireworks Book*, H. Formschneider. German, 1460–70.

6 *Left* Soldiers armed with hand firearms. From Diebold von Schilling's *Bern Chronicle* of 1480. City Library, Bern.

sap rises in a tree. Although known to the public primarily as a firearms expert, his versatility was demonstrated when his *Sportsman's Cookery Book* was published by *Country Life* in 1926, the same year that *A History of Firearms* appeared. It is hard to think of a greater contrast. Another entirely different type of work, his *Wildfowl and Waders*, illustrated by Frank Southgate, was later published by *Country Life* in 1928.

The cookery book became a minor classic, still eagerly snapped up by the connoisseur, and it marked the beginning of an association with *Country Life*. Some time before, probably in 1925–the date is uncertain–Pollard had become the sporting editor of the magazine *Country Life*. During the 1939 war, many of their records were destroyed and they now have no reliable information on his work for them.

Despite this diversity, however, Pollard's continuing interest through the mid-1920s was still in firearms identification and, in particular, in collaborating with Churchill in trying to develop a comparison-microscope for identifying weapon markings on bullets and cartridge cases. As he wrote later, work on objects of this size is not really microscopic but macroscopic, and the difficulties they had in obtaining or devising suitable low-power instruments and rigidly aligning them on an experimental basis were considerable. These difficulties were compounded by the need for perfect illumination and accurate photography. For acceptable evidence in court, very clear photographic prints would have to be produced; and even then their significance might not be readily comprehended by counsel or jury who were often hazy about the difference between an automatic pistol and a revolver, let alone the difference between the individual characteristics of similar weapons. In fact, although Churchill's evidence had hanged men before then, and Pollard's work was later to help in this direction, more than one defendant was lucky enough to get off the capital charge through the failure of prosecuting counsel to follow technical jargon and logic and to seize on crucial facts and their implications. But it was probably much more difficult in those days for the expert witnesses from all the specialized fields, not only of firearms but pathology, toxicology and so on, to explain abstruse points of evidence clearly in terms comprehensible to the non-technical or lay mind; for the lay mind is generally far better conditioned nowadays to accept simplified scientific or technical information. Not surprisingly, perhaps, there was at that time considerable public distrust of, and opposition to, the developing science of firearms identification–and not the least vociferous of the opponents had been George Bernard Shaw!

It should be mentioned that an independent firearms specialist was not only engaged as an expert witness by the prosecution or defence, as the case might be, to give evidence in court. In those days, an expert, usually Churchill in the Metropolitan area, would frequently be consulted during police investigation of firearms cases and charges might be made or not made according to his findings. Thus, Churchill, and Pollard, too, might be acting in a way for the 'defence' of a suspect before a charge was even considered. The same thing applies to the firearms specialists of the Forensic Science Laboratory today.

Frustratingly, success with the microscope was eluding the joint efforts of Churchill and Pollard. However, work on similar lines had been progressing in other countries. In Cairo, Professor Sydney Smith (later Sir Sydney), then the head of the medico-legal department of the Egyptian Ministry of Justice, had done a great deal of original work on firearms identification during the long series of political murders culminating in November 1924, in the assassination of Sir Lee Stack Pasha, the Sirdar of the Egyptian Army and Governor-General of the Sudan. In the course of this work Sydney Smith had successfully improvised a comparison-microscope which was certainly in use by 1924, if not earlier, and the assassins of the Sirdar were brought to book largely by the bullet evidence provided by him and his staff, and the comparison-microscope.

Pollard had got to hear of this and had written in 1924 asking in an oblique way for information (for press cuttings) not to Sydney Smith but to Arthur Lucas at the Government Laboratory, to whom he had previously written introducing himself and asking for a copy of rumoured published papers to help his work on the Abbé Delorme case. The papers he had heard of were probably Sydney Smith's book on Forensic Medicine first published in Cairo–*in Arabic*! If Pollard had got into touch with Sydney Smith, he and Churchill might have been saved a good deal of unrewarding work. On the other hand, Sydney Smith might well have preferred to reserve his material for his own purposes. As it was, Pollard seems to have got little information, though Arthur Lucas wrote saying he would look him up in England sometime in 1926.

In America, Major Calvin Goddard, of the Ordnance Reserve of the United States Army, had been working on the same problem. In 1924, he and Charles E. Waite, a criminal investigator, and their associates founded the Bureau of Forensic Ballistics in New York–it was later merged with the Scientific Arms Detection Laboratories of the University of Chicago. In February, 1926, Major Goddard published a paper in *The Military Surgeon* outlining *his* researches. During this time, a comparison-microscope had been successfully developed; and it was probably this design that Sydney Smith later obtained. Who first used the instrument for bullet work is not clear, and possibly no longer important; but it is clear that, as so often happens, development in different countries had been almost in parallel.

The importance of the comparison-microscope had been amply demonstrated. Accordingly, Churchill visited America early in 1927 to study the necessary techniques. With Pollard's assistance, he then drew up his requirements for a similar instrument which was built to his specifications. This, though still far from perfect, was usefully employed later in the Police Constable Gutteridge murder case.

In the field of firearms evidence in Britain, this was an historic case. On 26th September 1927, the constable had been found shot dead with what proved to be ·455 flat-nosed soft-lead bullets. Brutally, two more shots had been fired through his eyes as he lay dead or dying in the road. Later, in an abandoned stolen car, a fired ·455 cartridge case was found. This was recognised by the head of the C.I.D. (then Sir Wyndham Childs) as a pre-1914 Enfield case that had been loaded with a flat-nosed lead bullet. Also, in detailed examination, he noticed minute, pimple-like blisters in the cap–which would relate to tiny indentations in the standing breech of the gun that had fired it. Churchill and Pollard made several tests with the fired case and the crime bullets, which were badly deformed, to compare them with the test cases and bullets fired from various ·455 revolvers the police had found. Experiment was also carried out to determine the range of the shots from the pronounced blackening and powder tattooing that had been present on the body. Both black powder and smokeless loads had been used in the crime. In the event, it was established that two revolvers belonging to known criminals, ... Browne and . . . . . Kennedy, had been used and they were both subsequently convicted and hanged. The case was almost wholly dependent on technical firearms evidence and it can, in general, be said to have established the principle of firearms identification and evidence in British Courts.

Some years after the Gutteridge case, Major Sir Gerald Burrard stated in an article in *Game and Gun* that the firearms identification work had been done by the War Office. He appears to have got hold of the wrong end of the stick. War Office experts did test an enormous number of revolvers but it seems to have been largely corroboratory work. Churchill's photomicrographs and reports are on file. And Pollard's notes on the case were later read and approved by Churchill to my certain knowledge.

A state of feud had existed between Churchill and Burrard ever since the latter, as firearms correspondent of *The Field*, had adversely (and anonymously) criticized Churchill's 25-inch-barrelled sporting guns when reviewing his book *How to Shoot* in 1925 (the book that had been mostly written by Pollard!). Further, Burrard had not personally answered his numerous, indignant and remonstrative letters. Neither did *The Field* print all of them–the Editor closed the correspondence. Churchill retaliated with a privately printed brochure (a real 'blast of the trumpet') which was unambiguously entitled *Myself and The Field.*

Pollard, of course, was revelling in the background of all this; it gave great scope for his mordant wit and oblique humour. As sporting editor of *Country Life*, he had already joined in the squabble on Churchill's side. Churchill carried on the fight for some weeks on the back page of *The Shooting Times* in what were ostensibly advertisements. *The Field*'s correspondent remained anonymous, though his identity was an 'open secret'; but eventually a rather extenuating article on the subject by Burrard was printed in *Game and Gun.* This was Churchill's opportunity to let rip another snorting broadside in a second privately printed pamphlet. So it went on. By the time it all simmered down, all the editors concerned must have been heartily sick of it.

By the time that last postscript to the Gutteridge case appeared, Pollard was well established in his country home in Sussex enjoying the fruits of success and the traditional sports of the English country gentleman, hunting and fishing as well as shooting. Born and bred in London, he had become more the country gentleman in some ways than many a born country gentleman. But he still got through a great deal of work; book followed book, and article followed article. He had changed over to Eyre and Spottiswoode who published *Game Birds* (1929), *The Gun Room Guide* (1930) and *Hard Up On Pegasus*, on riding and hunting (1931).

His collaboration with Churchill was, of course, well known to the Metropolitan Police and to the Director of Public Prosecutions. When the notorious Elvisa Barney shooting case of 1932 had broken on the delightedly shocked and scandalized West End, it was Pollard whom the police called in while Churchill returned from abroad.

After a drunken quarrel, during an alleged struggle at 4 a.m., Mrs. Barney's little pocket revolver had 'gone off' and killed her subsidised lover. The London evening headlines were full of it. In contrast to all the titillating phrases was Pollard's report: '. . . she was the daughter of Sir John and Lady Mullens and had married an American called Barney. She had a mews flat in Williams Mews, Knightsbridge, which was furnished with a cocktail bar and a library of erotic literature. In addition to alcoholic stimulants there were birch rods. For some time this woman had been keeping a lover, Thomas Scott Stephen, and on May 31st in the early hours of the morning Stephen was shot through the left side of his chest with a ·32 (S & W) Harrington & Richardson. This weapon is almost impossible to fire accidentally as it has no external hammer, is solely double-action, and is also fitted with an intercepting grip safety. . . .

'At the trial at the Old Bailey, Sir Patrick Hastings, K.C., defending, took the line that it was a case of accident in a struggle.' (The trigger pull was about 14 lb. To show how 'easily' it could be fired accidentally, Hastings pulled the trigger rapidly several times in Court. It was said to have made his finger stiff. JB) 'The prosecution was led by Sir Percival Clarke and it was soon obvious that he was not at his best in criminal work. Evidence was called from Sir Bernard Spilsbury, Mr. Robert Churchill and Major Hugh Pollard. The jury, swayed by the advocacy of Sir Patrick Hastings, returned not a manslaughter verdict as had been expected, but one of "Not Guilty." The main interest of the case to firearms experts is that *it is an excellent instance of a jury being unable to assess evidence when under the spell of most able emotional advocacy* despite a very clear summing up by Mr. Justice Humphreys.'

Through those middle years of Pollard's there were many such cases. He was always on the go. But commuting to London in those days, especially by train from Haslemere, was a great deal more comfortable–and more elegant–than today. And he had his London clubs, the Authors' and the Savile. Despite his activity, there was still time for writing and his next book *Game Birds and Game Bird Shooting* was published in 1936.

In this year also, there was the most controversial, most misunderstood and mis-reported incident of his career–the Franco affair. At that time his closest friend, according to Mrs Pollard, was Douglas Jerrold, then Editor of *The English Review* and Chairman of Eyre and Spottiswoode. Another friend of Jerrold's, Luis Bolin, was the London correspondent of a Madrid newspaper. According to Bolin, he was impressed into service by his publisher, the Marquis de Luca de Tena, to act as an amateur secret agent and directed to charter an aircraft capable of flying from London to Casablanca in Spanish Morocco and then on to the Canaries to 'rescue' General Franco from virtual exile there. After chartering a de Havilland Rapide at Croydon, Bolin went to his friend Jerrold for help. As well as the aircraft, he required an English companion and a couple of blondes to fly to 'an unspecified spot' on the N.W. coast of Africa and disguise the flight as a party of rich tourists.

Jerrold thought of his friend Pollard, who would be just the man. So, together with Juan de la Cierva (of autogyro fame) who had advised on chartering and on 'tourist cover', they visited Pollard. Bolin describes him at that time as a British Major on the Reserve–which he wasn't–and a good-looking man of about forty-five with cool appraising eyes. 'Good-looking' may or may not have been a conventional journalistic tribute; it is hard to say. Pollard would then be forty-eight, and he could have very cool eyes! It was arranged that he and his daughter Diana and also Dorothy Watson, who worked on his farm, should go on the flight. It all seems as casually fortuitous as that.

Again according to Bolin, whatever Pollard guessed, he was not told the purpose of the flight at first. He was captivated by the mystery and hint of intrigue; and besides his friend Jerrold had vouched for Bolin.

Early on July 11th, the four of them took off from Croydon in the chartered Rapide, piloted by a Captain Bebb, on the first leg to Bordeaux. Re-fuelled there, they took off again. Unfortunately, the navigator had 're-fuelled' all too well and took them right off course. After an eventful flight over the mountains of Northern Spain and the delay of turning back to Biarritz to refuel–for Bolin dared not land in Spain!–they were forced to put down at Espinho, a small military airfield in Portugal. Any suspicion was averted by the presence of the girl 'tourists' and they were allowed to proceed the following morning. Arriving in Casablanca a day late, Bolin missed his contact and had to remain there to deal with 'exigencies'.

At Bolin's request, Pollard ('this suave English officer') flew on with Captain Bebb, and with the girls as tourists, to Las Palmas to make contact with a Dr. Gabarda in Tenerife and to offer to bring back to Casablanca any passengers he suggested. That night they made the last leg of the trip by packet-boat to Tenerife to meet Franco and arrange his secret departure. In the event, to avoid overloading the Rapide, Pollard and the girls did not return to Casablanca with it. Having helped to get the aircraft unremarked and unmolested to Las Palmas, they left it there and went home by ship.

Meanwhile, the aircraft returned to Casablanca with General Franco (who had been prudently transferred to Tenerife garrison duty by the newly elected People's Government) and with a few of his officers. From Casablanca, Franco and some of his staff then flew to Tetuán to lead the troops garrisoned there in the right-wing revolt against the duly-elected Government of Spain.

At that time in 1936, Pollard became decidedly Pro-Franco and, by this definition, anti-'red'. Long afterwards, he drafted a letter to Bolin saying that it had cost him 'materially a great deal in promotion and pay' but that he 'would do it again as it was right', for people in England did not understand things in Spain or Spanish thinking. To the end of his life,

Pollard was convinced (as was the grateful Franco) that he had 'helped Spain' on the grounds that the Popular Front Government had no chance of controlling the nineteen existing and sometimes conflicting political factions and preventing a civil war in any case.

Living in the country through the 1930s, Pollard, as a keen hunting man, became absorbed in the study of scent. Technical interest was the key to most of his activities. Given any new interest, his probing mind would fully clothe the subject by assiduous research. His game shooting, for instance, not only resulted in works on shotguns but also in a book called *The Biology of The Pheasant*. Not content with pondering the vagaries of scent, he set about determining the causes or constituents of 'good scenting conditions'. The result was a device he called his 'Scentometer' for correlating humidity, temperature and wind conditions to indicate the probable scenting conditions. Though a number were made and sold, it does not seem to have done very well. But he admits '. . . infallibility is claimed only by the Pope, the Bolshies and the Fascists. . . .' However, it all made one more book, *The Mystery of Scent* (1937), in which, I think, his humour is at its wittiest on the need for a hypothetical 'Standard Fox' and the need, for lack of an official unit of smell, of a suggested scale of 'deci-smells'. Despite the humour, it is still a most informative book.

These were good years for Pollard: he had a charming home, he was financially secure, he enjoyed the best of sport, and his work was in demand. Barely past the prime of life, he had the wiry figure of the horseman and swordsman, for amongst other things he had been a keen fencer, and he had seemingly inexhaustible energy. He pursued his objective with the pertinacity of a terrier–and, like a terrier, too, I imagine, he would bristle when crossed. His writing appeared not only in magazines and newspapers but also in anthologies and in The Lonsdale Library. He enjoyed being an authority. He had the self-confidence that enabled him to over-simplify amusingly: 'Shotgun ballistics are very largely a matter of polite convention', a reference to the inevitable compromises in a shot pattern between shot spread, density and energy. And no doubt it was out of this same self-confidence that he was one day to tell one of Scotland Yard's firearms experts that they knew 'nothing about it', which was neither forgiven nor forgotten! Some, who did not know him, saw it as arrogance, an impression which his dry, clipped manner and his sometimes cold blue eye of indifference did nothing to dispel. Yet he seems to have enjoyed a considerable social life and had many friends, some of them important and influential people, who appreciated his odd humour.

The outbreak of the 1939 war found Pollard a civilian, which did not please him. He had completed his time on the Reserve in 1938. At the age of fifty-two, he succeeded in getting back into the Army with an emergency commission as a Lieutenant in March, 1940, and was transferred to the Intelligence Corps (once more) in July. In a letter to a friend long after the war, he wrote that he 'had enjoyed the war' but had 'a devil of a time, of course, at the hands of our "reds". . . .' Many people with Socialist leanings were rather 'red' to Pollard's way of thinking and his temper, often explosive in any case, was likely to erupt in political argument.

He had been in Spain in 1940 for a negotiation on arms. Britain was desperately short of small arms of all descriptions. At home, Pollard and Churchill had been gathering in all the weapons they could track down, particularly continental calibres suitable for British agents. In Spain, according to Pollard, the negotiations were 'busted' by the collapse of France and the German breakthrough. Then he got wind of a consignment of arms that the defeated Republican forces had managed to take into France at the end of the Spanish Civil War.

'I am rather a good pirate in the best English tradition,' he wrote. 'There was rather a fuss about it but, while Gamelin was talking, I got the stuff to le Havre and across.' In this consignment, there were about 300 air-cooled Vickers machine-guns designed for the Russian service cartridge which had never even been unpacked. The guns were quickly modified for the ·303 cartridge and put usefully to work in the Battle of Britain.

According to records, Pollard was put on the Army's unemployed list in July 1941. But what he was really doing at that time is anybody's guess. For a while, during the Blitz on London, he was working with Churchill on methods of defusing unexploded bombs. Early in 1942, he was appointed to the Inspectorate of Armaments at Woolwich Arsenal with the rank of Captain. He served as Proof Officer, a post which suited his talents and with which, he said, he was delighted since anything to do with arms and ammo was his specialist hobby. He was also secretly rather proud of being the first non-regular to have the job.

Promoted to Major, he was appointed Deputy Inspector in 1945. He did not 'escape to active service', as he put it, until after D-day. Eventually, he records, he went with Patton's forces into Thuringia in technical intelligence on small arms. Here, he did another semi-piratical sort of job ('I had a lovely time!') and took out a great many arms and designs before the Russians moved in. Later, he was o/c Intelligence, Technical, in Vienna where, he wrote, he had to deal with anything from atoms to looters. The latter were troublesome. 'But,' says Pollard, 'in three weeks I stopped all the nonsense . . . with sawnoff shotguns. . . .'

When Pollard finally got home again, there was plenty of post-war crime to interest him. After the Antiquis murder case in 1947, Robert Churchill delegated most of his forensic work to Pollard. Churchill was bowing out; and Pollard went in his stead for the defence in firearms cases in Kenya and Uganda. He was finally released from Army service in April 1948, and was granted the honorary rank of Major. His letterhead 'Major Hugh Pollard, A.I. Mech.E., F.R.M.S., Expert on Firearms and Forensic Ballistics', gave a St. John's Wood address again. When he read of an interesting firearms case, he would write to the Chief Constable of the particular area to offer his services, but the day of the independent firearms expert was nearly over, except for acting for the defence in shooting cases or as a consultant in cases of accident or claims over faulty weapons and so on. The Home Office made other arrangements for firearms identifications and evidence in prosecutions.

Apart from other activities during the war, Major Pollard had completed another book, *British and American Game Birds*, with Phyllis Barclay-Smith, which came out in 1945. This seems to have been his last published book. But between 1947 and 1950, he compiled a vast work provisionally entitled 'Forensic Ballistics'. This was the sum total of his own firearms experience, and a great deal of Robert Churchill's. It was never published.

There were various contributory reasons for this. In the early 1950s, Pollard still had a fair amount of forensic work on hand–he was, for instance, the expert for the defence in the Craig and Bentley case in 1952. Churchill had had enough of crime weapons and was spending much more time in sporting shooting both at home and abroad. He had married again, very happily, and Pollard did not see nearly so much of him. Also, Pollard had moved down to Midhurst to spend his latter years in his beloved Sussex. In his mid-sixties, he could no longer drive himself on as he had done so often in the past; and he missed the stimulation of life in London, the British Museum Reading Room, and friends and facilities for all the editing still to be done. And most of all he missed Churchill to spur him on. The old fire-eater was slowing down.

In the country, too, there were all his other interests to tempt his time away. Like many before, and after, he found that the best place to be busy is a busy place. He had little financial incentive to write. The book was postponed. As the time passed he became very deaf. It was, perhaps, a result of the countless shots he had fired (for he hadn't always practised what he preached on ear protection) or maybe it was a legacy of that hellish bombardment long ago in Ypres. But he went out less; met fewer people. Then his almost lifelong friend and long-time colleague Robert Churchill, the stout hearted, the unshakeable witness, died in 1958. The horizon was closing in. The book, which had been conceived as a collaboration, was shelved.

Yet there had been one more task completed. Major Pollard had revised *A History of Firearms* during the late 1950s. His own personal copy was criss-crossed with innumerable amendments and there were many additional sheets of MS. It had all been carefully re-typed–in a nearby nunnery, of all places–some 600 pages, together with a further 100 pages of his revised List of Gunmakers. But the numerous new publications that began to appear in the 1950s had already made further revision necessary and this was beyond the scope of one man alone living quietly in the country. In 1959, he signed over all rights in *A History of Firearms* to Eyre and Spottiswoode as the basis for a completely new edition to be comprehensively revised by a team of the leading firearms writers under the editorship of Mr. Claude Blair. And Pollard's own revision was laid aside with 'Forensic Ballistics' to gather dust. Mr. Claude Blair eventually acquired the copyright and took the project to the Hamlyn Publishing Group. *Pollard's History of Firearms* is now being published by Country Life Books, an imprint of Newnes Books, which is a Division of the Hamlyn Publishing Group.

All this was implicit in the 'parcel of his papers' that his Executors had asked me to examine some time after they had received them from the Imperial War Museum where they had been sent from the Armouries, H.M. Tower of London, who had removed them and retained certain items for safe keeping when Major Hugh B. C. Pollard died aged seventy-eight in 1966.

For a time, burning the papers had been considered; and this might well have been done had not one learned gentleman taken to reading 'Forensic Ballistics' over his port and sandwich at lunch time and found it fascinating, and had not 'MacHastings' been consulted and had he not counselled otherwise.

That learned gentleman, the lawyer for the Pollard Trust, Mr. W. H. Betts, had urged me to visit Mrs. Pollard. She would, he had said, be delighted to talk to anyone interested in her husband's work. And so it proved. Although nearly eighty, she had met me at Haslemere, had waited an hour that cold, foggy morning because my train had broken down, and had then driven me to their last home in the house on the hill near Midhurst.

Surrounded by Pollard's possessions, his well-stocked library–a writer's library–his swords on the green-baize door panel, all that remained of his weapons collection (for '. . . they wouldn't even leave me one pistol . . .' she had complained), I began to perceive the domestic Pollard through her eyes. Still enthusiastic, almost girlishly enthusiastic, she gladly offered copies of Pollard's early works, long out of print, and a few more papers to take way to brood over. Strangely, there had been many gaps in her knowledge of his working life, things I had learned which she had forgotten or had never known because of his habitual reticence. And there were many things I forgot to ask that most loyal and tolerant of wives before it was forever too late. Now she, too, has gone. The sources of accurate personal information, one by one, have vanished away.

Then there had been the framed photographs, all along the wall. Had *he* hung them, I wondered? Pollard, the young soldier; Pollard, Military Intelligence; Pollard, the firearms expert; Pollard, the successful writer; one of Franco when young, autographed; Pollard, the prickly enigma, Knight of the Order of St. Anne, Chevalier of the Red Arrows of Spain; Pollard, the shooting man, the hunting man; Pollard, debonaire in glistening topper, something a shade sardonic in his smile. Pausing over the last, 'There he is,' Ruth Pollard had said softly, smiling her whimsical old lady's smile, gazing fondly yet with a chuckle, a curious hint of ambivalence, 'there he is . . . the old devil. . . .' There were so many aspects of Pollard, mere glimpses only, in all those old pictures and in forty pounds or so of dusty papers. Somewhere in all this, in some elusive and undiscovered combination perhaps, there would be the essential Hugh Pollard.

When there were no more papers–except for a few small sheets with the last, almost illegible and soon abandoned beginnings of letter drafts–many questions still remained unanswered. But the author no longer seemed so shadowy: he had emerged at least clearly outlined by his own industry.

JOHN BREWER

CHAPTER ONE

Early Firearms

Claude Blair

The Origins of Gunpowder

80, 82 The early history of firearms, in the modern sense of
83 the term,[1] is still obscure. The view, once widely held, that they are mentioned in the Gentoo (i.e. Hindu) Laws of 300 BC is based on a mistranslation, while other alleged early references to the use of firearms in India have been shown to be quite unacceptable. Recent research[2] suggests that a form of gunpowder was probably first used by the Chinese – but only for incendiary and pyrotechnic weapons – not later than the first half of the eleventh century AD. The evidence for this, however, is not absolutely reliable, for the text in which it is contained, the military treatise *Wu Ching Tsung Yao*, though originally completed in *c.*1040 is available only in a fifteenth century copy to which additions may have been made.[3]

The generally accepted view at the present time regarding the introduction of gunpowder in Europe is that the formula for its manufacture was brought here through the medium of Arabic alchemical treatises, possibly via Spain, in the first half of the thirteenth century. Again, however, the evidence is unreliable, for it has yet to be proved that the Arabs were acquainted with gunpowder at a date prior to its earliest recorded mention in a European document. Moreover, even if the Arabs did know of gunpowder before it appeared in Europe, it seems to be quite certain that they did not recognise its use as an explosive propellant, for all the available evidence points to the conclusion that the gun is a Western invention.

The earliest definite evidence for the existence of gunpowder comes from European sources of the thirteenth century. These are as follows:

1. The *Epistolae, Opus Majus* and *Opus Tertium* of Roger Bacon

Three works of the English philosopher and alchemist Roger Bacon (*c.*1214–92/4). The best known of these is the treatise *Epistolae de secretis operibus artis et naturae et de nullitate magiae,* which was probably written soon after 1257, and not later than 1265. At the end of Chapter XI occurs a famous passage containing what is widely believed to be a formula for gunpowder given partly as an anagram:

> Sed tamen sal petrae *Luro vopo vir can vtriet* sulphuris; et si facies tonitruum et coruscationem, si scias artificium.

Lt Col H. W. L. Hime[4] rearranged the letters of the words given in italics, which are meaningless as they stand, to read 'R[ecipe] VII PART[es], V NOV[ellae] CORUL[i], V ET', so producing the following translation of the whole passage:

> But take 7 parts of saltpetre, 5 of young hazelwood [charcoal] and 5 of sulphur; and so you may make thunder and lightning, if you know the trick.

The given proportions of saltpetre, charcoal and sulphur would produce perfectly satisfactory gunpowder, but it should be noted that there is apparently no known manuscript authority for the 'cipher', which is first recorded in a printed version of Bacon's works published in Paris in 1542. There is, in fact, considerable controversy among students of the history of science not only about its interpretation but also about its authenticity as one of Bacon's writings.[5] A fifteenth century manuscript[6] of the treatise in the British Library contains a completely

---

1 Various incendiary weapons, such as Greek Fire, used from Classical times onwards should strictly be included under the heading *firearms.* As those fall outside the scope of this book the term is confined here to weapons using the power of exploding gunpowder to propel a projectile. But see p. 425.

2 For a very full discussion of the evidence relating to the origins and early use of gunpowder the reader is referred to J. R. Partington, *A History of Greek Fire and Gunpowder,* Cambridge, 1960.

3 See, however, p. 426.

4 Lt Col H. W. L. Hime, *Gunpowder and Ammunition, Their Origin and Progress,* London, 1904, pp. 156–8.

5 See Partington, *op.cit.*, pp. 70–6; Lynn Thorndike, *A History of Magic and Experimental Science*, Vol. II, New York, 1923, pp. 616–91; George Sarton, *Introduction to the History of Science*, Vol. II, Baltimore, 1931, pp. 1036–8.

6 Sloane Ms. 2165.

different version of the cipher which has not yet been solved.

In the *Epistolae* Bacon does, however, refer to a material from which 'sound like thunder and flashes in the air can be made, indeed greater horrors than those produced naturally'. He gives no indication of the composition of this material, but two similar passages in his *Opus Majus* of 1267 and his *Opus Tertium* of 1266-8 leave little doubt that it was gunpowder. The more important of these, from the *Opus Tertium*, is as follows (translated from the original Latin):

> By the flash and combustion of fires, and by the horror of sounds, wonders can be wrought, and at any distance that we wish–so that a man can hardly protect himself or endure it. There is a child's toy of sound and fire made in various parts of the world with powder of saltpetre, sulphur and charcoal of hazelwood. The powder is enclosed in an instrument of parchment the size of a finger, and since this can make such a noise that it seriously distresses the ears of men, especially if one is taken unawares, and the terrible flash is also very alarming, if an instrument of large size were used no one could stand the terror of the noise and the flash. If the instrument were made of solid material the violence of the explosion would be much greater.

2. The *Book of Fires* of Mark the Greek (Marcus Graecus Liber Ignium)

This is a collection of recipes for various incendiary devices and compounds–including gunpowder–some of which go back at least as far as the eighth century. The identity of Mark the Greek, if he existed at all, is unknown, but the view, first put forward in the eighteenth century, that he lived in the eighth century cannot be accepted. The earliest known manuscripts of the *Liber Ignium* date from *c.*1300, and it is now considered that these represent compilations made from various sources at various dates, the gunpowder recipes having been added during the thirteenth century. These last deal with the making of rockets and crackers ('flying fire' and 'thunder') and contain no reference to the propellant powers of exploding gunpowder.

3. The *De Mirabilibus Mundi* of St Albert Magnus (d. 1280)

This work, which is a semi-magical scientific treatise, includes a number of recipes for incendiary and pyrotechnic devices. Two of these are the 'flying fire' and 'thunder' recipes exactly as given in the *Liber Ignium* of Mark the Greek from which they may well have been copied, though the converse is equally possible. It should be noted that the treatise is not certainly by Albert Magnus and its precise date is therefore in some doubt. No manuscript of it dating from within the saint's lifetime is recorded, so that even if his authorship were definitely established the possibility would still remain that the gunpowder recipes were later interpolations.

It seems clear from the above that although both the composition of gunpowder and its explosive properties were well known in Europe by the end of the thirteenth century its powers as a propellant, other than for rockets, were not. A study of the earliest–that is late-thirteenth century–Arabic sources containing references to gunpowder points to a similar conclusion for the Moslem world, with one possible exception. This is a copy, dated 1474, of an earlier Arabic treatise entitled *Collections Concerning the Various Branches of Art*, preserved in the Institute of the Peoples of Asia at Leningrad (Ms. C686). Included in a section dealing with incendiary devices is an account, with illustrations, of a primitive handgun called a *midfa*,[7] which consists of a wooden cylinder attached to a pole. It is described as being loaded one-third full with gunpowder and used for discharging arrows or bullets.[8] The importance of the device in the history of firearms depends entirely on the date of composition of the treatise in which it is described. If, as has been suggested by some writers, it was written at the very beginning of the fourteenth century it provides the earliest known evidence for the existence of guns, and the credit for their invention must almost certainly be given to the Arabs. But the evidence for ascribing the work to so early a date is merely that it cites a *Treatise on horsemanship and strategems of war* written *c.*1280 by Al-Hasan al-Rammāh (*d.*1294-5) and also mentions Ghāzan, Khān of Persia who died in 1304. Its date cannot therefore be regarded as firmly fixed, and it may well have been composed, or include material added, long after the early-fourteenth century.

Certainly all the other available evidence from Arabic sources would seem to point to the conclusion that guns were not used in the Moslem world until some years after their use is first recorded in Europe.

---

7 *Midfa* was a common term for a cannon in Moslem lands from the second half of the fourteenth century onwards. The term is discussed very fully by D. Ayalon in *Gunpowder and Firearms in the Mamluk Kingdom*, London, 1956.

8 The treatise also contains a description of another, and apparently quite impractical device for projecting arrows. It consists of a wooden rod drilled to contain an iron tube (also called a *midfa*) which was attached to it by a length of silk cord. A charge of gunpowder was placed behind the tube and an arrow in it. When the device was fired the tube was discharged with the arrow, only to be arrested by the cord, leaving the arrow to continue its flight alone.

The Earliest Guns

According to a tradition dating back in Germany to at least the beginning of the fifteenth century, guns (and in some versions gunpowder also) were invented by a German or Greek monk called Black Berthold (Berthold Schwartz, Bertholdus Niger). Varying dates for his invention have been suggested–some considerably later than those of the first recorded guns–but, in fact, no acceptable evidence for his historical existence has ever been discovered. On the other hand, the view put forward by a number of modern writers that he was a purely legendary figure–a kind of 'folk' inventor–is not based on any positive evidence either. The possibility exists, therefore, that the story of Berthold's invention contains an element of truth and, though it cannot be accepted as a historical fact, neither can it be dismissed out of hand as unworthy of serious consideration. The wisest course in the present state of our knowledge would seem to be to keep an entirely open mind on the subject.

The earliest firm date in the history of the gun is 1326.[9] On 11 February of that year the Council of Florence issued a decree to the effect that two officials should be appointed to the task of making iron bullets (or arrows) and metal cannon (*pilas seu palloctas ferreas et canones de metallo*) for the defence of the castles and lands of the Republic. Other documents of the same year in the archives at Florence record payments made to Rinaldo di Villamagna for cannon, iron balls and gunpowder.[10]

Some idea of the probable shape of the Florentine cannon can be obtained from an illustration of a gun,
88 the earliest known, in a contemporary English manuscript from the library of Christ Church, Oxford.[11] This is a treatise–*De Nobilitatibus, Sapientiis, et Prudentiis Regum*–on the duties of a king, written for Edward III by Walter de Milemete and dated 1327. Some of the illustrations in the manuscript show various siege-weapons. Included among them is one of a mail-clad soldier firing a cannon which rests on a support like a trestle-table, and from the muzzle of which a large arrow is issuing. The gun is shaped like a long-necked vase with a flared mouth and has a touch-hole on top to which the gunner is applying a piece of smouldering tinder attached to the end of a rod. There are no indications of any fastenings holding it to the trestle, or of a recoil-stop behind it.

The authenticity of the Milemete miniature as the earliest illustration of a gun has been doubted, mainly on the following grounds: **1.** It is suggested that the miniature was not included in the manuscript originally, but was inserted in a space conveniently left in the text long after this had been written. But, as was pointed out by the late M. R. James, the arrangement of the text points to its having been written round the illustrations and not vice versa so that the latter in fact date from slightly before the date on the manuscript, which is that of its completion.[12] **2.** It is further suggested that a gun of the shape shown in the illustration, with its narrow neck and bulbous powder-chamber, would have burst on ignition instead of discharging its projectile. Even if it did not burst, its recoil, in the absence of any fastenings or recoil-stop, would have blown it back off its trestle on to the gunner. The artist must therefore have drawn the gun from his imagination or from an imperfectly understood description of such a weapon.

This criticism of the drawing is based on the quite unjustified assumption that the internal shape of the gun was more or less the same as its exterior. It seems more reasonable to assume that the bore was cylindrical and that the bulbous external shape of the rear part of the gun was the result of the need for an extra thickness of metal over the powder-chamber where the charge exploded. All gun barrels are reinforced over the chamber, though to a much less exaggerated extent. At the time when the Milemete manuscript was produced, however, the power of gunpowder was probably enough of an unknown quantity to make excessive reinforcement seem necessary. Indeed, as recently as 1830 a bronze cannon of very similar external appearance to that in the miniature and with a cylindrical bore was produced in Japan.[13]

The absence of any fastening or recoil-stop for the cannon in the miniature is more difficult to explain. This may simply be carelessness on the part of the artist, or a stop may be concealed by the support but it is also conceivable that the low power of early gunpowder, coupled with the great weight of metal in the cannon, would have made any attachments unnecessary. A practical experiment made with a full-sized reproduction of the cannon would solve this problem.

9 For a discussion of a number of allegedly earlier references to guns none of which can be accepted, see Partington, *op.cit.*, Chapter 3.

10 It has been suggested that these records are spurious. For reasons given by R. Davidson in his *Geschichte von Florenz*, Berlin, 1896–1927, Vol. III, pp. 758–9; IV, i, p. 249; IV, ii, p. 21, they must be accepted as authentic.

11 Bodleian Library, Ms. Ch. Ch. Coll. 92, f. 70^{v}.

12 M. R. James, *The Treatise of Walter de Milemete, etc.*, Roxburgh Club, Oxford, 1913.

13 See A. Hoff, *Feuerwaffen*, Brunswick, 1969, I, pp. 60–65 and *Zeitschrift für historische Waffenkunde*, Vol. XV, (1937–9) pp. 139–40.

The other illustrations of military devices in the Milemete manuscript have every appearance of being accurately observed. It seems reasonable, therefore, to accept the illustration of the gun as an authentic representation of something that actually existed. It should be mentioned that a similar, though larger, gun is illustrated in another manuscript attributed to Milemete, formerly at Holkham Hall, Norfolk, and now in the British Library.[14]

For some reason that has yet to be satisfactorily explained, no other illustration of a gun dating certainly from before the very end of the fourteenth century has been noted.[15] For our information about firearms of this period we are therefore forced to rely almost entirely on documentary sources. After the Florentine references cited above the earliest known firmly-dated mention of firearms is contained in a receipt in the Bibliothèque Nationale, Paris, dated 2 July 1338, and relating to the issue by Thomas Fouques, 'garde du clos des galées du roy à Rouen' of 'un pot de fer à traire garros à feu, 48 garros ferrés et empanés en 2 cassez, une livre de salpêtre et demi livre de souffre vif pour faire poudre pour traire lesd. garros'.[16] The iron pot for shooting iron-shod arrows (*garros ferrés*) was probably similar to the guns shown in the Milemete manuscripts.

From *c.*1340 onwards references to firearms gradually become increasingly common in the records of the major countries of Europe, and it is clear from these that by the end of the third quarter of the fourteenth century the use of the new weapon had become general. A very thorough survey of the documentary material relating to the history of firearms in Europe during the fourteenth century was published by Bernard Rathgen[17] and no useful purpose would be served by entering into details here. Instead, we can consider very briefly a series of fourteenth-century accounts which, though they were apparently overlooked by Rathgen, give an excellent picture of the kind of development that was taking place all over Europe in this field.

The accounts in question are those of the English Royal Chamber, and in particular those of the Privy Wardrobe which was the chief armoury and arsenal of the English crown during the second half of the fourteenth century.[18] They are of particular importance for a study of this kind in that they are preserved in an almost unbroken sequence for the whole of the second half of the fourteenth century.

The earliest entry that probably relates to firearms is contained in an account covering the period 25 January 1333 to 31 July 1334 and simply records the purchase of a small quantity of sulphur and saltpetre. This was probably, though not certainly, for making gunpowder. The next payment of this type, which records the purchase of 10 lb of powder for the navy in 1341-2 is also doubtful, but in 1345 appears the first of a long series of entries in which guns are specifically mentioned. It refers to the repair of guns with arrows and pellets (*gunnis cum saggitis et pellotis*), a fact that would seem to indicate that these weapons had already been in use for some time.

In 1346 several orders were issued for the preparation and shipping to France of guns kept in the Tower of London. They were to be accompanied by storage chests, large and small lead pellets, pieces of lead for making pellets, and barrels of powder, saltpetre and sulphur. Some idea of the quantity of ammunition involved can be obtained from the fact that one order out of many was for no less than 912 lb of saltpetre and 886 lb of quick sulphur. The guns are sometimes described as having tillers (*cum telariis*), a term normally applied to the stock of a cross-bow, but here clearly referring to a gun-stock of similar shape. Two guns with tillers are specifically described as being large so it may reasonably be assumed that the others were fairly small, perhaps small enough to be classified as handguns, though the term itself is not recorded until much later in the century. This view is supported by the mention in one section of the account of 'hand engines called guns' (*manualia ingenia vocata gunnys*).

It is clear from the above that by 1346 firearms were no longer a rarity in England. The remaining accounts, covering the period down to January 1399, show an ever-increasing number of similar entries. The following are of particular interest.

1353: The material of which the guns are made is mentioned for the first time. The term used is *cupro* which, translated literally means copper, but it was applied loosely to brass and bronze at this time. It

14 Add. Ms. 47680.

15 See *Journal of the Arms and Armour Society*, Vol. VIII, (1974-6), pp. 234-7. The allegedly fourteenth century wall-paintings showing cannon in the church of St Leonardo in Siena actually date from the fifteenth century.

16 Victor Gay, *Glossaire Archéologique du Moyen Age et de la Renaissance*, Vol. I, Paris 1887, p. 76. The Italian chronicle of Juliane, which can probably be accepted as reliable, says that guns (*vasa* and *schiopi*) were used in 1331 in an attack on Cividale, Friule (Partington, *op.cit.*, p. 102).

17 Bernard Rathgen, *Das Geschütz im Mittelalter*, Berlin, 1928.

18 A very full study of the references to firearms in the accounts was published by T. F. Tout in 'Firearms in England in the Fourteenth Century', *The English Historical Review*, Vol. XXVI, 1911, pp. 666-702 (Reprinted in *The Collected Papers of Thomas Frederick Tout*, Vol. II, Manchester, 1934, pp. 233-75, and as a separate booklet, London, 1968). All the extracts given here are taken from this article.

appears throughout the accounts. The same account mentions, also for the first time, a copper mortar and an iron pestle, presumably for preparing gunpowder.
1361: Small guns mentioned.
1365: Large and small guns mentioned together.
1373-5: Payment for attaching handles to eight guns and ten axes from old stock '*ad modum pycoys*', that is in the manner of pikes or spears. These were probably hand-guns of the type described below.

This account also mentions for the first time guns made of iron, 'drivelles' (i.e. ramrods) of iron and firing-irons, together with latten (i.e. brass) moulds for casting pellets, and iron ladles, presumably for melting the lead. Some of the guns are described as being accompanied by 'pots', a term that probably refers to a separate chamber of the type described on page 30 below.
1382-96: This mentions stone shot for the first time, apparently for use with large cannon, lead pellets being reserved for the smaller ones. Wooden tampons are also mentioned, though it is not clear whether these were intended, as later, to close the muzzle of the cannon when they were not in use, or whether they were to be placed like wadding between the powder and the ball. It is interesting to note that this account includes arrows (quarrels) among the ammunition for firearms.

Of special interest in the account is the record of the issue, by writ of 7 November 1388, of 'three small cannon called hand-guns' (*iij canones paruos vocatos handgunnes*) together with three copper moulds for casting pellets and thirty-one large quarrels 'for small cannon'. This appears to be the first recorded use of the term *handgun*.

Most writers on early firearms have put forward the view that the first guns were fairly large pieces of artillery, and that the handgun did not develop until the second half of the fourteenth century. This seems unreasonable on grounds of common sense alone; moreover, as we have seen, there is documentary evidence suggesting the use of hand firearms as early as 1346. In fact, what is generally accepted
1 as the earliest surviving gun–excavated at Loshult, Sweden in 1861 and now in the National Historical Museum, Stockholm–was clearly designed to be used in the hand. Cast from a single piece of bronze and only $11\frac{13}{16}$ in long, it is formed like a flask swelling at the breech and narrowing until it is almost cylindrical at the muzzle, where there is a narrow moulding; the back of the breech is almost flat. Its external form, in short, is almost exactly like that of the two Milemete guns, for which reason it is generally dated to the first half of the fourteenth century. Its bore is tubular with a calibre of 1·41 in at the muzzle, tapering to 1·22 in before widening again to 1·41 in to form the powder-chamber. A circular touch-hole is drilled at right-angles into the chamber, and it should be noted that the mouth of this is countersunk to form a *pan*, for easier ignition of the priming powder, as on later firearms.

The Loshult gun shows no signs of any fittings for attaching it to a stock, but an explanation of the way in which this was probably effected can be obtained from a group of early guns in several Continental museums, notably that at Pilsen in Czechoslovakia. The date of these is uncertain, though they are clearly medieval, but it seems very likely, in view of their primitive form, that they were made during the fourteenth century or very early in the fifteenth century. They have short iron barrels–some little larger than that of the Loshult gun–polygonal in section and of more or less even thickness throughout. Each is set in a channel in the stepped forward end of a wooden stock, so that the flattened rear end butts against the back of the step. It is held in position by one or more iron bands, one of which is usually equipped with a flat, downward-projecting lug. This last, which acted as a recoil-stop when hooked over a parapet, led to the name *Hakenbüchse* (i.e. hook-gun) being applied to a gun fitted with it.[19] The term, as we shall see, later came to have a much broader connotation.

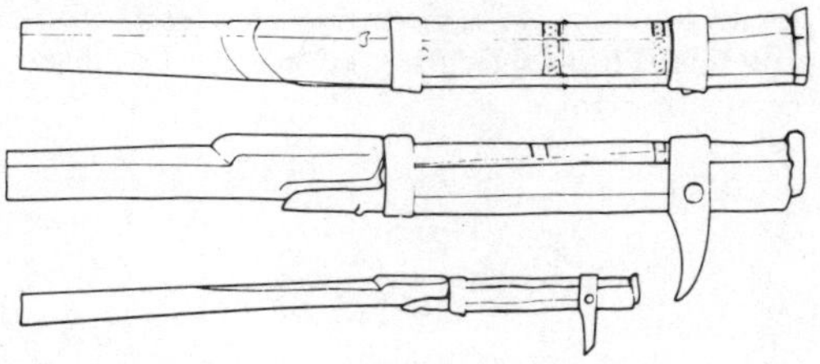

Handguns with iron barrels and wooden stocks. German, fourteenth – fifteenth centuries. City Museum, Pilsen.

The thick, heavy stocks of the Pilsen guns are of polygonal section where they support the barrel and for some distance to the rear of this. They then change to triangular section and, for the most part, splay out slightly to form a clumsy butt which was apparently designed to be held under the arm. Nearly all are quite straight, but a few bend down at a slight angle to the rear of the barrel.

Apart from the Loshult example only two guns that can be dated with certainty to the fourteenth

19 There can be no doubt that this is the origin of the word *Hakenbüchse* and through it of the English *Hackbut* and the French-English *Harquebus*. The illustrated inventory of the Landshut Arsenal, drawn up in 1485, for example, shows *Hagnpuchsen* and *Handtpuchsen* (i.e. handguns) which differ only in that the former have hooks. See *Zeitschrift für historische Waffenkunde*, Vol. I, 1897-9, pp. 282, 300-1.

century are known. Each is of bronze and consists of a polygonal barrel of normal cannon form, thickened over the chamber, and cast in one with a socket into which a wooden pole-like stock was fitted. It seems likely, in fact, that they are of the same construction as the English guns hafted '*ad modum pycoys*' mentioned above (p. 29). They are:

1. A gun fished out of the sea near Mörkö, Sweden at the beginning of the nineteenth century and now
2 in the National Historical Museum, Stockholm. It is decorated with religious inscriptions in German and Latin and on top, with the small bust of a man whose hair and beard styles indicate a date in the last quarter of the fourteenth century. It also has a hook below, and should therefore be classified as a *Hackenbüchse*. The touch-hole on top is countersunk to form a shallow pan for the priming powder. The total length is only $7\frac{19}{32}$ in and the calibre 0·82 in.

2. A gun excavated from the ruins of the Castle of Tannenberg in Hesse, destroyed in 1399, and now in the Germanisches Nationalmuseum, Nuremberg. It is larger than the Mörkö example and undecorated, but is otherwise of very similar form. It has a countersunk touch-hole and, a particularly interesting feature, the bore is constricted at the mouth of the powder-chamber to concentrate the force of the explosion. The total length is $12\frac{4}{5}$ in and the calibre at the muzzle 0·70 in.

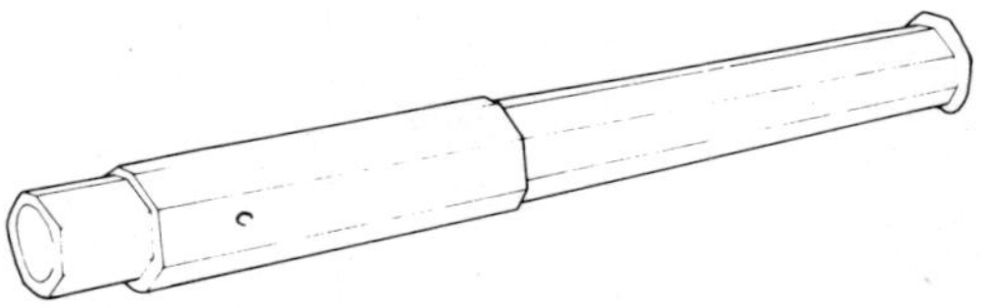

Bronze hand-gun from Burg Tannenberg, Hesse. German, pre-1399. Germanisches Nationalmuseum, Nuremberg.

A number of other examples of guns of the same general type as the above are known, some of which may date from the fourteenth century. It is not possible to be certain of this, however, as there is pictorial evidence to show that similar firearms remained in use until the second half of the fifteenth century.[20] These same fifteenth-century illustrations show that there were apparently three main methods of holding guns of this form when they were fired. The stock was rested on top of the shoulder, or tucked under the arm, or rested on the ground so that the gun sloped up at an angle. When the last method was used the barrel was often supporterted on a forked rest. In each case the gun was loaded down the muzzle and the charge was ignited at the touch-hole by means of a hot iron or a piece of smouldering slow-match held in the gunner's free hand or, in some instances, wielded by a companion.

Some surviving iron handguns, instead of being socketed for a wooden haft, are forged in one with a long, metal rod that performs the same function. A good example is provided by a gun in the Tøjhusmuseum, Copenhagen, which was excavated on the site of the Castle of Vedelspang (destroyed in 1426), in Schleswig. It is forged from iron into a single piece, except for a ring carrying a 'hook' that is apprently shrunk on to the barrel.

Fragments of two iron guns of the same form as the Vedelspang one, but of slightly different construction, were found in the precincts of Castle Rising, Norfolk, during the last century and are now kept in the Tower of London. They are 'built up' in a similar manner to a number of large medieval cannon, for example the fifteenth-century bombard known as Mons Meg at Edinburgh Castle. Each barrel consisted originally of a tube, made from a sheet of iron bent round, with shorter and thicker tubes separated by rings shrunk over it. A solid breech containing the chamber and made in one with an iron haft was welded on at the rear. They probably date from the fifteenth century.

Also found at Castle Rising was a bronze hand-cannon, now unfortunately missing, and another iron gun which, though possibly designed for use in the hand, is more likely to have been a piece of light artillery. It is constructed in the same manner as the other iron guns from the same source, but the breech is left open to receive the flanged lip of a separate wrought-iron chamber. Several chambers were found and each one was probably held in the firing position by a wedge inserted between its rear face and the stock of the gun.

The early method of igniting firearms, by means of a separate iron or piece of match, must, for obvious reasons, have been particularly inconvenient when applied to a handgun. At some unknown date in the late-fourteenth or early-fifteenth century the first semi-mechanical device for firing was produced, the matchlock. The earliest evidence of its use is provided by an illustration in a German manuscript
of 1411.[21] This depicts a man firing a handgun with 3
a long, pole-like stock to which is pivoted a lever of elongated Z-shape – the so-called serpentine – the upper end of which holds a piece of smouldering match. When the lower end of the serpentine, which served as a trigger, was squeezed or pressed towards the stock the match descended into the pan.

The form of lock just described is shown in illustrations as late as the last quarter of the fifteenth century, but no authentic example is known to

20 See *Zeitschrift für historische Waffenkunde*, Vol. I, 1897–9, pp. 138–9, 252–3.

21 Austrian National Library, Vienna, cod. Ms. 3069.

survive. It was a remarkable, if simple, invention, for it reduced the act of discharge, which had previously been the work of one hand, to a mere pressure of the forefinger, an economy of effort that has not been improved upon to date. The gunner now had two hands with which to aim and steady his piece, and this may be taken as the point where the true hand-gun develops out of the rudimentary stage when it was really only a miniature version of the field cannon fired from a carriage.

Though the first form of matchlock remained in use until nearly the end of the fifteenth century, two improved versions had been developed before this,
4 probably as early as *c.*1470.[22] Both were built round a flat lockplate that was screwed to the side of the stock, and each had a short curved serpentine or cock with jaws that held a match and which was dipped mechanically into the pan. On one form, the snap-matchlock, the cock was kept pressed into the pan by the action of a weak spring. Attached to the interior of the lockplate was a springy lever carrying a stud or sear which passed through a hole in the plate immediately below a projecting toe on the bottom of the cock: at its rear end it carried a button trigger that also projected through the lockplate or, in some instances, through a recess in the side of the butt behind the plate. When the cock was pulled back the sear caught over the toe and held it back from the pan. Pressure on the trigger withdrew the sear, so allowing the cock to carry the match into the pan. This form of lock seems to have gone out of general use in the second quarter of the sixteenth century, but examples dating from as late as the beginning of the seventeenth century are known. By this date the button trigger had generally been replaced by a trigger of modern form. (See p. 50.)

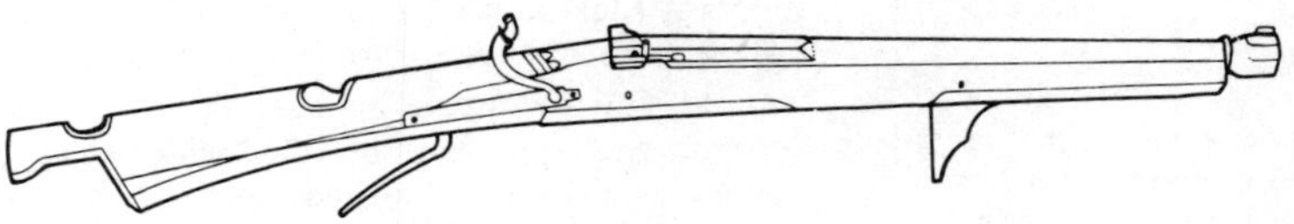

Hackbut with snap-matchlock. Swiss, fifteenth century. Historisches Museum, Bern.

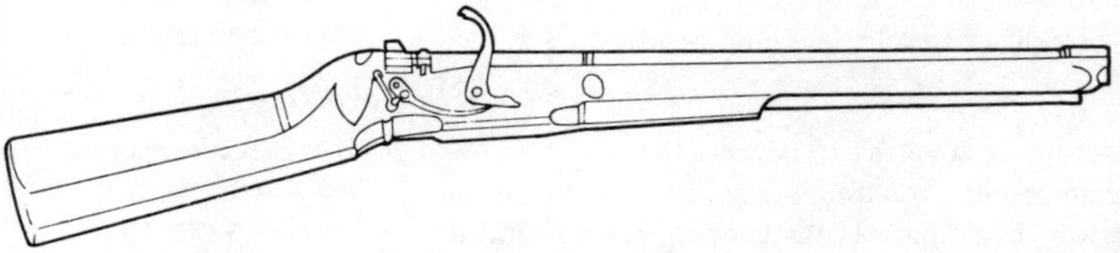

Hand-gun with snap-matchlock, on the butt the arms of Behaim of Nuremberg. German, *c.*1500. Hermitage Museum, Leningrad.

The second improved matchlock, the *sear-lock*, was very widely used until the early-seventeenth century. On this the mainspring acted in the opposite direction to that on the snap-matchlock and held the cock *away* from the pan. The spindle on which the cock pivoted was fitted on the inside with a tumbler connected to a system of interlinked levers operated by a lever-shaped trigger – like that on a crossbow – extending under the butt of the gun. Gentle pressure on the trigger lowered the cock, and its match, into the pan against the action of the spring: when the pressure was released the cock was withdrawn.

Two developments that may or may not have been connected with the invention of the matchlock can be conveniently mentioned at this point. The first of these was the introduction, probably in *c.*1400, of a pivoted, manually-operated, metal cover for the pan, designed to protect the priming-powder from the weather and also to make it possible for the gun to be kept ready primed. Secondly, from probably the third quarter of the fifteenth century, the touch-hole was normally drilled from the side and accompanied by a short projecting lug containing the pan: henceforth, the only exceptions to this arrangement were guns designed to be ignited by hand in the old way.

The introduction of a semi-mechanical ignition system made other improvements in the construction of the handgun worth while. The barrel became longer and more slender and, during the third quarter of the fifteenth century, the stock developed a form that for the first time began to resemble, if only remotely, that of the modern rifle. The butt was now flat and oblong, and could be held against the shoulder or, more usually, pressed against the cheek, when the gun was fired. Many stocks of this type are shown in the illustrations to Diebold Schilling's *Berne Chronicle* of 1474–83 and, in fact, it became more or 6
less the standard form until the 1530s. It is often called the 'Landsknecht stock' (*Landsknecht Kolbe*)

22 See *Zeitschrift für historische Waffenkunde*, Vol. I, 1897–9, p. 255.

because it is shown so frequently in contemporary illustrations of armed Landsknechts.

Before concluding this chapter three other developments of the fifteenth century can be mentioned briefly.

1. At some unknown date towards the end of the century the old method of attaching the barrel to the stock by bands was replaced by one that was henceforth almost universally used in Europe. A series of pierced lugs were now brazed or welded to the underside of the barrel and these were secured in recesses in the stock by transverse pins.

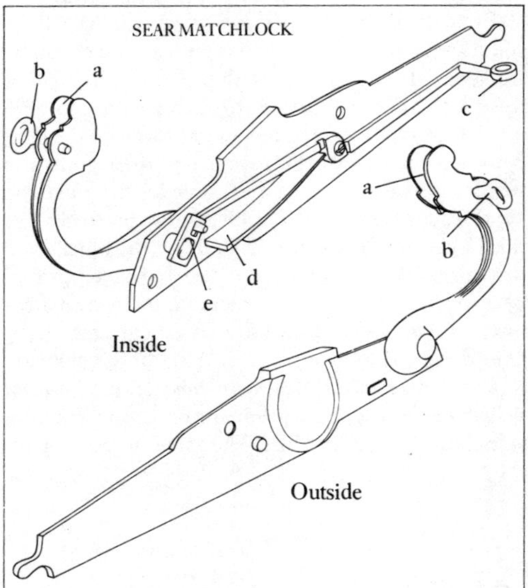

The sear-lever is linked at (c) to a long lever trigger like that of a crossbow. Upward pressure on this causes the opposite end of the sear-lever to move downwards against the action of the mainspring (d), so moving the tumbler (e) attached to the cock-spindle, so tipping the smouldering match held in the jaws of the cock (a & b) into the pan.

2. Again at some unknown date towards the end of the century a new barrel construction was introduced. Hitherto, apart from the built-up construction mentioned on page 30 above, the normal method of making a barrel had been to cast it in one piece if it were of brass or bronze, or forge it in one piece if it were of iron. Henceforth, the usual method was to make it first as a tube open at both ends and then to close the rear end with a screwed breech-plug. This method made the manufacture of iron barrels much easier and henceforth brass and bronze barrels gradually became less common on hand firearms.

3. It is possible, though by no means certain, that rifling was introduced at the end of the fifteenth century. This consists of a series of longitudinal spiral grooves in the inner surface of the barrel designed to impart a rotary motion to the projectile, so equalising any irregularities in its flight and lessening its tendency to deviate from a straight line. According to a 'tradition' that seems never to have been investigated the system was invented either in Vienna or Nuremberg in the late-fifteenth or early-sixteenth century. There seems to be good reason for locating the invention somewhere in the German cultural area as all the earliest known rifles are German. With one rather doubtful exception discussed below, however, all date from after *c.*1540,[23] so it would be unwise to place too much reliance on the 'traditional' date for the invention of rifling.

The exception mentioned in the last paragraph is a handgun of 'Landsknecht' type in the Smithsonian Institution, Washington.[24] On the stock is painted a single-headed eagle of the form used by the later Emperor Maximilian I as his coat-of-arms between 1498 and 1508. It seems reasonably certain, therefore, that the gun was made between those dates. The bronze barrel appears to be rifled with twelve very shallow grooves at the muzzle but, owing to corrosion, they cannot be traced further down the bore. This being so, and in the absence of other evidence, the gun can be accepted as the earliest known rifle only with very considerable reservations.

---

23 The earliest known firmly dated rifle is a German wheel-lock dated 1542 in the Tøjhusmuseum, Copenhagen (No. B. 277). See plate 13.

24 See the *American Rifleman*, March 1953, pp. 15-18, 75.

CHAPTER TWO

The Sixteenth Century

Claude Blair

During the whole of the period we have dealt with so far hand-firearms were regarded essentially as weapons of the common soldiery. They were rarely used by the upper classes, no doubt partly because of prejudice, but also because the troublesome lighted match made them unsuitable both for mounted use and for hunting. The gunsmith did not, therefore, receive the kind of patronage that made it possible for him to develop his craft into an art. The invention during the first half of the sixteenth century of purely mechanical means of ignition brought about a tremendous change. The upper classes began to use firearms both for war and – perhaps more important – for hunting, and they were prepared to pay high prices for the best workmanship. This meant that not only was the gunmaker able to experiment with technical improvements, but he was also able – indeed required – to produce finely-finished and finely-decorated arms. The history of the gunmaker's art, in the fullest sense of the word, therefore really starts in the early sixteenth century.

Systems of Ignition

It will be convenient at this point to give a short account of the mechanical systems of ignition referred to above before going on to deal with more general matters.

The Wheel-lock

10-17 This lock ignited the charge by means of sparks
21-37 struck from a piece of iron pyrites by a rotating
92-95 wheel, very much in the manner of a modern
278 cigarette lighter. In its developed form it consists normally of a flat lockplate with the wheel supported against its outer face by a bridle. The wheel-spindle passes through the plate and is linked by a short length of transmission-chain to one end of a powerful V-shaped spring attached to the inside of the plate. Also attached to the inside of the plate is a sear-lever consisting of an arm, pivoted horizontally and terminating in a small lug or sear which projects through a hole in the lockplate on to the back of the wheel. The lever is kept in this position by the pressure of a small spring. The outer end of the
wheel-spindle is squared for the attachment of a key 7-37
(spanner) by means of which the wheel can be 89-95
spanned, that is wound up. As the wheel is rotated 278-9
the transmission-chain winds round the spindle, so compressing the mainspring: after about three-quarters of a turn a recess in the back of the wheel comes opposite the sear which, under the pressure of the sear-lever spring, engages in it and so locks the wheel. Pivoted at right-angles to the plate at the rear end of the sear-lever is a trigger-lever with a spring that presses it towards the sear-lever. As the sear engages in the hole in the wheel the near end of the lever moves away from the lockplate so allowing a step in the trigger-lever to move under it and wedge it. Pressure on the trigger of the gun withdraws the trigger-lever, so releasing the sear lever. The mainspring is strong enough to overcome the sear when it is not wedged by the trigger-lever and rotates the wheel rapidly.

The wheel is so arranged that its rim passes through a slit in the bottom of the pan, which is normally attached to the top of the lockplate. This is usually equipped with a sliding spring-operated cover which, when pushed back, is held open by a catch. Pivoted to the outside of the lockplate in front or, more rarely, behind the wheel is an arm (*cock* or so-called *dog-head*) equipped at the top with a pair of screw-operated jaws which grip a piece of iron pyrites. The cock can be moved manually so that the pyrites rests against the wheel in the pan: it is held in this position or, when required, away from the pan, by the pressure of a V-shaped spring against its lower end.

The operation of a gun fitted with a wheel-lock is as follows. It is first loaded down the muzzle in the normal way and the lock is spanned. A small amount of fine gunpowder (priming) is then placed in the pan, the pan-cover is closed either manually or by pressing a release-button, and the cock is moved down until the pyrites rests on the pan-cover. Pressure on the trigger releases the wheel and as this starts to revolve a cam on its spindle strikes a lever attached to the pan-cover and forces the latter open, so bringing the pyrites into contact with the wheel. The resultant shower of sparks ignites the priming, which in turn

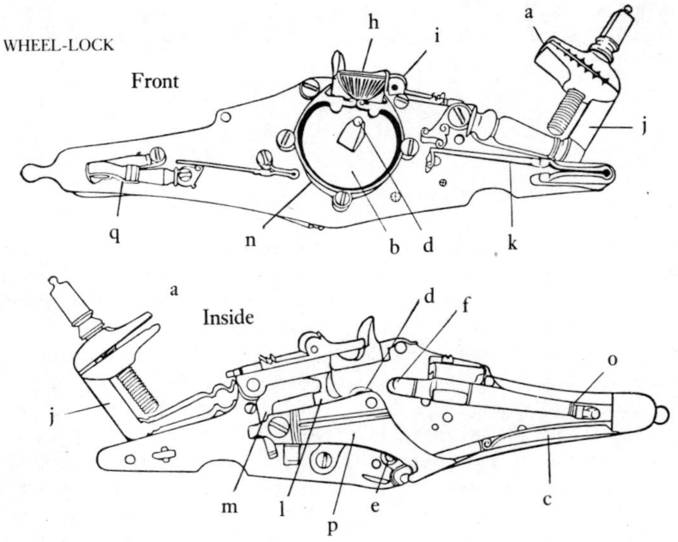

The wheel (b) is held by a bridle (n) on the outside of the lockplate, and rotates on a spindle (d), which is supported on the inside of the plate by another bridle (p) which also secures the lower arm of the V-shaped mainspring (c). The wheel-spindle and the mainspring are linked within bridle (p) by a short length of steel chain (e). A spanner is fitted to the squared end of the wheel-spindle (d) and the wheel is turned in a clockwise direction, so winding the steel chain (e) round the spindle. When the wheel has been turned through three-quarters of a revolution a recess in its rear face is engaged by the nose of a sear forming part of the spring-actuated, rocking, sear-lever (f) working through a hole in the plate, so locking it; the sear-lever itself is wedged by the trigger-sear (o) which is pushed under its rear end by a spring as its front end moves into engagement with the wheel. After the pan (h) has been primed in the usual way, the sliding pan-cover (i) is closed and the cock (j) is moved down manually until a piece of pyrites held in its jaws (a) rests on the cover; the cock is held in this position by a spring (k). Pressure on the trigger, which is pivoted separately in the stock, withdraws the trigger-sear (o) from behind the wheel-sear (f) and allow the wheel to rotate rapidly under the action of the mainspring. As this happens a cam forming part of the wheel-spindle strikes against a steel arm (l) linking the pan-cover to a pivot on the lockplate. The movement of the arms opens the cover, so causing the pyrites in the jaws of the cock to come into contact with the rotating wheel, so producing a shower of sparks to ignite the priming. A spring (m) serves to hold the pan-cover in the open or closed position. A safety-catch (q) can be made to engage with, and lock, the trigger-sear (o) when the lock is spanned. From a late-sixteenth-century German (?) lock in the Victoria & Albert Museum (No. M61-1912).

ignites the main charge through the touch-hole.

The origins of the wheel-lock are obscure, but it was probably invented by Leonardo da Vinci in *c.* 1500. The evidence for this is provided by two drawings of wheel-lock devices in the volume of Leonardo
7 manuscripts, known as the *Codex Atlanticus*.[1] It is not yet possible to date the drawings precisely, though it is generally accepted that they must have been executed at the end of the fifteenth century or very early in the sixteenth. If this is correct they provide the earliest known evidence for the existence of the wheel-lock mechanism.

One of the devices shown in Leonardo's drawing has a helical mainspring, and was probably intended only as a tinder lighter,[2] but the other is clearly a

1 *Codex Atlanticus*, Ambrosiana Library, Milan, fo. 56 v.b.

2 It should be noted, however, that a French (?) wheel-lock carbine of about 1540 in the Real Armería, Madrid (No. K.63) operates by means of a helical spring, very much in the manner of Leonardo's device. See *Zeitschrift für historische Waffenkunde*, Vol. XIII, 1932-4, pp. 226-7.

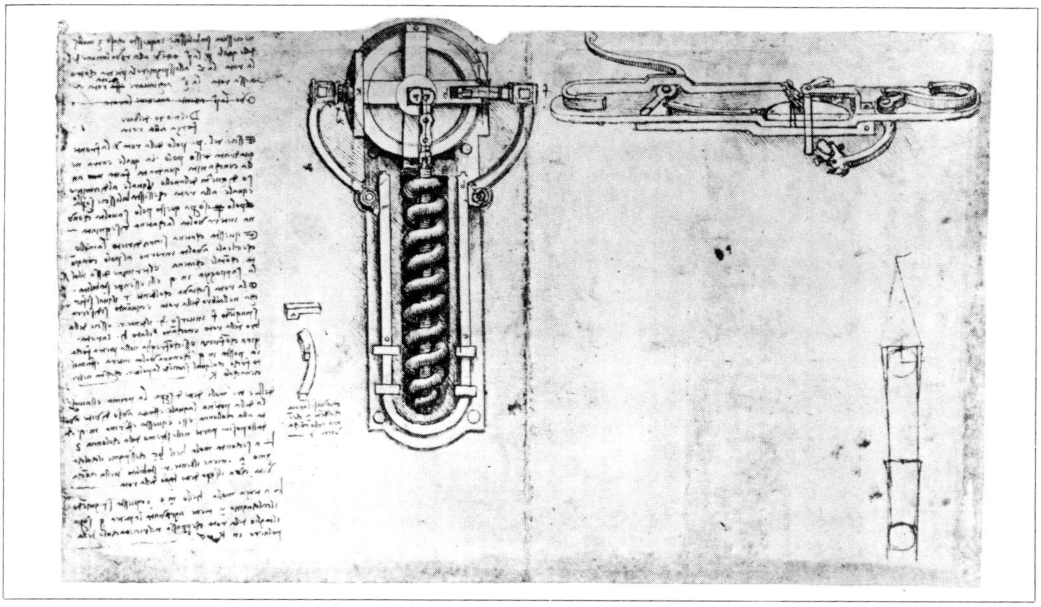

7 *Above* Designs for wheel-lock mechanisms by Leonardo da Vinci. From the *Codex Atlanticus*, probably early sixteenth century. Biblioteca Ambrosiana, Milan.

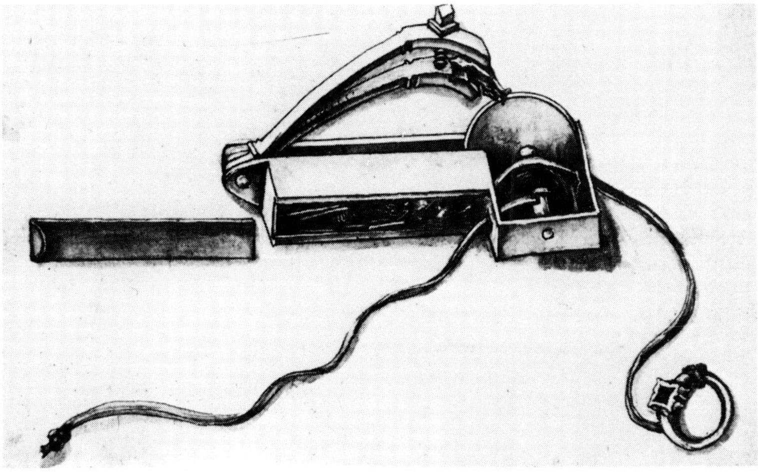

8 *Right*, *top* Drawing of a wheel-lock tinder-lighter from the Löffelholz Manuscript of 1505. Formerly Staatsbibliothek, Berlin.

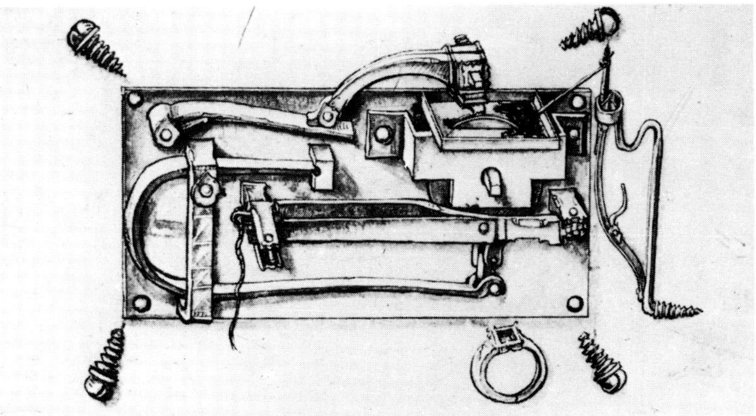

9 *Right* Drawing of a wheel-lock tinder-lighter from the Löffelholz Manuscript of 1505. Formerly Staatsbibliothek, Berlin.

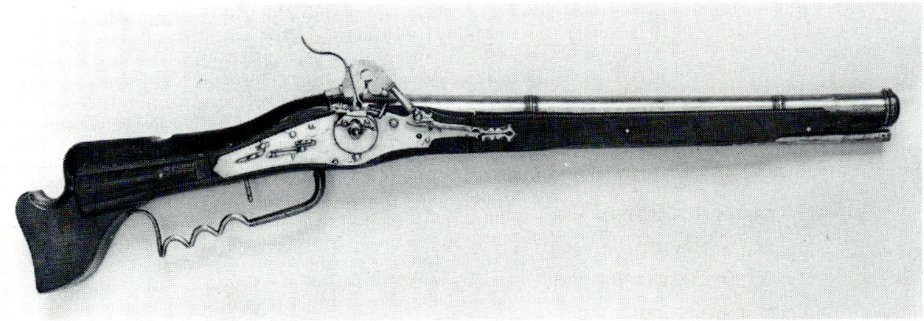

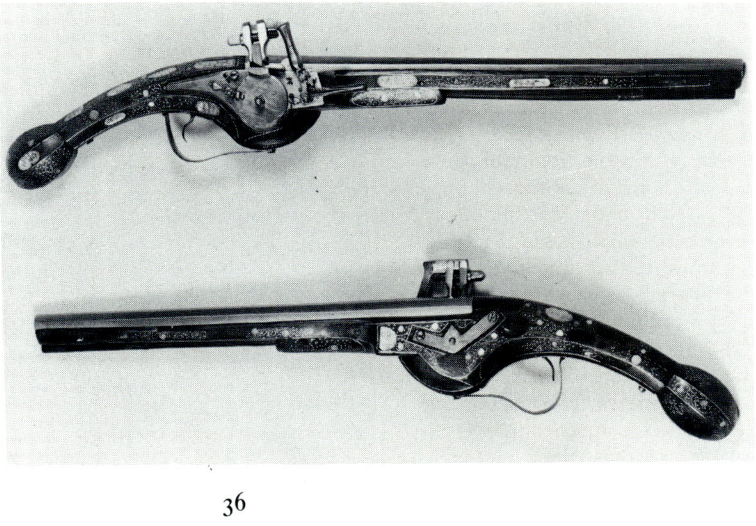

10 *Above* Combined wheel-lock gun and crossbow made for the Archduke Ferdinand of Austria. German (probably Nuremberg), between 1521 and 1526. Bayerisches Nationalmuseum, Munich.

11 *Right, top* Wheel-lock gun. The stock bears the arms and initials of Otto Heinrich, Count Palatine of the Rhine (d. 1559). South German (Augsburg), dated 1533. Bayerisches Nationalmuseum, Munich.

12 *Right* Pair of wheel-lock pistols, the stocks inlaid with brass wire and mother-of-pearl. French, *c.*1600. Formerly collection of Lord Astor of Hever.

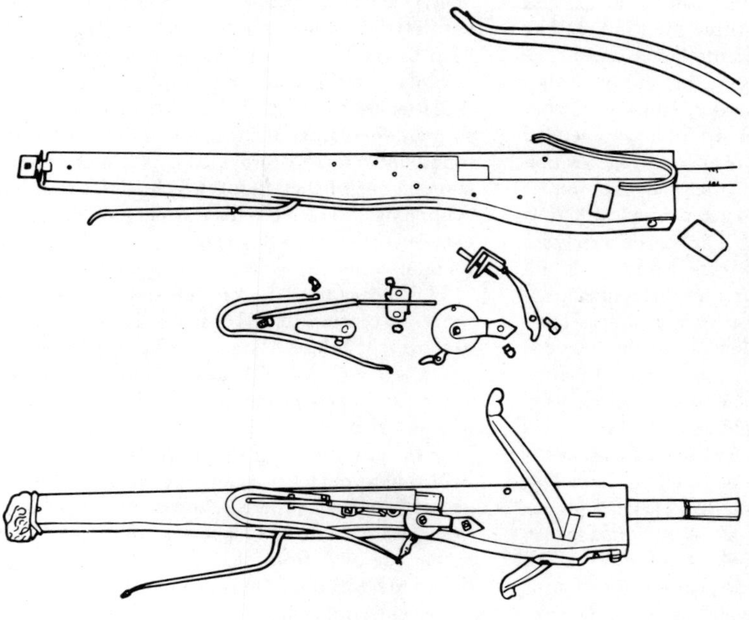

Two combined crossbow and wheel-lock guns, one dis-assembled, made entirely of steel. Italian, *c.*1510. Palazzo Ducale, Venice. (See pp. 38-9.)

gun-lock fitted with a lever trigger of the type described on page 31 above. It is shown obliquely from above with the pan and the upper half of the wheel omitted in order to display all the mechanism. This last is basically the same as that of all subsequent wheel-locks, though the sear mechanism is rather primitive and there is no device for opening the pan-cover automatically. Experiments made with a full-size modern reproduction of the lock show that it will work only after certain modifications have been made, a fact that suggests that Leonardo's drawing is an original design and not an illustration of an existing lock. This being so there is some reason for regarding Leonardo as the inventor of the system.

Against the view that the wheel-lock was invented in Italy is the fact that the earliest precisely datable information about the mechanism comes from Germany. Before the Second World War there was preserved, in the Stadtbibliothek, Berlin, a manuscript volume of drawings of mechanical inventions prepared by or for Martin Löffelholz of Nuremberg,
8-9 and dated 1505. Included in this were illustrations of two wheel-lock tinder lighters, of which one need not concern us here as it was operated manually by means of a thong wrapped round the wheel-spindle. The other, however, operated in very much the same way as the Leonardo lock, except that the sear was of slightly different construction and was released by pulling a cord attached to its free end. The mechanism is close enough to that of Leonardo's lock to suggest that it was probably derived from the latter, though, in the absence of a firm date for the *Codex Atlanticus* drawing, the possibility remains that the converse may have happened. Whether this is so or not there can be little doubt that wheel-lock firearms were being made in Germany at the time the Löffelholz manuscript was executed, for in 1507 Cardinal Ippolite I d'Este sent from Italy to Germany for 'a gun of the type that ignites with a stone' (*unam piscidam de illis que incenduntur cum lapide*).[3] This is hardly likely to have been anything other than a wheel-lock at such an early date.

The next earliest reference to what are presumably wheel-locks also come from Germany. In 1515 Laux Pfister of Augsburg accidentally shot a woman in Constance with a gun the lock of which functioned in such a way that when the firing-mechanism was pressed it 'ignited itself' (*so schlug es selb feur auff*).[4] Two years later, in 1517, the Emperor Maximilian I banned the use of 'self-striking handguns that ignite themselves' (*die selbschlagenden hanndtpuchssen, die*

3 A. Nyáry, 'A modenai Hippolit codexek', *Századok*, Vol. for 1870, Budapest, p. 679. See also C. Blair and J. F. Hayward, 'Die Rechnungs-bücher des Kardinals Ippolito d'Este im Staatsarchiv Modena', *Waffen- and Kostümkunde* Vol. 19, 1977, pp. 157-9.

4 For this and the other early references to the wheel-lock mentioned here see *Journal of the Arms and Armour Society*, Vol. III, 1959, pp. 221 ff; Vol. IV, 1962-4, pp. 187-8.

sich selbs zundten) within the Habsburg territories, following it in 1518 by a similar ban on the use and manufacture of these guns within the Empire. The reason for the ban is revealed in a letter sent to the Emperor on 16 March 1518, by the *Ausschuss Landtag* of the Austrian hereditary lands meeting at Innsbruck. This contains a list of recommended laws dealing with all types of offence, one section being directed against highwaymen and other similar criminals, including certain persons who 'carry guns secretly under their clothing'. The section concludes with the recommendation that the Emperor should make it illegal 'to carry or bear guns that ignite themselves and to make the locks anywhere'. The second recommendation clearly follows from the previous one for, by obviating the need for a lighted match, the invention of the wheel-lock made possible the production of a gun that could be carried concealed ready for instant use. It also made possible accidents resulting from the discharge of 'unloaded' guns!

The earliest known documentary evidence for the use of the wheel-lock in Italy is provided by an ordinance issued by the Duke of Ferrara on 14 November 1522. This forbade the carrying of arms in the streets of Ferrara, including 'stone or dead fire guns' (*scoppeti . . . da preda o da fuoco morte*). It can be seen, therefore, that if it were not for the existence of Leonardo's drawings of wheel-locks there would be good reason for accepting the traditional view, already current at the beginning of the seventeenth century, that the wheel-lock was invented in Nuremberg or Augsburg. But apart from the drawings there is a little more evidence in favour of the view that the lock was invented in Italy. This is provided by a group of three guns combined with cross-bows and fitted with wheel-locks of very primitive type, which are preserved with the remains of the Doges' armoury in the Palazzo Ducale at Venice.[5] The weapons are made entirely of steel and are all of closely similar design, though one differs from the others in decoration. In each case the barrel of the gun is enclosed within the tiller with its muzzle projecting out beyond the bow at the front and its pan, which has a pivoted manually-operated cover, projecting out on the right. The lock mechanism is attached directly to the right-hand side of the tiller, and consists of a narrow wheel, secured by a simple bridle, a large V-shaped mainspring, and a trigger that consists simply of a longitudinal lever, set between the arms of the spring, pivoted laterally and with its forward end terminating in a sear.

Basically, the wheel-lock mechanism found on the Venice cross-bows resembles very closely that of the more complex of the two tinder lighters illustrated in the Löffelholz manuscript of 1505. The main difference between the two forms lies in the method of pivoting the trigger-lever which on the tinder lighter, it will be recalled, is designed to be pulled outward by means of a cord attached to one end, whereas the levers on the cross-bows are squeezed inwards with the hand. In all probability, therefore, the latter are not much later in date than 1505. Some support for dating them tentatively to the period round about 1510 is provided by the etched decoration on one of them (Q2), which is of a type most commonly found on Italian armour of the second decade of the sixteenth century, though it is also found occasionally as late as the 1530s.

The subsequent history of the wheel-lock in sixteenth-century Italy is obscure. There are records to show that at least some of the Italian nobility (for example the Duke of Mantua) employed German gunmakers[6] who produced locks indistinguishable in style from those they had made at home, while from the last quarter of the sixteenth century, if not before, locks of German construction were produced generally in Italy. There is, however, some evidence to suggest that a form of lock with an external mainspring, derived from that described above, continued to be produced in Italy until the early years of the seventeenth century. The later locks had trigger mechanisms of normal type and were equipped with sliding pan-covers that opened automatically in the manner described at the beginning of this section. Similar locks were apparently made in Spain and Portugal in the early seventeenth century, while a variant, possibly derived through Hungary from Italy, is found on the birding-rifles known as Tschinke[7] that were made at Teschen during the greater part of the seventeenth century.

Where Germany is concerned a much clearer picture presents itself. The German gunsmiths usually marked their work and not infrequently dated it, and from 1530, when the first known dated example was made,[8] we have a long series of locks available for study. Earlier than any of these – and in fact the earliest datable example known – is the wheel-lock on a combined gun and cross-bow in the Bayerisches National Museum, Munich. The tiller of 10
the cross-bow is painted with the arms of the Archduke Ferdinand, later Emperor Ferdinand I, as used before he became King of Bohemia in 1526, together with his own initials combined with those of his

5 Nos. Q. 1, 2 and 3.

6 See J. F. Hayward, *The Art of the Gunmaker*, Vol. I, London, 1962, pp. 75-7.

7 See p. 96.

8 See p. 39.

9 The 'A' may, however, stand for *Archidux* which would make an even earlier date possible.

FRENCH-STYLE WHEEL-LOCK

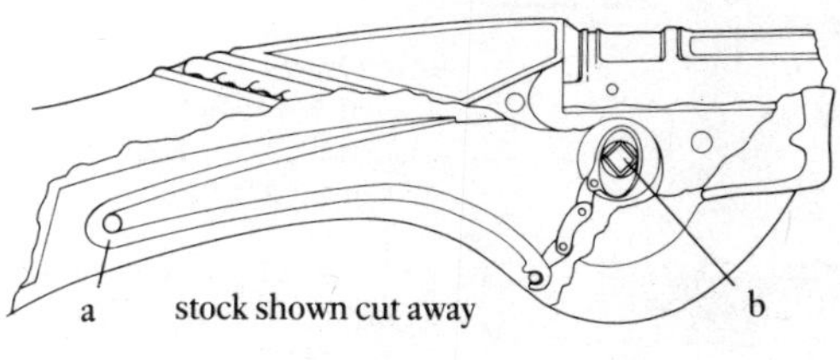

This operates in the same way as the wheel-lock of conventional construction (p. 34) but the mainspring (a), instead of being secured to the lockplate, is contained in a recess in the stock. The wheel-spindle (b) similarly, instead of being secured to the lockplate by a bridle, is loose and runs right through the stock: one end works, and is supported, in a hole in a metal bearing-plate (c) set in the stock on the side opposite to the lock, while the other passes through a hole in the lockplate into the wheel, which is itself supported by a bridle (not shown).

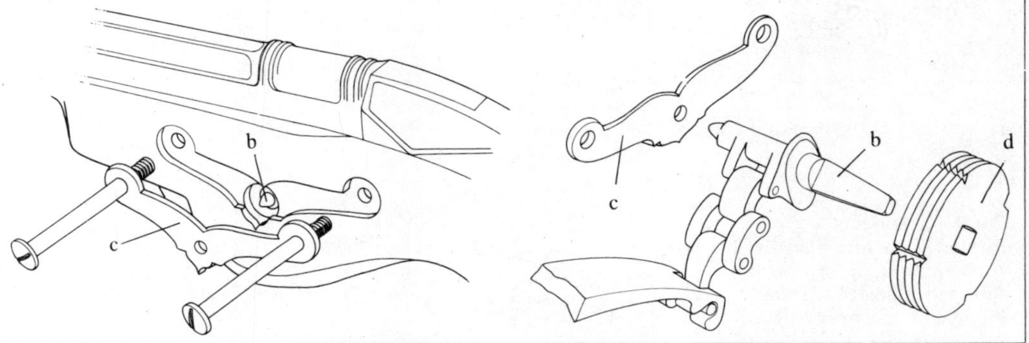

first wife, Anna of Bohemia,[9] whom he married in 1521: the whole can therefore be dated to between 1521 and 1526. The lock is a sophisticated piece of work and clearly represents a fairly advanced stage in the development of the wheel-lock. With the exception of the cock and cock-spring the mechanism is concealed inside the lockplate, the pan has an automatic cover and the sear-lever, which is operated by a press-button release at the rear end of the lockplate, consists of two interacting bars. Nevertheless, the large U-shaped mainspring and the slender curved cock, which unfortunately lacks its jaws, are reminiscent of those found on early Italian locks.

A distinctive feature of the lock of the Munich cross-bow lies in the form of the cock-spring which is sickle-shaped with the curved portion embracing the lower part of the wheel. This form of spring is found at a slightly later date on firearms bearing the Nuremberg mark, so it seems likely that it originated in that city, though it was probably being made elsewhere by the middle of the sixteenth century. The shape of the spring altered slightly as the century progressed and locks fitted with it can be dated approximately by reference to the following table:

*c.*1520–*c.*1535: Simple sickle shape.

*c.*1535–*c.*1545: The 'blade' of the sickle almost completely encircles the wheel, and the 'handle' springs out from it at right-angles.

*c.*1545–*c.*1555: As under the last, but with the 'handle' curving up where it joins the 'blade' and projecting upwards a little beyond the point of juncture.

The sickle-shaped form of cock-spring became uncommon after *c.*1555, though later examples are occasionally encountered.

The earliest dated wheel-lock is attached to a carbine in the Real Armería, Madrid,[10] which bears on the barrel the mark of Simon Marquart the Elder of Augsburg, together with the date 1530. Constructionally this is a fully-developed lock of the type described at the beginning of this section, even
including a safety-catch. The cock-spring is V- 11
shaped with its upper arm very much longer than the lower. This form of spring is found on a number of early wheel-locks bearing the Augsburg mark, and it has been suggested that it originated in that city. Whether this is so or not it was speedily copied elsewhere, and is commonly found, for example, on late-sixteenth and seventeenth century Italian wheel-locks. Elsewhere, a V-shaped spring with the lower arm slightly longer than the upper, or of the same length, was the one most commonly used after *c.*1550.

Another form of cock-spring found on German wheel-locks that should be mentioned is also V-shaped. Its distinctive feature, however, lies in the fact that it is secured inside the lockplate and acts on a tumbler attached to the inner end of the cock-pivot. It is found as early as 1537 on a pistol at Madrid[11]

10 No. K.32.

11 K.45.

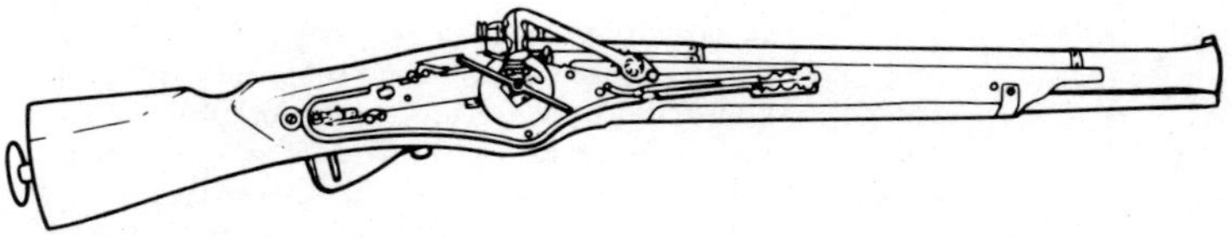

Wheel-lock carbine of the Emperor Charles V by Simon Marquart of Augsburg. The earliest dated wheel-lock. German, 1530. Real Armería, Madrid.

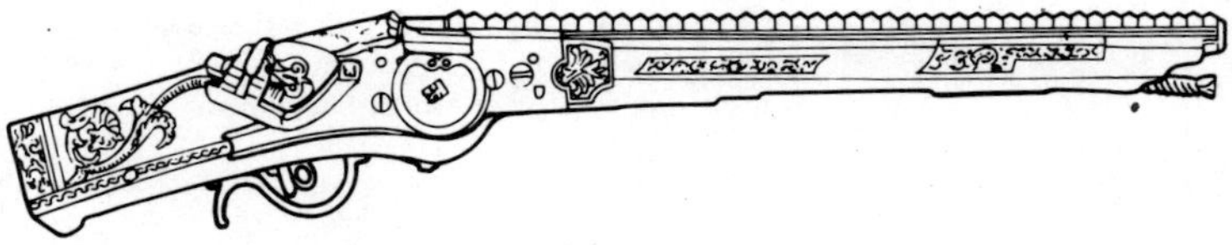

Wheel-lock pistol of the Emperor Charles V, the lock with a detached mainspring in the French manner. French, c.1540. Real Armería, Madrid.

Detail of the lock of a wheel-lock pistol, the barrel fitted with a tubular sight, the lock fitted with a wing-headed spanning key; the stock covered with panels of engraved staghorn; the stock inscribed VIVE BORGOVGNE and dated 1537. French. Real Armería, Madrid.

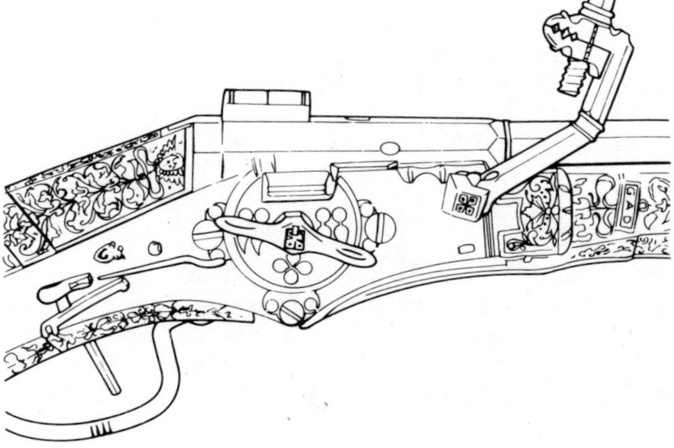

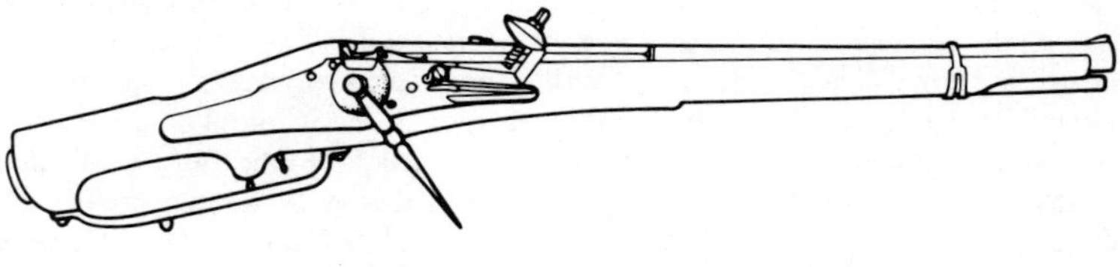

Wheel-lock carbine. On the barrel the mark of Peter Pech of Munich, on the back that of Leguisamon of Seville. Spanish, dated 1596. Real Armería, Madrid.

and was frequently used until c.1570, especially on firearms connected with Brunswick, when it went out of fashion, only to be revived again in the seventeenth century.

A very distinctive wheel-lock construction was used almost exclusively in France.[12] On this the mainspring, instead of being secured to the inside of the lockplate by a bridle, rests loose in a recess in the underside of the stock. The wheel-spindle, instead of being supported by a bridle, passes right through the stock and engages in a recess or hole in a bearing-plate attached to the side opposite the lock. This construction is found on a carbine (or pistol) of perhaps as early as c.1525 in the Musée de l'Armée, Paris, and another carbine of c.1540 at Madrid[13] which is probably, though not certainly, French but no other examples earlier than c.1570 are recorded. From this date on examples become increasingly numerous.

French gunmakers also produced firearms with

12 The only recorded example of this construction not connected with France is on a typical German ball-butted pistol of 1593 in the Victoria and Albert Museum (No. M 230-1919). It has the Nuremberg mark on the barrel.

13 K.62.

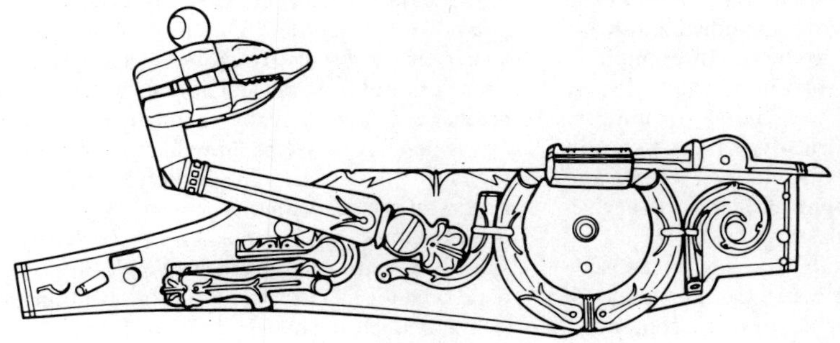

Self-spanning wheel-lock (detached). German (Nuremberg), *c.* 1540 Victoria & Albert Museum, London.

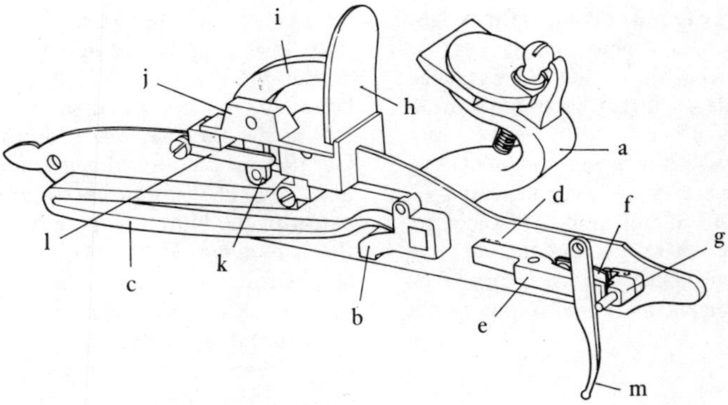

EARLY SNAPHANCE LOCK

When the cock (a) is pulled back the tumbler (b) attached to the inner end of its spindle presses up on the toe of the mainspring (c) and compresses it. When the cock has been drawn back far enough the nose (d) of the sear (e) is pushed through a hole in the lockplate by the action of the spring (f) and engages over its heel, so retaining it in the cocked position. The sear itself is wedged by the edge of the spring-actuated trigger-sear (g) which slips behind it. The steel (h) is made separately and pivoted on an arm (i) which works against a v-spring attached to the outside of the lockplate. The sliding pan-cover (j) is likewise made separately and works on a vertical pivoted arm bar (k) attached to the inside of the lockplate and secured lightly in the open or closed position by a flat spring (l). When the cocked and primed lock is fired pressure on the trigger (m), suspended in the stock causes the trigger-sear (g) to withdraw from behind the main sear (d) so allowing the mainspring, acting through the cock on the nose of the sear (d) to overcome spring (f) and so the cock falls. The flint (n) strikes the steel and forces it to pivot back: at the same time the tumbler (b) pushes a sliding bar (o) forward against the pan-cover pivot-bar (k), so causing the pan to slide open and uncover the priming.

locks of conventional form, as is demonstrated by a group of firearms in the Museo di Capodimonte, Naples (see p. 43) which are possibly the work of a Franche Comté maker who worked for the House of Savoy. These all bear the same mark, which also occurs on a snaphance gun in the University Museum, Oxford, but have locks variously of French and German construction.

At least one example of a German firearm–a pistol dated 1593 in the Victoria and Albert Museum (M230-1919)–is also recorded with a lock of French construction. This bears the Nuremberg mark and at first sight looks like a standard German *Puffer* of this period. A possible reason for its existence is that it was made for a French client as a specific order, since the maker did not avail himself of the one apparent advantage of the construction, the possibility of having a smaller lockplate and, in consequence a lighter stock.

In the remaining countries of Western Europe

the German form of wheel-lock seems to have been adopted with little modification and as a result the locks produced there are virtually indistinguishable from the native German products. An example of what probably happened elsewhere is provided by Spain. Here members of the Marquart family of Augsburg worked in Madrid during the sixteenth century[14] where they continued to use their mark of a sickle. A number of examples of their work survive, notably in the Real Armería at Madrid.

During the period *c.*1540 to *c.*1600 a few self-
33 spanning wheel-locks were made. On these the cock and the wheel were linked by cog-wheels and, sometimes, a ratchet. The action of pulling back the cock thus turned the wheel and spanned it ready for the next shot. This form of lock seems never to have been popular, presumably because of its complexity.

Finally, before leaving the wheel-lock, mention must be made of a device found on some of the earliest examples, for example a carbine dated 1531 at Madrid.[15] This is a cock with two sets of jaws placed back to back and made so that by rotating the head of the cock one or the other could be brought into operation. The purpose of the device was, of course, to provide a spare piece of pyrites that could be brought into action immediately in case of a misfire. It was not taken into general use but the idea was revived and adapted to the flintlock by Henry Nock and Sir Howard Douglas in the early-nineteenth century in England.

The Snaphance

17,279 The basic mechanism of this form of lock comprises a cock linked to a V-shaped mainspring, and a flat piece of steel (steel or hammer)[16] pivoted vertically over the pan. The cock, which is equipped with jaws to hold a piece of shaped pyrites or, more usually, flint, is pulled back against the action of the spring until it is held by a sear. Pressure on the trigger releases the sear and the spring causes the cock to fall forward sharply and strike the flint against the steel, knocking the latter backwards and so producing a shower of sparks which ignites the priming in the pan.

The term snaphance is derived from the Dutch *snaphaan* (literally *snapping-hen*). There can be little doubt that it was applied to this type of lock because of the action of the cock, which is in fact called *hen* (*Hahn*) in German and Dutch. The origins of the lock itself are obscure. It has been suggested that the 'stone or dead fire guns' mentioned in the Ferrarese ordinance[17] were actually snaphances but, though this is possible, it seems more likely that the phrase refers to wheel-locks. The earliest firm date in the history of the snaphance is, in fact, 1547, when it is mentioned as *fucile* (*archibusi . . . da fucile*) in a Florentine ordinance,[18] and as *snapplås* in a Swedish royal account.[19] The latter term simply means snap-lock and is clear enough, but the former requires some explanation. *Fucile* (French *fusil*, English *fuzee*) was applied as early as the fourteenth century to the separate piece of steel used for striking a spark to make fire, from a piece of flint. It continued to have this meaning but, from some unknown date in the first half of the sixteenth century, it came also to be applied to the snaphance lock–clearly because of the *fucile* against which the flint struck–and eventually to a gun fitted with such a lock.

Whether the snaphance lock originated in Italy, Germany or even Sweden it is at present impossible to decide. The earliest known example is fitted to a gun with the Nuremberg mark on the barrel in the Royal Armoury at Stockholm.[20] This can be dated on stylistic grounds to the middle years of the sixteenth century and there is every reason, therefore, for identifying it with one of thirty-five Nuremberg harquebuses recorded as being fitted with 'snap-locks' in the Swedish royal armoury at Arboga in 1556.[21] It would, however, be unwise to place too much emphasis on this second indication of an early connection between Sweden and the snaphance lock, for many German workmen are known to have been employed at Arboga at this time. Moreover, the construction of the Stockholm lock suggests that it probably derives from the German snap-matchlock described on page 31 above. The cock, which is formed as a pair of screw-operated jaws,[22] is long and flat and the back is extended at the bottom into a projecting lug (heel). When the cock is pulled back the

14 The name was later Hispanised to Marcuarte. For an account of the Marquarts see J. D. Lavin, *Spanish Firearms*, London 1965.

15 K.33.

16 The term *frizzen* commonly applied by collectors to this part of the lock seems to have been colloquial one only. Its more usual form appears to have been *frizzle*. H. L. Blackmore, 'Frizzen or Frizzle?' *Journal of the Arms and Armour Society*, December, 1980, pp. 47-56.

17 See p. 38.

18 A. Angelucci, *Catalogo della Armeria Reale*, Turin, 1890, p. 421.

19 Åke Meyerson, *Stockholms Bössmakerei*, Stockholm, 1936, p. 10, n. 21.

20 No. 1341.

21 Åke Meyerson, *Vapenindustrierna i Arboga*, Stockholm, 1939, p. 103.

22 It is interesting to note that the jaws of one of the tinder lighters in the Löffelholz Ms. of 1505 (p. 37) are of very similar form.

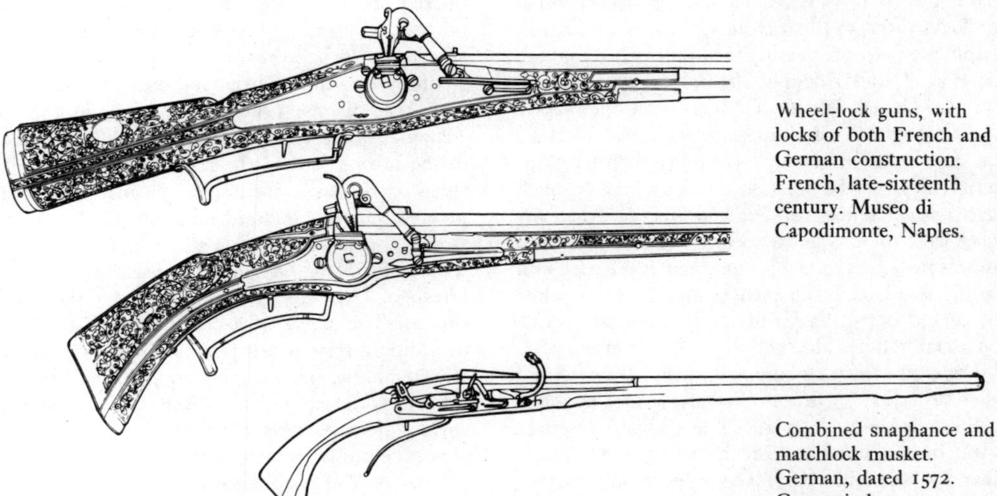

Wheel-lock guns, with locks of both French and German construction. French, late-sixteenth century. Museo di Capodimonte, Naples.

Combined snaphance and matchlock musket. German, dated 1572. Germanisches Nationalmuseum, Nuremberg.

heel presses down against the mainspring, which is mounted on the outside of the lockplate, and is eventually caught under a laterally-working sear which projects through the lockplate from the inside. Pressure on the trigger of the gun causes the sear to withdraw and the cock is snapped forward under the action of the mainspring, so striking the flint against the steel. The latter is attached to an arm pivoted just forward of the pan. The pan-cover, which pivots horizontally as on a matchlock, has to be opened by hand before firing.

The form of snaphance just described remained in use with very little variation in Russia and parts of Scandinavia until well into the seventeenth century, so that examples are frequently difficult to date. Both it and the more refined version that developed in the area of the Baltic during the seventeenth century[23] are in fact usually classified as 'Baltic locks' though, as already noted, the type may well have originated in either Germany or Italy.

The next firm date in the history of the snaphance is provided by four muskets preserved in the Saxon arsenals at Dresden and Veste Coburg, in the Germanisches Museum, Nuremberg and the Tøjhusmuseum, Copenhagen. They are equipped with combined match and snaphance locks and are dated variously 1571 or 1572 on the barrels. The snaphance mechanism here is very much more sophisticated than that on the Stockholm gun. The cock consists of a vertical bar, curved forward slightly, with the jaws at the top. The mainspring is attached to the inside of the lockplate and operates against a tumbler on the inner end of the cock-spindle. The sear, which is also internal, operates laterally as on a wheel-lock and engages in a recess in the tumbler when the cock is drawn back fully. The pan-cover slides backwards and forwards on a vertical pivoted arm which is itself linked to a longitudinally-moving bar attached to the outside of the plate: a 'toe' on the cock strikes the end of this bar as the cock falls and so causes the pan-cover to open automatically.

The provenance of the muskets is at present unknown. Their connection with Saxony has in the past led to their being called German, but it would be unwise to accept this view too readily. In the Pitt-Rivers Museum, Oxford, is a gun fitted with a slightly more advanced form of the same lock which bears a maker's mark also found on a group of wheel-locks of French construction at Capodimonte, Naples. All the snaphances may also be French.

The earliest recorded mention of the snaphance in England is contained in a document of 1580 preserved in the archives of St Paul's Cathedral, London. In this year the Dean and Chapter equipped nine light-horsemen for service in Ireland with, among other things, '9 cases of snaphaunces at 40s the peece'.[24] The use of the word 'case' here indicates

23 See p. 67.

24 *9th Report of the Historic Mss. Commission*, London, 1883, Appendix, p. 44. The use of the word snaphance in England suggests that the lock was introduced here from Germany or the Low Countries.

that the weapons were pistols. The probable form of the locks fitted to them is illustrated by an English snaphance petronel bearing the unidentified maker's mark, *R.A.* and a fleur-de-lis on lock and barrel[25] –in the Danish National Museum, Copenhagen. This is of particular importance because it bears the date 1584 in the fore-end, together with the initials *D.I.* of the stockmaker. The lock is much more refined in both form and construction than any other example discussed so far. The flat cock is of 'swan's neck' shape and is equipped at the rear with a projecting heel which engages under the sear when the cock is drawn back fully. The sear itself, which moves laterally, is attached to the inside of the plate and operates through an aperture; it can be locked when necessary by means of a safety-catch attached to the outside of the plate. The sliding pan-cover works on a pivoted arm on the inside of the plate: when the cock falls a bar linked to the tumbler pushes this forward, so opening the pan-cover. A distinctive feature of this lock is the small plate (fence) attached at right-angles to the outer end of the pan. Similar fences were especially popular in Britain in the late-sixteenth and early-seventeenth centuries.

A major development in the history of the snaphance was the combining of the steel and pan-cover into a single L-shaped piece, pivoted at the toe of the L to the front edge of the pan.[26] The origins of this form, which was extremely rare before the second quarter of the seventeenth century, are unknown. It occurs, however, on a detached combined wheel and snaphance lock, probably of Italian make, in the Artillery Museum, Turin, and on a lance combined with two pistols, probably Spanish, in the Real Armería, Madrid,[27] both of which are usually dated to the second half of the sixteenth century.[28] The steels on the lance are unusual in that they are not pivoted but slide forward when struck. A one-piece steel and pan on a pivot is also found on a pistol of *c.*1600 formerly in the Historisches Museum, Dresden. The shape of the lockplate and the stock of this are like those of a French wheel-lock, even including a false bearing-plate on the left, as for a wheel-spindle, and a supporting plate in front of the trigger for the end of a non-existent detached mainspring. The pistol can therefore be regarded as almost certainly French in origin.

The form of snaphance with the steel and pan-cover made separate could be rendered safe, even when the gun was loaded, simply by pushing the steel forward out of reach of the cock. Where the steel and cover were combined, however, some other means had to be devised to enable the gun to be carried with safety yet ready for instant action. On the lock at Turin the problem is solved by placing a small pivoted hook (back-catch, so-called 'dog') at the rear of the cock so that it can be engaged over the heel of the latter when it is drawn back, the locks on the Madrid lance are fitted with safety-catches operating on the sear-lever. The lock of the Dresden pistol, on the other hand, is fitted with two sears, one of which engages under the toe of the cock when the latter is drawn halfway back, giving the safety or

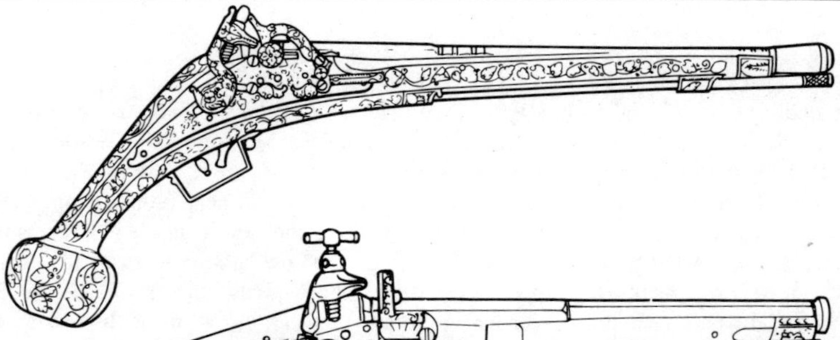

Snaphance pistol, English, dated 1593. Zámek Konopiště, Czechoslovakia.

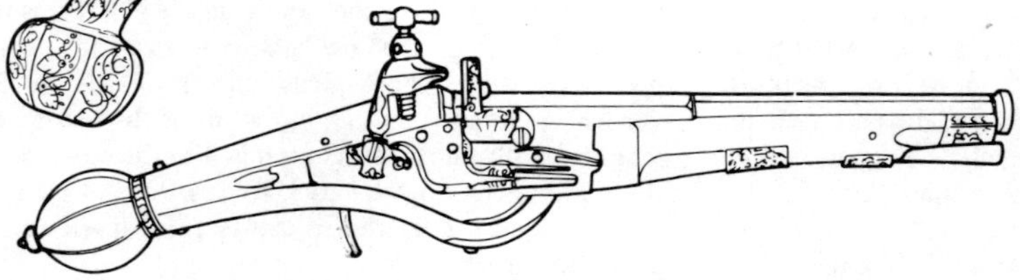

Snaphance pistol. One of the earliest known examples with steel and pan-cover combined. French, *c.*1600. Historisches Museum, Dresden.

25 A musket with a lock of similar form, dated 1588 and bearing the same marks, is preserved at Belchamp Hall, Essex. The stock bears the makers initials *R.I.* and *D.I.* See plate 279.

26 Many modern writers and collectors describe locks with the combined steel and pan-cover as flintlocks, irrespective of the form of the rest of the mechanism. I have, however, followed the late Dr Torsten Lenk here in confining the term to the type of lock described on p. 67.

27 No. I.20.

28 It should be mentioned that doubts have been expressed about the early dating of the Turin lock.

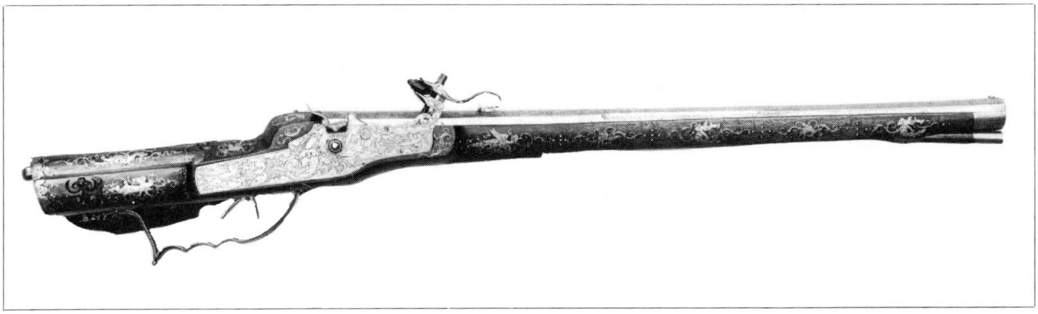

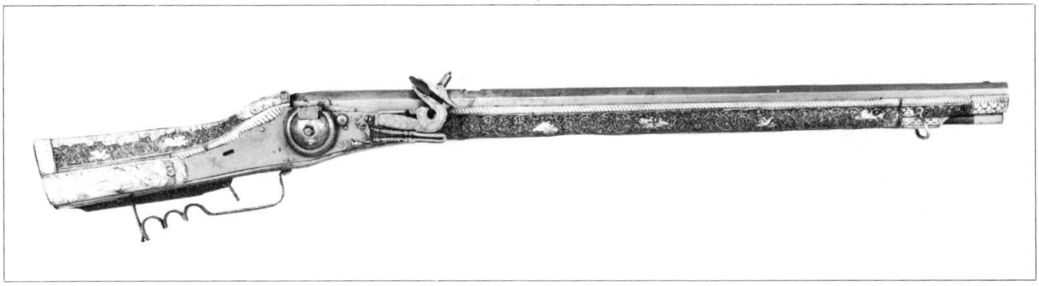

13 *Above, top* Wheel-lock with rifled barrel dated 1542. By Hans Ruhr, German (Coburg), *c.*1640. Tøjhusmuseet, Copenhagen.

14 *Above* Wheel-lock rifle, the staghorn stock inlays including the Saxon arms. On the lock the mark V.S. German (Saxon), *c.*1590. Tower of London Armouries.

15 *Right* Wheel-lock fitted with two cocks. Italian, late-sixteenth century. Castel Sant' Angelo, Rome.

16 *Below* Dagger with a wheel-lock pistol, the blade etched and gilt. German, *c.*1550. Formerly collection of Lord Astor of Hever.

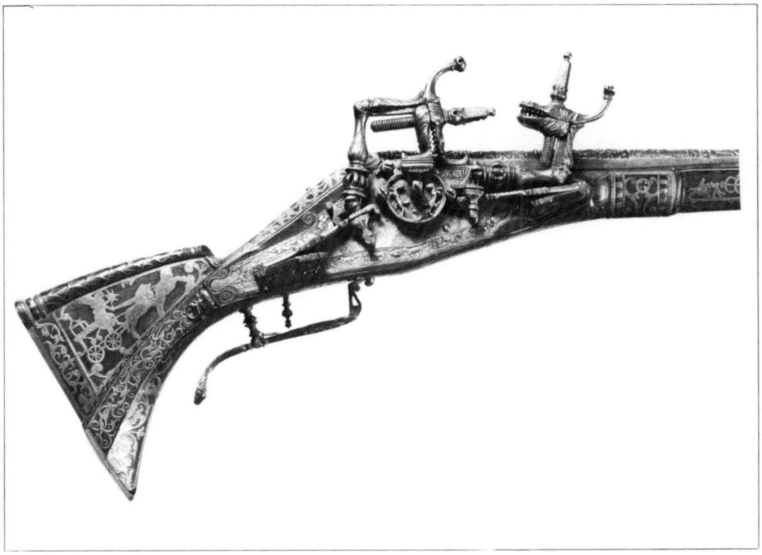

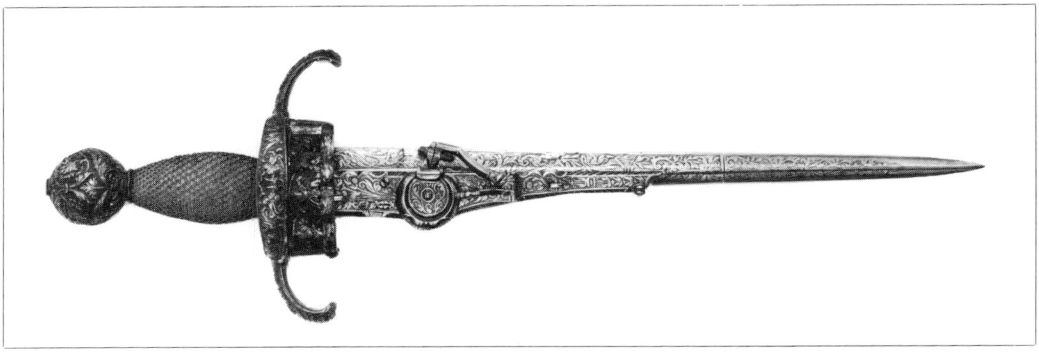

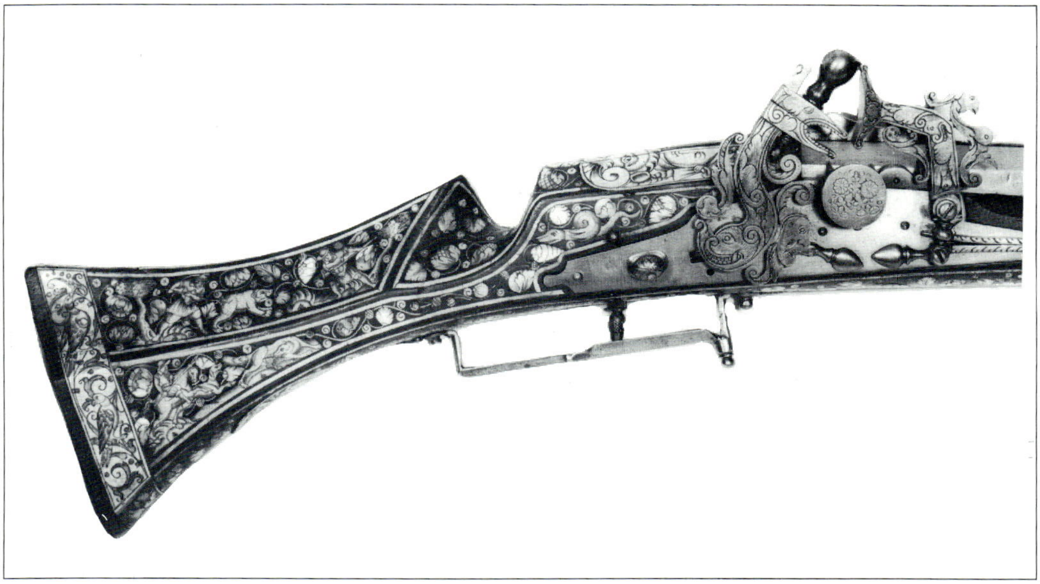

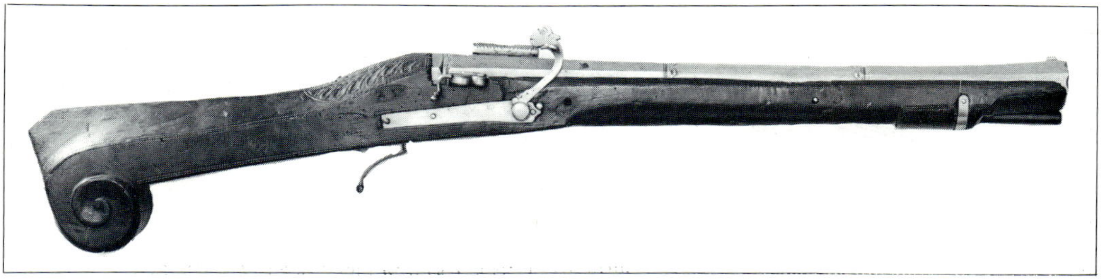

17 *Above, top* Snaphance gun, the stock inlaid with engraved staghorn. English, late-sixteenth century. Army Museum, Prague (formerly Schloss Konopiště).

18 *Above* Matchlock gun with carved stock. German, dated 1537. Bayerisches Nationalmuseum, Munich.

19 *Right* Engraving of musketeers with matchlock muskets, rests and bandoleers. From the funeral roll of Sir Philip Sidney, d. 1586, by Thomas Lant. Victoria & Albert Museum, London.

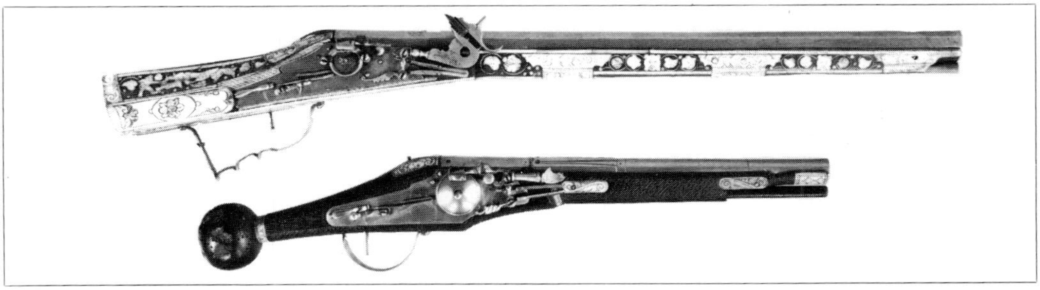

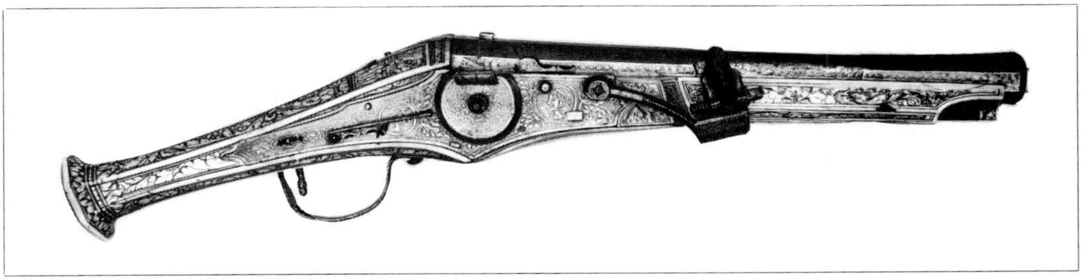

20 *Above, top* Double-barrelled wheel-lock pistol, the stock and butt inlaid with engraved ivory. Made for the Emperor Charles V by Peter Pech of Munich, *c.*1540. Metropolitan Museum of Art, New York. William H. Riggs Gift.

21 *Above, middle* (*top*) Wheel-lock sporting rifle, the stock inlaid with engraved staghorn. German, *c.*1600. Tower of London Armouries.

22 *Above, middle* (*bottom*) Wheel-lock holster pistol, the stained-wood stock stamped in imitation of staghorn. On the barrel the mark of Hans Stockmann. Saxon (Dresden), *c.*1600. Formerly Dresden Rüstkammer. Tower of London Armouries.

23 *Above* Wheel-lock pistol, the walnut stock inlaid with engraved staghorn panels. The barrel etched and inscribed with texts. On the breech-strap the date 1548. South German (Augsburg), dated 1548. Odescalchi Collection, Rome.

24 *Left* Officer from the bodyguard of Rudolph II by H. Goltzius, *c.*1587. The main figure is wearing powder and priming flasks, and carrying a matchlock gun and a forked rest. Victoria & Albert Museum, London.

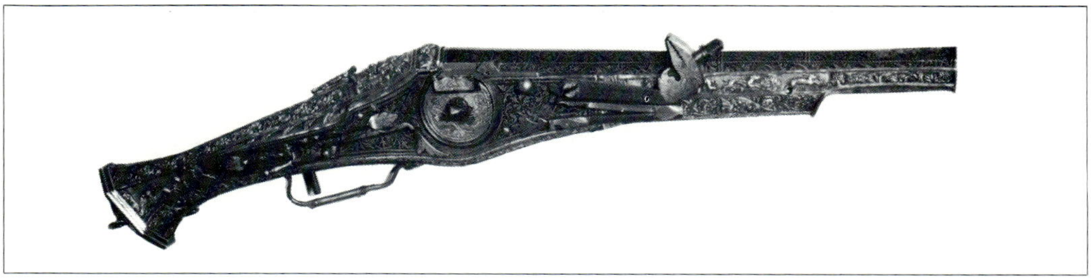

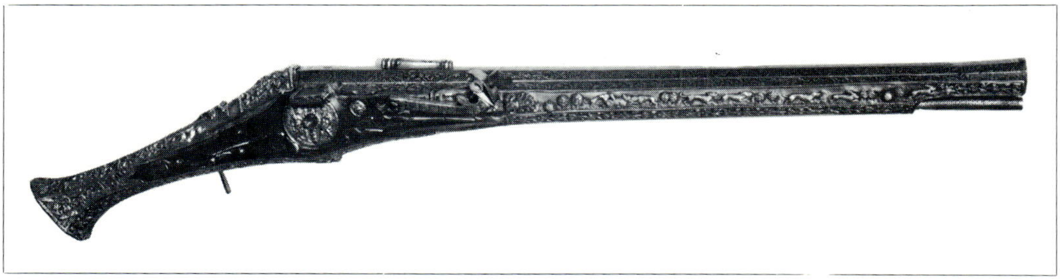

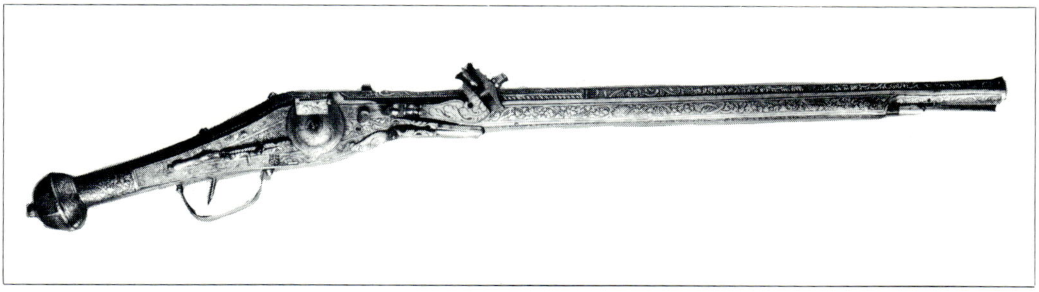

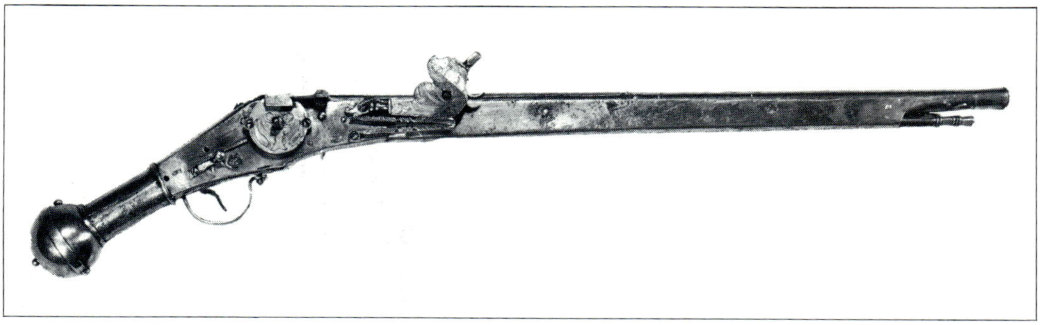

25 *Top* Short wheel-lock pistol, the stock covered with embossed silver sheets bearing the marks of Leipzig and an unknown goldsmith. Made for Heinrich VII Burgraf von Meissen (1536–72) and later in the possession of Archduke Ferdinand II (1529–95). German, dated 1555. Kunsthistorisches Museum, Vienna.

26 *Middle* (*top*) Wheel-lock pistol, the stock covered with silver sheets bearing the marks of Leipzig and an unknown goldsmith. Made for Heinrich VII Burgraf von Meissen. German (Leipzig), dated 1555. Kunsthistorisches Museum, Vienna.

27 *Middle* (*bottom*) Wheel-lock pistol, the stock of etched and gilt steel. Maker's mark B H and pair of spectacles on a shield. German (Nuremberg), dated 1562. Kunsthistorisches Museum, Vienna.

28 *Above* Wheel-lock pistol of steel. On the lock the maker's mark: a lion beneath H S on a shield. The grip was probably bound with cord originally. German (Nuremberg), 1560-70. Victoria & Albert Museum, London.

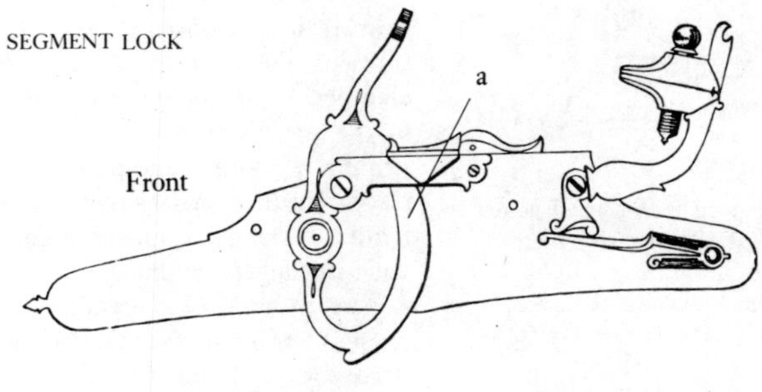

This operates in a similar manner to the wheel-lock except that the wheel is replaced by a steel striker shaped like the segment of a circle (a). This is operated by a mechanism similar to that actuating the cock of the early snaphance.

From an Italian lock signed and dated RAF.VERD. (i.e., Rafaello Verdiani) in the Tower of London Armouries, London (No. XII 1067).

'half-cock' position, while the other engages over the heel in the normal manner when the cock is drawn back fully.

The form of snaphance with the two sears, which is now usually called by the modern term *miquelet lock*, was widely used in Spain and Southern Italy until early in the nineteenth century. In its most characteristic form it has an external mainspring which, very broadly speaking, acts on the heel of the cock on the Spanish lock and on the toe on the Italian. It should be emphasised, however, that locks with both types of spring were manufactured in both countries.

The Segment Lock

This very rare mechanism was a kind of compromise between the wheel and snaphance locks. The form was similar to that of a wheel-lock, but the wheel was replaced by a steel segment or arc pivoted at the bottom. The pivot was linked on the inside of the plate to a mechanism like that working the cock of a snaphance, so that the segment could be pushed forward against the action of the mainspring until held by a sear. The operation was exactly like that of a wheel-lock, the only difference being that the sparks were struck from the pyrites by the curved top of the segment which snapped back when the sear was withdrawn.

The history of the segment-lock is still obscure. Moritz Thierbach, in his great work on the history of firearms, describes and illustrates several examples in German collections, at least one of which appears to be of late-sixteenth century date.[29] The lock may, therefore, have been a German invention. On the other hand, General A. Gaibi has suggested that the lock was the invention of Rafaello Verdiani (*c.*1580–*c.*1630), an Italian maker of mechanical devices who worked for the Medici in Florence.[30] The only known example of one of his locks–signed and dated inside *RAF.VERD.*1619–is in the Tower of London Armouries.[31] The solution of the problem of whether this was an original invention or merely an adaptation of an earlier device will have to wait until more detailed research has been carried out on the whole group of locks working on this principle.

The Rasp Lock

In this extremely rare mechanism sparks are struck from a piece of pyrites or flint by a straight metal rasp moving longitudinally. One of the few examples known occurs on a short handgun in the Historisches Museum, Dresden, which, because of an early tradition that it was invented by Berthold Schwarz, is usually called the 'Monk's Gun'. Made of blued iron it consists of a barrel of circular section, 11 in long and with a calibre of 0·43 in. It is thickened over the breech and the last three inches flare out slightly to form the muzzle. The front and rear of the muzzle and the breech are each encircled by an incised band formed of close-set Gothic 'I's while between the muzzle and the breech are two encircling rows of widely-spaced trefoils, also incised. On top of the breech is punched a mark, possibly that of the maker, consisting of three addorsed crescents.

29 M. Thierbach, *Die geschichtliche Entwickelung der Handfeuerwaffen*, Pt. I, Dresden, 1886, pp. 30-1.

30 See *Armi Antiche*, Vol. IX, Turin, 1962, pp. 126, 137-8.

31 No. XII. 1067.

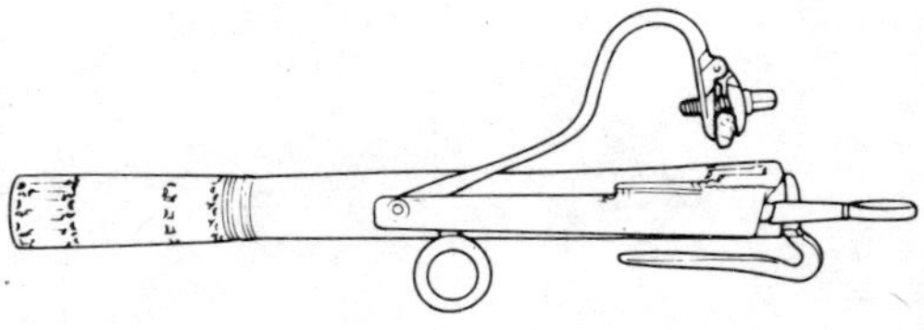

The so-called Monk's Gun. Engraved with a black-letter inscription. It is ignited by pulling a steel rasp which operates against a piece of pyrites, producing a spark. Formerly thought to have been made by the legendary inventor of firearms, Berthold Schwarz. German, late-fifteenth or early-sixteenth century. Historisches Museum, Dresden.

Attached to the rear end by a large rivet that apparently passes right through the bottom of the chamber, is a flat belt-hook bent so that it runs parallel to the underside of the barrel. Riveted to the left side is what is in effect an oblong box, $5\frac{1}{2}$ in long, with its rear end divided into a small compartment to form the pan. Pivoted in the forward end of the box is the cock. This has a long slender hooked neck terminating in a pair of screw-operated jaws that are pivoted together on a transverse pin, exactly like the jaws of the cock on Leonardo da Vinci's drawing of a wheel-lock.[32] Passing vertically through the bottom of the box and into the neck of the cock near the point where it is pivoted is a large screw-eye which can be turned to move the cock up or down. With the gun is a slender steel rasp of rectangular section, grooved longitudinally and slightly notched on one face, and terminating at one end in a ring. The front and rear walls of the pan are each pierced with a small central aperture through which the rasp can be pushed from the rear until stopped by the ring, in which position it extends almost to the cock-pivot.

In order to fire the gun it was first loaded and primed in the normal way. The cock was then screwed down until the pyrites in its jaws was clamped firmly against the grooved face of the rasp in the pan. The gun was then apparently simply gripped with one hand forward of the cock while the rasp was pulled back sharply by its ring with the other hand, so striking a shower of sparks from the pyrites and igniting the priming.

The Monk's Gun cannot be dated precisely at present, though the Gothic letters used in the decoration indicate that it is not likely to be later than the middle of the sixteenth century. Its lock may, as some writers have suggested, represent the first stage in the evolution of the wheel-lock, though this seems unlikely in view of the fact that it is the only example known that could conceivably antedate Leonardo's drawings. Until further evidence is available the wisest course would seem to be to regard the Monk's Gun as an experimental arm outside the main line of development of mechanical systems of ignition. The same applies to the two or three other examples of rasp-locks known, all of which date from the seventeenth and eighteenth centuries. These use a spring-actuated rasp in place of a wheel.[33]

During the sixteenth century and for much of the seventeenth century mechanical systems of ignition were employed chiefly on sporting guns, their military use being largely confined to pistols and to

32 See p. 34.

33 See Thierbach, *op.cit.*, pp. 27–30.

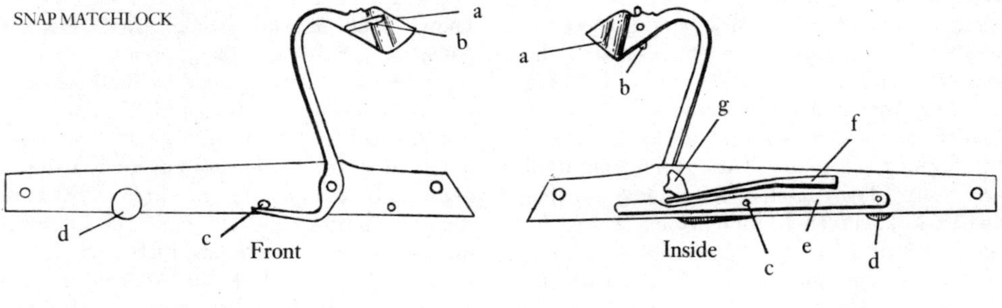

The jaws of the cock (a), which hold the match, are operated by a screw (b). The cock itself is pivoted on a spindle attached to a tumbler (g), on the inside of the lock-plate, against which a weak leaf-mainspring (f), operates. Set below the mainspring is another leaf-spring (e), secured at its forward end and carrying a stud-like sear (c) in the centre and button trigger (d) at the rear, both working through the plate. In order to cock the lock, the cock is pulled back until its heel (d) has over-ridden the sear (c) and the latter has sprung back above it, so securing it. Pressure on the trigger (d) withdraws the sear and allows the mainspring to snap the cock forward. From an early-sixteenth-century German lock in the Historisches Museum, Bern (No. 2211).

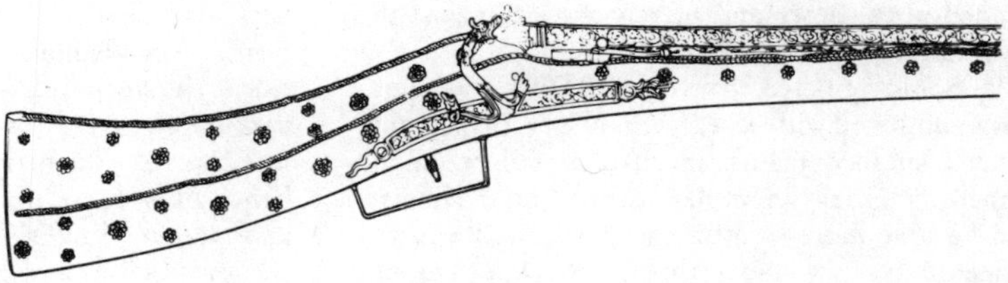

Matchlock gun. The stock covered with velvet and silver-gilt studs. Italian, *c.*1560. Kunsthistorisches Museum, Vienna.

the arms of specially equipped troops. Military long-guns, almost without exception, were fitted with matchlocks, no doubt because these were both cheap to manufacture and reasonably reliable in use. A number of sporting and target guns were equipped with matchlocks also, but surviving examples are comparatively rare.

The actual construction of the matchlock changed little during the sixteenth century. The snap-matchlock tended to go out of use after *c.*1550, though it is found on a small group of German target rifles dating from the late-sixteenth and early-seventeenth centuries.[34] On most of these the cock is slender and straight with an aperture, instead of jaws, for the match, while instead of a button release they mostly have set triggers of conventional form activated by pressing a button or pulling a cord. But from the middle of the century onwards by far the most popular form was the sear-matchlock of the type described above.[35] It survived until the second quarter of the seventeenth century, but from *c.*1590 onwards it tended to be replaced by a slightly improved mechanism, the *trigger lock.* On this the lever trigger attached directly to the lever on the inside of the lockplate that operated the cock was

34 See Arne Hoff, 'Late Firearms with Snap Matchlock', *Four Studies on History of Arms*, Tøjhusmuseet, Copenhagen, 1963, pp. 9-30. On a few of these rifles the trigger is replaced by a cord which is pulled to release the cock.

35 See p. 31.

Mounted figures with wheel-lock firearms, *c.*1570. Woodcut from Jost Amman's *Kunstbüchlein.*

replaced by a separate trigger of modern form, suspended in the stock and merely resting against the right-angled end of the lever.

It should be noted that the matchlock was sometimes combined with other forms of lock, presumably as an insurance against mechanical failure on the part of the latter. Examples are comparatively rare, and become more so after the third quarter of the sixteenth century. Nevertheless, the idea was not

Landsknecht loading a matchlock. German, *c.*1540. Woodcut by N. Meldmann of Nuremberg.

completely abandoned until nearly the end of the seventeenth century.

Long-guns

11 From about 1540 onwards, with the general adoption
14-15 of firearms by the upper classes, long-guns can be
17-21 divided into two groups according to whether they
24, 90
93-4 were intended for sporting or military use. The two
279 groups follow closely parallel lines of development,
340-44 and indeed often overlap but, in the main, until the
nineteenth century sporting firearms were generally technically in advance of those used for military purposes. As might also be expected, elaborate decoration and the finest workmanship are found almost exclusively on sporting arms.

Apart from the new lock-mechanisms described above and various experiments with breech-loading and repeating arms discussed in Chapters 6 and 7, the main developments in the history of long-guns in the sixteenth century relate to the form of the stock and, more particularly, of the butt. Before discussing these, two small, though important, technical innovations can be conveniently mentioned here. The first of these was the trigger of modern form, suspended on a pivot in a recess in the underside of the stock. It is first recorded on the wheel-lock carbine of 1530 at Madrid,[36] but thereafter it was fitted to the vast majority of wheel-lock and snaphance guns. From the beginning, except in Scottish and certain English firearms, it was invariably accompanied by a trigger-guard that was sometimes a simple semi-circle and sometimes angular: on German wheel-locks it was often indented for the fingers. The second innovation was the set-trigger, which seems to have been first used on firearms in Germany towards the end of the century. On this a small spring-mechanism was set by means of a button, a cord or an extra trigger. Very light pressure on the trigger proper was sufficient to release the mechanism, so causing a spring-operated lever to strike the sear-lever of the lock and actuate it mechanically.

The matchlock handgun with a rather flat oblong butt designed primarily to be rested against the cheek remained in use until well into the second quarter of the sixteenth century in Germany. Many engravings and woodcuts of the period show Landsknechts carrying guns of this type, whence the form of stock with which they are fitted is often called the 'Landsknecht stock'. A developed form, used occasionally during the second quarter of the century and apparently designed mainly to be rested against the shoulder, had a thick heavy butt with a pronounced semi-circular toe.

Though the typical Landsknecht stock went out of general use in the middle years of the sixteenth century, a new and important form had started to develop from it in the 1520s. This was the cheek-butt, often called the 'German butt' by collectors because it was used almost exclusively in the areas of German culture. In its earliest form, first recorded in the 1530s, it was simply a more shapely version of the Landsknecht type of butt, thickened and of rhomboid section so that it could be rested more comfortably against the cheek.[37] Usually a large spherical- or conical-headed screw was fitted to the rear end to protect the buttplate, which was normally of staghorn, when it was rested on the ground. On early examples the butt generally slopes down at a slight angle from immediately behind the barrel-tang, where it is often recessed to form a grip. Towards the end of the century this recess began to take the form of a distinct step, below which the butt

36 See p. 39.

37 On a very few early examples, for example the carbine of 1530 at Madrid, mentioned above, the butt contains a metal rod terminating in a disc which can be pulled out to form an extension. This could be rested against the shoulder.

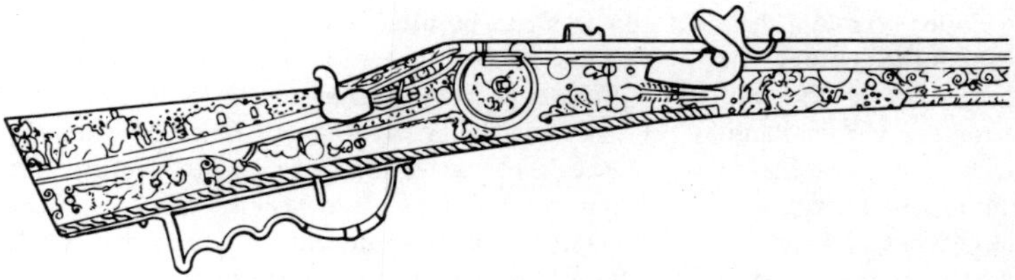

Combined wheel and matchlock gun. The stock bears the arms and monogram of Franz II of Saxe-Lauenberg. S. German, dated 1593. C. O. von Kienbusch Collection, Philadelphia.

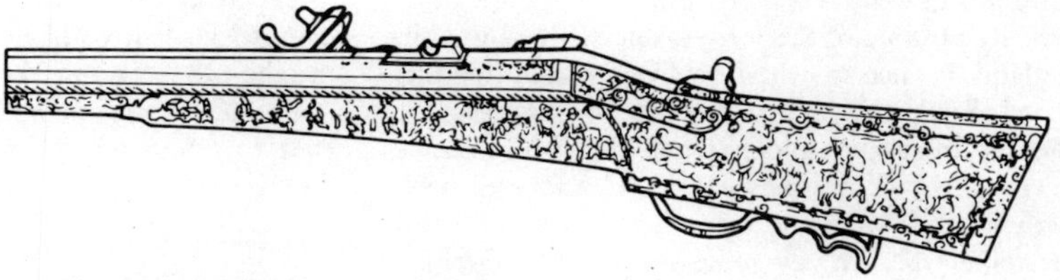

Stock of a wheel-lock gun. On the barrel, the mark of Stephan Klett of Suhl. S. German, dated 1583. C. O. von Kienbusch Collection, Philadelphia.

extended backwards almost parallel to the axis of the barrel. At the same time the left face was extended downwards and outwards to form a cheek-piece. This shape remained the usual one until the early eighteenth century on the majority of rifled sporting- and target-guns produced in Germany. It should be mentioned that the true cheek-butt appears never to have been fitted to military arms, presumably because it could not be used with the heavy charges of powder that were required to make firearms really effective on the battlefields of the sixteenth century and later.

The other forms of butt evolved during the sixteenth century were all used on military arms–some on sporting ones also–and were designed to be rested against the shoulder or chest. Their early history is still obscure, but it seems likely that all had a common origin in a type of butt found, for example, on a matchlock musket, probably of German make, in the Tower of London Armouries,[38] which can be dated to the second quarter of the sixteenth century. This is simply a Landsknecht butt that has been lengthened so that it can be rested against the shoulder or chest. It is possible that this form originated in Spain, for Sir Roger Williams in his *Briefe Discourse on Warre* of 1590 refers to muskets being 'streight stocked, after the Spanish manner'. The type of stock to which he refers was probably the developed form of that found on the Tower gun which appeared during the second quarter of the century. On this the butt sloped down at a slight angle and had a wide recess for the thumb of the trigger hand immediately to the rear of the barrel. During the 1580s there began a tendency for the upper and lower edges to follow slightly divergent concave curves and this led during the following decade to the development of the splayed or 'fish-tail' butt, formed like a truncated triangle with in-curved sides, its base towards the rear.

Another form of stock that had started to develop by the middle of the century had a down-curved butt that was rested against the chest. By *c.*1580 the curve had become very pronounced so that the outline of the gun was almost like that of a hockey-stick. The shape was an awkward one and apparently cumbersome to use and it barely survived to the end of the century. The type of light gun called a petronel,[39] because it was fired resting against the breast (French *poitrine*), was probably fitted with a stock of this kind, whence it is sometimes called a 'petronel stock'. Roger Williams[40] describes it as a stock 'crooked after the French manner to be discharged on the breast'.

Yet another type of stock had appeared, probably first in Italy, in about 1550. On this the upper edge of the butt followed a shallow concave curve with the lower edge almost parallel to it. The form seems to have been used mainly in Italy during the sixteenth century, but a rather similar shape of butt was used in Scotland and parts of Scandinavia throughout the greater part of the seventeenth century. Whether this was adopted as a result of Italian influence or developed independently is at present unknown.

Finally, mention must be made of a form of shoulder-stock that is first recorded on French sporting-guns of the 1570s. On this the rather

38 No. XII. 9.

39 The Spanish *pedreñal*, which refers to a type of wheel- or flintlock pistol, is thought to be derived from the late Latin *petrinus* (of stone) and to refer to the system of ignition. It is unclear whether or not the word is connected with *petronel*(see p. 56.).

40 *op.cit.*, above.

narrow butt curves down slightly from behind the barrel, the upper edge being convex and the lower almost parallel to it. A developed version, first recorded in Italy towards the end of the century, has a high comb running along the top of the butt immediately behind the grip for the trigger-hand. This version was also used to some extent in Germany during the period round about 1600.

Our knowledge of the various types of long-gun made during the first three quarters of the sixteenth century is extremely patchy. For example, we know virtually nothing of the form taken by those used in England, France and the Low Countries during this period. Such evidence as is available suggests that all these areas were under strong German influence down to *c.*1550, and may even have imported most of their firearms from Germany. Until the third quarter of the century some form of the German Landsknecht gun seems to have been used in most areas for military purposes. Sporting-guns were probably either variants of this or of the German cheek-butted type already discussed. During the third quarter of the century, however, we begin to read in contemporary sources of new types of military firearms. It is not easy to discover exactly what many of these were, for writers of the period often give conflicting information about them. They can best be discussed individually, the names given here being those current in England, though versions of most of them, or the same guns under different names, were used on the Continent.

The Musket

9 This was the heaviest of all military hand firearms and was invariably supported on a forked rest when fired during the whole of the period with which we are concerned here. According to the contemporary writer Martin du Bellay[41] 'les arquebouzes qu'on tiroit sur une fourchette' were invented at the time of the Battle of Ghiara in Italy, fought in 1521 between the forces of the Emperor Charles V and the Pope on the one hand and of Francis I of France on the other. Heavy bell-mouthed Landsknecht guns accompanied by forked rests are illustrated as early as 1530 in an engraving showing the entry of the Emperor Charles V into Bologna,[42] though we do not know whether these would have been called muskets at the time. According to Brantôme the musket was first used by the Duke of Alva in his Netherlands campaign of 1567: 'il fut le premier qui leur donna (à ses soldats) en main ces gros mousquets, et que l'on vit les premiers en la guerre et parmi les compagnies . . . et ceux qui les portoient, on les nommait Mousquetaires.'[42] It is likely, however, in view of the evidence given above, that Brantôme's remarks can be interpreted as referring only to the first use of the musket in north-western Europe.

Whatever the date of the introduction of the musket may be, it can be shown that by the beginning of the last quarter of the sixteenth century it was being taken widely into service all over Europe. Brantôme, for example, informs us that it was first adopted in France by Philippe Strozzi, Colonel General of the French infantry, in 1573.[42] Other countries seem to have speedily followed suit and by the 1580s the musket had become, with the pike, the chief European infantry weapon, a position it was to retain for the next two hundred and fifty years.

Cyprian Lucar, in his edition of Tartaglia's *Three Bookes of Colloquies Concerning the Art of Shooting* published in 1588, gives the size of a musket of the period in very precise terms.[43]

> . . . his Musket which shall be allowed for militarie seruice must be in length at least four foote,[44] and . . . the bore must be in Diameter $\frac{23}{30}$ of an ynch and in circumference two ynches and $\frac{43}{105}$ of an ynch, and . . . a due charge in gunpowder for his Musket is $\frac{3}{4}$ of that waight which a fit pellet of lead for the same Musket doth waye, and . . . such a due charge in gunpowder wayeth one ounce $\frac{3}{4}$ of an ounce 19 graines and $\frac{1}{2}$ of a graine of *auer de poize* waight . . . and . . . the diameter and circumference of a fit pellet for his Musket must always be somewhat less than the diameter and circumference in the bore . . . & . . . a fit pellet of lead . . . wayeth two ounces $\frac{1}{4}$ of an ounce, one dramme & six graines of *auer de poize* waight [i.e. just under seven balls to the pound]'.

Lucar's information cannot be accepted as anything more than a counsel of perfection that could hardly have been acted on precisely in the conditions of a period when standardisation was impracticable. There seems to be no reason to doubt, however, that all muskets would have approximated in size, and especially in calibre, to the figures he gives.

Muskets seem invariably to have been fitted with some form of stock designed to be rested against the shoulder for, as Sir Roger Williams[45] says:

> for the recoyling, there is no hurt, if they be streight stocked after the Spanish manner: were they stocked crooked, after the French manner,

41 See J. Hewitt, *Ancient Armour and Weapons in Europe*, Vol. III, London, 1860, p. 618.

42 *ibid.*, Plate 120 and p. 623.

43 Appendix, pp. 61-2.

44 The measurements of surviving muskets of the period suggest that this probably refers to the barrel only.

45 *op.cit.*, p. 53 above.

> to be discharged on the breast, fewe or none could abide their recoyling; but being discharged from the shoulder, after the Spanish manner, there is neither danger nor hurte.

Again no precise standardisation in the form of stock seems to have been attempted, but from the very end of the century the splayed butt seems to have generally supplanted all others.

Finally, it should be mentioned that arrows were sometimes fired from muskets when they were used at sea. Among naval stores at Rochester in 1595, for example, were 'Musket arrowes, 983 shefe, 6 arrowes: musket arrowes with fier woorkes, 109 shefe 4 arrowes'.[46] The last-named were presumably some form of incendiary arrow.

The Harquebus (Hackbut)

This term, which, as already noted, is a corruption of the German *Hackenbüchse*, appears to have been applied during the first half of the sixteenth century to any form of long handgun.[47] With the development of other types of gun in the second half of the century it came to be applied to the lightest form of military handgun. The harquebus was frequently used on horseback and by the end of the century it had apparently come to be what we should now call a heavy carbine. Lucar mentions in 1588,[48] that it threw a pellet weighing 1 oz.

The Caliver

This is the same word as *calibre*, that is the diameter of the bore of a firearm. The origin of the application of the term to a type of gun is given as follows by Edmund York in his *Order . . . for the Marshalling of the City of London* of 1588.[49]

> I remember when I was first brought up in Piemount, in the Countie of Brissacks regiment of old Bandes, we had one particular Calebre of Harquebuze to our Regiment . . . of which Words of Calibre, came first this unapt term which we use to call a Harquebuze a Calliver, which is the Height of the Bullet and not the Piece . . .

The Comte de Brissac was Governor of Piedmont between 1550 and 1559, so that the date of York's service with him can be established fairly closely.

York goes on to say:

> Before the Battell of Moungunter [Moncontour, 3 October 1569], the Prynces of the Religion caused 7000 Harquebuzes to be made all of one Calibre; which were called Harquebuse du Calibre du Monsieur le Prince. So as I think some men not understanding Frenche, brought hither the name of the Height of the Bullet for the Piece, which word Calibre is yet contynued with our good Cannoniers.

'Monsieur le Prince' was the Prince de Condé who was shot after the Battle of Jarnac (13 March 1569) some months before Moncontour, so the introduction of the caliver, if York is correct, may well have taken place in about 1568.[50] Certainly, the term *caliver* was in established use in England by 1568 for it occurs in an inventory of the goods of Dame Frances Talbot taken on 28 November of that year.[51]

In practice the caliver was a gun, fired without a rest, midway in weight between an harquebus and a musket. In 1590, for example, Humphrey Barwick in his *A briefe discourse concerning all manual weapons of fire* wrote as follows.[52]

> It is supposed by many that the weapon called commonly a Caliver is another thing than a Harquebuze whereas in truth it is not, but only a Harquebuze, saving that it is of a greater circuit or Bullet than the other is of: wherefore the Frenchman doth call it a peece de Calibre which is as much as to say, a peece of bigger circuit.

Cyprian Lucar writing in 1588[53] says:

> . . . his Caliver which shall be allowed for militarie seruice must be in length at least three foot and two ynches, . . . the bore . . . must be in Diameter $\frac{2}{3}$ of an ynch, and . . . a fitte pellet of lead for his Caliver wayethe one ounce $\frac{1}{4}$ of an ounce two scruples, and 12 graines of *auer de poiz* waight . . .

The actual shape of the caliver does not seem to have been fixed during the sixteenth century any more than was that of the musket, a weapon that it resembled closely apart from its size. The remarks above[54] about the shape of the musket therefore apply equally well to it.

The Currier

This was a form of gun–apparently mentioned only

46 Hewitt, *loc.cit.*, p. 683.

47 *Handgun* also appears in inventories of the period, for example Henry VIII's inventory of 1547 (*Archaeologia*, Vol. LI) but how it was differentiated from the harquebus is not clear.

48 *op.cit.*, Book I, p. 35.

49 Stowe, *Survey of London*, Edn. of 1754, Vol. II, V, XXXI, 570-1.

50 Brantôme, it should be noted, gives the credit for the introduction of the *harquebuzes de calibre* to Strozzi. See Hewitt, *loc.cit.*, p. 674.

51 *Archaeologia*, Vol. XX, p. 78.

52 *cf.* p. 80.

53 *Op.cit.*, Appendix, p. 61.

54 See p. 54 above.

in texts of the second half of the sixteenth century – of the same calibre as the caliver, but with a much longer barrel and taking a larger charge of gunpowder.[55] It was used without a rest.

The Petronel

As already noted briefly[56] this was originally a form of gun with a hooked stock so shaped that it could be rested against the breast (French *poitrine*, hence *poitrinal*).[57] In its fully developed form it seems to have appeared first in France in the middle of the sixteenth century, whence it was disseminated over the rest of Western Europe, reaching England in the 1570s. By this time the petronel seems already to have become a form of heavy carbine used mainly on horseback, a type of weapon to which the term *petronel* continued to be applied long after the hooked stock had gone out of use at the very end of the sixteenth century.

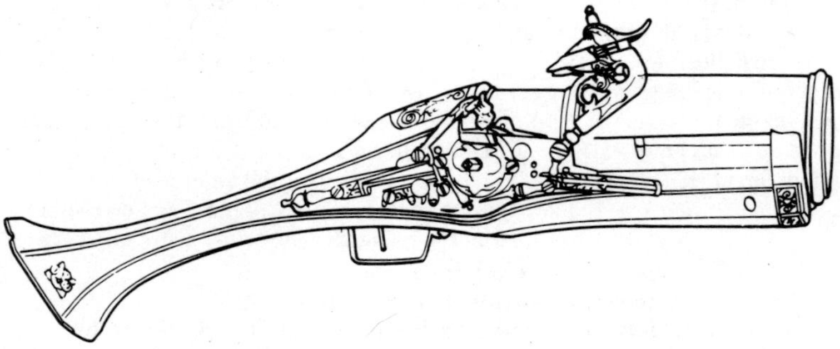

Hand mortar with bronze barrel. Mark of Nuremberg and that of the lock maker, GH over a pierced heart. German, *c.*1590. British Museum, London.

The Carbine

A short light gun for mounted use. It takes its name from the *carabins*, mounted harquebusiers raised on the Continent in the late-sixteenth century. The way in which the carbine differed from the harquebus in the late-sixteenth century is not certain and the terms seem, in fact, to have been interchangeable.

It should be noted that at a later date in England, where service arms were concerned, the term 'carbine' was applied to any gun of carbine bore, irrespective of whether or not it was for mounted use. In France, also at a later date, a *carabine* was a short light gun for mounted use with a rifled barrel.

Hand-mortar

This modern term is applied to a group of short-barrelled guns with very wide bores capable of throwing a grenade. A few specimens dating from the late-sixteenth century are known, but the majority of examples are of the seventeenth century and later.

The Birding Piece

From as early as *c.*1530 light, long-barreled guns were made for shooting at sitting birds. From the second half of the century they were sometimes rifled.

The Pistol

A number of surviving medieval hand-cannon are 12
small enough to be classified strictly as pistols. The 20-37
introduction of the true pistol, however, had to await 91-2
the invention of the wheel-lock[58], a device that made 336-9
possible for the first time the construction of a firearm that could be operated satisfactorily with one hand alone. The earliest pistols in fact appear with the earliest wheel-locks, while the only matchlock examples of European origin known to the writer are a unique revolving pistol of the sixteenth century at Venice[59] and a late seventeenth-century pistol, probably of eastern European origin, in the Suermondt Museum, Aachen.

The origins of the pistol are still obscure. The name is first recorded in the 1540s, usually as *pistolet*, but it has been suggested that it derives from the medieval Bohemian term *pišťala* (pipe whistle) which was applied to a light gun.[60] As no connection between the two words, other than their similarity of sound, has ever been established this seems

55 *Archaeologia*, Vol. XXVIII, p. 77.

56 See p. 55.

57 Victor Gay, *Glossaire Archéologique*, Vol. II, Paris, 1928, p. 230.

58 The matchlock pistols at the Tower of London, fitted with circular shields, which were made for Henry VIII, cannot be classified as true pistols.

59 Palazzo Ducale, No. N.30.

60 See Z. Drobna and J. Durdik, *Medieval Costume and Weapons*, London, *n.d.* [1958] pp. 57-8 and *Zeitschrift für historische Waffenkunde*, Vol. II, 1900-2, pp. 414-15.

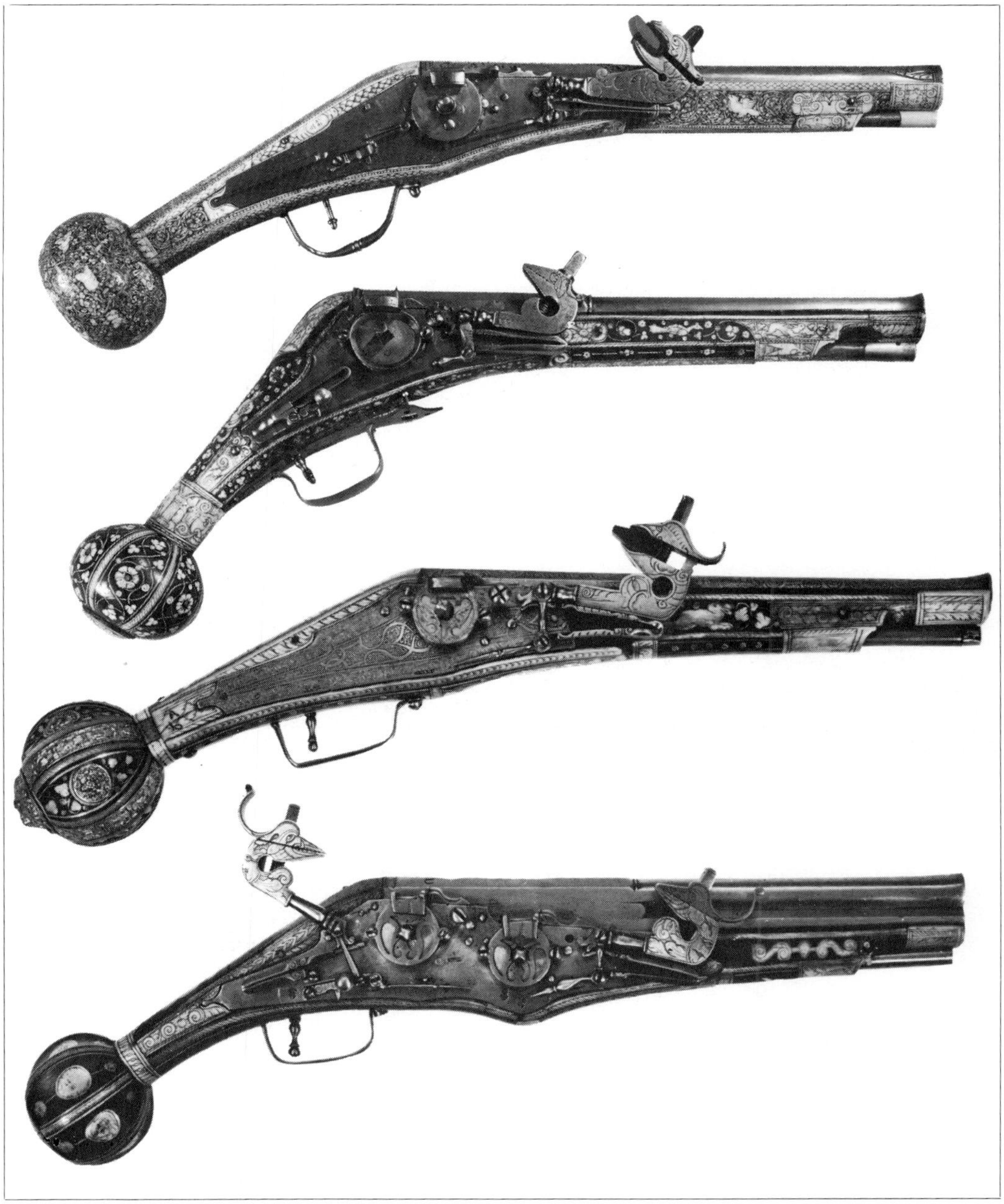

29 *Top* Wheel-lock pistol with ball-butt, the stock inlaid with staghorn, the barrel dated 1579. Victoria & Albert Museum, London.

30 *Middle* (*top*) One of a pair of wheel-lock pistols, the stock inlaid with staghorn; the barrel bears the marks of Augsburg, a hunting horn in a shield, and of the maker, probably Jäger. German (Augsburg), *c.*1580–90. Victoria & Albert Museum, London.

31 *Middle* (*bottom*) Wheel-lock pistol, the lock and barrel etched and gilt, the ball-butt mounted in gilt bronze. German (Nuremberg), *c.*1580. Tower of London Armouries.

32 *Above* Double-barrelled wheel-lock pistol, the stock inlaid with staghorn. German (Nuremberg), *c.*1580. Tower of London Armouries.

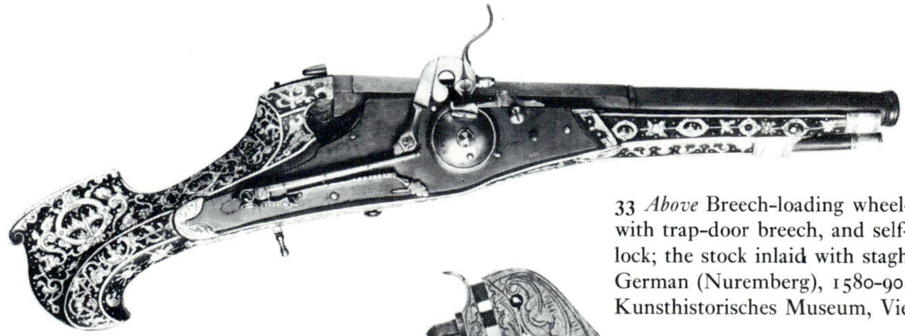

33 *Above* Breech-loading wheel-lock pistol with trap-door breech, and self-spanning lock; the stock inlaid with staghorn. German (Nuremberg), 1580-90. Kunsthistorisches Museum, Vienna.

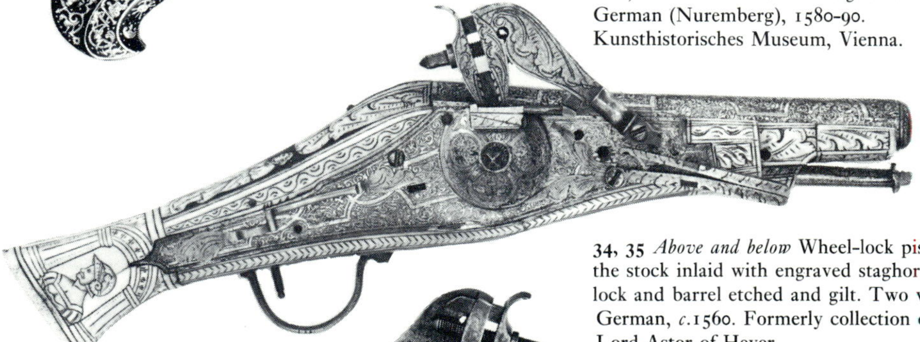

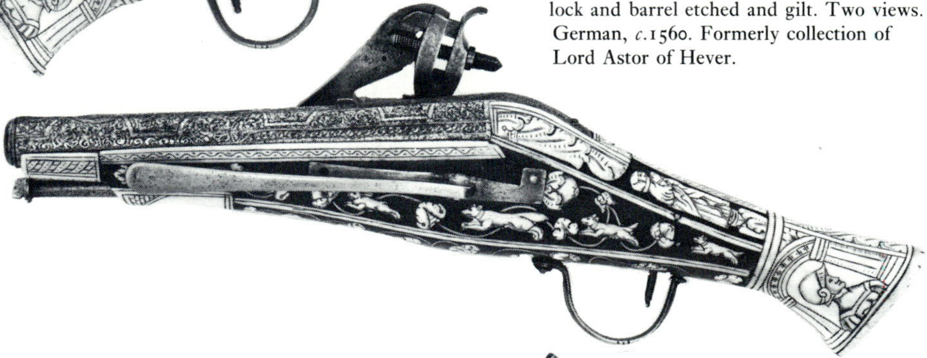

34, 35 *Above and below* Wheel-lock pistol, the stock inlaid with engraved staghorn, the lock and barrel etched and gilt. Two views. German, *c.*1560. Formerly collection of Lord Astor of Hever.

36 *Above* Wheel-lock pistol, the stock inlaid with engraved staghorn. German (Nuremberg), *c.*1590. Victoria & Albert Museum, London.

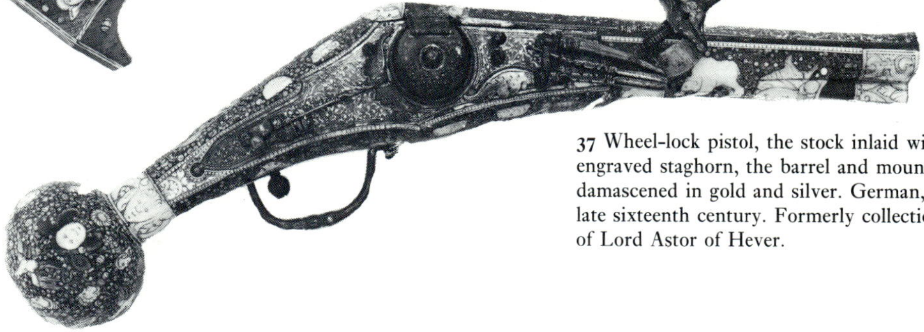

37 Wheel-lock pistol, the stock inlaid with engraved staghorn, the barrel and mounts damascened in gold and silver. German, late sixteenth century. Formerly collection of Lord Astor of Hever.

unlikely. A more probable derivation is from *pistolese*, the name of a kind of dagger made in Pistoia, which in France and England was changed to *pistolet*. That this was certainly the view at the time when the word was coming into general use is shown by the following passage in Henri Estienne's *Traicté de la conformité du language François auec le grec* which first appeared in Geneva in 1565 (the original is in French):

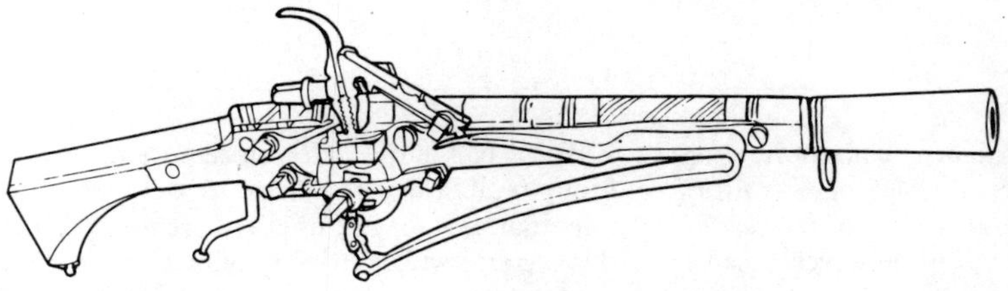

Wheel-lock pistol, the stock of engraved iron. Italian (?), *c.*1525. Germanisches Nationalmuseum, Nuremberg.

> At Pistoia, a little town that is a good day away from Florence, they are wont to make little daggers, the which, being imported into France as a novelty, were named after the place [of their manufacture] first *Pistoyers*, then *Pistoliers*, and in the end *Pistolets*. Some time afterwards, the invention of little harquebuses having come about the name of these little daggers was transferred to them.

Why the name for a dagger should have been transferred to the new type of firearm is unknown, though it is conceivable that it was because some of the latter also came from Pistoia where a firearms industry was already well established in the sixteenth century. Whether this is so or not, no evidence has yet been produced in support of the view that the pistol was actually invented in Pistoia, for the weapon itself was certainly in general use before the first recorded appearance of the words pistol or pistolet. In England the term 'dag' (also spelt *tack*) was used first, and it continued to be applied to some form of pistol, at present unidentified, until the early-seventeenth century.[61] In Spain the term 'saddle-harquebus' (*arcabuzillo de arzón*) was used to describe what we should call pistols as late as 1558 in the inventory of the armoury of the Emperor Charles V, known as the *Relación de Valladolid*. Similarly, in Italy the term 'little harquebus' (*archibusetto*) was used until late in the sixteenth century.

A small group of wheel-lock pistols with external lock-mechanisms of the type described as probably Italian[62] may date from as early as *c.*1525, though this is by no means certain. The earliest firmly dated pistols are German and date from the 1530s and 1540s, most of the surviving examples being in the Real Armería, Madrid, and it is in fact Germany that dominates pistol design throughout the remainder of the sixteenth century. All the early examples–including the Italian ones–are quite straight with their butts continuing the line of their barrels. Some are merely miniature long-guns with oblong butts, while others have grips like those found on contemporary maces, sometimes with indentations for the fingers. On this last type the grip usually flares slightly at the rear, is cut to a forked goat's foot or fish-tail shape, or terminates in a knob (pommel).

During the second half of the sixteenth century two main forms of pistol-stock were used. One of these has a fairly straight butt, set at only a slight angle to the line of the barrel and widening into a small polygonal pommel (at first quite small), into a goat's foot or fish-tail shape or, towards the end of the century, into what was in effect a miniature shoulder-butt like that on some contemporary muskets. The other form, which started to develop fully in *c.*1560, has the butt set at a much sharper–sometimes very sharp–angle to the line of the barrel and terminates in a spherical pommel that, during the period *c.*1570-*c.*1590, was often very large. The purpose of the pommel, which was normally held in place by glue and a peg, seems to have been to facilitate the drawing of the pistol from its holster: contrary to popular belief, it was not strong enough to be used as a club. This second type of pistol is often called by its German name *Puffer*: like the first type, however, it seems to have been made internationally in North-Western Europe, though its more exaggerated forms were probably confined to Germany. All these pistols are found with stocks of wood, of metal (usually iron) or of wood covered with metal, the last two constructions at this date being particularly favoured in Germany.

The majority of sixteenth-century pistols were

61 In the Henry VIII inventory of 1547 (*Archaeologia*, Vol. LI) *dag* and *tack* are the only words used to denote pistols. In Scotland *tack* was used as an alternative for *pistol*, applied particularly to the all-metal Highland form of the weapon, until the eighteenth century.

62 See p. 38.

Three-barrelled wheel-lock pistol of the Emperor Charles V. The barrels are rotated manually and are designed to fire steel darts. German (Nuremberg), *c.*1540. Ameria Reale, Turin.

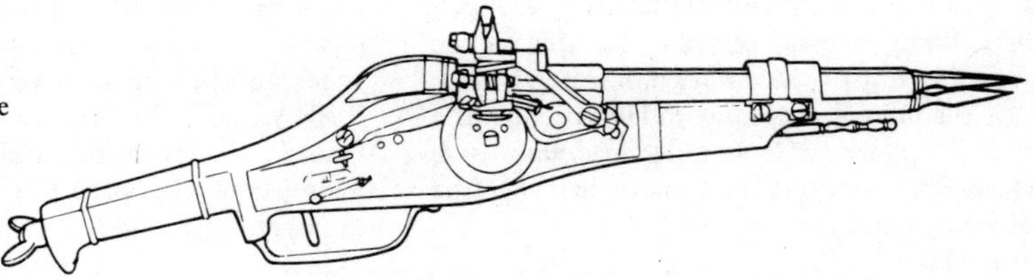

designed to be used by horsemen–both for hunting and for war–and were carried, sometimes as many as four at a time, in holsters attached to the saddle. From at least as early as *c.*1540, however, smaller pistols that could be carried at the belt were produced, and from the last quarter of the century both these and the longer forms of pistol were sometimes fitted with a long flat belt-hook on the side of the stock opposite to the lock. There is no evidence to show that any attempt was made to standardise pistol calibres at this early period but it is broadly true to say that before *c.*1580 most normal pistols had comparatively short barrels and large bores. At this last date, however, a new form of pistol appeared, probably first in France, with a long slender barrel of small calibre. The old butt-shapes were retained but they were now straight or else curved or sloped down only very slightly. The ball pommel was still the most frequently used type of terminal to the butt, but it now became pear- or elongated oval-shaped. It was this type of stock that was to supplant most others after *c.*1600.

Though the majority of sixteenth-century pistols were designed to fire round ball, a small number, all apparently German and dating from the period *c.*1535-50, fired iron darts. It is difficult to identify these where, as is almost invariably the case, they do not retain any of their darts, but it is likely that a very small bore is one of their characteristics. The best known of these pistols is the remarkable iron-stocked example made for the Emperor Charles V in *c.*1540, probably in Nuremberg, and now in the Armeria Reale, Turin.[63] This has three barrels rotated manually by means of a wing-nut at the end of the butt, and retains three of its iron darts, each of which is made in one with a rod that extends down the barrel as far as the charge. The lock is a wheel-lock with a double-headed cock and a sickle-shaped cock-spring.[64]

63 No. N.49.

64 Of the type described on p. 39.

By the end of the sixteenth century firearms were firmly established in Europe as weapons of major importance. It may be useful, therefore, to conclude this chapter with a brief account of their effect on warfare during the first three centuries of their existence.

Contrary to popular belief, the invention of the gun did not immediately bring about the downfall of the armoured knighthood of Europe. The art of the armourer did not attain its highest level of perfection until over a century after the appearance of the first guns, and its greatest period was from *c.*1450 to *c.*1550. Hand-firearms do not, in fact, seem to have played a prominent role on the battlefield until the Hussite Wars of 1419-34, and they did not even start to supplant the bow and the cross-bow as the chief military hand-projectile weapons until the second half of the fifteenth century. During the Italian Wars of the late fifteenth and first half of the sixteenth century, however, the use of firearms led to a complete revolution in military tactics and from this time onwards their supremacy over the older weapons was assured.

The slowness with which hand-firearms came to play an important part in warfare is not difficult to explain. In the early stages of their development the only advantages they had over the cross-bow and the long-bow were that they were cheaper to make than the former and could be used effectively with less training than the latter: as far as range, accuracy and rapidity of discharge were concerned they were at first markedly inferior to the older weapons.[65] Furthermore, the tactical application of hand-firearms must have been considerably limited for virtually the whole of the first century of their existence by reason of the fact that they had to be

65 Even as late as the end of the sixteenth century there were writers on military affairs who advocated a return to the long-bow on the grounds that it was a superior weapon to the musket. In 1776 Benjamin Franklin suggested that bowmen should be included in the newly-formed American army though his suggestion was not adopted.

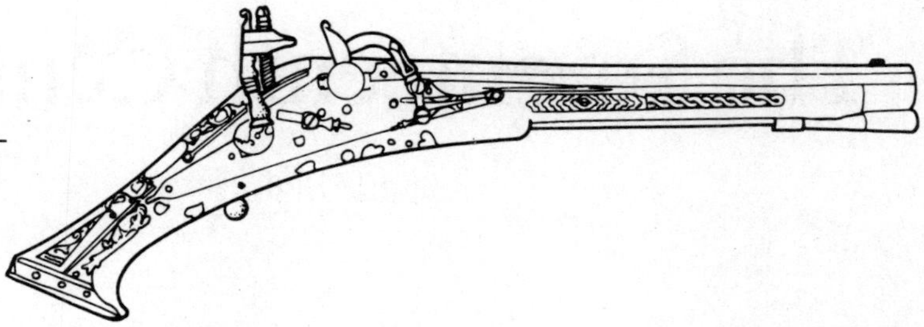

Snaphance pistol. Flemish or English, late-sixteenth century. Porte de Hal Museum, Brussels.

manipulated and aimed with one hand while the other was left free to use the piece of smouldering slow-match used for ignition. For this reason, as already noted, the invention of the matchlock was an event of major importance in the history of the development of hand-firearms, though it came into general use only slowly.

Another major factor, that was to lead in the sixteenth century to the final predominance of fire-arms over all other types of hand projectile weapons, was the development of more powerful gunpowder. The history of this development has not yet been studied in detail, but there seems to be little doubt that it resulted mainly from the introduction of the process of 'granulating' or 'corning'. The earliest gunpowder was what is usually known as 'meal' or 'serpentine' powder, that is to say it was literally powder, and when loaded in a gun barrel it formed a compact mass that burned relatively slowly. Corned powder, on the other hand, consists of comparatively large granules produced by compressing the meal into a hard cake and then forcing it through meshes of suitable size: when loaded the grains did not compress together and the resultant air-spaces between them produced much quicker ignition and, in consequence, a more rapid and powerful building up of gases behind the projectile.

The corning process was probably introduced during the second quarter of the fifteenth century,[66] though it seems to have been adopted only slowly, possibly because it produced powder that was too powerful for the firearms that were available at first. The extent to which it was used during the second half of the fifteenth century is uncertain, but it seems to have come into general service during the first half of the succeeding century. It is probably significant in this connection to notice that the first evidence of body-armour being reinforced or increased in weight to make it bullet-proof appears in *c.*1550, a date that also marks the real beginning of the decline of the armourer's art though fine-quality armour continued to be made for another century.[67]

---

66 See Partington, *op.cit.*; p. 154.

67 Another major factor that led to the disappearance of the fully-armoured horseman from the battlefield was the invention of the wheel-lock. This produced a revolution in cavalry tactics by making possible the production of a gun—the pistol—that could be used really effectively on horseback. The result was that from *c.*1540 onwards the heavily-armoured 'knights' who charged, formed in depth, with their lances were rapidly replaced by more lightly armoured pistoleers who advanced in line to fire their pistols at the enemy before weaving off sideways.

CHAPTER THREE

The Seventeenth Century

Claude Blair

38-111 The sixteenth century had been essentially a period
280 of experiment comparable to that following the invention of the percussion system in 1807. Gunmakers had sought, by a process of trial and error, to discover the most efficient forms of barrel, stock and lock that could be devised within the limits of the technology of the time: in short, to establish the basic principles of their craft. The advent of the seventeenth century produced no sudden violent change in the general lines of development that had been followed in the preceding century, but it marked the beginning of a period of consolidation. The most obvious sign of this was a general reduction in the number of different types of gun and, particularly, in the variety of stock forms. The shoulder-butt was generally adopted for long-guns, except in Germany where the cheek-stock survived, alongside the other, until the eighteenth century. By the second decade of the seventeenth century both pistols and long-guns had generally assumed basic forms that are recognisable as the direct precursors of those still in use today, and development for the next fifty or so years was to be concerned mainly with the refinement of these forms.

In the field of military firearms the same processes were at work, and they were undoubtedly stimulated by the Thirty Years War (1618-48) which created an unprecedented demand for weapons of all kinds. As the century progressed, military guns tended to become lighter and less unwieldy, while the growth of standing armies led to the appearance of regulation arms made to specifications laid down by the government either by private gunsmiths under contract or else in state arsenals. This did not result in standardisation in the modern sense of the term–the production methods of the time made this impossible–but it did have the effect of sharpening the lines of demarcation between military firearms and those intended for other purposes.

The development of firearms in the sixteenth century had been completely dominated by the great gunmaking centres of Germany, notably Nuremberg, Augsburg and Suhl. During the first half of the seventeenth century the lead was taken by the French gunsmiths and henceforth until the middle of the eighteenth century, when they were in turn supplanted by the English, theirs was the dominant influence on the design of firearms all over Europe. This was partly the result of the tremendous influence that the France of Louis XIV exercised on every aspect of European culture, but it also owed something to the fact that Louis XIII (1610-43) was passionately interested in firearms. We know from the diary of his physician J. Héroard that by 1611, when he was only nine years old, he already owned seven guns and that these had been increased to fifty by 1614. His patronage of native gunmakers must have had a tremendous influence on the development of the manufacture of the fine-quality firearms for which France was soon to become famous. The king's interest was not, however, confined to the weapons of his own day. He has, in fact, a good claim to being regarded as the first gun-collector in the modern sense of the term, and on his death in 1643 his collection of hundreds of guns included many antiques. Its importance for the study of French firearms has been very great indeed, for in 1673 an inventory of its entire contents was completed on the order of Louis XIV, while a further inventory was made in 1729.[1] Nearly every piece was stamped with its inventory-number–usually in the stock just in front of the trigger-guard–and so can still be identified despite the fact that the collection has been broken up.[2] A few weapons with elaborately decorated stocks were not marked in this way, but these can sometimes be identified from the detailed descriptions in the inventories.

The major technical invention of the seventeenth century was the flintlock, which appeared in France in the first or second decade. It was ultimately to revolutionise firearms design but, as its immediate

1 See J. J. Guiffrey, *Inventaire genéral du mobilier de la couronne sous Louis XIV*, Vol. II, Paris, 1886.

2 It seems to have survived intact until the French Revolution, but its subsequent fate is uncertain. It had certainly been broken up by the period immediately following the Battle of Waterloo and its surviving contents are now widely scattered, though many pieces still remain in the Musée de l'Armée, Paris.

impact was negligible, the seventeenth-century evolution of the lock-forms already current in the sixteenth century will be discussed first here.

Systems of Ignition

The Matchlock

58 A few fine-quality matchlock arms were made in the first half of the seventeenth century, notably target guns,[3] but the vast majority of private purchasers of firearms preferred to have them equipped with wheel- or snaplocks.[4] Where long-arms for the infantry were concerned, however, the matchlock was used almost exclusively, except for the equipping of certain special troops, until the end of the century (the British government, for example, did not abandon it finally until the early eighteenth century). The reasons for this are obvious. The lock was cheap and easy to manufacture and, having no complicated working parts, was mechanically very reliable. Moreover, the infantry tactics of the time, which involved bodies of men firing in unison at fairly close range according to a set drill, would have gained little from firearms equipped with more complex systems of ignition.

Throughout the remainder of its career the matchlock differed hardly at all from that described on page 31 above. The only major development, as has already been mentioned, was the introduction in about 1590 of the trigger-lock. It will be recalled that on the sear-lock, the lever on the inside of the plate to which the tumbler on the cock was linked was itself connected to a lever-like trigger that projected backwards under the butt. On the trigger-lock the latter was replaced by a trigger of modern form, separate from the lock, suspended in the stock on a cross-pin so as to engage in front of a right-angle projection on the end of the lever linked to the tumbler on the cock. This had a number of advantages: the lock could be removed for cleaning or repair without the necessity of detaching the trigger first; a trigger-guard could be fitted, thereby reducing the danger of accidental discharge; and the new trigger gave a better grip and an easier pull-off, and so an improved aim.

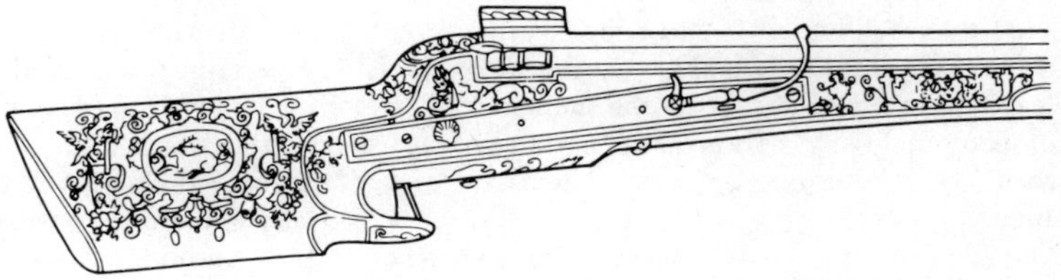

Snap-matchlock gun, the stock marked FF, the barrel by Christoff Dressler of Dresden. Saxon, dated 1607. Musée de l'Armée, Paris.

The trigger-lock very rapidly replaced the sear-lock and it is doubtful if any of the latter were made after *c.*1620. That some were still in use in England as late as the 1630s is, however, shown by the following entry in the list of gunmakers' rates embodied in a Commission appointed by the Privy Council in 1631 to inspect the arms of the Trained Bands:

> For furnishing and setting of a tricker lock in place of a sceare lock, with a handle [*i.e.* trigger-guard], tricker and tricker pynnes – 2s. 6d.[5]

The actual form of the lock changed very little during the seventeenth century, though there were minor variations, chiefly in the shape of the lockplate. This was at first usually flat and, on military firearms, shaped like a narrow oblong. On the few *de luxe* matchlocks of the period the oblong type of lockplate was sometimes replaced by one of rhomboid form. After about 1660 the lockplate was normally similar in shape to that of the contemporary flintlock.[6]

The Wheel-lock

The wheel-lock remained in wide use throughout 38
the first half of the seventeenth century, but during 42–5
the second quarter it began to be supplanted by the 57, 59 75–7
various forms of snaplock, of which the most import- 101, 102
ant was the flintlock. There were several reasons for 107, 110
this. First, the snaplock was both easier and cheaper to manufacture. This is demonstrated, for example,

3 Of the type described on pp. 50–51.

4 An apparently unique pistol of *c.*1680 in the Suermondt Museum, Aachen, is fitted with a matchlock. I have not been able to handle this so am unable to say whether the lock is original or a replacement, but the pistol itself has every appearance of authenticity. The style of inlaid decoration on the stock, which resembles that found on Tschinke (see p. 96), suggests an East European origin.

5 See J. N. George, *English Guns and Rifles*, Plantersville, USA, 1947, pp. 36–7.

6 See p. 74.

by the English gunmakers' rates of 1631, already quoted, where a pair of firelock (*i.e.* wheel-lock)[7] pistols are priced at £3.0*s*.0*d*. and a pair of snaphance ones at £2.0*s*.0*d*.[8] Secondly, the snaplock was easier to use and did not require a separate key, which might become lost, to prepare it for action. And, finally, it was much more reliable. Several seventeenth-century writers comment on the fact that if a wheel-lock was left spanned for too long a period it was likely to jam,[9] while on its lack of safety Randle Holme, writing in the 1680s, comments as follows:

> a wheel Lock for a pistall . . . These kind of fire locks with their spanners to wind up the spring of the wheele were onely in use for Troopers in the Late rebellion in tyme of King Charles I, Anno 1641, but now wholly layd aside as useless and dangerous, being the sudden death of many by fireing unawares, the party thinking them not to be wound up, when they have bine.[10]

Outside Germany the lock seems to have become rare after the 1640s and to have been discarded altogether by the 1660s.[11] In the area of German culture, however, though it does not seem to have been applied to pistols after the 1670s, it remained very popular, alongside the flintlock, for sporting and target rifles until well into the eighteenth century. The reason for this has never been satisfactorily explained and one can only assume that it was the result of some kind of sporting convention, analogous to the use of a fly in fishing when other forms of bait would be more effective.

The main lines of development of the wheel-lock during the early part of the seventeenth century were directed towards making it simpler and more compact. The domed wheel-cover disappeared during the first decade and henceforth this feature was normally quite flat, sometimes with pierced decoration. The ring-shaped substitute for the cover introduced during the sixteenth century remained in use, while in *c.*1600 another construction appeared in which the wheel was supported merely by one–or more rarely two–lugs attached to the plate. This form came into very wide use, though it never completely supplanted the flat cover and the ring. It was often carved to represent a figure or some other decorative shape. In Germany from the 1630s onwards the wheel was commonly placed on the inside of the plate, leaving a flat external surface, and after the middle of the century this became the normal construction. On pistols, with the widespread adoption of a slender curved butt in the second decade of the century, the French shape of lockplate came into general use. This was rather narrow, except in the centre where the lower edge curved down to take the wheel, and at the rear curved down slightly into a point. With it came a lightening of both the main- and cock-spring which extended also to the locks on long-guns, though these–except, of course, in France–retained a rather wide angular plate. On German guns, especially those fitted with a cheek-stock, this last developed a marked step at the rear to correspond to the step in the butt, immediately behind the barrel, which had started to come into use at the very end of the sixteenth century. In Italy the lockplate on both pistols and long-guns was normally of rhomboid form.

The actual mechanism of the majority of wheel-locks changed very little throughout the seventeenth century, though the peculiarly French construction with separate mainspring seems to have gone out of use after *c.*1630. The tendency towards simplification, already noted, did, however, lead very early in the century to the discarding of the safety-catch on the majority of wheel-locks. This was presumably because the lock could be rendered safe by keeping the cock away from the wheel, though Randle Holme's remarks quoted above suggest that this elementary precaution was frequently ignored. The automatic pan-cover release likewise was fitted less frequently after *c.*1630, though it seems never to have been discarded completely during the period under review.

In certain areas rather primitive-looking wheel-locks with external mainsprings–possibly derived from the 'Leonardo' locks described above[12]–continued to be made until well into the seventeenth century. They are of two main kinds, of which the one most commonly encountered is found on the distinctive group of birding rifles, known as *Tschinkes*, that were the speciality of the town of Teschen in Silesia.[13] This has a wheel-cover in the form of a horizontal curved bar and also a triangular cover for the rear end of the mainspring. It also differs from the standard form of lock in having a sear mechanism that has to be set before use by pressing a button that projects from the mainspring cover.

7 The term *firelock* was later transferred to the snaphance and flintlock.

8 George, *op.cit.*, p. 37.

9 e.g., John Vernon, *The Young Horseman*, 1644, p. 11.

10 Randle Holme, *Academy of Armory*, Vol. II, Roxburgh Club, London, 1904, Lib. III, Cap. xx, no. 49.

11 A curious revival of the system occurs on a pair of pistols by Le Page of Paris, dated 1829, in the Musée de l'Armée, Paris (No. M. 1698).

12 See p. 34.

13 See p. 96.

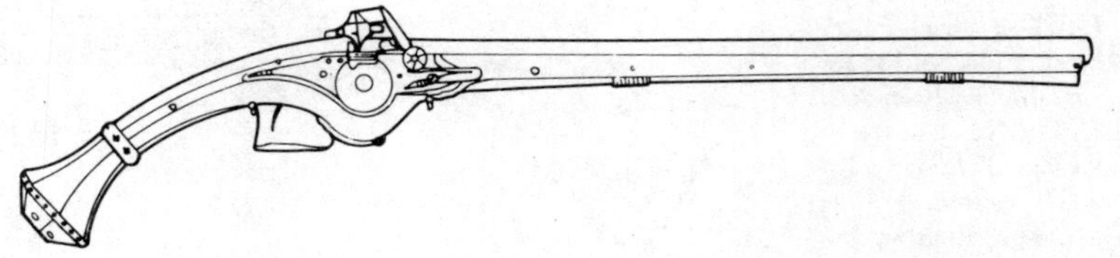

Wheel-lock pistol. French, *c.*1600. Wallace Collection, London.

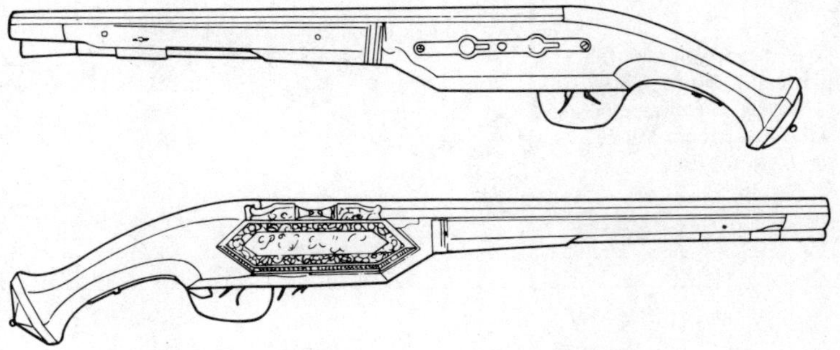

Wheel-lock pistol with enclosed lock, firing two superimposed shots, of the type invented by Pierre Bergier of Grenoble. French, *c.*1636. Probably No. 203 in the *Cabinet d'Armes* of Louis XIII. Musée de l'Armée, Paris.

The second type of lock with an external mainspring appears to be either Spanish, Portuguese or possibly Southern Italian in origin. The mainspring here is of a very distinctive shape, with the two arms coming together to form a V and then diverging into a ring, while the upper jaw of the cock is commonly fitted with a kind of hood that projects downwards over the neck. Surviving examples, which are rare, all appear to date from the first half of the seventeenth century.

As always, individual gunmakers in the seventeenth century produced locks of distinctive design that were not widely adopted. Self-spanning mechanisms, locks that were spanned from the opposite side of the stock, and hinged pan-covers that also served as pyrites holders are examples of this. Among locks fitted with the last-mentioned device reference must be made to the rare group, produced in Austria and probably also Bohemia in the second quarter of the century, with a vertical tubular 'chimney' attached to the cover to take the flash and smoke from the
40 priming away above the level of the shooter's eyes.

The only one of these individually-designed wheel-locks that calls for fairly detailed discussion here is that perfected by Pierre Bergier, a clockmaker of Grenoble, in 1634, and intended, according to the Louis XIII inventory, '*pour tirer dans l'eau*'.[14] This should not be taken to mean that the lock could literally be fired under water but merely that it would continue to operate in damp conditions that would have been sufficient to put an ordinary lock out of action. Bergier's secret was to enclose the mechanism of the lock behind the lockplate and at the same time to make all the parts very close-fitting. The hinged pan-cover incorporated a pyrites-holder and sealed off the priming when closed; the lock was spanned through an aperture, fitted with a hinged cap, on the other side of the stock; and the lockplate and other external mounts were made of gilt-bronze in order to prevent oxidation. In addition, the actual mechanism of the lock differed from the standard one in that it used a spiral spring like a clock, instead of the usual heavy V-shaped mainspring.

In 1635 Bergier presented Louis XIII with a gun fitted with one of his locks which fired four superimposed charges from a single barrel. The present whereabouts of this are unknown, but the description of it in the Louis XIII inventory shows that it was completed in 1634 and that it had a quadruple lock. In 1635, as a result of this gift, Bergier was granted, by royal letters patent, the monopoly of the manufacture of his invention in France, and he subsequently produced two other guns and a pair of pistols for the king, in collaboration with a lock-

14 See Charles Buttin, 'Pistolets de Louis XIII', *Armes Anciennes*, II, Geneva, 1957-9, pp. 75-83, on which the following account is based.

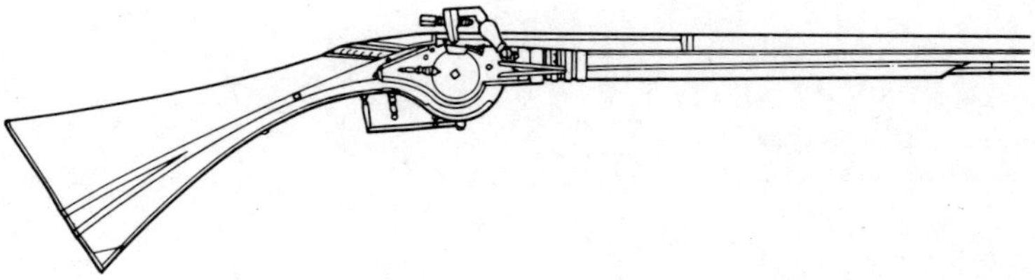

Detail of wheel-lock birding piece made for Louis XIII. French, *c.*1620. No. 5 in the *Cabinet d'Armes* of Louis XIII. Victoria & Albert Museum, London.

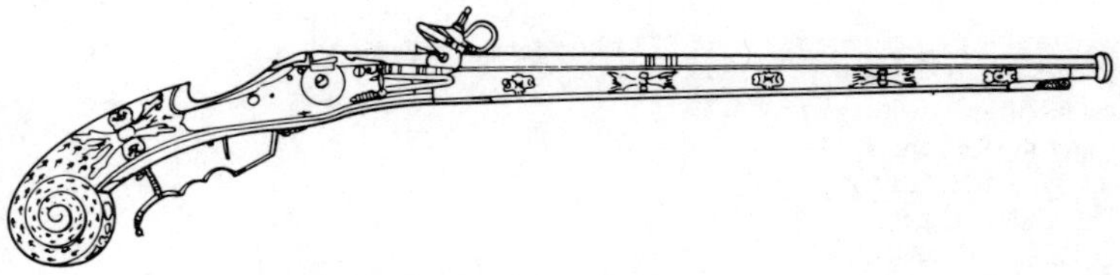

Wheel-lock gun with the devices of the Archduke Matthias, later Emperor. German, *c.*1600. Musée de l'Armée, Paris.

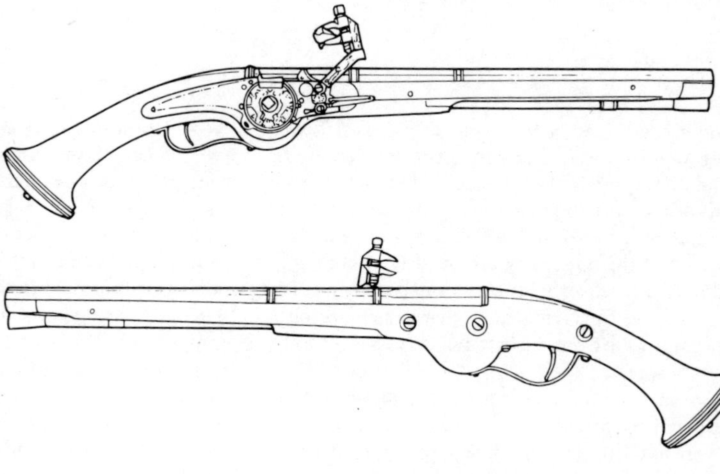

Pair of wheel-lock pistols, the barrels inscribed LAZARI COMINAZ. Dutch, *c.*1650. Victoria & Albert Museum, London.

maker of Montélimar, Pierre Chabroux. The pistols, which are preserved in the Musée de l'Armée, Paris,[15] are each equipped with a double lock to fire two superimposed charges from a single barrel. Another similar pistol by Bergier, in an English private collection, was included in the exhibition 'The Art of the Armourer' held at the Victoria and Albert Museum, London in 1963.[16]

Despite his patent of monopoly Bergier seems to have produced very few examples of his invention and less than five years later another maker, La Fonteyne of Mourgues, was manufacturing very similar pistols and claiming to be their inventor. A pair in the Army Museum at Prague are signed *Fai a Mouges par La Fontaine 1642* and a single pistol in the Wallace Collection, London[17] is signed *Faict a* 41
Mourgues par La Fontaine Inventeur. Nothing further seems to be known about this maker.[18]

15 Nos. M. 1659-60.

16 Cat. No. 271.

17 No. A. 1182.

18 R. E. Gardner, *Small Arms Makers*, New York, 1963, p. 279, records him as Muentain La Fontaine 'before and after 1640', of Morges in Switzerland, but gives no source for his information. Mourgues was, however, also the old French name for Monaco.

The Snaphance and Flintlock

Perhaps no aspect of the study of early firearms has given rise to more confusion than the different ways in which modern writers apply the terms 'snaphance' and 'flintlock'. There can be no doubt that, historically, the two words were used synonymously for any type of lock that operated by striking a flint against a steel, whatever the precise details of its mechanism. 'Flintlock', which is only recorded for the first time in 1683, in Turner's *Pallas Armata*, eventually became the standard term, 'snaphance' having become obsolete before the end of the seventeenth century.[19] Modern writers have, however, sought to apply the terms quite arbitrarily to two distinct forms of flint mechanism. Until the publication of Dr Torsten Lenk's great work *Flintlåset* in 1939[20] students followed the definitions laid down by Sir Samuel Meyrick in the early nineteenth century and called any flint mechanism that had the steel and pan-cover combined a flintlock, reserving 'snaphance' for mechanisms on which these parts were separate. Many collectors and writers still hold to these definitions, but others follow Lenk, who defined the flintlock as a snaphance that has the steel and pan-cover combined *and* a sear operating vertically to engage in two notches–giving respectively half-cock (safety) and full cock–in a tumbler attached to the inner end of the cock-spindle.[21] The definition has some historical justification in that this construction had virtually supplanted all other forms of snaphance at the time when the word 'flintlock' came into use and I have therefore adopted it here. All other forms of flint snaplock mechanism will be classified as snaphances irrespective of the construction of the pan-cover and steel. In addition, the modern term 'snaplock' will be used as a general one to cover both types of lock.

A detailed study of the snaphance lock has still to be made and its origins and the relationship between the various types in use during the seventeenth century are still obscure. Three main groups can at present be identified tentatively: the Scandinavian-Russian snaphance; the Netherlands, and related snaphances; and the Mediterranean or Miquelet lock.

19 The French word *fusil* (sometimes Anglicised to *fusee* or *fuzee*) was also used in England to denote a flintlock in the late seventeenth century. It later came to mean a light military flintlock gun; cf. also p. 42.

20 Torsten Lenk, *Flintlaset, dess Uppkomst och Utveckling*, Stockholm, 1939. All references to this work made here apply to the English edition: *The Flintlock: Its Origin and Development*, translated by G. A. Urquhart, edited by J. F. Hayward, London, 1965.

21 Some modern writers call this the 'true' or 'French' flintlock. See also pp. 73 and 107.

The Scandinavian-Russian Snaphance

This derives directly from the type of snaphance described on page 42 above and its most obvious characteristic is a long narrow cock with only a single–often very shallow–bend in it, and very deep jaws. The most primitive type, which was used generally in Scandinavia and Russia during the seventeenth century, and by some of the peasantry in those areas until the nineteenth century, differs little from the sixteenth-century prototype. It has an external mainspring, a sear that operates laterally through the lockplate to engage over a spur on the heel of the cock, and a simple pivoted pan-cover that had to be opened manually before firing. From the beginning of the seventeenth century two main types can be distinguished: the Norwegian–also used in Russia–on which the rear of the upper jaw of the cock is equipped with a short dowel that works in a hole in the fixed lower jaw, and the Swedish on which the upper jaw is dovetailed at the neck of the cock. A variant of the latter, usually referred to now as the 'Baltic lock', with the upper jaw shaped at the rear like a leaf bent halfway round the neck, also appeared in the middle years of the seventeenth century (p. 69).

A combined steel and pan-cover made its appearance on the Swedish lock as early as the 1620s but, as there was no half-cock mechanism, the steel was made so that it could be pivoted sideways to enable the gun to be carried in safety ready loaded and primed with the cock down. This construction was also adopted for the other locks, including those made in Russia, though the separate steel and hand-operated pan-cover continued to be made.

Guns with Swedish locks were also made in northern Germany and by German gunsmiths living in Sweden, possibly initially as a result of contacts between the two countries during the Thirty Years War. This German influence may perhaps account for the fact that the construction of finer-quality Swedish locks had become a little more sophisticated by the middle of the seventeenth century. The mainspring was moved to the inside of the plate, the jaws of the cock became shorter, and the spur on the heel was reduced in size and eventually disappeared altogether, when the sear was made to operate–still laterally–in a notch in the tumbler. This form of lock continued to be fitted to fine-quality guns in Sweden until *c.*1730, after which date it was generally supplanted by the flintlock. As previously noted, however, the form of lock from which it had developed continued to be made by provincial Swedish gunsmiths until well into the nineteenth century.

The Netherlands and Related Snaphances **47, 62 97–100**

The name Netherlands Snaphance is usually applied **105, 111**

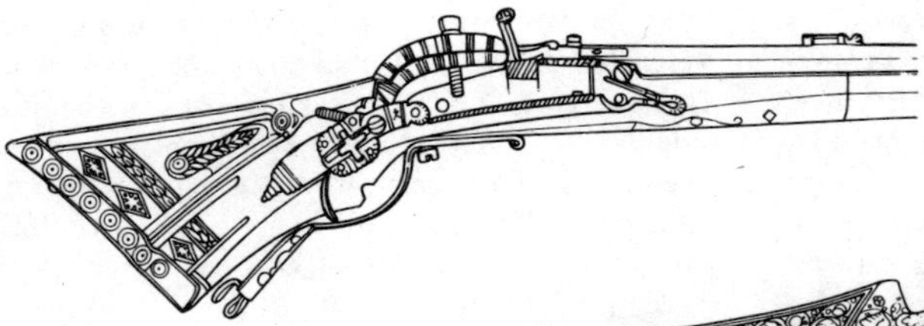

Detail of flintlock gun, the lock with a swivelling steel. Southern Swedish, *c.*1650. Livrustkammaren, Stockholm.

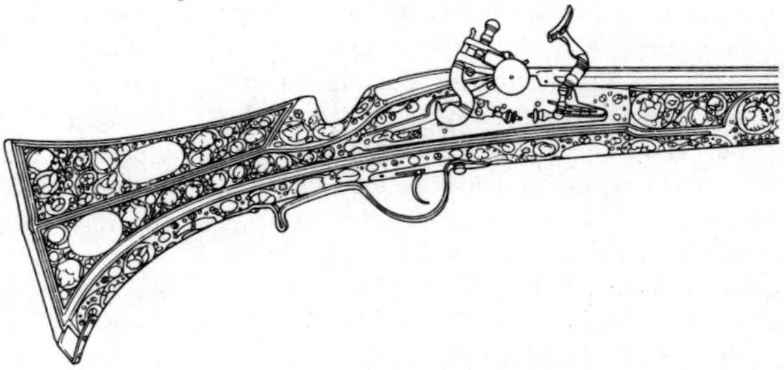

Snaphance gun. Dutch *c.*1620. Musée de l'Armée, Paris.

by modern students to the form of snaplock described on page 44 above. Its characteristic features are: a cock with a spur at the rear that engages under a laterally-moving sear working through the plate; a separate hinged steel held firm by a small V-shaped feather-spring attached to the exterior of the plate; a sliding pan-cover that opens automatically as the cock falls; an internal mainspring working on a tumbler attached to the cock-screw; a buffer attached to the plate in front of the breast of the cock; and a circular or polygonal fence at the side of the pan. Whether or not this form originated in the Netherlands is uncertain, though the fact that the word 'snaphance' applied to it in England is of Dutch derivation[22] suggests that it did, while it was certainly used widely in Holland during the first half of the seventeenth century. Nevertheless, the earliest recorded examples are English and Scottish[23] and it sometimes seems to have been known on the Continent at the beginning of the century as the *Scottish lock*[24]

Of all the forms of snaphance used during the seventeenth century this is the one that has been studied least, and the full limits of its distribution and the extent to which it influenced the design of other forms of snaphance in use during the same period are uncertain. When reading this section, therefore, it should be borne in mind that some of the lock types that I have linked with the Netherlands type may, in fact, have been developed independently.

The lock construction described at the beginning of this section remained in wide use, especially on military arms, in the Netherlands and in England until the middle of the century, and also enjoyed a certain amount of favour in France. Throughout this period the lockplate, which was secured to the stock by three screws, was normally flat, tapered towards the ends and with an almost straight lower edge. Another form had a plate like that of a wheel-lock with a lower edge that curved down in a semi-circle in the centre. It is found on only a very small group of Dutch and English firearms but both it and the 'standard' form of Netherlands snaphance were very popular in Russia, almost certainly having been introduced there by the Western gunsmiths who are known to have worked in the Kremlin Armoury during the seventeenth century.[25]

As early as the 1620s an improved version of the Netherlands snaphance appeared on which the pan-cover and steel were joined together to form an L-shaped feature. This necessitated the introduction of a half-cock (safety) mechanism as the lock could no longer be rendered safe, when primed, simply by disarming the steel. The best-known of these improved locks is probably the one usually called the 'English lock' by collectors because it is found on a considerable number of seventeenth-century firearms found in England. On the first version of this, recorded as early as *c.*1630-5 on a pistol formerly in the Renwick Collection at Tucson, Arizona, [26] the sear has a small projection on its underside which engages in a notch in the tumbler at half-cock. From *c.*1640-*c.*1680 an improved version was in use on

22 See pp. 43, 410.

23 I know of no snaphance of undoubted Netherland origin dating from before 1600. The example in the Rijksmuseum, Amsterdam, illustrated by Lenk (*op.cit.*, Pl. 1:2-3) was abandoned in Novaya Zemlya in 1597 by a Dutch expedition but may well have originated in Norway (cf. ibid., p. 14, n.25).

24 Count John of Nassau Siegen in his *Discours da itzige Teutsche Kriegswesen belangend* (Dillenburg Archives, Wiesbaden, No. K. 398) states that in 1608 dragoons had muskets with *Füer oder Schottische Schloss* (Lenk, *op.cit.*, p. 22). Also, a gun with such a lock is described in an inventory of Gustavus Adolphus of Sweden (d. 1632) as Scottish (ibid., p. 21).

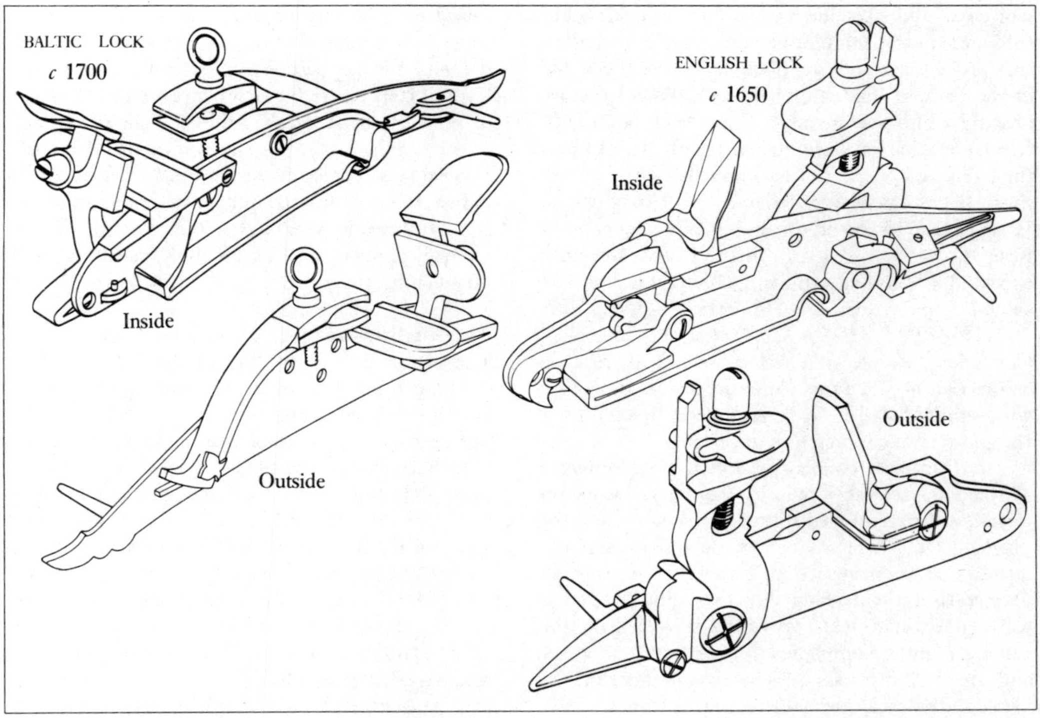

which the sear, though still working horizontally, engaged in the tumbler at full-cock also: this occurs not only on English firearms but on French, German and Netherlandish ones of the middle years of the century too.

All forms of the English lock are often fitted with a back-catch, a small pivoted hook that engages at half-cock in a notch at the end of the spur on the heel of the cock or, where the sear does not work through the plate, in the back of the body of the cock. This form of safety-catch was also commonly fitted to Continental locks, notably in Russia and Scandinavia, and its presence is no indication of English origin. Modern writers sometimes refer to this safety-catch as a dog or dog-catch, whence comes the term 'dog-lock' (also modern) often applied to a lock fitted with it, in particular the English variety.

As we have seen,[27] the horizontal sear engaging in the tumbler to give full-cock was already in use on the Continent in the 1570s. It is also found on a small group of German firearms of the late sixteenth and early seventeenth centuries – for example, on a Nuremberg revolving gun dated 1597 in the Tøjhusmuseum, Copenhagen[28] – and it may, therefore, have been German in origin. But the history of the snaphance in Germany – where it seems never to have been used widely – is so obscure that no definite conclusions can be reached on this point.

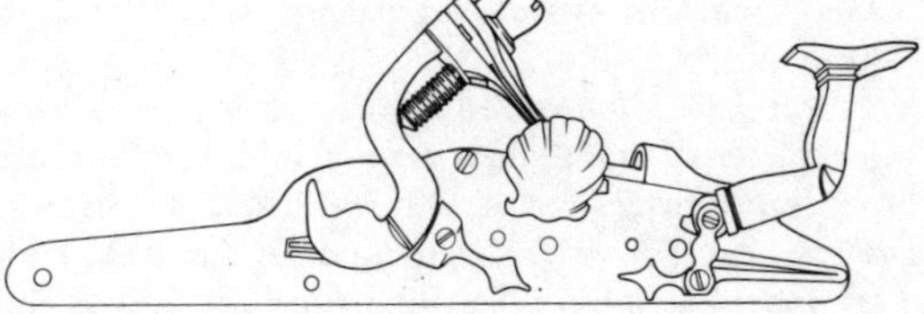

NETHERLANDS LOCK *c*.1630

Another variety of snaphance that probably derives from the Netherlands lock has a combined

25 *cf*. p. 73.

26 The pistol was sold at Sotheby's, London, on 12 November 1973 (Lot 14), when it was described as being made up from various different elements. The leading authority on English seventeenth-century pistols, Mr Ian Eaves, is, however, of the opinion that only the barrel is associated. See *Journal of the Arms and Armour Society*, Vol. VIII, p. 327, n. 105.
A gun fitted with a similar lock and dated 1619 on the stock is at Windsor Castle (No. 364). The lock was almost certainly substituted for an original matchlock at a later date.

27 See p. 42.

28 No. B. 294.

pan-cover and steel and a horizontal sear that gives full-cock on the tumbler and has a small extension that projects through the plate in front of the breast of the cock to hold it at half-cock. Its origins are obscure and it seems only to have been popular in Scotland, where it is found on pistols dating from the late seventeenth century onwards.[29] Apart from these it has been recorded on only two guns, of Western European origin and dating respectively from the 1630s and 1640s, in the Royal Armoury, Stockholm,[30] and on a splendid chiselled Italian lock signed and dated *PETRVS ANCINVS REGIENSIS F.MDCXXXXIII*, in the Odescalchi Collection, Rome.[31] Whether or not there is a connection between this construction and the somewhat similar 'Madrid' lock, popular in Spain during the eighteenth century,[32] is uncertain.

The European country in which the snaphance attained its greatest popularity was Italy. Two main forms were developed there of which one, the 'Roman' lock, is of miquelet type and is therefore discussed in the next section. The other was probably derived from the developed Netherlands lock, for it has a horizontal sear, providing full-cock on the tumbler, but accompanied by separate pan-cover and steel. Many examples have a buffer for the breast of the cock, normally springing from the base of the pan. Judging from surviving examples the lock appears to have been introduced in the third decade of the seventeenth century and was perhaps based directly on the English lock, for we know that English snaphances were greatly esteemed in Italy at this period. The Florentine gunmaker Antonio Petrini, for example, writing in *c.*1640 says 'Quanto alli fucile l'inglesi hanno portato la palma per bonta',[33] while as early as 1613 and again in 1615 the Venetians were purchasing snaphances in England.[34]

Some of the earliest Italian snaphances have lockplates of rhomboidal shape reminiscent of those on Italian wheel-locks. But by *c.*1640 a narrower form, like that on the contemporary flintlock, with its upper and lower edges almost parallel and its end rounded or bluntly pointed, had made its appearance. This remained in use with little variation until the end of the eighteenth century, especially in Central Italy where the snaphance seems to have had its greatest vogue. In the middle of the seventeenth century, however, a variant appeared: this had a vertical sear, copied from the flintlock from which, in fact, the lock differed only in having its pan-cover and steel made separately. The construction remained popular in Central Italy until the early nineteenth century.

The Mediterranean or Miquelet Lock

The term *miquelet* or *miguelet* was applied in Catalonia to irregular troops of mountain fusiliers who are supposed to have been equipped with guns fitted with a distinctive form of snaphance lock, which in consequence came to be called miquelet also [35] In fact, this application of the word seems to be a comparatively recent one and no evidence has yet been adduced to show that it was in use before the lock itself had gone out of fashion. I have, nevertheless, retained it here as a convenient term of classification.

The 'classic' miquelet lock has an external mainspring, two sears working through the plate to give respectively full and half-cock and a combined steel and pan-cover. It was employed throughout the Mediterranean area–whence it is sometimes called the 'Mediterranean' lock–but it is, above all, associated with Spain where it was virtually the only mechanism employed from the early seventeenth century to the beginning of the nineteenth century. The origins of the lock are still obscure, but it seems likely that it derived ultimately from the earliest form of snaphance,[36] which may have been introduced into both Spain and Italy by the German craftsmen who are known to have worked in both countries in the middle years of the sixteenth century. This, however, is only speculation and the history of the mechanism can only be traced with certainty from the beginning of the seventeenth century, by which date it was already almost fully developed.

The miquelet was made in two main basic forms, which are usually classified as Italian and Spanish from the countries in which they were most widely used, though neither was confined exclusively to one or the other. The first type was known as the lock *alla Romana* (i.e. 'in the Roman fashion')[37] and its use in Italy seems to have been confined largely to

29 See p. 416.

30 Nos. 1280 and 1333.

31 No. 1811-946.

32 See p. 116.

33 Unpublished manuscript of Petrini's *Arte Fabrile* in the Department of Arms and Armor at the Metropolitan Museum, New York. This differs from two other copies of the same treatise in the National Library, Florence, and the Tower of London Armouries.

34 *Calendar of State Papers*, Venetian, Vol. XIII, London, 1907, pp. 62-3, 70, 454.

35 Pollard, *History of Firearms*, London, 1926, pp. 35-6.

36 See p. 42.

37 Its seventeenth-century Spanish name was apparently *invención*, though during the eighteenth century it came to be called *alla romana*.

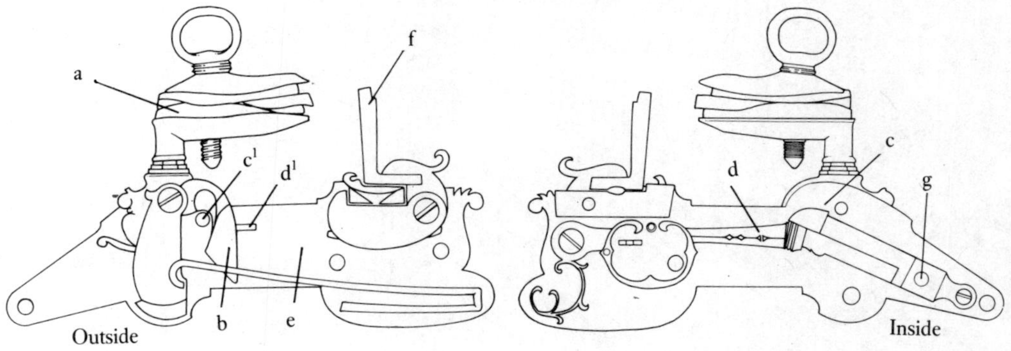

SPANISH MIQUELET LOCK (PATILLA).
The two arms of the sear (c & d) project through the lock plate in front of the cock (a), the toe of which has a blade-like extension (b). The half-cock arm ends in a stud (c^1) which engages under the angle of the extension, as shown in the drawing; the full-cock arm ends in a flat lug (d^1) which engages under the blade when the cock is pulled back fully. Both arms of the sear are withdrawn laterally when the trigger-lever (g) is pressed. The mainspring (e) presses upwards on the heel of the cock.

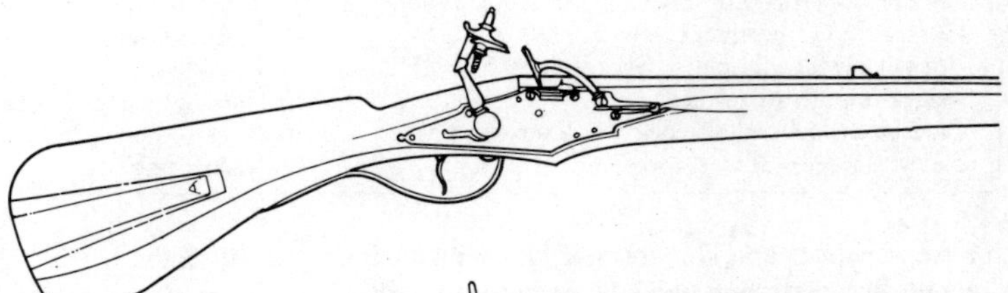

Detail of snaphance gun. French *c.*1630. No. 138 in the *Cabinet d'Armes* of Louis XIII. Victoria & Albert Museum, London.

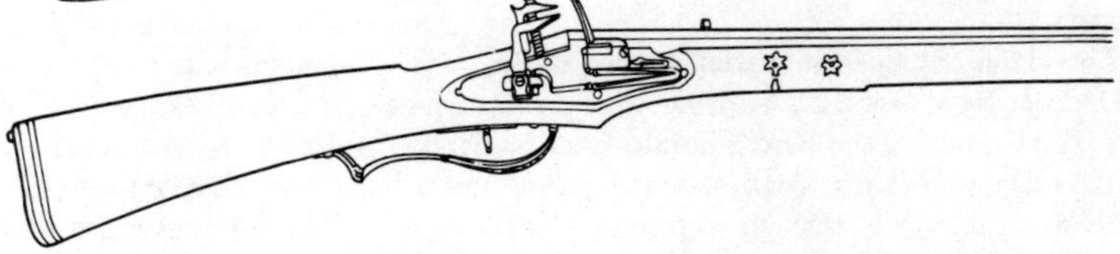

Miquelet gun, the barrel signed *Angone*, the stock HGH. Italian, *c.*1625-50. Schloss Schwarzburg, (Rudolstadt).

the central and southern areas of the country, though it was certainly manufactured in the northern gun-making centres also. It is characterised by having a mainspring that presses downwards on the toe of the cock, while its two sears give half and full-cock on the toe and heel of the cock respectively. The earliest known examples that can be dated with reasonable certainty were produced in the 1620s, but the detached lock in the Artillery Museum, Turin,[38] with miquelet *alla Romana* and wheel-lock combined on the same plate, may date from the second half of the sixteenth century. Whatever its date this seems to represent an earlier construction than the one described at the beginning of the paragraph, for full-cock is provided on the heel of the cock by a single spring-sear with a press-button release (missing) attached directly to it, a back-catch being provided for half-cock.

During the second quarter of the century the Italian miquelet was commonly mounted on a plate of rhomboidal form resembling that of the contemporary native wheel-lock. Thereafter the plate followed the outline of the flintlock[39] though its surface, because of the construction of the mechanism, always remained flat. The cock, with rare exceptions, had a slender straight neck of circular section, usually decorated with turned mouldings, and rather wide square jaws operated by a screw

38 See p. 44.

39 See p. 73.

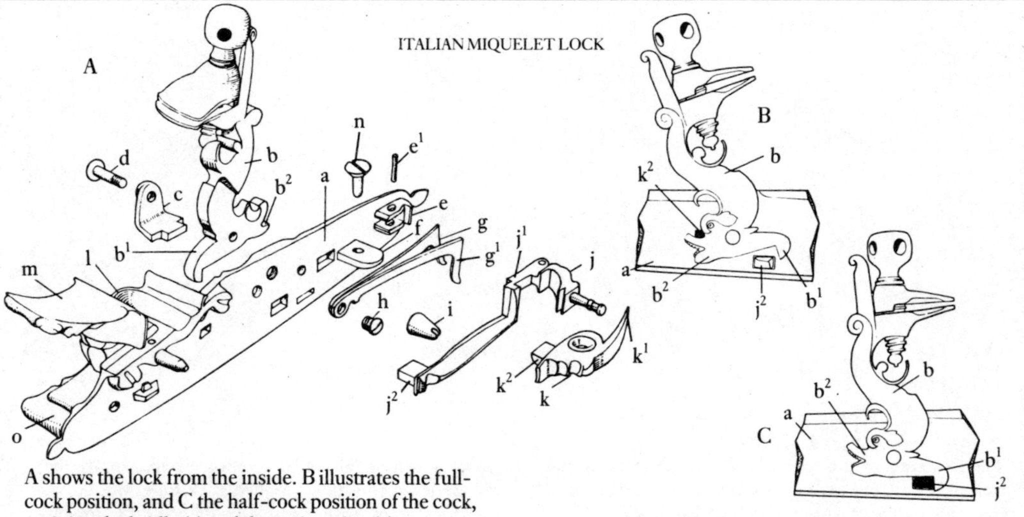

A shows the lock from the inside. B illustrates the full-cock position, and C the half-cock position of the cock, omitting the bridle (c) and the mainspring (o).

- a Lockplate
- b Cock with toe (b^1) on which the mainspring (o) presses and heel (b^2).
- c Bridle for cock
- d Cock pivot-screw (also serving to retain the bridle (c)), secured at the inner end by a nut (i)
- e Bracket to which the half-cock sear-lever (j^1) and trigger-lever (j) are pivoted
- f Bracket to which the full-cock sear-lever (k) is pivoted
- g and g^1 Trigger- or sear-spring
- h Screw for attaching (g) to the lockplate
- i Nut for securing the inner end of the cock-pivot (d)
- j^1 Half-cock sear-lever with angular recess in which the toe marked (g) of the sear-spring rests and sear (j^2)
- j Trigger-lever pivoted to the half-cock sear-lever (j^1)
- k Full-cock sear-lever with sear (k^2)
- l Pan
- m Combined steel and pan-cover
- n Pivot-screw for the full-cock sear-lever (k)
- o Mainspring

with a ring-shaped top. This form of lock remained in use with little variation until the early nineteenth century.

74 The classic Spanish miquelet, known in Spain as
256 the *patilla* lock, has a mainspring that presses upwards on the heel of the cock. The cock itself has large rectangular jaws with a ring-headed screw and a short straight neck of circular section decorated with raised mouldings. The long toe is down-curved and chisel-shaped at the end to engage with two sears that give respectively half and full-cock, the half-cock sear being deeply notched for additional safety. The face of the steel is made detachable so that it could be renewed when worn, and is deeply grooved vertically.[40] The lockplate is flat and has a marked 'waist' due to the fact that it widens at front and rear for the attachment of the mainspring and a bridle supporting the outer end of the cock-screw.

The origins of the Spanish miquelet, as already noted, are obscure. Documentary evidence shows that some form of snaplock was already in use in Spain as early as the 1570s.[41] A lance combined with a pair of snaplock guns in the Real Armería, Madrid,[42] already mentioned, may be as early as this, though its precise date is uncertain. In any event, the locks of the guns do seem to represent a prototype of the *patilla* for the cocks each have the down-curved chisel-shaped toe that is so characteristic of the latter. The single sear, however, gives only full-cock, while the combined steel and pan-cover slides back exactly like the pan-cover of a wheel-lock. This last feature, which appears to be unique to this weapon, coupled with the fact that the cock-jaws are exactly like those found on wheel-locks of the sixteenth century, would seem to support an early dating.

Apart from the above, no Spanish locks of miquelet type made before *c.*1625 have been identified and by this date the mechanism had almost achieved its final form. Three locks of this period by Simón Marquart the Younger, Lucas de Ros and Pedro de Santiago, mounted in wall-pieces in the

40 Grooved steels were used widely on all types of snaplock in the Near East, but in Europe they are found only very occasionally on locks made outside Spain.

41 See J. D. Lavin, *A History of Spanish Firearms*, London, 1965, pp. 148ff., where the whole history of the Spanish lock and its origins are discussed in detail.

42 No. I, 20.

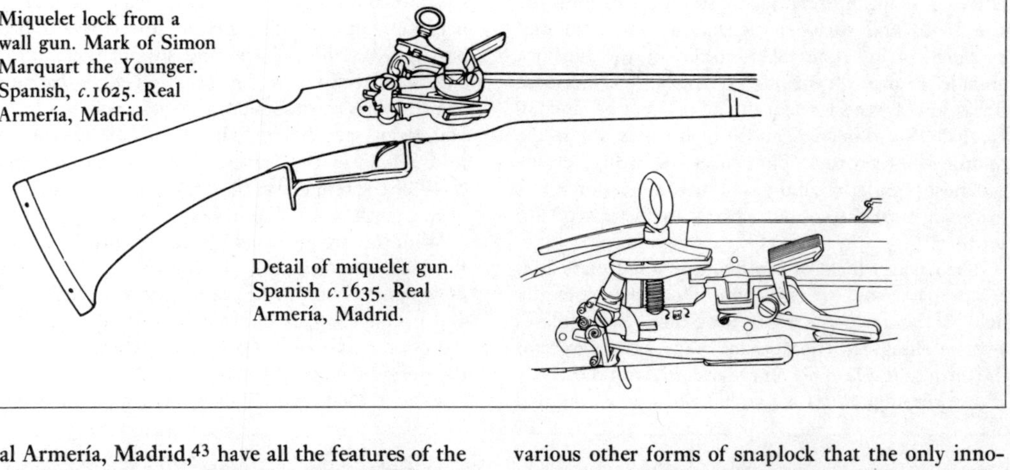

Miquelet lock from a wall gun. Mark of Simon Marquart the Younger. Spanish, *c.*1625. Real Armería, Madrid.

Detail of miquelet gun. Spanish *c.*1635. Real Armería, Madrid.

Real Armería, Madrid,[43] have all the features of the *patilla* lock except for the half-cock sear. This last had probably already appeared by the early 1630s, though the first definite evidence we have of its existence is provided by the descriptions of the various forms of miquelet in a book published in 1644, Alonso Martinez de Espinar's *Arte de Ballesteria y Monteria*. Thereafter the lock remained virtually unchanged until it was finally abandoned in the second quarter of the nineteenth century, so individual examples are often very difficult to date. In this connection it is worth noting that locks made before *c.*1650 commonly contain screws equipped with retaining-pins (*fieles*). Thereafter the pins were generally discarded, though used very occasionally to the middle of the eighteenth century.

Apart from the *patilla*, Espinar describes three other forms of miquelet used in Spain, the *agujeta*, *inuencion* and *calço*. It is not easy to understand precisely what he is describing, but James Lavin[44] identifies the second with the lock *alla Romana* previously described, the *agujeta* with a variant of this having a more complex sear-mechanism, and the *calço*–which he suggests should really be called *calzo atrás*–with a rare form of *patilla* in which the full-cock sear engages in a recess in the enlarged heel of the cock.

The Flintlock

46 The flintlock was defined by Torsten Lenk as a
48-56 snaplock with steel and pan-cover made in one and a
60-61 63-66 vertical sear engaging in two notches in the tumbler
68-73 of the cock-screw to give full- and half-cock respec-
103, 106 tively (Fig. p. 107). It will be obvious from what has
109, 280 already been said in the sections dealing with the various other forms of snaplock that the only innovation here lay in the construction of the sear. The invention of this mechanism, and with it of the first true flintlock, was ascribed by Dr Lenk to the Frenchman Marin le Bourgeoys (*d.*1634) of Lisieux in Normandy, and to a period before 1615. His evidence for doing so was, however, derived from the misreading of the mark on a flintlock gun formerly in the Renwick Collection, Tucson, and now in the Metro-
politan Museum of Art, New York. This was thought 48-9
to be that of Marin le Bourgeoys's brother Jean, who died in 1615. It appears, in fact, that it is of another brother, Pierre, who did not die until 1627. Since this is the earliest flintlock to which any kind of firm date can be attached, the date before which we know the true flintlock had been invented must be brought forward to 1627. It seems likely, in fact, that it was introduced in the early 1620s and that the le Bourgeoys family can still be given credit for its invention since some of the earliest examples are by them (for example, in the Musée de l'Armée, Paris, and the Hermitage Museum, Leningrad).[45]

Though by the second half of the seventeenth 46
century it had come to be generally accepted outside Spain that the flintlock was superior to all other known systems of firearms ignition, it did not, in its early days, spread very quickly. For the first twenty years or so of its existence it seems to have been made almost exclusively in the country of its origin, though, curiously enough, the armoury at the Kremlin, Moscow, contains a flintlock revolving pistol[46] alleged to have been made by Pervoucha Issaïev who

43 Nos. P.5, 10 and 14.

44 *op.cit.*

45 For the latest assessment of the problem of the origin of the true flintlock see W. B. Gusler and J. D. Lavin, *Decorated Firearms 1540-1870 from the Collection of Clay P. Bedford*, Colonial Williamsburg, 1977, pp. 3-6.

46 No. 8351.

worked there during the period *c.* 1616–*c.*1625. This, however, is quite exceptional, and it is not until the late 1630s and early 1640s that we begin to find evidence of any general adoption of the flintlock outside France. It begins to appear on German, Swiss and Netherlands guns at this period and on English, Scandinavian and Italian ones about the middle of the century. Thereafter it speedily became the most popular of all types of lock, a position it was to retain until the second quarter of the nineteenth century.

The earliest form of flintlock had a flat plate and, as was to be usual with this type of lock, was generally held to the stock by two screws only. Some plates were of elongated rhomboidal shape, others were of the form that was to become standard, with the upper and lower edges almost parallel and with a rounded point at each end. The cock was also flat, with a slender, slightly curved neck and was fitted over a square on the tumbler, the two being held together by a nut on the inside. As on the Netherlands snaphance, a small lug screwed to the external face of the plate acted as a buffer for the cock as it fell, but this feature disappeared in the 1630s. Thereafter its function was performed by a shoulder cut in the inner face of the cock which came into contact with the top edge of the plate.

By *c.*1640 the cock had become shorter and broader at the base and had started to assume the graceful swan- or goose-neck form that was to be used henceforth more than any other during the remainder of the flintlock's existence. From this date until about 1690 the weakest point of the cock, the neck, was often strengthened with a little scroll across the angle below the bottom jaw. In effect, the cock was pierced with a transverse hole for the lower end of the jaw-screw, so foreshadowing the throat-hole cock that was to be so popular for military firearms in the eighteenth and early nineteenth centuries.

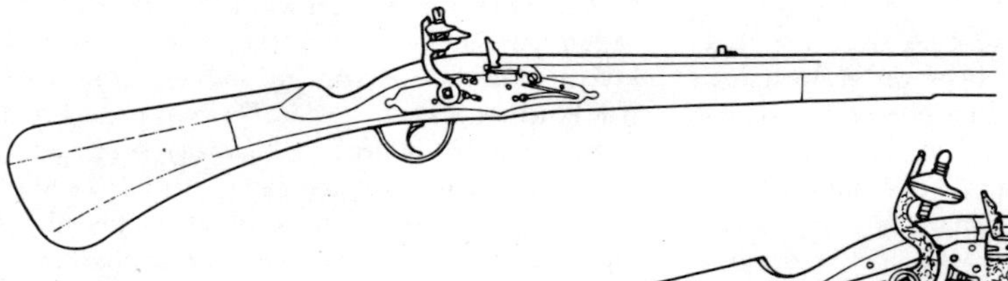

(*Left*) Detail of flintlock gun. French, *c.*1630. No. 139 in the *Cabinet d'Armes* of Louis XIII. Victoria & Albert Museum, London.

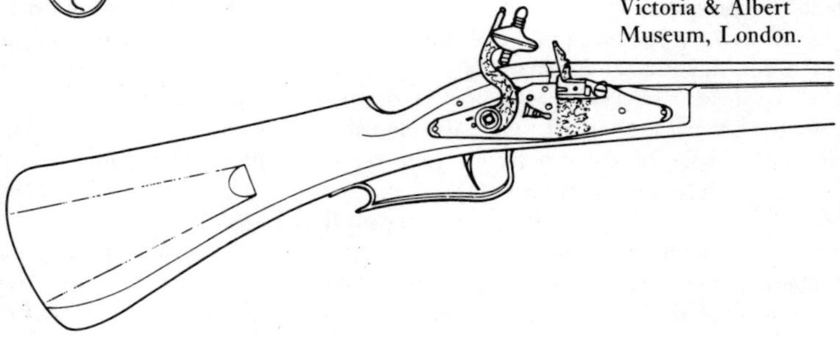

(*Right*) Detail of flintlock sporting gun, the lock engraved with foliage. French, *c.*1640. From the *Cabinet d'Armes* of Louis XIII. Tower of London Armouries.

In the middle of the seventeenth century two constructional improvements were introduced that soon became standard. The first of these was a bridle passing over the tumbler and supporting the inner end of the cock-screw. The other was the substitution of a simple screw to hold the cock in position instead of the transverse bolt held by a nut. This was threaded into a hole in the centre of the square and made possible the removal of the cock without the necessity of dismantling the whole lock.

With the introduction of these improvements the flintlock was mechanically complete and all future development was to be concerned with refinements and minor changes in form that left the basic construction unchanged. Only a few of these come within the period covered by this chapter.

From *c.*1660 the lockplate was commonly slightly banana-shaped with a concave curve along the bottom. At the same time a fashion, introduced in France as early as *c.*1630, for rounding both the cock and the external face of the lockplate became general. Designed to give increased strength, the fashion remained popular until the very end of the century – when flat surfaces began to come into favour again – and did not finally disappear until the second half of the eighteenth century.

On a small number of locks of the middle of the century the steel and pan-cover are linked to a tumbler acting on a feather-spring inside the plate. The normal system, however, was for the spring to be mounted externally, as on a snaphance, so that it pressed against a projection on the underside of the toe of the pan-cover. On the earliest flintlocks the steel, viewed in profile, had a marked outward curve on its front face (or breast) just above the middle. From the 1620s until the middle of the century it was either very narrow with a slightly rounded breast, or else shaped like a flattened triangle with a rounded apex just below the centre. The latter form became

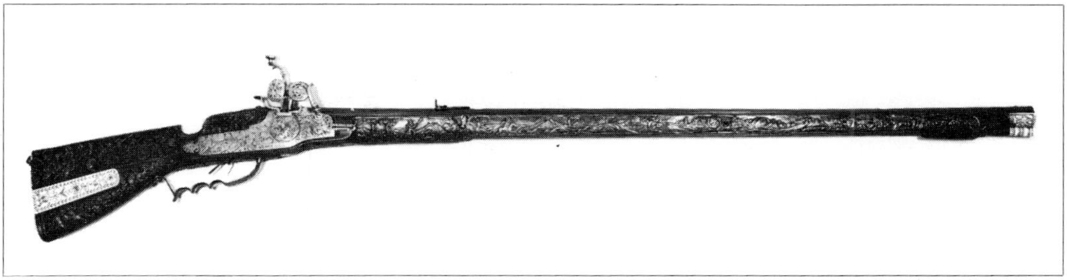

38 *Above* Large wheel-lock gun, the stock carved with hunting scenes, the lock engraved, the barrel inscribed HANS REINER ZU EGER and dated 1676. German Czechoslovakia (Eger), 1676. Victoria & Albert Museum, London.

39 *Above, left* Detail of a wheel-lock rifle (*Tschinke*), the walnut stock inlaid with staghorn and mother-of-pearl. German (Teschen), *c.*1650. Victoria & Albert Museum, London.

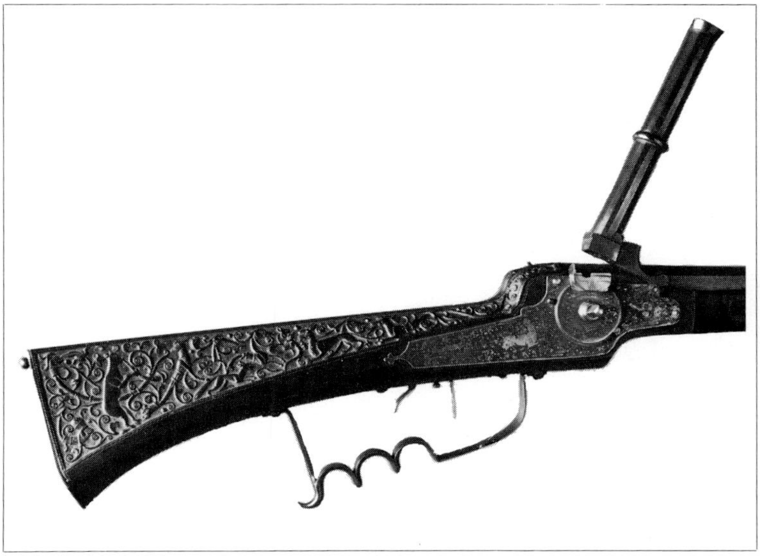

40 *Left* Detail of a wheel-lock rifle of the Emperor Ferdinand III (1637-57), the barrel signed HANS FASCHANG. The stock is by the Master of the Animal-Headed Scroll (*Meister der Tierkopfranke*). The 'chimney' is designed to lead away the smoke from the priming. Vienna, *c.*1640. Kunsthistorisches Museum, Vienna.

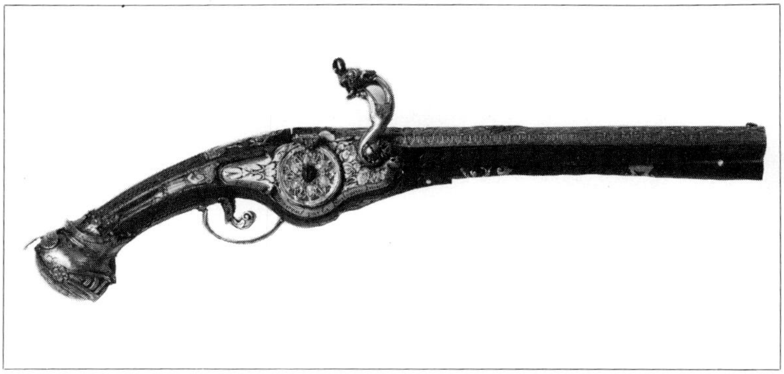

41 *Left* Wheel-lock pistol. Brass barrel, engraved and gilt. Inscribed around the base of the lockplate *Faict a Mourgues par la Fonteyne Inventeur 1645*. French. Wallace Collection, London.

42 Double-barrelled wheel-lock pistol, the barrel etched and gilt; single trigger. From the *Cabinet d'Armes* of Louis XIII (No. 237). French, *c.*1600. Victoria & Albert Museum, London.

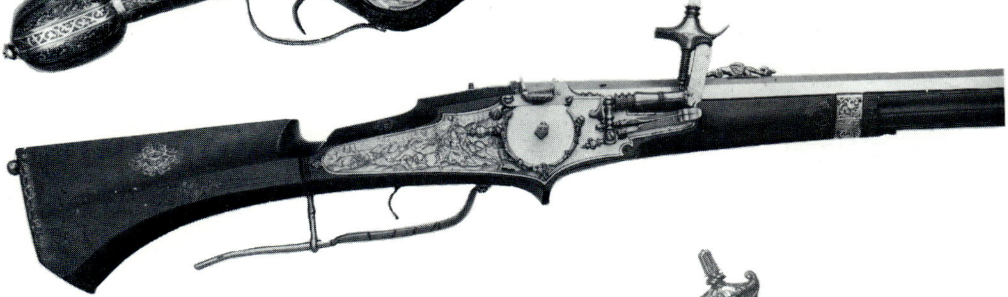

43 Detail of a wheel-lock gun, the mounts of chiselled steel. Italian (Brescia), *c.*1630. Tøjhusmuseet, Copenhagen.

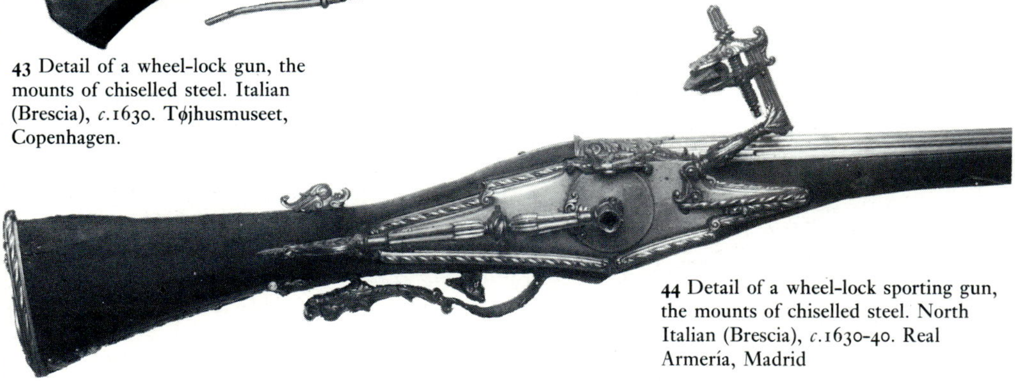

44 Detail of a wheel-lock sporting gun, the mounts of chiselled steel. North Italian (Brescia), *c.*1630-40. Real Armería, Madrid

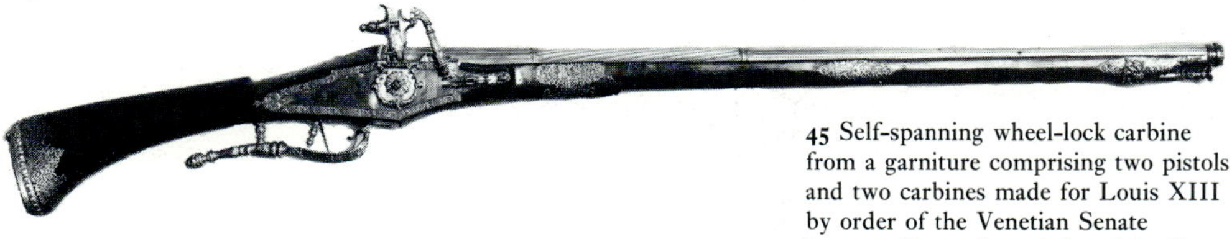

45 Self-spanning wheel-lock carbine from a garniture comprising two pistols and two carbines made for Louis XIII by order of the Venetian Senate between September 1638 and April 1639. The lock by GIOVANNI ANTONIO GAVACCIOLO: the barrel by LAZARINO COMINAZZI; the mounts and chiselled work by ANTONIO and CARLO GOSI and GIACINTO SECARDO. Italian (Brescia), 1638. Livrustkammaren, Stockholm.

46 Detail of a flintlock gun, signed *M. Le Bourgeoys a Liseul.* From the *Cabinet d'Armes* of Louis XIII (No. 152). Mounts of gilt bronze. French (Lisieux), *c.*1620-25. Hermitage Museum, Leningrad.

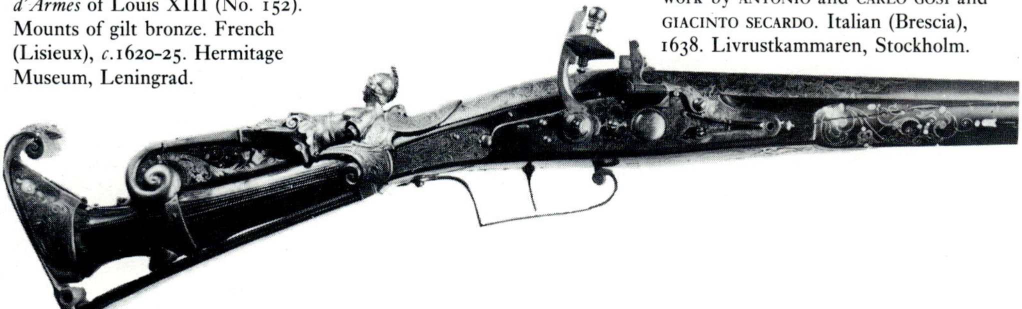

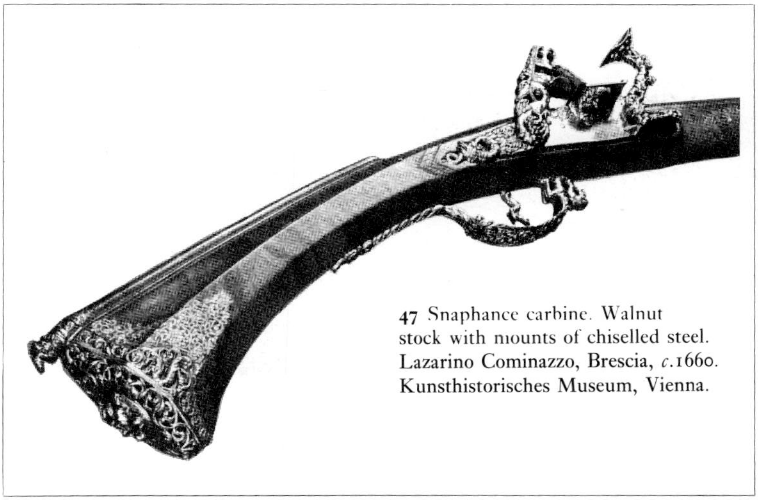

47 Snaphance carbine. Walnut stock with mounts of chiselled steel. Lazarino Cominazzo, Brescia, *c*.1660. Kunsthistorisches Museum, Vienna.

48, 49 *Below* Details of a flintlock fowling piece, the stock inlaid with engraved silver and mother-of-pearl, and a crowned L for Louis XIII of France. No 134 in the *Cabinet d'Armes* of Louis XIII. On the breech the mark of Pierre le Bourgeoys. One of the earliest known examples of the 'true' French flintlock gun. French, *c*.1620. Reverse and obverse views. Metropolitan Museum of Art, New York.

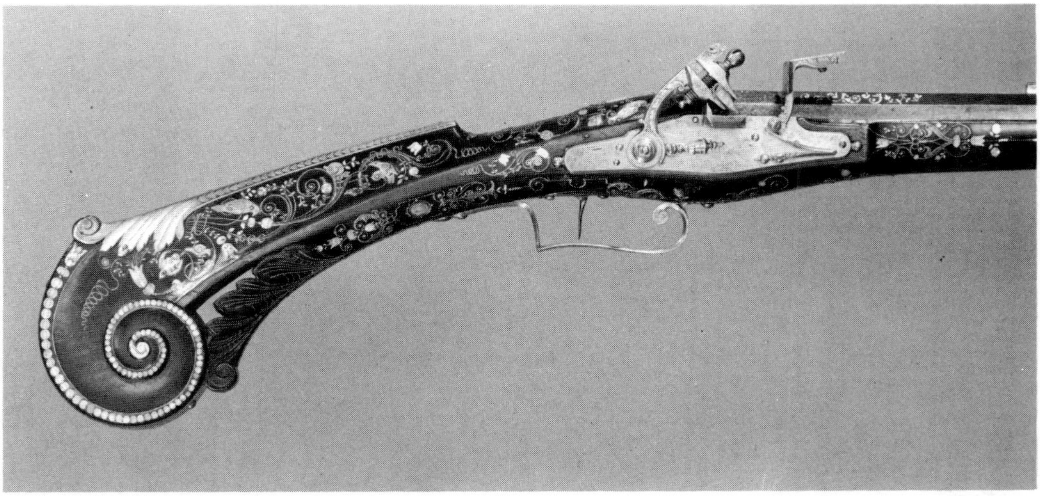

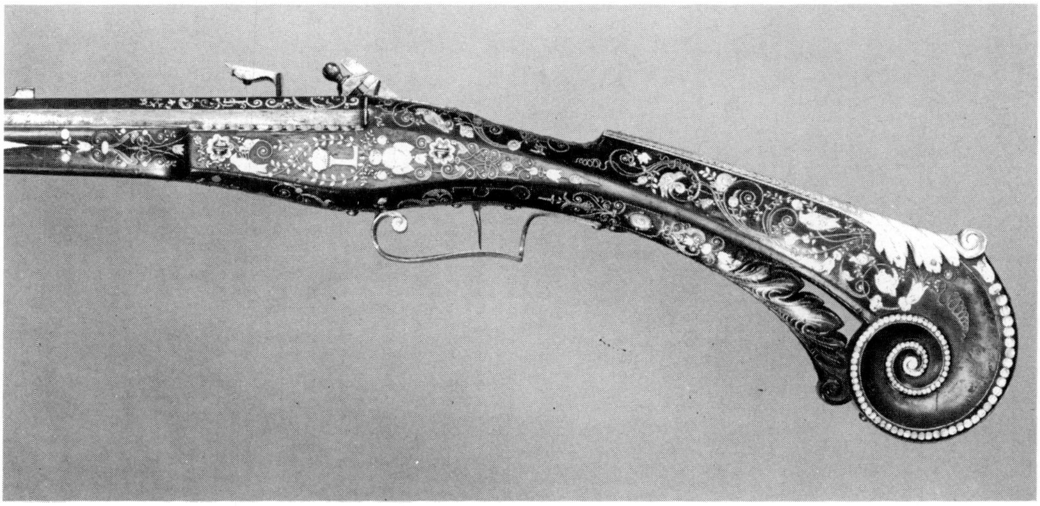

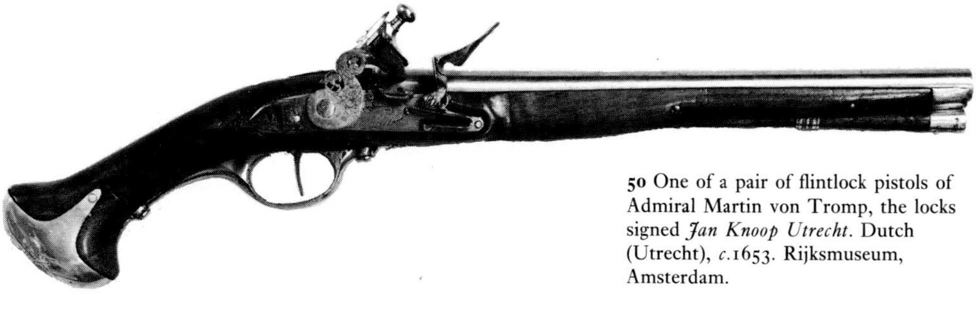

50 One of a pair of flintlock pistols of Admiral Martin von Tromp, the locks signed *Jan Knoop Utrecht*. Dutch (Utrecht), *c.*1653. Rijksmuseum, Amsterdam.

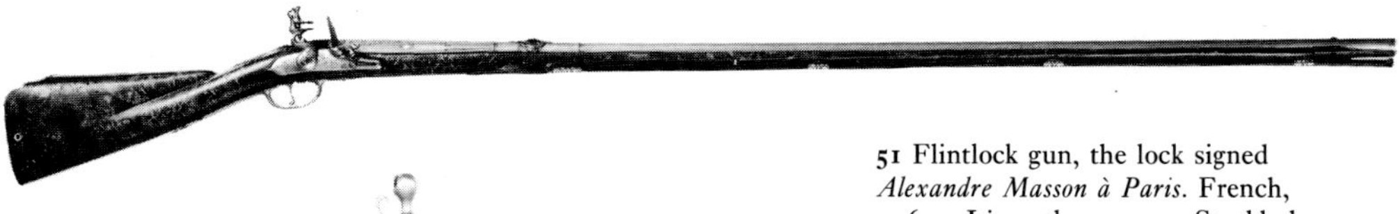

51 Flintlock gun, the lock signed *Alexandre Masson à Paris*. French, *c.*1670. Livrustkammaren, Stockholm.

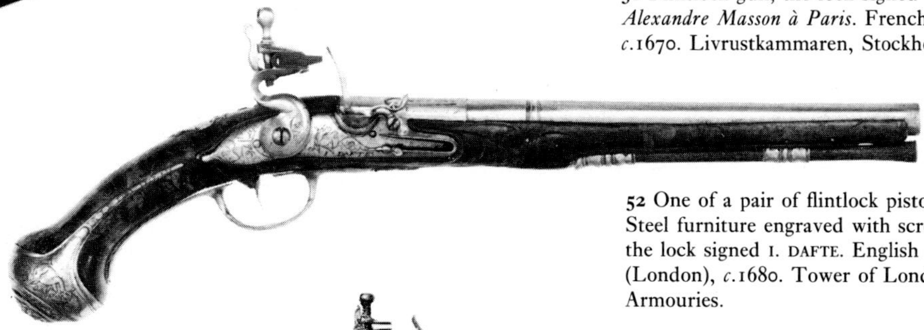

52 One of a pair of flintlock pistols. Steel furniture engraved with scrolls, the lock signed I. DAFTE. English (London), *c.*1680. Tower of London Armouries.

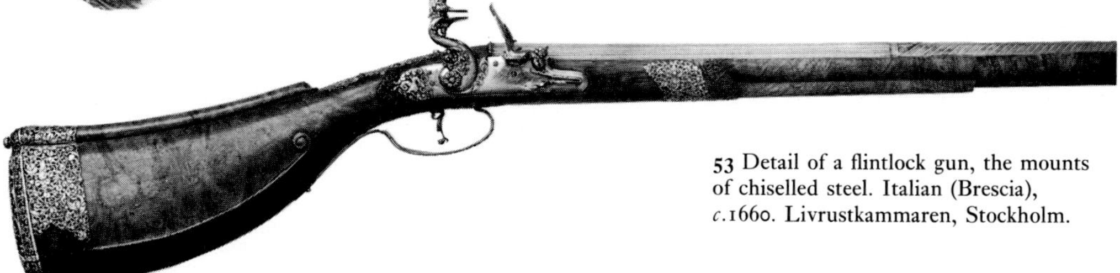

53 Detail of a flintlock gun, the mounts of chiselled steel. Italian (Brescia), *c.*1660. Livrustkammaren, Stockholm.

54 Flintlock fowling piece, the lock signed *Starbus Amsterdam*. Dutch (Amsterdam), *c.*1680. Livrustkammaren, Stockholm.

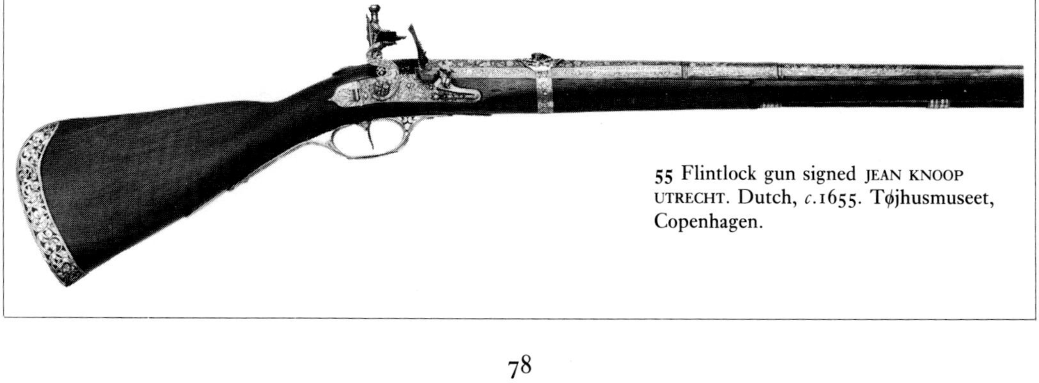

55 Flintlock gun signed JEAN KNOOP UTRECHT. Dutch, *c.*1655. Tøjhusmuseet, Copenhagen.

the normal one after *c.*1650, though the other survived until the end of the century. From *c.*1670 the tip of the steel was commonly bent slightly forward, while at the same time a small wart-like projection appeared in the centre of the breast. As the century progressed this last often developed as a decorative feature, sometimes taking the form of a mask, foliage or a grenade. Viewed from the front the steel was at first cut off straight or rounded at the top, but after *c.*1660 its shape was something like that of a tongue.

Two features that were to become common in the eighteenth century are very occasionally found on flintlocks of the second half of the seventeenth century. The first of these is the *detent* (p. 113), a small pawl attached to the tumbler and designed to prevent the sear from catching in the half-cock notch (or bent) as the cock fell. The earliest example known occurs on a pair of snaphance pistols of *c.*1660 by Antonio Venazolo of Brescia in the Wallace Collection.[47] It has been noted on a few French flintlock pistols of the last quarter of the century.

The other device was a safety-catch in the form of a sliding bolt on the inside of the lockplate that locked the tumbler in the half-cock position (p. 107). This again has been noted on only a very small number of pistols of the last quarter of the century.

Before leaving the flintlock reference must be made to a rare group of all-steel firearms, mostly pistols, dating from *c.*1640-50, which have the lock-mechanism mounted externally on the left of the stock. The cock, pan, pan-cover and steel are mounted on the right in the normal way, the cock-spindle being attached to the mechanism through the stock. The form of the pistols so resembles that of a group of all-metal pistols of normal construction made by members of the Cloeter family of Grevenbroich, south-west of Düsseldorf, that they have been generally assigned to the same workshop. It is worth noting, however, that a pistol of this type in the Polish Army Museum, Warsaw,[48] is signed on the barrel *HANNS EVCHORN ERINGEN*, the last word being the name of a town in Bavaria.

In concluding this section on systems of ignition reference must be made to a gun of *c.*1660–80 with a curious snaphance embodying a sliding cock, made by Mathias Kalthoff in Copenhagen[49] and to the fact that a few seventeenth-century segment and rasp-locks are recorded. It should be noted also that, as in the sixteenth century, a few makers still produced double locks – a second mechanism, sometimes of different type from the first, being provided as a reserve. The best known of these is probably the one attached to the *fusil-mousquet* introduced by Vauban into very limited service in the French army in 1688. This was a flintlock with an auxiliary serpentine for a match, a single pan being used for both. It appears to have been copied from the almost exactly similar musket introduced, also into very limited service, into the Austrian army in 1666 by General Montecuccoli.

47 Nos. A1191-2.

48 No. 59231 MWP.

49 Tøjhusmuseet No. B.478.

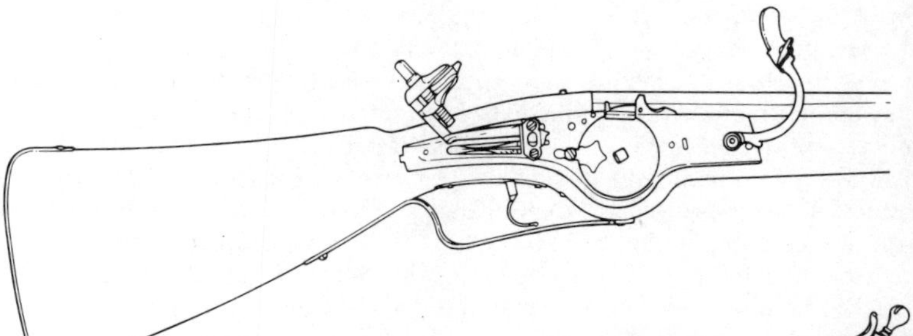

Detail of combined flintlock and matchlock musket on the Montecuccoli system. Austrian, *c.*1660. Heeresgeschichtliches Museum, Vienna.

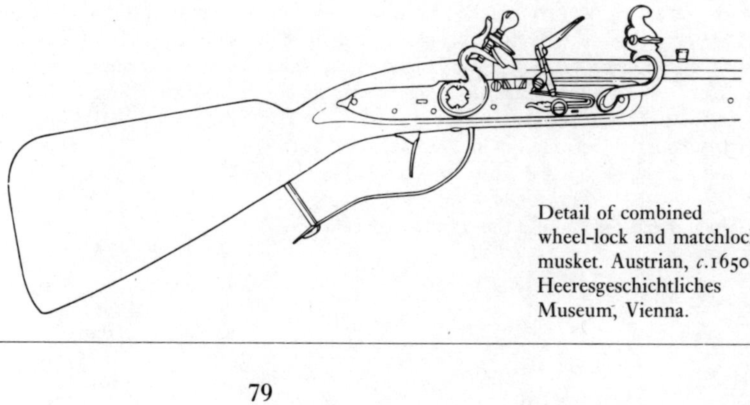

Detail of combined wheel-lock and matchlock musket. Austrian, *c.*1650. Heeresgeschichtliches Museum, Vienna.

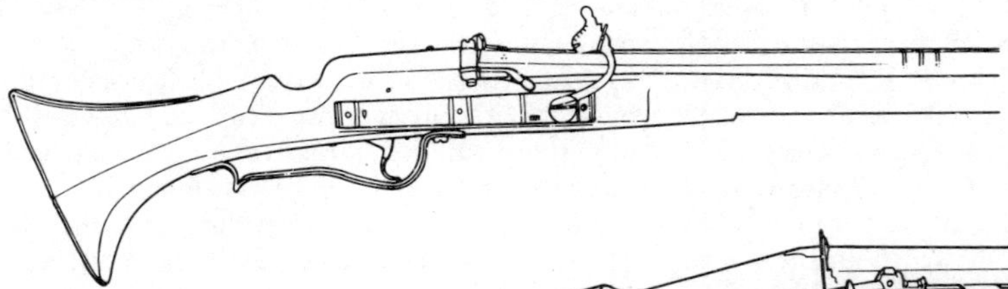

(*Left*) Matchlock musket. Swedish, *c.*1600. Kungl. Armémuseum, Stockholm.

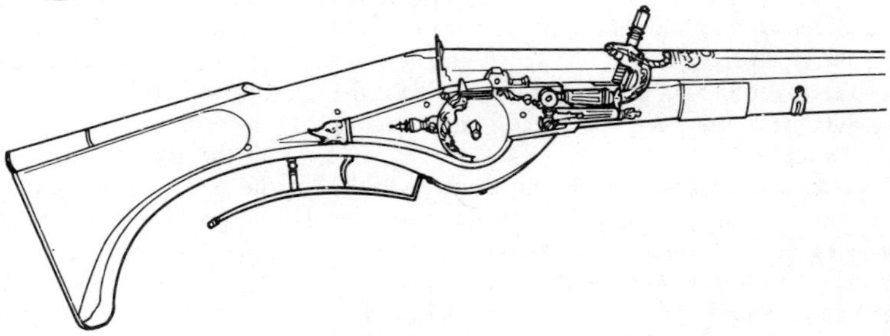

Detail of wheel-lock gun with Turkish barrel. French, *c.*1620. Probably No. 3 in the *Cabinet d'Armes* of Louis XIII. Victoria & Albert Museum, London.

Long-guns

38-40 As has been mentioned already, the history of fire-
43,45 46,47 arms became less complex in the early seventeenth
48-9 century. Where previously gunmakers had directed
51 their energies towards establishing the most satis-
53-8 factory forms for their products they now turned to
96 the problem of improving and refining the forms
101-4 they had selected. Where long-guns are concerned
107-10 143,317, the most important aspect of this trend lay in the
342 development of the shoulder-stock in conjunction
345-6 with the snaplock. The dominant role was played by France and, as with the flintlock, it was the French type of stock that was finally adopted everywhere in the form which still remains the standard one.

In the areas of Germanic culture the cheek-stock, accompanied by the wheel-lock, remained in use on certain arms until well into the eighteenth century. These were all hunting and target guns, almost invariably rifled, and, as previously noted,[50] one can only assume that they continued to be produced in a form that soon became antique because of some kind of sporting convention. This view is supported by the fact that the outline of these weapons changed hardly at all after about 1610, when the step in the stock behind the barrel which had begun to appear in the late sixteenth century reached its full development. Apart from this feature, stocks varied little from the sixteenth-century form,[51] and unsigned examples are often very difficult to date other than on the basis of their decoration.

Apart from the Germanic countries the cheek-butt seems to have been used only in Russia. Here a rather elongated form, usually fitted with a snaplock, remained in use throughout the seventeenth century.

The development of the shoulder-butt in the seventeenth century stemmed from two forms that had appeared in the second half of the sixteenth century. One of these was the fish-tailed musket-butt[52] and the other the combed butt that had appeared in conjunction with the French wheel-lock.[53] The former remained in use with little variation until *c.*1630. The latter, in the first decade of the century, became longer while the concave curve of its lower edge became much shallower.[54] In this form it remained in use with minor variations until the 1650s. As early as *c.*1620, however, a new shape of butt had started to develop under the influence of both of the earlier types of shoulder-stock. This had a rounded heel and toe, a low comb, flat or with a very slight concave curve on top, and on the underside curved down in a marked 'belly', while immediately behind the barrel the notch for the thumb found on the old fish-tail butt had developed into a shaped hand-grip which clearly foreshadowed the small of the butt found on modern gun-stocks.

The bellied form of butt remained popular in a wide area centring on France until *c.*1660, and in Central Italy survived until well into the eighteenth century. But as early as *c.*1640 French gunmakers began to modify its outline, making it narrower and more rounded while reducing the curve on the underside. By *c.*1660 it had developed a shape which was almost indistinguishable from that of a modern rifle. This was adopted all over Europe and has remained the most popular form of gun-butt ever since.

The fully-developed French shoulder-butt was

50 See p. 64.

51 See pp. 52-3.

52 See p. 53.

53 See pp. 53-4.

54 Some of the earliest flintlock guns had eccentric versions of this butt, pierced, rounded at the rear or with a projecting toe above.

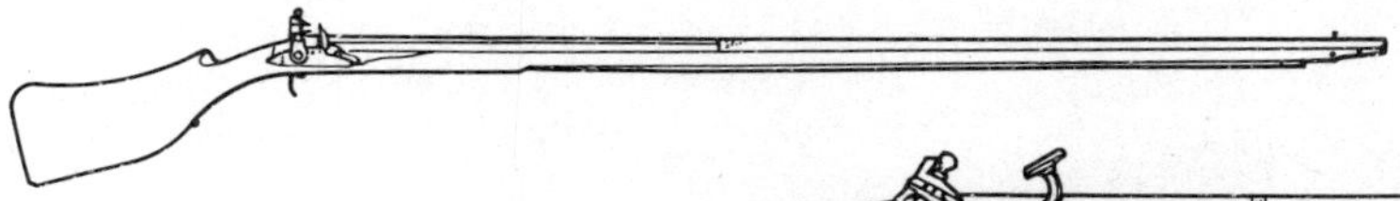

Flintlock gun of King Charles X of Sweden. Signed *Thomas à Paris*. French, *c.*1640. Livrustkammaren, Stockholm.

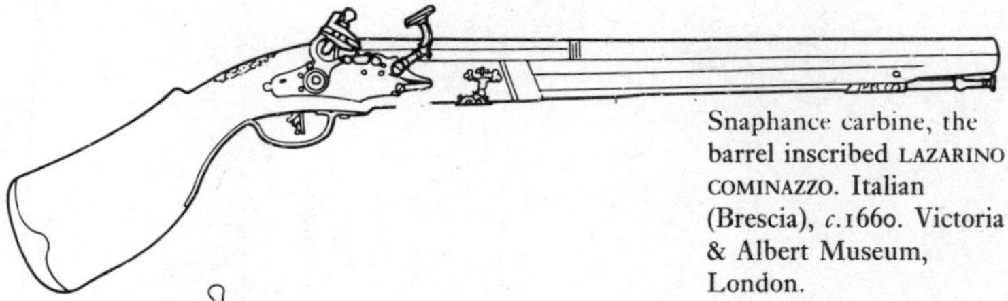

Snaphance carbine, the barrel inscribed LAZARINO COMINAZZO. Italian (Brescia), *c.*1660. Victoria & Albert Museum, London.

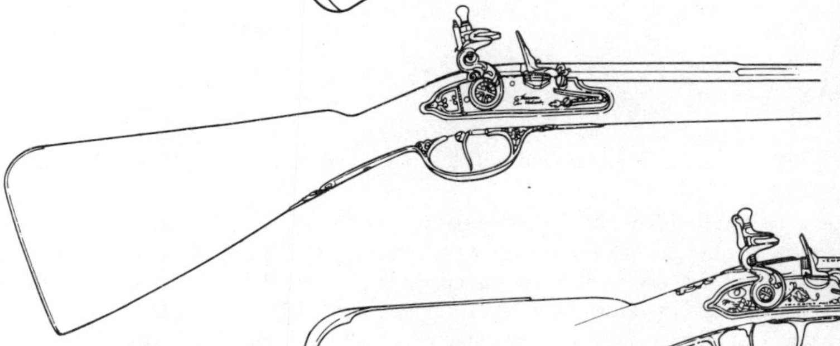

Detail of flintlock gun. Signed *Thuraine et L'Hollandois à Paris*. French (Paris), *c.* 1660. Tøjhusmuseet, Copenhagen.

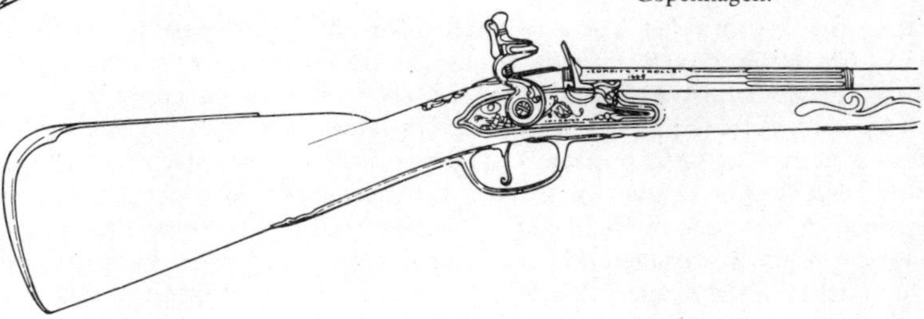

Detail of flintlock gun, signed THURAINE A PARIS and dated 1669. French. Tøjhusmuseet, Copenhagen.

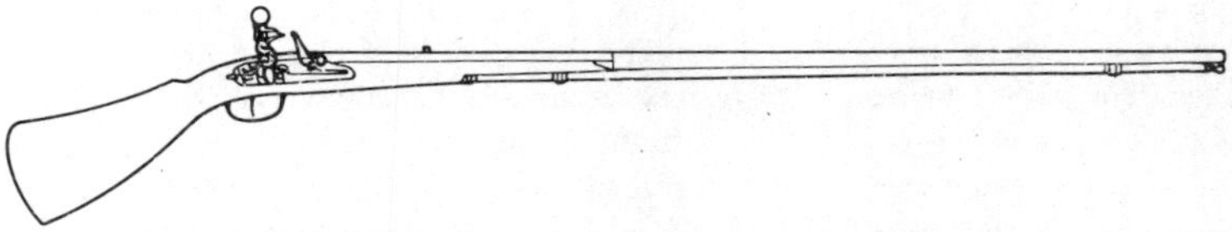

Sporting gun. Italian (Brescia), *c.*1660. Tøjhusmuseet, Copenhagen.

used everywhere in Europe, including Russia, but some areas had also developed their own forms that were often superseded only very slowly. In Italy, early in the seventeenth century, a long narrow down-curved butt had appeared. This had little or no comb and widened and thickened slightly towards the rear, where it was of oval section. It remained in use until the third quarter of the century.

In Spain a flat-sided, down-curved shoulder-butt with its upper and lower edges almost parallel, except at the rear where the lower edge turned down to form a rudimentary toe, had appeared at the very end of the sixteenth century. Early in the seventeenth century the toe became very pronounced, producing a form–often called the *Catalan stock* by modern writers–which was to enjoy a very wide vogue in the Peninsula until the early nineteenth century. On the firearms produced at Ripoll in Catalonia it was overlaid almost completely with thin-sheet metal, pierced and engraved with foliage.[55] Another distinctively Spanish form of butt appearing in the latter part of the century, was similar in outline to the developed French shoulder-butt but was rather thicker and with what was, in effect, a comb on the underside as well as on top, both being fluted.[56] This again enjoyed great popularity, especially in the Madrid area, until the early nineteenth century.

Finally, mention must be made of a distinctive form of butt used in Scandinavia in conjunction with the various local forms of snaplock.[57] These last were sometimes mounted in a cheek-stock of German type but they are more frequently found in a developed version of this. The butt is sloped strongly downwards and equipped with a very high triangular comb which starts immediately behind the barrel and projects well beyond the toe of the

55 In the manner described on p. 491.

56 It is difficult to accept that the example illustrated by Lavin (*op.cit.*, Pl. 68) with a lock dated 1648 can, in fact, be as early as this.

57 See p. 67.

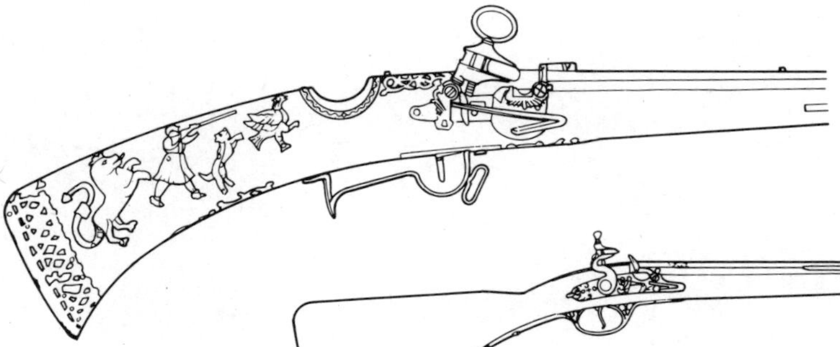

Detail of a miquelet gun. Spanish (Ripoll), dated 1693. Musée de l'Armée, Paris.

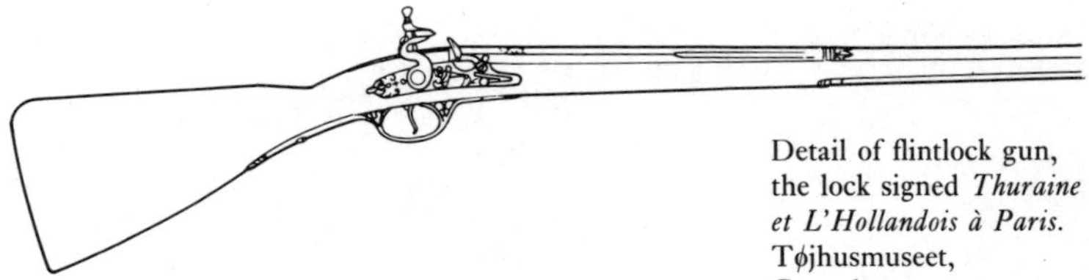

Detail of flintlock gun, the lock signed *Thuraine et L'Hollandois à Paris.* Tøjhusmuseet, Copenhagen.

butt so that the rear face has a marked backward slope. The purpose of this seems to have been to provide a butt which was both rested against the cheek and supported on top of the shoulder when the gun was fired. The form apparently appeared early in the seventeenth century and, with variations, remained in wide use in Sweden and Norway for about a century. In remote areas of these countries it survived until the nineteenth century.

All seventeenth-century guns were stocked to the muzzle unless the requirements of some special mechanism made this impracticable. Stocks were almost invariably of wood – Grenoble walnut being a special favourite for fine-quality arms from *c.*1630 – though steel or brass examples are encountered occasionally.[58] Normally, however, the metal parts of the stock were confined to the mounts – or 'furniture' as they were known in the seventeenth and eighteenth centuries – comprising buttplate, trigger-guard, side-plate (or nail-plate), escutcheon (or thumb-plate), ramrod-pipes and also a fore-end cap.

Until the seventeenth century the only standard furniture was the metal trigger-guard. Good-quality weapons, however, also often had a horn fore-end cap, sometimes accompanied by a horn protector for the end of the ramrod-groove that ran the full length of the fore-end, and a flat horn – or very much more rarely metal – buttplate. On cheek-stocks this last was usually equipped with a metal knob designed to protect the butt when it was rested on the ground. This type of furniture remained usual on cheek-stocks until the very end of the seventeenth century, after which date the more elaborate forms found on contemporary flintlock guns were sometimes adopted. The development of the furniture in the seventeenth century, as far as it affects long-guns, is therefore concerned almost exclusively with its application to the shoulder-stock. The lead was again taken by the French gunsmiths who were then followed by makers elsewhere in Europe. The most popular material for the furniture during the period covered by the following review was steel, but during the second half of the century silver and brass were increasingly employed.

From the first decade of the century a thin steel plate was commonly fastened over the rear face of the butt. In about 1620 the upper end of this was prolonged to form a short tongue, cut off straight, that extended over the heel of the butt. This form of plate remained in use until the end of the century, especially on military guns, but during the 1650s the French makers started to extend the tongue along the top of the butt. This tongue was at first quite short, but by the late 1660s it had assumed the form of an elongated triangle, usually with its sides cut into decorative shapes, which extended for much the length of the comb. This fashion survived until the 1690s, when the tongue became comparatively short again, though still retaining its triangular shape.

The development of the tongue on the buttplate in the 1660s was accompanied by a change in the contours of the plate itself. It became thicker and was moulded to the curve of the front of the shoulder, acquiring a distinct bump at the top which during the period *c.*1680–90 was occasionally very prominent. At the same time, on elaborate weapons, the edges were sometimes cut into decorative shapes and extended round the sides of the butt. In Italy, and especially in Brescia, deep cap-like buttplates of this kind, but without the tongue, were in use from *c.*1630 onwards. They were sometimes bordered by a separate band of elaborate steel filigree-work inlaid

58 The Brescian maker Stefano Siolo (Ciolo or Scioli) seems to have specialised in the manufacture of metal stocks. See *Wallace Collection Catalogue. European Arms And Armour*, Vol. II, 1962, pp. 583–4.

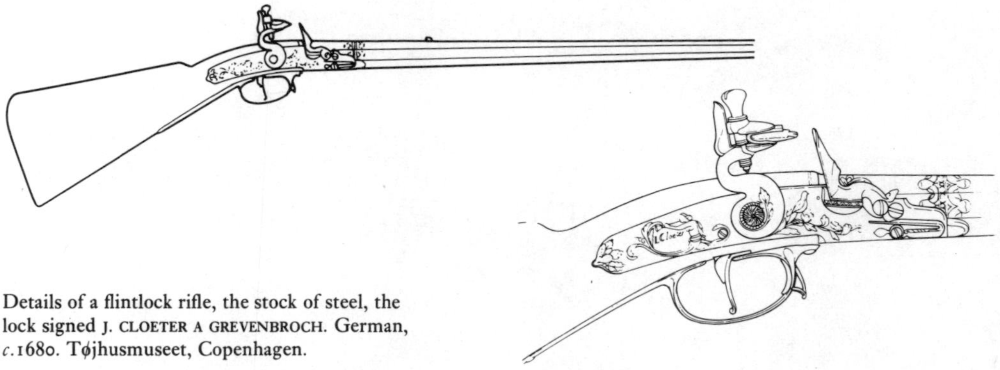

Details of a flintlock rifle, the stock of steel, the lock signed J. CLOETER A GREVENBROCH. German, *c.*1680. Tøjhusmuseet, Copenhagen.

in the wood, which made them appear even deeper.

From the beginning of the century the wood of the stock where it was pierced by the lock-screws was sometimes reinforced with inlaid horn or metal washers. This arrangement survived until *c.*1700, especially on cheek-stocks, but on flintlock arms from as early as *c.*1640 the washers were sometimes fitted with small decorative extensions. By *c.*1650 these had been linked so as to form a single S-shaped side-plate pierced for the lock-screws.[59] After *c.*1660 this feature became a standard one on flintlock and snaphance arms and, as the century progressed, it became increasingly elaborate. During the period *c.*1675–*c.*1700 plates were commonly carved and pierced to represent one or more convoluted serpents or dragons, or intertwined foliage involving grotesques, while an escutcheon bearing the owner's coat-of-arms, crest or monogram was also sometimes included.

The remaining furniture can be dealt with very briefly. The basic shape of the trigger-guard remained a simple semi-circle throughout the seventeenth century, except on the cheek-stock which retained the angular form, indented for the fingers. Metal ramrod-pipes appeared early in the seventeenth century and down to *c.*1640 were simple tubes, thereafter they were increasingly decorated with raised mouldings that became usual after *c.*1650. The escutcheon, a small decorative cartouche set in the butt behind the barrel-tang appeared in *c.*1660 and soon became standard. It was commonly engraved with the owner's coat-of-arms, crest or monogram. Finally, throughout the period under review the fore-end was sometimes protected with a simple horn or metal cap, usually quite plain. Its use seems to have been entirely a matter of individual taste and many of the finest guns do not have it.

The three main forms of barrel in use during the sixteenth century – circular section, circular section with an octagonal breech, and entirely octagonal – remained popular throughout the seventeenth century. The third of these was associated particularly with cheek-stocked firearms, but it is also found on some German guns with shoulder-butts. This type of barrel was usually thick and heavy in proportion to its length and with a small bore, now almost invariably rifled. The main exception to this generalisation is provided by the light birding-rifle known as a Tschinke,[60] which had a comparatively slender barrel of octagonal section.

The other two forms of barrel were the ones most widely used with shoulder-stocked firearms. From *c.*1620, under the influence of French gunsmiths, they tended to become lighter and more slender, until in the last quarter of the century the walls towards the muzzle became almost dangerously thin. The chamber, however, was always stoutly reinforced by thickening the metal round it, the line of demarcation between it and the barrel proper usually being indicated by a raised moulding. After the middle of the century the French commonly made this breech area of two or even three different polygonal sections, the rear one usually octagonal, and this fashion was soon widely adopted.

The normal material for the barrel throughout the seventeenth century was iron or steel, though brass

59 The early snaplock pistol at Dresden described on p. 44 has such a plate, but this is clearly because the stock is that of a French wheel-lock pistol which, of course, had a bearing-plate here. On the Marin le Bourgeoys gun in the Hermitage (p. 73) the side of the stock opposite to the lock is covered with a damascened steel plate, but its purpose is chiefly decorative and it seems to have no connection with later side-plates.

60 See p. 96.

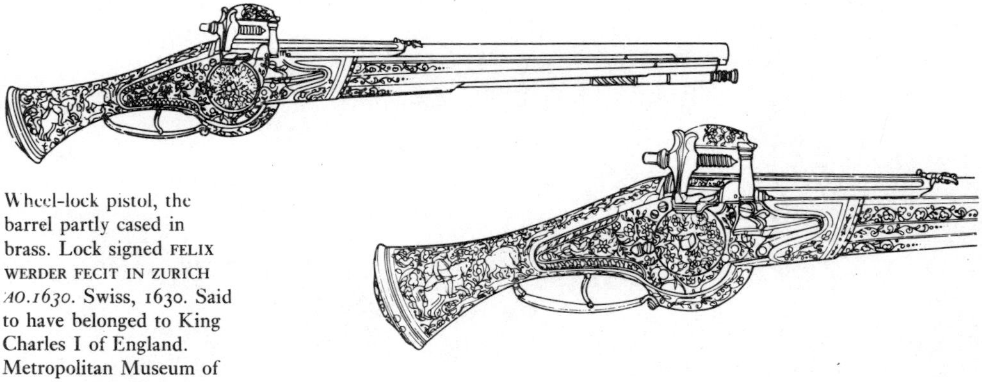

Wheel-lock pistol, the barrel partly cased in brass. Lock signed FELIX WERDER FECIT IN ZURICH *AO.1630*. Swiss, 1630. Said to have belonged to King Charles I of England. Metropolitan Museum of Art, New York.

was used occasionally, especially on blunderbusses and grenade-throwers, while the celebrated maker Felix Werder of Zürich made a speciality of very thin-walled barrels of hardened brass.[61] A magnificent pair of pistols in the Livrustkammar, Stockholm[62] and a gun in the Tower of London Armouries,[63] all made by Louis XIV's gunmaker
108 Bertrand Piraube in the late 1670s, have silver barrels, but these are quite exceptional. As in the sixteenth century, the normal method of attaching the barrel to the stock was by means of a vertical screw through the breech-tang and transverse pins passed through the fore-end into loops on the underside of the barrel. After the middle of the century the breech-screw, instead of passing through the stock from underneath, was normally inserted from the top. In Spain, from the same period, it became the practice to replace the barrel-pin with external bands (*capucines*), secured by spring catches, encircling the barrel and the fore-end.

Outside the areas of Germanic influence rifled guns seem to have been used only rarely before the end of the seventeenth century, and they were not to become common until nearly a century after this.[64] It is worth noting, however, that on 24 June 1635 one Arnold Rotispen considered it worth his while to take out an English patent for a device 'to rifle, cutt out, or screwe barrels as wyde or as close or as deep or as shallowe as shalbe required and with greate ease'. There are also records of the use of screwed guns by gamekeepers, fowlers and the like, acting as snipers at some of the sieges of the English Civil War.[65] These were clearly sporting weapons, as were the vast majority of rifled guns produced during the seventeenth century.

The rifle was, in fact, quite unsuited for general military use at this period. Its one advantage over the smooth-bore gun lay in its greater accuracy, and this was of no real significance in a system of infantry-tactics based on bodies of troops firing *en masse* at comparatively short range. Moreover, it was more expensive to make and, because the ball had to fit tightly, more difficult to load. For this reason the few specifically military rifles produced during the seventeenth century were intended for use by special troops only. The earliest of these appear to be a group of cheek-stocked wheel-locks in the Tøjhusmuseum, Copenhagen, made at Elsinore between 1611 and 1622 by Jørgen Dressler and Reinhardt Pasquier, probably for the bodyguard of King Christian IV. From 1631, when William, Landgrave of Hesse, raised a troop of riflemen,[66] select units similarly armed came into general, though limited, use in Germany. During the 1670s (probably in 1676)[67] Louis XIV ordered that eight men in each company of his bodyguard should be armed with rifled carbines. In 1679 he ordered that two men in each light-cavalry regiment, chosen from among the best marksmen, should be similarly equipped and placed at the forefront of the battle to fire at the enemy at long range. Finally, in 1690 he ordered that these men should be formed into separate

---

61 See A. Hoff in *Arms & Armor Annual*, I, Northfield, Ill., 1973, pp. 162–9.

62 Nos. 4072–3.

63 No. XII, 1619.

64 See p. 139.

65 George, *English Guns and Rifles*, p. 46.

66 L. Robert, *Catalogue des Collections Composant le Musée d' Artillerie en 1889*, Vol. IV, Paris, 1893, p. 16.

67 In this year the royal bodyguard was first armed with carbines. See G. Daniel, *Histoire de la Milice Françoise*, Vol. II, Paris, 1721, p. 148.

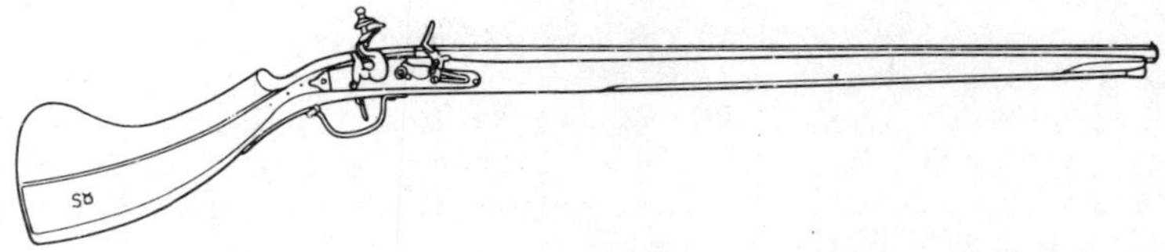

Snaphance birding piece. English, *c.*1620. Curtis Museum, Alton, Hampshire.

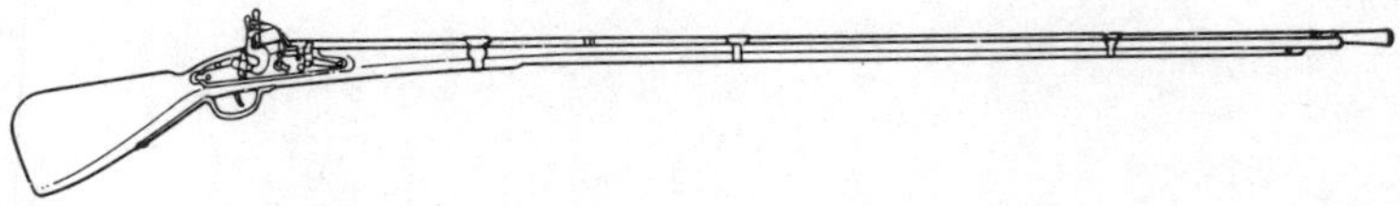

Long fowling piece. English, *c.*1640. Curtis Museum, Alton, Hampshire.

companies, one for each cavalry regiment.[68]

Before leaving the subject of the development of the gun-barrel reference must be made to two eccentric forms designed for sporting weapons. The first of these occurs on a few experimental arms made by the Danish maker Andreas Neidhart of Elsinore in the 1640s which have trefoil or cinquefoil bores.[69] They were probably intended to be loaded respectively with three or five small balls for shooting at sitting birds.

The other eccentric form was a rifled barrel containing a removable tube, also rifled, so that it could be used with two sizes of ball for large or small game. Only ten examples are recorded, of which five, all dated in the 1650s, are signed by Sigmund Klett of Ebenau, near Salzburg, two being inscribed *INVENTOR* after the signature.[70]

The various main types of long-gun in use during the seventeenth century can now be discussed briefly in alphabetical order. With one or two exceptions the terms used will be the English ones, so it should perhaps be mentioned that most of the weapons were employed all over Europe. Standardisation as we now understand the word was still unknown, however, and considerable variations in size and calibre occur. The measurements quoted from contemporary sources must, therefore, be regarded as approximations only. Unless otherwise stated it may be assumed that each type of firearm was fitted with some form of shoulder-stock.

Birding-Piece or Fowling-Piece

These terms were frequently used synonymously, but Randle Holme, writing in the 1680s,[71] makes a distinction between them:

> A cocking peece, or birding peece. The barrel of this is but short, and a small bore: and is the least of guns shott of with both hands, holding the Butt end (of this and the following guns) to the right shoulder, fireing it with the right hand, and supporting it with the left.
>
> A Fowling peece, is of seuerall length in the barrell from a yard and quarter, to 7 foot, or two yards, and a halfe long. The bore is generally in these guns, lest than a calever bore.

The precise difference between the two guns as far as their use is concerned is unclear. It seems probable, however, that the birding-piece was a light, small-calibre gun designed to fire a single ball at sitting birds and small game. This view is supported by the fact that when in 1652 certain London gunmakers were allowed to export 'Smale Birding peeces called Barbary Gunns' to the Barbary Coast permission was given on the grounds that the guns were 'soe smale boared as . . . to bee noe way usefull for ye service of the State'.[72] The screwed guns[73] used by fowlers during the English Civil War probably fell into this category, while a smooth-bored English example of *c.*1640 is preserved in the museum at Alton, Hampshire. An apparently unique French specimen in an English private collection has a rifled barrel with a calibre of only 0·187 in.

The fowling-piece appears to have been what we should now describe as a shotgun, and into this

68 On the use of rifled carbines by the French army under Louis XIV see Robert, *loc.cit.*; Daniel, *op.cit.*, p. 479; and *Gaya's Traité des Armes 1679*, edited C. J. ffoulkes, O.U.P., 1911, p. 29.

69 e.g. the Tøjhusmuseum, nos. B. 162-3.

70 See S. V. Grancsay, 'Cornell Klett, Hofbuchsenmacher', *The Gun Digest*, 9th Edn. Chicago, 1955, pp. 47-51.

71 *op.cit.*, p. 134.

72 H. L. Blackmore, *British Military Firearms*, 1650-1850, London, 1961, p. 26.

73 See p. 84.

category can be placed the majority of smooth-bore sporting-guns produced during the seventeenth century. It was widely believed that the longer the barrel fitted to this type of weapon the more effective it was likely to be, and it did sometimes attain the 'two yardes, and a halfe' mentioned by Holme. These 'long fowlers' seem to have been particularly favoured in both England and New England during the seventeenth century, though surviving examples are rare.

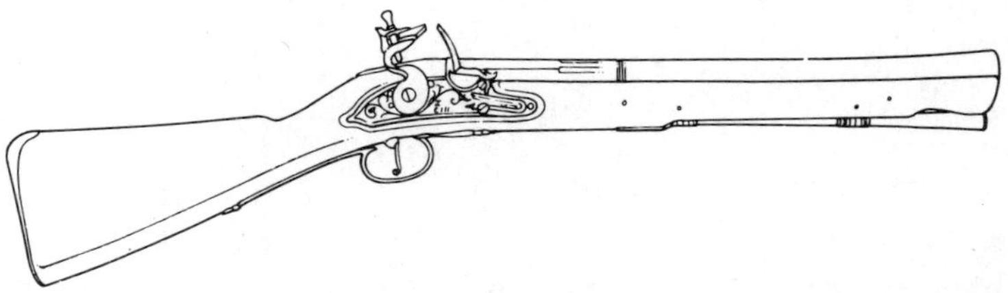

Flintlock blunderbuss. English, late seventeenth century. Tower of London Armouries.

Blunderbuss

Sir James Turner, writing in 1670–1 about carabineers, says 'some instead of carabines carry blunderbusses, which are short hand-guns of a great bore, wherein they may put several pistol or carabine balls, or small slugs of iron.[74] The term itself is derived, probably through the Dutch *Donderbuse*, from the German *Donderbuchse* (i.e. 'thunder-box'), a word used as early as 1348 to refer to cannon firing arrows.[75] When it first came to be applied to the type of gun described by Turner is unknown, but the classic blunderbuss's most characteristic feature, the flared muzzle designed in the erroneous belief that it would spread the shot, is first recorded on the engravings depicting Charles V's entry into Bologna in 1530.[76] There is no evidence to suggest, however, that the bell-mouthed muskets depicted there were intended to fire shot.

The wide-bored shotgun with a flaring muzzle to which the term *blunderbuss* is now invariably applied probably developed on the Continent, perhaps first in Germany and in Holland, during the second half of the sixteenth century. Its origins are, however, extremely obscure[77] and the vast majority of surviving examples date from after *c.*1650. It is first recorded in England in 1654 when '100 Brass Blunder Bushes' were included among arms carried by the Hispaniola Expedition of that year.[78] Thereafter, it became increasingly popular, especially as a defensive weapon for travellers, coachmen and the like, and also for use at sea. Both brass and iron barrels are found, varying in size from about 12 in to 24 in, though much longer examples are found on heavy wall-pieces.

The blunderbuss seems to have been produced chiefly in Southern and Western Europe, especially in England and Holland, being used hardly at all in Germany and the countries to the north and east. As noted by Turner it was loaded with shot and not, as is popularly believed, with bits of iron, tin-tacks, stones and any other miscellaneous missiles that happened to be handy.

Caliver[79]

This military long-gun survived until the English Civil War. At this time, with the introduction of a lighter form of musket and the abandonment of the musket-rest, it probably lost its separate identity. Randle Holme[80] says that it had not been generally used since Queen Elizabeth I's time 'but by some perticular persons and now it is an Instrument little known'. The first part of this statement is certainly incorrect for when in 1630 the English Council of War promulgated 'Orders for the general uniformitie of all sortes of armes both for horse and foote' they included the caliver, its dimensions being given as 54 in overall, 39 in barrel and bore of seventeen bullets to the pound rowleing in'.[81]

Carbine

This remained, as in the sixteenth century, a short light gun for mounted use. It was normally fitted with either a wheel- or snaplock, of which the

74 *Pallas Armata . . . written in the years 1670 and 1671*, London, 1683, p. 137.

75 Bernard von Rathgen, *Das Aufkommen der Pulverwaffe*, Munich, 1925, p. 23.

76 See p. 54.

77 It is first recorded by name (as *Donderbuss*) in Holland in 1598. See D. R. Baxter, *Blunderbusses*, London, 1970, p. 10.

78 George, *Guns and Rifles*, p. 59.

79 See p. 55.

80 *op.cit.*, p. 134.

81 Blackmore, *op.cit.*, p. 24.

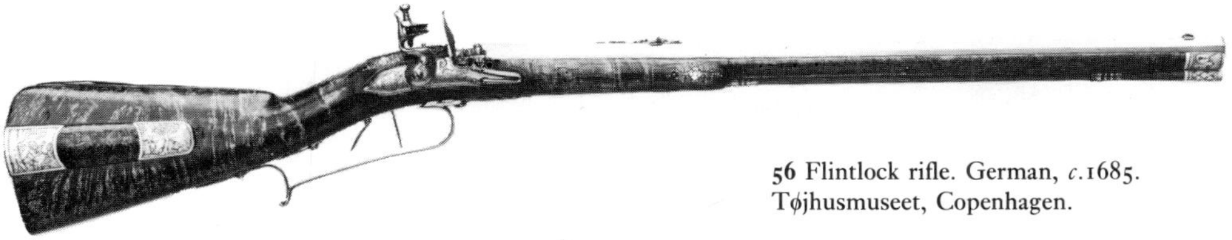

56 Flintlock rifle. German, *c.*1685. Tøjhusmuseet, Copenhagen.

57 Wheel-lock rifle (*Müllerbuchse*), the barrel signed *Gottfried Hahn*. German, *c.*1680. Tøjhusmuseet, Copenhagen.

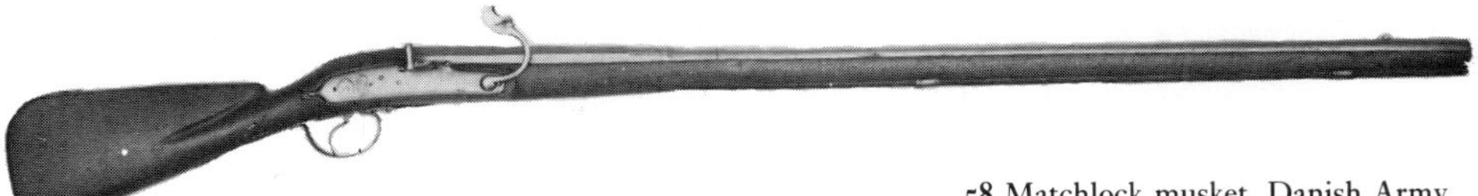

58 Matchlock musket. Danish Army Model of 1685. Tøjhusmuseet, Copenhagen.

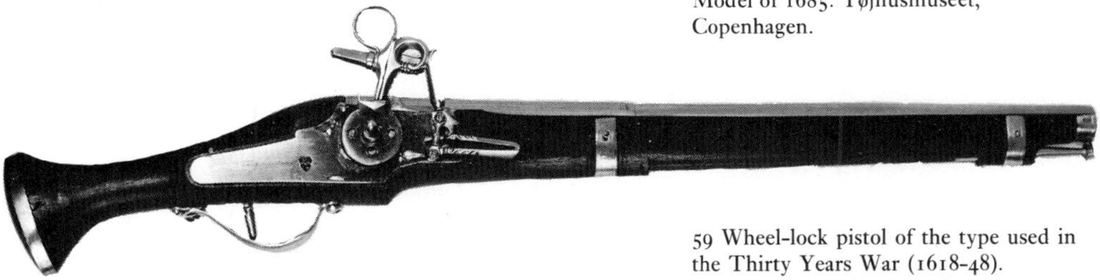

59 Wheel-lock pistol of the type used in the Thirty Years War (1618-48). German (Nuremberg), *c.*1620-40. Landeszeughaus, Graz, Austria.

60 Flintlock pistol, the lock signed *Jean Dubois À Sedan*. French, *c.*1660. Skokloster, Sweden.

61 Flintlock pistol, the lock signed *Jean Prevot A Mazy*. French, *c.*1640. Tøjhusmuseet, Copenhagen.

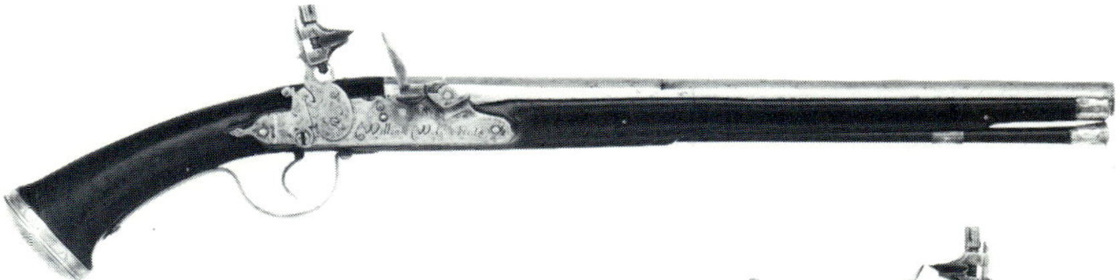

62 Pair of snaphance pistols, the furniture of engraved silver. The barrel bears proof-marks used under the Commonwealth and Protectorate (1649-59). Lock signed *William Wotson Fecit*. English (London), *c.*1650. Tower of London Armouries.

63 One of a pair of flintlock pistols belonging to Queen Kristina of Sweden (1633-54). By P. Thomas. French (Paris), *c.*1640. Livrustkammaren, Stockholm.

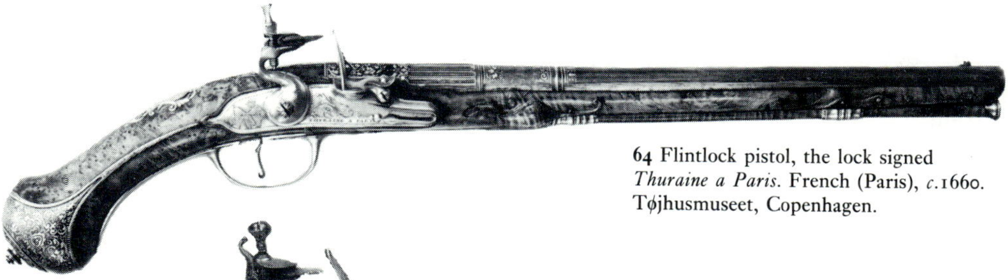

64 Flintlock pistol, the lock signed *Thuraine a Paris*. French (Paris), *c.*1660. Tøjhusmuseet, Copenhagen.

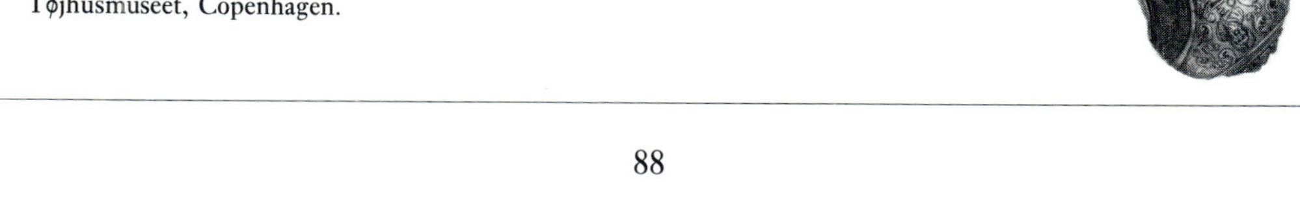

65 Pair of flintlock pistols, the stocks inlaid with silver, the locks signed *Chasteau a Paris*. French (Paris), *c.*1720. Tøjhusmuseet, Copenhagen.

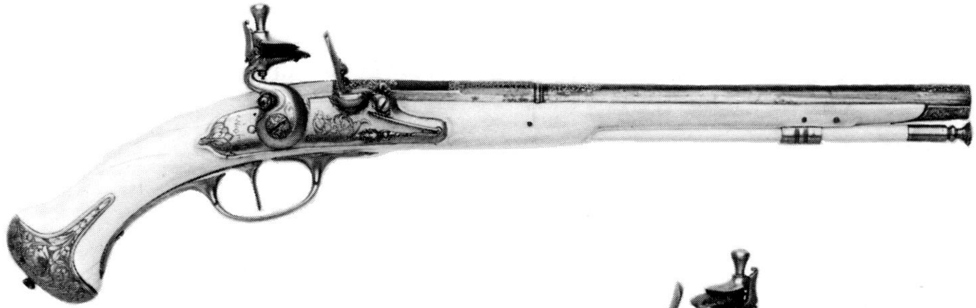

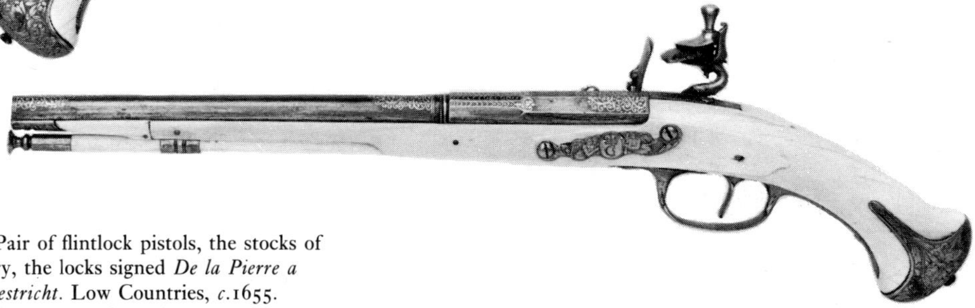

66 Pair of flintlock pistols, the stocks of ivory, the locks signed *De la Pierre a Maestricht*. Low Countries, *c.*1655. Tøjhusmuseet, Copenhagen.

67 Wheel-lock pistol, the butt in the form of a dog's head. Dutch, *c.*1650. Tøjhusmuseet, Copenhagen.

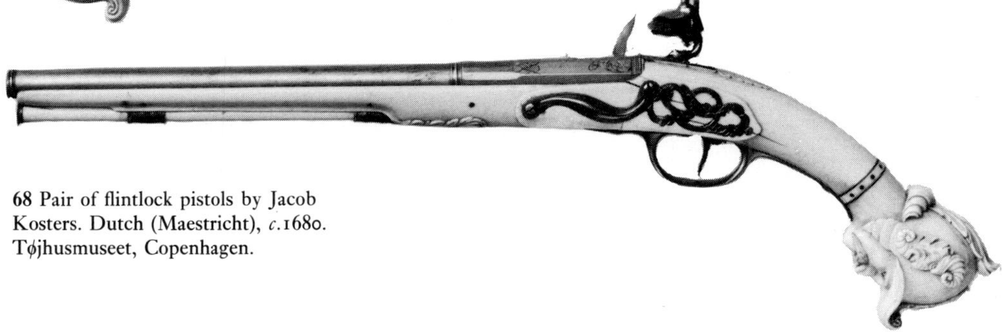

68 Pair of flintlock pistols by Jacob Kosters. Dutch (Maestricht), *c.*1680. Tøjhusmuseet, Copenhagen.

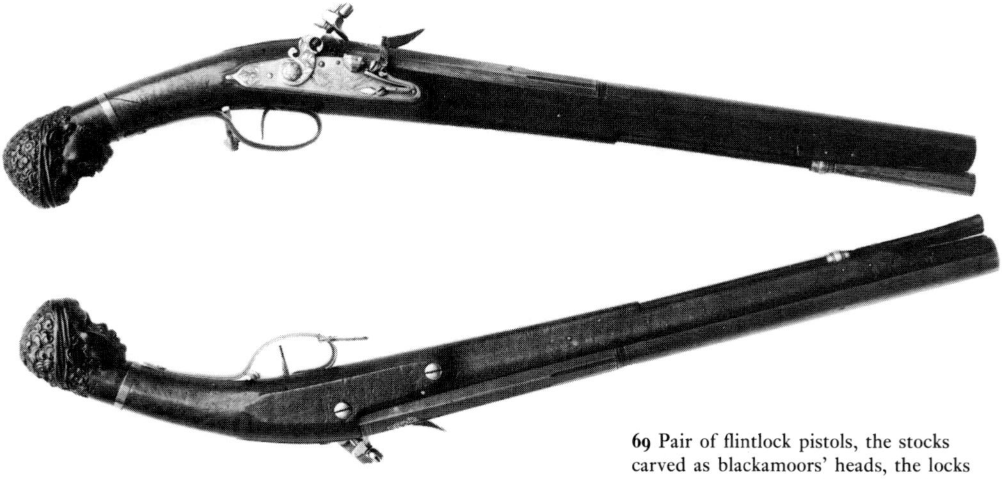

69 Pair of flintlock pistols, the stocks carved as blackamoors' heads, the locks signed *Devie*. French (Paris), *c*.1660. Historisches Museum, Dresden.

70 Flintlock pistol, one of a pair, the mounts of chiselled steel. Italian (Brescia), *c*.1660. Wallace Collection, London.

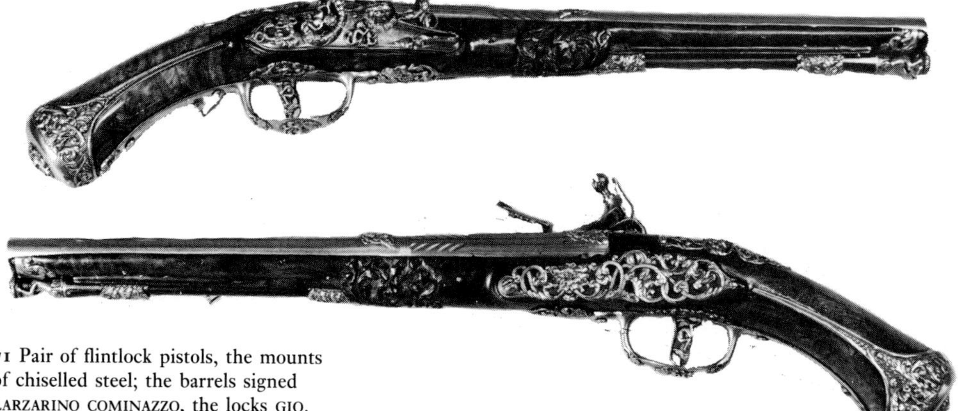

71 Pair of flintlock pistols, the mounts of chiselled steel; the barrels signed LARZARINO COMINAZZO, the locks GIO. BATTA. TIANI. Italian (Brescia), *c*.1690. Private Collection.

latter became increasingly popular from early in the seventeenth century. Randle Holme writes about it as follows.[82]

> A carbine, is an horsmans gun about a yard or more long in the barrell; this is hung by the mans side, in a belt ouer his left shoulder, and vnder his right Arme: with a sweel [swivel], or sweeth vpon it, which by the help of a spring in it, taks hold of a ring, on a side bar, or Iron rod screwd on the stock, the contrary side to the lock.

The English Council of War Order of 1630 gives the overall length of the 'Carbine or Petronel' as 45 in with a barrel of 30 in, and a bore of twenty-four balls to the pound. By the last quarter of the century English military carbines were being made with barrels of two standard lengths, 2 ft 7 in and 3 ft.[83] There were, however, wide variations in size in English non-military carbines and foreign carbines of all types, and it is not possible to lay down precise measurements within which a gun must fit to fall into this category.

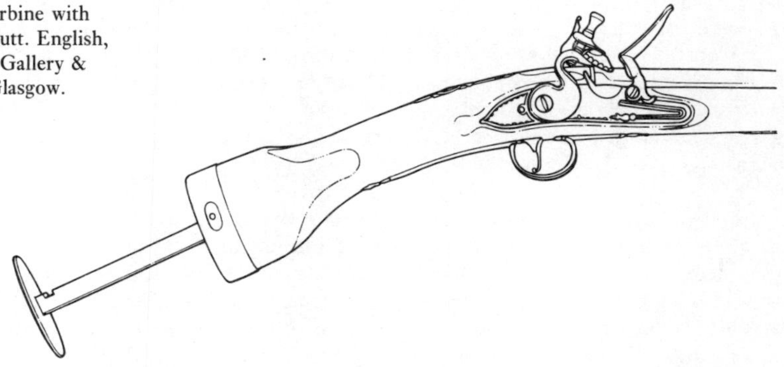

Detail of carbine with extending butt. English, *c.*1690. Art Gallery & Museum, Glasgow.

During the second half of the seventeenth century very short carbines were occasionally made with the buttplate attached to an iron bar concealed in the stock. This could be pulled out and locked to form an extension-butt, the idea apparently being to permit the carbine to be fired either like a pistol with one hand, or from the shoulder. Other carbines are found with folding butts, or with butts that can be divided into two, presumably for easy carriage and concealment.

Crabut

A term, found very occasionally in seventeenth-century English texts, referring to a firearm that has not been identified with certainty. According to Randle Holme[84] it was 'the least sort of a carbine'.

Dragon

A heavy-calibre carbine carried by dragoons, who were mounted infantry, and from which they are said to have derived their name, though the converse seems equally likely. The origin of the term is unknown and, so far as the writer is aware, no actual example of the weapon has ever been identified. The only definite information about its size noted so far appears to be that given by Gervase Markham in his *Souldiers Accidence* of 1625. Speaking of the equipment of the dragoons he says:

> and for offensive armes, they have a fayre *Dragon* fitted with an Iron worke to be carried in a Belt of leather, which is buckled over the right shoulder and vnder the left arme, having a Turnell of Iron with a ring through which the peece runneth vp and downe; and these *Dragons* are short peeces of 16 inches the Barrell, and full Musquet bore, with firelocks [i.e. wheel-locks] or snap-haunces: also a Belt, with a Flaske, pryming-boxe, key and Bullet-bag . . .[85]

It is worth noting that even if the dragon was the original firearm of the dragoons they are commonly referred to throughout the seventeenth century as being armed with muskets, carbines or musketoons. The last term, which is first recorded in 1627,[86] when *dragon* seems already to have been going out of

82 *op.cit.*, p. 134.

83 Blackmore, *op.cit.*, pp. 24 and 36.

84 *op.cit.*, p. 134.

85 G[ervase] M[arkham], *The Souldiers Accidence*, London, 1625. p. 43. Francis Markham in *Five Decades of Epistles of Warres*, London, 1622, Bk. IV, p. 133, refers to the late invented Dragoones 'being not aboue sixteene inch Barrell, and full musquet bore'. See also Hewitt, *op.cit.*, Vol. III, pp. 716-22.

86 See p. 94.

current use, was almost certainly synonymous with it.[87]

Fusil (Fusee or Fuzee)[88]

As early as 1629 *fusil* had already come, in France, to be applied to a snaplock or to a gun fitted with such a lock.[89] During the period with which we are concerned here it seems both in England and in France to have been used invariably with this restricted meaning.[90] In the eighteenth century it was commonly used in England to refer to a light flintlock musket carried by officers and sergeants, while in France, of course, it eventually became the standard general term for any long-gun.

Snaphance muskets were in use from the sixteenth century onwards,[91] but the first infantry to be regularly armed with them were almost certainly the troops appointed to guard artillery and ammunition-dumps, and the grenadiers, who required guns that could be carried slung, though ready for instant action, while they threw their grenades. When in 1671 Louis XIV raised a special *Régiment des Fusiliers* they were, as their name indicates, armed with fusils.[92] Only seven years later Gaya in his *Traité des Armes*[93] says that the fusils used by the 'Compagnies de Fusiliers & Granadiers' were of the same calibre and weight as muskets. His accompanying illustration shows that the only major difference between the two weapons was that the musket was equipped with a matchlock and the fusil with a flintlock.

When the English Royal Regiment of Fusiliers was raised in June 1685, a warrant addressed to the Ordnance ordering arms to be issued to them included '100 fusees, musket bore'.[94] Other records of the period describe these same weapons as 'Snaphance Musquets, strapped, with bright barrels of three foot eight inches long'. There can be little doubt, therefore, that *fusil* was used in England, as in France, to describe a gun equipped with a snaplock, a circumstance that accounts for the variation in the sizes of weapons described as fusils in contemporary records.[95] The situation is made more confusing by the fact that in England 'firelock' was also commonly used to describe a snaplock gun from the middle of the century onwards, if not before. Randle Holme,[96] for example, says that if a musket has 'a Lock that striketh fire, and so fireth off the Gun, then it ceaseth to be called a muskett, but hath the denomination of a Fire-lock'.

Hand Mortar

This weapon[97] continued to be used throughout the seventeenth century. The barrel remained virtually unchanged, but the stock and lock followed the development of those found on standard firearms of the period. A new form that appeared in the third quarter of the century resembled a short flintlock musket except that it had a detachable discharger-cup attached to the muzzle.

An extremely unusual form of hand-mortar, represented only by two specimens in the Tower of London Armouries,[98] was probably invented by John Tinker, an employee of the Board of Ordnance, in 1681. This is shaped like a flintlock musket but the butt divides into two halves on a hinge. The forward half is, in fact, a discharger-cup linked to the pan of the lock by a tube controlled by a shutter. The musket can either be fired in the ordinary way or used, in conjunction with a folding rest, as a grenade-thrower.[99]

Harquebus.

As already mentioned,[100] *harquebus* by the late sixteenth century, if not before, had come to denote a form of heavy carbine. By this date also the harquebusier had become the typical light cavalryman of Europe, a role he retained until the third quarter of the seventeenth century. Captain Cruso, in his *Militarie Instructions for the Cavallerie* of 1632, says that 'For offensive arms, he must have the harquebuse of two foot and a halfe long, (the bore of 17 bullets in the pound, rowling in,) hanging on a belt by a swivell, a flask, touch box, and pistols like the cuirassiers (as some writers have it)'.[101] The dimensions given here agree with those in the English Council of War Order of 1630, namely an

87 cf. Blackmore, *op.cit.*, p. 32.

88 The origin of this word is discussed on p. 42.

89 J. B. Giraud, *Documents pour Servir à l'Histoire de l'Armement*, Vol. II, Lyon, 1899, p. 81.

90 In England *fuzee* was also applied to a fuse for a grenade.

91 See p. 43.

92 Daniel *op.cit.*, Vol. II, pp. 434 and 533.

93 *op.cit.*, p. 25.

94 W. Wheater, *Historical Record of the Seventh or Royal Regiment of Fusiliers*, Leeds, 1875, p. 3.

95 See Blackmore, *op.cit.*, pp. 32-3, and E. Chambers's *Cyclopaedia*, 1728-51, sub *Musquet* and *Fuzee*.

96 *op.cit.*, p. 134.

97 See p. 56.

98 Nos. XII 260-1.

99 Blackmore, *op.cit.*, p. 35.

100 See p. 55.

101 Quoted by Hewitt, *op.cit.*, Vol. II, p. 712.

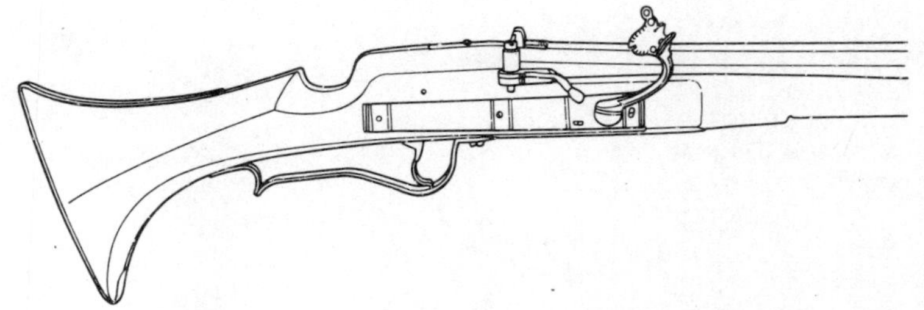

Matchlock musket. Danish, early-seventeenth century. Kungl. Armémuseum, Stockholm.

overall length of 45 in, a barrel of 30 in and a bore of seventeen bullets to the pound. Another version of the order lists the accessories as 'a key to bend it wch may hould tutch-powder and iron worke called a swifle to it', while the *Gunmakers' Rates* of 1631 give the cost of an harquebus with all its accessories as £1. 16*s*. 0*d*.[102]

As early as 1622 Francis Markham[103] says 'Harquebusses I cannot allow in this place, because they are grown out of vse, and can by no means make their encounter good when the Musquet is opposed against them.' The information given in the last paragraph shows that this statement is not absolutely correct, but there seems to be no doubt that the harquebus was going out of use in the 1620s. After *c*.1630 it is mentioned very much less frequently in contemporary records, the harquebusier henceforth being usually described as equipped with a carbine.[104]

Müller-Büchse

A German term, meaning 'Miller-Gun', first recorded in the eighteenth century, now applied to a form of German rifle equipped with a heavy, clumsy version of the French shoulder-stock. The type is first recorded in the 1660s and survived, in both wheel- and flintlock versions, until the early eighteenth century. The fact that eighteenth-century inventories of the armoury of the Electors of Saxony refer to *Müller-Büchsen* with both French (shoulder) and German (cheek) stocks indicates that the term was not then used in its present restricted sense. It has been suggested, with some probability, that it was originally applied to guns fitted with barrels made by Jost Lagemann of Vollmarshausen, Hesse (*d*.1666), who combined the trades of gunsmith and miller.[105]

Musket

The form of musket that had appeared in the closing years of the sixteenth century remained in use with little variation in form and construction until the 1630s. The dimensions laid down in the English Council of War Order of 1630, for example, are much the same as those given by Tartaglia in 1588,[106] namely, length 62 in barrel 48 in and bore twelve bullets to the pound.[107] The price of a musket and its accessories at this period, according to the *Gunmakers' Rates* of 1631, were as follows:

For a new musket with mould, worm and scowrer – 15*s*. 6*d*.
For a musket rest – 10*d*.[108]

During the 1630s the French form of shoulder-butt was adapted to the musket and with this came a general move towards lightening the whole weapon. The development that took place in England can be taken as giving a general picture of what was happening everywhere in Europe.

In 1639 the English Ordnance officers suggested that the musket-barrel should be reduced to $3\frac{1}{2}$ ft and the charge, to lessen recoil, to only half the weight of the the bullet instead of two-thirds. The Council of War accepted the recommendations in part and ordered 15,000 muskets, of which 5,000 were to have barrels $4\frac{1}{2}$ ft in length and a total weight of 14 lb, and 10,000 $3\frac{1}{2}$ ft barrels and a weight of 12 lb.[109]

The results of the Council of War's experiment are unrecorded, but it seems eventually to have led to the adoption of a lighter musket. This is indicated by the fact that the musket-rest began to go out of use in the 1640s. Lt Col Elton, writing in 1649, says that 'our rests are of little or no use to us in time of skirmishing; fit they are we confess in the Military

102 Blackmore, *op.cit.*, p. 24 and George, *Guns and Rifles*, p. 37.

103 *op.cit.*, Bk. I, p. 33.

104 C. H. Firth, *Cromwell's Army*, 4th edn., London, 1962, pp. 116–18.

105 See E. Haenel, 'Die Hessen-Cassler Müllerbüchsen un ihre Meister', *Festchrift Thierbach*, Dresden, 1905.

106 See p. 54.

107 Blackmore, *op.cit.*, p. 24.

108 George, *Guns and Rifles*, pp. 36–7.

109 Blackmore, *op.cit.*, p. 24.

Matchlock musket. Dutch, *c.*1660. The barrel bears English proof-marks. Tower of London Armouries.

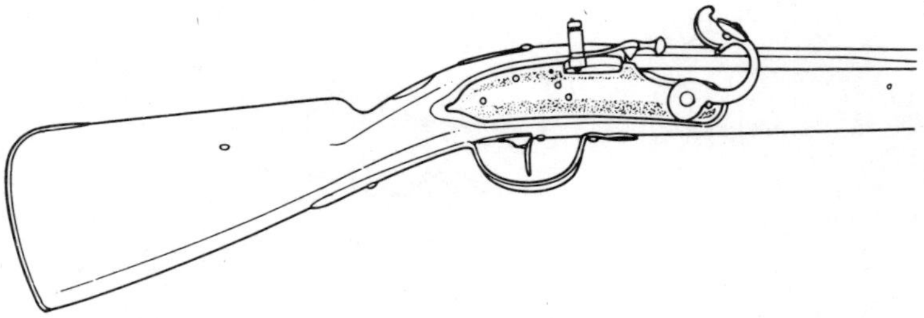

Gardens, but in time of battle both troublesome and cumbersome'.[110] A statute of 1662 dealing with the arming of the militia does not mention a rest as part of the equipment of a musketeer and implies, from the way it is worded, that muskets were being made much lighter than the authorities thought desirable:

> For the foot, a musqueteer is to have a musquet, the barril whereof is not to be under three foot in length, and the gauge of the bore to be for twelve bullets to the pound, a collar of bandeleers with a sword. Provided that all muster masters shall for the present admit and allow of any musquets already made, which will bear a bullet of fourteen to the pound, but no muskets which henceforth shall be made are to be allowed of, but such as are of the gauge of twelve bullets to the pound.[111]

By 1693, at the latest, a barrel-length of 3 ft 10 in had been adopted for the musket, and this was to remain standard for many years to come.[112]

Though snaphance muskets had made their appearance in the second half of the sixteenth century,[113] the matchlock remained the main weapon of the infantry until *c.*1700. But from early in the seventeenth century, and especially during and after the Thirty Years War, there is evidence of an increased use of snaphances by the foot-soldiers.[114] They seem at first to have been confined to special units and, as noted above,[115] were employed in particular by the companies whose task it was to guard the artillery and ammunition-dumps. This was undoubtedly because soldiers equipped with smouldering matches in the vicinity of open barrels of gunpowder constituted a very real danger, as many contemporary writers testify.[116] When the English Parliament raised the New Model Army in 1645, it included at least two companies of firelocks, who were distinguished from the rest of the infantry by tawny, instead of red, coats.[117] These, as we have seen,[118] were later formed into separate fusilier regiments, while at the same time snaplock muskets began to be taken into use by the navy and by some of the ordinary infantry units. From *c.*1670 onwards, the muskets issued to the British forces were divided roughly equally between snaphances and matchlocks, with the latter preponderating slightly at first. But not until the early eighteenth century was the matchlock withdrawn completely from service.[119]

Musketoon

A term, derived from the French *mousqueton*, first recorded in Sir Thomas Kellie's *Pallas Armata* of 1627:

> The Souldiers of the militarie yarde at *London* are taught to use a *Musqueton* or *demy Musquet*, with their *Pick* [pike], which hangs about their Neck in a Belt like a *carabine*, being two foot in length, and of full *Musquet* bore 12 bullets to the pound, but hauing a *snapwork*, it wil carie blanck as far as a *Musquet* which I haue sene: this *demy Musquet* they *charge* and *discharge* with as greate facilitie as if they had nothing to use but their peace: making their *Picks* as it were a *rest* vnto it.[120]

110 Firth, *op.cit.*, p. 79.

111 F. Grose, *A Treatise on Ancient Armour and Weapons*, London, 1786, pp. 112-13. Randle Holme (*op.cit.*, p. 135), writing in the 1680s, says that rests have been discarded 'by reason that the muskett is made much lighter than formerly but in the Artillery yards they exercise with them to this day'.

112 Blackmore, *op.cit.*, p. 37.

113 See p. 43.

114 See, for example, Josef Alm, *Armens Eldhandvapen*, Stockholm, 1953, pp. 90ff.

115 See p. 92.

116 See Firth *op.cit.*, pp. 86 and 88.

117 ibid, p. 88.

118 See p. 92.

119 Blackmore, *op.cit.*, pp. 32 and 37.

120 Sir T[homas] K[ellie], *Pallas Armata, or Militarie Instructions for the Learned: The First Part, Containing the Exercise of the Infanterie*, Edinburgh, 1627, p. 112.

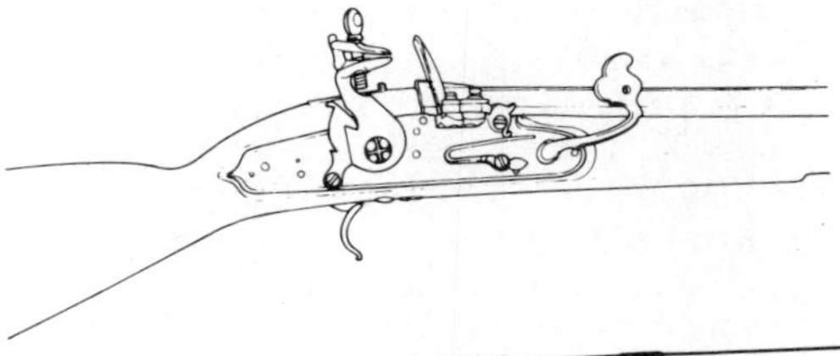

Detail of combined flintlock and matchlock musket. English, *c.*1690. An English version of the Vauban lock. Tower of London Armouries.

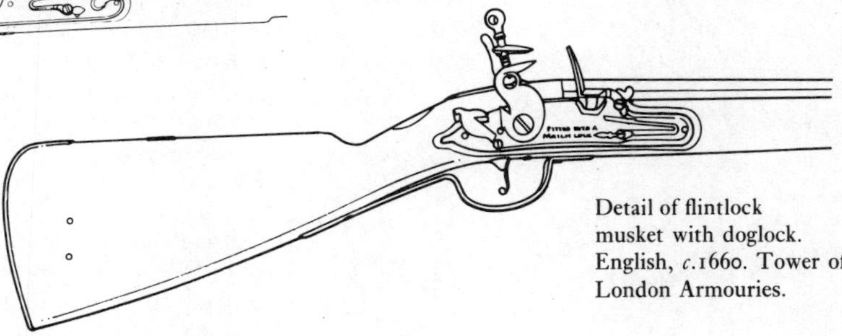

Detail of flintlock musket with doglock. English, *c.*1660. Tower of London Armouries.

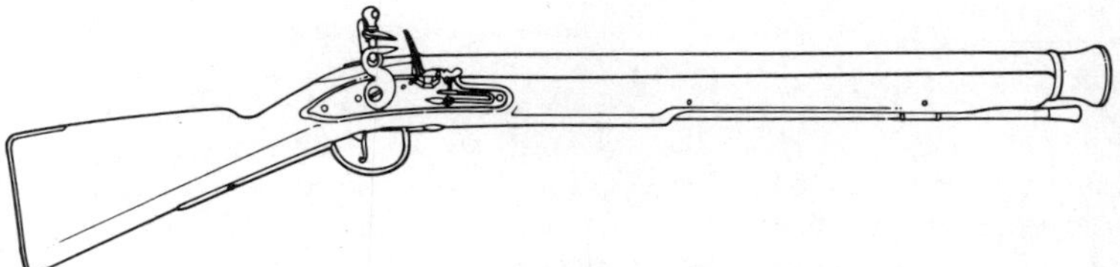

Musketoon. The brass barrel with proof-marks used under Charles II. English, *c.*1670 (Lock 1721). Tower of London Armouries.

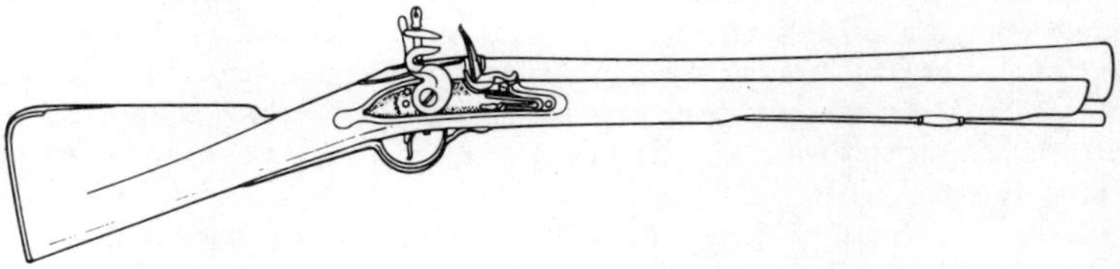

Sea-Service musketoon. English, *c.*1730 (the mounts late seventeenth century). Tower of London Armouries.

This description is so close to that given of the dragon by Gervase Markham in 1625[121] that it seems virtually certain that *musketoon* and *dragon* were synonymous.

Gaya's treatise of 1678[122] shows that a musketoon was still a heavy carbine, sometimes rifled, at this date. By the beginning of the eighteenth century, if not before, however, the term had come to refer to the smallest type of blunderbuss.[123]

Petronel

By *c.*1600 this term had come to refer to a type of carbine. The English Council of War order of 1630, for example, gives only one set of dimensions for the 'Carbine or Petronel',[124] which, coupled with the fact that the latter term seems to have gone out of general use shortly after this date, suggests that the two words were now synonymous. Randle Holme, however, describes the petronel as a kind of pistol.[125]

> The petronell, is a sort of pistall longer than the Holster pistall the barrell being longer than the foresaid by almost halfe the length. These were formerly horsmens pistalls and were (a case of them) hung on either side before the sadle. All these kind of pistalls are shott of with one hand, the other holding the bridle to guide the horse.

121 See p. 91.

122 *op.cit.*, p. 26.

123 Chambers, *op.cit.*, *s. musquetoon.*

124 See p. 91.

125 *op.cit.*, p. 134.

Tschinke

39, 104 A distinctive type of light, small-calibre wheel-lock rifle, intended for shooting at sitting birds, and produced in the Silesian town of Teschen, from which its name is derived. Its characteristic features are a butt of 'dog-leg' shape, designed to be rested

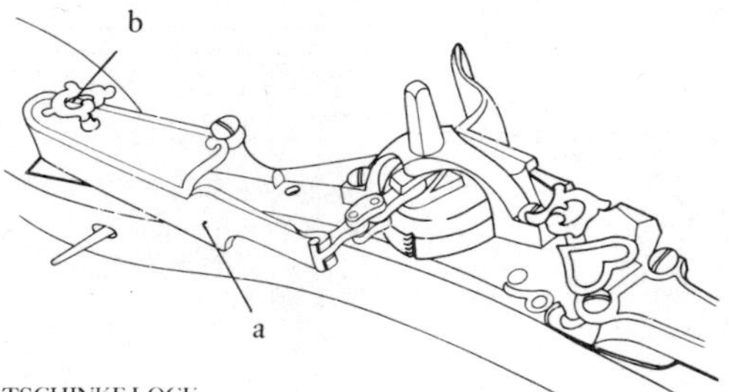

TSCHINKE LOCK

a External mainspring
b Button pressed when wheel is wound up to cause the sear to engage

This operates in the same way as the conventional wheel-lock (p. 34) but has its mainspring (a) mounted externally, and a sear-mechanism that has to be set by pressing a button (b).

against the cheek and at the same time supported on the shoulder, and a lock with an external mainspring that projects below the stock. Before it can be spanned the sear mechanism has to be set by pressing a button that projects from between the arms of the mainspring. Most examples have their stocks decorated with rather coarse inlay of engraved mother-of-pearl and staghorn and of brass wire.

The earliest record of the existence of a special Teschen type of birding-piece dates from 1580,[126] but all the actual examples known to the writer date from the second and third quarters of the seventeenth century.[127] During this period there appears to have been virtually no change in the form of the Tschinke and examples are therefore difficult to date precisely.

The term *Kurlandisch* is often applied to the Tschinke and, more particularly, to its distinctive form of wheel-lock, on the evidence of some of the early inventories of the Electoral gun-collection at Dresden. It was believed that this indicated that they were made in the province of Courland, but Dr Viktor Karger[128] has suggested that it is much more likely to refer to the work of the Teschen gunmaker Georg Kurland (recorded 1629-31).

It should be mentioned that the term *Tschinke* (*Teschinen*, *Tsechinken* or *Tesehkin*) continued to be applied to a gun with a very small calibre until the second half of the nineteenth century.[129]

Pistols

Throughout the seventeenth century pistols con- 50, 52
tinued to be used, as before, for personal defence, 59-75
hunting from horseback and, above all, as cavalry 105, 106
weapons. The outbreak of the Thirty Years War in 111
1618 produced a tremendous increase in production, especially of 'munition' pistols that were entirely functional, without ornamentation and with their furniture reduced to the minimum. As a result of this we begin henceforth to have a correspondingly larger number of surviving pistols available for study.

With the exception of the turn-off weapons,[130] the vast majority of seventeenth-century pistols were smooth-bored. All the lock mechanisms discussed previously in this chapter were applied to them, though only two matchlock pistols are recorded.[131] The wheel-lock pistol remained widely popular until *c.*1650, though outside the areas under German cultural influence it had already started to go out of use in favour of the snaplock long before. In Germany it lingered on until *c.*1680, though surviving examples as late as this are rare.[132]

Snaphance pistols, as we have seen, had been in use in England since at least as early as 1580.[133] A comparatively large number of examples survives from the early seventeenth century, so it seems likely that they had become common by that date, though they did not finally supplant the wheel-lock until the end of the Civil War. The *Gunmakers' Rates* of 1631 includes both forms:

> For a pair of firelock pistols, furnished with a key, mould, scowrer, worm, flask, and cases of leather, of length and boar according to the

126 Viktor Karger, 'Neue Teschner Beiträge zur Herkunftsrage der Tsechinken', *Waffen-und Kostumkunde*, Vol. VI, Munich-Berlin, 1964, p. 30.

127 Two Tschinkes in the old civic armoury at Emden in Germany are dated respectively 1558 and 1560 on the barrels. The stocks and locks, however, appear to be of seventeenth-century date. In the Finnish National Museum, Helsinki, is a rifle (No. 2341:1) with a lock which appears to be an early version of the typical Tschinke one and a stock which is midway in shape between the kind found on Tschinkes and the standard German cheek-stock. The barrel is dated 1607.

128 *op.cit.*, p. 32.

129 F. M. Feldhaus, 'Tesching und Flobert', Z.H.W.K., Vol. VIII, 1918-20, pp. 83-4.

130 See pp. 189-90.

131 See p. 56.

132 The French wheel-lock pistols of 1829 mentioned on p. 64 n.11 represents a deliberate revival of the system.

133 See p. 43.

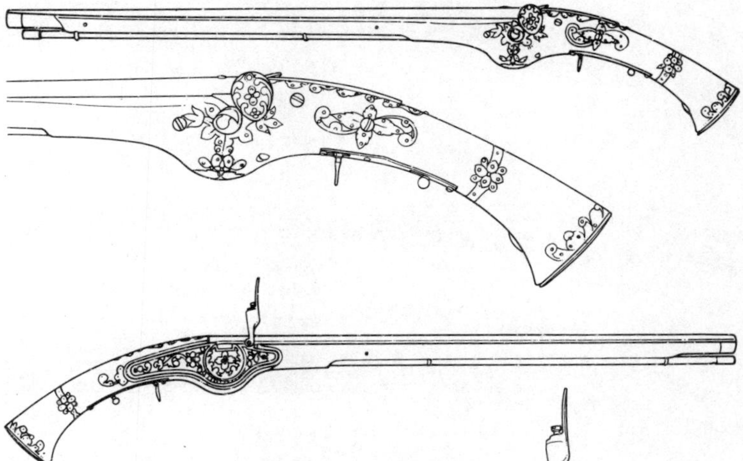

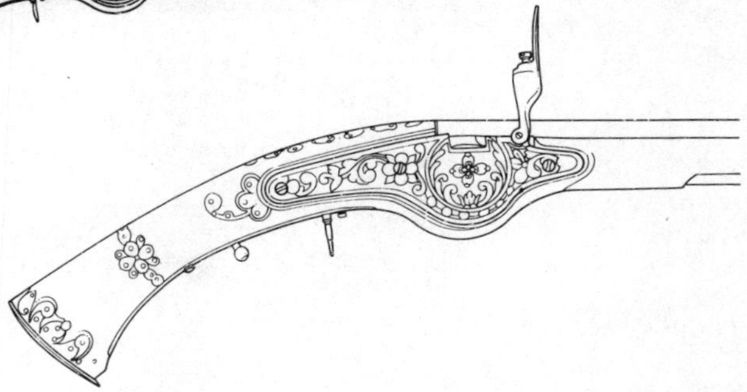

Pair of pistols with internal wheel-locks spanned from the opposite side, with details of stocks and mechanisms. Signed *Jacob Grell* ARTZBERG *1652*. Hermitage Museum, Leningrad.

allowance of the counsel of war £3. 0*s*. 0*d*.
For a pair of horsemans pistols furnished with snaphaunces, mouldes, worms, scowrer, flask, charger and cases £2. 0*s*. 0*d*.[134]

Robert Ward, writing in 1639,[135] gives the drill movements for loading and firing a pistol fitted with a wheel-lock (which he calls a firelock) and one fitted with a dog-lock. He prefaces his instructions on the latter with the remark that 'our English Pistolls differ from the firelocke Pistoll', a fact that suggests that the snaplock pistol was then used very little outside this country. The little evidence that is available does, in fact, indicate that such pistols did not start to come into wide use on the Continent until the 1630s, when the first recorded flintlock examples appeared. By the 1640s the flintlock pistol was well on its way to supplanting all other forms, except in Spain where, as with the long-gun, the miquelet reigned supreme until the nineteenth century.

The physical development of the pistol during the seventeenth century, broadly speaking, differed from that of the contemporary long-gun only in so far as changes in the form of the stock, and especially of the butt, were concerned. The barrel and the furniture, other than the butt-cap, were of similar design on both types of arm and it will not therefore be necessary to discuss them here in detail.

The long, slender form of wheel-lock pistol with a straight or slightly down-curved butt ending in an ovoidal pommel survived until the second decade of the seventeenth century. In about 1600, however, a new form had appeared, on which the butt merely widened at the end, where it was cut off straight or slightly rounded, and fitted with a metal butt-cap or a reinforcing ring. Shortly after this, with the general tendency towards making the lock smaller and more compact, the whole stock became lighter and the French form that curved down below the centre of the lockplate became widely popular. This shape had, of course, been designed to accommodate the peculiarly French form of wheel-lock with its detached mainspring, but it was now commonly used also with locks of normal construction.

The form of stock just described was the one most widely used on the wheel-lock pistol for the rest of its existence, though it should be noted that wheel-locks were also not infrequently mounted in stocks of the type described below in connection

134 George, *Guns and Rifles*, p. 37.

135 *Animadversions of Warre*, London, 1639, Bk. I, pp. 300-1.

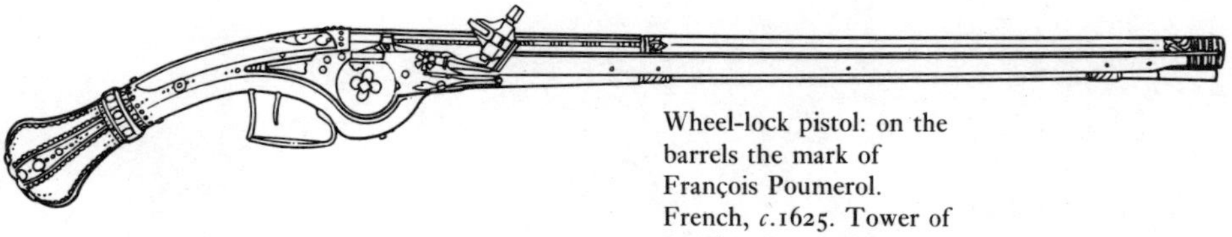

Wheel-lock pistol: on the barrels the mark of François Poumerol. French, *c.*1625. Tower of London Armouries.

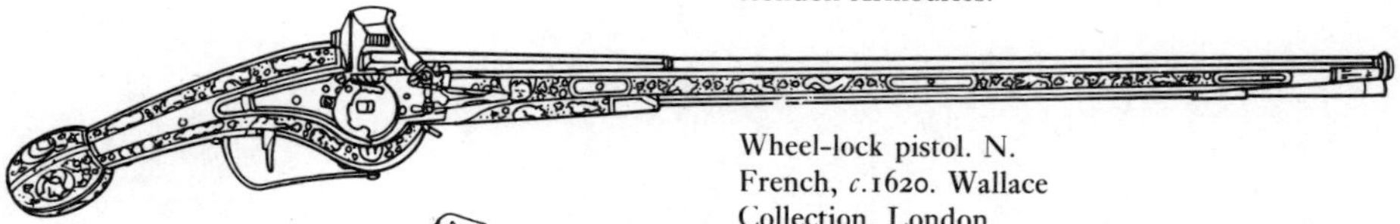

Wheel-lock pistol. N. French, *c.*1620. Wallace Collection, London.

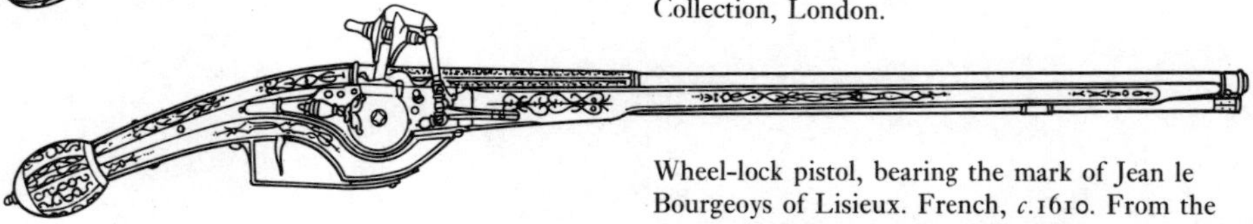

Wheel-lock pistol, bearing the mark of Jean le Bourgeoys of Lisieux. French, *c.*1610. From the *Cabinet d'Armes* of Louis XIII (No. 211). Wallace Collection, London.

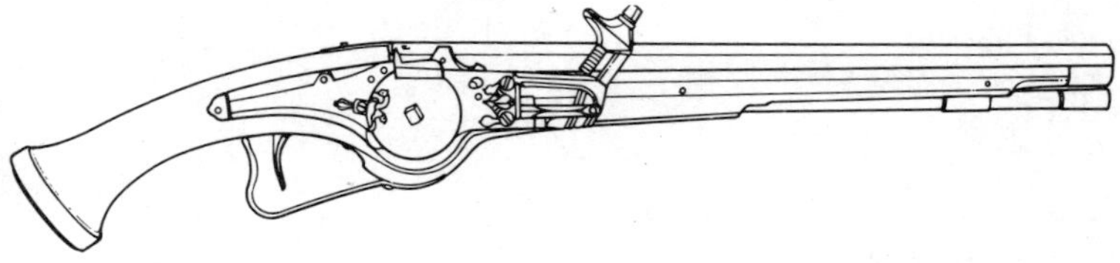

Wheel-lock pistol carried by Gustavus Adolphus of Sweden at Lützen (1632). German or Swiss, *c.*1630. Livrustkammaren, Stockholm.

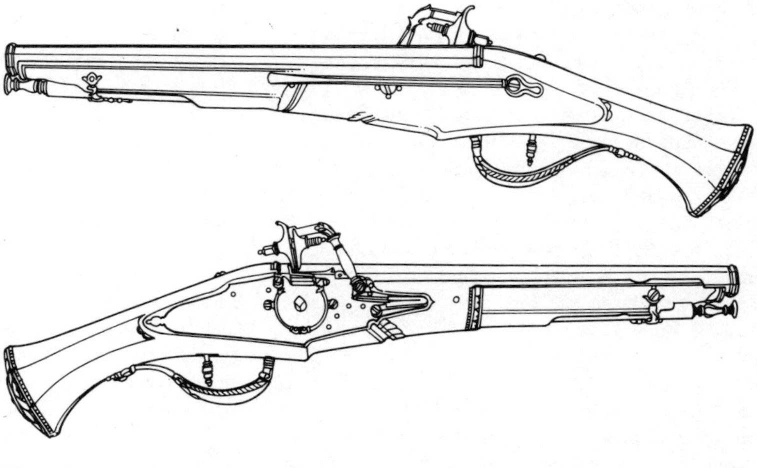

Pair of wheel-lock pistols with chiselled steel mounts. Italian (Brescia), *c.*1640. Victoria & Albert Museum, London.

with the flintlock. One major change that took place in the second decade of the century was a general reduction in the length of the barrel of the large cavalry holster-pistol. It is impossible to express this in terms of hard and fast figures but, broadly speaking, whereas previously barrels of 20 in–25 in had been common, 15 in–18 in now became the more usual length.

As previously noted, snaplock pistols seem, in the early seventeenth century, to have been used mainly in this country,[136] and all the examples known

136 On the whole subject of seventeenth-century English pistols see two important articles by Ian Eaves in the *Journal of the Arms and Armour Society*, Vols. VI (pp. 277–344) and VIII (pp. 269–329).

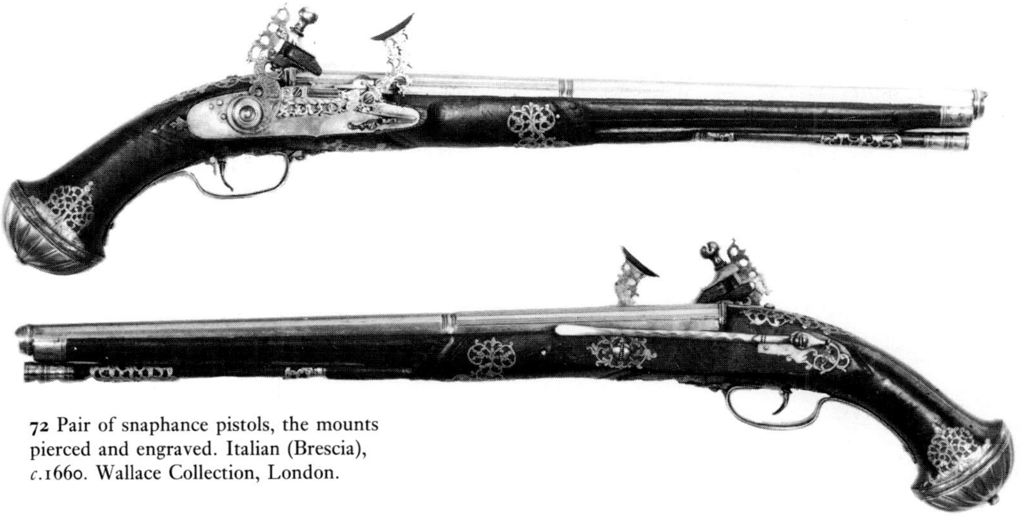

72 Pair of snaphance pistols, the mounts pierced and engraved. Italian (Brescia), *c.*1660. Wallace Collection, London.

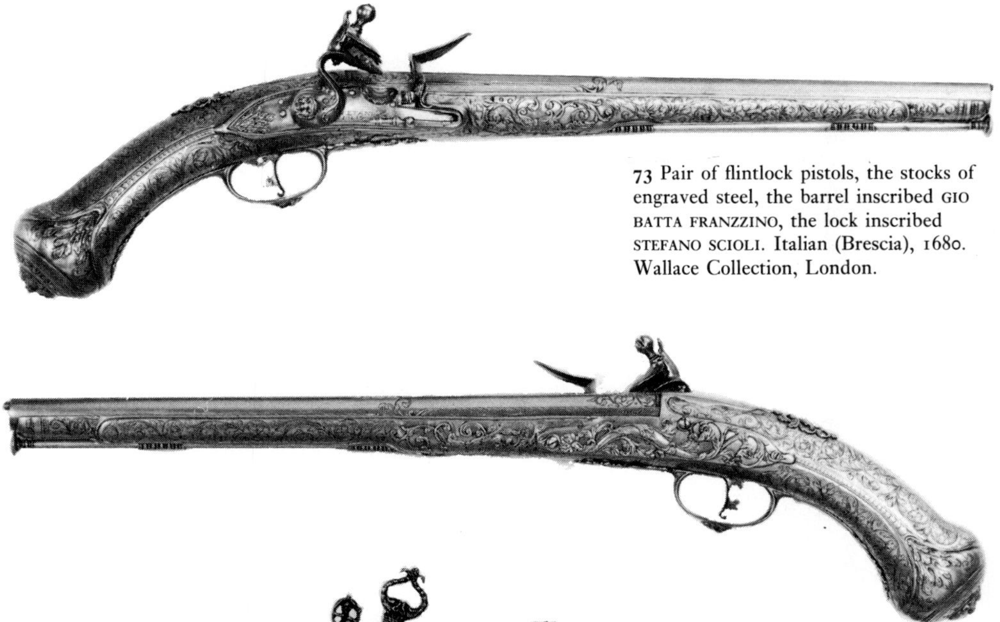

73 Pair of flintlock pistols, the stocks of engraved steel, the barrel inscribed GIO BATTA FRANZZINO, the lock inscribed STEFANO SCIOLI. Italian (Brescia), 1680. Wallace Collection, London.

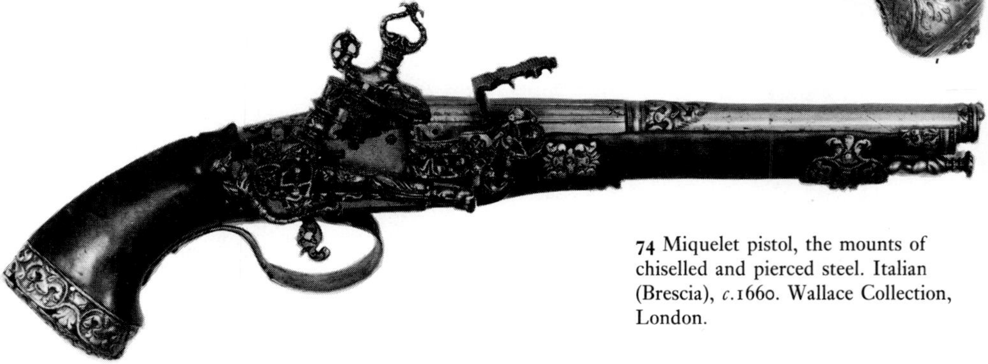

74 Miquelet pistol, the mounts of chiselled and pierced steel. Italian (Brescia), *c.*1660. Wallace Collection, London.

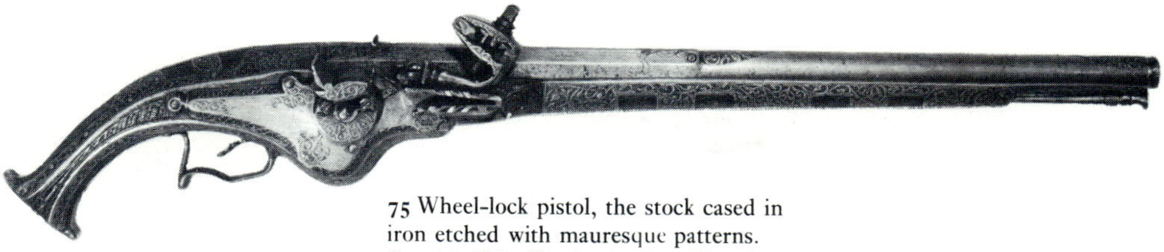

75 Wheel-lock pistol, the stock cased in iron etched with mauresque patterns. Spanish (Ripoll), dated 1614. Victoria & Albert Museum, London.

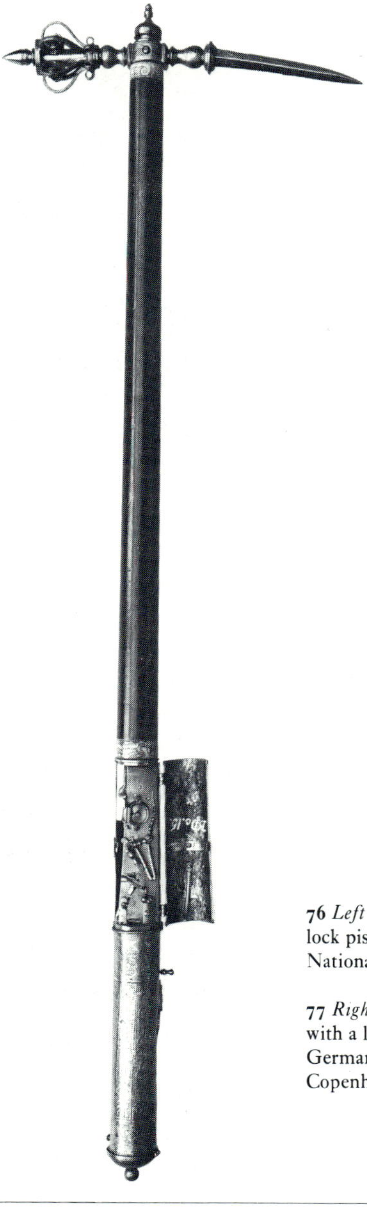

76 *Left* Hammer combined with a wheel-lock pistol. Polish, *c.*1600. Nationalmuseet, Copenhagen.

77 *Right* Wheel-lock pistol combined with a late-sixteenth-century axe. German (Augsburg). Tøjhusmuseet, Copenhagen.

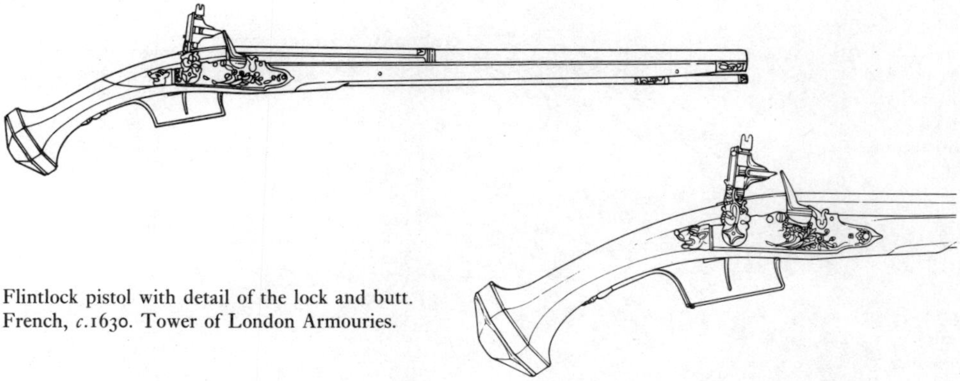

Flintlock pistol with detail of the lock and butt. French, *c.*1630. Tower of London Armouries.

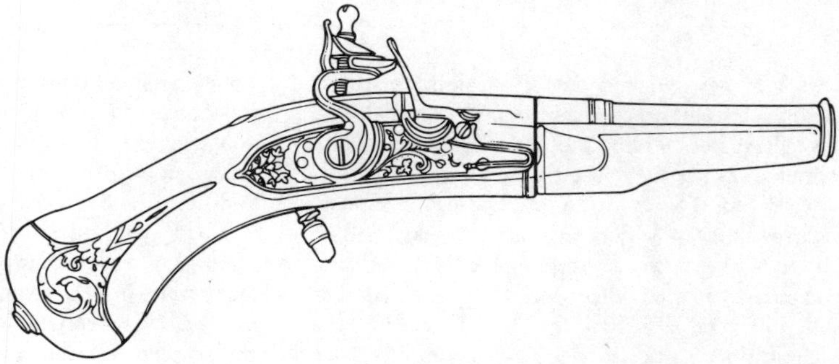

Turn-off screwed flintlock pocket-pistol, signed WINTLE. English, *c.*1660. Tower of London Armouries.

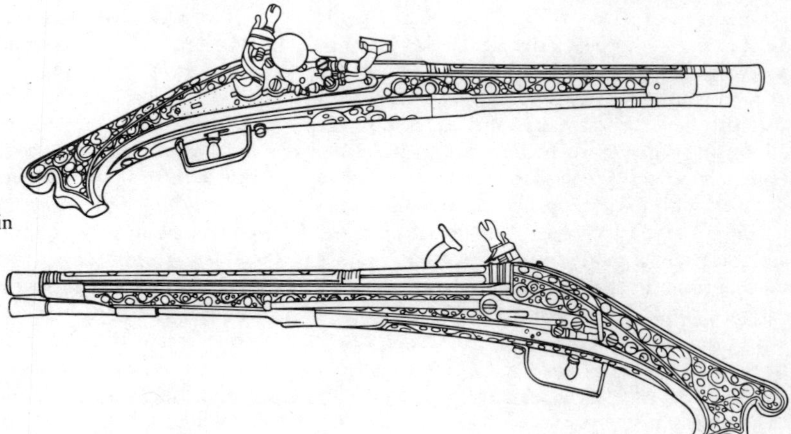

Snaphance pistols. English, *c.*1600. Kremlin Museum, Moscow.

to the writer are either English or Scottish with the exception of a pistol signed *HECTOR* in the Hermitage Museum, Leningrad, which may have been made in Antwerp. The types used in England and Scotland are clearly closely related, though precisely what this relationship is has yet to be elucidated. Scottish firearms are discussed separately in Chapter 14 and it will only be necessary here to make a brief comment on the English variety. The earliest examples of this, dating from the first two decades of the century have butts that slope down at only a slight angle to the line of the barrel and terminate in ovoidal pommels or, like examples in the Doge's Palace, Venice, and the Kremlin, are fish-tail shaped.[137] At some unknown date, perhaps in the 1630s, the straight or slightly-curved form of butt,

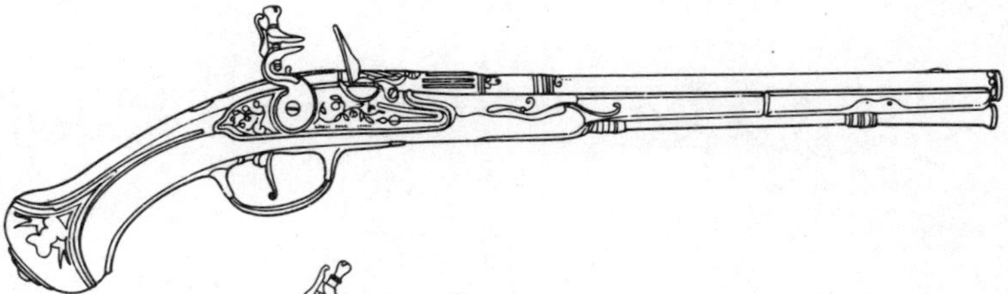

Flintlock pistol by Des Granges of Paris, commissioned by Baron Gyldenstierna of Sweden in 1668. Livrustkammaren, Stockholm.

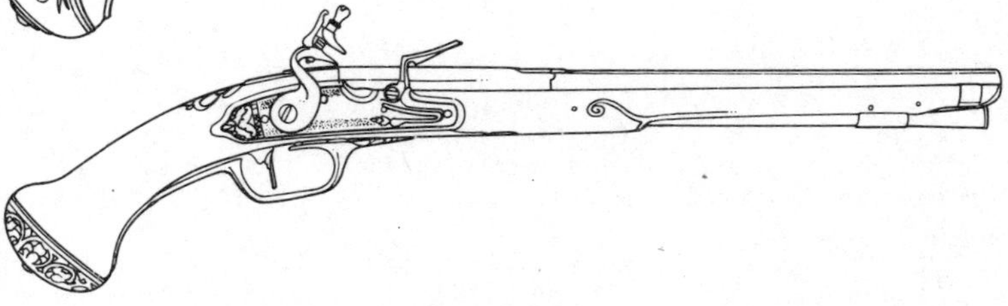

Flintlock pistol, signed H. BARNE. English, *c*.1650. Art Gallery & Museum, Glasgow.

widening at the end and cut off straight, like that used on contemporary Continental wheel-locks, seems to have been widely adopted in England. Many specimens, dating from the time of the Civil War, are preserved, for example, at Littlecote House, Wiltshire, some of which have an unusual form of lockplate with its lower edge shaped to a strong convex curve, as on a wheel-lock.[138] The Civil War period, however, also saw the introduction of the French flintlock stock described below and this stock soon became the normal one in England, as elsewhere.

As might be expected, the major influence on the development of the pistol during the seventeenth century was the flintlock and, as with long-guns, the lead in evolving new designs was taken by the French gunsmiths. The earliest recorded flintlock pistol is the Russian revolver,[139] which was allegedly made, presumably after a French model, between *c*.1616 and *c*.1625. This has a straight stock, widening at the end, and a curved lockplate, both based on those found on contemporary wheel-locks, and rather similar to those in the English pistols at Littlecote mentioned above. The Russian weapon must, however, be regarded as exceptional – at least in the present state of our knowledge – and the continuous history of the flintlock pistol can be regarded as commencing with a group of pistols produced in Western Europe, almost certainly in France, in the 1630s. These have butts of similar shape to that on the Russian pistol, but curving gently downwards and, as the locks have the narrow plates normally found with the flintlock construction, the stocks are more slender. The butts are either slightly domed at the end or cut off straight, and fitted with a metal plate or reinforcing ring.

The type of butt last described survived until the 1650s, but early in the preceding decade a new form appeared which was soon to supplant it. On this the rear end was strongly domed and fitted with a metal cap of corresponding shape held by a central screw with a button-shaped head which was sometimes pierced laterally for a turning-bar. Shortly before *c*.1650 the cap was extended up each side of the butt in two small triangular or rounded projections. These soon developed into spurs which grew longer as the century progressed until, by the mid-1660s, they extended almost the full length of each side of the butt. During the same period the outline of the end of the butt was softened so that, instead of widening suddenly, it swelled out smoothly into a rounded pommel. When the spurs of the butt-cap became long enough to hold it in position the central screw at the bottom was increasingly replaced by a peg, held by a pin or driven into the wood like a nail, with a wide head, either flat or profiled, which was commonly decorated with engraving or chiselling. This type of butt was the one most widely used for the remainder of the seventeenth century, though the butt-cap without spurs or with only rudimentary ones is occasionally found on fine-quality pistols as late as the 1670s and continued to be fitted to common military pistols until the nineteenth century.

Certain distinctive types of butt require separate mention. A few French, German and Dutch pistols of the period *c*.1630-60 have prominent pommels, often of ivory, metal or ebony, in the form of human, animal or bird heads. This type of pommel is associated particularly with the ivory-stocked pistols which were a speciality of the Dutch town of

---

137 A curious pair of early-seventeenth-century pistols in the Real Armería, Madrid (Nos. K. 215-6), have butts of this type and may be Scottish or English. The authenticity of the stocks has, however, been doubted.

138 A similar form also occurs on firearms made under Dutch influence, in the Kremlin Armoury.

139 See p. 73.

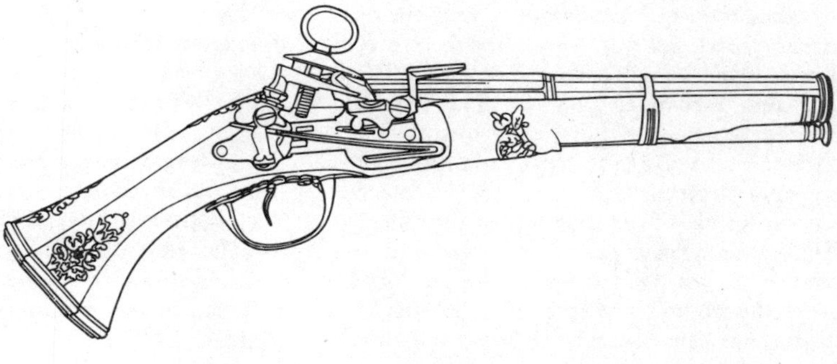

Miquelet pistol. Spanish, or Brescian in the Spanish manner, *c.*1650. Victoria & Albert Museum, London.

Maastricht, where they continued to be made, alongside pistols with ivory stocks of standard type, until almost the end of the century.

In Italy, a butt of angular section was used on both wheel and snaplock pistols during the period *c.*1630-60. It widened at the end where it was fitted with a faceted, slightly-domed metal cap. From the 1640s the French form of stock was widely used, though during the third quarter of the century, on Brescian pistols, the spurs were commonly replaced by separate inlaid panels of elaborately pierced metal. A distinctively Italian version of the French butt, found on Brescian pistols of *c.*1660-90, was of circular section, widening evenly towards the rear, where it was cut off straight and fitted with the usual cap. Finally, it should be noted that on many Italian pistols with the fully-developed French form of stock the pommel is much less protuberant than was the fashion elsewhere in Europe. This shape survived in central Italy until the early nineteenth century.

In Spain, a butt of the angular Italian form described above was used on miquelet-lock pistols during the period *c.*1640-60. From the middle of the century onwards, however, the French type of stock was generally adopted, except for the highly distinctive pistols produced at Ripoll in Catalonia.

The earliest recorded Ripoll pistols date from the first quarter of the seventeenth century and are wheel-locks, often with abnormally long barrels, so long, in fact, that some are carbines rather than pistols. All sizes have the same short, very slender curved butt of angular section with a small fishtail pommel. The whole stock is often covered with thin sheet-iron, etched with fine scrolling foliage involving grotesques and pierced in various places to show the wood beneath. At some unknown date, but probably in the first quarter of the century, the barrel was shortened and a butt equipped with a spherical or ovoidal pommel appeared. This was so short that the pommel had to be held in the hand when the pistol was used. At the same time the wheel-lock was abandoned in favour of the miquelet *patilla* lock.

These short, ball-butted pistols, like the long arms produced at Ripoll, normally had their stocks encased in sheet-iron, brass or silver, engraved and pierced with running foliage, sometimes with an underlay of coloured cloth showing through the apertures. A feature that seems to have been unique to arms made in Ripoll and in Russia is a leather tab, often covered with coloured cloth and trimmed with galloon, or embroidery, nailed to the side of the butt and projecting over the base of the cock. This was intended to prevent the fingers getting caught in the mechanism, a necessary precaution when the butt was so short. Another feature commonly, though not invariably, found on Ripoll locks is the geometrical arrangement of the striations on the insides of the cock-jaws.

Apart from these ball-butted weapons the Ripoll makers produced pistols with rather squat versions of the developed French stock, though rarely with butt-caps, and of the angular-section Italian butt. A local speciality, produced during the eighteenth and early nineteenth centuries, were blunderbusses fitted with a squat version of the contemporary French shoulder-stock, many of which are small enough to be regarded as pistols.

The Ripoll makers continued to produce pistols that varied very little from those evolved in the seventeenth century until their industry was destroyed, together with their town, by the Carlists in 1839. A few of their latest production make a concession to modernity in having percussion locks, but even these have mechanisms of miquelet type.

Finally, reference must be made to a distinctive form of butt which made its appearance at the end of the seventeenth century, though its use did not become widespread until the beginning of the next one. It is found almost exclusively on turn-off pistols[140] which, for constructional reasons, had metal bodies into which the butt fitted from the rear. The form of butt that was evolved for these was of circular section, curved and at first rather thick, swelling into a rounded pommel. The butt-cap, when fitted, had no side spurs but frequently had a short triangular tongue in the centre of the top edge.

The types of pistol used during the seventeenth century can be classified, according to their size, as holster, belt or pocket pistols. No hard and fast measurements can be laid down for any given category, though the presence of a belt-hook of course automatically identifies a belt-pistol, whatever its size. As a rough guide to general classification one can do no better than quote Randle Holme who, it will be recalled, wrote in the 1680s:[141]

> It is a pistall . . . this is a small gun discharged with one hand of which there are seuerall sorts, whose names are according to the bigness of them, as
>
> The pockett pistall, is the least of fire Armes, the Barrell of such peeces being from 4 to 6 Inches long.
>
> The Girdle, or belt pistall, is a degree longer in the barrell then [*sic*] the former; and is generally hung by the side; by a long peece of Iron screwed on the contrary side of the stock, to the lock. The barrells of such are from 7 to 9 or 10 inches long.
>
> The Troup, or Holster pistall, this is longer than the fore said by as much againe, the barrells of these being generall some 16, 18 or 20 Inches; all troupers haue two of these put into holsters fixed to their sadles, and brest plate of the horse on each side.

As noted above[142] Holme also includes the petronel among the pistols.

A few belt and pocket-pistols dating from the 1660s onwards and mostly of English origin have blunderbuss barrels for firing shot. They are always referred to as 'blunderbuss-pistols' by modern writers, but an advertisement of 1695 in the *London Gazzette*[143] suggests that the contemporary term was a *musketoon-pistol*:

> At his late Dwelling-House . . . are to be sold . . . Musketoons, and Musketoon Pistols

Where regulation military pistols are concerned we can turn again to the English records to provide a general impression of what was happening all over Europe.

The Council of War Order of 1630, already frequently mentioned, gives the over-all dimension of the pistol as 45 in, with a barrel of 18 in, and a bore of twenty-four bullets to the pound. In 1639 the Ordnance officers started experimenting with barrel-lengths and reported that a pistol-barrel of 16 in was as accurate as one of 18 in or 20 in. Nevertheless, the Board decided that the 18 in barrel should be retained.[144] At some unknown date between then and 1685, however, the barrel was reduced to 14 in, a length which was to remain standard until the eighteenth century[145]

Combined Arms

Only a very few authentic combined arms of seventeenth-century date are known. What was, however, to be the commonest of all weapons of this type made its appearance at the end of the century. This was a short sword of the type known as a 'hanger', with a flintlock pistol attached to the base of its blade and a trigger in its handle. Some of these weapons were probably designed for use by travellers, but the majority seem to have been hunting-weapons intended, like the modern explosive harpoon, to give a more completely effective *coup-de-grâce* to a wounded animal than was possible with an ordinary sword. A few seventeenth-century rapiers with pistols attached to their blades are also recorded but many of these appear to be modern pastiches. 76-7

The seventeenth-century combined weapon that is most frequently encountered, and even this is rare, is based on the long-handled, small-headed axe (*Czekan*) that was carried by the Polish nobles. This was combined with a flintlock pistol so that the barrel and its fore-end formed the top of the haft and was commonly decorated in a similar manner to the contemporary Tschinke, even to the inlay of the wooden parts. There can be little doubt, in fact, that the majority, if not all, of these axes were produced in Teschen also,[146] probably for an exclusively Polish market. All the examples known to the writer date from the second half of the seventeenth century and the early eighteenth century.

A rather more formidable axe combined with a flintlock pistol is preserved in the Tower of London

140 See p. 190.

141 *op.cit.*, p. 134.

142 See p. 95.

143 No. 3055/4. Quoted by the *Oxford English Dictionary*, *s. Musketoon*.

144 Blackmore, *op.cit.*, p. 24.

145 Ibid p. 36.

146 Karger, *op.cit.*, pp. 31-2, quotes a document of 1732 referring to the manufacture in Teschen of *2 Tschakanen . . . nach der Teschinischen art . . .*

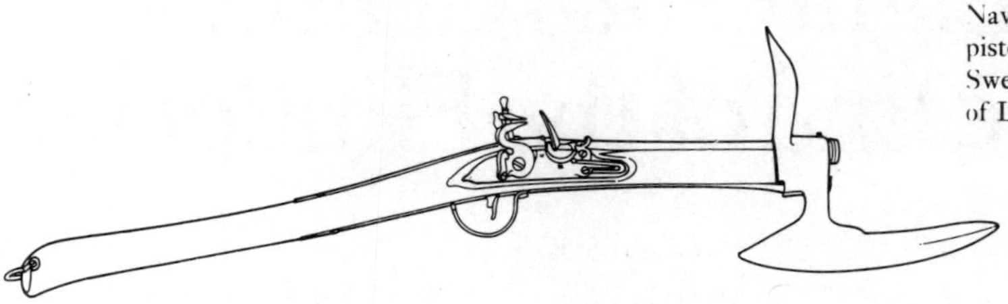

Naval flintlock pistol/boarding-axe. Swedish, *c.*1700. Tower of London Armouries.

Armouries.[147] Undecorated and unsigned, its origins and the purpose for which it was made are alike unknown, though it clearly dates from about 1680 and is probably of English workmanship. Its form suggests that it was intended for mounted use, so it may perhaps be an experimental arm produced as a precursor to an attempt to reintroduce the horseman's axe which had been widely used in England during the Civil War.[148]

Finally, reference must be made to the so-called 'warder's key'. This is a very large key with a touch-hole drilled into its barrel so that it can be used as a rudimentary small-bore pistol. The majority of examples encountered are probably modern forgeries, though the keys themselves are usually genuine, but one in the Instituto de Valencia de Don Juan, Madrid,[149] has every appearance of being authentic. This has a very compact miquelet lock concealed within its box-like bow, and a small press-button trigger at the rear. It bears two unidentified Spanish coats-of-arms and probably dates from the second half of the seventeenth century. The whole device is so impractical that one suspects that it was made merely as a curiosity.

147 No. XIV. 7.

148 Firth, *op.cit.*, pp. 117-18.

149 No. 169.

CHAPTER FOUR

The Eighteenth Century and the End of the Flintlock

H.L. Peterson

78-84 In Western Europe and America the eighteenth
113-17 century was the age of the flintlock. It was also an
119-21 era of specialisation. By 1700 the flintlock was already
123-6 almost a hundred years old and well established as
134
137-8 the dominant ignition system for almost all of
140, 142 Europe. This era was one of gradual refinement and
145, 257 perfection in contrast to the rapid and radical
259
260-8 innovations of the previous periods and the even
270-1 faster and more radical developments of the century
317, 320 to follow. The flintlock itself was brought to its
348-9 highest development. It was made stronger, faster-
351 acting, more reliable, and even partially waterproof. Its form was varied for specific purposes, and it was applied to an ever-increasing number of highly specialised guns including breech-loaders and repeaters.

Ranging from tiny pocket pistols to huge wall guns, each of these arms was designed to offer the most efficient performance for its particular purpose. No previous period in history could offer the prospective shooter such an array of sizes, types and models to choose from and none has surpassed it since. In pistols alone, for instance, a sufficiently wealthy gentleman might own a small pair for his coat pockets, a larger pair for his greatcoat pockets, a cased set to carry in his coach, another pair for his saddle holsters if he should wish to ride, and, after about 1770, a cased set for duelling if his honour should be impugned. His choice of long-guns would be equally extensive with specialised arms for self-defence, target shooting, hunting different kinds of game, or military service. Strictly military arms added to the variety, and so did those designed for naval service, commerce, and the like.

Despite this concentration upon the refinement and specialisation of flintlock arms, it should not be assumed that the earlier ignition systems had disappeared. The flintlock was indeed standard for most of Europe and America, but there were areas in which the people clung to their traditional weapons. In the Germanic lands, for example, wheel-locks were still being made as late as 1750. These included Tschinkes from the eastern areas as well as hunting and target rifles from Central Germany and Bohemia. In Spain the miquelet remained the popular gun-lock throughout the entire period, and it was not abandoned until the percussion system eventually superseded all spark-striking systems in the nineteenth century. Corsicans and Sardinians also clung to their miquelets, and so did the southern Italians. In Northern Italy, on the other hand, the flintlock was accepted readily – but the sophisticated Italian snaphance remained popular, too. Far to the north in Scandinavia the situation resembled that in Italy. Flintlocks were widely popular, but traditionalists and isolated groups held to the older snaplocks. In remote areas, in fact, the snaplock continued in use until almost 1900. Like the Spaniards, the Scots also preferred their traditional lock with its laterally-acting sear to the more refined flintlock. A few flintlocks were made in Scotland, it is true, but the majority of Scottish guns retained the older lock. Indeed, so strong was this preference, that even guns made in England for Scottish use often bore locks of the traditional type.[1]

There were other localised exceptions to the general rule of the flintlock, too, but these were the most important. Even these are not so significant as a listing might make them appear. Only in Spain, Corsica, Sardinia and Scotland was the flintlock largely excluded. Despite the presence and continued use of native mechanisms in Scandinavia, Germany and Italy, the flintlock was still the most popular ignition system in these areas. In the Low Countries, France, England, Ireland, and America it had no rival whatsoever.

Refinement of the Flintlock

By 1700 the flintlock was fully developed in the major mechanical sense. The vertically-acting sear, the double-notched tumbler, the combined steel and pan-cover, the external screw attachment of the cock and the shoulder buffer to arrest the cock's forward movement had all been devised and tested by years of use. Still there were improvements to come. For one thing, many locks, at least on long-guns, had been attached by three bolts or 'side nails' as they

1 See Chapter 14.

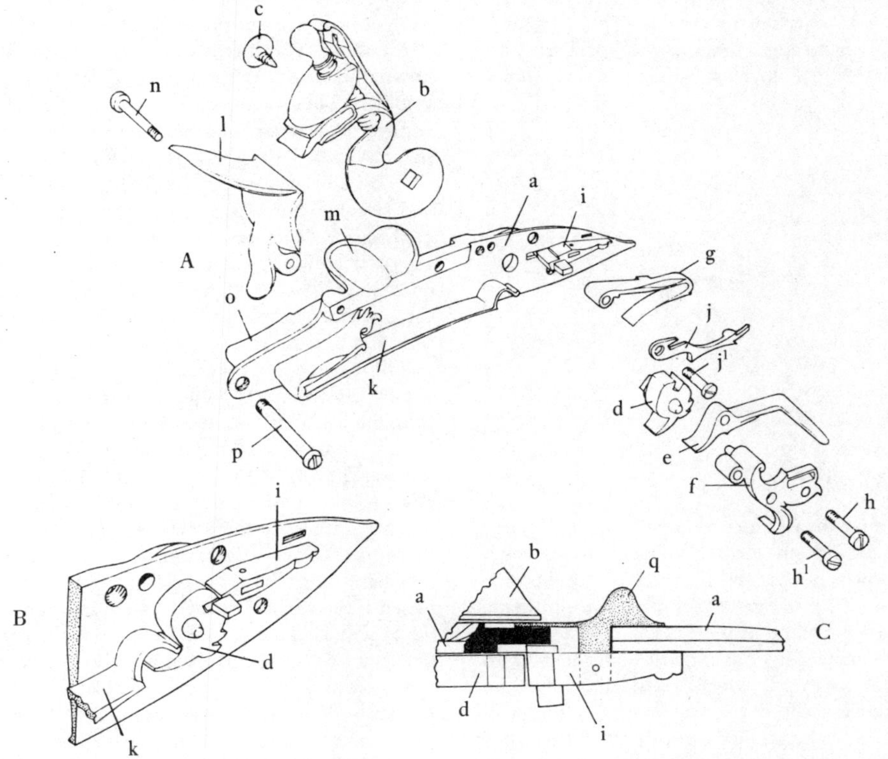

FLINTLOCK
- a Lockplate
- b Cock
- c Cock-screw, fitting into the squared end of the tumbler (d)
- d Tumbler. The projecting toe engages under the tip of the mainspring (k). The three notches, commencing at the top, are for the safety-catch bolt (i), and for giving full- and half-cock respectively on the sear (e)
- e Sear- and trigger-lever
- f Bridle supporting the tumbler and the sear-lever
- g Sear- or trigger-spring
- h, h[1] Screws for attaching (f) to the lockplate
- i Sliding safety-catch bolt
- j Safety-catch spring
- j[1] Screw for attaching (j) to the lockplate
- k Mainspring
- l Combined steel and pan-cover
- m Pan
- n Pivot-screw for the steel and pan-cover
- o Feather-spring for steel and pan-cover
- p Front screw for attaching lock to stock
- q External knob of safety-catch

Based on the lock of a gun of c. 1740 by Griffin of London, in the Victoria & Albert Museum (No. 128-1878)

were called at the time. Most collectors today call them lock screws. These bolts passed through the stock with the side or screw plate serving as a washer beneath their heads and engaged threaded holes in the lockplate. There was no need for this much strength. Two bolts were sufficient, and elimination of the excess bolt had begun late in the 1600s. The first quarter of the eighteenth century witnessed the complete disappearance of this surplus fastener. Custom dies hard, however, and so these years also offer a few locks which appear at first glance to be attached by three bolts. Closer examination, however, will reveal that the rear 'bolt' is a wood screw that serves no purpose whatsoever. It merely maintains the traditional appearance of the screwplate.

Attachment of the lock had been extra strong in the seventeenth century, but there were two places in which the earlier flintlocks had lacked strength. These centred around the pivots of the tumbler and sear on the inside of the lockplate and the pivot of the steel and pan-cover on the outside. To correct this situation, reinforcing brackets or bridles were devised and added to both of these stress points.

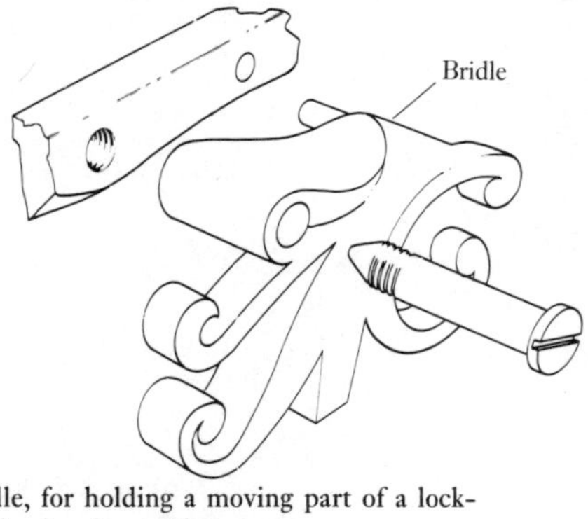

Bridle, for holding a moving part of a lock-mechanism in position.

The bridle for the tumbler and sear came first. Some exceptionally fine locks had offered this improvement as early as *c.*1650, but it did not become common until 1700. Even then, some cheaply-made locks omitted it. The bridle for the steel and pan-cover came next. This was formed by fashioning an arm on the pan itself which extended forward to provide support for the screw on which the steel pivoted. This external bridle appeared shortly after 1700 and quickly became popular for better quality arms. Cheaper arms, however, were still being made without it in the last quarter of the century.

With these improvements the flintlock had become as sturdy and dependable as it was possible to make it. But there were still areas for improvement. For one thing friction could be reduced and the action of the lock speeded. The first step towards this end was taken about 1770 by inserting a tiny roller bearing at the point of contact between the steel and the feather-spring. Sometimes it was attached to the steel, sometimes to the spring itself. Friction had always been intense at this point, and the new bearing enabled the steel to fly back and open the pan much more rapidly than it had before. The faster opening allowed the very first sparks struck from the steel to reach the priming powder in the pan. This not only speeded ignition but by opening the pan to the entire shower of sparks it also made ignition more certain. By 1785 this bearing had become common in England for good-quality civilian arms. It was not generally employed for military weapons. Outside Great Britain the popularity of the roller bearing was limited. American arms with imported English locks began to boast it after 1800, and locally-made pieces of high quality sometimes utilised it after about 1810. The best French gunsmiths such as Boutet and Le Page were quick to adopt the roller bearing, but elsewhere on the Continent acceptance appears to have been slight and sporadic.

A second area of friction in the flintlock was the bearing point of the mainspring upon the toe of the tumbler. This was eased by the insertion of a link connecting the two which not only reduced friction but eliminated the tendency of the mainspring to slip off its bearing point after the toe of the tumbler had become worn. Again, this seems to have been an English development and to have appeared at approximately the same time as the roller bearing on the outside. More than its external counterpart, the mainspring link was a symbol of quality workmanship. It was included only on the very best locks.

The closing decades of the eighteenth century which produced the roller bearing and the link, brought forth still another refinement of the flintlock. This was the so-called waterproof pan. One of the weaknesses of the traditional pan had been its susceptibility to dampness as drops of rain collected on the surface of the steel, ran down and leaked through the joint at the top of the pan to wet the powder within. The new waterproof pans boasted a raised rim over which the pan-cover fitted like the lid of a box. At the same time a groove or gutter between this rim and the fence at the rear of the pan was pierced with a small hole so that all water from the face of the steel would drain away. No device could protect the external flintlock and make it operable in a heavy rain, but the waterproof pan was effective for short exposures in far worse weather than would have been possible with the older design.

After *c.*1750 the *detent*[2] came into general use on fine-quality arms. The half-cock notch with which the designer of the detent was concerned had been created originally as a safety position. It was usually a deep notch with a strong lip, one from which the sear could not be released by a pull on the trigger. This worked reasonably well, but wear on the tip of the sear or on the lip of the notch could reduce the security of the engagement so that the gun might well 'go off half-cocked'. Because of this gunsmiths sought other devices to make sure that a gun could be carried, loaded and primed with greater safety. Approaches to the problem were restricted only by the individual designer's imagination, but five of them achieved enough popularity to be recognised as standard types.

The first of these safety devices in order of appearance was the back catch.[3] Interestingly, these catches survived as a supplementary safety feature long after the half-cock notch had appeared. They

2 *cf.* p. 79.

3 See p. 69.

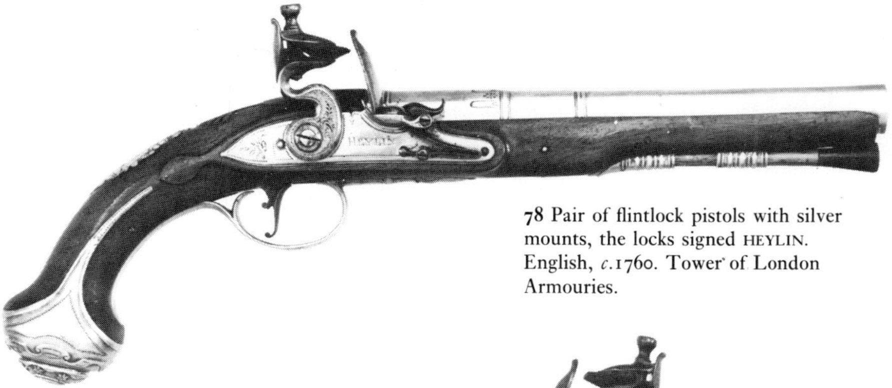

78 Pair of flintlock pistols with silver mounts, the locks signed HEYLIN. English, *c.*1760. Tower of London Armouries.

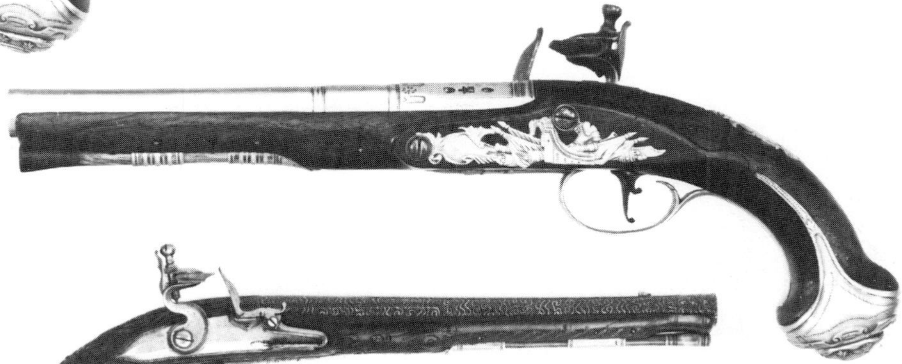

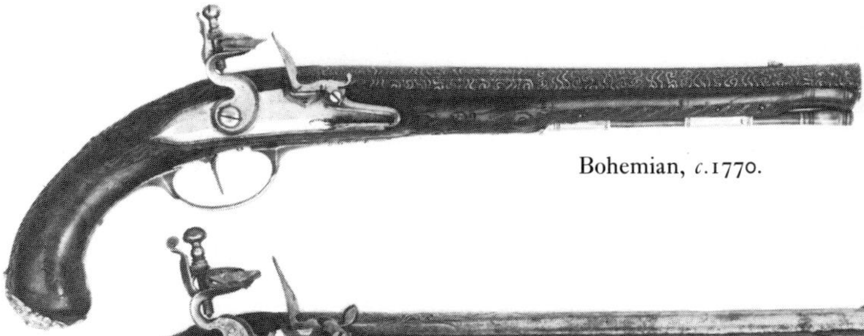

Bohemian, *c.*1770.

French, *c.*1730.

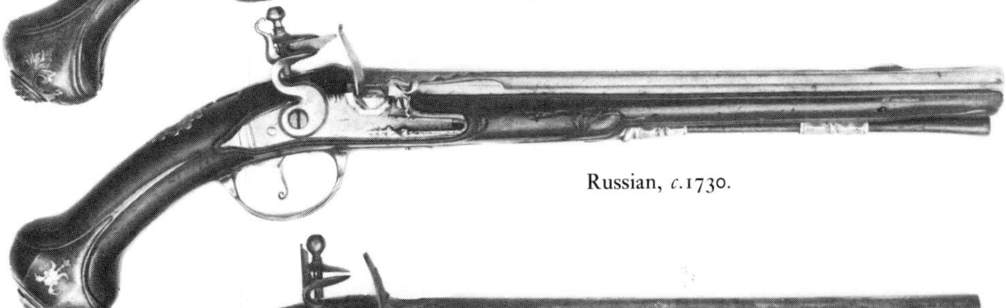

Russian, *c.*1730.

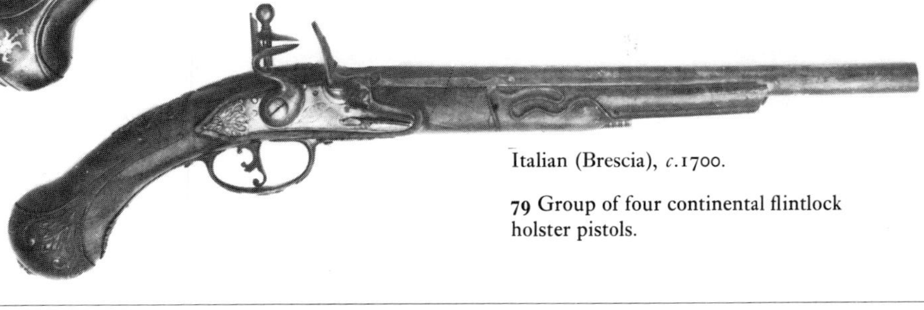

Italian (Brescia), *c.*1700.

79 Group of four continental flintlock holster pistols.

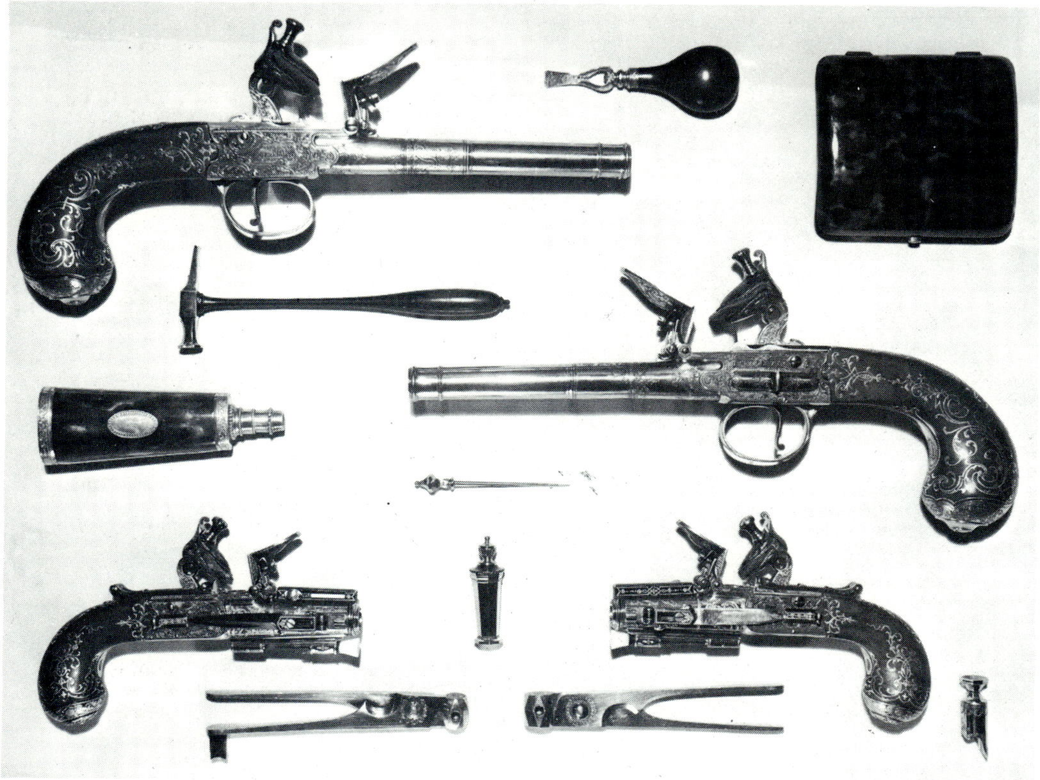

80 *Above* Set of two pairs of box-lock pistols with interchangeable barrels and accessories. (*Counter-clockwise from top*): screw-driver, hammer for refinishing the flint, powder flask, pricker and oil bottle (*lower middle*), two bullet moulds (*bottom*), patch cutter (?), and tortoiseshell case. Signed IACINTO XAVIER. Portuguese, dated 1799. City Art Museum, Saint Louis.

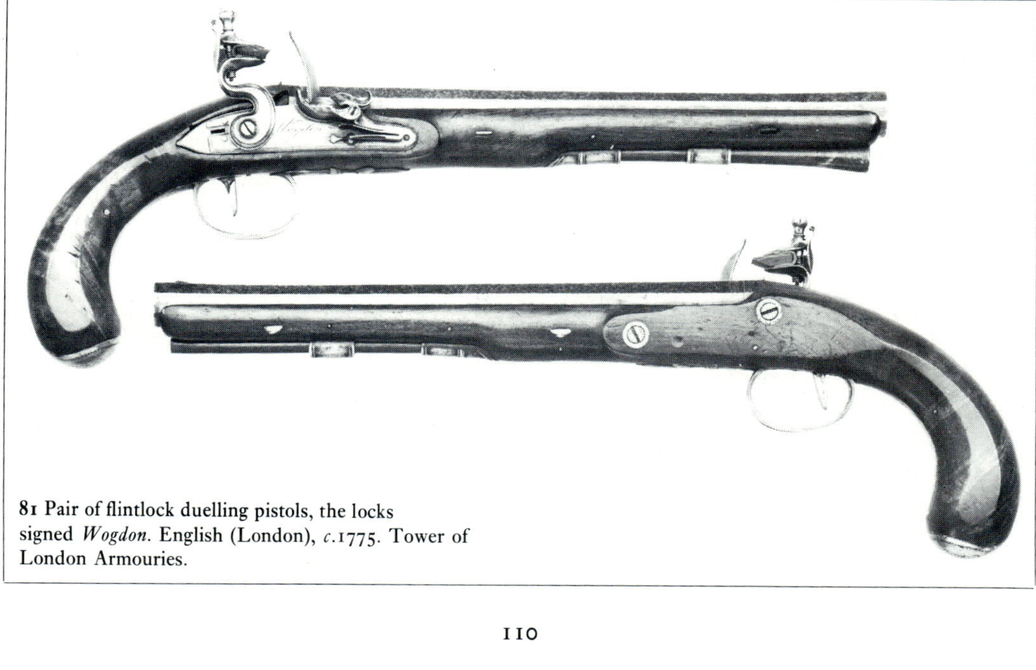

81 Pair of flintlock duelling pistols, the locks signed *Wogdon*. English (London), *c.*1775. Tower of London Armouries.

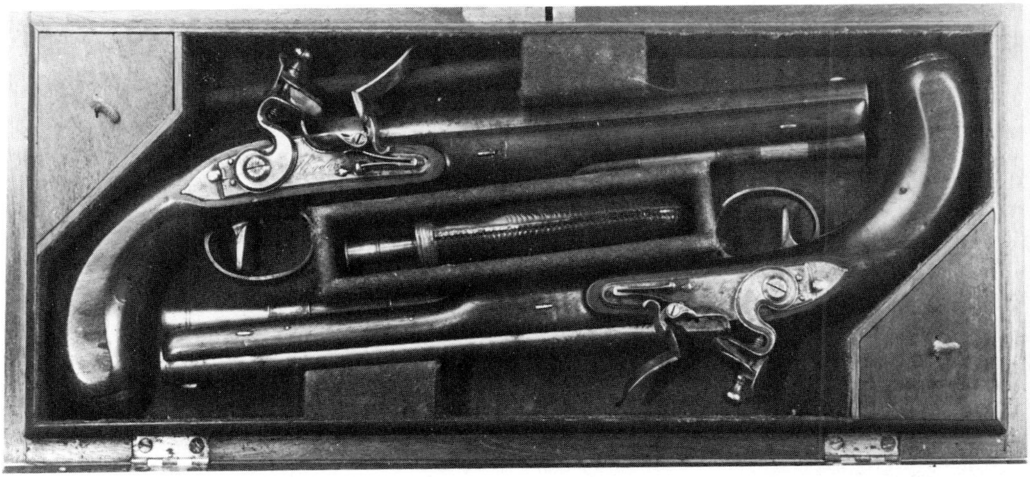

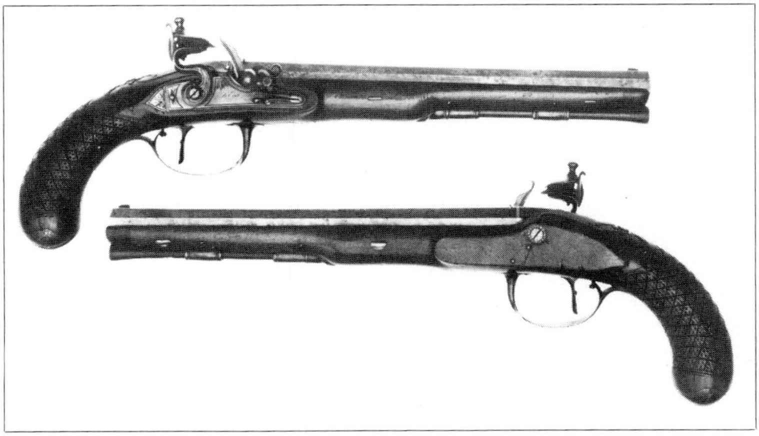

82 *Above* Pair of flintlock duelling pistols in original fitted case, the locks signed *Wogdon*. English (London), *c*.1780.

83 *Left* Pair of flintlock duelling pistols with octagonal barrels, the locks signed D. EGG. English (London), *c*.1785.

84 *Below* Cased pair of flintlock duelling pistols with octagonal barrels, the locks signed JOSEPH MANTON LONDON.

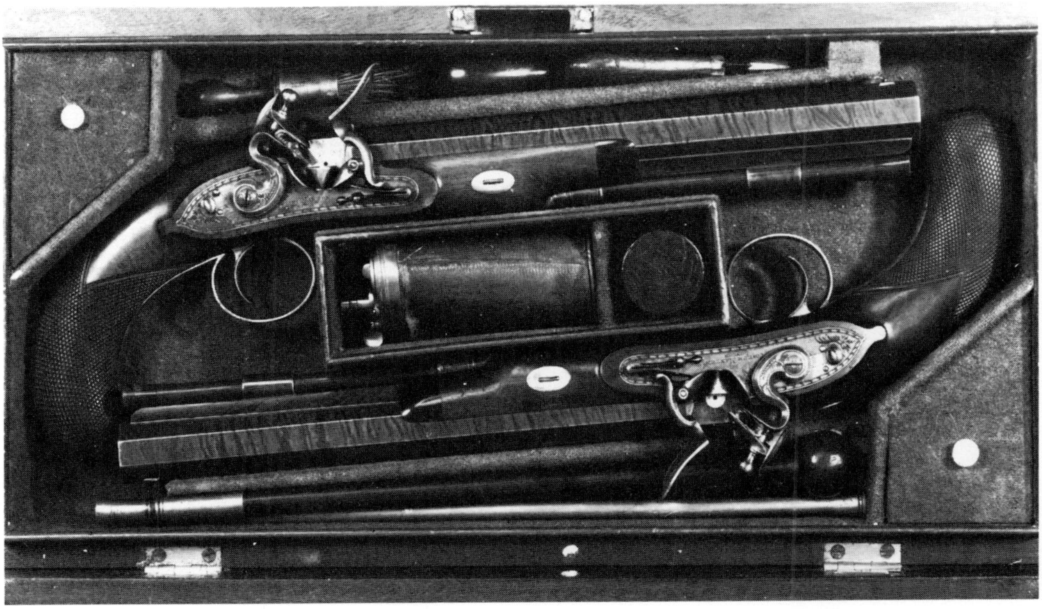

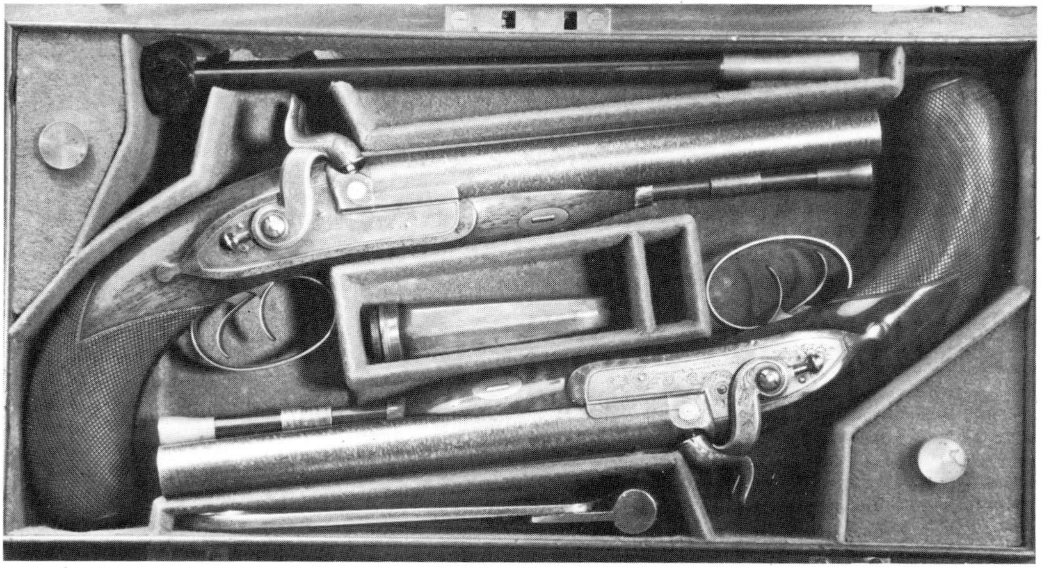

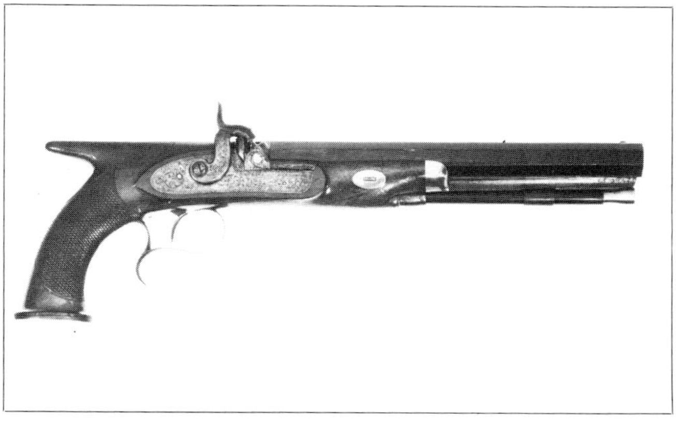

85 *Top* Pair of double-barrelled percussion pistols, with browned 'twist' barrels. In original case with accessories, by John Manton & Son, Dover Street. English, 1838.

86 *Above* Cased pair of percussion duelling pistols with accessories, the barrels by William Fullerd and the locks by Forsyth and Co. Patent Gunmakers. English (London), *c.*1830.

87 *Left* Saw-handled percussion duelling-pistol, the lock signed *Drake and Co. London*. English, *c.*1830. Tower of London Armouries.

are encountered occasionally throughout the entire flintlock period and well into the percussion era.

The second major safety device to appear was the sliding bolt. Usually this took the form of a narrow bar let into a recess of the lockplate behind the cock.

The pivoted detent (c) prevents the nose of the sear (a) becoming caught in the half-cock bent as the cock falls. The full-cock bent is at (b)

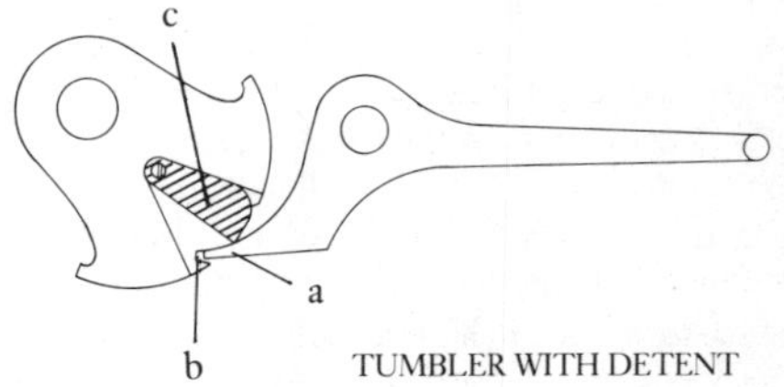

TUMBLER WITH DETENT

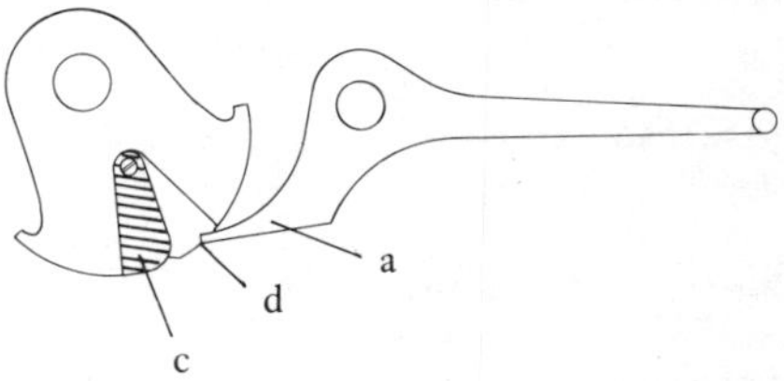

MANTON'S GRAVITATING STOP

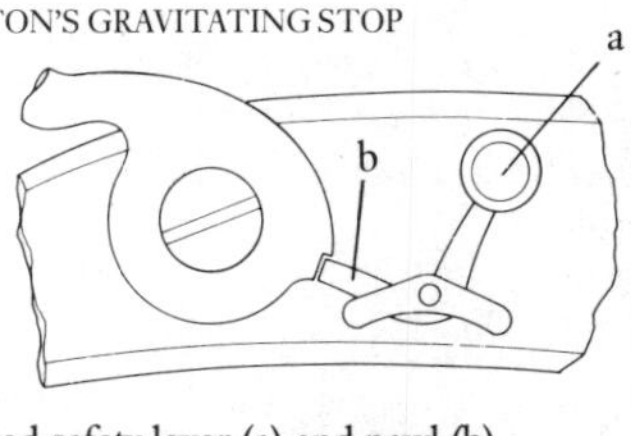

Weighted safety lever (a) and pawl (b)

By pushing on a raised lump at the end of the bar, the shooter could slide it forward to engage the tumbler and hold it rigid until he retracted the bar when ready to fire. Some of these bars engaged the cock directly instead of the tumbler. Prototypes of this form of safety appliance appeared as early as the third quarter of the seventeenth century, but its peak of popularity came after 1750 (Fig. p. 107).

Closely akin to the sliding bar in the lockplate was a safety device found on pistols with enclosed mechanisms and centre-hung cocks. In such arms a movable plate slid forward to engage a notch in the rear of the cock, and sometimes it locked the steel in a closed position also, thus offering a double safety. This device appeared about 1750 and remained popular to the end of the flintlock era, especially on pocket-pistols.

Still another sliding safety device involved the trigger-guard. On weapons equipped with it the guard could be moved forward so that a flange slipped into a notch in the trigger and prevented it from moving. Often a spring catch held the guard in one position or the other until it was released by pressure on a stud. Such trigger-guard safeties were especially popular for use on pistols during the first half of the eighteenth century, but they continued in use throughout the entire period.

The last of the major safety devices to appear was in some ways the most imaginative. This was the 'gravitating stop' patented by Joseph Manton of London in 1812. Manton was primarily concerned with the danger of a shoulder arm discharging accidentally as it was being loaded. In such a situation the piece with its butt on the ground and its muzzle up was normally already primed and the cock bent in the half-cock position from which a jar from the ramrod might possibly dislodge it at great hazard to the loader. To counteract this danger Manton designed a weighted lever and pawl attached to the lockplate in front of the cock. Whenever the piece was pointed upwards at an angle of 80° or more the weight activated the pawl so that it engaged a notch in the breast of the cock and prevented it from falling. When the piece was dropped to an angle closer to the horizontal, the pawl automatically disengaged and freed the cock. Despite the ingenuity of the device it never achieved widespread popularity. Dirt and grease could cause it to malfunction, and when working properly it made high shots impossible. Thus even guns which were originally equipped with it frequently had it removed.

While the mechanism of the flintlock improved, its external appearance also underwent changes. These stylistic variations are less easily defined than the mechanical features, but taken in conjunction with the construction of a lock they are useful for dating a specimen. Probably the two most important features for study in this connection are the lockplate and the cock. At the opening of the eighteenth century the typical lockplate was comparatively long. Much of this length comprised a pointed tail. Most often this tail began with convex curves as the top and bottom lines of the plate approached each other. Then a sharp concave curve at both edges produced an apical point or peak. Sometimes, however, the top and bottom lines approached each other and joined in a simple point without the additional peak finial. Almost always, with or without the finial, this point was below the centre line of the plate. The bottom line of the plate itself most often followed a concave line, sometimes slight, sometimes pronounced, while the surface of the plate might be rounded or flat with bevelled edges. As the century progressed the point at the tail of the lockplate became blunter, and it moved higher until it reached the centre line. By about 1800 the tail had become round, and all traces of the point had disappeared. Interestingly, the peak finial, though less common than at the beginning of the century, continued to appear on some specimens, even after the tail had become entirely rounded. The elimination of the pointed tail emphasised a trend towards shorter and generally smaller lockplates. The bottom line of the plate gradually straightened. The sharply concave line had largely disappeared by about 1750. After 1770 locks with absolutely straight bottom lines from front to curve at the tail are encountered. The surface of the plate also became flatter. After 1790 even a slightly rounded surface was rare. By 1800 the bevelled edge on the flat plates was hardly noticeable, and many locks were being made without any bevel whatsoever.

Among cock designs there were two basic forms, and both persisted throughout the entire period. These have been called the swan- or goose-neck and the throat-hole or reinforced patterns. Of these the goose-neck was the more popular, but the reinforced design gained greatly in favour after 1770.

At the beginning of the century the goose-neck cock had already reached its most graceful form with rounded breast and delicately curved neck. Its surface might be convex or flat with a bevelled edge. Generally speaking the convex surface was more popular for side-locks at least up to 1770. After that date flatter, narrower and more angular cocks began to appear which were totally bereft of grace and elegance. These were the most common of the goose-neck cocks after 1800 although such artists as Nicolas Noël Boutet still managed to produce elegant forms within the slender lines of the period.

The throat-hole cock first developed in the mid-seventeenth century, and its appearance at the beginning of the eighteenth century remained the same as it had been fifty years earlier. Its surface was completely flat, and it still often bore the notch at the back for the engagement of a back catch. For the most part its use was confined to simple military arms and to guns with enclosed locks. Shortly after the middle of the century the surface of those throat-hole cocks used for side-locks became convex for military arms and for a few civilian pieces. Most of the latter remained flat, but decorative details were added and more pleasing shapes appeared.

One other form of cock which developed about 1800 may also be mentioned as a type related to both the goose-neck and the throat-hole varieties. In this pattern the main body of the cock became a reverse C-curve with the jaws perched on top of it and the upper terminus of the curve swinging around to form almost a throat-hole cock in reverse. Such cocks seem to have been a French innovation, but they are also frequently found on fine English guns, especially those of Joseph Manton, and on other Continental firearms of good quality as well.

It should be noted as a word of warning that generalisations on the dating of stylistic changes such as those given above are always dangerous. Individual preferences for a given form sometimes brought it into use before its time or held it after the general taste had moved on. Changes in styles varied from area to area also. England and France seem to have been in the forefront as innovators and arbiters of taste during this era. Other Continental areas were more apt to cling longer to traditional forms, sometimes ignoring the new designs altogether. America normally followed British or French patterns but with a decided time lag of perhaps as much as ten or twenty years. There are also many other details of design and craftsmanship on these and other features of firearms which enable a specialist to identify the era and area of origin of a given specimen. A knowledge of these minutiae, however, comes largely from years of studying actual specimens and is well beyond the scope of a general work such as this. For the beginner the cock and lockplate shapes are the most important and the most easily explained as well.

Special Forms of the Flintlock

Most of the flintlocks to which these refinements in construction and changes in style were applied were side-locks. Normally they were situated on the right side of the piece opposite the breech of the barrel. There were other types of flintlock as well, however,

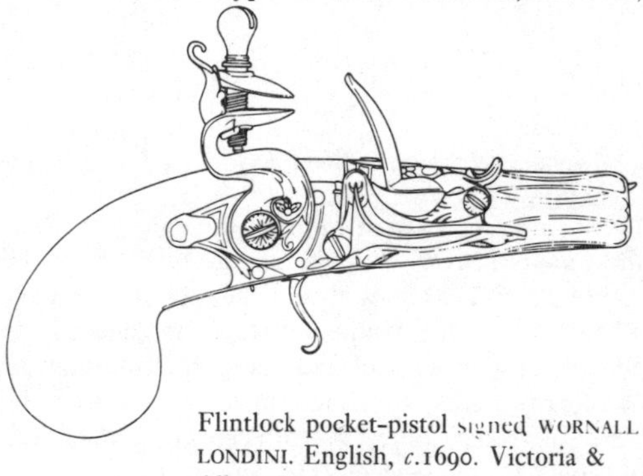

Flintlock pocket-pistol signed WORNALL LONDINI. English, *c.*1690. Victoria & Albert Museum, London.

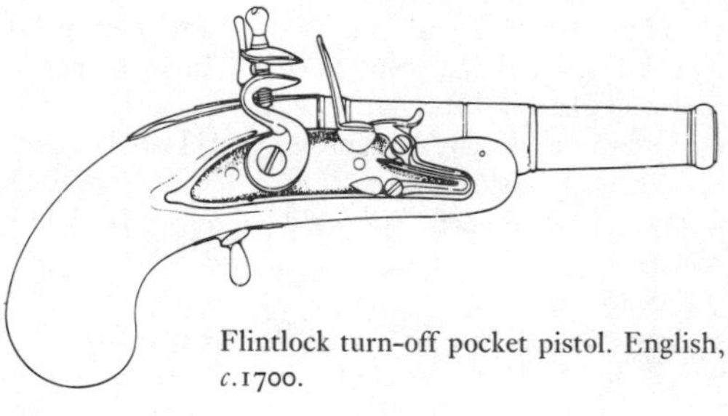

Flintlock turn-off pocket pistol. English, *c.*1700.

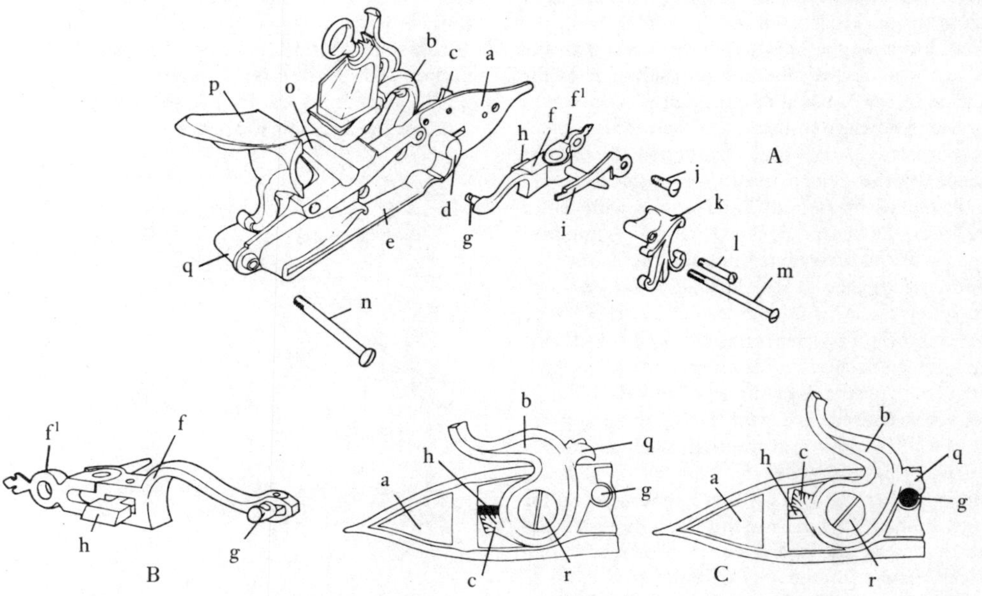

SPANISH MIQUELET LOCK OF MADRID TYPE
B illustrates the construction of the sear-mechanism and C the way in which the sears engage with the cock

- a Lockplate
- b Cock
- c Heel of the cock, engaging under the sear (h) for full-cock
- d Tumbler, over the squared end of which the cock is fitted and secured by a screw (r). Its toe engages under the end of the mainspring (e)
- e Mainspring
- f Sear- and trigger-lever pivoted to bracket (f^1) screwed to the lockplate
- f^1 Bracket
- g Half-cock sear engaging under projection (q) on the breast of the cock
- h Half-cock sear, engaging over heel of cock (c)
- i Sear- or trigger-spring
- j Screw for the attachment of the sear-bracket (f^1) and sear-spring (i) to the lockplate
- k Bridle for sear-lever (f) and tumbler (d)
- l Screw for attaching bridle (k) to lockplate
- m, n Screw for attaching lock to stock
- o Pan
- p Combined steel and pan-cover
- q Feather-spring for the steel and pan-cover
- r Cock-screw

Based on the lock of a pistol of c. 1750 in the Victoria & Albert Museum (No. M. 2804-1931).

and these special forms also deserve comment. One of the earliest of these was the so-called 'Queen
137 Anne' lock. It was characterised by a feather-spring placed with its apex directly behind the pan and pointing upwards. The short arm of the spring was vertical beneath this point while the long arm curved forward beneath the pan to offer a bearing surface for the steel. An offshoot of this lock found the feather-spring with its apex to the rear in exactly the reverse of the normal position. The purpose behind both designs was to shorten the lockplate and consequently the length of the stock necessary to hold it. This was especially important for pocket-pistols where both length and bulk were critical. The name 'Queen Anne' applied to locks of this sort is a modern collectors' designation probably arising from the large number of pocket-pistols with locks of this pattern manufactured in England during the first two decades of the eighteenth century and thus coinciding at least in part with Queen Anne's reign (1702-14). Actually the same sort of pistol had been made in England as early as 1680, and the type continued there until perhaps 1750. Also, while England produced the bulk of this type of pistol, its manufacture was not confined to that country. French and Flemish specimens are well known also.

Another type of flintlock designed primarily for
pocket-pistols was the enclosed or box-lock. In this 80
form of lock the entire mechanism was housed within a metal breech with the cock, steel and pan directly in the centre of the piece. Notches for the sear were cut into the cock itself, and the tumbler was eliminated. Once again this design reduced the necessary bulk of a pistol and at the same time eliminated

structures on the outside of the weapon which might catch in the pocket when it was drawn. Some of the earliest forms of the box-lock were made with the cock at the side, but mounted on the inside of the lockplate. A few isolated examples of this off-centre design are known from the second half of the seventeenth century, and they continued to appear occasionally throughout the entire flintlock era and into the percussion period. The box-lock with centre hung cock, however, achieved its real popularity about 1750, and it remained popular thereafter.

Both the 'Queen Anne' lock and the box-lock were widely used for a long period, but there were also a number of special forms of the flintlock that were confined to specific regions or used only briefly. Of these perhaps the most important was the 'Madrid lock', a bastardised form with the external appearance of the flintlock and internal mechanism of a miquelet. The advent of the Bourbon dynasty in Spain in 1700 created an interest in and demand for French modes. In firearms this brought forth the imitation of the outward appearance of the French flintlock. Externally the only differences discernible are the two holes in the lockplate for the noses of the sears to pass through to engage stops on the breast and tail of the cock. Internally there is a tumbler which serves as a bearing point for the mainspring, but the sears act laterally as they had in the true miquelet and engage the cock directly. This form of lock was popular only in Madrid where it was termed *a la moda* or *a las tres modas*. It continued in use there until the Peninsular War (1808-14).

In Germany during the second quarter of the eighteenth century there appeared a small group of guns with completely concealed flintlocks. A small lid in the top of the breech lifted up for priming and when closed its under-surface provided the steel. The cock was actually a flint vice driven by a spiral spring so that it would thrust forward when released by the trigger, strike a glancing blow against the lower surface of the lid and thus produce the sparks to ignite the priming. Two apparent triggers were provided within the guard. The forward trigger, however, was actually a cocking lever. Pressure upon it retracted the cock and compressed the spring. The rear trigger then acted upon the sear to release the cock and fire the gun.

Another ingenious, but little used, mechanism was the screwless lock. Two such locks were invented, both by English gunsmiths late in the century. Jonathan Hennem's lock was first in 1783. It replaced all screws except the cock-screw with pivots fastened by springs. Henry Nock devised a better version in 1785, and it was actually adopted by the British Ordnance for limited service. In Nock's system the moving parts were sandwiched between two plates in a form of box-lock. A catch at the front held the inner plate in position with all of the components upon their respective pivots or pins. It cost somewhat more than the ordinary lock of the period, and its advantages were somewhat esoteric, but it was one of the most ingenious and efficient flintlock mechanisms to appear.

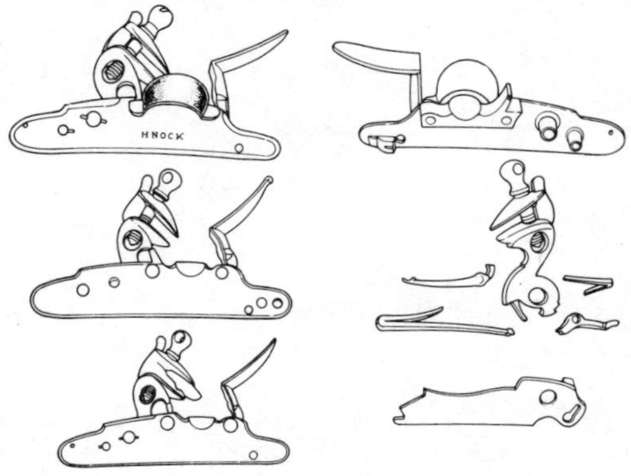

Henry Nock's screwless carbine and musket locks, English, *c.*1786. Private collection.

Probably the most unusual of all the special flintlocks, however, were those with the cock under the barrel. The theory, apparently, was to remove the cock from the line of sight and to shift the flash of the priming to a position where it would be less of a distraction to the shooter. Both German and American versions of this unusual arrangement are known, and the dates range from the mid-eighteenth century to the early years of the nineteenth. In these surviving examples the locks are of the box variety with centre-hung cocks. When the flint strikes the steel, the pan opens, and the priming powder actually begins to fall. It is ignited in mid-air by the sparks from the steel, and the resulting flash then burns upwards, setting off the main charge through the touch hole in a most unusual manner. Improbable as it may sound, modern experiments with such locks indicate that they actually work rather well. Despite such latter-day evidence, however, very few 'under-hammer' flintlocks appear to have been made. Certainly surviving examples are rarities.

Pistols

As noted previously, the pistols of the eighteenth century came in a wide variety of types and sizes. The smallest, of course, were those designed for the pocket. The trend towards small pistols that could be carried easily and unobtrusively upon the person had begun in earnest during the second half of the seventeenth century. The eighteenth century carried the development of such arms still farther and made the pocket-pistol a highly popular arm.

The earliest of these small guns normally were equipped with locks of the 'Queen Anne' pattern. Many, if not most, of them were also constructed with turn-off barrels.

137 The turn-off system[4] remained in use in the eighteenth century but was confined almost entirely to pocket-pistols and greatcoat or belt sizes. At about this time also wrenches were developed to assist in unscrewing turn-off barrels that proved recalcitrant through powder fouling or heat expansion. These handy tools came in two types. One was an external wrench in the form of a loop which slipped over the barrel and engaged a lug on the bottom near the breech. Such wrenches were frequently fashioned on one of the handles of a bullet-mould accompanying the pistol. The second type of wrench consisted of a plug which could be inserted into the muzzle of the pistol where its edges would engage grooves similar to rifling cut into the last quarter or half of the bore.

The pocket-pistol with the 'Queen Anne' lock and the turn-off barrel remained popular through most of the first half of the eighteenth century, though many specimens were also made with fixed barrels. About 1750 the box-lock surpassed the 'Queen Anne' in popular esteem. The barrels of these pistols, both the turn-off variety and those which were fixed, usually had decorative 'cannon' mouldings at the muzzle. As the century waned, however, these began to disappear, and the perfectly plain barrel characteristic of the early nineteenth century developed. At the end of the century also the trigger-guard was often eliminated and a folding trigger substituted. These triggers fit smoothly into a recess in the grips until the piece was cocked. Then they automatically snapped out, ready for use. A number of pocket-pistols, especially among those made after 1750, boasted two, three or four barrels which could be fired selectively. Another interesting feature, found on some fixed-barrel pocket-pistols of the mid-eighteenth century, were tiny bayonets which could be folded back against spring pressure and fastened with a catch.[5] When the catch was released these bayonets would spring forward and lock into position. Since they were often as short as two or three inches in length, however, it is difficult to consider them as a really useful adjunct to the pistol as a weapon.

Most pocket-pistols were equipped with wooden grips. In the so-called Queen Anne pattern these grips were rounded in section. One end fitted into the metal breeching which contained the lock and the chamber of the barrel. The other terminated in a butt cap, often of silver and normally cast in relief with a grotesque mask. Some of the early box-lock pistols had similar grips, but during the second half of the century the grips became flat on the sides, and the butt-cap was eliminated.

In addition to the usual pistols with wooden grips there were also some made entirely of metal. A few relatively large specimens of this genre were produced in England, but by far the greatest number were manufactured in and about Liège between 1750 and 1820. These latter pistols were mostly inexpensive arms, reasonably well finished externally but lacking in internal workmanship and formed of cheap materials. For sales reasons many bore names and addresses intended to disguise their real origin. London, Dublin and Paris designations were particularly popular, and one marking of *SEGALAS LONDON* appeared so often in so many different variations of spelling that it has become a collector 'type'. These all-metal pocket-pistols appeared in all the standard forms, single-, double, triple- and quadruple-barrelled, with trigger-guard, with folding trigger, with bulbous butt and with flat-sided butt. A special feature found on some pairs of all-metal pocket-pistols with turn-off barrels, however, was a pierced butt so designed that each gun could serve as a barrel wrench for the other. In this one instance, at least, the cheap little arms offered an advantage not available among their more expensive competitors.

The smallest of the pocket-pistols were made with barrels ranging up to 5 in long. These were intended to be carried in the pocket of a person wearing normal civilian attire. Somewhat larger pistols with barrels of 6 in or 8 in are often called great-

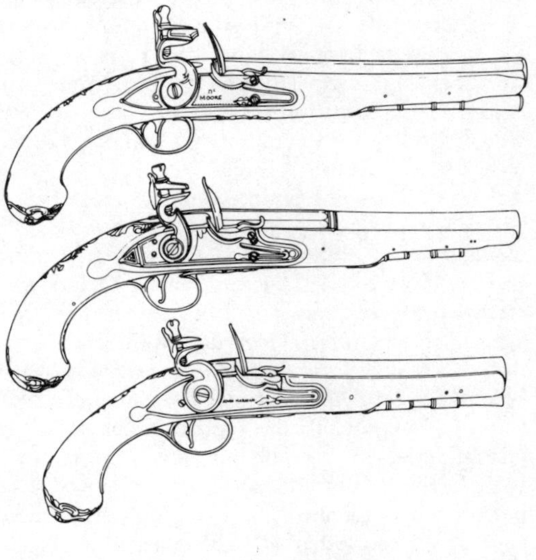

Three English flintlock holster pistols with hallmarked silver mounts. (*Top*) By Daniel Moore; London, 1766. (*Centre*) By T. Richards; Birmingham, 1774. (*Bottom*) By John Harman; London, *c.*1750.

4 See pp. 189–90.

5 See p. 510.

coat pistols or belt-pistols. Sometimes they are also known as travelling or coaching pistols. This latter designation is most often employed when the pistols are boxed in a special case for ease in carrying or storing. Such cased pistols could conveniently be carried by a gentleman with his other baggage and kept upon

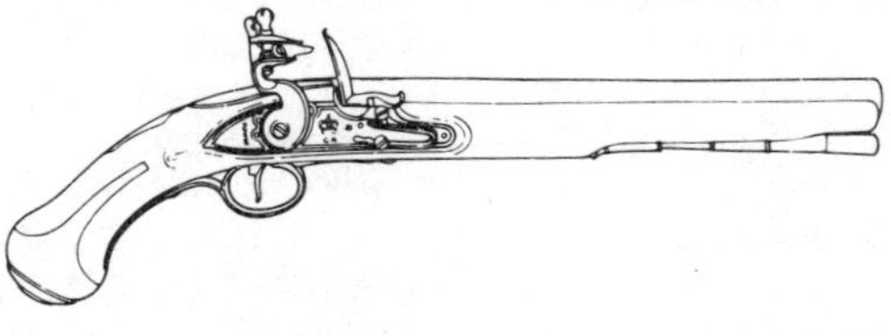

Flintlock heavy dragoon pistol, the lock marked TOWER and GR (crowned). English, *c.*1775.

the stage-coach seat so that their owner would be prepared to defend himself if attacked by one of the highwaymen who plagued travellers through much of the eighteenth century.

Until about 1770 pistols seem to have usually been sold in flannel bags but thereafter it became increasingly usual to pack them in cases that were both handsome and functional. They were made of wood, most often walnut, mahogany or oak, and lined with felt. Normally there were brass mounts, including a handle for carrying, an escutcheon plate on which the owner's monogram or crest might be engraved, and a lock. Within the case were compartments to hold the pistols, powder flask, bullet mould, loading and cleaning tools, prepared bullets, extra flints, and sometimes an oil can. Inside the lid there was often a large label identifying the maker. Sometimes, especially in Continental European casings, the boxes were designed to hold two pairs of pistols with their accessories. In these instances, one pair of pistols was usually of the small pocket variety while the other pair would be larger, either greatcoat or belt size or duelling-pistols.

Such duelling-pistols were another innovation of the eighteenth century. Firearms had been used for duelling almost from the first appearance of guns that could be handled with reasonable facility and accuracy. Swords, however, had been the favoured weapon for centuries. Then, during the mid-1700s the practice of wearing swords with civilian costume began to decline. At least partly as a consequence of this the pistol duel became more common. By 1770 pistols designed especially for the purpose were being made in England, and they developed into precision instruments. The barrels of the earliest specimens averaged 9 to 10 in in length. Usually they were round with a back-sight, a front-sight, and a flat along the top of the barrel to facilitate quick aiming. Calibres averaged 0·57 in. Stocks were full length, and the grip was shaped to give a secure hold. The whole weapon, in fact, was designed to function as an extension of the arm and to 'come up' and point naturally as the arm pointed. So skilful were the gunmakers in achieving this end that the natural pointing quality is frequently offered as the test of a good dueller.

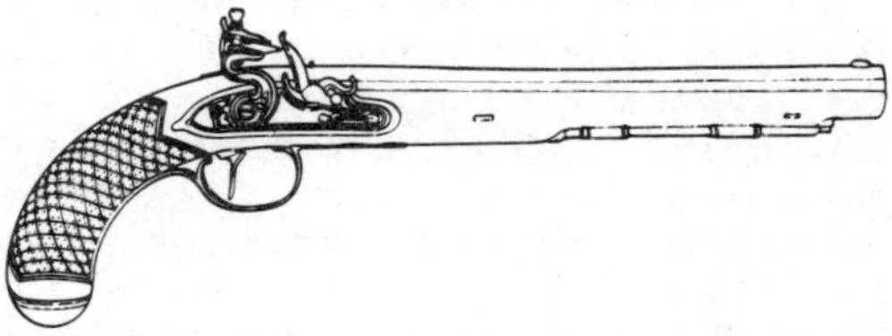

Flintlock duelling pistol by Durs Egg. English (London), *c.*1790.

The metal mounts of a duelling-pistol were reduced to a minimum. Brass, which was frequently used on other pistols, was eschewed for duellers. Silver mounts are encountered occasionally, but for most pistols blued iron was preferred. It did not flash in the light as the other metals did, and duellists regarded this as an advantage. Shiny metals might attract an opponent's eye or interfere with aiming. For this reason also the barrels of duelling pistols were almost always browned. The only bright metals that were tolerated were gold or, from about 1805, platinum bushings for the touch-holes, linings for the pan, or edgings to the breech. In these instances the areas were small, and the non-corroding metals improved the action of the guns. In duelling this was all-important. Appearance and decoration were secondary. Grips were sometimes chequered in later specimens, but this actually provided a firmer hold. Almost the only decoration regularly employed was a trace of engraving on the lockplate and the metal mounts.

As the years passed, the English duelling-pistol became even more efficient. The barrels became octagonal and heavier, making the weapon feel slightly muzzle-heavy. This was done on purpose to correct the tendency of a nervous duellist to shoot high. Fore-ends were made shorter as part compensation for the heavier barrels. Set or hair triggers became common. Shortly after 1800 a spur was added to the rear of the trigger guard to receive the middle finger and thus strengthen the grip, and at about the same time special saw-handle shaped butts were designed to offer an even steadier grasp. These were weapons superbly designed for their specialised task. They pointed almost automatically. Their mechanisms worked smoothly with a light touch so there would be no jerk, and they were accurate at the normal duelling ranges of thirty to fifty feet.

In France specialised duelling-pistols appeared

somewhat later than in England. The sword had remained the preferred weapon there until the Revolution. Then the social upheaval which followed militated against the development of such single-purpose arms. Thus it was 1800 or later before the French duelling-pistol appeared as a recognisable entity. Since its function was the same the French version of the arm closely resembled the English in many ways. It was apt to have a slightly larger calibre, however, and it was frequently rifled whereas most English duellers were smooth-bore. Spur triggers did not appear on French specimens until almost the end of the flintlock period, and set triggers were rarely employed.

Elsewhere in Europe and America there were no specialised schools of duelling-pistol design. Americans usually imported British pistols or copied

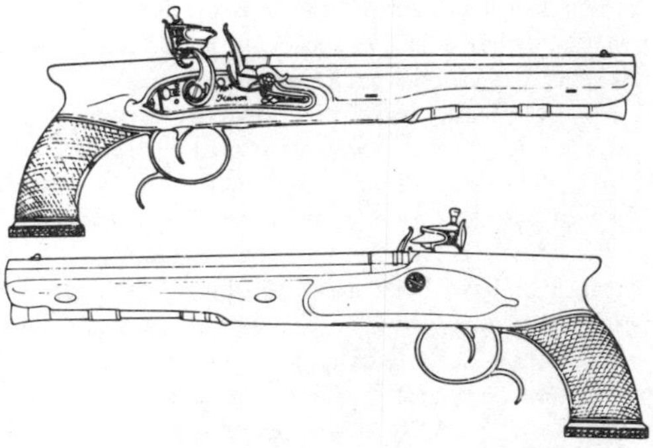

Pair of saw-handled flintlock duelling pistols by Hewson. English (London), *c.*1815.

British designs. Most Continental nations clung more tenaciously to the sword as the weapon of honour, and when pistols were used they were apt to be general-purpose arms.

Such general-purpose arms for any country could comprise the larger of the greatcoat, belt or travelling pistols, but they might also include an even bigger variety. These were full-stocked pistols with barrels ranging between 10 in and 12 in, possibly even longer in some areas of Continental Europe. Because they were designed to be carried in saddle holsters such arms have, over the years, come popularly to be called 'horse pistols'. These arms might be carried by any traveller riding through dangerous territory. Most often, however, they were used for military service.

Horse pistols were almost always stocked to the muzzle, and they followed the same evolution in design as other full-stocked pistols exclusive of duellers. For the first seventy-five years of the eighteenth century they had bulbous butts covered with large metal caps. In the centre of this butt cap was a separate convex boss, often ornamented with a mask or other embossed decoration. During the last quarter of the century the curve of the grips became sharper, and the butt became smaller until by 1800 there was often no swelling whatsoever. Butt-caps were frequently eliminated. In England and America the butts normally remained rounded or acquired a slight bird's-head form. Continental pistols tended to follow a French design that offered a flat-rimmed butt though both rounded and bird's-head forms were also manufactured. Once again, however, it should be noted that all generalisations concerning style changes should be accepted with reservations because of the factors of personal and local taste. There are always exceptions, and it is therefore necessary to consider mechanical features and manufacturing techniques as well as design in assigning a date to any given specimen.

Simpler, heavier versions of the horse pistol were issued to enlisted men of mounted units. Such

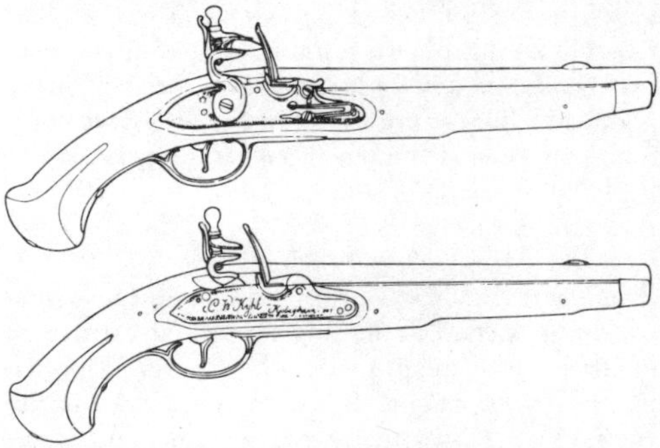

Danish flintlock military pistols: (*Top*) Model of 1806. (*Bottom*) Model of 1807. Tøjhusmuseet, Copenhagen.

martial pistols are a field of specialised study well beyond the scope of any general work. Numerous books have been written dealing with the evolution of such arms in almost all nations and the interested reader is referred to the bibliography for a listing of some of them. It is only possible to make a few general comments here. During the first half of the eighteenth

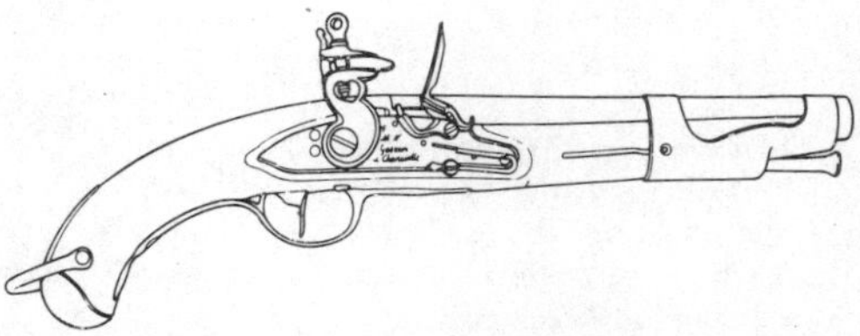

Flintlock cavalry pistol. French, Model of 1763. Musée de l'Armée, Paris.

century the issue pistols of almost all nations boasted bulbous butts, goose-neck cocks, and pin-fastened barrels. In the second half of the century France pioneered with throat-hole cocks and barrel-bands for its government model 1763 pistol. Thereafter both features are frequently encountered in the pistols of various nations. One other interesting detail which made its appearance for military pistols during the flintlock period was the detachable shoulder stock designed to give the pistol greater accuracy at long ranges. Notable examples of these were the Danish and Swedish models of 1808 and later variants, and the British Royal Artillery pistols of 1793, these latter being especially unusual because they were also double-barrelled. The Scandinavians also pioneered in the issue of rifled pistols to their mounted troops during this period.

In addition to the military pistols, most nations offered a comparable series for naval service. These arms shared most of the design features of the horse pistols, but in many instances they bore a distinctive structure not found on those weapons designed to be carried in saddle holsters. This was a belt-hook, a simple iron clip fastened to the left side of the stock. Other issue pistols were sometimes equipped with belt-hooks, notably those issued to Scottish highland regiments, but the great majority of such devices are found on weapons designed for naval service.

Muskets

Pistols were made in a great variety of forms during the flintlock era, but the single type of firearm made in the greatest quantity was the musket. This was the principal weapon of all of the armies of the civilised world in an era when a tremendous series of wars involved the major powers on battlefields of three continents.

The musket, as noted in Chapter 2, had appeared as a special type of firearm during the second quarter of the sixteenth century. The contributions of the eighteenth century lay in the standardisation of models, adoption of the bayonet and perfection of tactics for the weapon as well as minor improvements in the arm itself. The beginning of the century found many states still in the changeover from the matchlock musket to the flintlock. England had begun the shift during the reign of King James II (1685-88) and almost completed it under William and Mary (1689-1701). When Queen Anne ascended the throne in 1702 the Army itself was fully equipped with flintlocks, but the sea services and the militia still counted matchlock muskets among their armament. Even among the Army flintlocks there was a heterogeneity of models. Most of them were equipped with old style locks featuring flat throat-hole cocks and safety-catches (so-called dog-catch). Some were brass mounted, however, while others had iron furniture, and there were numerous additional variations in detail. Many authorities believe it was Anne, or rather her military authorities including John Churchill, Duke of Marlborough, who pressed for complete standardisation of the military musket and started the process which led to the appearance of the famous 'Brown Bess' during the reign of George I.

Few students agree on how the Brown Bess acquired its name. Some assert that the 'Brown' derived from the colour of the stock which had been black in previous models; others feel that it referred to the browned barrels of the later specimens. The 'Bess' may have been a corruption of the German *Büchse*, meaning gun, or it may simply have been a typical soldier's nickname for his weapon. All agree, however, that it was a sturdy and handsome weapon. In its fully developed form it was brass mounted, and the barrel was pin-fastened to the walnut stock. The calibre was a nominal 0·75 in for all, but the barrel length varied for different models. It was 46 in for the Long Land musket, often called the 'First Model', which was most common prior to 1760. During the 1760s the short land musket or 'Second Model' with a 42 in barrel became standard. The lock for both models had a goose-neck cock with a convex surface. Then, late in the century, the

The Long Land Musket (Brown Bess). (*From top*) Dated 1731; sealed pattern of 1746; Short Land pattern dated 1762; heavy dragoon carbine, *c.*1750. Tower of London Armouries.

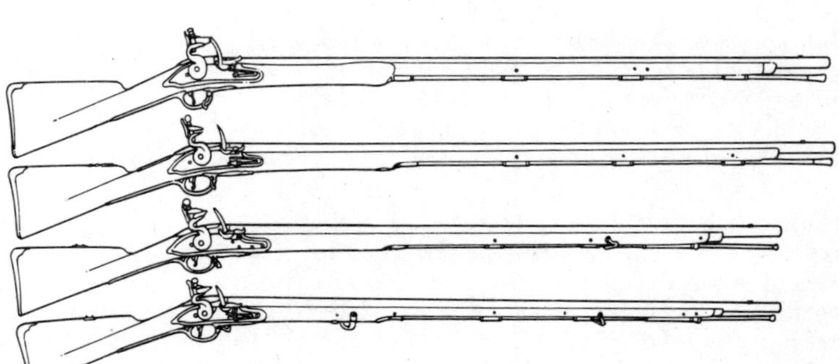

88 The earliest illustration of a gun. A miniature showing a soldier firing a gun, from the English manuscript '*De Nobilitatibus, Sapientiis, et Prudentiis Regum*' by Walter de Milemete, dated 1326–7. Christ Church, Oxford.

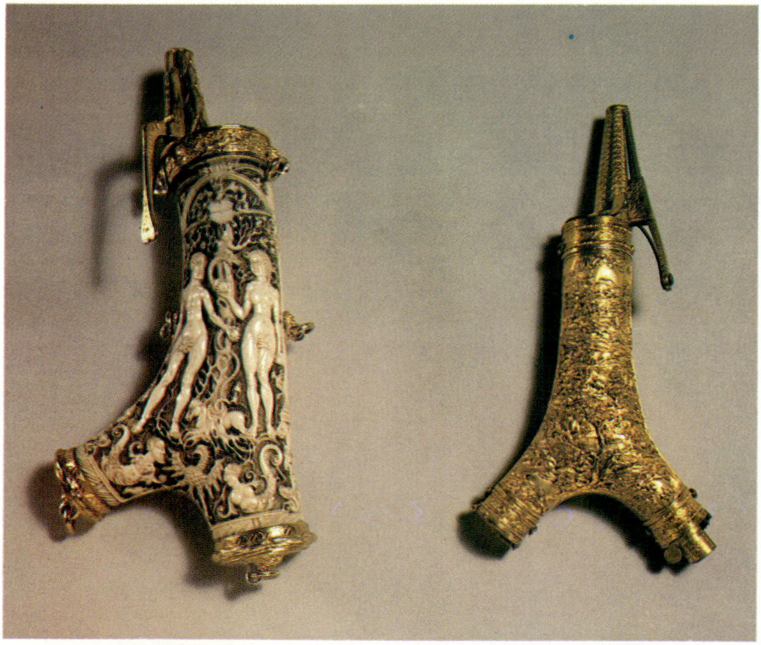

89 *Far left* Powder-flask, carved staghorn, mounted in silver-gilt; arms of the Zu Welpsperg family of the Tyrol. German (Tyrol), *c.*1550. Victoria & Albert Museum, London. *Left* Powder-flask, cast and gilt bronze. German, *c.*1550. Victoria & Albert Museum, London.

90 *Below* Matchlock gun, the stock inlaid with engraved staghorn; the lock and barrel chiselled and damascened. The stock by HANS PAUMGARTNER of Graz and dated 1570. On the butt-plate are the arms of Archduke Karl Von Steiermark (1540-90). Austrian (Graz). Kunsthistorisches Museum, Vienna.

91 *Right* Pair of wheel-lock pistols, the stocks overlaid with engraved staghorn and stained cow-horn; the barrels chiselled, blued and gilt. Barrels bear the Augsburg mark and that of a maker (Jäger?). German (Augsburg), *c.*1580–90. Victoria & Albert Museum, London.

92 *Below* Wheel-lock pistol, the stock inlaid with engraved staghorn. Butt set with silver roundels, *verre eglomisé* with the Sacred Monogram, a heart and sprigs of forget-me-knots, VERGIS MEIN NIT and 1581; the lock of chiselled steel. French, *c.* 1585. Tower of London Armouries.

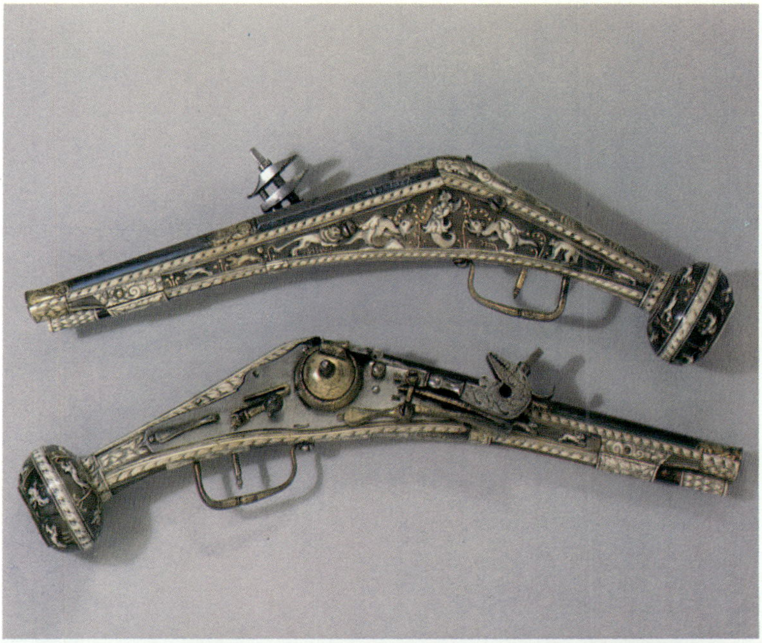

93 *Opposite, left*
Stock of a wheel-lock rifle, walnut inlaid with engraved staghorn; the barrel incised with HK at the breech and stamped I.B. underneath. Polish or Lithuanian, *c.*1600. Victoria & Albert Museum, London.

94 *Opposite, right* Detail of the underside of stock.

95 *Right* Detail from the underside of a wheel-lock rifle; the stock of carved ebony set with panels of carved staghorn, probably by Peter Opel of Regensburg. South German, *c.*1600. From the armoury of Prince Fugger at Schloss Babenhausen. Victoria & Albert Museum, London.

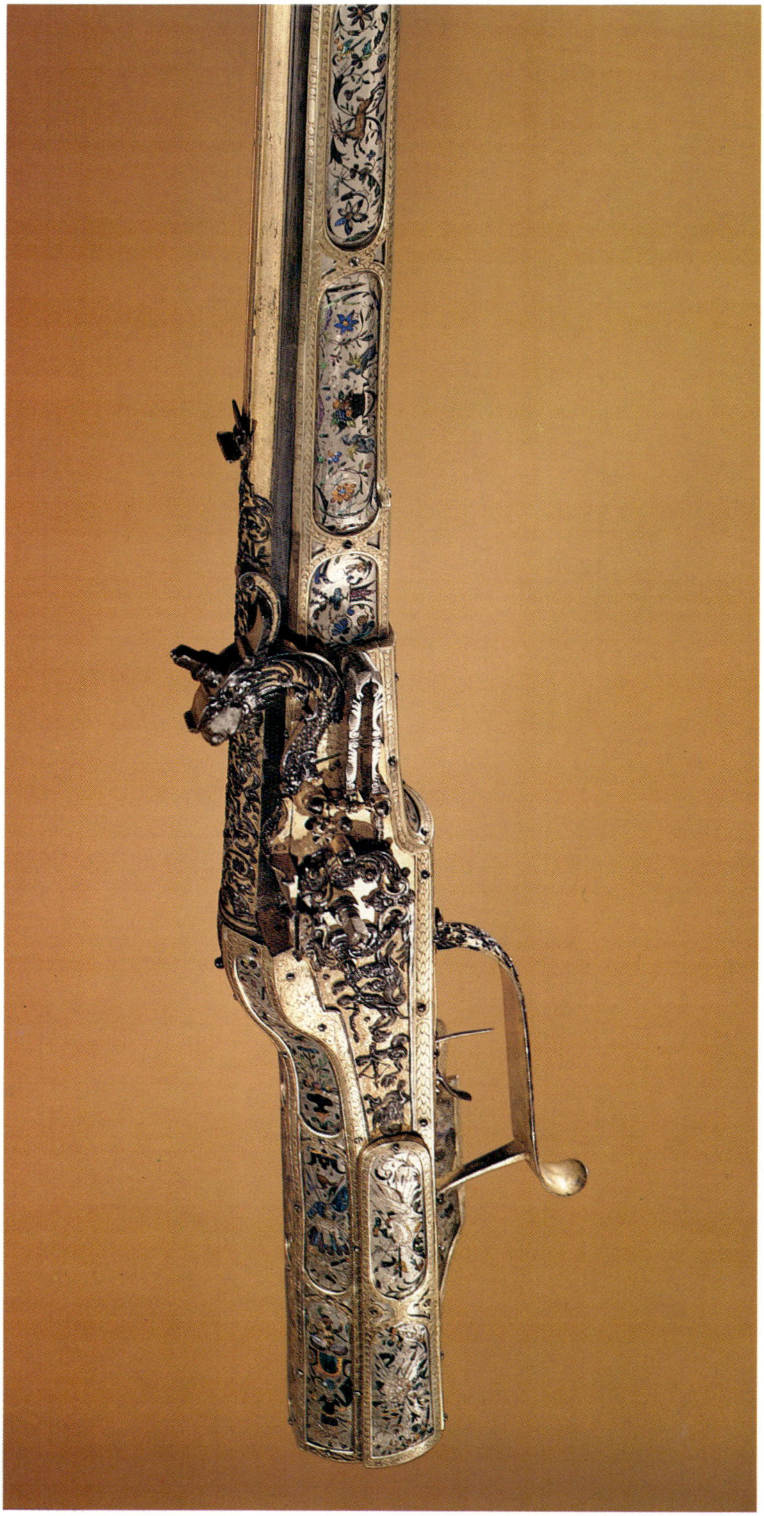

96 *Left* Detail of wheel-lock rifle of the Emperor Rudolph II (1576-1612), the stock mounted with enamelled silver plaques; the barrel and lock chiselled, blued and gilt. The mounts on the stock bear the mark of David Altenstetter of Augsburg. The chiselled steel-work is by Daniel Sadeler of Munich, *c.*1605. Kunsthistorisches Museum, Vienna.

97 *Opposite, top* Detail of snaphance gun, the stock and barrel of engraved brass with traces of gilding, the lock of engraved steel. The barrel and lock are dated 1624, the latter with the mark IL, attributed to James Low of Dundee. The pierced section at the end of the butt can be pulled out to form an extension. Probably made for Charles I, when Prince of Wales. Scottish (Dundee), dated 1624. National Museum of Antiquities of Scotland, Edinburgh.

98 *Opposite, middle* Pair of snaphance pistols with lemon butts. The stocks of brass engraved with strapwork and scrollwork; the barrels and fences are dated 1614. The lock-plates are stamped with the mark attributed to James Low of Dundee. The butt of each pistol can be extended by unscrewing the pommel and pulling it out on a steel rod. Scottish (Dundee), dated 1614. Private collection.

99 *Right* Pair of snaphance pistols, the barrels and stocks of engraved brass with traces of gilding, the locks of engraved steel. The barrels are engraved with the royal arms of France and the inscription LOUIS XIII ROY DE FRAC. The locks are stamped with the mark IL, ascribed to James Low. From the *Cabinet d' Armes* of Louis XIII. Scottish (Dundee), dated 1611. National Museum of Antiquities of Scotland, Edinburgh.

100 *Left* Detail of snaphance gun, the lock chiselled and engraved, the stock inlaid with engraved horn and mother-of-pearl. English or Dutch, *c.*1620. Musée de l'Armée, Paris.

101 *Opposite, top* Detail of wheel-lock target rifle, the stock inlaid with silver engraved with scenes of the chase, the lock chiselled and engraved; the stock is signed by HANS SCHMIDT of Ferlach and dated 1628. The cheek-piece is inlaid with the arms of Archduke Leopold V (1586–1632). The circular powder-flask is decorated *en suite*. Austrian (Ferlach), dated 1628. Kunsthistorisches Museum, Vienna.

102 *Opposite, bottom* Detail of double-wheel-lock gun, the walnut stock mounted in pierced and chiselled steel; inside the lock is the mark of Giovanni Angelo Gavacciolo; the barrel is signed GIO.BATT.FRANCINO. Italian (Brescia), *c.*1630. Victoria & Albert Museum, London.

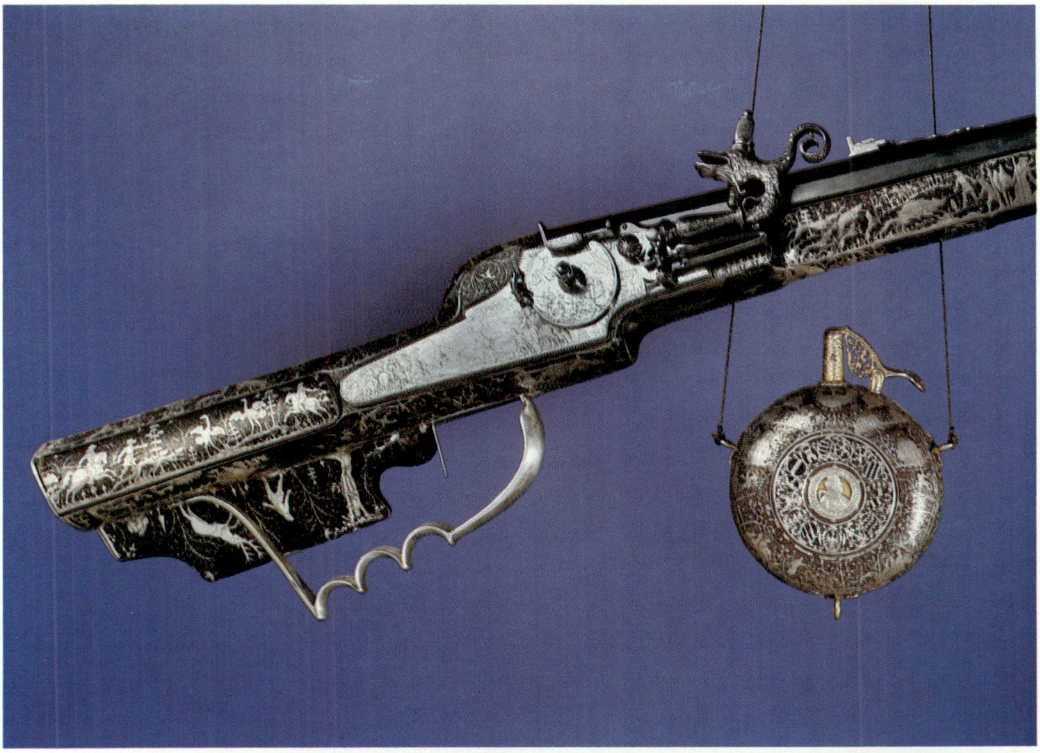

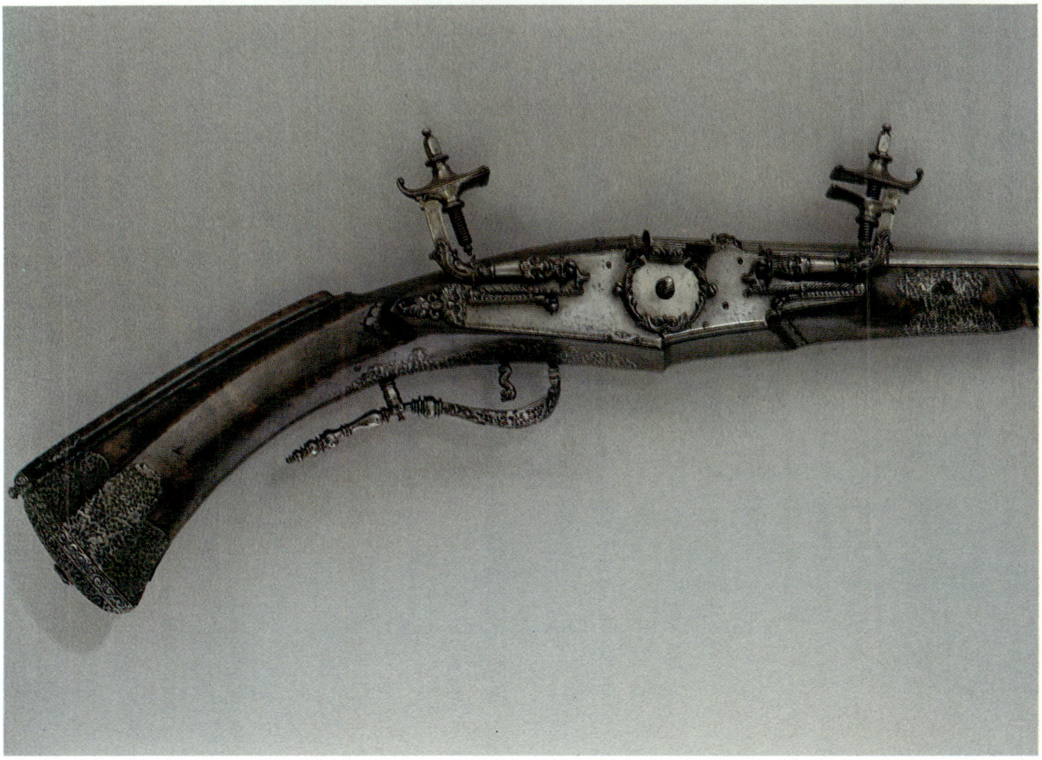

103 *Left* Detail of flintlock sporting gun, the stock inlaid with stained and engraved staghorn and brass wire; attributed to Jean Conrad Tornier of Massevaux. French (Alsace), dated 1646. Tower of London Armouries.

111 *Left* Pair of snaphance pistols, the stocks inlaid with engraved silver, the furniture of chiselled steel. Each pistol has an escutcheon chiselled with the portrait of a man and woman respectively, probably the owner and his wife. The barrels are signed underneath GIO.BATTA.FRANCINO and above ACQUA FRESCA. Italian (Bargi, nr. Bologna), *c.*1690. Private collection.

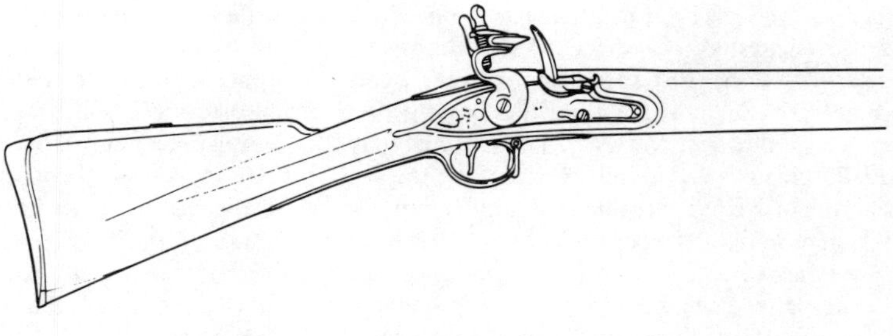

Detail of musket made for East India Company with the Company's ownership mark. English, dated 1793. Tower of London Armouries.

cheaply-made India Pattern musket, often called the 'Third Model' Brown Bess, with its 39 in barrel was adopted. Early examples of this last pattern retained the goose-neck cock, but soon a throat-hole cock replaced it. The brass mounts became smaller and cheaper. The stock was simplified, and the strength of the barrel was reduced. Even so, it remained a sturdy arm, giving good service until it was superseded by percussion cap muskets in the 1840s.

These were the muskets of the British Army throughout the great Continental wars of the eighteenth century, the colonial struggles in America and India, the Napoleonic Wars of the early 1800s, and the American War of 1812. American gunmakers copied the early models, Portuguese soldiers welcomed later versions, and the very last patterns saw action in the hands of Mexican troops as late as 1847.

Opposed to the Brown Bess in most of the major campaigns and battles of this strife-filled era were muskets of French design. The French began the standardisation of models at about the same time as the English, the first significant design being adopted in 1717. Unlike the Brown Bess which remained relatively unaltered during the years, the French muskets underwent a lengthy series of model changes, some major and some minor. The 1717 musket barrel was pin-fastened like the Brown Bess, and the lock bore a goose-neck cock. By 1728 the pins had been replaced by three barrel-bands. In 1763 the goose-neck cock gave way to a flat throat-hole type which became convex by 1777, the same year in which a brass priming-pan was added. Other changes were of lesser importance. These were the major alterations which brought the French musket to its most highly developed form. Its calibre of 0·69 in and the use of the bands for fastening barrel and stock together permitted a somewhat lighter arm than the British, while the corrosion-resistant brass pan offered a considerable advantage.

Like the Brown Bess, the French muskets exercised an influence well outside their homeland. American muskets from about 1777 until 1842 were patterned after the French flintlock models. Some Spanish muskets also followed the design as did those of some of the Italian states and to a lesser degree Austria.

Elsewhere in North and Central Europe muskets tended to be heavier than either the British or French patterns, and calibres were often larger. Also the goose-neck cock predominated over the throat-hole variety. In addition a special feature found only on muskets from this area was an elliptical brass front-sight. Both banded and pin-fastened models were manufactured among the German states. Perhaps the most readily recognisable of all were the Prussian muskets with their narrow butts and the extreme number of ten pins holding barrel and stock together. In Scandinavia the Swedes favoured the pin-fastening system until the 1770s, then switched to barrel-bands. Norwegians and Danes, however, clung to pins throughout the period.

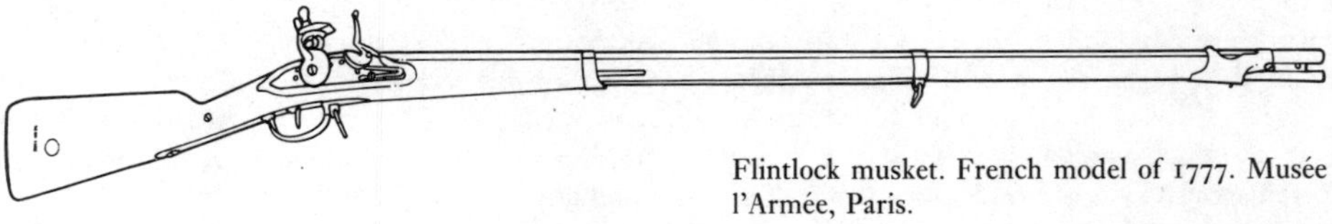

Flintlock musket. French model of 1777. Musée de l'Armée, Paris.

Apart from the guns themselves two external factors were of the utmost importance in guiding the evolution and shaping the use of the muskets of all nations. These were the paper cartridge and the socket bayonet; the latter is discussed in Chapter 18.

Like the bayonet, the cartridge had been invented well before 1700 (See p. 239.). In fact, Leonardo da Vinci had suggested its use for cavalry almost 200 years earlier. These first cartridges, however, consisted only of the charge of powder wrapped in paper. The bullet still had to be loaded separately. Gradually means were found for attaching the ball so that the cartridge became a complete unit in itself. Then, in about 1700, or perhaps a few years later, systems were developed for wrapping the ball inside the paper package with the powder charge. The British may perhaps have been first to adopt this type of cartridge. They used a cylinder of paper tied at the end holding the ball and twisted shut at the other end. In 1738 the French issued instructions for making a similar cartridge but called for fastening it with paste instead of string. By 1750 cartridges of one or the other of these types were widely used throughout Europe and America.

Either form of cartridge greatly speeded the loading of a musket, as did the introduction of the virtually unbreakable iron ramrod for military service, first by the Russians in 1718. The British started using it in the 1720s–and had adopted it fully by the beginning of the American Revolution–and the French in 1746. In practice the soldier bit off the twisted cartridge end just beyond the powder, poured a little into the pan of his musket for priming, and dumped the rest of the powder down the muzzle followed by the ball still wrapped in the paper which then served as a wad to hold the bullet in place when it was rammed home. Actually, it could all be done faster than it can be described. One English military treatise of 1768, in fact, states that no recruit was to be dismissed from practice until he could load and fire his piece fifteen times in three and three-quarter minutes, an average of one shot every fifteen seconds.

The combination of the bayonet and the cartridge made the eighteenth century musket a truly formidable weapon for its day. Tactics were quickly adapted to make the most of its advantages. The standard formation was the line of battle with soldiers lined up shoulder-to-shoulder, two or sometimes three ranks deep with an extra row a short distance behind to supply replacements for casualties and keep the ranks full. Such solid bodies of troops provided considerable firepower as the trained soldiers loaded and fired as fast as possible. Firing was done in volley by command. The men did not pick out individual targets but fired directly ahead or to the left or right oblique as ordered. The theory was to lay down a concentrated field of fire through which an attacking enemy would have to pass and to keep as dense a concentration of bullets in the air as possible. This theory prevails in warfare today.

If a charging enemy should manage to penetrate this hail of bullets, the solid lines of battle provided sufficient strength to meet the attack in hand-to-hand conflict. Here the bayonet was vital, and the opposing troops battled in much the same way their ancestors had with pikes for centuries before. Some commanders took especial pride in the ability of their men to meet steel with steel instead of relying upon firepower, and occasionally attacks were made with unloaded muskets, relying entirely on the bayonet. This was especially true of night attacks or pincer movements where there was a danger of firing upon comrades by mistake.

The flintlock musket offered strength, versatility and rapidity of fire. The one quality it did not offer was accuracy. As mass-produced weapons, some muskets were poorly bored. Even with the best, however, the balls were made to fit loosely so that they could be loaded quickly even after prolonged firing had fouled the bore. Most muskets were made without rear sights, and many lacked front sights as well. For formal battles, where speed of fire was the only real concern, this lack of accuracy was of little importance. There were some instances, however, when a soldier did need to aim. These included small actions with only a handful of men on either side, picket, flank or ranger duty. For such purposes it was desirable that a soldier should learn how to shoot well, and there are references to marksmanship practice with the musket during the eighteenth century. By general consensus, however, it was agreed that the best a good marksman could expect would be to hit a target the size of a man at 100 yards. Beyond that range an individual enemy would be relatively safe.

In addition to the full-scale musket, there were also shorter and lighter weapons for special troops or purposes. Officers frequently carried a light version of the musket called a fusil. So did light infantry and artillery men. Other short weapons for cavalry and artillery were carbines and musketoons, which were manufactured in a far greater variety of types and patterns than the full musket. Many but by no means all of the carbines had sliding bars and rings for carrying on a shoulder belt. Often the bore was slightly smaller than the standard for the musket, but in many instances the calibre was the same[6]. In fact, the only common feature of these arms was their short length.

Mention should be made of the latest British short flintlock cavalry carbine which was named after its supposed designer, General Henry Paget (1768-1854). One with a folding stock is recorded.

6 As noted on p. 56 the term *carbine* was used in the British forces to denote any gun of carbine bore (i.e. rather smaller than musket bore) irrespective of its length.

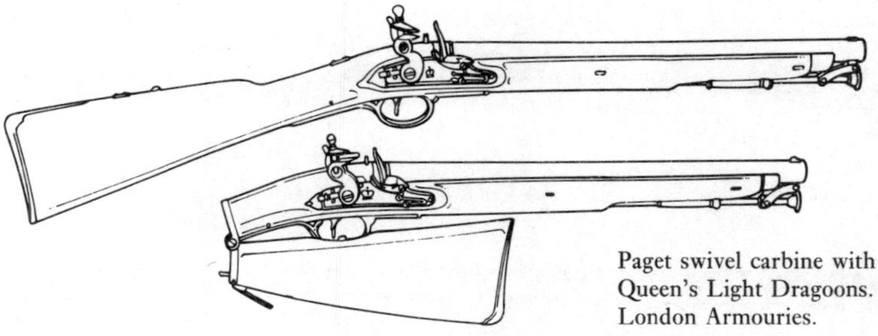

Paget swivel carbine with folding butt, of the Queen's Light Dragoons. English, *c.*1800. Tower of London Armouries.

Rifles

While the musket and its diminutive versions such as the fusil, carbine and musketoon remained the favourites with military men because of their rapidity of fire, another weapon offered the accuracy which these smooth-bores lacked. This was the rifle, an arm which had first appeared two centuries earlier. For all of the intervening years the rifle had been used primarily for hunting or for target shooting. The eighteenth century witnessed its début as a factor in warfare.

Ever since the invention of rifling, the centre of manufacture of such arms had remained in Central and Northern Europe. Rifles were known and occasionally produced elsewhere, but not in quantities comparable in any way to those made in Germany, Austria, Switzerland and parts of Scandinavia. Probably this was due at least in part to the fact that most of the big game for which rifles were especially useful could be found in these areas, while smooth-bores were adequate for the majority of animals hunted elsewhere.

By 1700 the hunting rifle of Central Europe had acquired all of the characteristics which marked it as a distinctive type throughout the succeeding 150 years until it was superseded by breech-loading arms. Collectors and students today designate the short German flintlock or percussion rifle a *Jaeger*. Indeed, even contemporary English and American usage often followed this practice. The name derived from the German word meaning 'hunter' both because this was the primary function of the weapon and because the men who used it most were the professional gamekeepers and foresters. Military riflemen in the service of the various German states were also known as 'Jaegers', again because of the rifle they carried and because many of them had been recruited from the ranks of gamekeepers and foresters.

The fully developed Jaeger rifle was a short weapon with a large bore. Barrel lengths averaged 30 in and calibres ranged between 0·55 in and 0·65 in. The rifling was deep and poly-grooved, externally the barrels were octagonal and almost always there was a slight flare at the muzzle. The sights usually consisted of a brass or white metal blade in front, and an open rear sight of iron. Set triggers were also often provided. The walnut stock was thick through the butt and often decorated with raised carving at the tip of the comb, on the cheek piece and around the mortises for the locks and mountings. A special feature of all such rifles was the butt-trap on the right side of the stock. This continued a feature normally found also on wheel-lock rifles. It was designed to hold extra flints and small tools or other accessories. Some writers have advanced the theory that this compartment was also used for the greased patches often employed by riflemen to wrap their bullets for loading. This may have been done on occasion, but the absence of grease stains in surviving specimens indicates that the traps were used primarily for other gear. Finally, there was usually a sling for ease in carrying: this attached to a regular sling swivel beneath the barrel in front and to a button on the bottom of the butt stock just behind the long trigger-guard. A complete average specimen weighed about $7\frac{3}{4}$ lb.

The Jaeger rifle was a good, efficient weapon. Its light weight and short barrel made it easy to handle in wooded territory while its large bore gave it good stopping power even against big animals. Moreover it was an accurate weapon, especially at ranges up to 200 yards. Like all rifles, however, it was slow to load, even with the patched ball which had been popular in Germany for almost a century.

The need for accuracy in some of the military situations mentioned above brought the rifle to the attention of professional soldiers everywhere. Units of riflemen were added to the armies of most of the German states during the first quarter of the eighteenth century. Norway armed its ski troops with Jaeger-type rifles as early as 1711, and Sweden adopted the rifle for limited use even earlier. Spain and Italy generally ignored the rifle as a military weapon. France had used rifled carbines the century before but made no effort to equip any infantry units with it, and England delayed the adoption of the

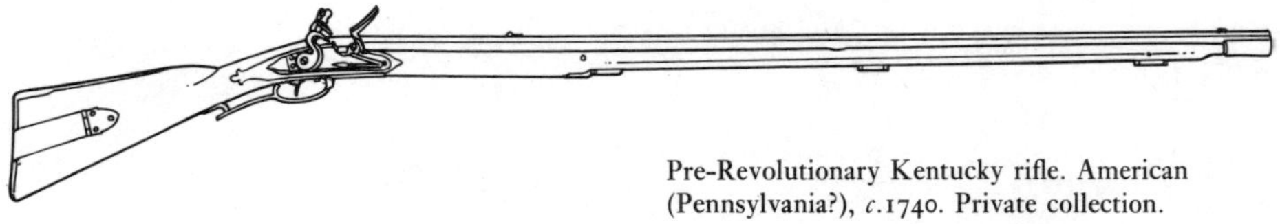

Pre-Revolutionary Kentucky rifle. American (Pennsylvania?), *c*.1740. Private collection.

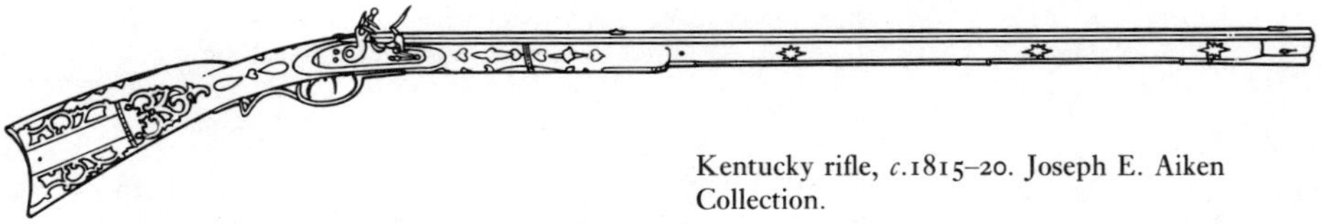

Kentucky rifle, *c*.1815–20. Joseph E. Aiken Collection.

rifle, even for limited purposes, until mid-century.

Meanwhile the German rifle had spread across the Atlantic Ocean to America. Settlers emigrating to Pennsylvania from Germany and Switzerland early in the 1700s took their rifles with them. In the wilds of the new country the traditional weapon evolved into an arm especially designed to meet the demands of its environment. The barrel was lengthened for accuracy at greater ranges, and the bore was decreased to conserve both powder and lead. In the process the stock also gradually altered in appearance, becoming lighter and more graceful. Usually it was made from the hard native curly maple rather than the traditional walnut. Also the butt-trap came to be used almost solely for greased loading patches and thus acquired in America the name of *patch box*. At first this feature retained the sliding wooden cover similar to that used on the Jaeger. Later, however, it was superseded by a hinged cover, usually made of brass, but sometimes also of iron or even silver. Finally, it became an entirely different sort of a gun, a long rifle known to its contemporaries as just that–a 'long rifle' or an 'American rifle'. After the battle of New Orleans in 1815 a popular ballad celebrated the feats of riflemen from Kentucky with such rifles, and all such weapons came to be called Kentucky rifles. There have been modern attempts to redesignate the arm the Pennsylvania rifle, on the grounds that this was the state of its origin and its greatest manufacturing centre. More recently, however, evidence has been adduced to suggest that it many actually have originated in Virginia or N. Carolina.

The evolution of the American rifle was not a sudden thing. It happened gradually over half a century. The longer barrels and slightly smaller bores were in general use by the 1740s, but the stocks were still straight and thick in the butt and the wooden patch-box cover continued to predominate. By 1750 enough of the evolution had occurred for the rifle to be considered distinctly different from its German ancestor. The next sixty years witnessed its full development, and in *c*.1780 started what has been called the 'Golden Age' of the Kentucky rifle. The calibre decreased to an average of 0·40 in to 0·45 in. The gracefully dropping butt with its sharply crescentic buttplate and the Roman nose of the comb all appeared in this era. Metallic inlays of brass, pewter, and silver, often engraved with designs, added surface beauty to the rifle's design. Then, after 1810, a deterioration began. Inlays and other surface decorations tended to become gaudy. The lines of the stock lost their graceful curves and became angular. The arm remained as accurate and as functional as before, but the beauty was gone.

It was this American descendant of the early German rifles that was destined to bring the rifle forcibly to the attention of the world's military powers. As noted previously, there had been regular rifle units in many of the armies of Europe, some of them dating back to the seventeenth century. These units had participated in some of the major Continental wars of the first half of the eighteenth century. In America colonial riflemen had fought in some of the engagements of the French and Indian War, and Great Britain had purchased rifles for issue to picked marksmen of various regiments serving in the wilderness. None of these instances of the military use of the rifle had aroused more than minor interest. It remained for the American War of Independence to focus really widespread interest in the arm. During that conflict the feats of rifle units at Saratoga and at King's Mountain reinforced widespread newspaper publicity on the American weapon.

The experiences of the War of Independence graphically illustrated both the advantages and disadvantages of the round-ball muzzle-loading rifle for military purposes. The slowness in loading and the lack of a bayonet were great weaknesses. Unless they were supported by regular infantry armed with muskets or protected by fortifications, riflemen could seldom stand against a determined attack. A charging foe could usually reach them before they had time to fire more than one or two rounds. Even if all these shots were superbly accurate they would not sufficiently weaken the attacking force in most instances to break the charge. Once actual contact was made the rifleman had no choice but to retreat since he had no defence capable of withstanding a soldier with a fixed bayonet.

On the other hand there were instances when the rifleman was superb. Supported by regular infantry and cavalry as at Cowpens and Guilford Courthouse, he could do a fine job of softening up an attack before giving way to the line troops for the final volleys and the hand-to-hand fighting. Acting as a sniper, a skirmisher or in an advance unit he could also prepare the way for a formal attack by weakening and demoralising the enemy. A few years later the War of 1812 provided, at the Battle of New Orleans, a fine demonstration of the way in which round-ball rifles should and should not be employed. There, American rifleman with a clear field of fire, a breastwork for protection, and regular infantry and artillery for support took a terrible toll of the attacking British forces. In that battle the British also had fine rifles, but they were out in the open under fire and with very small targets at which to shoot. In such a situation they were less efficient than the muskets carried by the bulk of their comrades. Their impression on the battle was almost nil.

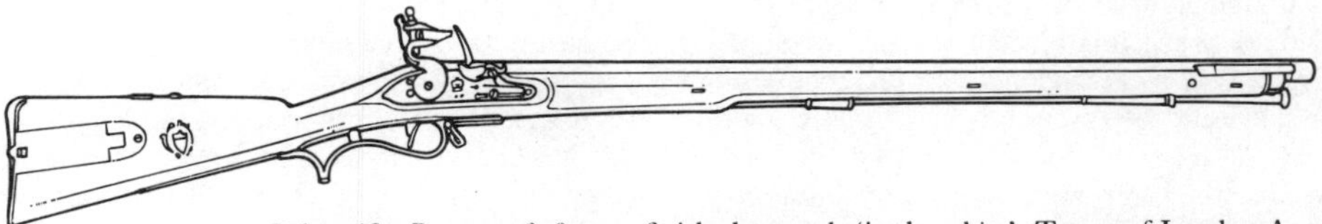

Baker rifle, Pattern of 1823, unfinished example 'in the white'. Tower of London Armouries.

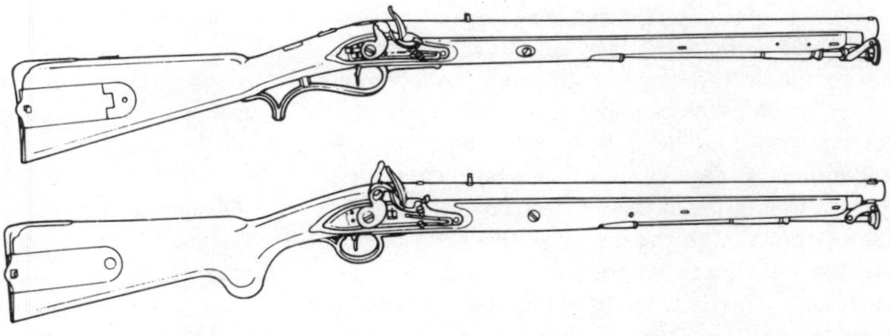

(*Top*) Baker cavalry rifle. English, *c.*1822. (*Bottom*) Baker cavalry rifle with pistol grip. English, *c.*1822. Tower of London Armouries.

As a result of these experiences a new emphasis was placed upon the rifle in military circles. Nations which did not already include riflemen in their military establishments added them, and those which did have them increased their number. Great Britain, experiencing a period of retrenchment following the American War, was slower to respond than most of her Continental neighbours. At first some rifles for British use were bought from suppliers on the Continent, but it soon became apparent that this was an unsatisfactory expedient. In 1800 the Board of Ordnance at Woolwich ordered extensive tests to develop an official British rifle. A wide variety of designs were examined–English, American and Continental–to find the most efficient type for military purposes.

In the end the Board chose a rifle made by Ezekiel Baker of Whitechapel, London. In all respects, except for the fact that it had a bayonet and boasted a hinged brass butt-trap cover, the Baker rifle resembled the typical short Jaeger of Germany. It weighed 9 lb and had a 30 in barrel with seven groove rifling that made only a quarter of a turn in the length of the bore. Such a slow twist made the piece easier to load because it reduced friction and collected less fouling. Also it produced a flatter trajectory for the ball, and this made aiming easier since the shooter did not have to compensate for so sharp a drop as he would have with a faster twist. From a military standpoint, one of the most important aspects of the Baker, aside from its bayonets, was the relationship of the ball to the bore. At first some rifles were made with musket bore. With these, however, it was necessary to use a mallet to seat a patched ball, and so they were soon abandoned. A carbine bore of 0·625 in was adopted, and the bullet was so designed that when wrapped in a greased cloth patch it would fit tightly, take the rifling and fly accurately. When loaded without the patch it would drop loosely down the barrel. This sacrificed accuracy, but it made the Baker almost as fast to load as the musket, and this was a decided advantage in the crucial moments of an engagement when the enemy was at point-blank range and precision shooting was not needed.

The Baker was an excellent rifle, and it performed well in battles on the Peninsula and in France. It continued in use as an official weapon until 1838 when it was superseded by the percussion Brunswick rifle. During this period it underwent a number of modifications. Many of these related to the bayonet. The first models were equipped with a 2 lb sword bayonet which tended to make the arm muzzle-heavy and difficult to shoot. In 1815 a socket bayonet with triangular thrusting blade was substituted, and finally in 1823 a spike bayonet compounded from the brass handles of the old sword bayonets and triangular blades from standard musket bayonets was introduced. There were also minor differences in the shape and size of the butt trap, the cock design which varied from goose-neck to throat-hole, and the design of the buttplate, but the rifle remained essentially the same throughout its entire history.

Interestingly enough, Americans were even slower to adopt an official military rifle than the British. In 1792 some rifles were purchased from various makers in Pennsylvania, but it was not until 1803 that an official model was adopted and put into production at the national armoury at Harper's Ferry, Virginia. Secretary of War Henry Dearborn was instrumental in the design of this new weapon, and under his guidance the rifle marked a decided break with American tradition. It was, in fact, far closer to the Baker rifle in appearance than to the Kentucky. The barrel was short, and the calibre was a substantial 0.54 in. The butt was straight, and the fore-end ran less than half way to the muzzle. This half-stock was designed to lighten the weight of the arm and make it easier to carry. For the same reason the forward two-thirds of the barrel were turned round. Only the breech was left octagonal in traditional rifle style. Strangely enough after the experiences of the War of Independence, the new rifle was not equipped with a bayonet. An American rifleman would still have to rely on regular infantry for support or try to defend himself with the knife and tomahawk with which he was issued for use as combination tools and side-arms.

Once the rifle was adopted as an official United States weapon, it was never again abandoned. Riflemen disappeared from the Regular Army from time to time, but there were always militia units equipped with the weapon from Federal stores. In 1814 the model of 1803 was altered slightly by the addition of a barrel three inches longer. In 1817 an entirely new rifle was adopted, and production began in 1819. This arm, called the 'common rifle' to distinguish it from the Hall breech-loaders (p. 201) which also commenced manufacture that year, more closely resembled the contemporary American musket, and hence owed much of its design to France. The lock was a close copy, though smaller, of the French infantry musket model of 1777, and the barrel and stock were fastened together by bands in the French manner. All mounts, including the hinged oval patch-box lid, were of iron instead of the traditional brass. It was a good sturdy arm, but still there was no provision for a bayonet. In this respect, Americans seem to have learned slowly. This new rifle was made entirely by private contractors rather than in a Federal armoury, and it remained the official muzzle-loading rifle until it was superseded by a percussion model in 1841. Even then, it continued in production until 1848.

Thus far, the emphasis has been placed on military rifles. The Jaeger, of course, had developed as a civilian arm for hunting big game, and the Kentucky rifle also was created to meet the wide range of requirements for a frontier people–hunting, recreation and personal defence. Both types continued in use for these purposes throughout the period. The Jaeger changed hardly at all. The Kentucky passed through the evolution mentioned earlier, then gave birth to a new type of rifle which blossomed into full development during the percussion era as the so-called plains rifle. These were shorter arms with half-stocks, more convenient than the long rifle for carrying on horseback. The calibres were larger, ranging between 0·45 in and 0·55 in because the game in the American West was bigger, and the soft iron barrels were made heavier, too, so they could withstand suitably powerful charges of powder. These were not graceful guns. They were chunky pieces with thick wrists and little or no decoration, but they were well-designed for their intended use. Aside from the drab appearance of these short rifles, the average viewer is probably most impressed with their weight. Flintlock specimens might weigh as much as 15 lb. Later percussion examples might be 2 or 3 lb heavier.

Both America and Europe produced other heavy flintlock rifles, however, and some of them weighed much more than these. Target shooting had been a popular sport in central Europe as early as the fifteenth century, and it remained so throughout the flintlock era. German emigrants to America carried enthusiasm for the sport with them, and both areas manufactured specialised rifles for such competition. The distinctive target rifle appeared first in Europe, and by far the larger number were made there. American specimens came later and were usually

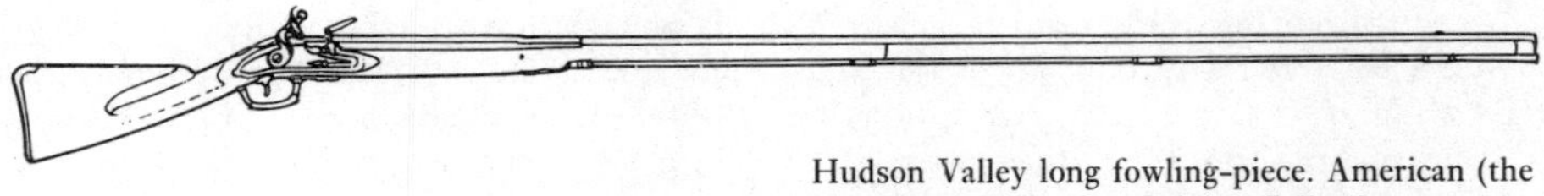

Hudson Valley long fowling-piece. American (the barrel Dutch), *c.*1690. Private Collection.

much simpler than the German variety. In fact, about the only features that the two had in common were the weight (up to 15 lb or possibly 18 lb for off-hand shooting; 30 lb to 45 lb for bench-rest matches) and the set triggers. Both shot exceptionally well, but the European arms excelled in finish and in such refinements as sights, a whole host of which were available. There were open sights with adjustable leaves for different distances, laterally moving sights to compensate for drift, peep sights, and even telescopic sights for precision shooting at long ranges. All of these refinements were known before 1700, and most of them were in use on target rifles from the very beginning of the period. Telescopic sights were perhaps less common than the others, though they are recorded as early as 1684,[7] while King Frederick the Great of Prussia mentions in his diary using a target rifle with such sights in 1737. Thus there were no real improvements or innovations among target rifles in the flintlock era. The only changes were those related to style and decoration.

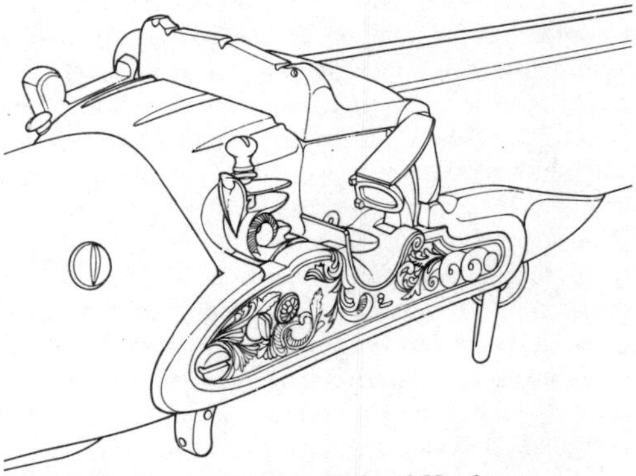

Detail of punt-gun. Used by Colonel Hawker on Southampton Water. English, *c.*1830. Wildfowlers' Association, Birmingham.

Fowling Pieces

Like target shooting, fowling was also an old and well-established sport by 1700. It continued to be popular throughout the remainder of the flintlock era, and a group of professional market fowlers appeared to supplement the ranks of the amateur birders and of the country folk who hunted birds to protect their crops and supplement their food supply. Generally, the two major types of fowling pieces developed during the previous century continued in use with some improvements and modifications. These were the long fowler, designed to take large numbers of birds at long ranges, and the short fowler, more popular for field fowling though also used for water birds. The major contribution of the period, however, was the development of the double-barrelled fowling piece as a practical and a popular arm. **120-24** **259**

The long fowler continued to be used most commonly along the coasts of England and Ireland and in America along the Hudson-Mohawk waterway and the coast of southern New England. There seems also to have been some use of a similar weapon along the coast of the Low Countries, but little or no employment of it elsewhere on the Continent. At the beginning of the period these huge guns remained much as they had been during the late years of the previous century. Barrels ranged up to 5 ft or even 6 ft in length and of perhaps seven, eight or nine bore. The only differences were stylistic which saw the stock, lock and furniture reflect the changing tastes of the years.

In England, however, the late years of the century witnessed a sudden change in the long fowler which produced a new type of gun. The weapon increased radically in size. The traditional long fowlers had

7 See p. 526.

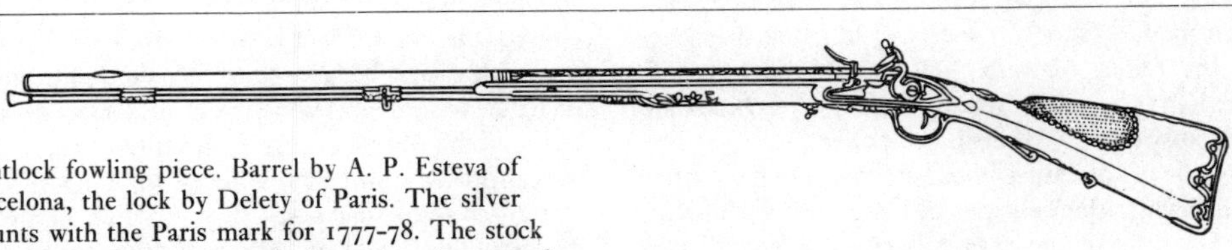

Flintlock fowling piece. Barrel by A. P. Esteva of Barcelona, the lock by Delety of Paris. The silver mounts with the Paris mark for 1777-78. The stock is fitted with a padded cheek-piece. French, 1777-78. Victoria & Albert Museum, London.

usually been fired from a rest of some sort, but the new gun required one, often a stanchion or even a fixed swivel. Bores were enlarged to $1\frac{1}{4}$ in or $1\frac{1}{2}$ in and the weight of the entire piece might run from 69 lb to 132 lb or even more. Sometimes these pieces were mounted in blinds, but more often they were placed aboard a canoe or punt and manoeuvred on the mud flats or over the coastal waters to approach flocks of water birds. When properly handled these punt guns brought down huge numbers of birds. A good shot might net twenty fowl, an excellent one forty, and with real luck the punter might bag even more.

Well after the advent of the percussion system for general purposes some punt gunners clung to the flintlock even though the detonating lock was more certain to fire in the damp conditions under which they laboured. The famous sportsman Colonel Peter Hawker even invented a double-barrelled punt gun with one percussion lock and one flintlock. According to his theory, if both barrels were fired at once, the percussion side, being quicker to ignite, would startle the flock, while the slower igniting flint side would catch the birds as they rose with wings spread, their most vulnerable moment. According to Hawker's own reckoning this weapon accounted for 14,000 birds before it was retired.

Among the short fowlers, important changes were few until late in the eighteenth century. The graceful, finely balanced arms of the late 1600s were continued with minor stylistic variations to reflect the changing modes and with the general improvements in the flintlock itself which were applied to all sorts of arms. Since these were often the guns of wealthy individuals some of them rank among the finest of decorated firearms, and their lines were among the most pleasing. Almost all of these fowlers were single-barrelled. A few side-by-side double guns were made during the early 1700s, but because of the long barrels required to burn a normal charge of powder efficiently these tended to be unwieldy and they failed to achieve popularity.

One of the principal reasons why efficient powder burning required a long barrel was the method by which it was ignited. In the normal flintlock the flash from the priming powder in the pan passed through the touch-hole and ignited the propellant charge at one corner. From there the combustion spread gradually through the rest of the charge. Gases formed in the very early stages of burning began to push the bullet forward well before the fire had reached the more distant areas of the charge. If all of the powder was to burn and add its force to the propulsion of the bullet, these areas had to have time to ignite while the ball was still confined within the bore. On the average a 40 in barrel was considered necessary for the usual charge in a smooth-bore, either fowling piece or musket.

More rapid ignition would alleviate this situation. It would also reduce the lag between the trigger pull and the actual shot, thus diminishing the distance by which the hunter needed to lead his quarry and so make aiming easier. Gunsmiths and sportsmen alike attacked this problem. In 1729 J. G. Leutmann described and illustrated what is now called the chamber breech, which had a conical termination of the bore with a fire-channel leading to the vent from the centre of its base. The flame from the priming powder would thus be led to the channel which would ignite and in turn direct its flash into the centre of the propellant charge in the bore proper. This system, which was later adapted by Joseph Manton in his patent of 1792, did indeed cause the propellant to burn more rapidly and gave a greater initial impetus to the ball. Guns with such chambered breeches could be made with shorter barrels and still hit harder than those with the more usual breech.

Another solution was provided by the ingenious London gunmaker Henry Nock with his patent breech of 1787. Nock also utilised a chamber in the breech plug, but he supplemented it with an 'ante-chamber' drilled cross-wise from the touch-hole and passing completely through the barrel. The far end of this hole was closed with a screw and the touch-hole itself was made as short and as narrow as possible. With the powder loosely confined in this ante-chamber, the flash from the pan produced an explosion rather than simple burning. Flame was thus transmitted from the ante-chamber to the chamber proper and on to the propellant charge almost instantly. So rapid were the successive explosions, in fact, that they sounded like one. The time lapse of the older chambered breech was eliminated, and all its good features were retained. With Nock's patent breech, guns shot quicker and hit harder as their loads burned more rapidly. Because of this rapid combustion barrel lengths could be reduced considerably. Instead of forty inches, thirty-two or even thirty inches were sufficient. Thicker metal could be used at the breech, thus permitting heavier loads (which would still burn within the shorter barrel lengths) and therefore greater range.

The effects of Nock's patent breech upon gun design were prompt and far-reaching. Other gunsmiths quickly developed their own adaptations of it, and soon almost all sporting guns made in England offered it in one form or another. Because they could shoot faster and harder, sportsmen found it possible to make more wing shots. The graceful dropping butts of the older fowlers made quick aim at high-flying birds difficult. Therefore butts became straighter and shorter so the guns could be brought up more easily. With the straighter stock it was convenient to have a support for the fingers of the right hand behind the triggers. Many English guns

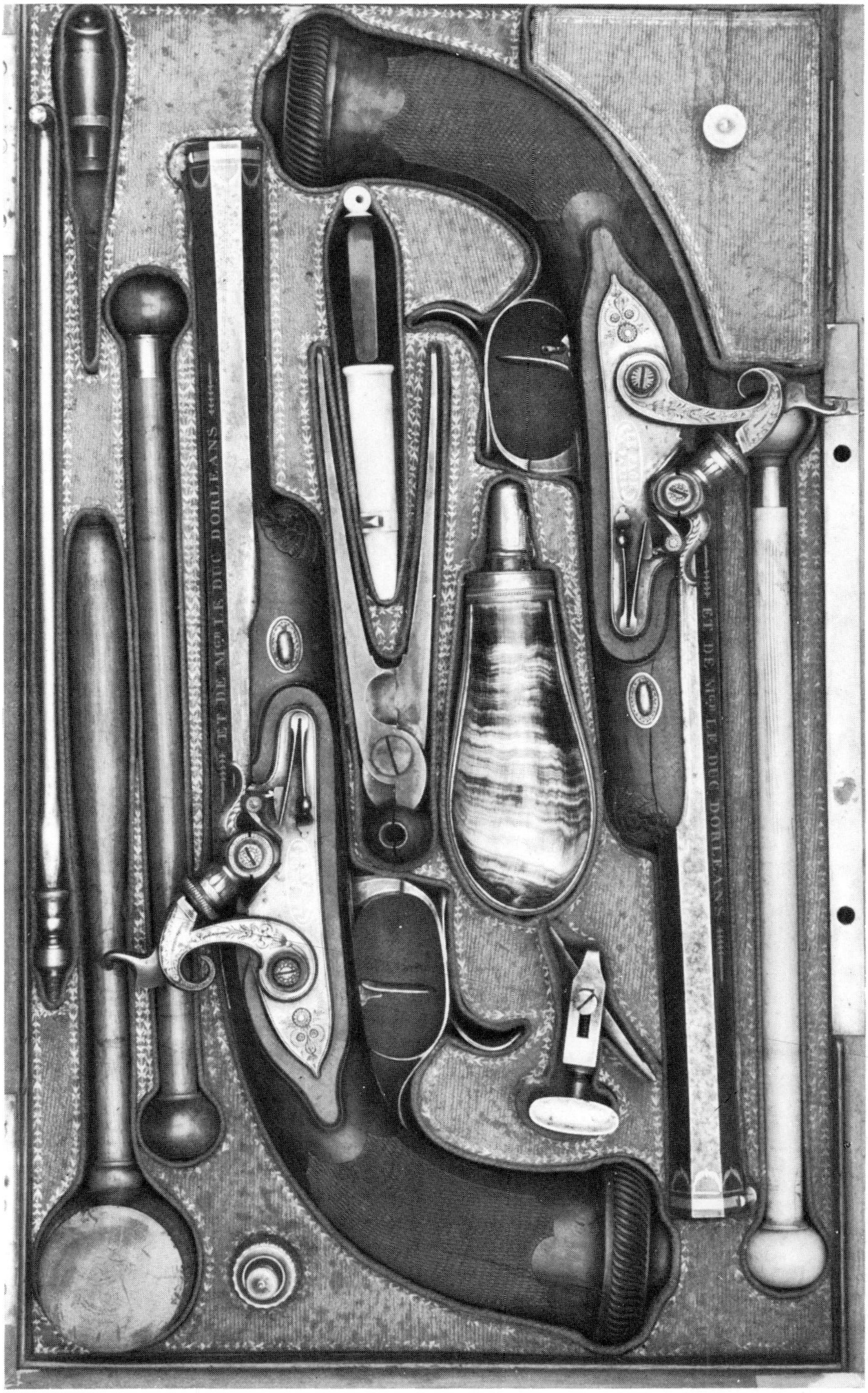

112 Cased pair of pellet-lock duelling-pistols signed in gold LE PAGE A PARIS ARQER. DU ROI ET DE MGR LE DUC DORLEANS, with all the original accessories except the screwdriver. French (Paris), *c.*1820.

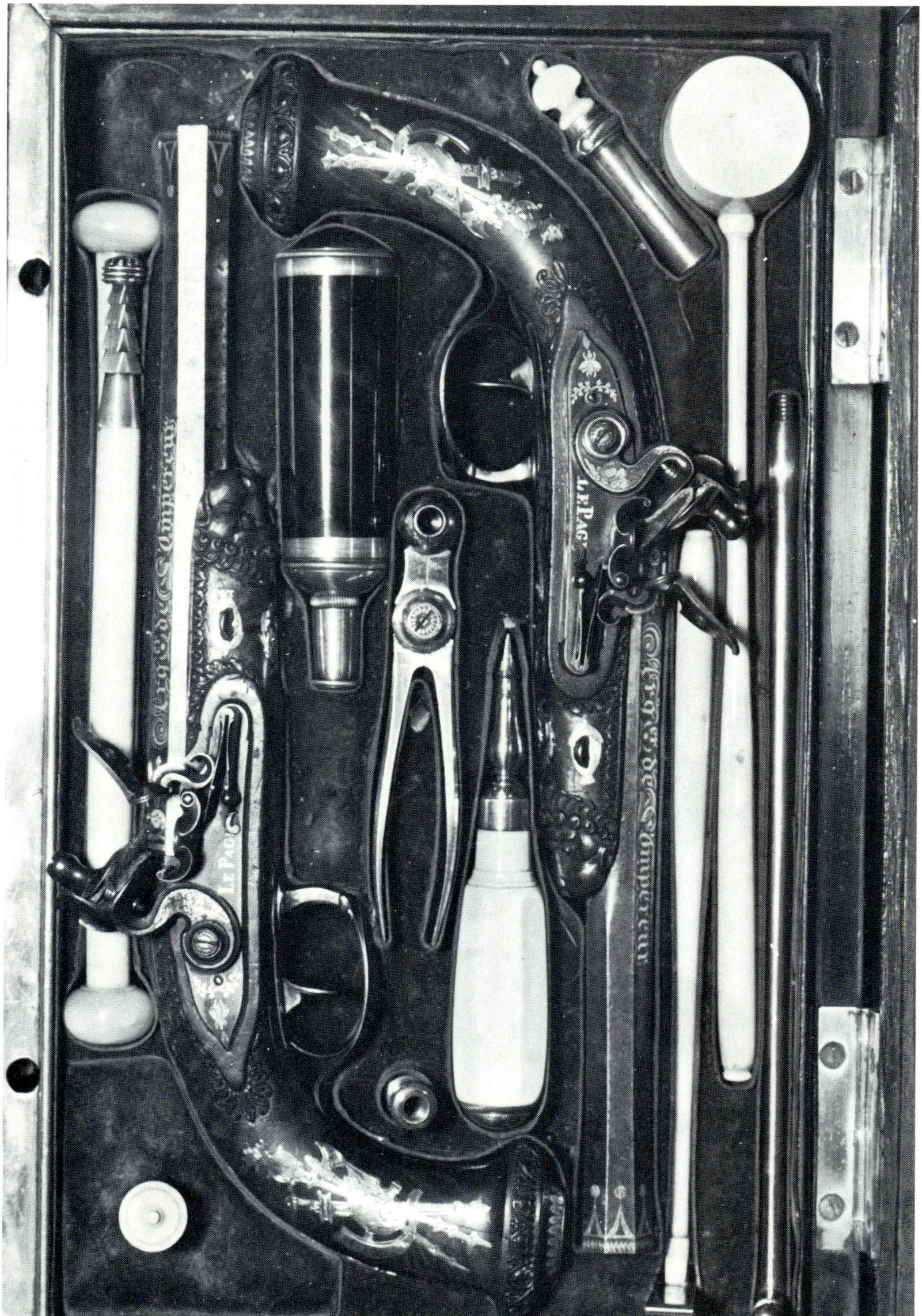

113 *Opposite* Cased pair of flintlock pistols with accessories, the locks signed *Le Page*. French *c*.1810.

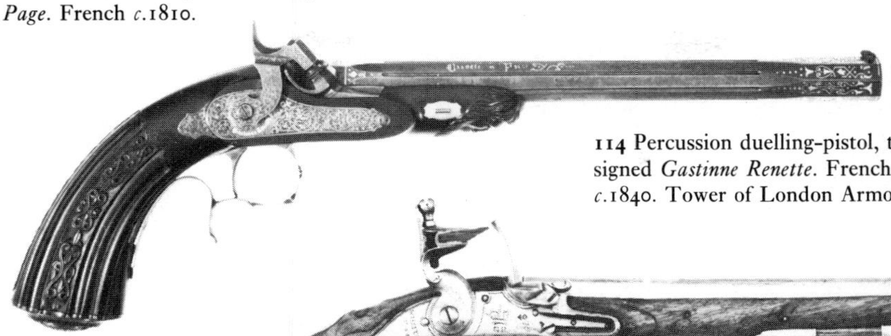

114 Percussion duelling-pistol, the lock signed *Gastinne Renette*. French (Paris), *c*.1840. Tower of London Armouries.

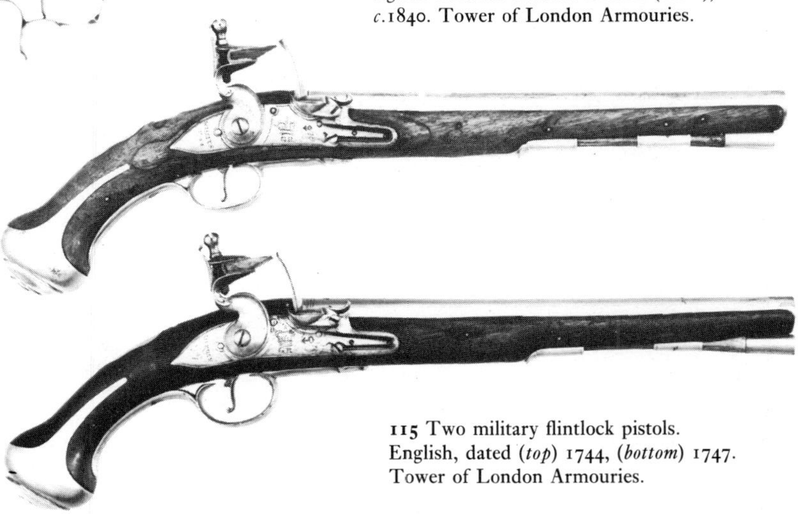

115 Two military flintlock pistols. English, dated (*top*) 1744, (*bottom*) 1747. Tower of London Armouries.

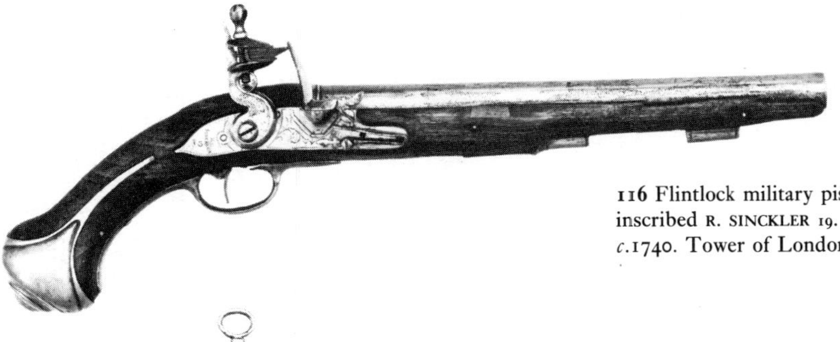

116 Flintlock military pistol, the lock inscribed R. SINCKLER 19. English, *c*.1740. Tower of London Armouries.

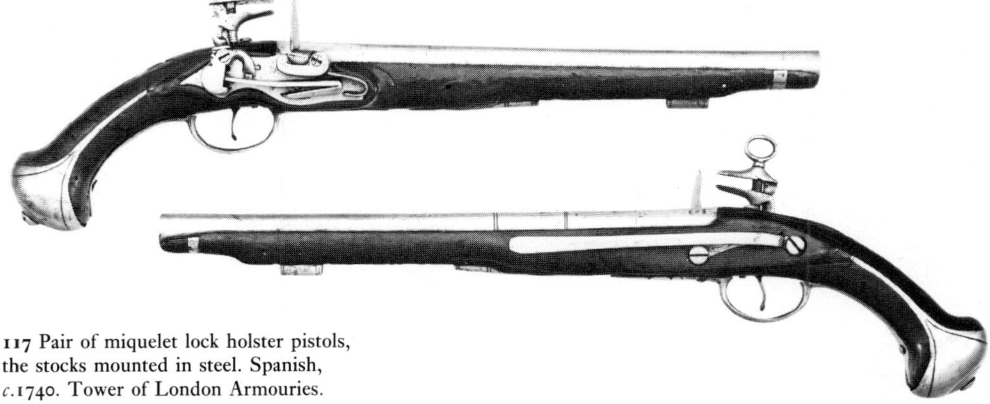

117 Pair of miquelet lock holster pistols, the stocks mounted in steel. Spanish, *c*.1740. Tower of London Armouries.

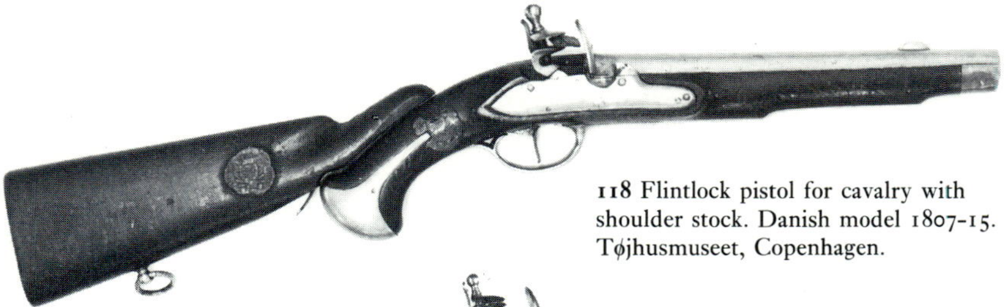

118 Flintlock pistol for cavalry with shoulder stock. Danish model 1807-15. Tøjhusmuseet, Copenhagen.

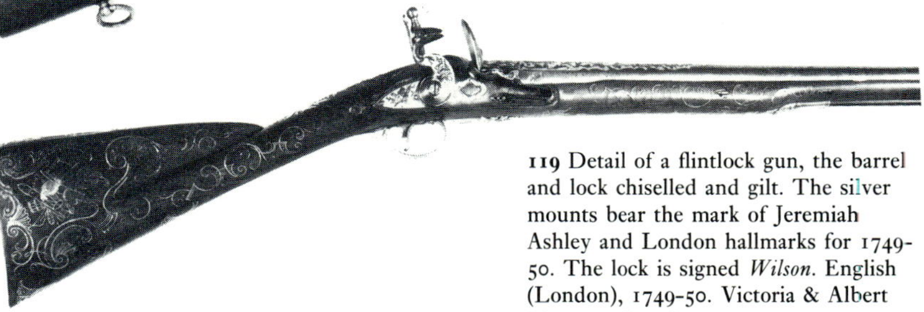

119 Detail of a flintlock gun, the barrel and lock chiselled and gilt. The silver mounts bear the mark of Jeremiah Ashley and London hallmarks for 1749-50. The lock is signed *Wilson*. English (London), 1749-50. Victoria & Albert Museum, London.

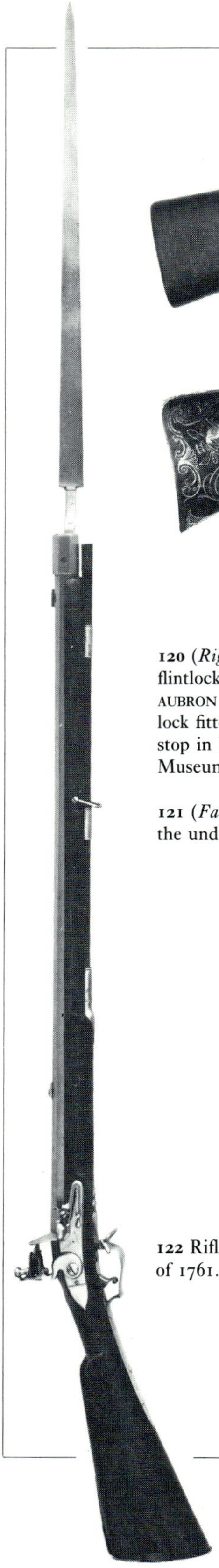

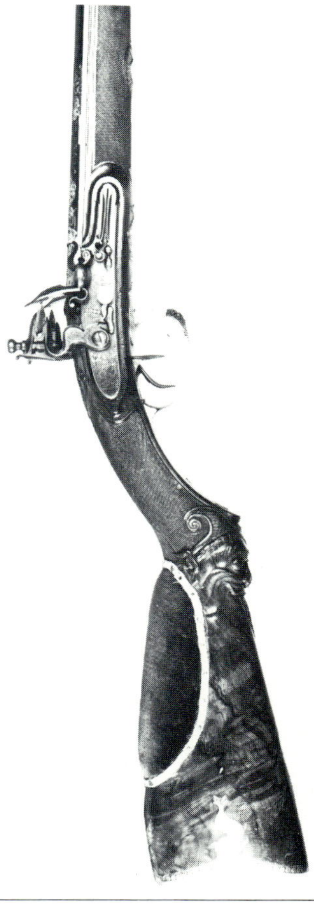

120 (*Right*) Detail of a double-barrelled flintlock fowling piece, the locks signed AUBRON A NANTES. French, *c.*1810. The lock fitted with Manton's gravitating stop in England. Victoria & Albert Museum, London.

121 (*Far right*) Detail of carved head on the underside of the stock.

122 Rifle and bayonet. Swedish model of 1761. Tøhusmuseet, Copenhagen.

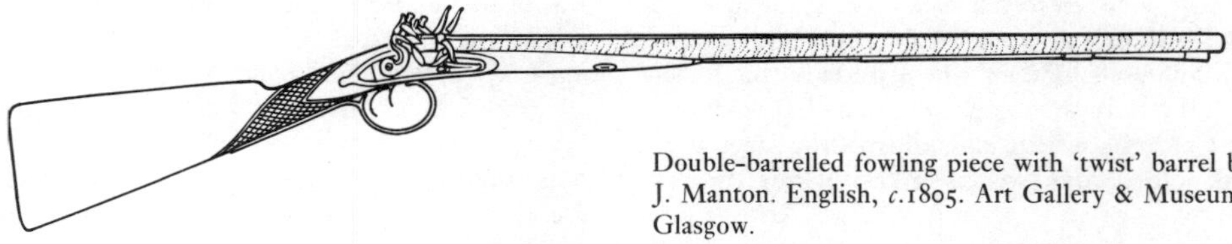

Double-barrelled fowling piece with 'twist' barrel by J. Manton. English, *c.*1805. Art Gallery & Museum, Glasgow.

provided this by extending the trigger-guard in a scroll while Continental makers, especially those in France and the Low Countries, often added a swelling to the stock itself, the forerunner of the modern pistol-grip. Frequently this protuberance was carved as an animal head for a major decorative element, even on cheap arms. On both English and Continental guns, and to a lesser degree on those made in America, the wrist or small of the butt was chequered to afford a better grip.

Most important, the shorter barrels made the side-by-side double gun practical. Sportsmen were delighted with the possibility of well-balanced arms that offered the opportunity for two quick shots, and the new double-barrelled shotguns quickly became popular. As a means for further reducing the muzzle weight of these arms, the full stock disappeared, and the half-stock fastened by one key became almost universal. Well before the end of the flintlock era the double-barrelled shotgun had attained the general architecture which characterises it today. Changes have come in ignition systems, loading methods and bore interiors, but not in overall design.

Still there was one weakness of the double gun that critics were quick to point out. It was accurate primarily at short ranges, perhaps thirty or forty yards. Further than that it tended to shoot low, and beyond sixty yards it was almost useless. Again an English gunsmith remedied the situation. Joseph Manton, one of the best known of all British manufacturers of flintlock sporting guns, invented an elevated sighting rib and obtained a patent on it in 1806. This was a rib fastened between the two barrels and thickened towards the breech so that it slanted slightly for its entire length. Sighting along such an inclined rib caused the shooter to elevate the muzzle of the piece more than he normally would with a flat rib. This made the shot a trifle high at short ranges but put it dead centre at longer distances. A properly thickened rib would place the target in the lower centre of the shot pattern at thirty to forty yards where the concentration was still sufficient to kill cleanly throughout the entire diameter and centred the target at fifty to sixty yards where the shot had scattered so widely that only a centre hit would be effective. Sportsmen hailed this device and considered it an innovation of the greatest importance in raising the effectiveness of the double gun. It was now the equal of the single-barrelled fowler in all respects, and it offered the advantage of an extra quick shot at the expense of only a few ounces of additional weight.

One other Manton improvement also added to the popularity of the double gun. This was a variation of Nock's patent breech which reduced the thickness of the breech in the area of the touch-holes where the pans jutted out on either side, thus making the arm slimmer and easier to handle. At the same time Manton cut a drainage hole vertically through the breech between the chambers so that any water from rain or splashes which collected on the upper surface of the gun would be carried off through this aperture instead of collecting in the grooves on either side of the sighting rib and possibly overflowing into the flash pans to wet the priming.

The half-stocked fowling piece, whether single- or double-barrelled, could be disassembled quickly into relatively short pieces. This fact led the gunmakers of the very early nineteenth century to design cases for carrying and storage similar to those made for pistols. Once again the case was normally of wood with internal compartments lined in felt or baize for the components of the gun and its accessories. In all respects it resembled the pistol case except for the size and the fact that the gun was carried in pieces rather than fully assembled.

The new percussion locks (Chapter 5) were applied to fowling pieces from the very beginning. In fact, the very first experimental lock was devised for a fowler by the Reverend Alexander Forsyth who was distressed by the slowness of the flintlock's ignition and the fact that the open flash from the pan sometimes startled his quarry. Nevertheless many of the more conservative sportsmen continued to prefer the flint fowling piece to the newer percussion arms so that both systems continued in common use until about 1825 in England and perhaps 1830 in America and the more remote areas of the Continent.

In addition to the mechanical improvements described above, there was one other major development in the manufacture of sporting guns during the late-eighteenth century. This was the widespread use of the *twist* or *Damascus* barrel. Once again the origin of the technique goes back to the previous century. Fine Damascus barrels were made in India and the Middle East well before 1650, but the first European description of the manufacturing technique did not appear until 1773[8]. In the Damascus or twist barrel alternate rods of iron and steel were welded, folded, and twisted in an intricate process before being flattened into a strip. This strip in turn was heated and wrapped spirally around a mandrel and hammer welded to form a rough barrel, which, in turn, was bored out, filed smooth and etched with acid to bring out the design formed by the fibres of varying hardness from the different metals. These twist barrels combined the hardness of steel with the toughness of wrought iron. Also the decorative effect of the etched patterns was highly prized. By 1800 most of the better sporting guns were being made with Damascus barrels, and English guns, especially, offered a subtle 'stub twist' which the celebrated gunmaker W. W. Greener noted[9] in 1835 was made by combining old horseshoe nails and chopped up coach springs in a ratio of about two to one for the basic strips. Sporting guns were not the only weapons to boast twist barrels, however. Fine pistols of the early nineteenth century were also frequently equipped with them.

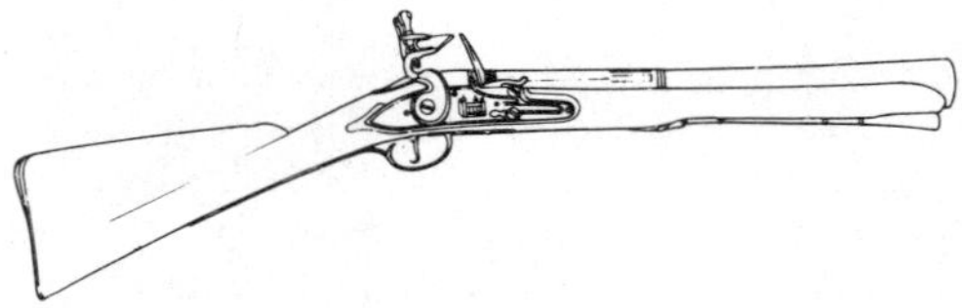

Flintlock blunderbuss, the lock engraved with a picture of the White Tower, by T. Hatcher, Master Furbisher at the Tower of London, *c.*1750–60. Tower of London Armouries.

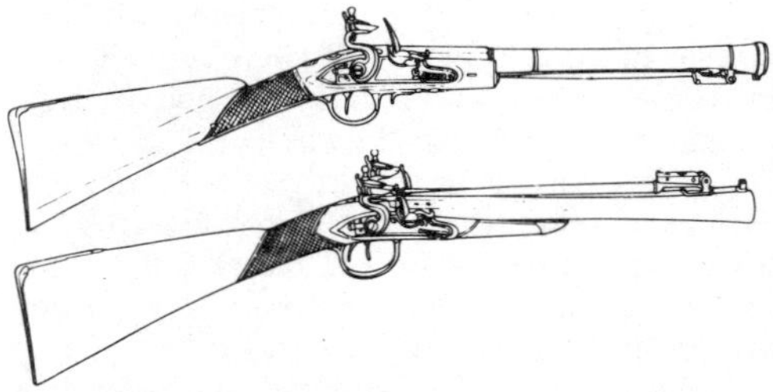

Blunderbusses with folding bayonets, one on top of the barrel, one under the barrel. English, *c.*1780. Tower of London Armouries.

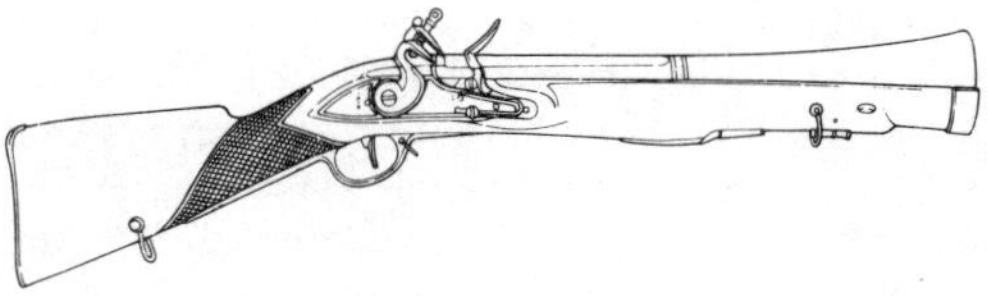

Flintlock blunderbuss made for East India Company. English, dated 1810. Victoria & Albert Museum, London.

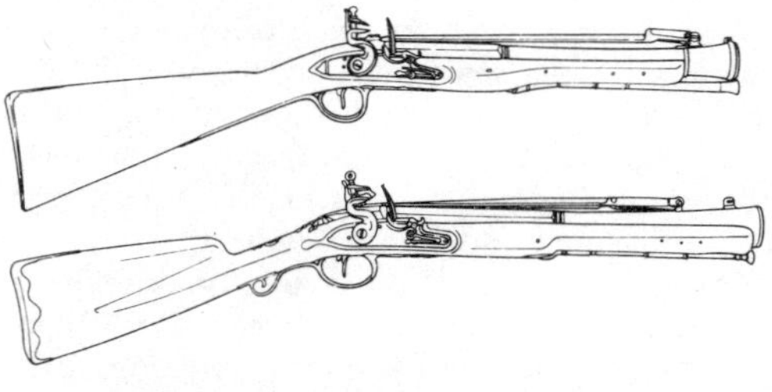

Flintlock blunderbusses, the top one with copper barrel and spring bayonet. Dutch, *c.*1790.

Blunderbusses

While the beginning of the percussion era saw the double-barrelled shotgun begin to assume its modern form, it also witnessed the demise of one of the flintlock era's most colourful weapons. This was the blunderbuss, an arm designed to scatter a large amount of small shot over as wide an area as possible and usually characterised by either an expanding bore or a bell muzzle or both. Though, as noted in Chapter 3, this interesting arm had developed in the seventeenth century, it was not until the eighteenth century that it became really popular, and while some wheel-lock specimens are known, it was almost always a flintlock weapon.

Dictionaries of the eighteenth century describe the blunderbuss as 'very fit for doing great execution in a crowd, to make good a narrow passage, door of a house, stair-case; or in boarding a ship'. It was a popular arm for stage-coach guards, toll-gate keepers and for household defence as well as for the military and naval purposes noted in the contemporary definition. The standard load consisted of as many buck-shot or pistol balls as would chamber conveniently and a charge of powder sufficient to the load and the breech strength. A large specimen of the type carried by coach guards might carry as many as twenty buck-shot with a charge of 120 grains of powder.

The typical blunderbuss of the early eighteenth

8 P. Wässtrom, 'Beskrifning pa damascherade skjutgevar af jarn och stal, *Kongl. Vetenskaps Akaaemiens Handlingar*, XXXIV, Stockholm, 1773, pp. 311–18.

9 W. Greener, *The Gun*, London, 1835, p. 23.

10 But see p. 86.

century was a relatively short gun. Its barrel was normally round throughout its length, expanding towards the muzzle and usually flaring in a bell. The calibre was large, perhaps 0·75 in at the breech, and the bore was usually cylindrical for a short distance before it began to expand. Some barrels were iron, but a large number were made of brass. As the century progressed the addition of a spring bayonet to the top or occasionally to the side of the barrel became common. Normally these bayonets were hinged and folded back until released by a sliding catch. Towards the middle of the century a type of blunderbuss with a longer barrel, a smaller calibre and a more pronounced bell became popular. Then, after 1750, and more especially after 1775, a shorter

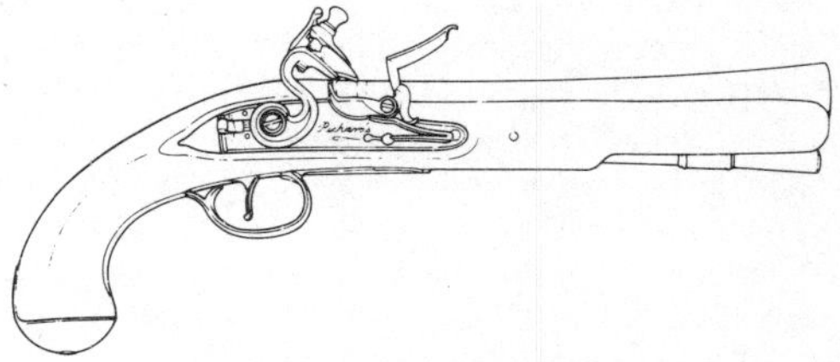

Flintlock blunderbuss pistol, signed RICHARDS. English, *c.*1780. Art Gallery & Museum, Glasgow.

form again became popular in England, but this time with a smaller bore diameter than that which characterised the blunderbuss of the early years of the century. These shorter English blunderbusses of 1775-1815 usually had octagonal breech sections, round chases, and heavy cannon mouldings at the muzzle. These generalisations about style do not always hold true; one finds blunderbusses of *c.*1800 with short round barrels and gradually flaring muzzles. It is safe to assert, however, that one almost never encounters the octagonal breech and the heavy always hold true, for one finds blunderbusses of *c.*1800 with short round barrels and gradually flaring from an early date, but they very rarely featured the heavily moulded muzzle.

The expanding bore and flaring muzzle of the blunderbuss were created with the thought that they would cause the shot to spread more rapidly than from the standard cylindrical bore. For this reason a great variety of flares and bell shapes are encountered as their creators sought rapid or slow dispersion. After 1750 elliptical muzzles were sometimes utilised in the hope that the shot would spread out in a horizontal pattern in the zone of maximum utility while the misses caused by pellets flying too high or too low would be eliminated. Actually all bell designs were based upon false ballistic theory. Shot can only spread out at a given rate, which is highly predictable. If the sides of the bore or the flare of the bell expand faster than this rate, they have no effect upon the shot whatsoever. Wide shot dispersion can best be obtained by a large bore at the breech where the balls are chambered, a short barrel and a gradually expanding bore. The bell, no matter what its shape, is completely superfluous. The English gunmakers of the eighteenth century gradually came to realise this and designed their weapons accordingly. This explains the shorter barrels of the late years of the century and the fact that the muzzle flare of these pieces is more apparent than real, being formed by the heavy mouldings which helped perpetuate the traditional exterior shape of the gun. At the same time the thickness of the barrel walls at the breech was also increased so that a heavier and thus more lethal load could be employed. The short barrel made this extra weight of negligible significance. Failing to understand the shot ballistics involved, many modern collectors have charged these late blunderbusses with being decadent forms. Actually, they represent the arm at its functional best.

In addition to the more common short shoulder weapons, blunderbusses were also manufactured as pistols and as swivel guns. The pistol form is quite rare, for it was a highly inefficient arm. The light weight required of any handgun combined with the heavy charge of shot necessary to fill the big bore produced a truly ferocious kick. At the same time the bores could never be made really big enough to make such a pistol noticeably more effective than its cylindrically bored counterpart. When found, such pistols normally have brass barrels, and both flare and bell are slight. Heavy swivel guns, on the other hand, were quite popular. Most often they were equipped with a yoke-type swivel for mounting on the gunwale of a ship or even of a small boat. These big guns had calibres ranging up to $1\frac{1}{2}$ in at the breech and could thus hurl a formidable quantity of shot. The navies of many nations in Western Europe and the United States adopted such blunderbusses, and merchantmen also found them useful. Sometimes these huge weapons had brass barrels similar to those found on pistols and shoulder blunderbusses, but most often they were iron.

The centre of blunderbuss manufacture was undoubtedly Great Britain. The Continental nations, notably France, Italy, and the Low Countries, produced large numbers of blunderbusses also, but they did not compare with Britain either in quantity or variety. Fewer blunderbusses were made in Scandinavia, Central Europe and Spain, and almost none were manufactured in America until after 1800, though many English specimens were imported for use there. In other areas, such as Turkey, Persia, and especially India, the blunderbuss was very popular, most often in short lengths, some of them actually pistol size and possibly designed for use in one hand. In these areas also the blunderbuss continued in use far longer than in Western Europe or America. A few blunderbusses with percussion locks, mostly military or naval models, were manufactured in these latter areas, and production ceased almost entirely about 1845. In India and the Middle East, on the other hand, flintlock blunderbusses have been made until very recent times. For some of these very late specimens the tourist market seems to have been the principal aim, but a few may have been intended for more lethal purposes.

Other Specialised Arms

In addition to the common arms such as pistols, muskets, blunderbusses, fowling pieces and rifles, the eighteenth century also produced a number of even more highly specialised arms. Some were designed for military or naval use; some were civilian. Some were made for law enforcement or the protection of property; others were built specifically for clandestine or even extra-legal purposes. Because of their limited objectives and usefulness, these specialised arms were made in far smaller numbers than their more popular contemporaries. Nevertheless they were all typical of their era and its inventiveness in the field of firearms.

The largest group of these minor weapons undoubtedly were those designed for use by the army and navy. The huge blunderbusses mounted on swivels have already been mentioned, but there were other similar weapons without expanding bores or flared muzzles. As a category these were known as wall guns, swivel guns, or sometimes as *amusettes*. All of these names were often applied to a species of small cannon, but they were adapted also to indicate guns shaped like shoulder weapons, only heavier, and designed to be fired from a fixed mount. All of these arms were equipped with a swivel resembling the modern rowlock. Sometimes it was attached to a band passing around the barrel, sometimes to a bar passing through the fore-end beneath the barrel and sometimes to trunnions actually fashioned as a part of the barrel as they were in cannon.

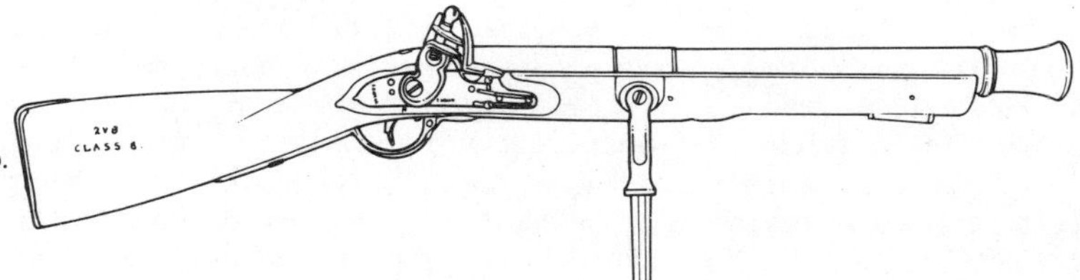

Swivel blunderbuss, inscribed T. FRENCH CANTON. American, *c.* 1790. Smithsonian Institution, Washington, D.C.

Such wall guns bridged the gap between small arms and heavy ordnance. They were relatively light and could be transported easily. They could also be mounted quickly and simply in a post sunk in the wall of a frontier fort, or hastily built earthwork, or in a stanchion of the gunwale of a ship or small boat. One man could easily load and fire such an arm as he would a musket, but the larger size afforded greater range and increased striking power. They were frequently used for commanding rivers or other narrow bodies of water when it was not possible to obtain cannon. Early forms of the wall gun, usually without the swivel, had appeared in the wheel-lock period which preceded the flintlock, and they continued in use in the percussion period which followed. The eighteenth century, however, witnessed the flowering of the type, and saw it reach its maximum popularity and its greatest variety.

Of all the various types of stocked wall guns, the blunderbuss was perhaps the most popular. It offered the greatest potential for anti-personnel purposes at short range. There were also a large number of wall guns resembling the contemporary musket, however. These offered more accuracy and longer range plus some effective anti-personnel work if a quantity of buck-shot were added to the usual ball. The longest range and greatest accuracy of all, however, were provided by the rifled amusettes. A number of these were manufactured at the Rappahannock Forge in America during the War of Independence. They weighed about 50 lb apiece, and ranged about 5 ft in length. Surviving specimens are bored to take a 4 oz ball, but there is one contemporary reference to a 2 oz model that could hit a half sheet of paper at 500 yards. Most wall guns were single-barrelled weapons, but there were a few with multiple barrels and a very small number of breech-loaders as well. Almost all nations of Europe as well as the United States recognised the stocked swivel gun as an official weapon for their navies if not also for their armies.

There were even more specialised flintlock

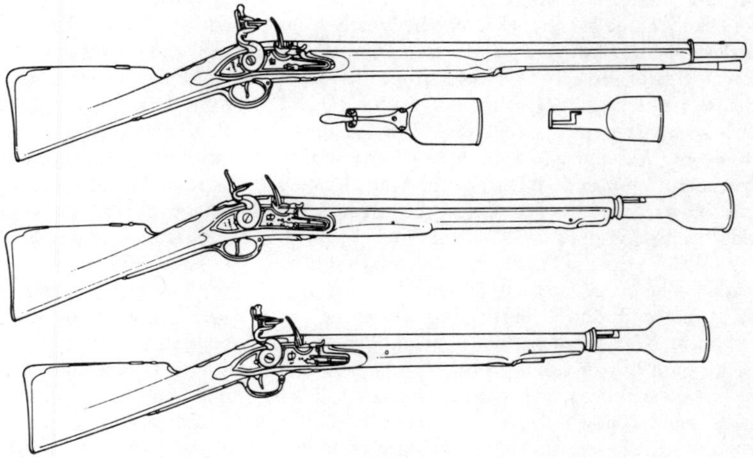

Flintlock grenade launchers (the cups for discharging grenades). English, *c.*1810. Tower of London Armouries.

weapons for military and naval use, however. These included the rocket launcher or hand mortar. Some eighteenth century versions of this weapon continued the tradition of the German wheel-lock models of the late sixteenth century with the short heavy barrel and grenade cup made in one piece and mounted on a stock. This is especially true of a group of such guns made in Switzerland and of some in France, the Low Countries and England. Nevertheless there was one new variant of the weapon. This comprised a musket with a barrel slightly shorter and heavier than usual and a detachable grenade cup that fastened in firing position with the same sort of stud and locking slot as the contemporary bayonet. Such grenade launchers are known to have been in use in England and on the Continent as early as 1728. Still, they suffered from the same drawback as the earlier models–it was necessary to light the fuse of the grenade before cocking and firing the musket with the propelling charge. A misfire or a delay of any sort remained a great hazard for the grenadier and those about him. For this reason grenade launchers of all sorts disappeared about the middle of the century and did not come back into use for over a hundred years.

While the grenade launcher disappeared during the flintlock era, another launching device made its first appearance at the very end of the period. This was the rocket gun. In 1808 Sir William Congreve designed the first successful war rockets to be produced in Europe. Mostly these were big affairs, fired from launchers or from boats as a form of artillery. Towards the end of the Napoleonic Wars, however, there seems to have been an attempt to adapt the rocket as an infantry arm as well as an artillery weapon. From this period a number of rocket guns, suitable for operation by a single soldier, survive in the Armouries of the Tower of London. Some have regular musket butts and were designed to be fired from the shoulder. Another

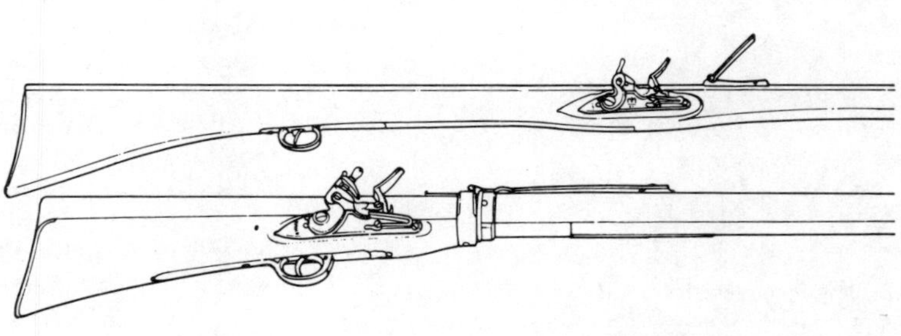

Details of flintlock rocket launchers, the locks inscribed with TOWER and GR (crowned). English, *c.*1815. Tower of London Armouries.

model is hafted and intended to be braced against the ground when discharged. Both types utilise standard musket or carbine flintlocks to ignite the propellant charge in the rocket, either directly from the flash pan or through a powder train. Some have flash shields to protect the shooter from the rocket exhaust; others do not, although such a shield would seem to be essential for safety. The close of the Napoleonic Wars apparently brought this interesting experiment to an end. When World War II called forth the 'bazooka' infantry rockets actually took the field; their beginnings date back to the flintlock period.

Flintlocks were used to fire cannon also as well as rockets. The usual method of igniting a cannon during the eighteenth century was to prime the vent with loose powder from a priming horn or insert a quill primer ready packed with powder and touch it off with a slow match held in a linstock or with a hot-burning portfire. The presence of the lighted match or portfire in the vicinity of spilled powder from priming or from cartridge bags was always a hazard, and thus designers constantly sought to eliminate it. Late in the eighteenth century a number of flintlock devices were invented with this purpose in mind. Some were large locks which could be set upon the breech of the cannon and fired by a lanyard. Others were shaped somewhat like the contemporary pistol and could be held in the hand. Such firing devices were more popular for naval use where the danger of fire was greater than for field artillery or siege guns. They never supplanted the linstock and the portfire for general use, but nevertheless they continued to be manufactured, especially in England, until the end of the flintlock era when they were converted to percussion locks and later supplanted by the friction primer.

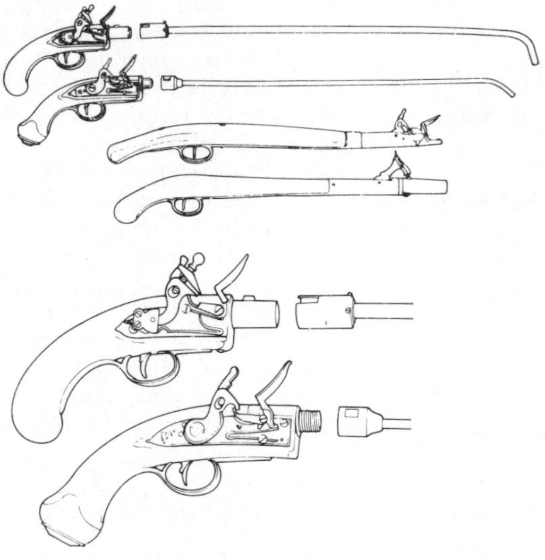

Cannon igniters, fourth from the top with a percussion lock, with details of butts, locks and attachment method of igniter tubes. English, c.1815-20. Tower of London Armouries.

Another concept which appealed to military and naval men was the production of a whole volley of shot from one gun. The blunderbuss offered this advantage, but there were other attempts to obtain it as well. The idea of a multi-barrelled weapon firing all its charges at once first appeared with the *ribauldequins* in the mid-fourteenth century,[10] (see p. 202) and later versions of the same weapon kept reappearing throughout most of the history of firearms, even into the modern cartridge era. The eighteenth century boasted two popular forms.

One of these forms grouped a number of barrels in a cylindrical cluster. Normally there was a central barrel with six other barrels gathered around it. Some guns had more barrels, some less, but seven was the most popular number by far. This may have been caused by the magical significance often attached to the number seven, but more likely it resulted from the fact that if all bores are equal, six is the most practical number that can be fastened around the central barrel. A few pistols were manufactured with such multiple barrels, but normally such volley guns were made as shoulder weapons.

The most famous of all such seven-barrelled volley guns were undoubtedly those made for the British Royal Navy by Henry Nock. James Wilson invented the weapon and presented it to the Board of Ordnance for trial on 29 July 1779. The Board considered it a practical arm but felt it would be of more use aboard ship than on land, and so they referred the piece to the Lords Commissioners of the Admiralty. At the direction of this body Henry Nock made two sample guns for testing purposes. Then, when it was decided to purchase these arms in quantity, Nock, with the experience obtained in fashioning the prototypes, was able to underbid other competitors and become the sole suppliers of these arms to the British Navy. Wilson was awarded £400 for his invention.

The manufacture of one of these volley guns was a complicated procedure. Each barrel was made separately. Then they were fitted and brazed together. The central barrel was threaded so that it could be screwed to a plug or spigot which contained a bell-shaped chamber connected to the touch-hole. This chamber fired the central barrel while holes radiating out from it in turn carried the flame to the outer barrels and fired them at almost the same instant. To produce these radiating channels, Nock drilled through from the outside of each of the barrels, cutting through both walls and then through the wall of the central barrel. The hole in the outer wall was

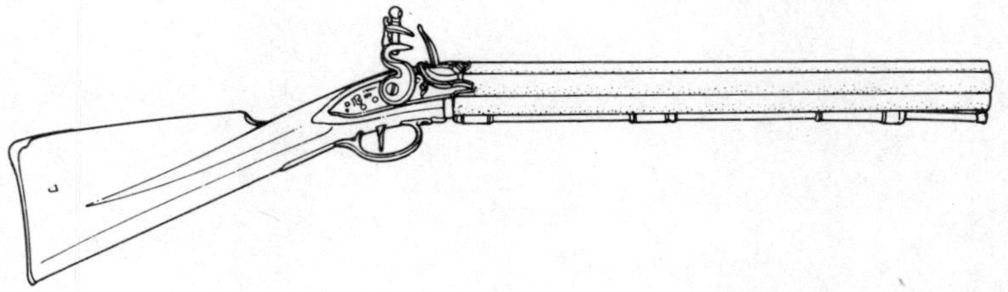

Seven-barrelled flintlock naval carbine by Henry Nock. Inscribed with TOWER and GR (crowned). English, *c.*1780. Tower of London Armouries.

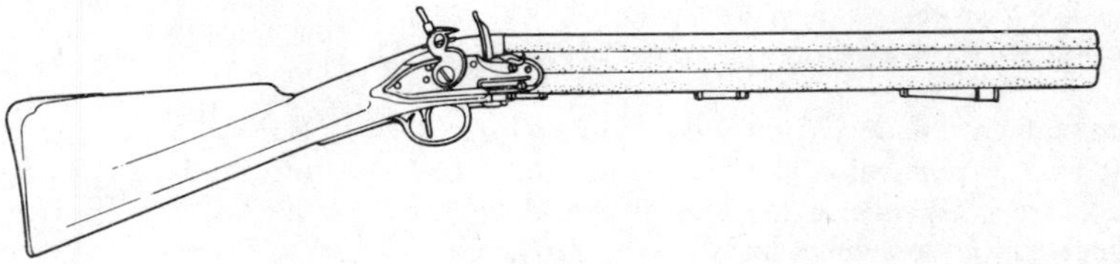

Second model seven-barrelled flintlock naval carbine by Nock, 1787. Inscribed with TOWER and GR (crowned). Tower of London Armouries.

then fitted with a screw plug to close and seal it. These plugs could be removed for cleaning out the channels which had a tendency to become clogged with powder fouling after firing a number of rounds. Complete arms were about three feet long and weighed twelve pounds. The two prototypes boasted rifled barrels and cost £15 apiece. The regular production models were smooth-bore and cost £13. In all, Nock produced some 655 of them for official use between 1780 and 1788.[11]

The Nock seven-barrelled volley guns had been purchased for use in the fighting tops of naval vessels. From such a position a sailor or marine could sweep the deck of an opposing ship. The angle was advantageous, and the volley fire from such a gun offered highly desirable firepower. Nevertheless there was also a fire hazard. It happened that men with guns in the tops sometimes set sails and rigging on fire and thus destroyed their own vessel. For this reason many British naval officers deplored the new weapon and refused to use it or any other gun for such purposes. There is an indication that the volley gun was used by Lord Howe when his fleet relieved Gibraltar in 1782, but it is very doubtful that they ever saw any other important service.

Interestingly enough, however, there was a civilian market as well as a military demand for such volley guns. In slightly reduced sizes they were manufactured for hunting wildfowl. Nock, in fact, produced a handsome silver-mounted specimen of his gun for King George III, now in the collection at Windsor Castle, and other English makers produced variations of it for commercial purposes. Most of these were seven-barrelled weapons, but some had five or six barrels, and a few had even more. The celebrated English sportsman Colonel Thomas Thornton was proud of one such gun with twelve barrels and even had his portrait painted holding it. His *pièce de résistance*, however, was a handsome twin-seven-barrelled monster offering a total of fourteen barrels,
now preserved in the Musée d'Armes, Liège. It is so 126
designed that it can be broken down into two seven-barrelled arms or both sets of barrels can be mounted and fired together. Surprisingly, the gun complete with all barrels weighs slightly less than the Nock naval volley gun, and it is equipped with a special handle on the fore-end to help support it in firing. These sporting versions of the volley gun were made on the Continent as well as in England, and they were sufficiently popular for many of them to be converted to percussion when that system became standard.

A second form of volley gun which acquired some popularity during the late eighteenth century was a pistol with four barrels splaying out from a common breech. Modern collectors call these 'duck's-foot' pistols because their shape somewhat resembles the splayed foot of that fowl. Normally these had box-locks, the centre cock firing all four barrels at once as the flash from the pan travelled through four separate channels to reach the various charges. The angle of dispersion between the two external barrels was not great, perhaps 20° was an average, but it still created a wide field of fire. Supposedly these arms were designed for prison guards and for ships' officers who might be faced with a mob of mutineers. A few, in fact, have naval motifs engraved upon them and some are also equipped with a belt-hook in the tradition of naval weapons. Such a pistol might well have been effective in facing a mob, especially from the psychological standpoint, but it was also bulky

11 See H. L. Blackmore, 'The Seven-Barrel Guns', *Journal of the Arms and Armour Society*, Vol. I, 1953-5, pp. 165-82.

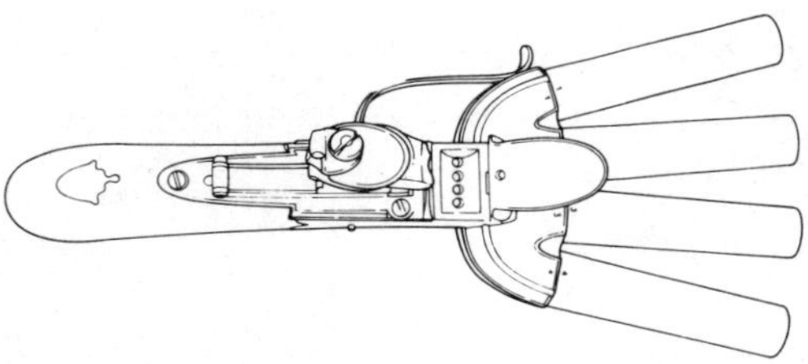

Flintlock 'duck-foot' or 'mob' pistol, signed JAQUES. English, *c.*1780. Art Gallery & Museum, Glasgow.

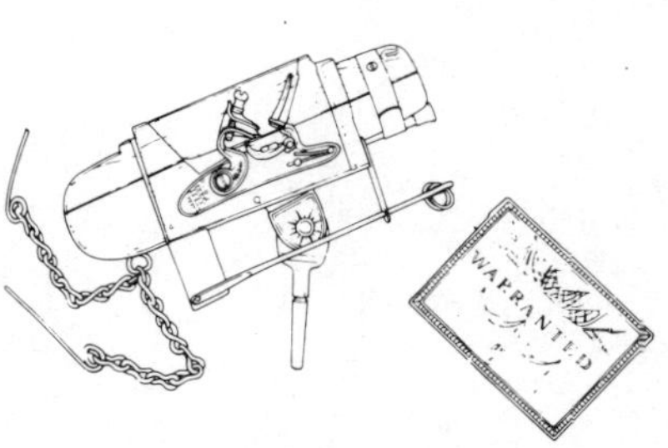

Trap gun with removable brass cover-plate to protect the lock. English, *c.*1800. Museum of Science and Industry, Birmingham.

and clumsy. The recoil was severe, and, of course, there was no possibility of isolating a single individual as a target. Anyone in the vicinity would be endangered, and sometimes this was a decided liability. For these reasons the duck's-foot pistol never became widely popular. Most specimens seem to have been made during the last quarter of the century with a few being manufactured after 1800. England seems to have been the centre and limit of their production.

There were other specialised, and slightly fantastic, firearms in the flintlock era besides these duck's-foot pistols. For one thing guns continued to be combined with other weapons as they had been in previous centuries, but the variety–and seeming impracticability–of the combinations became
127-8 greater. Flintlock pistols and sometimes even long-guns were concealed in walking-sticks or canes, added to truncheons or even united with such unlikely implements as table knives, forks and spoons. The combination of sword and pistol which had appeared long before continued in use. The most popular association, probably, was that of pistol and
129 hunting sword. Presumably this was designed to aid the huntsman who had approached a seemingly mortally wounded bear or boar to deliver the *coup de grâce* with his sword only to find the quarry still dangerous and able to attack. With his sword in his hand it would be difficult for such a hunter to draw a pistol, if indeed that weapon was not some distance away in a saddle holster. In such a situation a pistol readily available as part of the sword could be a real comfort. This was not the only use of such hunting sword and pistol combinations, however. Some military men favoured them and actually carried them as weapons in time of war.

A few of these combination arms were also designed for clandestine use. This was particularly true of cane or walking-stick guns which could be carried unobtrusively by a poacher but brought quickly into action if a good opportunity presented itself. Some of these cane guns were little better than pistols, but others offered detachable shoulder stocks that could be carried separately under the coat while the barrel served as the walking stick itself.

Such practices as poaching, grave-robbing to provide cadavers for anatomical research, and simple burglary also called forth specialised weapons to oppose them. Most popular, probably, was the so-called trap- or spring-gun. This was a flintlock with a barrel of the blunderbuss type completely encased in wood and usually with a tinned-iron cover to protect the lock from the weather. For a trigger there was an iron rod with a loop at its free end to which three wires could be attached. The gun itself was mounted on a swivel and set about a foot from the ground while the wires were run out across paths or other lines of expected approach within a limited arc in front of the piece and made fast. If a poacher or grave-robber should trip over one of these wires or springs as they were called, the tension on the line would first swing the gun in his direction and then fire it. Most of these weapons were designed to fire low and so wound rather than kill. Some, however, could be adjusted to point upwards at an angle and deliver a more lethal shot.

Most trap-guns of this variety were made in Great Britain, but there was another form of flintlock trap-gun which is usually associated with France and the Low Countries. Collectors today often call it a 'chicken thief' gun. This weapon was designed for protection against an intruder attempting to enter a door or window. It resembled the standard pocket-pistol with box-lock popular during the last years of the eighteenth century and the early 1800s. At the back of the grips, however, there was a screw clamp by which the piece could be fastened in position and aimed at the opening it was supposed to protect. It was thus immovable and could not rotate as the British spring-gun could. A lever pivoted on the front of the trigger-guard, or the under-side of the barrel, provided an attachment for a wire to the door or window. A tug upon it applied pressure to the trigger which moved in the usual manner. Unlike the British version which lasted for a brief period (the setting of such guns was made illegal in 1827), the French type continued in production into the percussion era, and some metallic pinfire cartridge specimens are also known.

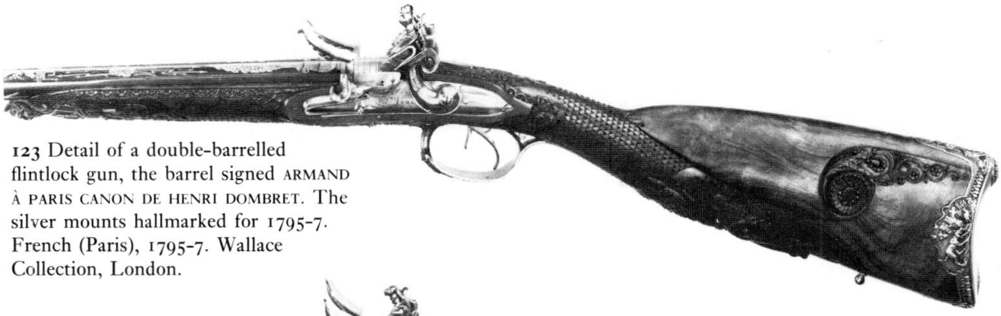

123 Detail of a double-barrelled flintlock gun, the barrel signed ARMAND À PARIS CANON DE HENRI DOMBRET. The silver mounts hallmarked for 1795-7. French (Paris), 1795-7. Wallace Collection, London.

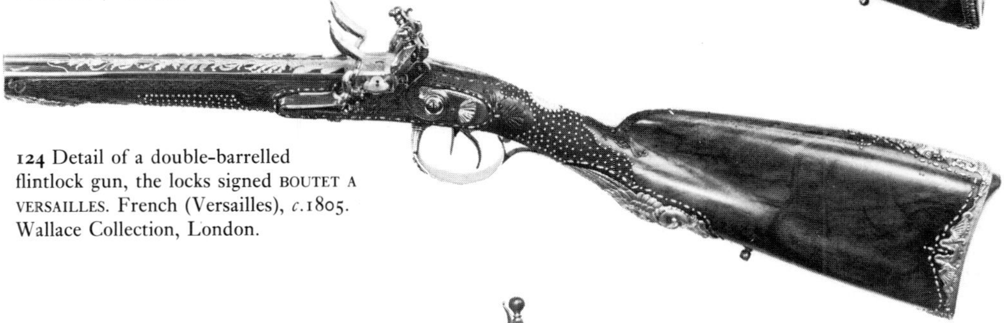

124 Detail of a double-barrelled flintlock gun, the locks signed BOUTET A VERSAILLES. French (Versailles), *c.*1805. Wallace Collection, London.

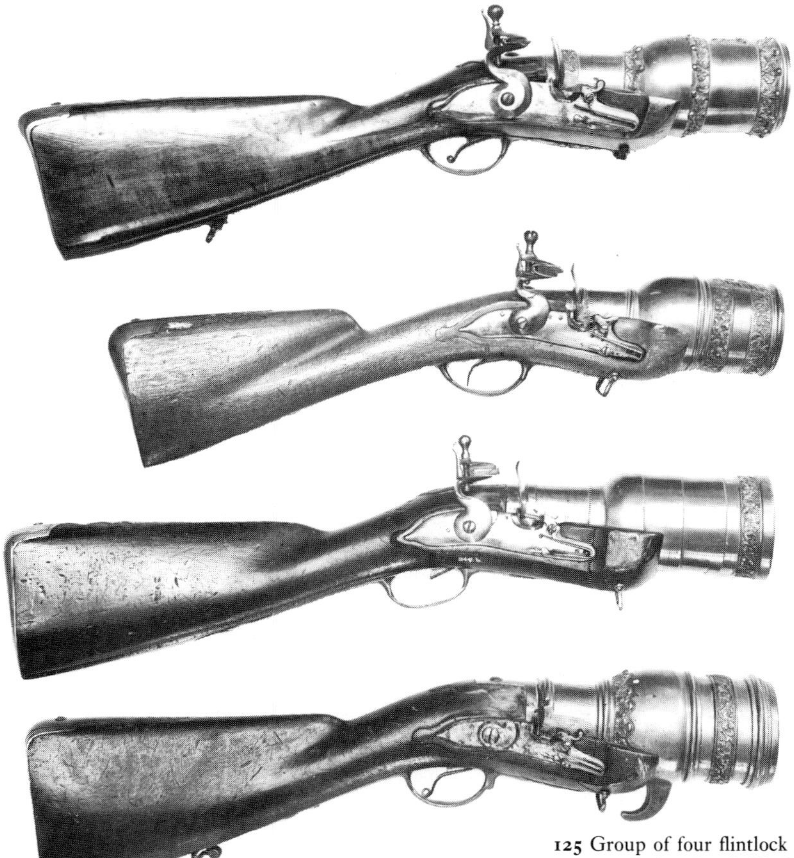

125 Group of four flintlock hand-mortars. Swiss, first half of eighteenth century. Historisches Museum, Bern.

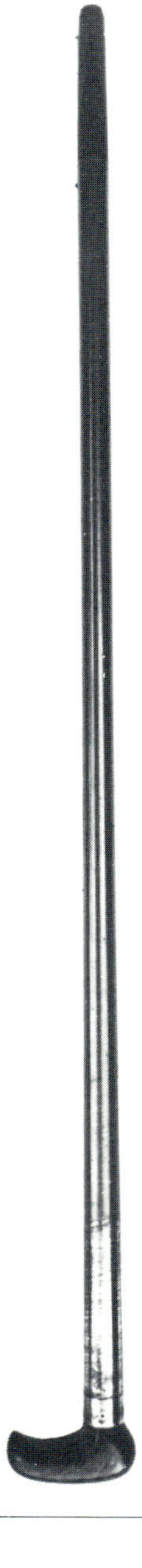

126 *Above* Detail of flintlock volley gun of Colonel Thomas Thornton with two sets of seven barrels. English, *c.*1790. Musée d'Armes de Liège.

127 *Far left* Flintlock walking-stick gun with shoulder stock. Mounted ready for use. English, *c.*1815. Private collection.

128 *Left* The gun converted for use as a walking stick.

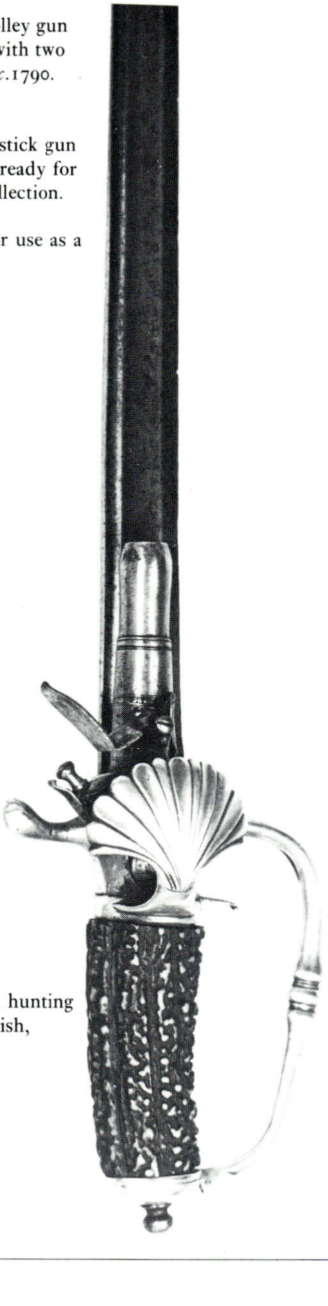

129 *Right* Detail of a combined hunting sword and flintlock pistol. English, *c.*1730. Private collection.

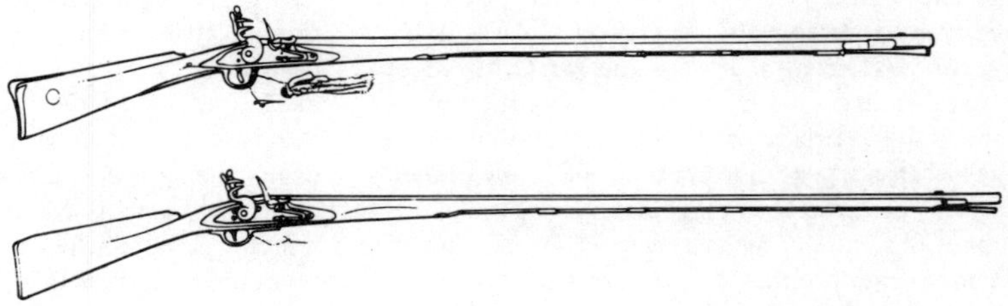

Flintlock trade guns. Belgian, nineteenth century. Tower of London Armouries.

A final form of fixed flintlock 'gun' designed to protect its owner from intruders or at least to warn him of their presence was the simple alarm gun. These devices fired no bullet but did set off a charge of powder by flintlock ignition. In some instances these alarms were activated by trip wires, but in others they depended upon more complicated mechanisms. Some were even incorporated into door or chest locks so that they would fire if a key were inserted and turned in what would seem, to the uninitiated, to be the proper way. In rare instances such lock-guns might fire a lethal charge, but in most cases they simply sounded a warning.

Last, but by no means least, among the specialised arms of the flintlock era were the trade guns designed for barter with the American Indian or the African native. Almost from the beginning of contact between the European and the aborigine there developed a trade in firearms despite sporadic efforts to ban or control it. Few of civilisation's goods were so highly prized by primitive people as the gun. It would separate him from his furs, his ivory, or his captive enemies more quickly than almost anything else, and so the Europeans were quick to take advantage of this situation.

In North America guns began to find their way into Indian ownership via the trade route early in the 1600s, but the numbers were small until the flintlock became standard towards the middle of the century. Thereafter the gun trade became brisk. At first any sort of gun was used for the purpose–as long as it could be acquired cheaply enough for a good profit. Then the Indian began to make known his preference for light pieces that he could carry through the woods more easily than the heavy muskets favoured by the colonists. By 1700 light fowling pieces of 0·56 in to 0·61 in calibre and 42 in to 48 in barrels were most popular among both French and British traders. About the middle of the century English fur companies and gunmakers produced a standard trade gun, and after 1763 when Great Britain gained control over most of North America it became almost universal.

This standard English trade gun is known by several names to collectors today. Most often it is called the 'North-West gun' or the 'Hudson's Bay gun' after the most prominent trading companies. Sometimes it is also called the 'Hudson's Bay fuke' (a corruption of fusil) or 'Mackinaw gun' after another fur trading company. Such trade guns are easily recognisable pieces. They are light with stock and barrel fastened together by pins. Especially characteristic are cast brass side plates shaped like dragons or sea serpents and large full trigger-guards, big enough for a man with a glove to insert his finger with ease. The ramrod pipes are ribbed, and the brass buttplate on the early specimens is thin and fastened by nails. The barrels are octagonal at the breech, round in the chase. The calibres are approximately 0·59 in and the barrel length ranges between 36 in and 48 in. About 1798 shorter barrels of 30 in were introduced and quickly became popular. A few better-quality flintlocks were made for trade or gifts to the Indians also. These were about 0·60 in calibre and distinguished by light engraving on the brass furniture, a silver escutcheon plate with an Indian head engraved upon it, and a good-quality flintlock with a roller bearing for the feather-spring. Since almost all known specimens of these better guns bear the broad arrow indicating government ownership, it is assumed that they were made for special presents to influential Indian leaders. In addition the Liège trade fabricated vast quantities of trade guns of common pattern, and the French also produced some. From *c.*1800 the Americans entered the market for their own Indian trade.

Even after the development of the percussion lock, and indeed of cartridge arms, the American Indian continued to prefer the Hudson's Bay flintlock. Caps and cartridges had to be purchased from traders. An Indian could make his own flint if necessary. Also a flintlock was easier to load on horseback than a percussion arm with its small cap. Thus the flintlock Indian trade gun continued in active commerce until the 1870s. Throughout its entire history it changed only slightly in the shortening of the barrel and in the switch to cast buttplates fastened by screws which occurred towards the middle of the nineteenth century. The Indian himself, of course, made many alterations in the gun once it was in his possession. Often he shortened the barrel still more for ease in use on horseback, and frequently he removed the buttplate to salvage the useful brass for some other purpose. Decorations of brass-headed tacks and rawhide wrappings completed the adaptation of the piece to his taste.

Central and South America created a different demand for trade guns because the game to be hunted differed and the objects of trade were mainly agricultural. Also the Spanish and Portugese were somewhat more reluctant to allow firearms to pass into the possession of the natives. Nevertheless some trade guns were fabricated for use there. Mostly they were cheap, light single- and double-barrelled fowling pieces manufactured in Birmingham or Liège. A few of the higher quality pieces boasted carved Indian heads on their stocks, but the others were indistinguishable except for their small bore and their lightness.

Africa offered ivory, spices, and above all the lure of slaves for the American markets, and so a commerce in guns developed at an early date. One English company obtained a Royal charter for the African trade as early as 1662, and the commerce flourished for more than a century. Even after the slave trade ended, there was sufficient profit to maintain a healthy trade with the Dark Continent. Guns figured among the standard items of exchange perhaps from the very beginning. Nothing is known about the design of the earliest of the firearms manufactured for shipment to Africa except that they were of exceptionally poor quality. During the first half of the eighteenth century, however, two distinctive types seem to have developed. These were designated 'male' and 'female', probably in reference to the gender of the slave they were designed to purchase. The male gun was of reasonable quality, usually being a reconditioned musket of early vintage or a newly assembled piece made up from surplus military parts. The female model, on the other hand, was a light gun with an exceptionally long barrel and a sharply curved 'fat bellied' stock of a pattern popular at the very beginning of the eighteenth century. Some of the barrels of such female trade guns were as much as 5 ft long, and the stocks of both types were often decorated with red paint, brass-headed tacks or even mirrors.

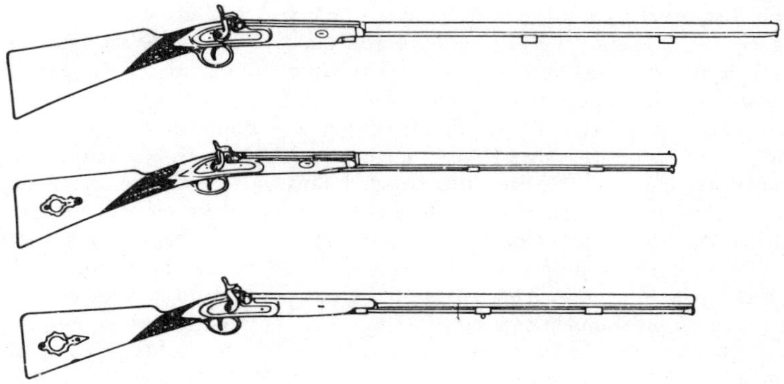

Muzzle-loading percussion trade guns, the lower two with butt-traps. English (Birmingham), *c.*1860. Museum of Science and Industry, Birmingham.

Many of these African trade guns were produced in England with Birmingham as the centre of manufacture. Hundreds of thousands were produced in Belgium also, however, and the makers of Liège utilised the surplus parts of guns from all parts of the world. As late as 1900, for instance, 50,000 obsolete percussion muskets left over from the American Civil War were shipped to Belgium for conversion to flintlocks for the African trade. Then World War I broke out. In its wake a different Africa emerged. The League of Nations established protectorates to replace many of the older colonies. New policies and attitudes developed in others. Trade methods and goods changed, and the old style trade gun vanished. With it the flintlock disappeared as a working arm. It is still being manufactured for hobbyists, but its era as a serious weapon at last was finished.

CHAPTER FIVE

The Percussion System

H. L. Blackmore

85-114 131 135-6 One of the first writers to deal with the principles of firearm construction, Giuliano Bossi, described in 1625[1] the various ways in which the gunmakers of his day had endeavoured to increase the range of their guns. Different types of touch-holes, chambers, breech-plugs and subsidiary barrels had all been tried with varying degrees of success. But he discerned that the basic principle of them all was simply to make all the powder of the charge ignite before the bullet left the muzzle. An even better way of achieving this, according to Bossi, was to fortify the gunpowder with antimony or a mercuric precipitate; and he noted with some satisfaction that:

> if you want to make a great shot mix in the charge of powder two or three grains of powdered gold precipitated with Aqua Fortis adulterated with sal ammoniac and congealed with oil of tartar. In France this powder is called the Fart of the Devil; because the spirits of these waters which are united with that gold have such power and strength to be positively astonishing. Because if you take ten grains of that powder and put them on a wooden table of no great strength, then set fire to it as you would ordinary powder, it will make more noise than a well-charged musket when it is fired, and have an effect which runs against nature. In so much that fire by its very nature flies upwards and seeks the air, but this fire strikes downwards and seeks the bowels of the earth, and breaks the table which is a perfectly true fact. The gun barrels that are fired with this gold must be strong and if you put in more than three grains there is a risk that they will burst.

Bossi's explosive powder was one of several known by the historic name of 'fulminating gold'. Samuel Pepys in his *Diary* for 11 November 1663 also noted the strange effect of this explosive material.

> Nov 11, 1663.
>
> At noon to the Coffee-house, where with Dr Allen some good discourse about physick and chymistry. And among other things I telling him what Dribble the German Doctor do offer of an instrument to sink ships; he tells me that which is more strange that something made of gold which they call in Chymistry *Aurum Fulminans* a grain I think he said of it put into a silver spoon and fired, will give a blow like a musquett, and strike a hole through the silver spoon downward without the least force upward.

Another fulminate, that of silver, was also known in the seventeenth century, and the German alchemist Johann Kunckel (1630-1703) is credited with the first preparation of fulminate of mercury. All these fulminates, however, were not only difficult to isolate but possessed a dangerous sensitivity to friction and shock, so that at first no practical use could be made of them as explosives. Nevertheless, throughout the seventeenth and eighteenth centuries, scientists persisted with their attempts to augment the power of gunpowder with a fulminating or some similarly acting chemical. In 1788 the French gunpowder factory at Essones was placed at the disposal of the chemist Claude Berthollet for the manufacture of a gunpowder composed of potassium chlorate, sulphur and charcoal. Although Berthollet was aware of the detonating qualities of the first chemical, safety precautions were not sufficient and the experiments were brought to an end by a disastrous explosion.[2]

It was not until Edward Howard, a Fellow of the Royal Society in London, published in 1800[3] the properties and preparation of mercury fulminate in great detail that the first real steps in the exploitation of fulminates could be taken. Howard's own experiments, like those of his predecessors, were directed mainly towards the successful employment of the fulminates in guns as the main propulsive power. In trials held at Woolwich for the Board of Ordnance, however, it was quickly established that no cannon

1 This was the year when his first book *Breve Trattato d' Alcune Inventione*, etc. was published in Antwerp. Wirt Gerrare in his *Bibliography* suggests that a MS version was in existence in 1616.

2 Deane's *Manual of Fire-arms*, London 1858, pp. 78-9.

3 *Philosophical Transactions of the Royal Society of London*, 1800, Pt. 1, pp. 204-33.

could withstand the explosion of a charge of mercurial powder necessary to project its shot. The experimenters failed completely to appreciate that the fulminates could be used as an effective means of setting off gunpowder. As far as small arms were concerned Howard described how a gun belonging to 'Mr Keir, an ingenious artist of Camden Town' was charged with thirty-four grains of fulminate instead of the normal charge of sixty-eight grains of gunpowder. When fired from the shoulder, Keir was not hurt but the patent breech of the gun, which was 0·4 in thick all round, was torn open and flawed in many directions, and the gold touch-hole driven out.

Such results and another premature explosion which destroyed his apparatus and severely injured him were enough to make Howard give up; or as he wryly put it, 'I must confess, I shall feel more disposed to prosecute other chemical subjects.' But other men were prepared to carry on his work, and one of these was the Reverend Alexander John Forsyth (1768-1843), the Minister of Belhelvie in Aberdeenshire, who had been following the experiments with great interest and had contributed an article 'On certain useful properties of the Oxygenated Muriatic Acid' to Nicholson's *Journal of Natural Philosophy* in July 1799.

As a keen sportsman Forsyth was well aware of the disadvantages of the flintlock – the uncertainty of the spark, a priming all too easily affected by damp, and, not the least, the time-lag between the ignition of the priming and that of the main charge. The interval of time which followed the tell-tale puff of smoke arising from the priming-pan was often long enough to enable the game to take warning and escape. With this in mind Forsyth set out to prove that the detonation of a fulminate or other percussion powder would not only ignite a charge of gunpowder but would do it so quickly that the two explosions would be coincident. By 1805 he had achieved this objective and had also managed to devise a percussion lock which could be used with safety on all types of gun.[4]

Several experimental locks were to be constructed but in its final form the Forsyth lock could be made by a simple conversion of an existing flintlock. No alteration was made to the interior of the flintlock but the priming-pan and steel were removed and replaced by a round plug with an internal channel leading into the touch-hole. Rotating round this plug was a steel box shaped like a small flat vase or scent bottle. The long neck portion contained a powder magazine sufficient for approximately twenty-five to thirty charges of priming. The other end held a sprung striking-pin. The scent bottle was first rotated so that the magazine was on top and deposited a few grains of percussion powder into a cavity on top of the plug. Then it was reversed so that the striker was in position just above the priming cavity. A hammer substituted for the old flintlock cock could then be pulled back and released

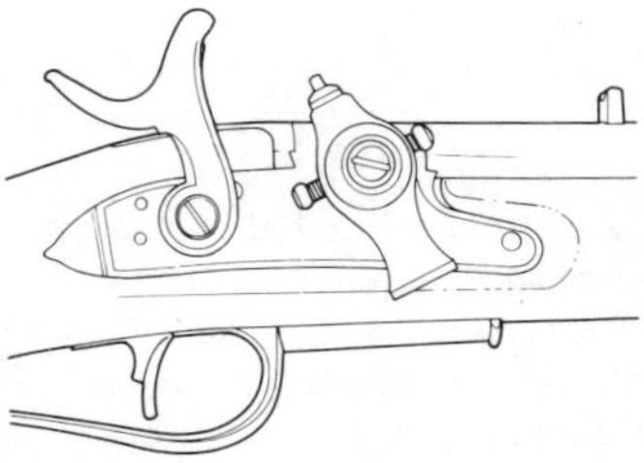

Detail of Forsyth's 1st standard percussion lock on a Baker cavalry rifle. English, *c.*1806. Tower of London Armouries.

by the trigger to hit the striker and detonate the charge.

Early in 1806, with the encouragement of his cousins, Henry and James Brougham, Forsyth brought his lock to London where he was introduced to Sir Joseph Banks and, finally, Lord Moira, the Master General of the Ordnance. The latter, perceiving the military potential of such a lock, suggested that Forsyth should continue his experiments in the Tower of London with official assistance in order 'to construct a Lock that would inflame a charge of Gunpowder with certainty which should be secure against damp and be used effectually and safely by the most awkward person.' Unfortunately the negotiations between the Master General and the inventor were conducted with the utmost secrecy so that no note of the proceedings was entered in the books of the Board of Ordnance, and the only official accounts of what transpired are to be found in a file of papers now in the Public Record Office, London.[5] This consists of Forsyth's letters and petitions for reward for his services written in the 1840s when he was over seventy and with his memory somewhat impaired, together with a précis of the affair composed by Ordnance officers who had no first-hand knowledge of the matter. Both sides of the story therefore must be accepted with some reserve.

Before the experiments began an unofficial agreement seems to have been reached between Lord Moira and Forsyth's legal adviser, Henry Brougham (later Lord Chancellor), to the effect that Forsyth

4 See W. Keith Neal & D. H. L. Back, *Forsyth & Co: Patent Gunmakers*, London, 1969, pp. 82 *et seq.*

5 Ordnance Inventions W.O. 44/625 No. 277.

should be given leave of absence from his ministry and an assistant appointed in his place, paid for by the Government. Any reward was to depend to a large extent on the saving of gunpowder that could take place if and when the lock was brought into government use. The first part of the agreement was honoured straight away and in July 1806 Forsyth was given an advance of £100 towards his own personal expenses. But when work commenced in the Tower Forsyth met with immediate difficulties. The Ordnance armourers viewed the new lock with distrust, and laboratory assistants seemed unable or unwilling to produce sufficient detonating powder, so that in the end Forsyth was obliged to do most of the work himself, helped by a civilian gunmaker, Joseph Vicars. The latter was hired specially for the occasion.

A gun-lock and a lock for a 3-pounder cannon were eventually produced and these were put to

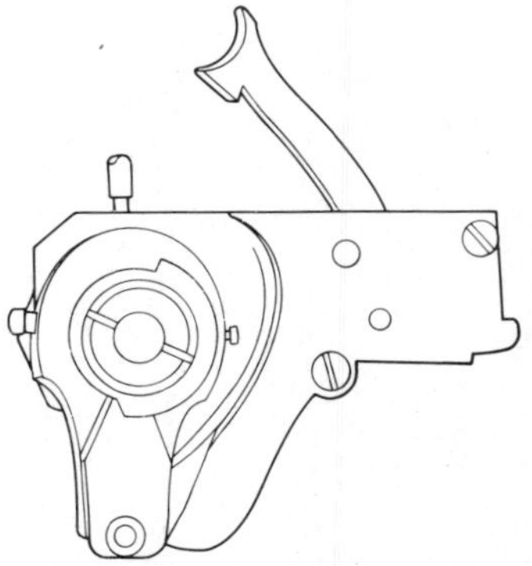

Detached experimental percussion lock for a cannon by Forsyth, *c.*1806. Tower of London Armouries.

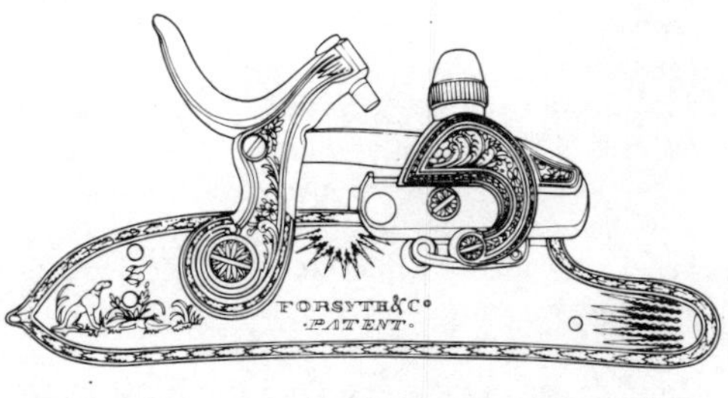

Forsyth's sliding-magazine fulminating-power lock, *c.*1813. The magazine is linked to the hammer.

trial by Colonel Thomas Blomefield, the Inspector of Artillery at Woolwich. While there is no official account of the result, Forsyth, in one of his petitions, explains that as he was then 'in a great measure unacquainted with the principle or rather the mechanical construction of the Percussion Lock upon which the saving of the Gunpowder depended, the experiment in a great measure failed and was reported to the Board of Ordnance as a failure'. He had been working on the assumption that a small charge of gunpowder fired by percussion was as powerful as a larger charge ignited by a flintlock. When the lock was tried on a musket, however, no such advantage was apparent.

Nevertheless, Forsyth was asked to continue and in March 1807 was given another £300 towards his expenses. At the same time he was asked–not unreasonably–to give some details of his outlay. Complying with this request, on the 29 April Forsyth sent in the following bill:

To paid the Workman appointed by the Superintendent at the Tower to assist in the experiments–Wages at 3 guineas per Week, from 9th January to 10th April–Rent of Shop for same time at 7/- per week, and expense of Materials used	£58.18.6
Stipend for one year paid to the Assistant by Lord Moira's desire....	£145. 0.0
My expenses in London for 1 year and expense going and returning from Aberdeenshire last Autumn, in order to arrange some matters with the Presbytery, and to obtain leave of absence	£400. 0.0
	£603.18.6

The balance of £203.18*s.* 6*d.* due to him was in fact paid in August of the same year and there appears to be no justification for his later statements that 'no remuneration was given him by Government, and even the promises as to his Clerical Assistant were not fulfilled'.

It is probable that at this point Forsyth realised that whatever the merits of his locks they would not achieve recognition in the military field. In sending in his bill he also enclosed a formal disclaimer from any official reward–'However much he may think himself entitled to remuneration from Government for his Invention, and for the time during which these experiments entirely occupied him begs permission to state that for the present he will bring forward no claim on that hand as the Hon Board of Ordnance had not thought proper to make any use of his invention.' This in effect cleared the way for the full application of a Patent (No. 3032) which he had been previously granted on 11 April, and which the Ordnance would have impeded had they adopted his invention. Not long after this a final severance with the authorities was made when a new Master General was appointed and Forsyth was notified that the official experiments were regarded as terminated.

It is probable that in all these moves Forsyth was acting on the astute legal advice of Henry Brougham. Certainly the wording of his Patent was most effective and it was drafted in such a way that it could be held to cover all methods of 'Discharging or Giving Fire to Artillery and all other Firearms, Mines, Chambers, Cavities and Places in which Gunpowder or other combustible Matter is or may be put for the Purpose of Explosion.' In 1808 he established a gunmaking business in London (Forsyth Patent Gun Company) in partnership with James Brougham and the *Morning Post* for 23 December carried this advertisement;

> To Sportsmen. The Patent Gunlock invented by Mr Forsyth is to be had at No. 10 Piccadilly, near the Haymarket. To those who may be unacquainted with the excellence of this invention are informed that the inflammation is produced without the assistance of flint and is much more rapid than in the common way. The Lock is so constructed as to render it impervious to water, or damp of any kind, and may in fact be fired under water.

The last may seem an extravagant claim, but, in spite of the Ordnance's adverse report, there is no doubt that when the lock was properly made and handled it was extremely effective and a great improvement over the flintlock. The sporting world was not slow to appreciate this and the following year the gunmaker Innes of Edinburgh (where Forsyth had also lodged a Patent), advertising in the Edinburgh *Evening Courant* of 6 May, was able to advise his clients that he could 'recommend with confidence double and single guns made on the Forsyth principle'.

The idea quickly spread to Europe where it was seized upon enthusiastically by the French gunmakers. The report made by Benjamin Delessert[6] to the *Société d'Encouragement pour l'Industrie Nationale* describes how the Parisian gunmaker François Prélat ('armurier fort habile et intelligent') received a Government licence to import a number of the Forsyth guns. Prélat also patented an exact copy of the lock on 17 April 1810. The following June another Parisian gunmaker Le Page took out a patent for a number of locks employing magazines of percussion powder with attendant strikers usually in a separate housing. In September of the same year de l'Étrange, a gunmaker of Versailles, patented several improved versions of these locks. The scene was thus quickly set for a great spate of experiments and inventions connected with the new percussion action, and the benevolent authorities in Paris were happy to set their seal on any new mechanical application of the system.

In Scotland and England it was another story. For many years Forsyth remained faithful to his original scent-bottle lock, and armed with his patent attempted to suppress any new kind of percussion lock. In 1811 he obtained an injunction against one of his own workmen, Joseph Vicars, who had invented a sliding magazine lock and had started a business of his own, prohibiting him from making percussion locks. Many of the great London gunmakers like Durs Egg, Joseph Manton, and Ezekiel Baker, proud of their achievements in the perfection of the flintlock, were at first scornful of the new lock, but on 29 February 1816 Joseph Manton was granted an English patent for a new kind of percussion lock in which the percussion powder or pellet was contained in a detachable and reloadable tube or plug, which fitted into the head of the hammer. With this lock there was no danger of a powder magazine blowing up, but there was the inconvenience of being obliged to carry spare plugs, a fresh one being necessary for each shot.

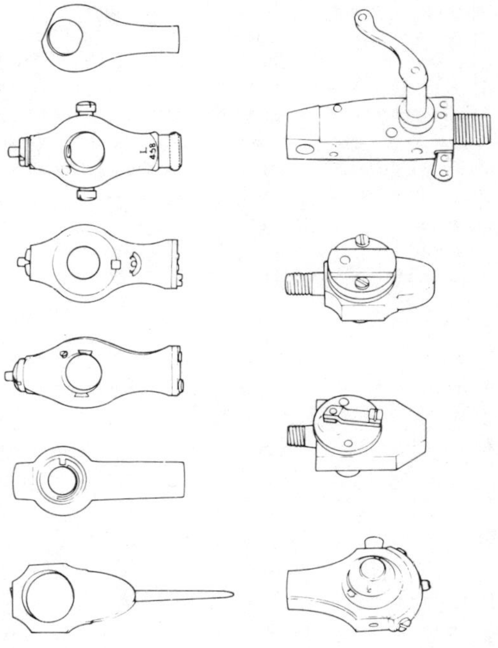

Various experimental examples of Forsyth's patent scent-bottle lock. English, 1806. Tower of London Armouries.

Immediately, Forsyth sought an injunction against Manton and began a series of legal actions which culminated in a hearing at the Court of King's

6 M. A. Paulin-Desormeaux, *Manuel de l'Armurier*, Paris, 1832, pp. 224-7.

Bench on 12 December 1818.[7] The defendant sought to justify his patent on the grounds that mechanically it was different from that of Forsyth's, but was told that it was a 'clumsy imitation', and lost his plea.[8] Encouraged by this case Forsyth took action against three other gunmakers in 1819–Levier, Isaac Riviere and Collinson Hall. The last-named, whose lock was awarded a silver medal by the Society for the Encouragement of Arts, Manufactures and Commerce in the same year, had gone to great lengths to perfect a percussion disc or patch. This was formed by two round, paper discs with a globule of detonating powder in between. The powder was actually a paste made of oxymuriate of potash, flowers of sulphur, powdered charcoal and gum arabic. The disc or patch was coated with wax and was inserted in the nose of the hammer where it was held by the adherence of the waxed surface. The general idea of the lock, whose hammer hit a metal cone or nipple screwed on to the barrel, was a direct copy of a lock patented in Paris by Prélat the previous year. Nevertheless the court ignored all this and held that Hall's lock infringed the Forsyth patent. A point which Hall had tried to maintain in his defence against Forsyth was that not only was his a different lock but that, in any case, the Forsyth lock was not a perfect piece of apparatus and had had to be modified outside the terms of its patent.

It is interesting to note what this modification was and the circumstances of its adoption. Forsyth in his patent had laid stress on the fact that his lock was not only water-tight but air-tight ('I do close the touch-hole or vent by means of a plug or sliding piece or other fit piece of metal or suitable material or materials, so as to exclude the open air, and to prevent any sensible escape of the blast or explosive gas or vapour outwards . . .'). In the legal disputes which followed Forsyth's counsel made much of this exclusion of the air as part of the proof of superiority of the Forsyth lock over its competitors. But when the lock was fitted to a rifle an unforeseen difficulty arose. The first to notice this apparently was the notorious Baron Random de Berenger. In his *Helps and Hints* published in 1835, he describes how in 1811-12, while practising at the Montpelier Shooting Ground in London, he encountered trouble in loading 'as my rifle had one of Forsyth's patent magazine percussion locks, and which, not allowing air thus rarefied to escape through the vent, caused my ball and ramrod to spring upwards again, not unlike the piston of an air-gun condenser'. He goes on to describe how he eventually persuaded Forsyth's foreman, Charles Uther, to drill a small air-hole or ventilator, which was found to improve the whole performance of the gun. Eventually these ventilators were fitted to all the Forsyth guns although this was, as de Berenger sarcastically commented, 'in hazardous deviation from the original grounds upon which the patentee founded his claims of the superiority of his invention'.

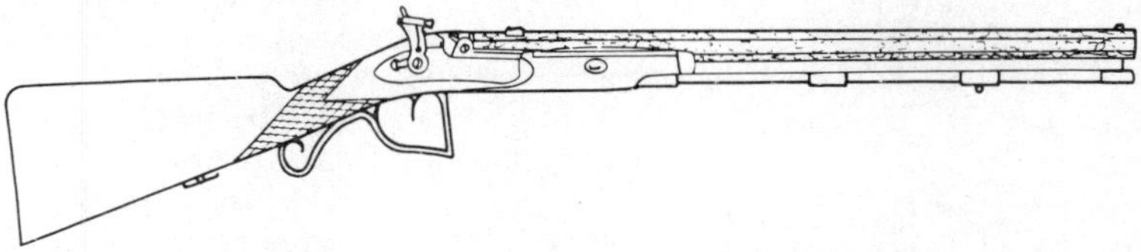

Rifle with Damascus-'twist' barrel and Joseph Manton's pellet lock, *c.*1830. Tower of London Armouries.

However, technical details did not seem to bother the courts, and so the other gunmaker Riviere tried a new tactic. He sought to prove that Forsyth was not the originator of the percussion lock, and produced witnesses who asserted that a lock on the same principle as Forsyth's had been invented by a clergyman called Butler, who resided at Okeford, near Blandford, Dorsetshire. This gentleman had communicated his ideas to two friends and a gunmaker called Symonds a short time previous to the dates when Forsyth took out and enrolled his patent. This plea met with as little success as the others, for the Lord Chief Justice gave a ruling that 'though many men might discover the same thing simultaneously, he alone was entitled to benefit by it who first communicated it to the public'.

In spite of the restrictions imposed by Forsyth, gunmakers in England, as in other countries, continued to experiment with, and to design, other forms of percussion locks. As well as the patch or disc detonator already mentioned, there were percussion pellets in which the fulminate was held together with wax or coated with iron oxide. Both types of detonators, however, because of their small size, were inconvenient to handle, and the pellets, in particular, had to be carefully stored against deterioration. The tube lock patented by Joseph Manton in 1818 was an attempt to overcome both

7 For a full account of this and other law suits see Neal & Back, *Forsyth & Co.*, pp. 171 *et seq.*; idem, *The Mantons: Gunmakers*, London, 1966, pp. 173 *et seq.*

8 *The Times*, 14 December 1818.

these disadvantages. This type of primer consisted of a small tube of copper less than an inch long filled with fulminate. In its most popular form the lock was arranged so that part of the tube could be thrust into the touch-hole, while the rest of it lay on a flat pan, held in position for the hammer blow by a

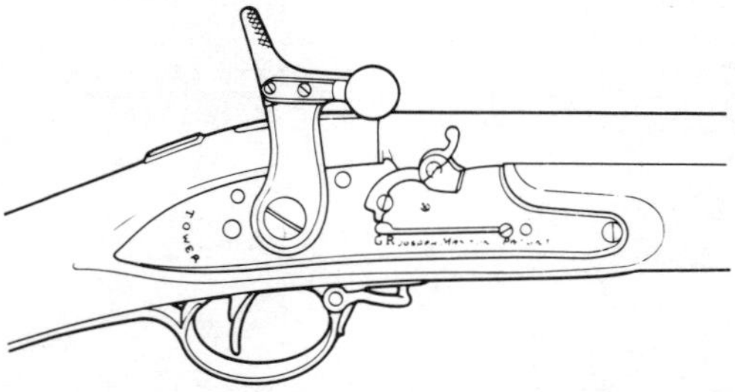

Detail of a New Land musket experimentally converted to a tube-lock system by Joseph Manton in 1834. A circular metal guard is screwed to the nose of the hammer to prevent the tube flying out sideways on discharge. Tower of London Armouries.

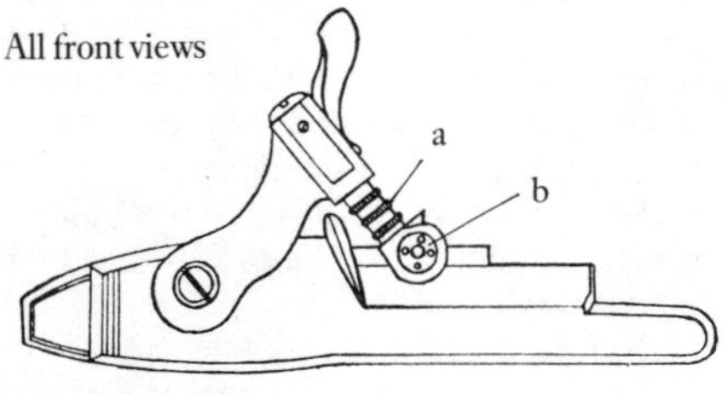

PILL OR PELLET LOCK

This has a percussion hammer which operates in the normal way but has a detachable tubular extension (a) containing a floating firing-pin which, when the hammer is down, coincides with a vent in the 'anvil' (b) on top of the lockplate. A pellet of detonating compound is placed in the tube, and when the hammer falls on the anvil this is ignited, and the flame passes through the vent into the powder charge. Patented by Joseph Manton of London in 1816 (Patent No. 3985). *The drawing is copied from the one in the patent specification.*

TUBE LOCK

This again has a percussion hammer which operates in the normal way but has a chisel-shaped striking edge. The detonator is a thin copper tube containing fulminate which fits into a vent in the side of the chamber, where it is secured by a hinged holder (a). The system was patented by Joseph Manton of London in 1818 (Patent No. 4285). *From the cock of a gun by Manton in the Tower of London Armouries (No. XII 1614).*

spring or cover. The main trouble with this lock, which gave excellent ignition, was the tendency of the tube to break and fly into the face of the shooter or his companion; a snag usually avoided by a shield fitted to the head of the hammer.

A logical development of the tube-lock was the tape-lock first patented in France in 1821 by Leboeuf de Valdehon. This, in effect, was another percussion magazine-lock, as the priming was contained in a long piece of straw which was housed underneath the barrel and was moved into position bit by bit, the hammer automatically cutting off a piece for each detonation. The *fusil de Valdehon* was quite an innovation as it was also a breech-loader and one of the first under-hammer guns.

What was to prove the most successful of all the percussion primings, the percussion cap, was a much simpler piece of apparatus. Shaped like a miniature top-hat and made of copper with the priming in the crown, it was placed on an iron cone or nipple screwed into the barrel and drilled with a communicating channel that led into the chamber of the barrel. Because of its universal adoption many gunmakers, writers and sporting personalities laid claim to its invention, and it is difficult now to decide who has the rightful claim.

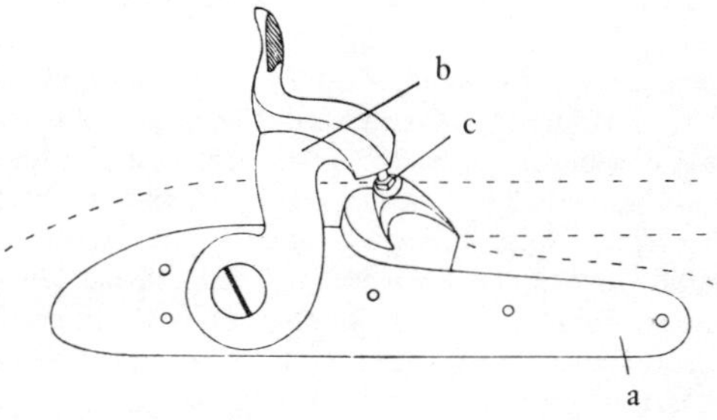

PERCUSSION LOCK
a Lockplate
b Cock (hammer)
c Nipple

Colonel Peter Hawker in the 6th Edition (1830) of his *Instructions to Young Sportsmen* describes the purchase of one of Joe Manton's pellet-lock guns in 1816 and his attempts to make a simplified version of it. He goes on:

> At last the plan of a perforated nipple and the detonating powder in the crown of a small cap occurred to me. I made a drawing of it, which I took to Joe. After having this explained, he said he would show me something in a few weeks' time; when, lo and behold! there was a rough gun altered precisely on my own plan! His factotum, poor old Asell, assured me that the whole job was done from my drawing. Thus Joe, who led the fashion for all the world, sent out a

> few copper-cap guns, and I know with some degree of reluctance. The trade, finding that he had then deviated from his own patent, adopted this plan; and it proved to answer so well that we now see it in general circulation.

A likely story, but it is significant that in the previous edition of Hawker's book, published in 1826, there is no mention of this incident.

Another claimant was the gunmaker Joseph Egg who, for many years, printed on his trade labels and engraved on his guns the legend 'Inventor of the Copper Cap'. His claim is supported by the fact that a percussion copper-cap musket of his making was tried by the Board of Ordnance at Woolwich in June 1820–the first authenticated trial.[9] In 1842, Captain Lacy, in *The Modern Shooter*,[10] confirmed that Egg had made the earliest claim to the invention and that he had had Egg's personal assurance that he had made the first copper cap 'out of an old penny-piece'. He goes on, however, to recount how James Purdey, who had been Forsyth's leading man in his early days, had told him that he was the real inventor.

> I was, said Purdey, sitting one evening with a friend named Prior, who had just returned from a very wet day's shooting; the detonating patches were then in vogue, and Prior complained that he found them too much exposed to be waterproof, and suggested the idea of enclosing them in some substance impervious to wet. Yes, replied I, inverting an empty tumbler, a metallic cap in this form, with a perforated peg to communicate with the charge. The day following, continued Purdey, at the request of Prior, I set out to work to realize this new idea, and, from the *tag* of an old umbrella, produced a brass cap, which was handed about for some time, and, a year or two afterwards, Mr Egg brought out the copper cap.

Another version of how Egg acquired the idea of the copper cap, and one probably nearer the truth, is given by Henry Wilkinson in his *Engines of War*:[11]

> Mr Egg, I believe, purchased it from Mr Roantree, a gun-maker at Barnard Castle, Durham, who had it from a workman employed by Mr Joshua Shaw, now residing at Philadelphia. I can trace it no further. Mr Shaw assured me that in 1814 he invented a steel cap, which, when fired, was retained to be primed again; that in 1815 he made a pewter cap, which was thrown away after using; and lastly, that in 1816, he used a copper cap precisely similar to those at present employed. He made application for a patent in England, but the solicitor to whom it was referred, decided that it could not be obtained without infringing Forsyth's patent then in force.

Joshua Shaw, who seems to have the strongest claim of all to the invention of the copper cap, was born in Bellingborough, Lincolnshire in 1776. Apprenticed to a sign-painter he grew into an artist of some distinction, exhibiting in London and Bath. His step-father, however, was a plumber and glazier, and to this association can be traced Shaw's first English patent in 1815 which was for an improved 'Glazier's Diamond'. We have only got his word that he was at the same time experimenting with percussion caps, but it is by no means improbable.

In 1817 he emigrated to the USA, supposedly in order to patent his invention. But it has been suggested that the real reason was simply the pique of a temperamental artist, disgruntled with what he believed to be unfair treatment of his work in London.[12] On his arrival in America he is said to have applied for a patent and to have been refused because he had not been resident for two years; but what evidence there is shows that he was not granted a patent until 19 June 1822. This, according to the 1829 *Journal of the Franklin Institute*, was for an 'Improvement in Guns and Fire-arms, which improvement consists in a priming head and cap applied to guns and fire-arms, for the purpose of priming and giving them fire, by the means of percussion, fulminating or detonating powders.' No copy of this patent has survived in the US Patent Office but when, in 1844, Shaw began negotiations with the US Government for a reward for his invention of the percussion cap, the Commissioner of Patents signed an affidavit confirming its title. In 1847 Congress passed an Act granting him $18,000 and in the same year he published the story of his invention in *A Sketch or History of the Copper Cap*.

The only concrete fact that arises from all this is that Shaw was granted an American patent for a percussion cap in 1822. But by this date the percussion cap was already well known in Europe and had already been patented there. Some doubt must still remain therefore as to who was the real inventor of the copper cap.

It first appears in Europe in a patent granted to François Prélat of Paris on 28 July 1820. This was a supplementary or *certificat d'addition* to his patent of 29 July 1818, which covered a lock in which the hammer held a portion of detonating powder in its

9 D. W. Bailey, 'Joseph Egg, Joseph Manton, and the Percussion Trials of 1820', *J.A.A.S.*, VII, Sept. 1971, pp. 60-72.

10 R. Lacy, *The Modern Shooter*, London, 1842, p. 39.

11 Henry Wilkinson, *Engines of War*, London 1841, p. 78.

12 Lewis Winant, *Early Percussion Firearms*, London, 1961, pp. 45-50.

nose and detonated it on a nipple or peg screwed into the barrel. Following closely on this, on 22 September 1820, was the main patent of another Parisian gunmaker, Deboubert, whose percussion cap (*chapeau en cuivre*) was primed with silver fulminate. The percussion cap is not mentioned in an English patent until 1823 (No. 4861, John Day of Barnstaple), which is strange when one considers that the Forsyth patent became obsolete in 1821 and one would have expected a rush to patent the various percussion locks known to be in use by then.

In fact the only immediate reaction in 1821 was the patenting by William Webster and William Westley Richards of two improved versions of the Forsyth scent bottle lock. The inference is that at this date the copper cap was but one of a number of devices none of which had shown any great merit over its fellows. This is borne out by the variety

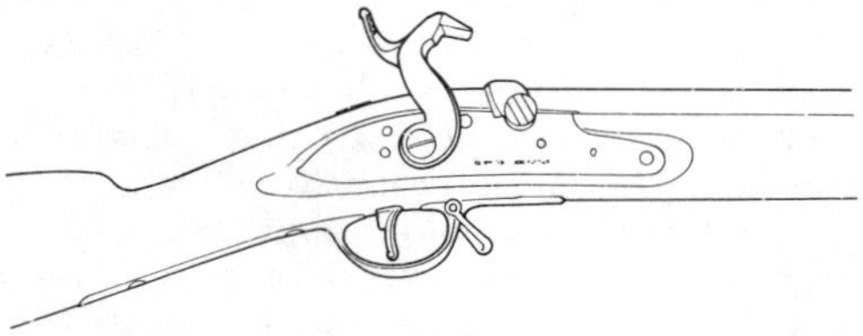

Detail of a Westley Richards tube-lock on a gun, *c.*1838. Tower of London Armouries.

of percussion lock patents taken out in France during 1820-1. As well as the cap locks of Prélat and Deboubert mentioned above, they were:

	Inventor	*Type*
1820	Gosset	disc
	Pottet	pellet and powder
1821	Moreau	pellet
	Dabat	pellet
	Pichereau	pellet
	Nicolas	powder
	de Valdehon	tape

At the same time several gunmakers were patenting modifications to the flintlock. There were simple conversions to a percussion lock like Puiforcat's French patent of 1821, or, as in the case of the 'Devolving Pan Lock', patented in England by Sampson Davis in 1822, locks which could be used with either flint or percussion ignition.

In a matter of two or three years, however, there was to be a drastic change. This is well illustrated by the treatment given to percussion primers by T. B. Johnson in his book *The Shooter's Companion*. In the first edition, published in London in 1819, although generous space is given to percussion locks and particularly to those of Forsyth and Manton, there is not one mention of a percussion cap. But in the second edition, published in 1823, the author not only spoke of copper caps with enthusiasm but prophesied that 'copper cap guns will unquestionably become general'.

To account for this sudden change of heart one must examine the work of the chemists and manufacturers responsible for the production of the percussion cap. In its early days it was an uncertain device. If the metal of the cap was too soft it would jam the hole in the nipple, if it was too brittle it was liable to fly into splinters with unpleasant results to the face of the sportsman. Another important point was the composition of the priming used in the caps. For some reason not readily apparent the use of fulminate of mercury had never gained any popularity, and the priming most favoured was a mixture of potassium chlorate, sulphur, charcoal, etc. – the so-called muriatic powder.[13] This varied in strength to a degree that the user never knew when he was going to get a soft misfire or a mighty bang which blew off the hammer. Another disadvantage of this type of primer was its strong corrosive effect (from the formation of potassium chloride) on the gun barrel and nipple.

In 1823, however, E. Goode Wright published his classic paper 'On the Substitution of Fulminating Mercury in place of the Detonating Compositions into which Chlorate of Potash enters as a Priming for Percussion Guns' in *The Philosophical Magazine and Journal*, and although some strong opposing views were forthcoming the manufacturing processes were immediately taken over and developed by the London chemist Frederick Joyce. In the following year, both in England and the United States of America, the new anti-corrosive caps received favourable publicity. The Franklin Institute of Philadelphia went so far as to hail them as a 'new discovery . . . made of a metallic preparation perfectly neutral' and Joshua Shaw wrote letters in their support. It is worth noting that in one letter dated 20 March 1829 he stated, 'I have been in the habit of using copper caps for at least thirteen years, and for the last seven years have manufactured and sold them at the rate of two millions annually.' In the space of a few years machines were produced to manufacture caps of standard size and weight in large quantities; the hammer of the percussion lock was hollowed out so that it formed a protective shield over the cap during firing, thus removing one source of complaint; and with these improvements the copper cap was soon recognised as the safest and surest of primers.

13 According to Deane's *Manual of Fire-arms* p. 89, Forsyth employed lycopodium, the highly inflammable powder contained in the spore cases of the club moss *Lycopodium clavatum*.

But there was no immediate rejection of all the other primers, for the small size of the cap still made it a difficult article to handle, and some gunmakers and inventors still held out hopes that one of the other primers in magazine form would prove a better proposition. Various attempts were made to improve the magazine powder-lock. In the Forsyth scent bottle lock the combined magazine and striker was obliged to rotate through 180° between the charging and striking position, and the movement of the hammer was independent. Most of the improvements were aimed at linking the two movements and reducing the time of charging. The most popular method, which was used by Forsyth himself, was to connect a sliding magazine to the hammer, the nose of which became the striker. When the hammer was pulled back the magazine slid back over a touch-hole, where it deposited the required priming. As the hammer descended the magazine was automatically pushed out of the way. According to Henry Wilkinson,[14] this action was the invention of Joseph Vicars, who, after his discharge by Forsyth, made the lock for the London gunmaker W. A. Beckwith. However, the action was patented in 1819 by Bruneel, a gunmaker of Lyons, France, and it was incorporated in a number of handsomely-decorated sporting guns and pistols by the Austrian gunmaker Joseph Contriner. In 1832 Colonel Francis Macerone writing in *Defensive Instructions for the People* was still recommending this type of lock as the best of the percussion magazine actions.

Another improvement on the Forsyth lock was the use of a swivelling magazine linked to the base of the hammer, so that the magazine moved in a small arc out of the way of the hammer as it fell. This lock was patented in France by Henri Pottet in 1820. A similar effect was achieved by the London gunmaker, William Green, who cut large teeth in the base of the hammer which engaged in opposing ones on the base of the swivelling magazine. Although the powder magazine lock scored over its competitors by the ease with which it could be made to deliver a number of shots with one filling, it suffered not only because of its complicated structure but because of the speedy deterioration of the percussion powder. In other primers the powder, whether muriatic or fulminate, could be weatherproofed by wax, varnish or gum arabic.

The percussion pellet treated in this way was particularly adaptable to magazine actions. In a lock patented by Joseph Egg in London in 1822 and in Paris in 1827, the pellets were confined in tubular magazines lying along the top of the barrel, being fed by gravity into the pan or touch-hole. A sliding cover protecting the pellet was withdrawn when the trigger was pressed. Joseph Manton's last patent of 1825 was also devoted to a pellet-lock with a tubular magazine, but it was too complicated, and Colonel Hawker prophesied correctly that 'it would not answer'. A magazine pellet-lock designed by a Winchester gunmaker T. H. Hayward, however, was considered sturdy enough in 1834 to take part in the trials organised by the British Ordnance department to choose a percussion lock for the British Army. Also in these trials was one of the few successful military single-shot pellet-locks. Invented by Joseph Manton and patented in 1834 by his son John Augustus (Joe was bankrupt at the time), the percussion pellet was contained in a wooden cone in the top of which was a striking pin. This construction overcame the difficulty of handling the tiny pellets individually but was discredited when it was found that the wooden holder was distorted by damp or heat.

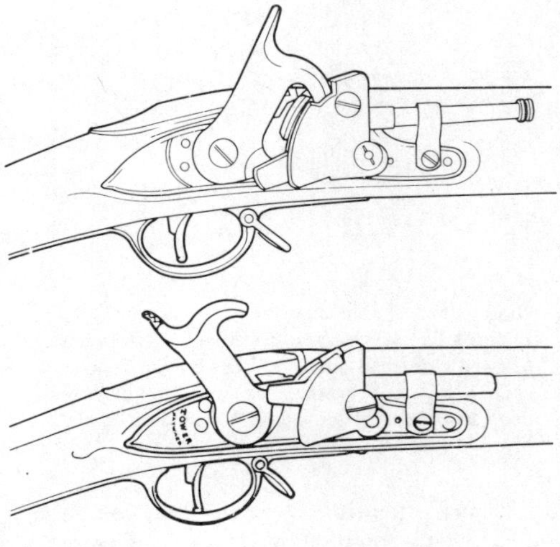

Details of Hayward's pellet-lock on a musket with hammer uncocked and cocked. English, *c.*1835. Tower of London Armouries.

In America the percussion pellet found a strong supporter in Dr Samuel Guthrie, one of the discoverers of chloroform. He, however, rebelled against the current trend and denounced the use of mercury fulminate on health grounds. In this he was supported by the eminent Belgian army physician Dr Van Broeck who warned against guns 'emitting mercurial vapours highly prejudicial to the health of the soldiers'.[15] Dr Guthrie's pills or pellets were composed of potassium chlorate mixed with gum

14 *Engines of War*, London, 1841, pp. 75-6.

15 Deane's *Manual of Fire-arms*, p. 89.

arabic and, with the help of some astute advertising, achieved considerable success. As a result there was a noticeable vogue for pill-lock guns, pistols, and even revolvers, in the USA during the 1830s. The simplicity of this primer was the main factor in its long life. As late as 1853 the brothers von Winiwarter

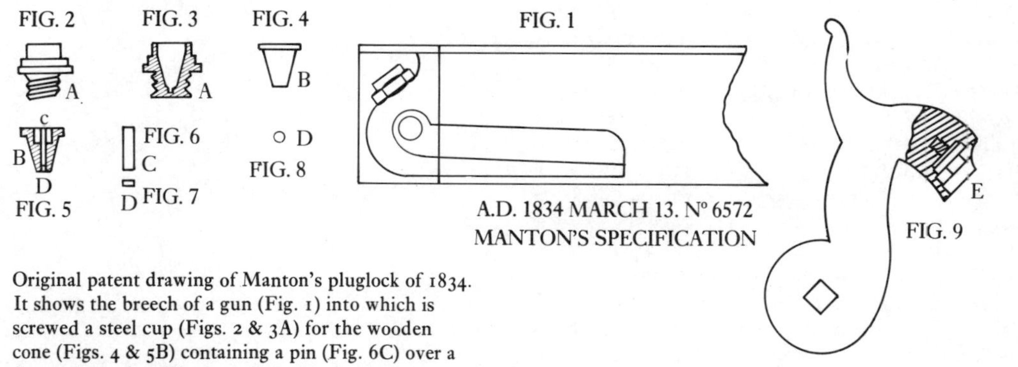

Original patent drawing of Manton's pluglock of 1834. It shows the breech of a gun (Fig. 1) into which is screwed a steel cup (Figs. 2 & 3A) for the wooden cone (Figs. 4 & 5B) containing a pin (Fig. 6C) over a detonating pellet (Figs. 7 & 8D). The head of the hammer contains a firing-pin (Fig. 9E)

of Vienna patented in England a complicated detonating composition which they advocated for use in pellet-locks.

The percussion-tube primer, because of its tendency to be blown out of the touch-hole, was probably the least liked of all the primers, although there was nothing wrong with its power of ignition. In a well-constructed lock, where it was held securely and covered on impact by a shield, it gave excellent results. The Austrian Army for this reason adopted a lock, invented by Giuseppe Console and modified by General Vincent Augustin, in which the priming tube was gripped by a heavy protective cover with a built-in striker. An unusual primer consisting of a steel tube of fulminate was patented by Westley Richards in 1831. This was placed vertically in a special nipple-like holder. The manufacturer laid emphasis on the ease with which it could be handled and 'the impossibility of unexploded material, or copper annoying the face and eyes – an inconvenience that often happens from the use of light, French, or badly manufactured caps'.[16]

While it was almost impossible to design a lock which incorporated a magazine of percussion tubes, the tape primer held out great possibilities in this sphere. The first of these locks was that patented by de Valdehon in 1821, but no specimen of it has been found and it is possible that the straw tube used to hold the priming proved to be impracticable. In 1834, however, the French urologist Charles Louis Stanislaus, Baron Heurteloup, designed a gun similar to the *fusil de Valdehon* in that the hammer had a combined cutting and detonating action on a long tube or tape of priming (*l'amorce continué*). Heurteloup's priming was encased in a tube of soft metal – an alloy of lead, zinc and tin – and was placed in the butt of the gun. The Heurteloup gun differed also in being a muzzle-loader and employing the normal side-lock. It was patented in France and England in 1834. The latter patent met with initial difficulties as it was discovered that a copy of the 1821 de Valdehon patent had been deposited in the British Museum Library, thus constituting a previous publication and invalidating the Heurteloup patent. An appeal was made to the Privy Council on the grounds that the de Valdehon invention had never been used and this was upheld by the passing of a special Act.[17]

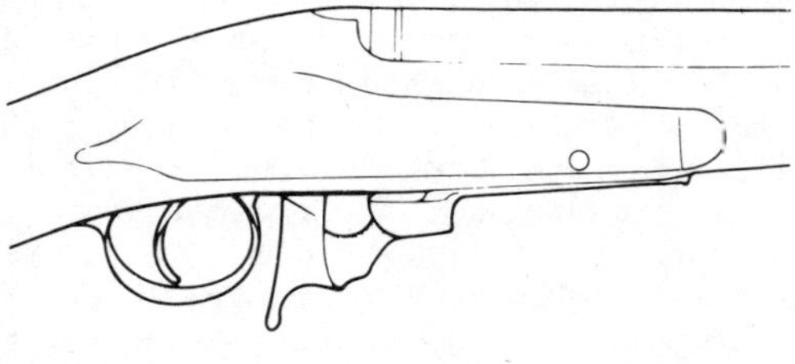

Heurteloup's under-hammer musket made for the 1837 trials. Tower of London Armouries.

As soon as the validity of his English patent had been established, Heurteloup unashamedly adopted several of the features of the *fusil de Valdehon*. His next model, although still a muzzle-loader, had an under-hammer action and the primer was placed under the barrel. An added refinement, removed

16 P. Hawker, *Instructions*, 9th edn., 1844, p. 85.

17 5 & 6 William IV c. 83.

from later models, was a toothed wheel which moved the primer automatically when the gun was cocked. He broadcast the virtues of this gun in a *Memoire sur les Fusils de Guerre* and gave it the intriguing name of *Koptipteur*.[18] Improved models were patented in France and in Scotland (1837), in Belgium (1838), in England (1839) and in the USA (1841). There were many apparent advantages to the *Koptipteur*. The under-hammer action was comparatively weather-proof and did not obscure the vision, and it was claimed that the upward blow of the hammer did not upset the aim as much as the conventional downward one. The tape priming was enough for seventy shots, it could be replaced in thirty seconds, and it was not so easily dislodged as other primings. These were all points which appealed to the military, and, in fact, a pamphlet was published in London in 1837 with the title *The Koptipteur and Copper Cap Muskets compared with respect to their efficiency for Military Service in every point of view*. But everything depended on the correct functioning of the gun under service conditions. The British authorities were not impressed and rejected the *Koptipteur* after trials in 1837 and 1842. However, it was adopted to a limited extent by the French, Belgian and Russian armies.

A Swedish version of the gun with a different type of under-hammer, invented by Major Gustaf Erik Fleetwood, the Director of the State Manufactory at Husquarna, in 1837, met with less success, the only known examples being three models which the inventor presented to the Danish King Frederick VI in 1838.

It is ironical that Heurteloup, who did not scruple to purloin other people's ideas – he was several times forced to publish disclaimers to his patents – was himself plagiarised in the end by an American dentist Dr Edward Maynard. The events leading to this were as follows. In 1839 a lock with a strip primer, coiled in a box in front of the touch-hole and detonated by a cutting and striking hammer *à la Koptipteur*, was patented in Paris by M. Martin. It could be easily fitted to the conventional side-lock, and Heurteloup was not slow to exploit its advantages. He incorporated it in another British patent of 1841 and in a Belgian patent of 1843 (under the name of Sigrist). A French patent on similar lines was taken out in 1842 by Augustin Thibert. There was, however, one great disadvantage with all these continuous primers, which were usually made with a strong chlorate of potash mixture. This was their susceptibility to a through-burning action, like that of a slow match, if the unspent portion of the tape was not fully isolated after the hammer blow.

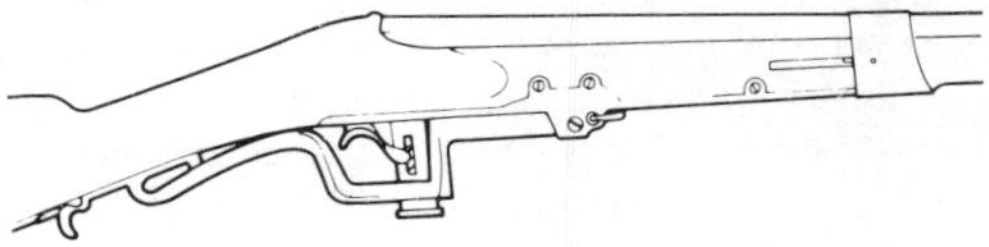

Percussion under-hammer gun with *Koptipteur* lock of Gustaf Fleetwood. Swedish, 1837. Tøjhusmuseet, Copenhagen.

This was where Dr Maynard came in. While utilising the general idea of the coiled primer on the lock, he designed a new form of tape and a lock to go with it. The Maynard primer consisted of a roll of two narrow strips of paper cemented together, enclosing small pellets of fulminating powder laid at regular intervals. This effectively stopped any tendency to through-burning although the action of the lock had to be carefully regulated to ensure that each pellet was properly seated for the hammer blow. Dr Maynard's first American patent taken out in 1845 refers to this as 'The mode of . . . measuring out the primers by the movement of the lock.'

As the paper primer took up much less room than the European metal tapes it could be comfortably hidden in a cavity cut in the lockplate between the hammer and the nipple. It was thrust on to the nipple from the movement of the hammer being cocked, either by a metal prong or 'finger', or by means of a cogged wheel. It was a much simpler and smaller device than any of the other automatic primers, and, once the initial teething difficulties had been overcome, the inventor was able to claim a number of very real advantages for his primer over the percussion cap. It was much cheaper, easier to make, faster to handle and safer to store and use.

Few people disagreed with the inventor, and the Maynard lock was fitted to muzzle-loaders and breech-loaders; flintlocks were converted to it; and even the smallest revolver was adapted to its use.

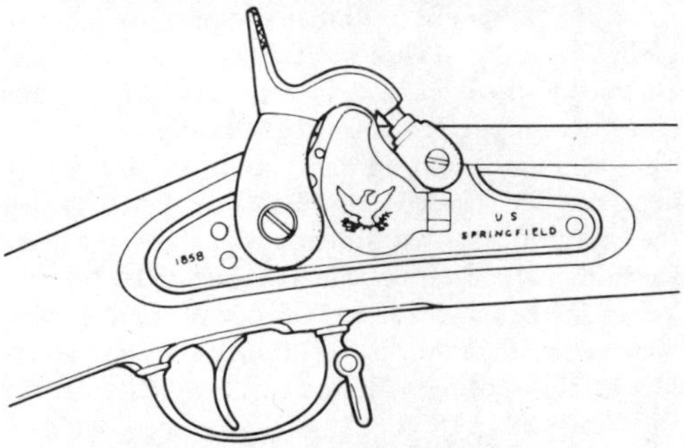

Detail of a Springfield Model 1855 rifle showing Maynard's tape primer. U.S.A., 1858. Winchester Gun Museum, Cody, Wyoming.

18 Derived from the Greek words for 'to cut' and 'to strike'.

The Maynard Gun Company, Chicopee Falls, and the Maynard Arms Company, Washington, were founded to manufacture special Maynard firearms, and, in 1854, after several thousand military arms had been made under his licence, the inventor sold the rights of his patent to the US Government for $50,000.

It was inevitable that he should have his imitators. In 1856 Lieutenant J. N. Ward patented in the USA and in England a lock in which the Maynard tape primer was employed in a magazine fitted into the head of the hammer. The Ward 'Priming-Cock'

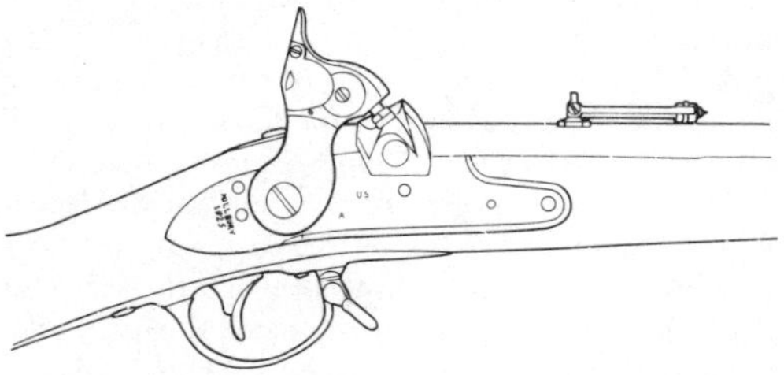

Detail of U.S. musket fitted with J. H. Ward's patent primer, *c.*1856; lock 1825. Winchester Gun Museum, Cody, Wyoming.

had a wide, heavy head with a recess on one side containing the roll of priming, which was brought into position by a spur or ratchet on the other side. A small number of US muskets were converted to this primer in 1859.

Another group of automatic primers to enjoy great success in the USA employed the percussion disc which had met with little favour in Europe. But whereas in England, France and Germany the disc primer had rarely been made of anything other than paper or cardboard, in 1852, the American gunmaker, Christian Sharps, patented an automatic primer using tiny discs of copper, each holding a charge of fulminate. These discs were contained in a vertical tube cut into the lock of the gun just in front of the hammer. Thrust upwards by a coiled spring the topmost disc was thrown off by a 'driver' attached to the hammer which detonated it as it fell on to the nipple. It was an ingenious action but, as Sharps pointed out in his patent, it was vitally necessary for the driver to throw the disc with just the right force so that it neither fell short nor overshot the mark. Sharps, who had patented a breech-loader in 1848 and was a mechanic of some genius, managed to obtain the perfect functioning necessary.
130 His breech-loading rifle fitted with his disc primer and modified with the R. S. Lawrence cut-off of 1859 (a device which could disconnect the disc primer and enable the lock to fire percussion caps) became one of the most effective guns to be used in the American Civil War. Afterwards it survived to do deadly service in the hands of buffalo hunters and other sportsmen.

Sharps was copied in his turn. In 1859 Jesse S. Butterfield and Simeon Marshall patented a 'New and useful Improvement in Self-Priming Locks'. This was another lock using fulminate-filled discs which were called 'wafer-primers' in the patent. A very similar mechanism to the Sharps was used, the sliding lever which Sharps called a driver being named in the Butterfield patent a 'carrier or conductor'. The latter was so arranged that when the hammer was raised it covered the vent and kept the main charge dry in adverse weather conditions. A distinguishing feature of the lock is the tubular primer-case which projects down below the lock-plate where it ends in a knurled knob. This primer was patented in England in 1858 by Joseph Lemuel Chester, and it was fitted to an experimental issue of Enfield rifles.

A very rare type of self-priming lock, which also used a disc or wafer, formed the subject of two US patents taken out by Jacob Rupertus in 1859. It appears to have been tried out mainly on pistols, with the magazine of discs either in the butt or in the rear of the hammer. In both instances the primer was fed into a cavity in the nose of the hammer instead of on to the nipple.

Attempts were also made to produce satisfactory magazine actions for percussion caps. The difficulty here was that the nipple was normally set at an angle on the barrel and some ingenuity was needed to design a mechanism able to seat the cap on it. Before Sharps produced his successful disc primer he patented in 1848 a 'Breech-loading and Self-Capping Rifle-Gun'. The capper of this rifle consisted of a round flat box with a brass lid containing a wheel notched to hold caps in its perimeter. When the breech lever was depressed the magazine wheel turned bringing a cap into position for the nipple on the sliding breech to pick up on its return to the loaded position. It is significant that Sharps fitted a cap primer only to the first model of his rifle.

Another cap self-primer which met with only a limited degree of success was patented by Alonzo Perry in the USA in 1855. His caps were kept in a tubular magazine which stretched from the butt-plate to the nipple on the cartridge chamber. Again it was the action of the moving breech which enabled the nipple to be capped.

On a muzzle-loader it was a more difficult proposition to get the cap on to a stationary nipple. When the nipple was screwed into the barrel at right angles to its axis as in the under-hammer guns, the usual arrangement was something akin to the *Koptipteur's* tubular magazine under the barrel, with caps replacing the continuous strip. This method appeared in Henry Wilkinson's patent of 1839 for an under-hammer gun; and as late as 1859 the London gunmaker Frederick Prince patented what was to all intents and purposes a *Koptipteur*, except that it was a breech-loader and when the hammer struck, it automatically took a cap with it on to the nipple. Two claws on either side of the hammer removed the spent cap when the gun was re-cocked.

With the nipple set at an awkward angle on the bolster of a barrel, it was easier to work a hand-operated priming magazine as in the Westley Richards patent of 1838. In this a tubular magazine was placed on top (and to one side) of the barrel in front of the lock. A smart movement of the thumb brought a sliding conveyor, holding a cap, to the open end of the magazine, where the cap was pressed down over the nipple. Concealed magazines were neater in appearance but not so reliable. Dezmaurel and Bessière of Paris patented in 1840 a magazine running through the butt and ending in a nozzle which moved over the nipple to deposit a cap when the hammer was cocked, and out of the way when the hammer fell.[19] In the 1832 French patent of Thomas Motte-Falisse of Paris it was the nipple which was made to swivel to receive the cap from a magazine.

Combining the priming operation with the cocking of the hammer was possible but was never a really satisfactory action. An example was the lock patented by Della Noce and Bianchi of Turin in Paris in 1854, and in London in 1865. They revived the carrier-moving-in-an-arc principle used in the Hayward pellet lock[20] and adapted it for percussion caps. This lock was actually fitted to some British Enfield rifles, but was never adopted on any large scale.

But although the percussion-cap lock in self-priming form never reached the prominence attained by the Sharps and Maynard disc- and strip-primer locks, the ordinary percussion-cap lock remained the standard work-a-day means of ignition both in the USA and in Europe. We have seen that by *c.*1830 the sporting world had generally recognised the superiority of the percussion-cap lock over the flint-lock. It was some time, however, before the military authorities were prepared to concede to this opinion. It was one thing for the sportsman to have his well-made gun or rifle converted to the new ignition, it was quite another for the armies of the world to discard the flintlock muskets which thronged their armouries in such profusion and in which they had placed their trust for nearly two hundred years. The extreme caution with which the military approached this move is well illustrated by the behaviour of the British Board of Ordnance and its advisory Committees. In the 1820s they examined tentatively several percussion locks submitted by various inventors but rejected them firmly 'feeling in full force the frequently repeated objection to the introduction of detonating powder in any shape'. But in 1830, alarmed at the news that France had started experiments with percussion arms, they began a long and laborious series of their own to establish which type of primer and lock to adopt; and it was not until 1838 that they finally decided on the percussion cap.[21] France, Sweden and the USA quickly followed suit.

It may be noted here that when the British Army decided to adopt the percussion system, Alexander Forsyth, the man who had started it all, petitioned for some award for his original invention. At first, in 1842, the Treasury made him a grant of only £200 as they contended that the lock used by the British Army was not invented by Forsyth but was 'rather a Lock of which he furnished the idea but which subsequent experience had rendered available for the Public Service' – a not unreasonable summing-up of events.[22] However, Forsyth, by then an old man still humbly devoted to his parochial duties in Belhelvie, had won public sympathy and in the face of a national press campaign the Treasury was forced to accede to the payment of a further £1,000. Tragically Forsyth did not live to receive this final act of official recognition.

The essential requirements of a military weapon were strength, simplicity and cheapness, and it was to just these standards that the single-shot percussion cap gun could be measured with great facility. At first the military bodies were mainly concerned with the conversion to percussion of the large existing stocks of flintlocks. Private gunmaker's experience with this type of work on sporting weapons was consulted. In nearly all cases the flintlock's steel, steel-spring and pan were removed, and the cock replaced by a hammer. The latter was set at such an angle that it would fall on the nipple either screwed directly on to the barrel or on to a projection on the side of the barrel. The easiest method was to screw a cylindrical plug into the touch-hole and mount the nipple on this. But it was found to be susceptible to the repeated blows of the hammer. The strongest conversion was obtained by brazing a lump of metal on to the barrel to form the seating for the nipple, known in the U.S.A. as a bolster alteration.

The construction of the old flintlock even in its

19 This primer was patented in England in 1842 by Alexander Rousseau.

20 See p. 169.

21 See H.L. Blackmore, *British Military Firearms*, London 1961, Chap. VIII. D. W. Bailey, *Percussion Guns & Rifles*, London, 1972.

22 ibid.

most advanced stage had always placed a limitation on the general design of the gun. Gunmakers soon realised that with the introduction of the percussion lock the way was now clear for a number of inno-

Day's patent truncheon pistol decorated with fine fluting. English, *c.*1825. Kingston-upon-Hull Museum.

vations and, indeed, a new concept of firearm design. The first of the new ideas resulted in a wider application of the under-hammer lock. The first patent for a percussion example of this type of lock was taken out by the Parisian gunmaker Gosset in 1820. The first English patent to show a percussion cap, that of John Day of Barnstaple in 1823, also incorporated an under-hammer lock of surprisingly advanced design. Composed of only two working parts, a hammer and a trigger, each motivated by a spring, it was small enough to be concealed in the handle of a walking-stick. When closed, only a small knurled knob indicated its presence. Firing was simple. The hammer, which was situated underneath the barrel and tubular stock, was pulled down until cocked by a sear and folding trigger which flicked down ready for release in the manner of the old flintlock pocket-pistol. A similar mechanism was fitted to a number of all-brass English truncheon-pistols. These so-called truncheons – their exact purpose is not known – are all stamped *DAY'S PATENT* and are all made to the same pattern with a handle or butt cast in the shape of an eagle's head. The lock was also fitted to hunting whips with a pistol concealed in the handle by the same maker.

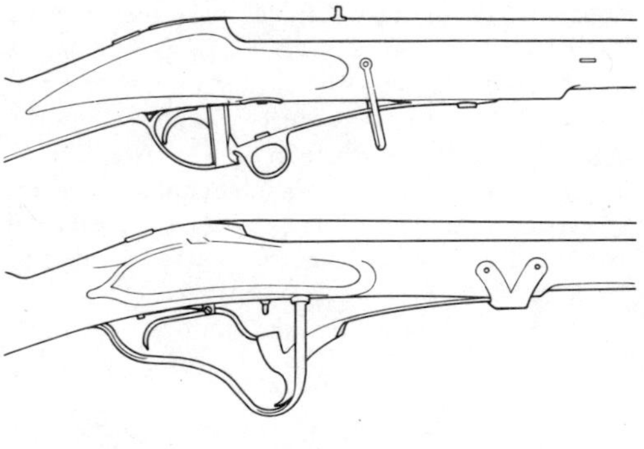

Details of two of Wilkinson's experimental under-hammer muskets. English, *c.*1839. Tower of London Armouries.

Under-action guns had been known in the flintlock era but were regarded as curiosities and only a few examples have been preserved. Day's patent under-hammer guns were the forerunners of a large number of guns and pistols which achieved a great popularity in the sporting world, and as personal weapons, because of their simple and effective construction. Single-shot guns with under-hammer locks were also made for military action. Denmark and Norway both adopted percussion guns with heavy, ring under-hammers based on the designs of the Danish gunmaker N. J. Løbnitz. A musket with a combined mainspring and under-hammer lock was submitted to the British Board of Ordnance by Colonel Whitelock, aide-de-camp to the King of Sweden, in 1835, and an almost identical weapon was patented by Henry Wilkinson, the London gunmaker, in 1839 (No. 8119). In his book *Engines of War*,[23] the latter recalls how, meeting with little encouragement in his own country, he sent one of these guns to the Emperor of Russia, who reciprocated with a splendid diamond ring. Wilkinson managed to reduce the number of parts in his lock to three by making the hammer and mainspring in one piece, the trigger-cum-sear with its spring being the other two. There were many variations to the ways in which the three or four parts of an under-hammer lock could be assembled. In some the mainspring, specially shaped for the purpose, became the trigger-guard; in others, a semi-circular hammer served the same purpose.[24]

Apart from the simplicity of its mechanism the under-hammer lock offered the user of a shoulder gun a shield for his eyes against splintering of the cap, an unimpaired view of the target and what was considered to be a quicker ignition, the nipple being screwed directly into the barrel. The last advantage was shared by guns which were supplied with the so-called side-hammer lock. William Moore, the London gunmaker, made a number of these for sporting purposes and he marked the lockplates *WILLIAM MOORE PATENT*, although no patent is registered in his name. Designers of the side-hammer lock sought to combine the advantages of the under-hammer lock with those of the conventional pattern which could be removed from the gun as one unit. Few English gunmakers seemed interested in departing from normal practices and engaging in the manufacture of these unconventional locks, but in the USA the side-hammer and under-hammer lock found a wide market. The American variety of the side-hammer lock, with its

23 1841 ed., p. 80.

24 See Herschel Logan, *Underhammer Guns*, Harrisburg, 1960.

130 *Above* Eight-bore flintlock elephant gun, the locks signed PROSSER LONDON. English (London), Model 1855. Tower of London Armouries.

131 *Above* Percussion pistol with under-hammer lock. This type of pistol was known as a 'bootleg'. American, *c.*1830. Smithsonian Institution, Washington, D.C.

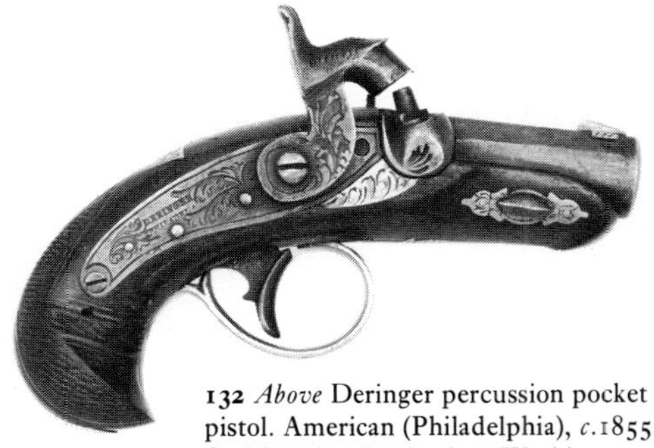

132 *Above* Deringer percussion pocket pistol. American (Philadelphia), *c.*1855. Smithsonian Institution, Washington, D.C.

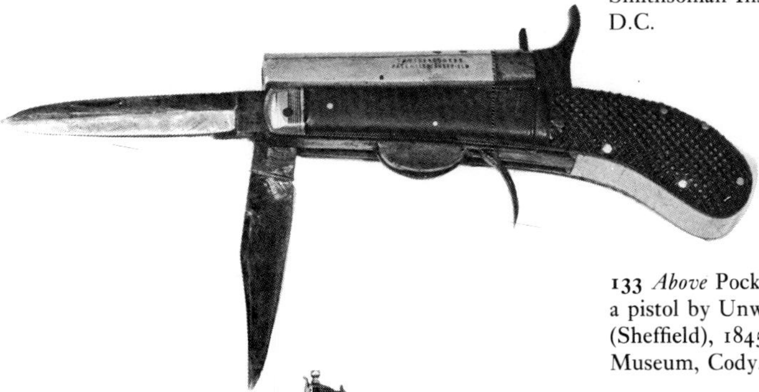

133 *Above* Pocket-knife combined with a pistol by Unwin and Rogers. English (Sheffield), 1845-62. Winchester Gun Museum, Cody, Wyoming.

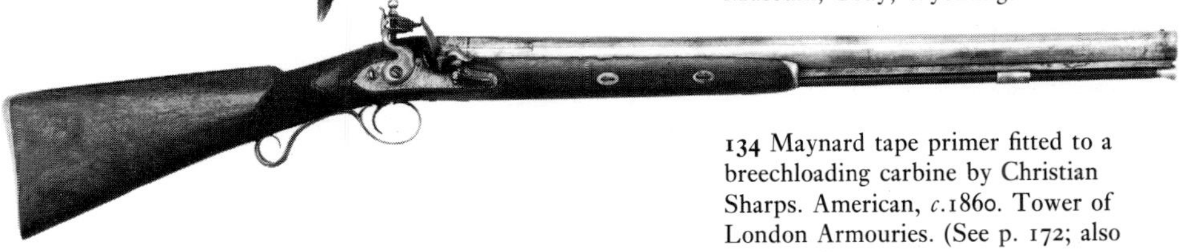

134 Maynard tape primer fitted to a breechloading carbine by Christian Sharps. American, *c.*1860. Tower of London Armouries. (See p. 172; also plate **164**.)

135 *Above* Five-bore 'Reid's' double-ribbed rifle by Alexander Thomson and Son of Edinburgh. Scottish (Edinburgh), *c.*1850. Tower of London Armouries.

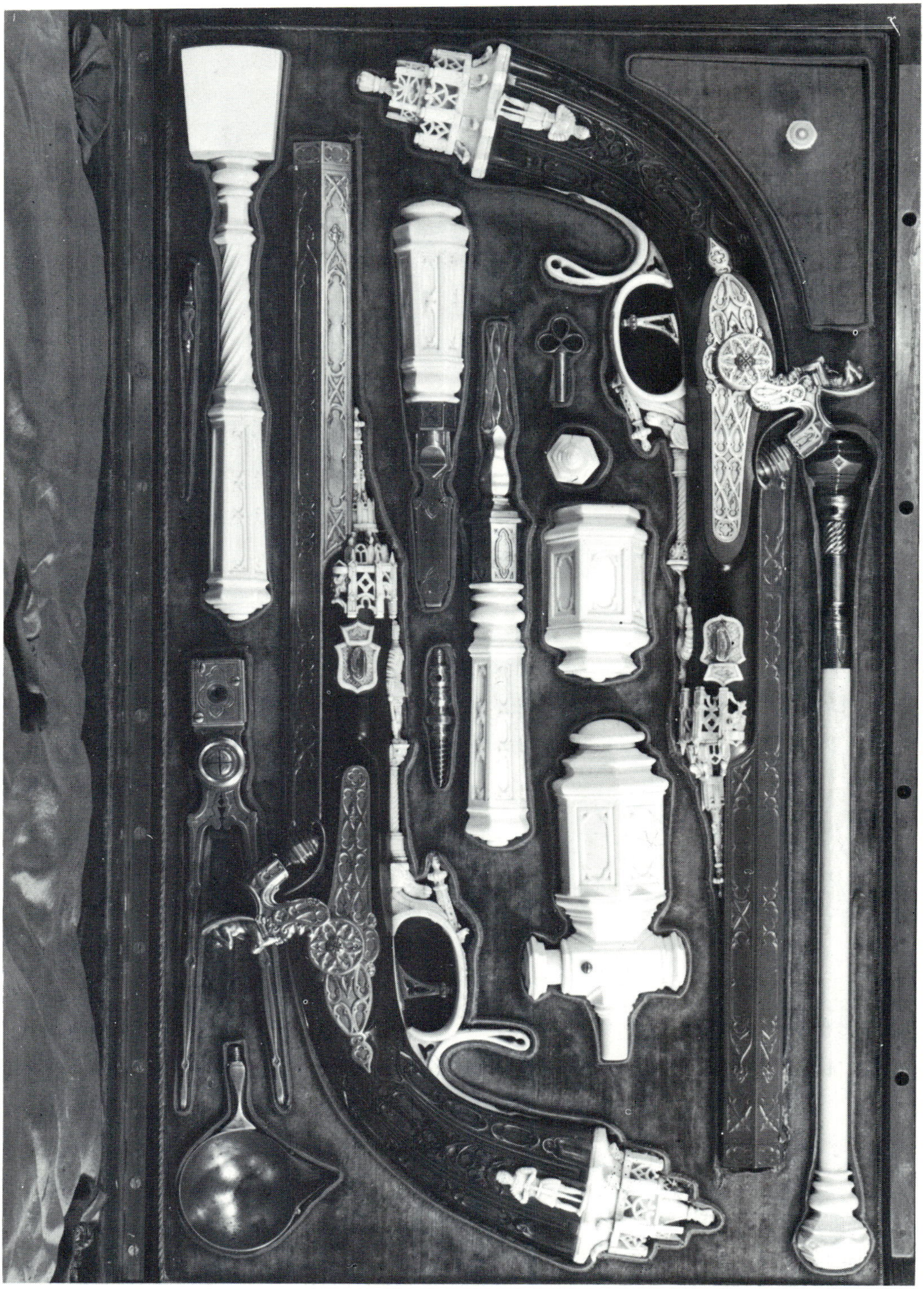

136 Pair of cased percussion target pistols in the Gothic taste, said to have been made for the Great Exhibition of 1851. Belgian (Liège). Signed under the barrels, CHARLES HONORE FECIT.

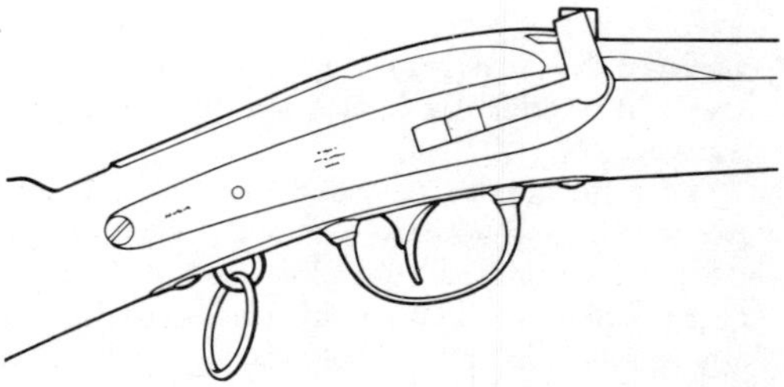

Detail of lock on a breechloading Navy carbine by Jenks. U.S.A., *c.*1847. Winchester Gun Museum, Cody, Wyoming.

bar hammer terminating in an ear-shaped projection used for cocking, became known as the 'mule-ear' lock. It was to the pistol maker that the under-hammer lock had most attraction. Because of its smoother outline and lack of cumbersome projections it could be carried with ease in the belt, pocket, holster or boot. It was the last item that was to earn for the weapon its American nickname of 'boot-leg' pistol, for, apart from being worn in
131 the side of a leather high-boot, it also resembled the latter in general shape.

While the under-hammer lock was the most noticeable innovation of the percussion cap system, there were other developments in the more conventional forms of lock, placed on the side and to the rear of the breech. The first reaction to the new system was the invention of a number of freak locks. Typical of these was the one Henri Pottet patented in France in 1824; a lock which was clipped into a vertical slot in the stock and could be easily removed to render the gun harmless. It was composed mainly of a U-shaped mainspring of which one end acted as the hammer and the other formed the pivot of a combined trigger and sear. This fetish for simplicity found its expression in the development of what became known as the back-action lock. As its name suggests all the working parts of the lock lay behind the hammer. With this kind of construction it was possible to devise locks in which the mainspring acted on both hammer and sear, or incorporated its own sear.

There were several advantages other than the reduction in the number of lock parts. The lock cavity, which in a side-lock or front-action lock, had to be cut out of that part of the stock already weakened by the intrusion of the wide breech-end of the barrel, could now be carved out of the wrist or grip of the stock. When the lock was screwed into position it acted in effect as a metal reinforcement. The back-action percussion lock also facilitated the development of the breech-loader and revolver as will be seen from a study of the chapters on those arms. It was adopted for the muzzle-loading arms of the French Army in the 1840s and was fitted to a number of new model arms of the British Army during the same period.

The old box-lock action found on so many of the pocket-pistols of the flintlock era was revived by Isaac Riviere, the London gunmaker, in his patent of 1825. In his percussion-cap lock which he fitted to both shoulder- and handguns the hammer and mainspring were fastened to the barrel tang whilst underneath a trigger plate supported the trigger, trigger-spring and guard. The two metal plates screwed together strengthened the stock at its weakest point and provided a reasonably weather-proof cover for the lock movement. Only the hammer

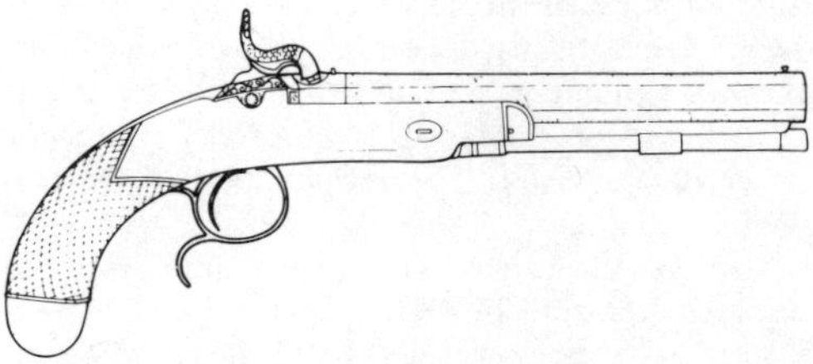

Duelling-pistol with 'twist' barrel and with Isaac Rivière's patent percussion lock of 1825. English (London), 1825-30. Tower of London Armouries.

on top and the trigger in its guard below were visible and thus Riviere described himself on his trade cards as the 'Patentee for the Guns without Locks'. A similar lock was patented by the Danish gunmaker N. S. Jessen in 1828.

This desire to protect the lock's interior from the weather was carried a step further by several gunmakers who designed guns with concealed locks. In most of these locks the internal mechanism had to be provided with an exterior cocking-lever or a dummy hammer. A sliding or hinged lid was also necessary so that the nipple could be capped. The first of the concealed lock mechanisms was patented in England by David Laurence and John Crundwell in 1829. They managed to dispense with the external cocking-lever, the gun being cocked when a sideplate holding the nipple was opened. In the guns patented by George Stocker and Joseph Bentley in 1839, cocking was effected by a dummy hammer on the side of the breech; and in another made by Baron de Berenger a large, clumsy trigger-guard was necessary to encompass a trigger and a cocking-lever.

Only experimental models of these guns seem to have been made but a number of fine double-barrelled shotguns with concealed locks were produced by the Birmingham gunmaker Charles Jones. In 1833 he took out two patents for locks of simplified construction. In the first one, No. 6394, he achieved the ultimate in simplification by fashioning the hammer, tumbler and trigger out of one piece of curved metal with the mainspring acting on a projection of it. In the other patent, No. 6436, the hammer is in one piece with the tumbler, and the trigger and sear move on the same centre. This was the action he used for his concealed locks. Locks of very similar design were patented in France by Joshua Scholefield in 1834 and by R. B. Cooper in 1839.

Perhaps the greatest effect of the introduction of the percussion cap was felt in the design of the pistol. The flintlock pistol was always of questionable value. As a personal weapon carried in the pocket it had more psychological value than any other. Even the duelling-pistol, whose vogue coincided with the last and best phase of the flintlock, was only effective in the hands of a practised marksman. In fact, according to some contemporary writers, it was better to rely on a sword or bludgeon for personal protection rather than a pistol. The introduction of the percussion cap altered all this.

Not many of the percussion pistols quite emulated the grace the beauty of the English flintlock duelling-
86-114 pistol but they were decidedly more effective. The pistol which was to prove this more than any other was the deringer, named after its inventor,
132 Henry Deringer Jr. The son of a Pennsylvanian gunmaker of the same name, he began his business in Philadelphia in 1806, where he won government contracts for the supply of flintlock rifles. Although it was not until 1845 that he received official orders for percussion arms, he was one of the first to adopt the new system, and he established a reputation for excellent percussion rifles and duelling-pistols.[25] To appreciate what followed one must recall the lawless social life of many of the American towns in the middle of the nineteenth century, when the majority of citizens carried loaded firearms or other weapons concealed about their persons. Here is an Englishman's description of the entrance to a gambling saloon in San Francisco in 1851.

> Several doorkeepers were in attendance to whom each man as he entered delivered up his knife or his pistol, receiving a check for it, just as one does for his cane or umbrella at the door of a picture-gallery. Most men drew a pistol from behind their backs and very often a knife along with it; some carried their bowie-knife down the back of their neck, or in their breast; demure, pious-looking men, in white neck-cloths, lifted up the bottom of their waistcoat, and revealed the butt of a revolver; others, after having already disgorged a pistol, picked up the leg of their trousers and abstracted a huge bowie-knife from their boot; and there were men, terrible fellows no doubt but who were more likely to frighten themselves than any one else, who produced a revolver from each trouser pocket and a bowie knife from their belt. If any man declared that he had no weapon the statement was so incredible that he had to submit to be searched.[26]

Among the miners, sporting gentry, gamblers, peace officers, and business men of the Western and the Southern states there was a large potential market for a pistol that was small enough to be concealed and worn without discomfort, but which would deal a deadly blow at close quarters. Deringer's answer to this need was the production of a single-barrelled pistol with a back-action percussion-cap lock, and neat walnut stock. The rifled barrel, which varied in length from one inch to six inches had a patent breech and a wide bore. The genuine pistols were stamped on the lock and barrel with the words
DERINGER PHILADEL^{A}. By the middle 1850s 132
the fashion of wearing this little pistol had become well established and it figured in several notorious murders, including the assassination of President Lincoln in 1865 by John Wilkes Booth. It became so popular in fact that many other gunmakers began openly copying it; large supplies were also imported from Liège. On some of these pistols the inventor's name was misspelt, possibly to escape any legal action, although Deringer had not patented his design. The height of absurdity was reached when one New York gunmaker advertised himself as a 'Rifle, Gun and Imitation Deringer Pistol Manufacturer'.

As well as the imitators of the deringer there were those who sought to improve on it. An example was the deringer with a hammer whose nose was adjustable to fire two superimposed charges in the barrel, after the 1855 American patent of Frederick Beerstecher. Another model of the deringer was equipped with the Butterfield patent magazine primer of 1855. But all of them, including the cartridge models which followed, continued to be known, even after the inventor's death in 1868, as the deringer[27].

The references above to the men carrying many bowie knives as well as pistols leads to another unusual weapon of the percussion period, the Elgin Knife Pistol. The idea of combining a firearm with some kind of blade was well known, and swords with pistols in the handle, and pistols with folding

---

25 John Parsons, *Henry Deringer's Pocket Pistol*, New York, 1952.

26 J. D. Borthwick, *Three Years in California*, Edinburgh & London, 1857, pp. 77-8.

27 Purists now reserve the term *deringer* for Henry Derringer's own, now rare, products, and *derringer* for the imitations. The former spelling is, however, used for both here.

bayonets had been common in the flintlock period. The popularity of the large hunting knife, immortalised by James Bowie at the Battle of the Alamo in 1836, led George Elgin of New York to patent in 1837 a combined percussion-cap pistol and cutlass knife. After some difficulty in establishing his patent in the face of similar claims by another inventor, R. B. Lawton, for an 'Improvement in the Pistol-

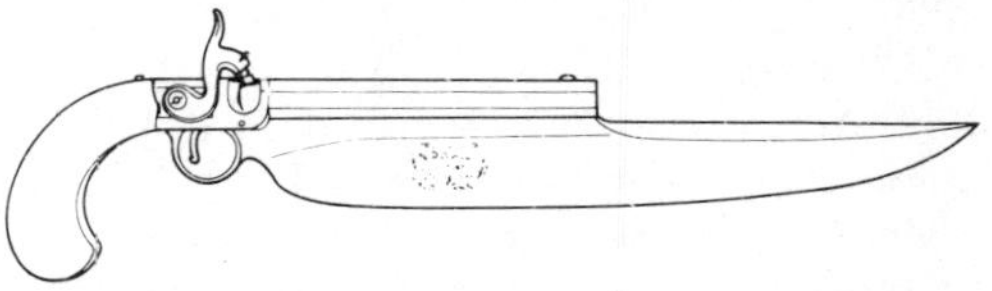

Elgin cutlass pistol, the blade signed by N. P. Ames, of Springfield, Mass. U.S.A., *c.*1840. Smithsonian Institution, Washington, D.C.

Saber',[28] Elgin won a small contract in the same year for the supply of 150 of his pistol-knives to the United States South Sea Exploring Expedition (1838-42). The pistols had a 5 in octagonal barrel of smooth 42-bore and the knife blade ('of the best shear steel') was 11 in long. A feature of the Navy pattern is a hand-guard, or knuckle-bow, connecting the trigger-guard to the butt-cap. This is not normally found on civilian models. The Elgin knife-pistol was not a success, and by the time the expedition had returned the inventor had gone out of business; one of the makers, Morrill, Mosman & Blair, was bankrupt, and another, C. B. Allen, had died.[29] Today, the surviving specimens of this ill-fated enterprise are much sought after by collectors.

Both the Elgin and the deringer pistols were products of the American way of life and they had no direct counterparts in Europe. But many of the small English pocket-pistols had large-bore barrels equivalent to the deringer. A maker who favoured this form of pistol was the firm of Rigby of Dublin. William and John Rigby also made all-steel percussion pistols which relied for their effect not on the power of a single large-bore barrel but on a group of three or four barrels. These barrels were ignited by a large circular hammer with a revolving striker which hit each nipple in turn.

Knife-pistols of smaller size than the Elgin were also popular in Europe. One type, made mainly in France, had a handle whose grips concealed the pistol mechanism. The two crossguards or *quillons* on one side acted as the hammers, the barrels lying on either side of the blade. Both hammers were released by a single folding trigger.[30] The majority of these knife-pistols bear the stamp *Dumonthier Brevete Btg*, but at least one specimen is engraved *W. Watson Inventor*. In the George F. Harding Museum, Chicago, one of these knives hangs from a finely-decorated waist-belt, obviously intended as a hunting weapon.[31]

The most widely known of the combination weapons was a pocket-knife variety made by the cutlery firm of Unwin & Rodgers of Sheffield,
England. Advertised as early as 1839[32] their so-called 133
'Life and Property Preserver' consisted of a large pocket penknife with a large folding blade and with a pistol barrel attached to the side. At the rear was a small hammer released by a folding trigger which, fashioned like a gimlet, could be screwed in to a doorpost and the pistol used as a burglar alarm if need be. Folded down one side was a long hook which also served the purposes of a handle and, when unscrewed, a ramrod. The makers stated that 'this instrument is capable of carrying a ball with sufficient force to kill at 50 yards distance' – a slightly optimistic claim one feels. This weapon was not patented in its original form in England but a cartridge version was patented in 1861[33] and similar knives were made by other makers. Later models were fitted with a container for caps and with a bullet mould.

With a gun-lock requiring such a small space at their disposal gunmakers and inventors could give full vent to their imagination and ingenuity, and the percussion-cap pistol was combined with a variety of objects. It was hidden in purses, cigar cases, the bottom of stirrups, the handles of whips and the buckles of belts, and it formed the basis of a large number of burglar alarms and animal traps which were patented on either side of the Atlantic in the 1850s and 1860s.

Arising out of the power of the percussion cap itself, a special group of arms, mainly pistols, was developed. William Greener, writing in *The Gun*[34] of his attempts to design an improved nipple, first noted that the percussion cap had the power to

28 There was yet another patent in 1837 issued to R. W. Andrews for a pistol whose barrels could be pulled off to reveal a hidden dagger.

29 C. Meade Patterson, 'George Elgin's Pistols', *The Gun Collector*, Madison, Wisconsin, No. 30. (Nov. 1949) pp. 349-80.

30 Prison warders in Norway were armed, for a time, with weapons of this type.

31 H. Gordon Frost, *Blades and Barrels*, El Paso, 1972, pp. 57-67.

32 Robson's *Commercial Directory of Sheffield*, 1839, Appendix p. 131.

33 An American patent was taken out by A. J. Peavey in 1865.

34 London, 1835, pp. 131-2.

discharge a bullet without the aid of gunpowder.

> I cut a piece of cork to fit the muzzle of a gun-barrel and charged it with a quarter of an ounce of lead, to cause it to give a greater resistance to the air, and when a cap was fired on the nipple it would just blow it out. I then put in the newly invented nipple, tried it, and the cork and lead were blown six yards from the muzzle.

This principle was used for the construction of special low-power saloon pistols for use in shooting galleries or homes where, in the confined space, the fumes of gunpowder were undesirable. Gastinne-Renette of Paris, whose own galleries were patronised by the great marksmen of the day, patented a breech-loading model of the *pistolet a capsule* in 1847. This had an internal hammer and nipple. A muzzle-loading pistol with an under-hammer lock firing an expanding bullet with the cap only was also patented in France by Cusson-Pourcher and Rossignol-Lefevre in 1850.

Apart from the production of these unusual types of pistol, the percussion system was responsible for alterations in the general design of the ordinary single-shot pistol. To begin with the percussion pistol followed closely the lines of its flintlock predecessors with the same kind of barrel, stock and furniture. The same national types of butt – the flat-butted French and Belgian, the rat-tailed Balkan, the ball-butted Caucasian, etc. – prevailed, and some of these were not discontinued during the percussion period. Specialised forms of butt, like the saw-handled or the duelling type with the extended trigger-guard, were reproduced again with percussion locks. But there was an increase in the use of the all-metal stock, and with the introduction of the back-action lock the wooden fore-end, except in the case of the very large pistol, was mainly discarded.

In Northern Europe and North America gunmakers favoured a plain, rounded butt with a pronounced curve. There was a steady decline in the use of decoration and the ornate cast butt-cap quickly became a small formal plate, often serving the purpose of a lid to a cavity for spare caps. On some military or naval pistols – the British Naval or Coastguard pistol is a good example – the buttplate was there only as an anchorage for a lanyard ring. In the USA new methods of construction used for the pepperbox revolver were applied to the pocket-pistol, the butt being formed by two wooden plates screwed together on each side of a metal frame projecting from the action. Many American single-shot pistols were also fitted with the distinctive top-action bar-hammer found on early pepperboxes. In France and Belgium, however, more traditional designs were maintained and there developed a fluted butt, ending in a heavy ornamental metal cap, which is a characteristic feature of these countries' arms.

The discouragement of duelling in the middle of the nineteenth century and the increase in the popularity of the revolver had its effect on the production of the larger percussion single-shot pistols. However many officers and sportsmen preferred a stout single- or double-barrelled pistol of large bore to the revolver. Sporting versions of these pistols are now often called 'howdah' pistols from the fact that they were carried, for defence, by hunters shooting tiger from the backs of elephants.

On the other hand the single-shot pocket-pistol remained popular throughout the percussion period and continued to be made long after the cartridge weapon had been perfected. The 1889 catalogue[35] of the Great Western Gun Works, of Pittsburgh, Pennsylvania, which advertised all kinds of modern cartridge shotguns, rifles and revolvers, also included 'the American Single Barrel Cap, Powder and Ball Pistol' with a choice of 2 in, 3 in and 4 in barrels and an iron or brass frame. A similar but cheaper pistol was still in production in Belgium up to the beginning of the Second World War.

In the general design of the shoulder gun the percussion lock also had its effect. Again there was an emphasis on the utility and efficiency of the gun rather than on its appearance. In the USA the single-shot percussion gun was still built on the traditional lines of the old Kentucky or Pennsylvania rifle, but the decoration was normally restricted to an ornamental surround to the butt box. In the 1840s the length of the barrel was shortened and eventually the fully-stocked pattern was replaced by a half-stocked one in the European fashion.

During the nineteenth century many of the German and Swiss emigrants to America brought with them the specialised form of rifle used in their national shooting festivals. In these competitions (*Schuetzenfest*) shooting was largely conducted from the standing, off-hand position, with no restrictions to the calibre, weight and length of the barrel. In the normal upright stance the marksman could not support the heavy weight of the barrels, so the left elbow was rested on the hip and the weight taken by the left hand with the fingers either outstretched or grasping a special palm rest screwed under the fore-end. The stock had to be specially shaped with a pronounced drop to the butt in order to bring the line of sight up to the eye. Heavy, iron buttplates ending in long prongs which gripped the shoulder also helped to steady the rifle. Adjustable aperture sights and double set-triggers completed the equipment.

35 Reproduced in *Gun Digest*, Chicago, 20th Edition, 1966, p. 251.

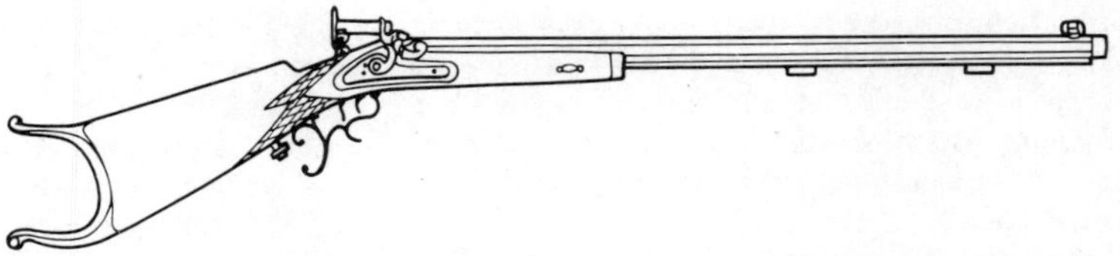

Schuetzen percussion rifle. German, *c.*1840. Milwaukee Public Museum.

Few percussion guns ever received the lavish ornamentation which was so often applied to the flintlock and wheel-lock firearms. But in the 1840s the widespread romantic movement fostered by the novels of Sir Walter Scott brought in the cult of the
136 Neo-Gothic, and the gunmakers of Paris, Liège and Prague began to produce highly-decorated firearms in this fashion for presentation purposes. The cased pair of duelling-pistols was an ideal subject for this exercise. Deeply-carved ebony stocks were contrasted with ivory inlays, and barrels treated to a lustrous black colour were highlighted with gold and silver. A pair of 'Gothic' pistols by Gauvain of Paris at the Paris World Exhibition of 1844 were much admired. Not content with this stylised form of decoration the gunmakers were next inspired by a series of designs published by the Belgian artist Charles Claessen in 1856,[36] in which the wooden and metal parts of the gun were sculptured with mythological, hunting or heroic scenes. Another school of engravers and etchers covered the entire surface of guns with an interwoven mixture of flowers, leaves, animals, etc. in a style known as the *genre vegétal*.[37]

So far the steps to perfect the percussion-cap lock and the resultant changes in the exterior design of pistols and long-guns have been noted. During the thirty years from *c.*1835-*c.*1865 in which the percussion system of ignition flourished, some very important changes were also taking place inside the barrel of the gun. At the beginning of the nineteenth century, when the first percussion experiments were being conducted, the flintlock military rifle was a specialist arm issued to small picked bodies of men who rarely fired at ranges exceeding 300 yards. There were conflicting views as to the number and shape of the grooves that were necessary to make up the rifling and to the degree of twist to which the spiral of rifling was subjected. In all cases the bullet was the same spherical shape as that used in the musket, and in order to make it grip the rifling it had to be carefully wrapped in a paper, cloth or leather patch and be forcibly rammed down the barrel. This did not guarantee accurate shooting as the ball needed to be only slightly off-centre in its packing to have its rotational stability upset when it left the muzzle. This state of affairs had prevailed since the first rifles had been produced and in the lifetime of the rifle–over 300 years–little or no progress had been achieved. The first progress was made in the early 1830s when the Hanoverian and Brunswick armies began experimenting with oval-bored rifles.

Oval-bored rifling in itself was nothing new. It had been advocated in 1729 by the Saxon Johan Georg Leutmann[38] and had been dismissed by the English writer Mark (formerly thought to be Henry J.) Beaufoy in 1808 as 'a very old invention, though quite obsolete in our time'.[39] The importance of the German trials lay in the typical thoroughness with which they were conducted–a report submitted to the British Board of Ordnance ran to seventeen volumes–and their effect on the other European powers. The British authorities who summarily rejected a Hanoverian oval-bored rifle in 1835 were just as quickly converted to the merits of a similar Brunswick rifle in 1836.

This Brunswick rifle, which had been developed by Captain Berner, Field Adjutant to the Duke of Brunswick, fired round or oval lead balls, and proved itself superior to a rifle with eleven grooves of conventional pattern then under consideration by the British Army. George Lovell, the Superintendent of the Enfield Small Arms Factory, who was in charge of the latter's experiments, then introduced some modifications of his own. The oval rifling was accentuated into a distinct two-groove section and a belted ball, wrapped in a greased patch, was designed to fit it. To facilitate loading two notches were cut in the muzzle of the rifle. The result was Lovell's Improved Brunswick rifle with a 30 in barrel of 0·704 in calibre sighted for 200 and 300 yards, which was to remain standard for British rifle corps from 1838-51. During the same period the Navy was supplied with a heavier rifle of 0·796 in calibre

36 *Recueil d'Ornéments et de Sujets pour Etre Appliqués à l'Ornementation des Armes*, Liège, 1856.

37 H. L. Blackmore, *Guns and Rifles of the World*, London, 1965, Nos. 501-4.

38 *Nachricht von gezogenen Büchsen*, Nuremberg, 1735.

39 'A Corporal of Riflemen', *Scloppetaria*, London 1808.

ranging up to 470 yards, and experiments were made with a large, breech-loading wall-rifle–a copy of a French model–all with the two-groove rifling making a complete turn in each barrel length.

There is no doubt that at the time of its trials the men taking part believed that it was more accurate than the flintlock rifle, particularly at long ranges; that the smoother form of rifling would wear better and that there was no difficulty in loading. The first premises may have been true but the statement on loading is now hard to understand, for when the rifle was put in the hands of the troops, loading became their bugbear; as one report put it 'the force required to ram down the ball being so great as to render a man's hand much too unsteady for accurate shooting.'

This was the perennial problem of the muzzle-loading rifle. If you increased the accuracy of the rifle by making the bullet fit tight, you made it more difficult to load. This could be overcome by introducing an oversize ball from the breech, but a trouble-free breech-loading action had yet to be thought of. The solution, as far as the muzzle-loader was concerned, lay in expanding the diameter of a ball *after* it had been pushed down the barrel.

The beginnings of this can be traced to attempts made during the eighteenth century to increase the rate of fire of a musket by dispensing with the rammer. After the powder charge had been poured down the barrel a loose ball was dropped down into the breech-end of the barrel where it was retained by a spike or by a narrowing of the bore, the butt of the musket being thumped smartly on the ground to seat the ball. In 1718 the French engineer Deschamps published several designs of chambered and coned breeches which would achieve this result.[40] Another great Frenchman, Marshal Saxe, in his *Rêveries*[41] resuscitated the idea for a special rammerless carbine he proposed to introduce–'ces fusils auroient un dez au fond ou secret pour qu'ils ne fussent pas dans la necessité de bourer leur charge.'

In 1796, a Major V. Gardner submitted the idea to the Board of Ordnance, this time advocating a spike driven into the breech-end of the barrel at right angles to the bore. It was not a practical idea and the gunmaker Henry Nock who was consulted substituted a chamfered sleeve or ring. Between 1810-13 an experimental issue of modified India-Pattern muskets was made to three regiments of Foot Guards. Reports of the trials show that the Nock muskets were not only fast to load but lost little of their velocity. They were finally rejected because of the difficulties of cleaning the breeches, a fault from which all specially chambered muzzle-loaders suffered.[42]

Up to this point the chambered breech had been considered mainly as an aid to quick loading on muskets, but its employment in sporting rifles as a means of obtaining a better ignition of the charge had not gone unnoticed. It was inevitable that sooner or later someone using a rammer in a chambered rifle would discover that two or three strokes flattened the ball as it lay on the rim of the chamber so that it expanded into the rifling. This was the basis of the rifle submitted by Gustav Delvigne to the French authorities as early as 1826. A proper trial of the Delvigne rifle was instituted at Vincennes in 1829, but only a weak charge was used in the rifle and the spherical bullets had only a slight windage, i.e. they were just small enough to roll down the barrel. The result was that although the rifle fired as fast as a smooth-bore musket at first, loading became increasingly difficult and after frequent firing a residuum of fouling collected in the chamber, which eventually forced the powder of the charge above the shoulders of the chamber. From then on a proper expansion of the bullet was only obtained at the expense of compressing the powder.

In 1833, therefore, Lieutenant Colonel Poncharra of the French Artillery proposed that the spherical bullet should be seated in a wooden cylindrical plug or *sabot* half the diameter of the bore in length. To this was attached a greased patch or *calepin* which did not reach as far as the bullet. Such a compound bullet had been tried before although not with any expansion of the bullet in view. It was patented and used in a rifled cannon by Joseph Manton in 1792[43] and it was given an official test in a tight-bored musket invented by Lieutenant J. A. Gillmore of the 3rd West India Regiment in 1815.[44] In 1823 a grooved lead ball with a wooden nose and base was submitted to the Board of Ordnance by C. Gillham.[45] It was rejected because it was feared that the force of the explosion would smash the wood sabot. In fact the wooden sabot of the Delvigne–Poncharra bullet was often smashed, not by the force of the explosion but by the blows of the rammer. Another disadvantage of this bullet was the complicated character of the cartridge which added to the difficulties of manufacture. Nevertheless it was an improvement over Delvigne's original design and in 1838 the first

40 *Machines et Inventions Approuvées par l'Académie Royale des Sciences*, Paris, 1735.

41 See Plate XV of the Amsterdam edition of 1757.

42 Blackmore *op.cit.*, 1961, pp. 247-8.

43 H. A. Baker, 'Joseph Manton's Cannon', *Journal of the Arms & Armour Society*, London Vol. IV, 1961-4, pp. 41-50.

44 Blackmore, *op.cit.*, 1961, pp. 156-7.

45 Public Record Office, London, W.O. 44/540.

experimental issue of the rifles was made by the French to the Duke of Orleans' *Chasseurs à Pied*. Further batches of the rifles were successfully tested in action in Algeria in 1840.

Other inventors were watching these events with great interest and, in 1839, that versatile character Baron Heurteloup took the opportunity to include in the specification of the English patent of his *Koptipteur* some improvements to 'a new system of loading rifled guns which has lately attracted public attention in France'. Heurteloup proceeded to describe the Delvigne system and pointed out, what was well known, that the ball after being expanded was often misshapen or did not fit the grooves properly. His remedy was as follows:

> In order to obtain the requisite figure of the ball to the grooves of a rifled gun I have shaped the bottom or breech of the barrel and the ramrod in a manner that the parts of the ball which correspond with the grooves are pinched between the projections placed at the bottom of the barrel, corresponding with the grooves and the projections of the thick extremity of the ramrod, whereby I force these pinched parts of the ball into the interior of the grooves.

In effect the hollowed end of the ramrod and the mouth or rim of the chamber, both cut with opposing indentations, acted as the two halves of a mould which produced a partly-cylindrical bullet with a grooved surface matching that of the barrel. Or at least that was the theory. In practice the cutting edges of the breech became corroded and fouled from the explosion of the charge and those on the rammer head were inevitably damaged by the wear and tear of the loading operation. Heurteloup did not help matters by recommending that the rammer should also act as a sliding bayonet.

No official cognisance was taken of Heurteloup's suggestions, either in England or in France, but it was at last becoming obvious that the spherical bullet was out-of-date. Delvigne himself, aware of the shortcomings of his system of loading, had already begun to experiment with various bullets of a cylindro-conoidal shape. In 1840 he patented an explosive bullet of this shape (*Balle-obus*) which had a flat base more readily expanded by the action of the rammer. The following year he patented a cavalry carbine with a back-action lock and a pistol grip. The barrel was equipped with a chamber breech and associated with this in the patent drawings were several different types of cylindro-conoidal bullets (*balles cylindro-coniques evidées*) with hollowed-out bases. One had a hard metal ball secreted in the base. How far Delvigne intended these bullets to be self-expanding by the action of the gases behind them is not clear, and he gained no official support for these proposals.

The French authorities were in fact still enamoured with his first system, and in 1842 a properly designed rifle with the Delvigne chambered-breech and a manually-expanded bullet known as the Pattern 1842, was officially adopted in place of the temporary model rifle Pattern 1840.

Another bullet-expanding system proposed by Colonel Thouvenin in 1844 also gained rapid recognition. In this breech there was no chamber, but a short steel pillar or *tige* was screwed into the centre of the breech-plug with its axis parallel to the bore. The length was adjusted so that there was just enough space round it to hold the powder charge. A solid bullet was dropped down the barrel in the usual way and expanded on the end of the pillar. It was a breech which could be fitted to any musket or rifle and any shape of bullet could be accommodated. The French Army chose one of cylindro-conoidal form with a groove or cannelure cut round its waist designed by Captain C. E. Minié. No patch was necessary as the bullet was dipped in a mixture of tallow and wax. Curiously enough a pillar breech was patented in France by Prélat and Doye in 1845, but their pillar or spigot was pointed and was intended only to hold a spherical bullet in position.

Although the powder space of the pillar-breech rifle was just as subject to fouling as that of the Delvigne breech, it was soon proved that the Thouvenin system gave an easier and more effective expansion of the bullet. It was officially adopted in France in 1846 and was widely copied in Britain and other European countries. In 1848, the London gunmaker Charles Lancaster registered it (No. 1418) under the Non-Ornamental Designs Act of 1843.[46]

In 1846 a different series of experiments took place in England,[47] the results of which should have shaken the complacency of military minds everywhere and most of all in Great Britain. The latest smooth-bore musket, the English Pattern 1842, was given a thorough trial under the most favourable conditions to ascertain exactly how far it would shoot and with what accuracy. A maximum range of between 650 and 700 yards was established at an angle of elevation of 5°, which meant aiming over a 100 feet above the target. At 250 yards ten shots directed at a target 11½ ft by 6 ft all missed, and at 150 yards only half scored a hit. Such was the official mind, however, that in 1849 the Select Committee of the House of Commons was assured that the maximum range of the musket was 'from 1,700 to 1,800 yards'. Nobody, however, was under any

46 Blackmore *op.cit.*, 1961, p. 241.

47 *Report of Experimental Musket Firing carried on at the Royal Engineer Establishment Chatham between 8 April & 8 May 1846.*

misapprehension about the accuracy of the musket and it was becoming obvious that it would soon have to be replaced by the rifle as the standard military arm. Every European power was now feverishly conducting experiments with rifles, but the initiative still lay with France.

The successful operation of the French pillar-breech rifle was enhanced by the use of a new projectile with a pronounced ogival nose, invented by Captain Tamisier. The cylindrical rear of the bullet was cut with sharp-edged cannelures under the impression that by creating an air resistance or drag on that part it would prevent the axis of the bullet from deviating from its trajectory. Yet another French officer – it will be noted how important was the contribution of French inventors to the development of the rifle – was experimenting with the bullet.

Captain Claude-Étienne Minié (1804-79), who in 1840 had patented a self-priming percussion-cap lock for the Delvigne gun, now re-examined Delvigne's idea for a self-expanding bullet. Into the hollow base of the bullet he inserted an iron cup which by being thrust further into the centre of the bullet would expand its walls into the grooves of the rifling. It was very difficult at this time for inventors to find out exactly what did happen to a lead bullet after firing, but there was no mistaking the positive action of the Minié iron cup, which in some cases was forced right through the soft lead body of the bullet by the action of the explosive gases. In 1849 Minié took out a patent for hollow bullets with plugs of zinc, wood, iron, copper or lead.

The Minié self-expanding bullet was an immediate and fantastic success. It seemed to be the panacea for all evils of the gun. There was no need for the gunmaker to worry about special breeches. The Minié bullet appeared to convert all rifles and many of the old muskets into accurate and quick-firing machines. The French Army adopted it and the inventor received from his grateful government the sum of 20,000 francs and a staff appointment at the Vincennes School of Musketry. Other countries were not slow in following France's example. The British, who were in the midst of some trials of their own, seized on it eagerly as a stop-gap solution. In 1851, 23,000 'Minié Rifled Musquets' were ordered and a substantial number of them were received from the makers in time to participate in the Crimean War. *The Times* correspondent at the Battle of Inkerman reported 'the volleys of the Minié cleft them like the hand of the Destroying Angel.' The new rifle, and the man whose name it bore, received the fame and acclamation of a popular idol. People forgot that Minié had taken but a small part in the experiments that had led to the rifle's development. It was in vain that Minié himself wrote to *The Times* on 28 April 1855 protesting that Delvigne had not received sufficient credit and asking that the rifle should be called the Delvigne-Minié. To the public at large the rifle, and indeed any rifle firing an expanding bullet, became known as the 'Minnie'.

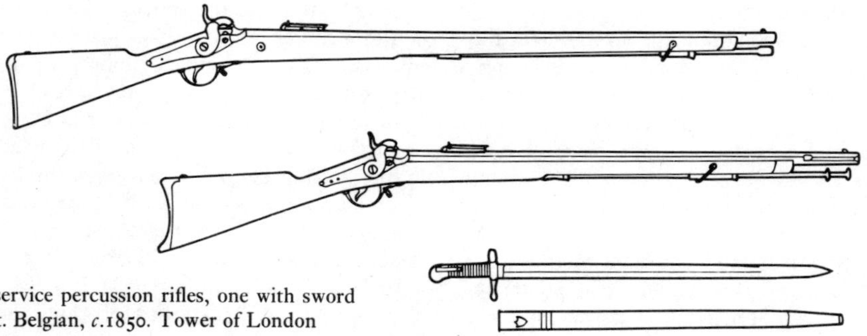

Minié service percussion rifles, one with sword bayonet. Belgian, *c.*1850. Tower of London Armouries.

As always when some new invention became successful and widely known there were those who claimed prior discovery. On the general principle of the self-expanding bullet the most persistent voice was raised by the English artillery officer Captain John Norton. He claimed to have started his experiments in 1818 and to have had an expanding bullet rejected by the British Ordnance Committee in 1823. All the evidence suggests, however, that his was an explosive shell designed to blow up on impact. It was an elongated hollow bullet, containing a small charge of gunpowder, and was ignited by a percussion cap on a nipple screwed into the nose. Any expanding properties it had, due to its hollow construction, were not emphasised by its inventor at the time and its rejection was due to the fact that under trial the bullet did not always hit the target nose first.

It is possible to go back much earlier than this and see in the writings of other experimenters the germ of the idea of the self-expanding bullet. One of Leonardo da Vinci's manuscripts[48] includes a drawing of a hollow cylindro-conoidal bullet. Mark Beaufoy in his *Scloppetaria* of 1808[49] illustrated a round-nosed elongated bullet with a hemispherical cavity in its base, and described it as follows;

Those balls are said to possess great advantages over the common ones: that is to say, they range farther and are more accurate. The reason assigned is, that during the ball's rapid course through the air, the latter in collapsing as the ball passes, gives it constantly a degree of impulse, *a posteriori*.

The first practical version of the self-expanding bullet – an oval-shaped bullet[50] with a conical plug – was produced by the English gunmaker William Greener in 1836. Although he considered it had more application to the smooth-bored musket than a rifle, a trial of the bullet was organised by a party of the 60th Rifles at Tynemouth in Northumberland. The report of the officer-in-charge, Major Walcott, was not a favourable one. The main fault seemed to be that the plug became detached from the bullet after leaving the barrel and, after an inspection by the Select Committee at Woolwich, the bullet was dismissed as 'useless and chimerical'. On Christmas Day 1841 Greener wrote to *The Times* to describe an improved version of his bullet with an iron plug in it, but he failed to awaken any official reaction. With the adoption of the Minié by the British Government, Greener campaigned for compensation and with the help of his Member of Parliament, Mr Scholefield, was eventually awarded £1,000 in the Army Estimates of 1857.[51]

The success of the self-expanding bullet did not result in the abandonment of all other projects. An English officer in India, General John Jacob, conducted single-handed a campaign for the adoption of a rifle of his own design. He was a remarkable man distinguished as a mathematician, mechanic, engineer, artilleryman and sportsman. In a town in Upper Scinde, India, of which he was the architect and which was named after him, Jacobabad, he built a rifle range with distances up to 2,000 yards long. Here, from 1845, he experimented with a number of different rifles built to his specifications by London gunmakers. Starting with the Brunswick as his pattern he first produced a four-grooved rifle firing a double-belted ball. From this he progressed to a double-barrelled rifle handling a cylindro-conoidal bullet which had a flat base and four rectangular studs on the side to fit the rifling. This was the rifle he recommended for military use in the fourth edition of his book *Rifle Practice* published in 1858 just before his death. Although the East India Government rejected his rifle – they were content to follow official patterns – a regiment raised by Jacob, known as Jacob's Rifles, was subsequently armed with these formidable rifles. The barrels were only 24 in long with a maximum range of 2,000 yards and were capable of firing an explosive bullet.

The Jacob rifle was not a weapon which could be placed in the hands of the common soldier, but it did prove the practicability of a rifle with a solid bullet which could out-shoot the Minié in range and accuracy if not in speed. The first flush of success for the Minié, in fact, was quickly over. It was soon discovered that the iron cup was a source of trouble. Unless it was seated exactly in the bullet its movement when fired was erratic. It could be forced to one side by the discharge, or be driven through the nose, and sometimes it did not move at all; all of which was reflected in the quality of the shooting. There were some writers, like John Boucher,[52] who dismissed the whole system of hollow bullets as a complete fallacy.

After extensive trials the British Board of Ordnance revised its ideas and put into production a rifle, the Enfield, which had a reduced calibre firing a round-nosed cylindrical bullet with a small depression in its base designed to expand without the aid of a cup. The London gunmaker Richard Pritchett was paid £1,000 for the use of this bullet in 1854, but it was remarkably similar to the one illustrated by Beaufoy in his *Scloppetaria* of 1808. In 1849 the French Army had tried out at Vincennes a similar bullet designed by Captain Fauconprit, but had then decided in favour of the Minié. In 1856, however, they reversed this decision and the French Minister of War decided against the use of a composite bullet with plug, wedge or cup. Instead a cylindro-conoidal bullet with a blunt nose and a triangular cavity in its base was adopted. On its surface was a single deep cannelure. The bullet chosen by the Belgian Army, known as the 'Peeter's ball' was even more unusual. The hollow cavity in its base had a conical projection called a *noyau* which was supposed to prevent the sides of the bullet from bursting and to steady it in flight.

48 British Museum, *Arundel MS 263*, f.54.

49 Plate II, fig. 4.

50 An oval bullet was described and illustrated by Leutmann in 1729, and advocated by Benjamin Robins in his *New Principles of Gunnery*, London, 1742.

51 W. Greener, *The Science of Gunnery*, London, 1841, pp. 299-300. *Gunnery in 1858*, London, 1858, pp. 343-53.

52 *A Treatise on Rifle Projectiles*, London, 1856, p. 20.

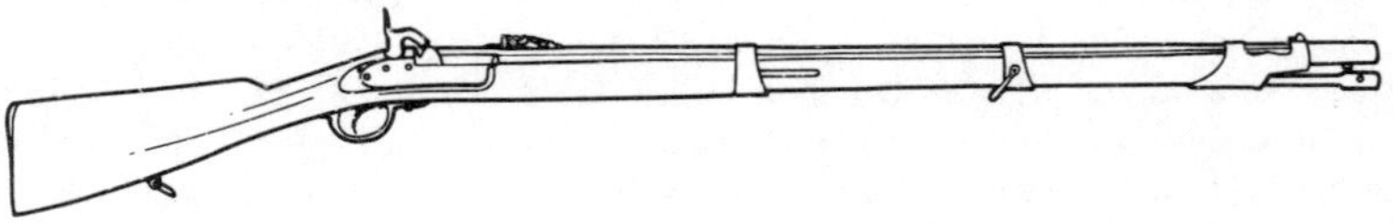

Oval-bore rifle by N. S. Jessen. Danish, 1851. Tower of London Armouries.

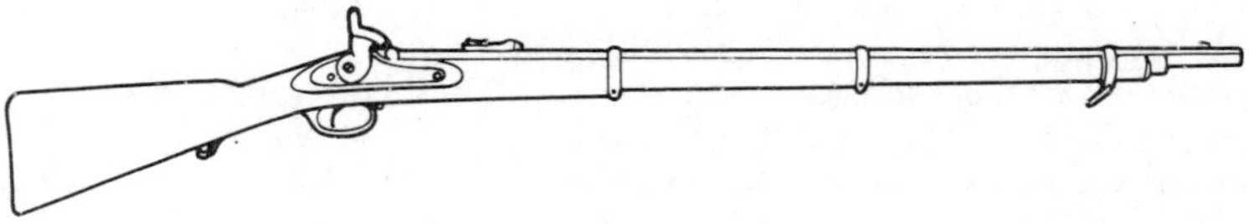

P/62 Whitworth rifle by Joseph Whitworth. English. Tower of London Armouries.

By the late 1850s, although most nations had adopted the rifle as the standard military arm, there was a considerable divergence of opinion as to the type of barrel and bullet to be used, and it is impossible to give a coherent description of the various weapons and their ammunition. The situation was summed up by Hans Busk in 1860[53] with these words:

> There is, amongst other things, much discrepancy of opinion on the question of calibre, librating, as it does, between the Swiss as the smallest (·41 inch), and the Swedish or largest, which is ·74 inch. In the number of grooves there is still greater diversity; in Brunswick, Oldenburg, and Russia, the two-grooved rifle is yet in use; in Wurtemburg, on the other hand, we find one with 12 grooves. These numbers 2 and 12, represent the extreme limits in military weapons; but the majority of those most in favour do not exceed three or four grooves. The number most generally adopted is *four*; rifles with *eight* are the next most numerous. With respect to the shape of the grooves there is great want of uniformity. Some are cut with sharp edges, others have them rounded off; the base of the groove being flat in some cases, concave in others. Nor is there less difference in the turn of the grooves. The longest is that used in Oldenburg where a twist of 6 feet 8 inches finds advocates. The Sardinians have adopted the shortest, one of 17 inches only. In America, France and Belgium, the grooves are progressive in depth; in Spain, Nassau, and Hanover, one rifle only has progressive grooves, the rest being all uniform. In some countries as in England, America and Switzerland, the rifles have neither *tige* nor chamber, and in others they are fitted, as has been seen, with both. This is the case in Prussia and Sardinia. Some rifles, as the Austrian, Belgian, and the French have a plug breech fitted with a *tige*.

One form of rifling not mentioned by Busk was the oval or elliptical type referred to by Beaufoy in 1808 and which had been converted to a two-groove rifling on the British Brunswick rifle. The true oval-bore with no grooves was patented by John Beaver in England in 1825 to give 'a more effective range to the charge of shot'. He did not apparently visualise it as a form of rifling. It was used for this purpose by the Danish gunmaker N. S. Jessen in a chamber-breech rifle which was rejected by the Danish Army in 1848.[54] In England Charles Lancaster who had been commissioned by the British Board of Ordnance to make an experimental number of his pillar-breech rifles with the standard two-groove rifling in 1846, now began to evince an interest in the special rifling. He took out a patent (No. 13161) in 1850 for a method of oval-boring guns but he clearly had in mind the exaggerated two-groove type at that time. Then Jessen sent one of his rifles to the Great Exhibition of 1851 in London. It aroused some interest and was purchased by George Lovell for the British Ordnance Board. In the same year Lancaster was taking part in official rifle trials with a version of his pillar-breech rifle with two-groove rifling. It is significant that the following year Lancaster changed over to the pure oval bore. This proved so effective that he was given an order to supply carbines with this rifling to the Royal Engineers in 1855.

Another unusual type of rifling, which gave the barrel a pentagonal or hexagonal section, was first suggested to the Board of Ordnance in 1843 by Robert Moore, a Sergeant-Major of the Royal

53 *The Rifle: and How To Use It*, London, 7th edn, 1860, p. 154.

54 Finn Askgaard, 'N. S. Jessens Ovalgevaerer', *Vaabenhistoriske, Aarbøger* VIIc, 1954, pp. 165-86.

Artillery. Also working on the same lines was Isambard Brunel, the famous civil engineer; but it was Sir Joseph Whitworth, the mechanical engineer, who finally patented and exploited its possibilities. Whitworth, with his experience of working to fine limits, was originally called in by the British Government to improve the standards of arms manufacture, but his experiments led him to try to discover the perfect form of rifle barrel. The result was a hexagonal rifling with a hardened-lead hexagonal bullet. An experimental number of these rifles was first made for government trials in 1857 and 1858. After decisively outshooting the Enfield rifle–it was still putting shots on a target at 2,000 yards which the Enfield could not touch–the Whitworth was given its first service trial, a batch of a 1,000 being made with 36 in iron barrels in 1862.

Enfield Service Short Rifles. From top: P/58 'Bar on Band'; P/56; P/58 Naval; P/61. Tower of London Armouries.

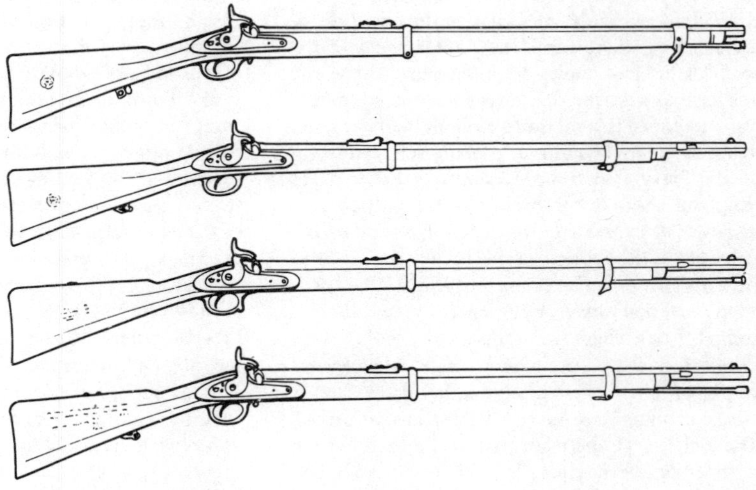

As this 1862 pattern proved promising, a further batch of rifles with steel barrels was ordered the following year, and these were issued to seventeen regiments for extensive trials in 1864.[55]

The words of John Boucher were now proving prophetic. In 1854 he had written 'if the bullet has length enough and fits properly, the *vis inertiae* of the fore part alone is quite sufficient to resist the onward movement of the latter part, until a sufficiency of the lead has been expanded into the grooves by the force of the expanding gases'.[56] It may be noted here that the Whitworth bullet had a length of 3 diameters compared with the Enfield's 1·81 diameters. However the Whitworth was itself to be challenged and finally beaten by the bullet designed by William Metford which was even longer, 3·02 diameters. Just as Boucher had predicted, the success of Metford's rifle, which had seven shallow grooves, was due to the way the bullet fitted the barrel, the maximum of fire check and the minimum of friction being created. The precision muzzle-loaders of Whitworth and Metford with their astonishing accuracy at ranges over 1,000 yards were never adopted officially because they became obsolete before they had passed the experimental stage. In the middle 1860s the military breech-loader arrived and the muzzle-loader was left in the hands only of the marksman and sportsman. Nevertheless the designs of William Metford successfully bridged the gap between the two systems of loading and his bullet and rifling remained in use until the introduction of cordite in 1891.

55 C. H. Roads, *The British Soldier's Firearm 1850-1864*, London, 1964, Chap. V.

56 *The Volunter Rifleman and the Rifle*, London, 1854, p. 71.

CHAPTER SIX

Early Breech-Loading Firearms

H.L. Blackmore

The breech-loader appeared very early in the history of firearms. This is not so surprising as it at first seems. The first pieces of artillery had little more than psychological value, and in the kind of warfare then prevalent, when gunners could be easily overrun or even out-ranged by cross-bow or long-bow, it was of the greatest importance to increase the rate of fire. Within a few decades of the introduction of firearms, then, there came the development of the breech-loader and multi-barrelled gun. From the terms used to describe these weapons in contemporary documents it is sometimes difficult to understand which particular class of gun is being referred to. In 1372 the Privy Wardrobe Accounts of Edward III of England show that a brass gun with three pots (*uno gonne de latone cum iij potz*) was sent to the defence of Calais. From the same accounts we hear of guns with two or more *capita* or *testes*.[1] The 'two-headed' cannon may well have been double-barrelled guns, but the guns with 'pots' were undoubtedly those of which there are several examples still in existence–although of later date.

These cannon were forged or cast in two pieces. In the earlier type the main part of the barrel of the gun, open at both ends, lay on its wooden bed secured by means of thongs or iron bands. The smaller part, or chamber, after being loaded was placed at the breech end of the barrel and wedged in position with a piece of wood. The mouth of the chamber was chamfered off to fit into the breech and the whole piece was prevented from recoiling to the rear by a block of wood, part of the wooden stand or carriage. In the later type of this breech-loader a stronger construction was achieved by making the housing for the chamber an integral part of the barrel forging. Movement of the chamber was checked by an iron wedge. This was a popular form of breech loader that continued in use up to the end of the eighteenth century and went under various names such as *base*, *patteros*, *perrier* or *sling*, etc.[2]

The earliest record of this type of breech-loader is found in the accounts of the Bailiffs of St Omer in 1342, in which are listed the artillery of the castle of Rihoult in Artois. One of the cannon which fired arrows with brass feathers and leather tampions was made in two parts, a barrel for the arrow and a separate chamber for the gunpowder. The latter part was loaded and placed at the end of the barrel where it was retained by a wedge called a *laichet*. The powder was apparently ignited by an iron rod heated in a charcoal fire.[33]

There was a third form of early breech-loader also cast or forged in two pieces, in which the breech chamber screwed into the barrel. The finest example of this form of construction is the Dardanelles Gun in the Tower of London. With these very large guns the great weight of the parts involved would seem to rule out any possibility that the breech end was unscrewed for loading. Separation of the gun into its two parts was necessary only to lighten the task of transportation. It is clear from some of the drawings of Leonardo da Vinci in the *Codex Atlanticus* c.1500-10, however, that smaller examples of this screw-chamber construction were used as breech-loaders. Where the chamber was too heavy for manual operation Leonardo suggests an ingenious rack and pinion mechanism to bring the chamber upright for loading once it had been unscrewed. He also illustrates a light field gun whose breech chamber is manually unscrewed, and then loaded with a cartridge. In another drawing the same gun is shown firing a dart with off-set feathers.

All the breech-loaders mentioned so far have been in the breech-loading artillery class and one of the first indications that a handgun was envisaged is a drawing in the *Codex Atlanticus* which shows a *Hackenbüchse* built like one of the turn-off breech cannon in miniature, with a tubular shoulder stock. Unless Leonardo intended this gun for use with the cartridge advocated by him ('a single fold of paper with the ball within') little advantage would be gained by its employment, for the time taken to unscrew it and load the chamber would have

1 T. F. Tout, 'Firearms in England in the Fourteenth Century', *The English Historical Review*, Vol. XXXVI, Oct. 1911, pp. 666-702. (Reprinted separately, London, 1968).

2 See H. L. Blackmore, *The Armouries of the Tower of London, I Ordnance*, London 1976, No. 196 and glossary.

exceeded that of the normal muzzle-loading procedure. It is possible, however, that with that far-seeing clarity of vision which distinguishes all his work Leonardo realised that the breech-loader unscrewing at the breech would accommodate an oversize ball which, by fitting the barrel tightly, would give a greatly improved performance over the muzzle-loader with its loosely-fitting ball.

Two drawings of Leonardo's[4] are of a breech-loading gun working on similar lines to the perrier. As far as can be judged its size would appear to bring it within the handgun range. The breech end of this gun has been left open and it also has a slot a few inches long cut into the top of the barrel. The tapered iron cartridge which is inserted into the chamber has a projection on its base, drilled with a touch-hole. This projection slides along the slot until fully inserted when a transverse wedge locks it.

Pre-dating Leonardo's drawings by a decade or two are some illustrations in a manuscript in the University Library at Erlangen.[5] These show breech-loading handguns working on the same principle as the perrier with their reloadable metal chambers. In one type shown the metal chamber lies in a trough at the breech in the same way as the larger artillery examples. A perforated projection underneath the chamber fits into a slot in the lower portion of the breech housing where it could be pegged into place. Chamber and barrel are held together in a simple butt-joint which would not have prevented an escape of gas, and so a projecting cover is fitted to the top of the chamber to protect the face of the shooter. In the second type shown in the manuscript the problem of obturation has been overcome by making the chambers small enough to be inserted into the breech end of the barrel. Each chamber is provided with its own touch-hole and cover, which, when the chamber is in position in the gun, can be ignited through an open slot in the side of the gun.

These, the first breech-loading handguns of the late fifteenth century, are known to us only by drawings, and actual examples of early breech-loaders only date back to the early sixteenth century. From then on, the efforts of gunmakers to produce a breech-loader which was both quick and safe to use with little or no loss of power resulted in a bewildering variety of actions which defies intelligible chronological description. For the purposes of this chapter the pre-percussion breech-loaders have been divided into those guns with movable barrels, movable breech plugs, detachable chambers, and pivoted chambers.

Breech-loaders with Movable Barrels

In this class the joining of barrel to breech was not confined to the screw-thread method already described. As we shall see there were many other types of join–slot, hinge, interrupted thread, bayonet catch, and so on–but the first successful breech-loaders of this category were in fact of the screw-thread variety. Only a few examples in the wheel-lock range appear to have been made, mainly because of the difficulty of altering the elaborate wheel-lock mechanism so that, in its usual place in the stock, it would permit the barrel to be removed without difficulty. On a wheel-lock gun by Michael Gull of Vienna, made in *c.*1650, now in the Kunsthistorisches Museum, Vienna[6] this has been done by placing the cock of the lock behind the wheel, allowing the lockplate and stock to be cut off abruptly underneath the join between barrel and chamber. The barrel is then simply unscrewed from the breech.

Wheel-lock turn-off gun by Michel Gull of Vienna. Austrian, *c.*1660. Kunsthistorisches Museum, Vienna.

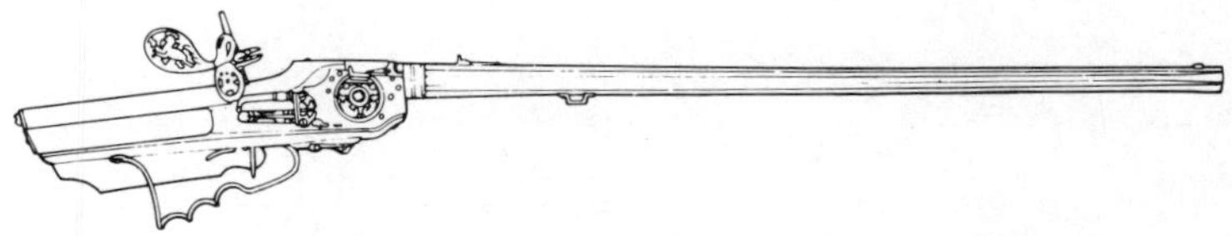

On a flintlock gun the length of lock in front of the touch-hole could be similarly reduced by reversing the spring of the steel–inside or outside the plate–so that it lay under the pan instead of projecting to the front. This was the method adopted by English gunmakers in the so-called 'Queen Anne' type of flintlock pistol, nearly all of which have barrels which unscrew for loading. This type of gun first appeared in the second quarter of the seventeenth century when both pistols and carbines are often fully stocked, the fore-end unscrewing with the barrel. When no fore-end is fitted the barrel is sometimes held to the body by a hinged link and running ring. This device was for the benefit of anyone obliged to reload on horseback to prevent loss of the barrel.

---

3 I. Fave, *Études sur le Passé et l'Avenir de l'Artillerie*, 1862, Vol. III, p. 77.

4 *Cod. Atlanticus*, f. 359b.

5 *Codex MS* 1390.

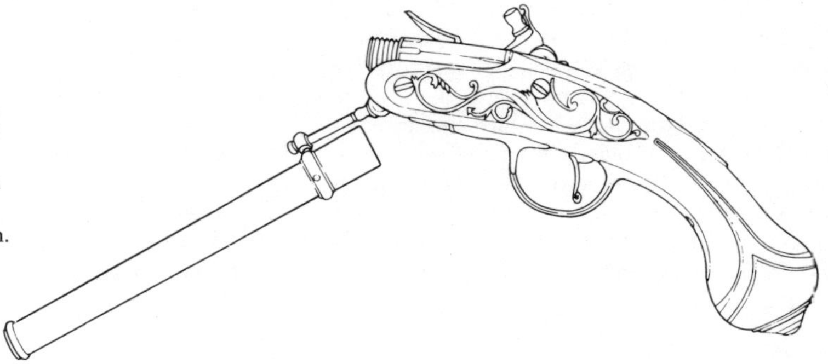

Turn-off flintlock pistol, the barrel unscrewed for loading Signed *Fisher*. English, late seventeenth century. Victoria & Albert Museum, London.

In the seventeenth century this type of pistol was in fact popular with cavalry officers. Contemporary descriptions of these pistols can cause confusion if the wording is not understood. Randle Holme in *The Academy of Armory*[7] of *c.*1680 explains that a pistol with a barrel that could be unscrewed was known as a 'turn-off' pistol and one that was rifled as a 'screwed' pistol. The turn-off pistol was particularly suited for rifling as it could fire an oversize ball. The latter was placed in the cup-shaped end of the chamber where it was held securely when the barrel was screwed back on to the breech. Loading was thus comparatively quick, no patch being necessary, and yet the pistol had the accuracy of a normal muzzle-loader which had been carefully and lengthily loaded with a patched ball. The accuracy of these pistols is well illustrated by the well-known story of Prince Rupert, who, on the occasion of the Royal Army halting at Stafford on 13 September 1642, put a bullet through the weathercock on the steeple of St Mary's Church with his 'screwed horseman's pistol'. On being challenged by his uncle King Charles, he repeated the feat with his other pistol.[8]

Although the heyday of the turn-off pistol occurred in England in the first half of the eighteenth
137 century when so many graceful silver-mounted specimens were produced, the use of this form of breech-loading action was carried on well into the nineteenth century although it was then mainly confined to pocket-pistols. The one difficulty with this type of pistol was the task of unscrewing the barrels, and it is interesting to note the different ways in which this was done. The majority of the guns and pistols had a square stud cut underneath the breech end of the barrel. A lever with a ringed end notched to fit over this stud could then be slipped over the barrel. If the barrel was octagonal instead of round then the wrench was shaped to a similar section. Another way was to file one of the handles of the pistol's bullet mould into a square key. Grooves, often mistaken for rifling, were then cut into the muzzle end of the barrel so that the corners of the key would take proper purchase. This method was most appropriate in multi-barrelled pistols whose barrels could not be grasped easily from the side.

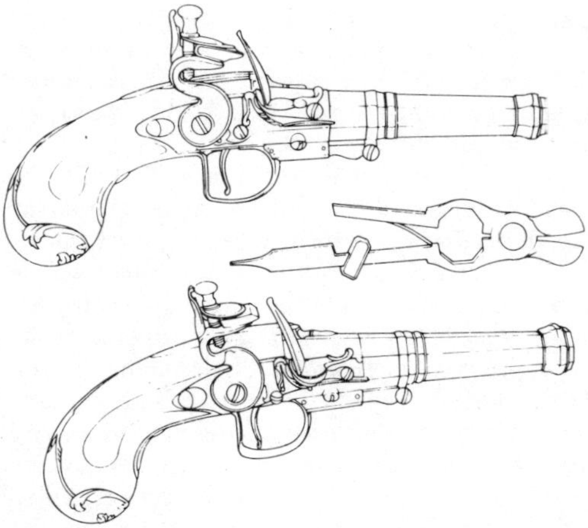

Pair of turn-off flintlock pistols, with combined barrel key and bullet mould. Barrel signed BARBAR. English (London), *c.*1720. Montagu Family Armoury.

With the realisation that the key or bullet mould was not always available, the exterior surface of the barrel was sometimes grooved longitudinally, and the owner had then to rely on the strength of his grip to turn the barrel. The most positive device was a

6 No. HGK.673.

7 Volume II, Roxburgh Club, London 1905, p. 135.

folding lever permanently attached to the underside of the barrel. If a folding bayonet was attached it was made to perform the same function. The French gunmaker Pottet took out a patent in 1818 for a flintlock breech-loading gun with a turn-off barrel. A wooden handle was fastened at right angles to the middle of the barrel where it acted as a fore-end grip as well. The barrel was attached to the breech plug by a quick thread so that it could be quickly detached by a turn of the handle. It was then suspended in a ring housing hinged to the fore-end so that it could be tipped up for loading. A gun of similar construction *c.*1760 signed *F. BERNIER*, is in the Tower of London.[9] The barrel has a tapered quick thread but does not tip up.

Perhaps the most beautifully made of all the turn-off barrel breech-loaders is the silver-decorated flintlock rifle made for George IV when Prince of Wales in *c.*1790 by Durs Egg. Now in the Mark Dineley Collection and apparently the sole surviving specimen of its kind, it has a hinged lever which, by a single turn, advances the barrel forward to uncover a loading aperture on the top, without separating it from the stock. It was an action which was, as J. N. George said, 'as nearly perfect as any which could be devised for a breech-loading flint rifle which must necessarily be loaded with loose powder and ball'.[10]

What may be termed a variant of the turn-off barrel action was the breech with an interrupted screw-thread, the fastest action of all. It was used on a breech-loader with a tip-up chamber made by Peter Duringer of Mainz in *c.*1660 and now in the Rotunda, Woolwich.[11] It is a gun with several unusual features including a combined matchlock and flintlock with a single trigger, and a large hinged knife bayonet. Thierbach[12] illustrates another gun with an interrupted screw-thread breech which he dates to 1740-60.

By the latter date gunmakers had tried all kinds of methods to lock and unlock the barrel from the breech with varying degrees of success. Quite a number of them–quick threads, interrupted screw-threads, interlocking studs, bayonet studs and spring catches–were included in the English patent taken out by the London gunmakers Thomas Wright and Charles Byrne in 1772. It is doubtful whether the majority of these actions were ever put into operation, but the last method mentioned, the spring catch, was tried on a number of occasions on breech-loaders where the barrel was simply pulled forward to open the chamber for loading. A French gun of *c.*1770 in the Tower of London[13] has a pull-out barrel that slides out along a projecting rod and is retained by a single spring catch underneath.[14] Thierbach[15] shows a gun whose barrel slides along its stock between the barrel-bands, after release from two sprung claws on each side of the breech. This gun is marked *SYSTEM SBORBORI 1770*. The breech chambers of both guns have coned mouths which make a reasonably gas-tight joint with the barrel.

One other type of breech action, which comes within the moving-barrel category is exemplified by a flintlock gun also illustrated by Thierbach.[16] The barrel is hinged underneath where it joins the breech and the two parts are held in line by a strong spring catch on top of the barrel. When this is released the barrel drops down in the manner of the modern shotgun. The chamber is reinforced and chamfered at its mouth but it is doubtful whether such an action could be satisfactory without the use of a metal cartridge. It is inscribed *INVENIT MARTIN GIZL ET FECIT. SALZBURG 1761*.

The moving barrel principle had its advantages, but its employment was obviously restricted by the weight and length of the barrel. There was also the tendency for the barrel to work loose in its housing, especially if it was a long or heavy one. From the gunmaker's point of view it was much preferable to secure the barrel to the stock and to open its breech by some simple mechanism, which did not disturb the strength of the whole gun. The simplest way of doing this was by inserting a screw plug into the breech end of the barrel in some convenient position.

Breech-loaders with Movable Breech Plugs

The earliest known example of such a mechanism is the detached barrel (probably from a matchlock gun) now in the Real Ameria, Madrid, which is believed to have been made by the Spanish gunmaker Cristóbal Frisleva in *c.*1570.[17] This barrel is drilled at the breech end with a vertical hole through which is threaded a screw-plug. The upper surface of the

8 J. N. George, *English Pistols and Revolvers*, Onslow County, North Carolina, USA, 1938, p. 17.

9 No. XII–259.

10 J. N. George, *English Guns and Rifles*, Plantersville, S. Carolina, 1947, pp. 181-3.

11 No. IX–7.

12 M. Thierbach, *Die Geschichtliche Entwickelung der Handfeuerwaffen*, Dresden, 1886-8, Plate 19, Fig. 474.

13 No. XII–1126.

14 H. L. Blackmore, *Guns and Rifles of the World*, London, 1965, No. 359.

15 Thierbach, *op.cit.*, Fig. 476.

16 *ibid.*, Fig. 477.

17 No. K. 352. See J. D. Lavin, *A History of Spanish Firearms*, London, 1965, p. 136 & Pl. 52.

latter is recessed to form a pan, and this in turn is drilled with a touch-hole which communicates with the chamber. The other end of the plug is shaped as a square nut which may have originally been fitted with some form of lever. In the Bayerisches National-museum, Munich, there is another detached barrel which can be opened at the breech by a lever-operated screw-plug. This is known to have been made by Freiherr von Sprinzenstein in 1593.

The introduction of the new multi-shot guns of the Kalthoff system (see Chapter 7) seems to have diverted the attentions of gunmakers during much of the seventeenth century and the next specimens of the screw-plug breech-loader do not occur until the late 1600s. One of these by Daniel Lagatz of Danzig in the Historisches Museum, Dresden, which can be dated to *c.*1690, is in fact a repeating gun with magazines of powder and ball in the butt. Charges are conveyed to the breech chamber by a moving breech-block operated by the trigger-guard. There is also a vertical screw plug with its own lever, which acts as a cut-out in front of the repeating mechanism, and if necessary converts the gun into a single-shot breech-loader.

In 1664 Abraham Hill, a Fellow of the Royal Society, took out a patent which embraced such diverse mechanical objects as carriages, washing machines, clocks, etc., and various breech-loading guns. One of these was 'another Gun that is charged and primed in like Manner at a Hole belowe the Sight or Visier, which is shutt with a Screw smaller below then above'. A wheel-lock rifle of *c.*1680 in the Victoria and Albert Museum[18] is perhaps an
110 example of this idea. The upper plane of the breech end of the barrel has been pierced with a threaded hole for loading. This is filled with a screw-plug surmounted by a square nut which is slotted to act as a back-sight. This type of screw-plug needed a key or wrench for removal and being only a small object could be easily lost in the field. Simple though it was from the constructional point of view it had such obvious disadvantages that it is surprising how many guns used it throughout the eighteenth and early nineteenth centuries, the plug being placed on top, underneath or at the side of the barrel.

In some instances the screw-plug was provided with a wing nut of sufficient size and strength to be moved by the fingers, but most makers recognised that the plug needed a permanently-attached lever placed in a convenient position for effective operation. With the Kalthoff guns as an example it is curious that the gunmakers took so long to realise that a movable trigger-guard provided the answer to their problems. One Danish gunmaker, Johan Merckel, produced a breech-loading rifle with a screw-plug which was turned by a separate, curved lever which, in the closed position, lay flush round the front of the trigger-guard.[19] Merckel was an apprentice of the famous Heinrich Kappel of Copenhagen and was admitted to the Guild of Master Gunmakers in 1706. It is doubtful whether his rifle can be dated earlier than *c.*1710.

The credit for the invention of a satisfactory screw-plug breech-loading system must go to the French engineer Isaac de la Chaumette. He was a man of many talents. In 1700 he had published, by the Royal Academy of Science in Paris,[20] the first of a number of inventions which ranged from military weapons–guns, bayonets and powder-flasks–to more prosaic objects like smokeless chimneys and unspillable snuff-boxes. His first invention related to a pair of holster pistols which could be joined together to form a carbine (*pistolet d'arçon dont on peut faire une Carabine*). This was done by giving one of the pistols a straight-through barrel open at both ends. A vertical screw plug joined to the front of the trigger-guard was threaded right through the barrel to act as a breech-plug. When it was desired to convert the pistols into a carbine, this plug was unscrewed and the muzzle of the other pistol was screwed into the rear of the breech. A highly doubtful arrangement which does not seem to have been tried, but it gave La Chaumette the idea for his next invention, which was a straightforward breech-loader utilising the screw plug and trigger-guard combination to control an opening on top of the barrel. He published the details of this gun, his *Fusil qui se charge par la culasse*, in 1704, and continued nearly every year until 1715 to produce some ingenious device for the approbation of his fellow scientists. A sporting gun with the screw-plug action of La Chaumette in the Musée de l'Armée, Paris, signed *C. Chasteau A Paris* and dated 1718, indicates that La Chaumette's work was not without recognition in his own country. But the first signs that it had met with any popular approval did not emerge until 12 August 1721.

On that date La Chaumette, who had emigrated to England, possibly as a religious refugee,[21] took out an English patent (No. 434) to safeguard 'Divers Engines, Machines and Instruments'. In the fashion of his time the wording was couched in vague and general terms. The breech-loading guns were

18 No. 124–1897.

19 In the Tøjhusmuseum, Copenhagen (No. B. 1140). Blackmore, *Guns and Rifles,* No. 387.

20 See *Machines et Inventions Approuvées par l'Académie Royale des Sciences,* Paris, 1735.

21 See David Agnew, *Protestant Exiles from France*, Edinburgh, 1886, Vol. II, p. 258.

referred to as follows:

> A cannon or piece of ordnance, which being charged by the breech through the barrel, is cooled by cleaning it and cleaned by firing it; it carries twice as far as those comonly in use and requires but halfe the quantity of powder and halfe the length of an ordinary cannon and does not recoyl; it is very useful especially at sea where the gunners will not be exposed as they now are in loading the guns and it may be fired ten times as often, which will render a ship or place unapproachable–fusils and pistols of the like make.

This allusion to the accuracy of the breech-loader and the cleaning action of the shot indicates that the employment of a slightly oversize tight-fitting ball was intended.

A few weeks after the grant of his patent La Chaumette announced in the London newspaper the *Daily Courant* for 27 October 1721, that

> a publick Tryal of the said Firearms is to be made at the Artillery Ground in Bunhill Fields, on Thursday the 2nd November next, between 10 & 11 in the Forenoon; and any Person desiring to be furnished with such Guns and Arms may enquire at White's Chocolate House, St. James's Str.

There is no report of this trial but that the breech-loaders were successful can be gauged from the fact that the Gunmakers' Company of London saw fit to call a special meeting on 5 December 1723, when a formal protest was registered against La Chaumette's patent 'for the sole makeing of a new invented hand-gun of which a considerable Quantitye had been made and more bespoke to the great prejudice of the Trade.'[22]

An attempt was made to prevent the guns from being proved and thus restricting their open sale, but some of the company's members were obviously engaged in their manufacture and only a limited embargo seems to have been enforced. The most noted maker of the La Chaumette guns was a compatriot, Bidet, also domiciled in London. Although not a member of the Gunmakers' Company he was, in fact, allowed to prove guns and appears in the Company's proof register from 1721-31. Several La Chaumette guns made by him are recorded, the outstanding example being the silver-decorated gun, probably made for George I of England, in the collection of the Duke of Brunswick, exhibited at the Tower of London in 1952.[23]

This gun incorporates several improvements on La Chaumette's original design; the plug has been cut with a quick thread so that one turn of the trigger-guard is sufficient to open the breech, and a removable stop has been fitted just behind the trigger to prevent the plug from being overturned and extracted in error. In screw-plug breeches where the latter event was possible some difficulty was always experienced during replacement of the plug in finding the right groove so that the plug was properly re-seated. Whether these important modifications are to the credit of the inventor or the gunmaker is not known, but an inscription on the barrel leaves no doubt as to the virtues of the inventor:

> *Carabine Nouvelle*
> *La Chaumette a produit ce foudroyant tonnerre*
> *De tout ses protecteurs on benira le sort*
> *Puisque c'est le moyen de terminer la guerre*
> *Et d'etablir des siecles d'or.*
> (New Carbine
> La Chaumette has made this terrible gun
> All its patrons will be blessed
> For it is the means of ending war
> and establishing the Golden Age.)

The inventor of the gun would also appear to be the author of the verse as a later poem refers to him as *géomètre, artilleur, poëte.*[24]

In his own country La Chaumette's chief protagonist or plagiarist, as the case may be, was none other than the great Marshal Saxe. This famous, naturalised Frenchman came to Paris in 1719 preparatory to taking up his first command, and it was no doubt at this time that he became acquainted with the new breech-loaders. Not having any great sense of modesty, he appears to have adopted them as his own invention. In his military memoirs *Mes Rêveries*, first published in 1757 seven years after his death, he advocated the use of La Chaumette's breech action in a cavalry carbine and in a light piece of artillery called an *Amusette.*[25] These breech-loaders were reputedly issued to the French Army and Navy, but no evidence supports this.

Gunmakers on both sides of the English Channel, however, continued to make sporting versions of the screw-plug breech-loader. Benjamin Robins in 1747[26] remarked on the fact that 'the rifled barrels

22 H. L. Blackmore, *British Military Firearms*, London, 1961, p. 81.

23 *Catalogue of an Exhibition of Arms, Armour and Militaria at the Armouries of the Tower of London*, 1952. No. 138.

24 Anatole de Montaiglon (Ed.), *Archives de l'Art Français*, etc. Paris, 1862, 2nd Series, Tom. 2.

25 In some editions of the book the Amusette is shown as a muzzle-loader but in the Amsterdam edition of 1757 both guns are clearly shown with screw plug breeches à La Chaumette.

26 'Of the Nature and Advantages of Rifled Barrel Pieces', read to the Royal Society in July, 1747. (Published as Appendix II in the second edition of the same author's *New Principles of Gunnery*, London 1805).

which have been made in England . . . are contrived to be charged at the breech, where the piece is for this purpose made larger than in any other part. And the powder and bullet are put in through the side of the barrel by an opening which, when the piece is loaded, is filled with a screw.' Nevertheless the breech-loader of this period was regarded with a certain amount of distrust. Diderot in the supplement to his *Encyclopédie* of 1777[27] commented on the La Chaumette action in particular–'Ces sortes de pieces sont ingénieuses & meritent un place dans un cabinet de curiosités, mais à la guerre, il faut des armes sûres & solides & c'est à ces qualités sur-tout qu'il faut s'attacher.' While he was writing these words another inventor was busy proving him wrong.

In March 1776 Captain Patrick Ferguson of the 70th Regiment took out a patent in London for a screw-plug breech-loader apparently identical to that of La Chaumette. The specification of his patent, however, shows that Ferguson made no claim to the main mechanism. In fact he made a reference to his prèdecessor's work with these words: 'something similar to this has been attempted, but has always failed for want of the following improvements, and indeed has never been seriously studied as an object of public utility, or rendered in any degree fit for service'.

Ferguson's improvements[28] consisted of: a projection under the barrel to house the plug when it was lowered; a smooth section cut across the threads of the plug where it formed the breech; vertical grooves cut into the threads; and a small reservoir, or hollow, behind the screw-plug. The first improvements had already been used by Bidet, but the last three, which were intended either to prevent fouling forming on the screw threads or to help clear them, were the really important measures. There is little doubt that excessive fouling of the screw-plug breech had foiled all previous attempts to popularise it. Just how effective were Ferguson's improvements can be judged by the reports of a trial of his rifle which were published widely in the *Annual Register, The Gentleman's Magazine* and most of the London newspapers in June 1776. Ferguson had had two rifles made for him by the London gunmaker Durs Egg, and he had first demonstrated their superiority over the musket for the benefit of Lord Townshend and other officers of the Board of Ordnance. Townshend then arranged for Generals Hervey and Desaguliers and other high-ranking officers to witness a full-scale demonstration on 1 June 1776. It was anything but the glorious First of June. The experiments were conducted on the marshes of Woolwich Warren near London in the face of driving rain and a strong gusty wind. The reports described how Ferguson:

> performed the following four things, none of which had ever before been accomplished with any other small arms; 1st He fired during four or or five minutes at a target, at 200 yards distant, at the rate of four shots each minute. 2dly He fired six shots in one minute. 3dly He fired four times per minute, advancing at the same time at the rate of four miles in the hour. 4thly, He poured a bottle of water into the pan and barrel of the piece when loaded so as to wet every grain of the powder, and in less than half a minute fired with her as well as ever, without extracting the ball. He also hit the bull's eye at 100 yards lying with his back on the ground; and, notwithstanding the unequalness of the wind and wetness of the weather, he only missed the target three times during the whole course of the experiments.

Ferguson's breechloading flintlock rifle, *c.*1775. Inscribed TOWER and GR (crowned). Morristown National Historical Park, New Jersey, U.S.A.

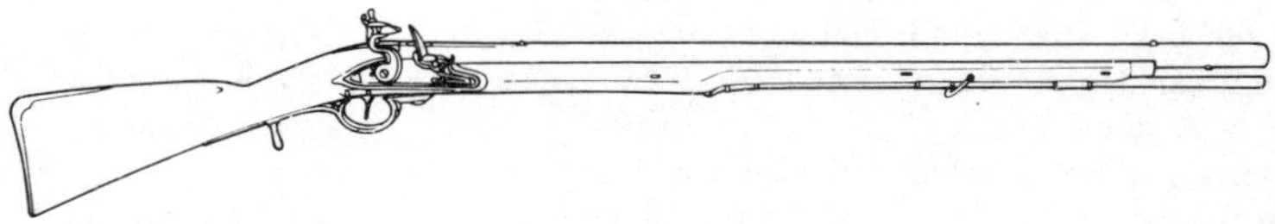

No one could fail to be impressed by these results, and the Board of Ordnance who had recently ordered muzzle-loading rifles from manufacturers in Germany and Birmingham, England immediately put in hand preparations for the manufacture of 100 of Ferguson's breech-loading rifles.

The intention was to arm a small detachment of men so that the rifle could be tested under active-service conditions in the American War of Independence then in progress. In February 1777 the detachment was formally raised at Chatham Barracks with volunteers from the 6th and 14th Regiments. Ferguson then took command and put his men through an intensive course of training. The Corps of Riflemen arrived in America in May 1777 and joined the army of General Howe. On 11 September they took part in the Battle of Brandywine, fighting

27 Vol. III, p. 163.

28 The patent also included other forms of breech action, an elevating sight and a new type of rifling.

in the vanguard of General von Knyphausen's column. Here they distinguished themselves and proved beyond doubt the qualities of their arms. Unfortunately Ferguson himself was wounded and with his temporary withdrawal from the campaign the Riflemen were disbanded and distributed among the light companies of other regiments. Ferguson recovered and subsequently became a daring leader of special corps until his death at the Battle of King's Mountain in 1780. As far as is known no more government-issue models of his rifle were made.

These events had not gone unnoticed in England and several London gunmakers, including the original maker Durs Egg, supplied volunteer companies with military carbines and also produced fine-quality sporting rifles of the Ferguson pattern. Some of these guns, probably made under licence from the patentee, are stamped with the letters *PF* under a crown. The majority of military models of the Ferguson rifle were intended as infantry weapons and were armed with a long socket bayonet, or a sliding bayonet, but the East India Company also ordered a small number of full-stocked breech-loaders from Henry Nock apparently for issue to their cavalry.[29]

There are no signs that the Ferguson rifle was reconsidered by the British Army on the outbreak of war with France in 1793, and one of the last specimens of the screw plug breech-loaders was made by the Norwegian gunmaker, Erik Larsen Svørsdal, in 1810. As Master Gunmaker of the Bergenhus infantry regiment he made a copy of the Ferguson and presented it to his king, Frederick VI, as his own invention. The screw-plug breech brought little advantage to the operation of the pistol apart from quick loading and only a few specimens of pistols made in the Ferguson pattern are known.

There were other types of movable-breech plugs apart from the screwed ones, although they never attained the latter's popularity. One of the first was a development of the Kalthoff magazine guns.[30] In some models of these guns rotation of the trigger-guard moved a rectangular breech-block in a horizontal plane at right angles to the line of the barrel. In the magazine guns its purpose was to convey charges of ball and powder from magazine to barrel, but, in a gun made by the Danish gunmaker Heinrich Kappel in *c.*1690, the complicated repeating mechanism was omitted and the breech-block left to perform the simple function of a single-shot breech-loader. When the breech-block was moved to the left by turning the trigger-guard, a loose part of the butt could be removed revealing the open breech end of the barrel ready for the insertion of the charge.

Of slightly earlier date and probably unique in its construction is the gun signed by Peter Diringer of Mainz, in the Bayerisches Nationalmuseum, Munich.[31] It has a round, loading aperture underneath the breech end of the barrel which is closed by a sliding push-in cylindrical plug. This is tight-fitting and is forced into position by a long lever hinged to the barrel which acts as the trigger-guard. A spring catch locks the lever and plug in position. Diringer seems to have had a good understanding of mechanical principles and he placed the fulcrum of this lever where it could convey the maximum thrust to the breech-plug. Other gunmakers who designed breeches with sliding plugs or blocks did not appreciate this. Many of them provided no leverage at all and the shutter had to be manipulated by the fingers or by a blow from a hammer, neither of which would have been easy once the breech had become fouled. Examples of these breech-loaders were made by Theiss of Nuremberg in *c.*1660[32] and by Montalembert in 1776.[33] La Chaumette published in 1705 a breech with a pull-down conical plug, kept in place by a spring shaped to act as a trigger-guard. Ferguson's patent also included two breeches with sliding pull-out lids.

Included in this section on breeches with movable plugs is another group with revolving breech-blocks or faucets. In these the plug has no motion other than a turning one, and is recessed or hollowed out to provide access to the barrel. A gun in Dresden, signed by Adam Knot,[34] appears to have been made on the La Chaumette system, but when the trigger-guard is turned to the front, the plug does not drop down. Instead a loading channel, which runs through the plug from its top to its side, is brought opposite the mouth of the barrel. Powder and ball can then be poured through the plug into the chamber. Reversing the trigger-guard brings the solid part of the plug into position to seal off the end of the barrel. A pair of pistols and a gun of similar design, signed *J. C. Peter à Carlsbadt*, are in the Smithsonian Institution, Washington.

In the Lorenzoni magazine action[35] the main part of the mechanism consisted of a cylindrical breech-block with a recess large enough to take the charge, revolving on a horizontal axis. This device was also

29 H. L. Blackmore, *Guns and Rifles of the World*, London, 1965, Nos. 399–403.

30 See p. 207.

31 Thierbach, *op.cit.*, Fig. 488.

32 W. W. Greener, *The Gun and its Development*, London, 9th edn. (1910), p. 109.

33 Thierbach, *op.cit.*, Fig. 487.

34 ibid., Fig. 486.

35 See p. 208.

adapted by some gunmakers for use as a single-shot breech-loader. A rifle of this kind was made for trial by the British Army in 1801. The rolling breech-block was connected to a long lever which lay alongside the barrel in the closed position. When the lever was raised vertically the breech-block revolved bringing the mouth of its recess or chamber opposite a loading aperture in the top of the breech housing.

Breech-loaders with Separate Chambers

In nearly all cases, breech-loaders which employed some form of movable breech-plug were by necessity charged with loose powder and ball. But from the sixteenth century onwards the use of paper cartridges for muzzle-loading military weapons at least was widespread, and the designers of breech-loaders were obliged also to cater for these accessories. This section of breech-loaders–those with separate chambers–were in effect cartridge arms.

It has been noted that Leonardo da Vinci designed guns in which a metal chamber or cartridge loaded with powder and ball was inserted in the breech. To lock the cartridge in position he employed the wedge as used in the larger guns, the perriers. This might function well with artillery but had its limitations on shoulder arms. Until the end of the eighteenth century designers of this type of breech-loader were concerned mainly with the problem of how to insert and withdraw these metal chambers with speed without endangering the security of the gun. The actual chamber or cartridge remained basically the same metal (brass or iron) cylinder closed at one end and drilled with a touch-hole.

The earliest specimens of breech-loaders with separate chambers are all due to the initiative of that great admirer of arms and armour, Henry VIII. In the Tower of London[36] are two guns believed to have been made for him. One is a carbine dated 1537 and bearing the initials *HR*, and the other is a long heavy gun stamped with the maker's mark of a *WH* over a fleur-de-lis. This may be the mark of William Hunt, a gunmaker who was appointed 'Keeper of the King's Handguns and Demi-Hawks' in 1538. Both guns have similar breech-loading actions. A hinged trapdoor on top of the breech lifts up to reveal a loading tray into which is dropped the metal cartridge. The latter is pushed into the barrel by a projection on its base, through which is drilled the touch-hole, fitting into a slot cut in the mouth of the barrel. The trapdoor, or breech-block, is then closed and locked by a catch.

Also in the Tower of London are a number of round shields, each with a breech-loading matchlock pistol in its centre, probably made for a royal bodyguard. The only clue to their date of manufacture is a letter of 1544 from Giovanbattista, a painter of Ravenna in Italy, offering to reveal to Henry VIII (on payment of passage money) a number of secret weapons including 'several round shields and arm pieces with guns inside that fire upon the enemy and pierce any armour.'[37] Apart from minor variations in design and construction the shields are all made of wood armoured on the outside with steel plates and lined inside with leather. Some still show traces of their original gilded decoration. The pistols have a pivoted lid at the rear which swings up for the insertion of the metal cartridge. A cock controlled by a small lever-trigger holds the match.

The hinged trapdoor breech was used on a number
of wheel-lock sporting guns, outstanding examples 33
of which are the beautifully decorated saddle-carbine in the Armeria Reale, Turin[38] and the gun with the self-spanning lock in the Wallace Collection, London.[39] As always with these early breech-loaders, pistol examples are exceedingly rare, but there is one in the Victoria and Albert Museum[40] by Hans Stockmann of Dresden, dated 1610, and another in the Museum für Deutsche Geschichte, Berlin.

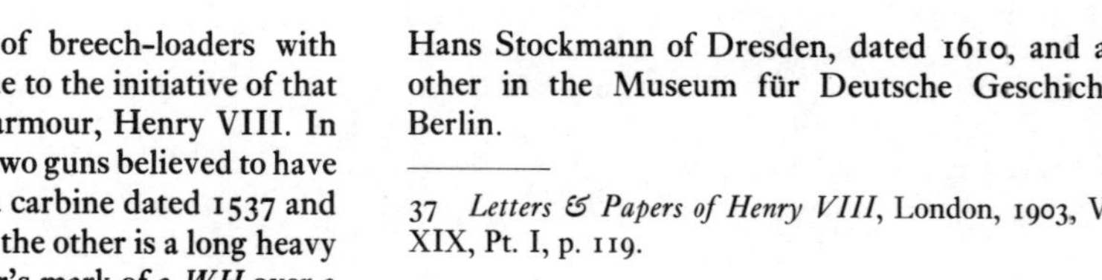

Detail of breech-loading carbine of Henry VIII. English, dated 1537. (Breech shown open; lock missing.) Tower of London Armouries.

36 Nos. XII 1 & 2.

37 *Letters & Papers of Henry VIII*, London, 1903, Vol. XIX, Pt. I, p. 119.

38 No. N.10.

39 No. A. 1081.

40 No. M641–1927.

Detail of breech-loading long-gun of Henry VIII. English, *c.*1537. Tower of London Armouries.

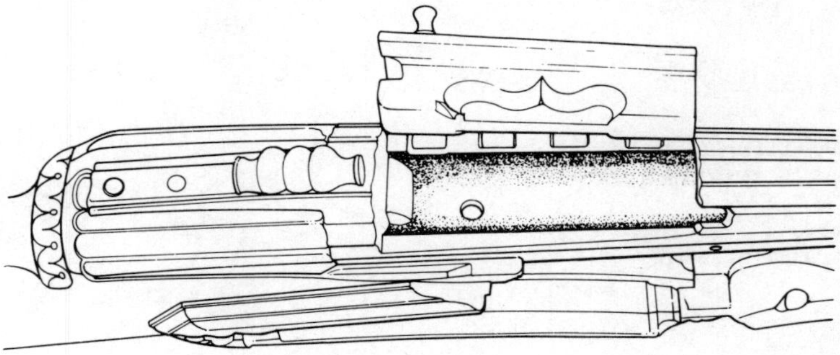

Detail of breech-loading wheel-lock pistol by Hans Stockmann of Dresden. German, *c.*1610. Victoria & Albert Museum, London.

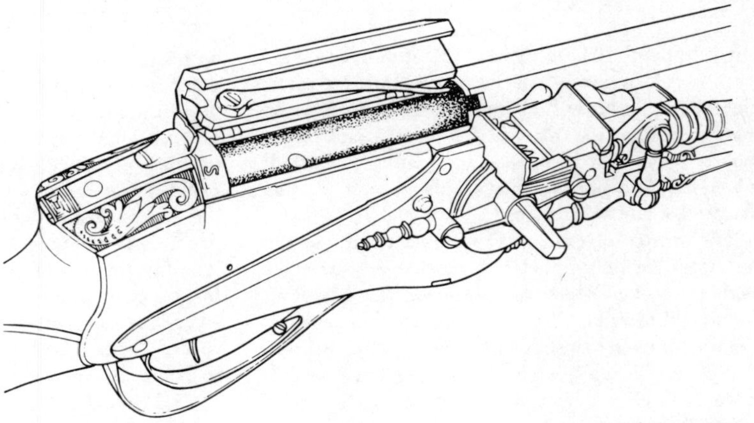

Matchlock guns were rarely considered worthy of a breech-loading action, but a long wall gun in the Bern Historisches Museum[41] has an open breech end into which is placed a substantial metal chamber or cartridge with a strong handle sticking out at the rear. It is retained by a large metal wedge which is thrust vertically through a slot in the rear of the cartridge down into a similar aperture in the stock. This gun dates from the early seventeenth century.

With the introduction of the flintlock and the construction of lighter stocks and barrels, another type of breech action to take metal chambers was developed. This was the so-called 'break-action' breech, in which the barrel was hinged at the breech and, when released, dropped down or moved sideways to open its breech for the cartridge. Examples of this type of breech action are to be found in all the national collections, but two of the most beautiful pieces may be mentioned. The first, which opens with a sideways motion and is a fine specimen of chiselled steel workmanship, was made by a member of the Acqua Fresca family of gunmakers in Bargi, near Bologna in 1694, and is now in the Birmingham City Museum. In more lavish style is the drop-down barrel gun in the Real Armería, Madrid.[42] This was made by Joseph Cano of Madrid in 1736 and was redecorated for Philip V in 1738 with gold and diamond embellishments to the value of 27,000 reales.[43]

The last gun was provided with a set of twelve spare chambers each with its priming-pan and steel. The gun thus became a rather clumsy edition of the modern shotgun, but with the additional weight of the all-metal cartridges. Opinions were divided as to whether the cartridges should have their own pan and steel. Some gunmakers, as in the Acqua Fresca gun mentioned above, fitted a magazine primer to the lock and used plain cartridges to obtain the same effect. One of the problems with these guns was the task of extracting the fired cartridge. If no pan was fitted it was difficult to pull

41 No. 2216.

42 No. K. 156.

43 James D. Lavin, *A History of Spanish Firearms*, London, 1965, p. 99. H. L. Blackmore, *Guns and Rifles of the World*, London, 1965, No. 418.

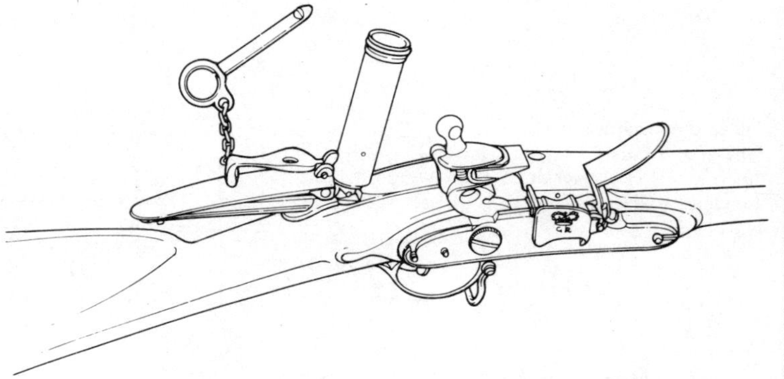

Detail of tip-up breech-loading musket by Henry Nock of London. English, *c.*1786. Tower of London Armouries.

out, although Nicolas Paris, the gunmaker who worked in Warwick in the late seventeenth and early eighteenth centuries, and made a number of most
138 ingenious firearms, produced a break-action gun whose brass cartridge was automatically ejected when the gun was opened. This is now in the Warwick County Museum.

The matter of extraction was dealt with in no uncertain fashion by Henry Nock on a breech-loading musket which he made for the Duke of Richmond in 1786. This had a separate, but captive, chamber hinged to a slide on top of the stock behind the breech. When this metal chamber was inserted it was locked by a vertical peg with a ringed handle on top. It is a clumsy-looking piece of apparatus but like most of Henry Nock's ideas it worked well. A quick upward and backward jerk on the ring immediately released and extracted the chamber, which was left in a convenient upright position for loading. This gun was one of the last to use the reloadable metal chamber or cartridge in this way.[44] The extra weight involved told against it and after *c.*1800 gunmakers concentrated on the use of paper and other expendable cartridges. These were, to start with, more applicable to the last section of breech-loaders in this review–those with pivoted chambers.

Breech-loaders with Pivoted Chambers

All the breech-loaders discussed so far have, with but minor exceptions, been loaded with loose powder and ball. Although Patrick Ferguson, for one, had proved that such guns could be made to function with speed and safety, there was always an inherent delay in charging a firearm with powder from one flask, priming from the same or from another, and then loading a ball from still another container. Loose powder also brought with it the hazard of accidental explosion. Military authorities, therefore, favoured the breech-loader which could take the standard paper cartridge used with the muzzle-loading guns. The first breech-loader to be successfully adapted for this purpose was of the type in which the breech end of the barrel is separated from the main portion, and is pivoted so that it will tip up or move sideways to expose the mouth of the chamber.

This kind of action can be traced back to Leonardo da Vinci's cannon whose breech unscrewed and tipped up for loading. It was a mechanism which defeated the efforts of gunmakers to incorporate with the wheel-lock, and the first handguns with such breeches do not appear until the second half of the seventeenth century. The 1664 English patent of Abraham Hill[45] included a 'New Way of Makeing of a Gun or Pistoll the Breech whereof Riseth upon an Hindge by a Contrivance of a Motion from under it, by which it is also let down againe and bolted fast by One and the same Motion . . .' An example of this breech is found on the flintlock gun now in the 139
Tower of London[46] made by John Bicknell of London, who was one of Hill's contemporaries. The rear end of the breech is pivoted and connected to a long lever trigger-guard. When the tip of this is released from a catch on the stock and thrust down, the front of the chamber rises for loading. Chamber and barrel fit together with a simple slanting butt-joint, which, although under pressure from the lever when closed, would have allowed some of the gases of the explosion to escape.

44 After the introduction of percussion ignition the old-style metal cartridge with a percussion nipple screwed in its base was revived for a short time. It was also used on the Roper repeater of 1866.

45 See p. 192.

46 No. XII–1617.

In following the course of development of the pivoted-chamber breech the main interest lies in the different methods adopted for preventing this escape of gas. Peter Diringer of Mainz[47] attempted it by joining the two parts together with an interrupted screw thread. In Diringer's gun, which dates not long after that of Bicknell, the barrel and fore-end after unlocking are thrust forward in their holding bands to allow the chamber to spring up. As has been commented on before, however, the introduction of any movement to the barrel immediately weakened the strength of the whole gun, a serious matter in military models. For this reason probably the only pivoted-chamber breech-loaders to be adopted in any quantity were those in which the gas escape from the joint was largely ignored.

The first of these was invented by Giuseppe Crespi, a watchmaker of Milan in 1770. He used the slanting butt-joint of Bicknell's gun but locked it together with a hinged lever which engaged under two lugs on top of the breech casing. The rights of this invention were bought by the Austrian Army for 1,500 ducats, and carbines using his system were issued to the cavalry. Examination of surviving specimens of these carbines shows that as they became well-used the gas escape was in many cases excessive enough to burn the wooden stock. It was little wonder that in 1779 the carbines were withdrawn. In the 1790s, probably because of a shortage of firearms, they were re-issued to the city militia of Vienna for a brief spell of service.[48]

In 1784 the London gunmaker Durs Egg was commissioned by the Duke of Richmond to make two exact copies of the Crespi carbine. After initial difficulties in proving the strange breeches, an experimental batch of thirty carbines was ordered from Egg. They were made in three different barrel lengths 2 ft 4 in, 2 ft 9 in, and 3 ft 2 in, half being rifled and the remainder left smooth-bore. Two unusual features of their design were the special flintlocks of the so-called screwless pattern and their long spear bayonets. The Egg carbines were issued for extensive trials by the Light Dragoons in 1786. The conflicting reports received from the regiments in 1788 and the unfavourable news of their progress in Austria led to the abandonment of the whole scheme.[49]

The last significant appearance in England, during the flintlock period, of the pivoted breech-loader came in 1817. In that year Urbanus Sartoris, who was a merchant by trade, patented in London and Paris a breech-loader in which barrel and chamber were joined by an interrupted screw-thread. It was a direct revival of Peter Diringer's action and the only refinement that Sartoris added was a folding handle on the barrel to help manipulate it. Unfortunately for the inventor it was the wrong time to market a new firearm. The aftermath of the Napoleonic Wars had left the military authorities with thousands of unwanted arms on their hands. There were also the first signs that the flintlock was to be replaced by the precussion lock. Although Sartoris patented some minor modifications to the breech-loader in 1819 he succeeded in winning orders only for a few sporting models and for some carbines and rifles for Volunteer troops. In 1826 he was forced into liquidation.

But meanwhile in America two other inventors working on similiar lines had agreed to join forces. John Hancock Hall of Portsmouth, Maine and William Thornton of Washington took out a joint patent in 1811 for a breech-loader with a tip-up breech chamber to be used on both guns and pistols. The Hall breech-loader,[50] as it became known, differed from all its predecessors in that the chamber and flintlock were incorporated in one breech-block. This was a neater arrangement than the others but no attempt was made to seal the gap between barrel and chamber, and the gun became notorious for its gas leakage. Nevertheless, after the war of 1812, extensive tests of the gun were organised and it was adopted as an official US rifle in 1819–the first
breech-loader to be made a standard issue weapon. 140
The strange thing is that it was not the escape of gas which seemed to worry the soldiers, but the large hook catch used to lock the chamber in position, which hung down under the stock, galled their shoulders and became entangled in their equipment.

The Hall breech was applied to several military models, the majority of which were manufactured at Harper's Ferry Armoury under the supervision of the inventor, who devised special machinery for their mass production, though some were also produced under contract. The principal model was a 0·52 in calibre rifle but carbines were also produced. In 1833 a Hall carbine became the first US martial arm to be converted to the percussion-cap ignition. It was a significant step. While breech-loaders like the Crespi and Hall depended on the flintlock, with its need for a separate supply of priming powder, little real progress could be made. It was the introduction of the percussion system which enabled the breech-loader finally to gain ascendancy.

47 See p. 191.

48 F. H. Baer, 'The First Effective Military Breech-loaders,' *Art, Arms & Armor*, I, Chiasso, 1979, pp. 458-77.

49 H. L. Blackmore, *British Military Firearms*, London 1961, pp. 87-89.

50 R. T. Huntington, *Hall's Breechloaders*, York, Pennsylvania 1972.

CHAPTER SEVEN

Early Repeating Firearms

H.L. Peterson

Loading a gun before each shot is a time-consuming process, even for a breech-loader with modern self-contained cartridges. With loose ammunition and muzzle-loading firearms it frequently took so long that a man could count on only one shot at his target. Thus the advantages of having a gun that could fire several successive shots after each loading quickly became apparent. Almost from the beginning designers sought to produce such weapons. For more than three hundred years they pursued this goal in many varied and ingenious ways until the metal-cased cartridge finally provided the key to complete success. With one major exception the present chapter traces the history of the attempts to produce repeating arms before the perfection of the self-contained cartridge. The revolver, which developed into a practical weapon even without fixed ammunition, is discussed in other chapters as a topic in itself.

One of the most obvious ways to obtain extra shots from a gun was to increase the number of barrels. The ribauldequins which appeared during the second quarter of the fourteenth century are regarded by some authorities as the earliest examples of this approach. The usual ribauldequin is believed to have consisted of a group of parallel barrels fastened to a frame with their touch-holes aligned so that they could be fired almost simultaneously by applying the lighted match or coal to a train of powder laid across them. When fired in this manner they were really volley guns rather than repeaters. Some ribauldequins, however, offered several tiers of barrels that could be brought into firing position in successive stages and so could perhaps be considered the earliest of the repeaters.[1]

The use of multiple barrels was so obvious, and so simple, that the principle has continued in use almost without a break from the fourteenth century to the present. There have been double-barrelled shotguns and rifles, sometimes with the barrels side-by-side; sometimes one above the other. Upon occasion two smooth-bore barrels have been combined with a rifled barrel to produce a three-barrelled gun, and there have been other combinations as well offering the shooter a choice of bores as well as additional shots. Pistols, too, have been made with multiple barrels. The earliest surviving specimens date from the sixteenth century, but the greatest period of popularity began during the eighteenth century. Flintlock pistols with two, three, four or even more barrels were made in considerable quantity as weapons for self-defence. Shortly after the appearance of the percussion system the pepper-box with its rotating barrel-block superseded the fixed barrel types, but a final renaissance of popularity for the multi-barrelled pistols came still later in the era of the metallic cartridge and continued into the present century.

Most of these multi-barrelled arms were designed to fire one load after another at the choice of the shooter. In the case of arms offering different sizes or types of bore, it was necessary for the user to select the proper barrel to fit the situation in which he found himself. In arms offering several barrels of the same type, the firing order was usually automatic. Such individual shots could be achieved in many ways. Separate gun-locks for each barrel offered one of the most obvious methods, and it is still used today for many double-barrelled shotguns and similar arms. Providing movable barrels that could be brought under a fixed lock was another method, and it has been especially popular for over-and-under rifles and shotguns whether ignited by flint or percussion. Two other methods, which were especially popular for pocket-pistols during the flintlock era, were the divided priming-pan and the valve or tap action. Sometimes, in fact, both methods were employed on the same arm. In the divided pan a partition or partitions created two or even three separate compartments, each connected by a touch-hole to a different barrel. A split pan-cover could then be adjusted to expose only one compartment at a time to the sparks struck by the flint from the steel, thus firing only one barrel at a time. In the tap action, each pan or pan compartment was connected by separate touch-holes to two or more barrels. A

1 It is not certain, however, that the earliest firearms ribauldequins included guns. See A. V. B. Norman's comment in *Journal of the Arms and Armour Society*, Vol. VIII, pp. 236-7.

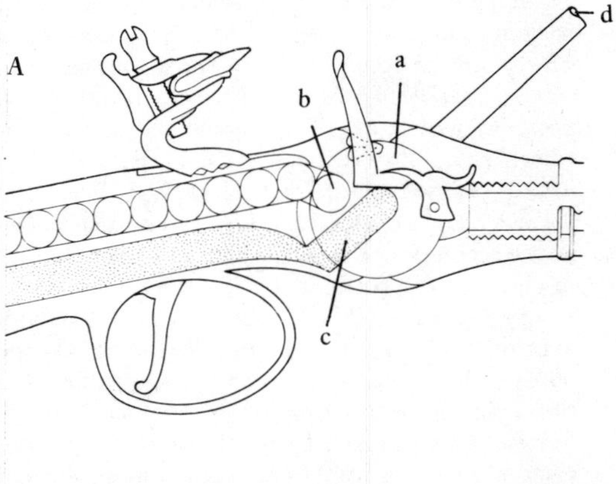

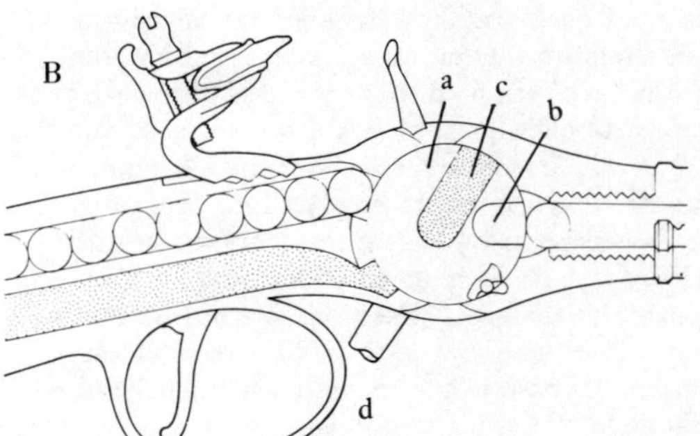

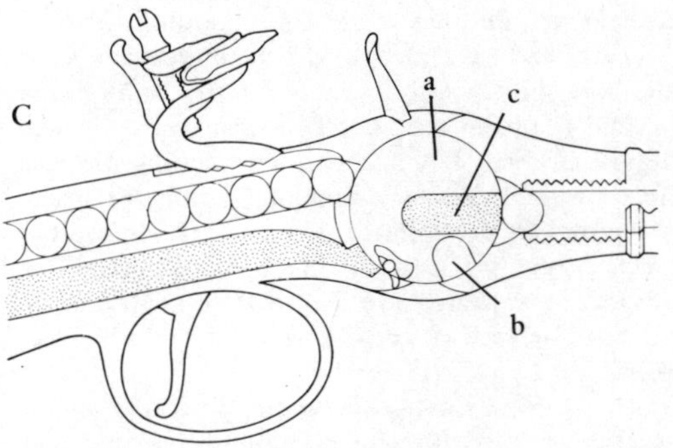

THE OPERATION OF THE LORENZONI/COOKSON REPEATING MECHANISM (See p. 208.)

The drawings show a section through the breech part of the butt with the lock partly cut away. After firing, the mechanism is in the position shown on bottom drawing except that the cock and steel are down. To load the gun or pistol fitted with the system it is held muzzle down and the cylindrical breech-block (a) is rotated backwards by a handle on the left side (d) to the position shown in drawing A. As this happens, the pan-cover is closed by a cam and the cock pushed back to the half-cock position by an arm, while the pan is primed from a small magazine (not shown) attached to it. The block contains a powder-chamber (c) and a ball-recess (b) which, when in the top position, are gravity-fed with a charge of powder and a ball respectively from tubular magazines in the butt. The powder-chamber is partly blocked by a cross-bar so that it does not pick up a ball as it passes the mouth of the ball-magazine. The block is next rotated forward again and, as it reaches the position shown in middle drawing, the ball drops into the breech of the barrel. It is finally returned to bottom position, in which the chamber containing the powder-change is stationed immediately behind the ball ready for firing.

manually operated valve opened the hole to the barrel selected by the shooter. The final major method for firing a number of barrels selectively developed during the percussion era and involved the use of movable hammer-faces or firing pins.

All of these firearms with two or more barrels did indeed offer a shooter additional shots for each loading. Some of them, in fact, worked very well. Yet all suffered from one common drawback: every barrel that was added increased the weight and awkwardness of the piece. When such additional barrels offer the extra choice of different bores the advantage has sometimes outweighed the increased bulk. Thus such arms are still being manufactured and used. When it was simply a matter of providing additional shots of the same size and type, the arrangement was not so satisfactory. The ideal was a gun that would fire numerous shots through a single barrel, thus avoiding the drawbacks of weight and unwieldiness that were unavoidable with extra barrels. Such a gun would be a true repeater with each charge utilising the same action and barrel as opposed to the multi-shot category described above in which different barrels, and sometimes different actions, were provided for each load.

The search for such a true repeater began at least as early as the sixteenth century, and in general it followed three principal lines of development: the revolving cylinder, the use of super-imposed loads, and the magazine. The revolver, which may actually be the oldest of all the repeaters, is often considered as a separate weapon and, as already noted, is discussed elsewhere in this work. The evolution of the other two approaches therefore provides the basis for this study of early repeaters.

Of these two remaining systems the earliest was undoubtedly the use of super-imposed loads. Definite documentary evidence can be found for its employment in Germany as early as the beginning of the fifteenth century, and in 1580 John the Almain wrote a recommendation for one of his German countrymen stating that he could make an harquebus 'that shall containe ten balls or pellets of lead, all the which shall goe off, one after another, haveinge once given fire'.[2] Collectors today often refer to this as the Roman candle system because of the way one shot follows another after a single ignition until all loads have been fired. In its simplest form such guns utilised bullets pierced completely through, and the holes filled with a fuse compound. A number of powder charges would be placed in the gun barrel, each separated by one of these bullets so oriented that the hole with its fuse ran directly from one charge to the next. When the foremost charge was ignited, either by a lock or by a powder train or match, its flash would theoretically light the fuse in the hole of the bullet immediately behind it. This would burn through and set off the charge behind in a chain reaction that would continue until the final load was fired. Needless to say the bullets had to fit the bore tightly. Otherwise the flashes would pass around the balls and set off the successive charges almost at once. The necessity for aligning the fuse holes properly and for ramming home the tight-fitting bullets necessitated slow and careful loading. Such a gun had to be prepared for firing well in advance of expected use. Normally it could not be reloaded in action and so was useless after one firing.

Almost from the beginning gun designers sought to alleviate this situation by adding a second gun lock in the normal position with its own touch-hole. Once the super-imposed loads in such a piece had been fired, it could be loaded and used like any other firearm of its era. It is not known whether John the Almain's friend made guns with such a second lock, but there is evidence that the system was employed at least as early as 1534, the date on a two-shot wheel-lock gun of German manufacture utilising this two-lock system in the Frank E. Bivens collection, Los Angeles. In the same collection is a Nuremberg gun of *c.*1590-1610 taking sixteen charges. In this instance the forward lock fired the first nine shots while a safety catch prevented the wheel of the rear lock from turning and a solid bullet or wad stopped the chain reaction at that point. Then a tube filled with a priming compound, and connecting the pan of the rear lock with another touch-hole part way up the barrel, allowed the shooter to fire a second series of six shots Roman candle fashion. This left a single shot still in the breech which could be fired by sliding a gate in the pan to one side and exposing a third touch-hole in the normal position, repriming the pan and respanning the wheel–or as a final refinement using a lighted match in a serpentine provided on the lockplate. Thereafter the arm could be loaded and fired as a normal single-shot weapon until the owner had the opportunity to re-charge it as a repeater.

Few Roman candle arms offered so many methods of firing–and so many opportunities for careless and possibly disastrous errors. Many, however, did offer the choice between multiple loads and single loads. For some two hundred years inventors in various parts of the world would offer such arms as new and wondrous weapons which would revolutionise warfare. Usually they were granted patents, and often their proposals would be considered seriously by military boards–and sometimes they would even be adopted, apparently without any realisation that the system had been in use with little success for many years. Charles Cardiffe of England, for instance, obtained a patent on the super-imposed load system in 1682 and offered to make 'musketts, carbines, pistolls, or any other small fire-arms to discharge twice, thrice or more severall and distinct shotts in any single barrel and lock with one primeing and with double locks, oftener reserving one or more shotts til occasion offer which hitherto by none but himself hath been invented or known. . . .' Earlier, the Italian Giuliano Bossi, who lived part of his life in the Netherlands, specialised in the manufacture of the two-shot superimposed wheel-lock guns and wrote and published two pamphlets (in 1625 and 1629 respectively) describing this system and its advantages.

Almost a century later in America, Joseph Belton of Philadelphia notified the Continental Congress in April 1777 that he had just discovered a method for converting ordinary small arms to fire up to twenty such super-imposed loads and thereafter remain capable of being loaded with a paper cartridge and fired as usual but that he had kept this invention a dark secret until the enemy 'should be maid to know it in the field, to their immortal sorrow'. Congress authorised Belton to manufacture a hundred such muskets for test purposes, but the British capture of

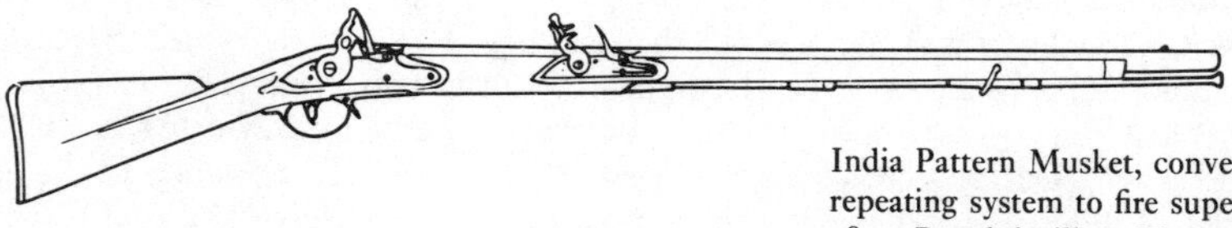

India Pattern Musket, converted to the Chambers repeating system to fire superimposed shots. English, 1815. Royal Artillery Museum, Woolwich.

2 D. R. Baxter, *Superimposed Load Firearms*, Hong Kong, 1966, pp. 36-7.

Philadelphia a few months later apparently ended that enterprise.

Within forty years, however, another American, and in fact another Pennsylvanian, named Joseph G. Chambers, claimed the invention of such a system as his own and succeeded in obtaining a patent on it on 23 March 1813. Furthermore he succeeded in interesting both the Commonwealth of Pennsylvania and the United States Navy in placing orders for his arms and in actually using them during the War of 1812. In all, 850 muskets, rifles and pistols were ordered along with a number of seven-barrelled swivel guns which would fire 224 shots each. Following the war these interesting arms quickly disappeared, and they are known today only through documentary references and two surviving specimens–a swivel gun in the Musée d'Armes in Liège and a musket in the Rotunda at Woolwich. Interestingly, the musket found its way to England when John Bland, one of the men who had helped manufacture the Chambers gun in America, came to Great Britain after the war and attempted to interest the British Ordnance in the system. Having had considerable experience with this sort of weapon in the past, the British had no desire to become involved with it again, but retained a sample.

Yet the Roman candle system continued in use elsewhere. The Danes developed an arm employing it during the Napoleonic Wars. They called it an *espingole*. Once again it was considered a highly secret weapon, and details about it were concealed until 1844. At that time the great Danish arms designer Nicolai Johan Löbnitz became interested in the possibilities of such a repeating arm and developed a number of refinements for it. He increased the number of barrels and arranged them in two tiers, much like some of the ancient ribauldequins, and he designed new ammunition for ease and precision in loading. In October of 1850 he demonstrated a twenty-barrelled version of the gun which fired some 300 shots at a time. Despite the fact that it required three-quarters of an hour to load, and could not be used without full charges, Danish officials were enthusiastic, and the espingole became an official arm of the Danish Army and Navy for more than two decades before it was superseded by more efficient repeating arms using metallic cartridges.

These were the most common arms manufactured on the Roman candle principle. There was, however, one unusual and interesting variant of the system which is found on some German wheel-lock pistols and carbines of the early seventeenth century. These were four-barrelled weapons with all four barrels fastened together in a single rectangular barrel block which was mounted in the stock with an angle at the top instead of a flat. Thus, when one looks at the muzzle, it gives the appearance of a diamond or lozenge shape with one barrel in each angle. In these interesting weapons the wheel-lock fires a single shot from the barrel closest to it. As the gases and flame from this charge reach almost to the muzzle, a channel leads a flash from them to the other lateral barrel on the left side of the block which is filled with powder to form a columnar fuse. As this powder burns backwards towards the breech it passes channels connecting with the upper and lower barrels and sets off super-imposed charges which have been loaded in them. Since the left-hand barrel in this arm provided the fuse, special pierced bullets were not required, thus reducing the cost of ammunition. It was necessary, however, to load with great care so that the various powder charges would align with their respective channels to the columnar fuse. The average pistol of this type fires fifteen shots, the carbines proportionately more. The popularity of such arms could not have been very great, yet five or six are known to have survived, and there may well be more which have not been recognised as repeaters and have been classified incorrectly as four-shot volley guns.[3]

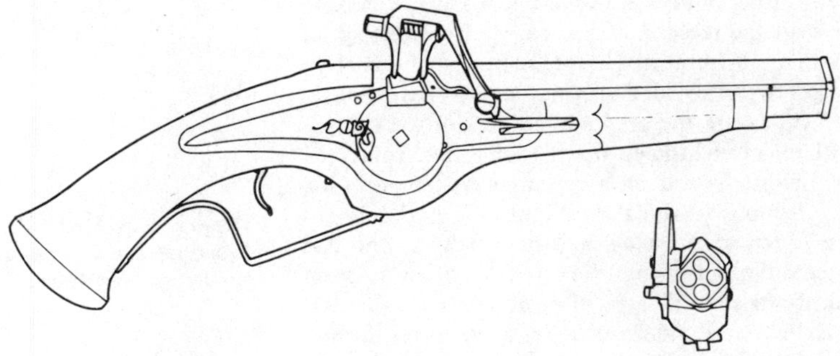

Multi-shot 'Roman Candle' wheel-lock pistol with four barrels and detail of the front of the muzzle. German, *c.*1650. A. C. Carpenter Collection.

3 See *Journal of the Arms and Armour Society*, Vol. IV, pp. 93-96.

Of all the various Roman candle guns only the Chambers and the espingole seem ever to have been manufactured and used for military or naval purposes. Considering their many drawbacks it is surprising that any of them achieved this success. The difficulties of loading have already been mentioned as one defect, but there were others, equally serious. For one thing, it was impossible to stop a series of shots once it had begun until the last charge had been fired. If a man should drop or otherwise lose control of his weapon after he had pulled the trigger he was a menance to his comrades and even to himself. And there were other possibilities for accident and malfunction as well which greatly outweighed any advantages the arm might have in average combat situations.

There was one way to overcome this drawback, while still obtaining extra shots through the use of super-imposed loads, and gun designers recognised it almost from the beginning. A touch-hole could be provided for each charge and either multiple locks or a movable lock could be used to provide separate ignition. Pierre Bergier of Grenoble made two-shot wheel-lock pistols and four-shot harquebuses during the 1630s with separate wheels, pans and touch-holes for each shot–but with a single trigger.[4] All employed super-imposed loads in a single barrel, the tight-fitting bullets and wads serving as fire stops to prevent the ignition of one charge from setting off the one behind it. Three ramrods of different lengths were provided with the four-shot harquebuses to help assure the proper alignment of the charges with their touch-holes. In 1780 John Aitken obtained an English patent on a repeating system utilising super-imposed loads and a sliding lock. At the close of the American Revolution Joseph Belton, who had offered the Continental Congress a musket made on the Roman candle system to decimate the British, travelled to London in 1784 to offer his former targets an improved system with a sliding lock and a separate chamber which could apparently be removed for loading. The Board of Ordnance was not interested in the invention after giving it a trial, but at least a small quantity of his arms including muskets, pistols and carbines were made by Belton in partnership with the London gunsmith William
142 Jover, and some were purchased by the East India Company. Isaiah Jennings of America patented a rifle with a sliding lock in 1821, and the State of New York actually purchased 520 specimens, manufactured by the gunsmith Reuben Ellis. Four years later Jacob Mould patented a similar arm in England, and it was manufactured both in flint and percussion.

These were only a few of the better known

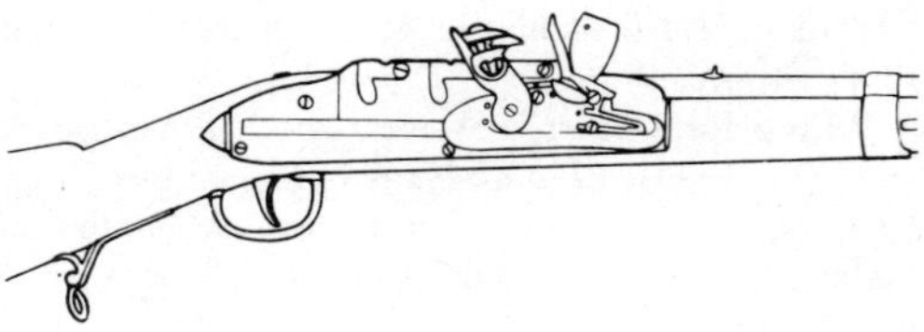

Detail of sliding lock on superimposed-load rifle by Isaiah Jennings. American, *c.*1821. Smithsonian Institution, Washington, D.C.

instances of the use of super-imposed loads and sliding locks. There were a great many more. All of them suffered from the delicacy of their mechanism, especially the devices which fastened the lock in its successive positions and in the various forms of rod connectors between the trigger and the sear. There was also the danger of sliding a lock too far in a moment of stress and so firing a charge from an intermediate position in the column with resultant excessive strain on the barrel and recoil against the shooter. These factors, plus fouling, and the ever-present need for special care in loading to align the charges properly, prevented any of these multiple-load arms from achieving popularity.

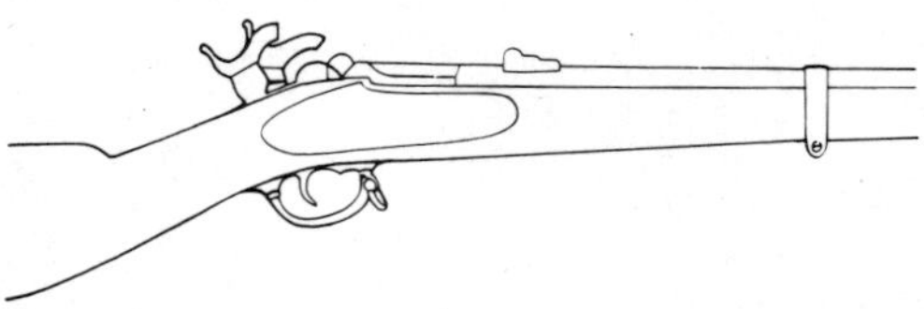

Detail of U.S. Model 1863 musket with side-by-side lock firing two superimposed charges. By John P. Lindsey of New Haven. Smithsonian Institution, Washington, D.C.

Arms firing only two or three super-imposed loads had far fewer problems. Separate fixed locks could be provided. Sometimes all that was necessary was a separate hammer, pan or priming channel or even a hammer nose that could be adjusted. All of these systems were also tried and manufactured in one form or another. Best known, perhaps, were the Walch revolvers described in Chapter 11 and the two-shot percussion pistols and rifled muskets invented by John P. Lindsay of New York in 1860. None of these systems, however, managed to achieve really widespread acceptance, again probably because of loading difficulties and the fear of firing the rear shot first.

The real answer lay in feeding the individual shots into the barrel one at a time from some repository outside. In revolvers a cylinder of individual chambers provided this repository. In

4 See p. 65.

other arms it took various forms which have been designated by the generic name *magazine*. Such magazines might be in the butt, in the fore-end, in a special receptacle under the action or almost any place attached to the arm so long as they held the necessary store of powder and shot until they were required in the chamber. They could deliver the components separately or together. It made no difference as long as bullet and powder arrived in proper order and condition for firing. During the course of their history magazine repeaters took all these forms and even added a few wildly impractical types such as the chain feeds and harmonica, or lateral containers of charges, which passed through the breech.

No one knows exactly when or where the first magazine repeater appeared, but it was undoubtedly some time shortly after 1600. There are no provable references to such guns before that date, and there is every evidence that a number of systems were in production over a wide area of Europe before 1660.

One of the earliest of these repeaters was apparently developed in the vicinity of Solingen, Germany, probably during the 1630s. Students today call it the Kalthoff system after the family of gunsmiths most closely associated with its manufacture. There was an exodus of Kalthoffs from Solingen before 1640, and thereafter the manufacture of their type of magazine repeater spread throughout Europe as members of the family dispersed and taught the mechanism to their apprentices. Thus Wilhelm Kalthoff obtained a patent on the system in Paris in 1640. Peter Kalthoff received a Dutch patent in 1641, then moved to Denmark where he worked until his death in 1672. Caspar Kalthoff travelled to London where he set up shop, and his son, Caspar, Jr., moved on to Moscow. Other makers of the system included H. Bartmans, Cornelis Coster, Cornelis Kant and Jan Flock of the Netherlands, Harman Barne of London, Henrich Habrecht, Alexander Harting and various
143 members of the Klett family of Austria, Berselli of Rome and Cousin of Paris.

The first gun of the Kalthoff system which may be identified by date was made by Peter Kalthoff in Denmark in 1645 and now reposes in the Tøjhusmuseum in Copenhagen. In this specimen the trigger-guard is rotated in an arc of 180° to operate the action. There are actually two magazines, one in the butt for powder and another in the fore-end for bullets. A carrier attached to the trigger-guard receives a charge of powder from the butt magazine and carries it forward as the guard is rotated. At the same time a box-shaped breech-block moves from left to right to pick up a bullet and deposit it in the chamber before the powder charge in the container on the trigger-guard reaches the extreme forward position and is poured into the chamber behind it. The same action of the trigger-guard primes the pan from a small third magazine and spans the wheel of a wheel-lock or cocks the action of a flintlock, depending on which ignition system is employed. About fifty guns of this type survive in the Tøjhusmuseum, Copenhagen, and all but two are flintlock rifles. The remaining two are wheel-locks. They are believed to have been issued to the Danish Foot Guards and used in the siege of Copenhagen in 1658 and 1659 and again during the Scanian War of 1675–9. If this is indeed true, they would undoubtedly represent the first magazine repeating rifles ever issued for military purposes.

Variations of this earliest form of the system included arms utilising a cylindrical breech-block rotating on a vertical axis instead of the box-shaped block and a form with a cylindrical or quarter-cylindrical block rotating on an axis parallel with the line of the bore. Another variation of the Kalthoff system is believed to have been invented by Sigmund Klett about 1650 and manufactured by various
members of the Klett family of Salzburg. In his 144
adaptation the trigger-guard, instead of carrying the powder charge itself, activated two cylinders set on vertical axes, one at the front of the chamber, one at the rear. The anterior cylinder turned to receive a ball from the bullet magazine in a hole with which it was pierced laterally and then turned back to align this hole with the bore. The rear cylinder filled with a charge of powder from the magazine in the butt, then turned back to deposit this powder in the chamber and serve itself as the breech face. This was a more complicated and delicate mechanism than the original system from which it was adapted. Yet at least seven arms (four rifles and three pistols) utilising it are known to have survived, and others are known through historical references.

There is no documentary evidence to indicate whether any of these Kalthoff repeaters worked efficiently. The large number of surviving specimens plus the widespread extent of their manufacture would seem to indicate that they did indeed work and that they were at least relatively dependable. The difficulty, of course, lay in their extremely complicated mechanisms. There was an intricate system of gears, links and springs which had to be fitted carefully, and all parts were interdependent. If any one part jammed or failed, the whole piece was useless until a skilled gunsmith could be found to fix it. Both the delicacy and expense of such arms prevented them from ever becoming standard military weapons or highly popular sporting arms. Interestingly enough, the later examples of the system tended to become more and more complicated and thus less and less adaptable to general use.

A second magazine repeating system which

appears to have developed in southern Europe a quarter-century later than the Kalthoff was simpler and even more widely used over a far longer period of time. Students today usually call this system the Lorenzoni in reference to the Florentine gunmaker Michele Lorenzoni (see p. 203) who has often been credited with inventing it, though it is by no means certain that he did. In America, however, many collectors still call it the Cookson system since the first specimen discovered and published in the United States bore the name of the English gunsmith John Cookson. Like the Kalthoff, the Lorenzoni boasted separate tubular magazines for powder and bullets plus a small priming magazine on the lock. In the Lorenzoni, however, both the principal magazines were in the butt, and it was a movement of a lever on the left side of the butt rather than the trigger-guard which loaded, primed and cocked the piece. The key to the Lorenzoni repeater was the cylindrical breech-block which rotated on an axis set across the line of the barrel. In it were two cavities. When the gun was held muzzle-up and the lever pulled back as far as it would go, one cavity aligned with each butt magazine. As the piece was turned muzzle-down, one cavity picked up a ball and the other filled with a measured charge of powder from the supply in the butt. Returning the lever to its forward position moved first the ball and then the powder to the chamber as it primed the pan and cocked the action. The necessity to raise and lower the muzzle plus the longer movement of the lever made the Lorenzoni a slower arm to fire than the Kalthoff. At the same time, however, it was a simpler and stronger system and therefore less expensive and less apt to get out of order.

It was undoubtedly these last factors that led to the relatively wide dispersion of the system and its long period of manufacture. As noted above, the Lorenzoni was probably invented in Italy during the third quarter of the seventeenth century. Certainly it first appeared somewhere in Southern or Central Europe about that time. A specimen by Giacomo Berselli of Bologna and Rome in the Musée de l'Armée, Paris, appears to date from the 1660s or 1670s. Guns made by Lorenzoni himself existed at least by 1684 and perhaps considerably earlier. The Augsburg gunmaker Wetschgi claimed the invention in an inscription of a pair of repeaters made about 1700 and in the Musée de l'Armée, Paris. As early as the 1680s, however, the English
109 gunsmith John Cookson was producing examples of the system, and soon a number of other English makers began to manufacture it. By 1766 circumstantial evidence indicates that it was being made in America by John Pim of Boston, and by 1756 there is definite evidence that an American, John Cookson, perhaps a relative of the English maker of the same name, was indeed manufacturing guns on this system in Boston. This already represents a century of use for the device, but it was by no means the end. H. W. Mortimer of London was still making Lorenzoni repeaters in *c.* 1800, but as far as is known, he was the last maker to produce the system.

Because Michele Lorenzoni's name does not appear on the earliest surviving examples of the revolving breech-block magazine system, there is considerable doubt that he actually invented it. He was, however, actively interested in the design and manufacture of breech-loaders and repeaters of various sorts, and this has led students in the past to attribute still another magazine system to him. In this repeater, two external tubular magazines are located beneath the barrel, and the whole assemblage is rotated against a fixed breech-block to load.

Flintlock pistol with three hand-rotated revolving barrels, signed *Lorenzoni*. Made for Cosimo III de Medici or a member of his family. Italian (Florence), *c.* 1680. Victoria & Albert Museum, London.

Lorenzoni did indeed manufacture arms utilising this mechanism, but the earliest known example formerly in the Renwick Collection, Tucson, Arizona, is signed by T. Lefer *A Valenza del Po* Italy and dated 1668. Another Italian specimen, in the Armeria Reale, Turin, contemporary with those made by Lorenzoni, is signed by Giorgio Pietro Callin in Genoa and dated 1684. Thus all evidence strongly indicates an Italian origin during the third quarter of the seventeenth century. In some quarters, however, the mechanism is known as the *Système Chalembron* after a gunsmith in the French arsenal at Pondicherry, India, who manufactured a number of repeaters of this type a hundred years later. There has even been a tendency in recent years to denote this system as the Lorenzoni-Chalembron in an effort to avoid confusion with the so-called Lorenzoni repeaters described previously.

By whatever name it is called, the magazine repeater with a rotating barrel assemblage was never so popular as that with a revolving breech-block. It was more complicated to manufacture and therefore

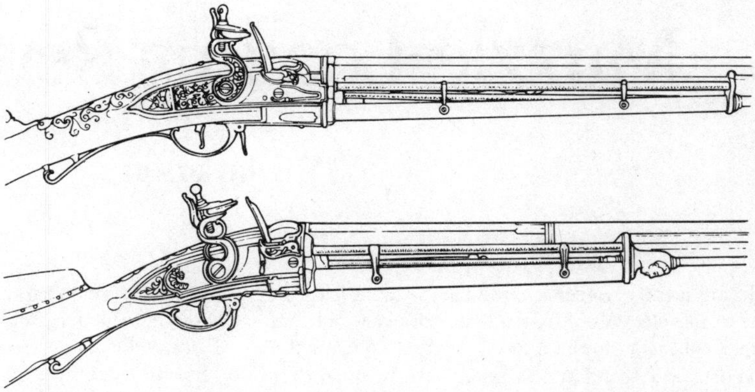

(*Top*) Detail of silver-mounted flintlock 'Lorenzoni' magazine-gun, signed CHALEMBRON A PONDICHERRY. Franco-Indian, *c.*1780. From the collection of King George III.

(*Bottom*) Detail of native Indian-made copy of above system. Dated 1802/3. Both Collection of H.M. The Queen, Windsor Castle.

more expensive. Also the exposed magazines were more susceptible to damage and, at the same time, they made the arm clumsier to handle.

In the simplest versions of this repeater, there were two tubular magazines beneath the barrel, a long one for powder and a shorter one for bullets. To load, the shooter held the gun muzzle-up and rotated the barrel assemblage in a clockwise direction. This brought first the powder magazine and then the ball magazine past the chamber opening in the fixed breech. As each passed, a cam forced open their mouths to allow a fixed amount of powder and then a ball to drop into the chamber. Reversing the rotation of the assemblage brought the barrel back into line with the chamber, and the piece was ready to prime and fire. A catch locked the barrel in line with the chamber. More complicated versions of this system introduced a third tube below the barrel. In these examples the powder magazine was placed near the muzzle of the piece in the centre line of the barrel. The shorter ball magazine and an empty tube of equal length were fixed closer to the breech and parallel to each other. As the assemblage was rotated the empty tube formed a connection between the powder magazine and the chamber, allowing a measured charge to drop down into the chamber. This extra step assured that there could be no direct connection between the powder magazine and the chamber and thus added an isolation factor for safety. A tiny port also allowed any loose powder that might remain in the conveyor tube to drop out so that it would be entirely empty. The bullet magazine functioned in generally the same fashion as on the simpler specimens except that the ball dropped into a special recess in the breech-block instead of directly into the chamber. From this recess it was pushed into the barrel by a spring-activated plunger as the assemblage was returned to its original position. In these more complicated arms, the act of rotating the barrel assemblage normally cocked and primed the piece as well.

Of all the magazine repeating systems developed during the two centuries which elapsed between the 1630s and the 1840s only these three forms achieved any real success. Other mechanisms were invented and tested. Some worked with at least a modicum of success, but in general production was limited to a few experimental models. The Kalthoff with its rotating trigger-guard, the Lorenzoni with its revolving breech-block and the Lorenzoni-Chalembron with its external tubes and rotating barrel assemblage were at least manufactured on a commercial basis over a wide portion of the civilised world, and some even saw military service. Real success awaited the development of self-contained metal-cased ammunition in the nineteenth century.

CHAPTER EIGHT

Muzzle-Loading Revolvers

A.W.F. Taylerson

146-55 272 Although the revolver is not a complicated firearm, the terminology used by students does vary and can cause confusion to the unwary reader. Accordingly, it is proposed to define one or two basic terms as they will be used here, and in Chapter 11.

The word 'revolver' is now normally used in describing pistols which have a short cylinder, or cluster of charge chambers, revolving behind a conventional barrel. This restriction in the use of the word is comparatively modern in England; as late as 1851, the *Illustrated London News* found it necessary to explain this type of firearm to the British public as distinguished from the picture then commonly accepted. For the United Kingdom, at that time, the term was usually applied to multi-barrelled revolving pistols, here called 'pepperboxes', in which no separate barrel was embodied.

In describing the lock mechanism of revolvers or pepperboxes, the terms 'self-cocking', 'single-action', and 'double-action', will be used. A self-cocking revolver is a weapon in which the whole firing cycle is accomplished merely by pulling the trigger, and no provision is made for the hammer to be cocked by the thumb. A single-action revolver, on the other hand, is cocked by the thumb pressing down upon the spur of the hammer and then fired by pulling the trigger. Double-action arms, as the name suggests, have locks which permit use as a self-cocking mechanism, but can be cocked by the thumb at will.

It is appreciated that some readers may quarrel with this division (some American collectors regard the terms 'self-cocking' and 'double-action' as interchangeable), but such a difference of opinion merely emphasises the need for an explanation of the manner in which the terms are used here. For the purist, the use of 'double-action' in the sense here preferred is hallowed by its use in William Tranter's British Patent No. 1913 of 1856.

The barrels of the earliest multi-shot hand firearms were fixed in their stock, and fired in turn by a hand match; however, small cannon had been radially mounted on a turntable by the beginning of the fifteenth century, and it can probably be assumed that the first multi-barrelled hand-rotated small-arms appeared at some time after 1500. The earliest recorded actual example, however, appears to be a three-barrelled matchlock, revolving pistol in the Palazzo Ducale, Venice, which has been almost certainly identified in an inventory of 1548. The barrels are rotated by hand, a spring catch serving to lock each in turn in the firing position.

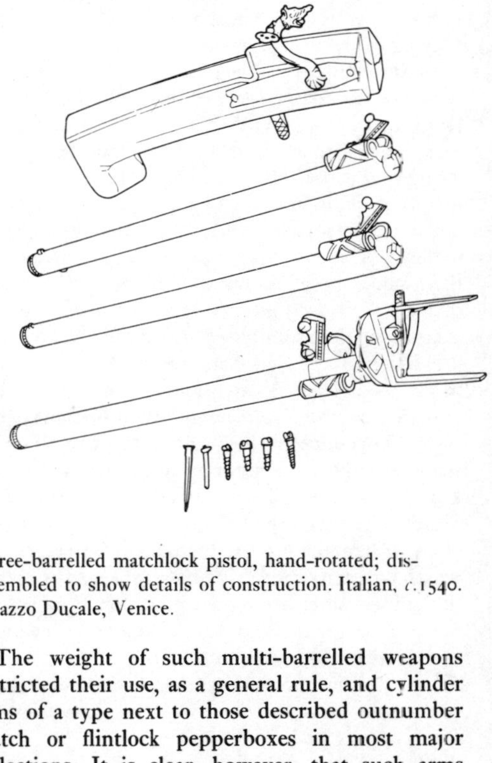

Three-barrelled matchlock pistol, hand-rotated; dis-assembled to show details of construction. Italian, *c.*1540. Palazzo Ducale, Venice.

The weight of such multi-barrelled weapons restricted their use, as a general rule, and cylinder arms of a type next to those described outnumber match or flintlock pepperboxes in most major collections. It is clear, however, that such arms enjoyed a limited popularity in the East, and three-, four- and five-shot matchlock pepperbox pistols and guns from India or Japan have survived, and can be dated to the seventeenth and eighteenth centuries. The Musée de l'Armée, Paris, also holds a double-barrelled hand-rotated matchlock gun from the *Cabinet d'Armes* of Louis XIII, which dates from about 1620, and shows that European interest in the multi-barrelled design was quite slow to die. In the

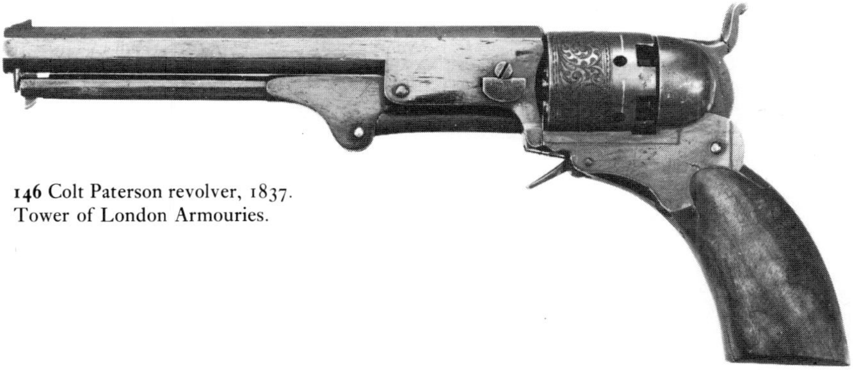

146 Colt Paterson revolver, 1837.
Tower of London Armouries.

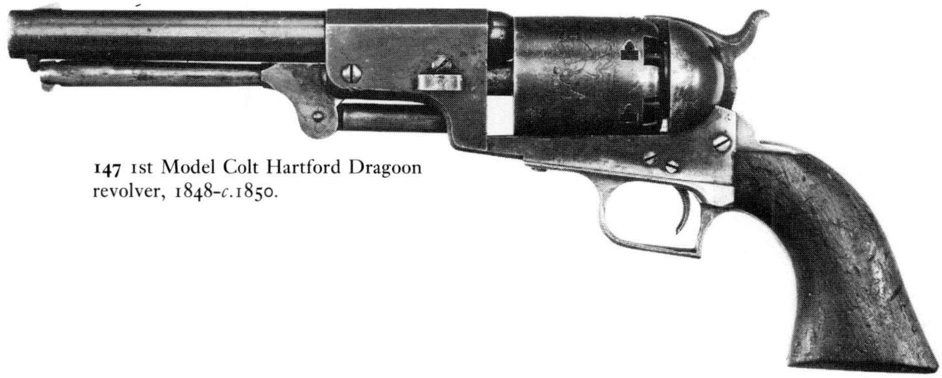

147 1st Model Colt Hartford Dragoon revolver, 1848-*c.*1850.

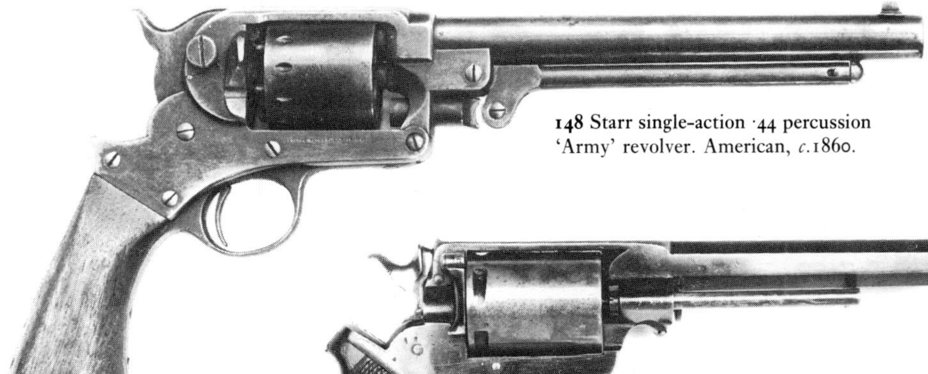

148 Starr single-action ·44 percussion 'Army' revolver. American, *c.*1860.

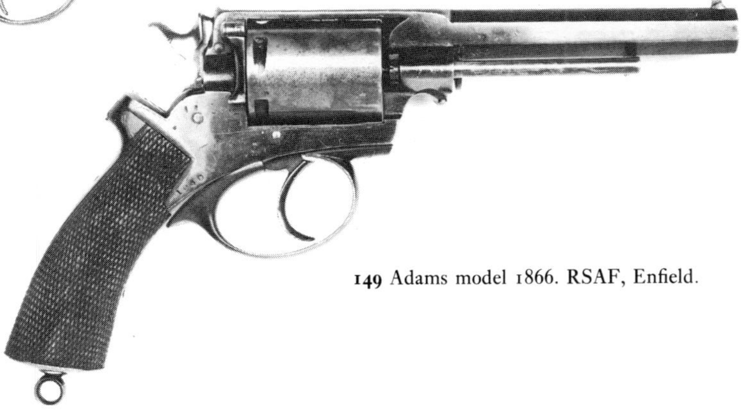

149 Adams model 1866. RSAF, Enfield.

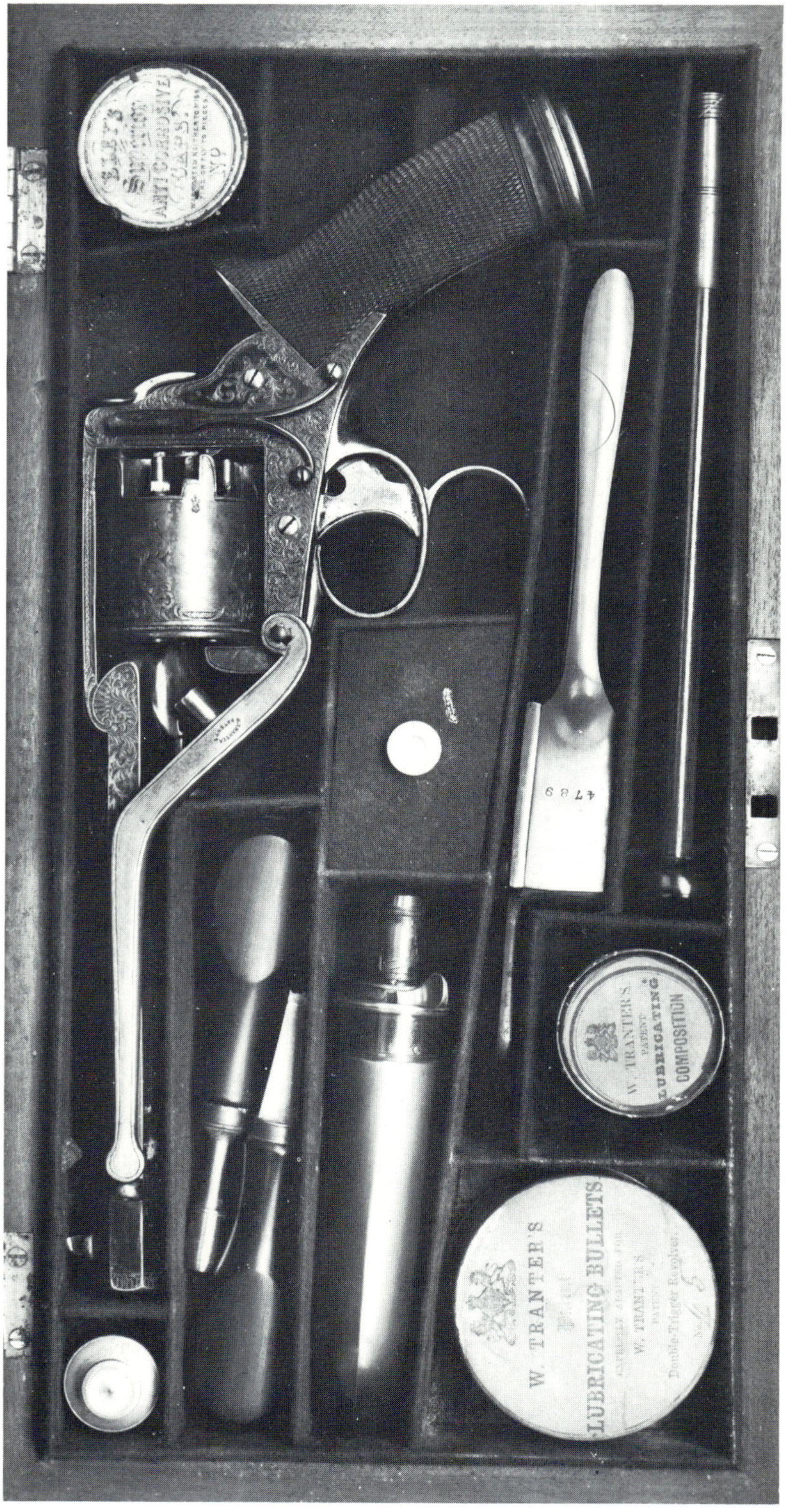

150 W. Tranter's double trigger revolver in case, 1855. Birmingham Museum of Science and Industry.

double-, and occasionally triple-barrelled form known as 'turn-over' or 'Wender' it in fact survived for pistols until well into the nineteenth century.

At an uncertain date prior to 1600, the single-barrelled cylinder firearm emerged as a viable weapon. A five-chambered, hand-rotated matchlock wall gun, made before 1627, in the Palazzo Ducale, Venice, has a $33\frac{1}{3}$ in barrel of 1·58 in calibre and can scarcely be regarded as a small-arm, but the existence of such a weapon hardly argues that it was unique.

It is also clear that other systems of ignition were applied to cylinder arms from an early date. A six-chambered wheel-lock petronel in the Tøjhus-museum, Copenhagen, is dated 1597, and a beautiful six-shot pistol carbine snaphance lock lies in the Kremlin Collection, Moscow, and can be dated about the same period.

As to the use of true flintlocks, Thomas Anquetil[1] described a five-shot flintlock revolver gun, signed *Lehanne*, which he dated around 1600, while a similar weapon noticed by Anquetil was actually dated 1632 and bore the maker's mark of a fleur-de-lis between two Hs; this latter gun (then in the collection of M. Leroy, of Brussels) is probably that numbered IX.71 in the Porte de Hal Museum in Brussels. The cylinders on both guns were hand-rotated, but the Lehanne arm was distinguished by a separate pan for each chamber.

John Deane[2] added another three-chambered flintlock shotgun to the list, fitted with a 'Spanish lock' carrying the mainspring outside its lockplate. His illustration of the gun showed separate steels protruding around the cylinder (or 'rotatory breech', as he termed it), but the weapon probably dated from nearly a century after the other two guns.

Detail of twelve-shot matchlock revolving gun. German, late sixteenth century. Germanisches Nationalmuseum, Nuremberg.

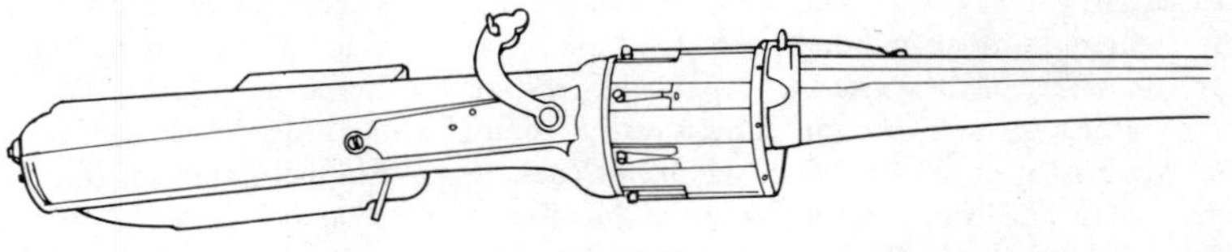

Although certainly not the earliest revolver, a series of pistols by a Swiss, James Gorgo, were made in London towards the end of the seventeenth century and offer an interesting departure from the conventional design. In Gorgo's revolvers (which resembled the turn-off holster pistol of that period) the barrel was not properly aligned with the chamber on firing, the bullet being funnelled into the barrel on discharge. The cylinder, bored with three chambers, was manually rotated and fired by a flint side-lock on which the steel operated a priming powder-magazine as it was closed; pressing up the trigger-guard released the cylinder for rotation.

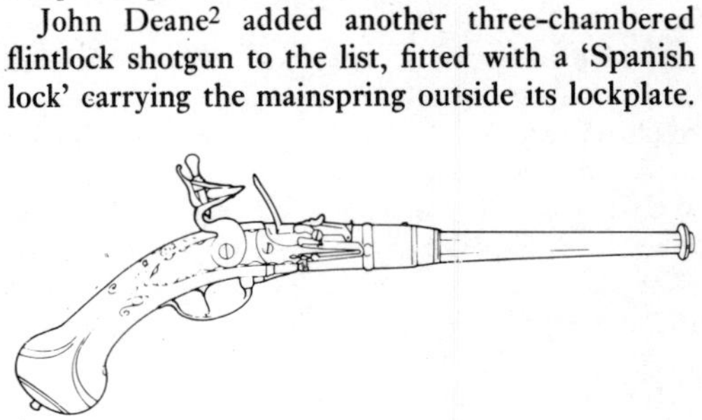

Three-chambered flintlock, hand-rotated, by J. Gorgo, London, *c.*1690. W. Keith Neal Collection.

Certainly ante-dating Gorgo's revolvers is one of snaphance type, which was in the Royal United Services Institute, in London, for many years, and was described in detail by the late J. N. George.[3] This pistol, which dates from about 1680, has now been transferred to the Tower of London Armouries; it is made almost entirely of brass, weighing $6\frac{1}{4}$ lb at an overall length of $21\frac{1}{2}$ in.

The pistol is of 0·500 in calibre, and a six-chambered cylinder is mechanically rotated by the action of cocking the side cock. Each chamber carries a separate priming-pan, over which a sliding pan-cover fits, and a single steel serves to ignite the priming when the lid is knocked forward by the falling cock. As in revolvers of two centuries later, each chamber is bolted in alignment with the barrel at the instant of firing. On the strength of a very similar carbine in the Milwaukee Public Museum, signed by J. Dafte of London, the unsigned pistol was attributed to the same maker by J. N. George.

Many snaphance or flintlock guns and pistols of similar appearance are in the major museums of both America and Europe (for a number of makers in England, France, Germany, Russia and Spain tackled such designs in the period 1670–1740), but few embody the unique feature of mechanical rotation for their cylinders. As will presently appear,

1 *Notice sur les Pistolets Tournants et Roulants, dit Revolvers*, 1855.

2 *Manual of the History etc., of Firearms*, 1858. John Deane borrowed freely from Anquetil, in compiling this work.

3 *English Pistols and Revolvers*, 1938, pp. 144–7.

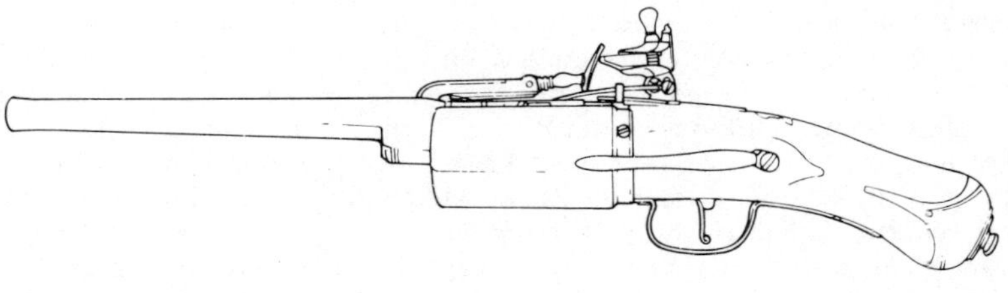

Single-action, six-chambered snaphance. Perhaps by John Dafte of London. English, *c.*1680. Tower of London Armouries.

hand-rotation of cylinder or barrel-cluster obtained until late in the 1830s, although a pair of mechanically-rotated flintlock pepperbox pistols[4] prove at least one maker of the period as capable of tackling the principles of such rotation. These pistols rotate their barrels (by a gear-train) in the act of cocking their cocks, and were made by J. G. Kolbe, a Suhl gunmaker, who worked in London between 1730 and 1737.

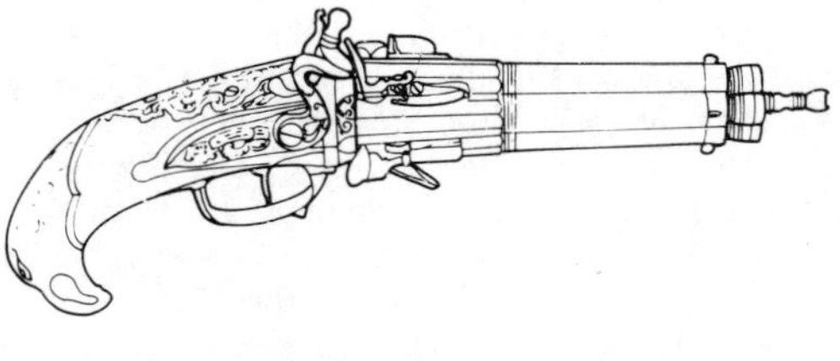

Four-barrelled flintlock, hand-rotated, by Mathias Bramhofer of Augsburg, *c.*1750. Metropolitan Museum of Art, New York.

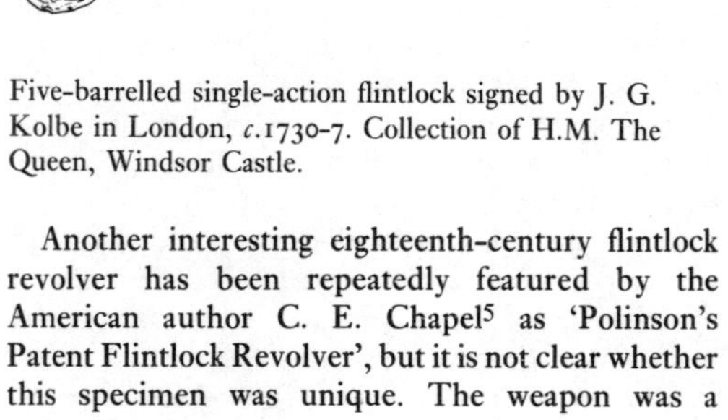

Five-barrelled single-action flintlock signed by J. G. Kolbe in London, *c.*1730-7. Collection of H.M. The Queen, Windsor Castle.

Another interesting eighteenth-century flintlock revolver has been repeatedly featured by the American author C. E. Chapel[5] as 'Polinson's Patent Flintlock Revolver', but it is not clear whether this specimen was unique. The weapon was a conventional flintlock, with hand-rotated cylinder; a frail wooden fore-end protruded along the underside of the barrel and carried a normal ramrod. Polinson appears to have worked in London towards the close of the eighteenth century, but no English patent of the period seems relevant to this weapon.

Far better known than the arms mentioned above are those small flintlock pepperboxes with hand-

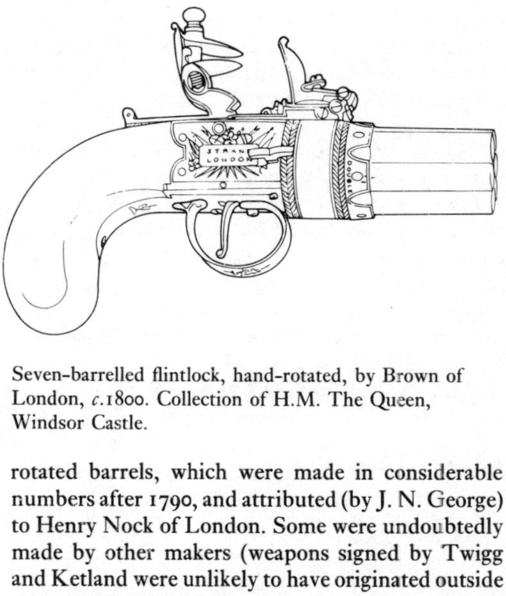

Seven-barrelled flintlock, hand-rotated, by Brown of London, *c.*1800. Collection of H.M. The Queen, Windsor Castle.

rotated barrels, which were made in considerable numbers after 1790, and attributed (by J. N. George) to Henry Nock of London. Some were undoubtedly made by other makers (weapons signed by Twigg and Ketland were unlikely to have originated outside their workshops), but many bear the names of gunmakers poorly equipped for such manufacture; the names of Pooley & Co., Hunter and Nicholson appear in this latter category.

In these weapons, six small-calibre barrels are grouped about a seventh, and all are screwed home upon a solid circular breeching. The barrels are unscrewed with a muzzle-key for loading, exactly as for a conventional turn-off pocket-pistol, and are normally about 3 in long and of 0·32 in calibre. Protruding from the rear of the breeching is a spindle, crowned by a heavy toothed wheel, and this spindle can be inserted or withdrawn through a hole in the standing breech of a large centre-cock

4 Nos. 798 and 807 in the Armoury, Windsor Castle.

5 *The Gun Collector's Handbook of Values*, 1947 and 1951 editions.

pistol-action. Inside the lock-case of the weapon is a long flat spring, with a roller bearing on the barrel end, and this engages the teeth on the breeching spindle. On rotating the barrels by hand (against the tension of this spring) the barrels are thus held in alignment with the steel and cock for firing.

Drilled in the circumference of the breeching are six small priming-pans, normally surrounded by a gunmetal sleeve to retain their powder; this sleeve is attached to the breech of the pistol, and also carries the steel. Priming was done with the breeching home in its sleeve, via the open steel, but the barrels and breeching can be readily withdrawn from the lock-case by turning home one thumbscrew (which pushes the tensioning spring off the breeching spindle) and loosening another which holds the breeching tight against the standing breech.

It should be clear from this description that one of the priming-pans has to serve two barrels. The centre barrel is appropriately connected to another, by a priming passage, and permits double-discharge at a moment dictated by the user's fancy, or by the chance positioning of the barrel cluster at the commencement of firing.

In the light of an article in *The Gun Collector*[6], it is clear that Henry Nock also signed at least one carbine on the pepperbox system but that he used another system for priming this weapon. The gun illustrated and described had six 18 in barrels brazed into the bundle round a spindle, and discarded the system of loading (used in Nock's pistols) by unscrewing the barrels from a breeching. A side flintlock was fitted, which embodied a priming magazine in the steel, and the barrels were hand-rotated (to the right), but were locked by a ratchet and pawl similar to a clock escapement. The weapon was in 59 bore, and weighed 9 lb 13 oz at an overall length of 33½ in.

The magazine-primer was formed by thickening the steel, and fitting a small lid at the top, giving access to a hollow interior. At the bottom of this cavity was a transverse rotating pin with a groove running along its length. By an ingenious linkage the groove in the pin turned up to receive a priming charge when the steel was open, and turned over to drop the charge into the pan when the steel was shut down. The vents leading to the barrels were covered by a solid silver band, in place of the gunmetal sleeve used for the pistols.

Although twice signed by Henry Nock, the weapon carried a barrel maker's mark *EB* between the proof marks of the London Gunmaker's Company, and it has been suggested that this may have been the mark of Ezekiel Baker, the well-known gunmaker working in the Whitechapel Road during the early 1800s. The suggestion has some support, in Baker's known earlier association with Nock, and, if the identification is correct, it could date the gun prior to the establishment of Baker's own business in the late eighteenth century.

The priming mechanism used has been seen in other weapons, including a pair of heavy-calibred pistols, signed by Fowler of Dublin and dated 1811, which were once in the collection of the late Major R. H. S. Brown of London.

Major Brown also drew the attention of collectors in *The Gun Collector*[7] to another system of priming for flintlock pepperboxes, in a four-barrelled pistol by Isaac Pratt, who worked in Throgmorton Street, London, during the first decade of the nineteenth century. It is possible that the system was imported from abroad, since an identical primer has been found upon a seven-barrelled pepperbox (in the collection of Sam E. Smith) signed *Mairet aux Ponci*, a signature that refers to Jean Henri Mairet (d.1772) of Ponts-de-Martel, Neuchâtel, Switzerland.

In both of these weapons a side-lock was fitted, and the rear of the breechings carried inset priming-pans covered by a sleeve in the same manner as the Nock pistols. However, since the lock was on the side of the pistol, it was necessary to shake or throw the priming powder sideways under the steel each time the barrels were turned by hand. This could be done by turning the barrels sharply, or by rapping the pistol once they had been turned. To prime, the weapon was held lock-upwards and the powder poured in past the open steel.

The Mairet pepperbox has a thumb-catch on top of the frame, which releases the barrels for rotation, but it anticipated the Nock pistols in using a double discharge for firing the central barrel; of 0·31 in calibre, the barrels are 4¾ in long.

Ingenious as all these weapons were, they can only be regarded as evidence of superb craftsmanship by men well paid to take the necessary time and pains in their construction. For examples of early revolvers made by ordinary workmen, little can be quoted prior to the middle of the 1830s.

An early example of an attempt to reach this ideal was made in England by an American named E. H. Collier who patented a really effective flintlock revolver during 1818. An equivalent American patent was secured by Captain Artemus Wheeler, and French protection was taken by Cornelius Coolidge.

Arguments have continued over the years as to which of these men actually designed the weapons protected by these patents, and although they are known in England as 'Collier' arms, it is a matter of record that Wheeler built muskets and carbines

6 Issue 17.

7 Issues 16 and 19.

under the American patent, which were tested by the US Navy in 1821. The United States National Museum Collection, Washington, features two types; one model was a pepperbox carbine with seven $12\frac{1}{2}$ in barrels, and the other was a true revolver musket with a 4 in, seven-chambered cylinder, and a 32 in barrel. Both versions were smooth bored in the standard service rifle calibre of 0·525 in and both were hand-rotated.

Pending further discoveries, it seems best to accept Collier's own testimony as to the rights of the three men in the basic invention. In a famous law case, of 1851, between Samuel Colt and the Massachusetts Arms Company, Collier stated that the other two men were also Americans and that the English patent in his name was sought as partly communicated to him by a foreigner. By inference, it seems clear that Collier improved upon Wheeler's revolver and manufactured that improved version. Coolidge apparently bought an interest in the Collier variant, and his French patent was a straightforward copy of the English specification.

Collier revolvers were made as pistols, rifles or shotguns, and were principally flintlocks. In later years some persussion weapons appeared and there is often doubt as to whether these arms were made for this system of ignition, or converted to it.

As with the Nock carbine, all of Collier's flintlock arms had a single priming-pan and steel which served each of the five chambers, in turn, through small vents drilled in the cylinder wall. A magazine primer fitted to the steel dispensed with the need to re-prime after each shot, the lock being simply cocked and the steel shut down into the pan. Collier apparently tried two mechanisms in these priming magazines, one of which had a linkage quite similar to that described earlier for the Nock carbine. The other used a similar roller base to the magazine, but had three priming grooves instead of one. On this system a ratchet at the end of the roller engaged a projection on the fence, as the steel was shut, and this rotated the roller one-third turn to deposit priming in the pan.

The most satisfactory feature of the Collier arms was the method adopted for obtaining a gas-seal, between chamber and barrel, on firing. The mouth of each chamber was countersunk, and fitted over a male chamfer at the rear end of the barrel. By designing the cylinder with a fore-and-aft movement on its supporting spindle, it could be pulled back off the barrel (once the weapon had been cocked) and then hand-rotated to bring the next chamber into alignment. Contact between chamber and barrel was ensured by a helical spring at the rear of its spindle, and a wedge, operated by the falling hammer, locked the cylinder against any recoil on discharge.

As Collier originally designed his weapons, the cylinder was to be automatically rotated by a coiled spring. The idea was apparently conceived by Wheeler, and involved the mounting of this spring at the rear of the cylinder spindle. With the chambers loaded, and the weapon cocked, it was then necessary to rotate the cylinder manually, in an anti-clockwise direction, until the spring was in tension. Once this had been done, the act of cocking after firing withdrew the cylinder from engagement with the barrel, permitted it to spin the next chamber into alignment, and released the cylinder to snap forward again on to the end of the barrel.

Collier's firearms exist in some numbers today, but no specimen is known to embody the mechanically rotated cylinder. On a few weapons evidence has been observed to suggest that they were originally made up to embody it, and a seven-shot revolver was demonstrated at Woolwich (in 1819) with the mechanism working. However, as Collier himself put it (in giving evidence in the Massachusetts Arms Company law case): 'I wanted to get rid of all superfluous parts, and left the spring out; that is I considered the gun better without it.'

The Board of Ordnance test, at Woolwich, may also have contributed to the decision for abandoning the rotary mechanism. The Commandant of the Garrison reported to the Duke of Wellington (then Master-General of Ordnance) that the mechanism was not new in principle, although very ingenious. However, he added that the committee considered it 'by far too complicated and expensive to be applicable to the Public Service'.[8]

Like many other inventors, Collier seems to have pinned his faith upon the securing of service acceptance for his invention. It was difficult and expensive to make and he obviously felt that an official order for his arms would serve as a useful basis for commercial production.

Undeterred by the lukewarm report, and subsequent official delays in publishing it, the inventor secured another test at Woolwich, again before a Committee of Artillery Officers, in 1824. On this occasion he produced a percussion rifle built with the mechanically-rotated cylinder, and proceeded to fire one hundred rounds in twenty-nine minutes. Seventy hits were obtained on a target one hundred yards distant, and a subsequent five-round discharge at 200 yards was accomplished without missing.[9]

This test (and an earlier unofficial demonstration before the Duke of Clarence, at Chatham) was not successful in arousing official interest and might be unrecorded today were they not (with that of 1819)

8 Public Record Office: W.O. 44/623. My thanks are due to the late Mr. S. B. Haw for this reference.

9 H. L. Blackmore, *British Military Firearms*, pp. 251–2.

quoted in two rare Collier broadsheets, in the James L. Mitchell Collection, Atlanta, Georgia. Thereafter, Collier turned to the civilian market, for which he made rifles, shotguns and pistols; the former were fitted with percussion or flintlocks (apparently at the customer's choice), but the revolvers were almost universally of the latter type.

During the greater period of this British manufacture, Collier used two addresses, the second of which often appeared upon his arms. For about a year he was soliciting orders from 6 Herbert's Passage, off the Strand, but after 1825 he moved to 54 Strand, under the style 'Collier & Co., Gunmakers'.

Despite this claim, there seem grounds for doubt as to whether he actually made the rifles, shotguns and pistols that bore his name. Deane stated flatly that the cylinders for Collier arms were made by Mr Evans, of 114 Wardour Street, Soho, in 1821-2. If this man (a noted designer of arms-making machinery) made these components for the arms used at the second Woolwich demonstration, it seems fair to assume that he continued to do so when Collier turned to the civilian market. Evans himself later claimed to have made complete Collier flintlock arms in 1822, and Mr S. B. Haw (who has studied Collier's activities in detail) is inclined to accept the plain, early arms as having been made by this man.[10] Both Haw and the late J. N. George seem inclined to accept Rigby, or one of the other leading Irish makers, as responsible for the later, more decorative weapons.

The scale of Collier's operations is not clear. Giving evidence in the famous law case, already mentioned[11] he spoke in impressive numbers and suggested manufacture of from fifty to a hundred of the mechanically rotated guns alone. His evidence was suspect, but if his claim to have sold £10,000 worth of arms through two merchant houses was true, he must have made quite a number of rifles and shotguns. Collier alleged making one consignment through the East India house of Bazette, Farquhar, Crawford & Co., and one through another firm, on an advance payment of twenty-two guineas for each weapon. Whether this figure, or the mentioned selling price of sixty guineas for some arms, is accepted, the total output must have been impressive for a firearm so complicated. It seems not impossible that as many as four hundred arms of all types were produced.

After 1827, Collier moved to 3 North Piazza, Royal Exchange, but seems to have achieved little good by the transfer. In the years that followed he appears to have reverted to his original career of civil engineer, and to have concentrated his attention first upon marine boilers and later upon patented machinery.

He returned to America in 1850, and appeared for the defence in the Massachusetts Arms Company law case earlier mentioned. Dickerson, Colt's attorney, was able to produce 'several boxes' of his guns (to demolish the claim that he had used the mechanically-rotated cylinder in numbers), and this act can be read equally to support the view that many were made and sold, or that those which were made sold slowly.

It is difficult to offer dimensional details upon Collier's arms, for these differed markedly. Rifles were made in calibres as large as 0·55 in, and 20 bore shotguns were another line; the pistols were made in only small numbers, but when encountered are likely to be of smooth-bore, with 6 in barrels in 44 bore. A variant revolver in 60 bore with a 4 in barrel, in the Tower of London, is serially numbered '1', and may be the only example of the type.

At least one coaching blunderbuss, of most attractive appearance, formerly in the J. N. George Collection, was made and marked *E. H. Collier Patent No. 9*. The weapon held six shots, and had a bronze cylinder chamber in 0·625 in calibre. The 14 in barrel carried a folding bayonet beneath it, and flared out to 0·695 in at the muzzle. A ramrod was concealed in the underpart of the gunstock. In important particulars it closely resembled the 'No. 1' revolver, for the cylinder was unfluted on both weapons, and the side-cock worked inside the lock-plate. In later Collier arms the cock was conventionally mounted on the outside, and many were fitted with a plate covering the chambers in front. This doubtful improvement may have been intended to prevent the charges from being jarred out of the chambers. In the event, it seems likely to have prompted multiple discharge by deflecting the flash into adjacent chambers.

Some contemporary copies of Collier arms were made, a very fine German flintlock rifle in the collection of Dr Prentiss D. Cheyney being particularly noteworthy. This rifle (dated 1824) has double set-triggers, and the 0·56 in calibre barrel carries the legend *L. Kolb Zögling des Königl Gewerbe Institutes zu Berlin*. The Students' Room at the Tower of London Armouries harbours a 20 bore percussion shotgun marked *Collier's Patent*, but retailed by Edwards of London. It does appear possible that some Coolidge guns were made with the mechanically-rotated cylinder, although specimens are now wanting. In the Massachusetts Arms Company case such a gun could not be produced by the defendants, but the type was distinguished from

10 'The Revolver (1819)', *The Marksman*, July and September, 1950.

11 Samuel Colt *v* The Massachusetts Arms Company, 30 June 1851, Circuit Court of the US, District of Massachusetts.

the manually-turned models by referring to it as 'Coolidge's', or 'the French gun'.

Opinions upon the worth of Collier's weapons obviously varied in his own day, but it is worth noting that one of the broadsheets earlier mentioned was endorsed by Samuel Nock, W. A. Beckwith and Thomas Mortimer, all well-known London gun-makers. The inducement for their support is not recorded, but it would be charitable to assume that they could recognise a satisfactory design when they saw it.

Before leaving the subject of these early revolving cylinder arms, weapons made in the East must be noticed. No detailed break-down of types is practicable, since the makers followed their fancy in each case. Most of these firearms were three- or four-shot matchlock muskets, with crude 'cylinders' built up from long sections of barrel tube; however, an excellent six-chambered musket in the late C. G. Vokes's Collection (which is signed *Devanagri* and dated 1689) shows that weapons of superior quality and fire-power were made. Apparently originating from Persia and India, the stocking and detail of such guns followed the taste of more conventional native weapons, and simple 'tricker' locks are normally found.

Flintlock arms of similar type were also made in the East at a later period. They were distinguished from the more sophisticated weapons of Nock or Collier type by their long cylinders and smaller fire-capacity. Three or four shots were normally available, and, since there was a separate steel and pan for each chamber, they were awkward both in appearance and in handling. If they had an advantage over the weapons named, it lay in the use of the long tubes from which the cylinder bundle was constructed. By such arrangement, the firer's hand and wrist were well behind the flame leaking out between barrel and chamber on discharge.

Although these revolving arms are mentioned here in the context of the first quarter of the nineteenth century, they must not be associated with that period alone. As earlier mentioned, the matchlock ignition was applied to Indian and Japanese pepperbox arms during the seventeenth and eighteenth centuries, and whilst the conservatism of Eastern buyers could have produced matchlock and flintlock cylinder arms long after such locks were obsolete in the West, there is no proof that the cylinder design was not available in the East with these pepperbox arms.

It is natural to identify the appearance of revolving arms in large quantities with the introduction of the percussion cap and the ascendancy of the American designer, Samuel Colt. However, it would be a pity to overlook some of the firearms using other types of fulminate ignition.

An interesting series of pill-lock revolving rifles was made in America, under a patent of 1829, held by J. Miller of Brighton, New York. The inventor allowed his patent to expire, and manufacture passed into the hands of William Billinghurst, at Rochester, New York.

The Billingshurst rifles were very beautifully made and seem to have reached an English market, if specimens in British collections today are any guide. Fitted with a single-action side-lock and a seven-chambered, hand-rotated cylinder, they presented a fragile appearance in lacking any strap connecting the long barrel to the action body. Barrel, cylinder and frame were joined solely by the stout arbor upon which the chambers turned. Small percussion-pills were inserted into wells drilled into the cylinder, at points where a percussion nipple might be expected, and were crushed by a nose on the hammer. A simple spring latch indexed the cylinder in line with the barrel, but it is a measure of the care lavished in manufacture that some Billingshurst rifles had their chambers rifled to match the barrel. A rare variant arm had an additional shot barrel beneath the rifled tube, which also served as an arbor on which the cylinder turned. Elijah Snell, G. A. Brown and A. A. Sizer made rather similar guns, the latter preferring the conventional nipple and cap.

The percussion tube may seem an unlikely choice for any revolving arm, but at least three makers toyed with its use. A superb pair of single-action tube-lock revolvers were made by Le Page of Paris, closely modelled upon the second type of Collier revolver. The cylinders were hand-rotated and propped up to the barrel in the same manner, and percussion tubes were clipped into vents (drilled at right-angles to the chamber) and smashed against the side of the cylinder by the falling hammer. A Birmingham maker, Joseph Rock Cooper, patented a self-cocking pepperbox, fired by such tubes, in January 1840. The point of the design was that the tubes were inserted centrally to the bores, giving a very strong and certain ignition, but no specimen of such a weapon is known to exist today. The Genhart pistol[12] was another revolver using these tubes, and although the mechanism was complicated and expensive to make, rifles as well as handguns are found in collections.

However, ingenious as these weapons undoubtedly were, the percussion cap ousted them all. Attempts to find an alternative ignition continued long after the conventional muzzle-loading revolver was established, but the rarity of specimens requires the briefest of notice.

David Edwards, of Zanesville, Ohio, patented a frail, but bulky, pill-lock revolver in 1839. It threw

12 See p. 330.

back to the early flint revolvers in carrying a wooden fore-end and ramrod beneath the barrel. Years later, G. T. Bousfield (an English patent agent) secured a British patent for an un-named principal, in which fine particles or seeds of a detonating compound were used to fire a revolver of Colt type. The patent lapsed in 1860, and no trace of any specimen arm remains today.

Jesse Butterfield and Jacob Rupertus (both Americans) patented disc-primer mechanisms in 1855 and 1859 respectively. The Butterfield revolvers fed the detonating disc or wafer from a tubular charger to the vents in the cylinder; Rupertus fed this wafer to the hammer nose, by which it was carried forward and smashed against a special nipple.

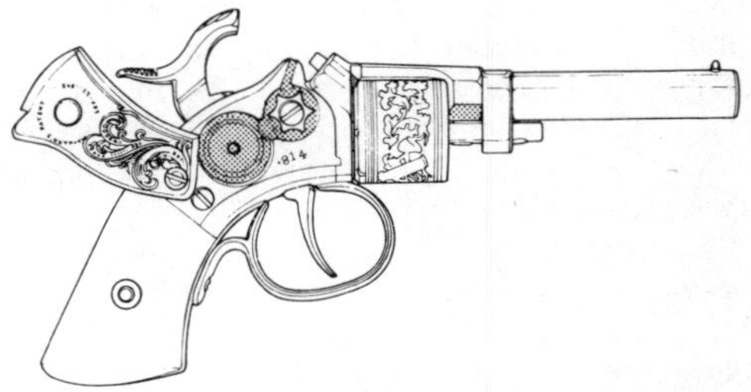

Massachusetts Arms Co. six-shot, single-action 0·32 in. cal. revolver, *c*.1858. The cylinder is rotated by gears. The example fitted with a Maynard tape-primer magazine (shown open and empty.) Smithsonian Institution, Washington, D.C.

Another ignition system of immense popularity in America was also applied to a few revolvers made by the Massachusetts Arms Company. The Maynard tape primer was an oversized roll of paper caps, fed to the percussion nipple by a wheel feed. Whether employed in military rifles or pocket revolvers, a single-action lock was used; cocking the hammer served to wind a primer forward under the hammer. The revolvers were single-action, with side-hammers for the larger (0·31 in calibre) pistols, and centre-hammers in the smaller 0·28 in calibre arms; their cylinders were rotated by hand, after pressing up a small button in the trigger-guard. As was normal for arms using the Maynard tape primer, a hinged door on the right of the frame gave access to the feed-wheel mechanism for renewal of the tape. On the smaller arm, only one nipple was fitted, being screwed into the revolver-frame and communicating fire to the chambers via tiny vents at the rear of the cylinder. If the reliability of Maynard primers in long arms was echoed in these revolvers, they must have been satisfactory enough, but offered no real advantage over the readily obtainable copper cap.

Whilst on the subject of these oddities, it is in order to notice the arms of two other Americans, although specimens normally encountered were designed to use the copper cap.

J. W. Cochran, of New York City, invented a 'many chambered and non-recoil rifle', in 1837, on which a flat drum-like cylinder (with nine radially bored chambers) revolved on top of the action body and was fired by a single-action under-hammer. The top-strap could be raised and a fresh 'turret' or drum substituted in seconds. A few seven-shot pistols of 0·36 in calibre were also made, and are sometimes described as 'Monitor' pistols today. The name springs from the gun turret of a famous Civil War battleship, which closely resembled the hand-rotated drum of Cochran's arms. C. B. Allen (of Springfield) made the arms in America, and a few rifles were made in England, by Wilkinson of London, under a patent secured by Moses Hill, also in 1837, presumably upon the inventor's behalf.

P. W. Porter patented a rather similar type of arm in 1851, but the radial chambers revolved in a vertical plane and were operated by an under-lever similar to that used on the later Winchester rifles. This lever also cocked a 'mule-ear' or side-swinging hammer. Eight- and nine-shot rifles were made (some as pill-locks and some as true cap-lock arms), but only a single specimen of the Porter pistol is believed to exist. One patent model had an automatic magazine feed of loose powder and ball from a container mounted over the top of the drum. It appears that even the inventor could see the danger inherent in this design, and it was not produced commercially.

All of these weapons are rare today, as compared with the next type of revolving firearm to be considered. This arm, the self-cocking percussion pepperbox for conventional caps, was made in considerable numbers.

With rare exceptions, later to be noticed, these pepperbox pistols all had their barrel-cluster machined and drilled out of solid stock, and were fired by a long bar hammer on top of the frame. This hammer was operated entirely by the self-cocking lock mechanism, and struck nipples protruding at right angles from the breeches of the cluster.

In the majority of British weapons a circular shield protected the nipples from any accidental blow (which might have ignited a cap), and no partitions or fences were erected between the nipples. As a result of this omission, the flash from one cap occasionally set off its neighbour. This must have been annoying but not particularly dangerous, since all the barrels were free for such discharge; in a revolver, where the front of the frame might be facing a prematurely discharged chamber, this sort of incident was rather more serious.

The self-cocking lock mechanism of these British pepperboxes was ingenious and entirely effective for the purpose intended. On some weapons, the blow of the hammer was inadequate to discharge the small, rather sensitive percussion caps specially produced for such arms, but this failure was better laid at the door of the spring-maker, or assembler, than with the designer of the mechanism.

The bar-hammer was cranked just below the point of pivot, carrying a link to the mainspring on one side of the tail and a pivoted hook at the other. This hook was forced down into engagement with a bent or notch on top of the trigger. When the latter was pulled, it turned about its own pivot and the notch dragged the hammer hook forward. This, of course, pulled upon the lower end of the hammer, and raised the long bar upwards, on top of the frame. At the correct point, a cam on the rear of the trigger forced the hook up and out of engagement with its notch, and the hammer was driven down on to the nipple by a mainspring.

The mechanism for turning the barrel cluster was rudimentary, but sufficiently accurate for a revolving arm which merely required that a nipple be brought roughly beneath the round, flat-bottomed striker on the end of the hammer. The lever rotating the barrels is commonly called a 'hand', and will be so described here and in Chapter 11.

The hand was a long lever, lying along the right side of the action body, loosely secured by a screw set into the frame. A light spring, bearing on the rear of the hand, urged this lever into engagement with rotating teeth cut at the rear of the barrel cluster. By means of a pin passing transversely through the top of the trigger, the hand was lifted as the trigger was pulled and turned the barrels through one-sixth of a revolution. The loose pinning of this hand permitted it to ride down over the rotating teeth, when the trigger was released (and swung forward again by the trigger spring), so that it was correctly positioned for the next shot.

On all but the cheapest pepperboxes, a small bolt was linked to the trigger, and thrust forward to lock the barrels at the firing position. It was withdrawn when a trigger spring restored the trigger to its normal position.

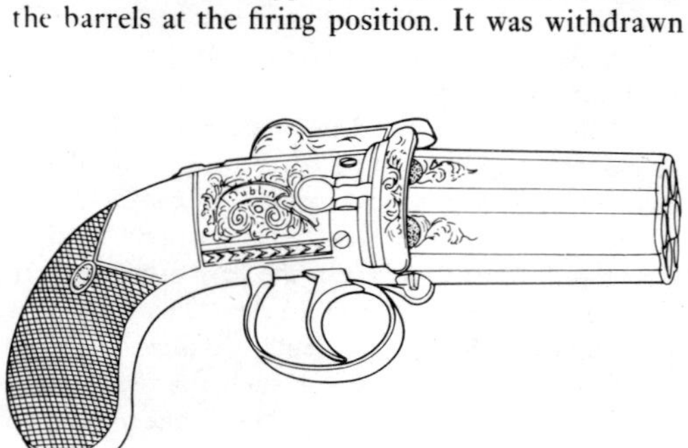

Six-barrelled self-cocking percussion pepperbox by Rigby of Dublin, *c.*1845-50.

For most of these arms, it was unnecessary to remove the barrels for loading. However, the cluster could be unshipped by turning out a large, cheese-head screw in the end of the arbor on which the barrels turned, and pulling it forward off the pistol. On a few pepperboxes by William and John Rigby, of Dublin, the barrels could be released by pressing in two studs, one of which protruded at each side of the frame and just behind the nipple shield. These Rigby pistols were most beautifully made, as six-shot, 0·32 in calibre pocket weapons. A sliding safety latch was normally present, which raised the hammer clear of the nipples, and their barrels were smooth-bored.

Despite the wide variety of names appearing on British pepperboxes, the weapons give every indication of centralised manufacture for their main components; frames were made of German silver, brass, or case-hardened iron, but the use of standardised casting patterns is always suggested upon examination.

The reader should not accept this suggestion as meaning that the parts of various weapons can be interchanged, but only as a proposal that the British pepperbox was a standard 'trade' line. The weapons could be purchased from the chief Birmingham suppliers, like Cooper & Goodman, Hollis & Son or Pryse & Redman, their frames already engraved with the retailer's name and address; such weapons might already have been finished and proved by the supplier, or be supplied 'in the white' for completion and proof by the purchaser.

Curiously enough, the original designer of the self-cocking mechanism used in British pepperboxes remains unknown, even today. No relevant English patent can be traced, and the most tentative dating of the invention is difficult to make. When George Stocker and Joseph Bentley patented the nipple-guard for such weapons, in April 1839, their drawings clearly illustrated a standard lock mechanism, but their patent laid no claim to it. In such circumstances, it can be safely assumed that the lock design had passed into the public domain and was beyond English patent-protection, even by such an early date. This state of affairs could have arisen if the idea was copied from imported weapons, or if it had been already patented abroad.

On the latter point, it is known that an American pistol manufacturer, Ethan Allen, applied for an American patent on a self-cocking pistol lock mechanism in 1837, and although his design was first used in single-shot pocket arms, there are grounds for belief that it was not long afterwards adapted to revolving pepperbox pistols.

Since Allen began to produce pepperboxes around

1838 (in partnership with Charles Thurber, after 1840) at Grafton, Massachusetts, his series of arms warrants first attention. Subsequently, Allen & Thurber operated factories at Norwich, Connecticut and Worcester, Massachusetts, but his arms varied only in detail and remained popular until the end of the American Civil War. One American authority,

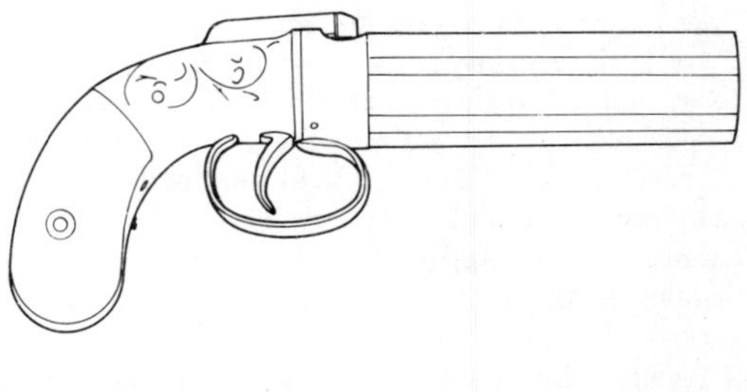

Allen & Thurber six-barrelled, self-cocking percussion pepperbox. U.S.A. 1847-65.

C. W. Sawyer,[13] assigned the following dates to the periods of manufacture at Grafton (1837-42), Norwich (1842-7) and Worcester (1847-65), which are valuable in helping to date Allen pistols marked with a manufactory name.

Fortunately for the collector, Allen's pepperboxes differed considerably in detail over the whole series, although examination of weapons made at any one factory is unlikely to yield any great difference apart from that of barrel length. As one example, the earlier weapons had a rib machined out of the metal between each barrel, but this gave way to a plain, shallow groove during the period the factory was at Worcester.

In the majority of cases, a nipple shield was screwed on to the action body, and not cast integrally with it in the manner adopted for British arms. Some later frames were cast with rudimentary shields, but towards the close of manufacture (when the firm had become Allen & Wheelock) that refinement was dropped altogether, and the nipples protected by sinking them into deep wells in the barrel breech.

In similar fashion, the original six-shot model was ultimately discarded in favour of compact four- and five-shot pistols, more suitable for the pocket. As earlier mentioned, the barrel lengths varied and can serve as a visual guide to the probable bore. Short-barrelled arms were made of 0·28 or 0·31 in calibres, whilst barrels over $5\frac{1}{2}$ in were normally bored for a 0·36 in ball.

Unlike many English pepperboxes, the Allen series all used butt-straps cast integrally with the frame. Two wooden butt-cheeks (varnished, but unchequered) were secured by a cross-screw and sometimes carried an oval silver plate let into the wood. The early weapons hung badly in the hand, being rather abruptly sloped at the butt, but later arms were greatly improved by curving the butt at a more conventional angle.

In normal course, Allen pepperboxes (whether of Grafton, Norwich or Worcester manufacture) are marked both with the appropriate firm name, and with a patent reference; usually, this reference is to Allen's 1837 lock mechanism patent, but occasionally the date 1845 recognises a later patent by him, covering barrel rotation. The words *Cast Steel* are frequently present, and the frames were engraved with a pattern of coarse curlicues until almost the close of production in 1865.

Variant Allen and Thurber arms are occasionally encountered. The trigger-guard on the heavier models sometimes carries a finger-bow or spur to help in steadying the barrel mass, whilst a few pistols dispense with guards altogether and use a ring-trigger. Some hammerless weapons were also made, specimens appearing with and without trigger-guards.

Any model can be encountered bearing a distributor's name, the firms of A. W. Spies & Co., J. G. Bolen, and E. K. Tryon being the most common; such arms must be distinguished from the various imitations of Allen pepperboxes, some of which bear a striking resemblance to the parent arm.

Amongst the better-known imitations are those by W. W. Marston, and by the Manhattan Fire Arms Manufacturing Company, both of whom were

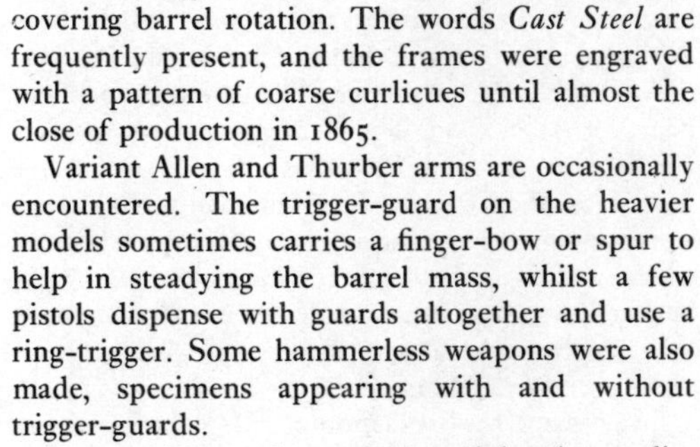

Marston's patent, six-barrelled percussion pepperbox.

based in New York. Marston (whose arms may be stamped *W. W. Marston & Knox, Marston & Co.*, or *W. W. Marston*) copied the short-barrelled Allen, but riveted his nipple shields on to the frame instead of screwing them there. The Manhattan arms were slightly better-made, and the firm also produced a three-barrelled pepperbox in some numbers; this pistol had a top bar-hammer, like an Allen, but the barrel cluster was rotated by hand.

13 'American Percussion Pepperboxes', *Antiques Magazine*, Oct. 1926.

Less common than these Allen imitations, were a series of bar-hammer pepperboxes by Pecare & Smith, of New York; Jacob Pecare and Josiah M. Smith patented these arms in 1849, and they are principally noteworthy for a trigger which folds up into the frame when not in use. These arms were four-barrelled, of 0·31 in calibre, and may be found with iron or brass frames. The partners also made a ten-shot pepperbox, of 0·28 in calibre, which is now extremely rare. A folding trigger was used, but a curious vertical hammer (working in and out of the front of the frame) replaced the bar-type; the 4 in barrels of this model were entirely shrouded by a long sleeve anchored to the frame, and it was exhibited at the Great Exhibition at London, in 1851.

Amongst other American bar-hammer pepperboxes of Allen type, 0·31 in calibre pistols marked *Union Arms Co.* and *The Washington Arms Co.* are noted for their rarity, but were conventional in construction and operation. Another pepperbox (in the same category) was marked *Phenix Armoury*; it is believed to have been made in a new Marston factory, after destruction of the original during the New York Draft Riots of 1863.

In England, the bar-hammer, self-cocking pepperbox achieved calibres and finishes quite unknown to the American makers, but differed little in mechanical detail. An American pepperbox exceeding 0·36 in calibre was quite unusual, but British pepperboxes in full 20 bore (0·615 in) calibre are still sufficiently common to appear in private collections. Some beautifully-engraved arms, in this calibre, were sold by George & John Deane (of 30 King William Street, London Bridge) with a cluster of five barrels, 5½ in long; such pistols measured nearly 11 in in length, and were often fitted with a belt-hook for carrying them about. The purpose of luxury arms in this calibre is obscure (although they may have been made for sale to naval officers), but some plain weapons are believed to have been issued in the police service.

It would be difficult to list even the principal retailers of British pepperboxes, for the names of such famous makers as *C. & H. Egg*, *Samuel Nock*, *Charles Lancaster* or *W. A. Beckwith* appear upon weapons indistinguishable from those signed by men of lesser renown. The better class of pistol commonly had a one-piece butt, finely chequered and with a cap-box in its base, but cheaper arms followed the same practice as that adopted in America, and sported two separate wooden cheeks on integral straps.

Little attempt was made to improve the construction or design of these pistols. In all qualities, the left-hand frame plate was a separate component, secured by a screw which could fail and allow the plate to drop off, whilst arms with separate butts required additional pins to secure the top frame plate and strap. In deference to the Colt patent covering such features, few makers fitted partitions between the nipples, but some Rigby arms were made on this design, using a vertical hammer behind horizontal nipples.

J. R. Cooper, B. Cogswell and W. Tranter all secured patents, or Registered Designs, protecting improvements to the top hammer mechanism, but there is little evidence that the devices were ever adopted, even by their inventors. Cooper's improvements related to rotation of the barrels, whilst Cogswell designed a magazine for feeding caps on to each nipple; Tranter's idea was to re-design the link connecting mainspring and hammer in such a fashion as to eliminate the need for any trigger spring.

Another idea involved the provision of a 5 in stabbing blade, which would be attached to the pistol. In this better-known embodiment, the blade could be screwed into the end of the arbor upon which the barrels rotated, but a less handy weapon had a blade permanently attached to the base of the butt. History fails to relate how these weapons were to be carried (when thus garnished), and it is unlikely that many were made. Unfortunately, it is comparatively simple to make up and mount daggers of this sort, and a number of modern forgeries have come on to the market in recent years.

There is little to be said of the cases used with the better qualities of pepperbox, or the accessories included with them. A pincer-type, single-cavity iron ball-mould was normally provided, and a brass or wooden ramrod (with a worm under the tip) was included for loading or withdrawing the charges. On a few pepperboxes the weapon was loaded by removing the barrels and using the arbor as a rammer, but a separate rod was preferred by most makers.

The only unusual tool included in an ordinary case was the nipple key, which had a head suitable in shape only for use on pepperbox nipples. On conventional gun or revolver nipples, a square (or two flats) was formed immediately below the cone, and this was engaged by a suitable square or notch on the nipple key to turn the nipple in or out of its socket. The pepperbox nipple had no engaging surfaces of this sort, but was made with two notches on the circular skirt upon which it seated. The key therefore had two prongs or tines formed at its head, which engaged the skirt to turn the nipple. On some Bentley arms only a single notch was formed in the skirt, to mate with a single stout tine on the tool. Both types of key were fragile, and are often broken when encountered.

With the Belgian maker, J. Herman, as a striking exception, there is little evidence that the bar-hammer pepperbox found favour on the Continent, a quite distinctive under-hammer design having appeared there around 1837. This *Mariette* mechanism was immensely popular; it also appeared in England as the 'Cooper' pepperbox, and in America as retailed by Blunt & Syms of New York. The

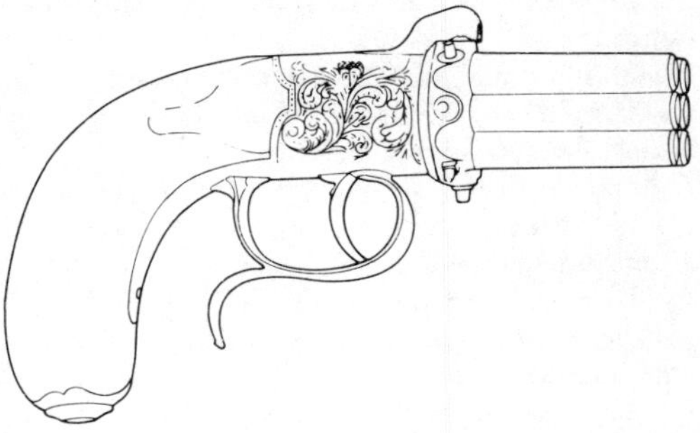

Eight-barrelled self-cocking percussion pepperbox by Arnold of Liège, *c.*1850.

Cooper weapons were undoubtedly made in England, but there is evidence to suggest that the American arms may have been imported and not made there. J. R. Cooper had a sales outlet in New York, around 1850, and could have arranged such importation. Against this view can be set almost identical pistols marked *J. Post's Self-Acting Set* or *J. Post Self Acting Pistol*, which acknowledge an American patent, of 1849, in that name.

The Mariette or Cooper pistol operated an under-hammer striking upon the lowest nipple instead of that uppermost. The barrel-rotating hand was identical to that used in the bar-hammer weapons, but the hammer (hung upside down) was dragged back by a hook linked to the trigger in this mechanism. This hook engaged a notch on the underside of the hammer to effect the cocking.

Two striking features of the weapon lay in its use of nipples screwed home in line with the bores, instead of protruding at right angles like the bar-hammer pepperboxes, and in their separation by fences or partitions to lessen the danger of multiple discharge.

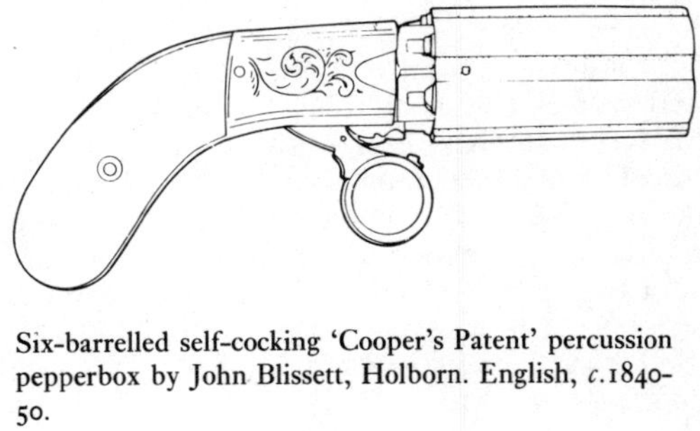

Six-barrelled self-cocking 'Cooper's Patent' percussion pepperbox by John Blissett, Holborn. English, *c.*1840–50.

These horizontal nipples were a specific claim in J. R. Cooper's English patent of 1840, and their use accounted for the appearance of a legend *J. R. Cooper's Patent* (or, less commonly, *J. R. Cooper, Patentee*) on the frame of the pistol. Elaborate lock mechanisms for these arms were also claimed in the patent, along with an idea for screwing nipples into the breeching from in front, but neither refinement was actually used in Cooper's pepperboxes.

The majority of these pistols were pocket weapons measuring about 8 in overall, with six 3½ in barrels in about 0·38 in calibre. Brass, iron, or German silver, were used in making their frames, and the arms were seldom particularly well finished. A few fancy pistols were made, with 4¾ in barrels and grotesque mask butts, but even here the workmanship can only be regarded as adequate. It was unusual for any Cooper pepperbox to be fitted with a nipple shield, the horizontal cones and protective partitions making this an unnecessary refinement.

The comparable American arms by Blunt & Syms of New York also lacked a nipple shield. One leading American authority[14] has advanced the theory that these arms originated through an employee, John Zettler, who made up a pattern arm for a customer who never returned for it. As earlier mentioned, the background of these arms is confused, and their

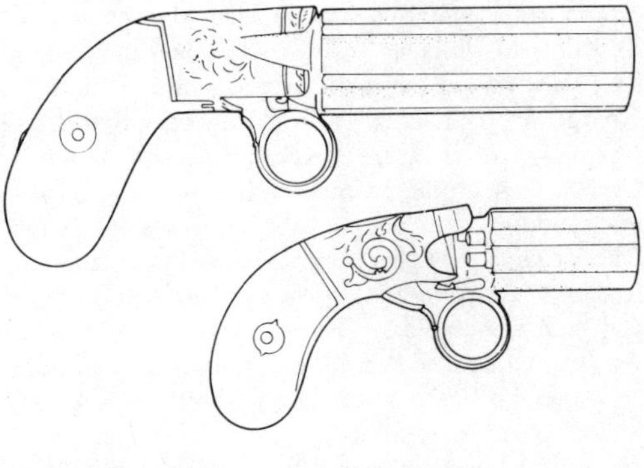

Blunt & Symes six-barrelled self-cocking percussion pepperboxes. U.S.A., *c.*1850. Saunders Memorial Museum, Berryville, Arkansas.

importation from abroad seems probable, if the maker's ability to sell through a 30 per cent *ad valorem* customs duty can be accepted.

A typical Blunt & Syms pistol was of 0·31 in calibre, with barrels varying between 3¾ in and 4¾ in in length, and had no nipple shield. This omission (matched in the Cooper arms) was remedied in the J. Post weapons and also dealt with in

14 W. H. B. Smith, *National Rifle Association Book of Small Arms*, Vol. I, 1942.

a series of unsigned pepperboxes whose origins are obscure. Post completely shrouded the nipples in his 0·31 in calibre pistols, but the unsigned arms merely extended the top edge of the frame into a peak or cowl protecting the uppermost nipples. Some of these latter pistols had saw-handle butts, and large 0·36 in calibre versions with 7 in barrels were made.

Belgian-made pistols on this under-hammer system were usually marked *Mariette Breveté*, but were distinguished by the method for loading them. Each barrel was notched at the muzzle, and could be unscrewed from the breeching (by a key) so that powder and ball might be inserted in a suitable breech cup. As in the Nock flintlock pepperboxes (or conventional turn-off pocket-pistols) a tightly fitting ball could be loaded in this fashion.

The barrels of these Belgian arms were often of twist-iron, exhibiting a most attractive figure in the metal, and were normally of fairly small calibre and short length. The number of barrels varied widely, four or five being normal, but grotesque pistols with twenty-four barrels (grouped as fifteen about an inner core of nine) were also made.

Some top-hammer pistols were also made in Belgium, which can be confused with the Mariette weapon at a casual glance. These pepperboxes have the screwed barrels and ring triggers of the Mariette, but the lock is adapted to strike the topmost nipple. Such arms, which acknowledged the patents of T. Lhoist or J. Herman, were matched in England by a rare pepperbox sold by the London house of George & John Deane. It is unlikely that these weapons, which were marked *Deane's Improved Central Fire Pistol*, were actually made by Deane, but no specific source of supply can be suggested. The arms had sights fitted to them (an unusual feature in a pepperbox), with a conventional trigger and guard. A typical specimen was 8 in long, with six $3\frac{1}{2}$ in barrels machined integrally and in 70 bore.

A variant percussion pepperbox now keenly sought by collectors has a single-action lock. Such arms occasionally present difficulties in classification when the barrels are hand-rotated, since they then approach the function of turnover pistols. The view generally accepted is that arms with a single hammer may be regarded as pepperboxes, whilst multi-barrelled pistols with two hammers are left in the other category.

In England, such arms were not greatly favoured. One or two of the Nock flintlock pepperboxes were converted to percussion, and present a grotesque appearance. The nipples were unshielded and protruded around the breech in a most dangerous fashion. Even to lay such a pistol on the table invited accidental discharge. Another type of pistol with a folding trigger and five small-calibre hand-rotated barrels, had a central hammer and a circular nipple shield. The ramrod was lodged in the centre of its barrel cluster.

Joseph Lang, a gunmaker in the Haymarket, London, produced a few single-action centre-hammer pepperboxes on which the barrels were mechanically rotated by cocking the hammer. It is not impossible that the Lang revolver (later to be noticed) was developed from this design. Although beautifully made and mechanically reliable, these six-barrelled pocket arms made little headway against the self-cocking pistols.

Another British pepperbox, the Budding, is included here although it can hardly be described as a conventional single-action pistol.

The Budding barrels were hand-rotated, and it may be one of the earliest of the British pepperboxes. The nipples were mounted horizontally, like a Cooper, but the firing mechanism consisted of a simple bolt sliding in the underside of the frame. This bolt was propelled by a coiled spring and was cocked by the finger-piece protruding through a slot in the bottom of the frame.

Two models of the Budding were made, one of which had a conventional trigger and guard. The other version dispensed with a trigger, the cocking piece being drawn back against spring tension and pressed into a notch on the side of the groove. To fire this Budding it was necessary to press the spur sideways out of its notch, and allow the bolt to fly forward.

Barrels and frames were made of bronze, the weapons being normally Birmingham proved and marked only *Budding, Maker*. It was necessary to remove the cluster of five barrels in order to re-cap these pistols, which normally measured $7\frac{1}{2}$ in overall and were of 150 bore calibre.

Although eccentric in design, the weapons were very well made, and much discussion has taken place as to their date and the identity of their maker. The researches of an English authority, W. Keith Neal, have now established that Edward Budding (a machinist at Thrupp Mill, near Stroud) was the maker, probably around 1830.[15] Whether he designed these arms, or not, remains to be demonstrated.

In America, the series of four- or six-shot single-action pepperboxes by Benjamin and Barton Darling are considered desirable by collectors. The arms were made from about 1836, first at Bellingham, Massachusetts, and later at Woonsocket, Rhode Island. Crude in appearance, but reliable in operation, the arms were made entirely of iron (save for the wooden butt), and had centre hammers and conventional trigger-guards. A stout nipple shield was fitted, and a few late weapons had mechanically-rotated

15 *Guns Review*, May 1962.

barrels. Very similar weapons, made almost entirely of brass and signed *J.Engh IEH*, *AGS* and *AIS* are now known to have been made in Sweden.[16] In any version, the calibre was commonly around 0·30 in and barrel lengths varied between $3\frac{3}{4}$ in and $4\frac{1}{2}$ in.

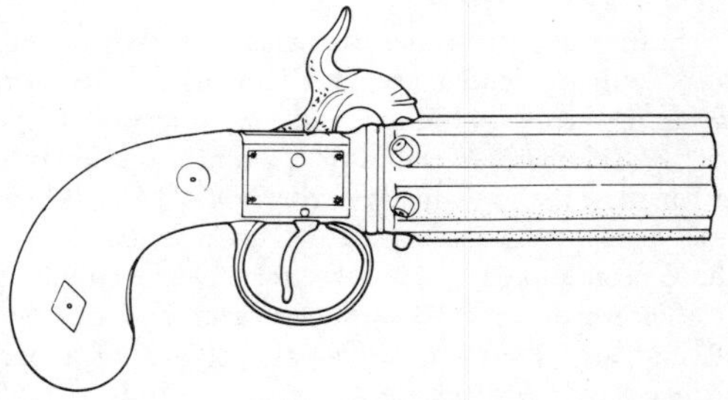

Darling six-barrelled hand-rotated percussion pepperbox. U.S.A., *c.*1836. Late W. M. Locke Collection.

A very different type of single-action pepperbox, six-barrelled, and with an underhammer, has also been attributed to the Darling brothers. The pistols had no trigger-guards, and some barrel clusters were mechanically rotated, but the arms were not signed and this identification is tentative.

A rather more sophisticated underhammer pepperbox was sold by Bacon & Co. of Norwich, Connecticut. Thomas J. Bacon was a late arrival in this field, and it is unlikely that these 0·30 in calibre, mechanically-rotated pepperboxes appeared before 1852. In many aspects, they suggest manufacture by Allen, to Bacon's design, although they are single-action and have no trigger-guards.

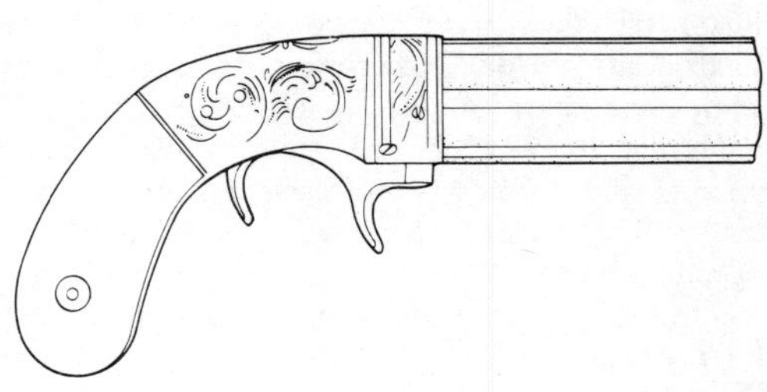

Bacon six-barrelled single-action percussion pepperbox. U.S.A., *c.*1860. Late W. M. Locke Collection.

A single-action pistol, with a really striking resemblance to the Allen weapon, was made by Stocking & Co. of Worcester, Massachusetts. The top barhammer was used on these arms, but a long thumb-spur was naturally fitted, and the six barrels were mechanically rotated.

The Stocking pepperbox was made in 0·28 or 0·31 in calibres, and in barrel lengths varying from $3\frac{1}{2}$ in to $4\frac{1}{2}$ in; a few 0·41 in weapons were a notable exception to the American preference for small calibres in such arms. Many of the weapons acknowledged a patent of 1848, but the detail protected is unknown. Like the Allen pistols, the nipple shield was screwed to the frame, and trigger-guard or butt-cheek details parallel those of the self-cocking weapon.

Stocking six-barrelled single-action percussion pepperbox. U.S.A., *c.*1850. Late W. M. Locke Collection.

Continental manufacturers must be assumed to have made single-action pepperboxes, since a variety of such arms were available during the opening years of the metallic cartridge revolver, but specimens are hard to find. At least one series were made for needle-fire ignition, in which a long needle (linked to the hammer) passed through the paper cartridge to strike a percussion cap embedded behind the bullet. These were four-barrelled pepperboxes, with screw-off barrels in 0·31 in calibre, and were engraved *Rissak Patent*, although proved in Belgium.

Before turning to the true revolver, one type of multi-barrelled pistol remains to be noticed, although some collectors quarrel with its inclusion amongst pepperbox arms.

In these pistols, the barrel cluster is fixed, and the hammer nose revolves. The weapon is found only in a rare series of all-metal arms, normally signed by Irish makers, and in a few wooden-butted pistols signed by Englishmen. Since specimens signed by William and John Rigby, of Dublin, are the most common, the type is now often described as a 'Rigby' pistol.

The weapons had barrels bored in a solid cluster of three or four, and the single-action, centre hammer carried a circular plate on its nose. Each barrel had a separate nipple, and the plate could be turned to strike a fresh cap after the hammer had been cocked. The metal butt had a finger hole through it, by which the weapon could be better gripped for

16 See Eric Ashede, 'Småländske Mässingsvapen', *Samlarnytt*, No. 7/8, Stockholm, August, 1963, pp. 3-4.

use as a club after firing. For such a purpose, to quote the late Major Brown, this weapon would be 'frightfully effective'.[17]

In America, a rather different type of pistol on this principle was developed under the patents of George Leonard (of Shrewsbury, Massachusetts) round about 1850. The inventor made a few early specimens, near Boston, which were four-barrelled arms in 0·31 in calibre. An improved, five-shot, series with saw-handled butts were later produced by the Robbins & Lawrence Co. of Windsor, Vermont.

Leonard's pistols all had fixed barrels, and an internal striker cocked by a ring trigger and fired by another trigger above it. The nipples were mounted in line with the bores, which last were unusual (for a pepperbox) in being rifled.

On early arms, the barrel-cluster was unscrewed from the frame for capping but, in the Robbins & Lawrence version, the barrels tipped down on a hinge for this purpose. In deference to the difficulty in loading rifled barrels, the cluster unscrewed forward of the breech for the charges to be inserted. Barrel lengths varied between $3\frac{1}{2}$ in and $4\frac{1}{2}$ in, and the Vermont pistols were available in 0·28 in or 0·31 in calibre.

Again, evidence is wanting that the Continental makers turned out weapons on this system. However, one ingenious variant of the fixed-barrel pepperbox was made by the Belgian, J. Herman. In this four-barrelled pistol, a folding trigger operated the self-cocking mechanism to trip four hammers in succession. A pistol almost as bizarre was patented in England, during 1853, by Richard and Charles John Jones of Birmingham. In these arms, the barrels were arranged one above the other in such a manner that their nipples faced a self-cocking hammer in a concave arc. The hammer was mounted on an arm connected to both ends of the mainspring and struck each nipple in succession down the curve.

One other rare Continental pepperbox was made in France, by Le Page of Paris. This maker was renowned, among other things, for pistols firing superimposed charges from a single barrel. A few superb six-barrelled, twelve-shot pepperboxes were made on this system, using the ring trigger, self-cocking mechanism of J. Herman. Magnificently cased and finished, the accessories included means for loading six balls, and six powder charges, simultaneously.

A peculiar American firearm, patented by John Couch and Henry North, in 1859, is sometimes mistaken for a pepperbox pistol on casual examination, but was actually intended for use as a trap-gun. This pistol had six barrels bored in a solid cylindrical block, but only one nipple with which to fire them. No conventional hammer was fitted, a large circular plate (propelled by a coil spring) served this purpose, and fired all barrels simultaneously.

The weapon could be fixed to a tree or post, and any animal (or human being) who blundered into a wire attached to the trigger received the six charges in one blast.

In turning to consider the true cap-lock revolver, it is both just and reasonable to consider first the weapons made by Samuel Colt, of America. It has been fashionable for more than a century to quarrel with the view that his was the first true revolver, and many weapons antedating his original design have been quoted by his detractors. Deane cited the Collier weapons, with Continental arms by Devisme, Rissac and Herman, whilst the claims of other Americans (Whittier, Nichols and Childs *et al.*) must press hard upon any claim for such priority.

However, when all the evidence has been examined, the most hardened iconoclast must accept the grudging acknowledgement of John Deane that '. . . as a revolving firearm, his [Colt's] pistol was a great and leading step in advance'.[18]

Samuel Colt was born at Hartford, Connecticut, in July 1814, and secured his first US revolver patent in February 1836, after prudently filing for British protection (necessary to establish novelty of invention there) in the previous October. The vital feature of these patents was the claim for rotating the cylinder by a 'lifter and ratchet' motion, and of locking it for discharge by a key.

In order to finance manufacture, Colt parted with most of his interest in the invention, and 'The Patent Arms Manufacturing Company', of Paterson, New Jersey, began to make his revolving arms with the not inconsiderable capital of $75,000. Unfortunately, the arms proved unexpectedly expensive to make and, the demand proving far from brisk, the company became insolvent by 1843.

During its brief history, the company made pistols, rifles, shotguns and carbines under Colt's patent. The arms are rare today, and much fancied by collectors.

The pistols were particularly notable in having 146
folding triggers. Their locks were single-action, and the cylinders were rotated by a hand linked to the hammer, when the latter was cocked. Unlike later Colt revolvers, the frames were not a solid forging, but were painstakingly constructed from a number of small parts. The barrels, however, established a pattern for Colt revolver assembly in years to come, and were fixed to the pistol frame by a cross-wedge passing through barrel lug and cylinder-axis pin to lock the barrel, cylinder and frame into one. No top strap connected barrel to frame.

17 *The Gun Collector*, No. 23, July 1948.

18 *Manual of Fire-Arms*, London, 1858, p. 109.

These pistols were five-chambered, with partitioned nipples horizontally aligned with the bores, and were made with barrel lengths ranging from $4\frac{1}{2}$ in to 12 in and in calibres of 0·28 in, 0·31 in and 0·36 in. On most of the series no ramrod was fitted, and the barrel had to be removed to use patented tools for charging the chambers. Revolvers are sometimes found fitted with a lever rammer beneath the barrel, and this may be factory work or done in later years at the buyer's instance.

The Paterson long-arms came in two versions. A hammerless design was cocked and revolved by a ring lever in front of the trigger, and made as a rifle (in 0·34 in, 0·44 in and 0·69 in calibres), in six-, seven- and eight-shot variants with barrels of 30 in or 32 in. A centre-hammer series of rifles and carbines were made in calibres of 0·44 in, 0·47 in, 0·53 in and 0·56 in, in company with six-chambered 20 or 30 bore shotguns. Both designs were made with and without lever rammers, and both were purchased in small numbers for US Army tests; the ring-cocked rifles saw service during the Seminole War in Florida around 1838, with a few of the revolvers, and were credited with some success by Colonel W. S. Harney, who ordered them.

On the failure of the Paterson Company, Colt salvaged his patent rights from the wreckage, but made no attempt to resume manufacture for some years. However the outbreak of the Mexican War aroused interest in his pistols, one Colonel C. A. May demanding their supply at the instance of General Taylor. No Paterson pistol being available to copy, Colt re-designed his revolver in collaboration with Captain Samuel Walker of the Texas Rangers and produced the Army Model of 1847. In every aspect, this weapon set the pattern of Colt revolvers until 1873.

The 1847 pistol (known as the 'Walker' Colt, to modern collectors) was made in the arms factory of Eli Whitney, at Whitneyville, Connecticut, under Colt's supervision. It was a very heavy weapon (4 lb 9 oz) measuring $15\frac{1}{2}$ in overall, with a 9 in barrel and six chambers in 0·44 in calibre. Unlike the Paterson arms, the Walker had a trigger-guard, a really powerful lever rammer beneath its barrel, and a frame forged in one piece. The lock was single-action, and the barrel was keyed to the cylinder pin as for the earlier arms.

Whitney had been a pioneer in the production of arms with interchangeable parts, and the Walker pistol was the first Colt arm on this principle. Colt adhered to this method of manufacture when, in 1848, he set up his own factory at Pearl Street, Hartford, the town of his birth. In the same year he received another US Government order for a
147 lighter version of the Walker pistol, and these Model 1848 'Dragoon' revolvers bore upon their cylinders legends acknowledging their military connection; in normal course, a scene of fighting between soldiers and Indians was roll-engraved upon the cylinder, and the letters *U.S.M.R.* were sometimes added in recognition of the 'Mounted Rifle' units to whom the military version was issued. In the same 0·44 in calibre as the Walker, this six-shot Dragoon weighed only 4 lb with a $7\frac{1}{2}$ in barrel and an overall length of 14 in.

In the scramble to produce his 1847 Army revolvers, Colt took time to consider the civilian market and designed lighter belt and pocket models for production when the opportunity offered. Towards the end of 1848, a five-shot, 0·31 in calibre, pocket revolver went into production. Barrel lengths of 3 in, 4 in, 5 in, and 6 in (invariably octagonal, in distinction from the round military shape) were available, but the lever rammer was not supplied.

From these arms came the remarkably popular 'Pocket Model of 1849' which was made in 0·31 in calibre, as a five- or six-shot revolver with a lever rammer beneath the barrel. In England a superbly

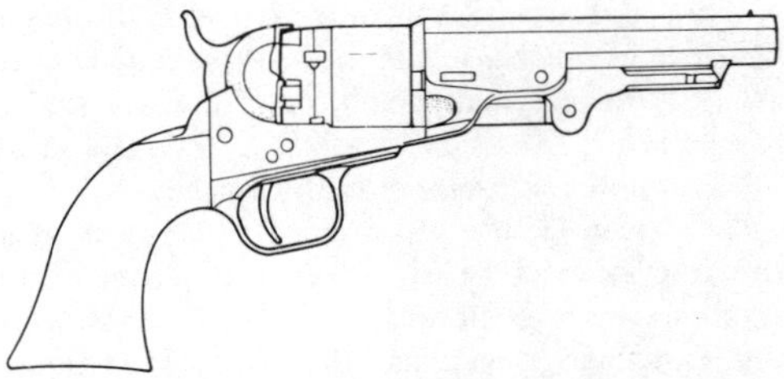

Colt Model 1849 pocket revolver. Tower of London Armouries.

detailed patent of June 1849 claimed improvements to the 1835 protection, and covered or disclosed most of the principal features in the 1848 and succeeding models. Particular claim was laid to the rotation of the cylinder by a hand linked to the hammer and bearing on rotation teeth at the rear of the cylinder. A keyed barrel frame assembly was noted, along with the see-saw cylinder bolt which tipped in and out of engagement with notches in the cylinder wall, as the hammer was cocked. The lever rammer was also protected.

To follow the 1849 revolver came the 'Navy' Model of 1851. This was again a single-action, six-chambered weapon, but in 0·36 in calibre and with a 7 in barrel. It achieved a popularity rivalled by few firearms, selling widely in the commercial market, and being bought for service issue in both America and England. The cylinder was roll-engraved with a naval battle-scene, and the words *Engaged 16th May, 1843*, the work being signed by W. L. Ormsby, a noted steel engraver. Despite this decoration, it seems likely that the 'Navy' name came from its calibre of 0·36 in, rather than its decoration.

All muzzle-loading Colt revolvers carried their inventor's name and address stamped upon the barrel, and the Navy pistol can be found bearing all those used after 1849. *Address Sam'l Colt, New York City, Address Col. Sam'l Colt, New York, U.S. America* appeared upon American revolvers, and *Address Col. Colt, London* upon those made in the London factory.

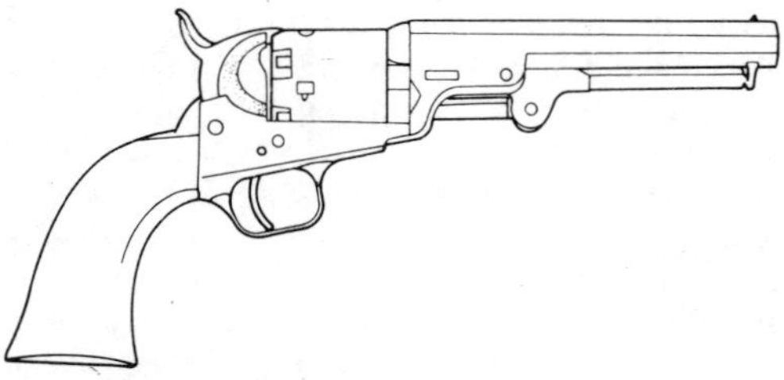

Colt Pocket Model of Navy Calibre (1853). Tower of London Armouries.

In 1855, Colt moved his factory to its present site on the Connecticut River, near Hartford. Although the series of muzzle-loading revolvers made at that factory form a fascinating subject for detailed study, they present (with one exception) little variation of sufficient note for attention in these pages.

The 0·36 in calibre was applied to a pocket arm with a cylinder rebated at the rear diameter to accommodate it to the smaller frame. E. K. Root, a Colt employee, developed their first solid-frame revolver, with a top strap connecting barrel and frame. This pistol is now known as the 'Model 1855', and had a single-action lock (with a hammer mounted on the right of the frame) and a stud-trigger without guard. Five-shot models, with plain or fluted cylinders, were made as pocket arms in 0·265 in and 0·31 in calibres.

These arms were probably made two years after the model date now given to them, and are quite rare in England. It seems possible that they were not offered here before 1865, since their solid frames were an infringement of the English patent of Robert Adams, to be noticed later. Their appearance also heralded another attempt, by the Colt Company, to enter the market with revolving long-arms. The Root mechanism was applied to rifles, carbines, muskets and shotguns, but the series were never particularly popular. An American Ordnance Office Report, of 1864, dealt with the performance of these rifles during the Civil War. The terse comments noted these rifles as 'too delicate and complicated. Require too much care. Stocks snap easily. Too long and cumbersome for cavalry.'[19]

The Root model carbines were made in 0·36 in, 0·44 in and 0·56 in calibres, with barrels as short as 15 in and as long as 21 in. The rifles added 0·50 in and 0·40 in to these calibres, and extended the barrel lengths to 31 in. The muskets (of 0·56 in calibre) and the shotguns (of 0·60 in or 0·75 in calibre) were naturally somewhat more stout than the carbines. Five- or six-shot models were made (the extra chamber being discarded for the heavier calibres) and long-arms were identical with revolvers in using a cylinder-axis pin that was inserted from the rear of the frame. This pin turned with the cylinder, the locking bolt engaging notches on a disc at the rear end of it.

Following these Root model revolvers came pistols built to the old keyed-barrel assembly, but with improved rammers. Formerly, the lever had been hinged to the barrel lug, but the improved rammer 'crept' on teeth which engaged holes drilled in the underside of the barrel. The first of these improved weapons (which all had rounded barrels) was the Army Model, of 1860; this was a six-chambered arm in 0·44 in calibre and with an 8 in barrel. Plain and fluted cylinders were made for it, and many revolvers were adapted for optional use with a detachable carbine stock. A 'New Model'

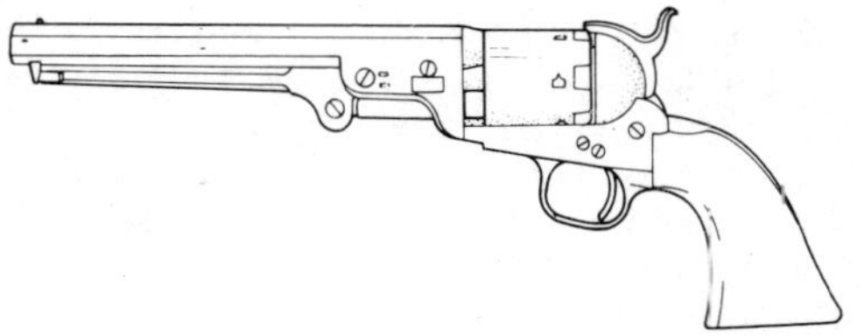

Colt six-shot single-action percussion holster or belt revolver, 'Old Model Navy' or 'Model of 1851'. Made at Hartford 1850-73, and in London 1853-6.

0·36 in calibre Navy pistol of similar appearance followed in 1861, and a particularly graceful (but very similar) 0·36 in 'New Model' Police revolver closed the Colt percussion revolver series in 1862. Colonel Samuel Colt had died in January of the same year.

Colt's London factory has already been mentioned, but although only the Pocket Models (of 1849) and the Navy pistols (of 1851) were made there, the establishment formed an important landmark in the history of British arms manufacture.

The inventor had exhibited his arms at the London Exhibition of 1851, where their utility contrasted strongly with the more decorative arms exhibited by most makers. He claimed that their manufacture by machinery made all parts fully interchangeable, and secured the Telford medal for

19 Ordnance Memo. No. 5, *Proceedings of Ordnance Board Convened Sept. 12, 1863*, Washington, 1864.

151 Double-trigger 0·44 in percussion revolver by William Tranter, after his patent of 1853. Tower of London Armouries.

152 Daw double-action percussion ·442 revolver, *c.*1860.

153 Self-cocking ·45 percussion revolver by William Westley Richards after his patent of 1852. Private collection.

154 Deane Harding. RSAF, Enfield.

155 W. J. Harvey's Patent Revolver *c.*1855. Tower of London Armouries.

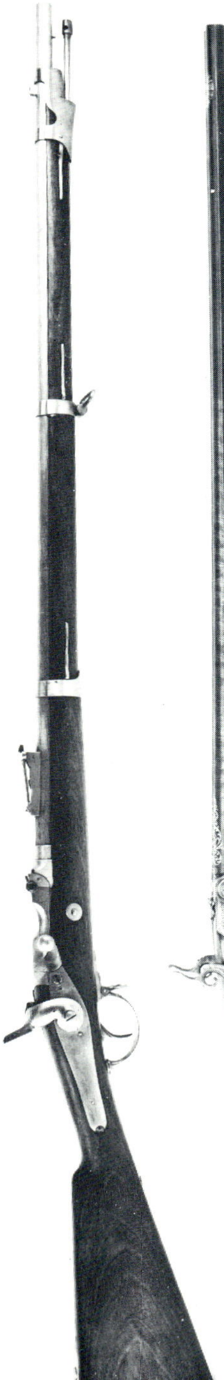

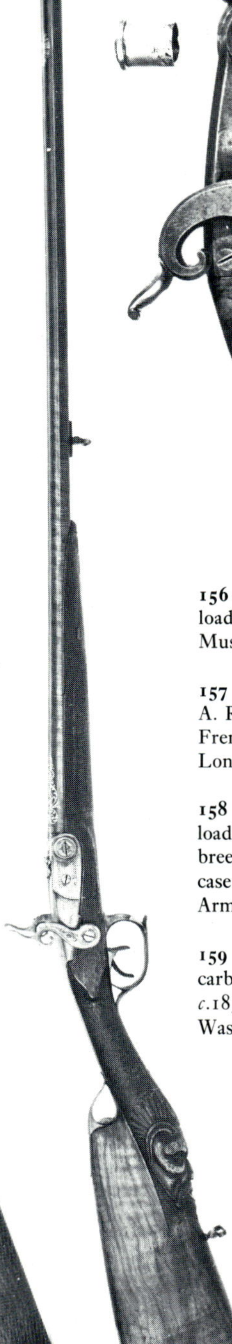

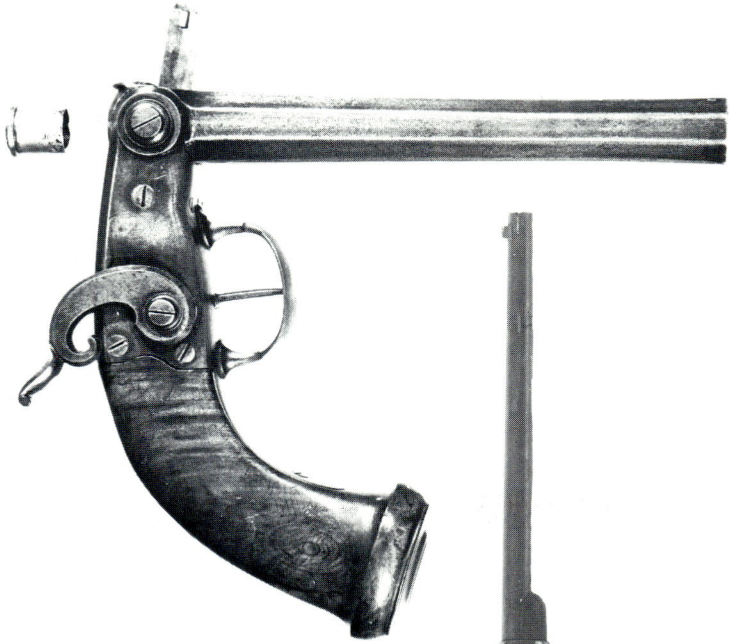

156 *Far left* Braendlin-Albini breech-loading military rifle. Belgian, *c.*1868. Musée d'Armes de Liège.

157 *Left* Double-barrelled gun made by A. Renette after the Pauly design. French (Paris), *c.*1815. Tower of London Armouries.

158 *Above* Detail of Pauly breech-loading centre-fire pistol, showing breech open and original brass cartridge case. French, *c.*1818. Tower of London Armouries.

159 *Right* Gilbert Smith breech-loading carbine with tilting barrel. American, *c.*1856. Smithsonian Institution, Washington, D.C.

a lecture upon the subject, given to the Institute of Civil Engineers in November 1851.

Exactly what prompted the decision to open a factory in London may never clearly be known. There is some evidence that the step was taken to bludgeon America's Congress into granting an extension of his US master patent, under the threat of withdrawing manufacture overseas. More probably, the step was taken in order to show the British Government that firearms could be manu-

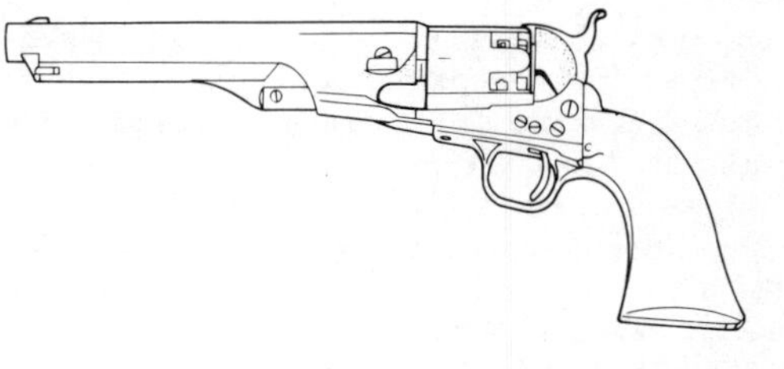

Colt single-action .44 Army percussion revolver, Model of 1860. Tower of London Armouries.

factured with fully interchangeable parts, by using the Colt machines and production methods. Obviously enough, to secure the prize of supplying service rifles by hundreds of thousands, the opening of this demonstration plant was a reasonable step.

Whatever the reasons, premises off Bessborough Place, near Vauxhall Bridge, were leased in 1852 and put into production in 1853. An American, Charles Dennett, was the first manager, but an Englishman, Charles Manby (who was also Secretary of the Institution of Civil Engineers) acted as Colt's English adviser. The plant was lavishly equipped with machinery, and 200 unskilled hands were employed under the supervision of American personnel from the Hartford works.

Colt's system was immensely unpopular with the British gun-trade, who decried both his methods for making guns in this fashion, and the possibility of making interchangeable parts by it. Initially the chances seemed fair, for Colt's evidence was respectfully received by the Parliamentary Committee examining the interchangeable principle, and a British Navy contract for 4,000 Model 1851 revolvers was secured in March 1854. As the Crimean War operations progressed, further orders called for another 5,500 pistols for the Navy, and (in December 1854 and August 1855) two further contracts meant 14,000 weapons for the British Army.

These revolvers were standard 0·36 in Navy Colt pistols with $7\frac{1}{2}$ in barrels and are curiously rare today. They bore the London barrel address, often with a *WD* and broad arrow on the barrel lug, and some appear to have had the naval scene deliberately erased from their cylinders. Another series can be encountered, which were apparently supplied from America; these arms bore only the *Enfield* stamp on their wooden butts, but had the American barrel address and high L-suffixed serial numbers. Their date of supply is uncertain, but they probably were for post-1864 Colonial service.

Promising as this start had been, the London venture did not prosper for long. Labour troubles and the success of a competing British revolver, the Beaumont-Adams pistol, finally brought matters to a head. Eventually, satisfied that his Hartford factory could supply demands from every quarter, and disappointed in his hopes for service rifle contracts, Colt withdrew from the field and closed his plant at the end of 1856.

Apart from the service arms already described, commercial Navy pistols were produced in fair numbers, along with the Pocket Model of 1849 in 4 in, 5 in and 6 in barrel lengths. After closure of the factory, a sales establishment was maintained at 14 Pall Mall, London. Colt percussion arms continued to be sold until 1872, and although most of them carried the American barrel address, all models can be encountered with the London legend engraved upon them. One weapon, the Dragoon or Old Model Army 0·44 in revolver, may have been assembled at the London factory from Hartford parts; despite the existence of a few specimens with London barrel addresses, the general concensus of opinion is against complete manufacture there.

As a result of its popularity, the Colt revolver was imitated or improved by a number of American and Continental manufacturers; a crude version of the 1851 Navy pistol was made in Russia (at the Tula Arsenal), but no British manufacturer saw fit to copy the Colt weapons, even when British patents lapsed.

In America, two firms made notably close imitations. The Manhattan Fire Arms Company (of Newark, New Jersey) produced five-shot versions of the 1849 and 1851 Colts, under patents of 1859 and 1864, one model of which had a spring plate interposed between hammer and nipples; the Metropolitan Arms Company of New York imitated the 1851 Navy and 1862 New Police. In all cases, the cylinder engraving differed markedly from the naval scenes or stage-coach hold-ups on the genuine arms.

A rare pocket revolver marked *London Pistol Company* was made by the Manhattan Arms Co., under an American patent of 1859 which the company held from Joseph Gruler and Augustus Rebetey of Norwich, Connecticut. For many years collectors were inclined to view these arms as made in London, out of parts abandoned by Colonel Colt when he shut down his factory there. The researches of an American, Sam E. Smith, uncovered the true facts.[20]

Confederate gunmakers also copied Colt's pattern during the American Civil War, although these arms were made in very small quantities. Official producers were at Augusta and Columbus, Georgia, but a large privately owned factory near Macon produced the Griswold & Gunnison revolvers in satisfactory quantities, from late 1862 until November 1864. These latter arms were 0·36 in calibre versions of the Colt 'Dragoon', but the majority of makers imitated the Navy pistol, such arms by Leech & Rigdon (later Rigdon & Ansley) being amongst the best and made successively at Memphis, Tennessee, Columbus, Mississippi, and Greensboro, Georgia. Amongst the lesser gunmakers, George and David Dance of Texas made 0·44 in and 0·36 in calibre revolvers now greatly valued for their rarity. Whilst resembling small-scale Dragoon revolvers in general appearance, the weapons lacked any recoil shield behind the nipples.

In Belgium, the Colt revolver was widely imitated in the keyed-barrel series (including the Paterson type), but the Root model was not copied. Colonel Colt actually had a Belgian equivalent to his 1849 patent, but was never able to suppress the makers who infringed upon it. Under Belgian law he was required to arrange manufacture in order to keep his patent, and this was arranged through Devos-Sera, of Liège, and Sainthill of Brussels. In general, Belgian copies (licensed or otherwise) resembled the Pocket or Navy Colts quite closely, and were often marked *Colt Breveté*. The standard of workmanship was rarely better than mediocre, even on the better quality arms by Gilon, Herman or other leading gunsmiths.

Curiously enough, the revolver which caused the legal fracas between Colonel Colt and the Massachusetts Arms Co., as an infringement of the famous patent on mechanical rotation of the cylinder, did not resemble a Colt revolver in any particular.

The offending pistol was produced by D. B. Wesson (through the company) under patents of Edwin Wesson, an elder brother. It was a six-shot weapon, with a single-action lock and the barrel linked by a hinged strap to the top of the action body. Cocking a side hammer rotated the cylinder anticlockwise by bevel gears, and the cylinder was removed for reloading by tipping up the barrel on its hinge. The relevant patent for the cylinder rotation was US Patent 6669 of 28 August 1849.

The Massachusetts Arms Company refused to regard this pistol as an infringement upon Colt's patent. Reasonably enough, they took the view that Colt's patent protected one method of mechanical rotation, and Wesson's patent covered another. Colt, on the other hand, claimed protection for mechanical rotation of the cylinder as an invention in itself. On his view, any system of mechanical rotation was an infringement of his patent and he took the Company to court.[21]

The case began in June 1851 and dragged over two years before Colt's claim was upheld in the teeth of attempts to prove that Collier (and other makers) had produced mechanically-rotated revolvers before Colt had secured his patent. Eventually Colt's attorney accepted an offer of $15,000 to settle the matter in his client's favour. Thereafter (until the expiry of Colt's patent in 1857), the Massachusetts Arms Company revolver (or 'Wesson & Leavitt', as it was also known) was produced only with a hand-rotated cylinder.

Imitators apart, the Colt revolver faced formidable competition in other American revolvers, of which the most considerable were arms by Remington, Savage, Starr and Whitney.

The Remington series were made at Ilion, New York, as an extension of the rifle manufacturing operations of E. Remington & Sons, and, upon the expiry of the Colt master patent, Fordyce Beals (already the inventor of a revolver made by Eli Whitney) joined under firm and designed the Beals Pocket Revolver under patents of 1856 and 1857. The series comprised five-shot, single-action pocket revolvers in 0·31 in calibre, with a distinctive hand working outside the action body; a second model (1858-60) discarded the original trigger-guard, and was later modified to use a lever rammer.

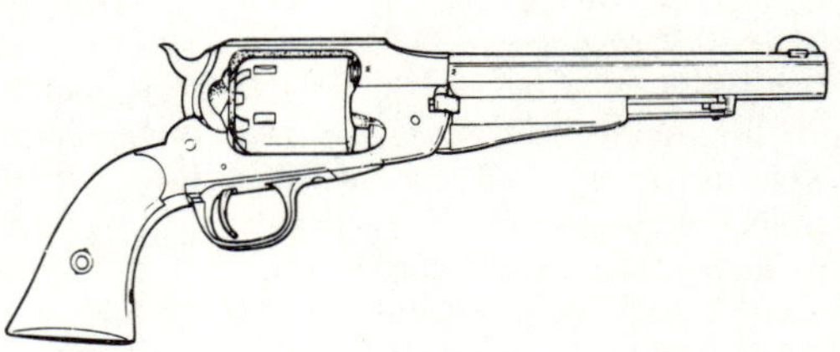

Remington New Model Army (1863).

At the close of this series, Beals designed a big 0·44 in calibre single-action Army revolver with an 8 in barrel and a conventional trigger-guard; about 3,000 specimens were made, but a very similar 0·36 in calibre Navy revolver (also six-shot) proved rather more popular.

These early weapons gave way eventually to a Model 1861 revolver, in Army and Navy calibres, which was followed by improved 'New Model' pistols on the same pattern. This last series endured until 1875, in company with a double-action pocket

20 *The Gun Collector's Letter*, No. 5, 25 December 1946.

21 See note 11 above.

revolver patented by Joseph Rider, of Newark, Ohio, in 1859. These Rider pistols had a peculiar cylinder, with a mushroom-shaped bulge at the rear in which the nipples were embedded. Crude in appearance, they proved reliable, and production continued until 1888. A New Model 0·36 in calibre single-action Belt Pistol proving popular, the Rider double-action lock was applied to the same design, and the Remington series of percussion revolvers was closed, with two final models, in 1863. Like all Remington percussion revolvers, these were solid-framed arms with separate octagonal barrels screwed into the frames. A single-action 0·36 in calibre New Police revolver was extremely popular, but over-shadowed by the success of a five-shot single-action New Model Pocket revolver with a stud trigger. A smaller quantity of 0·36 in and 0·44 in calibre rifles (with 24 in, 26 in and 28 in barrels) were built on the New Model frame, but it is believed that Remington discarded the detachable carbine stock favoured by Colt.

The competing revolvers of E. T. Starr were
148 produced under patents of 1856 and 1861, as manufactured by the Starr Arms Company, of New York. Two 0·44 in calibre Army models and a 0·36 in calibre Navy pistol were made under the patents, all of which had a removable screw on the right of the frame which permitted the barrel to be tilted on a hinge for removal of the cylinder. One of the Army pistols was single-action with an 8 in barrel, and the other was a double-action weapon with a 6 in barrel. Navy revolvers are now rare, but closely copied the double-action Army. Nearly 48,000 Starr revolvers were sold to the Union forces during the American Civil War.

The Savage revolvers were designed under patents of 1856 and 1860, by Henry S. North, and made by Edward Savage at Middletown, Connecticut; all were six-chambered arms in 0·36 in calibre, with highly distinctive lock mechanisms. The early model had a double trigger (shaped like a figure-eight), whilst the later arms had a large trigger-guard fitted in addition to the double trigger. In both versions the lower trigger turned the cylinder (and cocked the hammer), and the upper trigger fired the weapon. As the lower trigger was pulled back, the cylinder backed off the rear of the barrel and slid forward again (after rotation) to accomplish a gas seal. Some 11,000 of the Savage Navy revolvers went to the Union forces. A weapon similar in operation, but using a single-action lock, was patented and manufactured by C. H. Alsop, about 1862.

Eli Whitney's revolvers were made near New Haven, Connecticut, and the series are best remembered for the fine 0·36 in Navy and 0·31 in pocket revolvers built upon the same principle as the Remington single-action holster arms. Over 11,000 Navies were sold to the Union forces. Fordyce Beals worked for Whitney, before joining Remington, producing a weapon known to modern collectors as the 'Walking Beam' revolver. In this pistol, no hand rotated the cylinder against teeth cut at its rear; instead a lever (shrouded on the outside of the frame) was linked to the hammer and 'walked' the cylinder round by engaging in notches cut on the rear circumference of it. Whitney also produced some solid-framed revolvers with manually-rotated cylinders; in these arms, a second trigger (in front of the trigger-guard) released the cylinder for rotation.

Other American revolver manufacturers produced arms of merit, but in smaller quantities than the giants so far mentioned. Amongst the more noteworthy were pistols by Allen & Wheelock, of Worcester, Massachusetts (single-action, solid-framed, with trigger-guard serving as a rammer lever. Model 1858); Cooper Firearms Mfg. Co., of Frankford, Pennsylvania, (double-action Navy revolver of Colt type. Model 1863); B. F. Joslyn, of Stonington, Connecticut, (single-action, side-hammer Army revolver. Model 1858); C. S. Pettingill, of New Haven, Connecticut, (concealed hammer, self-cocking Army and Navy revolvers. Model 1858); Rogers & Spencer, of Willowdale, New York (single-action Army revolvers, under A. T. Freeman's patent of 1862); Springfield Arms Company, of Massachusetts (single-action Army and Navy revolvers, some with side-hammers and a separate trigger for rotating the cylinder. Made under James Warner's patents of 1851 and 1857).

Before leaving the American field, note should be made of three percussion revolvers which were on the lunatic fringe of design. The Edgar & Smith revolver had nine chambers, which were aligned in threes with the three barrels, and fired, three shots at a time, by a side-hammer. J. Walch's revolvers (patented in 1859) were ten- or twelve-shot pistols, firing superimposed loads from each chamber by double hammers; all were single-action arms, the earliest models sometimes having two triggers, the later arms having but one unguarded trigger. Revolvers by the Confederate designer Doctor (later Colonel) J. A. F. Le Mat were made in France and Britain during the American Civil War, but can be justly regarded as American in conception, for the design was patented there in 1856. The Le Mat 'grape shot' revolver (as it came to be known) was a single-action pistol with a smooth-bore shot barrel serving as an axis upon which the cylinder turned. Both cylinder and shot barrel were fired by the same hammer, which had a movable hammer nose to strike the appropriate nipple. Most of the percussion weapons (later, pinfire and centrefire versions were made) had nine chambered cylinders in 0·42 in calibre, and a shot barrel of 0·63 in calibre, although some smaller weapons were also produced. About one thousand Le Mats were made for the Confederacy, and an unknown quantity were made for the civilian market along with a few carbines of similar design.

As a result of two World Wars, it is now rather difficult for the average British collector to form any idea of European progress in the design and manufacture of percussion revolvers. Immense collections (notably at the Musée d'Armes at Liège) reveal a bewildering variety of these arms, but little evidence to support claims for large scale manufacture.

In France (about 1855) the Parisian maker Devisme developed a fine single-action revolver, which is sometimes found in a rifle version. These weapons (in 0·36 in or 0·44 in calibre) had an external cocking lever for an internal firing pin which struck horizontal (and partitioned) nipples. Many of these arms had pillar breeches on the Thouvenin system, the bullet being hammered down on to a vertical stem (*tige*) in the chamber to expand it against the chamber walls. Another French revolver by Houillier & Blanchard was, like the Devisme, purchased during the American Civil War but details of it have not survived. A strange self-cocking pistol of Porter type, its ten radially-bored chambers fired by a lateral hammer and percussion-pills, was developed by S. A. Noel in 1865.

In Belgium, perhaps the best known native designs were those made by Comblain of Liège. The simon-pure Comblain was probably invented about 1854, since Anquetil[22] reported seeing the prototype 'in the white'. It was a single-action five-shot revolver, built up like the Navy Colt, but with a side-hammer. Both holster and pocket models were made, all with horizontal partitioned nipples and a rack-and-pinion rammer beneath the barrel. At the instance of a Brussels manufacturer, Mangeot, a self-cocking model was developed; this too had a hammer at the side, with a peculiar safety catch mounted beneath it, and a simple push-rod rammer hung on a swivel beneath the barrel.

Two designs from outside Belgium which were probably made at Liège, were the Haaken-Plomdeur and the Loron revolvers. The former (a mish-mash of ideas by other designers) was a small-calibre six-shot pistol with a side-hammer and a single-action lock; the nipples were slanted into each chamber, and the tumbler had three cocking bents upon it. The Loron (by a Versailles maker) was a self-cocking revolver, chambering five bullets which embodied a fulminate charge.

Apart from the true Colt copies mentioned earlier, the Belgian makers produced a number of improved arms of roughly similar appearance. Double-action revolvers by David Herman were amongst the best, commonly in 0·31 in calibre, but some extraordinary ring-trigger arms on the J. Herman pepperbox principle were also made. Charlier, also of Liège, made pistols which embodied the combination trigger-guard and rammer mentioned in regard to the American Allen & Wheelock revolvers; this maker was probably one infringer of a Belgian patent on the Colt lever-rammer, since some of his weapons embodied a palpable copy of it.

In England, the most considerable revolvers were made to designs by Robert Adams, Joseph Bentley and William Tranter; the gun trade also produced some unpatented weapons that were popular in the cheaper price bracket.

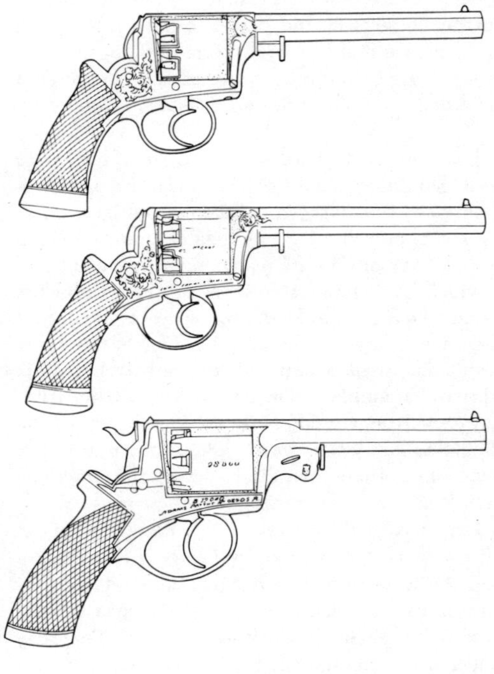

(*Top*) Deane-Adams Model of 1851 (so-called 'Dragoon') J. Bell Collection.
(*Centre*) Deane-Adams Model of 1853, 'hesitation' action. The Late R. & P. A. Bedford Collection.
(*Bottom*) Beaumont-Adams, Model of 1855. Formerly D. A. Nie Collection.

Robert Adams's revolver (patented in 1851) was a sturdy five-chambered self-cocking pistol with barrel and solid frame forged in one. The inventor was manager for the London house of 'George & John Deane', and a gunmaker of some note; his pistol was shown at the Great Exhibition and aroused great interest as a native competitor to the Colt revolvers shown there. As a result of the publicity for revolvers in general, a partnership was

22 *Notice sur les pistolets tournants . . .*, 1855.

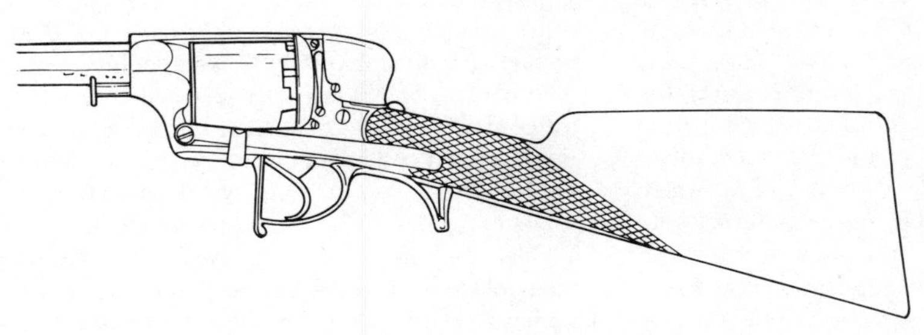

Detail of Deane-Adams five-shot revolving rifle, made under British patent of 1851.

established between the inventor and the John Deanes (Senior and Junior) for the promotion and manufacture of Adams's pistols. For this purpose a factory was established at Weston Street, Bermondsey, and a modest number of revolvers were produced in 38, 54 and 120 bore calibres, with $7\frac{1}{2}$ in, $6\frac{1}{4}$ in and $4\frac{1}{2}$ in barrels respectively. Later, rifles and shotguns were made in small numbers.

Despite its self-cocking mechanism, Adams's revolver proved reliable enough to undergo service tests against a comparable Colt, the first of which occurred, at Woolwich, in September 1851. The eventual decision to buy Colt pistols for the British Navy probably stemmed from a mistrust of any self-cocking lock under stress of combat, and the lack of any loading ramrod in the Adams. Where Colt used a powerful lever rammer, which seated the bullets beyond any chance of being jarred from the chambers, the Adams was loaded with a wadded bullet pressed home by the thumb.

Despite this service adoption set-back, Adams's revolvers sold so well that the London factory was unable to keep pace with demand. William Tranter, of Birmingham, made extra weapons under licence, and there is also evidence that Joseph Brazier (of Wolverhampton) and Hollis & Sheath (of Birmingham) also made them, as well as several licensees in Belgium. In all events, the lack of any rammer was made good by both Adams and Rigby, in 1854, with the patenting of simple lever rammers that lay along the side of the pistol frame when not in use.

Adams attempted to remedy the self-cocking lock by a mechanism patented late in 1853; this lock could not be cocked by the thumb, but was arranged to 'hesitate' just before the hammer fell, and allow deliberate aim to be taken. Few arms were made on this principle, the difficulty being more satisfactorily settled on the purchase of a lock patent secured by Lieutenant F. B. E. Beaumont, R.E., in February 1855. This improved Adams revolver (which could be cocked by the thumb as a result of including an extra sear above the hammer) was ordered for test by the Ordnance and bought for service issue to oust the Colt.

This success in securing an initial order ended the association of 'Deane Adams & Deane', for Robert Adams transferred his services and patents to a new company (formed by City merchants) with a larger factory at Henry Street, Bermondsey. A few Beaumont-Adams revolvers were made under the 'Deane Adams & Deane' label, usually fitted with Adams's rammer, but after 1856 the revolvers either bore the new *London Armoury Company* name, or (if retailed by others) were stamped *L.A.C.* in recognition of their source. These pistols were fitted with an improved lever rammer, patented by the company's superintendent, James Kerr, in 1855. This lay along the side of the barrel, and the weapons also had a sliding safety-catch and cylinder-pin release patented by Robert Adams, in 1854.

The company made these arms in 38, 54 or 120 bore calibres, and 80 bore pistols are also known; only five chambers were used, by virtue of the original Adams cylinder bolt. This was a lump on top of the trigger, which engaged partitions between the horizontal nipples, and its use prohibited addition of a sixth chamber. The association with this company did Adams little good, for he was ousted from the position of manager and returned to his own business in 1859. He apparently retained some patent rights, and sold Birmingham-made Beaumont-Adams revolvers from his address at 76 King William Street.

The London Armoury Company became a major

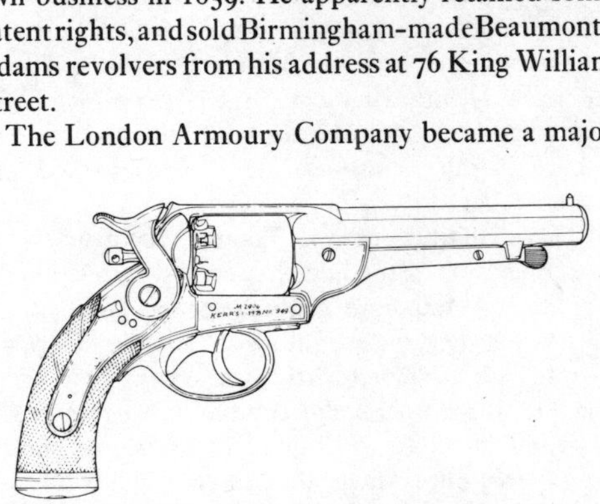

Kerr's five-shot, double-action 0·442 in., Army revolver, 2nd Model of 1859. Made by the London Armoury Company and with retailer's name, Edward Paton of Perth. Tower of London Armouries.

rifle manufacturer, and moved to new premises in Old Ford Road, Bow, in 1863. They continued to supply the Beaumont-Adams revolver (in 54 bore, with a $5\frac{3}{4}$ in barrel) to the British services until the company was wound up in 1867. During this period they also made two models of a percussion revolver patented by James Kerr, in 1858 and 1859, which were five-chambered pistols in 54 and 90 bore calibres. The earlier model was single-action, but this and the later version had side-hammers and very simple locks that could be removed from the two-piece solid frame like a conventional gun-lock. Never officially approved, the weapons were popular by reason of the robustness and simplicity of construction and nearly 1,000 of them went to Confederate forces during the Civil War. A Spanish copy was also supplied to the Spanish navy during 1862.

The Beaumont-Adams revolver was also made, under licence, in America and in Belgium. The version by the Massachusetts Arms Company was offered in 0·36 in and 0·31 in calibres, and although 0·44 in calibre versions have been rumoured, no specimen appears to have survived. Belgian weapons, the best of which were by Francotte and Mangeot, varied greatly in quality, and some were made with bronze frames. A creditable copy of the original self-cocking 1851 Adams was also made by Ancien & Cie, Dandoy, Francotte and Pirlot Frères.

William Tranter, an important trade manufacturer at 14 St Mary's Row, Birmingham, produced his own series of revolvers, which were licenced under the 1851 patent of Robert Adams as to their solid barrel and frame assembly. Tranter's contribution in this series was the famous double-trigger mechanism which he patented in 1853. Pulling the lower trigger (which protruded through the bottom of the trigger-guard) cocked these pistols and rotated their cylinders; the piece was fired by pulling the upper trigger. Tranter's early revolvers (with a detached one-piece rammer) acknowledged Adams's patent on their frames and were largely retailed by Deane Adams & Deane; later arms (the last of which had a permanently attached rammer) merely bore a licence royalty number and were marked *W.*
150 *Tranter's Patent*.

151 These double-trigger Tranter revolvers were extremely successful, and were widely retailed in 38, 54, 80 and 120 bore calibres to the close of the percussion period. A double-action single-trigger pistol (with a characteristic stud on the rear of the trigger, which operated a thumb-cocking sear) was patented in 1856, and added to the series shortly afterwards, but is the less common of the two types. Tranter took over Adams's master patent from the dying London Armoury Company (in 1863) and some of his later pistols and shotguns reverted to an earlier practice and were marked 'Adams's Patent'.

Joseph Bentley (of Liverpool and Birmingham) is conceded an important place in the history of British revolver manufacture, but the extent of his influence is difficult to mark. A series of coarse self-cocking arms (often unsigned) are attributed to him under his patent of 1852, in which a see-saw safety catch on the hammer nose could be set to hold the hammer clear of capped nipples. The Birmingham house of P. Webley & Son are credited with manufacturing many of these 'Webley-Bentley' revolvers, a few in 54 bore but the greater number as 80 bore pocket weapons. More rare now are self-cocking and double-action revolvers marked *Bentley's Patent* and made under the 1852 patent (or another of 1857). These were superior in finish, but delicate in their mechanisms.

The Birmingham gun trade produced one revolver that remains extraordinarily difficult to date. This pistol used the old pepperbox action-body and lock mechanism, but substituted a short cylinder (with vertical nipples) for the old barrel cluster. A conventional barrel, sometimes smooth-bored, was screwed to one end of the cylinder axis pin, but on arms of better quality, a strap was added to join barrel to frame on the underside. A single-action variant, with a long thumb-spur, was made by (or for) T. K. Baker of London, after 1852.

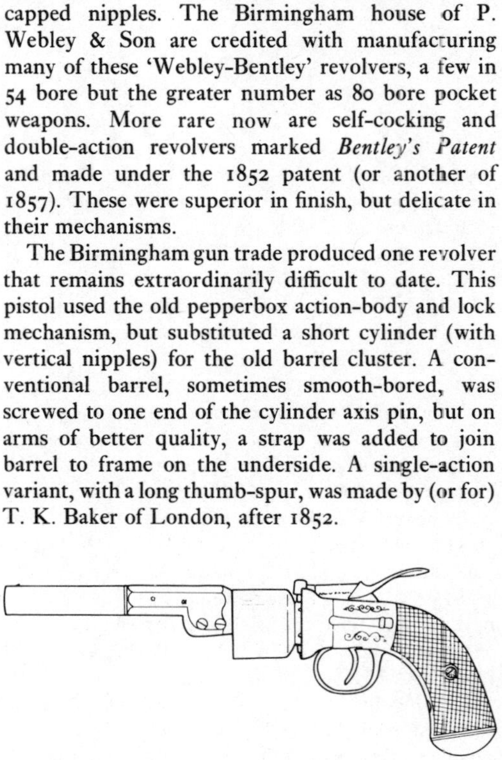

Baker's Patent six-shot single-action percussion. English, c.1852-5. J. B. Bell Collection.

J. N. George termed these pistols as 'transitional' arms, implying that they came between the pepperbox and the true percussion revolvers of Colt or Adams. Others have suggested that they were converted pepperboxes, but this theory bears little examination. It seems more probable that the trade

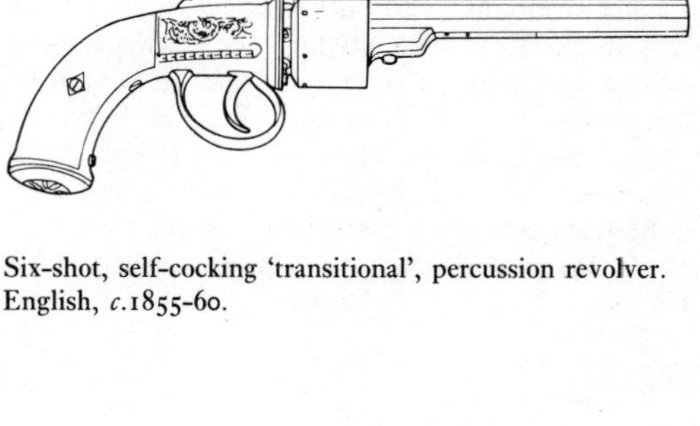

Six-shot, self-cocking 'transitional', percussion revolver. English, c.1855-60.

wished to tap demand for revolvers arising from the 1851 Exhibition successes of Colt and Adams, and used existing pepperbox foundry patterns and forging dies to produce these cheap bar-hammer pistols. A few weapons of superior quality were made, some of them being cased with companion pepperboxes to give the lie to any theory that one superseded the other. In America, rather similar arms were made under the 1854 patents of Josiah Ells, and by Allen & Wheelock.

John Deane claimed another English revolver as present at the 1851 Exhibition, although the catalogue fails to reveal its presence. This Lang pistol was a single-action revolver, with a centre hammer off-set for easier sighting, and a gas-seal cylinder (of Collier type) which was mechanically rotated by a pepperbox-type hand. The nipples were set verti-

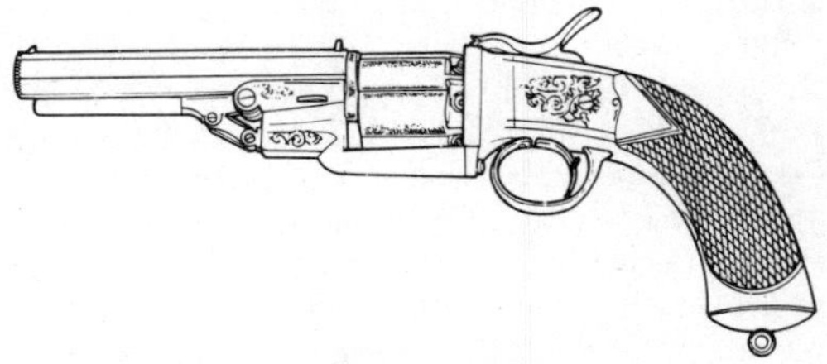

Six-shot single-action percussion, .442 calibre, by J. Lang of London, *c.*1855-60. J. B. Bell Collection.

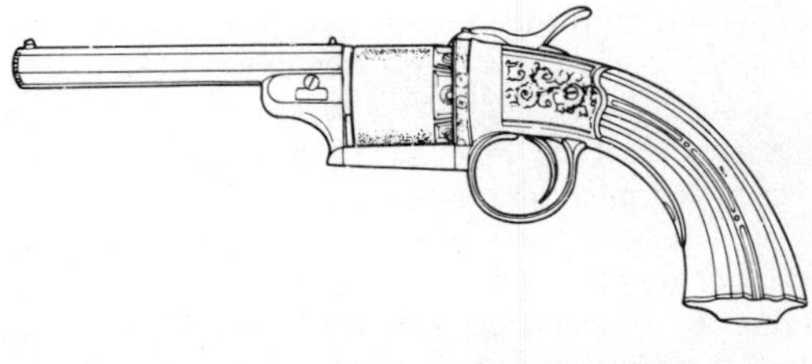

Six-shot single-action percussion with fluted walnut butt, .36 calibre, by J. Lang of London, *c.*1855-60. J. B. Bell Collection.

cally to the chambers, and the barrel was keyed to the cylinder-axis pin like a Colt pistol. This arm was never patented, and was imitated by Witton & Daw, and Parker Field, two other London makers. On some Lang weapons, the reciprocating cylinder mechanism was discarded, and nipples were inclined at an angle of 45° on later Daw pistols. The latter maker, George H. Daw, also had a most
152 attractive double-action revolver made for him, under their patent of 1855, by Charles Pryse and Paul Cashmore of Birmingham and West Bromwich.

The Birmingham house of P. Webley & Son took little interest in the actual manufacture of revolvers until after 1856. In that year, James Webley (elder brother to Phillip) died suddenly in the course of manufacturing a series of fine single-action trade

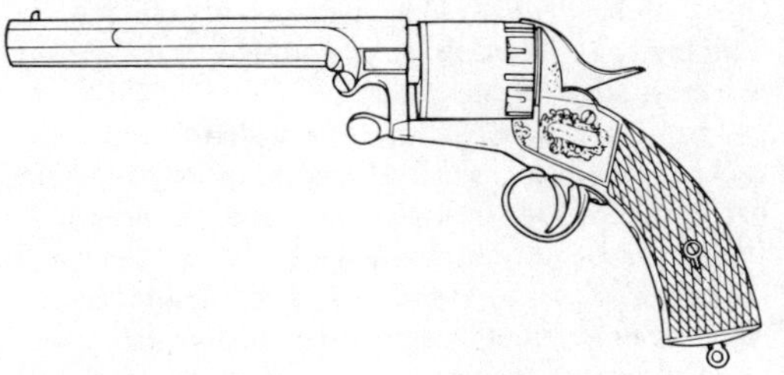

James Webley five-shot, single-action, percussion Holster or Belt revolver. 'Longspur' third model, *c.*1855. Tower of London Armouries.

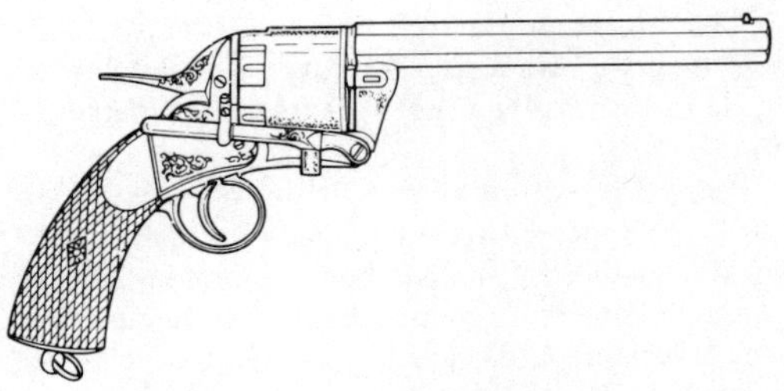

James Webley 'longspur', second model, *c.*1855-60. Tower of London Armouries.

revolvers under a patent of 1853. These arms, known to modern collectors as the 'Long Spur' Webley after the distinctive cocking spur on the hammer, were made principally as five-chambered pistols in 48 bore and 60 bore holster or belt-sized embodiments. A few six-chambered 120 bore pocket arms were also sold. In earlier pistols, the barrel was hinged to the frame and some folding rammers were mounted to lie along these frames; in a later series, the barrel was screwed on to one end of the cylinder pin, and locked by a butterfly screw in the forward end of the frame.

On his brother's death Phillip Webley continued manufacture, and added another version, with a top strap between barrel and frame, around 1858. At about the same time, he began to produce a double-action series (with locks after Bentley's patent of 1857), in which the barrel and top strap were keyed to the cylinder pin in Colt style. At the close of the percussion period these arms were re-designed, having a solid frame into which the octagonal barrel was screwed.

Amongst the British percussion revolvers of lesser renown were the Harding, Harvey, Moore & Harris, 153
Pennell and Westley Richards.

The Harding, a five-chambered double-action revolver with a quickly dismantled two-part frame, 154
was promoted by Deane & Son (of London Bridge) as a 54 bore and 120 bore competitor to the Beaumont-Adams. The weapons were made for

them, under William Harding's patents of 1858, by Tipping & Lawden, Pryse & Redman, and Calisher & Terry, all of Birmingham.

The Harvey series were six-chambered self-
154 cocking revolvers, normally in 60 bore with 5 in barrels, and had a totally enclosed 'hammerless' action. The lever rammer could be readily detached to serve also as a screwdriver and nipple key, on the later weapons, but a few early pistols had saw-handled butts and no rammers. Both rifles and pistols appeared, which were beautifully made (under patents of 1853 and 1854), but it seems unlikely that W. J. Harvey actually produced them at his Exeter premises.

The Moore & Harris revolver was a frail self-cocking arm, with a reciprocating gas-seal cylinder, made in Birmingham under its inventors' patent of 1852.

Pennell's revolvers were provisionally patented in 1853, and appeared as both pistols and rifles. A slab-sided flat-topped action body (sometimes only marked 'Patented') concealed another hammerless lock mechanism. Curiously, the lock was not the subject of Pennell's patent, which protected the method of dismounting the barrel and a peculiar detached rammer.

The Westley Richards revolvers (under W. W. Richards patents of 1852, 1854 and 1855) were made as single-action or self-cocking pistols and are now extremely rare. The single-action pistol attempted a similar improvement to that in the later Kerr weapon in mounting all lock components on a separate lock-plate. All self-cocking arms had side-hammers, and a peculiar gravitating safety stop which held the hammer off the nipples until the trigger was pulled. Both versions had their barrels connected to the locks by a hinged top strap only, and a rack-and-pinion rammer (protected by the patent of 1854) was mounted on the left side.

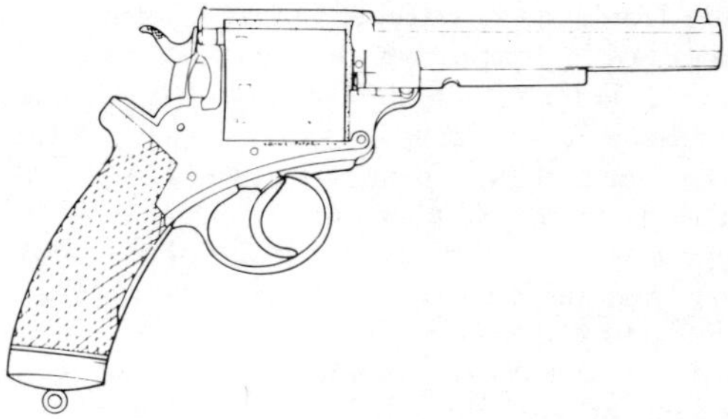

Double-action John Adams', Model 1867 Army revolver (Mark II) in .450 centre-fire calibre.

Other British percussion revolvers were made in small numbers, under the patents of John Adams (1857 and 1861), T. Bailey (1858), H. Ball (1858), R. Brazier (1858), C. Reeves (1857 and 1858), and C. E. Wallis (1863). John Adams's revolvers were double-action arms, with a two-piece frame expressly designed for slotting out by circular cutters; Bailey's pistol was an attractive side-hammer design, rather similar to the Root Colt; Ball's revolvers were operated by a rocking trigger guard; Brazier's double-action revolvers used Robert Adams's patented solid frame, with a most intricate lock mounted on a circular plate on the side of the action body; Reeves made more weapons for other makers than those under his own patents, but produced a few solid-framed double-action revolvers with a sliding inspection plate to the lock, and a quick-thread cylinder pin; Wallis's revolvers, which are now extremely rare, were crude weapons with vertical nipples and a bar hammer of pepperbox type. Each chamber was double-loaded, and a sliding striker on the hammer struck first one row of nipples, and was then moved to fire the rear charges.

CHAPTER NINE

Breech-Loading and Repeating Firearms 1810-1870

H.L. Peterson

Cartridges

130 Even the most successful of the breech-loaders firing
156-67 loose ammunition left something to be desired. The
269 Chaumette and the Ferguson offered fast operation, a tight seal, and reasonable freedom from the troubles of powder fouling. Still, there was an inherent delay in loading any firearm with powder from a horn or flask, priming from the same or a separate container, and loading the ball from still another container or pouch. Also loose powder always presented more of a hazard of accidental explosion. If breech-loaders could be devised to use cartridges, it would reduce this danger and greatly speed loading. In addition it would assure uniform loads no matter what the breech system. These were the desiderata that spurred gun designers throughout the Western world to seek to develop breech-loading systems that could utilise fixed ammunition. The final discovery, which was that the metal-cased cartridge offered the most effective breech seal, came almost as a surprise bonus rather than as a primary goal of the search.

At the beginning of the period covered by this chapter cartridges of a kind had already been used for a very long time for muzzle-loading firearms. The word *cartridge* is itself an Anglicisation of the French *cartouche*, a roll or cornet of papers, or the Italian *cartoccio*. Leonardo da Vinci seems to have been the first to mention paper cartridges[1] and there is little doubt that they were well known by the middle of the sixteenth century, and were commonly used thereafter for fine-quality arms (see p. 514). For military long-guns, from at least the beginning of the sixteenth century until the second half of the seventeenth, gunpowder was commonly carried in made-up charges in bandoleers (see p. 509). These were prone to accidental ignition and were also inconveniently slow in use, so, during the Thirty Years War, the great Swedish general King Gustavus Adolphus (d.1632) introduced paper cartridges in their place as one of his successful methods of increasing the rate of musket fire, to be followed by other countries. One of the advantages of the cartridge was that it provided the ball with a ready-made piece of paper to act as a wad to take up the windage, as explained in the following passage by John Vernon in 1644:[2]

> . . . you shall finde in your Crattreg case a turned wooden pin which you must take, having cut lengths of white paper something broader than the pin is in length, and rowle the paper on the pin, then twist one end of the paper, and file it almost full of powder, then put the bullet on top of the powder, twisting that end also . . . now when you come to lade your carbine or Pistols with these Cartreges, you must bite off that end of the paper where the powder is, powring it into your Carbine or Pistol, then put in that bullet and some of that paper will serve for a wad after it and Ram home . . .

In some of the earliest cartridges of this kind the ball appears to have been held by its sprue, which was left on for this purpose, but by the eighteenth century it was invariably placed inside the paper covering. The method of using this type of cartridge was usually to bite off the end opposite to the ball and pour the loose powder down the barrel to be followed by the paper-wrapped ball.

Little change in the design of the cartridge was effected in the flintlock era but the introduction of the percussion system marked the beginning of a period of experiment in the design of ammunition that was to last for much of the nineteenth century. Bullets evolved from simple spheres to cylindro-conical projectiles in a variety of forms. The tied or pasted paper wrappings of eighteenth century cartridges were joined by a host of other materials before the rigid copper or brass case became standard. And finally the primer, which had always been external since the beginning of firearms, was moved inside to make the cartridge a single self-contained unit, something that the invention of the percussion system made possible for the first time. Through most of the evolution the developments seem to have been aimed at making the cartridge a

1 E. MacCurdy, *The Notebooks of Leonardo da Vinci*, London, 1938, Vol. II, pp. 194-5.

2 See John Vernon, *The Young Horseman*, 1644, p. 10.

sturdy, easily handled object; one that could be carried safely without undue danger of breakage or hazard of explosion and which could be seized by the fingers and inserted into the breech with very little thought and manipulation. Some designers did think of using the cartridge case for a gas seal, even those who worked with separate primed types. The quest thus centred as much on understanding the possibilities of the cartridge in the matter of obturation as on finding a suitable casing material.

Most of the cartridges used with such breech-loaders as the Crespi, Sartoris and Hall,[3] and in all the percussion period systems, were combustible. Some were wrapped in paper which had been treated with nitrates to make it burn more readily. Others were cased in linen, animal intestine known as gold-beater's skin, or, in the case of some revolver cartridges, collodion. Sometimes the ends were cut off in loading, but in others the flash from the primer was expected to set the wrapping on fire and so ignite the powder within. Another group of cartridges used slightly more durable materials for casings. Some were made of metal foil wrapped in paper. Some were cardboard, some hard rubber, and a few were actually metal. Then the base was either made of nitrated paper or pierced with a hole to admit the flash. All of these, both fully or partially combustible or pierced, are today designated as 'separate primed' because the spark or flash for ignition was provided by a flintlock or one of the percussion primers completely separate from the cartridge.

The real advances in the history of ammunition lay with those cartridges which included a primer. First and foremost of the figures associated with these developments was, of course, Johannes Samuel Pauly, whose all-brass and brass-headed cartridges are described below. Not only did Pauly add a centrefire primer to the cartridge as early as 1812, but he also recognised the use of a rimmed head for a gas seal. The weakness of Pauly's cartridges, however, was the exposed primer in the *bassinet*, as he called the recess for it in the base of the cartridge. It was too easily knocked out, too vulnerable to the elements. Others shared the same trouble, and some were worse. The Galy-Cazalat, patented in France in 1826, for instance, used a similar base depression to the Pauly for a fulminate primer but, instead of a pierced metallic case, utilised one made of parchment or leather which was not nearly so strong and offered no gas seal whatsoever. In 1829 another Frenchman, Clement Pottet, invented a metallic cartridge that offered either a base depression for fulminate or a nipple for a standard percussion cap. This was a good strong cartridge, but the loose primer was still a handicap until, in 1855, Pottet improved his design by cutting threads in the inside of the base depression and screwing a cap-like primer into it. The result was to all intents and purposes the modern external primed centrefire shotgun shell. This improvement came twenty-six years after Pottet's first patent. Meanwhile there had been many other developments.

For one thing there was a serious effort to move the primer to the inside of the case. One avenue of approach was the pinfire cartridge patented by Casimir Lefaucheux in which a percussion cap was placed inside the metal case and detonated when a pin, which projected from the opposite side, was struck by the hammer and driven against the cap. An early version of this cartridge was covered in Lefaucheux's 1835 addition to his 1832 patent for a tipping-barrel breech-loader described below. Eleven years later his compatriot Houiller obtained a French patent on an improvement which held the cap firmly in place in the centre of the cartridge head, instead of resting relatively loosely on one side. He also secured the pin more firmly. This brought the pinfire cartridge to its highest development. It functioned well, but the exposed pin was a weakness, subject to breakage and accidental discharge. An attempt was made to move the pin inside and protect it under a bulge in the cartridge case, but this expedient never became popular. The form with the exposed pin was made until late in the century.

Another approach was to place the primer or propellant charge in the base of the bullet itself. Johan Nikolaus von Dreyse's needle gun described later used such a cartridge with the primer nestled in the base of the projectile and requiring the firing pin to pass through the powder charge to reach and detonate it. John Hanson and William Golden obtained a British patent in 1841 for a bullet with a fulminate in its base cavity that supplied both primer and a weak propellant charge; in America a similar bullet cartridge was used in the Volcanic repeating rifles and pistols of 1854.[4] None proved entirely satisfactory. The need for penetrating the powder charge in one and the weakness of the other were drawbacks.

In France there was one other notable use of a detonating compound for a propellant. The Flobert cartridge of 1849 was little more than a bullet inserted in the open end of a percussion cap, the priming covering the whole base. In 1850 C. H. Houllier obtained a *certificat d'addition* to his French patent of 1846 which included a cartridge in which the priming encircled the rim and this can be regarded as the forerunner of the rimfire cartridge. It was useful for indoor target ranges but little else.

Interestingly, almost all of the major strides in the

3 See p. 201.

4 See p. 256.

early development of self-contained cartridges were made either by Frenchmen or by men who had worked in Paris. Pottet, Lefaucheux, Houiller and Flobert were all French. Pauly and von Dreyse had both worked in Paris. It remained for two Americans, Horace Smith and Daniel B. Wesson to achieve the next major breakthrough and develop the rimfire cartridge as it is known today. In their cartridge there was a distinct rim around the head. Also encircling the head was primer in the form of a ring of detonating compound where it was in a position to be crushed by the hammer against a rebate at the base of the chamber. The rim was one improvement over the Flobert and Houiller cartridges. The second was the addition of a propellant charge of powder. Smith & Wesson patented this new cartridge in 1860, having previously manufactured one in which the priming covered the whole of the base. For a short period rimfire cartridges were used for large calibre sporting and military arms up to 0·58 in which is believed to have been the largest rimfire cartridge ever made on a regular basis. Now the system is used primarily for 0·22 in cartridges and other small calibre weapons. The reason the larger calibres were eliminated lay in the fabrication of the metal case. It was impossible to produce a case strong enough to withstand the pressure from a heavy charge and yet soft enough to be indented easily by the hammer of the gun. Even the large calibre rimfire cartridges were of necessity relatively weak.

An escape from this predicament was offered by the centrefire cartridge. Pauly's cartridge had pointed the way. Pottet's work had improved it in 1829 and again in 1855[5] when the same maker patented in France a paper cartridge with a brass head containing a central percussion-cap set over an anvil. This was still further perfected by another Frenchman named Schneider in 1858. The Schneider cartridge was introduced into England by G. H. Daw in 1861, and it quickly became the standard for shotgun ammunition.

In the meantime, many other English, French and American designers were making strides in developing centrefire metal-cased ammunition. Charles W. Lancaster of Great Britain offered a gas-tight drawn-metal cartridge in 1854 that was fired by indenting the soft metal of the head. Since the cases could not be reused, it was too expensive for popular appeal. The American G. W. Morse obtained a series of patents between 1856 and 1858 which covered most of the major features of the centrefire cartridge as it is now made, but final perfection waited for the patents of Colonel Hiram Berdan of the United States and Colonel Edward M. Boxer of Great Britain, based on the Schneider-Daw cartridge, in 1866, in which a drawn-brass case was employed. Both offered internal reloadable primers and set the standards for all modern centrefire cartridges. Interestingly enough, the British Boxer type is the only form manufactured in the United States today while the American Berdan is by far the most popular system in Europe.

The advent of successful rimfire and centrefire cartridges brought the era of the muzzle-loader to an end. The safe, easily handled ammunition, which also solved the problem of the gas seal, made any number of breech-loading and repeating systems possible. The only burdens left now to the gun designer were to provide a simple, sturdy method of opening and closing the breech, that would not get out of order easily and that would offer sufficient strength for the power of the proposed charge, and also to find a satisfactory repeating system.

A SELECTION OF EARLY CARTRIDGE CASES

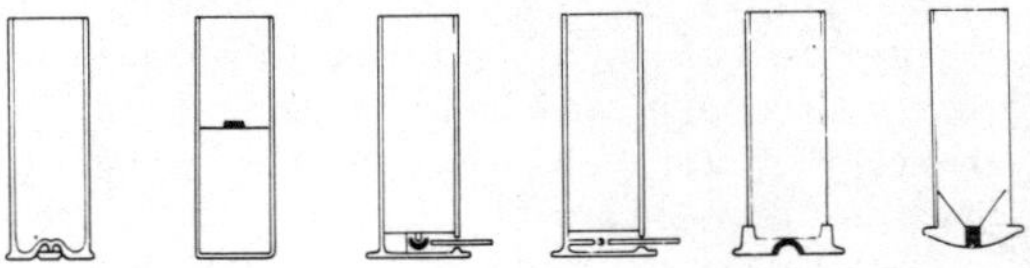

(Left to right)
C. Fusnot external cap on one-piece base; English of 1868. Dreyse needle-fire, 1847. Houllier pin-fire, 1846–50. Paper case, brass base; Casimir Lefaucheux, 1835. Cup-shaped central primer for diagonal striker; Casimir Lefaucheux, 1847. Paper case, brass base with fulminate 'rosette'; S. J. Pauly, English, 1816.

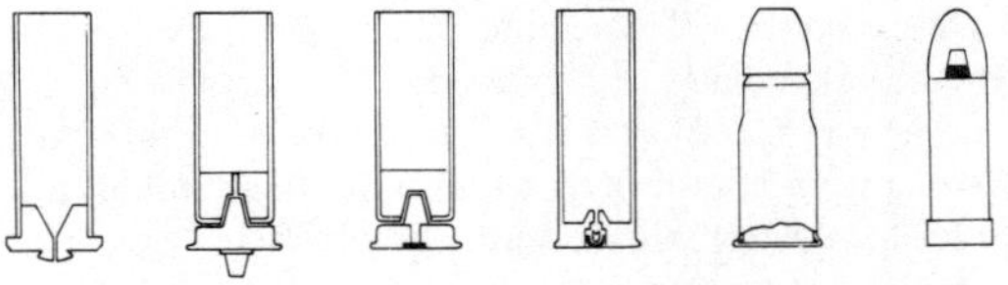

(Left to right)
Paper case, brass base for 'rosette'; English patent 1816 (as shown in patent drawing). Pottet, 1819. Paper case, screw-in metal base; Pottet, patent 1829. Metallic base with primer and separate anvil; Pottet, patent 1855. Copper case, rim-fire, for Spencer Repeating Rifle; Smith & Wesson, patent 1860. Paper with wadding base for Westley Richard's Terry's or Greene's breechloaders, *c.*1865.

Breech-loaders

Because the search for an efficient breech-loader was so widespread and because communications were highly irregular, there is almost no evolutionary pattern to their development, at least during the years prior to 1850. Men working thousands of miles

5 It is worth noting that a centrefire revolver was patented as early as 1844 in France by Michalon.

apart developed similar designs independently. Occasionally these discoveries occurred at almost the same time. Often there was a time differential of a quarter of a century or even more. Key inventions were passed unnoticed by gunsmiths who knew of them, only to be rediscovered years later by other designers who could and did adapt them to their weapons. For these reasons the present section does not attempt to tell the story of the development of percussion and self-contained cartridge breech-loaders as a steady chronological progression of integrated ideas and inventions. Instead the major breech systems are discussed typologically, and the most important examples, whether early or late, are described under these headings. It would be impossible to discuss every different mechanism found among these breech-loaders. There were far too many. They were born of a highly fertile era that has been almost unparalleled before or since for the variety and complexity of the breech actions which it spawned. Those selected have been the most popular, the most significent for their impact on gun design, or for their classic typology. It is hoped that they will convey an accurate and understandable picture of the many approaches by which inventors sought to make the dream of a self-contained cartridge breech-loader become a reality.

Pivoted and Tipping-breech Types

This type, already discussed in Chapter 6, continued to be used into the percussion period. As noted in Chapter 6 the Hall system was converted to percussion in 1833. In that year a Hall carbine with percussion-cap lock became the first US martial arm to boast the new ignition. Throughout its history the Hall infantry rifle remained unchanged, except for some conversions to percussion. The carbine, on the other hand, underwent a number of modifications with different calibres and butt traps. Most important of all, however, there were various latch designs in an attempt to correct the difficulties that the original hook stud had caused. The last pattern of the Hall carbine was put into production in 1843. Both rifles and carbines of the Hall pattern were used in the Seminole War, various Indian engagements on the frontier, the Mexican War, and even the American Civil War. A further matter of interest related to them is the fact that they are the first firearms in the world to be manufactured with completely interchangeable parts. Hall also designed the system of machines, templates and gauges which made this industrial triumph possible. In addition to the military models, sporting rifles and a very few pistols were also made as Hall breech-loaders. Most of these were manufactured in the period between 1811 and 1817 when Hall became actively engaged in work for the US Government, but at least one sporting rifle of about 1830 is known with interchangeable breech-locks that offer both flint and percussion ignition. It appears to have been a production-piece by a Pennsylvania maker, and there were undoubtedly more of them.

Word of the Hall rifle spread to Europe. In Norway an army officer and gun designer named Frederik Wilhelm Scheel read a general description of it and decided to adapt the tipping chamber to a new arm he was working on. In Scheel's gun, however, the chamber was activated by a lever on the right side of the piece and an eccentric axle which caused it to move backwards before tipping up. A forward movement of the lever reversed the movement. Scheel's chamber could thus be necked down at the mouth and actually inserted into the rear of the barrel for a tighter seal than was possible with the Hall or its predecessors, the Crespi and Egg. This action resembled and may well have been adapted directly from the work of the Danish inventor Nicolai Johan Löbnitz who had just developed a breech-loader employing the same mechanical principles in a reverse manner: the barrel moved to expose the stationary chamber. In 1838 Scheel's gun, complete with an under-hammer percussion lock, was presented for tests by a Royal Commission established to propose new firearms for the Norwegian Army. One hundred rifles were tested by an infantry battalion in 1842, and later that year the Scheel was adopted as the official arm for the whole Norwegian Army. It thus became the first breech-loader to serve as the single standard military firearm for any nation. It was a good, sturdy arm. There was some gas leakage, but apparently it was not objectionable. Over the years it was manufactured in several different models and lengths. The original calibre of 16·8 mm was reduced to 11·7 mm in 1860. Then, when the Remington metal-cased cartridges were adopted for the Norwegian service in 1867, the best of the remaining Scheels were modified to fire the new ammunition.

An entirely different approach to the tipping chamber was invented by William Mont Storm and 156
patented in the United States on 8 July 1856. A British patent followed in 1857, and a United States reissue on improvements was granted in 1867. Little is known about Mont Storm personally, but he is believed to have been a Belgian. In his system the chamber was pivoted on a top axle at its forward end. When opened for loading it passed through an arc of 180° and lay upside down on top of the barrel with the opening to the rear. This meant that the cartridge had to be loaded powder end first in a manner that at first would seem to be backwards. Unfortunately there was a tendency for shooters to forget to make the necessary mental adjustment, and this, as much as anything, contributed to the Mont Storm's lack

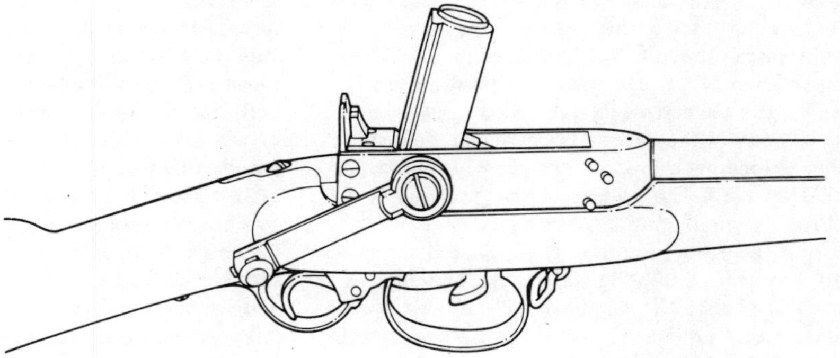

Breech mechanism of Scheel rifle, Model of 1842. Norwegian. Tøjhusmuseet, Copenhagen.

of success. Good features of the system included a breech seal involving an expansion ring and a locking bolt connected to the hammer tumbler so that it acted automatically to fasten the chamber securely in place. The United States purchased the right to convert 2,000 muzzle-loading muskets and rifles to Mont Storm breech-loaders in 1858 and at least 400 were so altered at Harper's Ferry prior to the Confederate capture of the armoury in 1861. The Mont Storm also attracted much favourable attention in England where it was employed for sporting-rifles and shotguns and was awarded a silver medal in the 1862 Exhibition. In addition a sealed pattern was produced in 1865 for the manufacture of 3,000 for trials in the British Army, though nothing came of this as a result of the development of the metallic-cartridge Snider system.

These were the most important of the tipping-chamber breech-loaders. There were literally dozens of others. The French government adopted a breech-loading wall gun with such a system in 1831 and the British Ordnance considered it also. In the United States there was the Lindner system of 1859 with a threaded sleeve to seal the breech joint in a manner somewhat reminiscent of the Sartoris, the Milbank breech of 1862, the Burghart, the Gross and others even less successful. Other nations could add to the list almost indefinitely.

Tipping-barrel Types

All of the tipping-chamber breech-loaders so far described used the standard combustible cartridges of the era. Priming was supplied separately by a flintlock in a few, by percussion caps in most. The earliest of the more important tipping-barrel systems, however, heralded a new era with a self-contained cartridge embodying all the elements of priming, propellant charge and missile. The inventor of this very advanced arm was Johannes Samuel Pauly, a Swiss working in Paris where he obtained a patent on his arm in 1812. Two different breech systems were covered in this patent. One was a long-gun with top-lever opening. The other was a pistol with a barrel that tipped down for loading when a spring catch on the left side of the barrel was released. The really important features of both arms, however, was the cartridge they were designed to employ. It was the rimmed, soft brass head of this cartridge that was designed to expand under pressure and form the gas seal that was so important to any breech-loader. This is the key feature employed by all breech-loaders today, but at the time it seems to have passed almost unnoticed. In the Pauly cartridge the priming was placed on the outside of the cartridge head. A small depression in the centre of the head, which the inventor called a *bassinet* or *pan* in an analogy to the priming-pan of a pre-percussion arm, was filled with a percussion priming compound and tamped firmly so that it would not fall out. A tiny hole in the centre of the bassinet led to the propellant charge within. In firing, a pin driven by the external cocking arm or 'hammer' struck this compound and detonated it. Because this priming was external, it represented a weak point in the design. Loaded weapons had to be carried at half-cock because of the danger of the firing pin disturbing the compound and causing it to fall out if the hammer were left at repose in its safest position. Also there was a chance for these primers to be dislodged simply by jarring one cartridge against another in carrying. Some of Pauly's cartridges were made entirely of brass. Others utilised brass heads with wrapped paper sides similar to modern shotgun ammunition.

There were probably more Pauly pistols made than either the rifles or shotguns with the lifting breech described later. Certainly more have survived, some military, some purely civilian. Some were manufactured by Pauly himself. Others were made 157
by different gunsmiths, primarily in France, England and Denmark, but probably elsewhere as well.

In 1814 Pauly obtained an English patent for a breech-loading gun operating in the same way as that patented in 1812 except that the striker was replaced by a spring-operated fire piston. This was an old device that utilised the heat generated by the sudden compression of air in a syringe to produce fire. In Pauly's gun the narrow jet of hot air served to ignite the priming in the base of the cartridge, for which either detonating compound or a pinch of gunpowder could be used. Examples of Pauly firearms fitted with this form of ignition are extremely rare.

After the Pauly, the next chronological tipping-barrel system of importance was undoubtedly the Danish Löbnitz. Nicolai Johan Löbnitz of Copenhagen was a prolific inventor. His tipping-breech system patented in 1833 was only one of a number

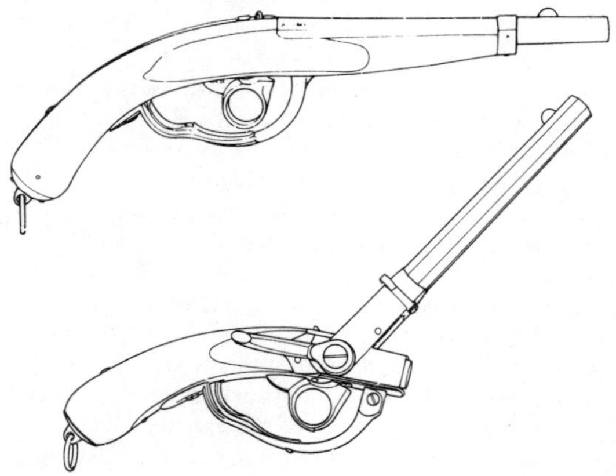

Löbnitz breech-loading pistol. Danish, *c.*1833. Tøjhusmuseet, Copenhagen.

obtained during his lifetime. The Löbnitz greatly resembles the Scheel, which was apparently copied in part from it, but in this instance the breech and chamber remain stationary while the barrel moves forward and then tips to expose the mouth of the chamber for loading. The side lever and eccentric axle, which open the breech, also close it, tipping the barrel down and then sliding it backwards so that the necked mouth of the chamber is inserted into the base of the barrel for a tight seal. Löbnitz arms of this pattern never seem to have been made in large quantity, though they were issued to Danish Hussar regiments between 1848 and 1855, and only a few specimens are known to survive. It is principally important for its apparent influence upon Scheel whose arms were used extensively in Norway.

By far the most common of the tipping-barrel breech-loaders, however, were those in which the barrels tilted down for loading, then closed again against a standing breech. Indeed this breech system was probably the most popular single approach to the entire problem of devising a successful single-shot breech-loader. The United States alone granted more than a hundred patents covering variations of this system between 1837 and 1873. For those guns firing combustible cartridges, or those hard-cased cartridges not designed to afford obturation in themselves, the principal problem was, of course, an effective breech seal. In many, the solution was found in a lever-and-link arrangement which moved the barrel forward before tilting it, in much the same action Scheel and Löbnitz achieved with their lever and eccentric axle. This permitted the same necking or coning of either the breech or barrel for insertion into the other, and a number of early breech-loaders made use of this device. Others relied on expansion rings, flanges, or similar devices. These latter types did not require the barrel to move forward and back, and so they often utilised simple hinge joints to permit the tipping.

A typical example of a breech-loader which passed through stages in which it attempted to obtain a breech seal both by an expansion ring and by a cartridge case was the Smith carbine patented by
Gilbert Smith of the United States in 1856 and 1857. 159
In the first of these a thin flange of metal at the very rear of the barrel was designed to push back tightly against the breech under pressure from the powder gases and so form a seal. It did not work as expected, and in Smith's next attempt he designed a gun with the joint in the centre of the chamber. At the same time he selected a cartridge cased in India-rubber or metal foil and paper. These cartridges were not self-primed and so were pierced with a hole in the centre of the head to admit the flash from the standard percussion cap. In loading, the cartridge was pressed into the recess in the breech with the bullet protruding. When the barrel was raised back into

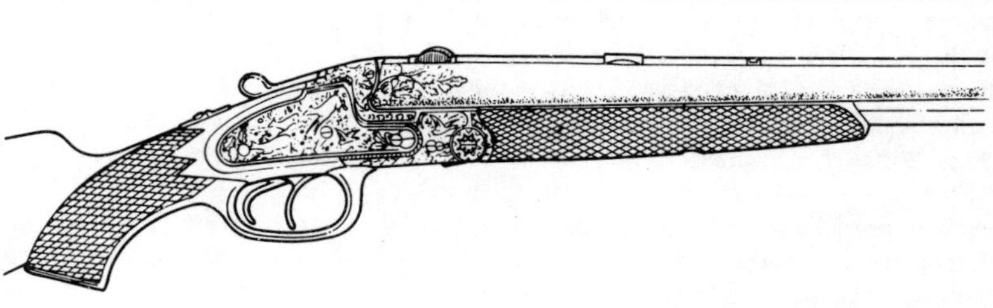

Double-barrelled shotgun with top locking lever. German, *c.*1860. Tower of London Armouries.

position the bullet slipped into its base. A spring catch on the barrel snapped over a lug on the breech and held the two together. It was Smith's theory that the cartridge walls would expand under pressure from the gases and push outwards in all directions against the centrally located joint. This system functioned much better than the previous one. More than 30,000 Smith carbines were purchased by the Federal Government for use during the American Civil War, and the system was reputedly considered by several European governments as well.

Edward Maynard, the American dentist, whose inventions in the fields of both dentistry and firearms brought him world-wide recognition, produced a tipping-barrel breech-loader at almost the same
160 time as the Smith. Patented in 1856 and 1859 it was an even better arm because it utilised a cartridge with a solid brass case and a wide rim. The solid case and the wide rim permitted the breech joint to be placed at the rear of the chamber in the usual manner. Extraction of the empty case was easy, and the seal was good. Ignition was provided by a standard percussion cap in most models instead of the tape primer for which Maynard is most often remembered in firearm circles. A small hole in the centre of the cartridge base permitted entry of the flash from the cap. The breech itself opened and closed by the lever action of the trigger-guard, which thrust the base of the barrel upwards.

The Smith and the Maynard were typical of the better tipping-barrel breech-loaders firing separate primed ammunition which saw widespread use in America during the Civil War. Even when they were invented, however, they were obsolete. Advances had been made in Europe which were to lead to the principal design still in use today for double-barrelled shotguns. Pauly, of course, had pointed the way. He was followed by the elder Lefaucheux (Casimir) of Paris who patented an action very similar to the modern shotgun breech in 1832. Three years later he obtained a supplementary patent covering the breech action and a self-primed cartridge to be used
161 in it. In this breech system the barrel was hinged and tipped down to load in the modern manner. It was locked in firing position by a lever on the underside of the breech, which moved laterally to engage a slotted lug on the bottom of the barrel.

More important was the cartridge. Like the Pauly, it had a brass head and a paper or cardboard case. Inside the head lay a percussion cap resting against one of the brass walls with a pin poised above it and protruding through the head on the opposite side. When the gun's hammer struck this pin it drove it against the cap and exploded it, thus setting off the powder charge. Collectors today call such cartridges 'pinfire'. They were the first successful internally primed type. (Pauly's cartridge had included a primer, but the compound in the bassinet had still been technically outside.) The soft brass of the cartridge head afforded a good breech seal, and the new gun was well received.

There were still drawbacks. The external pin on the cartridge was frail and subject to accidental blows. The single grip of the locking lug on the barrel was weak, and the lever under the breech was unhandy. Successive years and inventors brought improvements. By 1860 a T-shaped lug for the barrel had appeared to offer a more secure lock, and by 1878 a snap closure opened by a lever at the top of the breech had become popular. For greater safety this lever also activated a bolt which passed laterally through a hole set in a vertical lug at the top of the breech. Thus the new shotguns offered two or three locking devices to secure the closure in a foolproof manner. Mechanical extractors had also appeared, and in many instances the hammers had been enclosed to produce the modern double-barrelled single-loading shotgun in all its major features.

Sliding-barrel Types

Another method of opening a gun's breech for the insertion of a cartridge was to slide the barrel forward. Normally this involved a track on which the barrel could move, a stop at the forward end, and a latching system to hold barrel and breech together for firing. A number of the arms which are often classified today as sliding-barrel types could just as well be classified as tipping-barrel forms, since they are activated by a lever-and-link arrangement utilising the trigger-guard, which causes the barrel to move forward and then tip. The American Gibbs and Gallager carbines typify this design, and it is a matter of definition whether they are classified here or in the previous section with the Löbnitz. In both instances the joint between the breech and the barrel involves the insertion of a narrowed portion of one into the other. In the Gibbs the breech has a neck which fits into the barrel; in the Gallager the rear of the barrel is coned to fit into the breech.

There were, however, breech-loaders in which the barrel simply slid forward and did not tip. Perhaps the best of these was invented by Frederic Prince of London in 1855. In this simple, but sturdy, percussion-cap weapon, the barrel was moved by a bolt or arm which projected below the fore-end. When the breech was closed this arm rested against the front of the trigger-guard where it was held in place by a spring catch. Two lugs on a conical projection of the breech also engaged slots in the rear of the barrel for further security. To open the breech, the shooter released the catch on the trigger bow, pulled the arm to the right to free the lugs on the breech, and then shoved it forward. The Prince rifle was officially tested at the School of Musketry at Hythe

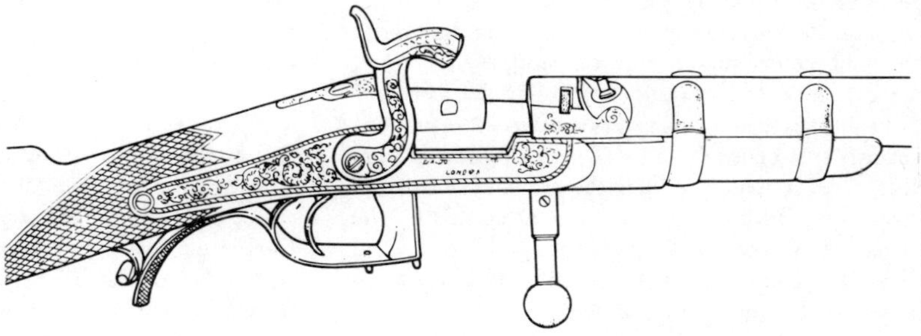

Detail of Prince breech-loading cartridge rifle, Model of 1855. English.

by the British Ordnance in 1855, and it performed very well indeed. It was durable, accurate and rapid-firing. In an unprecedented move twelve of the best-known London gunsmiths signed a testimonial stating that it was beyond comparison the best breech-loader they had ever seen, and technical writers generally wrote approvingly of it.[6] Still it failed to receive favourable notice from the military authorities, and was not adopted for service.

There were many other breech-loaders with sliding barrels. In Britain in 1860 Eugène Lefaucheux, son of Casimir, the inventor of the pinfire shotgun, patented an action in which the barrel was moved forward and back by a rack-and-pinion.[7] Schroeder, Salewski and Schmidt patented another rack-and-pinion action in the United States in 1856, and patents for twenty-eight other guns with sliding barrels were granted in that country between 1852 and 1871. Best known, perhaps, was that granted to Christian Sharps in 1859 and applied to his four-barrelled pocket-pistol, the only sliding-barrel breech-loader to be manufactured in quantity and to achieve real popular success. In one of the most unusual types, noted on an unmarked French shotgun, the barrels are positioned on a long pin which juts from the breech and are locked in position by a key or wedge, which also bears a loop for a sling. To load, the key is withdrawn, the barrels moved forward a short distance on the pin and turned 90°. Only one barrel may be loaded in this position so that a complete 360° turn must be made before the arm is fully loaded and the shooter is ready to slide the barrels back and lock them in place for firing.

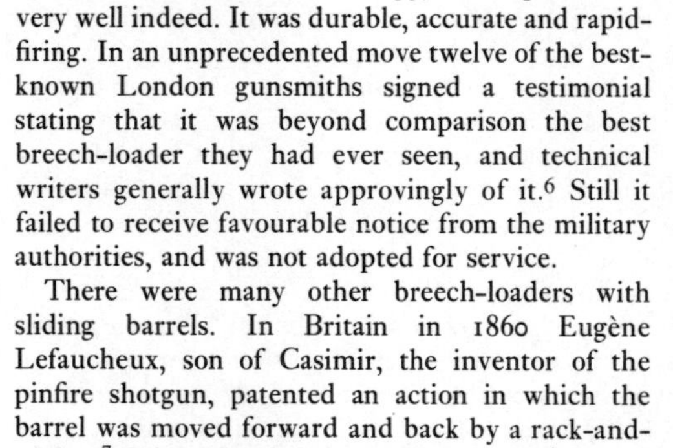

Sharps four-barrelled pistol. U.S.A. (Philadelphia), *c.*1870. Smithsonian Institution, Washington, D.C.

Top-lever Types

Far simpler than the sliding-barrel systems were those which relied upon a top lever to open a hinged breech. The first and classical form of this action is found in Johannes Samuel Pauly's patent of 1812. Unlike the pistol with its tipping barrel described earlier, which was also covered in this patent, the long-arm featured a hinged breech-block raised and lowered by a top lever terminating in a loop. When the breech was closed this lever lay along the wrist of the stock, and the loop nestled against the nose of the comb, where a spring catch held it in position until released by finger pressure when the shooter wished to open the breech once more. This breech system was not especially tight, but it had no need to be. The base of the barrel was chambered and rebated to take the Pauly rimmed cartridge with its brass head on which the designer relied for a breech seal. With the cartridge thus providing its own obturation, the breech joint itself was not required to be gas tight. Another interesting feature of the Pauly design was its long firing-pin. This pin was connected to the tumbler of the external cocker, which somewhat resembled the usual percussion-cap hammer. Perhaps one reason for the length of these firing-pins was the fact that the lifting breech of the Pauly gun was long and hollow to receive the small amount of gas that would inevitably escape through the tiny hole connecting the primer in the bassinet of the cartridge head with the propellant charge inside. Vents in the sides of the breech then permitted this gas to dissipate.

6 Deanes' *Manual of History and Science of Fire-Arms*, London, 1858, p. 184.

7 British patent of 17 February 1860 (in the name of J. H. Johnson).

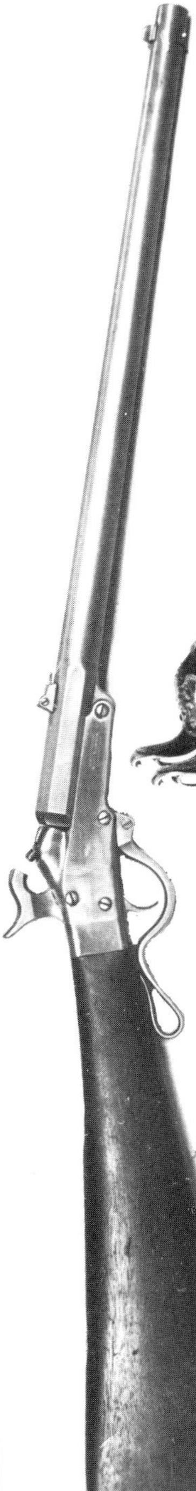

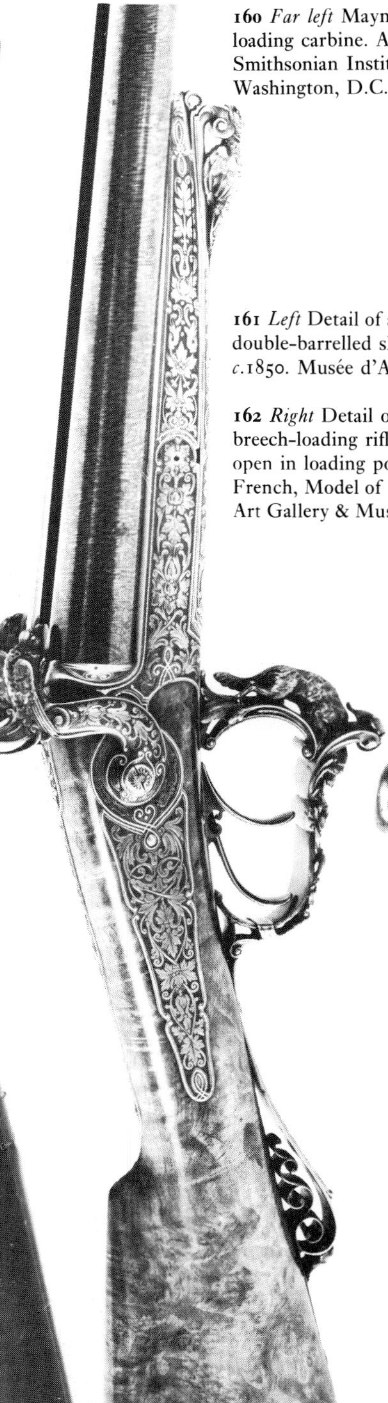

160 *Far left* Maynard breech-loading carbine. American, *c.*1860. Smithsonian Institution, Washington, D.C.

161 *Left* Detail of a Lefaucheux pin-fire double-barrelled shotgun. French, *c.*1850. Musée d'Armes de Liège.

162 *Right* Detail of a Chassepot breech-loading rifle with breech open in loading position. French, Model of 1868. Glasgow Art Gallery & Museum.

163 Greene underhammer bolt-action rifle. American, *c.*1857. Smithsonian Institution, Washington, D.C.

164 Sharps carbine. American, Model 1853. Smithsonian Institution, Washington, D.C. (See also plate **134**.)

165 Remington centre-fire pistol with 'rolling block' breech. American, *c.*1870. Imperial War Museum, London.

166 Werder breech-loading rifle, Model 1869. Tower of London Armouries.

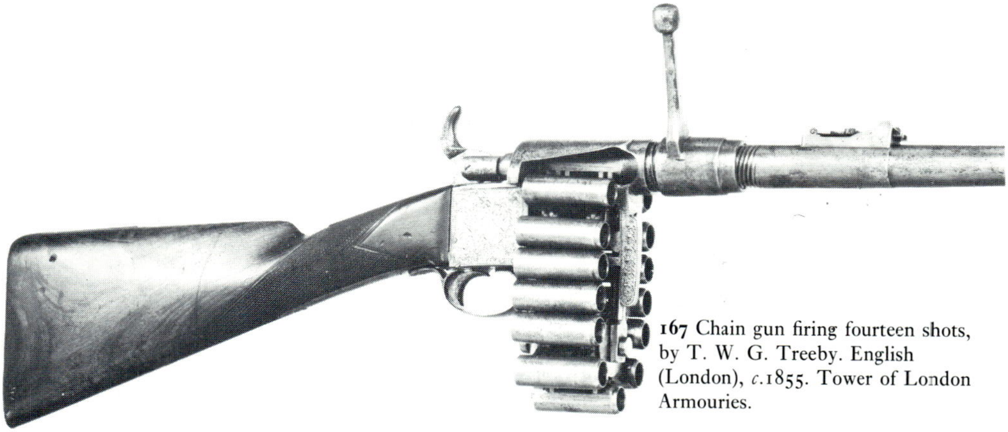

167 Chain gun firing fourteen shots, by T. W. G. Treeby. English (London), *c.*1855. Tower of London Armouries.

Both rifles and shotguns were constructed on Pauly's principles, and they performed exceptionally well – when handled by trained and careful shooters. Their drawbacks lay in the need for care in handling. They were not rugged enough for the usage a military, or even a sporting, arm is frequently called upon to withstand. There was also the danger of the loss of the external priming in the cartridge head previously mentioned. These reasons, plus the greater cost of the Pauly as compared with standard muzzle-loading arms, caused the French Ministry of War to reject it as a military weapon, and its sales as a sporting arm were never great. Thus the Pauly guns disappeared from the scene. It was not until Casimir Lefaucheux's patent of 1832, mentioned above, that the really important feature of the self-obturating cartridge reappeared.

Although the cartridge feature of the Pauly dropped from use, the top-lever system of breech closure continued. In France some of them followed Pauly's design exactly but used combustible cartridges and standard percussion-cap ignition. These could not have been very efficient because the Pauly breech seal was not tight and because the length of the breech required a long channel for the flash to follow from the cap to the charge. At least one such French percussion-cap double-barrelled shotgun, formerly in the Winant collection, is known bearing Pauly's name even though the inventor himself had long since moved to England.

An American percussion-cap breech-loader with a top lever, which saw some use in the American Civil War, was invented by Benjamin F. Joslyn and patented in 1855. This was more than forty years after Pauly's patent, but some of the features are remarkably similar. The lever with a loop at its tip, for instance, lies along the wrist of the stock when the breech is closed and latches against the nose of the comb. The Joslyn breech, however, was much shorter than the Pauly, and it was much tighter. Expanding gases from the powder charge in the paper cartridge used in the early Joslyn pushed back against a breech plug in the form of an inverted cone. As this cone moved backwards under pressure it expanded two encircling rings so that they formed an effective gas seal. After the shot a spring returned the breech plug to its original position. These top-lever Joslyns were used in limited quantity during the first two years of the American Civil War. A later cartridge breech-loader also invented by Joslyn, but without a top lever, saw much wider action.

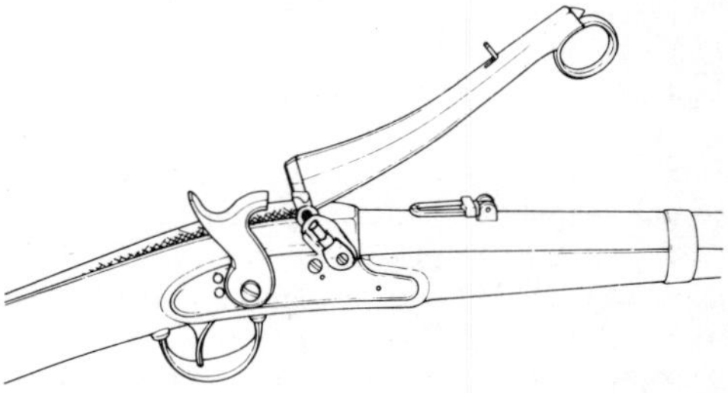

Detail of a carbine fitted with the capping breech-loading action patented by Benjamin F. Joslyn of Worcester, Mass. on 28 August, 1855.

Sliding Breech-bolt Types

Closely allied with the top-lever breech-loaders was a whole series of arms in which a hinged lever of one sort or another activated a sliding bolt to open and close the breech aperture. Since most of these levers lay along the top of the barrel or wrist of the stock they were in a sense top-lever arms. The distinction is made here, however, between the simple opening and closing of a hinged breech and the action of moving a bolt forward and back which usually required a link in addition to the lever. Guns utilising this method of breech closure were both more numerous and more generally successful than the simple, hinged-breech types.

A good example of this system is found in the British Westley Richards 'monkey tail' breech-loader of 1858, sometimes described as the best percussion-cap breech-loader ever produced. Like the top-lever types described above, the lever of the Westley Richards pattern lay along the wrist of the stock when the action was closed. It was, however, far shorter than either the Pauly or the Joslyn. Attached to it was a plunger, or breech-bolt, which moved in and out of the chamber when the lever was lowered or raised. The forward end of this bolt was made of brass and shaped to fit the chamber as closely as possible. Its rear end butted against an extension of the barrel for extra strength, if gas pressures within the barrel should require it. A special feature of the Westley Richards was its ammunition. This was wrapped in paper in the usual manner for a combustible cartridge. Its unique feature, however, was a stout greased felt wad at the base. This wad remained in the chamber and served as an auxiliary breech seal when the piece was fired. As the next cartridge was seated by the sliding bolt it pushed the wad from the previous load ahead of it and drove it through the bore when it was fired, thus providing an automatic cleaning action. Because of it the Westley Richards arms were able to fire a phenomenal number of rounds without trouble from powder fouling.

The Westley Richards 'monkey tail' achieved a well-deserved success. A few rifles of this pattern were issued to British infantry, and the carbine version became the standard cavalry arm until it was replaced by the Snider metallic-cartridge model.

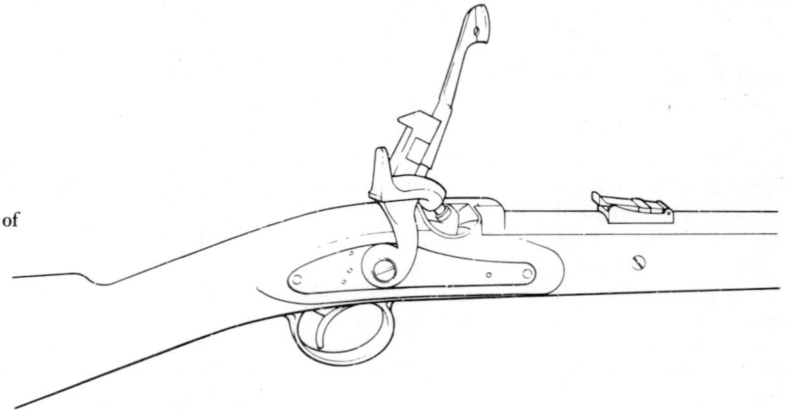

Westley Richards 'monkey tail' breech-loading carbine, Model of 1866. English.

Even then, the Westley Richards carbine continued in use for yeomanry for many years. A few rifles of this pattern were issued to Canadian troops, and the Portuguese government adopted it for military purposes. In addition, the Westley Richards action also enjoyed considerable popularity among sportsmen, and some pistols were made.

In America, a percussion-cap breech-loader patented by James H. Merrill at almost the same time as the Westley Richards operated in a very similar fashion. In the Merrill, however, the lever lay along the top of the barrel and latched on the base of the rear sight. Thus its motion was exactly opposite from the Westley Richards. Also the Merrill paper cartridge lacked the felt wad as an auxiliary gas seal and relied entirely upon the copper tip of the sliding bolt for obturation. It was thus not quite so efficient as the British weapon. Nevertheless some 14,695 Merrills were purchased by the Federal Government during the Civil War, along with 770 rifles. In addition, some 14,000 existing muzzle-loading rifles are believed to have been converted to the Merrill system during the war, and still other Merrills were purchased by states and individuals during the conflict.

Some arms with sliding breech-bolts had levers below instead of on top. One such action was patented by W. W. Marston of the United States in 1850. In his system the trigger-guard of a long-gun, or a special lever which lay along the front of the grips of a pistol, could be pulled forward to retract a breech-bolt and open a slot in the side of the receiver for the insertion of a cartridge. Like the Westley Richards cartridge, this one also had a greased wad at the base, this time of leather, to help provide a seal and to act as a cleaning swab when pushed through the bore ahead of the next shot. Marston arms were manufactured as rifles and shotguns as well as military pistols, but never in large quantities.

A final type of action with a sliding breech-bolt might almost be classed as a bolt action. Indeed, had it been invented twenty years earlier it would undoubtedly have been classed by most students as a transition piece between the types listed above and the true bolt actions described later. This was the Terry breech-loader patented in 1856 by William Terry of Birmingham, England. This interesting weapon employed a hinged arm on the right side of the breech which pivoted laterally and could then be pulled back. With this action it retracted a sliding breech-bolt and opened a loading hole in the side of the breech just behind the hammer. A cartridge could

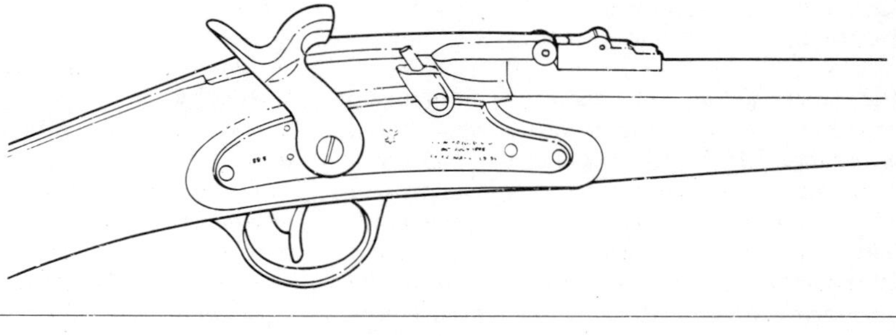

Merrill breech-loading carbine. U.S.A., *c.*1855. Smithsonian Institution, Washington, D.C.

be inserted in this hole and the bolt slid forward again to push the cartridge into the chamber. When the arm was folded back into place along the side of the breech a lug engaged a slot for locking purposes and the tip of the lever arm fitted into the loading hole. When the cartridge was properly seated its side was opposite the channel from the percussion nipple, so that the flash from the cap ignited the powder charge in the centre. Like the Marston and the Westley Richards, this cartridge also had a greased wad at its base which helped the coned head of the breech bolt form a tight seal and which also performed the same cleaning and lubricating functions claimed for the two previously described arms.

The Terry, apparently, was an excellent arm, and the greased wad worked efficiently both as a seal and a cleaner. In one test made aboard HMS *Excellent* in 1858, a Terry carbine fired a total of 1,800 rounds without cleaning, an unheard of achievement for a black powder arm of that era. Some Terry carbines were purchased for experimental issue to selected cavalry units in Great Britain, and more were purchased for use by Confederate troops during the American Civil War.

Bolt-action Types

The Terry approached the bolt action in mechanism, muzzle-loading, with the firing-pin attached by a link to a percussion lock of more or less standard form, but then the inventor, who had worked for Pauly in Paris during his youth, developed his bolt-action breech-loader.

In all essentials the action of the Dreyse gun is the same as that used today. A rigid arm is raised and pulled back to open the breech, then pushed forward and down to close it. One difference from present systems, however, is the need to release a thumb latch manually before opening the bolt and replace it after the bolt is closed, which cocks the action. Another variation is the lack of an extractor, since the Dreyse cartridge was combustible and left no case in the chamber. All later changes have been merely refinements of this original system.

Despite the fact that the breech seal was bad and leaked gas severely and that the slender firing-pins tended to bend and break, the Dreyse needle gun achieved great success. Within a few years after its invention it was being tested in the Prussian Army. In 1848 it was first issued officially. The spectacular success of German troops in the short wars with Denmark and Austria were popularly attributed in large part to the new gun, and it achieved a reputation that was well merited until it was used against the Chassepot.

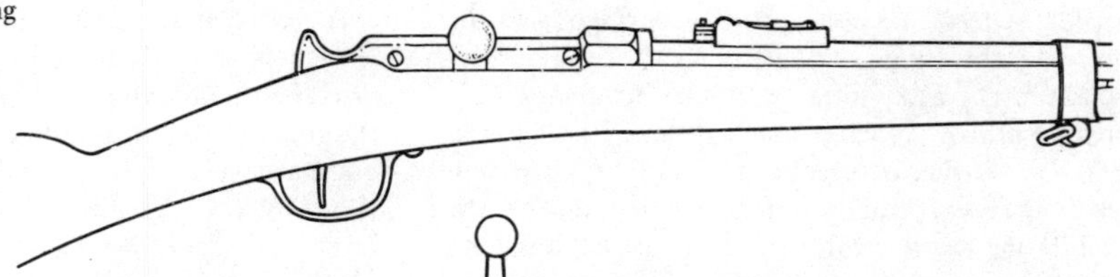

Chassepot breech-loading rifle, French Model of 1866. Art Gallery & Museum, Glasgow.

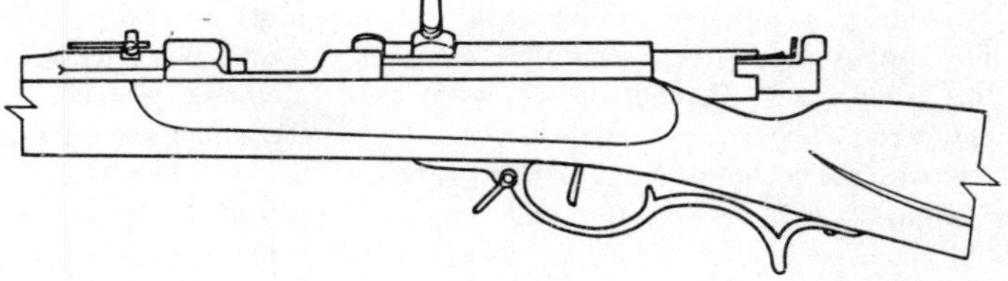

J. N. von Dreyse military needle-fire rifle, Prussian Model of 1841.

but credit for the invention of the classical mechanism is usually given to Johann Nikolaus von Dreyse of Sömmerda, Prussia. He evolved his action in 1841, fifteen years before the Terry. The key to the Dreyse system was its cartridge, a paper-wrapped self-contained unit with the primer resting on the base of the bullet. To detonate it, a long, sharp, needle-like firing-pin had to pierce the wrapping, pass through the powder charge and crush the primer against the bullet. Because of this firing-pin Dreyse arms came to be called 'needle guns'. The first types of 1828 were

Other nations developed similar arms; for example, the one patented by George Kufahl in London in 1852. But the best of these later bolt-action needle guns was undoubtedly the Chassepot, adopted by the French Army in 1866. This rifle,
invented by Antoine Alphonse Chassepot in 1863, 162
greatly resembled the Dreyse, but in some respects was superior to it. The primer, an inverted percussion cap, lay at the very base of the cartridge instead of nestling against the bullet. Thus a shorter firing-pin could be used. Also a rubber disc temporarily

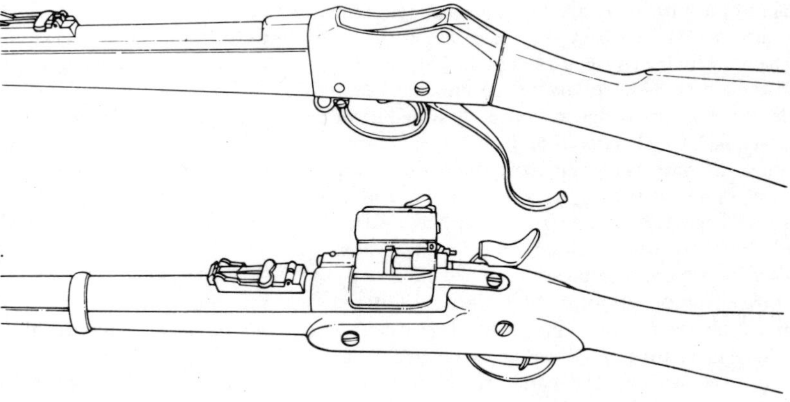

(*Top*) Detail of Martini action. See page 254. (*Bottom*) Detail of the breech-loading system patented in 1859. By Jacob Snider of Baltimore. See page 254.

gave a far more efficient breech seal as the expanding powder gases pushed it back against the bolt head. On the adverse side firing-needles required frequent replacement, as did the rubber obturators. In all tests the Chassepot performed excellently and, following the disastrous Franco-Prussian War, captured French rifles were even altered to fire cartridges and issued to German troops. The Chassepot remained the standard French arm until 1874 when it was modified to fire a metallic centrefire cartridge and became known as the Gras rifle.

America also produced the under-hammer, oval-bored bolt-action patented by Lt. Col. J. Durrell Greene in 1857. Its combustible cartridge used the bullet for obturation, being loaded with the powder section first. The initial shot was loaded with a separate bullet. An extension rod on the bolt seated the bullet forward before the next round was inserted. The U.S. government purchased 900 during the Civil War; more went to Russia, serial numbers suggesting a total production of around 3,000.

The most important bolt-action design was, of course, that produced by Peter Paul and Wilhelm Mauser of Oberndorf. Developed partly in Germany and in Liège with the encouragement of the Remington agent, Samuel Norris, between 1867 and 1870, the first official model of 1871 combined a self-cocking and self-extracting bolt having only three major components, with the calibre and rifling of the Chassepot, which had proved much superior to the Dreyse. This first Mauser saw limited service as late as the First World War, but was succeeded in 1886 by the Model 71/84, an eight-shot tubular magazine rifle. The Model 1898 action formed the basis for more military and, possibly, sporting-rifle actions than any other design. Some were periphcially modified locally to satisfy national pride, but ultimately some form of Mauser action was accepted by thirty-five countries, with some remaining in service today.

Types with Movable Breech-blocks

Paralleling the development of all of the types of breech-loaders described previously was another whole group which provided access to their chambers by a movable breech-block. In some the breech-block could be lifted. In some it dropped. In a few it tipped, and in a very few it rotated. Arms with movable breech-blocks were among the very first types designed for use with fixed ammunition, and at the very close of the period several were altered to fire the new, self-primed, metal-cased cartridges. One or two of the actions developed during this period are, in fact, still used today.

A very early example of an arm with a rising breech-block is described and illustrated in W. W. Greener's famous book.[8] The present whereabouts of the gun are unknown, but the author attributed it to a gunmaker named Theiss in Nuremberg and dated it about 1804. In this flintlock weapon a button-headed lever pivoted on the forward end of the trigger-guard could be pushed up to open the action by raising a breech-block set in a vertical mortise above it. This block was pierced with a hole the same diameter as the bore of the piece, and when it was fully raised the hole and bore were aligned. The stock immediately behind the breech was grooved so that a cartridge could be readily inserted into the bore. To close the action the user simply drove the breech-block back down again. According to Greener this system leaked gas badly and was discontinued. Certainly surviving examples are scarce, if indeed there are any.

A much more successful example of a breech-block moving in a vertical mortise is found in a weapon invented by the American Christian Sharps in 1848. The Sharps breech-block was activated by
the trigger-guard, which was pivoted at its forward 164
end and so formed a lever. The earliest of the Sharps

8 *The Gun and its Development*, 1907, p. 109.

actions had a slanted breech with the breech-block moving at an angle. In 1859 the mortise was made perpendicular to the bore. Gas seals were provided in the earlier models by a fixed platinum ring in the face of the breech-block. After 1859 this was changed to a steel plate which expanded and pressed tightly against the base of the barrel under pressure from the powder gases. During the percussion period Sharps rifles and carbines were equipped with automatic primers: Maynard tape primers in the models of 1851 and 1855, disc primers in the models of 1852, 1853, 1859 and 1863. A cutting edge on the top of the breech-block sheared off the end of the paper-wrapped cartridges customarily used and thus exposed the powder within to the direct flash from the primer.

The Sharps action was a very good one and exceptionally strong. The soldiers who used it during the American Civil War praised it as the finest single-shot breech-loader of the conflict.[9] When metal-cased self-contained cartridges became popular at the close of the War the Sharps was adapted to use them, and later single-shot cartridge rifles, such as the British Farquharson and Henry (patented 1865), the Winchester and the Stevens, continued to employ it. It is still used today for some anti-tank weapons and other arms requiring exceptional breech strength.

Another breech-loader of the American Civil War offers an excellent example of a breech-block which tips or tilts. This is the Gwyn & Campbell, patented by Edward Gwyn and Abner C. Campbell in 1862, often confused with the earlier similar looking Cosmopolitan carbine in which these partners also had an interest. In the true Gwyn & Campbell the trigger-guard, which serves as a lever, has an ingeniously eccentric forward terminus. When the guard is lowered, this end rotates and first moves the breech-block backwards to disengage its necked section from the chamber and then tips it downward so that its grooved top forms an inclined plane down which the shooter can slip a cartridge into place. Raising the guard returns the breech-block to its closed position. Only two moving parts are required to produce this rugged breech action. The insertion of the necked portion of the breechblock into the chamber affords a reasonably good breech seal, and modern tests have shown the gun to be both dependable and accurate.

A third breech-loader of the American Civil War era exemplifies an action with a rotating, or rolling, breech-block. Ambrose E. Burnside, later to achieve distinction as an army commander in the war, invented the system in 1856. Again the trigger-guard serves as a lever to roll the breech-block backwards and downwards in an arc and exposes a chamber in the block itself for the insertion of a cartridge. Returning the trigger-guard to its proper position rolls the block back into place and seats the bullet and the forward rim of the cartridge in the barrel. A key feature of the Burnside action was the special cartridge the inventor designed for it. It was metal cased and tapered from bullet to base where it was pierced for the flash from a conventional percussion cap. The chamber in the breech-block was tapered correspondingly. Thus even though the user had to insert the cartridge base first there was no chance for him to err as there had been in the Mont Storm or the Smith. The metal sides of the cartridge, covering the joint between the breech-block and the base of the barrel, afforded a good seal in a manner very reminiscent of the second model Smith carbine which was its contemporary and a frequent competitor. The Burnside underwent several modifications and improvements which altered the locking system holding the breech in place, changed the shape of the hammer, and so on, but the basic breech action remained the same. It was an excellent arm, and next to the Sharps it was the most widely used single-shot breech-loader of the American Civil War.

The moving breech-block system was widely used in conjunction with fixed ammunition, as already noted. Many variations were produced in both Europe and America and only a few of the most important can be mentioned here. Some of these were variants of the needle gun, like the system patented in London in 1852 by Joseph Needham which incorporated what was, in effect, a bolt, though it was secured at the back on a hinge. The breech was opened by turning a small projecting handle on the bolt towards the top. This retracted the bolt slightly on a thread thereby disengaging its head from the breech, and permitted the whole to be lifted up and turned back on its hinge. A combustible centrefire cartridge was then fed manually into the breech and the bolt was returned to its position. The striker, a long spring-operated needle, was contained inside the bolt and was cocked automatically when the breech was opened and closed.

More popular than the needle action was that in which the breech-block contained a spring-loaded striker which was itself struck by a hammer of conventional form when the gun was fired. Probably best of all these was the rolling-block action patented in the United States by Leonard Geiger of Hudson, New York in January 1863, and subsequently improved and manufactured on both guns and pistols
by the Remington Arms Company. The action 165
consisted simply of a vertical block, pivoted at the lower end in a recess in the frame in front of the hammer. It could be rolled back manually for the

9 It should be mentioned here that one model used in the Civil War had a coffee grinder built into the butt for camp use.

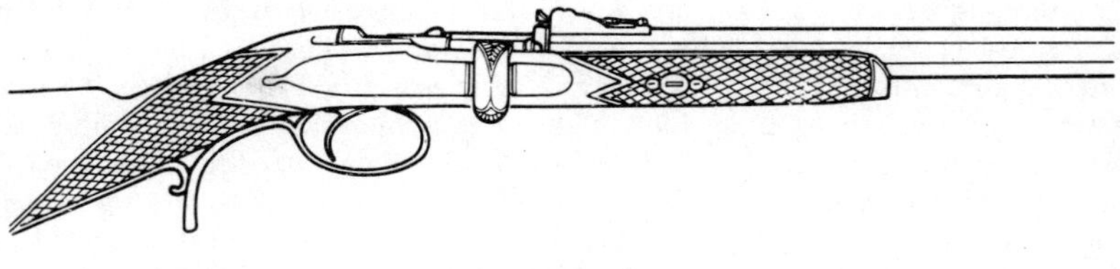

Detail of needle-fire breech-loading target rifle by J. Needham. English, c.1860. Tower of London Armouries.

insertion of a metallic rimfire cartridge and incorporated an extractor for spent cases. It was automatically locked as the hammer fell.

Other types used a breech-block that could be hinged sideways–as on the Henry VIII guns[10]–or forward to open the breech for the insertion of the cartridge. This system had the advantage of being easily applicable to the conversion of existing muzzle-loading arms to breech-loading, and was used by a number of governments for this purpose.

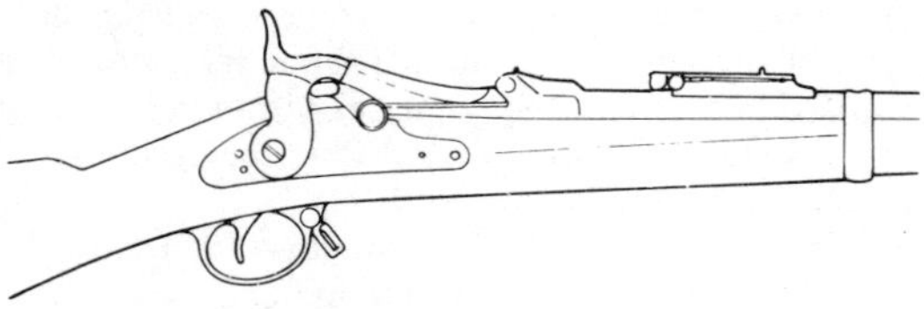

Detail of Allin Model 1884 breech-loading rifle. U.S.A. Tower of London Armouries.

The most famous (with a sideways opening block) was probably the one patented in 1859 by Jacob Snider of Baltimore,[11] which was adopted officially by the British government in 1865, and in a slightly modified form by the French in 1867 (Fig. p. 252). The US government in 1865 adopted a system with a forward opening block patented in the same year by Erskine S. Allin of the Springfield Armoury. A somewhat similar system patented in the US by Hiram Berdan in 1866 was also used both in America and Spain, while another patented in the same year by Isaac M. Milbank, was adapted by Professor Amsler of Schaffhausen and used for converting the muzzle-loading rifles of the Swiss Army. Another system of the same type, the Albini-Braendlin was adopted for the Italian Navy in 1866 and in 1867 for the forces of Belgium.

Another type of action used a breech-block that was pivoted laterally at the rear end. To open the breech the block was tipped downwards into a cavity below it in the frame and the cartridge was loaded manually. On most examples the block has a gutter-shaped recess on top to guide the cartridge into the breech. The system from which all others of this kind stem was patented in the United States by Henry O. Peabody in July 1862 and manufactured by the Providence Tool Company of Providence, Rhode Island. This took a metal-cased rimfire cartridge, the breech being opened for its insertion by depressing an under lever that also formed the trigger-guard. A hammer on a back-action lock of normal type had also to be cocked manually before the gun could be fired.

Similar to the Peabody were the systems devised by General B. S. Roberts, U.S. Army, adopted by Serbia in 1870 and that by J. L. Werder of Nurem-

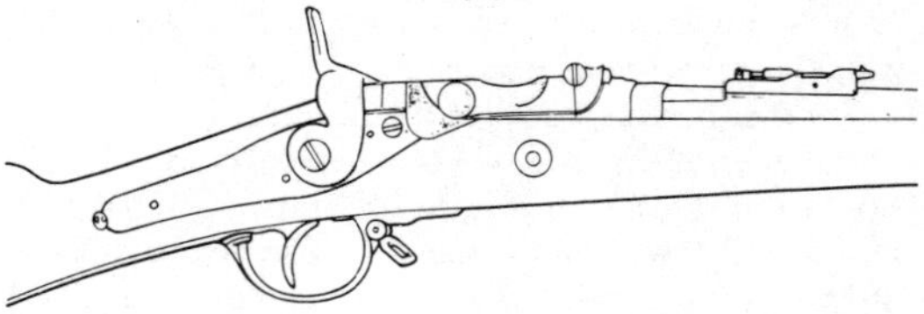

Detail of Albini-Braendlin breech-loading rifle. Belgian, 1868. Tower of London Armouries.

berg, adopted by the Bavarian army in 1869, and later 166
by the Austrians also. Its most famous offspring was, however, the one developed by the Hungarian-Swiss Friedrich von Martini and patented in England in 1868 (US 1869) (Fig. p. 252). The major improvement embodied in this lay in the replacement of the hammer-activated striker by a self-actuating one cocked automatically by the opening and closing of the breech. The Martini action used in conjunction with the system of rifling invented by Alexander Henry of Edinburgh produced the Martini-Henry rifle which was adopted officially by the British government in 1869.[12]

Early Cartridge Repeaters

Magazine Repeater

The appearance of the self-contained cartridge solved at once the problem arising from the use of loose powder, both for the main charges and priming,

10 See p. 198.

11 See pp. 259–60.

12 For a fuller description see pp. 260–1.

Berdan breech-loading rifle. Russia, dated 1870. Tower of London Armouries.

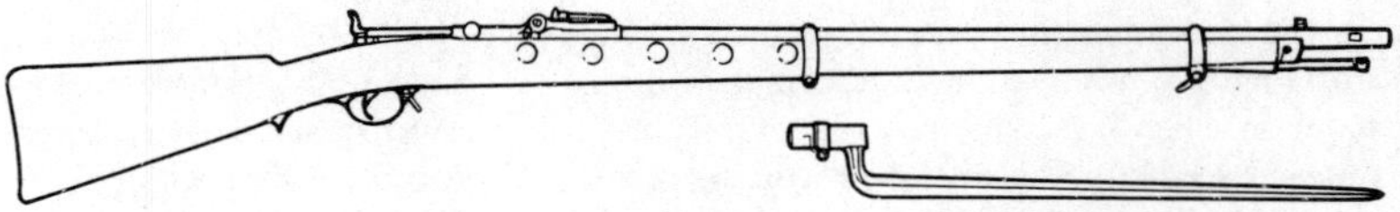

Peabody breech-loading rifle, Model of 1862. U.S.A. Tower of London Armouries.

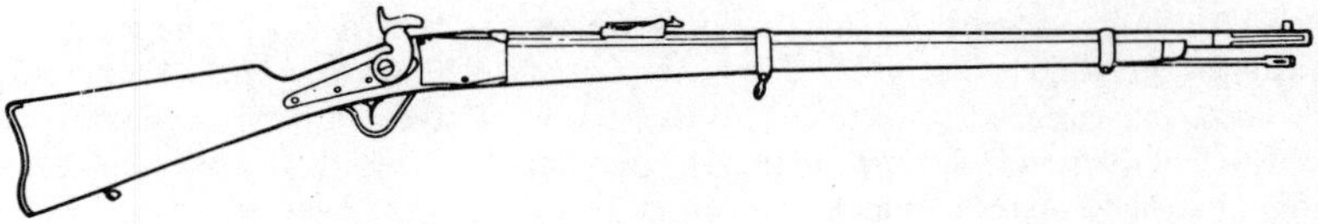

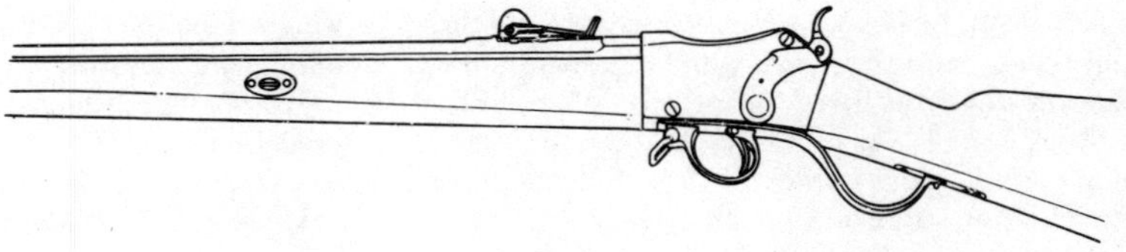

Martini breech-loading rifles. (*Top*) Swiss, 1868. (*Centre*) English Martini-Henry, 1874. (*Bottom*) English M-H MK.IV fitted with quick-loader.

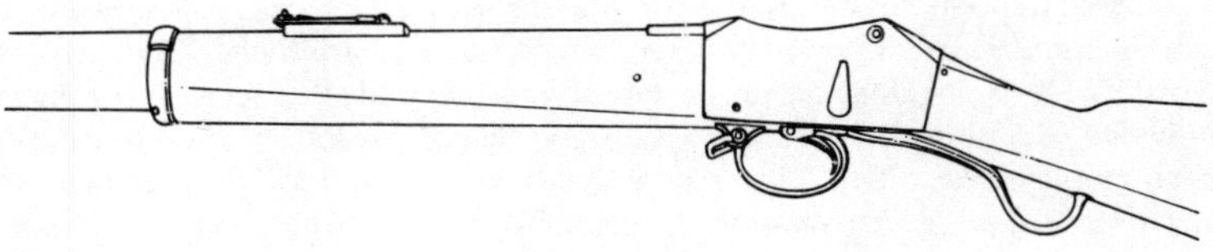

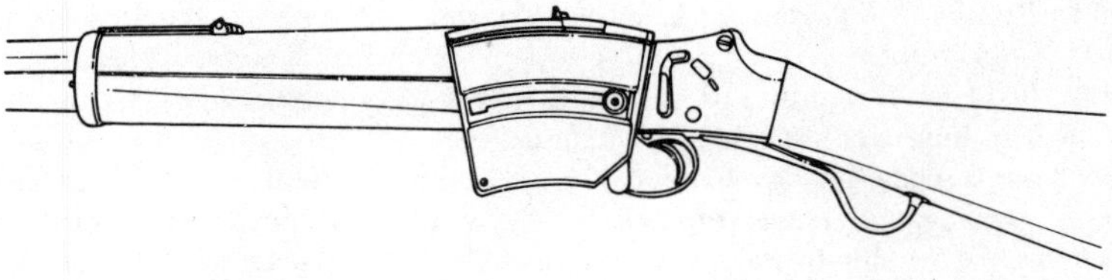

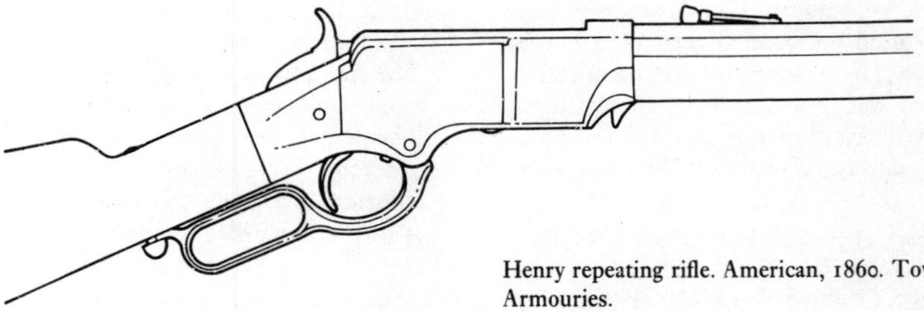

Henry repeating rifle. American, 1860. Tower of London Armouries.

that had hitherto made the development of a really satisfactory magazine repeater so difficult. As it happened, the development of the magazine cartridge repeater was itself inhibited by the fact that, at almost the moment when it became possible, the future of the repeater seemed to lie with the revolving system which, as described in Chapter 8, Samuel Colt's invention had made very much a practical proposition. Gunsmiths nevertheless continued to experiment with magazine repeaters, though few of those produced within the period covered by this chapter had even limited success, the two major exceptions being the Henry and the Spencer, discussed below.

The credit for the invention that led to the first successful cartridge magazine repeaters must be given to the American Walter Hunt. In 1847 he applied for United States patents for a hollow conical bullet containing its own propellant charge and for a twelve-shot repeating rifle with a tubular spring magazine under the barrel for use with it. The bullet, or 'Rocket Ball', as it was called, was granted a patent in 1848 and the gun in the following year entered in the name of Stephen Taylor, acting for a foreigner, presumably Hunt. Both were also subjects of an English patent in 1847.

Hunt's 'Volitional Repeater', as he called it, was too complex to be successful, but in the year that he received his US patent for it another patent was granted to Lewis Jennings for an improved version of it with a rack-and-pinion breech action. Jennings was an employee of a New York model-maker and machinist, George A. Arrowsmith, to whom Hunt had assigned his patents. All the patents were then immediately acquired by a New York financier, Courtland Palmer, and the rifle was put into production by Robbins & Lawrence of Windsor, Vermont, a firm of gunsmiths.

In 1854 Horace Smith and Daniel B. Wesson patented an improved version of the Jennings gun – embodying a toggle-link lever action – together with a pistol working on the same principle.[13] They were taken into partnership by Palmer and, in the following year, together formed the Volcanic Repeating Arms Company at Norwich, Connecticut, to manufacture the arms. These were fitted with a tubular spring-loaded magazine under the barrel into which the loaded bullets – similar to Hunt's but with their own priming – could be inserted through a cut-off at the front, opened by swinging the muzzle sideways. The mechanism was operated by moving a lever, which also served as a trigger-guard, down and forward. This caused a breech-block (breech-pin) to move backwards while a platform, originally in line with the rear of the magazine, moved up to position a bullet behind the chamber. Reversal of the process moved the block forward to thrust the bullet into the chamber and also straightened a toggle-shaped wedge linked to the back of the block, thereby locking it. Firing was by means of a hammer which struck the breech-block a blow that was hard enough to jerk it forward so that a blunt striker on its front end set off the detonator in the base of the bullet.

Smith and Wesson sold out their interests in the Volcanic company in the year of its foundation. No doubt they soon realised that the venture was not going to be a success, and, in fact, the firm went into liquidation in 1857. Its assets were then acquired by one of the shareholders, a shirt manufacturer of New Haven, Connecticut, named Oliver F. Winchester, who formed the New Haven Arms Company to continue manufacturing the Volcanic arms.

Winchester, at first, had no more success than his predecessors. He was, however, fortunate in having as his factory superintendent Benjamin Tyler Henry, a skilled gunsmith who had been associated with the Hunt-Jennings repeater and its successors since the Robbins & Lawrence days. In October 1860 he obtained a US patent for an improved version of the Volcanic rifle of which the most important part consisted of '. . adapting the arm to the use of a solid ball, enclosed in a metal cartridge, thus greatly increasing the power and certainty of the fire of the arms'. The cartridge was a rimfire one and could be made in much larger calibres and with a much greater charge of powder than was possible with the 'Rocket Ball' type of ammunition. A further improvement was the introduction of a spring-loaded striker – still hammer-actuated – working through the breech-pin.

The New Haven Arms Company now turned its attention exclusively to the manufacture of the new rifle, which had a brass frame and was marketed as Henry's Patent Repeating Rifle. Its first appearance coincided very neatly with the preparations for, and the actual outbreak of, the American Civil War in 1861, which produced an unprecedented demand for firearms. The Henry rifle was an instant and phenomenal success, so much so that the firm had difficulty in meeting orders. In their publicity hand-outs[14] they claimed that it could fire sixty shots a minute from a sixteen-shot magazine:

> The size now made is 44-100 inch bore, 24-inch barrel, and carries a conical ball 32 to the pound. The penetration at 100 yards is 8 inches; 400 yards 5 inches; and it carries with force sufficient to kill at 1,000 yards. A resolute man, armed with one of these Rifles, particularly if on

13 An Italian copy of the pistol, the Venditti, was long thought to be a possible prototype. See E. Marciano, 'The Final Word on the Venditti-Volcanic Controversy', *Arms & Armor Annual*, Vol. I, Northfield, Ill., 1973, pp. 308-14.

14 See for example, the poster reproduced by William B. Edwards, *Civil War Guns*, Harrisburg, Pa., 1962, p. 160.

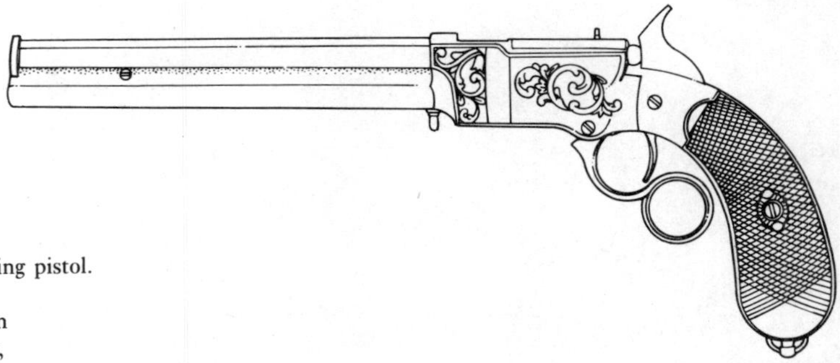

Volcanic repeating pistol. U.S.A., *c.*1855. Winchester Gun Museum, Cody, Wyoming.

horseback, CANNOT BE CAPTURED.

In 1866 Winchester reorganised the New Haven Arms Company and altered its name to the one that it has retained ever since, the Winchester Repeating Arms Company. This event coincided with the production of the first Winchester rifle, the model 1866. It was basically the same gun as the Henry but incorporated several refinements devised by Nelson King, of which the most important was a loading-gate permitting the magazine to be loaded from the rear end. A second model, the most famous of all Winchesters, followed in 1873 and was produced alongside that of 1866. This was designed for a series of rim and centrefire cartridges and had an iron, instead of a brass, frame.

The chief rival to the Henry and Winchester repeaters was the gun patented in the United States in March 1860 by Christopher M. Spencer, which likewise benefited from the Civil War. This had a spring-loaded tubular magazine for seven rimfire cartridges in the butt and a rolling-block breech mechanism, operated by an under lever, which transferred the cartridges to the chamber and also incorporated an extractor for spent cases. One slight disadvantage in comparison to the Winchester was that the lock, which was a back-action one with a side-hammer, had to be cocked manually. This was, however, more than outweighed by the strength and simplicity of the Spencer action.

In 1861, after raising enough capital to start a factory, Spencer submitted a rifle for testing by the US Navy. The test, which took place on two mornings in June of the same year, was extremely successful, the gun firing 500 rounds, without cleaning, at rates that never fell below seven shots in ten seconds and only misfiring once. The result was a rather disappointing order for only 700 rifles for the Navy. In November of the same year, however, tests were carried out by the Army and these tests resulted in an initial order of 10,000 Spencer rifles with sword bayonets.

Spencer, in the meantime, founded the Spencer Repeating Rifle Company in Boston, Massachusetts, which continued to manufacture his firearms until 1869. A certain number were also produced by the Burnside Rifle Company of Providence, Rhode Island, under a contract of June 1864. Both rifled carbines with a length of 39 in, and rifled muskets, with a length of 47 in were produced, principally in 0·52 in calibre. They were improved by the invention of the Blakeslee cartridge-box, designed to carry from ten to thirteen extra loaded magazines, and by the introduction in 1865 of a cut-off, invented by Edward M. Stabler, which permitted them to be used as simple single-shot breech-loaders, while retaining the magazine in reserve to be brought into instant action if necessary.

Of the success of the Spencer there can be no doubt and it is said to have been called the 'horizontal shot tower' by the Confederate soldiers. It has been estimated that something over 100,000 rifles and carbines were manufactured by the Union forces, but in the efficiency that made this possible lay the downfall of the Spencer Company. The end of the Civil War placed an enormous surplus of the arms on the market and virtually killed any demand there may have been for new ones, particularly in face of competition from the Henry, which was more successful as a sporting and all-purpose saddle rifle. In 1869, therefore, the Spencer firm was put up for auction, when most of its assets were acquired by Winchester.

Other American repeaters of the period that should be mentioned are the Ball & Lamson of 1864 and the Warren R. Evans of 1869. Both had tubular magazines and lever-actuated breeches. They were produced only in small quantities.

In Europe many makers designed magazine repeaters but, lacking the stimulus of a major war, none achieved great success in the period covered here. Among them can be mentioned those of Victor Colette of Liège (1855), Franz von Dreyse of Sömmerda (1868) and W. Krutzsch (patented in

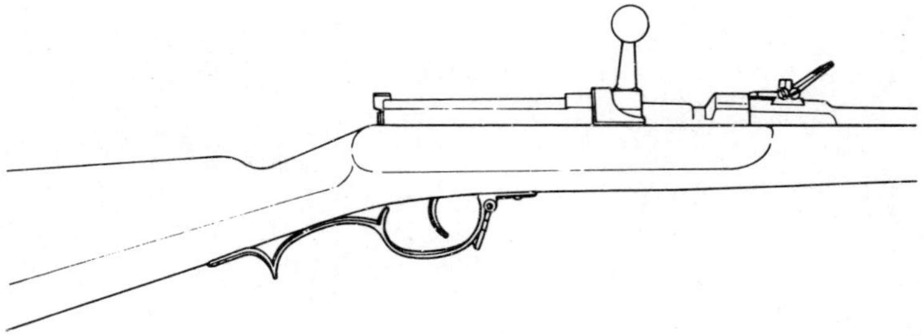

Detail of Spenser repeating rifle, Model of 1867. U.S.A.

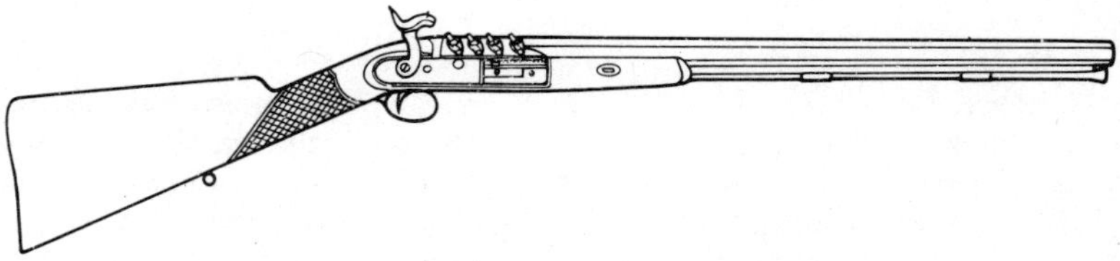

Captain Ritso's patent percussion gun with sliding lock firing four superimposed shots, by W. Mills of London, *c*.1830. Tower of London Armouries.

England in 1866). The most significant was the thirty-shot, 10·4 mm calibre rifle, invented by the Swiss Friedrich Vetterli and taken into service in the Swiss army in 1868. It had a tubular magazine under the barrel and a bolt action somewhat similar to that still in wide use today. It was the first bolt-action repeater to be adopted as an official service arm by any nation.

Other Repeaters

As before, multi-barrelled arms continued to be made in the period covered here, the most popular form having two barrels. The superimposed load system also survived into the percussion era. In 1825 Jacob Mould obtained a British patent for a system with a sliding lock–either flint or percussion–not unlike the Jover and Belton one mentioned on p. 206. A number of arms based on this patent are known, for example in the Tower of London Armouries–marked *CAPT. RITSO'S PATENT*, probably indicating that Mould had disposed of his patent. Other makers who patented superimposed load firearms, some using cartridges, were the Frenchman Claudius Ramel (1824), Jean Luzier (1827), de Lancry and Charoy (1831) and Gardon, Aubrey and Robert (1839). The only one to achieve any success was the Luzier system which was taken up by John P. Lindsay of New Haven, Connecticut, who had worked with Walch on his superimposed load revolvers.[15] In 1860 he obtained a US patent for a single-trigger mechanism operating two hammers which he embodied in a series of percussion pistols, called the 'Young Americans', which fired two superimposed charges from a single barrel. The pistols, some models of which had two triggers, had a limited success in the early years of the American Civil War, while in 1863 Lindsay received a government contract for 1,000 rifles working on the same principle. But though the prototype had behaved well under trial the rifle did not stand up very well to battle conditions and no others seem to have been produced.

In conclusion, brief reference must be made to a group of repeaters that are neither strictly revolvers nor magazine guns. The best known example of the system was patented in London in 1855 by T. W. S. Treeby and embodied a series of steel chambers linked to form an endless chain which passed sideways behind the breech. Each chamber was brought to the top in turn for firing by a percussion lock of normal type. A somewhat similar design, but using 0·22 in rimfire cartridges, was patented in the US by H. S. Josselyn in 1866. At about the same date a French maker, Guycot, produced a number of guns and pistols in which a belt of cartridge-holders revolved longitudinally behind the barrel in a covered body. The holders were loaded one at a time through a slot in the top of the body. Pressure on the trigger turned the belt until a cartridge was pointing into the breech, retracted the firing-pin, retracted an inner barrel until it covered the cartridge, and then released the firing-pin. None of these weapons achieved any real success. However, in the course of time the main line of firearms development had already passed them by.

15 See p. 233.

CHAPTER TEN

Firearms other than Revolvers and Automatic Pistols 1870-1918

C.H. Roads

68-227 It is impossible in a single survey to cover the developments that the gun, or rather long-arm, underwent between 1870 and 1918. The mere fact that there was a division between rifled and smooth-bored arms dictates a double approach. So disparate was the development of these two classes of weapons that their only substantial technical common ground would seem to lie in sporting double rifles. Rifles shaped the course of military history in the half century covered by this chapter, so it is to the military rifle that precedence must be given in any consideration of design. The development of match- or target-rifles, so interestingly interconnected with that of military rifles, is next discussed and a survey of sporting-rifles is also included. The second section of this chapter outlines the history of the shotgun from the hammer breech-loader at the time when rebounding locks were invented to the hammerless ejector almost indistinguishable from that so highly prized today. No chapter on the history of firearms during the period concerned could omit at least a glance at the genesis and development of automatic arms. By 1915 the machine-gun was the master of the battlefield and enormous efforts were being made to reduce it to a more portable form. The third section of this chapter is therefore subdivided into three: in it there are brief outlines of the development of the machine-gun, the machine-carbine and the automatic rifle. The final section covers the relatively minor subject of pistols with fixed mechanism.

Long-guns

Rifled Arms

In 1871, the year that Great Britain adopted the ·45 Martini-Henry rifle for the armament of her forces, Prussia selected the ·433 Mauser as her
168 official arm. These facts are well known to almost all who find any interest in the development of firearms: what they are less likely to know is that also in 1871 Metford, the greatest of nineteenth-century English rifle designers, at last produced a military breech-loader that really would shoot straight. Yet the significance of Metford's achievement is at least as great as that of Mauser or Martini. On the face of it Metford had won only the 1,000 yards Duke of Cambridge competition at Wimbledon whilst Mauser had won himself a major contract from the Prussian government. In fact their achievements were complementary: one had mastered the first obstacles in producing the ideal military action or, breech-mechanism, the other was well on the way to producing a combination of barrel and ammunition that would make effective rifle fire at 1,000 yards a tactical reality. When, between 1886 and 1887, Great Britain rather suddenly decided to abandon 0·402 in as her prospective calibre and go instead for 0·303 in Metford, through the remarkable extent of his practical experience, was able, at very short notice, to supply the Government Committee with the correct proportions for the grooving, the pitch of rifling, the shape and dimensions of the entry and the clearances for the cartridge so accurately that no improvement could be effected whilst the type of propellant remained unaltered. It is impossible to study the breech-mechanism in isolation from the barrel and ammunition, they are much too closely interdependent: it must always be remembered that their separation is merely a working convenience.

Great Britain for all this did not, in 1869, adopt the Metford, or rather, as it might have been, the Westley Richards-Metford. She chose instead the Martini-Henry (officially adopted in 1871), and with that decision opened one of the biggest arms controversies Parliament has ever seen. To understand the pattern of small arms development in Great Britain in the 1870s and 1880s, one has first to look at the sixties and, in particular, at the Snider and the Martini. In the previous chapter the multitude of breech mechanisms that emerged on the scene from the 1850s onwards has been outlined across the international scene, now an explanation is due as to why the systems which were actually adopted were as apparently crude as the Snider and the Mont Storm.

The Snider breech action was designed by Jacob Snider, an American, as a means of converting the vast stocks of existing muzzle-loaders to breech-loading. By 1864, the advantages of breech-loading were being demonstrated to the world in an unmistakable manner. The victories of the Prussians over the Danes in Schleswig-Holstein and the superiority of forces armed with breech-loaders in the American Civil War induced the British military authorities to invite ideas on converting their muzzle-loaders–the final spur came when they heard that the French had already decided on the same action. Of the forty-seven inventions submitted by 20 September 1864, only eight had sufficient merit to be taken seriously. William Mont Storm's forward and upward hinging breech-block action with side-lock striker was successful and a pattern was sealed for the manufacture of 3,000 for troop trials in September 1865. In 1864 the Storm's advantage over the Snider was that its skin cartridge ammunition was a relatively known factor and it was available: in 1865 the boot was on the other foot. Snider and Boxer of the Royal Laboratory had together improved their metallic, centrefire ammunition to such an extent that, when supply difficulties mounted over the provision of Storm's, they took over and the Snider was adopted.

There was nothing startling about the Snider breech mechanism. It consisted of a simple cylindrical block hinged longitudinally on the right hand side and traversed by a rod striker. This transmitted the blow from the hammer of the side-lock directly to the percussion cap in the base of the cartridge. Extraction was effected by pulling the whole block, when open, to the rear, and ejection was achieved by tipping the weapon upside down. In the earlier models there was no breech retaining catch as such but, though one was not ordinarily necessary, it was possible for the blast from a cartridge case, which ruptured near the base, to blow the breech open violently. The Mark III Snider had an effective catch fitted. The Mark I unmodified Snider is rare–it can be identified by the fact that there are no markings on the breech at all–and it has, amongst other early features, a rounded section countersink for the early brass Pottet style cartridge base; later models all have a squarish section countersink for the squared iron cartridge base adopted on 29 November 1866.

By February 1867, 150,000 Snider conversions had been completed for the British Army, by 1869 it was being said officially that the success of the arm exceeded 'the most sanguine expectation'. Snider, unfortunately, did not live to see this success and indeed at the time of his death had received only £1,000 of the £2,700 he claimed: in the end the authorities relented and paid the balance to his widow in November 1869. The Snider breech mechanism with the Snider-Boxer cartridge gave the 0·577 in Pattern 1853 Enfield rifle, and its many associated models in carbine length, a new lease of life. It was not, however, even at the time the competition was launched, regarded as anything more than a stand-by measure whilst a more perfect, entirely new arm was produced. The success of the Snider complicated the task of the authorities in finding a successor. Their first attempt to launch a new competition completely floundered. Some makers felt slighted over the Snider, others, with justice, accused the government of stealing ideas and many were convinced of unfairness somewhere. A new attempt, made in October 1866, looked for quite a high performance and extremely durable single-shot small-bore rifle and offered a £1,000 prize as a main inducement with £600 for the best breech mechanism. There was great interest in Great Britain, Europe and America. By June 1867 109 designs had been submitted.

The most promising rifles in the British trials of 1867 were considered to be the Albini-Braendlin, Burton 1 and 2, Fosbery, Henry, Joslyn, Martini, Peabody and Remington. All failed to measure up to the exacting specification that had been laid down but the best was found to be the Scottish Henry. Heavy charges and loads of two and three bullets eliminated the American Joslyn and Remington but the Peabody was sunk by the non-arrival of the correct ammunition from America. Martini's rifle impressed the committee who believed it was hamstrung by inferior ammunition as well as plagued by the French authorities who held it up on its way from Switzerland. It was not, however, an entirely bad start for the Martini and in the new trials of 1868 it began to move ahead.

Perhaps the most interesting aspect of these British tests was the clash between block and bolt systems. Of the bolt actions tried most could be induced to malfunction with bad ammunition and quite dangerously too. One of the adjudicating committee members, Sir Henry Halford, suffered a severe hand injury at Wimbledon in 1867 through the premature explosion of a hypersensitive cartridge in a bolt-action rifle. Thus though the Carter & Edwards bolt-action rifle could not be faulted mechanically, and put up a most creditable overall performance, it was condemned for the sins of its class. The committee felt they could look only at the block actions and this soon meant either the Martini or the Henry. Westley Richards' block-action rifle was, for some obscure reason, withdrawn by its designer and there were no other serious rivals. The Martini rifle, made at Enfield, triumphed. It had less parts, was of simpler form and eliminated the old side-lock which was felt to be somewhat vulnerable to seizure in very damp conditions. There was very little in it in fact: as late as 1874 the Martini-Henry might have been superseded by one of its immediate rivals but, somehow, it was not. It was an interesting weapon in many respects, breaking new ground with many features but by no means brilliant in basic conception.

It was, first, a small bore of 0·45 in calibre and had a rifling of Henry's design. Basically this was of a shallow seven-grooved type, which he patented in 1860; it fired a bottle-necked rolled-brass cartridge loaded with a heavy, 480 grain, hardened lead bullet. The recoil was punishing, though the bullet's muzzle velocity scarcely beat 1,300 ft/s. By the standards of 1870 it was, however, accurate, unless the comparison is made against Metford's military breech-loaders. Martini's breech action consisted of a block pivoted laterally at its rear end which, in its upper position, closed the breech so that a striker in it could impact the centrefire cartridge and, at its lower or open position, provided a loading platform and guide for the cartridge. The block was opened and closed by a long lever hinged laterally immediately to the rear of the trigger-guard. A sharp downwards motion on this lever lowered the block, cocked the striker within it, and actuated, by its bell-crank design, an extractor ejector. On the right side of the action there was a cocking indicator but production versions of the Martini-Henry have no safety of any kind, not even in half-cock position. It was quite revolutionary that a coiled spring was employed with the striker, and the divided stock also had many opponents; but the earliest difficulties that were encountered with it concerned the trigger mechanism. It was soon found that sand could lodge in the bent and prevent safe sear engagement. If the rifle did not discharge itself as the breech was closed, the trigger was hair set. So dangerous was the Martini-Henry in its early years that troops on service in Ireland were not allowed to carry their rifles loaded. In Parliament the Lords condemned it but the Commons decided to put up with it and it remained.

Today, from the collector's angle, any officially made British Martini with a non-standard length lever, safety-catch or long action for the early pre-bottleneck cartridge is rare, whilst even the later Enfield-made general issue rifle, regardless of its very minor mark changes, is scarce since most of these rifles were later converted into ·303 Martini-Enfields.

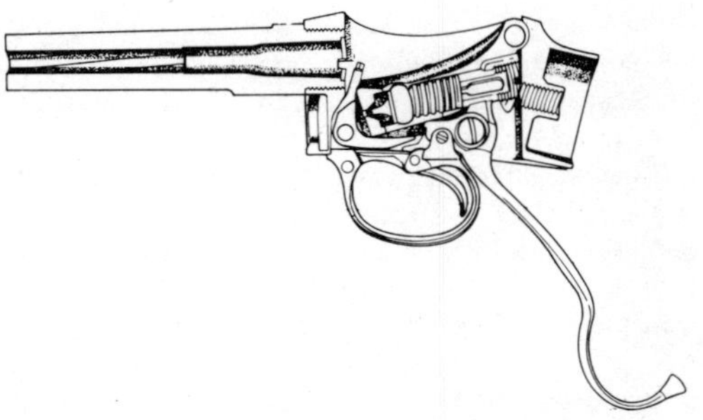

An instructional cut-away of the Martini action, showing the action of lever and breech-block and the location of the firing pin. RSAF Enfield.

In terms of military rifle breech-mechanisms the coincidence of the adoption of the Martini and the Mauser in 1871 is one of considerable fascination. The basic idea behind the Martini action was very sound though in its detailed design, as has been seen, it was poorly conceived. The internal layout of the Martini lock was about the worst that could have been devised to facilitate extraction and ejection, a fact which was not to pass unnoticed by the British army in Egypt a few years later. In Westley Richards's version of the Martini an improved lock arrangement, outwardly almost undetectable, entirely overcame these problems but it was too late for the British authorities, though not entirely so for Westley Richards himself. He was able to claim part responsibility for the action and shared with Martini the royalties obtained from the Martini. It is not, however, the detail of the Martini lock which is really relevant in this context. What is significant is that the British army in 1871 adopted a breech-loading mechanism that was almost impossible to convert into a repeating or magazine arm whereas the Prussians had chosen a design eminently suitable for conversion.

When placed against the background of international arms development the British choice seems even stranger. The Swiss had been officially manufacturing the magazine rifle known as the Vetterli since 1867 although it took them some years to go into anything approaching quantity production. The Austrians had adopted, in 1869, a bolt-action tube-magazine rifle of Fruhwirth's pattern for their gendarmerie while from America there was plenty of evidence of the military potential of the magazine rifle in such arms as the Henry and the Winchester. In addition, the American Spencer repeater, which had made such a reputation for itself in the American Civil War, had been tried, admittedly unofficially, by units in the British army in Canada. Yet the British authorities, usually so concerned not to concede anything in the military effectiveness of their equipment that they could not, for example, shorten a rifle without what amounted to a tacit international agreement that the other great powers (particularly France) would do likewise, shut their eyes to the future. The only conclusion that can be drawn is that they placed an absurd degree of significance on a premature explosion which occurred to Sir Henry Halford when firing an experimental bolt-action breech-loader.

The 11 mm bolt action rifle which Mauser supplied to the Prussian government from 1872 marked a far greater step forward in development from the Dreyse needle rifle than the 1898 Mauser did. The Model 71 Mauser lacked an ejector–but was fitted with a claw-type extractor on the left side of the bolt and also automatic cam cocking, which retracted the firing-pin at the first movement of the bolt, removing the risk of breakage and eliminating the danger of the cartridge being prematurely discharged in the process of feeding and before the breech was closed. The bolt also had a safety-catch incorporated in the cocking-piece. The Model 71, in contrast with the needle rifle had, therefore, a self-cocking, safety centrefire action locked strongly, if not ideally, at the rear by the handle bearing on the receiver. Considerable quantities of this model were manufactured by Mauser's themselves, by the German official manufactories at Erfurt, Amberg, Danzig and Spandau, and by the Austrians at Steyr. So much did the design impress contemporaries that this rifle was sold to China, Japan, Honduras and the Transvaal.

models, had a most distinctive appearance but basically did not materially differ from the simple bolt-type action of the Mauser, Berdan II and other contemporaneous models. The Italians soon initiated experiments to see how their Vetterlis might be adapted for magazine loading. Though they were not very successful and not alone in their quest – the Swiss were also investigating the same problem – they were attempting something unusual. Almost without exception the other European powers were thinking only in terms of single-loading or, at the most, quick-loader attachments to existing arms. For most of the seventies the many nations that had placed their faith in block-type actions had no real cause for alarm.

Austria had the rotating block ·433 Werndl and Bavaria the falling block Werder in service. Norway,

The Dutch Beaumont rifle of 1871 was unique in using a V-spring in the bolt to power the firing pin. RSAF Enfield.

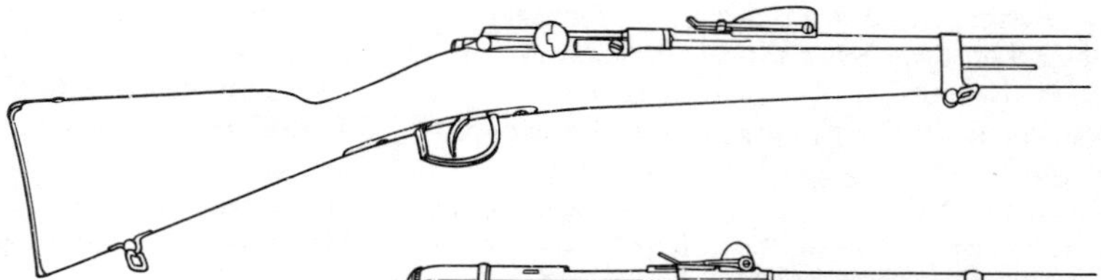

The Swiss Vetterli of 1868 was the first rifle to combine the turnbolt action with the metallic cartridge. It was later adopted by Italy. RSAF Enfield.

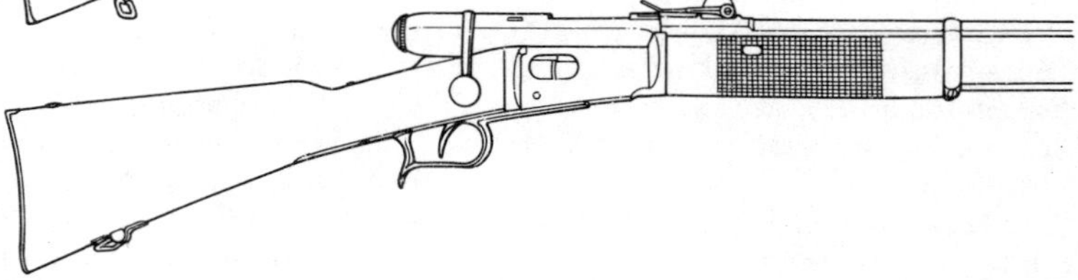

The Franco-Prussian War had been fought with needle rifles on both sides and whatever else it had demonstrated it had shown the superiority of that weapon over the other types available. Prussia was not long in putting her house in order and in 1873 France began to alter the Chassepot to handle centrefire ammunition. In 1874 she went one step further
169 and in the Gras conversion adopted a rifle which at least put her on a parity in armament with Prussia. Other nations were also deciding that the bolt action offered a solution to the problem of finding the best breech action. As early as 1871 Russia and Bulgaria adopted the Berdan II of 0·42 in calibre. Almost at the same time Holland introduced a 0·433 in bolt-action rifle, the Beaumont, in which a V-mainspring was incorporated into the bolt handle in a manner not so dissimilar from that by Norris in 1867 and by Manceaux in 1869. In other respects the design did not significantly differ from that of the 1871 Mauser. Also in 1871, the Italians decided to equip their forces with a 0·408 in centrefire version of the Vetterli. The Vetterli, in both the Swiss and Italian

Sweden, Denmark, Spain and Egypt all opted for the Remington rolling block. Belgium and the United States had not officially advanced beyond a simple turnover-block or trap-door action, the Albini-Braendlin and Springfield respectively. Serbia relied on the falling block Roberts and Turkey and the 0·45 in Peabody-Martini in service. Great Britain, officially at least, so little regretted the choice of the Martini that as late as 1886 her Small Arms Committee felt able to recommend the retention of the Martini modified only by being given a longer lever to aid ejection!

There is, of course, when considering these block actions and, in particular the Martini, Field and others of a similar type, a real danger of anachronistic judgement. The fault of which the British authorities were guilty in the seventies and early eighties was not wrongly judging these block action *vis-à-vis* their contemporary bolt-action rivals but in not foreseeing future developments. The Martini and the Field and similar actions were undoubtedly much superior to contemporary bolt actions in speed and ease of

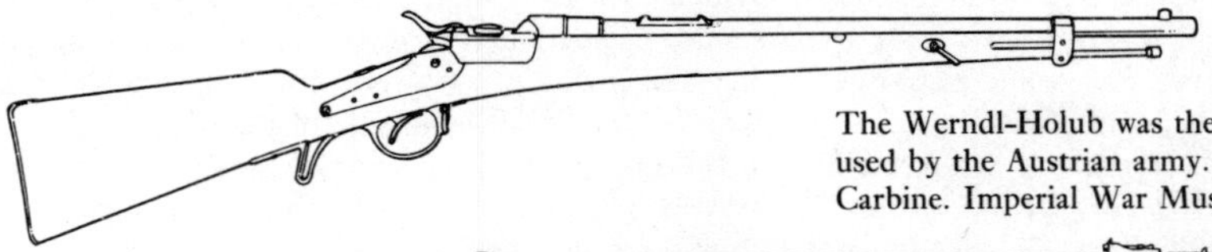

The Werndl-Holub was the last single-shot rifle to be used by the Austrian army. This is the Model 1873/77 Carbine. Imperial War Museum, London.

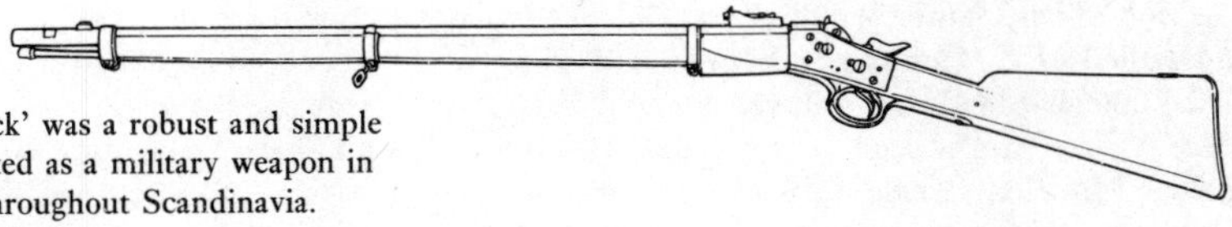

The Remington 'rolling-block' was a robust and simple mechanism which was adopted as a military weapon in Spain, Greece, Egypt and throughout Scandinavia. Imperial War Museum, London.

loading. Not even with clip-charging magazine-loading bolt actions could the rate of fire of the rising block Soper, for example, be exceeded, or even equalled. It has recently been fashionable to cast doubt on the Soper's sixty rounds a minute but this performance is well documented, if one troubles to examine contemporary records. The Soper, which
170 was first patented in 1865, and considered a number of times by the authorities in their search for an improved military action, had a long lease of life. In the seventies it was often used for long range and sporting shooting and was a subject for patented improvements as late as 1877. The Martini's forte was, to a considerable extent, the fact that it loaded so easily. This is the virtue that has enabled it to survive even to the present day in modified form for small-bore target shooting.

In 1877, at the Battle of Plevna, the Turks so convincingly demonstrated the military advantages of a repeater or magazine rifle that most of the great powers began to feel that it was no longer possible to ignore this development. The weapon, which was largely responsible for Russian casualties amounting to about 30,000 men, was the Winchester of 1866. A year later, in 1878, the French reacted to the extent of adopting for their Marines an 11 mm magazine
171 rifle of the Kropatschek pattern with a brass tubular magazine under the barrel of sufficient capacity to accommodate six cartridges. In its bolt action it closely resembled the Gras and a magazine cut-off was fitted so that it could still be used as a single loader. In Great Britain there was no visible reaction. To an extent she could detach herself from the Continental arms race and, understandably, she was in no hurry to add another arm to the list of those already in service which could easily pose serious supply problems in the event of a general war. Of course, she was not alone in this and there had been a period ten to fifteen years earlier when this problem was even more acute. Even so, in 1877, economy, convention, tradition and, perhaps, military efficiency had led (at a time when the Infantry of the Line, Rifle Brigade, Guards, Royal Marines and Royal Navy were armed with the seven-groove 0·45 in, 4 ft $1\frac{1}{2}$ in long, Martini-Henry) to the Militia, Volunteer Corps and some Indian native infantry regiments being equipped with the three-groove 0·577 in, 4 ft 7 in long, Snider-converted long Enfield; to the Royal Marine Artillery, sergeants of Militia and Volunteer Corps and other Indian native infantry regiments using the five-groove 4 ft $\frac{1}{2}$ in long, Snider-converted short Enfield; to the Royal Artillery, Army Service Corps, Militia and Volunteer Artillery having the five-groove 0·577 in, 3 ft $4\frac{1}{2}$ in long, Snider-converted Artillery carbine; to the Cavalry, except the Lancers who still had the old 10 in barrelled muzzle-loading Enfield pistol, carrying the five-groove 0·577 in, 3 ft $\frac{7}{8}$ in long, Snider-converted Cavalry carbine; and to the Royal Engineers employing the oval bore 0·577 in, 3 ft $11\frac{1}{2}$ in long, Snider-converted Lancaster carbine. Admittedly some of these Snider converted weapons were just on the point of being declared obsolete but no one could deny that a situation unfavourable to the introduction of a new pattern arm existed.

A magazine rifle which had a tubular magazine under the barrel, and even one in which it was in the butt, suffered from the not inconsiderable drawback that there was a changing point of balance. This not only made the weapon rather unpleasant to handle but also was bound to give the arm a varying 'zero'. In other words, such a rifle could not have satisfactory long-range performance. In addition, a tubular magazine was not easily loaded in a hurry. It marked, therefore, an important step forward in design when, in 1879, Lee introduced a vertical box-magazine. It was not the first. In British Patent No. 483 of 1867 Walker, Money and Little described a vertical box-magazine beneath the bolt and fastened into the stock in which six cartridges could be placed and from which they would be fed by a 'false bottom pressed upwards by a spiral spring'. In 1873 Rodier and Bates patented a manual lever-loading pistol which contained a similar vertical box-magazine. But nothing seems to have come of these early suggestions of the idea. However, Lee was not the only person seriously in the field. Both Mauser and Mannlicher were also investigating similar magazines, indeed Clark patented in Great Britain for Oesterreichische Waffenfabrik-Gesellschaft a rotary box-magazine, the 'Spitalsky' magazine, in March 1878, fourteen months before Lee applied for his British patent. The rifle which Mauser produced in 1881 for Serbia, and called the Milovanovitch, was still a single loader but in 1884, after an experimental model in 1882, Mauser introduced a tube-magazine version of their Model 1871 rifle. Considerable numbers of this pattern rifle went into service in the German armies and a somewhat similar arm, though with a locking lug as well as the bolt handle to lock the bolt against the receiver, was adopted by the Turks in 1887. It was therefore Mannlicher's privilege to demonstrate to Europe the advantages of a box-magazine and he did not stop there. The logical improvement was the packet, or clip, loading of ammunition and this he introduced in 1885.

The Europe to which Mannlicher demonstrated his new rifle was one remarkably committed to the tube-magazine. Apart from those already mentioned, in 1881 Switzerland had finally officially adopted a tube-magazine Vetterli, whilst as late as 1886 France decided on the Lebel and a year later still Norway and Sweden on the Jarman. When in 1886 Austria adopted a 0·433-in bore Mannlicher she was the first
172 European nation to issue a box-magazine rifle. In America Lee was not in the financial position needed for the power salesmanship of his box-magazine rifle but his 1879 rifle did achieve a limited market. It was not until 1888, however, that Lee really achieved full success with his magazine, when Great Britain adopted it for her new rifle.

Mannlicher had had a wide experience of different forms of military magazine rifles when, in 1886, his country adopted his arm. In his model of 1880 he had introduced a remarkable multi-tube butt-magazine arm. This had three tubes united to form a single rotating unit with a total capacity of fifteen cartridges. In succession, therefore, the operation of the bolt feed fed one cartridge from each of the three tubes. Loading was accomplished through the open action. There was another version of this rifle, for the German Mauser 71 cartridge which had four magazine tubes giving it a 20-round capacity. In 1881 Mannlicher produced a box-magazine rifle of a remarkably advanced design. It had a long, detachable, vertical, but raked, box-magazine beneath the action. The rake served the very essential purpose of ensuring that there could be no jams through the rim of the upper cartridge overlapping that of the round below it. The bolt was of two-piece construction with distinct and diametrically opposed locking lugs near its rear end. The next year saw a rifle launched which had a similar, though somewhat simplified, bolt but with a tubular magazine under the barrel in the fore-end. The same basic rifle design was also produced in 1882 with a gravity-feed box-magazine attached to the upper right hand side of the receiver. Such a magazine had an obvious advantage in that it could be kept 'topped up' with the minimum trouble to the firer, even if there was trouble when the laws of gravity were defied. Mannlichers were not the only magazine rifles of rather exotic specification–there are many fascinating experimental arms in existence of Martini-type fitted with somewhat similar magazines–and no coverage of the magazine arms of this period would be complete without a mention of the Austrian Schulhof of 1882 in which almost the entire interior of the butt was devoted to a cartridge magazine of very considerable capacity.

In 1884, in the same year that Germany was re-arming with the tube-magazine Mauser 71/84, Mannlicher introduced an entirely new bolt-action rifle. It was of a straight-pull type. By this is implied that the operation of opening and closing the breech was accomplished by a straight pull and push on the bolt handle. The bolt was made in two pieces, with the rear of the front section moving inside the hollow front of the rear section. The lugs, which actually lock the breech, were at the rear of the front portion of the bolt and thus some way back from the breech. The portion of the front section which fitted inside the rear section of the bolt was cut with helical or curved grooves and the interior of the sleeve of the rear section in which it was contained had matching helical ribs. Pulling back on the bolt handle at first moved the rear of the bolt without the front section, then the helical ribs and grooves engaged and the front section rotated 90° anti-clockwise to free its locking lugs. The striker was cocked in much the same manner, and held cocked by the rear of the trigger mechanism engaging the bent, as in conventional turn bolt actions. The 1884 Mannlicher was also remarkable for its improved, detachable, gravity-feed magazine. Probably the main reason for this rifle's lack of success was that it was chambered for an odd type of cartridge which tended to give trouble when pulled straight back without primary extraction.

In 1885 Mannlicher produced a new rifle of great importance and interest in that it was the first to use a clip-charging system for the magazine though of a different type from that which, introduced in the 1886 model, was to become one of the stock features of the Mannlicher. In this 1885 model a spring-loaded lever threw the clip upwards and out of the weapon on the bolt being opened after the last cartridge had been fired; in the 1886 model the floor of the magazine was in part cut away so that the clip dropped through it when the last round had been expended. The 1885 Mannlicher employed an extraordinary

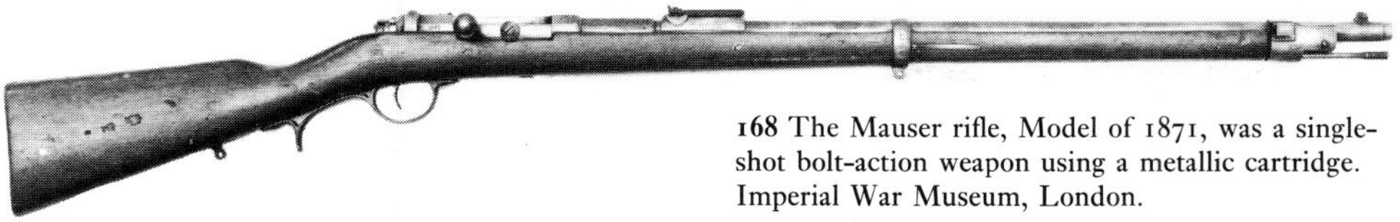

168 The Mauser rifle, Model of 1871, was a single-shot bolt-action weapon using a metallic cartridge. Imperial War Museum, London.

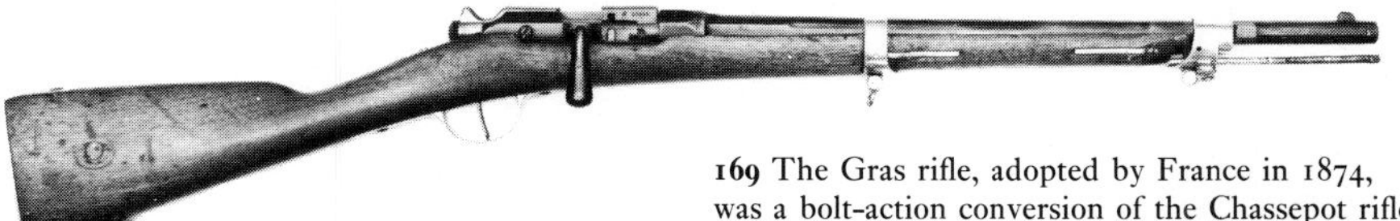

169 The Gras rifle, adopted by France in 1874, was a bolt-action conversion of the Chassepot rifle, using a metallic cartridge. Imperial War Museum, London.

170 The Soper rifle of 1866; the thumb-lever opens the breech and ejects the spent cartridge. RSAF, Enfield.

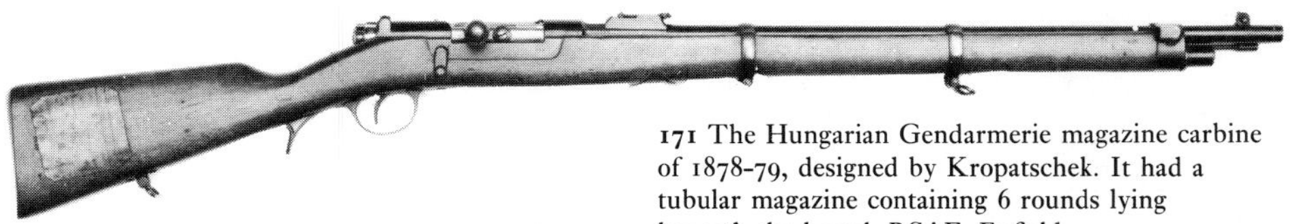

171 The Hungarian Gendarmerie magazine carbine of 1878-79, designed by Kropatschek. It had a tubular magazine containing 6 rounds lying beneath the barrel. RSAF, Enfield.

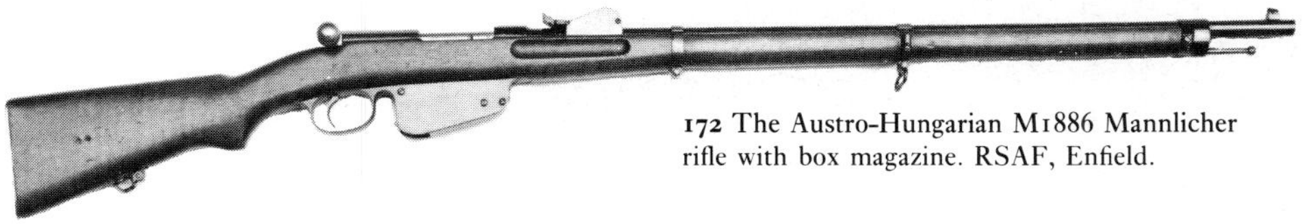

172 The Austro-Hungarian M1886 Mannlicher rifle with box magazine. RSAF, Enfield.

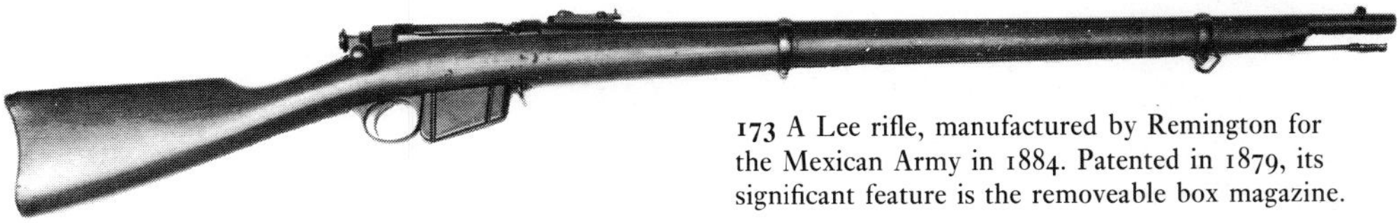

173 A Lee rifle, manufactured by Remington for the Mexican Army in 1884. Patented in 1879, its significant feature is the removeable box magazine.

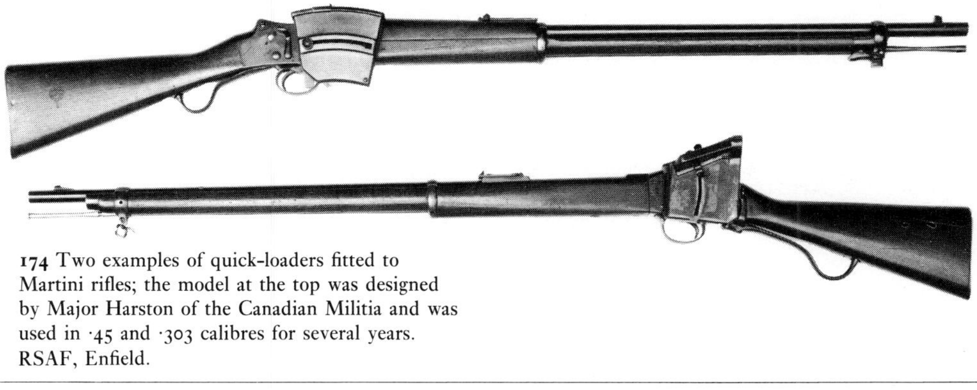

174 Two examples of quick-loaders fitted to Martini rifles; the model at the top was designed by Major Harston of the Canadian Militia and was used in ·45 and ·303 calibres for several years. RSAF, Enfield.

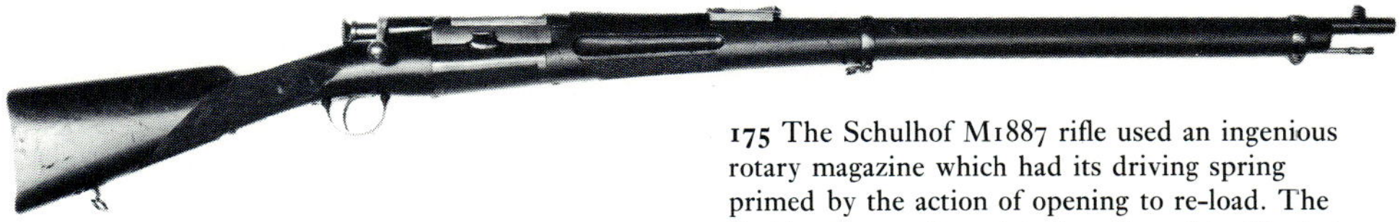

175 The Schulhof M1887 rifle used an ingenious rotary magazine which had its driving spring primed by the action of opening to re-load. The Serbian Army planned to introduce this rifle, but abandoned it as too complicated for field service. RSAF Enfield.

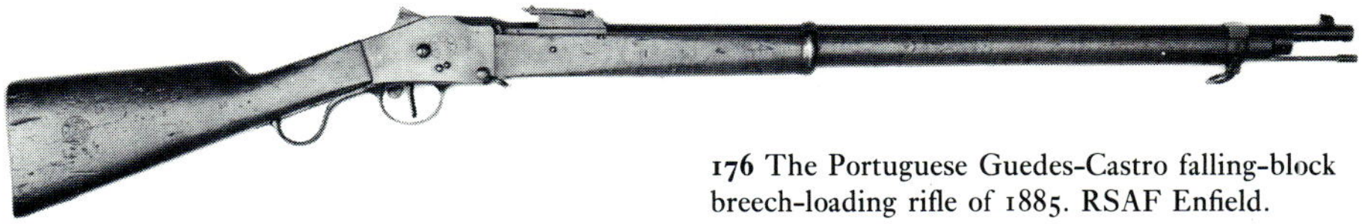

176 The Portuguese Guedes-Castro falling-block breech-loading rifle of 1885. RSAF Enfield.

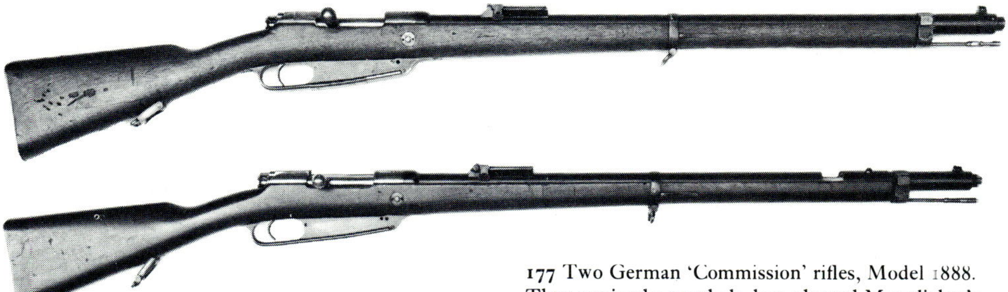

177 Two German 'Commission' rifles, Model 1888. They retained a turnbolt, but adopted Mannlicher's clip loading system. RSAF Enfield.

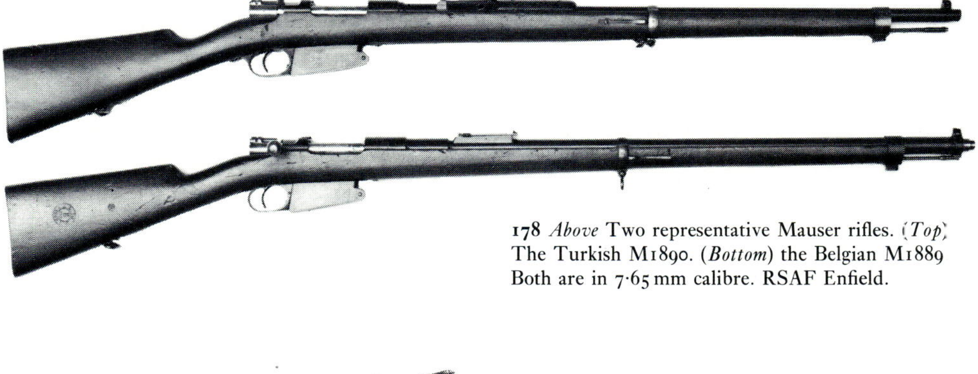

178 *Above* Two representative Mauser rifles. (*Top*) The Turkish M1890. (*Bottom*) the Belgian M1889 Both are in 7·65 mm calibre. RSAF Enfield.

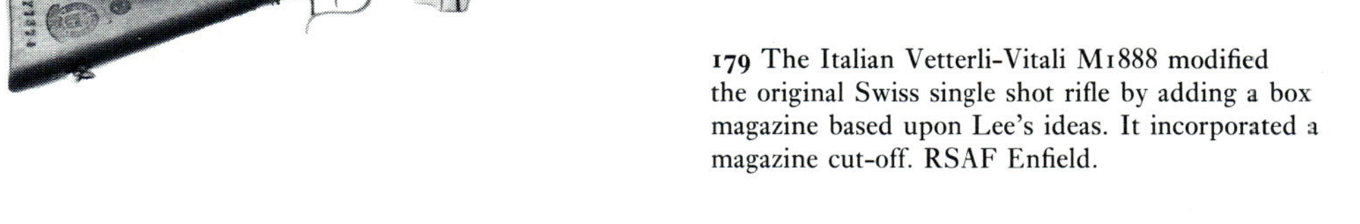

179 The Italian Vetterli-Vitali M1888 modified the original Swiss single shot rifle by adding a box magazine based upon Lee's ideas. It incorporated a magazine cut-off. RSAF Enfield.

form of two-piece straight-pull bolt with a hinged locking block on its underside. The locking block was so attached that it could be forced to move up or down by the action of inclined ribs formed on a wedge-shaped block integral with the bolt handle. At its lowermost point of travel the locking block engaged in a recess cut in the receiver. When the bolt was fully withdrawn the locking block was cammed right up clear of the receiver. The two-stage movement of the bolt in part, at least, compensated for there being no equivalent of primary extraction, as resulting from the cam action of a turning bolt being moved upwards, but this was an undesirable state of affairs in a bolt which was locked only on one side by a single lug. It was not a question of safety but one of unbalanced strain and erratic vibration impairing accuracy. However, the action worked well enough for it to be adopted in the 1886 pattern Mannlicher, which was that officially adopted by Austria in 11 mm calibre. These clip-loaded Mannlichers could not, by their construction, utilise a magazine platform sprung upwards by a coil or W-spring. They relied instead on a spring lever which bore directly on the underside of the bottom cartridge and which, rising between the sides of the clip, continued to bear on the bottom round until the magazine was empty. The clip was prevented from rising by a catch at the back of the magazine cutaway. The limited depth of the magazine meant that only five cartridges could be accommodated but with the new clip this was not the disadvantage it would earlier have been. This rifle, which survived in Austrian service for many years, in fact until the end of the First World War, was 52 in in overall length, weighed 9 lb 15 oz and had a 31·7 in barrel, rifled clockwise with six grooves on a pitch of one turn in 28·4 in.

Mannlicher's apparent preoccupation with spring box- or tube-magazines did not mean that he had abandoned the idea of a rotating-box type. In his model of 1887, which used the bolt action of his 1882 tube-magazine arm, he developed this style magazine to quite a level of efficiency. It was the first of the later famous Mannlicher-Schoenauer and, like later models of this type, had a release catch to allow the cartridge-separating drum centrepiece to revolve to empty the magazine rapidly, but comparatively few rifles of this model were made. In 1888 he produced a rifle which combined this rotatory magazine with the 1884 straight-pull action and, remarkably, managed to provide a clip loading facility.

Although Mannlicher spent so much time exploring various combinations of bolt style and magazine type, not one of his arms made before 1888 had a forward-locking bolt. This was important since it is the only really satisfactory way of guaranteeing that, on firing, the breech is secure and the cartridge does not move back appreciably. Meanwhile other manufacturers and experimentalists were also facing the problems that stood in the way of designing a really efficient military rifle. The principal limitation was that of the propellant. Black powder could be compressed and fairly high velocities achieved but nothing could be done to reduce the smoke it produced in burning. In 1870, when the Soper was fired at a rate of sixty rounds a minute, it was observed that the target was visible only for the first ten or a dozen shots. It was difficult, therefore, to see how the effectiveness of fire could match its rapidity. Moreover, because of the smoke from black powder, there was no chance of those who first opened fire in action concealing their positions from the enemy.

Attempts to find a substitute for black powder for blasting and general explosive use had been going on for decades. In 1846 Schonbein reported that a nitrated cotton burnt without smoke and appeared to have properties which might permit its use in small arms. France appointed a commission to look into the discovery and the other great European powers also put similar investigations in hand. Curiously, a further step forward by a Brunswicker, Dr Hartig, in 1847, for all its promising nature came to nothing as did most other attempts except that of a Captain Schultz in Berlin who, in about 1864, discovered an excellent smokeless powder for shotguns. It was not suitable for use in rifles and neither was anything else that was tried until Volkmann, about 1870, patented a powder called *Collodin*. But for the closure of his works in 1875 by the Austrian government to protect their official monopoly in the manufacture of gunpowder he might have been the first to succeed. As it was, in 1884, a French chemist named Vielle produced the first successful rifle nitrocellulose powder. His second type, designated *Poudre B*, became the first smokeless powder to be adopted by any power. France was not slow to turn the discovery to her advantage. In 1886 she became the first country to issue a small-bore, high-velocity rifle to her forces.

The Lebel was less remarkable in other respects than it was for its 8 mm (0·315 in) calibre and remarkable long-range performance. It was an eight-round capacity tube-magazine rifle, 4 ft 3 in long, weighing 9 lb $3\frac{1}{2}$ oz. The barrel was $31\frac{1}{2}$ in long and rifled with four shallow concentric grooves on a left-hand spiral of one turn in 10 in (30 calibres equivalent). The bolt was of the normal turning type but remarkable for the fact that the locking lugs were on the bolt head as close to the base of the cartridge as they could be placed. In this respect the Lebel also broke new ground. The Lebel's small calibre, and its remarkable velocity, were the consequences of the adoption of the new *Poudre B*. Not only was this smokeless but it was far more powerful than black powder. Less powder

The French Lebel of 1886 combined small calibre with smokeless powder. Imperial War Museum, London.

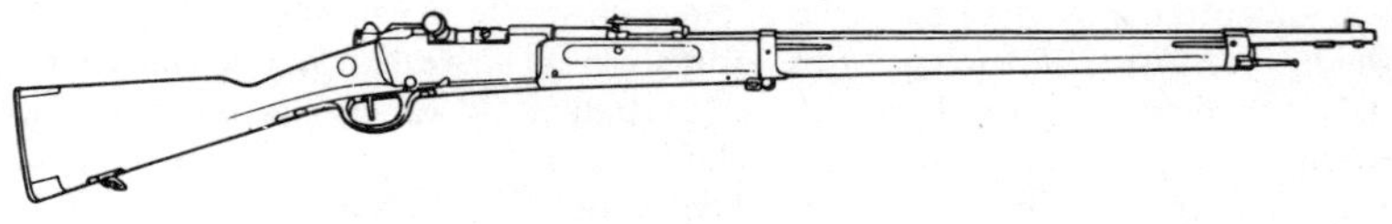

by volume produced very much more power so that the French were able to reduce the calibre and thus lighten the ammunition. The soldier was therefore able to carry more ammunition, and what he had was effective at ranges far beyond the maximum previously thought possible. France had, by this move, definitely regained from Germany the lead in arms design.

The French were not long allowed their lead. Other powders with similar properties were soon available. In 1888 Nobel began the production of *ballistite*, which was a compound nitroglycerine/nitrocellulose powder. The British Explosives Committee were not blind to Nobel's work and experimented with nitroglycerine and acetone as a solvent for guncotton though they did not, as did Nobel, use camphor to harden the grain since changes in the ballistic properties of the powder were an undesirable by-product. As a stabilising and anti-fouling additive they included a little vaseline. Although there were serious deficiencies in much *cordite* (as the British powder came to be known) of early manufacture these problems were ironed out and an excellent powder of remarkable stability, giving superb shooting, ultimately resulted. It did however have, and still has, one grave disadvantage as compared with nitrocellulose powder–the flame generated by the burning powder rapidly eroded the bore. Even today the number of rounds that can be fired through a British service rifle barrel without erosion likely to impair target accuracy appreciably amounts only to a few hundred. But a discussion of cordite and its properties is, in terms of the development of the British army's rifle, somewhat premature since it was not introduced until 1891.

The introduction of the Lebel into France in 1886 at last struck a responsive note with the Naval authorities. They had for some years been urging the need for a magazine rifle. The British Small Arms Committee from 1883 had had within its terms of reference the duty to consider 'the desirability or otherwise of introducing a magazine rifle for naval or military use, or both'. The committee examined many rifles, including quite a number of foreign origin, but only three were deemed to merit extensive trial. They were, the Lee magazine rifle, an improved Lee rifle with a Bethel Burton magazine mounted high on the upper right hand side of the receiver, and the Owen Jones magazine rifle. All three rifles were, in the 1885 trials, fitted with 0·45 in calibre Henry barrels: only the two Lee rifles survived into the 1887 trials and for them they were fitted with 0·402 in Metford barrels. The committee decided in favour of the Lee with Lee's magazine. While matters were at this point news came in that the Swiss had reduced the calibre of their rifle still further, to 7·5 mm. Already the new British choice of calibre, the 0·402, looked more of a large than small bore. It was decided to reduce the calibre again. Though there was as yet no British smokeless powder available 0·303 in calibre was selected and William Metford laid down the detailed form, measurements and tolerances for the rifling, lead and chamber. Thus, quite early in 1888, 350 rifles of a type soon to be known as the Lee-Metford, with Lee's action and magazine and Metford's shallow segmental rifling was issued for troop trials. The ammunition on which the new weapon relied also owed much to foreign designers.

The only way to long-range performance and, in particular, to a flatter trajectory was by increasing velocity. A flatter trajectory had the obvious military advantage that errors in estimating distances were of less importance and that the area under effective fire at any one sight setting was larger. But at a muzzle velocity of about 1,800 ft/s the surface of a lead bullet, even if alloyed and paper wrapped, begins to melt when fired. With the type of compressed black powder charge adopted for the Lee-Metford a velocity of about 1,850 ft/s was attainable. The only way in which more power could be harnessed was by jacketing the bullet. The idea of plating or coating a lead bullet with metal was not new, as a glance through the records of the British Ordnance Select Committee for the 1860s will confirm, but the reason for which it had normally been done in the past was to remove the risk of the surface of the lead oxidising seriously under poor storage conditions. In 1875 a Swiss, Major Bode, produced a design for a bullet jacketed to accept higher velocities but the real advance was made in 1881 when another Swiss, Major Rubin, Director of the Government Laboratory, produced a copper-jacketed bullet able to withstand not only the effects of high velocity but also the very considerable torque associated with the steep rifling pitch of a smaller-bore weapon. This latter requirement stemmed from the fact that in a reduced-bore rifle the weight of the projectile could only be kept at a reasonably heavy level by increasing its length. If the bullet did not have sufficient weight, velocity would fall off rapidly and there would be no acceptable long-range performance. But a long, heavy bullet could only be kept stable by imparting to it a considerably higher speed of rotation than was necessary in the older type of rifle. Rubin was not content to stop with the ammunition. He went on, in 1883, a year ahead of Mannlicher, to design a straight-pull bolt-action rifle with a detachable, vertical box-magazine. In spite of its merit (it was in a later form adopted by the Swiss) it was rejected, and Portugal in the Steyr, Austrian-made 0·315 in calibre Guedes-Castro single-loaders became the first nation to use the Rubin jacketed small-bore bullet. Portugal had therefore in 1885 the curious distinction of being at once the country to adopt the last block action militarily accepted and the first to employ a compound bullet. In Great Britain Metford and Halford were keenly aware of Rubin's work and its importance in what they were trying to induce their authorities to do. In some of their earliest experimental 0·303 in compound bullets there was still a tendency for the surface of the lead to melt, in spite of the jacket. However, they increased the thickness of the jacket and, in February 1889, the first government 0·303 in compressed black powder cartridge was officially introduced. It was loaded with $71\frac{1}{2}$ grains of powder and the bullet with a nickel jacket, except over its base, weighed 13·9 grams (215 grains). It was felt that the exposure of the lead core at the base was an aid to the setting up or expansion of the bullet and permitted the use of a bullet smaller than the diameter of the barrel taken from groove to groove. The cordite round, which came in in 1891, had a similar bullet but with a cupro-nickel jacket and a muzzle velocity of 1,970 ft/s.

Great Britain in 1888 had chosen to overlook the excellent clip-loading designs of Mannlicher, and
172 had ignored the forward locking feature of the Lebel. In 1886 Austria had rather surprisingly preferred Mannlicher's rather awkward hinged locking-block, straight-pull action to his excellent, if conventional, turning-bolt design and in 1888 she perpetuated her choice by issuing an 8 mm small-bore version of the 1886 rifle. Until 1890 a compressed black powder charge was used, giving a muzzle velocity of about 1,750 ft/s, with the introduction of a nitrocellulose powder this went up to 2,035 ft/s. The 8 mm barrel was, at 38·9 in, fractionally longer than that of the 1886 model. It was rifled with a clockwise twist of one turn in 9·84 in. But, for all its theoretical drawbacks, this rifle proved sufficiently attractive also to be adopted officially by the Bulgarians and Greeks.

The year 1888 also saw the issue of a German small-bore rifle. The lead that France had taken in 1886 was not long allowed to remain. A German Army Commission was specially charged with the production of a suitable rifle. Mauser himself was so tied up with a large Turkish contract for his model 1887 rifle that he was not in a position to thrust his services on the Commission and they did not consult him. On the whole the Commission looked more to Mannlicher's models for general construction, though they adopted a modified form of the Mauser 71/84 bolt. In one important respect, however, the bolt differed from those previously used by Mauser: it had forward-locking lugs. The box-magazine was very like that of the Mannlicher and was designed for clip loading with the discarding of the clip through the partly cut away bottom of the magazine. The cartridge for which the rifle was designed was a rimless 7·9 mm one, inspired by Rubin's demonstrations of the practical advantages of this style of case; the bullet had a nickel steel jacket and the charge was, of course, of smokeless nitrocellulose powder. The neck shape of the cartridge case was well designed, not too abrupt in its bottleneck form which would have made manufacture difficult, and yet sufficiently pronounced to ensure a positive head space location, for, with a rimless case, one gained the advantage of avoiding jams through rims locking together at the expense of not having a rim to give precise head space. The Commission rifle, which measured 48·8 in overall and which weighed 8·4 lb, was fitted with a 29·1 in barrel rifled clockwise with four grooves making one turn in 9·45 in. In external appearance perhaps the most distinctive feature was the tubular barrel jacket, which protruded from the top band (at the upper end of the fore-end) almost to the muzzle. The rifle was manufactured widely, by most of the German official manufactories, by the Austrian Steyr arsenal on contract for the Germans, by a number of outside German firms including Haenel, Schuler, Loewe and Schilling and by the Belgian firm of Schriever. A carbine version was mechanically identical but measured only 37·4 in overall and was stocked virtually to the muzzle. It is not difficult to see from this description that, in adopting this rifle, the Germans had once more taken the lead internationally in the armament of their infantry. All that others could do was to try to catch up.

The adoption of the Commission 88 rifle did not deter Mauser from continuing the improvement of his own rifle. In 1888 he submitted a box-magazine 7·65 mm calibre rifle to Belgian trials but it was with the rifle with which he replaced it in 1889 in the same trials that he really improved on the Commission 88 design. This rifle had a forward-locking, one-piece bolt and introduced a new system of charger loading.

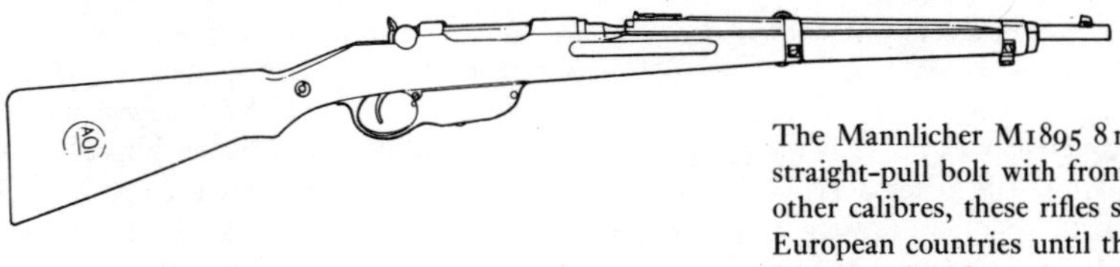

The Mannlicher M1895 8 mm calibre rifle used a straight-pull bolt with front locking lugs. Converted to other calibres, these rifles stayed in use in many European countries until the late 1940s. Imperial War Museum, London.

Mannlicher's clip system had been open to the objection that if the clip was bent or corroded it might be very difficult to load. With the Mauser charger the rounds were stripped, by a single movement of the thumb, straight into the magazine from the charger as it was gripped in a guide on the receiver bridge. The Mauser magazine therefore scored over the Mannlicher in that the bottom of the magazine was closed against the entry of dirt and water, and in that it could at any convenient time be topped up with loose rounds. The rifle was adopted by Belgium in 1889 and manufactured by Fabrique Nationale at Herstal and at the Belgian state manufactory in Liège. It was not produced by Mauser themselves, although it was in the First World War, by Hopkins & Allen of America and by a Belgian refugee factory in Birmingham, England. This rifle was 4 ft $2\frac{1}{4}$ in overall, weighed 8 lb $\frac{1}{2}$ oz, and had a 30·67 in barrel rifled with four grooves on a right-hand spiral making one turn in 9·842 in. The rimless 7·65 mm cartridge was loaded with 37 grains of a nitroglycerine/nitrocellulose powder and the bullet, which weighed 219 grains attained a muzzle velocity of 2,034 ft/s. Outwardly the most distinctive characteristic of the model was, perhaps, the forward bulge in the lower front of the magazine. Two carbine versions of the model were produced, one markedly shorter than the other. In 1916 a further, and somewhat modified, 1889 carbine was introduced.

In 1890 Turkey invoked the clause in her contract with Mauser which entitled her to claim the completion of the balance of her massive order of 1887, for 500,000 rifles and 50,000 carbines, in the last pattern introduced. Although part of the order had gone to Ludwig Loewe & Co. Mauser's found themselves in the end producing 280,000 rifles and carbines to a pattern known as the 1890 Turkish. This was an improved version of the Belgian model of 1889. The main improvement lay in the abandonment of the long, outer metal barrel handguard. The barrel had frequently started to rust inside the metal tube handguard but the principal objection to this type of guard was that, when damaged by rough handling, the barrel itself could be subjected to sideways pressure, which inevitably shifted the shooting zero and often impaired accuracy. There was no denying the need for a handguard – rapid fire with high velocity could soon heat the barrel to a very high temperature – so there was no alternative but to adopt a short wooden guard. As the heat generated in firing could appreciably expand the barrel lengthwise and disturb the bedding of a taper barrel nicely fitted into a wooden stock the exterior of the barrel was given a stepped outer contour with the necessary relief in the stock just ahead of each step – a feature which was retained on later models. A number of other detailed improvements were also made to the action and sights.

Mannlicher, in 1890, brought out a straight-pull rotatory action with forward-locking lugs not so unlike his 1884 model. The weapon to which it was fitted was a cavalry carbine and had what was by then the standard Mannlicher clip-loaded vertical box-magazine. An extremely similar Mannlicher carbine was adopted by the Swiss in 1894 for their cavalry, but it used a special Swiss designed box-magazine and clip. This straight-pull action was finally brought to its highest level of efficiency in his model of 1895. The 1895 rifle, which was extremely similar in mechanical detail to the 1890 carbine, was widely adopted. It was issued as the standard Austrian military rifle and was still that country's main infantry armament in the First World War: Bulgaria and Greece also made it their standard rifle. By the use of better quality steel the total weight of the arm was about $1\frac{3}{4}$ lb less than that of the previous model. Overall it measured 4 ft 2 in and was fitted with a 30·12 in barrel, rifled with four grooves on a clockwise spiral making one turn in 9·842 in. The calibre was 8 mm, the cartridge was rimmed, and the steel-jacketed bullet, which weighed 244 grains/$\frac{1}{2}$ oz, reached a muzzle velocity, driven by $42\frac{1}{2}$ grains of nitrocellulose powder, of 2,034 ft/s. The magazine, which was the usual fixed vertical box of Mannlicher type, held five cartridges and was clip loaded. Perhaps the most distinctive outer characteristic of the rifle and action was the curving spur-like upward extension to the cocking-piece which, incidentally, allowed instant manual re-cocking of the action for a second attempt in the event of a misfire. It is worthy of note that, in this comparatively refined form of straight pull action, primary extraction, earlier a difficulty with this type of action, was achieved by the cam shape of the end of the recesses in the receiver in which the bolt locking-lugs engaged.

The Italians, who had in 1887 added a fixed verti-
179 cal box-magazine to their Vetterlis to create the Vetterli-Vitali chambered for a 10·4 mm centrefire cartridge, in 1891 adopted the Carcano. This rifle, which is often loosely called a Mannlicher and which
180 was the standard Italian rifle in the First World War, and for long after, was actually more a Mauser. The breech action was a Mauser with forward-locking lugs modified by Paraviccini and Carcano at Turin; the magazine was of Mannlicher type and the split receiver was of modified Mannlicher design. A 36·2 in long carbine version, sometimes with a folding bayonet as a permanent feature, was also produced. The rifle was chambered for a 0·256 in (6·5 mm) rimless cartridge in which a charge of 30 grains of *ballistite* imparted a muzzle velocity of 2,395 ft/s to its 163 grain cupro-nickel jacketed bullet. In one respect only could it be said that the Carcano was inadequate and that was in a point of safety. The firing-pin and striker was retained in the bolt by a single small lug. If the cap was ruptured by the striker there was a possibility, even if remote, that this lug might yield to the force of escaping gases and the firer be injured by the separated bolt component. The rifle's overall length was 4 ft $2\frac{3}{4}$ in and, at 8 lb $6\frac{1}{2}$ oz, it was only an ounce heavier than the 1895 Austrian Mannlicher. The $30\frac{3}{4}$ in barrel was clockwise, progressively, rifled with four grooves starting at a pitch of one turn in $19\frac{1}{4}$ in and culminating at the muzzle in one of one in $8\frac{1}{4}$ in. This idea of progressive rifling was by no means new, Metford was a staunch champion of it. He claimed that it eliminated any tendency for the bullet to strip, imparting as it did 'equal increments in rotation in equal times'. Metford's contribution to military rifles has already been noted. In the 1870s his rifles established a reputation of being unbeatable in their shooting qualities. He was not a person to rest on his laurels and kept himself abreast of developments both in America and on the Continent. He soon assimilated the discoveries of Vielle and Rubin and continued to lay down vital specifications for rifling, interior barrel dimensions and cartridges. Concentric rifling itself, which most of the powers adopted, was of his design though his name became more closely attached to his system of segmentally grooved rifling. Great Britain was not alone in her choice of this system. Denmark also adopted it, though with a nitrocellulose loaded cartridge, in the 1889 Krag-Jørgensen and Japan in her Year 38 pattern rifle of 1907.

The 1889 Krag was an unusual rifle in more than one respect. The bolt had only one forward-locking lug and the magazine was of a fixed horizontal box design loaded from the right-hand side through a hinged loading gate. Cartridges thus travelled across the width of the rifle beneath the action which they entered from the left-hand side. In spite of its curious design the magazine could be loaded either by charger or with loose rounds. The barrel was encased in an outer tube guard which gave the muzzle an appearance like that of the 1889 Belgian Mauser. At 4 ft $4\frac{3}{4}$ in it was one of the longest military rifles in issue of its period and, for that matter, at 9 lb $11\frac{3}{4}$ oz it was probably the heaviest. It was fitted with a 32·9 in barrel of 8 mm calibre, rifled with six grooves on a right-hand spiral and making one turn in 11·811 in, which, by the standard of the new small-bores, was quite slow. The cartridge it fired was rimmed and loaded with a cupro-nickel jacketed (237 grain) bullet. The propellant was nitrocellulose. Although it is tempting to look from the choice of a single locking-lug for proof of its inadequacy in long-range shooting, it gained a reputation for itself as a good target arm. In 1910 slight modifications, including the addition of a safety-catch, were made but, in one form or another, it remained the Danish service rifle for many decades. The Danes were not the only nation to be attracted by its specification. Norway in 1894 adopted a 6·5 mm rimless version of the Krag-Jørgensen of an appearance very similar to the Danish model, except that there was no barrel outer jacket and a Mauser-type bolt safety was fitted. It, too, in both rifle and carbine form was still in

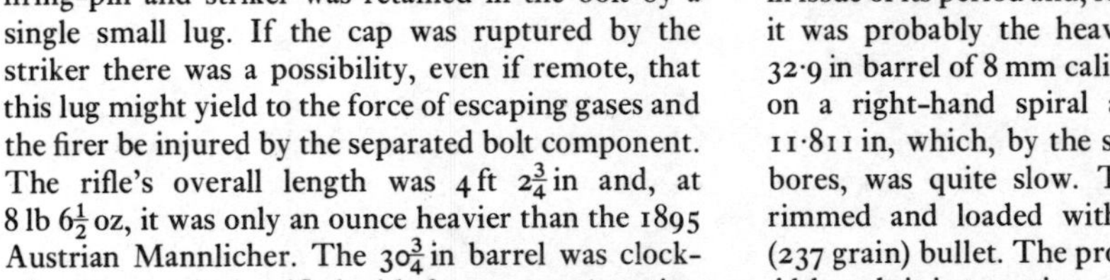

A Danish Krag-Jørgensen sniping rifle, Model of 1928. Notice the extremly heavy barrel, for accuracy, and the side magazine. Smithsonian Institution, Washington, D.C.

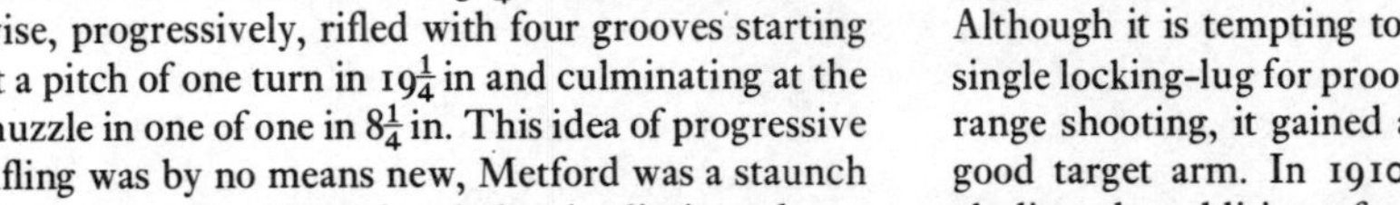

The U.S. Army's Krag-Jørgensen rifle of 1898. Imperial War Museum, London.

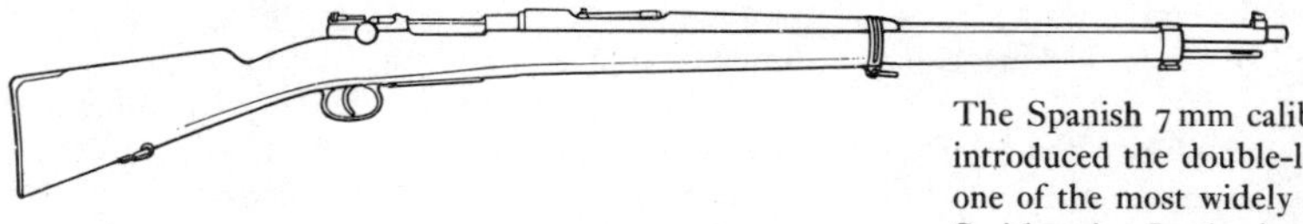

The Spanish 7 mm calibre Mauser M1893 introduced the double-line magazine and became one of the most widely adopted Mauser designs. Smithsonian Institution, Washington, D.C.

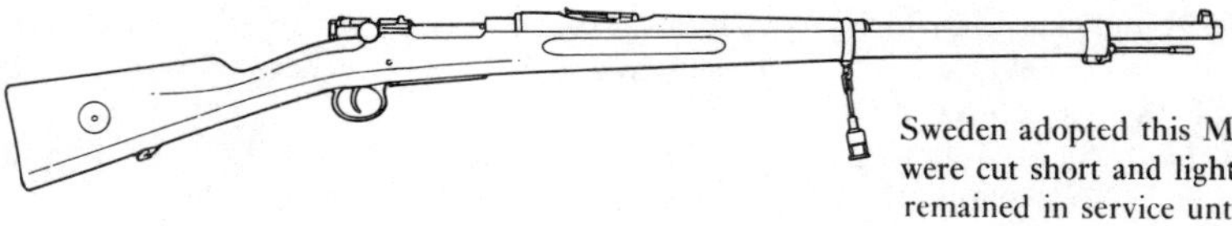

Sweden adopted this Mauser rifle in 1896; most were cut short and lightened in 1940. They remained in service until the 1950s. RSAF Enfield.

issue in 1918. The United States of America was also much impressed by the Krag-Jørgensen. Remarkably, in their Ordnance Board trials of 1890, it was selected from fifty-three competing arms. Certain modifications were made to the original. On the American arm, for example, the loading gate hinged downwards instead of forwards but in a ·30-40 calibre it was adopted as the model of 1892. A number of models followed rapidly but in the 1898 pattern the Americans produced a good quality reliable rifle of considerable accuracy if comparatively low ballistic performance.

In Austria Mannlicher was still not happy that he had produced the ultimate in military, magazine, bolt-action rifles. Nor, for that matter, was Mauser, and the French were certainly not content that their tube-magazine Lebel lacked the facility for clip or charger loading. In their Berthier carbine of 1892 (nominally 1890) the French gave their cavalry the benefit of Mannlicher's clip-loading system into a box-magazine, though otherwise the design was similar to the Lebel. The capacity of the clip was at first only three rounds but later it was raised to five. The French infantry had to wait much longer for improvements to their arm. Some similar modifications were made to the rifle in 1907 but, on a general basis, were not undertaken until 1915-16. Mannlicher also made the Romanians take note of his improvements to the rifle. In 1890 he designed an excellent and very strong split receiver-bridge turning-bolt action which the Romanians adopted in 6·5 mm rimless in
181 1893. This action had the now usual twin forward-locking lugs. In the extremely remote contingency of their shearing these lugs were so designed that the bolt handle would still hold the breech only partly open by bearing against the front of the split receiver-bridge. Since the bolt was hollowed by drilling from the front it had the minimum rear opening and therefore the maximum safety factor. A short separate head in front of the locking lugs was therefore needed to close the bolt's interior. This rifle, which was the official Romanian arm of the First World War, was 4 ft $\frac{1}{4}$ in long, weighed 8 lb $12\frac{1}{2}$ oz and had a $28\frac{1}{2}$ in barrel, rifled with four grooves, clockwise, on a pitch of one turn in 7·87 in. The 159 grain bullet, driven by 36 grains of nitrocellulose powder, had a velocity of 2,400 ft/s. A carbine version of this arm was also produced.

In 1895 the Dutch adopted a new Mannlicher model extremely similar to the Romanian. The calibre was still 6·5 mm but the cartridge, in fact, differed slightly in its dimensions and performance. A simpler ejector was adopted but the most obvious distinguishing external features are a strengthening rib, which on this Dutch model extends along the outside of the bolt from the base of the bolt handle, and a smooth exterior surface to the magazine whereas the Romanian arm had had a marked, reinforced rib along the exterior lower, side surfaces of the magazine. The Dutch rifle was a little heavier and longer than the Romanian but its 31·12 in barrel had identical rifling. As with the Romanian model there was a corresponding carbine version. The excellence of the Dutch Mannlicher action led to its wide employment as a target weapon. Today it still remains the favourite action of most long-range British match riflemen with, probably, its main rival the Mauser of 1898.

Mauser, after his Turkish model of 1890, produced an almost identical design for Argentina in 1891. A similar weapon was rejected by Spain in 1891 after troop trials. An improved experimental model of 1892 did well but not quite well enough to defeat the Krag-Jørgensen in the American trials of 1892. The 1893 model Mauser favourably impressed Spain and went down just as well with the Turks. Both countries adopted it. Compared with earlier models it was improved by a double column magazine and a simplified safety-catch. The calibre adopted by Spain was 7 mm, and by Turkey 7·65 mm. The Turkish model, unlike the Spanish, had a magazine cutoff. When Brazil, in 1894, also adopted the Mauser there was no chance of Mauser manufacturing them themselves; their full production was already bespoken. Ludwig Loewe and Fabrique Nationale therefore undertook their production, the former in addition to the massive share in the Spanish contract that they already had in hand. In 1895 further orders flowed in, largely from South American countries but also including Boer South Africa, China and Persia. From 1894 Sweden began introducing the Mauser, adopting it generally in 1896 with the model which, most distinctively, had a right-angled cocking-piece projection. It used the same 6·5 mm cartridge as the Norwegian Krag-Jørgensen. With this high level of international recognition for the Mauser it was not surprising that Germany herself began to think about replacing the Commission 88 rifle. After a long series of experiments, Germany in 1898 adopted an improved Mauser which, in time, became the most widely known and highly esteemed of all Mauser models.

The 98 Mauser was most obviously improved by being designed to cock on the opening action of the bolt. Since, in this arrangement, the effort required for cocking coincided with that required for primary extraction Mauser enlarged the bolt's diameter at the point where the cocking cam was cut so that the cam operated more easily. The front of the receiver, where the locking lugs engaged and into which the barrel screwed, was made of more generous proportions to increase its strength. It most effectively shrouded the bolt head and thus increased the safety of the arm. The extractor was improved but the generous tolerances in the fit of the bolt in the receiver when partly or fully withdrawn, though excellent from the point of view of military efficiency under poor conditions, gave the action a rather sloppy feel. These were not the only improvements compared with previous issue models but they are the most important. From the safety angle the bolt was cut away with two generous holes to allow for the rapid escape of gas if the primer should be pierced by the striker and, toward the rear, just in front of the bolt handle, the bolt had a safety lug which would abut against the rear face of a recess in the receiver in the event of the main forward-locking lugs shearing. This rifle was produced in endless versions and manufactured, almost without exaggeration, by the million. It was the rifle of the German army in the First World War and, in the eyes of both the British and the American authorities, so disturbingly efficient that they felt constrained to imitate it, or, at least, imitate its best features. In the German army rifle version it was 4 ft 1 in long, weighed 9 lb 4 oz and had a charger-loading, fixed, vertical, box-magazine with a five-round capacity. The barrel was 29·1 in long, rifled with four grooves clockwise with a pitch of one turn in 9·39 in and chambered for a 7·9 mm rimless cartridge, loaded with $40\frac{3}{4}$ grains of nitrocellulose powder and a 227 grain cupro-nickel coated, steel jacketed, bullet. The muzzle velocity was 2,093 ft/s. The torrent of Mauser models for foreign countries increased rather than abated with the arrival of the new model.

In the Spanish-American War the Americans gained practical experience of what it was like to be opposed by the Spanish Mauser; from the Boer War the world saw that the Mauser was an excellent military weapon and from the Boxer rebellion the Mausers made sure that the world realised that the new 98 Mauser had passed its baptism of fire with flying colours. The Americans closely studied Mausers they had captured in the Spanish war and sifted the other evidence that came in. In 1900 they produced their first 'Mauser' and in 1904 began to issue a new model known officially as the Short Magazine Rifle, Model 1903. As British arms often collected the name Enfield so this soon began to be known as the 'Springfield'. It was of 0·30 in calibre 182
and had a staggered, vertical fixed, box-magazine, charger loaded, with a capacity of five rounds. In overall length it was 3 ft 7·22 in, weighed $8\frac{1}{2}$ lb and had a short 23·79 in barrel, rifled with four grooves clockwise on a pitch of one turn in 10 in. The differences between it and the 98 Mauser were slight. There was a cocking-piece that could be manually retracted to allow a second attempt at firing a misfire, a cut-off for the magazine and a two-piece, in place of a one-piece, firing-pin. The sights on the arm were

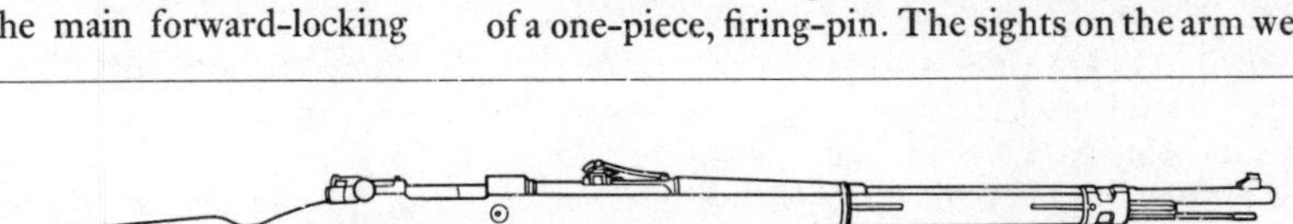
The German Army's Gewehr 98 Mauser rifle in 7.92 mm calibre. Smithsonian Institution, Washington, D.C.

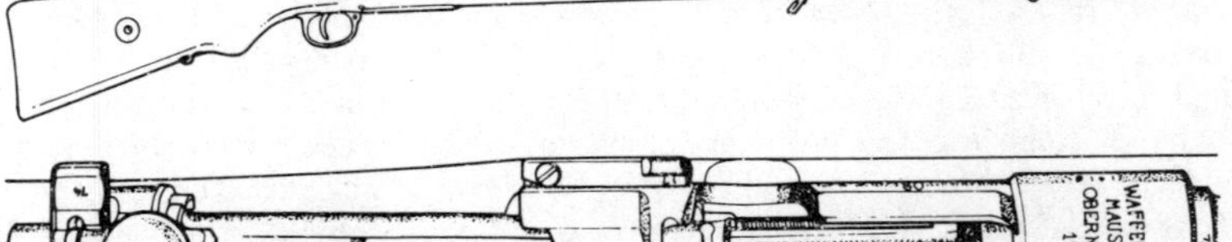

Detail of the German Gewehr 98 Mauser. Smithsonian Institution, Washington, D.C.

elaborate for a military rifle and allowed the firer to set wind corrections. The Americans were able, with the success of the Springfield, to discard their Krags and their Navy to abandon their 6 mm (0·236 in)
183 Lees. In fact, the Lee was actually dropped before the Springfield was introduced, as its straight-pull action was not able to withstand very high breech pressures safely. The Lee had an extraordinary locking system through a form of wedge, quite different from that used on the rotary straight-pull type of action. It had marked a step forward in the American service only in so far as it was their first rifle to use clip-loading. It was also interesting that it was rifled segmentally with six grooves in the Metford style. The Swiss, on the other hand, when they decided on a straight-pull action, had more success.

The Schmidt-Rubin was first accepted by the
184 Swiss authorities in 1889 and, in 1893, a slightly modified version with a shorter action replaced it. The action was of a most distinctive appearance with a looped handle, a rearward extension of the striker, projecting from the rear of the bolt. It was most unorthodox in that the locking lugs were on a bolt sleeve, which extended roughly to the extent of covering the rear half of the bolt proper. To make the breech support even less satisfactory the locking lugs were at the rear of the bolt sleeve. A stud engagement between the bolt handle and helical grooves in the bolt sleeve caused the latter to rotate to engage or disengage the lugs in recesses in the receiver. The action was not at all satisfactory from the point of view of cartridge support. In the 1893 (96) modified model the lugs were strengthened but it was not until 1911 that the action was substantially improved. The measure taken was the moving of the locking lugs to the front of the bolt sleeve but they were still some $3\frac{1}{2}$ in or more from the bolt head. The 1893 Schmidt Rubin had a detachable, vertical, box-magazine with a capacity of up to twelve 7·5 mm (0·293 in) calibre rimless cartridges. It was charger loaded. The rifle measured 4 ft $3\frac{1}{4}$ in overall, weighed 9 lb $13\frac{1}{2}$ oz, and was fitted with a 30·7 in barrel, rifled clockwise with three grooves. The bullet weighed 213 grains and was of unusual construction. It had a steel head and a paper-patched body. Its muzzle velocity with 29 grains of nitrocellulose powder was 1,940 ft/s. In 1900, with the introduction of a short rifle 3 ft $7\frac{1}{8}$ in long, minor changes were made to the rifling and, in due course, a nickel-plated, steel jacketed bullet was adopted, but the velocity, at 1,920 ft/s, remained much the same. It should be noted the barrel was about $7\frac{1}{2}$ in shorter, so it would seem that, although the charge was up to 30·7 grains, there was not sufficient length of bore for the maximum muzzle velocity to be reached.

Yet another nation favoured a straight-pull action and that was Canada. Sir Charles Ross filed his first patent for a straight-pull action in April 1893; his next, which followed in 1896 was for a very different form of straight-pull action. His first arms were manufactured in London by Lancaster in 1897. In his model of 1900 he was almost duplicating the bolt mechanism of the Austrian straight-pull action carbine. The Canadians, in 1901, officially tried the Ross and in 1902 contracted for an initial batch of 12,000. His first military model was that of 1903, or Mark I. It was fitted with Harris's box magazine which, though not of a type which could be loaded by clip or charger, had a lever extension to its platform to allow a handful of cartridges to be dropped straight into the magazine. Naturally, with the rimmed 0·303 in round, care had to be taken to ensure the correct relative positioning of the rims. The rifle, which had an overall length of 4 ft $\frac{5}{8}$ in, weighed 8 lb and was chambered for the British 0·303 in round. The Mark I was not actually issued until 1905 and then it was not a success. The Mark II rifle, which replaced it from 1906 onwards, had a redesigned bolt action in which cocking was accomplished on the withdrawal rather than the closing movement of the bolt. The locking lugs of early Rosses have the appearance of interrupted screw threads taking the form of three small lugs on either side of the bolt head. It is interesting to note that Mannlicher, in a rare 6 mm experimental model rifle of 1896, used a turning-bolt action with four small rather similarly arranged lugs either side of the bolt head. In the Mark II Ross the locking lugs are of an orthodox form, one either side of the head of the bolt. The necessary rotatory motion to lock and unlock the breech was imparted to the bolt head by meshing spirals in the outer sleeve and bolt proper. In 1910 a Mark III model came in. In this the interrupted screw-thread type locking lugs were re-introduced. The magazine was changed to a more conventional box form, charger loaded. The back-sight of the Mark III rifle was mounted on the receiver rather than the barrel. It is of interest that, although the Ross was chambered for the Mark VI 0·303 in cartridge, interior dimensions differed slightly from those of the British Short, Magazine, Lee Enfield; its actual bore was 0·300 in against the Enfield's 0·303 in.

The British authorities learnt much from their experience in the Boer War. They found that the cavalry disliked their short carbine version of the Lee Enfield as they claimed that it did not have the long-range performance necessary to match the Mauser. The idea of a shorter, lighter version of the Lee Enfield actually dated from before the Boer War but matters were speeded up by Lord Roberts's insistence from South Africa that a lighter, more handy, rifle common to both cavalry and infantry was needed. The Lee Enfield had not, in any case,

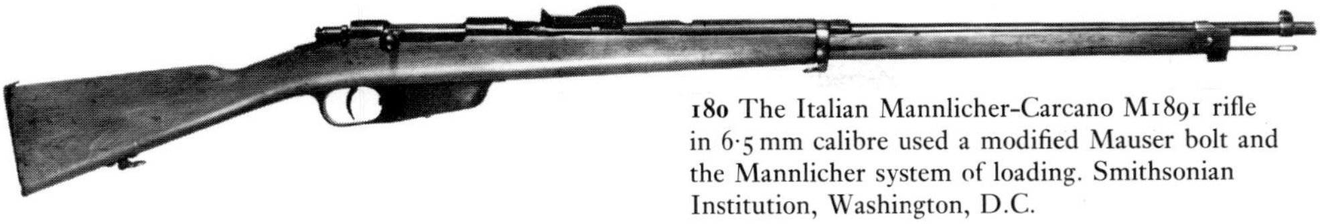

180 The Italian Mannlicher-Carcano M1891 rifle in 6·5 mm calibre used a modified Mauser bolt and the Mannlicher system of loading. Smithsonian Institution, Washington, D.C.

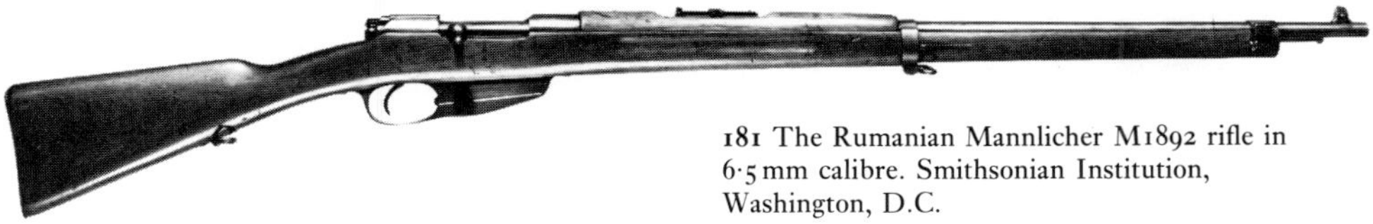

181 The Rumanian Mannlicher M1892 rifle in 6·5 mm calibre. Smithsonian Institution, Washington, D.C.

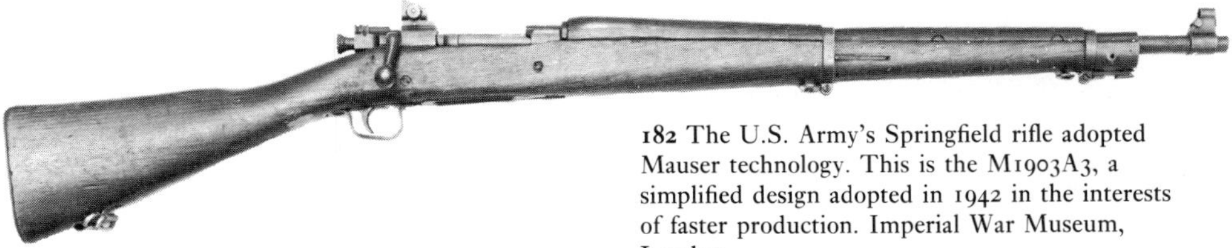

182 The U.S. Army's Springfield rifle adopted Mauser technology. This is the M1903A3, a simplified design adopted in 1942 in the interests of faster production. Imperial War Museum, London.

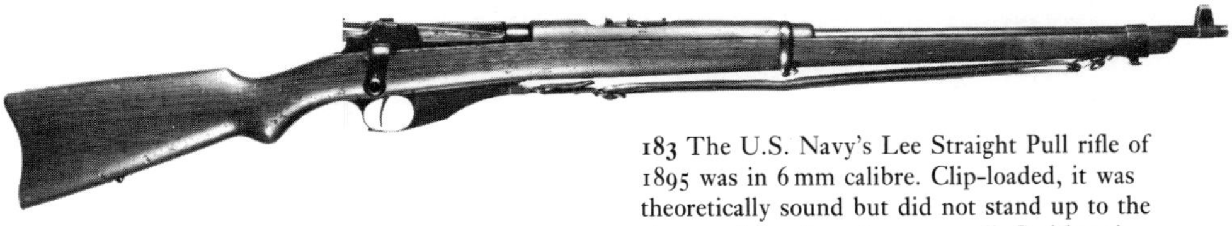

183 The U.S. Navy's Lee Straight Pull rifle of 1895 was in 6 mm calibre. Clip-loaded, it was theoretically sound but did not stand up to the rigours of naval service very well. Smithsonian Institution, Washington, D.C.

184 The Swiss Schmidt-Rubin was probably the longest-serving straight-pull rifle. (*Top*) The rifle of 1889. (*Bottom*) The M1911 carbine. RSAF Enfield.

185 The British Lee-Metford Mark I rifle, combining James Lee's bolt and magazine with rifling by William E. Metford. Imperial War Museum, London.

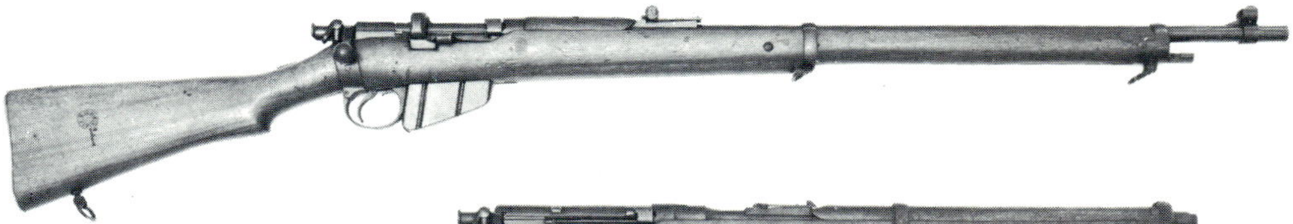

186 Lee-Enfield rifles. (*Top*) Long, Mark I, adopted 1895. (*Bottom*) Carbine, Mark I, adopted 1896. Imperial War Museum, London.

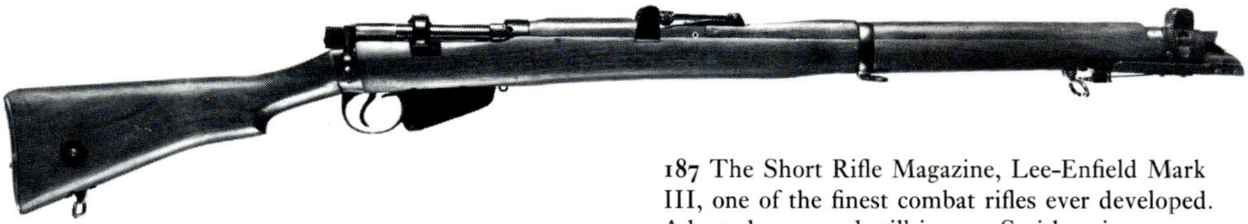

187 The Short Rifle Magazine, Lee-Enfield Mark III, one of the finest combat rifles ever developed. Adopted 1907 and still in use. Smithsonian Institution, Washington, D.C.

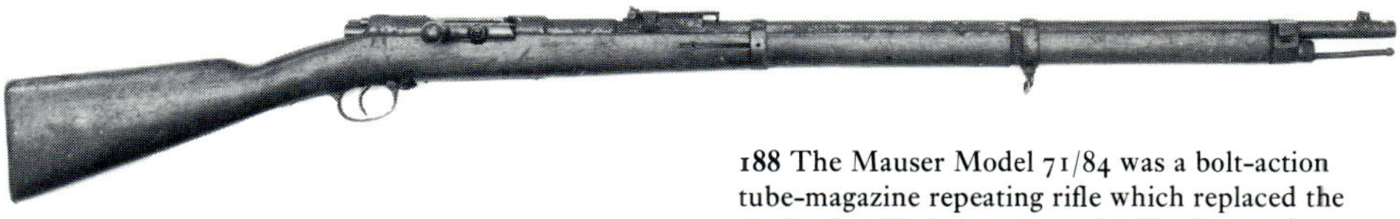

188 The Mauser Model 71/84 was a bolt-action tube-magazine repeating rifle which replaced the single-shot Model 71. Imperial War Museum, London.

189 German 13 mm calibre Mauser bolt-action rifle, developed in 1918 as an anti-tank weapon. Imperial War Museum, London.

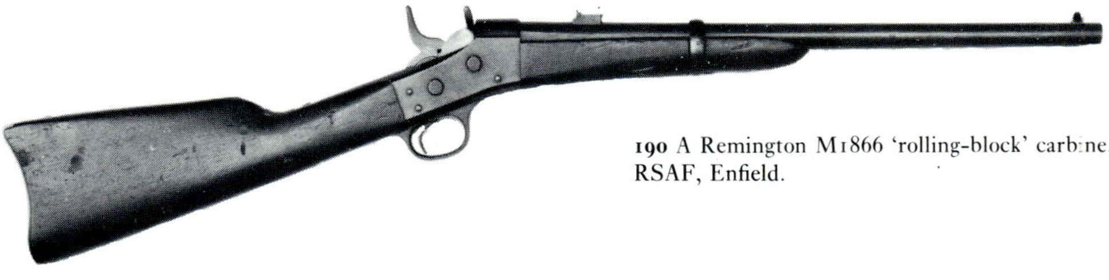

190 A Remington M1866 'rolling-block' carbine. RSAF, Enfield.

191 A 'rifle battery' of Lee-Enfield SMLE Mk III rifles, complete with elevation and traverse controls, for use in the trenches of the First World War. Imperial War Museum, London.

192 Field's patent dropping-block breech mechanism, dating from 1873. The block is operated by the lever on the underside. Tower of London Armouries.

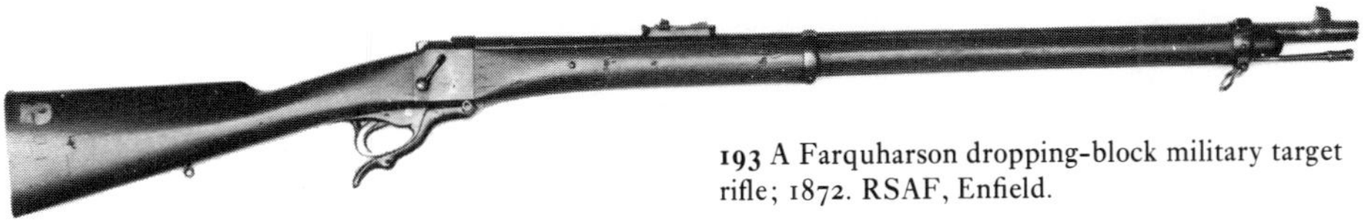

193 A Farquharson dropping-block military target rifle; 1872. RSAF, Enfield.

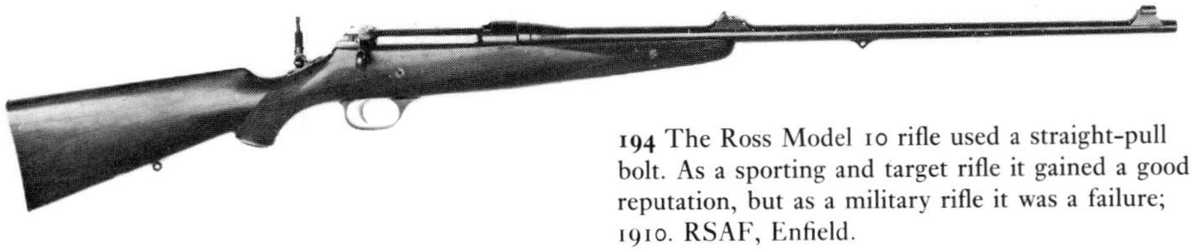

194 The Ross Model 10 rifle used a straight-pull bolt. As a sporting and target rifle it gained a good reputation, but as a military rifle it was a failure; 1910. RSAF, Enfield.

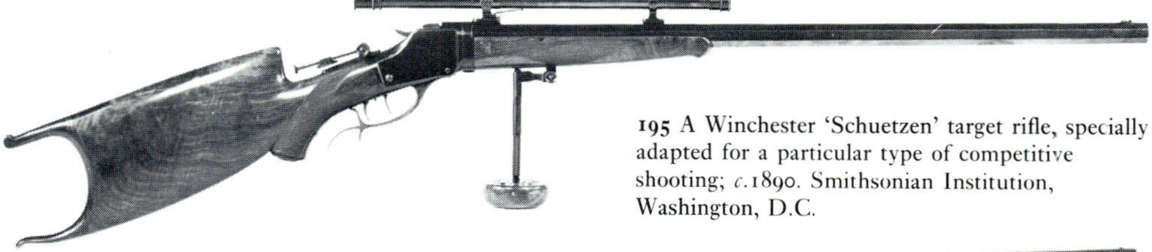

195 A Winchester 'Schuetzen' target rifle, specially adapted for a particular type of competitive shooting; *c*.1890. Smithsonian Institution, Washington, D.C.

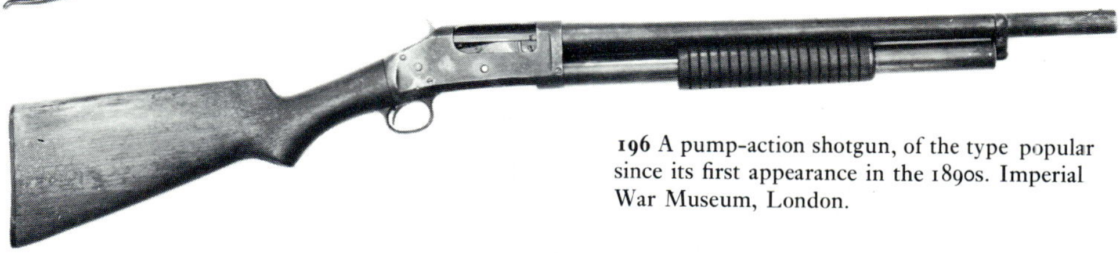

196 A pump-action shotgun, of the type popular since its first appearance in the 1890s. Imperial War Museum, London.

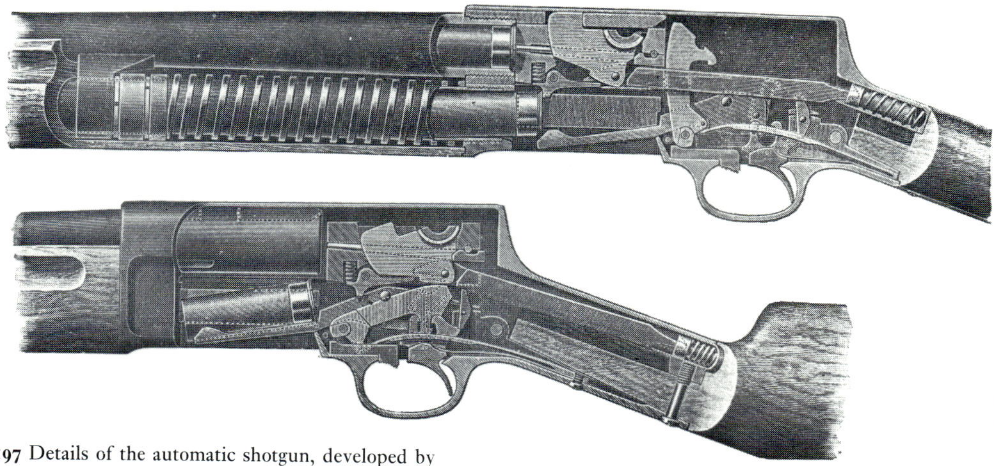

197 Details of the automatic shotgun, developed by John M. Browning and using the long recoil system of operation; *c*.1903. (*Top*) Position of parts when action is closed. (*Bottom*) Position of parts when action is open.

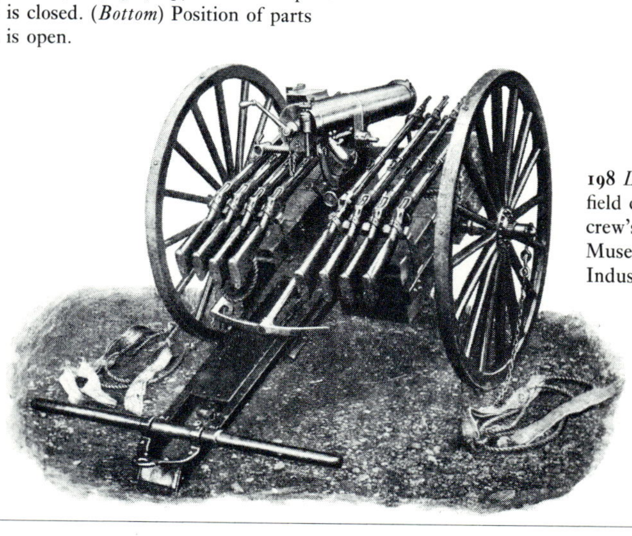

198 *Left* The Gatling Gun on field carriage (with racks for crew's rifles), *c*.1875. Museum of Science and Industry, Birmingham.

remained unchanged since its first issue in 1888. In its first form as the 0·303 in Lee Metford, it had survived substantially unaltered until 1892. The
185 Lee Metford Mark I had measured 4 ft $1\frac{1}{2}$ in overall, weighed $9\frac{1}{2}$ lb, and been fitted with a 30·2 in barrel, rifled anti-clockwise with seven Metford segmental grooves with a pitch of one turn in 10 in. It had a magazine capacity of eight rounds and a cover over the bolt to restrict the entry of dirt. Like its predecessor it had a divided stock, a form of construction which might aid repair and facilitate fitting the weapon to the individual soldier but which had, nevertheless, weaknesses which discouraged most other countries from using it. In British service complaints about butts working loose from shrinkage were endless.

The introduction in 1892 of a wider, larger capacity magazine to hold ten cartridges in two columns was the main reason for the new rifle being designated Mark II but there was still no move to follow the Continent and adapt the action for charger loading. In 1895 the Lee Enfield Mark I arrived because a new form of rifling, better able to resist the cor-
186 rosive action of cordite, was introduced. In this the grooves, five in number, were straight-sided and flat-bottomed, concentric as it is termed, and deeper by 0·002 in. The pitch remained the same. There were, of course, carbines for the cavalry and later for the artillery. In 1896 the cavalry carbine began to be made with the Enfield rifling. It was not, however, until 1898 that reports really began to mount about the inconvenience of reloading the magazine with single cartridges. Troops in action on the North-West Frontier of India considered this the chief drawback of their arms. From South Africa the complaint was heard again. There were, of course, many other complaints from South Africa but this was not surprising when one recalls that rifle engagements often took place at ranges between 1,500 and 2,500 yards.

The Small Arms Committee investigating complaints in June 1900 had reached the point of talking about the need for an entirely new rifle. In their listing of the defects of the Lee Enfield the action was severely criticised. They did not like the lugs, nor the cocking of the bolt on its forward movement. They had obviously been influenced by the design of the Mauser and Mannlicher. It was, however, officially recognised that too much expense and dislocation would be occasioned by a complete change. A short version of the Lee Enfield with charger loading was put on troop trials. Modifications followed and in December 1902 the Short, Magazine, Lee Enfield, the S.M.L.E., was officially introduced for both infantry and cavalry. The new arm was 3 ft $8\frac{9}{16}$ in long, weighed 8 lb $2\frac{1}{2}$ oz, and had a $25\frac{3}{16}$ in barrel rifled as in the longer weapon but for the fact that the grooves were slightly deeper towards the muzzle than at the breech. In keeping with the military needs of the time it retained the long-range dial sight of its predecessor graduated to 2,800 yards. The rifle was not welcome in all quarters. It was undoubtedly less accurate at very long range than the long Enfield. Indeed only at about 1,000 yards, through a certain characteristic which compensated for varying velocity in its ammunition, did it tend to outshoot the long Enfield. The barrel with which the S.M.L.E. was fitted was too light for really consistent and accurate performance. The version of the S.M.L.E., which was that which generally saw the British army through the best part of both World
Wars, was the Mark III which was approved on 187
26 January 1907. The main respect in which it differed from the Marks I and II was in its charger-loading arrangement. The sliding charger guide, fitted to the bolt head, was abandoned and in its place a bridge charger guide adopted. With the short rifle at last established, some of the long Enfields were converted to the new specification whilst others were given a charger guide bridge over the receiver.

The Lee action, as embodied in the Lee Enfields, was by 1907 almost, though not quite, the only representative of a rear locking action in military use anywhere. From the base of the cartridge to the locking lugs was no less than $4\frac{1}{8}$ in but, at least there were two lugs and one of these was so massive that there was little danger to the firer. The idea of a new weapon, perhaps on the well-proved lines of the Mauser, did not die with the introduction of the S.M.L.E. From 1910 the Small Arms Committee actively investigated the matter. A calibre of 0·276 in was chosen and the American Springfield taken as a guide to what was required. By 1913 one thousand of the new 0·276 in rifles had been issued for troop trials. However, problems with the ammunition, and with extraction, took time to cure and the war broke out before they could be completely solved. These trials did, nevertheless, have an important consequence. In the war when the British forces required more rifles than could be produced in this country, arrangements were made for the Winchester, Remington and Eddystone factories in the USA to produce the Enfield Mauser in 0·303 in calibre. As the P'14 it was widely used in both World Wars and adopted as a British Army sniper rifle. In turn, when America entered the First World War and wanted large numbers of rifles with the minimum delay it was a fairly simple matter for her to manufacture the P'14 in 0·30 in calibre. The P'17 resulted. Probably the most noticeable departure from later Mauser design in both the P'14 and the P'17 was the choice of an action in which, as in the Lee Enfield, the striker was cocked as the bolt was closed. It was argued, and in the eyes of many the war proved the contention, that this style Mauser action could be operated at a higher rate of fire than the Mauser 98. These rifles were rather too straight-stocked for many firers but otherwise, with dimensions very similar to other rifles of the period, were not particularly exceptional.

Developments which occurred to rifle design after 1894 do not amount to anything approaching those which packed the decade before that date. The history of the military rifle after 1894 is principally that of the reactions of the various powers to what was available and of how they eventually themselves adopted the improvements which leading arms designers had demonstrated. And these designers themselves in many cases began to devote more of their time to the development of automatic weapons. This situation certainly existed until 1905. In that year, however, Germany published the results of experiments designed to increase the range of her rifle substantially. The secret of German success lay in the adoption of a pointed bullet, *Spitzgeschoss*, hence the letter S to denote it. They found that a much lighter, pointed bullet and heavier powder charge gave them a velocity of about 2,882 ft/s, as compared with 2,093 ft/s from the old, round-nosed bullet. The powder was also slightly improved. The flatter trajectory from the spitzer bullet represented so much of a military advantage that other nations hastened to follow suit. By 1908 France, Russia and the USA had introduced pointed bullet versions of their cartridges: Great Britain followed with her Mark VII bullet in 1910.

Two English observers, writing in 1909, could not help remarking that it was only an historical accident that the pointed bullet had not been developed in the late 1870s. Some American match riflemen had, in the Palma Trophy match at Creedmoor in 1877, been very successful with pointed bullets. Metford examined the American bullets and decided that their advantage lay more in the steep slope of the shoulder than in the actual point. After various experiments Metford accordingly adopted an altered bullet for his rifles which had a somewhat more pointed appearance than the earlier and very blunt form. This new bullet was that which became the accepted standard and model for military bullets until the German rediscovery of the merits of a point nearly thirty years later.

When war came in 1914, and the rifles which the various powers had adopted were matched in battle, the only conclusions that could be drawn from the comparison did not entirely coincide with those forecast. The British Lee Enfield proved itself a remarkably durable and efficient military arm capable of a very high rate of fire even under appalling conditions. So good, in fact, that in the opening battles of the war the Germans believed themselves to be opposed by troops provided with a far higher proportion of machine-guns than was actually the case. If, as was undoubtedly true, the Lee Enfield proved itself superior to the Mauser 98 as a general-purpose rifle at least the Germans had no failure to compare with the collapse of the Ross. Before the war was a year old questions were being asked about it in the House. By June 1915 over 3,000 Canadians, or more than a third of the Canadian Division in France, had succeeded, by hook or by crook, in unofficially re-arming themselves with Lee Enfield rifles. The interrupted screw thread locking lugs of the Mark III Ross were undoubtedly rather vulnerable to the entry of mud and sand but it appeared that its extraction troubles were more due to wide manufacturing tolerances allowed in the production of British 0·303 in ammunition. With Canadian ammunition, which was not at the time available, it was expected that the Ross would have functioned more smoothly. The British army commander, Field Marshal Sir John French, therefore withdrew the Ross in June 1915 pending an investigation but it continued in use in the 2nd and 3rd Canadian Divisions. There was a top level exchange of messages between Canada and London when Haig complained of the failure of the Ross in action on 1 May 1916. The evidence strongly suggested that the relieving of the chamber, which had followed the 1915 complaints, had not entirely overcome the difficulty. It was the end of the Ross in France as a general-purpose rifle, and shortly after it was withdrawn from frontline service. As a sniping arm it was difficult to beat. With a Ross fitted with a telescopic sight Private MacDonald of the 90th Rifles shot no fewer than forty-two Germans between March 1915 and 3 January 1916 when he was killed by a bursting shell. A fair indication of the excellence of the arm in this role.

The Russian soldier was not likely to be in the position of the Canadian to criticise his rifle. There

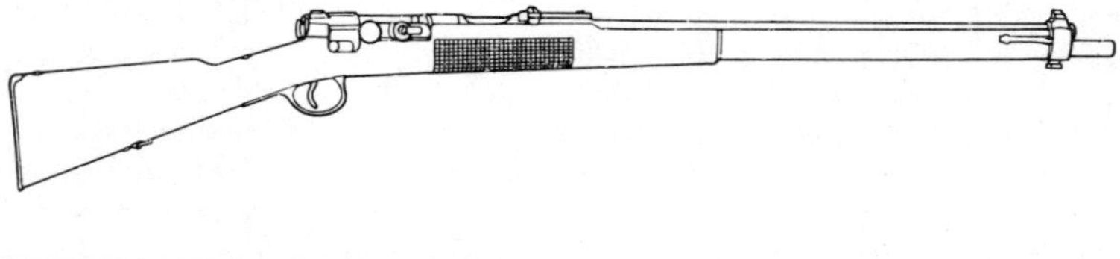

The Japanese 1887 Murata magazine rifle. Smithsonian Institution, Washington, D.C.

were periods of the war when he was lucky to possess one at all. The Russian '3 line', or Nagant, was a clumsy weapon weighing $9\frac{3}{4}$ lb and almost 4 ft 4 in long. As the Mosin-Nagant, it had been adopted in 1891. The bolt, which was unnecessarily complex in construction, was, with the action, of the design of a Russian Colonel S. I. Mosin. Nagant, a Belgian, was responsible for the magazine. The bolt had forward-locking lugs but they locked in position to left and right rather than the usual above and below the base of the cartridge. The front and rear portions of the bolt were entirely separate units linked through a special connecting bar. The locking piece, which was so formed that manual cocking was possible to deal with misfires, turned with the bolt as it locked, which was quite unusual. Uniquely the five-round box-magazine had an interrupter. This made it impossible for two cartridges to be fed towards the chamber simultaneously. The calibre was 7·62 mm and the $31\frac{1}{2}$ in barrel was rifled clockwise with four grooves making one turn in $9\frac{1}{2}$ in. The rimmed cartridge was loaded with a 214 grain cupro-nickel jacketed bullet and with a charge of 33 grains of pyroxiline propellant reached a velocity at the muzzle of 1,927 ft/s. The effectiveness of the rifle at long ranges was impaired by rather crude sights, whilst the small of the butt was too thick for good control of the arm. A pointed bullet with improved performance came into use in 1908.

It is of interest to look at the rifle with which this was opposed in the Russo-Japanese War. The Japanese had first equipped themselves with a single-shot, turning-bolt Murata of 11 mm calibre. This had weighed 9 lb 10 oz, and measured 4 ft $3\frac{1}{2}$ in overall. In 1887 they adapted the design to take a tube-magazine and reduced the bore to 8 mm. Ten years later the Murata was discarded in favour of a Mauser-style arm developed by a certain Colonel
188 Arisaka. It shared with the Ross the unfortunate property of being so designed that it was possible to misassemble it with dangerous consequences to the firer. The calibre of this Arisaka Mauser was 0·256 in or 6·5 mm, semi-rimless and its 163 grain copper-jacketed bullet had a muzzle velocity of 2,286 ft/s. The Russo-Japanese War saw the arm redesigned. In 1907 it emerged as the Year 38 pattern. It was only 1 oz lighter and $\frac{3}{4}$ in shorter than the 1887 Murata, but its performance, even with a round-nosed bullet, was incomparably better. The rifling was Metford segmental, four grooves on a right-hand pitch of 7·875 in and claimed muzzle velocity was 2,396 ft/s. This rifle remained the standard arm of the Japanese forces until long after the First World War.

The failure, under battlefield conditions, of the Ross rifle has already been mentioned. Attention has also been focused, as it deserves to be, on the practical excellence of the Lee Enfield, but the First World War had more influence than this on the specification of the military rifle. In particular it revealed the need to simplify externals so as to facilitate mass production. In this direction, admittedly, the First World War saw only the beginnings of the revolution in form which the Second World War was to witness. Such work as decorative or marginally functional milling on the cocking piece of the S.M.L.E. was severely curtailed or dropped altogether. Outlines were simplified and finish suffered. Occasionally, but not frequently, since few things are more detrimental to a soldier's morale than the structural or material failure of his principal arm, the standards for the quality of materials were relaxed. In a somewhat similar manner specifications altered, slowly reflecting the different character of the war. The ultra-long-range sight was abandoned and the magazine cut-off was dropped. Trench warfare, of the type which evolved on the Western Front, did not call for markmanship at 2,500 yards: countries had begun at last to realise that ammunition was not a commodity that could be rationed in a total war. But, at the same time that the rifle itself was being simplified, its regular application was being extended. The appearance of armoured vehicles as a regular instrument of war called for counter-defensive measures and one of these was the development of the anti-tank rifle.

To the student of arms it seemed like the 189
renaissance of the rampart gun. The Germans took the lead in this field by developing massive bolt-action rifles in calibres up to 0·6 in. The rifle also became, more than ever before, the universal arm. Groups were mounted together and fired as batteries. Grenade cup-dischargers, known for centuries, assumed a new importance and even wire cutters were conveniently mounted, when required, at the muzzle. Few would quarrel with the view that the First World War, which saw the emergence of the machine-gun and the tank as serious elements in the arsenal of war, saw also the apogee of the rifle's importance in military history.

The Match Rifle

In 1872 at Wimbledon, then the centre upon which all British marksmen gathered for their Annual Meeting, a match was shot between a team of five armed with military breech-loading rifles and a team armed with muzzle-loaders. Each man fired thirty shots at 1,000 yards and those with muzzle-loaders won by a margin of 15 points per man over their opponents. Four of the breech-loading rifles had Metford barrels and one a Henry so they represented the best then available in military breech-loaders. But muzzle-loading rifles had reached such a pitch of perfection that, when it was accuracy alone which

counted, they were still unbeatable. It was not a position which was likely to be tenable indefinitely. Within two years the challenge came from a breech-loader from America. In the autumn of 1874, in an international rifle match shot at Creedmoor, New York, between an Irish team armed with Rigby muzzle-loaders and an American team with breech-loaders victory went to the latter by a margin of three points. In fact it was a hollow victory. It could be viewed only as a triumph for the muzzle-loader which was shot in a normal manner; the American breech-loaders had to be wiped out after every shot. Not until 1881 did the breech-loader really begin to oust the muzzle-loader. Two years later the British National Rifle Association woke up to dangers inherent in the American habit of wiping out and banned it for both muzzle-loaders and breech-loaders since the fashion had become almost universal in 'Any' rifle competitions at Wimbledon. With this decision match riflemen in Great Britain returned to a situation where such improvements were seen as having a practical application to military arms. Almost all these early breech-loading match rifles were of a falling-block type. Indeed the block action almost completely monopolised match rifle design until 1897 when, once again, it was felt that the differences between match rifles and service rifles were likely to become great if new conditions were not introduced. Of American match rifles the most popular and successful makes were Remington and Sharps, naturally in falling-block single-loaders. Much the most outstanding of British
193 rifles was the Gibbs-Farquharson-Metford though it had powerful rivals in the Deeley-Edge-Metford, the Webley-Wyley, the Fraser and the Rigby-Banks. There were a number of other similar rifles which enjoyed some following in the 1880s, prominent amongst which were the Field-Rigby, Field-Turner and Ingram, but the key to success lay in the choice of barrel and that had to be of Metford's design. At least that is the only lesson that can be read into the results of the Wimbledon Meetings between 1870 and 1896.

The secret of Metford's system lay in its combination of a hardened lead bullet with ultra-shallow rifling grooves. To prevent lead being deposited in the bore the bullets were paper-wrapped and were so sized and of such a form that the paper was sufficiently incised by the rifling to drop away from the bullet immediately on its emergence at the muzzle. While it was important that the bullet did shed its paper before it was more than a very short distance from the muzzle it was equally important that the paper was not discarded before the bullet reached the muzzle or even in loading. The rifling grooves were intentionally shallow to afford fouling the minimum hold and to prevent the bullet, on setting up, from losing its intended aerodynamic form. The bullet was alloyed with antimony and tin, since tin on its own, which had before Metford's day been normal, imparted to the bullet the undesirable property of softening with age, or more correctly, of being inconstant in its hardness since such an alloy goes through a sequence of changes in this respect. Of course Metford also believed that the form of his bullet aided rapid, but not excessive, set-up and, particularly, that the progressive pitch on which his rifling was cut minimised undesirable surface stresses on the bullet. Possibly the feature of his system on which he was least insistent was a segmental section to the rifling grooves.

The fact that there was marked outward similarity between most of the falling-block actions in use in the 1870s and 1880s should not be allowed to obscure the fact that mechanisms were improved and new and lighter designs introduced. There is a real difference between, for example, the comparatively primitive, if superbly made, Henry of the early seventies which is no more than a mildly refined Sharps and the Rigby-Banks of 1884 (patented in 1882) with its ingenious internal hammer mechanism which incorporated a means of ensuring the withdrawal of the striker, and thus the opening of the breech. In other designs which depended on a spring to withdraw the striker it only needed the striker to stick forward in the fired position through dirt, fouling or a broken spring, or some similar circumstance, and the rifle was rendered useless since forcing the breech open would, at the least, ruin the striker. The rifle also represented an advance in design in that through the positioning of the back-sight on the heel of the butt, it recognised the consequences of the warping or movement of the butt on the rifle's sighting and endeavoured to minimise this risk by adopting an arrangement of increasing the substance of the rearwards extension of the action within the butt. This had the attendant advantage that the heavy tube served as an ideal and weatherproof housing for the main spring.

The positioning of the back-sight on the heel of the butt became general practice in the early 1880s with the almost complete switch from shooting in the prone to the back position. A few British marksmen even as early as the eighteenth century had previously used the back position, but the then customary position of the back-sight on the small of the butt made the posture an extremely uncomfortable one. American marksmen of the late seventies favoured the supine position and it caught on at Wimbledon to become so popular that, when a member of the English team in 1912 adopted the prone position in the Elcho International match, it was thought to be the first time for thirty-five years. The extremely elaborate sights used on match rifles of this period came in with the Whitworth muzzle-loading match rifle about 1862 but, though generally made on similar lines, they reflect the individuality of their makers. In general the back-sight consisted of a long tangent leaf with a slide moved up or down by a long threaded screw which passed through it. There was an aperture eyepiece which, on some sights, also served to lock the slide at the desired elevation. A vernier scale made the setting of this easy and precise: wind allowance was set on the fore-sight which consisted of an interchangeable element mounted in a frame. These elements varied in form according to the whim of the firer from a bead or aperture to calipers or a bar. A small spirit level was usually fixed to the fore sight to eliminate the possibility of canting the rifle. From the 1860s attempts were made to make the back-sight adjustable for wind but without achieving any popularity. Curiously, when breech-loaders became general there was no rapid change-over to wind adjustable back-sights. As late as 1900 Fraser of Edinburgh was the only maker actively promoting this type of sight. Its convenience was undeniable and it slowly came in: the advantage in being able to make one's last correction for wind only a second or so before firing could not be ignored. Finally, in 1905, magnifying sights were permitted and with this regulation, which gave the firer the choice of anything from a Galilean adaptation of the old sights to a full telescope, sights reached what is so far the ultimate in their development.

There is not the space to go into the mechanical detail of the various match-rifle actions at length. The Sharps action had the distinctive feature of being operated by a lever formed from the trigger-guard itself; the Remington had a block similar to the Sharps but was operated by a side lever. The Deeley-Edge action made by Westley Richards in its early forms of 1873 and 1878 was not much of a success: the action of this name which achieved high popularity came into use about 1882. This was lighter than its predeccessor, had better extraction and a side lever instead of an under lever formed of the trigger-guard and plate. The close link between military and match rifles is emphasised by the neat manner in which a universal model of this rifle could be converted from a military rifle to match simply by adding long-range sights of a slightly modified type marketed by Westley Richards for the purpose.

The military Field action looked rather like the Martini, had a side lever and, in the eyes of the British military authorities, sufficient merit in 1884 to reach the drawing board as a possible successor to the Martini. As a match rifle it had a vertically-sliding block operated by forward movement on a side lever. Fraser's own action developed from the Field was similar but used a rearwards, downwards pressure on the side lever to open the breech. The Webley-Wyley, which was first produced in 1879, had an external hammer and the operating lever prominently placed on the right of the vertically moving sliding block action. The hammer was cocked as the breech was opened by turning the lever to the right but could also be thumbed for a second strike in the event of a misfire. None of these actions, however ingenious, could match the Farquharson in popularity. It was, of course, like most of its rivals, a derivative of the Sharps action first patented in England in 1852. Though it will be found in a number of slightly different versions the basic design, of a vertically-sliding block drawn downward to open the breech by a vertical link pivoted on the operating lever close to its fulcrum with an internal block hammer cocked by a horizontal link in the same movement, remains the same. The lever was positioned underneath the action and pivoted at its front end to the front of the trigger-guard. Its downward movement also acted through an intermediary lever on an extractor arm at such a mechanical advantage that there was unusually powerful ejection.

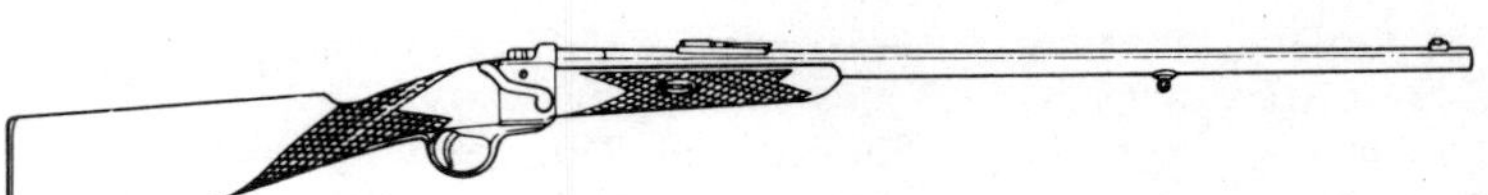

The Deely-Edge vertical sliding block rifle of 1884. Deely was a London gunmaker who was largely responsible for, among other things, the automatic ejection feature in shotguns. Tower of London Armouries.

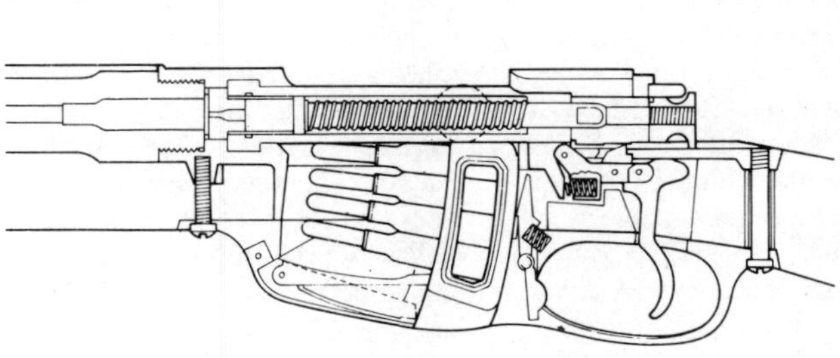

Cross-section of the action of a Mannlicher Rumanian Model 1892 military rifle.

Bisley 1897 saw the introduction of an upper limit of 0·315 in on calibre size but this did not lead to the adaptation of these block actions to the new calibre. They might have been the better choice if they could have been considered against the Martini in 1869 but, by 1897, they were obviously an anachronistic survival. Competitors turned to various bolt actions, including the Lee Metford, which showed that it could shoot very well, and the Mannlicher with a 0·256 in barrel. The Mannlicher, in fact, established quite a reputation and became the most popular arm in spite of its light bullet being rather blown about by the wind. Under such conditions these small-bores were not as accurate as the old 0·461 in black powder Metford rifle at the traditional distances of 800, 900 and 1,000 yards. Not until about 1907 was scoring really comparable with that of the 0·461 in and the improvement of the small-bore then was principally due to the adoption of a pointed bullet. In 1909 scores went further ahead but this was due to the introduction of a 0·303 in cartridge with a case of the size of the 0·375 in, giving the bullet a higher muzzle velocity. The new ammunition developed by the King's Norton Company proved too powerful for the Lee action and the Mauser generally replaced it. This final success, as it proved to be, of the forward-locking action in match rifle design at last spurred a British firm to the production of an action of this general type. Driver and Norman of the Birmingham Small Arms Company patented their system in 1907. It was a strong, cleverly-conceived action with forward-locking recesses so placed that they could very easily be cleaned. As it was designed as a single-shot action much of the receiver, which in a military design is cut away, could be left untouched for additional strength. Perhaps because Mauser, Mannlicher and Ross had already captured the market few were made and B.S.A. (British Small Arms Company) did not try to develop it into a military design. In 1912 the Ross 0·280 in swept the board – it had made its first sensational appearance in 1908 – and with the
194 popularity of its cartridge the straight-pull Ross became a very popular weapon at Bisley. The war, however, which broke so soon after the Bisley Meeting of 1914, proved that though the Ross was a good choice for the sniper it was not suitable as an infantryman's arm.

At intervals through much of the period under consideration the Americans participated in long-range matches with England, Scotland, Ireland, Canada and Australia, though often only two or three countries were represented. However, when the series started in 1874 it marked the introduction of a new form of shooting into America and one which, after almost dying out there between 1890 and 1901, finally succumbed before the First World War. The Americans developed their match shooting in rather different directions. Off-hand shooting and rested shooting were the most popular. Standing shooting was especially popular with immigrants from Central Europe. For this heavy Schuetzen rifles were made which differed from long-range match rifles in having much heavier barrels to give a steadier pos-
ition when shooting standing with the elbow rested 195
on or near the hip. It should not, however, be thought that standing shooting was confined to Schuetzen shooting. It was generally popular and most firing at ranges of up to 200 yards with military rifles was done either in this or in the kneeling position. The development of the Schuetzen rifle is therefore more a matter of the physical form of the entire weapon and its stylistic variation than one of mechanical importance. In bench-rest shooting this was even more the case though there were varying degrees of specialisation evident. In extreme instances such arms could weigh as much as 50 lb to 60 lb. In some classes of rest shooting telescope sights were used and muzzle-loading was preferred.

Off-hand, or as it is known today, positional, shooting, was on the Continent the premier form of target shooting. As the military rifle was improved, and new design features accepted, they found their way into target rifles. Schuetzen rifles dominated shooting in most of Europe with 300 metres established as almost the only distance. Some time before the turn of the century match conditions, of forty shots standing, forty kneeling and forty prone, as they still survive today, became the accepted norm. With their pronounced butt-hooks, palm rests and hair triggers these rifles, as those in America, were about as far removed from what was militarily practicable as it was possible to get. Certainly such arms could have little influence on or importance in the development of serviceable military arms.

The Sporting Rifle

The sporting-rifle was not likely to be the Cinderella in the application of technical improvements. Such rifles were made by the leading gunmakers for wealthy clients who had no wish to fall victim to the large game they sought to shoot. Metford, for example, spent much time on the design of sporting-rifles and the Farquharson-Metfords which Gibbs of Bristol produced were amongst the finest single-shot sporting-rifles anywhere obtainable. The sporting-rifle could, and did, benefit by advances introduced for match shooting and certainly did gain enormously from improvements in military arms and ammunition, but it also developed in its own right. There was freedom to choose the most effective ammunition at the comparatively short ranges involved and there was almost no limit on the money that could be put into producing the most perfect weapon. The most effective ammunition was that which had the flattest trajectory, thus minimising the difference in the point of impact of the bullet consequent on varying distance and which, at the same time, killed most cleanly. It was not therefore surprising that some English gunmakers in the 1850s began to develop a form of sporting-rifle of fairly large bore firing a comparatively light cylindro-conoidal bullet with a large charge of powder. The Express rifle, as it was soon called, had arrived. By the early 1880s it had been developed to such a degree that many gunmakers considered the minimum qualifying velocity for an Express was 1,750 ft/s. These black powder Express rifles were not normally used at ranges greater than 150 yards so that they could be sighted in such a manner that the point of impact did not differ by more than $4\frac{1}{2}$ in in elevation at any range up to this distance. In calibre these rifles rarely dropped below 0·400 in and were more normally between 0·450 in and 0·577 in. A few were in single-barrel form with a Farquharson or similar action but the double rifle was almost universal. The smaller bores of about 0·450 in to 0·400 in were thought excellent for deer, for dangerous game at least a 0·500 in was preferred, whilst many sportsmen insisted on a 0·577 in, which might weigh as much as 12 lb in double form. The bullets these rifles fired were of a hollow-point type with immense stopping power. The rifles themselves naturally differed in detail from maker to maker but were normally rifled with a fairly slow pitch of about one turn in 40 in to 50 in. A high standard of accuracy was frequently attained. In the *Field* trials of 1883 the winning 0·450 in Express by Holland & Holland had an average deviation of five shots from each barrel of only 1·45 in at 150 yards.

For elephant, and similarly thick-skinned dangerous game, the Express rifle fired too light a bullet. Though not essential – an Express rifle with solid bullet could be used – there was quite a following for a very heavy rifle in 8 or 4 bore, or, occasionally, 10 or 12 bore. The comparison of remaining velocity and striking energy at 150 yards between an Express rifle and a heavy rifle is most interesting. A 0·450 in Express with 322 grain bullet had a remaining velocity of 1,335 ft/s and a striking energy of 1,274 ft lb. This increased with a 0·577 in Express with a 591 grain bullet to a striking energy of 2,169 ft lb, though the remaining velocity at 1,286 ft/s was lower. A heavy rifle of 8 bore with an 862 grain spherical ball was in much the same class with a remaining velocity of 1,038 ft/s and a striking energy of 2,069 ft lb. The 4 bore with an 1,882 grain, or almost 4 oz, conical bullet was in a totally different class. Its massive bullet at 150 yards had a remaining velocity of 1,091 ft/s and a striking energy of no less than 4,969 ft lb – enough to stop a charging elephant.

In the early 1880s Express and similar rifles were constructed very much on the lines of a hammer shotgun. The locks were almost always of back-action type as this avoided the need to cut away part of the breech and consequently weaken the gun to accommodate bar-, or forward-action locks. The most popular breech action was the 'double grip' which consisted of an under lever lying along the outer contour of the trigger-guard. The breech was opened by moving the lever anti-clockwise to the right. This turned a form of screw from engagement with the breech and allowed the action to open by

A typical double-barrelled 'Express' sporting rifle.

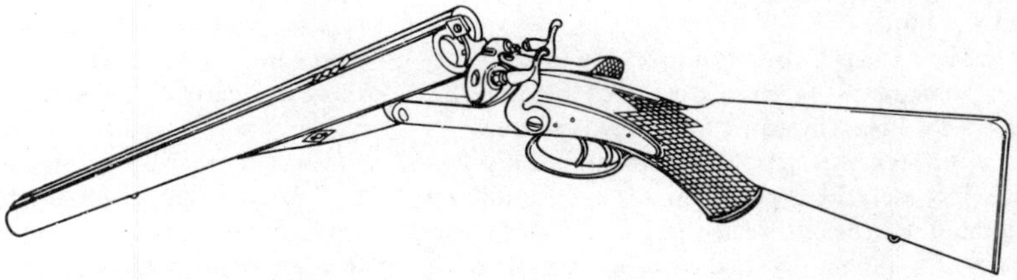

Another example of a double-barrelled sporting rifle. Imperial War Museum, London.

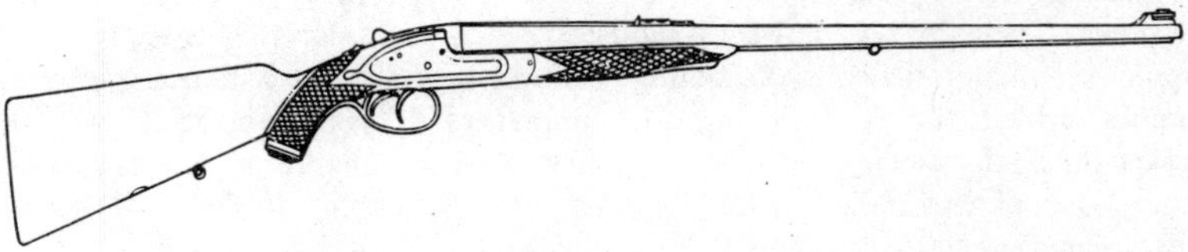

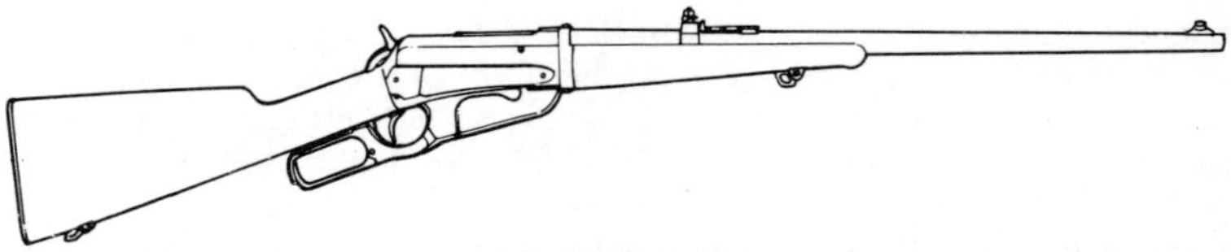

Winchester Model 1895 sporting rifle. Imperial War Museum, London.

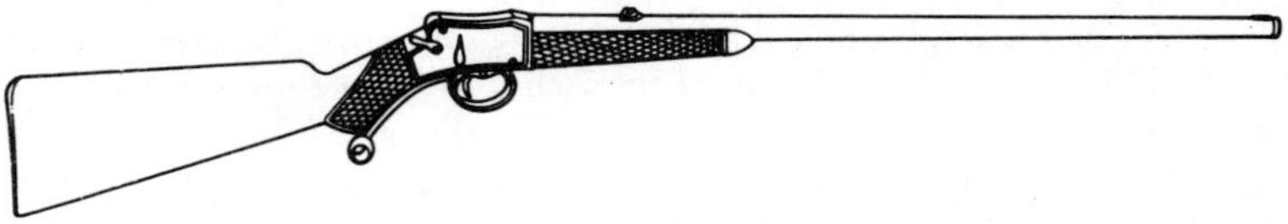

A .310 calibre 'Rook Rifle', a peculiarly English weapon.

drawing down on its hinge. The action could be further strengthened by an extended rib or 'doll's head' on the rear breech face of the barrels engaging in a recess cut in the standing breech. Apart from the great weight of the barrels and their leaf sights these rifles differed in style from most shotguns only in that they had pistol grips and a cheek piece on the side of the butt.

By the late 1880s Express rifles had followed shotgun improvements to the extent that hammerless actions were being fitted to most new weapons. As maker after maker designed and introduced his own hammerless lock the types likely to be encountered proliferated. By the outbreak of the First World War double rifles physically had reached the level of development at which they still are today though competition from magazine arms was not then as intense. The challenge from magazine arms came with the development of the high-velocity, small-bore military arm. The Mauser, Mannlicher and Mannlicher-Schoenauer slowly established their popularity in the smaller and medium calibres in versions which the leading English gunmakers marketed. High-velocity, small-bore bullets were found, when given a hollow or lead exposed nose, to expand enormously with a most disruptive effect on striking an animal. By 1900 it was only a matter of time before this principle was generally adopted for sporting-rifles, and jacketed bullets and smokeless propellant became widespread. The sporting-rifle of the first decade of this century was therefore increasingly becoming the Mauser or Mannlicher, with magazine, firing a high-velocity jacketed bullet. Its advantages, for lesser game, were obvious and it had the edge in cheapness as a double rifle was, by its construction, expensive to produce. For large and dangerous game the double rifle with improved ammunition retained its popularity. It guaranteed a second and, perhaps, vital shot simply by a second pressure on a trigger.

As the new, small-calibre, high-velocity rifles took over the role of the Express rifles the Expresses with their improved performance removed the need for the old heavy 12, 10, 8 and 4 bores. By 1900 such an improvement had been effected that the striking energy of the 0·450 in, for example, was double that attained with the same calibre in the early 1880s whilst the new 0·577 in loaded with cordite fired its 750 grain bullet to almost the same striking energy at 150 yards as had the old 4 bore. In the new, magazine, small-bore sporting rifles perhaps the most dramatic debut was that of the 0·280 in Ross. When it was introduced in 1908 it was the first rifle to reach a muzzle velocity of 3,000 ft/s. The success of this cartridge was to a large extent due to F. W. Jones, whose importance in match-rifle ammunition development in this period was considerable. The Ross's success was enduring. Other makers soon followed the 0·280 in with their magnum cartridges of which perhaps the most famous was the 0·375 in Magnum introduced by Holland and Holland in 1912, which fired a 235 grain bullet with a muzzle velocity of 2,800 ft/s.

It was to be expected that Mannlicher and Mauser could not be allowed to enjoy the monopoly of the market of those who wanted a magazine sporting rifle. Probably their most successful rival was the Winchester, in a variety of calibres from 0·405 in downwards. The Model 1895 Winchester action made a very useful and efficient sporting weapon. It was sold by a number of English and Anglo-Indian gunmakers and often stocked in an English style. There is no denying the fact that so stocked, without the concave American butt plate which so positively locates the arm in the shoulder as the lever is operated, it was not easy to guarantee a smooth second, or succeeding, shot. It was also, even in 0·405 in calibre, though nominally in the heavy medium bore class, actually, with its comparatively light 300 grain bullet and moderate 2,200 ft/s muzzle velocity, not quite in the dangerous thick-skinned big game category.

Not every sportsman was always after elephant or even deer, and rifles designed solely for rook or

199 French soldiers with a Montigny Mitrailleuse; *c.*1870.

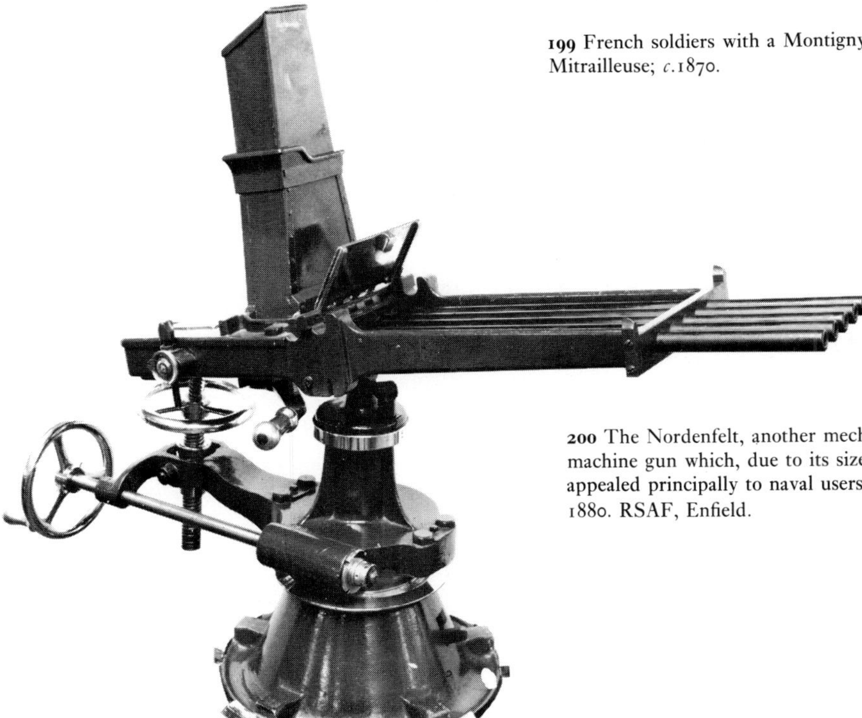

200 The Nordenfelt, another mechanical machine gun which, due to its size, appealed principally to naval users; 1880. RSAF, Enfield.

201 Hotchkiss British 'Machine Gun, Cavalry, No 2 Mark I' of 1914. RSAF, Enfield.

202 A German Maxim gun, Model of 1908, without its tripod mounting. Imperial War Museum, London.

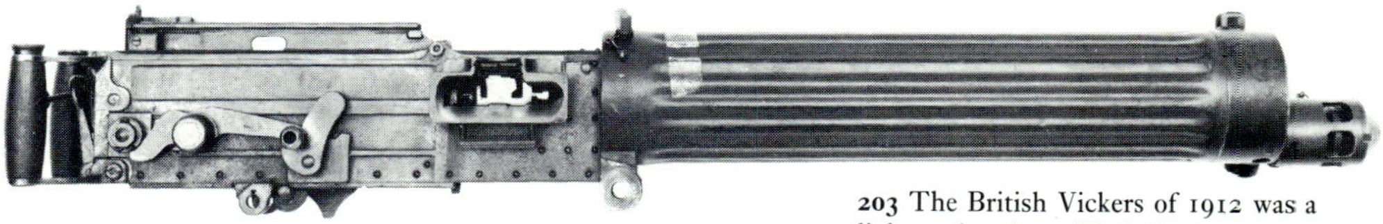

203 The British Vickers of 1912 was a lightened and modified Maxim type which remained in first-line service until the 1960s. Imperial War Museum, London.

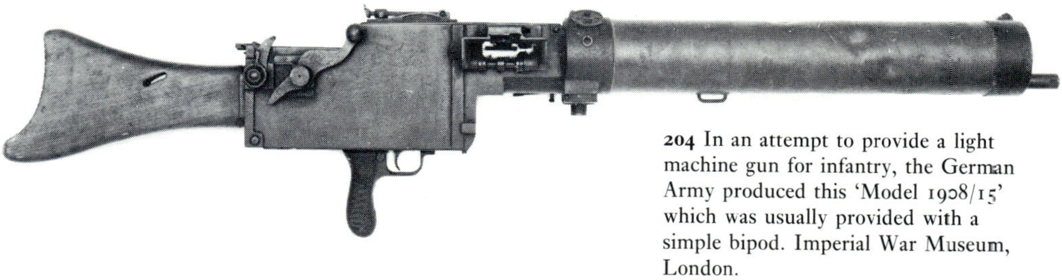

204 In an attempt to provide a light machine gun for infantry, the German Army produced this 'Model 1908/15' which was usually provided with a simple bipod. Imperial War Museum, London.

205 The Mondragon automatic rifle 1907, devised by the Mexican General Mondragon and manufactured in Switzerland. RSAF, Enfield.

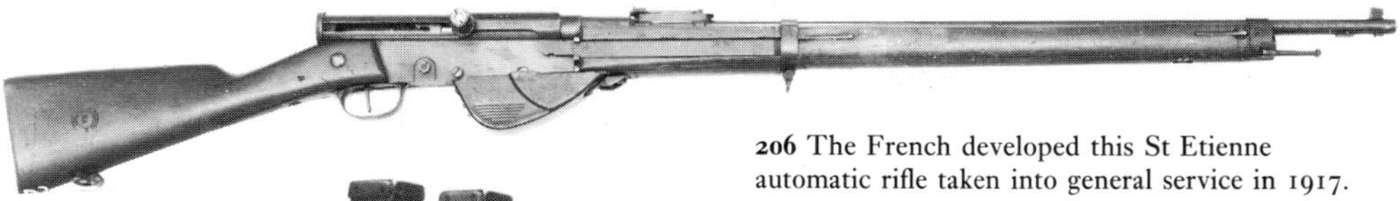

206 The French developed this St Etienne automatic rifle taken into general service in 1917.

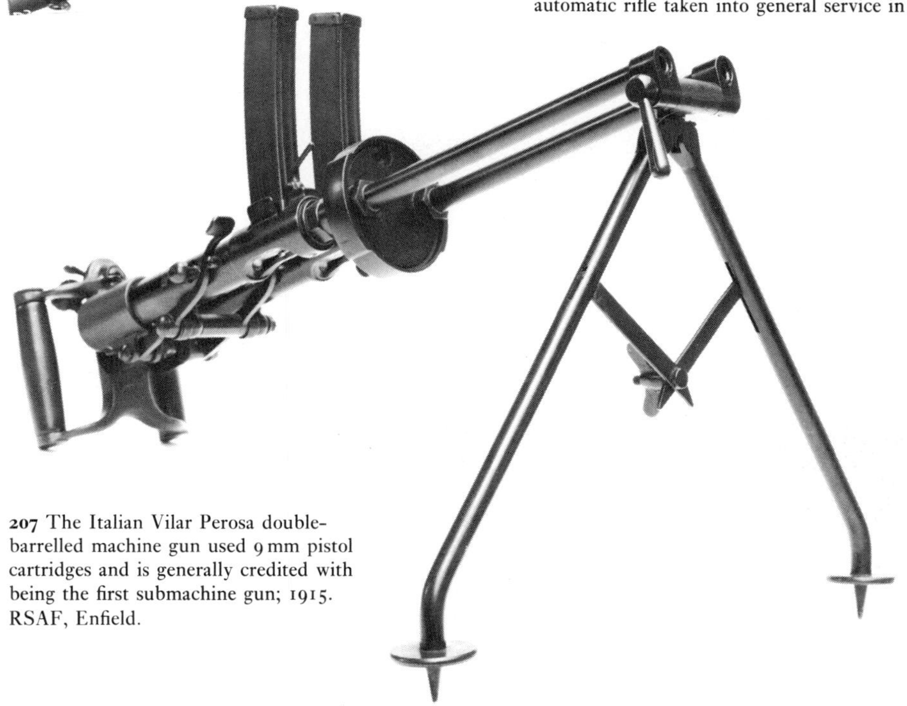

207 The Italian Vilar Perosa double-barrelled machine gun used 9 mm pistol cartridges and is generally credited with being the first submachine gun; 1915. RSAF, Enfield.

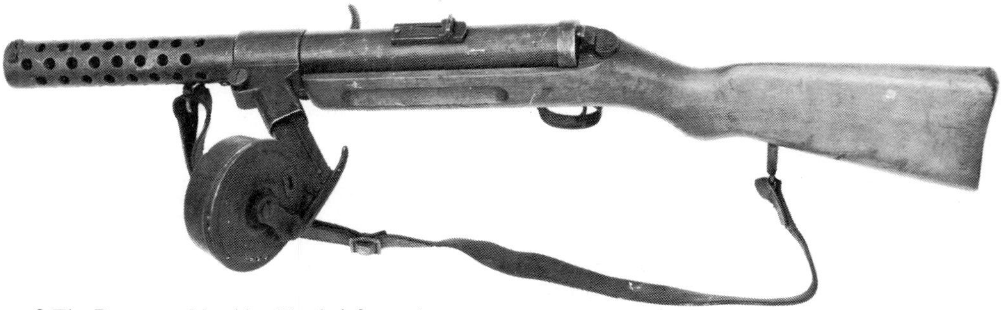

208 The Bergmann Maschine Pistole '18 was the first weapon to be tactically handled in the way which has come to be accepted as the submachine-gun role. Imperial War Museum, London.

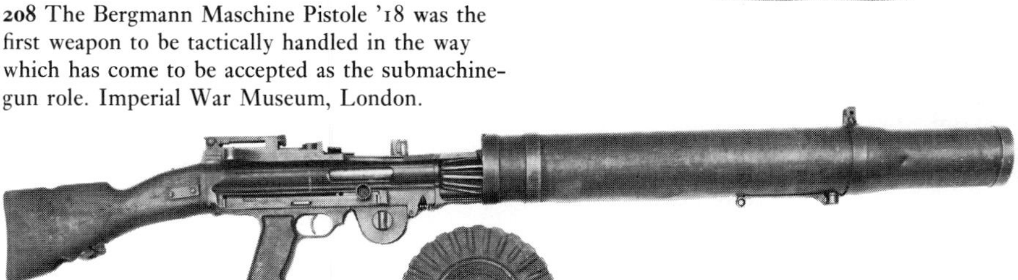

209 The Lewis light machine gun, with its 47-round drum removed and the cooling vanes visible; *c.*1914. Imperial War Museum, London.

210 The Colt-Browning 'Potato-Digger' machine gun of 1895. Imperial War Museum, London.

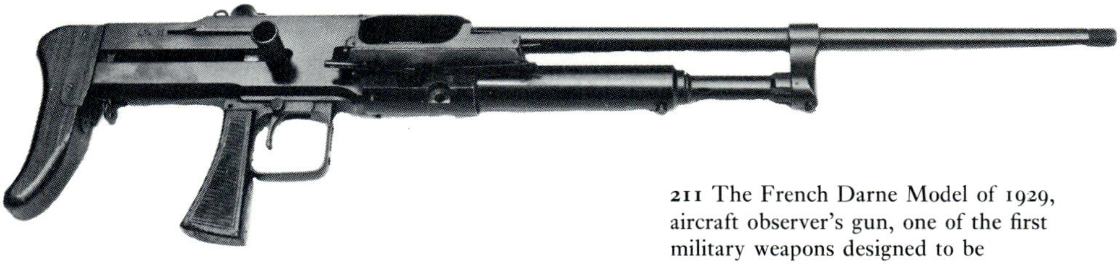

211 The French Darne Model of 1929, aircraft observer's gun, one of the first military weapons designed to be expendable. RSAF, Enfield.

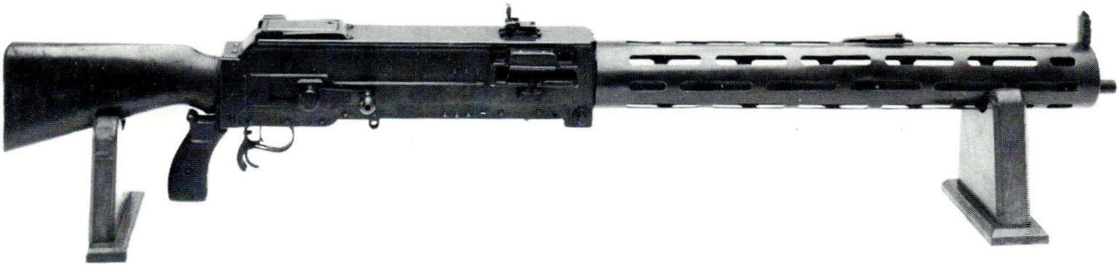

212 The German Parabellum aircraft machine gun was a lightened and air-cooled version of the Maxim, developed in 1914. RSAF, Enfield.

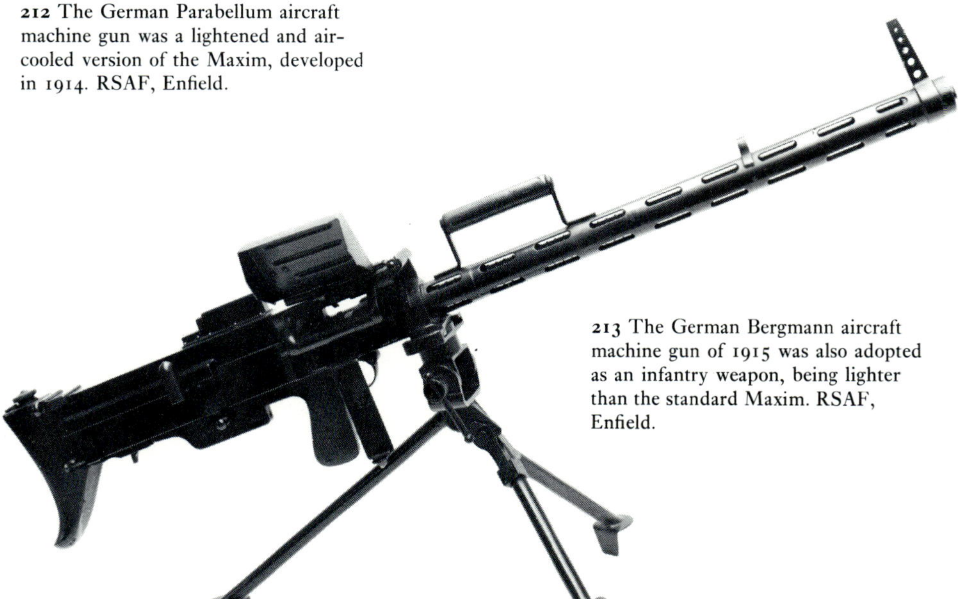

213 The German Bergmann aircraft machine gun of 1915 was also adopted as an infantry weapon, being lighter than the standard Maxim. RSAF, Enfield.

rabbit existed from the beginning of the period under review. In the 1870s some makers constructed them on the Snider principle, others on the Martini or some similar action. The calibre was almost invariably 0·360 in or 0·380 in. They enjoyed sufficient popularity at rooks and similar quarry to induce leading makers to produce fine quality small-bore arms which, in time, following the pattern of improvements to larger calibres, were often of hammerless design. In 1883 Holland and Holland introduced a new 0·295 in rook rifle of improved accuracy. This led to other small calibres such as the 0·320 in and 0·300 in. In America even smaller calibres, of 0·22 in or 0·25 in, were quite popular for small game and gallery alike. Colt, Marlin, Winchester, Ballard, Stevens and many other firms turned out excellent rifles in calibres up to 0·32 in. The popularity of small-bore shooting, especially as a target sport, was further encouraged by the increasing use of the Morris tube. This was basically a liner fitted within the barrel of a service rifle. It was first introduced for the Snider and continued for the Martini and 0·303 in: its usual calibre was 0·230 to 0·297 in. The 0·22 in gradually replaced this 0·23 in bottle-neck cartridge and, well before 1914, was the accepted small-bore calibre. Greener and Bonehill and others converted thousands of old Martinis to 0·22 in and a new 0·22 in rifle of modified Martini form was introduced by B.S.A. There were many that scorned these small-bore rifles and maintained that they were almost useless as training aids for military rifle shooting but, in spite of opposition, miniature rifle shooting, as it was then known in Great Britain, continued to increase in popularity as a sport in its own right.

The Shotgun

The development of the shotgun between 1870 and 1918 was, to a most remarkable extent, devoid of basic invention yet it was at the same time characterised by a wealth of individuality in design and innovation. The improvement of the shotgun within this period was considerable but almost entirely in consequence of the exploitation of inventions, or rather features already in existence. The choke-boring of barrels to concentrate shot patterns had probably been known to some makers for decades and, in any case, it was patented by William Pape in 1866. A public demonstration of choke-bore guns in competition with the best cylinder bores in New York led within a few years to this almost revolutionary improvement being recognised by all as an established feature of the shotgun. Smokeless powder of the type first produced by Schultze had slowly come into use from the late 1860s, being introduced into Great Britain by Dougall, and E. C. powder, even less troublesome, soon followed.

Hammerless breech-loaders were no new idea: Demondion's arm of 1831 was of this type but the first hammerless gun using modern-type cartridges was probably that of Daw of London, patented in 1862, which was itself an improvement of Schneider's action of 1861. It was too clumsy to show any real advantage over a hammer gun and was never popular. In 1871 Murcott, also of London, patented a design in which an internal hammer was introduced on to an otherwise fairly conventional side lockplate. In 1874 Gibbs and Pitt of Bristol went a stage further in designing a hammerless action which was more efficient, through not allowing themselves to be tied too closely to conventional lock layout. Needham, also in 1874, patented an improved hammerless action but it was the privilege and outstanding achievement of Anson and Deeley a year later, in 1875, to design and patent a hammerless action of so perfect a form that it remained throughout the period, and even to the present day, the basic action for cheaper guns. As Anson and Deeley were employees of Westley Richards their action was marketed by that maker. The cheapness of their action, its convenience and undoubtedly higher safety factor soon led to the discontinuance of various schemes for automatic cocking for hammer guns which were developed by some makers in this period. It did not, however, lead to the abandonment of attempts to convert the side-lock itself to hammerless action.

The first really successful hammerless side-lock was that designed by W. Scott of Birmingham and patented in 1878. It had a number of advantages over the Anson and Deeley box-lock. There was an automatic safety bolt or interrupter which almost entirely eliminated the danger of a jar or jolt firing the gun. Under royalty arrangements the design was manufactured by a number of makers, including Holland and Holland. In 1880 Beesley of Purdey's patented a bar-action side-lock which was of so successful a design that it has remained Purdey's choice for their guns right through to the present time. Within a few years dozens of designs or, more often, variants on the basic designs were patented by different makers including Woodward of London in 1877, Tisdall of Birmingham in 1880, Lang of London in 1877, Woodward of Birmingham in 1881, Greener of Birmingham in 1879 and Dickson of Edinburgh in 1880 and 1882. This last gun was possibly the most difficult to define as it was neither a box-lock nor a side-lock. Known as Dickson's Patent 'Round' action it was of peculiar construction in that the lock mechanism was carried directly on the trigger-plate and thus inserted from below.

As time passed it became more evident that, apart from the occasional special action, all designs were either of a box-lock form, in which locks as they formerly existed were dispensed with and the firing mechanism housed behind the false breech, or they were of one or other variety of side-lock. The side-lock was strongest when the minimum of the breech was cut away: there was therefore much to be said for it in back-action style in which the mainspring, instead of being forward of the tumbler, was behind it. There were a few makers who made back-action locks with a plate, outwardly resembling a bar lock, and this gained an aesthetic advantage without the structural drawback of the cavity for a forward main-spring. The great advantage of the side-lock was its lightness, as it avoided the mass of metal housing the action in a box-lock, but to gain the full benefit from a side-lock a high standard of workmanship was essential.

The idea of the automatic ejection of fired cases on the opening of the gun was first developed into a practical design by Needham but in its early form, either as made by Needham himself or by Lancaster, there was an unsightly lump under the action. Neither of these early applications of ejection from the late seventies or early eighties worked sufficiently well to gain real popularity. The first ejector to achieve a foothold was Greener's, which he patented in 1881 and applied to his treble-wedge-fast 'Facile Princeps' box-lock gun. In 1884 Deeley patented an ejector mechanism for the Anson and Deeley lock but he subsequently managed to improve on it in 1886 and 1888. It could also be applied to side-locks and established for itself long-lasting popularity. A few years later Beesley secured a patent on a somewhat simpler ejector mechanism which he sold to Holland and Holland and which became later widely known as the Southgate ejector. The Deeley and Southgate ejectors secured a sizeable portion of the market for themselves but did not, by any means, achieve a monopoly. There was also the Baker ejector and Boss, Lancaster and Dickson soon fitted excellent ejectors of their own peculiar design to their own guns.

Later in the period self-opening actions began to be introduced by some of the leading makers and most also felt obliged to offer a single trigger mechanism for the client who found such an arrangement more convenient than two triggers. Not all guns, of course, were double-barrelled, Lancaster in the early 1880s had some success with a four-barrelled arm and even applied this hammerless system to rifles. There were others in which the barrels were in an under-and-over arrangement. Later in the period such guns were revived and were produced by the leading makers; of them probably the finest were made by Woodward. But if there was little variety possible in the arrangement of the barrels the same was far from true in their construction.

Though steel for gun barrels had been pioneered by Berger & Co. in the mid-century its quality was difficult to guarantee. In consequence, most guns were made with a barrel of iron and steel wound around and formed on a suitable mandrel. These damascus or twist barrels existed in a number of clearly defined patterns according to their precise composition and structure and were often of great beauty. As the price of steel barrels, such as Whitworth's and Krupp's fluid compressed steel, came down so their use became more general, but, for some guns, damascus or twist persisted until the end of the period.

Quality, in terms of craftsmanship, might remain relatively constant through the period, or for that matter through the century, but the shotgun had in

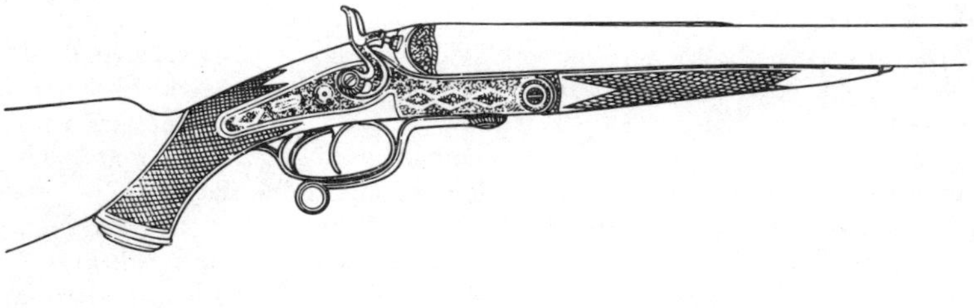

(*Left*) Detail of the 'Paradox' gun, a shotgun with the last few inches of the bore deeply rifled; it can be used with shot or with a solid bullet, *c.*1900. Paradox guns can be found in 8-, 10-, 12-, 16- or 20-bore. Imperial War Museum, London.

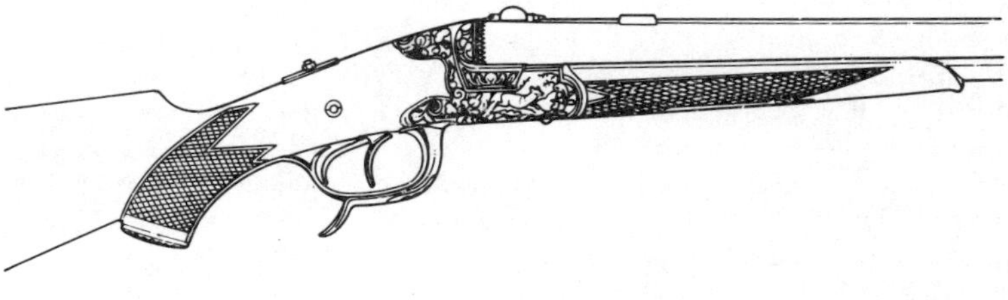

(*Right*) Detail of a 'Drilling', a double-barrelled shotgun with a third, rifled, barrel centrally below the shotgun barrels.

these forty years undoubtedly undergone remarkable mechanical refinement. As was to be expected the same was true of closely related combination arms. The *drilling*, or double-barrelled shotgun with a third and rifled barrel beneath, also progressed from hammer to hammerless design though it did not represent the only attempt at combining the features of a rifle and shotgun in a single weapon. Apart from double-barrelled arms with one smooth and one rifled bore, which were popular in South Africa, there was also the Paradox gun. This could be used to fire a special projectile to which a spin was imparted by a very short section of the bore in the choke itself, which was rifled. It was introduced by Holland and Holland in 1886 and was the invention of the Colonel Fosbery who designed the famous automatic revolver. It patterned extremely well with shot and was undoubtedly a better answer to the dual purpose arm than Lancaster's oval-bore rifle which, rather earlier in the period, had been promoted as possessing the same properties.

The history of the development of the shotgun in this period is one which can be written almost without reference to what was happening outside Great Britain. What British gunmakers failed to do for military rifle actions they more than made up for in shotgun design. But reference must be made to a form of shotgun which was emerging in America and which, in international terms, was at a later date to acquire considerable importance. This was the repeater, or pump-action, gun, obviously closely re-
196 lated to rifled arms operating on similar principles. One of the earliest successful American multi-shot shotguns was the Spencer which had a tubular magazine beneath the barrel and a sliding fore-end 'pump' action. This gun, though popular in America, did not appeal to the British sportsman, which is not very surprising as, by the mid-1880s, a good English double-barrelled hammerless ejector gun was capable of a rate of fire of at least thirty rounds a minute. A Winchester under-lever shotgun came out in 1887 and another, but of pump-action, followed in 1893.

In 1897 a new model pump-action shotgun, further proof of Browning's contribution to the Company's success, was introduced. Improvements to their shotguns continued to appear and, in 1912, Winchester brought out a hammerless repeating shotgun. Other leading American arms companies also manufactured repeating or ordinary shotguns, though where they were in direct competition with the finest products of English gunmakers they could not, and did not, manage to achieve parity in quality or lightness or artistic merit. Amongst the most important American manufacturers of shotguns in the period were Stevens, Remington, Colt, Parker, Smith, Ithaca, Marlin, Burgess and Savage. Some of the styles of gun they produced, though perhaps overshadowed by the English side-by-side double in the period under consideration, were later to acquire wide international acceptance. This is especially true of the automatic and of the under-and-over double. In these fields probably no single individual contributed more than did John M. Browning whose long-recoil action automatic and under-and-over shotguns achieved remarkable success.

Automatic Arms

The advances made between 1870 and 1918 in the design of long-arms to obtain automatic fire were more dramatic than those in any other direction. Though odd ideas were occasionally promoted for automatic, multi-shot or volley fire there were, in 1870, really only two valid approaches to the production of a machine-gun: one was mechanical and the other battery style. In the American Civil War a Captain Williams of the Confederate army had designed a quick-firing one pounder operated by turning a handle, which moved the breech-block backwards and forwards. In spite of the fact that it relied on paper cartridges it functioned with sufficient reliability to see some service in that war. The battery approach could either be on revolver lines or on those in which a large number of barrels, often in a single block, were loaded with a plate, or similar arrangement of cartridges, to be fired in succession or in volleys. A representative of this type was the Vandeberg volley gun, in which the barrels were massed within a jacket with an external appearance somewhat resembling a cannon. In 1870 probably the two most outstanding examples of these two classes of machine- or battery-gun were, respectively,
the Gatling and the Montigny. The Gatling was a 198
cleverly-designed, well-made gun of such merit that it was eventually adopted, to some extent or other, by a number of countries, including Great Britain and Russia, as a military arm. In its later form it was so successful in its application of a direct mechanical drive to the essential operational sequence of loading, cocking, firing, extracting and ejecting that it survived beyond the turn of the century. Indeed, with motor drive a rate of fire of 3,000 rounds per minute was attainable. In comparison with the Gatling, the
Montigny Mitrailleuse enjoyed very limited success 199
but it is of importance as probably the earliest attempt to combine the merits of rapid fire with those of accurate fire. In 1870 Metford spent months in Belgium as a technical consultant on the interior design and manufacture of the necessary barrels. The improved Montigny with Metford's barrels, which was purchased by the British Government for experimental work, was capable of effective fire at 1,000 yards, an outstanding performance at this date. The Montigny was probably the last battery gun to be seriously tested for military employment: the suc-

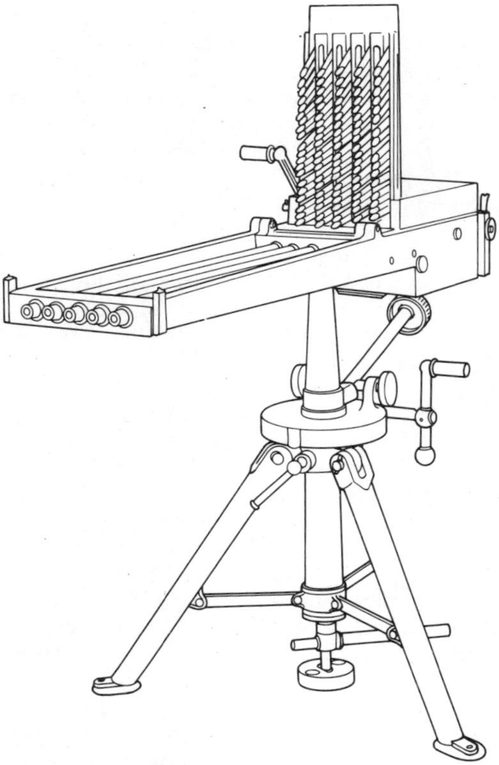

The Gardner machine gun, a mechanical weapon which was extensively used by the British Army and Navy in the 1880s.

cess of the Gatling, on the other hand, was, not surprisingly, the spur for renewed efforts to perfect a lighter and more portable weapon designed on similar lines.

Prominent amongst those who produced manually-powered mechanically-operating machine-guns was another American named William Gardner. His guns were twin-barrelled and lighter and thus more suited to land as well as naval use. The Royal Navy adopted them and they were used in the Sudan in
200 the 1880s. The Navy also issued a single-barrelled Nordenfelt, but it was probably more widely known in Europe in a four-barrelled version. The gun was of the design of a Swede, Heldge Palmcrantz, and, in 1 in calibre, was in use in British service, alongside existing Gatlings in 0·45 in and 0·65 in calibre, from 1880. However blind the powers were to the military potential of the machine-gun they were very concerned to have the best machine-gun available for the close-quarter protection of ships. At about the same time that Great Britain chose the Nordenfelt,
201 France, Russia, Holland, Denmark, Greece and Germany decided on the Hotchkiss. This revolving-style, mechanical machine-gun was also the invention of an American though one who had settled in France. It superficially resembled the Gatling but, in fact, was mechanically very different. As the extent to which it was adopted in Europe suggests, it possessed decided merit; in particular, it excelled over its rivals in accuracy of fire, penetration and durability.

It was left to another American, Sir Hiram Maxim, and one, as his title suggests, who settled in England, to replace, in the operation of a machine-gun, manual or external power with power generated by the exploding cartridges themselves. In 1883 he successfully operated a Winchester 1866 lever-action rifle by harnessing its own recoil through a lever linkage. He also toyed with the idea of utilising the force of the gases generated by the burning charge, a Patent No. 606 of 1884 covers this, rather than recoil but soon decided to concentrate on the latter. In his patent No. 3178 of 1883 he covered the application of his ideas not only to the Winchester, but also to the Peabody Martini, and in a bolt gun with a circular magazine. The first appearance of his toggle-breech arrangement, the essence of his fantastically successful machine-guns, was in his patent No. 8242 of 1884, in which it was illustrated as applied to a rifle. Although he experimented with many other designs for automatic pistols and rifles it was for this action applied to the machine-gun that he achieved international fame. So well did he work out the basic design that, from the date of its first public appearance, the mechanism underwent no change of substance. The British military authorities were most impressed by this arm and Maxim accepted official advice to make the form of the components of his machine-gun compatible with disassembling the mechanism without the use of tools. The gun was fed by a belt of ammunition, was water-cooled and fired the 0·45 in Martini-Henry cartridge. In 1889 the British Government finally adopted the Maxim, which Vickers made for the inventor in 0·303 in calibre and, in 1891, actually began issuing it. In the two years which had elapsed since the first British order for trial guns Maxim's invention had been put through its paces on the Continent. The Kaiser, who personally watched a demonstration at Spandau, was so impressed that he decided on its adoption by Germany though this did not in fact take place until 1899. By 1914 Germany had over 12,000 of these machine-guns in issue or available for issue to her forces. The Russians, too, were impressed by the demonstration of the Maxim that they witnessed in 1887 and subsequently adopted it. The Austrians, on the other hand, bought a few for experiment but ultimately decided on the Schwarzlose. The Maxim was not long in demonstrating its advantages in a practical fashion. It was appallingly effective in its first field use in the 1893-4 Matabele War and, in

1895, scarcely less so in the Chitral Campaign on the North-West Frontier. In the Boer War both sides made use of it in different forms with such effect that it is difficult to understand why it did not subsequently go into wider issue in British service. The Russo-Japanese War confirmed the supremacy of the Maxim over one of its main competitors, the Hotchkiss. It was only logical that its employment and the intensity of its deployment would increase sharply after this until, without exaggeration, it could be said that the Maxim was one of, if not the, key weapons on both sides during the course of the First World War.

The Maxim toggle lock has a close affinity with that later applied by Borchardt and Luger to pistols.[1] It was a long-established design when Maxim first employed it, dating back, in American usage, at least to the 1840s. It was to be found in the 1850s in the Volcanic rifle and in the Henry rifle of 1860. There is thus a clear link between its development in the Winchester of 1866, Maxim's automaticising of that weapon and his own 1884 machine-gun machanism. The mechanism required careful manufacture in good quality materials but these requirements were not difficult to meet by 1890. For adequate strength and durability when handling service rifle ammunition Maxim's design necessarily involved a rather bulky and heavy construction. The British Maxim of 1889 weighed about 60 lb and, even when Vickers in 1912 brought out their Mark I
203 version with a pressed-steel water jacket in place of the original cast bronze one, it still weighed 34 lb. The German 1908 Maxim of 7·92 mm calibre
202 weighed 44 lb without its tripod mounting, and even their light-weight version, the MG08/15 with bipod rest, weighed $36\frac{1}{2}$ lb. There was, therefore, clearly an incentive to design an equally reliable automatic weapon which could genuinely be carried and operated by one man, perhaps an arm which might ultimately replace the bolt-action rifle.

The most promising line of development towards this end was early seen to be by developing gas operation. Paulson, whose name has already been mentioned in connection with the early suggestion of a gas-operated revolver, also in 1885 patented the idea of gas operation applied to a Martini-Henry rifle. In 1891 Maxim, whose 1884 patent had first covered a design for a gas-operated arm, also patented gas operation applied to a Martini. In spite of the early appearance of these designs, none of them seems to have reached a stage of even limited production. The first really successful gas-operated automatic rifle was the Browning and that did not appear until the closing stages of the First World War. It was found easier to harness recoil. This way some early automatic rifles succeeded in achieving sufficient reliability to gain at least a footing in military armament.

Of this class of automatic rifle one of the earliest designs was that which von Mannlicher produced in 1885 and which, in most significant respects, anticipated those features which in Browning's machine-gun so largely contributed to its success. It was a short-recoil arm pioneering a pivoted accelerator for accelerating the movement of the breech-block once unlocked. The lock itself was made and broken by a locking block engaging and disengaging with the underside of the breech-block. The introduction of smokeless nitrocellulose powder with a more sustained pressure improved the chances of achieving reliable automatic breech operation. Mannlicher, in 1891, introduced two modified automatic rifles based on his early design but, in spite of their merit, could find no market for them. He did not allow this to deter him from further improvements. In 1893 he demonstrated two different kinds of hesitation lock which, though only experimental, undoubtedly later influenced other designers and, in 1894, he produced yet two more automatic rifle designs, though this time characterised by blow-forward actions. From both the 1893 and 1894 actions Schwarzlose clearly derived some of the features found in his later machine-guns. Mannlicher had still far from exhausted the possibilities in automatic rifle design. In 1895 he made a locked-breech arm, operated by gas through a piston, which was in many respects the forerunner of the Garand automatic rifle, which very much later was to go into American service. Five years later, in 1900, he introduced another design of related type but with a revolving box-magazine and short stroke piston which anticipated the design features later characteristic of the Lewis gun. Mannlicher's record in the field of all arms development places his achievement at least on the level of that of Browning and Maxim, indeed, in many respects he outshines all other designers.

Where Mannlicher was experimenting, Mauser also made his mark but it was not until 1898 that he was prepared to unveil his first automatic rifle. When he did, it was revealed as of gas-operated, short-stroke piston, locked-breech type. Four years later he produced both a long-recoil, lock-breech design and a gas-operated rifle with a muzzle gas-trap. Neither type was successful. Many others in this period tried their hand at producing an acceptable military automatic rifle but no one met with any success until a Mexican, General Mondragon, in 1908 205
evolved a gas-operated, locked-breech rifle which functioned well under reasonably clean conditions and which did not immediately rule itself out on the

1 'Lock' is used here, and sometimes in Chapter 12, in the sense of a locking device. For an explanation see p. 340.

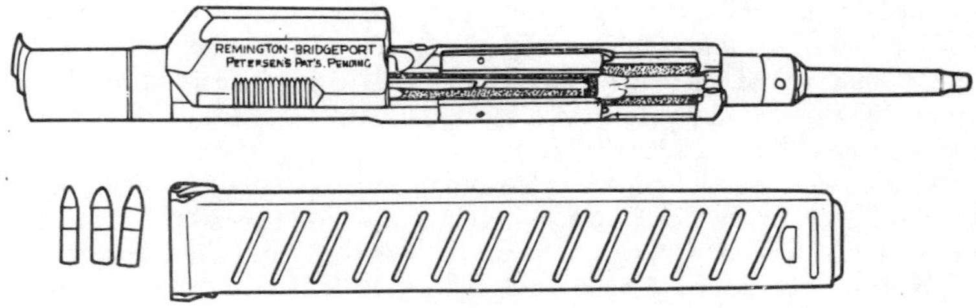

The American 'Pedersen Device' aimed at converting a standard .30 calibre rifle into a rapid-firing trench warfare weapon.

grounds of weight or extreme expense of manufacture. No doubt it owed its success, at least in part, to its Swiss manufacturers, the Société Industrielle Suisse of Neuhausen. In the first year of the First World War the Germans issued at least some of these automatic rifles to the crews of aircraft; the earliest recorded serious military employment of automatic rifles. It was the French, however, who gained the distinction of being the first power to issue automatic rifles for general use in the field. From 1911 they experimented with different designs which led, in 1917, to the St Etienne rifles which actually went into service. They were gas-operated and had a rotating lock breech-block; cartridges were con-
206 tained in a box-magazine. The Browning locked-breech, gas-operated, automatic rifle, to which reference has already been made, was first tested publicly in Washington in February 1917. Winchester started production in February 1918 and by September 1918 American troops armed with them were in action in France. It was an undoubted success as a military arm and a signpost to the future. Though most of the other great powers were similarly investigating the possibilities of automatic rifles, other than the Americans, only the French, and, to a very limited extent, the Germans issued them in the First World War.

The war also saw the emergence of the machine-carbine or submachine-gun. This was an offspring of the semi-automatic pistol and therefore used pistol ammunition. The first successful submachine-gun was designed by B. A. Revelli, an Italian, and
207 was called the Villar Perosa after the company that first manufactured it. Although it was originally intended for use in aircraft, the patent dates from 1914, the machine-gun ousted it in that role almost before it could be brought into use. However, the Italians for some time made use of it in general field service though its rate of fire, of about 3,000 rounds per minute, made it very unsuitable. This very high rate of fire resulted from its unusual design of two barrels, magazines and mechanisms. Even loaded it weighed only $14\frac{1}{4}$ lb and, as the operator could fire either one or both barrels, it was fairly flexible. The breech employed a hesitation lock through a breech-block which turned slightly, whilst camming action also delayed it slightly. The importance of this weapon really lies much more in the fact that it pioneered the military use of the submachine-gun than in its own merit—with such a high rate of fire it was almost impossible to hold on to any target long enough to have any effect.

The Germans were convinced by the Villar Perosa that the experiments, in which they had been engaged since early 1917, to investigate the potential of automatic versions of the Mauser and Luger when fitted with long barrels, shoulder stocks and large-capacity magazines, were not likely to produce as effective a military weapon as an arm designed specifically as a submachine-gun. At the Suhl works of Bergmann, H. Schmeisser, after many experiments, designed an exceedingly simple and effective blowback carbine with the general appearance of a small rifle. It shot the 9 mm Parabellum cartridge and relied only on the weight of its breech-block to retard the opening of the breech. A recoil spring returned the block and ammunition was fed into the side of the receiver from a snail magazine. It went into
issue late in 1918 as the MP 18, or *Maschinen Pistole* of 208
1918, though it was sometimes called the Bergmann Muskete, but, as the end was by this time close, the Germans were not able to develop its use.

The last year of the war also saw the production of the Pedersen device, a unit designed to seat in the receiver of the Springfield rifle in place of its bolt and thus convert it into a semi-automatic weapon firing a 0·30 in pistol type cartridge. The Americans were over-optimistic in their estimation of the military practicability of a system which depended on interchanging a number of components and carrying two types of ammunition. In spite of the great secrecy which attended its manufacture and preparation it was never issued and almost all the thousands of devices made were destroyed after the war. In contrast to the Pedersen device the military importance of the American Lewis gun was considerable.
Through its testing in that role in June 1912 it had 209
the distinction of being the first aerial machine-gun.

The basic design of the Lewis gun was actually the invention of McClean but many of the features characteristic of the better known versions of this weapon, such as its cooling system and rate of fire regulator, were the contribution of Lewis himself. An experimental Lewis was first fired in 1911 and, with its light-weight, drum magazine, and gas-operated design possessed a remarkably advanced and attractive specification in comparison with contemporary machine-guns. Lewis failed to attract American Government orders and went to Europe. His gun was first manufactured in Belgium but later produced by B.S.A. of Birmingham. With the outbreak of the war the advantages of the Lewis, the first really successful portable machine-gun, which, even if not entirely original in design, was a practical example of a light-weight, gas-operated, locked-breech weapon, were immediately recognised by the British. It was much more rapidly manufactured than the Vickers and was remarkably versatile. From very early in the war British aeroplanes began to make use of it. Later, with incendiary bullets, it proved extremely effective against Zeppelins. Tens of thousands of Lewises were made for British use and saw service in all theatres of the war. They were rather liable to jam but they still gave sterling service even under extremes of sand and mud. Evidence of its military worth and its suitability to manufacture under wartime conditions is to be seen in the fact that, at one time or another, the Lewis has been officially used, apart from Great Britain, by the United States, Belgium, Holland, Portugal, France, Russia, Japan, Italy and one or two other smaller countries.

In examining the development of automatic rifles and submachine-guns and, in particular, in having considered already the light-weight Lewis gun it might seem that the first fully successful design of a gas-operated machine-gun has been dismissed as insignificant. Certainly Browning's design, which became the 1895 Model Colt machine-gun, did not 210
have the same significance as Maxim's recoil-operated gun. It did, however, have a design of such merit that in some countries it survived in service until long after the end of the First World War. The United States Navy bought a few of this model but not many; at the time of America's entry into the war in 1917 she had only 158 of them. The 'potato digger', as it was popularly termed, was employed as a training arm by the United States in the war but used in action only in a modified pattern converted by Marlin to more orthodox operation. In this re-designed form, which was the work of A. Swebilius, the Marlin was produced for both ground and aircraft use and proved an effective weapon. Simultaneously with Colt's development of this machine-gun Hotchkiss were working on what was later to become the first successful gas-operated gun using a piston system.

The first gas-operated Hotchkiss, which was announced in 1895, was the result of Benét and Mercié's development of an Austrian, von Odkolek's, initial design. It had a locked breech operated from the movement of a piston itself set in motion by gas tapped from the barrel striking its head. The barrel was of very heavy construction and air-cooled; cartridges were fed by means of strips holding them in a more rigid fashion than a belt. In 1896 the American Navy tried the arm but, though it was rejected, certain improvements to the basic model indirectly resulted. The new model of 1897 found sufficient favour with the French to be adopted on a very small scale but cooling difficulties were not adequately surmounted until 1900, when improved barrel fins were introduced. The Japanese became the first power to adopt the Hotchkiss on a wide scale. However, their employment of it in the war of 1904–5 showed that it was not as satisfactory a military weapon–especially in its feed arrangements–as the Russian Maxim against which it was pitted.

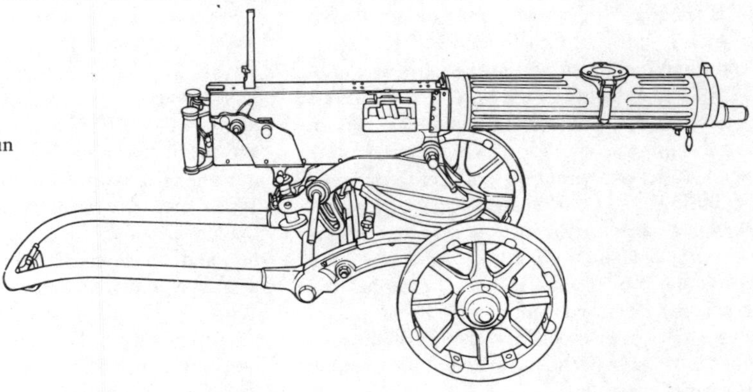

The Russian Maxim Model 1910 machine gun of the unique 'Sokolov' wheeled mounting. RSAF Enfield.

The 8 mm calibre Hotchkiss machine gun, standard weapon of the French Army throughout the First World War. RSAF Enfield.

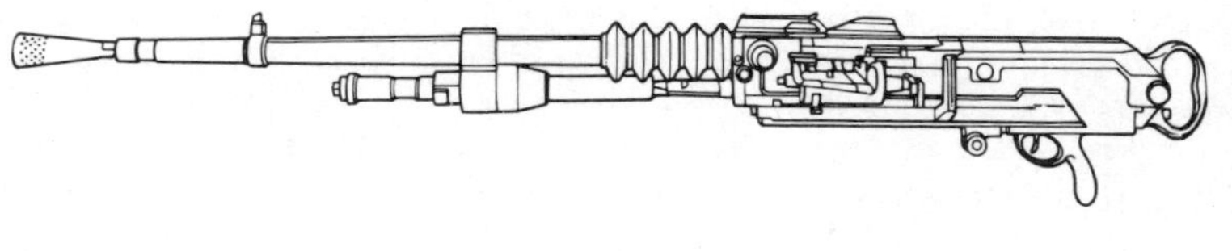

It seemed to many that, if the comparatively slight weaknesses of the Hotchkiss could be overcome, a real rival to the Maxim might emerge. Unfortunately most modifications of the basic design added to, rather than subtracted from the defects. In 1905 the French government produced the Puteaux and, a little later, the St Etienne, in which the operation of the gas piston was pointlessly (and most misguidedly) reversed, followed. Both were later superseded in French service by the 1914 Hotchkiss, which was very similar to the 1897 model. This model was manufactured in considerable quantities in the First World War and proved itself to be a very effective military arm. Far more so than another product of the Hotchkiss Company, the Benét-Mercié or Hotchkiss Portative, which, introduced in 1908, was later adopted to some extent by the Americans. The 1914 Hotchkiss was chambered, as were all the machine-guns that have so far been considered, for the corresponding rifle cartridge, in this case the 8 mm Lebel. The First World War seemed to reveal a requirement for a long range machine-gun and Hotchkiss, accordingly, begun the production of an 11 mm version of their gun. This proved successful and particularly useful for dealing with observation balloons.

The successful Lewis, gas-operated, machine-gun has already been mentioned but there were at least a few other gas-operated machine-guns brought out before the end of the war, though none acquired anything like the importance of the Hotchkiss and Lewis. The French-designed and manufactured
211 Darne, which came into very limited use from 1917, was even more the forerunner of the light-machine-gun, which was to flower in the Second World War, than the Lewis. It was also in anticipation of certain future developments in that it was of remarkably simple construction without a single forged component. Unfortunately, it went too far in the quest for cheapness as its quality was so low that it impaired its efficient functioning. Even so it was quite remarkable in conception. It had a gas-operated breech action locked by a shoulder of the gas piston camming the breech-block upwards and into engagement in a recess in the receiver and was capable of a very high rate of fire.

The First World War saw the inception also of many other machine-guns operating on a recoil system. One of the most successful of these was a German weapon called the Parabellum which was, in essence, a skilfully lightened version of the Maxim. 212
The firm responsible for its introduction just before the war was D.W.M. of Berlin, the manufacturers of the Luger pistol. With a weight of only about 22 lb the Parabellum was an obvious candidate for use in aircraft. Fokker developed an arrangement to permit the Parabellum to fire through a rotating propeller and this machine-gun proved so successful that it became the main German aircraft armament. Not all designers adhered so closely to the Maxim toggle-breech lock. Theodor Bergmann in 1902 first put on the market a short-recoil operated, locked-breech machine-gun. Minor alterations were made 213
in 1903 and 1910 but little else was required, so perfect was the first production form. Bergmann's machine-gun was especially outstanding for its advanced metal-link belt-feed and for its quickly interchangeable barrel system, a most surprising feature in a water-cooled gun. The breech-lock was made by a locking block and broken, after the barrel had travelled to the rear about a half an inch, by it being cammed downwards to release the breech-block for its further rearward movement. The whole gun had a most compact form. Indeed it possessed such qualities that it seems amazing that it did not go into widespread use in the war. It certainly saw service but did not manage even to complement, much less oust, the Maxim.

Another German, recoil-operated, machine-gun which saw service in the First World War was the Dreyse, the design of Schmeisser and the product of Rheinische Metallwaren und Maschinenfabrik A. G. of Düsseldorf. The basic design was patented in 1907 and produced in models of 1912 and 1918. Though it somewhat resembled the Bergmann in external appearance, it was internally very different. In particular, it utilised an accelerator to raise the rate of fire and an internal hammer-firing arrangement, neither of which features appeared in the Bergmann. While the Germans principally relied on the Maxim, the Austrians put their faith in the Schwarzlose. This machine-gun, which was first manufactured in quantity at Steyr in 1905, was quite unique in successful designs of the period in that it functioned on

214 The Austrian Schwarzlose machine gun, one of the few heavy guns to use the blowback action with success; 1907. RSAF, Enfield.

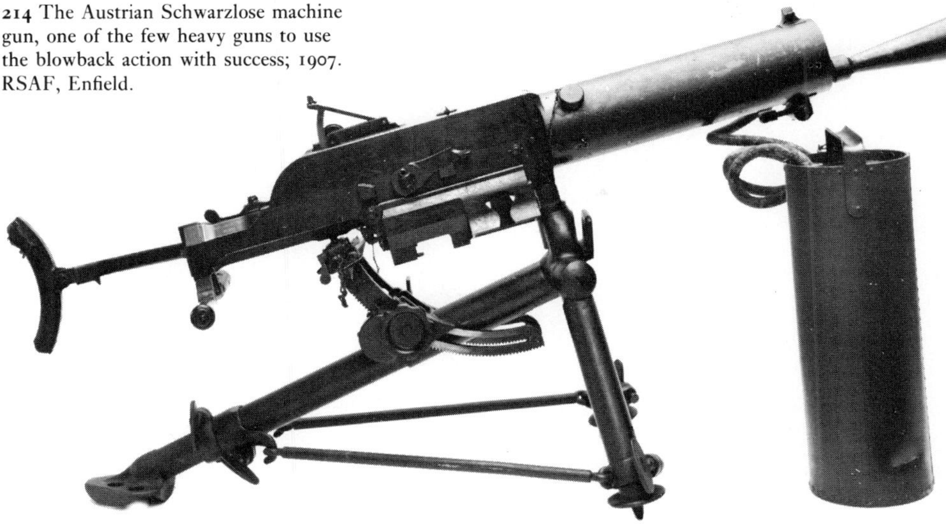

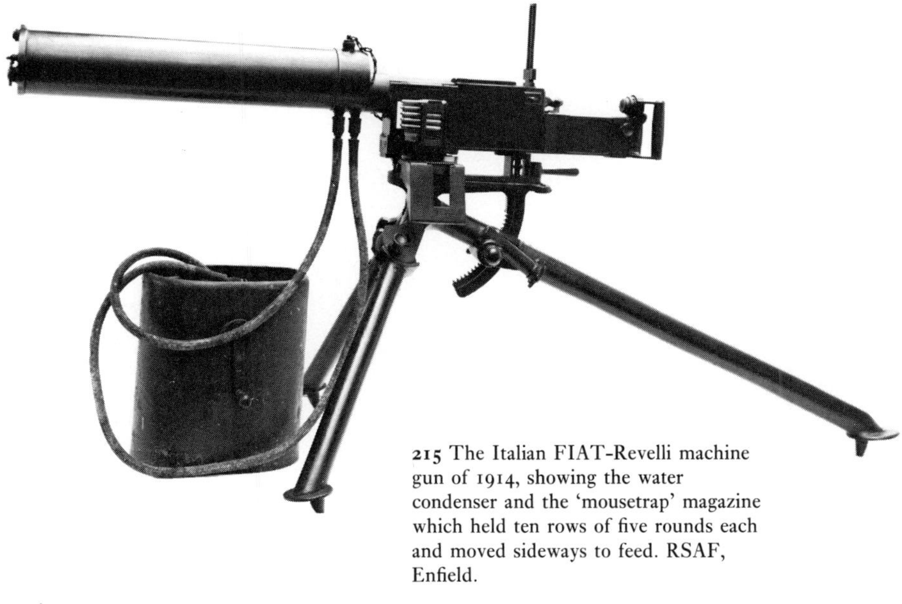

215 The Italian FIAT-Revelli machine gun of 1914, showing the water condenser and the 'mousetrap' magazine which held ten rows of five rounds each and moved sideways to feed. RSAF, Enfield.

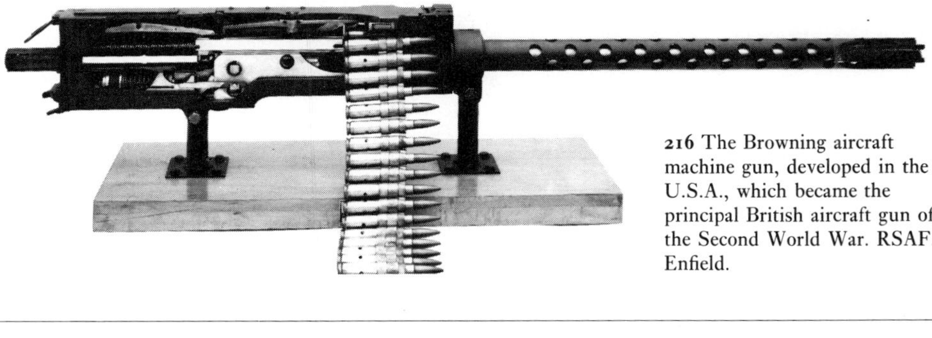

216 The Browning aircraft machine gun, developed in the U.S.A., which became the principal British aircraft gun of the Second World War. RSAF, Enfield.

217 The French Chauchat or CSRG light machine gun; 1915. Imperial War Museum, London.

218 The Italian Breda Model 37 heavy machine gun was extremely reliable, bu used an unusual feed and extraction system; 1937.

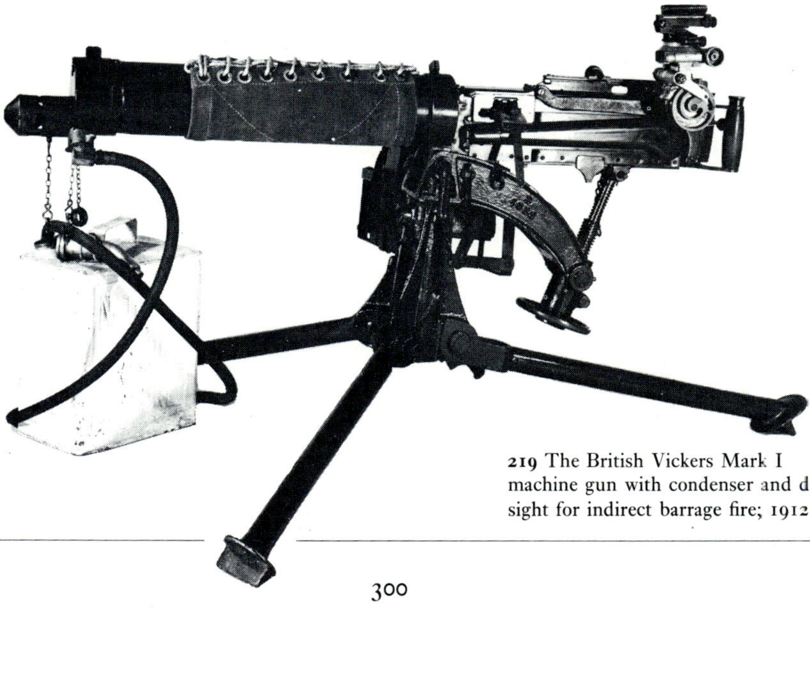

219 The British Vickers Mark I machine gun with condenser and dial sight for indirect barrage fire; 1912.

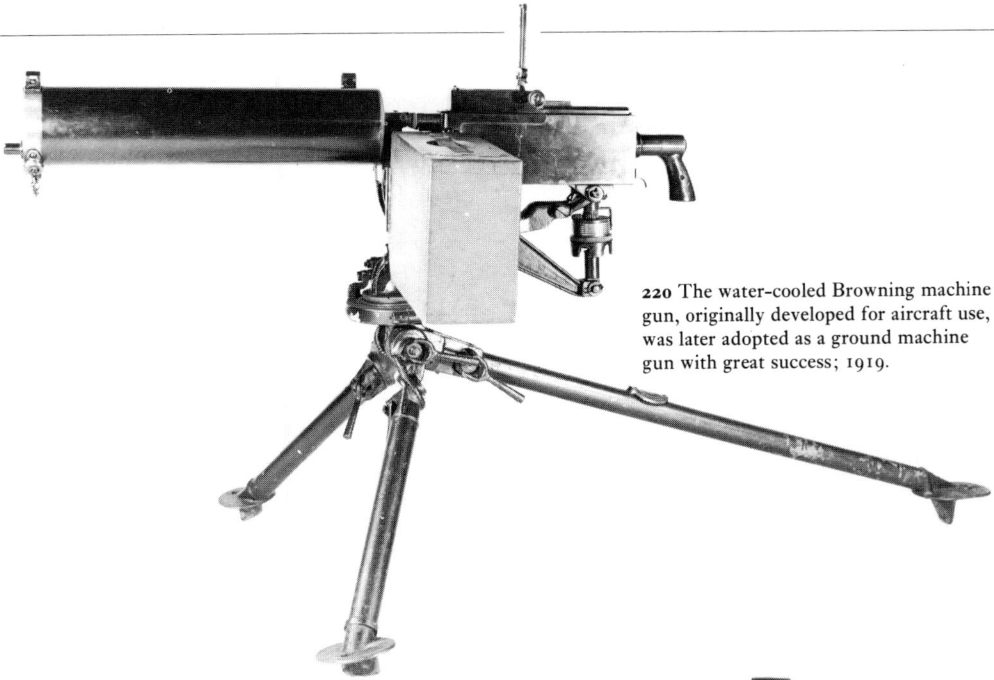

220 The water-cooled Browning machine gun, originally developed for aircraft use, was later adopted as a ground machine gun with great success; 1919.

221 An American Stevens 'Old Model' single-shot target pistol in ·22 calibre; 1864. Smithsonian Institution, Washington, D.C.

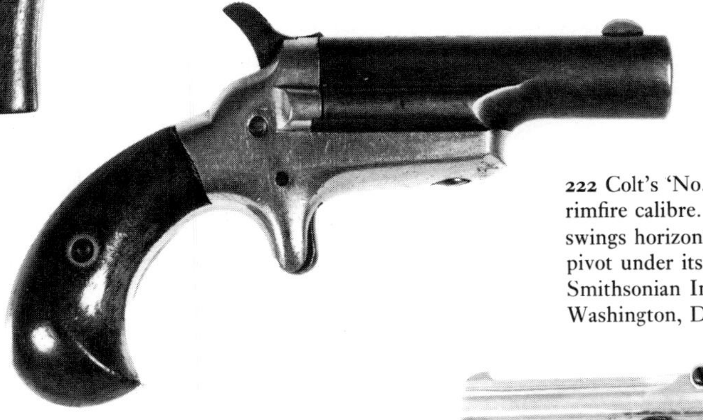

222 Colt's 'No. 3 Deringer' in ·41 rimfire calibre. In this version the barrel swings horizontally about a vertical pivot under its midpoint; 1871. Smithsonian Institution, Washington, D.C.

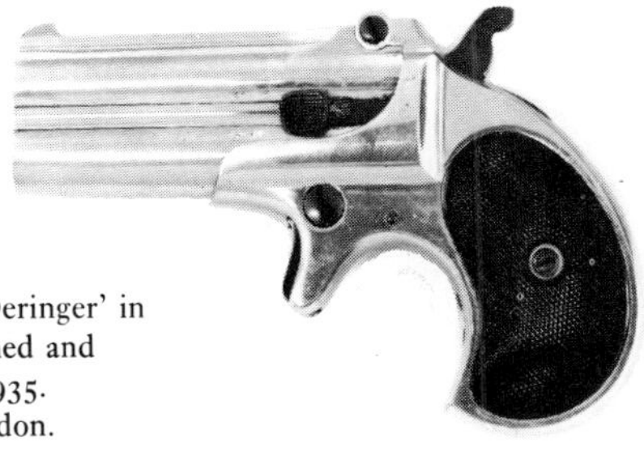

223 A Remington 'Double Deringer' in which the barrels are unlatched and swung up to re-load; 1866–1935. Imperial War Museum, London.

224 A 'Sharps' four-barrelled pistol, in ·23 rimfire calibre, made in Birmingham by Tipping & Lawden; 1854. RSAF, Enfield.

225 Lancaster double-barrelled pistol, in ·476 Enfield calibre; *c.*1885-1900. Imperial War Museum, London.

226 A Shatuck 'Unique' palm-squeezer pistol, with four ·22 barrels. Carried concealed in the hand, it was fired by squeezing the lower part upwards; post 1906. Smithsonian Institution, Washington, D.C.

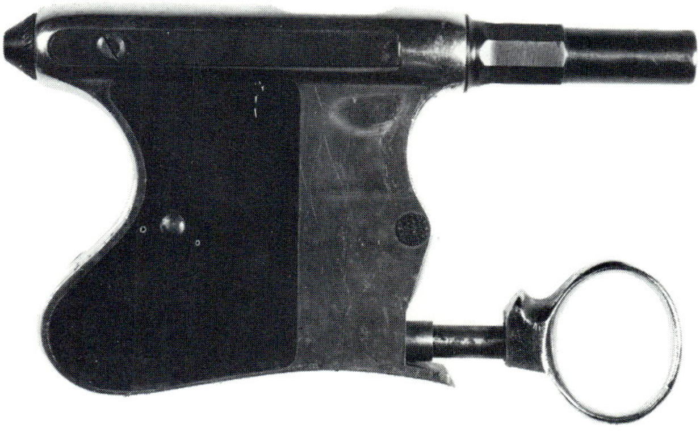

227 The 'Lampo' palm-squeezer pistol in 8 mm calibre. Made by Tribuzio of Turin in the late 1890s. Smithsonian Institution, Washington, D.C.

a retarded blowback system. The design had its drawbacks: in its early forms the only way of preventing cartridge cases from being extracted so rapidly that the base was separated from the body was by forced lubrication of the cartridge as it was chambered. Breech opening was retarded by putting the breech-block at a mechanical disadvantage in compressing a powerful recoil spring. In the Model of 1912, in which it was found possible to drop cartridge lubrication, the retarding arrangement almost assumed the form of a toggle action.

The French did not rely entirely in the war on the Hotchkiss, they also used a curious locked-breech machine-gun which had been developed by a commission and was consequently known either as the Chauchat, after the chairman, or C.S.R.G., after the
217 initial letters of the surnames of the members. It operated on the same long-recoil system that the Hungarian Frommer used for pistols. But it was not suitable for application to machine-guns and this the French and Americans, who carried these guns, found out the hard way, though, admittedly, much of the trouble experienced with the arm was due to very poor standards in manufacture. The Italians, on the other hand, in the Perino machine-gun, as early as 1901 possessed a basically sound and attractively elaborated design, in many respects superior to the Maxim, but somehow failed to put it into production. In 1914 they adopted the hesitation-lock Revelli which had the unique distinction of
215 being operated by both recoil and blowback. The origins dated back to 1908 and it was tested in America in 1911. It was manufactured by Fiat of Turin and survived in Italian service until well after the war.

One of the last designs of machine-gun to come out of the war was the Browning, which was adopted by the Americans under the designation, Model 1917. Two qualities which particularly commended it were the comparative ease with which it could be manufactured and its capacity for long sustained fire. Though some tens of thousands were manufactured in the last stages of the war they scarcely reached the front in time to undergo exhaustive testing in battle conditions. The gun functioned on the short-recoil principle and had a breech locked by a vertically-moving lock: an accelerator aided the last part of the breech-block's rearward travel. One other Browning machine-gun came out in the last months of the war and that was in 0·50 in calibre. The large calibre French Hotchkiss, to which reference has already been made, had demonstrated the value of this class of machine-gun. General Pershing himself took an interest in the move to develop the ·30 Browning into an arm of larger calibre but the war was over before the gun and its ammunition were ready for use in the field.

Other Pistols (excluding revolvers)

There is a very noticeable tendency with some collectors and students of arms to see the development of the pistol, from the time that the metallic cartridge comes in, as, first, the history of the revolver, and then, from about 1900, that of the automatic pistol with, of course, an element of the survival and even, in some measure, the improvement of the revolver. It needs no more than a visit to the pistol range to demonstrate the fallacy of this statement. The single-shot pistol survives to this day as the first and only choice for some forms of shooting as, above all else, its comparatively simple mechanical specification, and therefore durability, confer on it, when well-made, an excellent level of accuracy of fire as well as complete dependability. These are qualities valued by others as well as the marksman; indeed it was for this reason that the breech-loading single-shot pistol was so long dying in military and quasi-military circles. Long before 1871 there were American breech-loading revolvers, with the extra virtue of their rapidity of fire, available for the soldier yet, in that year, a 0·50 centre-fire Remington, rolling-block, Army, single-shot pistol was launched, an 8 in barrel companion arm to the 1867 Navy pistol of similar design. In Great Britain too the Westley Richards single-shot, breech-loading, combustible cartridge pistol was far from dead though, admittedly, not many of these arms were produced in the 1860s. Militarily there were two very adequate reasons why the single-shot pistol retained attractions: it was cheap to manufacture and so obviously a defensive arm that those to whom it was issued could be reasonably relied on to discharge their over-riding obligations or concentrate on the preferred arm. Artillery drivers, for example, were, in the 1870s and 1880s, not always fortunate enough to carry a pistol or even an arm at all as they were expected to give their full attention to their horses, while the trooper might be expected to put his trust in his lance or sword rather more than in his firearm if he carried a single-shot pistol instead of a revolver or carbine.

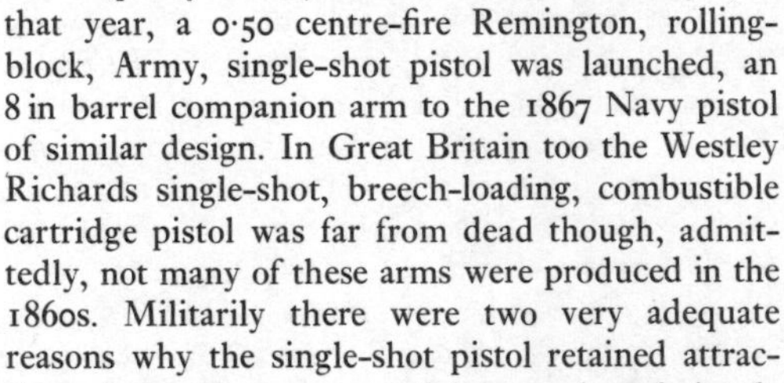

Single-shot c.f. pistol with Remington 'rolling-block' action. Adopted as a weapon by the U.S. Navy (1867) and Army (1871) and also sold as a target weapon. Imperial War Museum, London.

By the 1890s the Remington rolling-block pistol had become a purely target arm, the model of 1891 was available in no larger calibre than ·32-20. In Great Britain, and in Europe too, the single-shot pistol was by this date only a target arm. This does not, of course, mean that the target use of the single-shot pistol chronologically succeeds that of its military employment. To a large extent they were contemporaneous. The Flobert cap pistol for target shooting indoors was probably the earliest metallic cartridge pistol and first appeared in France in 1849.

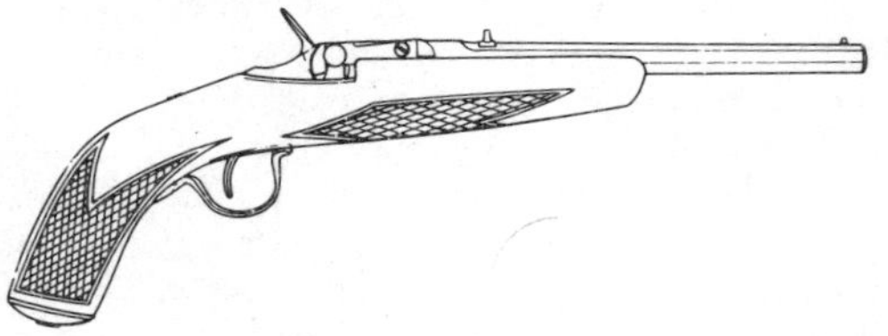

Flobert single-shot rimfire target pistol. French, second half of nineteenth century. Smithsonian Institution, Washington, D.C.

These pistols, shooting a bulleted breech-cap of small calibre and low power, became immensely popular and were widely manufactured in France, Belgium and England until well into this century. Naturally they appear in varying qualities–some very poor indeed–but may readily be identified by the absence of an orthodox breech closure, which is, in effect, provided by the hammer and by the presence of a trigger-like under lever in advance of the trigger-guard which allows the breech to be opened by dropping the barrel on its transverse hinge on the forward part of the frame. The use of the 0·22 in RF long rifle cartridge in a single-shot target pistol was
221 pioneered about 1886-7 by Stevens. Smith & Wesson in 1891 issued their combination revolver or single-

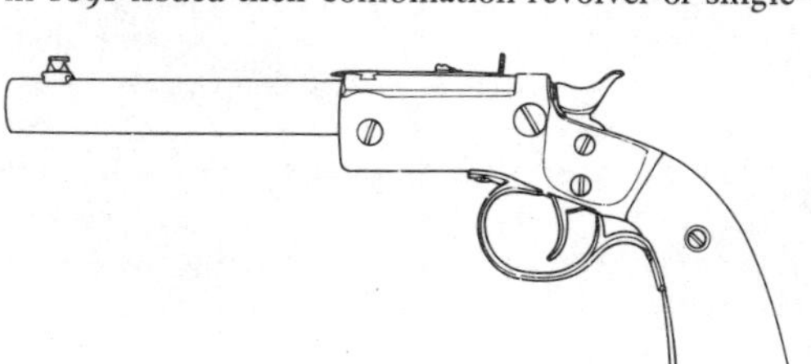

Stevens 'Gould' model target pistol in .22 calibre. Imperial War Museum, London.

shot pistol. This was a fine target-shooting set. As well as a 0·38 in single-action revolver there was a choice of 0·22 in long rifle, 0·32 in S & W or 0·38 in S & W single-shot barrels and a pair of oversize target grips. Webley followed suit in Great Britain in 1909 with a 0·22 in RF target pistol of very neat design in which the downward and forward movement of the trigger-guard unlocked the breech to allow the barrel to be hinged down. So successful was this pistol that it was still in production sixty years later with only the most minor modifications. It is perhaps worth noting that Webley's did not suddenly turn to small-bore pistols, they had had a great deal of experience with a series of Morris Tube single-shot adaptors in their various 0·455 in and 0·476 in revolvers. This highly successful form of adaptor

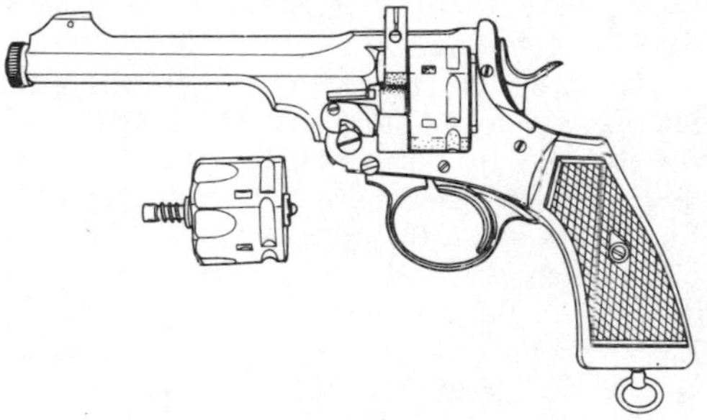

Webley .455 calibre service revolver with the cylinder replaced by a .22 calibre adapter unit held in place by a screwed bush at the muzzle. Imperial War Museum, London.

dated back to the early 1880s and originally used the 0·297 to 0·230 in long Morris cartridge. Similar devices were also produced by Wilkinson and Kynoch-Mullineux. In 0·22 in RF long rifle form they have remained popular until long after the period with which we are here concerned.

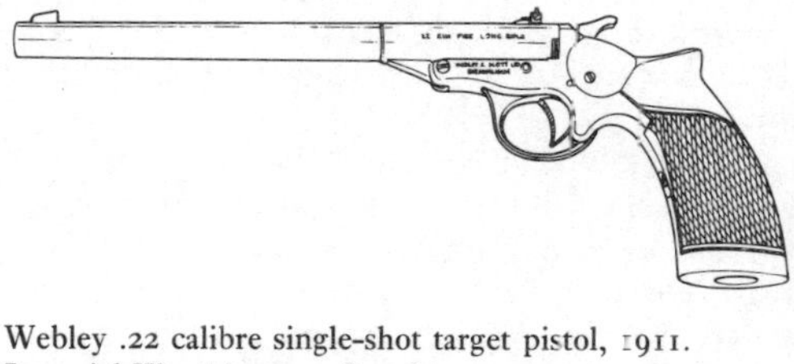

Webley .22 calibre single-shot target pistol, 1911. Imperial War Museum, London.

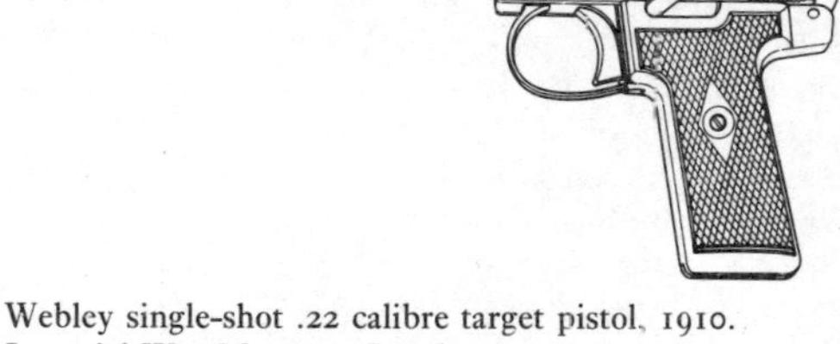

Webley single-shot .22 calibre target pistol, 1910. Imperial War Museum, London.

The field of single-shot target pistols was not entirely dominated by Webley and Smith & Wesson. Stevens, as has been noted, indeed anticipated them with a number of models of a true 0·22 in RF, long rifle, long-barrelled target pistol. There was the Diamond Model No. 43 available with either a 6 in or 10 in barrel, and first marketed in 1888. From about 1869 Stevens had made many different single-shot pistols in different barrel lengths and calibres, including some which could quickly be fitted with skeleton stocks to convert to 'pocket' rifles. The model which remained longest in production was the Lord No. 36, introduced in 1880, though only later available in 0·22 in RF long rifle, and not discontinued until 1911. In 1888 the Conlin No. 38 followed and survived until 1903; the Gould No. 37 was even shorter lived, running only from 1890 to 1903; and the Offhand No. 35 also available in 0·22 in long rifle as well as, like the others, in a variety of other small calibres flourished briefly only from 1907 to 1916. To these pistols Smith & Wesson's Perfected Model of 1909 was a very serious rival and one which generally prevailed at the top level of competition. It was inevitable that single-shot target pistols would, at some stage, attempt to borrow design features from the automatic pistol: in America this did not happen until Stevens brought out their Model 10 in 1919, to be followed by Smith & Wesson's Straight Line in 1925 but in England Webley tried it before the First World War. The 1911 0·22 in Webley target pistol fitted with either a $4\frac{1}{2}$ in or 9 in barrel was, in fact, of a rather unusual design. It might be termed a self-cocking and, occasionally, self-ejecting pistol. It did not utilise the recoil to feed a fresh cartridge into the breech, that the firer was expected to do by hand when he closed the slide. In theory at least the fired case was blown out of the chamber and clear of the gun as the slide opened; in practice it often had to be pulled out with a hand ejector.

There were certainly a large number of different manufacturers of long-barrelled, single-shot target pistols: many on the continent of Europe as well as those in Great Britain and America. But as a group, and in spite of a rare Belgian 12 mm PF with under-hammer action, their weapons of this general type do not demonstrate the mechanical variation, and therefore interest, of the other major group of single-shot, single-barrelled pistols – that of self-defence pocket arms. Without a doubt the most celebrated in this class is the Colt Deringer but it is by no means the only representative of this group. The true Colt Deringer was in any case preceded by Moore's and there were other arms made by, or to the designs of, Marlin, Remington, Williamson, Stevens, Conn and Webley.

The Colt No. 1 National Deringer was that patented by Daniel Moore in 1861-3 and mechanically distinguished by its breech-opening action in that the barrel rotated to the left to expose the chamber for reloading after an automatic ejector

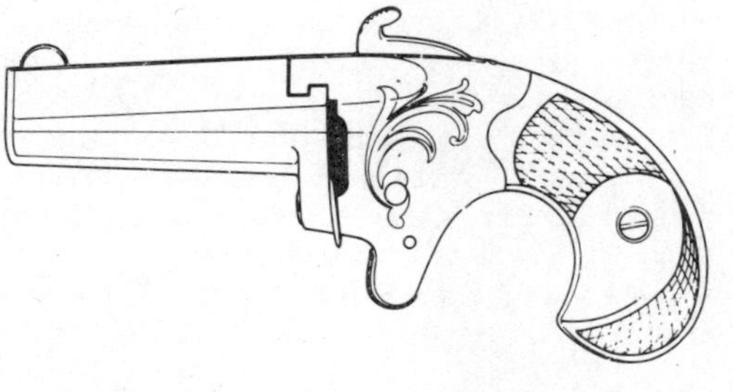

Colt 'No. 2 National Deringer' in .41 rimfire calibre, 1870/72 to *c*.1890. RSAF, Enfield.

had operated. This fired a 0·41 in short RF cartridge as, normally, also does the Colt No. 2 National Deringer. The Second Model principally differs from the First in having conventional wood or other appropriate material grips whereas the First Model was of all-metal construction. The other small, single-shot pistol of this kind produced by Colt was based upon a patent of Thuer. Known normally as the Colt Deringer No. 3 it was mechanically different 222
from the Models 1 and 2 in that the barrel swung sideways to the left to eject the spent case and permit reloading. It was produced in greater quantity than either of the other models so that it is markedly more common today though manufacture of the First Model continued until about 1890. Marlin marketed a series of three deringers, the 'Never Miss', in 0·22 in, 0·32 in and 0·41 in and another the 'Victor' also in 0·41 in and Hopkins & Allen, as well as their own 0·22 in RF Deringer, produced under Marlin's patent another 0·41 in deringer known as the 'XL Deringer'. All had side-swinging barrels similar to the Colt No. 3. Stevens, with one exception, limited his deringer-styled single-shot pistols, including 'The Gem', to 0·22 in short RF, but his Vest Pocket pistol chambered a 0·30 in short RF cartridge. In England Webley experimented with 0·41 in deringers very similar in form to the Colt Thuer but its rarity today suggests that comparatively few were made.

Perhaps the oddest single-shot small pistol was the Webber squeezer, patented in 1905. It had a simple cylindrical outline with a collar trigger that one drew towards one to cock and discharge the striker but in spite of its small size it was chambered to take a 0·32 in CF cartridge.

With the Remington real interest is injected into this group of pocket single-shot pistols. The Remington-Rider Deringer in 0·17 in calibre was absurdly small, it entirely merited its original name of 'parlor pistol'. Few were made and manufacture lasted only a few years in the 1860s; a successor in 0·22 in calibre survived until at least 1877. The most memorable features of this small pistol are the curiously shaped butts and detachable breech pieces.

Strangely, the outline of this, perhaps smallest of cartridge deringers, is slightly reminiscent of what must be the largest single-shot pocket-pistol, the Second World War 0·45 in ACP Liberator pistol, of the cheapest construction for quantity production for the arming of resistance forces in occupied territories. It was another pistol known also as the Remington-Rider, in 0·32 in RF calibre, and patented in 1871 which goes a stage further than any of the

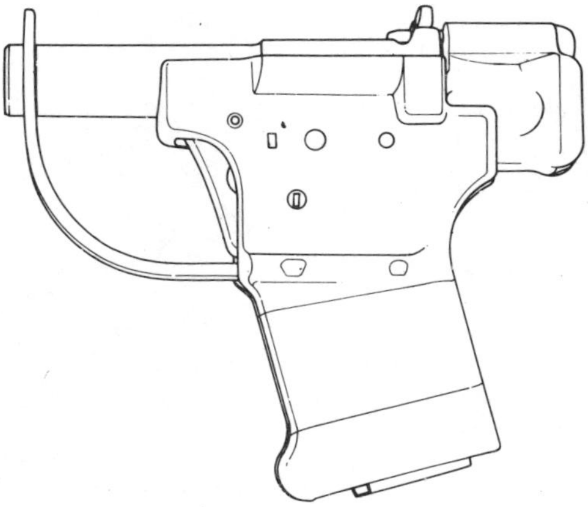

British 'Liberator', .45 calibre single-shot pistol. Made for use by resistance groups during World War II. Imperial War Museum, London.

pistols so far discussed in firepower potential. This single-barrelled pistol is mechanically cocked by pulling the breech-block tang to the rear, the case extracted and ejected and a new cartridge presented from the five-shot tubular magazine which lies beneath the barrel. Forward pressure on the breech-block tang completes the cycle by chambering the round. Its rarity again suggests that the system was more convenient in theory than practice. A harder and more certain punch, for the customer who wanted to keep a shot in reserve, was afforded by the Remington double Deringer, an arm which achieved
223 remarkable popularity, selling over 150,000 between 1866 when it was launched and 1935 when it was discontinued. This eleven-ounce, 0·41 in pistol was the invention of William Elliot, one of Remington's employees. The barrels were arranged one above the other and hinged at the top to move upwards for loading. A single extractor ejector was manually operated by a stud on the left side in the concave between the two barrels. The breech was unlocked by a lever pivoting on the right side of the frame just above the stud trigger. The hammer's nose alternated between the upper and lower positions. Modern firing tests have shown that, if aim is taken a little lower than required for a revolver, this deringer was easily capable of hitting a man every time at fifteen yards. Remington's may have discontinued their over-and-under deringer but others keep the pattern alive–a near replica in 0·22 in SLLR was until recently made in Germany by Rohm of Sontheim (Brenz).

The Remington system for over-and-under-barrelled pistol operation was by no means the best or the only one; indeed an examination of a number of these weapons will show that the movable trigger nose was rather too easily damaged. A more durable arrangement for pocket-pistols was foreshadowed in such percussion pistols as makers Reilly or Smith of London turned out in the 1830s and 1840s. An internal plunger-type striker fired the upper barrel and the barrels were then rotated by hand through 180° for the second shot. Woodward of London registered this design, adapted to rimfire cartridges, on 4 February 1863. His pistols are often very heavily silver plated with handsome bone handles. The barrels rotate anti-clockwise for loading on the right side where the frame is suitably indented. Webley also made a similar pistol: calibres used by the two makers range from 6 mm PF to 0·44 in. These pistols are very flat, especially in the smaller calibres and lie almost invisibly in the pocket.

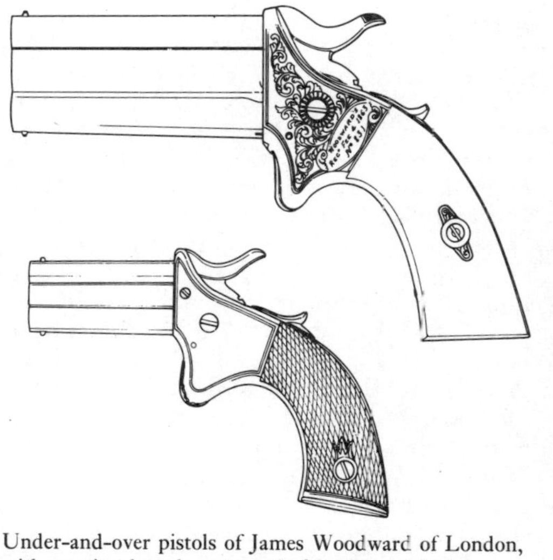

Under-and-over pistols of James Woodward of London, with rotating barrels, patented 1863. Imperial War Museum, London.

Side-by-side, double-barrelled, cartridge pocket-pistols are decidedly uncommon. Most seem to be 7 mm or 8 mm PF and of European origin. The traditional percussion lock form might be adhered to, as in a $2\frac{1}{2}$ in barrelled example with concealed erecting trigger, London proved and with breech unlocking lever sideways-swinging under the barrels. Delvigne's Belgian design of slightly more compact form, with near vertical grip, possessed some inter-

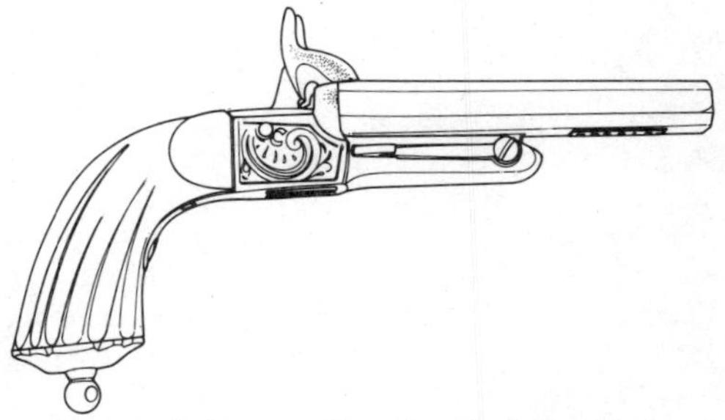

Double-barrelled 9 mm calibre French pinfire pistol. Third quarter of nineteenth century. Smithsonian Institution, Washington, D.C.

esting features: the two barrels, together with the rod trigger assembly, rotate clockwise to the right to be loaded at 90° to the closed position and the barrel unit is held in the correct firing position, which brings the rod trigger into alignment with the two sears, by a hook-ended removable rod which serves also as an ejector and trigger-guard. Thus a 3 in barrelled pistol has an overall length of only 4 in and no more depth than a conventional arm of similar calibre. In spite of the fact that pocket-pistols of this kind exist, the double-barrelled pistol is normally encountered in much larger size. As a 0·410 in shot pistol it still commonly survives today, directly and obviously descended from the double-barrelled flintlock horse or holster pistol of the eighteenth century. When W. W. Greener in 1883 compiled the fourth edition of his famous volume *The Gun and Its Development* he saw fit to include double-barrelled breech-loading pistols of the kind he termed saddle-pistols in 0·577 in calibre. He explained that they were often used for buffalo-shooting in America and were carried in pairs in saddle holsters so that it did not matter if they weighed $3\frac{1}{2}$ lb a piece. Their actions were similar to those then in vogue for shotguns with rotating under-lever or side-lever action and hammer locks. Barrel length was about 6 in and the Snider cartridge they chambered was charged with a spherical ball and $1\frac{3}{4}$ drams of powder.

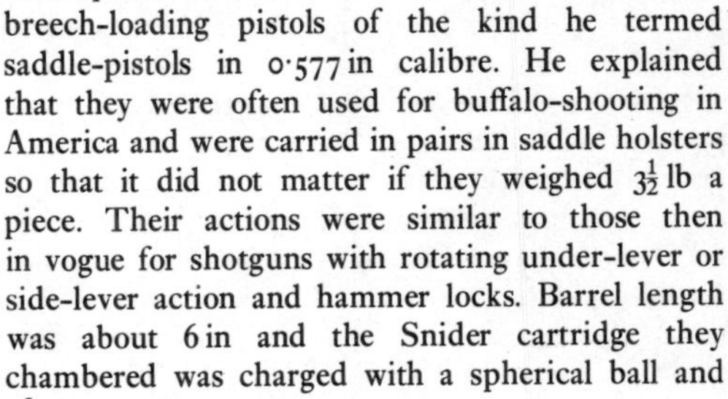

Belgian double-barrelled .60 calibre pinfire pistol. Third quarter of nineteenth century. Smithsonian Institution, Washington, D.C.

These are the pistols that have today somehow acquired the name 'howdah' pistols–an Indian flavour has replaced the American! There is, of course, no secret of their being carried on expedition by big game hunters and explorers such as Sir Samuel Baker. They certainly continued to be made by the leading London makers until the end of the period under review and, as such, exhibited the improvements in lock design that shotguns also show. Bland, for example, made a singularly attractive,

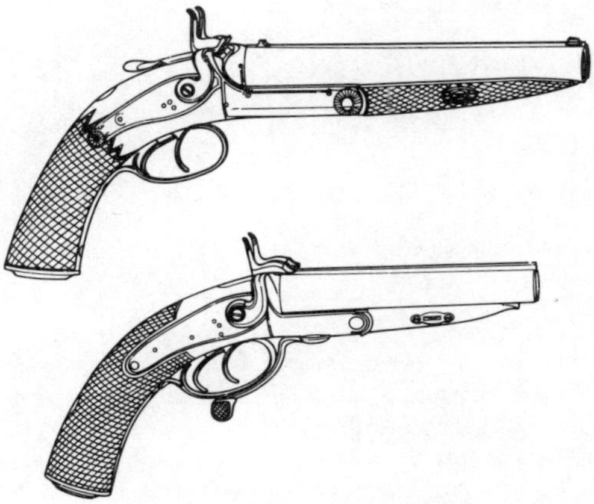

Double-barrelled, saddle or 'Howdah' pistols. (*Top*) C.f. by Moore & Grey, London, *c.*1880. (*Bottom*) Pin-fire by Harkom, Edinburgh, *c.*1875. Tower of London Armouries.

$9\frac{1}{2}$ in long, double-barrelled 20 bore pistol with hammerless front-action side-locks and single trigger, self-setting safety located, in shotgun style, on the top just to the rear of the top lever and saw-handled butt. Firing it is quite an experience, indeed the recoil is more severe than that of any other pistol that the author has shot but, in appearance, with its very high grade workmanship and materials, it attracts in a way that few modern pistols do. Of the earlier period a typical specification is that of a double-barrelled 0·577 in, side-lever hammer pistol with $6\frac{1}{2}$ in bands, all steel fore-end and engraved back-action locks made by Wilkinson–who probably produced as many of these arms as any maker. It should not be inferred that all double-barrelled pistols of this period fall necessarily into the pocket or saddle class, others can be encountered but they are rare. Holland & Holland of London about 1870, and perhaps to an individual order, made a double-barrelled, top-lever, rifled back-action, hammer pistol with non-rebounding locks, in as small a calibre as 0·36 in but it was more usual, and even with Charles Lancaster, for the double-barrelled pistols of this period to be of 0·577 in calibre. It is uncommon to find a Lancaster double-barrelled pistol of so conventional a form and perhaps only because it antedates the introduction of his design for multi-barrelled pistols that later almost became his hallmark. For all that his 0·577 in over-and-under pistol is a considerable rarity, it is decidedly more common in 0·476 in or 0·455 in calibre. The distinctive feature of these hammerless pistols is their revolving striker mechanism which fires each

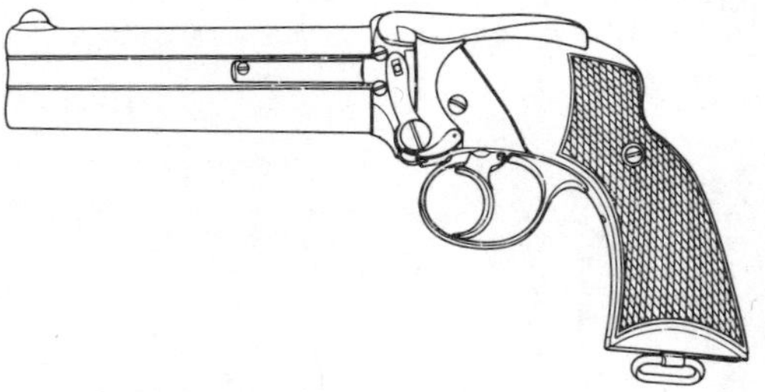

Lancaster 'hammerless' four-barrelled pistol in .577 Snider calibre. English, *c.*1885-1900. Tower of London Armouries.

barrel in turn. The extractor is housed in the depression between the barrels on the left side and functions very powerfully. All the Lancaster 0·577 in pistols the author has seen, and that amounts to only three, have conventionally shaped revolver butts; in 0·476 in or 0·455 in they are invariably fitted with bird-head butts. It is interesting to note that there was more than adequate strength in the 0·577 in pistol for a conversion to 20 bore, if the owner desired it, as, apparently, did the one-time possessor of pistol No. 8424. Lancaster, who invariably rifled these pistols on his oval bore system, never produced them in quantity. He was far too successful in the promotion of the four-barrelled version.

The construction of the Lancaster four-barrelled pistol is extremely similar to that of the double-
224 barrelled pistols. They are almost always in 0·455 in or 0·476 in calibre but a smaller 0·380 in version is known and others are believed to have been supplied to special order. Manufacture started soon after 1881 and ran on for about twenty years. Minor alterations were made, barrel latches went through three different shapes, very rare features of a trigger-guard spur or a shoulder stock may be found, and an alternative version was available with a cocking trigger projecting downwards through the trigger-guard. This had the virtue of making the arm quite easy to shoot, even to near target accuracy, since it lessened the trigger pressure by about ten pounds. These pistols were very well-made and serious rivals of the revolver as officers' weapons in the African and Indian minor wars of the late nineteenth century. Their ability to handle the government 0·455 in cartridge, in fact, kept them in occasional use right through the period and even into the Second World War. Lancaster's are not the only large calibred, four-barrelled pistols, they were also made in London in the 1880s to Martin's patent–the Mitrailleuse Pistol–and to Bland's but so few were produced that these arms are exceedingly rare today.

At this time a smaller calibred four-barrelled pistol 225
was enjoying considerable popularity. It was the Sharps pepperbox and, based on a patent of 1859, had been in production since the early 1860s. Apart from the features which usually vary between any large and small calibred pistol, it differed chiefly from the Lancaster in having a hammer action and achieving the rotation of the striker in the nose of the hammer itself. Again there are many minor variations in detail and a number of sizes of frame. The largest calibre used was 0·30 in but more commonly it was 0·22 in RF. In England this pistol was made under licence by Tipping and Lawden of Birmingham, who added a 9 mm version to the range of calibres. A few were made by Webley's after they took over Tipping and Lawden in 1877 and some English ones carry the name of the retailer rather than that of the manufacturer. There is also a distinctive model, usually in 0·32 in calibre, with bird-head grips. The basic design was very widely imitated on the Continent, often with interesting modifications and variations. Amongst the best known were pistols by Grünbaum of Austria and H. Biedermann, some of them reaching quite large calibres, up to 12 mm, and, of course, in a very close replica form, manufactured by the Navy Arms Company of Italy, the weapon still lives on. For all its wide popularity the Sharps did not enjoy a monopoly of the four-barrelled pocket pistol market, even in the United States. There was a Starr pistol patented in 1864 though derived directly from a design patented in 1856. It principally differed from the Sharps in that the striker-rotating mechanism was separate from the hammer and, therefore, interposed as a unit between the flat-faced hammer and the breech. There were other

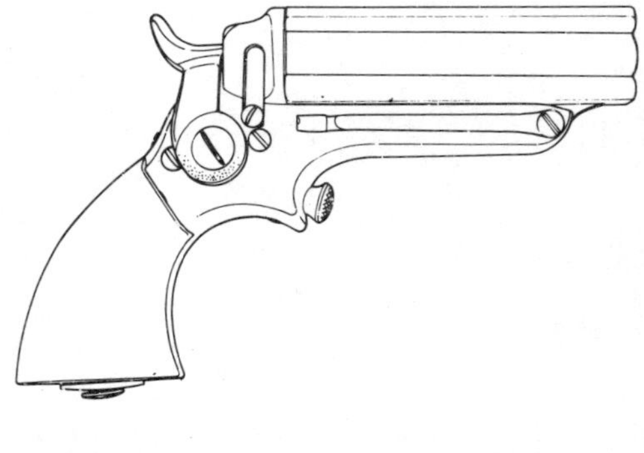

Four-barrelled Deringer by E. T. Starr of New York, 1864-67. Smithsonian Institution, Washington, D.C.

differences too. The barrels tipped down for loading rather than slid forward as in the Sharps and the trigger, generally, took a button rather than conventional stud form. Again many variant forms exist to the extent that five models have been identified.

It was Oscar Mossberg who, in 1906, patented a form of 0·22 in four-barrelled pistol which, dimensionally, went below the pocket class of arms. This novelty palm-pistol, later known as the 'Shattuck
226 Unique' also used a revolving firing-pin located, in this case, in the breech-block. Comparatively few were made but, even so, a 0·32 in version was marketed and so too was a very rare 0·30 in one. Production ceased about 1915 but it was not the end of Mossberg's association with the small four-barrelled pocket-arm. In 1919 he launched his own firm with a new design, the 0·22 in Mossberg

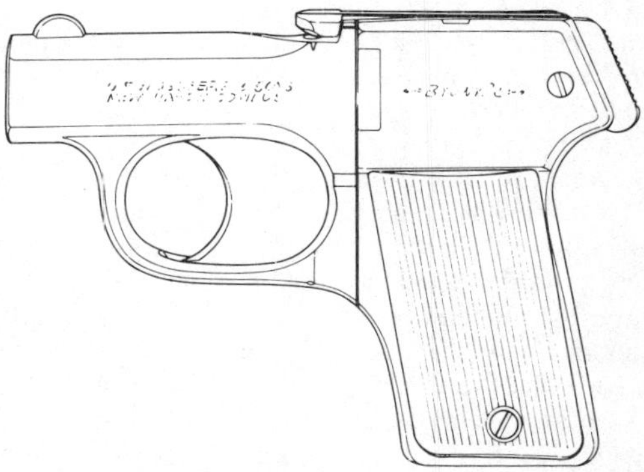

The Mossberg 'Brownie', a four-barrelled .22 calibre pocket pistol made to resemble an automatic, patented in U.S.A. in 1920. Imperial War Museum, London.

Brownie, and enjoyed quite a success with it. By 1932, when the model was discontinued, about 37,000 of these pistols had been manufactured. Outwardly the Brownie looks like a small pocket automatic pistol but the application of downwards pressure on the catch which extends to the rear at the top of the grip causes the whole barrel unit and trigger mechanism to drop forward. There was a rotating striker and a very curious steel-strip, manual extractor housed in the main frame. In Europe a rather different approach to a four-barrelled pocket pistol design was to be found. Of German origin the Reform pistol in 6·35 mm calibre has its four barrels drilled, the one above the other, in a vertical arrangement. As its double-action hammer action is functioned the barrel block is moved upwards, successively firing the four shots. A clever system of interconnecting gas-ports between the barrels utilises the gas of the barrel being fired to eject the case in the chamber just fired so that at the end, only the one

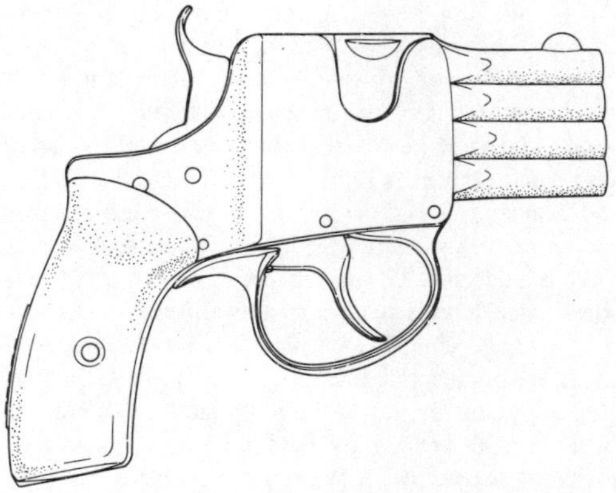

'Reform' pistol in 6.35 calibre patented in Germany in 1906 by August Schüller of Suhl. The block of four barrels moves upward as each is fired in turn. Smithsonian Institution, Washington, D.C.

case has to be ejected manually when the barrel block is removed for reloading. Another German four-shot arm, also usually chambered for the 6·35 mm cartridge, is the 'Bar' pistol. This has a cartridge-block taking four cartridges and fires two shots in succession through its over-and-under barrels before the firer turns the block through 180° to take his third and fourth rounds. Yet another 6·35 mm four-shot pistol was the hammerless European 'Regnum' in which the whole barrel-block, the bores arranged vertically one above the other, hinged down for loading. The enclosed hammer fired the four rounds in succession on sequential trigger pulls.

Naturally not all pocket-pistols of the cartridge era were single-, double- or quadruple-shot. There were three-shot arms and others affording five or more rounds successively. The Scheintod pistol,

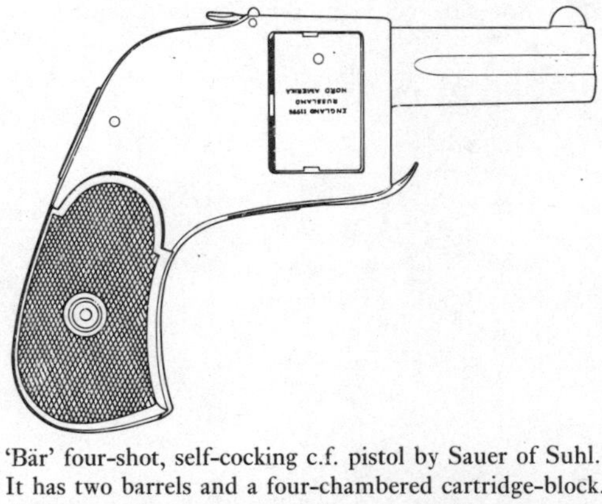

'Bär' four-shot, self-cocking c.f. pistol by Sauer of Suhl. It has two barrels and a four-chambered cartridge-block. After firing the top two chambers the block is reversed. Patented by B. Behr of Zürich (later Hamburg) in Britain in 1898 and U.S.A. 1899. Smithsonian Institution, Washington, D.C.

rather like the Regnum, had three barrels superimposed but was intended to fire special 0·410 in cartridges loaded with snuff, presumably somewhat discomforting, and the Marston, an American arm, also had the same barrel configuration. This latter arm, made under patents of 1857 and 1864, had an indicator on the right hand side of the frame to show which barrels were unfired. The Marston pistol is usually encountered in 0·32 in calibre but other calibres exist. Even when more than three or four shots were needed there was still a fairly wide choice of systems. Sharing some of the virtues of the flat Reform pistol the Jarre, made under French patents of 1862 and 1873, may be found in a number of different capacities. Although the barrel block with

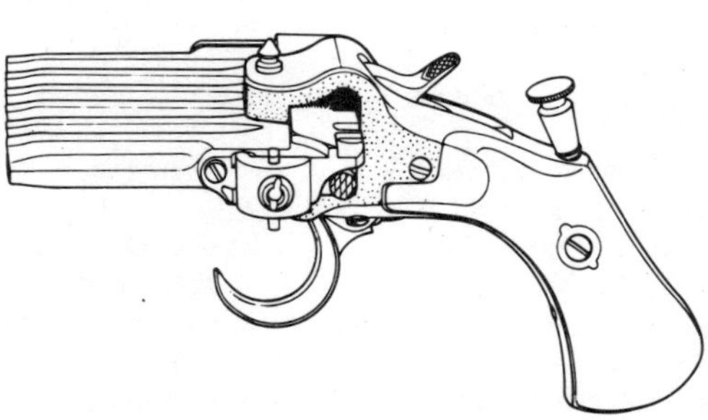

Jarre's 'Harmonica' pistol, model patented in France (and also U.S.A.) in 1873. The barrel block moves sideways for successive shots. Smithsonian Institution, Washington, D.C.

up to ten barrels is carried flat in the frame, the pistol operates with it in the horizontal position, transporting it sideways to discharge the cartridges successively. The barrel block was removed for loading and the cartridges themselves retained in their chambers by a plate. The distinctive appearance of the block gave the arm the name by which it is generally known, which is the Harmonica Pistol.

The Sharps pattern of pistol as manufactured by Grüenbaum and others was readily adapted to six shots and often made in this capacity; calibres were usually 0·300 in or 0·320 in RF. A very rare Italian pepperbox went even further. It had eight barrels divergently bored and could be fired in two four-shot volleys or in one eight-round fusilade. A special clip to allow the loading of all eight barrels in one movement helped keep up the rate of fire. But this is very much the odd weapon out, for those who needed compact firepower a revolver was the more obvious choice, unless they wanted a concealable arm. In this area, apart from the Mossberg Shattuck Unique, that has already been mentioned, though choice was limited there were a number of possibilities. The French Gaulois, by a squeezing action chambered and fired five shots successively in a manner mechanically not so dissimilar from that of the Remington-Rider pistol already noted. It used an 8 mm cartridge and did so very efficiently and, with a maximum thickness of only $\frac{5}{8}$ in, fitted quite inconspicously into the pocket. The French Merveilleux was a similar arm utilising a special 6 mm cartridge. In yet another French squeeze pistol, the Rouchouse, there was similar mechanical functioning – namely, in no way dependent on the recoil or gas from the discharge of the round – but the barrel was moved back over the round rather than the round being pushed forward into the barrel. The mechanical mode of operation of these arms had the virtue of rendering them immune to the consequences of defective cartridge – another squeeze cleared the useless round and a fresh one was chambered and fired. A final example of this small class of repeating pistols is the Tribuzio, invented by an Italian of that name in
Turin in 1890. It was of all-metal construction and 227
outwardly characterised by a ring trigger rather than the bar of the Rouchouse or Gaulois.

228 Detail of pinfire revolving rifle, 1864. See also plate **272**.

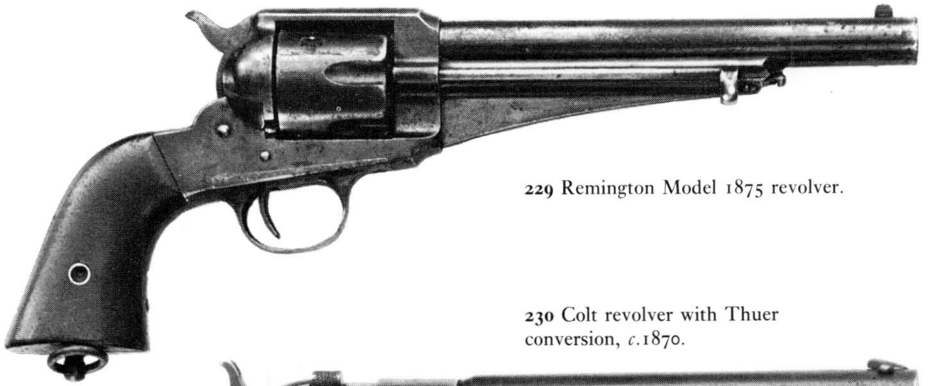

229 Remington Model 1875 revolver.

230 Colt revolver with Thuer conversion, *c.*1870.

231 *Right, top* Pocket pistol with self-cocking lock by Devisme of Paris, *c.*1860. Tower of London Armouries.

232 *Right* Double-action rim-fire pocket pepperbox revolver with folding trigger by Devisme of Paris, *c.*1860.

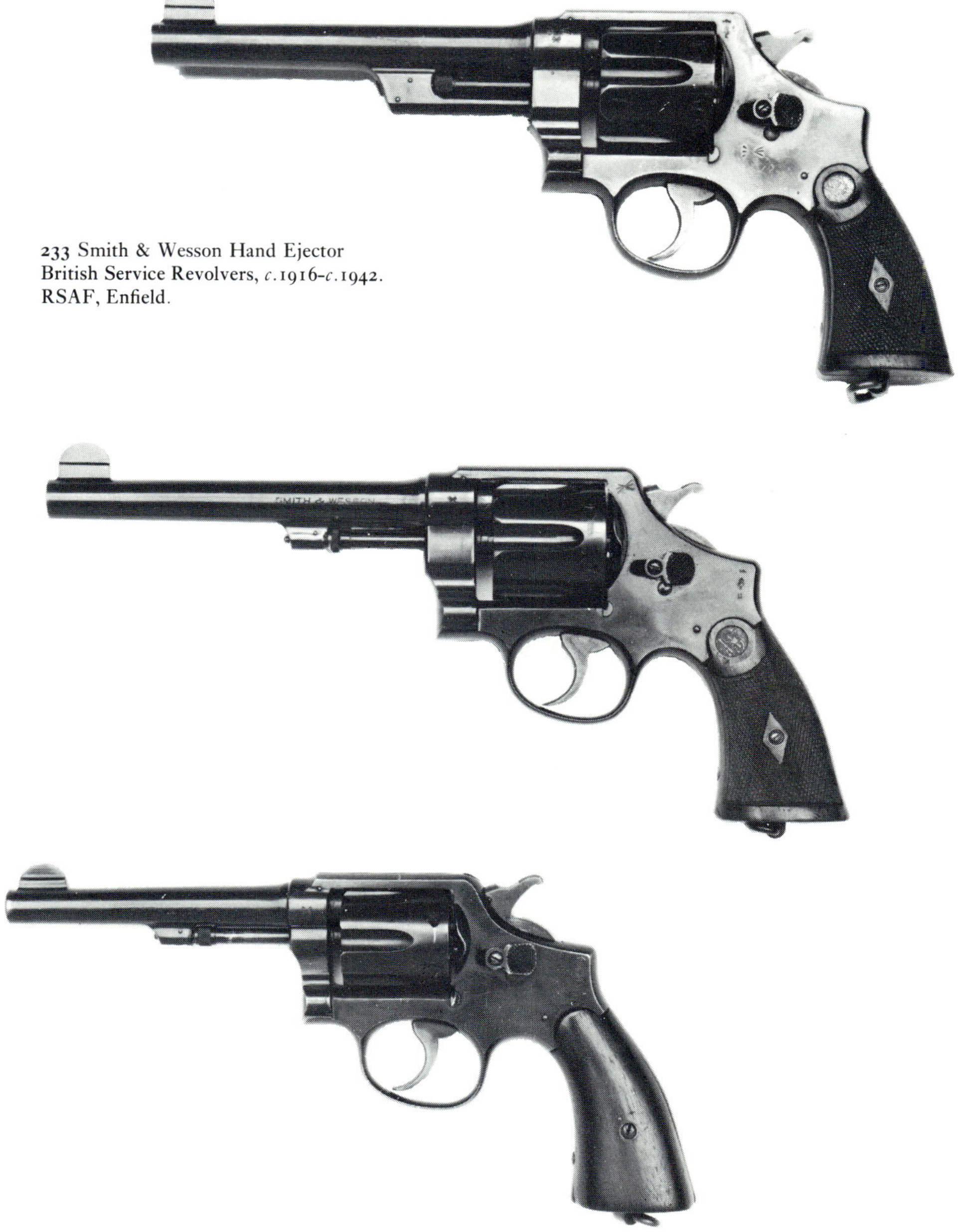

233 Smith & Wesson Hand Ejector British Service Revolvers, *c.*1916-*c.*1942. RSAF, Enfield.

CHAPTER ELEVEN

Cartridge Revolvers down to 1918

A.W.F. Taylerson

228-47 Metallic cartridge cases were applied to revolving
272-3 arms in a surprising variety of forms, but three systems of ignition–pinfire, rimfire and centrefire, described in Chapter 9–found principal favour and enable this chapter to be split into appropriate sections of study.

It must be appreciated that the revolvers to be described in relation to each type of cartridge progressed side by side, and that none of the rounds was obsolete at the close of the period under study. Some variant metallic cartridges, which were used in revolvers, will be noticed in these pages against the principal ignition system from which they deviated.

Pinfire Revolvers

The first revolving pistols to use metallic pinfire cartridges were multi-barrelled pepperbox arms, and they were first introduced in the late 1840s. The French gunmaker, Casimir Lefaucheux (inventor of the pinfire cartridge), patented the application of metallic pinfire cartridges to such an arm, in France, during 1846, and exhibited his pepperbox at the Great Exhibition, in London, during 1851.

Two types of self-cocking lock-mechanism were used in these arms, which are now quite rare, and the makers did not always sign their products. As would be expected, some weapons did bear the name of Lefaucheux and these were normally underhammer pistols, using the Mariette lock popular for many Continental percussion pepperboxes.

The Boissy pistols used a top hammer, but otherwise resembled the Lefaucheux arms. Ring triggers were used by both makers (as they were by others who did not sign their pistols), and no barrel-cluster seems to have been fixed upon as a standard. The nearest approach to a standardised weapon was reached by Boissy, who produced a four-barrelled, 12 mm pistol in some numbers.

Unlike the later gate-loaded pepperboxes, these early arms could only be loaded, or unloaded, by removing their barrels completely. Normally this was accomplished by unscrewing the retaining nut on the tip of the barrel-axis pin and removing the barrel-cluster, but some weapons retained the original Mariette system and required that each barrel be unscrewed separately from the breeching, the cartridge slipped backwards into its chamber, and the barrels then re-seated with the key or wrench provided for that purpose

Despite the obvious inconvenience of such systems, they appear to have endured for several years. Certainly, no gate-loaded pinfire revolver was patented in England until April 1854.

To succeed these necessarily elaborate weapons came the more compact *coup de poing*, or 'fist pistol' as it was termed in England. The exact date of this introduction is uncertain, but such arms were featured by Devisme of France at the Paris Universal Exhibition of 1867, and regarded then as something of a novelty. As a type they spread like a disease, and there can have been few British or Continental retailers who did not stock the cheap, small calibre, pocket version. For house protection, or in the hands of travellers, they enjoyed real popularity and were barely obsolete by the turn of the century.

The fist pistol owed little in appearance to the weapons previously described, for its smooth-bore barrels were machined as a solid component and loading was normally accomplished through a hinged gate at the right of the breech. However, some manufacturers still clung to an earlier feature, and made pistols in which the whole barrel group was removed for loading or ejecting the preferred 7 mm cartridge. Commonly, these pepperboxes had a self-cocking mechanism, and a folding trigger (without guard) favoured by Lefaucheux. A simple rod-ejector could be unscrewed from the butt for expelling the cartridges via the loading-gate, and no safety device of any kind was normally present. Almost identical weapons were made with Lefaucheux's double-action lock-mechanism, and a conventional spur on the hammer permitted the weapon to be cocked by thumb.

As a group, these fist pistols owed their compactness to a re-designed action-body, to their small calibre, and to the folding trigger.

In the earlier Mariette weapons, the whole of the lock-mechanism and action-body were behind

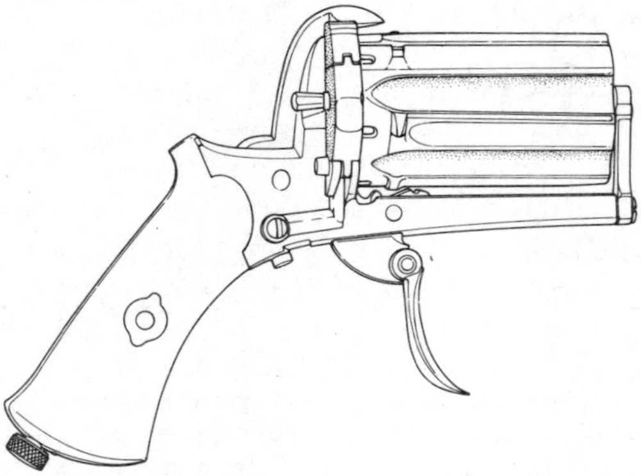

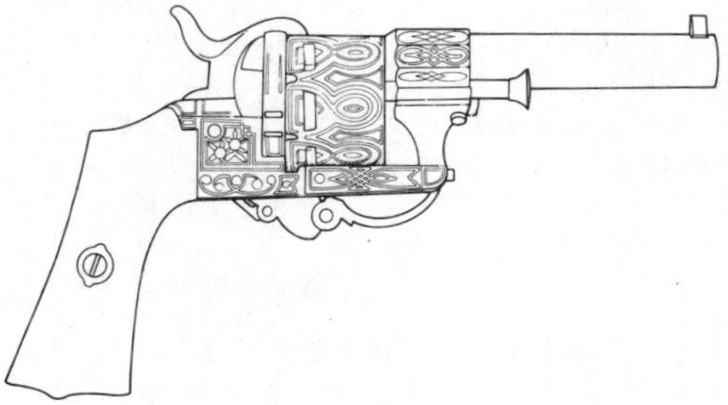

(*Top*) Pinfire pepperbox revolver. French, *c.*1850.
(*Above*) Pinfire pocket cylinder revolver. Deluxe model decorated with gold and silver damascening and ivory grips. Belgian, *c.*1850.

the barrel-cluster, but these later pistols avoided the bulkiness of such an arrangement. Their action bodies embraced the barrel group and supported its axis pin at each end, with the trigger hung below the breech end of the barrels. Given a common barrel length of a scant 2 in (in the 7 mm version), it can be appreciated that these pepperboxes measured less than 6 in in overall length. A comparable Mariette pistol bulked this by 2 in, and weighed considerably more. Identical weapons were made for the 9 mm and 12 mm cartridges, but the weighty bulk of their barrel groups made them less popular than the smaller pistols.

The first pistols seldom bore acknowledgement to any maker, and their proof marks give little guidance to their probable manufacturers. Weapons almost identical in appearance may bear the proofs of Liège, Birmingham, or even London, and the names occasionally appearing upon their butts are those of known retailers. In a casual listing of twelve 7 mm fist pistols, only two were retailer marked (one by F. T. Baker, of Fleet Street, and the other by F. Hill & Son, of Sheffield), and the proof marks split evenly between Liège and Birmingham. One of the Belgian weapons carried the mark of a Liège manufacturer, A. Francotte. But the stamp on this gun was hidden from view unless the butt-cheeks were removed.

In the circumstances, these arms are best regarded as 'trade' weapons, made by the larger British, Belgian and Austrian manufacturers for others to retail, but a few refined weapons can be associated with individual firms. Two Liège makers, L. Dolne and J. Delhaxe, produced distinctive fist pistols which embodied knuckledusters and dagger blades, while Francotte developed some curious 5 mm weapons during the bicycle boom of the 1890s. These pistols fitted into the ends of the handlebars, and could be quickly withdrawn for use.

As a firearm, the fist pistol can be dismissed as trivial, but it ranks with the cheap 'Suicide Special' revolvers made in America during the seventies and eighties of the last century. No would-be comprehensive collection of revolving arms can omit a weapon for which there was a demand so manifest.

To consider the true revolver, as adapted for the pinfire cartridge, it is necessary to turn to the activities of another Frenchman, Eugène Lefaucheux, son of Casimir, whose work upon pinfire pepperboxes has already been mentioned[1]. On 15 April 1854, Eugène took out a French patent for a breech-loading revolver to use these cartridges, and the design must have taken most manufacturers by surprise, for J. H. Johnson (a London patent agent) was able to secure British Patent No. 955 on 27 April of the same year without apparent opposition. Johnson did not reveal the name of his client, but the pistol shown in his 'Complete Specification' included most features of the pinfire revolver patented by E. Lefaucheux, and the latter was almost certainly Johnson's principal in this application for protection.

The pistol is revealed in the patent specification as a six-chambered, gate-loaded, single-action weapon, with a sliding cylinder-bolt thrust forward into recesses at the rear of the cylinder by the act of cocking; a rod-ejector was the right of the barrel.

Collectors of Lefaucheux revolvers will be familiar with the practice (on some early weapons) of boring the chambers slightly conical, and this is specifically mentioned in Johnson's patent. Taken in alliance with the distinctive weapon and cartridge shown in his drawings, it seems just to attribute the patent to E. Lefaucheux without argument.

The single-action Lefaucheux pinfire revolver was not merely popular with army officers and civilians, for a 12 mm version was adopted for the French naval service (as the Model 1858) and manufactured at St Etienne until 1873. This model also saw limited service in the Union Army, during the American Civil War, and was adopted as a troopers' revolver in Scandinavia. It has been reported (although no specimen could be traced) that the

1 See p. 313.

French finally altered their stocks of this naval revolver to use a centrefire cartridge, and that they re-issued it in 1873 with the lock modified to operate in double-action, after a new design by E. Lefaucheux. Such a conversion must have been costly (but not impossibly so), and was probably carried out to prevent logistical difficulties over ammunition, arising from the issue at that time of a new solid-framed, double-action, centrefire revolver to the French navy.

The single-action Lefaucheux revolver enjoyed considerable popularity and was copied faithfully in Liège and Spain, but the double-action versions are now better known and still exist in large numbers.

An exact date of appearance for the first double-action Lefaucheux arms is not known, but double-action Lefaucheux revolvers were included in the Norwegian service issue of 1864 and suggest that the design was well established by that date. Certainly the improved arm attracted civilian buyers, and it was produced in every size, quality, and available pinfire calibre. The service revolvers retained their trigger-guards, but the more popular weapons substituted a folding trigger. The origins of this refinement are also obscure, but weapons will be encountered with acknowledgements to Lefaucheux engraved upon such triggers, to suggest his association with this device.

To most eyes, now long accustomed to the solid frames of modern revolvers, the Lefaucheux pistol (whether double- or single-action) appears fragile and unhandy, with its heavy barrel secured on the end of the cylinder axis-pin, and the frame screwed together in several pieces, but the inventor applied his construction to an extraordinary variety of revolving arms.

At the Paris Exhibition of 1867, he showed a double-barrelled, twenty-shot, revolving rifle in which twin hammers were provided to fire the two circles of chambers in the cylinder. Another exhibit was a sabre embodying one of his revolvers in the hilt, and detachable skeleton stocks were offered with some of his weapons. These latter arms were accepted as gendarmerie weapons in several countries, and readers who served in Egypt during the two World Wars may remember seeing them in issue.

During the period, revolving pinfire rifles and
228 shotguns appeared in some quantities, and it is plain that other makers produced such designs, as well as their original inventor. It seems unlikely that any English maker was interested in this field, but arms marked *Fabrique-Royale de St. Etienne, Roland* and *F. W. Raul* stand in at least one famous collection to prove the efforts of other men. Such freaks seldom evidence a serious study of function or design, and are normally over-grown versions of the pistols that sired them. Frequently an elaborate trigger-guard served to keep the user's wrist well clear of the gas-leak between chamber and barrel.

The next serious advance in pinfire revolver design occurred around 1870, when the one-piece frame or action body became common in every quality of weapon. The original system of using a separate barrel was never abandoned, but the practice of building up the frame by screwing together small pieces of metal now ceased. The revolvers of this type most popular with collectors are twelve-chambered, and were made in 7 mm, 9 mm and 12 mm calibres to a closely standardised pattern. The cylinders were fully fluted (in place of the normal rounded shape) and also machined-out internally to reduce their weight. The lock was a simplified version of the double-action mechanism used in the Gasser (Austrian) service revolver, and the flat spring safety device used in that weapon was also duplicated.

Greener noticed these arms contemptuously, in 1871, but described them as ten-chambered. The present writer has not seen such a weapon, but there is no reason to doubt the accuracy of that author's observation. Freak revolvers of this type chambered twenty cartridges, and it is fair to assume that other variants existed.

The twelve-chambered pistols were usually numbered, and a variety of names appeared upon their barrels. Unfortunately, few of these names are of firms known to be capable of making such arms, and (as with the fist pistol) both Belgian and Birmingham proof marks are found. Pistols so similar argue for a centralised place of manufacture, and a likely Continental source (for France, at any rate) was the Fabrique Royale at St Etienne.

In England, the Birmingham house of P. Webley & Son catalogued a twelve-chambered model, but trade suppliers of their magnitude need not actually have made such arms. The manufacturing pattern in Birmingham was based on the free interchange of such specialised lines, and the revolvers could have been made for Webley by other firms, or even imported (as to the major components) from France or Belgium.

In London, the wholesale house of Adams & Co., in Finsbury Place, sold weapons identical to those offered by Webley. The 7 mm Adams weapon of this type had a $5\frac{1}{2}$ in rifled barrel, and a fluted cylinder only one inch long. The double-action lock mentioned above was fitted to the pistol, which could be loaded through a hinged gate on the right of the breech, and an ejector rod was mounted on the barrel in line with this gate. Sighting could only be done with the hammer cocked (since the rear sight consisted of a notch in the hammer lip), and, at an overall length of 10 in, the weapon weighed 23 oz when unloaded. This typical pistol was proved in

Birmingham, but showed no significant difference when compared with similar arms bearing the proof marks of Liège.

Two major defects were recognised in all the pinfire revolvers so far described, namely the poor method of assembling barrel to frame, and the bad cylinder bolt. As to the first, the established system was to screw the barrel onto the end of the cylinder-axis pin and then to lock it into position with an indexing screw turned through the front of the barrel lug and into the frame.

Such a design may be easy to make but it has one obvious inherent defect, and these weapons were easily rendered useless by any blow capable of bending the cylinder-pin, or even through wear on the appropriate threads caused by normal dismantling. The poor system of bolting the cylinder in alignment with the barrel could also cause damage. Obviously enough, if the weapon was fired with its cylinder and barrel misaligned, the latter sustained a heavy blow from the bullet on discharge.

The surprising fact remains that few manufacturers made any attempt to remedy these defects, and pinfire revolvers expressly designed to avoid them are rare.

Greener[2] illustrated a seven-shot weapon, in 1871, with a top-strap connecting barrel to frame, and this version was catalogued in 7 mm, 9 mm and 12 mm calibres by P. Webley & Son, of Birmingham. As a rule, these robust weapons carried a conventional rod-ejector but some were fitted with a quite different device for emptying the chambers. In these arms, the ejector-rod was T-shaped, the long stem serving as the cylinder-axis pin and the cross-head lying vertically against the front of the frame. When unloading the weapon, this cross-head was pulled forward (which withdrew the cylinder-axis pin) and the cylinder removed from the frame. A short chain connected the cylinder to the pistol, preventing loss, and had enough slack to enable the cartridge cases to be punched out of each chamber against the lower arm of the ejector rod. This had a retaining collar on the other arm, which slid along the barrel.

It would be satisfactory to suggest an original source for these solid-framed pinfire revolvers, but again we are faced with a mixture of British and Continental markings. Thus a typical seven-shot, Birmingham proved revolver bears, internally, the stamp of a Liège maker, Auguste Francotte.

The poor cylinder-bolting system used in pinfire revolvers was seen to be unsatisfactory during our period, but no action was taken by the manufacturers to parallel those improvements made in other types of revolver.

In nearly every case the sole means of indexing each chamber in alignment with the barrel was by a small lump on top of the trigger. When the latter was pulled right back, this lump rose through a hole in the floor of the frame and engaged a series of lugs standing proud on the rear circumference of the cylinder. On a tight pistol, the cylinder could not be accidentally rotated when the action was cocked, since this trigger lump prevented rotation one way whilst the hand (thrust against the rotating teeth) prevented the cylinder from backing off. However, it will be appreciated that this union was easily deranged by normal wear and tear on the soft metal used in manufacture, or by rust, dirt or congealed oil adhering to the working parts. Given their presence, it became all too easy for the cylinder to fail in aligning chamber to barrel, or to move out of alignment when the pistol was cocked.

No attempt was made to double-bolt the cylinder, and this defect was attacked by a different means. In essence, the method adopted was to arrange for the hammer to miss the firing pin on the cartridge if the latter was not correctly aligned with the barrel.

Alexander Guerriero, of Genoa, originally recognised the defect and patented a suitable correction in 1863, which consisted of a removable cap fastened to the rear of the cylinder. This cap covered all the cartridges, and the hammer could only reach the firing-pins through appropriate slots in the periphery of the cap; as a result, if the cylinder failed to align accurately, the hammer nose hit the protective cap instead of the cartridge. Guerriero's system was not adopted in full by others, but some makers accepted his line of approach by narrowing the width of the hammer nose. If the cylinder then failed to line up accurately, the narrow hammer missed the cartridge-pin altogether.

In general, it is true to say that the pinfire revolver saw little technical improvement after the various refinements mentioned above, until (in the last quarter of the nineteenth century) a simplified double-action lock mechanism was adopted by virtually every maker, in place of the Gasser-type, or Lefaucheux, locks earlier mentioned. This new lock was a simplified version of a well-known, military

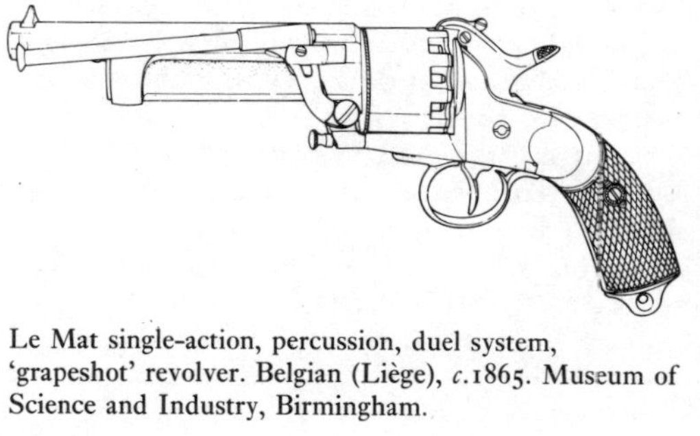

Le Mat single-action, percussion, duel system, 'grapeshot' revolver. Belgian (Liège), *c*.1865. Museum of Science and Industry, Birmingham.

2 *Modern Breech-loaders*, London, 1871.

revolver, lock mechanism, known as the 'Nagant', and is still used in many cheap revolvers. However, pinfire revolving arms served as the test-bed for some truly weird ideas.

The well-known Le Mat double-barrelled 'grapeshot' revolver appeared as a pinfire during the late 1860s, in both 12 mm and 9 mm versions, but the central shot-barrel continued to be loaded from the muzzle and fired by a percussion cap. The inventor controlled manufacture of his patented revolver, and these pinfire weapons normally acknowledge his name with that of the retailer. However, Liège-proved weapons were made which bear no acknowledgement whatsoever.

Apart from the notoriously fragile hammer nose (which was hinged to fire either barrel at choice) the Le Mat pinfires were stoutly built and possibly less liable to be knocked out of true than the conventional pistols. However, the single-action lock mechanism was despicably fashioned and easily crippled by careless handling.

Some other pinfire revolvers were also made with two barrels which had two concentric rows of cartridges in their cylinders, but unlike the original Lefaucheux revolving-rifle design (shown at Paris in 1867). these revolvers used a single hammer. In a well-known twenty-shot version of the Le Page house (of Paris and Liège), two beaks on the hammer nose fired shots alternately from the two rows of ten chambers. In an eighteen-shot variant by another maker (twelve chambers encircling an inner row of six), the hammer had a conventional nose for the cartridge-pins at the outer periphery of the cylinder, and operated a vertically sliding member in the standing breech to fire the inner chambers.

One or two attempts were made to increase firepower without the complexity and bulk of a double-barrelled weapon. Major W. C. Dowell[3] has unearthed an interesting pocket pinfire revolver in which the cylinder swings out sideways for easier loading, and an interesting method for cartridge extraction was proposed by the Belgian maker, Polain. On Polain's revolver (patented in England in 1865) the barrel was drawn forward in loading, and carried with it a plate forming the front of the cylinder; attached to the rear of this plate were short cartridge tubes, and the forward withdrawal of these tubes revealed loading ports in the sides of the chambers. Cartridges were loaded through these ports into the cartridge tubes, and the barrel was then pushed back so that the cartridge pins came under the hammer for firing. A conventional rod-ejector was fitted to use in removing cases that stuck in the loading tubes. However, it was apparently hoped that most of the cartridges would simply fall out of the cylinder ports when they were opened.

The combination of a revolver with some other weapon or appliance was as popular an idea with manufacturers of pinfire arms, as it was with makers of rim- or centrefire pistols.

The Lefaucheux revolver sabre has already been mentioned[4], and quite a number of the Paris exhibitors of 1867 showed similar arms. A number of the Liège manufacturers offered military swords thus enriched, and *couteaux de chasse* with revolvers were available at prices between 45 and 50 francs. The British official observer at the Exhibition noticed the arms of H. Dresse-Ancion, Laloux et Cie, M. Lambin and Lepage & Chauvot, but he also remarked that the Italian collection included these weapons as being greatly favoured by officers in that army. The fad was not taken up by British officers, but Birmingham-proved pistol-swords are known.

Given a sabre with a revolver embodied in the hilt, it was natural for the idea to be applied in pinfire revolvers for the civilian market, and weapons adapted to carry a heavy knife blade enjoyed considerable popularity in France. Such pistols must be carefully distinguished from those made by Dolne or Delhaxe, mentioned earlier. The latter were small calibre fist pistols, suitable for concealment in a pocket, but the arms of concern here were genuine revolvers of substantial size and calibre.

They were made in France by Lefaucheux and Dumonthier and in Liège by makers who remained anonymous. Both double-action and self-cocking mechanisms were used, and the blade was embodied by two methods. Commonly, the barrel and blade were forged as one, and the rifling bored through a heavy reinforce on top of the dagger. This barrel-blade was conventionally mounted by screwing it onto the end of the cylinder-axis pin, with a locking-screw at the forward end of the frame. In a less common weapon, the blade was made separately and pinned into a slot on the underside of the barrel. A scabbard was normally provided with either variant.

Some of these revolvers were very heavy, and six-chambered, 12 mm arms with a 12 in barrel-blade are not uncommon. Since all were built on the Lefaucheux open frame, it needs little imagination to picture their value as a pistol after a few heavy blows had been struck with the blade. The smaller 7 mm or 9 mm weapons were probably a rather more satisfactory weapon for the long term, but the handler today remains in real doubt as to whether pistol or blade was supposed to lead.

Around the turn of the century, the last debased embodiment of this idea came out of Belgium in a tiny 5 mm self-cocking revolver embodied in a large clasp knife. These were neatly made, but the imagi-

3 *The Webley Story*, London 1962.

4 See p. 315.

nation lurches slightly in attempting to picture a man carefree (or foolhardy) enough to carry a revolver bristling with six firing pins amongst the other trivia in his pocket.

Another rare pocket revolver had been patented in 1877, by Oliver Frankenau of Frankfort-am-Main, Germany, and requires notice amongst weapons of this kind. 'Frankenau's Purse Pistol' was originally conceived as a pepperbox pistol embodied in a metal wallet or purse, measuring about 4 in by 2 in by 1¼ in. Apparently the muzzle-blast from this contraption caused damage when it was fired, and the versions found in collections today are true revolvers, albeit extremely short-barrelled. A separate rod-ejector was fitted into the lid. The weapon had a simple self-cocking mechanism, and was permanently mounted in the compartment reserved for it. With the purse gripped in one hand, it was possible to reach a folding trigger and to discharge six 5 mm pinfire cartridges through a port at the revolver muzzle. Normally this port was shut, and the revolver virtually free from detection; however, when the folding trigger was freed from its retaining hook a lid over the port snapped open automatically.

It is not clear how many of these odd little weapons were made, but serial numbers suggest that several hundred were manufactured under Frankenau's patents. Liège proof marks predominate on surviving specimens, but both London and Birmingham proof marks may appear.

There is some temptation to regard pinfire revolvers as of little account, and the extraordinary range of cheap firearms produced for the various cartridges does lend credence to this view.

Around the turn of the century Francotte's Nimrod Gun Manufactory at Liège offered ten different sizes and quality of pinfire revolver, but all were cheap, folding-trigger weapons, with crude double-action locks. They contrast sharply with other varieties of revolver offered by that firm, and it is some indication of the price paid to the manufacturer that Charles Osborne & Co. Ltd., of Birmingham, could offer the 7 mm version at 7*s.* 6*d.* each, wholesale, in 1908. By 1912, their competitors, Joseph Bourne & Son, had cut this price to six shillings, and it is unfortunate that so many collectors identify the pinfire revolver solely with such trash.

These debased arms cannot detract from the overall record of success which the pinfire revolver achieved. In calibres ranging from 15 mm down to the tiny 5 mm round, these pistols were sent to every part of the world, and if any doubt their ability to function satisfactorily under normal handling, it is a matter of record that some Lefaucheux revolvers purchased by Norway in 1864 gave such good service that they were considered for re-modelling and re-issue in 1898!

Rimfire Revolvers

'The cartridge contains the ignition in the rim, but is liable to misfire,' wrote W. W. Greener in 1871[5]. The relevant weapon was the 'Smith and Wesson's American Revolver', and for collectors of revolving handguns that name will always be associated with this metallic cartridge.

Horace Smith and Daniel Baird Wesson patented a rimfire cartridge on 17 April 1860, a decade before Greener's words were published and three and a half years after they had joined in partnership. This was not their first appearance as patentees for pistol ammunition, but an earlier cartridge patented by them (in 1854) had proved too difficult and expensive to manufacture, and it is believed that few arms were ever manufactured to use it. The partners began to manufacture revolvers early in 1857, and it is necessary to give some attention to their preliminary negotiations in order to explain the appearance, in America, of certain variant rimfire cartridges and revolvers during the 1860s.

Smith and Wesson formed their partnership in anticipation of the final expiry, in 1856, of Samuel Colt's US master-patent. This covered the revolver with a mechanically-rotated cylinder, and they proposed to manufacture such arms with the added refinement of metallic cartridges embodying their own ignition.

Both men were experienced gunmakers and shrewd businessmen, and the long successful monopoly enjoyed by Colonel Colt, under the protection of his patent, apparently spurred them to follow his example. By means still unknown, the partners learned of an 1855 American patent held by another gunmaker, named Rollin White, which contained a claim for '. . . extending the chambers through the rear of the cylinder for the purpose of loading them at the breech from behind . . .' This patent actually protected a peculiar repeating firearm designed to use a leather-based paper cartridge fired by the conventional nipple and percussion-cap.

Lesser men than Smith and Wesson might have been tempted to ignore this patent, trusting to the novelty of their own proposed design to defeat any infringement proceedings by White. Such action might have arisen, in respect of the bored-through chambers needed to use their own metallic cartridge. However, the partners were obviously convinced that although their own design was sound it would be pirated by other makers, and they chose to ignore the existence of earlier patents teaching the principle of the bored-through chamber. Generous terms were offered to Rollin White and the partners duly became sole assignees of his patent as to the bored-through

5 See note 2.

chamber feature. Under the assignment, White bound himself to act against any who infringed this vital feature.

On the expiry of the Colt patent, the first Smith & Wesson revolvers were made and marketed, as the seven-shot 'No. 1' pistol. The cartridge used was a short 0·22 in round, and its soft copper case gave the partners certain design problems later mentioned. This pistol set the basic pattern of Smith & Wesson revolvers for many years. The barrel was hinged to the forward end of the top frame-strap, and, releasing a spring catch beneath it, permitted the barrel to be tipped up vertically. The cylinder could then be removed and the cartridge cases punched out against a rod protruding from the front of the barrel lug. A single-action lock was fitted to these arms, and the short trigger was partly sheathed in the frame without a guard. When the hammer was pulled back in cocking, it operated a bolt in the top frame strap and freed the cylinder to rotate.

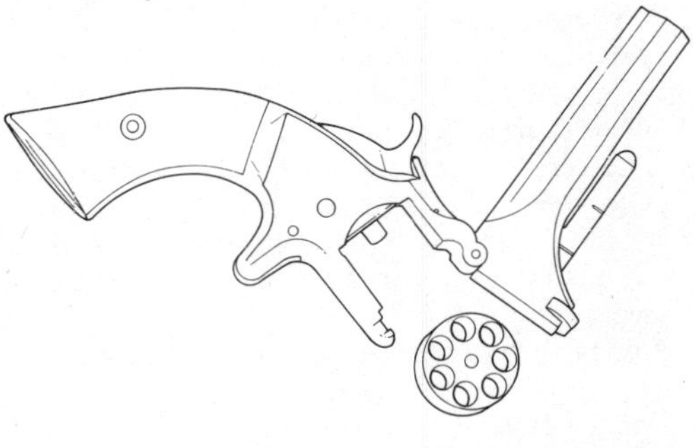

Smith & Wesson, 'No. 1', seven shot, single-action, r.f. revolver. Barrel tipped up to show method of removing. Breech broken for removal of cylinder for loading. 1860–68. Tower of London Armouries.

As earlier stated, the small rimfire cartridge used in these revolvers required a design feature in the cylinder peculiar to this series alone. The difficulty to be overcome lay in the tendency of the soft cartridge-heads to bulge on firing and to jam cylinder rotation by fouling the standing breech. Smith & Wesson's approach to this problem was to make the revolver cylinder with a rotating recoil-plate at the rear. This plate carried the ratchet which rotated the cylinder, and turned as one with the latter component. It supported the cartridge-heads and prevented jamming. In successively refined versions, Smith & Wesson used this system until 1859, when the plate finally disappeared from their pistols. This did not signify an end to the difficulty with bulging cartridges (the partners were involved in litigation for several years over an alternative remedy), but marked a recognition of the need to eliminate some of the more fiddling details from their weapons.

The partners were not, of course, alone in this difficulty. The British maker, William Tranter, used similar plates to a design patented in 1865, and another Birmingham maker, F. A. Braendlin, had an alternative design which was sometimes marked with his name. These British recoil-plates were commonly fitted to centrefire revolvers, but the jamming which they were intended to remedy was identical to that faced by Smith & Wesson.

The No. 1 Smith & Wesson revolver was an immediate success, and despite its tiny calibre thousands were sold during the American Civil War. The basic design went through successive modifications too detailed for notice here, and was also adapted to a six-shot, 0·32 in rimfire No. 2 pistol, in 1861. This was very similar in appearance

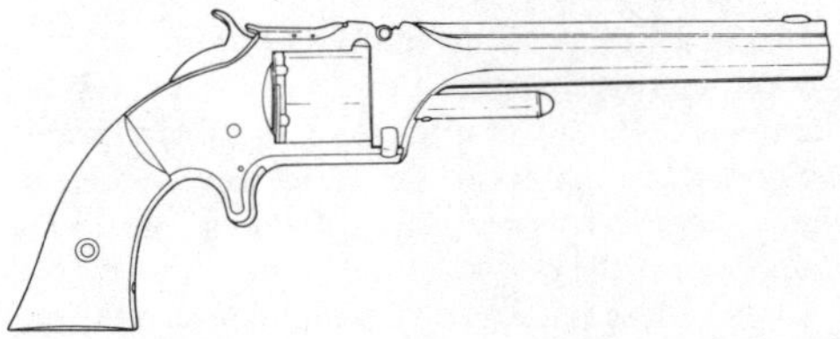

Smith & Wesson, 'No. 2', six-shot, single-action, r.f. revolver. 1861–74. Tower of London Armouries.

to the Model No. 1, but obviously larger in size. Barrels were available in 4 in, 5 in or 6 in (against the 3 in barrel of the No. 1), and a wrought iron frame replaced the brass used in that of the smaller pistol. This weapon achieved a popularity matching that of the pocket revolver, and saw limited unofficial use during the American Civil War. A five-shot version with a 3½ in barrel was introduced in 1865, as the Model 1½, and the round cylinders and flared butts began to give way to a fluted design in the former and the famous 'bird's-head' shape in the handle.

The last of these top-hinged revolvers left the factory in 1881, obsolete at last in the face of improved weapons manufactured by their own creators.

Until the close of the Civil War, Smith & Wesson were far too busy to concern themselves with markets outside the United States. So heavy was the domestic demand for their revolvers that the order books were frequently closed for months at a time, and customers were eager to accept even blemished arms.

Inevitably, other makers sought to compete with Smith & Wesson for this market, and it was here that the partners' foresight in acquiring the bored-through cylinder rights, from Rollin White, paid handsome dividends.

Ethan Allen appears to have been the first offender, and had a good run for his money. He began to produce a seven-shot, single-action, 0·22 in calibre revolver around 1859, and was not brought to book until ten years later. The offending revolvers were made under two patents secured in 1858, and were solid-framed arms with their hammer mounted at the side of the lock. They were made by Allen & Wheelock, at Worcester, Massachusetts, and their confident inventor actually patented an improved cylinder-bolt in 1861, in the face of Smith & Wesson's proceedings.

Five other makers of rimfire revolvers were also brought to heel by the indefatigable White.

The Bacon Manufacturing Company (at Norwich, Connecticut) had produced a 0·38 in rimfire 'Navy' revolver, with a solid frame from which the cylinder was partly removed to eject the cartridges. This weapon had a $7\frac{1}{2}$ in barrel, was single-action, and weighed a hefty 34 oz.

In 1862, Rollin White succeeded in infringement proceedings against one competitor, and the Bacon Company sensibly came to terms with Smith & Wesson. In the event, the latter were sufficiently impressed to purchase this infringing arm in an effort to meet the heavy demand for such revolvers.

Daniel Moore, a firearms manufacturer at Brooklyn, New York, was another infringer of the White patent, producing one unusual, single-action, pocket revolver in which the barrel and cylinder tipped sideways to clear the frame and permit cartridge ejection by a separate rod carried under the barrel. At a casual glance the weapon resembled a Colt muzzle-loading revolver.

Lucius W. Pond, of Worcester, Massachusetts, produced one of the few really heavy American rimfire revolvers. This was a six-shot, single-action 0·44 in calibre pistol, regrettably similar to Smith & Wesson arms in adopting a tip-up barrel.

Both Moore and Pond revolvers were sold by Smith & Wesson, under press of need, but they confined these purchases to the 0·32 in calibre arms which would accept the same cartridges as their own No. 2 pistol.

E. A. Prescott (also of Worcester,) produced a single-action 0·38 in 'Navy' pistol with a solid frame. It resembled Pond's revolver in appearance, but had a trigger-guard and solid frame in contrast. An injunction was issued against Prescott's use of the bored-through cylinder, and he ceased manufacture until the expiry of White's patent.

James Warner (who should have known better, as a neighbour in Springfield) produced a number of revolvers based on a patent of 1857. They differed little in appearance from his percussion revolvers, apart from using a 0·30 in rimfire cartridge, but Smith & Wesson bought the weapon to satisfy one of their customers, after Warner had come to terms with them.

The Manhattan Firearms Manufacturing Company, of New York, were the firm responsible for the surrenders mentioned above. They had been rash enough to manufacture copies of the Smith & Wesson No. 1 revolver, which were retailed by certain dealers. Rollin White brought suit against those selling the arms, for infringement of the bored-through cylinder feature in his patent. The success of this action (and the tenacity with which the proceedings against Allen were pursued) convinced the other infringers that Smith & Wesson must be placated.

As a result of the various purchases and royalty settlements with Rollin White, many of the Bacon and other revolvers bear the master-patent date of *April 3, 1855* on their cylinders, or are stamped *made for Smith & Wesson.*

Faced with this victory by Smith & Wesson, it became clear to competing manufacturers that conventional rimfire revolvers were barred until the expiry of White's patent in 1869, and it is that recognition which prompted the design of variant loading systems or 'sport' cartridges peculiar to America during these years.

The conventional method of loading from the rear of the cylinder being barred by White's patent, competing manufacturers could only insert their cartridges from the front or at the side of that component.

Lucius Pond, his lesson well learnt, stuck to the conventional rimfire cartridge but used a weird cylinder to handle it. His 'Separate Chambers' revolver (made under patents by other men) was a single-action, solid framed, pistol with a sheath trigger, and was made in both 0·22 in and 0·32 in calibres. The rear of the cylinder was solid, except for a slot penetrated by the hammer nose, and each chamber contained a withdrawable sleeve bored to accept the rimfire cartridge. On the side of the cylinder axis pin was a rearward pointing ejector rod, and the sleeves were successively drawn forward out of the chambers to rest on that rod. A cartridge was then dropped into the chamber and the sleeve pushed back in to embrace it. On firing, the hammer nose crushed the cartridge rim against the rear of the sleeve, and the empty case was knocked out by the ejector rod when the sleeve was withdrawn for reloading.

Frank Slocum, of Brooklyn, also clung to the conventional cartridge, and his single-action 0·32 in revolver was sleeve-loaded like the Pond weapon. The relevant patent antedated the Vickers protection on the Pond cylinder by some months, and the five 0·32 in cartridges were actually loaded sideways into troughs cut in the cylinder walls. As with the Pond, the Slocum cylinder was penetrated at the rear only by the hammer-nose, and proper cartridge chamber-

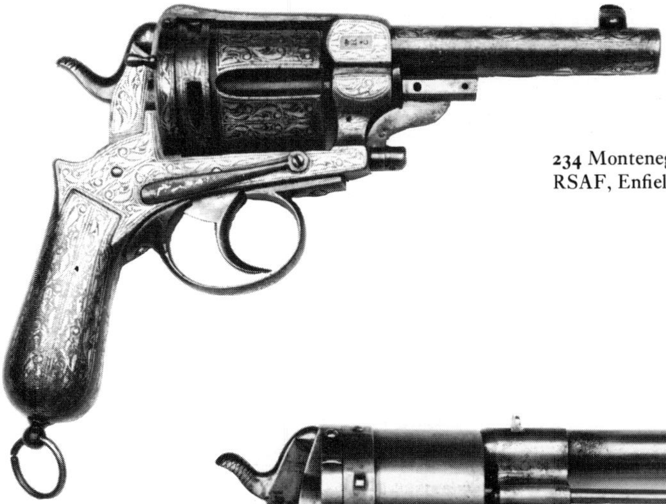

234 Montenegrin Gasser, *c*.1890. RSAF, Enfield.

235 Austrian Gasser service revolver, Model 1870. RSAF, Enfield.

236 French service revolver, Model 1873. RSAF, Enfield.

237 German service revolver, Officer's Model 1883, cal. 10·55 mm. RSAF, Enfield.

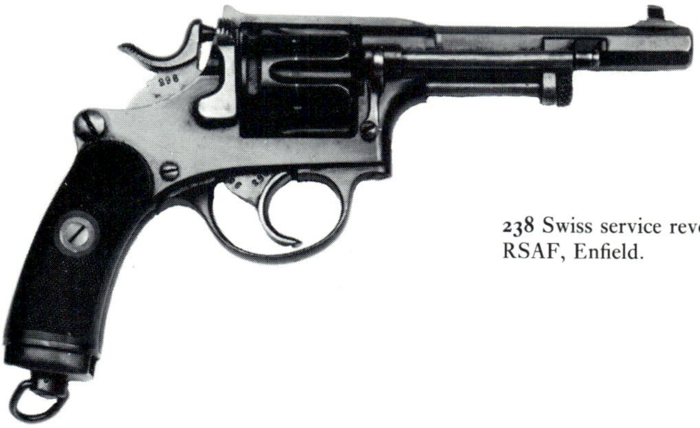

238 Swiss service revolver, Model 1882. RSAF, Enfield.

239 French service revolver, Model 1892. RSAF, Enfield.

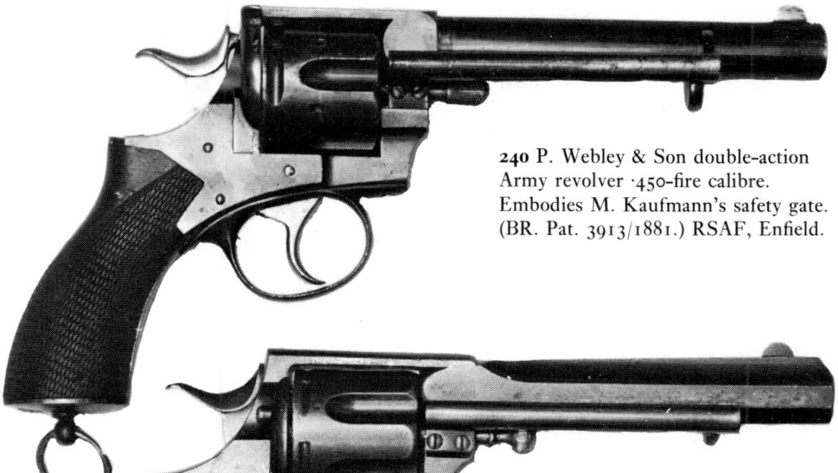

240 P. Webley & Son double-action Army revolver ·450-fire calibre. Embodies M. Kaufmann's safety gate. (BR. Pat. 3913/1881.) RSAF, Enfield.

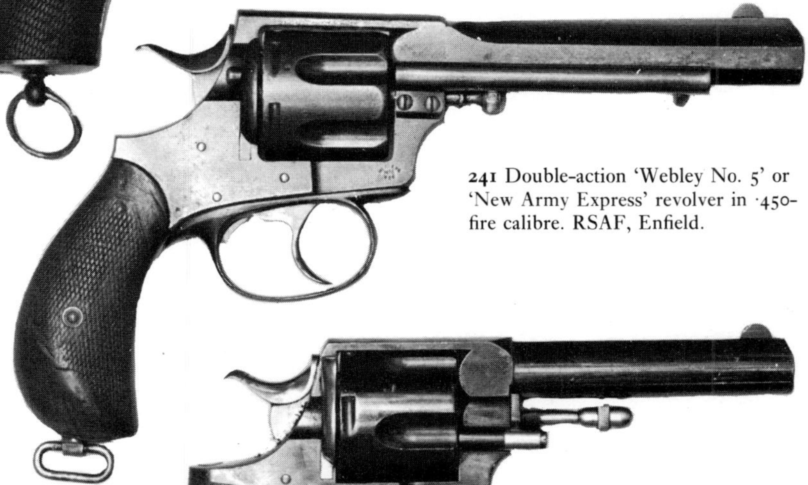

241 Double-action 'Webley No. 5' or 'New Army Express' revolver in ·450-fire calibre. RSAF, Enfield.

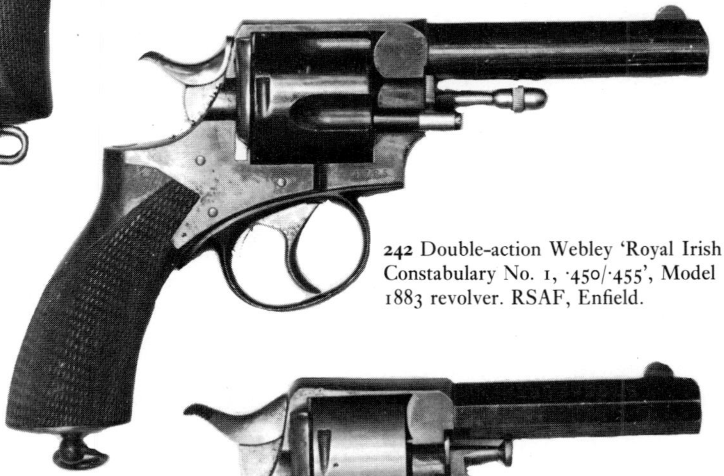

242 Double-action Webley 'Royal Irish Constabulary No. 1, ·450/·455', Model 1883 revolver. RSAF, Enfield.

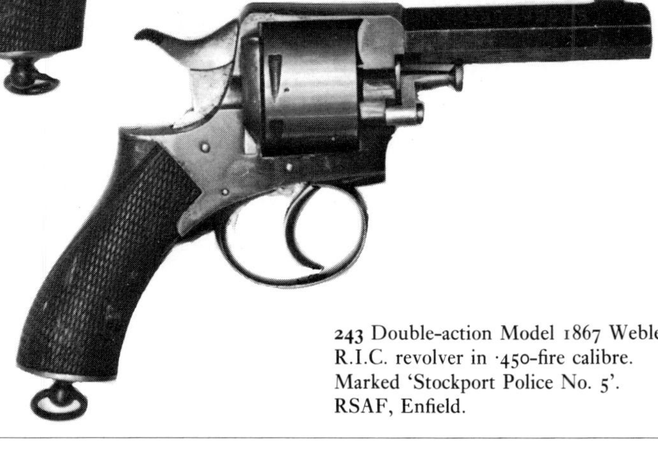

243 Double-action Model 1867 Webley R.I.C. revolver in ·450-fire calibre. Marked 'Stockport Police No. 5'. RSAF, Enfield.

244 Colt Double Action Army Model 1878. Tower of London Armouries.

245 Colt 'Lightning' revolver of 1878. Tower of London Armouries.

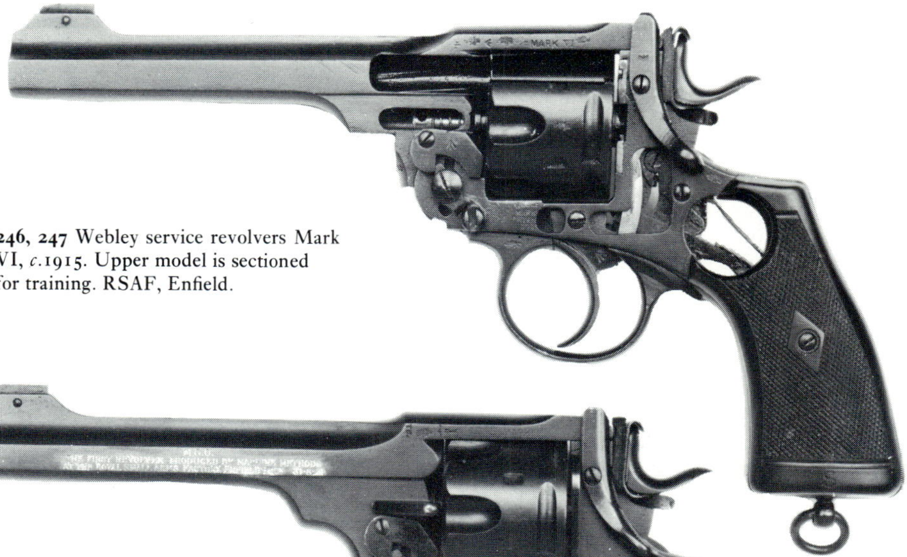

246, 247 Webley service revolvers Mark VI, *c.*1915. Upper model is sectioned for training. RSAF, Enfield.

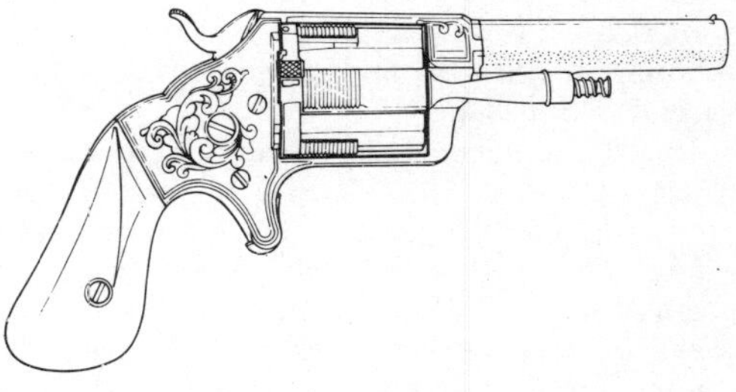

Slocum five-shot, single-action, front-loading revolver by the Brooklyn Arms Co., U.S.A., 1863-7. The chambers can be opened at the sides for insertion of the cartridges.

ing tubes were drawn forward to allow insertion of the cartridges. The revolver is rare, and is usually marked as manufactured by the *Brooklyn Arms Co.*

Both the Pond and Slocum revolvers appeared about 1864, and were matched by weapons designed to evade White's patent in another way. The makers in this instance discarded the true rimfire cartridge and developed rounds that could be pushed into the cylinder chambers from in front. In essence these cartridges were of the rimfire family, since their ignition was folded into the metal case. The largest and most reliable revolvers on this system used the 'cup-primer' cartridge. This round lacked a rim, of course, and had a straight case with a dished-in base. The hammer nose struck through a small aperture at the rear of the cylinder and hit the edge of the cavity base. The Plant Mfg. Co. of Norwich, Connecticut, made single-action revolvers in 0·42in and 0·36in calibre for the cup-primer cartridge and occasionally threw in an alternative percussion cylinder with cased arms, but nearly all surviving specimens acknowledge the New York house of Merwin & Bray as their distributors.

The arms normally found are solid-framed, have no trigger-guards, and embody a rod-ejector in a housing at the rear of the cylinder. This could be thrust forward through the hammer-nose aperture in the cylinder to eject the cases, and was patented in 1864. The earlier models lacked this refinement, and used a top hinged frame, like a Smith & Wesson revolver, from which the cylinder was removed to eject the cases against a rod fixed under the barrel.

A miniature version of the Plant revolver was made by the Eagle Arms Company of New York, and the design was belatedly patented in England, during 1868, by Hotchkiss and the Plant brothers.

Another type of front-loading pistol appeared during 1864, and is now known as the 'teat-fire' revolver after its cartridge. In this round, the detonating compound lay in a small round 'tit' protruding from the rear of the case and was smashed in a small aperture at the rear of the cylinder. Daniel Moore, through *Moore's Patent F.A. Co.* of Brooklyn, produced six-shot, single-action 0·30in calibre revolvers to use these cartridges (which he had patented), but later assigned his rights to the National Arms Co. who continued the series. He also used a slightly different cartridge with a flat teat, developed by an associate called Williamson.

Obviously enough, the unloading of a teat-fire cartridge by any rod striking at the rear was too dangerous to contemplate. The extractor eventually adopted was a modification to the loading gate. This, of course, swung at the front of the cylinder, and was adapted to hook forward a cartridge when opened.

More than a score of patents were secured during the currency of Rollin White's protection, all of which aimed at using metallic cartridges in a chamber closed at the rear. Enough has been said to indicate the usual line of approach, and it remains only to notice two extraordinarily dangerous ideas before returning to the conventional weapons.

In 1865, Silas Crispin patented a peculiar cartridge with its fulminate in a band round the belly of the case. A 0·32in revolver was actually developed (by the Smith Arms Co. of New York) to use this cartridge, in a cylinder formed in two parts. The barrel tipped down for loading and carried three quarters of the cylinder with it. Cartridges were then inserted, and the barrel tipped back to unite the cylinder and embrace the cartridges fore and aft of the detonating band. The hammer reached over the rear part of the cylinder to strike the primer band.

In the same year, Frederick Newbury, of Albany, New York, patented a front-loading 'improvement' to the Smith & Wesson revolver. Unbelievably, he proposed to use a rimfire cartridge which would have its loaded rim swaged into shape by pressure from the loading lever!

All good things must come to an end, and Rollin White's patent was no exception. Protracted efforts were made to obtain an extension after 1869, the last of which failed a decade later, but the bored-through cylinder was regarded as within the public domain from the formal expiry date, and conventional rimfire revolvers poured on to the market. Few of them offered any noteworthy advantage over the Smith & Wesson design, and the solid frame was almost universally adopted for their construction.

Amongst the better arms of this description were those made by E. Remington & Sons, of Ilion, New York. Long renowned for a superb series of muzzle-loading percussion revolvers, the firm showed little interest in metallic cartridges until a bare two years before the expiry of White's patent. By sensible negotiation, they then arranged for several thousand of their New Model (1863) Army revolvers to be converted from 0·44 in percussion to 0·46 in rimfire. This work was done by Smith & Wesson, the prin-

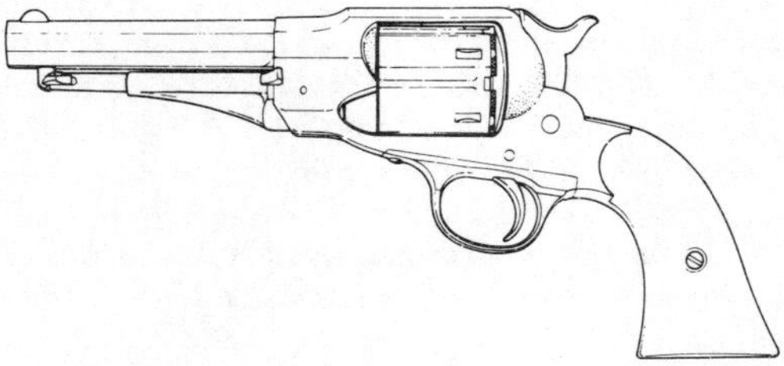

Remington six-shot, single-action percussion New Model Police Revolver, 1863.

cipal change being in the substitution of five chambers in place of the original six. The resultant weapon weighed 46 oz, with an 8 in barrel and the original single-action mechanism.

Apart from these arms, the Remington company later produced their own conversion system and sold under it arms which they catalogued as 'Improved Army' (0·46 in) and 'Improved Navy' (0·38 in) revolvers. In these pistols (unlike the Smith & Wesson conversions) a thick spacer plate was fitted between the breech-end of the cylinder and the frame. A rod-ejector was now provided on the right of the barrel and a proper loading gate prevented cartridges from slipping backwards out of their chambers. The equally famous belt and pocket revolvers were converted on similar systems, and such arms were sufficiently popular to remain
229 in Remington catalogues until 1888.

The Remington company's indifference to the metallic cartridge revolver, during the 1860s, is curious. Early in that decade they manufactured rimfire pepperboxes under the patents of William H. Elliott, and other deringers and rolling-block pistols evidence their skill in the application of metallic ammunition to handguns.

The Elliott pepperboxes were self-cocking pistols operated by ring triggers. One of them (a six-shot, 0·22 in calibre arm) had its barrel-cluster turned by a stud in the mechanism riding in zigzag grooves cut at the breech and was produced in limited numbers during 1861-2. This was followed by a weapon with a fixed barrel-cluster (in 0·22 in or 0·32 in calibres) in which the firing-pin revolved to strike successive cartridges.

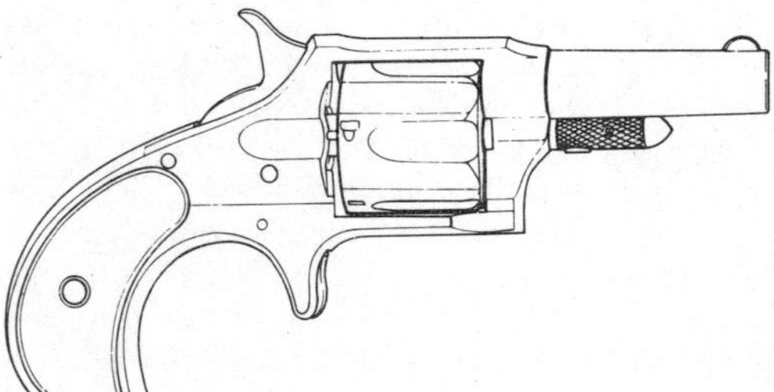

Remington five-shot, single-action, r.f. 'New Line' No. 4 revolver, 1873. Tower of London Armouries.

In 1873, Remington also began to produce new rimfire revolvers. These 'New Line' pistols were produced under the patent of W. S. Smoot, which protected the method of forming barrel, frame and guard strap in one forging. The No. 1 revolver was in 0·30 in calibre, the No. 2 was in 0·32 in, the No. 3 was principally built in 0·38 in rimfire, although some centrefire weapons were made, and the No. 4 was available in 0·38 in or 0·41 in versions.

These revolvers were developed from 1873-88,

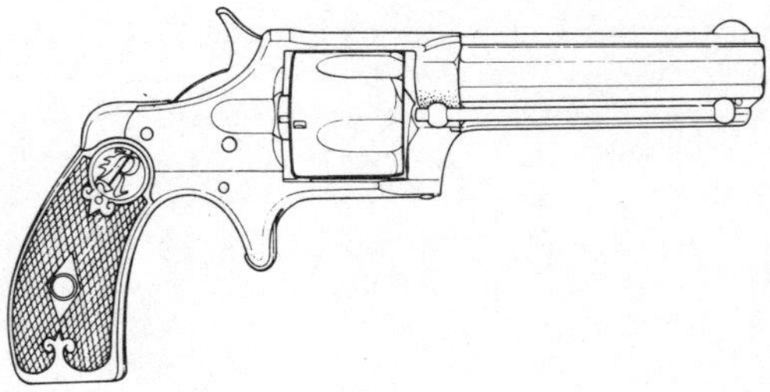

Remington five-shot single-action, r.f. 'New Line' revolver No. 3, 1875-88. Tower of London Armouries.

and all were single-action, five-chambered arms without trigger-guards. The last model lacked an ejector rod and (like the No. 3) had its barrel as a separate component screwed into the frame. In 1878, the Company produced a 0·22 in pistol similar to the New Line No. 4, which was their last rimfire revolver. It was seven-chambered and retailed under the trade name 'Iroquois'.

The other major firm balked by White's patent was the Colt's Patent Fire Arms Mfg. Co. of Hartford, Connecticut, and their approach to the use of metallic cartridges echoed the canny business sense of their competitors at Ilion. Saddled, after the Civil War, with a large factory equipped to make revolvers on an obsolete barrel and frame assembly, the company took no precipitate action. Various conversion systems were applied to their muzzle-loading revolvers and are noticed in the section upon centrefire pistols, but a brace of rimfire models were deliberately built to the old assembly. One was 0·44 in calibre, single-action, six-chambered holster revolver, and the other was a 0·22 in pocket arm. The larger Colt resembled an 1860 percussion revolver, but differed in that it was actually made from new parts with a rod-ejector mounted to the right of the $7\frac{1}{2}$ in barrel.

These revolvers appeared about 1872, and were soon followed by a fresh line of single-action, pocket, rimfire arms, known as 'House Pistols'. These were all solid-framed, and none had trigger-guards. Calibres ranged from 0·41 in down to 0·22 in and cartridge capacity varied between four and seven rounds.

A rather similar series to that by Remington next appeared, as the 'New Line' Police or House revolvers, which had flared butts in place of the earlier 'bird's-head' shape.

When the famous single-action 'Frontier' Colt of 1873 appeared, centrefire cartridges were those principally used in it. However, it is thought that about 2,000 pistols were made in the four principal rimfire calibres.

Colt interest in the rimfire cartridge lapsed thereafter, and their only fresh application during the period occurred in 1911, when the 'Police Positive' (Target Model) became available in 0·22 in short, long and WRF calibres. This revolver was a six-chambered, double-action pistol, with a solid frame from which the cylinder swung out sideways (on a crane) for cartridge ejection. Other models on this principle were introduced prior to 1918 and may be encountered in 0·22 in rimfire calibre. Since these 0·22 in models were not catalogued until after the First World War they are ignored here.

In the decade following the expiry of White's patent, a flood of cheap solid-frame, rimfire revolvers was dumped on the American market. Many were by reputable makers, and the names of the Bacon Manufacturing Co., Forehand & Wadsworth, Harrington & Richardson, and Hopkins & Allen, appeared upon the more sound designs. Most of these arms were mediocre in quality, whilst some were truly vile, but the type is of definite interest as evidencing ability to produce a working firearm that could be retailed for as little as 70 cents.

The name 'Suicide Special'–the connotations of which are obvious–was apparently first applied to the type in an article by D. McConnell in the *American Rifleman* for February 1948. It is commonly used broadly for any low-quality small revolver made for mass sale during the second half of the nineteenth century. Specialist collectors, however, confine it to a specific form of cheap, single-action American pocket-revolver of this period. Its characteristics are a spur trigger, a solid frame, which does not break for loading, and a cylinder held in place by a central pin that can be withdrawn from the front of the frame and used as an ejector. It often bears crudely engraved decoration.

The variations on the basic types were enormous, especially in finish and decoration. They were sold under dashing trade names like 'Bull Dozer', 'Marquis of Lorne', or 'Tramps' Terror', and bore no acknowledgement to any maker. This coyness was appropriate to an arm which sometimes merely pretended to be rifled.

On a plane of higher quality came copies of the original Smith & Wesson top-hinged design, and 0·22 s by J. M. Marlin (of New Haven), or I. J. Clark (of Philadelphia) were representative of the type.

The next major advance in rimfire design came again from Smith & Wesson, in the shape of the No. 3 self-extracting revolver patented in 1869. Unlike their earlier weapons, this pistol was hinged at the lower end of its frame and ejected all the cartridges automatically, when broken open, by a star-shaped extractor buried in the rear face of the cylinder, which was racked upwards (by a gear wheel engaging teeth in the extractor stem) as the barrel was tipped down.

The revolver was first marketed about 1871 (based on extractor patents by Gibson, Rodier and Dodge), and is now better known to collectors as the 'American' model. It acquired this name after being altered (from the original rimfire design) to use centrefire cartridges, at a time when it became necessary to distinguish it from a 'Russian' model.

Once having adapted this big single-action cavalry revolver to use a centrefire round, Smith & Wesson might have been expected to drop the rimfire ignition for their heavy-calibre arms, but the demand for that cartridge would not die. The No. 3 went to both Mexico and Turkey in some quantities, chambered for the Henry 0·44 in rifle cartridge, and a small quantity of the 'Russian' revolvers were similarly adapted (in 1877) for the latter government. This customer was so satisfied that 5,000 rimfire New Model No. 3s were ordered two years later.

However, these were really arms to special order, and their makers continually urged acceptance of centrefire cartridges. In 1874 the firm had discontinued the rimfire Models 1 and $1\frac{1}{2}$, and filled orders thereafter from stocks (or by the use of sub-contractors) until 1881, when the last No. 1s were sold off.

Until 1902, the rimfire cartridge was then ignored by Smith & Wesson. In that year, however, their Model 'M' Hand Ejector revolver appeared in 0·22 in rimfire calibre, as a seven-shot, solid-frame pistol with a double-action mechanism. Like the equivalent Colt revolvers, this arm had a cylinder which swung out to the side for ejection of the 233
cartridges.

This Hand Ejector went through two further model refinements (the last embodying a hammer rebound), and was followed by the 0·22–32 Heavy Frame Target Revolver of 1911. As the name suggests, this was really another model (the ·32–20 Hand Ejector, centrefire, model of 1903) adapted to use barrel and cylinder suitable for the rimfire cartridge, and it is the last Smith & Wesson revolver of concern here.

Whilst the predominance of American designs in this field must be accepted, the collector can expect to encounter some interesting British and Continental revolvers for these rimfire cartridges.

In England, one of the first firms to adopt the round for revolvers of respectable size and quality was the London house of Deane & Son, at London Bridge. John Deane junior patented an ingenious adaptation of the Harding percussion revolver, in 1862, and versions for the 0·442 in and 0·32 in cartridges were made for the firm in Birmingham.

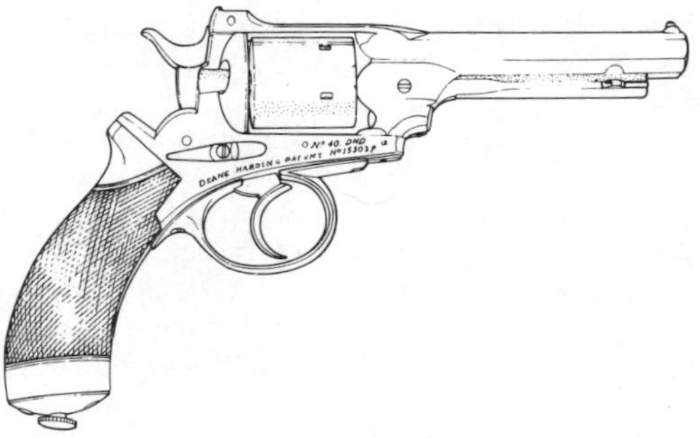

Deane-Harding six-shot, double-action rim-fire revolver, Model of 1862. RSAF Enfield.

'Deane's Patent Revolver' had a hammer-nose suitable for percussion-caps or metallic cartridges, thus a rimfire cylinder (and a recoil-plate) could be inserted in place of the muzzle-loading component. The arms are rare now, and were dropped around 1870 in favour of centrefire designs by other makers.

For most collectors, however, the British rimfire revolver will always be linked with the name of William Tranter, a director of the Birmingham Small Arms Company and a substantial manufacturer of revolving arms. The marking *W. Tranter's Patent* appeared upon both single- and double-action arms, but it is rare for any weapons to have been sold under his name and address. Normally, their barrels were engraved instead with the trading style of a retailer. The single-action revolvers were only made in the small rimfire calibres of 0·230 in or 0·320 in, and were commonly seven-chambered. Both had solid frames (with a removable inspection plate on the left) and a partly sheathed stud-trigger without guard was used. The smaller model frequently had a bronze frame, and both versions were fitted with octagonal barrels screwed into the weapon as a separate component.

Their maker apparently conceived these pistols in 1862, but the relevant patent on their butt construction was not sought until the following year. The lock mechanism was extremely simple and even today it is uncommon to find a specimen in which any component has failed under normal use.

Tranter's solid-framed, double-action arms were predominantly for centrefire cartridges, but rimfire ignition was adopted for some five- and six-chambered revolvers in 0·442 in, 0·380 in, 0·320 in and 0·230 in calibres. Such arms were featured in his patent of 1863, with the lever ejector used in the largest model, but the lock mechanism most frequently used was not patented until 1866. This was really a refinement upon his single-trigger percussion revolvers, and the characteristic stud at the back of the trigger was retained on many pistols to operate a

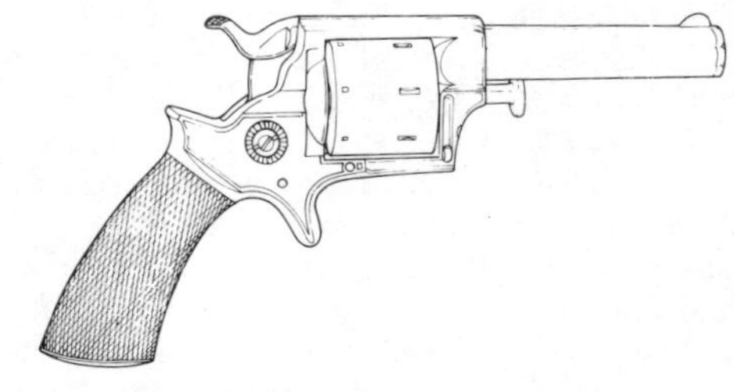

Tranter seven-shot, 0·32 in., single-action, rim-fire pocket revolver, Model of 1863. On the barrel a retailer's name, J. Veisey & Sons. Tower of London Armouries.

bottom sear at the rear end of the frame.

Rimfire revolvers by Tranter are rarely easy to date. The single-action weapons may have had a serial number range of their own, but the double-action pistols appear to have been numbered in with the more common centrefire weapons. However, the full range of cartridges were still available in the late 1880s, and it is safe to assume that the rimfire series of Tranter revolvers endured until his retirement in 1885.

British competition for Tranter lay principally with two other Birmingham makers, Tipping & Lawden or P. Webley & Son. Both firms made a few really heavy single-action rimfire 'Army' revolvers in the early 1860s, but their more common models were in 0·230 in or 0·320 in calibres.

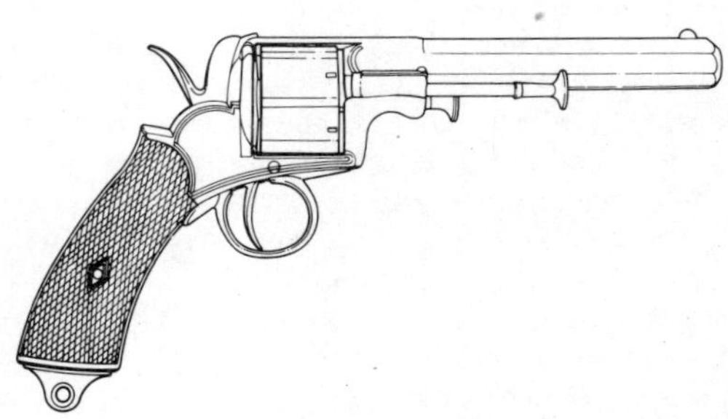

Webley six-shot single-action rim-fire 'Army' revolver, c.1860. Tower of London Armouries.

The Webley firm were large suppliers to the trade, and seem to have been able to offer copies of almost any promising design. Versions of the Smith & Wesson tip-up models have been attributed to them, although normally not marked with any maker's name, and a line very similar to the Tranter single-action series was sometimes marked *Webley's Patent*. Another interesting little revolver in 0·230 in calibre had a double-action lock, with a ring trigger, and appears to have been copied from a Continental design.

Tipping and Lawden were absorbed by P. Webley & Son in 1877, and had a long history of activity in revolver manufacture for others. Their interest in rimfire arms stemmed from the competing Sharps four-barrelled pocket-pistol, which they made under licence, and a pocket rimfire revolver, based on the Smith & Wesson pattern but not a slavish copy, was also turned out.

P. Webley & Son may have continued production of some of the Tipping & Lawden revolvers after taking over the business, and it is certainly difficult to believe that they manufactured all the revolvers that they sold. Some of their early double-action, solid-framed pistols (sold under the trade-names 'The Pug' and 'The British Bull Dog') were made in 0·44 in rimfire embodiments, but other arms often attributed to the firm bore no name or marking now traceable to Webley. In this category were big, double-action, solid-framed holster revolvers (in 0·44 in calibre) which sported a lever ejector along their barrels, similar in appearance to that favoured by Tranter.

The famous series of Webley hinged-frame, self-extracting revolvers are considered in the next section, and the company produced few rimfire versions during the period of concern here. These weapons could be fitted with Morris Tube adaptors (to use the 0·297 in, 0·230 in centrefire round) and Webley developed their own single-cartridge tube adaptor, in the 0·22 in rimfire calibre, about 1905. However, for men who preferred to practise with fully functioning service revolvers in this calibre, a few weapons were expressly made with suitable chambers and barrels, from about 1900. They were probably based on an earlier design which Webley made for the Wilkinson Sword Company of London.

In considering Continental developments of the rimfire revolver, the British student is severely hampered by a lack of available specimens of arms of better quality.

The ubiquitous fist pistol was adapted for this cartridge within a few years of its appearance as a pinfire arm, and less sophisticated pepperboxes with single-action locks were made in some numbers. The fist pistols came in 5 mm, 7 mm and 9 mm calibres (the smallest cartridge being often applied to an eight-barrelled weapon), but the single-action arms were rather more substantial, and generally claimed some patented feature under the style *Mariette Breveté*. This legend is found on pistols of different qualities (calibres 5 mm, 7 mm and 9 mm) with barrel clusters varying in length between 2¼ in and 7 in. Commonly, these barrels were rotated by hand and proved at Liège.

Equally common were the later Belgian and Spanish copies of Smith & Wesson tip-up revolvers,

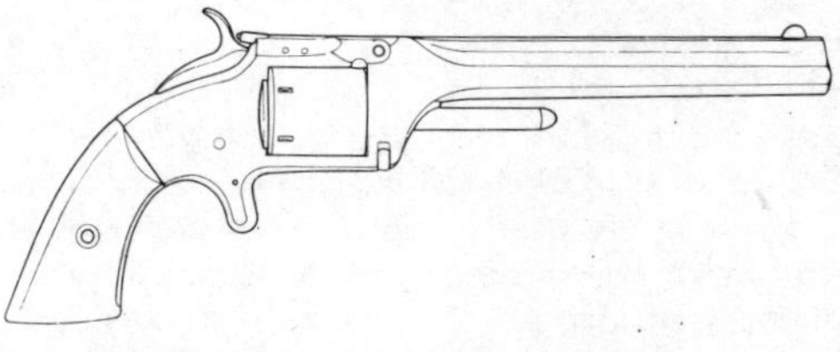

Six-shot, 0·32 in., single-action version of a Smith & Wesson revolver, with Birmingham proof-marks and retailer's name, W. R. Rape, Newcastle-on-Tyne. Probably made by P. Webley & Son, 1865–6. Tower of London Armouries.

in 0·22 in and 0·32 in calibres. In normal course, the cheaper specimens were marked only *Acier Spécial* or *Acier Fondu*, but exact copies were also made. The fitting was often appalling, although some weapons of superior quality could be found, and the existence of true Smith & Wesson revolvers (retailed by official agents to the company) can make identification difficult. Even the American barrel legend was reproduced on some copies.

This sort of piracy was not confined to the early pistols, and the No. 3 Smith & Wesson revolver (with its developments) appeared in rimfire versions from Belgium, Germany, and Spain.

Perhaps the most numerous Continental revolvers for the rimfire cartridge were the miniature, or pocket-sized, double-action weapons with folding
triggers. Little can really be said of them that has 232
not already been said of the equivalent 'Suicide Specials' in America. Francotte, of Liège, made them in various qualities, and varieties popular in Germany and France used a self-cocking mechanism with the hammer completely shrouded by the action body. Many of the trade names under which these arms were sold contrasted nicely with those favoured by the Americans. Joseph Saive's 'Le Mignon' (a 0·230 in, six-shot, Bull Dog-type *revolver de dame*) was made at Liège and demonstrated quite a different sales approach to that which prompted *Hard Pan* upon a roughly equivalent US weapon.

For service issue, the rimfire cartridge found favour in American revolvers sold to the governments of Egypt, Mexico and Turkey, but was apparently adopted by only one European nation.

The first Swiss army revolvers appeared in 12 mm and 9 mm calibres, which were later re-designed as the 10·4 mm Chamelot, Delvigne & Schmidt, Model of 1872. This weapon was a solid-framed, rod-ejecting, double-action pistol which proved satisfactory enough to endure until 1878. In that year a centrefire round was adopted, and the rimfire revolvers were altered to use it.

Centrefire Revolvers

It is possible to argue the priority of date for a number of cartridge revolvers as the first to use a centrefire round. A small revolver by Michalon of France used a front-loading centrefire cartridge, patented in 1844, and Captain Genhart (a Swiss artillery officer) patented a revolving pistol using another cartridge of this type, in 1856. Genhart's firearms had turret magazines (with radially-bored chambers) which turned on top of the action-body, and they fired metallic cartridges primed by a detonating tube at the rear.[6]

Lack of space prohibits concentration upon this matter of priority, as it must also curtail remarks upon cartridge construction. For the purposes of these pages, the classic centrefire round (with a separate percussion cap embodied in the base) must be lumped in with the 'inside primed' varieties, in which the detonating compound was sandwiched between the base and a disc (or other anvil) secured by cannelures pressed in the sides of the case.

This over-simplification accepted, two French revolvers present a likely claim to early production in our period. Both the Perrin and the Raphael pistols were in 12 mm calibre, and saw use in the American Civil War; the former used a rimmed cartridge loaded from the rear of the cylinder. The Raphael weapon (a double-action, six-shot revolver, like the Perrin) had rimless cartridges, and the two-part cylinder had to be removed for loading and extracting.

Neither of these side-arms was particularly satisfactory, but the thick-rimmed Perrin cartridge (patented in England during 1859) was extremely successful. Years later it was used in Galand's revolvers, and the Parisian firm of Perrin et Cie produced a single-action revolving rifle (about 1870), which used the 12 mm round and proved to be quite sturdy and reliable.

By the Paris Exhibition of 1867, the centrefire cartridge was well established for use in Continental revolvers, but was not accepted by the British Army until the following year.

In America, the round leapt ahead for every type of weapon except the revolver. The reason lay, of course, in the Smith & Wesson monopoly earlier noticed in the remarks upon Rollin White's patent for the bored-through chamber. Until the US Army expressed a preference for the No. 3 revolver in a centrefire model, the partners kept to rimfire designs and balked efforts to use the alternative.

Until the 1869 expiry of the White patent, various attempts were made to produce front-loading centrefire cartridges, (just as in the case of rimfire ammunition) and one of the better-known systems was patented on behalf of the Colt company.

Alexander Thuer's US patents of 1868 and 1870 protected mechanisms for converting muzzle-loading percussion revolvers to shoot a metallic centrefire cartridge and also covered the equipment for loading it. The rear of the muzzle-loading cylinder was turned-off in a lathe, leaving a central stem upon which to slip a conversion ring containing a firing-pin and an ejector button. The cartridges were pushed into the chambers from in front, and the revolver hammer struck the firing pin to explode each round. When all the cartridges were empty, the conversion ring could be rotated to bring the ejector button under the hammer which was then 'snapped' successively to knock each case forward out of the chamber.

Thuer's system was principally applied to the single-action Model 1860 Army Colt, but other 230
models have been found converted to it. All the pistols are rare, and there is good authority for the view that most of them were converted in London, through the Colt depot there.

Ingenious as it was, Thuer's system was too complicated for commercial success, and the Colt Company wasted no further time upon it after the expiry of White's patent. As earlier mentioned, the Colt revolvers produced after 1869 were to the old system of construction (with separate barrels secured by a cross-key) and closely resembled the percussion weapons upon whose components they were based. Initially they used C. B. Richards's system (patented in 1871) for fitting a rod-ejector in place of the old lever rammer, and a conversion breech-plate with an integral firing-pin. This looked rather similar to a Thuer ring, but embodied a loading-gate to permit insertion of 0·44 in centrefire flanged cartridges from the rear.

Slightly later (with the stock of 1860 revolver components exhausted) a simplified Richards-Mason conversion was developed, dispensing with the integral firing-pin and simplifying the ejector housing. Very similar components were used on smaller 0·38 in revolvers based on the older 1851 'Navy' and 1862 'Police' models. The sturdy 'New Line' pocket revolvers described in relation to the rimfire cartridge, appeared around 1873 (in 0·32 in, 0·38 in

6 See p. 218.

and 0·41 in centrefire versions), and older designs by Remington, Whitney and other makers were adapted to the centrefire round.

English manufacturers, unhampered by the Rollin White patent, got away briskly once the 'Boxer' revolver cartridge had been sufficiently developed. This was a round markedly different from those produced in America or on the Continent, where the brass or copper case was drawn to shape (by dies and punches) as one component. Colonel E. M. Boxer (of the Royal Laboratory, Woolwich) patented a rifle cartridge in 1866, which had an iron base fixed to a cylinder of coiled brass, and this was developed into a 0·450 in revolver round using a solid-drawn brass body to which the iron base was riveted. The cartridge was approved for British service revolvers late in 1868, and adapted to take a brass base-disc nine years later.

The 0·450 in service revolvers for which this ammunition was principally intended were based on the patents of John Adams (the London gunmaker), which had been secured in 1857, 1861, 1866 and 1867. These pistols were also available in better finishes for the civilian market, and a limited number of Beaumont-Adams Model 1857, service percussion revolvers were also converted to use this cartridge.

John Adams's Model 1867 revolver was a big ($11\frac{1}{2}$ in) six-chambered, double-action revolver with a $5\frac{3}{4}$ in barrel. At a casual glance it appeared to

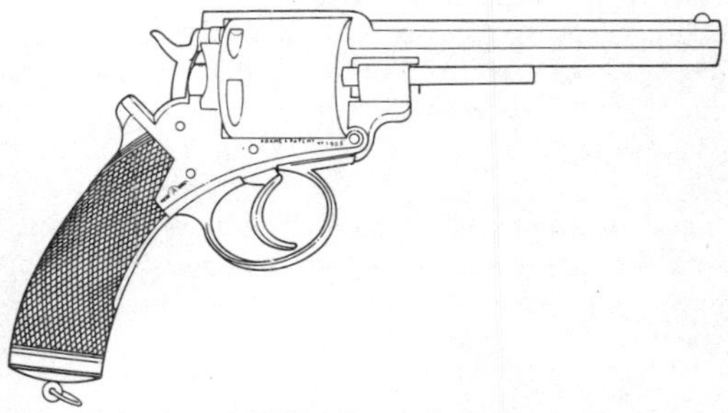

Adams, six-shot, double-action, c.f. service revolver, Model 1867. Museum of Science and Industry, Birmingham.

be solid-framed, but the action body was in fact a separate component secured to the barrel and cylinder frame in the manner patented by its inventor. A loading-gate was hung at the right of the breech, and the first weapons were fitted with a rod-ejector mounted on the right of the barrel lug. This rod was soon secured by an ingenious click, which only permitted the rod to be thrust into the chambers when the cross-head was turned out from beneath the barrel. In 1872, Adams patented an improved ejector rod (mounted on a swivel at the front of the frame) which was housed in the cylinder-axis-pin. This rod was used on Mark III Service revolvers, and was fitted to the models sold commercially.

Adams's Patent Small Arms Company, Limited was formed in 1864 to promote John Adams's patents, and a factory was established in the Strand, for that purpose. It seems probable that the company was also responsible for converting the old Beaumont-Adams percussion revolvers for the services. This was an elaborate conversion, requiring a new cylinder for the 0·450 in cartridge, and the weapons had loading-gates and ejector rods, of the type patented by John Adams in 1867.

The Model 1867 revolver was superseded, in 1880, by the Enfield pistol later to be noticed, and the Adams company passed into other hands. Such revolvers as were made thereafter bore the Strand address, but the company name changed slightly to become Adams's Patent Small Arms Manufacturing Co.

Solid-framed, rod-ejecting Service revolvers were much in vogue during the 1870s, and most of the Great Powers adopted such pistols. However, an important exception lay in the armies of Austro-Hungary, where the Gasser revolver found favour. This Model 1870 pistol was a legacy from the past 234-5
in its frame design, but proved surprisingly robust in issue. The big *revolver du troupe* Gasser measured nearly 13 in in length, and chambered a reduced-charge version of the 11 mm Werndl carbine cartridge. The double-action lock was quite complicated, and the barrel was a separate component mounted (in Lefaucheux style) on the end of the cylinder-axis pin. For infantry officers, a smaller 9 mm version was produced as the 'Gasser-Kropatschek'.

Italy was one of the first powers to adopt a solid frame revolver, and accepted a central-fire version of the Swiss Chamelot, Devigne et Schmidt weapon in 1874. This was a six-chambered, double-action pistol in 10·4 mm calibre, and was one of the first service revolvers with a large removable side-plate giving access to the lock.

The French navy adopted such a revolver in 1870
and the army followed suit, in 1873, by adopting a 236
Chamelot Delvigne revolver chambered for an 11 mm cartridge. In the next year, a refined model was introduced for issue to officers, and had a fluted cylinder against the plain cylinder for the troopers' pistol. Both weapons had locked rod-ejectors attached to their barrels in suitable sleeves.

Holland and Belgium opted for rather similar revolvers, with double-action locks designed by
Nagant of Liège. The Dutch weapon had no rod- 237
ejector fitted to it (a separate rod was attached to the holster), but the Model 1878 Belgian officers revolver had a rod-ejector designed by Nagant. This component was mounted on a rotating sleeve

around the barrel, and could be withdrawn from its seating in the cylinder axis pin to eject the cartridges from the cylinder. The Belgian Nagant also had a dismount system by which the trigger-guard could be tipped down to take tension off the springs, and permit field stripping of the lock.

As earlier mentioned, the Swiss converted their Model 1872 revolvers to use the 10·4 mm centrefire cartridge in 1878, and they introduced a new weapon (for the cavalry) in the same year. This was an advanced design (by their own Stabsmajor R. Schmidt) with a hinged sideplate giving access to the double-action lock, and a rod-ejector designed by Warnant. The most noteworthy feature of Schmidt's lock lay in extending the lower limb of the mainspring to serve as both hammer-rebound and trigger-spring. Rudolph Schmidt was prolific of firearms inventions, and a high velocity, small-calibre revolver to his design was adopted in 1882,
238 for issue to officers of the Swiss army.

The Germans came late to the scene, and did not adopt a revolver for cavalry issue until 1879. This was a 10·6 mm arm designed by a committee, and a lighter model (for officers) was produced as the Model 1883. Both revolvers were six-chambered, with single-action locks and no rod-ejector. The cylinder-axis pin served to eject the cartridges out through the loading gate, and they were a rare service revolver of the period as they were fitted with a safety catch. This consisted of a pivoted lever on the left rear of the frame, which bolted the hammer when turned down.

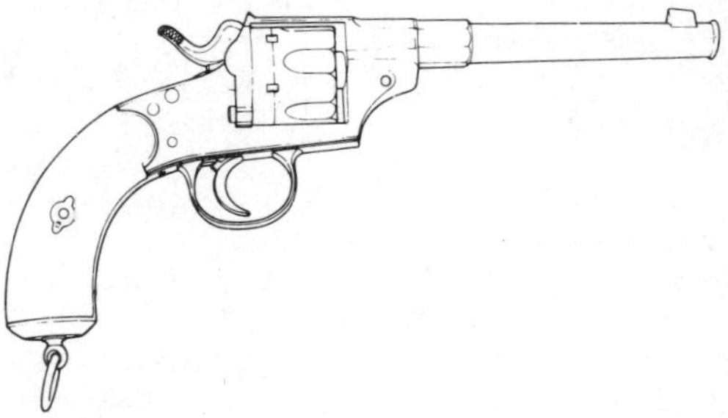

German government single-action, c.f. service revolver, Model 1879. RSAF, Enfield.

The only other major power to adopt single-action service revolvers was the United States, which ordered the Model 1873 Colt 0·45 in as a cavalry side-arm, until the early 1890s.

This was a six-chambered, gate-loaded revolver, with a tubed rod-ejector on the right of the barrel. It had a solid frame into which the barrel was screwed, but clung to the old tradition in having the butt straps and trigger-guard screwed to the frame as

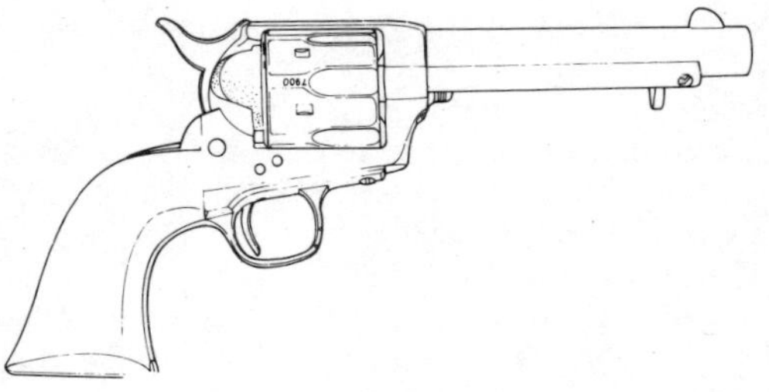

Colt six-shot, single-action, c.f. 'Frontier' revolver, Model 1873. Tower of London Armouries.

separate components. It was immensely popular throughout our period, and was also made for the civilian market in all the principal centrefire calibres and with barrel lengths ranging from $3\frac{1}{2}$ in to 16 in. The original cavalry arm favoured the $7\frac{1}{2}$ in barrel, but some were shortened to $5\frac{1}{2}$ in.

The 'Frontier' Colt, as the ·44–40 pistol was commercially known, was also available in target grades (sometimes with a flat-top frame), and was sold in competition with a single action 'Bisley' revolver after 1896. These Bisley Colts had re-designed butts, hammers and triggers, which earned an enviable reputation for the arm as a target revolver.

During 1877 and 1878, the Colt company began 244-
to produce their first double-action revolvers. The 'Lightning' series used a built-up butt assembly, like the Model 1873, but were fitted with bird's-head butts. They were six-chambered revolvers in 0·32 in, 0·38 in and 0·41 in calibres, and had delicate lock mechanisms which were easily deranged. The Model 1878 'Double Action Army and Frontier' revolver was a larger weapon, which had the frame and butt straps solid-forged to the bird's-head shape. On the left of the action body was a small circular inspection plate, secured by a screw which had to be turned clockwise to loosen it.

The double-action lock mechanism of these big revolvers gave constant trouble, but the Colt company persevered with it and managed to secure a Phillipine police order in 1902. This later series had larger trigger-guards and triggers than normal, and was fitted with a 6 in barrel in 0·45 in Colt calibre. It is often described, amongst collectors, as the 'Alaskan' model, on the theory that the large trigger-guard assisted use in a gloved hand.

In England, during the 1870s and 1880s, civilian revolvers for the centrefire cartridge came principally from the Birmingham houses of P. Webley & Son, or William Tranter.

Philip Webley had converted some of his solid-framed percussion revolvers to take an optional centrefire cylinder in the late 1860s, and had also catalogued some cheap self-cocking arms based on

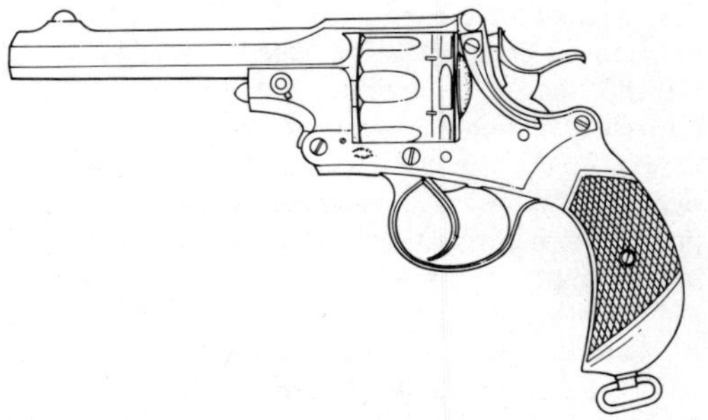

Webley-Kaufmann self-extracting ·450 revolver. Incorporating patents of 1880 and 1883. Tower of London Armouries.

percussion components, but the firm began to produce really important designs after 1867.

The Royal Irish Constabulary were formed in
243 1836, and adopted a Webley revolver as their issue sidearm in 1868. This weapon was thereafter sold as the 'R.I.C.' model and was taken up by various Colonial forces, as well as achieving enviable sales in the civilian market. The weapon was a solid-framed, double-action, 0·442 in calibre pistol, gate-loaded, and with a $4\frac{1}{2}$ in barrel screwed into the cast iron frame. It was fitted with a slender rod-ejector mounted and housed like the later Nagant design, and had a smooth cylinder with small locking notches near the muzzle-end. P. Webley & Son, who made this revolver for the heavy British cartridges (0·430 in, 0·442 in, 0·450 in, 0·455 in and 0·476 in), also chambered some weapons for the 0·44 in or 0.45 in American calibres, and Continental makers also produced the design in large numbers.

So popular were these weapons (and the rather
242 similar 'British Bull Dog' series), that an improved Model 1883 was produced and sold under a suitable designation, as the '83/450' and the '83/455', or the 'R.I.C. No. 2. ·320' or 'No. 5 ·360 Express'. These were all five-shot developments of the original 1867 design, and had fluted cylinders. A big six-shot 0·450 in/0·455 in R.I.C. No. 1 was also produced to modernise the old design (it was available with $4\frac{1}{2}$ in or 6 in barrels), and a special 0·450 in M.P. model, with a $2\frac{1}{2}$ in barrel, was adopted by the London Metropolitan Police in November 1883.

These models, with the Webley No. 2 Pattern 'British Bull Dog' (in 0·450 in, 0·380 in, 0·32 in calibres) were still catalogued in 1914, but were missing from the first post-war catalogues.

About 1881, Webley also began to produce an
241 'Army Express' series, which subsequently developed into the 'New Army Express' revolver. These arms were apparently intended as a counterpart to the Colt, Model 1878, double-action Army and Frontier revolvers earlier mentioned, and were six-chambered pistols, with $5\frac{1}{2}$ in barrels in 0·455 in or 0·45 in Colt calibres. Most of the weapons had a double-action lock mechanism, but a few single-action models were made for Colonial service.

The competing revolvers by William Tranter petered out, as a series, on his retirement in 1885. Their inventor was an active patentee and his arms were normally marked *W. Tranter's Patent* on their frames. Many of his revolvers were identical to the rimfire models earlier mentioned, which is to say that they were six-chambered, solid-framed arms using Tranter's patent double-action lock and having a rod-ejector (patented in 1868) lying beneath their barrels.

Tranter's British Patent of 1868 also protected a type of hammer used only in one series of his centrefire revolvers. In this weapon, a separate, spring-loaded firing-pin was mounted in the frame for striking by a rebounding hammer, and the firing nose of that component was shaped to shield the pin against any accidental blow.

Although preferring the 0·320 in, 0·380 in, 0·430 in and 0·450 in calibres for his pistols, Tranter also made revolvers for the 0·500 in cartridge. Commonly these were scaled-up versions of his 1868 revolver (lacking the firing-pin refinement), but a few weapons were made with very short cylinders, to use a less punishing cartridge than the big 0·500 in Eley revolver round.

These Tranter arms were very beautifully made, and retained one rather old-fashioned feature in ignoring the fluted cylinder. Some solid-frame Tranter revolvers had this refinement, but it is comparatively rare.

It will be appreciated that all the solid-framed revolvers so far described were slow to load, or to empty after use, and attempts to speed up these functions continued to be made until the turn of the century.

The most tempting ejection system, for the theorist, was to expel each cartridge case from

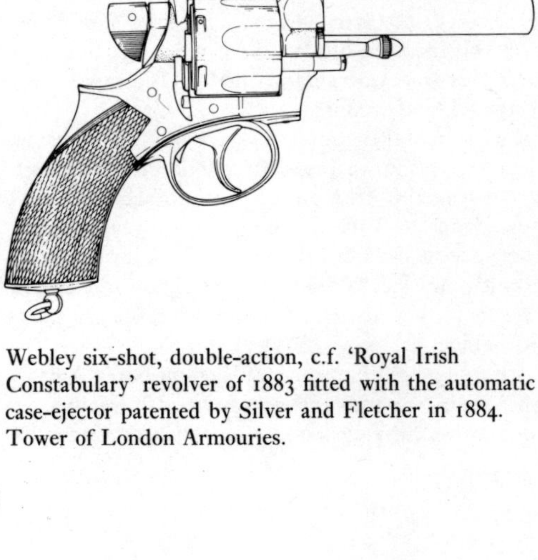

Webley six-shot, double-action, c.f. 'Royal Irish Constabulary' revolver of 1883 fitted with the automatic case-ejector patented by Silver and Fletcher in 1884. Tower of London Armouries.

the cylinder by some means connected with firing the succeeding round. Sederl (in 1880) and Messrs. Fletcher & Silver (in 1884) patented British systems in which the brow of the falling hammer struck one end of a hinged lever in the pistol frame and caused the other end to flick the neighbouring, 'one o'clock', cartridge out of its chamber. Similar devices were patented by Krauser, in Switzerland, and by Praunegger & Schmidt during 1896. Other systems tapping gas on firing, or using weighted rods jerked into the chambers by the recoil of the pistol were also tried. None of these devices was really successful, although some Webley Model 1883 revolvers were fitted with Fletcher & Silver's ejector.

The best known methods for simultaneous cartridge extraction are the hinged-frame designs, personified by the Webley or older Smith & Wesson revolvers, and the solid frame with cylinder swinging out to the side for cartridge extraction. The revolvers of Colt or Smith & Wesson remain today the leading embodiments of this system.

The hinged-frame revolver extracted all the cartridge cases simultaneously, when the barrel was unlatched and tipped down on a hinge at the lower forward end of the frame. The type must be distinguished from early Smith & Wesson pistols, discussed under the rimfire cartridge, in which the barrel was hinged at the top of the frame. Here the cartridges were punched separately from their chambers, after complete removal of the cylinder.

Attempts were made to use this top-hinged system in alliance with simultaneous extraction of all cartridges, but these pistols are now rare which suggests only a limited production. The Belgian gunmaker Spirlet produced such a revolver in 1869, whilst William Tranter of Birmingham patented three suitable extractors in 1868 and 1869. In Spirlet's pistol, tilting up the barrel cammed the hammer back to half-cock, and permitted a button on the forward end of the barrel lug to be tapped against a saddle, or any other hard object. This pushed back a star-shaped extractor in the rear face of the cylinder and ejected the cartridges by their rims. The Tranter revolvers were similar in construction, but their extractors were operated manually, either by a lever or by rack-and-pinion.

The true hinged-frame revolver did not appear as a self-extracting weapon until about 1869, although such a system of frame assembly had been patented in England (by Vail, an American) six years earlier. There seems little doubt that the honour of priority lay with Smith & Wesson, but the claims of Captain Tackels (a Belgian infantry officer) press hard upon this point.

The single-action Smith & Wesson No. 3 American Model has been earlier described in relation to the rimfire cartridges for which it was originally designed, and it is enough to say of it here that the extractor mechanism was patented in England during 1869, and that the first US Army order for the centrefire version was secured late in 1870. Subsequently, the arm was modified by Colonel G. W. Schofield, USA, who patented (in 1871) an improved latch pivoted on the frame instead of the barrel-strap, and (in 1873) an improved extractor to dispense with Smith & Wesson's gear-wheel mechanism. This officer was successful in securing service adoption for his modified pistol in 0·45 in calibre.

Around 1871, Smith & Wesson secured the first in a series of large orders from the Russian government. The pistol was a variant of the No. 3 weapon, and

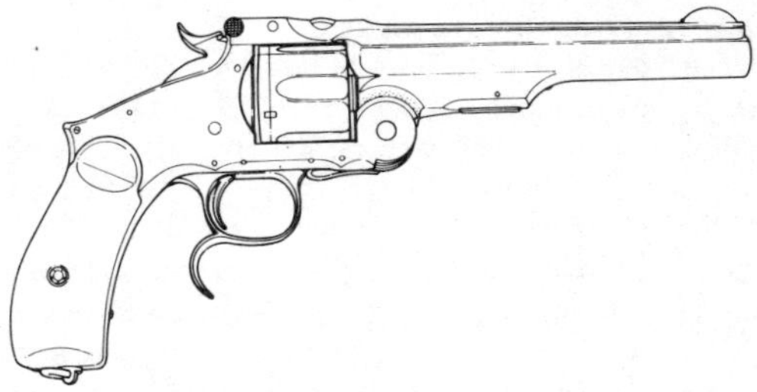

Smith & Wesson six-shot, single-action, c.f., hinge-framed 'Russian' revolver, 1873-78. Tower of London Armouries.

was known as the 'Russian Model'. A special 0·44 in cartridge was developed for it, and proved so satisfactory that it served as a target cartridge for many years after completion of the orders that sired it. During production of these Russian Government arms (which continued until 1877) the weapon went through various modifications, a series with saw-handled butts and finger rests beneath the trigger-guard being one most striking to the eye. A very substantial order for identical weapons was later placed (by the Russians) with Ludwig Loewe of Berlin, and Liège-proved copies are also known.

The popularity of these large models prompted enquiries for pocket versions, which the company met in 1876 with a 0·38 in, single-action pistol (in 3¼ in, 4 in and 5 in barrel lengths) now popularly known as 'the baby Russian', and with a 0·32 in calibre model of 1878. These weapons were the first Smith & Wesson revolvers to have hammers automatically rebounding off the cartridge heads, and no model with a trigger-guard appeared until 1891.

After completion of the Russian Government contracts, Smith & Wesson produced a 'No. 3 New Model' single-action 0·44 in revolver, which reduced the number of lock parts and ultimately embodied a simplified extractor mechanism (invented by J. H. Bullard, an employee) rather similar to that used in the Schofield weapon. This new model also became available in ·44–40 and ·38–40 Winchester calibres, was sometimes chambered for the 0·450 in Eley cartridge, and ultimately developed into one of the most beautiful target revolvers ever made when (from 1887) the ·32–44 and ·38–44 target cartridges were applied to it. The series were still catalogued by Charles Osborne (then British agent for Smith & Wesson) in 1909.

Equal in popularity were the double-action, hinged-frame Smith & Wesson revolvers, which were introduced during 1880 as five-shot pistols in 0·32 in, 0·38 in and 0·44 in calibres. Their principal patented features lay in the double bolting of the cylinder, and they were manufactured in considerable numbers until 1910.

The last of the Smith & Wesson hinged-frame designs was their 'Safety Hammerless, New Departure' pistol, introduced in 1887. These revolvers had a self-cocking lock, with the hammer completely shrouded within the action body, and a safety-lever embedded in the rear butt-strap. Unless the pistol was correctly gripped, it could not be fired by pulling the trigger, and the ingenious lock could not be accidentally operated by any fall or blow. In 0·32 in and 0·38 in Smith & Wesson calibres, these arms sold as successively improved models, and in large numbers and were not discontinued until long after 1918. A 0·44 in calibre version was planned, but never produced, and Continental imitations (not copies) of the pocket arms were also attempted.

In turning to European successes with the hinged-frame, self-extracting weapon, we have Captain Tackels's design of 1871, as the probable first starter. J. N. Cuttat[7] termed this pistol as the *revolver à bielle*, and it was a double-action weapon with a star-shaped extractor similar to that used by Smith & Wesson. The extractor was operated by a cam (*la bielle*) jointed to the frame hinge instead of the American rack system. The lock was rather complicated, considerable ingenuity being devoted to sealing the mechanism against entry of water or fouling.

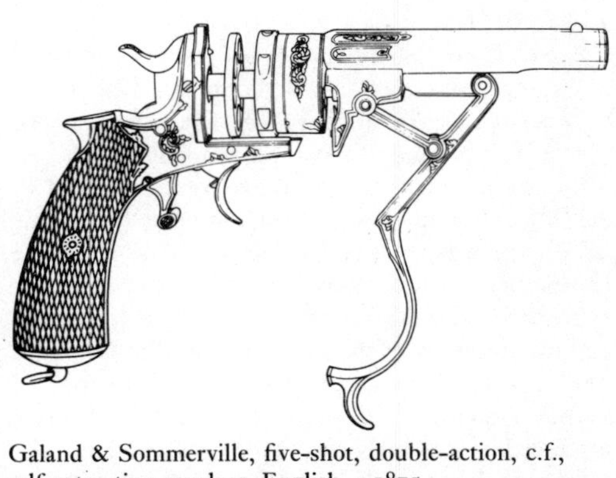

Galand & Sommerville, five-shot, double-action, c.f., self-extracting revolver. English, *c.*1875.

The leading competitor to Tackels's revolver can be conveniently noticed here, although its extractor was not operated by breaking open the pistol about a frame hinge. C. F. Galand (of Paris and Liège) patented this self-extracting revolver, in which the trigger-guard could be swung forward on a hinge attached to the underside of the barrel, during 1868. By an appropriate linkage, this movement pulled forward the barrel and cylinder, thus withdrawing all the cartridges, simultaneously, by a disc extractor connected to the rear of the cylinder.

Galand's revolver (a runner-up to the successful Chamelot Delvigne in the Swiss revolver trials of 1871) was made in 12 mm and 7 mm versions, for the Perrin welt-rimmed cartridge, and was adopted by the Russians at about the same time as the Smith & Wesson cavalry arm. A British patent was secured jointly by the inventor and A. Sommerville, of Birmingham, under which protection some 0·450 in and 0·380 in revolvers were made. These British pistols used an ejecting lever latched at the front of the frame, and had lock mechanisms of Tranter-type with a stud on the rear of the trigger to operate a bottom sear. The Continental Galand used a different lock.

It is not easy to identify the first hinged-frame design to appear in England, nor to suggest its inventor. Dowell[8] identifies a revolver of this type by P. Webley & Son under the invention of E. Woods and dates the weapon around 1870. No traceable British patent appears to exist, but the revolver gives every indication of manufacture at this early date. In this Woods revolver, a long lever was hung on the left of the breech and unlatched the barrel when pressed forward by the thumb. The pistol then broke open in conventional style to operate a star-shaped extractor in the rear of the cylinder.

Following this weapon , came a series of revolvers with barrel latches operated by press-levers on either side of the frame, which are now commonly described as 'Pryse' revolvers. The honour for their invention is accorded to Charles Pryse the Younger, of Aston, Birmingham, through his British patent of 1876, but their origins seem Belgian under examination. Pryse's patent only related to the cylinder bolt (engaging in slots machined round the circumference of the cylinder), and although his drawings showed some features of the design attributed to him, he disclaimed the lock-mechanism as being 'of the ordinary kind' and did not even illustrate the characteristic barrel latch.

However, these Pryse revolvers were extremely

7 *Les Armes à Feu Portatives*, Paris, 1877.

8 See note 3.

successful, for the last model did not appear until around 1890 and every popular British calibre was supplied, from 0·320 in to 0·577 in. The versions most common in England have the lock disclaimed by Pryse, featuring a rebounding hammer and a sear tail protruding through the rear bow of the trigger-guard. Later, a more advanced design was produced by Francotte of Liège, dispensing with the lower sear and trigger-spring in favour of a long rebound lever operated by the lower limb of the mainspring. These arms were proved and retailed in England, and were still catalogued by the larger trade houses up to 1914.

Whilst producing the British version of the Pryse weapon, P. Webley & Son linked up with another

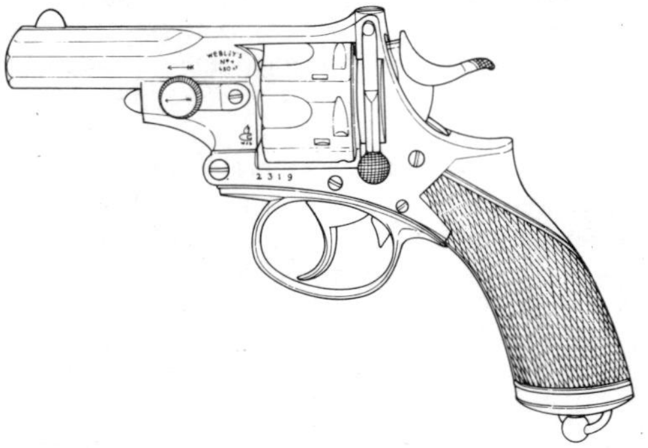

Webley's No. 4 Revolver ('Webley-Pryse'). Six-shot, double-action, c.f., hinged-frame, self-ejecting. Post-1876. Tower of London Armouries.

Continental designer and began to produce the 'Webley-Kaufmann' series of self-extracting revolvers. These were six-chambered 'Army-sized' pistols, with an inspection and stripping plate on the left of the frame. Apart from their superb finish and beautiful Kaufmann locks, the most striking feature of the Webley-Kaufmann and Improved Government revolvers lay in their barrel latches. The for-
240 mer pistol used a three-piece button-latch embedded
in a reinforce at the rear of the top strap, as patented by Kaufmann in 1881. The later revolver, which was warmly approved by both Bond and Walsh (in 1884 editions), had the same bolt operated by a thumb lever, an improvement patented by Henry Webley in 1883.

Kaufmann also contributed to a service revolver approved for the British army in 1880. This 'Pistol Revolver B.L. Enfield', attained Marks I and II as a six-chambered arm in ·455/·476 calibres, and was intended to replace the solid-framed 0·450 in Adams. In some aspects it was a most unfortunate choice, and few contemporary writers have a good word to say for it.

The ejection system was designed by Owen Jones (of Philadelphia) and was a compromise between the conventional hinged-frame extractor and earlier methods like that of Galand. When the barrel was unlatched and tipped down, the cylinder was drawn forward along its axis pin to leave the cartridges behind, hooked by their rims on a star extractor fastened to the breech of the frame. Jones secured British patents of 1876 and 1878 for this method of extraction, and it worked well.

The lock mechanism of the Enfield was patented by Kaufmann & Warnant (a Liège gunmaker) in 1878, as a development of a de Mouncie design, and in it the lower limb of the mainspring was extended past the hammer, to power a swinging plate operating trigger and pawl. The pistol was made at the Royal Small Arms Factory, Enfield, and was issued also to the Navy and the Mounted Constabulary of Ireland and Canada. The series was obstinately maintained in production until 1889, but various modifications to the lock showed that the design was unsatisfactory from the start.

To succeed the Enfield, the government purchased the Webley Mk I service revolver, in July 1887, and this six-chambered pistol (produced to chamber 0·476 and 0·455 cartridges) replaced such manufacture in private hands for the remainder of the period.

Service adoption of this Webley revolver was probably sparked off by Tranter's retirement, and the fine series of six-chambered 'W. G.' pistols produced by P. Webley & Son from 1885 onwards. These were made in both Army and Target versions, with lock and barrel latch patented by Henry Webley and W. J. Carter. This lock mechanism was not used in the Mk I pistol, but the famous Webley 'stirrup' barrel-latch was used thereafter in the whole series of British service revolvers.

The Mk I (with a 4 in Metford-rifled barrel) had a pronounced prawl or lump on the top butt strap, and 'parrot-beak' grips. It was followed by the
Mk II (1895), Mk III (1897), Mk IV (1899), Mk V 246
(1913) and Mk VI (1915), but only minor changes were made to an eminently satisfactory design prior to the Mk III.

Apart from these service designs, the Webley & Scott Revolver & Arms Company Ltd. (as it became in 1897), sold a small 0·38 in revolver with 3 in, 4 in, 5 in and 6 in barrels available at choice. Although for civilian sale, these were engraved as the 'Mk III', and were followed, in 1898, by a smaller 0·32 in weapon (which was available also as a hammerless design) known as the 'W. P.' model.

Continental makers favoured the hinged-frame design, but many of the arms produced in Belgium, France or Germany were little more than copies of leading American models. Levaux (a French firm) produced some early 0·450 in and 0·380 in self-extracting arms with a tall spur-operated barrel latch of rather weak design, and Francotte (who manufactured a considerable range of hinged-frame arms) developed a peculiar top-hinged series which extracted automatically as the barrel tipped up. These revolvers were also sold in England (under the trade mark 'The Stanley') and some huge weapons were made for the long 0·450 in Montenegrin cartridge.

Apart from low quality arms sold as of 'Smith & Wesson type' or on the 'system Smith & Wesson', a number of excellent hinged-frame revolvers of medium quality and small calibre were made in America, by Harrington & Richardson or Hopkins

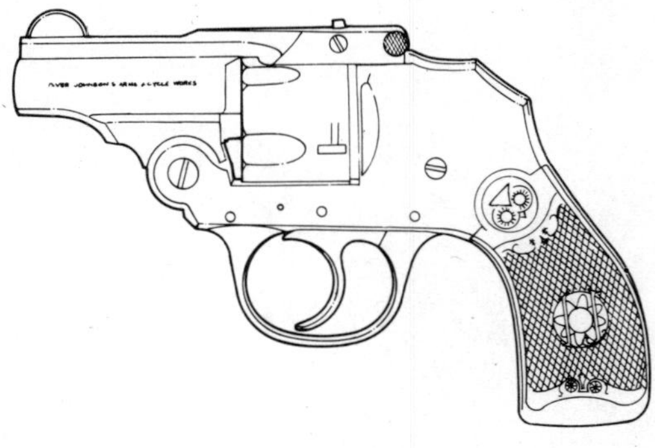

Iver Johnson hinged-frame revolvers, *c.*1896.

& Allen (both of Worcester, Massachusetts) and by the Iver Johnson Arms & Cycle Works, of Fitchburg, Massachusetts. The Hopkins & Allen pistols (see Fig. p. 339) had their hammers mounted on an eccentric pivot, and a firing-pin could only be struck when the trigger was pulled; Iver Johnson used piano wire springs and an ingenious bar on top of the cylinder pawl. This bar formed a bridge or anvil between hammer and firing-pin and made accidental discharge by blow, or fall, impossible.

During the years that the hinged-frame revolver was in development, the solid-frame design also progressed.

One interesting British design was patented by J. Thomas, of Birmingham, and was developed on a modest scale into the mid-1870s. The double-action, gate-loaded pistol was made with a long cylinder-aperture in the frame, and twisting the barrel permitted the cylinder to be pulled forward, until a star extractor fixed to the breech-face pulled the cartridges from the chambers. An interesting, but unconnected, development of the idea was produced by Merwin & Hulbert, of Brooklyn, New York. Their revolver (patented in 1878) was made as a heavy, single-action 0·44 in Army revolver in which the barrel was turned over to extract the cases in a manner similar to the Thomas. However, unlike

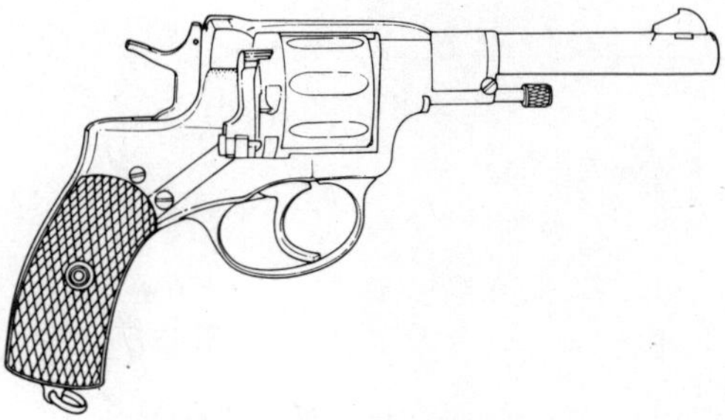

Seven-shot, double-action, c.f. revolver with device providing a gas seal between the chambers and barrel. Nagant of Liège, Model 1895. RSAF, Enfield.

the latter, it had no solid frame although a top strap was fitted to an improved model in the early 1880s.

An unusual solid-frame revolver was patented by Nagant of Belgium, in 1894, and adopted by the Russians in the following year. Externally, it differed little in appearance from the big Belgian officers' revolver of 1878, but was chambered for seven small-calibre high-velocity cartridges of special type. This 7·62 mm round had the bullet seated completely within its long case, and the cylinder moved to-and-fro upon its axis to seat the mouth of this cartridge in the end of the barrel on firing. The intention was to eliminate loss of gas (and muzzle velocity) at the junction of chamber with barrel, and in the standard $4\frac{1}{2}$ in barrel length a velocity in the order of 1,000 ft/s was achieved, against a velocity of 725 ft/s in a conventional pistol. The arm remained in issue until the Second World War.

Pieper, another Belgian, attempted to improve the Nagant by making a version with cylinder swinging out to the side for simultaneous (manual) cartridge extraction, but this design was never successful. The same maker produced a commercial revolver for the '7·62 mm Russe' cartridge, which resembled the Nagant closely but lacked a gas-seal mechanism.

The swing-out cylinder, with a button-operated extractor, was the leading refinement to solid-framed revolvers and was widely used after 1890. Why the major manufacturers were so slow to adopt it remains a mystery, for designs had been patented in America during 1865 (by W. Mason, an employee of the Remington company, which apparently made it in limited numbers), and in England, during 1869, by Captain Albini of the Royal Italian Navy.

The Colt Company tinkered with improved designs by W. Mason, but used other patents in their first swing-out cylinder pistol, the 0.38 in double-action 'Navy Revolver', model of 1889. These arms differed externally from later designs in having no locking slots on the outside of the cylinder, and a 0·41 in version was available on the civilian market.

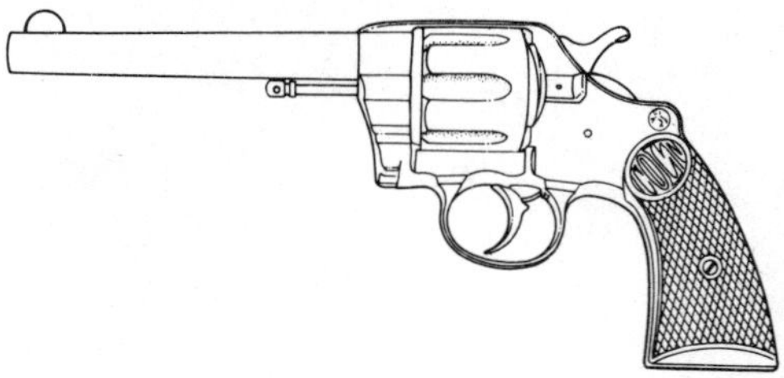

New Colt Army double-action .38 revolver. Model of 1896. RSAF, Enfield.

In 1892, the company introduced the more robust 'Army and Navy' series (0·38 in and 0·41 in calibres), which were successively improved until discontinued in 1908. The second modification, in 1894, provided hammer and trigger locks, and the ·32–20 WCF and 0·38 in Special calibres were later made available. A rare 'Marine Corps' 0·38 in model with a 6 in barrel was produced in limited numbers, between 1905 and 1908.

Many beautiful revolvers followed these pioneer versions, and bore their model name engraved upon their barrels, as the 0·32 in 'New Pocket' or 'Pocket Positive' (1895-1905); the 0·32 in 'New Police' (1896-1905); the 'Police Positive' (in 0·32 in and 0·38 in calibres, from 1905) and 'Police Positive Special' (from 1907); the magnificent 'Army Special' or 'Official Police' models (in ·32–20, 0·38 in Special and 0·41 in Colt calibres, from 1908), and the 'Officer's Model' series, in 0·38 in Special calibre, which developed from them.

Various modifications to the basic design were made prior to 1918, the 'Positive Safety Lock' (an intercepting bar to prevent firing unless the trigger was pulled) came in about 1905, and cylinder rotation settled down to a clockwise revolution. Possibly the most famous revolver of the series was Colt's 'New Service' pistol, which appeared in 1897 and achieved Standard, Target, Army & Navy, and Marine Corps models in calibres from 0·38 in to 0·476 in Eley cartridge. The last development, prior to 1918, was to chamber the arm to accept the 0·45 in Automatic Colt Pistol cartridge (in two semi-circular clips) as the Service Model of 1917.

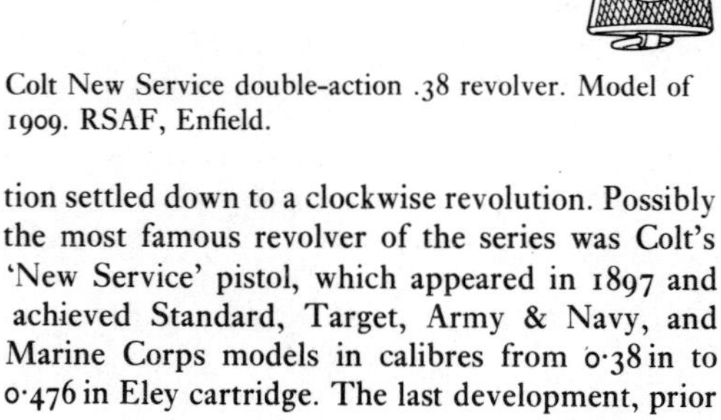

Colt New Service double-action .38 revolver. Model of 1909. RSAF, Enfield.

Smith & Wesson, well satisfied with the success of their hinged-frame revolvers, took some time before introducing a swing-out cylinder design, although the weapons eventually acknowledged a string of patents between 1884 and 1895. The first of these arms (the six-shot 'Hand Ejector' (1), First Model) appeared in 1896, and was chambered for the 0·32 in S & W long cartridge. It threw back to earlier designs in having a cylinder bolt pivoted in the top frame strap, and worked by the hammer when being cocked. It was succeeded (in 1903) by an improved model which ran to six changes by 1917. Barrel lengths of 3¼ in, 4¼ in and 6 in were available.

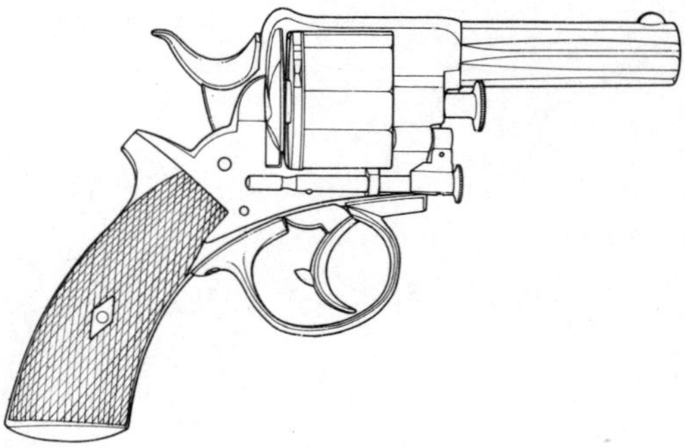

Double-action .450 'Constabulary' revolver, fitted with W. Tranter's ejector-rod, patented in 1868. Tower of London Armouries.

Introduced in 1899, and equally popular, were the Hand Ejector Winchester series to chamber the light ·32–20 rifle cartridge developed by the famous rifle manufacturers. This six-chambered revolver was refined in 1902, and again in 1905, achieving its seventh model change in 1915. The initial year saw also the introduction of a six-shot Hand Ejector M & P (Military and Police) 0·38 in calibre pistol, which was purchased by the US Army and Navy. The model only lasted until 1902, but sired a series of improved revolvers, of which the five-chambered 'Regulation Police' model, of 1917, was a fine example.

Smith & Wesson also produced a superb heavy calibre series as the Hand Ejector, New Century Model. Manufacture began in 1907 (in 0·44 in S & W Special, originally, with other 0·44 in, 0·450 in and 0·455 in calibres later available), such arms being popularly known as the 'Triple Lock' or 'Gold Seal' revolvers. The first name sprang from an additional bolting feature for the crane upon which the cylinder was swung. The weapon was made in

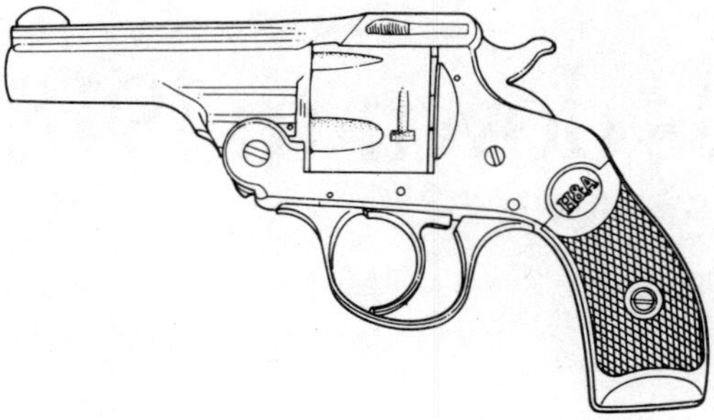

Hopkins and Allen hinged-frame revolver, *c.*1898.
(See p. 337.)

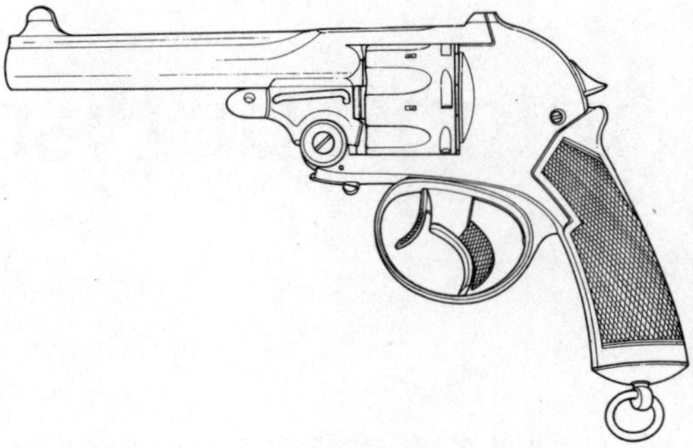

Double-action .476 Kynoch revolver incorporating H. A. Schlund's patent. Tower of London Armouries.

4 in, 5 in, 6½ in and 7½ in barrel lengths, and 5,000 were purchased (in 0.455 in Mk II calibre) for the British Government during 1914. The extra lock was abandoned during the First World War, but the model is still greatly fancied.

A Second Model Hand Ejector (in 0·44 in S & W Special calibre) appeared in 1915, and a Model 1917 revolver was also produced to chamber the 0.45 in ACP cartridge, held in the same clips as those developed for the comparable Colt pistol.

Continental copies of Colt or Smith & Wesson swing-out cylinder pistols were numerous, and often badly made. Pieper (Belgium) and Genschow or Pickert (Germany) versions were amongst the best, but one or two excellent Spanish and South American arms were damned by a stream of rubbish turned out by anonymous makers.

The French Army adopted a side-swinging cylinder design, as the *Modèle d'Ordonnance 1892*, which chambered a special 8 mm cartridge (with a copper-jacketed bullet) of modest striking energy and muzzle-velocity. This revolver was six-chambered, with a 4·5 in barrel, and weighed about 30 oz. Unlike the Colt and Smith & Wesson arms, the cylinder swung out to the right for loading or extraction, and the entire left-hand side of the frame could be turned out on a hinge to give access to the lock.

CHAPTER TWELVE

Automatic Pistols down to 1918

C.H. Roads

The field of design variation in the automatic pistol (or, in other words, a pistol which reloads and recocks itself after a first manual initiation), open to the ingenious engineer is almost limitless. To this the files of the London Patent Office bear abundant evidence as volumes of similar physical size successively cover fewer each year. Basic design, on the other hand, suggests three broad classifications; arms with a locked breech, those with an unlocked or blowback operation, and those with a measure of hesitation in the operation of the breech-block. Or, in lay terms, arms in which, on firing, the mechanism stays locked to the barrel, those in which the force of the explosion is allowed, without check, to push back the mechanism and, thirdly, those where there is some arrangement to retard or delay the separation of the breech-block from contact with the barrel and chamber[1]. The mechanical means by which the locking and unlocking of the breech are achieved have given scope to great ingenuity but almost as much thought seems to have been devoted by those producing low-powered, simple blowback pocket-pistols to the task of achieving individuality in outward appearance. This is readily understandable. There is no need to expend time and effort in locking the breech unless the power of the cartridge makes it necessary. Exactly where a blowback action ceases to be a practical proposition is very much a matter of opinion, depending on such factors as the measure of accuracy required, comfort to the user in firing, quantities of ammunition to be carried etc. Hiram Maxim in 1897 used a simple blowback unlocked breech for calibres as large as 0.455in and the Spanish, in the Astra, have used it for the fairly high power 9mm Parabellum cartridge, but more normally the line would probably be drawn at about 7.65mm or 0.32in.

In an automatic pistol the agency for the automatic operation of the breech mechanism, for the extraction and ejection of the fired case, for the cocking of the action and for the chambering of the new cartridge is almost invariably recoil, or more correctly, recoil and the energy of returning springs. This is, perhaps, one of the most marked differences in operation between heavier automatic weapons and pistols. The alternative is, of course, gas operation but with the short length of barrel used in a pistol this becomes exceedingly difficult to employ. Attempts have been made, indeed some of the earliest designs for an automatic pistol were on this principle. In 1886 there was Paulsen's patented idea for a gas-operated revolver which probably did not get off the drawing board and in 1892 the Clair brothers of St Etienne in France filed a patent for a gas-operated self-loading pistol, which had a tube magazine in the butt for the 8mm revolver cartridges which it fired. This pistol could not be called a success, only a small number were sold, but an even less successful endeavour to use gas operation is to be seen in Mclean's pistol, Patent No. 6298 of 1898.

If the Clair brothers' pistol failed to prove the possibilities of gas operation for automatic pistols it did not fail to provide the French with an opportunity to claim the first successful automatic pistol in the sense that it was the first available to the public. There are claims that the Clair brothers were working on the design from the early 1880s but no direct evidence is available of their activities until 1889. There is nothing yet discovered to prove that their pistol emerged before the Schönberger which in 1892 was first made by Österreichische Waffenfabrik at Steyr. This Austrian arm, which was derived from Laumann's patents of 1890, 1891 and 1892, was the first successful automatic pistol offered to the public. It did not sell as well as its design suggests it might because the certainty of its functioning depended so directly upon the quality of the cartridge it used. This was a fairly high powered 8 mm bottlenecked cartridge. Though this round was, in many senses, modern, the manufacturers had yet to reach that state of development that they could maintain variations in velocity within a reasonable bracket.

It is, in fact, more remarkable that it had proved possible, within so short a time of Veille's discovery of smokeless powder and Rubin's introduction of a jacketed bullet, to utilise these discoveries to make the production of a successful automatic pistol a practical proposition. Once the Schönberger pistol had revealed the tremendous possibilities now for

248 A Steyr-Mannlicher automatic, Model 1901, in 7·63 mm calibre. Smithsonian Institution, Washington, D.C.

249, 250 Two models of the Mauser Military automatic: (*Top*) Model of 1896 with the 'cone' hammer. (*Bottom*) Model of 1898 with the 'ring' hammer. Imperial War Museum, London.

251 The Colt Model 1908, Browning-designed, automatic pistol in ·380 (9 mm Short) calibre. RSAF, Enfield.

252 *Above* The service automatic pistol: (*Top*) the Remington M1911A1. (*Centre*) the Colt M1911A1. (*Bottom*) the 'Commander' lightweight model in 9 mm Parabellum calibre. Imperial War Museum, London.

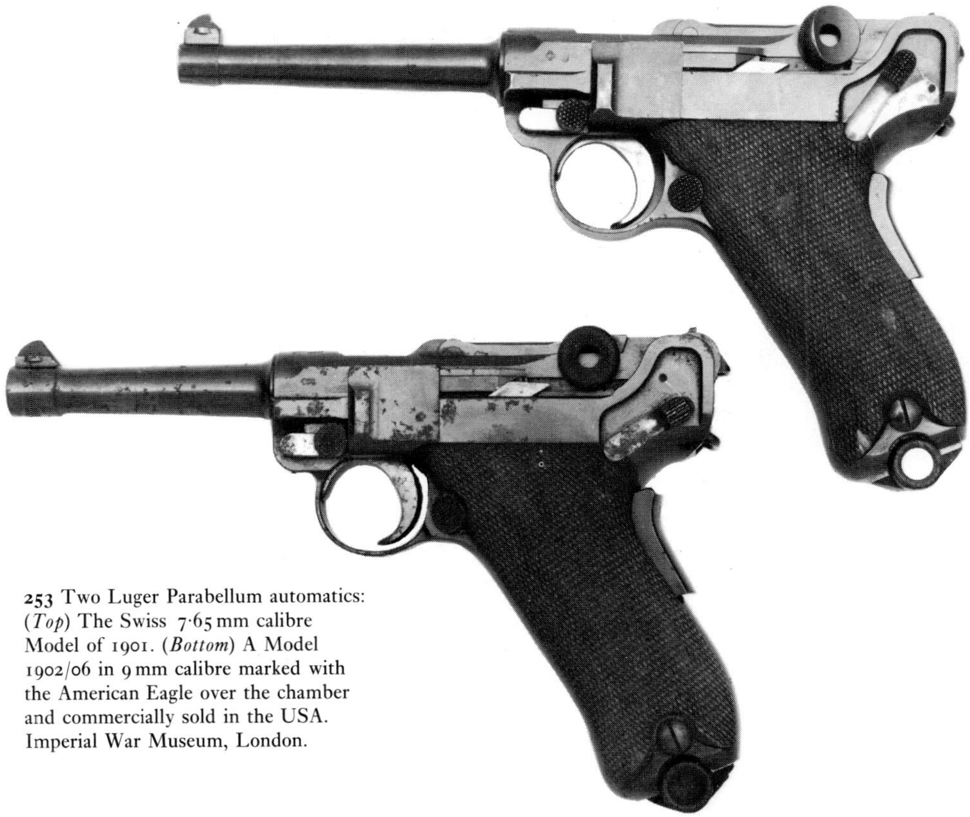

253 Two Luger Parabellum automatics: (*Top*) The Swiss 7·65 mm calibre Model of 1901. (*Bottom*) A Model 1902/06 in 9 mm calibre marked with the American Eagle over the chamber and commercially sold in the USA. Imperial War Museum, London.

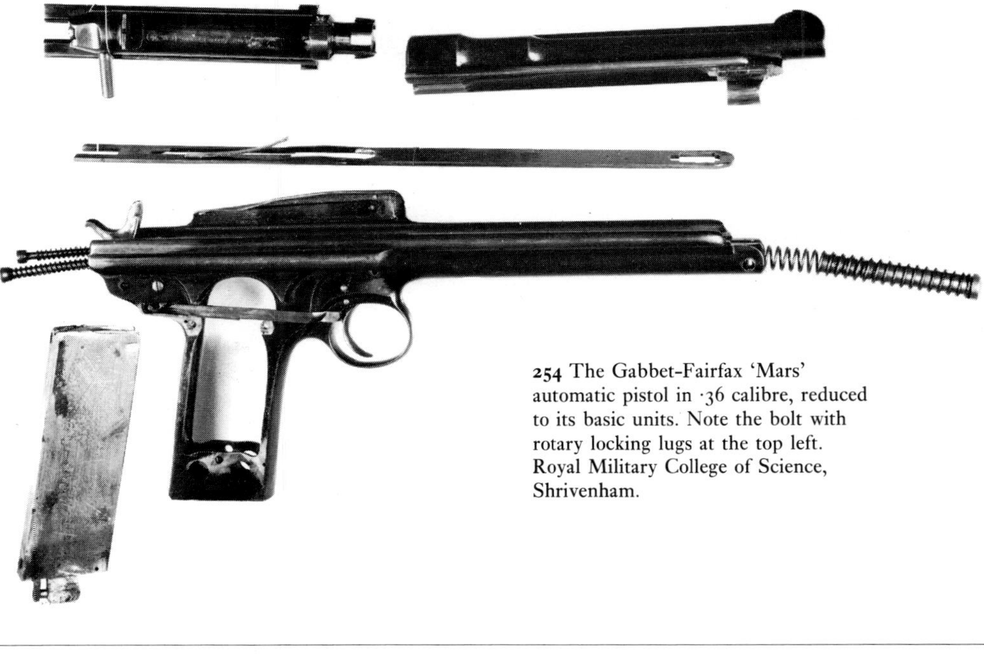

254 The Gabbet-Fairfax 'Mars' automatic pistol in ·36 calibre, reduced to its basic units. Note the bolt with rotary locking lugs at the top left. Royal Military College of Science, Shrivenham.

255 A group of Webley & Scott automatics. (*Top*) The ·32 calibre of 1905 with safety alongside the hammer. (*Left*) The ·32 calibre with external hammer. (*Below*) The 9 mm calibre High Velocity with safety grip. (*Below, left*) The ·32 calibre external hammer Police of 1906 with frame safety. Imperial War Museum, London.

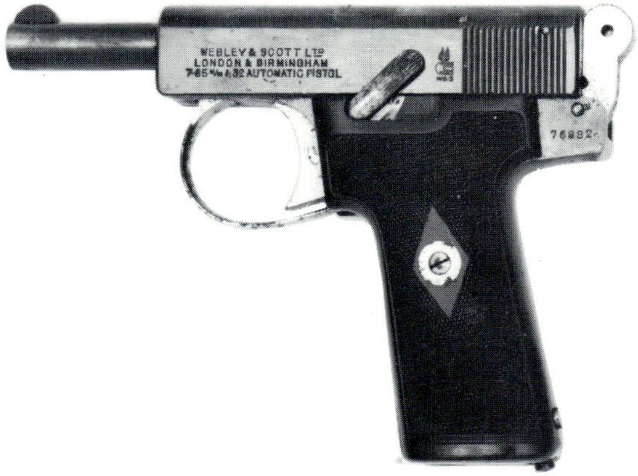

the first time open to pistol designers it was inevitable that there would be a flood of inventions. It was equally certain that there would be only a limited number of approaches to a pistol which handled well, shot straight and functioned reliably. By 1913 the ground had pretty well been covered and more than once in most cases. During the First World War, as was to be expected, certain designs were found wanting and dropped. Others underwent modifications which revealed, for example, the impact of logistic problems and those associated with mass production. By 1918 the forms which the automatic pistol had assumed were virtually those which exist today. Comparatively very little has happened in the last six and a half decades.

The twenty-six years with which we are here concerned, the period between 1892 and 1918, more logically divides into periods of experimentation and of consolidation on the year 1902 than on 1913. By 1902 most of the main designs had emerged or had been foreshadowed. The Mauser, the Mannlicher, the Luger, the Browning, the Webley Fosbery, the Schwarzlose, and the Bergmann were all emerging or had just evolved. In other words, automatic pistols using most of the main forms of breech-lock had passed through the stage of experimentation by 1902. There were certainly famous names in automatic pistols still unheard: the Savage, the Webley, the Glisenti and the Beretta are only a selection; but this in no way invalidates the fundamental division that can usefully be made at about 1902, just ten years after the year in which the Schönberger was first made and in which Andrea Schwarzlose patented his first design.

Schwarzlose, who was later to be responsible for a number of very interesting and successful weapon designs, in this pistol, of which only a very few specimens were produced, employed an action which superficially was rather reminiscent of the Remington rolling block. The cartridges, nose downwards, were contained in a magazine under the barrel. The breech-block and hammer were on a common axis and together pivoted back as the barrel recoiled so that they cocked the hammer and ejected the fired case. At the same time a cartridge carrier swung the next round through 90° and into alignment with the chamber. The cartridge was chambered as the working parts returned to their normal positions under the influence of a coiled spring housed in front of the magazine and underneath the barrel. Schwarzlose had certainly produced an interesting action but possibly not quite so important a one as that in the Schönberger pistol in which the barrel was fixed and the breech unlocked by a rearward movement of the striker caused by a deeply countersunk primer, in the specially designed cartridge case, moving against it. Although the Schönberger pistol was, in this sense, unorthodox it was otherwise fairly conventional with a coil mainspring and a trigger mechanism very similar to that of the Romanian Mannlicher revolver of 1892. The magazine was in front of the trigger-guard and was clip loaded. This pistol was of such quality of manufacture and materials, in the true tradition of the Steyr works, handled so very satisfactorily and was so well designed, that it was most unfortunate that ammunition could not be procured of an equal standard.

Although the Schönberger pistol was marketed in a small way on the Continent it did not reach England. The first to be put on sale in this country and to achieve real commercial success was the invention of an American, H. Borchardt, but manufactured by Ludwig Loewe in Germany because the inventor was unable to find in America the financial backing he required. Curiously its advantage over the Schönberger lay chiefly in its cartridge; it was very difficult to use as a pistol and needed the detachable shoulder stock with which it was sold.

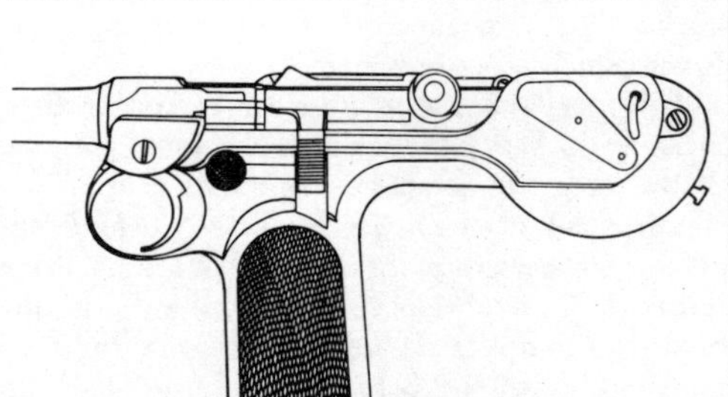

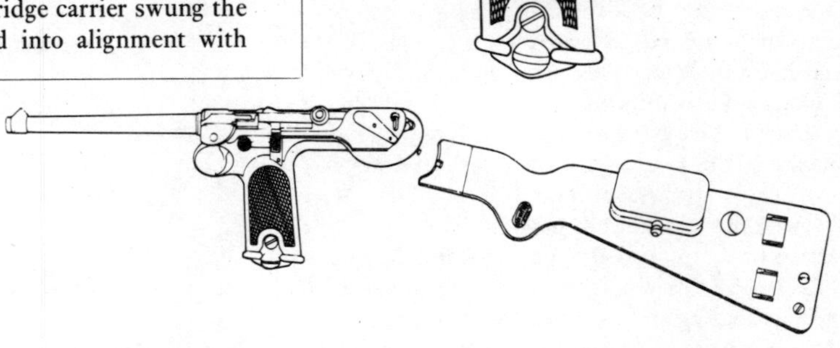

Borchardt pistol, 7.65 mm, with shoulder stock and detail. Smithsonian Institution, Washington, D.C.

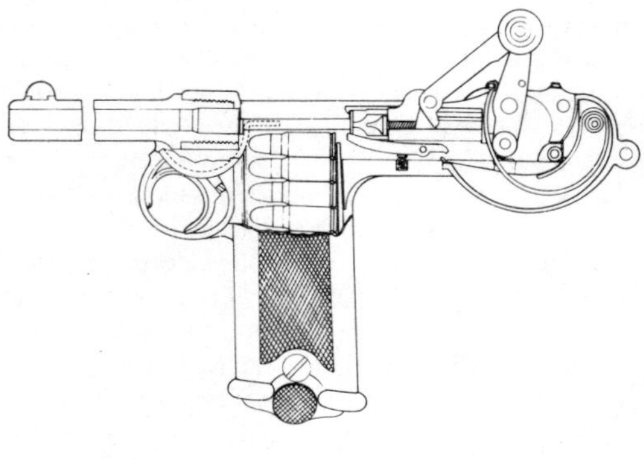

Mechanism of the Borchardt pistol at full recoil.

A glance at its outward appearance explains its awkwardness. Borchardt used a locked breech with a rising toggle and housed its flat-coil recoil spring in a massive projection well to the rear of the firer's hand. There was no doubt about the strength of the lock[2]; it was one of the strongest ever employed but the same enthusiasm could not be raised for the recoil spring which was very difficult to adjust to the correct tension. It was the first pistol to have a removable magazine in its butt and was, when one recalls that it was offered to the public in 1894, capable of incredible accuracy of fire with the shoulder stock attached. Its 6½ in long barrel contributed to this but credit must also be given to Borchardt, who himself worked at Ludwig Loewe's factory, for the excellence of detailed design and manufacture. The cartridge, which later was developed into the famous 7·63 mm Mauser, was of remarkable quality and, by the standards of the day, unprecedently consistent in performance.

This toggle-joint form of breech-locking arrangement works very simply and is absolutely positive. A two-piece arm, jointed at the middle and pivoted at either end, normally lies flat directly behind, and in line with, the axis of the chamber. When the barrel recoils the breech-block rides back with it thus ensuring complete closure whilst the bullet is travelling down the bore. As the entire assembly continues further back the centre joint of the two-piece arm is forced off-centre by two lugs in the receiver-frame which flexes the joint and permits the block alone to continue the rearward movement to extract and eject the fired case. It is clearly a prerequisite of this system that the joint's axis pins are of top quality steel and accurately fitted. There were only two other marques of pistol in which this type of action was employed, the 1905 Ross and the Luger. Whilst the first may not, the second certainly does, justify an understanding of the toggle principle.

At least one of the earliest designers of automatic pistols was convinced that a locked breech was not a basic requirement. Theodore Bergmann, whose works were at Gaggenau in Baden, clearly saw the possibilities of a simple blowback action and low power cartridge in a pocket-sized pistol. His first patent dates from 1893, but within a short time he was marketing in three calibres, 5 mm, 6·5 mm and 8 mm, a pistol which is known as the 1894 Model Bergmann. Though numerous varieties of these pistols can be found, some even with hair triggers, heavy barrels and target sights, there is a very marked similarity in external appearance. They all had external hammers, the same pattern of ordinary, single-action, revolver-lock, the magazine in front of the trigger and provision for a most distinctive form of clip loading. This last feature was, perhaps, the point most criticised about these pistols for, though it seemed to confer the advantage of very rapid loading it did in practice prove to be very troublesome. It was particularly apt that, in a pistol which shot so well, the barrel was easily removable for cleaning. The combination of propellant and fulminate in use at this period was extremely corrosive and rapidly ate away the rifling if the barrel was not properly cleaned. In view of the great advantages that these weapons offered over any other available at this period to those whose requirement was for a readily portable arm, it is not surprising to find that they proved very popular and that many of these German pistols continued in use until the 1930s.

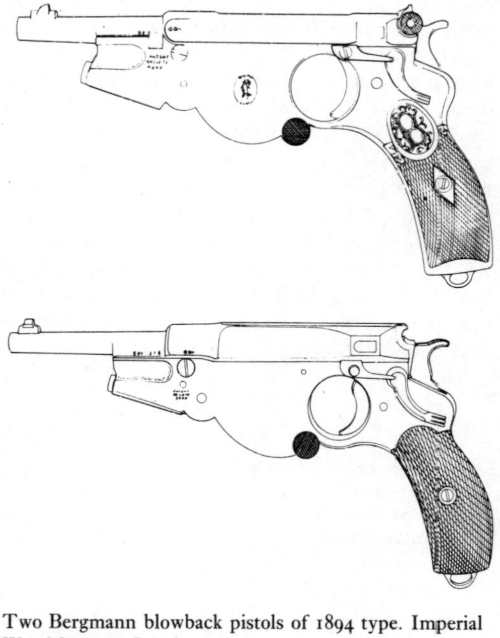

Two Bergmann blowback pistols of 1894 type. Imperial War Museum, London.

In 1894 Ferdinand R. von Mannlicher patented a rather different form of unlocked action. It was a blowback action in which the breech was fixed and the barrel was the moving component. There are slight variations of design but basically they are similar; in all the barrel moves forward to eject the fired case and, on its returning movement, chambers the next cartridge. The firing mechanism either took the form of an ordinary, double-action, revolver-lock or it needed to be cocked by hand each time so that the weapon was not a genuine automatic pistol – if in any case that term can be used, for what Americans call an automatic pistol is more usually in this country known as a semi-automatic pistol.

In December 1896 Hiram Maxim and L. Silverman filed a patent (No. 29836) for a quite remarkable automatic pistol which, equally remarkably, was never commercially produced. It possessed only four working parts, used a one-piece frame, receiver and trigger-guard, and with a simple blowback action handled high-powered, and even rimmed, cartridges. There is no doubt that in construction it was one of the simplest automatic pistols ever conceived. Examples exist to take the 8 mm Schönberger, the 7·65 mm Borchardt and the 0·455 in Webley revolver cartridge. It was outstanding for its handling. The grip was raked so that the pistol pointed naturally and, as the diameter of the tubular receiver was only a little larger than that of the barrel, the line of sight was exceptionally close to the top of the hand. Almost as outstanding was the ejection opening cover-plate which reciprocated with the breech-block and thus helped to exclude the entry of dirt and foreign particles. To tap off some of the surplus energy from the high-powered ammunition which might be used in this pistol Maxim bored two gas escape ports, one either side of the breech. The mystery remains unsolved why it was not commercially produced. The only plausible theory that has been suggested was that it was too much in advance of its time.

In 1897 Theodore Bergmann launched his first military pistol, one designed for a special 7·65 mm cartridge and covered by Patent No. 17251. It was not adopted by any country for its forces and sold rather poorly, with the result that it is very seldom encountered. It possessed more merit than this might suggest. It employed a locked breech of very unusual yet effective design in which the breech-block was unlocked from the barrel by a lateral movement caused by its encountering a projection in the action body. In general appearance this pistol closely resembled his earlier pocket-pistols but a sensible double tier magazine of more conventional design had replaced the earlier special pattern. The feature of a gas-escape hole at the side of the breech was retained. The back-sight, graduated to 1,000

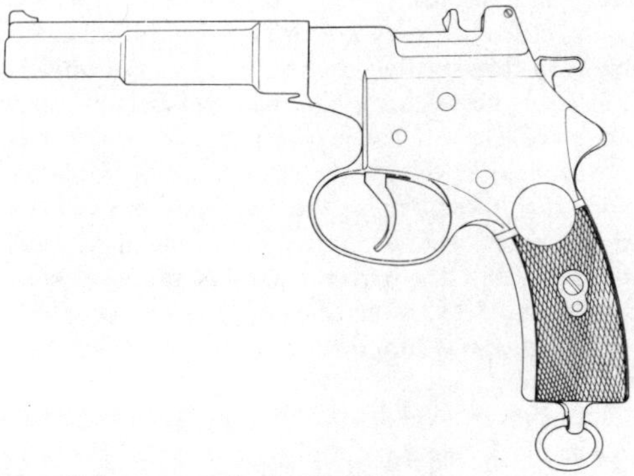

Mannlicher automatic pistol of 1894.

metres, reminds one that the pistol was intended to take a shoulder stock for long range work.

There were, however, other Bergmanns which were more successful, if rather less satisfying in other respects. One of these, produced in Spain and Belgium from 1897, probably achieved the distinction of being the smallest locked-breech automatic pistol ever produced. It was chambered for a 5 mm bottlenecked cartridge which later became known as the 5 mm Clement. In its type of action it was very closely related to the Mauser: after a short recoil the forward barrel lug forced back a rocking wedge which disengaged it from a notch cut in the under surface of the breech-block. The workmanship and quality of material do not approach that of Bergmann's made under the designer's name at his Baden factory; in fact, they are much more reminiscent of the Belgian-made Bergmann Simplex of about the same period. Unlike the Charola-Anitua, however, the Simplex had an unlocked blowback action. It shot an 8 mm cartridge of rather low quality, but which was later developed into the 7·65 mm or 0·32 in Colt automatic pistol cartridge. This has since become the most generally used of all pocket automatic cartridges. As might be expected the double, or staggered column, magazine which was used on the 1897 Bergmann military pistol also appeared in this pistol.

Bergmann pistols which are the most commonly encountered today are those which were adopted by various powers as official arms. One was adopted as the Danish side-arm in 1905: another version was a Greek official weapon. This design dates from 1903 and has also been used extensively as a police and military arm in Belgium, Spain and the Balkans. Chambered for 9 mm Bayard Long or 9 mm Mars cartridge, they have an overall length of about 10 in though the barrel is normally only about 4 in long. Many of these pistols will be found which were manufactured by the famous Belgian establishment of Pieper at Herstal and which therefore carry the trade name Bayard. Others will be found of German manufacture but they are in no sense interchangeable with those of Belgian origin. The most obvious differences between the German and Belgian made Bergmann-Bayard lay in the rifling of the barrel, four grooves in the former against six in the latter, and in that in the Belgian the barrel and its extension are machined from a single piece of metal whereas, in the German, the barrel is screwed into the extension. With most versions of the Bergmann a shoulder-stock holster was supplied rather like that used with the Mauser.

The breech was locked by the square section breech-block being secured by a vertically-moving locking-block in a square slot in the barrel extension. When the action is closed this locking-block sits on the frame and through its hollow interior lies the breech-block. On the underside of the breech-block is a wide lug with two flanking shallow recesses. This lug engages in a matching recess in the lower interior surface of the hollow locking-block. As the barrel, breech-block and locking-block recoil rearwards locked together the bevelled upper rear surface of the locking-block strikes the front of the roof of a tunnel in the rear of the frame which is made to take the recoiling breech-block. This causes the locking-block to drop down into a shallow recess cut at this point in the frame. The locking-block is thus disengaged from the breech-block which is then free to continue to the rear to perform the usual cycle of operations. There was an external hammer operating like a single-action revolver which struck a very long, light, firing-pin running through the length of the breech-block.

Andreas Schwarzlose followed his very distinctive 1893 design with another of an extraordinary character which he patented in 1895. In this the breech lock was effected by a turning barrel but the design was probably never taken up. Three years later he patented a design in which the breech was locked by a rotating breech-block. This Model 1898 Schwarzlose pistol was also important for a feature, later to be generally accepted, which it pioneered. On the firing of the last round the magazine follower pushed up a catch which held the breech open, thus warning the firer that he needed to reload and enabling him to do it with the minimum loss of time. However, the most interesting point about this weapon was its locking system which, after the disappearance of this pistol, re-emerged in the German MG 34. Its operation may simply be described as one in which, after recoiling together for about half an inch, the breech-block is unlocked from the barrel to continue rearwards on its own by its lugs being rotated from engagement with the recesses at the rear of the chamber. This rotation was imparted to the breech-block by means of its guide ring sliding in a helical slot. The 1898 Schwarzlose handled so well that one could, perhaps, overlook the error in adopting so short a sight base when it would not have been too difficult to have utilised the overall length of the pistol. It was not very successful from the commercial point of view probably because it was so easily put out of action by dirt and foreign matter. It was also rather prone to the consequences of wear to its many rather complex working parts. When clean, well-lubricated and in good condition it was a very comfortable pistol to shoot and quite an accurate one with the contemporary Mauser 7·63 mm cartridge. It was sold in America by Bannerman of New York under the trade name 'Standard'. In Germany it sold so badly that the manufacturers still had large stocks in 1905. Russian revolutionaries bought the entire remaining stock for the 1905 rising but lost a great many through confiscation at the frontier. The Imperial authorities (who did not look a gift horse in the mouth) issued the confiscated arms to their police forces. Most surviving specimens are therefore to be found either in Russia or in America.

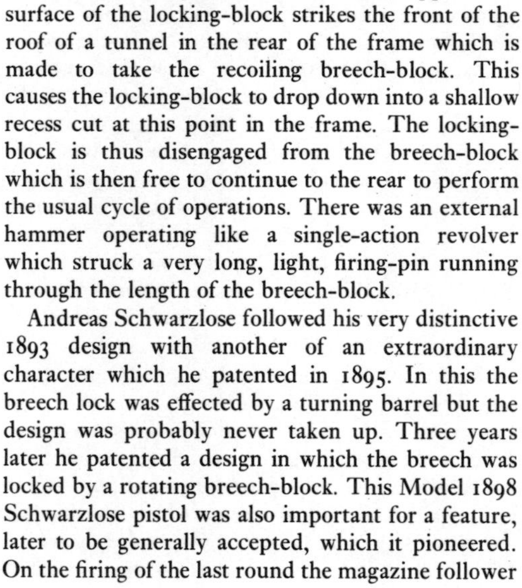

Schwarzlose 7.63 mm military pistol of 1898.

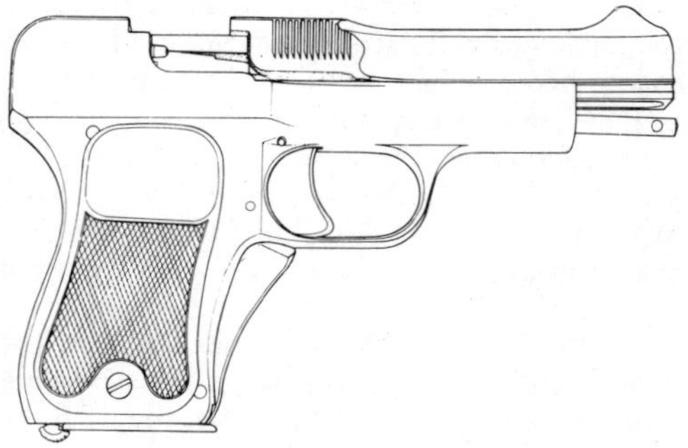

The Schwarzlose Model 1908 blow-forward pistol. Imperial War Museum, London.

The Schwarzlose pistol which did achieve world-wide sales was an extremely interesting blow-forward action arm of 1908, rather reminiscent of the 1894 Mannlicher, which was chambered for the

0·32 in automatic pistol cartridge. It is unique in that it is the only blow-forward pistol which has been a commercial success. It is also probably unique in its internal long-nosed hammer which directly struck the cap of the cartridge. There was no lock on the breech: a recoil-spring housed in the forward portion of the frame below the barrel returned the barrel to the breech face. A special magazine presented a cartridge to the chamber as the barrel returned to the closed position but the system was not as foolproof in feed as a good conventional blowback. Recoil was unpleasant to the firer both as the barrel went forward, and as it, on return, struck the breech face. But for all its faults this is a really remarkable weapon and one not unworthy of its great designer.

Mannlicher's pistol of 1894 was not really a success but those that he designed later in the decade were destined to have very different careers. One of them gained the distinction of being the first automatic pistol to have been seriously submitted to trial by a leading power with a view to its adoption. It is, however, very easy to confuse the three later Mannlicher pistols produced in this period. First, there is the model of 1900 which was the one patented in 1898; secondly, there is the model of 1901 which is a modified version of that of 1900 and was the one which was rejected by the Austrian authorities in 1905 and, thirdly, there is the model of 1903 which, in outward form, rather resembles the Mauser but which was, in fact, first manufactured at the Steyr works in 1896.

The 1900 Mannlicher pistol was intended to use a special 8 mm cartridge but it seems to have been issued in a form chambered for the 7·63 mm Mannlicher cartridge, which is almost straight-sided and very different from the bottleneck shaped 7·63 mm Mauser cartridge. The pistol employed a simple blowback action so devised that there was a braking influence on the opening of the breech. Such an arrangement was presumably necessary with a cartridge which, though considerably less powerful than the Mauser, still had a muzzle velocity of about 1,050 ft/s with an 85-grain bullet. The magazine was in the grip but was loaded with a clip through the top of the frame. The braking effect upon the breech-block was achieved by using the upper arm of the mainspring to hold a cam into a notch out in the under surface of the breech-block slide. The other arm of the V-mainspring hooked on to the right-hand fork of the hammer which was external; the other fork engaged the nose of the sear. The pistol gained a considerable reputation for its fine trigger pull which went well with its generally good handling qualities. There was an interesting type of cartridge release on the magazine by means of which the pistol might be emptied in an instant.

All that has been said about the Mannlicher model 1900 pistol applies to that of 1901 except that it was 248
manufactured only for the 7·63 mm Mannlicher cartridge. The differences between the two models are slight; the frame is of exactly the same dimensions in both arms. The 1900 model is three ounces lighter and has a $5\frac{1}{2}$ in rather than a $6\frac{5}{16}$ in barrel. Overall the earlier model measures $8\frac{3}{4}$ in against $9\frac{5}{8}$ in for the other. In keeping with its slightly smaller measurements the grip of the 1900 model is just over half an inch shorter. There should be no difficulty in distinguishing between these two models nor should there be any hesitation over identifying genuine Steyr-made pistols from the many imitations which were turned out in Spain. For the 1901 model pistol was extremely popular. It was widely carried by officers in the Austro-Hungarian Army and equally appreciated outside the Empire. Thousands of low-grade imitations were turned out in Spain for export to South America. The workmanship and materials of these pistols is as poor as that of the genuine ones made at Steyr is good.

The Model 1903 Mannlicher, or as it more correctly should be termed, that of 1896, had a breech which was locked by means of a 'prop-up' piece. Almost at the same time, and apparently quite independently, Mauser and Mannlicher chose a prop-up type of breech-lock but there the similarity ceases. Mannlicher used a locking piece pinned and bushed to the barrel extension to lock the breech-block by bridging the gap between it and a steel flat in the frame. When the barrel and block have recoiled rearwards about $\frac{1}{3}$ in the locking piece clears its retaining flat and thus the breech-block is unlocked, freeing it to travel back on its own. The pistol in external appearance is not unlike the Mauser of 1898, especially in its magazine being in front of the trigger-guard, but this resemblance should not trap anyone into using the 7·63 mm Mauser cartridge in it. Since the pistol will chamber the Mauser cartridge this is a real danger. The Mannlicher is much too light in construction for this powerful cartridge. Though the pistol is of the usual excellent Steyr quality and workmanship the Mauser cartridge operates the breech-block so violently that it can damage the rear of the receiver. The manufacturers intended the pistol to be used with a special version of the 7·63 mm Mauser cartridge with a light load.

On the right-hand side of the pistol there is an external cocking lever. This instantly shows whether the arm is cocked or not and immediately enables the firer to give misfires a second strike, which is very often effective. The pistol's internal hammer operates through a slot in the bolt locking piece. It is neat in conception and execution but the way in which the external cocking lever moves backwards and forwards with the cycle of operation is rather disconcerting. There is no mechanical difference between the three different forms in which this pistol appeared, namely, as a pure pistol, as a pistol with tangent sights graduated to 400 metres and convertible to carbine use with a shoulder stock, and as a fully-stocked permanent carbine. Normally a special charger taking six cartridges was used for loading the magazine but there are variations of this pistol which have detachable magazines loaded by a clip through the top of the action. The breech-block has a projection on the front end of its upper surface so that the firer could manually retract it to permit loading and cock the action for the first shot. The safety-catch, pointing to the rear, lies just above the level of the grip so that it can be released easily by thumb pressure on the small oblong plate which caps it.

This pistol has, in short, a very distinctive appearance. There should be no difficulty in recognising it. Normally it has a $4\frac{1}{2}$ in barrel, an overall length of 11 in and a total weight of $2\frac{1}{4}$ lb. In spite of its many good features and the popularity which it achieved in certain areas, it was never competitive on the military front. Commercially it was launched after the 1896 Mauser had established itself and there is no doubt that it was in many ways, and especially in carbine form, markedly inferior to that weapon.

The Mauser came into existence in the same year
249-50 as this Mannlicher pistol. The Mauser patent is No. 959 of 1896, though the pistol was not put on the market until 1898. It was and still is a truly remarkable arm. It was undoubtedly the first really successful automatic pistol. It was so well thought out that the basic design needed no subsequent modification, though the pistol remained in production until about 1945. It is very widely distributed all over the world. Such popularity is soundly based for, though it makes a very uncomfortable pistol, it is extremely reliable and capable of a very high rate of accurate long range fire – that is if its holster stock is attached. Paul Mauser did not come fresh to the field of arms design. He was already fifty-eight years old and since 1865 had been very active in the improvement of rifles. He had established a family concern at Oberndorf which was already very well known and had designed several revolvers. In the 1896 pistol he achieved a thoroughly practical, positive breech lock without using any pins or screws in the design. It worked on a short recoil system with a prop-up type of locked breech and took the 7·63 mm Mauser cartridge which was specially designed for it. It was the first pistol to appear on the market with a hold-open device for the breech operating when the last round has been fired though, as has been noted, the lesser known 1898 Schwarzlose also possessed this feature.

The pistol may be divided into five main parts; the barrel which is integral with its extension, the breech-block, the frame including magazine housing which contains the trigger mechanism and with which the grip is integral, the lock assembly and the magazine assembly. The frame has two ribs, one either side on its top edges, which engage in guide channels on the lower edges of the barrel extension. The lock assembly has a retaining catch keyed into its under surface which serves to hold together the pistol's main parts. The end of this retaining catch or latch just projects to the exterior immediately above the rear face of the grip.

In stripping the weapon the first step is to depress a plunger in the frame which locks the magazine floor plate into position. The plate may then be slid forward and out of the frame and will bring with it the magazine spring and platform. With the hammer cocked the action retaining latch is pressed upwards. This permits the separation of the barrel and extension and lock assembly from the frame. The lock assembly can now be lifted from engagement with the barrel extension and breech-block. The locking-block will normally come free from the lug on the underside of the extension, on which it loosely fits, in the same action. The breech-block cannot be removed from the barrel extension until the striker has been withdrawn which then will permit the breech-block retaining key, which projects through the slotted side of the block and through the right side of the barrel extension, to be released. The striker and its small coil spring are extricated from the square-section, hollow breech-block by the use of a suitable blunt pointed instrument to depress the rear end of the striker whilst its small retaining plate is slid upwards and clear of the end of the breech-block. The breech-block retaining key is removed by slight pressure forwards to disengage its rear ledge which is otherwise held in engagement with the wall of the barrel extension by the recoil spring. Once the breech-block retaining key has been removed the recoil spring will shake out of the breech-block.

The complete stripping and reassembly of the lock assembly, which comprises the lock frame, breech locking-block, hammer, sear, sear lever, sear spring, safety-catch, mainspring with two plungers and rocking coupling, and lock retaining catch is straightforward provided that one uses a screwdriver blade to compress the mainspring. Pressure is actually applied to the curved end of a small coupling which makes direct contact with a small cylindrical plunger fitting into the end of the coil mainspring and provided with a lug to ride in a slot guideway cut in the underside of the lock assembly frame. The disconnected safety is removed by pivoting it until it is at least at 45° to the position when operative. This brings a small retaining lug on the integral axis in line with its release slot in the lock frame thus permitting it to be lifted off the side of the assembly. The hammer is the last part to be removed. This is done by pressing out its axis pin, which avoids being the only pin in the design only by having a 'V'-shaped sear spring made integrally with it and thus serving, as it were, as its head. Both the assembly of the lock and that of the pistol are logical and very simple with a screwdriver. The only point which can be a little difficult is the retention of the mainspring by its coupling. This, however, is not difficult if a thin-bladed screwdriver is used to compress the mainspring and the coupling pressed into its seating with its convex surface facing outwards. When the screwdriver is withdrawn light pressure on the coupling will revolve it on its axis projections and seat it fully. It should, perhaps, be noted that the front end of the lock frame is positively located in the main frame by a lip which engages in a recess about half an inch above the tail of the trigger spring: at the rear the lock frame has two small projecting lugs which fit into corresponding slots cut into the rear edge of the main frame. The retaining catch which works off the rear spring locks the lock frame into the main frame.

The cycle of events that is initiated by pressure on the trigger when the arm is loaded, the hammer cocked and a round in the chamber, is as follows. The nose of the trigger rises, overcoming the resistance of its flat spring, and moves the sear lever upwards against the pressure of its spring. As the sear lever is keyed into the rear it pivots that part upwards. This releases the sear from engagement with the bent on the hammer which falls to hit the end of the striker and thus detonate the round. The barrel, breech-block and block locking-piece recoil rearwards locked together by the engagement of two lugs on the top of the locking piece in two recesses cut across the undersurface of the breech-block. As this recoil takes place a tooth-like lug projecting downwards from the front of the locking-piece bears against the rocking coupling in the lock frame and begins to compress the mainspring. At the same time the lower rear lug of the locking-piece moves down the working face of a lug on the lock frame until it rides over it and drops down. This action is controlled and facilitated by the manner in which the locking-piece rotates against the rounded concave form of the front of the lug which locates it on the underside of the barrel extension. The increasing upwards pressure on its tooth-like lower lug, as the mainspring exerts a counterpressure to recoil, tends to pivot the locking-piece downwards so that, when it is free to drop, it disengages its locking lugs very smartly from the recesses in the breech-block. The breech-block, now unlocked, continues to move back to compress the recoil spring and cock the hammer. As the block reaches the rear limit of its travel the ejector, which is simply a small lug on the upper front extremity of the lock frame and which runs along a groove cut in the underside of the breech-block, strikes the base of the fired cartridge case, to this point held firmly by a spring extractor-claw inlet into the top of the block, and ejects it. When the recoil spring takes over and the breech-block goes forward it feeds the top cartridge in the magazine into the chamber. At the same time the mainspring, which is under considerable compression with the hammer cocked, exerts through the rocking coupling a strong pressure on the tooth-lug of the locking-piece. More positively the lower rear lug of the block locking-piece rides up the inclined face of the projecting lug on the lock frame, a movement which is assisted by the contour of the front of the locking-piece in engagement with the concave surface of the lock frame immediately to the rear of the ejector extension. The breech is locked positively the moment the locking lugs on the locking-piece have re-engaged with matching recesses on the breech-block.

Although the basic design of the Mauser, established in 1896, remained unaltered, slightly differing models have been produced in the passage of time. The original model, which was first offered to the public in 1898, had a $4\frac{3}{4}$ in barrel, including the chamber. Its next most distinctive feature was, probably, its non-adjustable V back-sight. It has a large hammer terminating in a heavy, concentrically-ribbed, boss pierced by a very small hole so proportioned that the back-sight was visible only when the hammer was cocked. The safety-catch was pressed down to engage in the safety bent on the hammer. This original form did not survive long. Within a year the length of the barrel was increased to $5\frac{1}{2}$ in and a tangent back-sight, graduated from 50 to 700 metres, shortly after 50 to 1,000 metres, was mounted on the barrel extension. Otherwise no changes were made. It was this pistol which was often carried in the Boer War and which Sir Winston Churchill used so effectively at the Battle of Omdurman. In 1905 a 4 in barrelled model was introduced. Only a small number were made. Apart from its short barrel the arm may be readily identified by the fact that it had a five-shot instead of the usual ten-shot magazine, a smaller grip, a magazine bottom plate catch operated from inside the trigger-guard and a plain V back-sight. It did, in fact, also have a large-headed hammer pierced by a large hole encircled by two concentric grooves, but this alone cannot be taken as identifying this model as it came into use on the normal model fairly early on, with pistols bearing serial numbers somewhere in the mid-12000s.

These early models all have 4-groove rifling with a

right-hand spiral. Setting aside the very first model and the short-barrelled one of 1905 they were all made with $5\frac{1}{2}$ in barrels, tangent back-sights, long extractors measuring about $1\frac{11}{16}$ in and a safety-catch which operates with a downwards movement but, once this has been said, it is the minor differences which attract attention and which particularly seem to fascinate collectors. Many pre-1914 pistols bear the name of the retailer engraved along the barrel, very often that of Westley Richards who had the British agency for this pistol. Not surprisingly examples may be found with fore-sights dovetailed to permit lateral adjustment and the tangent back-sight leaf engraved, more usefully for serious shooting, from 50 to 500 yards, a modification which embraced lower sides to the ramp. On a few the graduation was from 100 to 300 yards, with or without the words 'Mauser Cartridge 303', presumably a curious endeavour to make the arm seem related in its ammunition to the Lee Enfield rifle and hence enhance its appeal in this country.

Pistols with the large-headed style hammer, pierced with a large hole, were very slightly wider across the wings of the breech-block but, initially, in other respects remained unchanged. The last of the 4-groove pre-1912 pistols anticipate some of the changes which become typical of the 6-groove model of that year. Up to this time the striker had been retained in the breech-block by a neat sliding plate dovetailed into position. This arrangement was dropped and the striker was redesigned to retain itself in position by the bayonet engagement of lugs formed integrally with its head. At the same time the trigger, which had formerly comprised a separate unit, was altered so that it was mounted directly in the frame. This change is easily detected by glancing into the trigger-guard. The earlier models show quite a large opening in the frame for the trigger in its separate unit; pistols made after this time have only the smallest piercing of the frame, just large enough to admit the width of the trigger itself. In a third small alteration made at this time the mainspring plunger was given a long projection pierced to take the rocking coupling instead of having it lying in front of it. It is also noticeable that at about this point in production, i.e. about serial number 22000, standardisation in the graduation of the back sight came in–virtually all sights are graduated to 1,000 metres and the 300- and 500-metre variants vanish.

At about the same time as these minor improvements and measures of simplification were being introduced a very noticeable change was made in the exterior machining of the frame. It was decided to leave it flat and not to machine recesses. The new appearance could not, however, have met with general approval since it was soon abandoned. As a result Mausers of this distinctive appearance are quite scarce since only about 7,000 to 8,000 were made. This period of production also saw two other changes made which help to set the pattern for the later 1912 model. In the first, the back-sight tangent leaf, instead of being pinned with a normal axis pin, was constructed with two small lugs to engage in the top of the barrel extension by being hooked under projecting loops against the pressure of the back-sight spring. The other change was the dropping of the facility of being able to lock the breech-block at the rear of its travel by operating the trigger so that the released hammer acted as a stop against the underside of the block. In earlier models this arrangement, of being able to lock the breech-block back independently of the magazine platform, was very useful in cleaning. In late flat-sided pistols with their round-headed hammers the small matching recess, into which the top of the hammer fitted, was abandoned. It is interesting to note that earlier boss-headed hammers had had a marked projection at their end to engage against the forward end of the short lug designed to roll back the hammer.

In 1912 6-groove rifling was introduced, still with a right-hand twist but readily identified even in a very worn barrel by the narrowness of the lands. The extractor was shortened to about $1\frac{1}{4}$ in in length and the safety-catch altered so that the pistol is made safe by an upward movement of the lever. The new safety was so designed that it could be applied with the hammer cocked as well as in the fired position: the earlier type could only be made safe with the hammer down. The front plunger of the mainspring was further modified by being given a tail. This projected through the underside of the lock frame to make contact with the sear lever and act as a disconnector. Whilst the plunger was pressed rearwards by the rocking coupling this extension prevented the sear lever from being moved upwards by the trigger. The lug on the under surface of the breech-block, which forced back the hammer, was extended almost to the rearmost locking recess. As with immediately preceding pistols the hammer will not lock the breech-block to the rear.

Probably the most distinctive feature of the 1912 model was its new hammer style–the head was pierced by a small hole bordered by two grooves concentrically cut. The sides had returned to the recessed panel type, the new trigger arrangement was continued, as also was the new striker retaining system, the new method of securing the back-sight leaf and the $5\frac{1}{2}$ in barrel length. The manufacturer's name and address appeared on the right-hand side of the frame and the serration on the wooden grips was more finely cut. Throughout the manufacture of this pistol occasional arms were fitted, presumably at special request, with plastic grips but weapons made before 1918 so furnished are not common. The

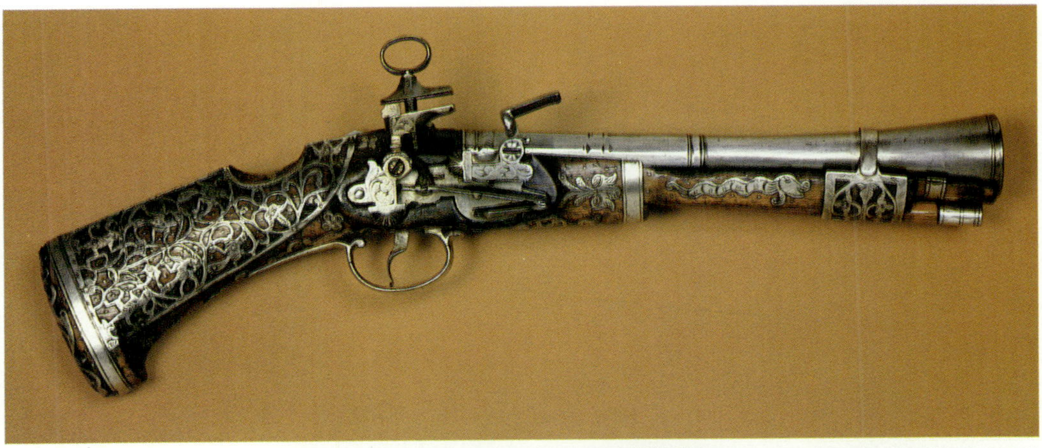

256 *Above* One of a pair of miquelet pistols, the stock inlaid with engraved silver and fitted with the name of the owner DN ANTONIO BIHALOUS. Spanish (Ripoll), *c.*1700. Victoria & Albert Museum, London.

257 *Right* Detail of a miquelet gun, the mounts of pierced and chiselled brass. Sardinian, *c.*1700. Tower of London Armouries.

258 *Left* Pair of flintlock pistols, the walnut stocks mounted in chiselled and engraved steel, inlaid in gold, the ramrods tipped with ivory; the barrels signed NICOLAS BIS MADRID. Probably made for Philip V of Spain. Spanish (Madrid), *c.*1720. Tower of London Armouries.

259 *Opposite, left* Detail of a snaphance sporting gun, the carved walnut stock mounted in chiselled steel; the lock chiselled and engraved; the barrel partly covered with embossed silver. Italian, *c.*1740. Birmingham Museum and Art Gallery.

260 *Opposite, right* Flintlock sporting rifle, the walnut stock inlaid with engraved gilt-brass; fitted with a Turkish barrel of chiselled and gilt watered steel; the lock signed GRIFFIN. The brass escutcheon engraved with the arms of John, Lord Carmichael, 3rd Earl of Hyndford (1701-67). English, *c.*1740. Victoria & Albert Museum, London. (See also plate **261**.)

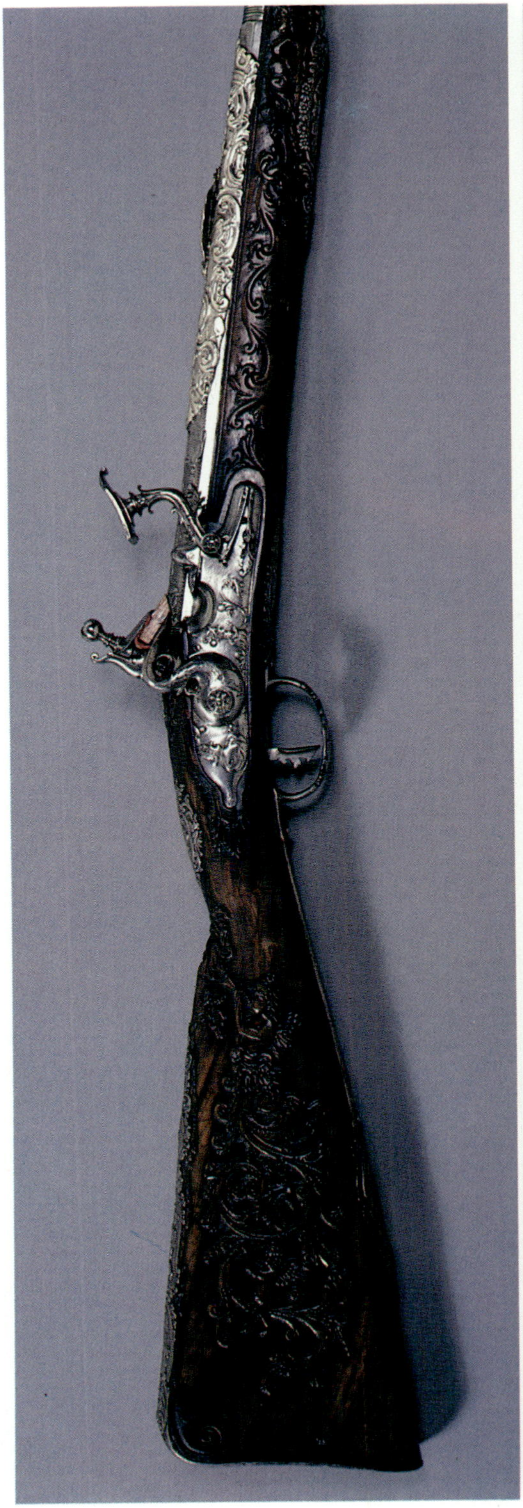

261 *Left* View of the top of the breech of plate **260**.

262 *Opposite, top* Air gun, the carved walnut stock, with built-in butt air-pump, inlaid with silver, the flint lock of chiselled and gilt steel; the brass barrel, formerly silvered, is also mounted in silver at the breech and contains the air-reservoir; the lock is signed KOLBE; the barrel is signed KOLBE FECIT LONDINI for J. G. Kolbe, who originated in Suhl (Thuringia), Germany. The silver mounts are proabably the work of G. M. Moser. English (London), *c.*1735-40. Probably made for King George II. Victoria & Albert Museum, London. (See also plates **263**, **264**.)

263 *Opposite, bottom* Detail of stock showing a lion and an eagle.

264 *Left* View of cast silver trigger-guard. (See plates **262**, **263**.)

265 *Opposite, top* Pair of double-barrelled flint-lock pistols with turn-over barrels; the stocks mounted in engraved silver; the locks and barrels signed W. BAILES, the latter also with two gold-inlaid marks. English (London), *c*.1750. Tower of London Armouries.

266 *Opposite, bottom* Pair of flintlock pistols, the stocks inlaid in silver; the furniture, locks and barrels of chiselled and gilt steel. The lock plates are signed in cyrillic script TULA 1752; on each barrel is the monogram of Empress Elizabeth of Russia (1741-62). Part of a garniture made for the Empress. Russian (Tula), dated 1752. Tower of London Armouries.

272 *Right* Revolvers (*top to bottom*): Remington Army revolver, New Model of 1874; Colt Root percussion revolver; Colt percussion revolver Navy Model 1861; Colt pocket revolver No. 239, made in London, Model of 1857; Colt New Line revolver, Model of 1875.

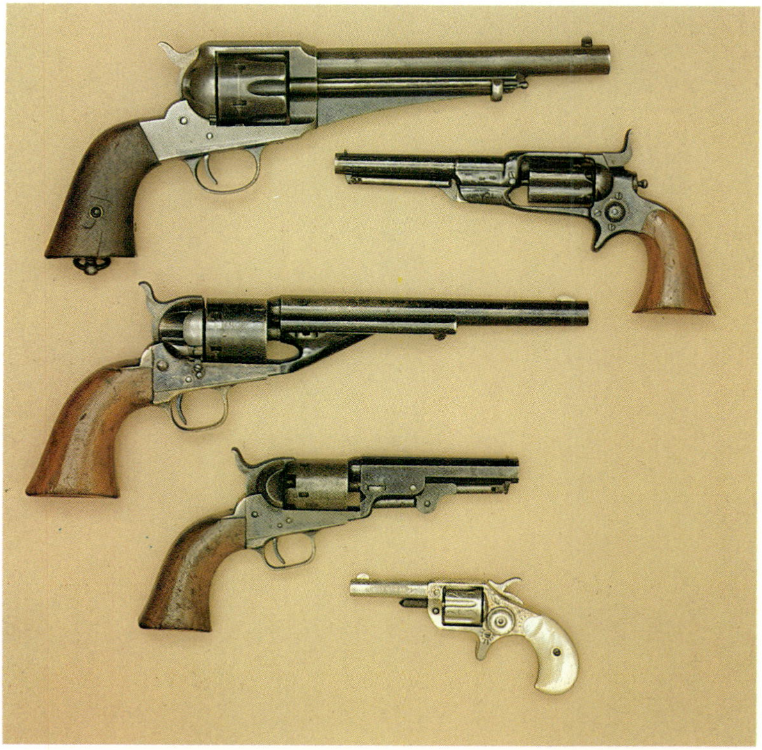

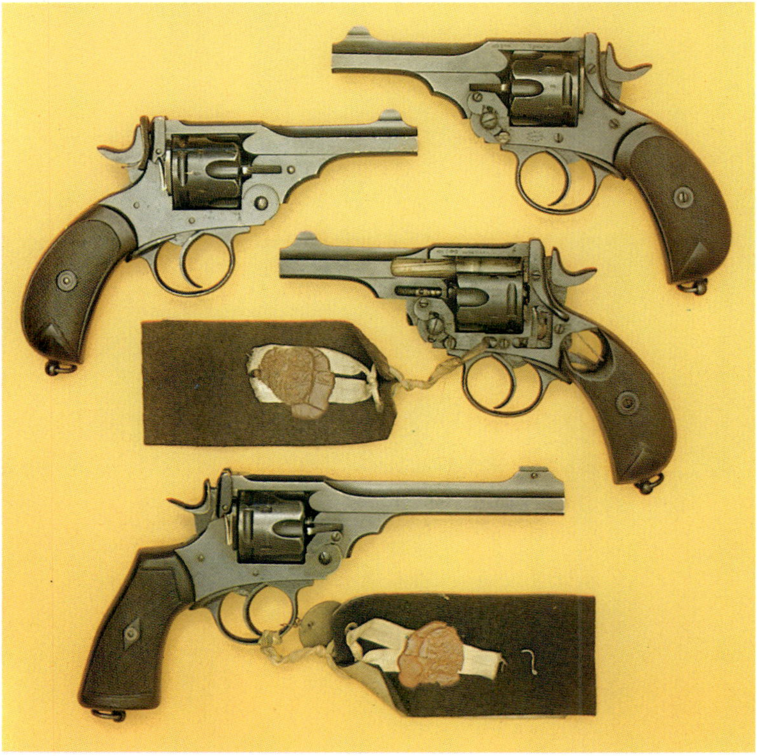

273 *Right* Webley revolvers (*top to bottom*): Mark III of 1897; Mark I of 1887; Mark III, a preliminary Model marked 'Approved 24/7/1900' Mark VI of 1915.

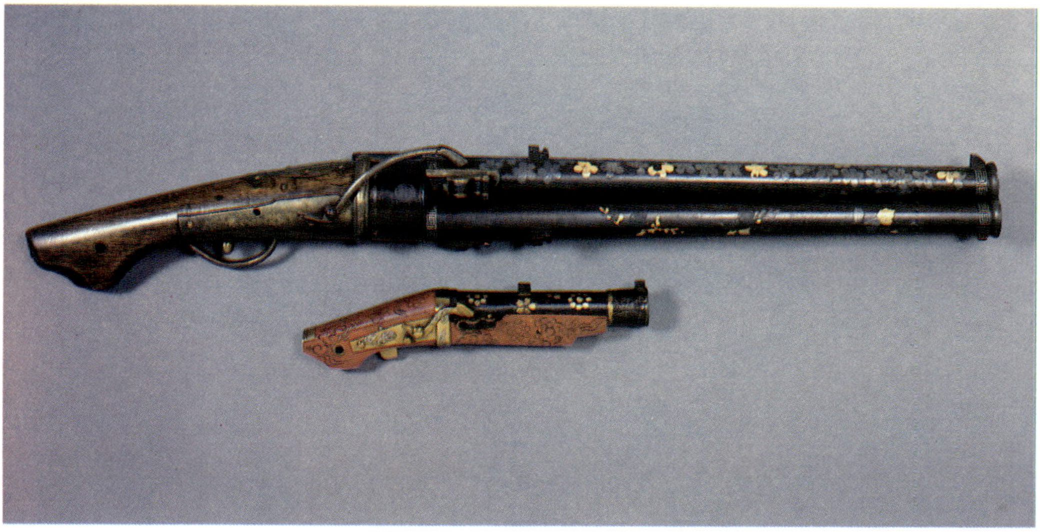

274 *Opposite, top* Submachine guns. (*Top*) Presentation Model UZI, *c.*1952. (*Bottom*) Standard Form, *c.*1952. Modern Israel.
275 *Opposite, bottom* Matchlock revolver (*top*) with three barrels, inlaid in gold and silver in the manner of the Hayashi School of sword-guard makers who worked for the Hosokawa family. Japanese, late seventeenth century. (*Bottom*) Brass-mounted matchlock pistol, the lacquer stock and the iron barrel engraved with flowers and the latter with the badge of the Hosokawa family. Japanese, late eighteenth century.
276 *Above* Miquelet carbine, the stock mounted in brass and steel; the barrel signed 'MUHAMMAD'. Albanian, dated 1794.
277 *Below* Miquelet gun, the stock mounted in ivory, silver-gilt and mother-of-pearl, the metal parts gold damascened; the barrel inscribed *The Work of Ahmad*. Turkish, eighteenth century. All (except **274**) Victoria & Albert Museum, London.

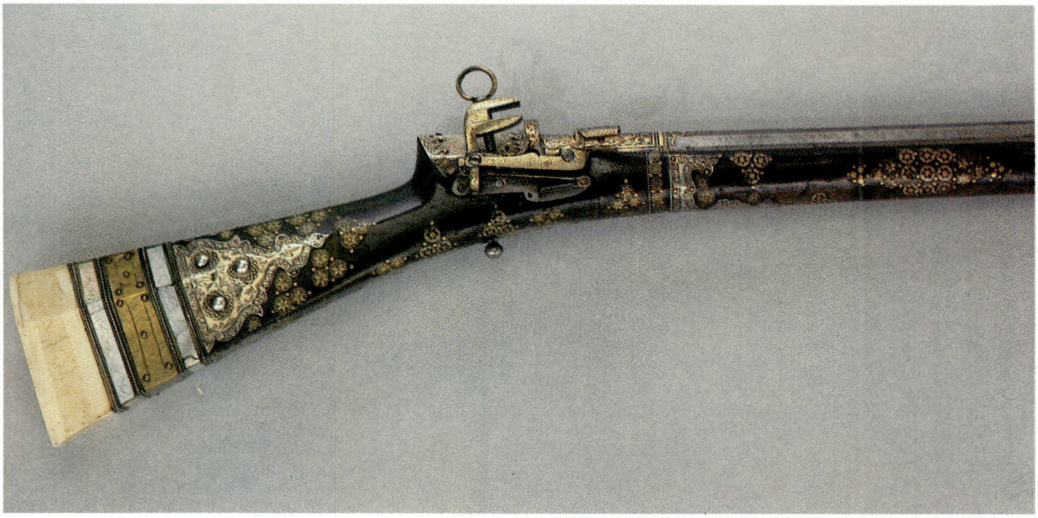

278 *Left* Wheel-lock pistol. Lock and barrel damascened in gold and silver. Wooden stock inlaid with engraved staghorn. Powder flask of wood inlaid with engraved staghorn, mounted in iron and damascened in gold and silver. Traditionally, made for Sir William Harris of Shenfield House, Margaretting. From Belchamp Hall, Essex. English, *c.*1580. Private collection, on loan to the Victoria & Albert Museum.

279 *Opposite, top* Snaphance musket, the wooden stock inlaid with engraved staghorn, the mounts of iron. Traditionally, made for Sir William Harris of Shenfield House, Margaretting. From Belchamp Hall, Essex. English, dated 1588. Private collection, on loan to the Victoria & Albert Museum, London.

280 *Opposite, bottom* One of a pair of flintlock pistols, the stocks inlaid with silver; the barrels chiselled and overlaid with gold; the chiselled locks signed MONLONG LONDINI. Pierre Monlong was Gunmaker-in-Ordinary to William III for whom the pistols were probably made. English (London), *c.*1690. Tower of London Armouries.

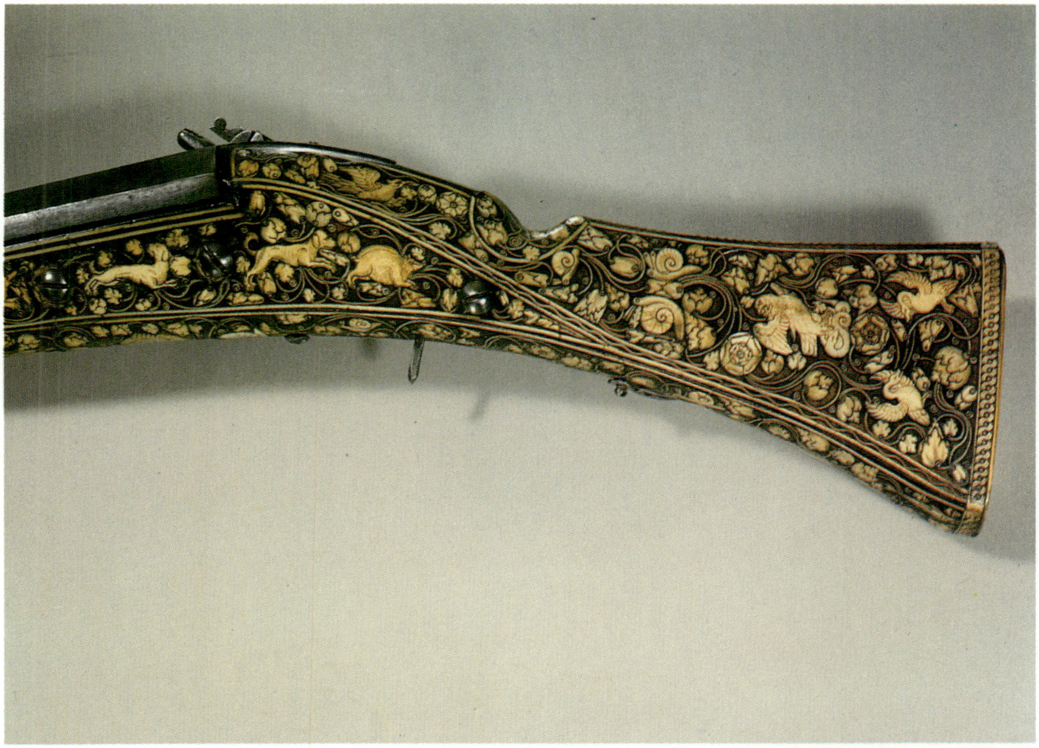

281 The Smith & Wesson Model 629, built from stainless steel and chambered for the powerful ·44 Magnum cartridge. This gun is thought by many to represent the zenith of revolver design.

back-sight was graduated from 50 to 1,000 metres but, in some cases, as with the preceding model, the 900 distance was omitted. On Model 1912 pistols of later manufacture the safety-catch has a solid knurled head instead of being hollowed out as in all earlier pistols. This change seems to have been introduced at about serial number 285000. It was this model which was produced on a large scale in the First World War and which is today by far the most common type. In those of wartime manufacture a rather drab finish prevailed but a high standard was still maintained in the quality of the materials and in the machining.

All these models, except possibly the short-barrelled version of 1905, were sent out by the manufacturers complete with a holster stock. The value of this attachment has already been stressed, as without it the pistol is difficult to handle and tends to shoot very high. The stock, which served as a holster when the pistol was not in use, has a metal tongue which slides into a groove machined in the pistol's back-strap. A spring catch at the lower end of the tongue automatically secures the stock. It is worth noting that the tang is numbered to correspond with the pistol: provided that the correct stock is used the fit should be quite tight, with little play.

All the Mauser pistols to which reference has so far been made were chambered for the 7·63 mm Mauser cartridge. In 1908, however, Mauser produced a 9 mm version chambered for a special 9 mm cartridge of extremely high power. It was straight-sided instead of being bottlenecked like the 7·63 mm calibre and imparted to its 128 grain bullet a muzzle velocity of about 1,300 ft/s. This larger calibre model was produced with the export market in mind. Many were sent to South America and the East, and others found their way to Turkey and the Balkans. With the exception of the calibre this pistol exactly resembled 7·63 mm models of contemporary manufacture.

In 1916 the Mauser works started the production of their 1912 model pistol in a new version for the 9 mm Parabellum. The reasons for the introduction of this new calibre are not difficult to discover. There was by this stage of the war a pressing need for more arms and a need to simplify rather than complicate the supply of ammunition. The Mauser factory was already producing its own pistol though not in the official calibre. It was much simpler for it to alter the calibre of the arm than to re-tool to make the official Pistole 08. There were only three differences between this 9 mm Parabellum Mauser and the normal 1912 model. The first was that the interior of the barrel was appropriately enlarged, the second that the graduation of the back-sight was only to 500 metres, in keeping with the lower powered cartridge, and the third, the appearance of a large '9' deeply incised in the grips and painted red. As these pistols were produced officially for the German government they bore the official proof markings. This Mauser was by no means the final variation produced but it was the last to appear until the decade after the war.

There is no need to prefix the following observations on the pistols of J. M. Browning with an eulogy of his contribution to firearms development. His name is almost a household word and the imprint of his ingenuity lies upon everything from pocket-pistols to heavy machine-guns: there was not much to which he would not try to apply the principle of automatic operation. It is estimated that he was granted at least 128 separate patents. Browning's interest in the application of automatic operation to firearms seems to date from about 1889 but it was not until 1897 that he patented a design for an automatic pistol. A pistol covered by Patent No. 22455 of 1898, and chambered for the 0·32 in ACP, or 7·65 mm, cartridge, appeared in 1899. By July 1912 F.N., the manufacturers, were celebrating the production of the one millionth pistol of this type, so successful was the design. Patent No. 9871 of 1897 had covered five different semi-automatic pistol mechanisms and, though four of them were ephemeral, the fifth emerged as the 1900 ·38 Colt. By 1900 Browning's pistols were well on the way to the tremendous success that they enjoyed, either as 'Brownings' produced by Fabrique Nationale of Liège, in Belgium, which shared the world market or as regular models of the Colt. Though the name Browning does not invariably appear on his arms of Colt manufacture, Colts through this period produced no pistols which were not of Browning's design. The old Model 0·32 in Browning was the basic type for almost all blow-back pocket-pistols and as such deserves some notice. Its overall length was about $6\frac{3}{4}$ in, that of the barrel 4 in, the weight was 22 oz and the magazine capacity seven or, occasionally, six cartridges. The pistol had a unique construction in that the recoil spring was housed in a tunnel above the barrel. Pressure on the recoil spring was transmitted to the breech-block through a guide rod pivoted on an intermediary lever, the top end of which, projecting through the top of the slide, served as a cocking indicator. The lower end of the lever served also to cock a striker-type firing mechanism. This form of construction had the advantage of permitting a very shallow form for the pistol. There was another and slightly larger version of this pistol which was about $7\frac{1}{5}$ in overall with a barrel $4\frac{3}{4}$ in, a magazine capacity of eight cartridges and a total weight of 27 oz.

In 1900 Colt produced the first high-powered Browning pistol, the 0·38 in ACP Sporting Model. It was one of the earliest really reliable automatic pistol designs and the first to be produced in the

United States on a commercial scale. It had the added advantage of clean lines and handsome Circassian walnut grips. In 1902 the new design made its second appearance, this time in a military model. In general form this Model L ·38 military pistol closely resembled its predecessor but magazine capacity was increased from seven to eight rounds, the butt was made squarer, hard rubber became the usual material for the grips, a slide stop to hold the action open after the last round had been fired was fitted and a lanyard loop was attached to the butt. The pistol did not long remain unmodified. In 1906 the chequering of the slide was moved from the front to the rear and its style changed from one of fine right angled squarish serration to coarse vertical cuts. With serial number 34000, in 1908, a spurred hammer replaced the former round-headed one and, about 1909–10, with number 37000 the prancing colt motif on the left rear of the slide lost its enclosing circle. The fact that serial number 37000 had been reached in only about eight years did not indicate the manufacture of that many pistols. In 1902 the numbers started at 14999 and worked backwards to 11000, which was reached about 1905-6: then, curiously, the numbering recommenced with 31000 and became conventional, though from this point it was concurrent with the Pocket Model which had started with number 16000.

A Pocket version of the Model L military pistol was first issued in 1903. It was extremely similar in appearance to the Sporting Model but, with a $4\frac{1}{2}$ in instead of 6 in barrel and a weight of 2 lb exactly, against about $2\frac{1}{4}$ lb for the Military Model, it was rather more convenient to use and, in fact, proved sufficiently popular to remain in production until 1927. The Military Model survived a little longer, until 1928, but the Sporting Model lasted only until 1908. All these models operated on the same principle applied through almost identical component form. The barrel was attached at both ends by links to the frame. These were so formed that the barrel could move rearwards about $\frac{3}{16}$ in and so that the first part of this movement took place without the barrel being pulled downwards by the links. This ensured that the three transverse lugs on the top of the barrel remained in engagement with three cuts in the underside of the top of the slide all the time that the bullet was in the barrel. The breech was thus locked while the bullet was travelling down the bore and until the slide had travelled to a point when the links pulled the barrel downwards to disengage the barrel lugs from the slide. The slide alone then continued to the rear, compressing, through the slide locking cross key, the recoil spring which was housed in a tunnel below and parallel to the bore. The usual operations of ejection and cocking occurred and the slide, under the influence of the recoil spring, moved forward to feed in a new cartridge and push the barrel forwards and upwards to lock the breech. The removal of the slide assembly was accomplished extremely simply by pressing in the plunger, visible just below the muzzle, and pulling out the slide locking cross key. The weak part of this design was clearly the slide locking cross key: if sheared there was nothing to save the firer from the slide as it flew rearwards off the frame. With the cartridge for which the pistol was intended, the 0·38 in ACP with a velocity of about 1,070 ft/s, there was no danger in a pistol in reasonable condition. However, if modern high-powered ammunition developing a velocity of about 1,300 ft/s is used the firer is definitely hazarding himself.

The 0·38 in automatic cartridge was not, even at the time the Military L Model pistol was introduced, popular in military circles. Its performance in the Philippines in the form of the 0·38 in Long Colt round had seen to that. It is, therefore, no surprise to find the Browning Colt appearing within a very few years, in 0·45 in calibre. This was the 1905 Military Model pistol which so closely resembled its 0·38 in antecedent that very little need be said about it from the point of view of operation. As with the

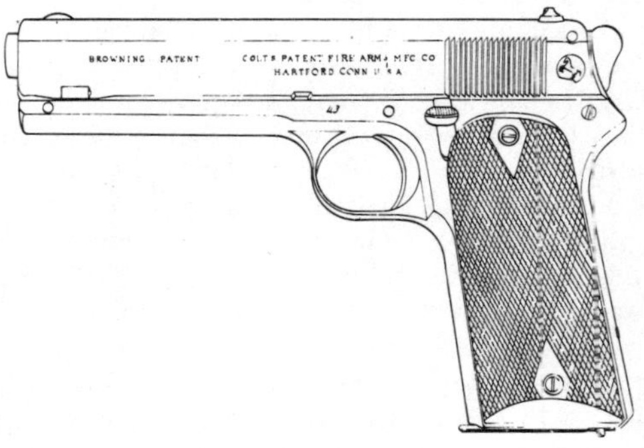

Colt M1905 .45 automatic. RSAF Enfield.

0·38 in it had no other safety device than a floating firing-pin, or in other words, a firing-pin which did not quite span the gap between the hammer, when down, and the cap. This pistol, sometimes known as the Old Model, continued in production until 1913. It had chequered walnut grips, a rounded or spurred hammer, according to the date of manufacture, and a 5 in long barrel. The ejector was rather more streamlined and lighter than that of the 0·38 in. The lanyard loop was abandoned, though it still appeared on a very rare variant which was marketed in London, and a few pistols were experimentally fitted with grip safeties. Magazine capacity at seven rounds was one down on the 0·38 in Military Model. The pistol weighed about $33\frac{1}{2}$ oz and measured $8\frac{1}{2}$ in overall.

For the United States Government competition

of 1911 a new and improved version of the 0·45 in automatic pistol was developed. Known as the Model of 1911 this pistol has achieved a very wide circulation and is still, basically, the pattern of pistol in use in the service of the United States and a number of other countries. In principle it worked in the same manner as its 0·38 and 0·45 in predecessors. In detail, a single link at the rear of the barrel and two lugs on the top of the barrel were found to be desirable simplifications of the basic design. The slide was so formed that it could be taken off the frame only to the front, this totally eliminated the danger of the slide blowing back towards the firer. By giving a single component the function of the barrel link anchor and slide stop the general design was not only tidied up but stripping without the aid of tools was greatly facilitated. The force of the recoil spring was therefore not transmitted to the slide by a cross key but through a short arm integral with a barrel bushing which took the place of the front link. As with the earlier model there was a disconnector protruding into the path of the slide. This ensured that the breech was properly closed when the pistol was fired: if the breech was not closed the disconnector was under pressure from the slide and the hammer locked. When the breech was closed the disconnector was accommodated in a recess in the underside of the rear of the slide.

Other innovations in the 1911 design were the inclusion of a safety-catch, the standardisation of a grip safety and the replacement of the old leaf mainspring by one of the more modern coil type. A magazine catch operated by a stud in the left side of the frame replaced the old type which projected from the bottom of the butt and a lanyard loop again became a standard feature. The barrel length and overall length remained the same as the Old Model 0·45 in but the weight of the pistol went up to almost $2\frac{1}{2}$ lb. Two series or types of the pistol were, and still are, produced, the Commercial and the Government: most pistols were chambered for the 0·45 in ACP round but, during the war, for British use many were produced to handle the 0·455 in Webley self-loading cartridge.

The measure of success enjoyed by the N.B. Browning Model 1900 encouraged Colts to ask Browning to design a simple fixed-barrel, blowback pocket-pistol for them. The outcome was the Colt Model M 1903 0·32 in ACP pistol which was so successful that an identical pistol, but in 0·380 in calibre, followed in 1909. The million mark had almost been reached by these pistols, too, when their production was stopped in 1941. The F.N. version of this design was chambered for the 9 mm Long Browning. This was extremely similar to the Colt except that the slide stop was on the right-hand side of the action and the hold-open device could be released by easing the slide further to the rear instead of by the usual operation of a thumbpiece. It was, of course, larger in size, weighed 2 lb and measured 8 in overall, in keeping with its role as a military or police pistol as opposed to that of a pocket weapon; the Colt weighed only $1\frac{1}{2}$ lb and had been $1\frac{1}{4}$ in shorter. It is perhaps also worth observing that the F.N. pistol had a 5 in barrel against the Colt's 4 in and that the Belgian-made arm had a magazine capacity of seven against the American's eight cartridges. The recoil spring was housed under the barrel and operated in a manner not very dissimilar from that found in the Colt M1911 ·45. The firing-pin did not function as the striker in the M1900 but was struck by a hammer, completely concealed within the rear of the frame. The hammer was cocked by the breech-block section of the slide running over it and thus rotating it on its axis pin until it was caught and held by the sear. A disconnector device, of the type employed by Browning on so many of his pistols, ensured that the pistol could not accidentally start functioning as a fully automatic weapon. The barrel was locked into the frame by means of lugs and grooves superficially resembling those of the 0·38 in and 0·45 in Colt military pistols except that they were on the underside of the barrel and functioned as a permanent lock instead of one designed to hold only whilst the bullet was still in the bore. In other words, in this blowback action the barrel was securely locked to the frame of the pistol and not to the slide.

In 1905 F.N. began the manufacture of a small, pocket Browning in 6·35 mm or 0·25 ACP calibre. Colt followed suit in 1908. This small pistol enjoyed such success that F.N.'s production alone exceeded a million: in America about a half a million were made. It had the distinction of being the only Colt to be fired by a striker, as opposed to employing hammer operation in one form or another. Production of the Colt continued until 1941 under the factory designation of Model N. It was only $4\frac{1}{2}$ in in overall length and weighed a mere 13 oz. The F.N. was very similar to the Colt but for a few totally insignificant differences: the barrel, for example, was $2\frac{3}{32}$ in long against 2 in for the Colt whilst the rifling had a right-hand as opposed to a left-hand twist. It should, perhaps, be noted that a magazine safety was not fitted to the Colt version until pistol number 141000. Mechanically the pistol was very similar to the Model of 1903 except that the breech-block portion of the rear of the slide was drilled to accept a striker assembly. It had a grip safety, a magazine safety and a disconnector, respectively ensuring that the pistol could not be fired unless it was held correctly, and the magazine in place and the breech fully closed. As it has been copied more widely and in greater quantities than probably any other weapon

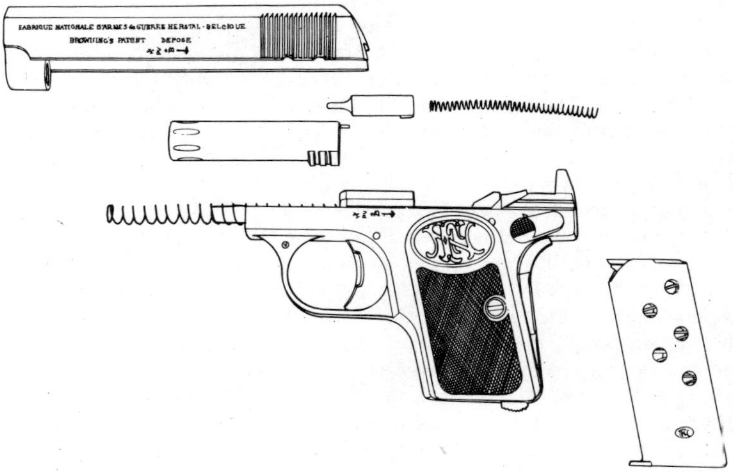

Browning Model 1906 automatic pistol broken down into basic elements. RSAF Enfield.

it is of interest to know these main details of the original arm.

It was but a logical step to reproduce this neat and effective design in a larger calibre. This the F.N. Model 1910 Browning in 7·65 mm calibre almost did. The only significant way in which this pistol, which was manufactured only by F.N. and which was not put on the market until 1912, differed from the 0·25 in arm was in its placing of the recoil spring around the barrel instead of beneath it. It still, therefore, amounted to a simple blowback pistol, incidentally with all the safety features of the smaller model. An identical version, but for the fact that it took the 9 mm Short Browning cartridge, was also produced. It weighed, in 7·65 mm calibre, $20\frac{1}{2}$ oz, was 6 in long and was fitted with a barrel $3\frac{1}{2}$ in in length. It enjoyed such success that by 1935 over a million had been manufactured and, as with the smaller calibre pistol, there were endless imitations to be found.

Rivalling 'Browning' in frequency in general usage is the name 'Luger'. The arm which Georg Luger developed from the Borchardt has become one of the best known of all weapons. Of the Luger there are innumerable variations – too many in fact for the authors of the two volumes totally devoted to the Luger, which have to date appeared, to cover completely. There is therefore little chance that this brief survey will be able to make any claim to comprehensive coverage. Borchardt's toggle operation has already been described; Luger's important improvement was the simplification of the form of the recoil spring. In the early models of the Luger the recoil spring was of a leaf type but in 1904 a spiral coil spring was substituted. Its location, in the rear part of the grip frame, remained the same. It is also true to say

STAGES IN THE EVOLUTION OF THE LUGER-PARABELLUM PISTOL

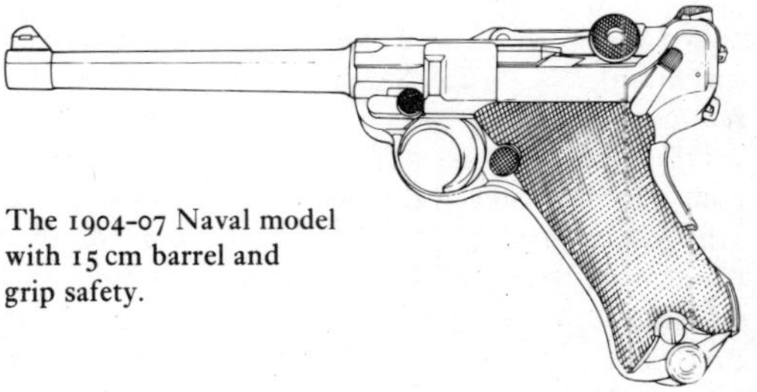

The 1904-07 Naval model with 15 cm barrel and grip safety.

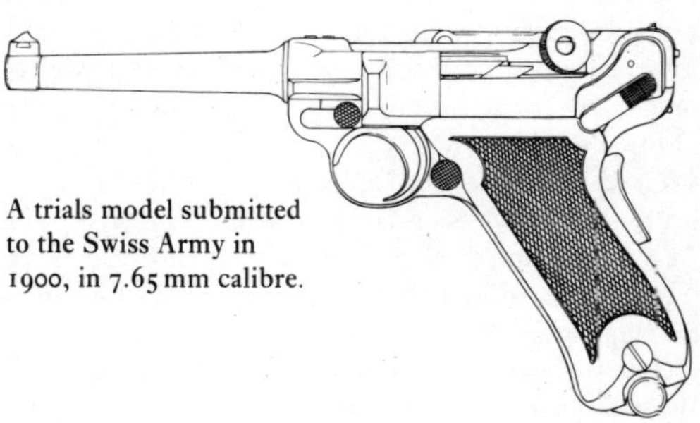

A trials model submitted to the Swiss Army in 1900, in 7.65 mm calibre.

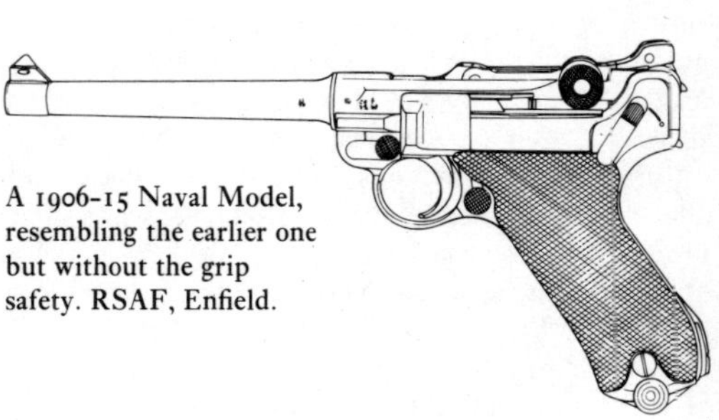

A 1906-15 Naval Model, resembling the earlier one but without the grip safety. RSAF, Enfield.

that the calibre of all early Lugers was 7·65 mm, and not until well after the period at present under consideration did 9 mm become standard. Very few Lugers indeed were made in other calibres. Very occasionally a conversion, either temporarily or permanently, to 0·22 in may be encountered; two pistols were definitely made in 0·45 in ACP and there are occasional rumours of a 0·32 in ACP Luger. By far the most significant variation in the Luger is that associated with the different recoil springs, for the differences accompanying these two springs amount to the two types of mechanism often known as the 'Old' and 'New' Models.

Outwardly the most conspicuous difference between the Old and New Models, the change-over of which occurred in 1906, lies in the toggle knobs. In the earlier version they are cut away towards the rear: from 1906 the knobs are left entire and finished with circumferential knurling. The earlier pattern toggles had incorporated a lock but it was found unnecessary as, even without it, the breech was securely locked at the moment of firing. As well as discarding the toggle lock the designers introduced a new extractor of more substantial construction, activated by a coil spring. The new extractor carried the word *Geladen* (loaded) on its left side. Other external differences between the two models included the adoption of a narrower trigger-guard, 0·47 in against 0·59 in; the widening of the trigger-piece from 0·33 in to 0·43 in and the raising of the flat upper surfaces of the rear toggle link so that it was no longer flush with the top of the receiver.

With all these differences, even if individually minor, there is no difficulty in distinguishing between the Old and New Models: where trouble begins to occur is in the often more subtle differences between models of different years for different governments by various makers. Luger himself had introduced his pistol to the general public with a model known as the 1900 Commercial. As a military weapon it began its long career as early as April 1901 with its adoption by the Swiss government. This first Luger was designed for the 7·65 mm Luger cartridge and fitted with a barrel only $4\frac{3}{4}$ in in length so that the overall length of the arm was kept down to 9 in. The manufacturers were D.W.M. (Deutsche Waffen und Munitionsfabrik) of Berlin who continued to produce all the earlier models of this famous pistol. The only difference between the 3,000 weapons of which the Swiss took delivery and the other Model 1900 pistols was an engraved Swiss cross in a sunburst over the chamber. The third model, which carried the year 1900 in its designation, is commonly known as the American Eagle Model though it was not, by any means, the only Luger model which bore the eagle. In 1901 the American government bought 1,000 of these pistols. They were experimentally issued to the cavalry but appear not to have been enthusiastically received and were withdrawn by 1905. It is not possible to distinguish between these pistols and other American Eagle Lugers which entered the country at the same time for it is estimated that the total production of this model amounted to between 6,000 and 8,000.

In 1902 the first improvement on the original
commercial design appeared. The principal change 253
was the adoption of a new cartridge, that later to become universally known as the 9 mm Parabellum. The new barrel length adopted was only 4 in and the rifling was changed from four to six grooves. Comparatively very few of these pistols were made: it was almost as if the 1,100 manufactured, which were either 'Commercial' or 'American Eagle', were a semi-experimental issue designed to gauge market reaction.

Two years later, in 1904, Luger scored his greatest success to date in his endeavours to sell his pistol to the German armed forces. In the form of the Naval Model of 1904 the German Navy adopted a weapon of 9 mm calibre with a 6 in barrel and a two-position back-sight graduated for 100 or 200 metres. The action was Old Style with a flat, recoil spring and toggle lock but the toggles were nearer in appearance to the style which was to come in in 1906 than to the cut-away variety which had previously been employed. Very few of these arms seem to have been made and most of those which have survived were at a later date, probably about 1920, and in common with some later Naval models, modified in various ways, including cutting the barrel down to 4 in. It is worth noting that, for the first time, the extractor, which partly protruded so that its sides became visible when there was a round in the chamber, was marked with the cautionary word *Geladen* (loaded). This model was the first to standardise a stock lug as a regular feature: it was, in fact, issued to the German Navy with a detachable flat shoulder stock.

In 1906 the New Style came in for all models and by this date the number of models was really proliferating. The Luger was catching on in other armies. The Portuguese and the Bulgarians, the Brazilians and the Dutch certainly entered into contracts for these pistols whilst the Swiss and Americans and German Navy began to take delivery of new pattern Lugers. There was also, of course, a Commercial Model. Known as the 1900/06 Model it had a 4 in long barrel of 7·65 mm calibre. There was a grip safety but no stock lug. The sights were of the plainest kind, lacking elevational adjustment and the lever safety still continued to carry no word indicative of which position was safe. The toggle, naturally, as on almost all Lugers of their manufacture, bore the initials *D.W.M.* Estimates of the number of these pistols made vary from 4,000 to 6,000.

Identical with this model, except that it was engraved over the chamber with a cross on a sunburst, was the Swiss Model of 1906. Similar also was the model for the Swiss Police with a cross on a shield. The American Eagle version was again identical except that an eagle was substituted for the cross. The Brazilian was not, however, distinguished by a distinctive chamber marking, which was in fact plain, but by the word *Carregada* (loaded) to be found on the extractor. The Portuguese Army model had a similar extractor but was clearly distinguishable by Manuel II's monogram, a device of a crowned M with entwined 2, engraved over the chamber. The Bulgarian version which boasted the full Bulgarian coat-of-arms, including supporters, on its chamber, departed only from this rigid pattern in having the lever safety marked in Cyrillic letters with the Bulgarian word for 'fire'.

The year 1906 saw also the beginning of the production of a series of 9 mm models which, because they closely resemble that of 1902 except of course that they are New Style, are often known as the Model 1902/06. They are easily distinguished by their 4 in long, 9 mm barrels, with four-groove rifling, as well as by their grip safety and absence of a stock lug. The version intended for commercial sales in America had the usual eagle over the chamber: the Brazilian, as with the 1906 7·65 mm version, is identified only by the extractor bearing the word *Carregada*. The Dutch also had a plain chamber, but the safety lever was very distinctively marked with the word *Rust* and an arrow pointing upwards. From the date on the barrel we can tell that although these pistols are of the 1906 Model they could not have been produced until about 1916, as this is the earliest date noted. In military use, for which they were intended, a brass plate was affixed to the left side of the frame so that the designation of the unit to which the pistol had been issued could easily be seen. The Portuguese Army version was marked exactly as their 7·65 mm version: the Portuguese Navy was very similar except that a crowned anchor replaced Manuel's crowned monogram. The Russians also took delivery of some of these 1906 Model Lugers in 9 mm. The chamber carried a device of two crossed rifles and the extractor the Russian word for 'loaded', in Cyrillic characters. The safety catch marking, though also in Cyrillic, was actually the Bulgarian word for 'fire'. In every other respect these pistols were like the other 1906 models.

Extremely similar in appearance to the 1902/06 models were the 1904/06 Navy pistols. Like the 1904 Naval Lugers they had a 6 in, 9 mm barrel and a distinctive rear sight graduated for 100 and 200 metres. Three versions of this model are to be found: all are completely New Style and have a grip safety, stock lug and no markings over the chamber. The wooden bottom of the magazine was of a distinctive appearance with concentrically ringed finger piece. In the version first manufactured the word *Gesichert*, meaning 'safe', was stamped in the lower part of the depression fashioned to accommodate the travel of the safety lever. Later these pistols were mostly altered so that the word *Gesichert* appeared in the top of the depression for the safety lever and the lower stamping was erased. Those manufactured after the first 8,000 were stamped only with the safety marking in the upper part of the lever's depression. As these were weapons intended for the German Navy they were proof marked with the letter *M* for *Marine* with a crown over it. A smaller quantity, which were proofed with a crowned *N* indicating that they were for commercial sale, had the word *Gesichert* stamped in the lower portion.

In 1907 two Lugers were specially made in 0·45 in ACP calibre for American Army trials, which were intended to find the pistol most suited for adoption. The fact that the Luger was unsuccessful must soon have been forgotten, for the next year, at last, the German Army adopted it as its official side-arm. The Pistole 08, as it was thereafter known, was very similar to the 9 mm Model 1902/06 except that the grip safety was abandoned. From 1910 onwards the date appeared over the chamber and from 1914 the stock lug reappeared. The monopoly of D.W.M. was at last broken and the Royal Arsenal at Erfurt was licensed to manufacture the 08 Model. On the toggle the word *Erfurt* was stamped with a crown over it. With its 4 in, 6-groove barrel this is today by far the most common Luger and is often found in its original holster complete with a spare magazine and screwdriver-cum-loading-tool. A few of the original 1908 Model Luger were made for commercial sale and a very few, as it would seem from the number surviving, for the Bulgarian Army. The Bulgarian has the same markings in Cyrillic on the extractor and near the safety lever as on the Model 1906 pistols intended for that country but, instead of the full coat-of-arms over the chamber, it has a small shield, crowned, bearing a rampant lion on the toggle link. The D.W.M. trademark, in consequence, was displaced and appeared over the chamber. Uniquely, the lanyard loop was placed on the bottom of the butt, just above and to the rear of the magazine opening.

In 1908 a new version of the Naval pistol appeared. The only really noticeable difference was the discarding of the grip safety. A few of this model were commercially proofed for sale on the open market. In 1914 the chamber began to carry the year of manufacture, which continued until 1918. The date also appeared on the side of the pistol just above the locking bolt and quite frequently also on the side of the fore-sight block.

In 1914 a long-barrelled version of the Model 08 pistol was produced for issue to the artillery and machine-gun units. It was fitted with an 8 in barrel carrying its own tangent back-sight graduated to 800 metres. This was so constructed that as the range was increased the sight moved progressively to the left to compensate for the increasing drift of the bullet since the rifling was cut with a clockwise spiral. The pistol was carried in a holster to which was attached a flat shoulder stock and was sometimes used with a snail magazine taking thirty-two rounds. On some of these pistols the fore- or back-sight or both sights were fitted with a screw adjustment to allow zeroing. The chamber was dated with the year, from 1914-18: the most common date appears to be 1917. Like the Pistole 08 this model was also manufactured at the Royal Arsenal at Erfurt.

This was by no means the end of the development of the Luger. Such pistols manufactured after 1919 show almost as much variety of type as those made before that date. Other firms began to manufacture it and other nations found in this weapon the answer to their side-arm requirements. Some of these weapons, such as the Krieghoff Lugers and those made by Mauser for the Persian government are as superbly finished as any that are likely to be encountered but they belong to a period when new ideas were beginning to be tried and when the Luger was at last beginning to show its years. In comparison, however, with many other makes of semi-automatic pistol, the Luger was, and remains, timeless; which is more than can be said, for example, of the Webley pistols which were introduced at about the same time as the Luger.

Chronologically it is the Webley-Fosbery which must first be considered. This was introduced to the public at Bisley in 1900 whereas it was not until 1904 that Webleys marketed an automatic pistol and then only in very small numbers. The inventor of the Webley-Fosbery, Colonel G. V. Fosbery, V.C., was no newcomer to the field of firearms. As early as 1865 he had interested himself in the pattern of breech-loading rifle most suited to the British army, and had been a designer and staunch protagonist of the explosive bullet before it was banned in 1868. In fact between 1866 and 1891 he took out thirteen patents for improvements to small arms. In his new automatic revolver Fosbery at last backed a winner, perhaps because it was so conservative and yet so efficient an innovation. The weapon still handled the same cartridge as the service revolver, (the 0·455 in government cartridge), it still looked like a revolver and yet it was possible to shoot it accurately at the rate of a round a second.

He did not produce the design overnight. In 1895 he patented an automatic mechanism for a revolver of similar design to the Colt. The cocking of the hammer and the rotation of the cylinder were both achieved by the rotation of the hammer-axis pin, itself the consequence of a short lever, projecting externally at 90° to its axis, striking a fixed stud on the non-recoiling frame. Cylinder rotation was taken off the turning axis pin through a pawl. The design, though simple and ingenious, was apparently not very satisfactory. The following year he patented an improved arrangement within what is obviously a Webley or Webley-influenced revolver. In this the hammer was cocked on recoil by an internal roller-

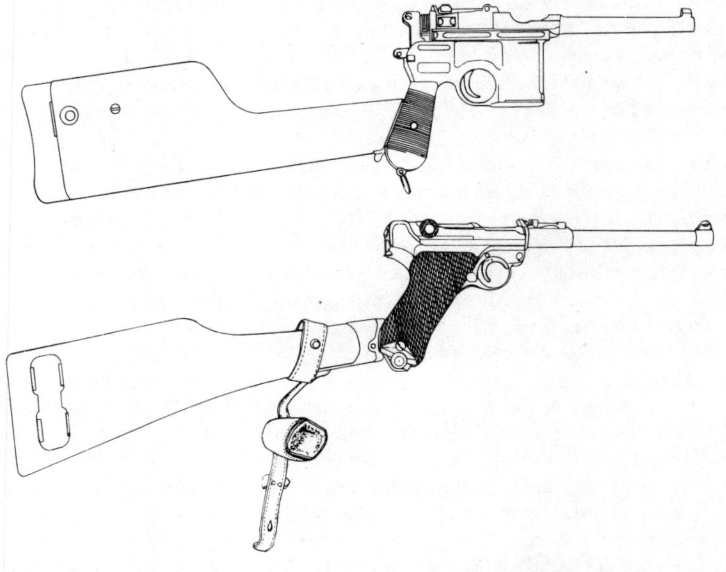

Pistols with shoulder stocks: (*Top*) Mauser military. (*Bottom*) Parabellum 'Artillery' model. Imperial War Museum, London.

ended spur running down the inclined inner surface of the upper rear grip frame thus revolving the hammer rearwards about its axis. The cylinder was still rotated by a linked pawl but the linkage was made more resilient. Fosbery also altered the trigger construction so as to eliminate the possibility of the mechanism operating fully automatically. In October 1896 Fosbery covered two new alternative, but closely related, schemes for cylinder rotation in his Patent No. 24155. In the first, pins or pegs were fixed to the exterior surface of the cylinder in such positions that, on recoil, they pressed against a cam projection and caused the cylinder to rotate. In the alternative arrangement a zigzag groove took the place of the pins, and a spring pin on the fixed frame in the groove the place of the hinged cam. It was this latter design which Fosbery was to develop and use for all production pistols.

Not all Webley-Fosbery automatic revolvers were chambered for the service 0·455 in cordite cartridge. Some of the earliest were intended for a 0·450 in black powder round and others for the 0·38 in Colt automatic pistol cartridge. In spite of the many small differences which exist between the production Fosberys which still survive they all work on the same general principle. The upper part of the revolver, including the barrel and cylinder, recoils on guide ribs independently of the rest of the weapon. This allows a stud on the lower frame, in engagement with a zigzag path cut in the outer surface of the cylinder, to rotate the cylinder so that the next chamber comes into alignment with the barrel. Half the cylinder rotation takes place on recoil and the remainder as the action returns to its forward position. This rearward movement also pushes the hammer back until the sear engages in the full cock bent. The moving parts are returned to their forward, and normal, position by a recoil spring positioned low down in the butt and operating through a long lever. Loading and extraction are effected in precisely the same manner as with an ordinary Webley revolver. Cocking the hammer for the first shot is necessarily manual but in the event of a misfire the hammer, which was generously chequered to afford an easy grip, could be grasped, pulled firmly to the rear and then released. This would, of course, both re-cock the action and bring a fresh cartridge into alignment with the barrel. Simple thumbing of the hammer would allow a second attempt at firing the same cartridge.

In type, examples of the Webley-Fosbery may be divided into two main groups, those, a few hundred in number, manufactured in 1901, and the remainder. Outwardly the main distinguishing feature is probably the different arrangement for securing the cylinder. In the first model components identical with those to be found on the Webley Mark IV

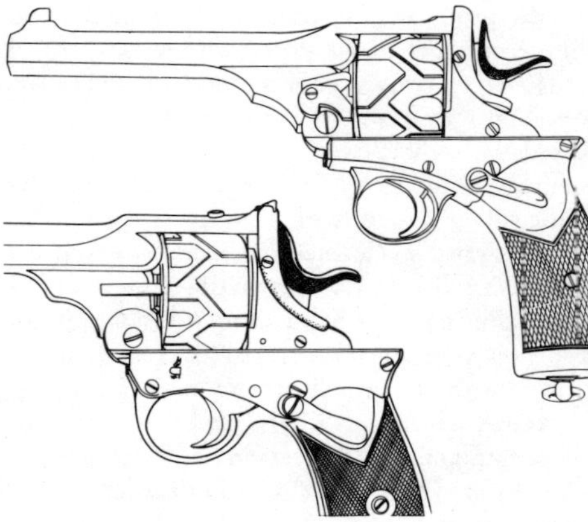

Webley-Fosbery Automatic Revolvers; (*Top*) Model 1901. (*Bottom*) Detail of Model 1902. Imperial War Museum, London.

revolver were utilised: later a much neater form was adopted whereby the cylinder was released by depressing a stud in the top strap, an arrangement which left the side of the revolver uncluttered. Both models have a guide to eliminate the possibility of the front of the cylinder snagging the mouth of the holster but, in the 1902 model, the head of the axis pin presented only the minimum surface area. Slightly less noticeable was the machining of the rear of the cylinder so as to reduce weight. This was obviously soon regarded as an unnecessary refinement and avoidable expense and, in the 1902 model, these surfaces were left intact. A closer examination of the two models will also reveal other differences, including, in the 1901 model, the fact that the backstrap is not, as later, made in one piece with the lower body of the revolver.

Amongst other features which underwent modification between the production of the two models was the accommodation of the trigger-guard and trigger assembly. After being a separate unit attached to the lower body it was, in the 1902 model, integrated with the body. The introduction of a one-piece butt also saw the abandonment of a coil return spring in favour of a V-spring. The preference shown by most English makers for V-form springs was no new development: the extraordinary choice of a coil spring in the 1901 model is what needs explaining. The awkward hooked form of the safety-catch on the 1901 model not surprisingly vanished, to be replaced by a much more streamlined lever.

These differences, between the early and later model Fosbery, are common to both the 0·455 in and the 0·38 in calibre versions. There were, however, two other rather striking differences between the 1901 0·38 in revolver and all other models. The cylinder of the 0·38 in had a stepped down reduction in the diameter for roughly the forward third of its length, which meant, of course, that the zigzag cylinder rotation grooves occupied less of the surface area of the cylinder and had a rather different appearance from other models. The safety-catch was rather distinctive in that it had a rounded knurled finish.

The barrel length of most Webley-Fosberys was 6 in but a target variety of $7\frac{1}{2}$ in is not uncommon. The 0·38 in models are extremely rare and all examined, or records of which have been seen by the author, have 6 in barrels. The 0·455 in, on the other hand, is known in a 4 in barrel length and in versions with a high barrel top rib or with a bird's head butt. All these varieties are exceedingly rare as is also a version chambered for the Colt 0·45 in cartridge, which competed unsuccessfully against various other pistols and revolvers in the United States service trials of 1906-7. At one time the company was seriously considering the production of a 0·32 in calibre Fosbery. An announcement, in fact, appeared in the technical press, but no example has ever been noted.

Webley's actually had their first experience of automatic pistols before they launched the Fosbery though the weapon in question, known as the Mars pistol, was the invention of a certain Gabbett-

Gabbet-Fairfax 'Mars' automatic pistol, .36 calibre. RMCS, Shrivenham.

Fairfax. The emphasis must be placed on 'experience'
254 as it was not until 1906 that this pistol was put on sale. However, the Mars, which was produced in 8·5 mm, 0·38 in and 0·45 in calibre, besides being of massive construction, was of remarkable design, giving its locked breech very considerable strength. There were, in fact, four large, symmetrically placed, lugs on the breech-block, which turned to apply the lock, which was not broken until the barrel and breech-block began the return movement from the point of furthest recoil. The cartridge for the 8·5 mm was an exceptionally powerful one imparting to the bullet a muzzle velocity of about 1,750 ft/s, that for the 0·38 in model with a muzzle velocity of 1,640 ft/s could penetrate twelve 1 in deal boards against $8\frac{1}{2}$ in with the 0·38 in Colt auto of 1902. Though the design of this pistol, with its extraordinary trigger mechanism and many other unusual features, invites closer study, its great rarity – rarest of all is a 0·38 in model with 12 in barrel and detachable shoulder stock – through so few being produced, must qualify this record. Its real significance lies in the experience from its design and manufacture that Webleys gained. The first true Webley automatic pistol was that produced in 1903. Naturally, with a 0·455 in cartridge the breech was locked. Two arms, one either side of the action, engaged lugs on the barrel. The hammer was external, in many ways resembling the style that was later to become almost the hallmark of Webley pistols. Very few of these pistols were made and none were put on the market.

The 1904 model 0·455 in automatic pistol is also more accurately classified as a prototype though a few were marketed. The design has clearly moved measurably nearer that later to become so familiar in the 1912 model but the breech was locked by a separate locking bolt. As the pistol was of very massive construction this worked well; so well, in fact, that in shooting almost the entire recoil was absorbed by the mass of the moving parts. Further improvements were soon made to the pistol and it was decided to modify the ammunition to allow simpler and more certain feeding. After an interim stage with what was still a rimmed cartridge, a semi-rimless design was adopted and survived to become that issued with the later naval model.

In the model brought out in 1906 the breech lock at last evolved into that which was to become, and remain, the distinctive feature of the larger Webley automatic pistols. The breech of the barrel is of heavy, square section with opposing vertical faces of this block made with inclined ribs to engage in matching grooves cut in the interior of the slide. Rearward movement of the barrel and slide led to the barrel moving down until a large but shallow rectangular lug, on the top of the square into which the barrel was formed at the rear, had disengaged itself, from a matching opening in the top of the slide, to allow the breech to recoil to the rear. The breech was closed and the lock held by the force of a very powerful V-spring acting through a lever on the breech-block. One of the great advantages of this design of mechanism was that the barrel could be detached without any need to remove the mainspring or any other assembly. There was, as almost invariably on Webley automatic pistols, an external hammer which, in this model, was on its left side, cut away to accommodate a safety-catch. In spite of the fact that six years passed before a new model was introduced, the 1906 model 0·455 in automatic pistol is a rare collector's item.

The 1912 model, which almost always carries the additional designation of 'Mark I', very closely resembled its predecessor. Perhaps the most obvious difference is that the fore-sight was made integrally with the barrel rather than being secured by a band and was much more square cut when viewed from the side. A lanyard ring appeared on the bottom rear of the butt, a grip safety generally replaced that on the hammer and a separate catch on the left above the grip was introduced for releasing the slide. In the 1906 model a stud, protruding through the right side of the breech-slide, had served both as a slide release and also linked the barrel and slide together. In the new model a long pin running right through the slide, and known as the recoil lever bar and breech stop, fulfilled this role. Though not externally apparent the 1912 model had fewer inclined barrel ribs, four against six, clearly a measure to reduce costs.

On 19 May 1913, this pistol was adopted by the Royal Navy and also for issue to the Royal Marines. It seems that these pistols were numbered starting from 1, as opposed to those intended for the civilian market which, apparently, began at about No. 100000. The Naval arms may most easily be distinguished by the letter *N* following *Mark I* but they also bear government proof marks and were dated both on the top of the action and on the right side of the frame at the rear, just below the slide, with the last two digits of the date preceded by an apostrophe, e.g.*'13*. Not infrequently these dates disagreed with that in full which was stamped on the left side of the slide. An examination of a large number of these pistols shows that the abbreviated date more accurately tallies with the serial number and therefore, presumably, more exactly records the date of manufacture than that on the left side. It is worth noting also that military models were numbered on the underside of the frame, in front of the trigger-guard, whilst civilian models carry their serial number on the left side of the frame close to the hammer axis.

Concurrently with the manufacture of the Naval pistol Webley's also made a special model, often, though not always, identified by a lightly stamped *No. 2* after *Mark I*. This was intended for Royal Horse Artillery and Royal Flying Corps use, being especially suitable for such employment through the provision made for a shoulder stock, the adoption of a rotating drum sight graduated to 200 yards, and the addition of an extra safety on the hammer. It followed the normal Mark I specification in having two positions for the magazine; at the first notch the magazine did not feed but acted simply as a floor to the action so that cartridges could be single loaded quickly and there was a normal fully home position for an emergency requiring the seven rounds in the magazine rapidly. The groove for the shoulder stock, which was flat-sided, was machined out of the lower frame just below the left grip. The back-sight drum, which was itself cut away with the back-sight notch, could be revolved so as to set either 50, 100, 150 or 200 yards by pressing its right end, which protruded on the right through an ear-like upward extension of the frame made to accommodate it. The drum was spring loaded and on the left side was fashioned with a small V-shaped lug which engaged in the notch corresponding with the range setting required. These pistols were numbered concurrently with the ordinary model. The earlier ones carry the date 1913, possibly these are from the small order manufactured for the trials which the R.H.A. ran in March 1914, but most appear to be of later manufacture and to be dated 1915. All the examples of this variety that the author has seen which are stamped with the bare *Mark I* without *No. 2* following it have serial numbers under 6000. This accords with the evidence from reports from Webley's Annual General Meetings that these specifically Army 0·455 in automatic pistols were manufactured in two contracts, a small trial one and a larger one later. It must be observed, however, that today this model, with or without the *No. 2*, is distinctly rare.

It is of interest that these 0·455 in automatic pistols, both military and civilian, are to be found without distinction with wooden or bakelite grips. The existence of one civilian pistol in the collection of the Imperial War Museum, London, with both Birmingham and government proof marks suggests that there may have been occasions when urgent government requirements were made up only by raiding stocks of those intended for the civilian market. Another unusual pistol in the same collection, numbered 111576, and in every way conforming to the civilian specification is, nevertheless, fitted with a safety-catch on the hammer and yet another civilian pistol numbered 120850 (in the military position, and in this it is not unique,) has the extremely unusual legend, rather as that on the 0·38 in HV pistols, *Webley & Scott Ltd. London and Birmingham ·455 Automatic Pistol* stamped on the left side of the slide.

The 0·455 in was not the only Webley automatic pistol to employ a locked breech. The actions of the 1910 and 1913 Models of the 0·38 in calibre High Velocity pistol were very similar to that of the 0·455 in, differing appreciably only in so far as they had internal rather than external hammers. These pistols were designed for the 0·38 in Colt ACP cartridge which developed a muzzle velocity of about 1,100 ft/s. The lanyard loop was of a flattish rectangular form made, apparently, integrally with the bottom of the frame below the left grip. The head of the slide release catch on the 1910 pattern

COMMERCIAL MODELS OF THE WEBLEY & SCOTT

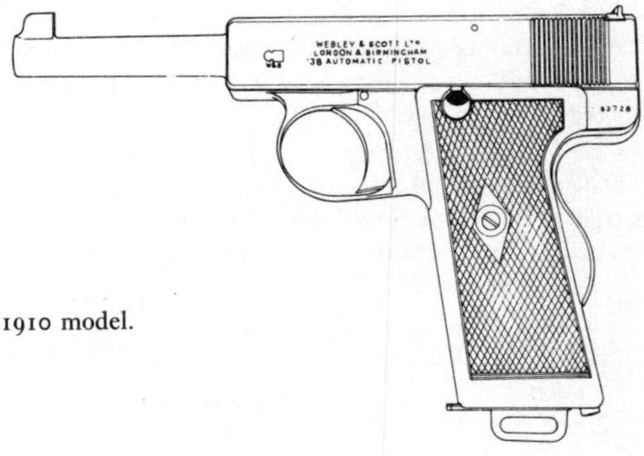

1910 model.

1913 model.
Imperial War Museum,
London.

was of much more spherical form than that of the larger calibre pistol. In the 1913 Model the catch in this form disappeared; in its place was substituted a long lever, pivoted at its front end, which served a number of purposes. As the grip safety had also vanished it acted as a safety, being applied by being moved to a horizontal position. By pressing down on this lever stripping the pistol might be begun, by moving it upwards the breech slide was released so that the action closed under the influence of the recoil spring. All 0·38 in HV pistols noted have borne serial numbers in the 60000s and all of the Model of 1913 numbers in the 66000 range.

All other models of the Webley pistol, whether 0·38 in, 9 mm, 0·32 in or 0·25 in have comparatively straightforward blowback actions, mostly with external hammers. The 9 mm (Browning Long) Model of 1909 was by far the most closely related in general appearance to the locked-breech pistol. It boasted a grip safety and rather massive proportions but it looked to the lighter calibres in the rounded form of the top of the breech slide. The 9 mm pistol was in production from 1909 to about 1930; whether by coincidence or not is not known but all examples the author has examined have serial numbers in the 110000s. The 0·380 in pistol is the biggest of the small pistols only in calibre, for it outwardly seems to resemble the 0·32 in automatic of 1906 in size and in every significant detail. In common with the ordinary 0·32 in model of 1906 it has a back-sight formed simply by grooving the top of the slide. All serial numbers noted have been in the 66000 range.

The 0·32 in or 7·65 mm automatic pistol first 255
appeared in 1905. It had a fixed barrel but one which was, interestingly, secured to the frame by means of a hinged trigger-guard so that pulling the trigger-guard forward released it. The safety was placed on the left side of the hammer itself in a manner somewhat reminiscent of those 0·455 in pistols which possess this feature. The slide was very rounded along the top and the back-sight notch was cut in a semi-circular push-across plate with knurled periphery. In 1906 a new model was brought out with a lever safety on the left side of the breech slide and, therefore, with a plain hammer. Quite a number of other changes, mainly stylistic, were made, but the bold serrating of the rear of the slide to allow an easy grip in opening the action must have been very welcome after the painful and inadequate knurled back-sight of the 1905 model, which, in the absence of anything else, was intended to serve this purpose. The 1906 Model found sufficient favour to be adopted in 1911 by the City of London and Metropolitan police forces and by many other forces in the country. Police pistols retained a back-sight very similar to that in the 1905 model whereas others, intended for the ordinary customer, had a plain groove in the top of the slide. Model 1905 pistols seem to be numbered up to about 1500 and 1906 model arms seem to continue to a figure of over 200000. Occasionally these pistols are found with broad arrow marks reminding one that they were issued, even if in limited quantities, to certain service personnel such as, in the Second World War, to officers in Naval Mine Disposal Squads.

The 0·25 in model of the Webley with external hammer was launched some time after 1906. It was quite unremarkable in design and closely followed the lines of the 1906 0·32 in model with the trigger-guard serving as a barrel release lever. There were no sights at all. In 1909 a hammerless model was marketed but almost the only remarkable thing about this model was that, though enclosed, it still had a hammer type of firing mechanism. It did, however, have sights. A very similar version was manufactured under licence for the American market by Harrington & Richardson.

When in 1908 it adopted the Luger as the official pistol for the army, the German Government did not gain the distinction of being the first major power to adopt a semi-automatic pistol; the Austro-Hungarian Empire had already taken this step. They had, a year earlier, adopted the 8 mm Roth-Steyr for their cavalry. Like the Luger, the Roth-Steyr had been in existence for about eight years at the time of its introduction, since its design stems from patents taken out between 1898 and 1900 by G. Roth and K. Krnka.

The Roth-Steyr was a well-made weapon with a locked breech and at least two striking mechanical features. The breech was locked and unlocked by the rotation of the barrel through about 90°, which was

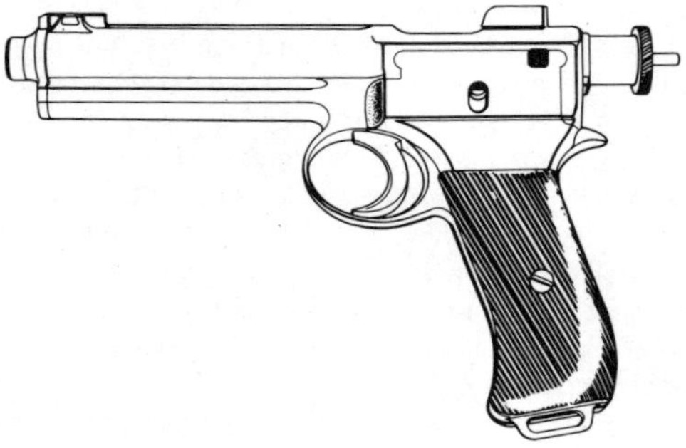

Roth-Steyr 8 mm pistol, *c.*1908. Imperial War Museum, London.

sufficient to disengage two opposing lugs, machined towards the rear, on its exterior, from the interior of the forward portion of the breech-block which extended forward to accommodate it. A removable nosecap, which served as a forward bearing for the barrel was internally cut with helical recesses to take two small lugs near the muzzle of the barrel. These also served to check the rearward movement of the barrel once the lock with the breech-block was broken. A downward projecting lug on the front of the breech-block retained the recoil spring which was housed beneath the barrel.

This design, with a floating barrel retained by a quickly detachable nosecap, permitted the almost immediate removal of the barrel for cleaning. Literally all that had to be done was to press across to the left a retaining key fitted through the top rib, at a point where it was enlarged to carry the front-sight, and pull the nosecap and barrel clear of the breech-block and frame. The trigger was even more ingenious. It operated, in fact, in a quasi-double-action fashion with all that that means in safety terms. Not until the 1920s, with the Le Français and later with the Walther P'38, does one again see an applica- of this principle, though then it is employed in a choate form. In the Roth-Steyr the first pressure on the trigger simply drew the striker to the rear, a second and heavy pressure released it, but the striker had to be cocked separately. For the first shot, which was necessarily a manual operation and, of course, for the loading of the arm, there was a very generously proportioned cocking-piece at the rear of the breech-block to grasp. One has only to try the trigger with its heavy creeping pull to understand why the theoretical advantages of this system were not much appreciated by many users.

The Roth-Steyr was principally an arm of the Austro-Hungarian Cavalry: the Austrian Landwehr carried the 9 mm Steyr pistol of 1911, sometimes called the Steyr-Hahn, or hammer Steyr. Unlike the

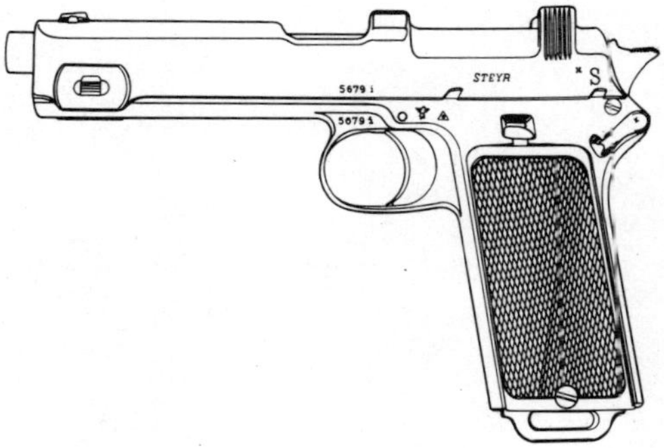

Steyr M1912 9 mm pistol. Imperial War Museum, London.

Roth-Steyr, which was manufactured at both the Steyr arsenal and Fegyvergyer, Budapest, the Steyr-Hahn was made solely at Steyr. Though this pistol is outwardly very different from the Roth-Steyr its locking system is not at all dissimilar. In fact, with an external hammer and an external appearance strongly reminiscent of the Colt of 1911 it is a rather interesting weapon.

The action was very readily dismantled, simply by withdrawing a flat pin at the lower front end of the frame – very similar to that on the 1902 Colt 0·38 in Model – which served both to transmit the force of the return spring to the slide, to close the breech and also to attach the slide, and with it the barrel, to the frame. The slide was cut away in its interior just ahead of the ejection opening with two curving recesses made to accommodate two short helical lugs on the top of the barrel. As recoil occurred the barrel was rotated about 50° clockwise through the engagement of a long helical lug on the underside of the barrel with a matching recess in the top of the frame, just above the trigger mechanism. This was just sufficient to disengage the two lugs on the top of the barrel from the corresponding recesses in the breech slide, permitting that assembly to continue to move to the rear to effect the usual cycle of operations. A short transverse lug on the underside of the barrel, to the rear of the long helical one, served as a positive check on the barrel's recoil once the unlocking action was complete. It is interesting to note that, as the barrel was rifled, the torque from the bullet passing through the bore tended to apply the lock even more positively.

Loading this pistol was not quite as straightforward as it might seem. Cartridges were pressed into the magazine from above from a clip, as in the 1896 Mauser, but the breech had first to be locked open by ensuring that the safety-catch hooked into a notch cut in the lower left rear edge of the slide. In contrast, unloading might be accomplished so easily that the unfired cartridges were scattered some distance away from the firer. All that was necessary, once the slide had been locked back, was pressure on the slide release catch and the platform rose to expel in one sweep the entire contents of the magazine. The cartridge used by this pistol was peculiar to it, the 9 mm Steyr. The bullet was steel jacketed and driven with a muzzle velocity of about 1,100 ft/s.

The Steyr-Hahn, though an important and finely made pistol, perhaps lacks the interest and attraction of the Luger. There is not the same wealth of variation, nothing like the profusion of models. Certainly there was a Romanian issue and there are examples to be found with '08' stamped on the slide indicating that, in the Second World War, they were rebarrelled for the 9 mm Parabellum cartridge, but that is more or less the scope of variation in this pistol. The barrel was always, or so it seems, 5 in long and the overall length $8\frac{1}{2}$ in.

The Roth-Steyr and the Steyr-Hahn were not the only Austro-Hungarian pistols to use a breech-lock dependent upon rotation. In the Frommer Stop 1912 pistol it was the rotation of the forward portion of the breech-block which made or broke the lock. The Roth-Frommer had earlier, in 1901, utilised the same long recoil system, namely, one in which the barrel and breech-block remained locked together throughout recoil so that all operations, extraction, ejection and chambering the new round necessarily took place on the return movement. In this 1901 pistol, which was chambered for an official, low powered 7·65 mm cartridge, a locked breech was hardly necessary nor indeed was it essential in a smaller version of the Roth-Steyr which was also chambered for this 7·65 mm cartridge.

The Frommer most commonly encountered, the
283 model of 1912, was an external hammer type pistol chambered for the 7·65 mm cartridge and in this form was one of the official issue pistols to the armed forces of the Austro-Hungarian Empire. Its construction was most unusual in that the entire upper portion of the pistol comprised merely a static extension of the frame and was not, as it may appear to be, a slide. Inside it the barrel travelled backwards and forwards; above the barrel to the front lay the barrel return spring and, to the rear, the breech-block return spring. The breech-block, which was accommodated inside the rearward extension of the barrel, was at its rear end extended upwards to unite with a guide rod which ran through the centre of the return springs. Throughout the rearward movement of the barrel the breech-block remained firmly locked to it by its forward rotatory portion. On the return movement of the barrel the front of the breech-block rotated anti-clockwise to unlock the barrel and allow it to go forward. Since, at this point, the breech-block was halted, continuing barrel movement effected extraction and ejection of the fired case. The final $\frac{1}{16}$ in, or so, forward movement of the barrel released the breech-block, which flew forward to chamber the next round. As it met the rear of the barrel the front section of the breech-block was, by its lugs in their engagement in the recesses in the barrel extension, rotated clockwise to lock the breech. In initial loading this unusual design limited the consequence of manual traction of the breech-block to its sliding rearwards within the barrel extension, in which, in fact, it was splined to prevent the rotation of its main portion. This pistol was, in short, of a remarkably complex design and, though it appeared to work well, it was extremely vulnerable to complete immobilisation by the denting or distorting of its very light upper frame. Frommer pistols may be found in 0·380 in ACP calibre and there is also a more pocketable version of the 7·65 mm, known as the Baby, as it was rather less than $4\frac{1}{2}$ in in overall length against $6\frac{1}{2}$ in for the official issue version.

At about the time of the outbreak of the First 284
World War the Japanese forces adopted the Nambu automatic pistol. This employed a breech locked by a locking block hinged in the barrel extension and normally in engagement with a recess in the underside of the breech-block. On the recoil the barrel and extension moved to the rear and the breech-block remained locked in position until the locking block reached the point where the frame was cut away. It then dropped and the breech-block was free to continue towards the rear. Through the frame being cut away it was possible to observe the downward and unlocking movement of the locking block as the barrel was pressed to the rear. Rather curiously the recoil return spring was housed in a parallel tunnel, lateral extension of the frame on the left side of the action and linked across to the breech-block through a cocking piece at the rear. Also arranged in a side-by-side, rather than the usual under-and-over alignment, were the sear and bent for striker release. As if these features were not unusual enough, the trigger unit was dovetailed into the front face of the butt frame and was thus removed by being pushed downwards. Directly beneath the trigger unit when assembled in the pistol was to be found a grip safety, unusually placed to the front of the grip.

The Nambu was chambered for a special bottle-necked 8 mm cartridge of moderate to low power. In fact, the chief criticism of this arm is that its ammunition was inadequate in performance for military purposes. There are a number of variants which may be encountered: one particularly striking model has the lower rear butt frame cut to accept a shoulder-stock-cum-holster of Mauser style. As the pistol was only about 9 in overall the shoulder stock was on the small side but this drawback was most ingeniously overcome by an internally concealed extension sleeve which could be pulled out to lengthen the weapon. Many of these pistols manufactured in peacetime were quite beautifully finished, giving the weapon a most attractive appearance.

In some ways superficially resembling the Nambu is the Glisenti which, in the model of 1910, became an Italian official service arm. Outwardly it was

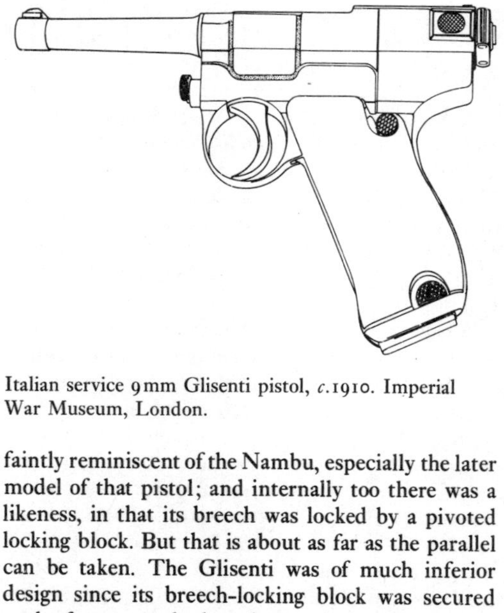

Italian service 9 mm Glisenti pistol, *c.*1910. Imperial War Museum, London.

faintly reminiscent of the Nambu, especially the later model of that pistol; and internally too there was a likeness, in that its breech was locked by a pivoted locking block. But that is about as far as the parallel can be taken. The Glisenti was of much inferior design since its breech-locking block was secured to the frame not the barrel extension and rotated to release the breech-block rather than being on a pivot to drop clear of it. The only possible connection between the two designs is that the Glisenti was probably one of the antecedent types considered by the Japanese in originating the Nambu. This is more than possible, in fact, since the Glisenti dates from 1906 with conceivably even earlier beginnings in a design produced by two Belgians, Haensler and Roch about 1905. The Glisenti is rather a problem in so far as its ammunition is concerned, for it is chambered for a special 9 mm cartridge, just a trifle shorter and appreciably less powerful than the 9 mm Parabellum. It will, in fact, shoot the 9 mm Parabellum round but, as the locking system is basically weak and there are many high-velocity sub-machine types of 9 mm Parabellum cartridge about, those who fire the Glisenti indiscriminately with any ammunition that it will chamber run a great risk.

The Glisenti is quite common as it was in issue to Italian naval and military formations in both World Wars. Overall it measures about $8\frac{1}{4}$ in; army models have plain chequered grips, those for the navy, grips carrying a heraldic device. The barrel extends to the rear in a square section machined to accept a breech-block of similar section. As the arm was designed so that the left sideplate might easily be detached the barrel extension slides on a rib integral with the frame only on the right side. This was a serious source of weakness as the side plate was not sufficiently securely attached to ensure that it could not work loose and jam the action. On recoil the barrel and breech-block moved to the rear locked together by a transversely pivoted locking block. When this had been carried about 20° to 30° past the vertical towards the rear by the recoiling parts the lock was completely broken because the block was by then, through its rotation on a fixed point, below the level of the breech-block. As the barrel could not return to its forward position until the locking block was seating itself in its recess in the breech-block the new cartridge had to be fed into the chamber at a slightly earlier point in the sequence of functioning. The only way that this obstacle could be surmounted was by providing what were, in effect, two sears, but at least this dispensed with the need for a disconnector to avoid accidental automatic fire. A grip safety was fitted on the front of the lower frame beneath the trigger-guard. The magazine, with grips attached to the platform, was particularly easy to load. Beneath the left grip a small tool for dismantling the striker from the breech-block was concealed. The pistol, on the right side of the frame, was stamped with its serial number, and with the letters F.A.B., the date of manufacture and a crown encircled.

The Glisenti was not the most popular of side-arms and, from 1915 onwards, was supplemented in the Italian service by the 9 mm and 7·6 mm Berettas. These Beretta pistols were well-designed simple blowback arms with internal hammers. There was nothing to check the opening of the breech but the mass of the moving parts and the recoil spring. Mechanically they were quite unremarkable as were scores of other blowback action pistols which were produced in the first and second decades of this century. In Great Britain, as has already been noted, Webley used an unlocked breech on all their smaller calibre models; in Germany Walther, from 1908 onwards, produced a series of small blowback pistols. Mauser, similarly, from 1910 onwards marketed a range of blowback pistols and Sauer & Sohn also

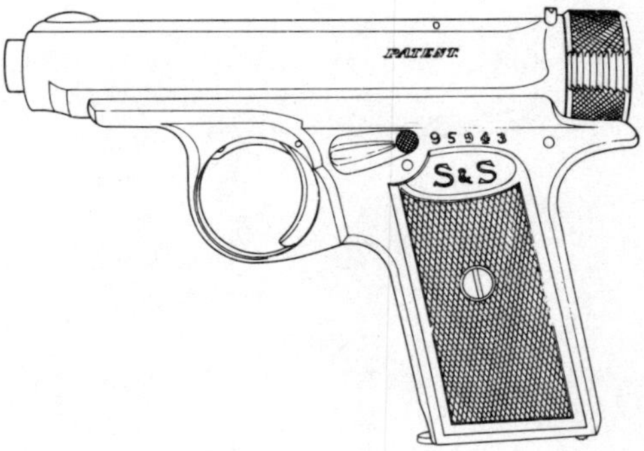

Sauer 7.65mm Model 1913 pistol. Imperial War Museum, London.

made 6·35 mm and 7·65 mm blowback pistols.

Not all blowback pistols were designed for cartridges of 7·65 mm or lesser calibre, Webley and F.N., it is to be recalled, produced 9 mm blowback pistols for the low-power Browning Long round and Dreyse, Rheinische Metallwaaren und Maschinenfabrik of Sommerda, even made such a weapon to accept the 9 mm Parabellum cartridge. The Dreyse pistol appeared during the First World War and in external appearance closely followed the lines of the smaller 0·32 in Dreyse pistol. As it was not practically possible to increase the weight of the moving parts to

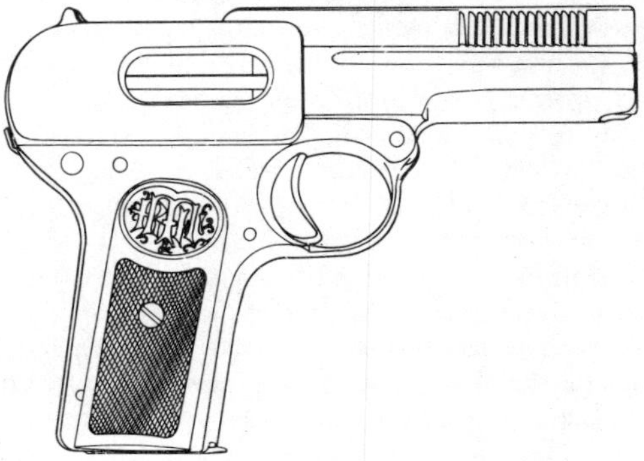

Dreyse pistol 7.65mm of 1907. RSAF, Enfield.

moderate the recoil the course of adopting a very powerful recoil spring was that taken. Along the top of the breech slide was fitted, almost as a lid, a long cocking lever pivoted at its front end so that its rear extremity could be pulled outwards from the slide to an angle of about 30°. When this was hinged upwards the movement freed it from the recoil spring lug so that the slide could easily be drawn to the rear, which compressed the striker. The action was closed by pushing the cocking lever forward, which compressed the mainspring, and by folding the lever to the slide, which re-engaged its lug with that of the recoil spring. Unfortunately it was quite possible for the cocking lever to be thrown out of engagement with the recoil-spring lug by the shock of the discharge and the arm to be put out of action. It is not therefore surprising that sales of this pistol were so small that it is today quite rare.

Another German blowback pistol of some interest is the F. L. Selbstader, named after its manufacturer Fritz Langenhan of Suhl. It was officially issued to certain German military personnel in the First World War though it was chambered for the ordinary 7·65 mm pistol cartridge. Its peculiarity lay in the extraordinarily easy take-down arrangement which, by turning a single milled screw, enabled the firer to remove the slide and breech block. Externally it rather resembles the F.N. Browning of 1900 and, measuring $6\frac{3}{4}$ in overall, it was quite sizeable. However it was its principal virtue which was its own chief enemy. The single screw could work loose and out of engagement in firing and, if it did so, the breech-block, which was separate from the slide, was blown back violently at the firer. The Germans also issued officially another blowback 7·65 mm pistol, known as the *Beholla*, but this was of straightforward design.

Steyr of Austria and Pieper of Belgium, in concert, produced in 7·65 mm an enclosed-hammer blowback pistol, known as the Model of 1908. In 1910 Pieper introduced a 0·380 in (9 mm short) version: there was also a 6·35 mm model. This 1908 weapon was chiefly remarkable for its tip-up barrel, a very convenient arrangement for cleaning but actually intended to allow its occasional use as a single-loader. Pistols of this type of early manufacture dispensed with an extractor. If the pressure of gases failed to unseat the case it was not difficult to open the barrel, by depressing a lever on the left side of the frame, and push out the recalcitrant case.

In the United States the automatic pistol which, apart from the Colt, survives today in quantities from the period under consideration is undoubtedly the Savage. It is equally true that it cannot be dis-

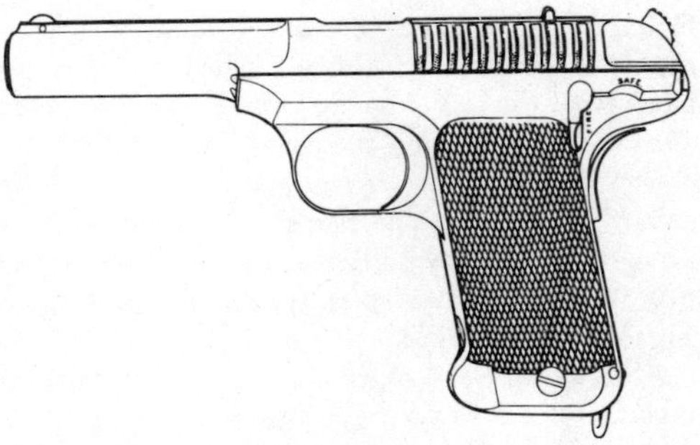

The American Savage .45. Smithsonian Institution, Washington, D.C.

missed as a simple blowback. The breech was locked by the barrel rotating a mere 5°. Its locking lug disengaged so rapidly that to some an action existed for which 'hesitation lock' is the only adequate description. The Savage was patented in 1905; in 1906 a 0·45 in version was manufactured and was one of the competing arms in the United States Army Trials of 1907. It was not successful and was not put on to the market until 1909, when a model with an exposed cocking piece in 0·32 in ACP calibre appeared. In 1910 'hammerless' versions in 0·32 in and 0·380 in calibre were introduced and new models in both calibres appeared in 1917. The 1917 model has a cocking piece with a spur type of thumbpiece replacing the rounded type on the 1910 model with exposed cocking piece. The butt on the 1917 was given a more splayed form so as to provide a better grip. A 0·25 in ACP model with simple blowback action was also produced by Savage. Although reference is frequently made to 'hammer' or 'hammerless' types of the Savage the firing mechanism was actually of striker type–the cocking piece was merely a means of drawing back the striker to the cocked position. In Savage pistols of an enclosed or 'hammerless' type there was a grip safety. The breech lock was effected by a small cammed lug, machined on the top of the barrel at the rear end, which engaged with a slot cut in the interior surface of the slide. As the rear quarter of an inch of the barrel-locking lug was cut with a steep left-hand pitch and the barrel was attached to the frame by a lug on its underside the recoil of the slide turned the barrel anti-clockwise. The lock was broken when the lug reached the straight portion of the groove in the slide. The Savage is of interest also in that its trigger mechanism was of very unusual design, permitting fine adjustment but not without a real risk of the gun firing automatically.

Much less is heard today about the early Smith & Wesson 0·35 in automatic pistol though it was a weapon of unusual design. There was no barrel slide but simply a breech-block. To allow this to be drawn easily to the rear, prior to its going forward to chamber the first round, a spring-loaded release catch could be pushed in to free the block from the recoil spring. There was also a most unusual arrangement of hinging the barrel at the rear of its long extension to a post rising from the rear of the frame. The barrel was released at the for cleaning, etc., by pulling down the trigger-guard. For all these interesting features, its action was of simple blowback type.

Almost at the end of the war, in 1918, Remington introduced a 0·380 in ACP automatic pistol to the design of J. B. Pedersen. It used a type of hesitation lock. The breech-block, which consisted of two parts, was mounted in the rear of the slide. After the

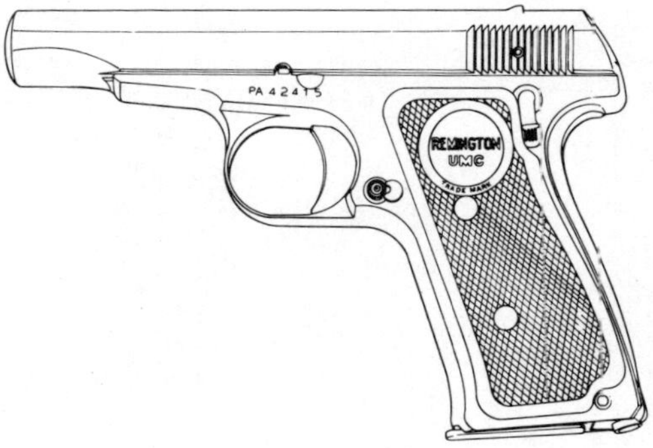

Remington .380 pistol. Imperial War Museum, London.

first $\frac{3}{16}$ in of recoil the shoulder of the movable portion of the breech-block struck an abutment in the frame. The slide, to which the effect of recoil had already been imparted by what amounted to a short power stroke of the breech block, continued rearwards alone until an incline on the slide engaged an incline on the block and lifted the rear end of the breech-block out of engagement with the frame. The slide and breech-block then recoiled together normally to carry out the usual sequence of operations. One effect of this arrangement was, of course, that extraction was in two stages; the first stage by gas pressure and the second by mechanical means. The pistol's main distinctive feature for many users was its exceptionally comfortable and well shaped grip, the product of considerable experimentation.

By 1919 there was little that had not been tried in automatic pistols and there were scores of models to choose from. The automatic pistol had not eclipsed the revolver but if one looked around it was now possible to find a pistol to suit any side-arm requirement. No real purpose is served by giving a catalogue of the blowback pistols that were on the market though there are some, such as the Lignose, with unusual features. The Great Powers were already committed to certain general specifications and to certain manufacturers because they guaranteed the most practicable design in combination with the highest standards of workmanship and the best quality materials. In Chapter 13 the principal developments of the post-1919 period are briefly recorded and it will immediately be seen that there are almost no newcomers to the manufacturing field and certainly very little if anything that could be called new in basic design. If the names Browning, Luger, Webley, Mauser and Mannlicher seem to dominate this survey it is for the simple reason that their products did dominate the period. And because examples are so frequently encountered it is their place in the pattern of arms development which tends to be of interest to most people.

282 Two Webley & Scott 6·35 mm calibre automatics. (*Above*) The Model of 1909 with internal hammer. (*Left*) The Model of 1910 with external hammer. Imperial War Museum, London.

283 Two Rudolf Frommer automatics: (*Above*) the 'Stop' 7·65 mm calibre of 1912. (*Left*) the 'Baby' of the same date and calibre. These pistols employed a complex 'long recoil' system of operation. Imperial War Museum, London.

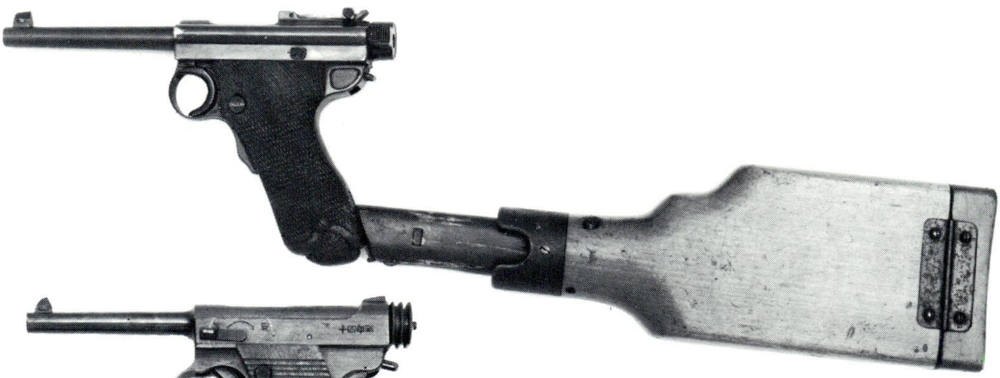

284 Two Japanese service 8 mm automatics: (*Left*) The '14th Year Model', 1925. (*Above*) The original '4th Year Nambu' model, 1915, with shoulder stock. The 14th Year model has an enlarged trigger-guard for use with gloves. Imperial War Museum, London.

285 Two Beretta automatics: (*Far right*) The 7·65 mm calibre Model of 1915/19 which was an improvement on the Model of 1915 patents; 1913. RSAF, Enfield. (*Right*) the first automatic pistol produced by this company. Imperial War Museum, London.

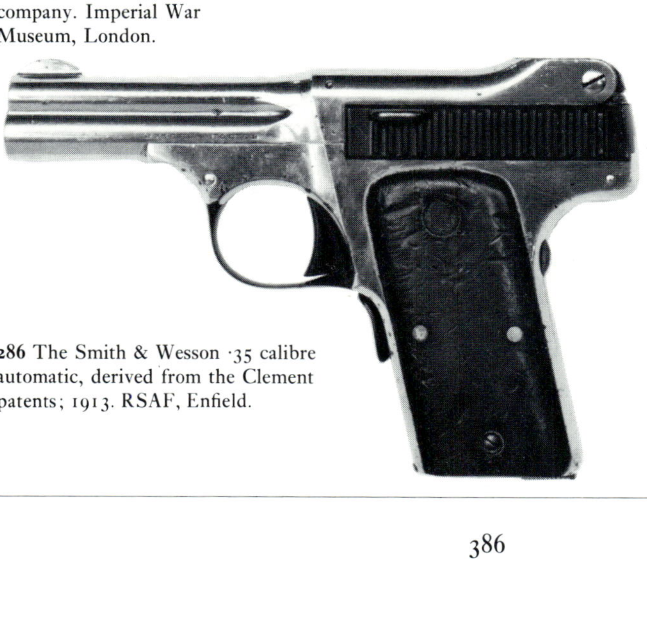

286 The Smith & Wesson ·35 calibre automatic, derived from the Clement patents; 1913. RSAF, Enfield.

ꩰ CHAPTER THIRTEEN ꩰ

General Survey of Firearms: 1918 to the Present Day

C.H. Roads with additional text by Ian Hogg

74, 281 The forces which have had their effect upon the
87-313 design and manufacture of arms since the end of the First World War have been those same ones which, in these decades, have transformed almost all upon which we gaze or with which we are concerned. The never ceasing tide of technological improvement and the wider and more even distribution of wealth have left their mark on the design of everything from the machine-gun to the match rifle. There are all the time fewer people able to pay high prices for top-class hand craftsmanship and fewer craftsmen willing to shut their eyes to the attractive vistas which modern technical advances offer to those with their basic skill and ability. At times, of course, economic necessity has been the over-riding factor, as when Germany in the last year or so before her collapse in the Second World War developed a fascinating range of utility arms. But these are all factors which one would expect to condition the development of arms or motor cars or aeroplanes or indeed anything of a similar nature. What is surprising about the evolution of arms since 1918 is that they have scarcely evolved. In many respects they have been improved, very frequently they have been simplified, and often new combinations of accepted features have proved more satisfactory than those first selected, but nothing to stand comparison, even remotely, with the introduction of the metallic self-contained cartridge case or the discovery of smokeless powder has transpired.

The Second World War, like the first, had the effect of accelerating the rationalisation of arms. Some, like the Boys Anti-Tank Rifle simply ceased to have a *raison d'être*–tank armour quickly became so thick that it was impervious to the projectile fired by such a weapon–and died. Others, such as ultra lightweight arms for parachutists and infantry operated anti-tank bomb projectors were developed either from existing arms or by applying devices and arrangements in use in other fields. Necessity, as well as being the mother of invention, could and did drive nations to press into service anything upon which they could lay their hands. The fantastic variety of weapons with which the British Home Guard equipped itself from home or overseas sources bears ample witness of this. The Germans, in turn, were obliged to utilise whatever they could most easily obtain. Under these circumstances they produced designs for arms which could be produced in almost any workshop, however simply equipped; they substituted laminated wood for traditional walnut and they even manufactured cartridge cases out of steel as they could not procure adequate supplies of copper. This policy of producing the best arms possible with the facilities and materials available to one or two standard calibres had much to recommend it over the alternative of 'any arm, and the ammunition will turn up from somewhere'. Of course, the comparison between the situation of the British in 1940 and the Germans in 1944 should not be too closely drawn: the threatened invasion of the British Isles seemed so imminent that anything but ready-made arms appeared likely to be too late.

The Second World War saw a continuation of the rather bizarre situation of the United States privately producing in the Smith & Wesson the finest revolver anywhere manufactured yet, at the same time, depending upon the Colt automatic pistol. Great Britain with only a limited production capacity for Webley automatics remained an enthusiastic champion of the revolver, almost the only power to do so. She had, however, soon after the First World War decided that a saving in weight and a gain in efficiency might be achieved by substituting 0·38 in for the long

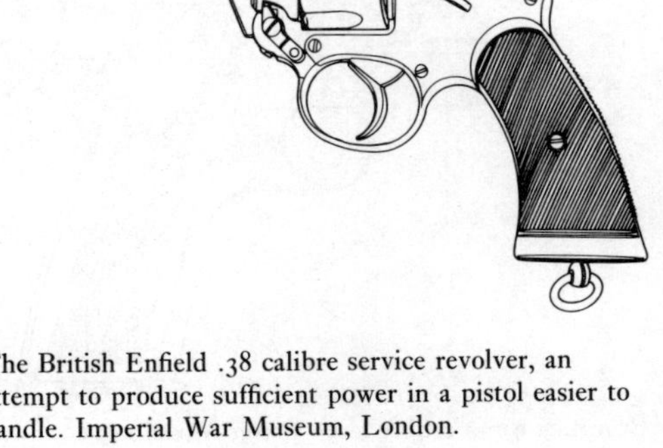

The British Enfield .38 calibre service revolver, an attempt to produce sufficient power in a pistol easier to handle. Imperial War Museum, London.

established 0·455 in calibre. The name Enfield reappeared with the 0·38 in revolver, or Pistol No. 2 as it was officially designated, but, throughout the war, there was such a demand for revolvers that the old ·455 remained in issue. Both revolvers were extremely serviceable arms with considerable stopping power and gained enviable reputations for durability. A double-action only, combless version of the ·38 revolver, theoretically an excellent high-speed short-range arm, was also issued during the war.

The Germans also still had in service their official side arm of the First World War, the Pistole '08, or Luger, but as a primary arm it had been superseded
287 by the Walther P'38. One of the great attractions of the Walther design, as compared with the Luger, was that it was much cheaper to manufacture. It also had a double-action trigger mechanism allowing a rapid fire by pressure on the trigger even though the hammer was down. This design was of value, also, in allowing an immediate second attempt, very often successful, at firing an apparent misfire. It had a breech locked by a swinging block, differently positioned but not so unlike that on the Mauser 1896 pistol. After the barrel and side had recoiled about half an inch, a plunger rod on the rear of the barrel extension was depressed by coming up against the frame. This cammed a simple locking block downwards about a forward pivot and released the breechblock, which was locked by the engagement of lugs on the upper surface of the locking block in slots cut in the forward part of the slide. The mechanism was very simply contrived and did not require a high grade surface finish to function reliably.

In spite of the criticism that can be levied at the potentially unsafe nature of the safety arrangements in the P'38 it marked, in the view of many, the most important advance in military pistol design since 1918. A strong rival, however, is to be found in the Browning High Power or Model of 1935. This was Browning's last modification of the design which had earlier been employed in the Colt Model of 1911. Progress in the simplification of both the form of the slide and that of the breech lock is most noticeable. The separate opening, for access to the recoil spring in the front of the slide, was eliminated; the swinging link on the barrel was replaced by an ingenious slotted lug on the underside of the barrel below the chamber which engaged with a cross-bar cam in the frame. The locking arrangement itself, of two rib-like lugs on the top of the barrel engaging in matching recesses cut in the upper interior of the slide, remained the same but the new arrangement at the rear provided a far more rigid mounting for the barrel. This pistol was later adopted as the Canadian official pattern and by the Chinese; more recently it has been issued to the British forces. One of its principal practical advantages over most other types is its large magazine capacity of thirteen rounds. The double-column magazine also contributes to the pistol's appeal in another way: the resulting large grip gives the arm an exceptionally comfortable feel and the firer excellent control over it. It was very easy to strip for field cleaning and foolproof in assembly.

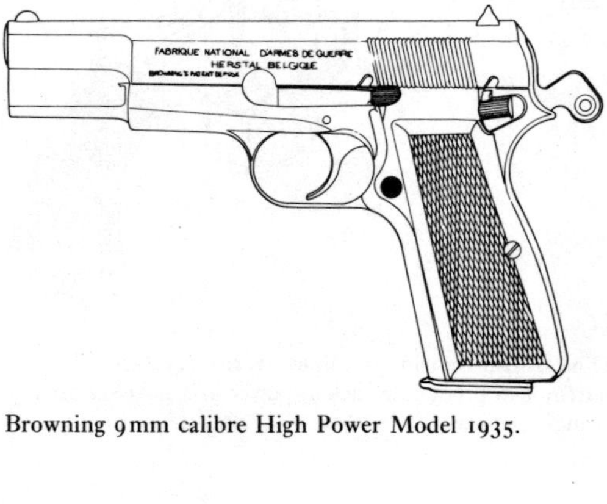

Browning 9mm calibre High Power Model 1935.

Though only a few countries actually adopted the Browning High Power military pistol a number of others did not scruple to copy its significant design features. The Poles in their Radom followed Browning's design closely and the French MAS found inspiration in the same source. The 1930 Russian

The Soviet Tokarev 7.62mm calibre automatic Model TT33, based on Browning's design and firing a cartridge derived from the Mauser 7.63mm calibre model. Imperial War Museum, London.

Tokarev also utilised Browning's locking system, though in its firing mechanism it was rather individual. This Russian redesigning of a Browning pistol was remarkably successful in simplifying the form of components and in reducing costs. Moreover, it was achieved not at the expense of the military properties of the arm but rather with advantage to its field employment. One of the most recent pistols to be introduced basically of Browning 8T design is the Swiss P-210. This incorporated the best features of the Tokarev with those of the original Browning HP. The most interesting feature of this weapon is the manner in which interchanging the barrel and recoil spring – the work of only a few moments – can convert the calibre from 9 mm Parabellum to 7·65 mm or vice versa.

Many countries since the First World War have been content with simple blowback pistols. The Italians, for example, gave their Berettas a new look
288 in 1934 and the Spaniards in the Model 400 Astra produced a really catholic 9 mm blowback arm which would safely fire almost any 9 mm cartridge. The German firm of Walther dramatically modernised its range of small blowback pistols, the Models
289 PP and PPK were stylistically futuristic, whilst the

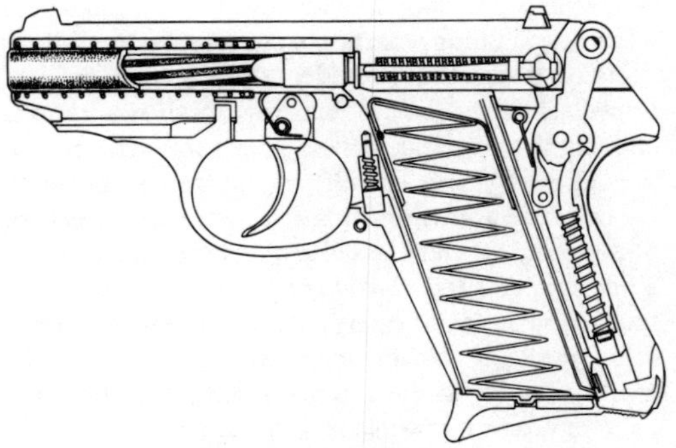

The workings of a simple blowback pistol, shown here by the Walther PPK 6.35 mm calibre model. Based on drawing in Walther handbook.

Mauser H SC was closely related both in style and in its double-action trigger mechanism. A few countries, apart from Germany, however, neither adopted blowbacks nor imitated the Browning. The Japanese redesigned their Nambu, though they adhered to the same general locking arrangement. This 1925 model retained the old and rather ineffective 8 mm calibre but was in many respects simplified. An interesting variety had an enlarged

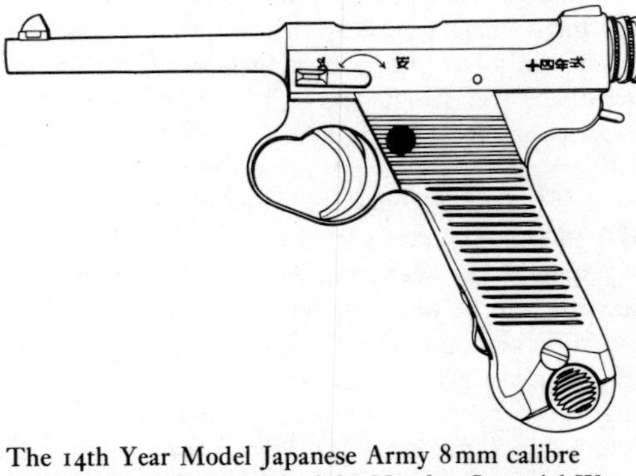

The 14th Year Model Japanese Army 8 mm calibre pistol, a simplified model of the Nambu. Imperial War Museum, London.

trigger-guard to allow a gloved finger access to the trigger. In most examples likely to be encountered the finish was rough and not comparable with the best to be found in the early model. The Finns and Swedes both adopted the Lahti pistol which, out- 290
wardly at least, was rather reminiscent of the Luger. Its locking breech, however, was quite different. The barrel extension rose at the rear to form a chamber above the breech-block. In this a locking block was housed which was cammed in and out of engagement with recesses in the top of the breech-block. Most unusually in a pistol there was an accelerator which, on being struck by the barrel, imparted an accelerating motion to the breech-block as it moved to the rear. An internal-hammer type of firing mechanism was used. The design of the Lahti was extremely sound and very safe for any 9 mm cartridge but undoubtedly expensive to manufacture. One other unusual military pistol design that has emerged since 1918 must be given passing mention. It is the 1928 French Le Française which, though of blowback operation, had a curious dichotomy between the firing mechanism and all other operations. But double-action operation of the firing mechanism through the trigger independent of the motion of the slide had the usual drawback that the trigger was not as pleasant to use as on conventional arms.

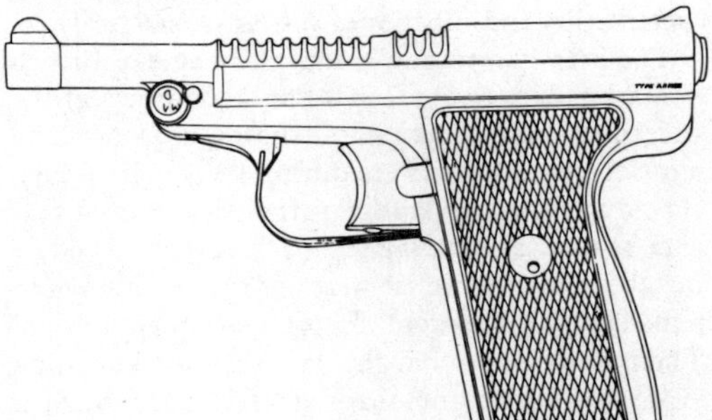

The French 'Le Francais Type Armee' 9 mm calibre pistol, submitted for military test in 1928, but not adopted. Imperial War Museum, London.

The survival of the Mauser 1896 military pistol until quite recently in military or police service in various parts of the world was, at the same time, a reminder of the sterling qualities of its basic design and a pointer to the greater military utility of a submachine-gun or machine pistol as compared with a pure pistol. The form in which the Mauser proved most enduring was with optional selection of automatic fire, an open-bottomed magazine cavity to take a full-length submachine-gun type magazine and, of course, a detachable shoulder stock. It was the only really successfully marketed pistol to have its magazine in front of the trigger and, in many ways, its continued popularity was due to this peculiarity. The basic pattern 1896 Mauser in this altered form was known as the Model of 1932 and it was manufactured in Germany, and also in Spain, under the name Astra. In China it was especially popular and there made to some extent in 0·45 in calibre. Though it was quite possible to fire short controlled bursts of automatic fire with this weapon it was expensive to manufacture and certainly of unnecessarily complicated design.

Probably the two most famous machine carbines, or if it is preferred, submachine-guns, were the
291 Thompson and the Sten. The Thompson, the earlier, was far closer to the Mauser in spirit of conception than the Sten, which was virtually its antithesis. The Thompson was first offered to the public in 1921. In its original form it employed a hesitation lock but one which imposed so mild a check upon the opening of the breech that it was barely clear whether the rate of fire increased if the inertia wedge block was temporarily discarded. The amount of machining in the Thompson's manufacture made it extremely expensive, but in the 1920s, in fact until 1928, it achieved sales all over the world because it had no commercial rival. Later models, which saw service widely with both American and British forces in the Second World War, were of simple blowback construction and functioned just as satisfactorily.

292 The Sten gun was an indirect outcome of British military failure to appreciate the significance of the widespread introduction of submachine-guns by most of the major powers during the 1930s. When, almost too late, the British authorities realised that in close quarters fighting submachine-guns could be matched only by similar weapons they attempted to remedy the situation. Enormous quantities of Thompsons were bought in America but their expensive but in the 1920s, in fact until 1928, it comparatively complex construction put them at a disadvantage under rough and, particularly, sandy conditions. The British need for a sub-machine-gun that was so simple that it could be made almost anywhere and yet which would function reliably,
293 made them turn to the German MP38 but even that was too complex to copy closely under the conditions prevailing. What ultimately emerged and which, in its breech-block and magazine arrangement was a close imitation of the German Schmeisser 28 II, was still something unique. The Sten gun was the ultimate product, manufactured, so it was rumoured, for only a few shillings a weapon, and yet in performance in battle generally proved more satisfactory than the Thompson, which could cost more than £50. So satisfactory a design was it that the Germans in turn themselves copied it and it remained in service with some units until the 1950s, in only a slightly improved form, the Mark V. The only real objections that could be made about the Sten were that the magazine spring had so little temper that every few days magazines had to be unloaded for the spring to be stretched, as otherwise there would be serious feed troubles. The recoil spring was also liable to fail to hold the breech-block, if the butt of the arm were bounced on the ground, from travelling far enough to the rear to feed a round. If the unsuspecting soldier was unlucky and a loaded magazine was in position with 'auto' set the fixed firing pin ensured that a burst of fire was the instant and shattering sequel.

The weapon which had most impressed the British authorities responsible for the development of the Sten gun was the German MP 38. This neat weapon had the appearance of an elongated pistol, especially when the shoulder stock extension was folded forward. The folding stock itself was a novel and highly practical feature in a submachine-gun. The Haenel Works of Suhl, which were responsible for the development of this arm, were also breaking new ground for this class of arm in their adherence to a purely metal and plastic construction. It is easy to fault on grounds of safety, e.g. there was no proper safety catch; it was disturbing to fire because of the amount of play in the extended butt; it would often fail to function if grasped by the magazine rather than by the receiver with the forward hand; the magazine fitted too loosely into its housing and its mouth was easily displaced in relationship to the path of the breech-block; the bottom positioning of the magazine also made the arm difficult to fire in the prone position when very low cover was all that was available. But for all these faults it was an outstandingly versatile arm which could be used as a pistol or a carbine. It represented a most satisfactory compromise between a specification of sufficient imagination to produce a versatile arm and a weapon which was both reasonably cheap to manufacture, adequately finished, and reliable and durable in use. The German parachutist was very well served by it and so too were those armoured fighting vehicle personnel who carried it where a pistol would have been more orthodox. During the Second World War it was only to be expected that America and Russia would be forced to recognise the military and economic advantages of the new generation of submachine-guns inaugurated by the MP 38 and confirmed by the Sten. The American
M3 managed to steer a middle course in quality and 294
manufacture between the two earlier weapons. It is not difficult to see how it soon acquired the unofficial name 'grease gun', from the ratio of visible unadorned barrel to markedly cylindrical receiver. The butt was more like the MP 38 than the Sten in being retractable but was pulled out rather than hinged round from its retracted to its extended

position. It is interesting that, though this weapon followed American practice in being made for the ·45 ACP cartridge, it actually weighed less than the 9 mm MP 38 and only just over a $\frac{1}{2}$ lb more than the Sten. By the simple arrangement of interchanging breech-blocks and barrels the M3 could be converted to 9 mm Parabellum operation and thus be made fully acceptable in Europe. Russian submachine-guns in the new style originate with the
295 PPSH model of 1941 but this was further improved in 1942, and in 1943 the PPS model emerged, very much in general appearance, and especially on account of its style of skeleton folding butt, reminiscent of the MP 38. Though, of course, of simple blowback type these Russian submachine-guns showed considerable independence in approach to the method of applying the basic system. A muzzle brake, furnished by a forward extension of the barrel jacket, was an interesting feature of the arm and certainly a thoughtful one since the rate of fire, at 650 rounds per minute, was 100 or more rounds higher than that of the MP 38 or Sten and even those weapons needed close control on automatic fire. The Russian submachine-guns were all designed for a Russian 7·62 mm cartridge.

Among the many other countries that have designed simple cheaply manufactured submachine-guns one of the most prominent is Australia. One of
300 her designs was the Owen which was most distinctive in appearance through the unusual positioning of its box magazine directly above the receiver, an arrangement which naturally required offset sights. The Austen was undoubtedly an even better arm which most successfully incorporated the best features of both the MP 38 and the Sten. The Schmeisser-style butt was adopted in an improved more rigid form. The German breech-block and recoil spring were also preferred but the Sten was the source of the design for the receiver and side-mounted magazine. Though all these blowback submachine guns relied for barrel cooling on the most simple arrangement of the breech remaining open between shots so that air could easily circulate through the barrel, the provision, in the Austen, for the rapid change of barrels was a feature which many welcomed. In a later version of the Austen a receiver of cast aluminium for simpler production was introduced, but not without considerable redesigning of the weapon to transfer to a rear extension of the barrel the bearing surfaces previously provided by the receiver. The Mark II Austen may appear to signpost the future but, in fact, it was really tangential to what has, since the Second World War, proved to be the line of development from the Sten and similar arms. The Patchett, or Sterling, as now
301 in use in the British service is reasonably typical of recent progress.

The Sterling clearly owes much in its design to the simpler forms evolved during the war but, at the same time, it equally reflects the circumstances of its being a weapon produced in peacetime. It is well made, well finished, but still simple and reasonably light and, with a folding butt, as versatile as any weapon in its class. Certain components, such as the butt, are more sophisticated than those which were normally encountered on earlier arms but they are in no way unnecessarily elaborate. The Sterling was, and still is, like all other submachine-guns or machine carbines, an arm designed for close quarters use, with 200 yards the maximum distance envisaged.

It was, perhaps, inevitable that the Second World War would see a reaction to the proliferation of types of arms, reminiscent of that which occurred very early in the century when a single short rifle was introduced as a measure to merge the old infantry rifle and cavalry carbine. A prerequisite of a weapon which might take on the roles of the rifle, submachine gun and pistol was that it fired a cartridge of reduced rifle rather than improved pistol characteristics. In 1941 the Germans brought in a 7·92 mm short cartridge which was just like a shortened standard rifle cartridge and still loaded with a streamlined bullet. After many trials, in 1943, they introduced a weapon which they called a machine-pistol but which was, in reality, a short rifle cum submachine-gun.

The MP44 version of this arm had a specification 302
which really did compare with what might be expected in a dual- or triple-purpose gun. Most significantly it had a fully-locked breech, gas operated, and was capable of either single shots or fully automatic fire. The sights allowed settings from 100 to 800 metres and, naturally, air cooling was employed. Magazine capacity was 30 rounds and the overall length of the arm was kept down to 3 ft $\frac{3}{4}$ in. The Germans undoubtedly succeeded in producing an efficient arm which could be used, on the one hand, in place of a conventional rifle or an automatic rifle, or, on the other, in lieu of a submachine-gun or pistol. Unfortunately, the idea did not, in practice, commend itself as much as it might seem to in theory. The Americans, in 1941, had tried a very
similar line in producing their M1 carbine. This also 303
fired with a locked breech and used gas operation. It was chambered for a 0·30 in cartridge firing an 110 grain bullet at 1900 ft/s, in other words, its performance did not as easily stand comparison with that of a standard military rifle as did the later German arms using the 7·92 mm short cartridge. It was consequently sighted only to 300 yards and in this model intended solely for single shots. It certainly had the virtue of being light, its weight was a mere $5\frac{1}{2}$ lb and a special model, the M1A1, was fitted with a folding skeleton-butt making it even easier for the

parachutist to employ. The M2 model, which could be fired automatically if required, was further developed into an M3 carbine which was sighted only with an infra-red telescope sight. The fact that other nations have not generally followed this line of arms development suggests that, for all the talk of rifle fire being a military requirement only up to about 300 yards, with perhaps occasional use to 500 yards, there is still a feeling that good performance at 600 yards or further guarantee an excellent performance at shorter range. It is also clear that the standard rifle cartridge already satisfactorily served both machine-gun and rifle and that, in consequence, the elimination of the rifle would not see a corresponding simplification in ammunition requirements. The 7·62 mm NATO cartridge is assuredly now much shorter than the old First World War rifle cartridges but still large to be contained in magazines in the quantities required in a machine-carbine cum rifle. It also might be argued that the 7·62 mm NATO cartridge has already gone so far in the direction of lightening of the bullet that long-range machine-gun performance has been impaired. If the 144-grain bullet in the NATO round is directly compared at 1,200 yards with a 173-grain bullet loaded into the same case the advantage of the latter is most marked. It would, in short, seem likely that any further reduction in length in the 7·62 mm cartridge, to make its use in an M1 type weapon more practical, would be at the expense of machine-gun performance.

The inter-war years saw no magical substitution of an automatic rifle for existing bolt-action types. Indeed, the Second World War was very much, from the infantryman's point of view, so far as his primary arm was concerned, an extension of the First World War. The need to re-design the form of components used in the Short, Magazine, Lee Enfield to make it more suitable for modern methods of mass production was recognised. This was done in the Mark VI version which, in due course, emerged as the new No. 4 rifle. Apart from taking the opportunity to change over to an aperture back-sight and to fit a heavier barrel–the lightness of the S.M.L.E.'s barrel had tended to jeopardise its shooting properties–very little else was done. And this was the rifle with which the British forces were slowly re-equipped through the 1930s and through most of the Second World War itself. The German Mauser 1898 underwent a somewhat similar, if less drastic, face lift. The Russians, too, saw the Second War through with the bolt action Mosin Nagant as their basic infantry weapon. This apparent inertia in the improvement of the rifle does not, in fact, do justice to the endeavours that were being made by many countries to find a really satisfactory automatic rifle and put it into as general issue as possible. The Americans won the race, if it ever really amounted to that. By the end of the war their Garand had entirely replaced the bolt-action Springfield.

The Garand semi-automatic rifle, the M1 rifle as 304
it was designated, fired from a breech locked by the rotation of a breech-block so that its lugs engaged in matching recesses on the receiver. It accepted the ·30 US rifle cartridge and was loaded with a special 8-round clip through the top of the action in a manner similar to the Mannlicher though the ejection of the clip was upwards rather than through the bottom of the magazine. The Garand was sighted to 1,200 yards, a practical maximum for the employment of direct rifle fire in all but the most skilled hands, and since it was a rifle rather than a machine-gun or pistol it could be fired only in single shots. This also avoided the need for any special arrangements for cooling.

Between the wars the British arms firm of Vickers, whose name is forever recurring in the whole field of arms design and production, produced experimentally Pedersen's automatic rifle. It used a toggle 305
and operated more as a hesitation lock than as a fully locked breech. It failed, however, without cartridge lubrication, to avoid a serious risk of base separation on the first and rather violent expulsion of the case from the chamber. The British armed forces did not therefore find themselves in the embarrassing position of being compelled to ignore a successful military design produced by a British firm–a situation which almost certainly would have arisen judging from the British Government's inability to appreciate the significance of the development of the submachine-gun in the same period and from the spirit of complacency and self-congratulation abroad

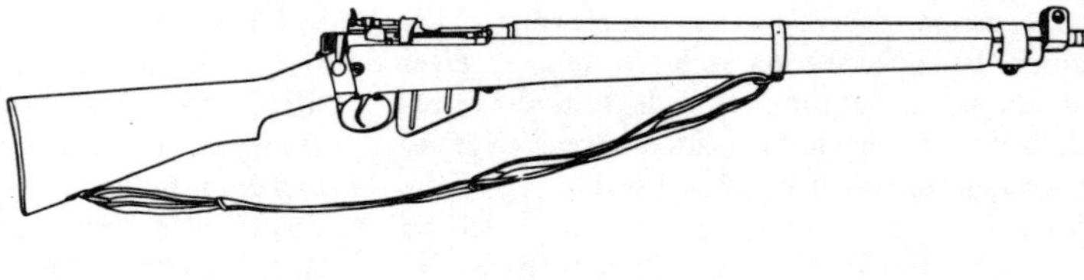

The Lee-Enfield Rifle No. 4, developed in order to facilitate mass-production and which armed most of the British and Commonwealth armies in the Second World War. Imperial War Museum, London.

that the Lee Enfield had in the First World War demonstrated itself to be undoubtedly the fastest and most serviceable type of military bolt-action rifle.

The Russians were far more conscious of the military potential of semi-automatic rifles. Even in the First World War they had been experimenting with different ideas and in 1936 they first issued, on a restricted basis, the Simonov rifle. It had a locked breech and was gas operated but was too compli-
306 cated. In 1938 an improved arm, the Tokarev, followed and this was modified in 1940. The Tokarev was rather too light in construction for all conditions of service but sufficiently successful in its use on the Eastern Front to make the Germans facing it very much aware of its merit. The 1941 German semi-automatic rifles, which were consequently developed, varied in type but used a muzzle-trap to harness the gases. Neither the W nor the rare M type were very satisfactory. With one weighing almost 11 lb and the other $11\frac{1}{2}$ lb they were very heavy and, though the breech was securely locked, subject to derangement through the accumulation of gas fouling. The Gewehr 42, which was developed as a parachutist arm, was an interesting compromise between an automatic rifle and light machine-gun. Whilst it drew heavily upon accepted design features it was novel in execution and at $10\frac{1}{2}$ lb reasonably light. It rather fascinatingly combined in its specification a bayonet and a bipod, and the American Johnson Light machine-gun's arrangement of firing with the breech closed on single shots for accuracy and open in automatic fire for cooling, with the breech lock of the Lewis. The Gewehr 43 was clearly in the line of development of the pure automatic rifle. It represented a considerable improvement on the 41. It relied on a more conventional form of gas operation and a neater breech-lock and block. The weight of the arm was reduced to under 9 lb and its reliability under active service conditions immeasurably improved. Setting aside the different unit of measurement, as with the Garand the Gewehr 43 was sighted to 1,200 metres and was air cooled since only single shots were available. The provision made for a telescope sight and the absence of a bayonet mounting indicate that the Germans viewed the use of this arm more as a supporting weapon than as an arm for assaulting infantrymen. The Gewehr 43 was reasonably well made but still required accurate internal machining. It was not, therefore, an arm suitable for mass production at very high speed in a country already severely hit by war. By 1944 Germany wanted something much simpler and she found it in a design first suggested by Haenel in 1942.

The Volksturm Gewehr that Germany put into front line service in 1945 was one of the most remarkable weapons of the war. The unprecedented simplicity of manufacture evinced in its design still gives to this arm great importance. In that it dispensed with almost all the machinery normally used in arms manufacture it could be produced clandestinely almost anywhere under almost any conditions. The form of breech-lock it employed was so original that it does not easily fit into the usual scheme of classification. It appears to be a blowback weapon but the fact that it handled the 7·92 mm short rifle cartridge shows that it was no ordinary blowback system. A special tubular jacket, containing barrel and breech-block, was used to check the rearwards movement of the latter on the opening of the breech. The jacket itself was checked from running easily to the rear by the use of gas tapped through gas ports a short way from the muzzle. This gas was so directed against the front interior of the jacket that it tended to move forward, thus countering the breech-block's otherwise violent rearward displacement. In many respects the Volksturm Gewehr was one of the most interesting designs to emerge from the Second World War and undoubtedly the most original of an important group of automatic rifles.

It is clearly impossible here to deal at any length with the many experimental arms which almost invariably link main models. The British automatic rifle known as the E.M.2 was of rather unorthodox form, but conventional in its gas operation. For all the intense controversy that raged over the essentially political reasons for its being discarded in favour of a common NATO arm it must be regarded as of transient importance, though the more recent American Armalite semi-automatic rifles imitate its interesting combination of back-sight and carrying handle. The rifle which the British army adopted in its stead, the

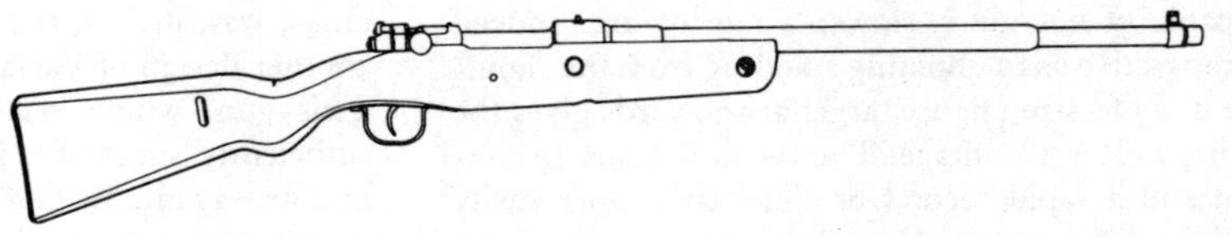

The 'Volkssturm Gewehr' was an emergency rifle design produced in Germany in the closing months of the war and intended to arm local Home Guard units. Smithsonian Institution, Washington, D.C.

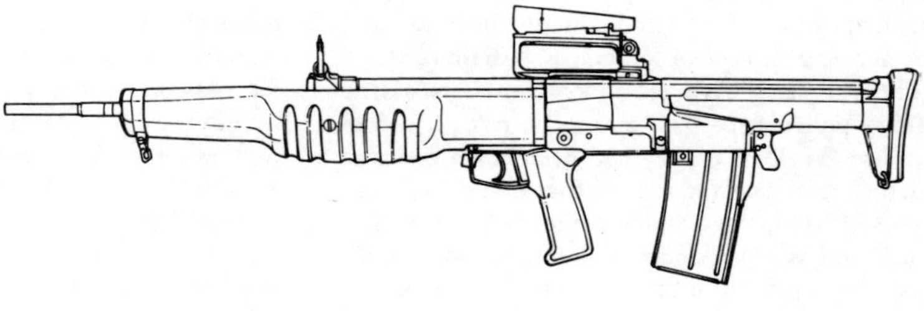

The British EM2 experimental rifle in 7 mm calibre, a 'bullpup' design in which the breech lies alongside the firer's face. RSAF, Enfield.

308 Belgian F.N., is one, however, which very distinctly falls into the other category. The basic idea for this rifle, which was designed by an F.N. engineer by the name of Saive, originated in an earlier pattern arm dating back to 1940. In its later form it has gone into issue in rather more than thirty countries including, beside Great Britain and many of the major Commonwealth and ex-Commonwealth countries, West Germany, Israel, Belgium and the Netherlands.

There is no doubting the reliability inherent in this Belgian design and its short-range accuracy of fire has long since been demonstrated but, if a direct comparison is made with, for example, the British No. 4 service rifle, the comparison does not show as much in favour of the more modern arm as might be expected. The large magazine vertically placed beneath the F.N. prevents the firer adopting as low a position as can be achieved with the No. 4, which can easily be fired, even with considerable precision, from a very low position, taking advantage of any cover available, perhaps not more than a slight fold in the ground. The F.N.'s magazine is also most inconveniently positioned for those with rather short arms. Indeed, for such individuals it is very difficult to find a comfortable, effective position. Compared with the No. 4 the action is so long that a short butt, the remedy for short-armed soldiers with the bolt-action weapon, may only have the effect of allowing the sight to bruise or more seriously damage the firer's face. Without any doubt the No. 4 rifle is more accurate if compared through the ranges to 600 yards and, probably, in the hands of an expert, capable of not much slower a rate of fire. Indeed comparative snap-shooting standing from the shoulder at a life-sized figure target at 100 yards gives the No. 4 a clear advantage. The recoil is easier to control and a rapid second or third shot more easily delivered. Of course the emphasis is inevitably on the firer having been trained to a high level of efficiency. The military advantage of the automatic rifle lies in the fact that it substitutes mechanical or automatic operation for that dexterity which it requires months of training to possess and retain subconsciously under any battle conditions.

Anyone who has helped to bring a Vickers medium machine-gun into operation, or even more so who has had the task of carrying the tripod, will most emphatically endorse the practical advantage of the light machine-gun. In the form of, for example, the Bren there was little that the Vickers could do which the lighter weapon could not attempt and it weighed only about 22 lb. The Bren was 309
derived from a Czech design, the ZB26, largely the outcome of work by the two Holek brothers, and gained its name from a combination of the two towns, Brno and Enfield. It was so satisfactory a weapon that it was still in service forty years after it first came into use. In its standard form this gas-piston-operated machine-gun was fired from a bipod which could easily be folded flat when, for instance, the gun was used from the hip. A tripod weighing about 30 lb converted the Bren into a medium machine-gun for such tasks as firing on fixed lines at night, whilst a monopod transformed it into a reasonably effective anti-aircraft weapon. The gun could quite easily be fired at a rate of four magazines a minute and be kept in action at this pace by changing barrels. It was the work of a few seconds only to exchange barrels and it was supposed not to harm a hot barrel totally to submerge it in water, if it was at hand, for rapid cooling. The ·303 rimmed case led to a very curved form of magazine and that, from its top mounting, to the use of offset sights. The Bren was far from the only product of Czech designers in this period.

The BESA, a British 7·92 mm Second World War machine-gun for such applications as mounting in tanks, was, in fact, the Czech ZB 53 machine-gun, another design of Vaclav Holek introduced in 1937. This gun, which was also gas operated, proved sufficiently successful for a 15mm version also to find its way into British service. In some respects the design was unusual; in its cocking arrangement it was without an imitator. Though there were other Czech designs of merit and importance, as the ZB 50 of 1932, it was the Germans who really set the pace in the development of machine-guns between the wars. The Versailles Treaty had the effect of channeling German arms design and production through

287 The German Walther Pistole '38, which replaced the P'08 Parabellum in 1942 since it was easier to mass-produce. Imperial War Museum, London.

288 The Italian Army's Beretta Model of 1934 in 9 mm Short calibre, which replaced the less-reliable Glisenti. Imperial War Museum, London.

289 The 7·65 mm calibre Walther PPK (Polizei Pistole, Kriminal) designed for plain-clothes detectives but widely adopted by the Luftwaffe and by German staff officers. Imperial War Museum, London.

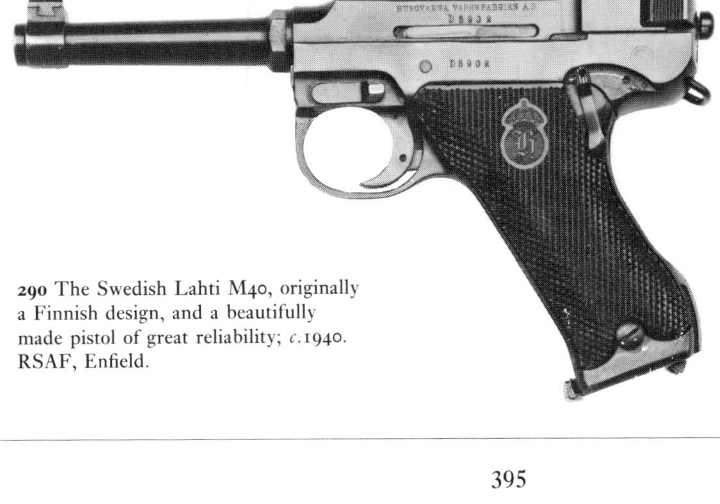

290 The Swedish Lahti M40, originally a Finnish design, and a beautifully made pistol of great reliability; *c.*1940. RSAF, Enfield.

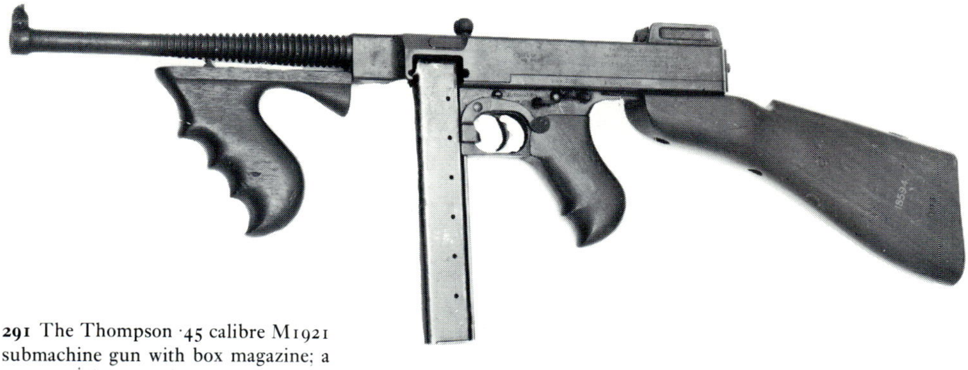

291 The Thompson ·45 calibre M1921 submachine gun with box magazine; a 50-round drum could also be fitted. Imperial War Museum, London.

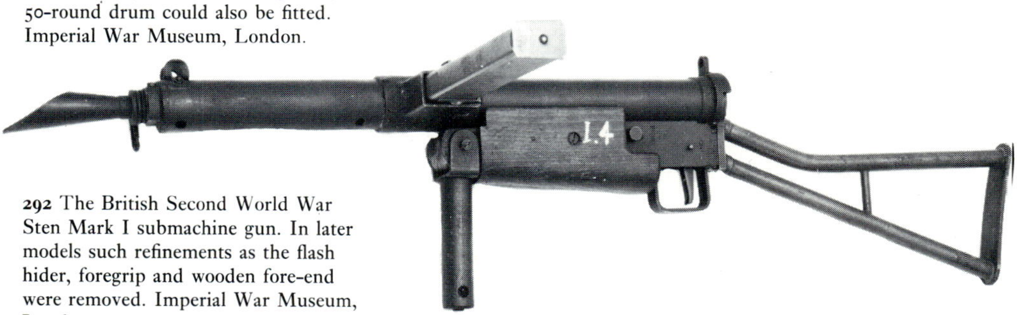

292 The British Second World War Sten Mark I submachine gun. In later models such refinements as the flash hider, foregrip and wooden fore-end were removed. Imperial War Museum, London.

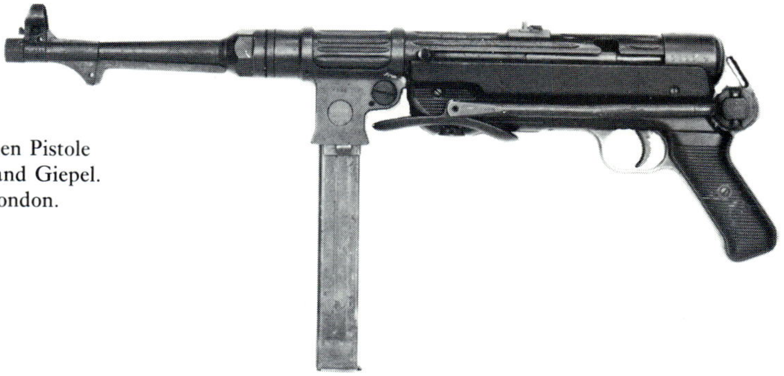

293 The German Maschinen Pistole '38, designed by Vollmer and Giepel. Imperial War Museum, London.

294 The American submachine gun M3, commonly called the 'Grease Gun' from its shape. Normally in ·45 calibre, it could be rapidly converted to a 9 mm calibre if necessary. Imperial War Museum, London.

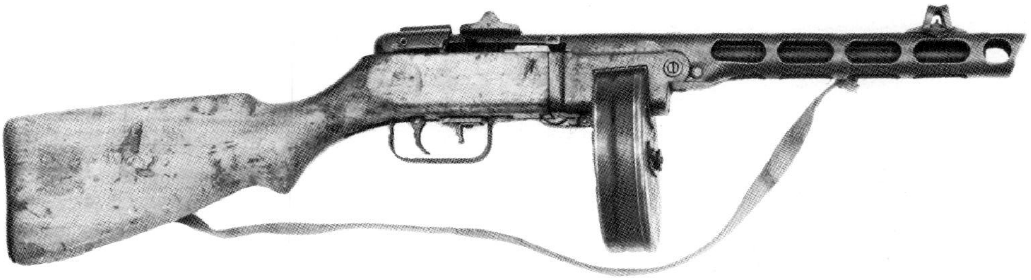

295 The Soviet PPSH 41 submachine gun in 7·62 mm calibre, an immensely robust weapon of which several million were made during the Second World War. Imperial War Museum, London.

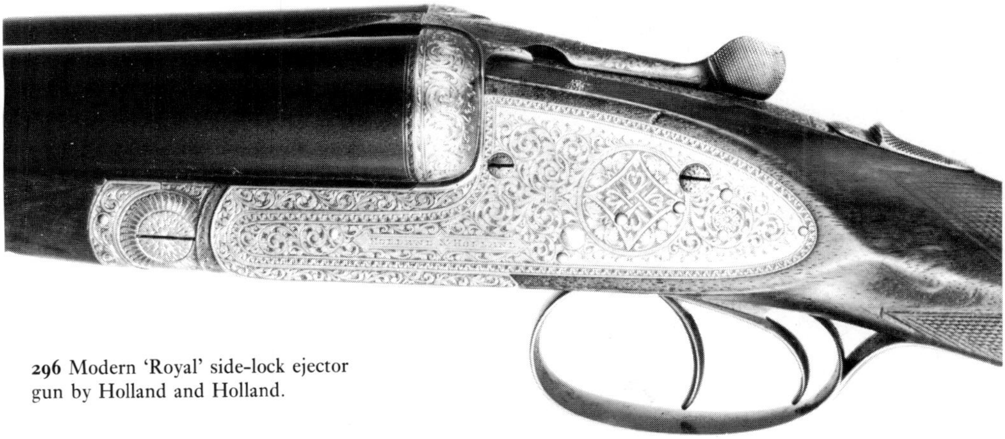

296 Modern 'Royal' side-lock ejector gun by Holland and Holland.

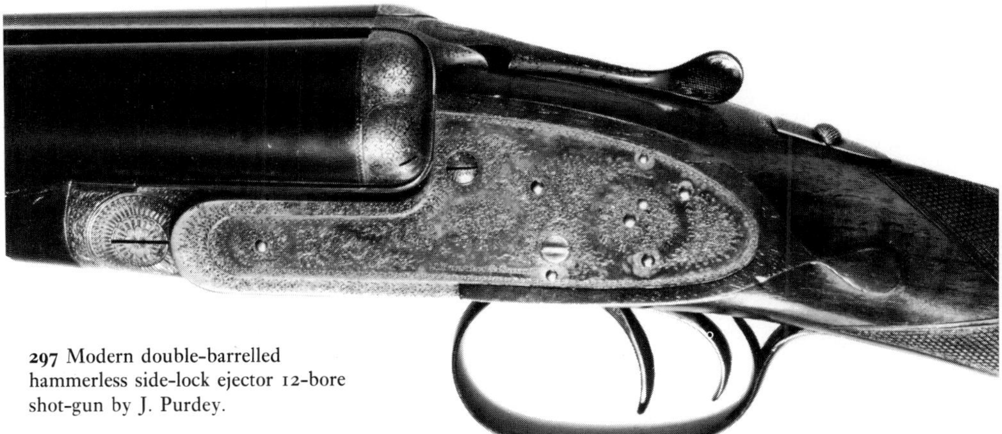

297 Modern double-barrelled hammerless side-lock ejector 12-bore shot-gun by J. Purdey.

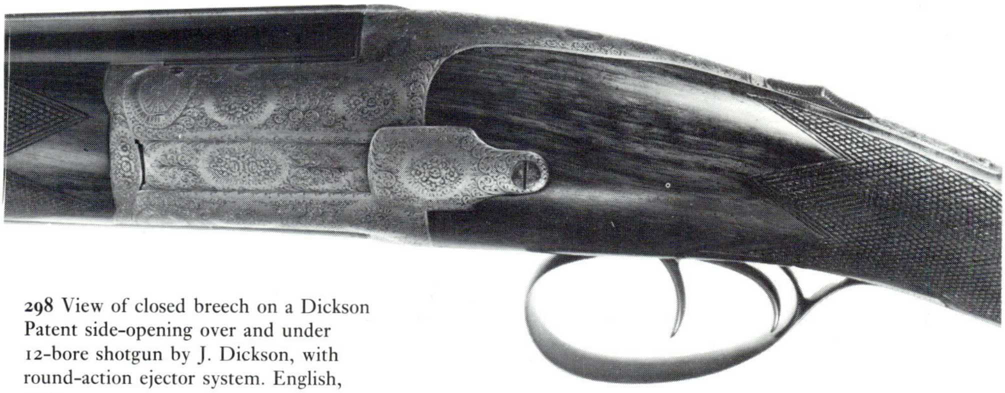

298 View of closed breech on a Dickson Patent side-opening over and under 12-bore shotgun by J. Dickson, with round-action ejector system. English, 1952.

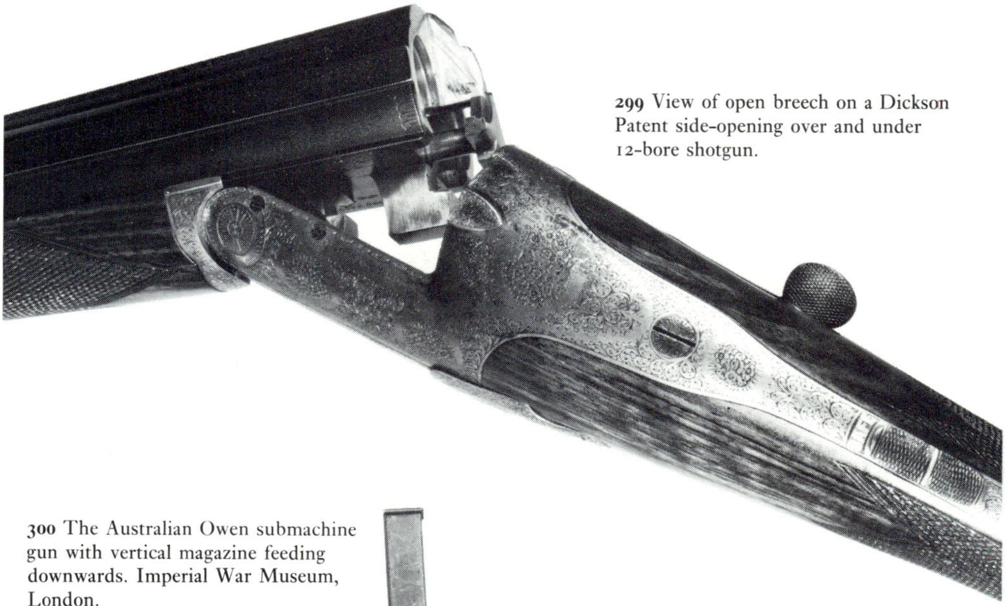

299 View of open breech on a Dickson Patent side-opening over and under 12-bore shotgun.

300 The Australian Owen submachine gun with vertical magazine feeding downwards. Imperial War Museum, London.

The Besa 7.92 mm calibre Tank machine gun, a Czech design adopted by Britain. Imperial War Museum, London.

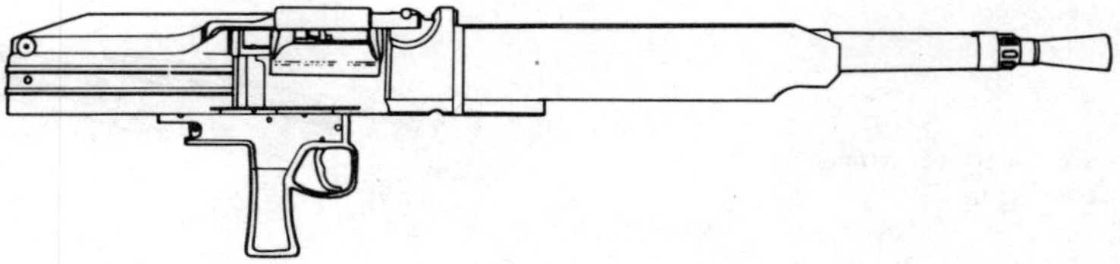

such foreign based outlets as Solothurn in Switzerland. Various models, prominent among which were those of 1929 and 1930, achieved some success but it was the official German model of 1934 which really became celebrated. It was designed as a general purpose machine-gun handling the standard 7·92 mm cartridge and was, in this sense, also a consequence of the Treaty of Versailles since that had banned German manufacture of heavier conventional machine-guns. It represented no revolutionary step forward in design but merely an improvement of basic mechanisms, already expatiated, by
310 Mauser, Maxim and Mannlicher. The MG 34 went into service in 1936 and was subject to later modification, particularly in the model known as the MG 81 which was a version intended for use in aircraft and therefore possessing an accelerated rate of fire.

The machine-gun which stands in the development of this class of weapons in much the same light as the MP 38 or Sten stands in the evolution of the
311 submachine-gun is undoubtedly the MG 42. This German gun was not a revelation of new theories in design but a most outstanding manifestation of a successful utilisation of modern manufacturing techniques. Almost incidentally it was also a brilliant combination of proved features from earlier designs. The secret of its success lay in the use of pressings rather than machine components. Grunow, an acknowledged expert in this field, revolutionised arms production by applying techniques perfected in other fields of industry. Although initial production was at Grossfuss, Dobeln, this arm was later manufactured by a number of German arsenals. The MG 42 had a somewhat parallel history but fell into the LMG/automatic rifle category. It was the product of Krieghoff of Suhl and almost as outstanding an exposition of the utilisation of pressed components as the MG 42. It was a gas-piston-operated gun somewhat on the lines of the Lewis.

It is possible to catalogue the unorthodox features to be found in the numerous machine-guns which, since 1919, have found sufficient favour to go into service somewhere in the world but it would reveal very little that was entirely new in conception and be quite out of place in this brief survey. The Russian Degtyarev light machine-gun, for example, which weighed only about 19¼ lb unloaded, was most unusual in its class in employing belt feed; the Czech Model 52 light machine-gun will accept either a conventional box magazine or belt. However valuable these features may be militarily they are still minutiae, so indeed in this context are the improvements in the general purpose
machine-gun (G.P.M.G.) of Belgian design which 312
is believed to represent a sufficient advance on the Bren and Vickers to replace those two arms in the British service. For the Belgian FN G.P.M.G. is really no more than a modified Browning automatic rifle. Its appeal stems from its detailed construction from which it derives remarkable versatility. It will, for example, fire any military rifle cartridge, below a certain length, merely by changing to the appropriate barrel. In a most pertinent way the properties that make this F.N. arm the machine-gun of the sixties and the Bren that of the thirties are epitomes of the changes that have occurred in the whole field of arms design since 1918.

A comparatively recent development of interest from the United States is the emergence of a military

The German 'Fallschirmgewehr 42' parachutist's rifle, a remarkable design of selective-fire rifle using full-power 7.92 mm ammunition. Imperial War Museum, London.

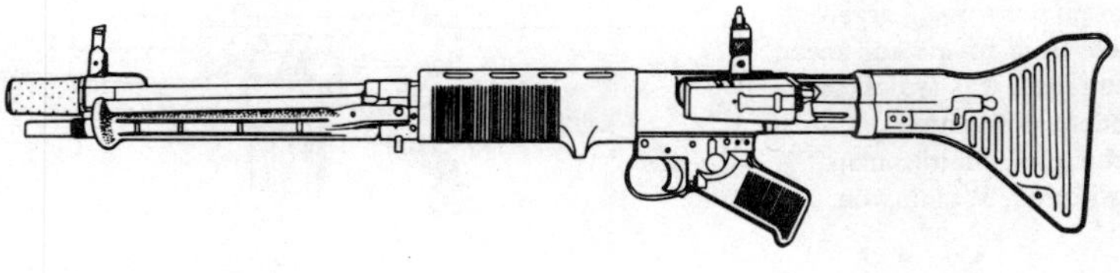

Soviet Degtyarev Model DP machine gun.

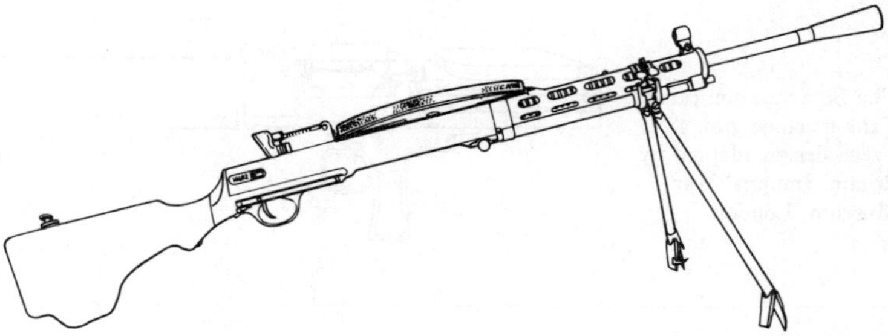

self-loading rifle of particularly light-weight construction firing a bullet of only 0·223 in or 5·56 mm calibre. The AR-15, as it is known, is a product of the Armalite Division of the Fairchild Engine and Airplane Co., though some arms are actually manufactured by Colt, and weighs as little as 6 lb, even with a 20-round magazine attached, so extensively are aluminium and plastics used in its construction. The muzzle velocity of its 55-grain bullet is in the order of 3,200 ft/s. The Armalite AR-15 is extremely unusual in that it is gas operated but avoids the use of a piston. It was even more unusual in military arms, when it first appeared in 7·62 mm NATO calibre, in its use of a steel-lined aluminium barrel. Later a steel barrel was substituted as the weight advantage of a bi-metal one was so slight. In still later arms of this pattern, or rather of the AR-15, the cocking handle was removed from the top of the action to the rear of the receiver. The AR-15 saw considerable use in United States service in Vietnam, where it proved itself a first-rate military arm. As its small-bore bullet has shown itself to possess more than adequate powers of penetration, the major reservation that many must have appears invalid.

Exactly the point reached today in military small arms development in the experimental establishments of the great powers is impossible to establish. It is no secret now that combustible plastic, cartridge cases have been tried successfully in certain arms. A success probably in large part due to the practicability, with manufacturing equipment of the present day, or producing breech obturation by mechanical closure. It is also known that disintegrating projectiles have been tried with real effect and acceptable accuracy at short range. Infra-red scope sights are now quite commonplace and silencers an established feature of even submachine-guns required for special purposes. Of course, military arms are not the only class of weapons which have benefited from recent advances in metallurgy and from the ever widening range of plastics. Sporting and target arms have also undergone an eye-catching face lift.

Revolvers have changed extremely little in the last half century. They have become much less a military and increasingly a target or sporting arm. Aluminium frames and cylinders have been tried but, as the tendency has been to go for more powerful cartridges, they have made little real headway. In America traditional designs have remained firm favourites, some nineteenth-century ones have even stood revival. At the same time, however, manufacturers have devoted themselves to the specialist perfection of the revolver. Police and similar bodies, especially in America, have so much valued the reliability and versatility of the revolver that short-barrelled, covered-hammer types have continued to be developed. Cartridges can fail and the automatic pistol cannot, as can the revolver, replace a defective round instantly with a fresh one. Equally a suitable revolver can be fired from almost any attitude or any place, even from inside a small pocket or when still passed through the loop of its own lanyard, holding

The Armalite rifle introduced the .223 cartridge into military use. Largely made from plastic and metal stampings, it is typical of modern production techniques. Smithsonian Institution, Washington, D.C.

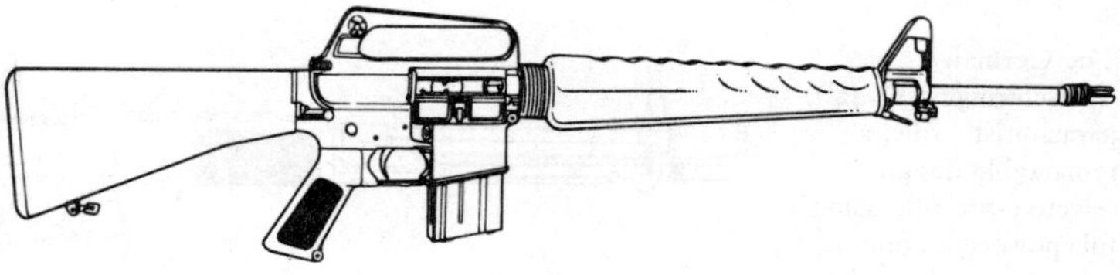

The Beretta .22 calibre 'Tipo Olimpionico' pistol, representative of the specialised weapon required for international competition. Note the balance weight below the barrel and the muzzle compensator. RSAF Enfield.

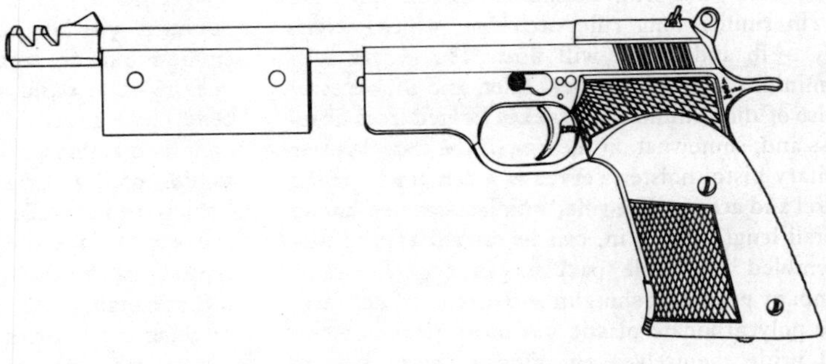

it tight round the waist under the skirt of a jacket, whereas the slide operation of an automatic pistol needs room to the rear. Others have found in the revolver (when fitted with a telescope sight) an effective and challenging short-range stalking arm. To many, a 'scope-sighted' revolver is, perhaps, a symbol of the modern generation of small arms, though present-day small-bore free pistols with their glove-like grips or 0·22 in rapid fire target pistols with their elaborately shaped muzzle weights must run it close.

Target rifles have undergone parallel improvement. One rifle most vividly illustrating this is the B.S.A. Martini-International Mark III which is in the direct line of development of the old Martini service rifles which were converted to 0·22 in. in the early years of the century. The International, which weighs $14\frac{1}{2}$ lb and is fitted with a completely redesigned action giving full adjustment to the trigger and very powerful ejection, does not, for all its refinement, succeed in looking quite so imposing as some of its rivals, especially those designed also for standing and kneeling shooting. Target rifles, such as the Anschutz, with elaborate thumb-hole stock, fully adjustable palm rest and butt hook, and interchangeable trigger mechanisms, represent a really remarkable level of sophistication though their derivation from earlier Schuetzen rifles is very apparent. In contrast, a 0·22 in rifle with simple single-shot bolt action for occasional sporting use can weigh as little as 4 lb and use a nylon stock. Fine walnut is now an extremely expensive commodity and increasingly reserved for top grade sporting, rather than target, arms.

Free rifles of the type made by Schultz and Larsen, Hammerli, Anschutz, Finnish Lion and a number of other Continental makers are also to be found in centrefire calibres. As the cost of such weapons can reach several hundred pounds the popularity of full-bore free rifle shooting is, in many countries, rather restricted. In Great Britain full-bore target shooting with other than military type or sporting rifles is limited to long-range match rifle shooting. The modern form of these rifles differs very little from that in use just before the outbreak of the First World War. Galilean sights are still dominant but telescope sights, often of American manufacture, have now reached such a level of durability and precision that they can safely be employed at ranges up to 1,200 yards. Match rifles made for use in the back position are still much more common than those for prone shooting though the latter have made some headway in the last decade. Increasing leisure and rising affluence leave their mark in greater individuality and more widespread experimentation in match rifle shooting just as they do in allied forms of target shooting such as bench-rest. It is, however, impossible to consider these variations in this context. What the arms companies can sell the public is of greater relevance and, amongst the dozens of rifles that can be bought over the counter, one of the most interesting is the Armalite AR-7 Explorer.

The Armalite 'Explorer' rifle being packed into its hollow butt-stock for carriage. RMCS, Shrivenham.

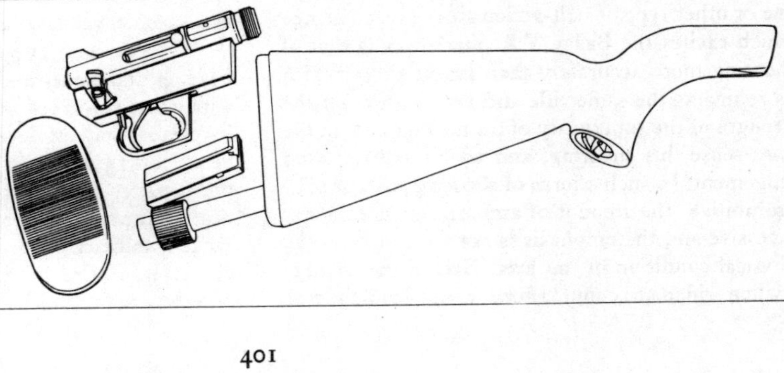

The AR-7 is a semi-automatic rifle, handling the
314 0.22 in rimfire long rifle cartridge, which weighs only $2\frac{3}{4}$ lb and which will float. The barrel is of aluminium alloy with a steel liner, and the receiver is also of aluminium. The stock is formed from fibreglass and, somewhat on the line of the 1896 Mauser military pistol holster, serves as a container for the barrel and action. The rifle, which assembled has an overall length of $34\frac{1}{2}$ in, can be carried around disassembled in a single 'pack' $16\frac{1}{2}$ in long. The same company produce a shotgun with a stock of unbreakable polycarbonate plastic but most manufacturers still pride themselves on offering their shotguns with walnut stocks. The popularity of automatic and slide actions is a dominant feature of American shotguns. While this is soundly based upon the cost advantage of such designs it cannot be said to enhance the lines of the shotgun. The use of substitutes for wood in these arms is therefore more understandable than in double-barrelled guns of either side-by-side or under-and-over construction. Understandably the currency of best quality English side-by-side doubles is rather limited but they, at least, yield nothing to the best guns of the last century in quality and appearance.

It needs little perspicacity to see that the division between military and target or sporting arms is growing wider all the time. Of course there are many points of contact. Mention has only to be made of the American Model 1911 0·45 in automatic pistol or of the British No. 4 SR(a) or (b) rifle as reminders of this contact. There is, however, no denying the fact that, whilst lessons learnt in the design of the AR-15 may be of considerable value in the production of survival arms for the civilian market, or those learnt in the manufacture of the Sterling submachine-gun may be of use to those requiring a police-type single-shot carbine, there is a vast gulf between the free or target rifle and the military self-loading arm. The fundamental difference is extremely simple and very obvious; the paramount military requirement is rapidity of fire while the dominant civilian requirement is accuracy. There are exceptions, but, generally, this is true. In Great Britain the army now carries the F.N. 7·62 mm self-loading rifle but civilian marksmen still compete for the Queen's Prize with one or other type of bolt-action rifle. The challenge which excites the Bisley T.R. marksman is that of shooting more accurately than his neighbour with more or less the same rifle and ammunition on the strength of the superiority of his holding and, in the pure sense, his shooting, and on his skill in wind judgement. In such a form of shooting costs are not prohibitive–the amount of ammunition fired is not excessive and the emphasis is not too much on the physical condition of the firer. Even if the average civilian rifleman could afford a self-loading rifle costing three times as much as his present arm it is doubtful whether he would want to pay for the ammunition he would be bound to expend in military-style rapid shooting. The alternative of a benevolent government providing F.N. rifles and unlimited ammunition is not only most unlikely but would entail a surrender of that independence of outlook and attitude which characterises marksmen and would have the unacceptable consequence of eliminating the elderly and infirm. Thus, inevitably and inexorably, the military and civilian aspects of shooting are drawing apart and their arms are becoming more divergent. The extent to which this present tendency can or will continue is difficult to forecast but in many countries, where the ties between military authorities and civilian marksmen organisations are strong and vitally important if shooting is to remain a popular sport, a serious dilemma is inevitable.

In terms of basic firearms design the past half century has been a period of comparative stagnation though not more so than over similar periods in the pre-nineteenth century era. Recent years have seen the almost universal introduction of non-corrosive primers, which take the sting out of cleaning arms and undoubtedly contribute considerably to the life of the average gun. The mere fact that this is a development of a form of ignition first introduced over a hundred years ago underlines the insignificance of attempts to harness electrical ignition to small arms. The continued improvement of metal, powders and plastics offers hopes of the wider production of almost indestructible weapons of extremely light weight but, perhaps, nothing looks more interesting in its potential for future development and general application than the Gyrojet.

The rocket is a military weapon of considerable antiquity and, even in a comparatively portable form, no novelty. MB Associates of California have, however, in their ·50 calibre Gyrojet handgun, which was first announced in 1965, succeeded in producing a weapon which may have a wide potential. The use of small rocket projectiles in the place of ordinary cartridges has the merit of allowing an extremely simple loading and firing mechanism. The elimination of recoil is also an advantage but at the price of a very low muzzle velocity. Provided that the enemy or quarry is at least 15 yards distant full velocity can develop and penetration is more than comparable with most revolvers and pistols. Unfortunately, in its present state of development the object needs to be at least 15 in in diameter at 25 yards to be within the capacity of the arm to strike it. If therefore a negligible protective or offensive value at very short range is militarily acceptable and if the conspicuous character of the rocket ignition flash is not too revealing the Gyrojet stands, at the present time, as an alternative to a military semi-automatic pistol or revolver. For all its deficiencies, and they are slight considering the measure of evolution that it represents from orthodox arms, the Gyrojet is one of the most interesting developments of this century and may be a pointer to the future.

Firearms in the 1970s

Technical advances in firearms during the last ten years have not thrown up much in the way of new principles of operation; the tendency has been more toward adaptation of weapons to fit specific roles and rationalisation of designs to suit the economic climate.

Taking the case of pistols first, we have seen an interesting reappearance of the machine-pistol idea. The automatic pistol adapted to full-automatic fire so as to function as a species of submachine-gun has appeared at various times since the Mauser imitations made in Spain in the late 1920s; it has rarely been a success because its combination of light weight and a high rate of fire has invariably produced an uncontrollable weapon. In the 1960s a number of automatic rifles appeared with a 'burst-fire facility', a selector mechanism which permitted a rapid discharge of three to five shots for a single pressure of the trigger. This was claimed to increase the chance of hitting whilst reducing unnecessary waste of ammunition. The idea does not appear to have prospered on rifles, but in the middle 1970s it appeared in the Heckler & Koch VP70 pistol. This was a conventional blow-

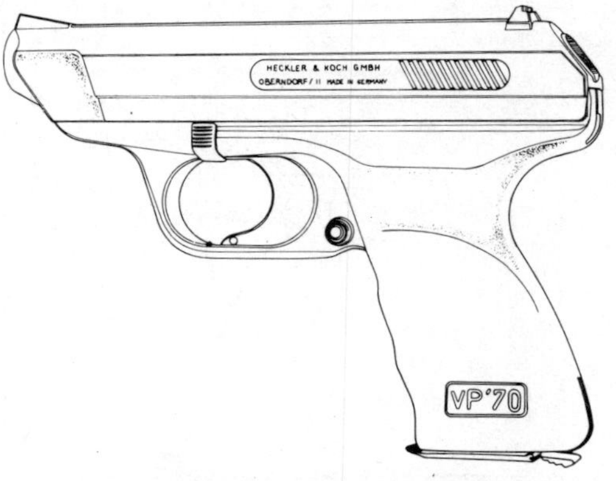

Heckler & Koch VP70 9mm calibre pistol uses plastic-coated steel for its frame in order to reduce maintenance demands. Heckler & Koch GmbH., Oberndorf.

back design chambered for the 9mm Parabellum cartridge and with an 18-round magazine in the butt. In the hand-held mode it functions as a normal pistol, but by attaching an accessory shoulder-stock a selector mechanism is automatically activated which provides for firing three-round bursts at a cyclic rate of 2,200 rounds per minute. Limited numbers are reported to have been bought by various South American governments, but widespread adoption will depend upon the results of various acceptance tests now in progress with various of the major armies of the world.

Economic factors are illustrated by the current SIG-Sauer pistols. The SIG company is well able to manufacture pistols of the highest quality; their P–210 is still ranked among the finest pistols in history. But they are severely restricted in their overseas sales by the controls on weapons traffic set up by the Swiss Government. They have therefore allied themselves with the well-known German manufacturers, J. P. Sauer & Son of Eckernförde. SIG produce the designs while Sauer manufacture the pistols and, due to the less restrictive market regulations in West Germany, sell them throughout the world. In fact, the designs have several features of pre-war Sauer pistols in them, notably the ability to use a thumb-lever to cock or safely let down the double-action hammer. These SIG-Sauer pistols are robust and efficient military and police weapons available in a variety of calibres.

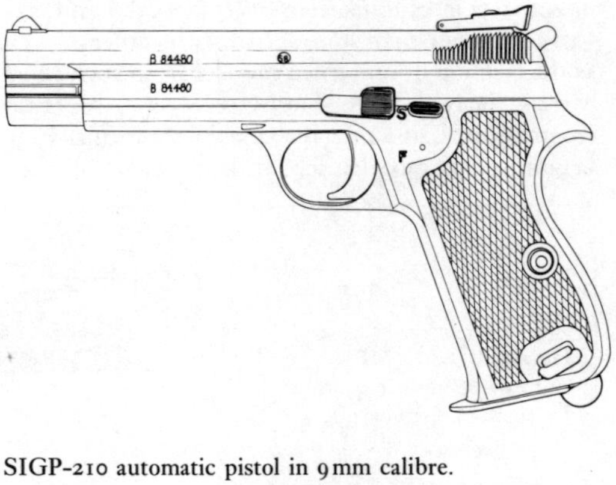

SIGP-210 automatic pistol in 9mm calibre.

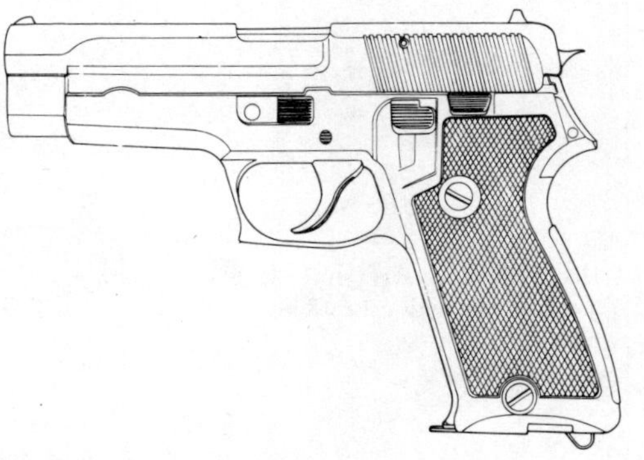

SIG-Sauer P220 service pistol, a combination of SIG and Sauer design, built in Germany to simplify marketing and export problems.

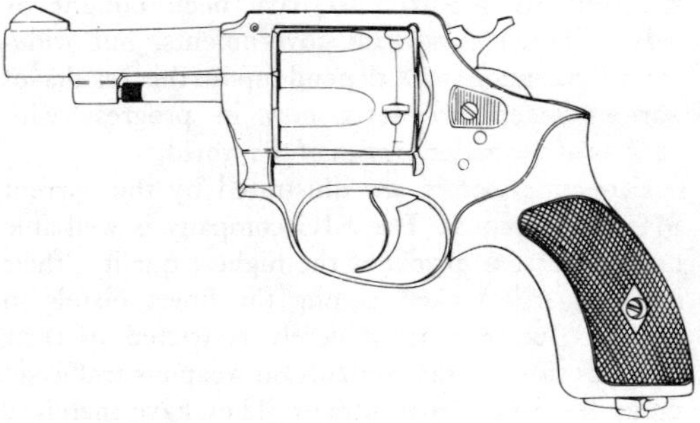

New Nambu 60

The civilian shooting scene has witnessed a remarkable rise of interest in 'combat' or 'practical' pistol shooting contests, in which speed, agility and accuracy in various simulated 'combat situations' are at a premium. This has, in consequence, led to a sudden rush of lightweight and compact pistols in the heavier 'combat' calibres. Short-barrelled revolvers for police use are no novelty, but these were usually to be found in 0·38 in or less, whilst the 0·44 in and 0·45 in calibres were solely available in long-barrelled models. In spite of ballistic problems, such as the ejection of unburned powder from such short barrels, heavy-calibre 'snub' revolvers are fairly commonplace, and now the smaller companies have begun to look more closely at the prospect of compact semi-automatic pistols. Thus, the USA has seen the arrival of, for example, the Detonics 0·45 in, a compacted variant of the well-known Colt M1911A1 pattern. Only 6·75 in long, with a 3 in barrel, and weighing 31·5 oz, the magazine of the Detonics carries six rounds of standard ·45 ACP ammunition. Another approach to this question of miniaturisation is found in the (also American) Semmerling LM–4 0·45 in pistol. This, though it resembles a semi-automatic, is actually manually operated; after firing one shot the slide is manually thrust forward to eject the spent case and then pulled back to chamber the next round from the 4 round magazine. In many respects it parallels the action of the 1908 Schwarzlose 'blow-forward' pistol. The LM–4 is a mere 5·2 in long and 22 oz in weight, and it seems doubtful that anyone will manage to produce a 0·45 in weapon much smaller than this.

The difficulty which arises with these compact pistols is that the recoil energy, which is proportional to the ratio between bullet weight and pistol weight, rises to somewhat high levels, and it takes considerable skill and practice to be able to shoot accurately and consistently with them. It used to be said that the Colt M1911A1 was a hard pistol to learn with, and that weighed 48 oz; the prospect of firing the same cartridge out of a pistol weighing less than half that is not one to be contemplated lightly.

The last ten years has also seen the gradual decline

Heckler & Koch MP5A3 submachine gun in 9mm Parabellum chambering.

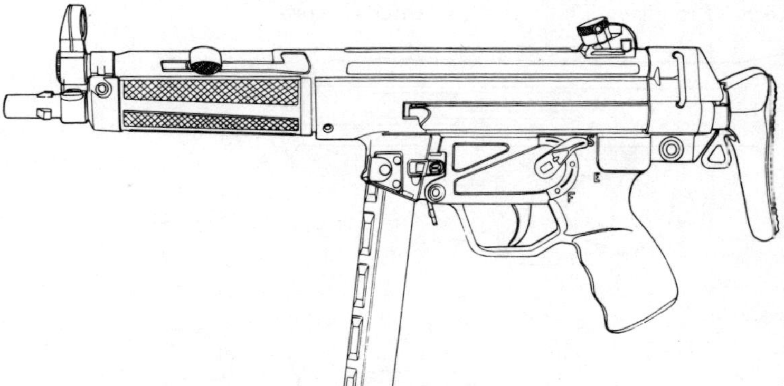

Heckler & Koch KH33A3 5.56mm rifle with collapsible butt.

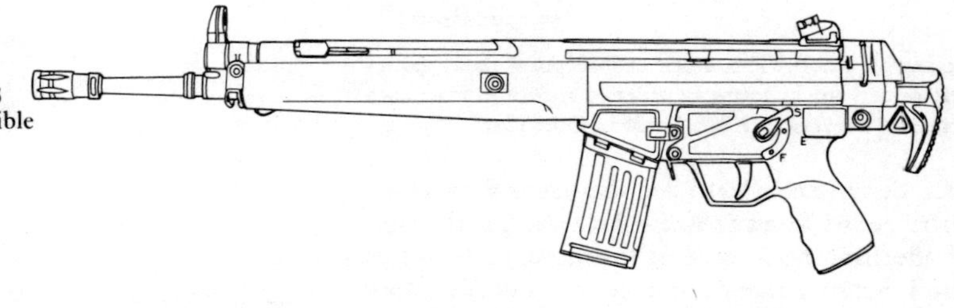

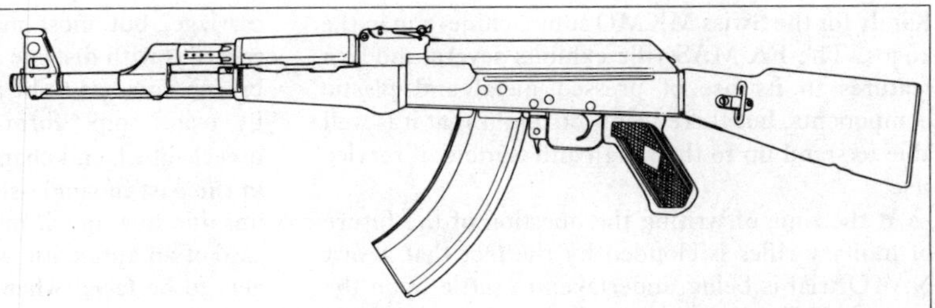

The Soviet AKM Kalashnikov assault rifle in 7.62 mm calibre, a variant of the original AK developed with mass-production in mind. RSAF Enfield.

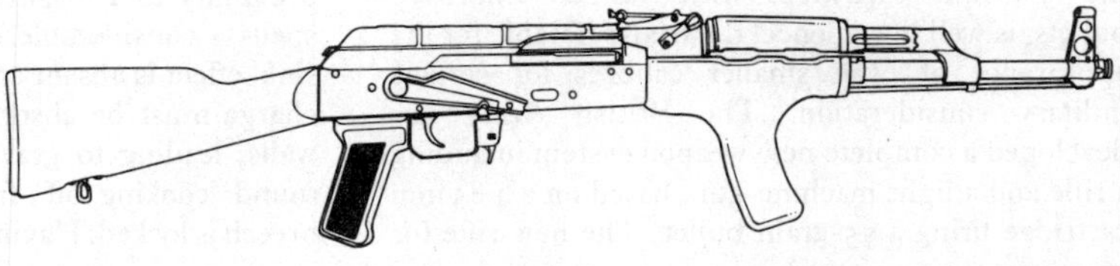

Indicative of the narrow margin between assault rifle and submachine gun is this East German variation of the Soviet AK rifle, fitted with fore-hand grip. RSAF Enfield.

of the submachine-gun. Although one or two new designs have been put forward, none appear to have been accepted for service or put into serious production and, in general, the major forces of the world have relegated the submachine-gun to the reserve. The reason for this has been the concurrent rise in importance of the assault rifle; in many cases these rifles weigh little more than a submachine-gun and are of similar size, and they can function equally well in either the rifle or the submachine-gun role. In the Soviet Army the AK and AKM rifles have completely replaced the formerly ubiquitous submachine-guns, and some Warsaw Pact armies have even gone so far as to fit forward hand-grips to their AK rifles to complete the illusion. An interesting compromise is shown by the Colt
315 'Commando' 5·56 mm weapon: this is variously called an assault rifle or a submachine-gun and is nothing more than the standard Colt-Armalite 5·56 mm AR–15 rifle reduced in length and with a telescoping butt to make it even smaller. The barrel is reduced to 10 in, and with the butt collapsed the whole weapon is only 28 in long. It is thus short and compact enough to be handled as a submachine-gun yet it fires a bullet which is acceptable as a rifle round to medium ranges. A very similar weapon, also based on the AR–15 rifle, is the Atchisson Submachine Gun, but this is chambered for the 9 mm Parabellum cartridge. This allows the weapon to be even shorter, with an overall length of 24 in, but of course it lacks the 200–400 yard range capability of the 'Commando'.

In the rifle field the 5·56 mm cartridge has become virtually the standard for assault rifles. Among the interesting designs which have appeared in the 1970s are the Israeli 'Galil', the Finnish Valmet M71/S, the Italian Beratta 70/223, the Spanish CETME Model L and the Swiss SIG SG540. All these are more or less conventional gas-actuated weapons of normal appearance, in contrast to the French FA MAS 5·56 mm rifle which is currently being issued to the French Army. This is a 'bull-pup' design in which the breech is located almost at the rear of the stock and thus under the firer's cheek. Such a configuration allows the maximum length of barrel for a given length of rifle and permits a compact design of weapon. Operation is by a delayed blowback system using a bolt moving in a bolt carrier and controlled by a delay lever, a system with some points of resemblance to that developed by

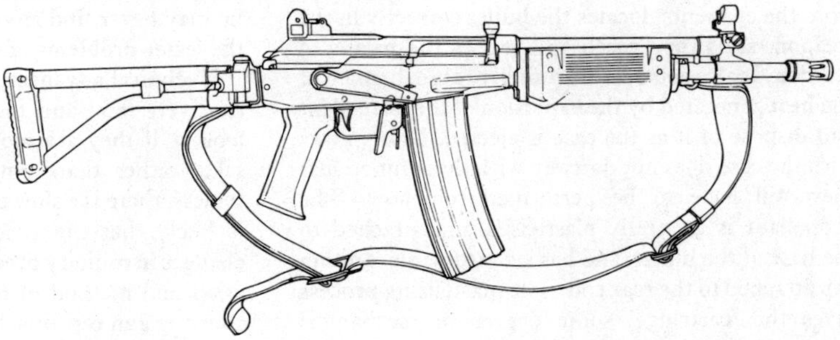

The Israeli Galil 5.56 mm assault rifle; this is the 'SAR' type with short barrel and folding stock; others are the 'ARM' with bipod and long barrel, and the 'AR' with long barrel. Masami Tokoi.

Kiraly for the Swiss MKMO submachine-gun in the 1930s. The FA MAS rifle exhibits several modern features in its use of pressed metal and plastic components, but there seems no doubt that it is well able to stand up to the rough and tumble of service use.

At the time of writing the question of the future of military rifles is clouded by the fact that a vast NATO trial is being undertaken to settle upon the next NATO generation of infantry weapons. While the 5·56 mm cartridge, with various improved bullets, is well in evidence, the trial is notable for the appearance of even smaller calibres for serious military consideration. The British Army has developed a complete new weapon system including a rifle and a light machine-gun, based on a 4·85 mm cartridge firing a 55-grain bullet. The new rifle (or 'Individual Weapon') is, like the French FA MAS, a 'bullpup' design, is extremely compact (30 in long and 8·5 lb in weight), robust and accurate. Gas-operated, it can be fired either at single shot or automatic and is provided with a robust low-power optical sight. No figures as to accuracy or range have been released, but it has been officially stated that the performance of the new cartridge is well in excess of NATO requirements.

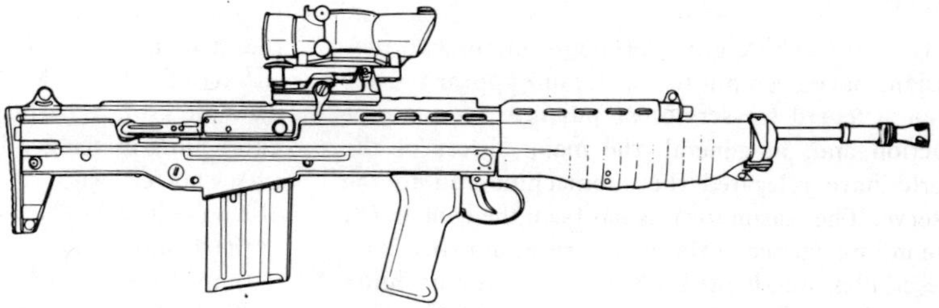

British 4.85 mm 'Individual Weapon' automatic rifle.

Even more innovative is the German entrant in the trial. This is a rifle firing a caseless 4·7 mm round. The caseless cartridge idea has been widely promoted for forty years or more but there are immense practical difficulties in its way. The conventional brass (or steel) case serves several purposes; it contains the propellant, preserves it from the elements, locates the bullet correctly in the weapon, seals the breech and carries the means of ignition. It also acts as a 'heat sink' to absorb much of the heat generated by the explosion of the propellant and dispose of it as the case is ejected. Doing away with the case does not do away with these functions; they still have to be performed somehow. The propellant is generally plasticised and attached to the base of the bullet, and has a consumable ignition cap attached to the rear end. The plasticising process gives the 'cartridge' some degree of mechanical strength to withstand the stresses of loading and carriage, but most military (and civil) authorities regard it with distaste as a fire hazard. Sealing of the breech now has to be accomplished by the weapon, by using some form of expanding seal between breech-block and chamber; this has proved difficult in the past in single-shot weapons, and we can well imagine how much more difficult it must be in the case of an automatic weapon. There are grave dangers to be faced when the question of misfires and hangfires arise; opening a hangfire breech in close proximity to a magazine full of uncased cartridges spells a considerable hazard. And finally the 'heat sink' effect is absent and all the heat of the exploded charge must be absorbed by the weapon chamber walls, leading to grave danger of a freshly-loaded round 'cooking off' from induced heat before the breech is locked. Having said all this, the fact remains that if the German Army are sufficiently confident to enter such a weapon into a serious and major trial, then they must have gone a very long way to solving all these difficult problems.

In the sporting arms world the last ten years have not exhibited very much that is new. As already noted, 'practical' pistol shooting enjoys popularity, while trap and skeet shotgun shooting is undergoing what can only be called a boom. Black powder shooting, using either genuine old weapons or some of the many modern replica pistols and rifles currently made is also extremely popular. Shotguns and blackpowder weapons are less severely regulated at the moment than more powerful arms and thus the average enthusiast, who is reluctant to go to immense trouble to own a high-powered rifle which he may never find anywhere to shoot, will settle for the lesser problems of owning one of these.

Technical advances in firearms design are, today, relatively few; and those which appear frequently look as if they are modifications for modification's sake, rather than genuine improvements. Nevertheless, there is a slow current of improvement and it is likely that the 1980s may see some significant changes in military firearms in the way of miniaturisation and method of manufacture. The hand-built sporting gun remains, but in the military world, that type of weapon has gone for ever.

301 The British Sterling submachine gun which replaced the Sten and has been adopted by several other countries throughout the world; 1954. Imperial War Museum, London.

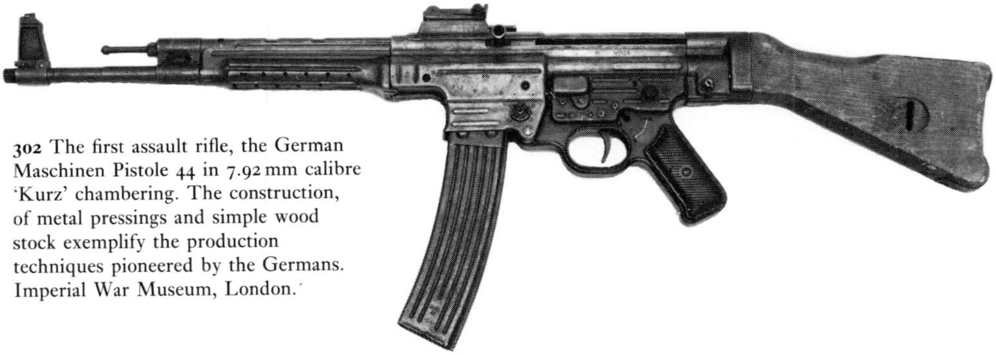

302 The first assault rifle, the German Maschinen Pistole 44 in 7.92 mm calibre 'Kurz' chambering. The construction, of metal pressings and simple wood stock exemplify the production techniques pioneered by the Germans. Imperial War Museum, London.

303 The American Carbine M1, a light rifle intended to replace the pistol carried by weapon crews and second-line troops with something more efficient at longer ranges. Imperial War Museum, London.

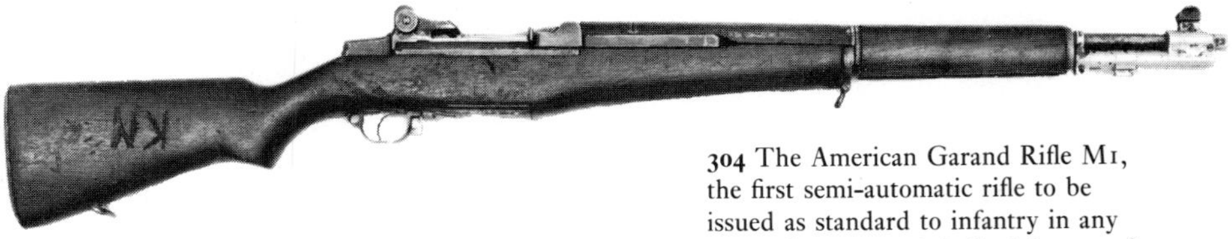

304 The American Garand Rifle M1, the first semi-automatic rifle to be issued as standard to infantry in any army. Gas-actuated, it fired from an 8-round clip. Imperial War Museum, London.

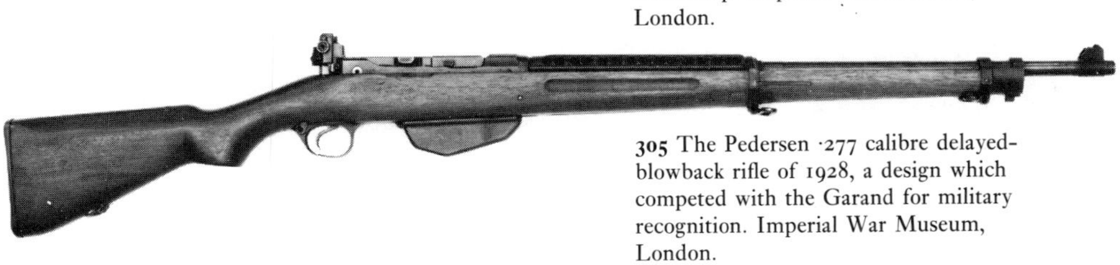

305 The Pedersen ·277 calibre delayed-blowback rifle of 1928, a design which competed with the Garand for military recognition. Imperial War Museum, London.

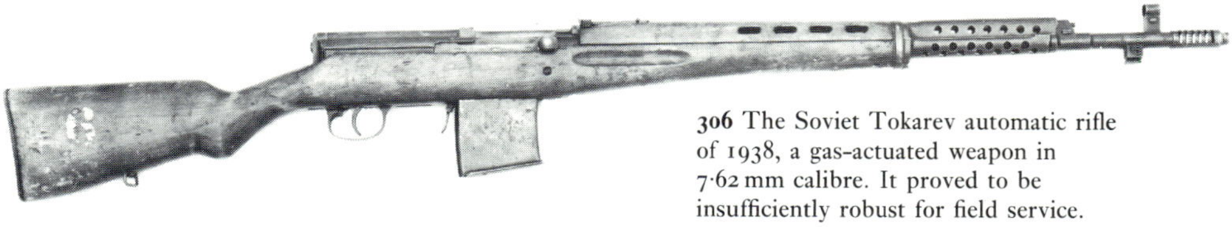

306 The Soviet Tokarev automatic rifle of 1938, a gas-actuated weapon in 7·62 mm calibre. It proved to be insufficiently robust for field service. Imperial War Museum, London.

307 The German Gewehr 43, a gas-actuated automatic rifle which was principally used as a sniper's weapon. Imperial War Museum, London.

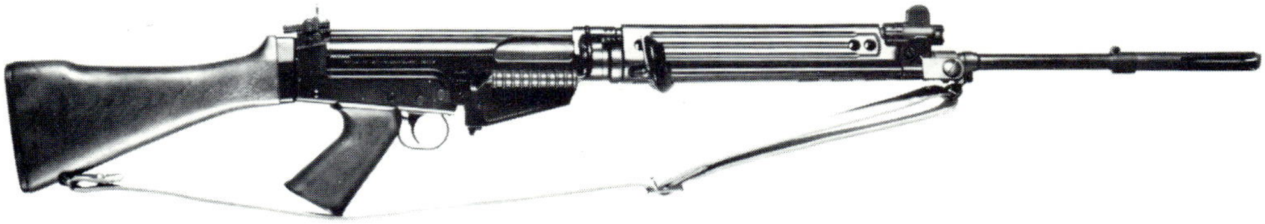

308 The Belgian FN *Fusil Automatique Légère* in 7·62 mm calibre has become one of the standard military rifles of the world. This 1958 version, with bipod, was used by the Austrian Army. Smithsonian Institution, Washington, D.C.

309 The British Army's Bren light machine gun, designed in Czechoslovakia, was among the finest weapons of its class ever seen; 1937. Imperial War Museum, London.

310 The German MG 34, with bipod for use as the squad automatic weapon. Belt-fed, the straight-line layout reduced the amount of 'climb' during firing. Imperial War Museum, London.

CHAPTER FOURTEEN

Scottish Firearms

W. Reid

97-99 In Scotland, as in any country whose record of
316-20 internal disorder more than matched the turbulence of her relations with powerful neighbours whose encroachments were resisted and independence preserved only by force of arms, the personal ownership of weapons was a matter of need rather than of luxury. Handguns of sorts were in use there in the early years of the sixteenth century but the form they took and the places which supplied them have still to be identified. Recent research suggests, however, that some, at least, were like the Hakenbüchse described on pp. 29-31[1]. Obviously the earliest were match- and wheel-locks but no example of either mechanism survives although there are frequent references to the use in Scotland of muskets fitted with *lunt-* or *rowet-works*.[2] These were respectively matchlocks and wheel-locks, the vernacular terms deriving from the German *Luntenschloss* and the French *platine à rouet*. Both seem to have been almost completely superseded by the earliest version of the Scottish snaphance lock by about 1600, but the reliable and less expensive matchlock continued in military service until after the Restoration. Its dependence on a supply of match gave it a positive advantage to an authority wishing to preserve the internal security of the state. Most of the readily available match could be held in arsenals only to be issued at the command of the government, thus controlling the amount of shooting in a country that was never quite free of strife. Between issues the militia, forming the greater part of the military forces, retained its muskets which were relatively harmless after the annual allowance of half a pound of powder and two pounds of match was spent. This advantage of the matchlock was mentioned in correspondence between Whitehall and the Lords of the Privy Council of Scotland as late as 1668.[3]

The early references to the firearms carried to *wappenschaws*, periodical musters at which sheriffs inspected the arms and armour of their neighbourhoods, and the laws of the 1560s[4] promulgated to restrict the carrying of arms and the affrays that they caused, mention *pistolettis*, *dagges*, and *culverings*, widening the field to cover all *utheris gunnis or ingynis of fyrewerk*. In these contexts the culverin was not the artillery piece shooting a ball of $5\frac{1}{2}$ in, diameter, but probably the matchlock hackbut mentioned elsewhere, a heavy cast bronze barrel mounted on a stout wooden stock. But whatever its

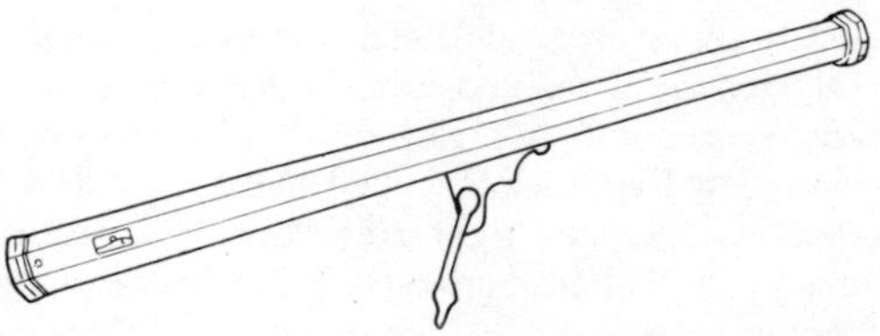

Bronze hackbut, found in Lough Neagh. French, early-sixteenth century. A type used in Scotland. National Museum of Antiquities of Scotland, Edinburgh.

form any man caught carrying it in certain towns and cities was liable to the death penalty unless he was a servant of the king or a soldier in the royal service. The exact forms of the above-mentioned classes of weapon are conjectural but by 1600, when Balfour of Burleigh went to 'Flanders and brought home a great quantity of arms',[5] most of it troopers' armour, the form of at least one style of pistol was well established and examples have been preserved in the Tøjhusmuseum, Copenhagen, in the Historisches Museum, Dresden, in the Armouries of the

1 See, for example, D. Caldwell (ed.), *Scottish Weapons and Fortifications*, Edinburgh, 1981, pp. 78-82.

2 For example, in the *Breadalbane Inventory of Plenishings*, Scottish Record Office, Register House, Edinburgh: 'Compt of the graith qlk patrik Mcalbyre porter of balloch hes within the place thairof maid at balloch the xj day of februar 1600.' *cf.* n.10.

3 *Register of the Privy Council of Scotland*, Volume II (Third Series), p. 469.

4 *Register of the Privy Council of Scotland*, Volume I, p. 593.

5 *Register of the Privy Council of Scotland*, Volume VI (First series), pp. 18, 181, 365, 669.

Tower of London, and elsewhere. The earliest are a pair at Dresden, dated 1598 on the fences of the characteristic Scottish right-hand and left-hand snaphance locks, each of which is stamped with a maker's mark of a cross fitchy flanked by the letters *I* (?) and *K*.

The early form of the Scottish snaphance lock used on the Dresden pistols is based on a lockplate of brass or steel, usually engraved with decorative patterns, frequently stamped with the maker's initials, and occasionally fretted at each end. On the outside of the lockplate is the pan with, on the earlier examples, a hexagonal fence that later became circular. There is no half-cock on these locks and at full cock the nose of the sear passes through the lockplate to engage over a hooked spur at the lower rear of the cock. Pressure on the trigger, which is invariably lobate and turned from a single piece of metal at this date, withdraws the sear and allows the cock to fall. Through a rod connected to the tumbler the sliding pan-cover is opened to expose the priming. A buffer on the lockplate prevents damage to the cock from overstriking. Locks of this form continued in use from some time before 1598 until well into the last quarter of the seventeenth century.

The barrel, with its back-sight raised out of the metal of the breech, and engraved mouldings at the muzzle and at intervals along its length, is equally characteristic. The wooden stocks of these pistols are early versions of the 'fish-tailed' stock mentioned below, fitted with flat steel belt-hooks, and already off-set to left and right respectively (a Scottish feature) but without butt-caps. The fully-developed form is exemplified by other pistols at Dresden. These are dated 1611 and marked *A-M*. Another pair in the Tøjhusmuseum is dated 1602 and bears the maker's initials *IL*. The stock is of the type known to collectors of Scottish arms as 'fish-tailed', the butt being very flat from side to side and flaring towards its end which is finished with a scrolled butt-cap of brass or silver engraved with floral patterns. The fore-end and the region of the stock around the lock is angular, almost a pentagon in section, another characteristic which continued, like the short, lobate trigger, on the great majority of Scottish pistols made in the succeeding two centuries, as well as on many guns. The stocks of these early survivors were of wood, often Brazil wood although walnut (*wanut trie*) was also common, but as early as 1611 they were being made from thin brass sheet. In the National Museum of Antiquities of Scotland there is an exceptionally fine pair of that date with the *IL* mark on the locks and, on the barrels, the arms of France and Navarre with the inscription *LOVIS*
99 *XIII ROY DE FRAC.* Louis also owned one of the four early sporting-guns made in Scotland which have survived in an almost complete state.[6]

The mechanism, the stock design and the engraved decorative patterns of these and another half-dozen in British and American collections, the latest dated 1631, are so similar as to suggest that all were made in one centre of production. There are variations, for instance some barrels are of brass and others of steel, and the lockplates were also made in both metals, but these differences seem to be inconsequential. Like the wood-stocked group and the two early sporting-guns described below, the brass-stocked pistols may well have been made in Dundee, a fact which serves to underline how very little is known about the products of the remainder of the country during the years before 1670. If the craftsmen ever committed any designs to paper or his purchases were ever described in detail by a customer, no record has so far appeared to thrill the antiquary and frustrate the collector whose ambition might be to have one of everything. For no Scottish pistols other than the fish-tailed variety have come down to us from before 1613.

By this time the gun trade in Scotland had settled down in the pattern which was to continue with little variation for more than two centuries. In a number of towns the metal-workers' craft guilds, the Hammermen's Incorporations, had long been established and it was quite natural that, in Dundee at least, their members produced native dag- and gunmakers as a separate craft by 1587. While the best Continental firearms of the day were often the combined efforts of several craftsmen, each a master worker, the Scottish gun and pistol seem to have been made during their best period in one workshop under the direction of a single master who sold direct to his customers either from his booth or at local fairs. In the places where there was a craft guild the master was invariably a guild brother, for he could not sell his products without having first associated himself with the mystery. But other fine makers worked in small towns and villages where one would like to think that the absence of the deacons' supervision resulted in no lowering of standards. It may even be that the production of firearms in quantity at Doune, Perthshire, at a later date arose from the arrival in the village of skilled makers wearied by the restrictions on their activities which they experienced in the guild-dominated cities which were the major arms production centres. Even a place as tiny as Glenelg on the north-west coast of Inverness-shire provided a market for a maker of such undoubted ability as John Campbell, whose name and village are engraved on the lockplate of a pistol in Warwick Castle. There is also evidence that major gunsmiths worked for important landowners, clan chiefs and members of the aristocracy whose houses

6 See p. 412.

Snaphance pistol with gilt brass stock. Dundee, dated 1624 and 1628. Art Gallery & Museum, Glasgow.

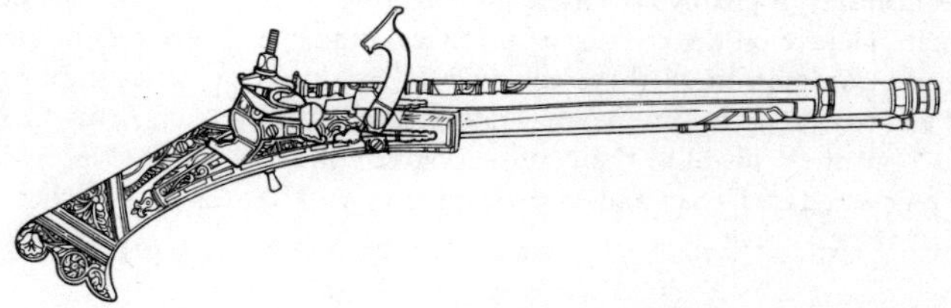

were a poor country's equivalent of the German princely and ducal courts which were the patrons of such artists as the Paumgartners, the Stoplers and David Altenstetter.

Falling within the dates of the fish-tail series with wooden stocks is an extremely rare group of which the writer has seen only four specimens: a pair with right- and left-hand locks, and two singles. All are similar to one another and to the fish-tail series except that their wooden butts are rather thicker and terminate in a faceted ovoid pommel reminiscent of certain wheel-lock pistols made on the Continent around the same period. None is dated, but the initials *PH* on a pair in the Nationalmuseum, Copenhagen, may stand for Peter Hamilton, dag-maker in the Edinburgh Canongate between 1596 and 1630. The initials of another maker who worked in the same district, Robert Mossman, appear on the lockplate of a similar pistol. The date 1626 is engraved on the breech of the weapon which was once in the collection of the late Charles E. Whitelaw, the outstanding expert on Scottish weapons to whom all modern students owe an incalculable debt. Whether the *PH* and *RM* pistols are of Edinburgh make is by no means certain, but, if they are, we can claim knowledge of only two towns out of the many where firearms were made in the first decade of the seventeenth century.

The wood-stocked pistols with oval butts may connect with a larger group with all-metal stocks and ovoid pommels, some of which retain a number of the stock characteristics we met in the Dresden fish-tail pair. The earliest, with the arms and initials of Count Axel Oxenstierna (1583-1654) are in the Livrustkammare, Stockholm.[7] Their locks are dated 1613 and are stamped with the initials *JA* which could indicate that they were made by one of two Dundee craftsmen called John Alison. The very long barrels are of gilt brass and the main surfaces are engraved with an elegant pattern of foliage enclosed by strapwork, all in the Celtic style. Two other similar pairs in the same magnificent collection are dated 1627 and 1629 respectively, and a fourth pair dated 1614 in the collection of R. T. Gwynn has
98 the initials *IL* which have already been mentioned and which may be those of James Low, yet another Dundee maker. The Gwynn pair has the unusual feature of pommels which unscrew and extend some 14 in on a stalk to form butts that allow them to be fired from the shoulder. Others of this group are rather less imposing in length but still interesting. All seem to originate in Dundee, whether they are steel-stocked like another with the *IL* initials now in the National Museum of Antiquities of Scotland, dated 1624, or brass, like an outstanding piece in the National Museum in Krakow dated 1635 and with an unidentified coat of arms [perhaps of the Brisbane family. *Ed*] accompanied by the initials *IB*. It is stamped with the initials *RA* of the maker, perhaps Robert Alison of Dundee. The pommels of the group vary in the detail of their shapes and some include piercing in their decoration, notably two of the pairs in the Livrustkammare[8] which appear to be by the same hand although only the former is stamped *IL*. The latest pistol of the type is a fragment consisting of the brass stock with faceted pommel and a very corroded early flintlock of *c*.1650, in the Tower Armouries.[9] It is of very poor quality and although it is included here with Scottish pistols, it was in fact excavated in Ireland and is much coarser in finish than any other Scottish pistol which has been recorded from this period.

Some of the group retain their touch-hole prickers, each with a pierced cubic knob at the end. These screw into the extreme end of the butt. Up to the middle of the period of the ovoid butts, some of which are almost spherical, the stocks remained rather angular but thereafter there was a softening of the lines particularly on the underside of the fore-end.

Of four all-steel pistols from the middle of the seventeenth century, of an unusual type, a pair and a single in the National Museum of Antiquities of Scotland may come from the same workshop. The fourth, in an American private collection, is similar in form but has some differences in detail. All have the later form of snaphance lock in which the sear engages on the tumbler and there is no half-cock.

7 Nos. 1726, 1727.

8 Nos 39/71 and 5685-6.

9 XII–1682.

The Edinburgh pistols are engraved with their date of manufacture on the circular pan-fences. Unusual features common to all three are their lobate butts and a narrow loop below the fore-end to take a ram-rod. The single pistol in the National Museum and the pair are dated 1647 and 1650 respectively. The pair, which was found during the demolition of a Glasgow house in 1844, also has the initials *TB* of an unidentified maker. The American-owned pistol is undated, the initials *LA* which are engraved on the lockplate are more likely by their style to be those of an owner than a maker.

The locks of the three National Museum of Antiquities of Scotland pistols are similar to those on what is probably the least attractive form of Scottish pistol, which developed shortly before 1660. It has a distinctly slab-sided stock with, at the butt, two inward turning scrolled horns between which was screwed a touch-hole pricker. The pricker had been in use since the earliest pistols and was to remain a standard fitting. An unidentified portrait dated to *c.*1660 by John Michael Wright in the Scottish National Portrait Gallery shows a young man in highland dress wearing a pistol of this type, of which there are dated examples in the Tower Armouries (166?), the Musée Historique, Neuchâtel (1678) and elsewhere (1662, 1678). A number of writers have suggested that these slab-sided ram's horn pistols evolved from the graceful fish-tail type but no direct relationship can be traced.

Metal stocks such as these, in both the earlier and later forms, were made in one piece from the correct thickness of brass or iron sheet cut to a pattern and then shaped with hammers to its final form when the joints were brazed and the stock was ready for the attachment of the butt terminals whether they were ram's horns, heart-shaped or ovoid pommels, or the little balls which replace the curling horns on one unique specimen. On the slab-sided ram's horn butts the horns were usually curled extensions to the end of a flat plate brazed in to close the box-like open end of the butt. The round triggers and the heads of the prickers were made from two small hemispheres of silver, or rarely of brass, which were soldered together and slipped on to the iron triggers or the pricker tangs which were then riveted over.

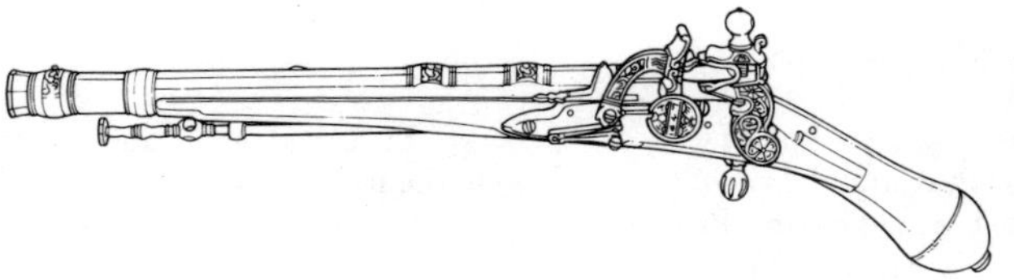

Steel-stocked snaphance pistol. Scottish, dated 1647. National Museum of Antiquities of Scotland, Edinburgh.

Mr Claude Blair draws attention to four detached sixteenth-century gun-barrels with similar features in an important paper, read to the American Society of Arms Collectors and published in that society's *Bulletin*, Spring 1975. There is little doubt that they are of Scottish origin and between them they represent the earliest surviving elements of firearms from that country as they are dated 1583, 1585, 1589 and 1595. Although their decoration does not help to confirm that they were made in Scotland three of the four bear the coat-of-arms, monograms, names, or combinations of the three which link them with Scotsmen of rank. Yet another sixteenth-century barrel, now in the National Museum of Antiquities of Scotland, dated 1599, has the initials and coat-of-arms of Sir Duncan Campbell. The 1599 gun, like one of the others referred to above, includes the 'pot of lilies' device from the coat-of-arms of Dundee in its decoration, suggesting strongly that it is the 'lang hagbute that wes maid in Dundie, gilt with the Lardis armis' listed in a Breadalbane inventory of 1600.[10]

These early barrels reveal varying degrees of sophistication in their decoration, which includes elaborate patterns engraved on inlaid silver and gilt copper. Their motifs bear a stronger resemblance to those found elsewhere in Europe than they do to Scottish traditional styles but there can be little doubt that some, if not all this group of five barrels, originated in Dundee.

Surviving examples of sporting guns made in Scotland fall into three distinct types. Two are quite local, the third is so close to those made south of the border that it requires only passing mention here.

Two complete examples of the earliest of the specifically Scottish types have been recorded and both had famous owners. One now in the Tower Armouries belonged to King Louis XIII of France (1601-37), who was perhaps the first great collector of firearms. The other was made for a famous Scot, Sir John Grant of Freuchie (1596-1637), and bears its owner's initials, coat-of-arms and title on silver plates on the butt and barrel. The Grant gun was the

10 C. Innes *Black Book of Taymouth*, Edinburgh, 1855, p.337. *cf.* n.2.

property of the late Countess of Seafield and was kept at her home, Cullen House, in Banffshire; it is now in the National Museum of Antiquities of Scotland, Edinburgh. It is engraved on the fence with the date 1635 but that may be the date at which the pan was replaced as the gun resembles very closely the smaller weapon from Louis's armoury which is dated 1614. Both guns were made in Dundee and are stamped with the initials of their makers. On the lock and barrel of the Armouries gun are the initials of Robert Alison and on the lock of the Grant gun those of Andrew Philp. Both men worked in the Angus burgh between *c.*1596 and *c.*1627.

The guns are stocked with Brazil wood (*Guilandina echinata lam. spreng.*) which is an expensive, close-grained red wood which seems to have achieved a certain popularity with the Scots for fine gunstocks and even for small items of furniture. One also finds pistols of about 1600 with stocks of Brazil, which was given its own rate in a list of the Customs duties charged on goods imported into Scotland in 1612: 'wood called Brissel or Fernando buckwode the hundreth weght xxiiij li.' This was a remarkably high rate compared with the twenty pounds and twelve pounds charged respectively on boxwood and ebony.[11] By a coincidence, one of the few contemporary descriptions, in an inventory of 1600, is of a 'gilt piece wt the lairds armes that come out of Dundee stockit wt brissell.[12] As initials on any firearm could belong to more than one maker it is invaluable to have some confirmation of the place of origin of Sir John Grant's gun among the decorative elements on its stock. Inlaid in silver on each face are unsophisticated representations of equestrian figures, hounds, and the ubiquitous fish that occurs in Northern symbolism. More important, the butt carries the coat-of-arms of Dundee, 'azure a pot of lilies argent' with the supporters 'two dragons vert their tails knotted below the shield.'

Both guns have full-length, silver-capped fore-ends and butts which slope downwards very slightly before curving upwards to the rectangular, silver caps which form the buttplates. The stocks are angular in section, the butts extremely narrow from side to side. Each has a trigger-guard, an unusual fitting on any Scottish firearm of the traditional types, to protect the short baluster trigger. The butt of the slightly later Grant gun is carved with a series of shallow flutings, a feature that developed and was emphasised on later Scottish guns and rifles. To date, no evidence has been found which gives more than a suggestion of the origin of the characteristic Scottish stock shapes, but it seems likely that they evolved in Scotland from types that were common to England and Scotland half a century or more before these two were produced in Dundee. They may well be quite untypical of the arms made elsewhere in the kingdom, telling us nothing about Scottish guns in general and only a little about those of Dundee.

Their similar snaphance locks, based on brass lockplates, are virtually identical in construction and material with those on the earliest Scottish pistols described above, some of which also share their Brazil wood stocks. Between them they form one of the rarest and most unusual groups of firearms to evolve in Western Europe. They confirm the opinion held by Dr Arne Hoff and others that the further one travels from the centre of a firearms production area towards its perimeter, the more aberrants from the mean one finds in the design, materials, decoration and construction of the local products.

The dates of the Louis XIII and Grant sporting guns bracket two Scottish guns which have come to light in the past few years. Their stocks share the extremely unusual feature of being made entirely from sheet brass. One in the Tower Armouries, which has had its original lock replaced, bears on its barrel the partly-obliterated date 1612, 1615 or 1619.[13] The other, in the National Museum of Antiquities of Scotland, is dated 1624 on both barrel and the original lock which also bears the mark 97
attributed to the remarkable Dundee maker James Low.[14] These brass guns are so similar in style that they seem almost to be a pair. The barrels resemble that on the Louis XIII gun of 1614 but their butt design is closer to that of a modern gun, and follows a style that was only beginning to come into fashion in the early years of the seventeenth century. The brass, originally gilded, is almost entirely covered with engraved strapwork, foliage, rosettes and fern-leaf, key and chevron patterns. Pairs of addorsed 'C's on the butt of the Tower gun resemble those found on objects once owned by King Charles I, suggesting that the gun was first owned by the young Charles when he was still Prince of Wales. The royal association is supported by the presence on both guns of a movable extension to the butt shaped and fretted as a royal crown. The extension on a notched slide moves in a socket within the hollow butt and can be locked in one of six positions by a spring catch. Similar adjustable butts are also found on the long brass pistols mentioned above and on at least

11 *The Book of Customs and valuations of Merchandises in Scotland* 1612, quoted in Cosmo Innes, *Ledger of Andrew Halyburton,* Edinburgh, 1867.

12 Breadalbane Inventory, see note 2 above.

13 William Reid 'A Prince's Gun from Dundee', *The Connoisseur*, p. 163 (1966), 148-50.

14 Stuart Maxwell, 'A Brass Sporting Gun Dated 1624', *Proceedings of the Society of Antiquaries of Scotland,* 1974-5, p. 215-218.

one other gun, but of English type, bearing the arms of the Spens family of Scotland.

There is a gap of some years from Sir John Grant's gun, dated 1635, to the next approximately datable Scottish firearm other than pistols. Like so many other Scottish weapons it conveniently bears the arms and initials of its owner, James, fifth earl and first marquis of Montrose, Buchan's 'candidate for immortality', who died for treason on an Edinburgh scaffold on 21 May 1650. The breech is engraved with the partly illegible date 16??, the early snaphance lock has its maker's initials *IS* under a crown of three points. The main difference between it and the Grant gun is that the Montrose weapon has the fully developed Scots stock with a deeply curved butt carved near its upper edge with a series of deep flutes. Above the lock the wood is notched for the thumb in a way that is also found in the earliest Scottish guns and which continued until the end of the seventeenth century although not common abroad. From the Montrose gun of *c.*1645 to the years when the international gun-stock was fully established in Scotland the trigger-guard is unknown; many guns have flared, faceted muzzles on barrels inlaid with brass or silver panels, and most have butt-caps formed like shallow, rectangular boxes to fit over the flat-section end of the butt.

In the National Museum of Antiquities of Scotland where the unrivalled Seafield collection of Scottish guns is now preserved, is the finest Scottish long-arm to survive: a superb silver-mounted rifle of 0·79 in calibre dated 1667 on the barrel and 1671 on the lockplate. The barrel also bears the initials and coat of arms of Ludovic Grant (?1650–1716), grandson of Sir John Grant whose gun is described above. On the stock are carved shallow, interlaced and delicate fern patterns, and on the silver mounts, of exceptional quality, are engraved simple but effective floral and foliar ornaments that retain something of the feeling for design found on Scottish tomb and cross sculpture of the Middle Ages. The variation in the dates on lock and barrel may be accounted for by the lock's having been replaced or repaired during the gun's working life. The pans on Scottish locks of this type are almost invariably detachable to allow of their replacement when powder burning, scouring and corrosion left them unfit for further service. At least one gun in the same collection has a pan which has been holed and is ready for replacement, and the renewal or re-use of parts is exemplified by two other guns from Castle Grant, both fitted with stocks which are almost certainly by the same hand as Ludovic Grant's. One is a little carbine whose barrel has the usual silver plaque with Sir John Grant's initials and is probably the weapon described in an inventory of 1720 as 'Sir John Grant's little gun'. It must date from before the laird's death in 1637. The other is dated on the barrel 1637 and bears the arms of George Mackenzie, second earl of Seaforth. Traces of gold in the barrel's engraved decoration points to this being 'Seaforth's gilt gun' also named in the 1720 inventory. There is every reason to believe that both were re-stocked around 1667–71, the dates on Ludovic's gun discussed above, and were the work of an outstanding, if as yet unknown, stockmaker.

Ludovic Grant, 'that Highland Saint of Mighty Majesty', replaced the old names for his seat—Freuchie and Bellachastel—with the new name, Castle Grant, in 1694 on the erection of his lands to the Regality of Grant. The second of the old, replaced names appears on the lockplate of an unusually long gun inscribed in a graceful script *Bellachastel/ Gulielmus Smith*, suggesting that Smith worked at the castle as the laird's personal gunmaker. As early as 1845 it was said that there was a hereditary family of workers in metal called Smith who were employed at Castle Grant, but there do not seem to be any surviving records to confirm the tradition. We know that certain Scottish gentlemen did have their own

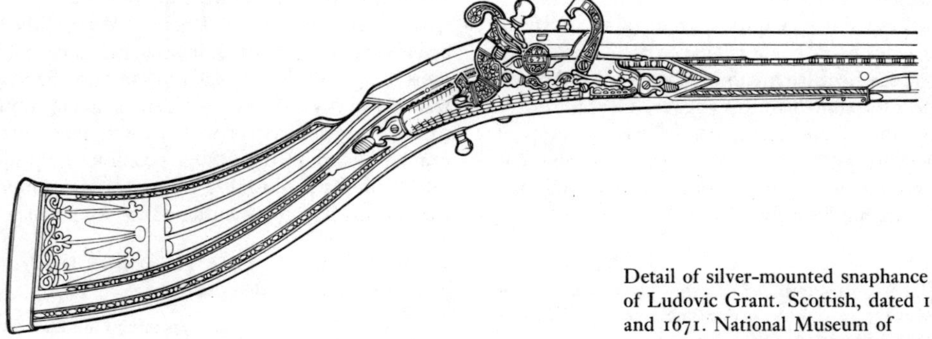

Detail of silver-mounted snaphance rifle of Ludovic Grant. Scottish, dated 1667 and 1671. National Museum of Antiquities of Scotland, Edinburgh.

gunsmiths from such references as Sir Hugh Campbell of Cawdor's order to an Inverness merchant in 1677 to supply a consignment of goods from Holland.[15] The delivery was to include fifty or sixty musket barrels which the laird planned to have stocked 'at hom for weapon guns to our watch and militia let them not be too long or too havy for a man to travell with his othir waponis, and be ordinar musket bor or rather less . . .' The size and weight were very important. Scottish fighting men, both regulars and fencibles, were described by William Sacheverell in his account of a visit made to the Isle of Mull in 1688 as being armed with a dirk, a pair of pistols, 'a round target on their backs, a blew bonnet on their heads, in one hand a broadsword and a musket in the other. Perhaps no nation goes better armed.' When a bullet bag and powder flask are added one does not have to wonder why Cawdor restricted the size and weight of the musket barrels. Even a minor saving in weight and awkwardness could be of vital importance after an army had covered sixty miles on foot in thirty-six hours–with fighting on the way–as Montrose's men did at Dundee.

Smith of Bellachastel signed the lock of Seaforth's gun in a different script and the uncommonly academic form for a Scottish craftsman *ME FECIT GULIELMUS SMITH* and dated it 1674. It is probable that the lock of another musket dated 1675, of a unique turn-off, breech-loading rifle of 0·68 in calibre, both from the Seafield collection, and of a plain musket of 0·80 in calibre dated 1690 in the Tower Armouries may indicate that they too were made by Smith. The full, rather stylish signature may have been reserved for the finest products of his workshop.

Like those late guns with the initials *GS*, by far the majority of the remaining score or so are fitted with snaphance locks although a few were modernised by the fitting of a combined pan-cover and steel. There are no examples of this type of weapon recorded which can be dated later than 1690.

The latest dated gun bearing any trace of Scottish characteristics to be recorded at the time of writing, although it has more in common with the contemporary English fowling piece than with the Scottish gun of the seventeenth century, is dated
317 1703 and signed on the lockplate *IO. STUART*. It still has a subtle suggestion of a curve to the butt, below which is a small floral carving in the Scottish tradition. Stuart (whose place of work is unknown) was one of the best Scottish pistol makers of the late seventeenth century and early eighteenth century, and apparently specialised in the all-steel pistols with heart-shaped butts, associated with the East coast, discussed below.[16] The lock of this gun is almost exactly similar to that on a number of Stuart's products, notably that on the unrestored pistol of a pair from the Seafield collection. The pistols are dated 1701 and engraved on a silver strip on each barrel *GRANT OF THAT ILK* for Ludovic Grant, eighth of Freuchie and first of Grant.

This important sporting gun, now in the collection of R. T. Gwynn, is the only known example of Stuart's having ventured into the field of shoulder arms, but the rarity of Scottish firearms of that date other than pistols suggests that great quantities of muskets, carbines and perhaps even rifles were confiscated after the risings of 1715 and 1745. The more easily concealed pistols could disappear into the thatches and cellars of houses throughout Scotland. Such weapons as have been preserved, whether intact or as restocked barrels fitted with new mounts and locks like the 'Spotted Gun' owned by Major John Stewart of Ardvorlich, form too small a sample to have much statistical validity in the assessment of Stuart's or any other maker's output.

Scottish weapons and their accessories are quite distinctive, the powder-horns no less than the firearms with which they were used. The typical Scottish powder-horn survives in some numbers in lengths from ten to twenty inches, all made from curved yellow-grey cow or bull horn which was flattened after it was soaked in hot water. This flattening, although intended primarily to make the horn a more convenient shape when it was being carried, also resulted in two good surfaces for the application of the decoration which is quite as characteristic as the shape. For the most part it consists of engraved geometric designs, scrolls, heraldic devices and foliate patterns of considerable complexity. The finest are exceptional pieces of engraving with the deeply-cut lines blackened the better to show the patterns. Their best period lay between *c*.1650 and *c*.1750 and many are dated, bear the name or the initials of their owners, long mottoes in English or Gaelic, and occasionally the name of the maker. On some, two or more dates indicate that they were used by more than one generation of hunters or soldiers. One bears the information that it was carved by its owner, Lieutenant MacDonald, while he served at Shelburn, Nova Scotia, in 1786. A splendid specimen in the Glasgow Art Gallery and Museum has the arms and motto of Lord Lovat and the date 24 July 1683.

Few still retain their original mounts, which consisted of a pewter, brass or silver nozzle–where the carved spout of the horn was not considered grand enough–and a plug of the same metal or of wood or horn. On the concave, upper edge of the horn are two

15 *The Book of the Thanes of Cawdor*, 1236-1742, The Spalding Club, Edinburgh, 1859, p. 335.

16 See p. 416.

or three small loops, either carved in the horn or formed by metal staples, that secured the shoulder sling. The leather strap was the most perishable element of the horn and only one complete specimen is recorded. It is of very narrow leather armed with iron rivets. Nothing is known of any powder flask or horn that may have been used in Scotland earlier than the flat horn which was itself largely superseded by 1770, when the copper flasks that were being turned out in such quantity in the workshops of Sheffield and Brimingham began to come into the country.

In the seventeenth and eighteenth centuries the bandolier also saw service in Scotland. The little chargers, occasionally of a variety of metals, as well as of wood, were slung from a crossbelt that was narrower than was common in England and abroad. There was nothing to save the charger from being discarded when it fell out of use as it had none of the aesthetic appeal of the engraved horn. Unsigned, undated and lacking any heraldic significance, there was little about them with which a history, factual or romantic, could be associated. One isolated example is preserved in the National Museum of Antiquities of Scotland.

The narrow strap that carried the horn and the equally narrow bandolier strap are paralleled in the diagonal strap on which pistols were carried when they were not worn on the waistbelt. The strap hanging from the left shoulder can be seen in a number of military portraits of the third quarter of the eighteenth century.

It is as well to record that Scottish firearms are found with a number of technical differences associated with the same basic style of stock. For example, dated pistols with heart-shaped pommels are found in the short space of ten years with both flintlock and snaphance mechanisms, and variations occur within each class. The snaphance locks have discoid fences and a horizontal sear that engages in the tail of the cock, but even this simple action is varied by the method of the connection. There are examples in which the sear engages over the hooked tail of the cock, through a pierced slot, or merely into a hidden recess on its inner surface. Moreover, some have a 'dog-catch' acting as a safety device by hooking into the back of the cock. The flintlocks, using the term in its most commonly used sense of a lock working on the flint and steel principle with a combined steel and pan-cover, have even wider variations in their actions. So far as it is possible to trace the development of pistols with locks of this class, the earlier flintlock, like the snaphance locks, have the horizontal sear engaging the tail of the cock to qualify them as snaplocks according to the definition set down by the late Dr Torsten Lenk. Later examples have the lock that established itself as the typical Scottish form in which, at half-cock, the horizontal sear engages quite high on the breast of the cock. At full-cock a projection engages the tumbler. A relatively small number of pistols have a flintlock of the international type. This seems to be a north-eastern variant which did not achieve general acceptance until the closing years of the eighteenth century when the Scottish pistol trade was on the decline.

Pistols with pommels of the so-called heart-butt type evolved in the third quarter of the seventeenth 318

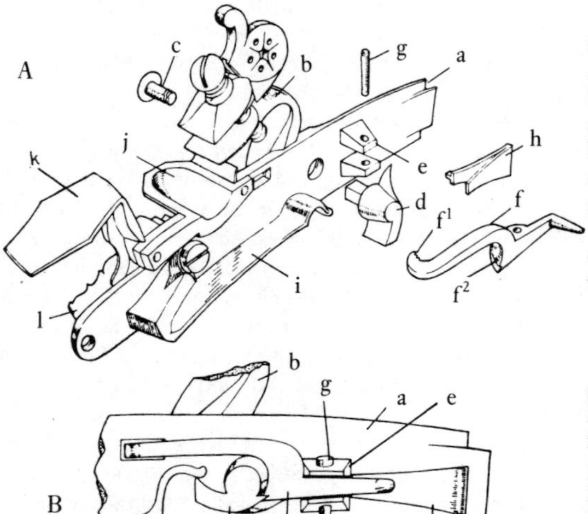

SCOTTISH SNAPHANCE
A illustrates the mechanism in the fired position
B illustrates the mechanism at full-cock
- a Lockplate
- b Cock
- c Cock-screw
- d Tumbler with bent which, at full-cock, engages with the full-cock sear (f^2). See fig. B
- e Bracket to which sear-lever (f) is pivoted on pin (g)
- f Combined sear- and trigger-lever with full-cock sear at (f^2) and half-cock sear at (f^1). The latter works through the lock-plate to engage with the breast of the cock
- g Sear-lever pin
- h Sear- or trigger-spring
- i Mainspring
- j Pan
- k Combined steel and pan-cover
- l Feather-spring for the steel and pan-cover

Based on the lock of an eighteenth-century Scottish pistol (No. 1425A-1874) in the Victoria & Albert Museum

311 The German MG 42 was designed with an eye to rapid production. It has been re-adopted by the Bundeswehr. Imperial War Museum, London.

312 The 'General Purpose Machine Gun' can be used as the squad light automatic or for sustained tactical fire. Designed by the Belgian FN Company, it has been widely adopted throughout NATO and other countries. RSAF, Enfield.

313 The Heckler & Koch VP70 pistol with butt stock attached, in which combination it can fire three-round bursts for each pressure of the trigger. Heckler & Koch GmbH., Oberndorf.

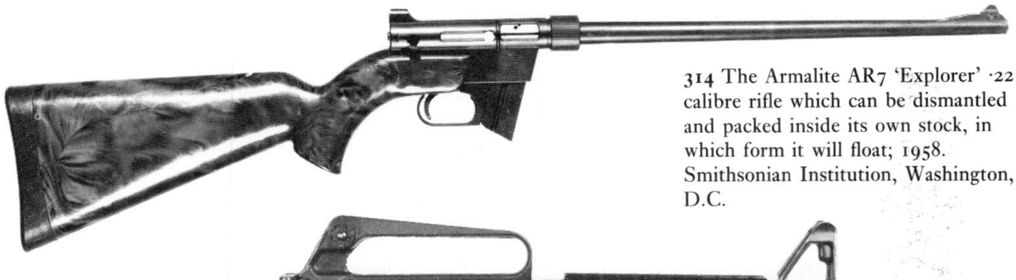

314 The Armalite AR7 'Explorer' ·22 calibre rifle which can be dismantled and packed inside its own stock, in which form it will float; 1958. Smithsonian Institution, Washington, D.C.

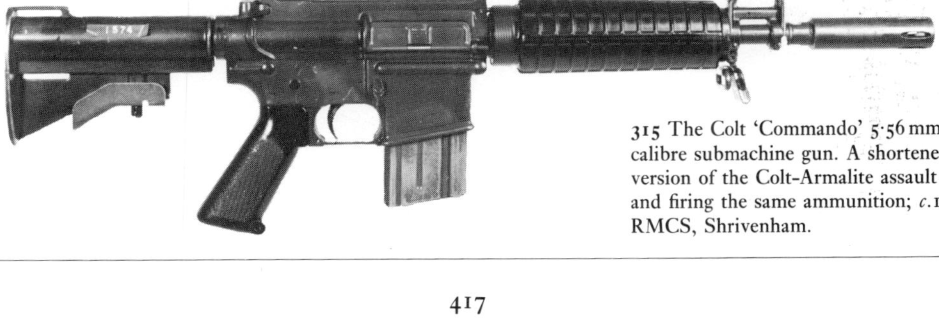

315 The Colt 'Commando' 5·56 mm calibre submachine gun. A shortened version of the Colt-Armalite assault rifle and firing the same ammunition; *c.*1965. RMCS, Shrivenham.

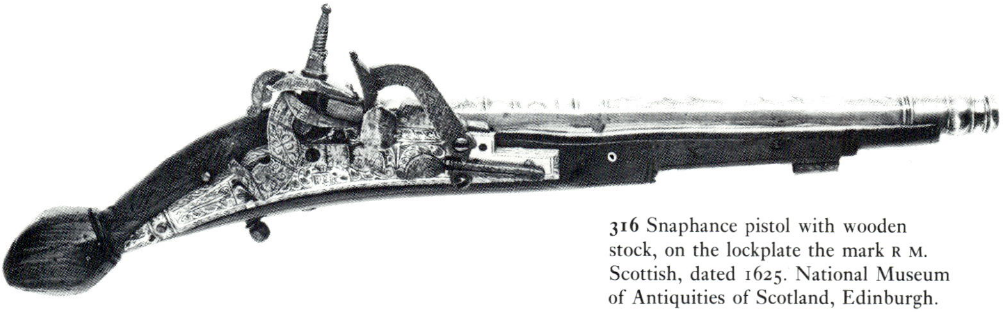

316 Snaphance pistol with wooden stock, on the lockplate the mark R M. Scottish, dated 1625. National Museum of Antiquities of Scotland, Edinburgh.

317 Detail of a flintlock gun, the lock engraved and signed IO STUART. Scottish, dated 1703. Private collection.

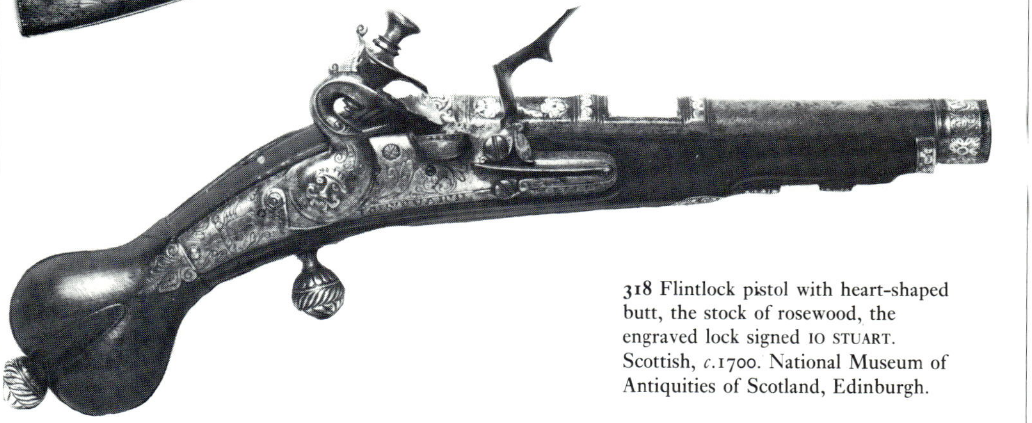

318 Flintlock pistol with heart-shaped butt, the stock of rosewood, the engraved lock signed IO STUART. Scottish, *c.*1700. National Museum of Antiquities of Scotland, Edinburgh.

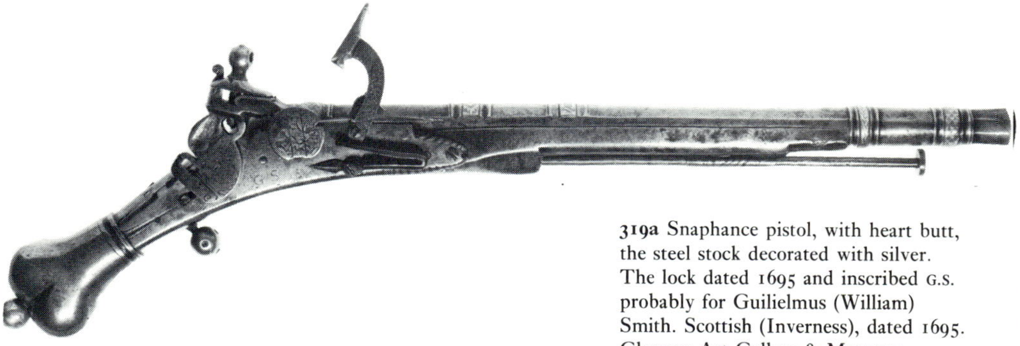

319a Snaphance pistol, with heart butt, the steel stock decorated with silver. The lock dated 1695 and inscribed G.S. probably for Guilielmus (William) Smith. Scottish (Inverness), dated 1695. Glasgow Art Gallery & Museum.

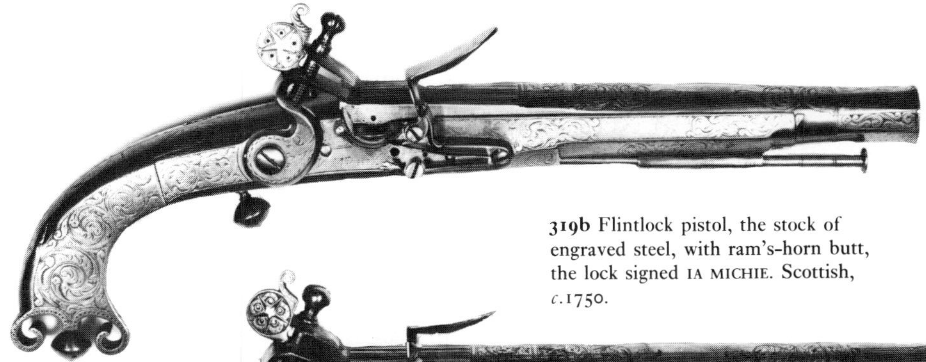

319b Flintlock pistol, the stock of engraved steel, with ram's-horn butt, the lock signed IA MICHIE. Scottish, *c.*1750.

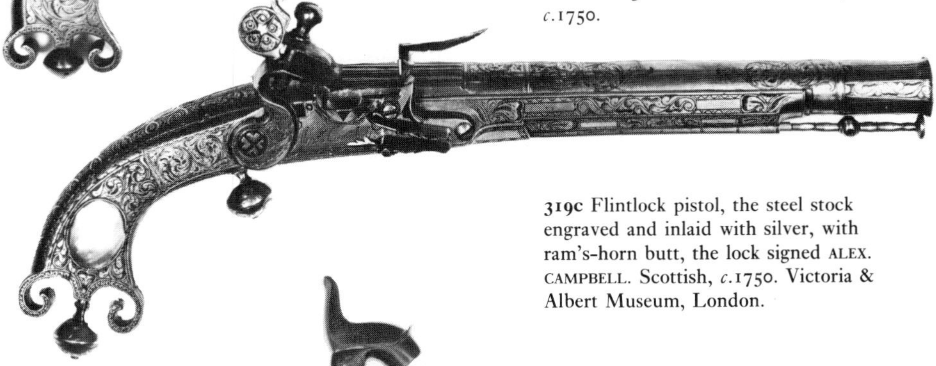

319c Flintlock pistol, the steel stock engraved and inlaid with silver, with ram's-horn butt, the lock signed ALEX. CAMPBELL. Scottish, *c.*1750. Victoria & Albert Museum, London.

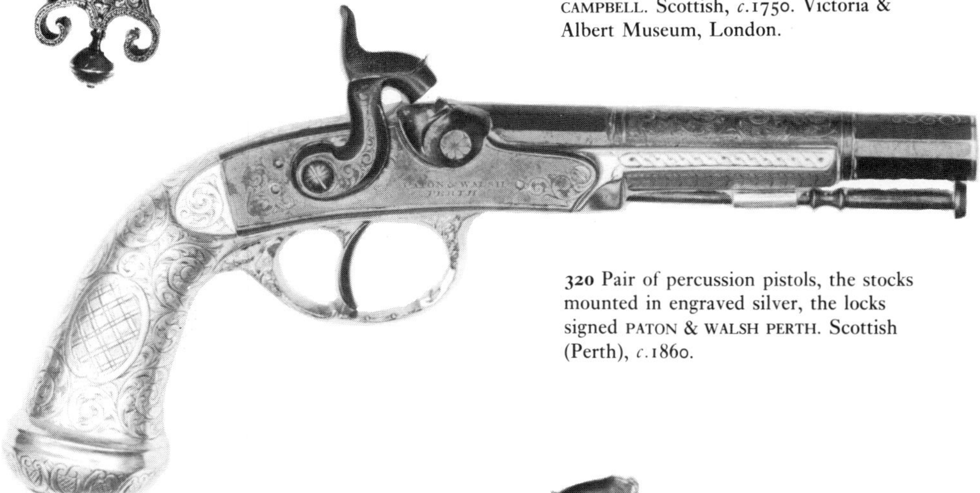

320 Pair of percussion pistols, the stocks mounted in engraved silver, the locks signed PATON & WALSH PERTH. Scottish (Perth), *c.*1860.

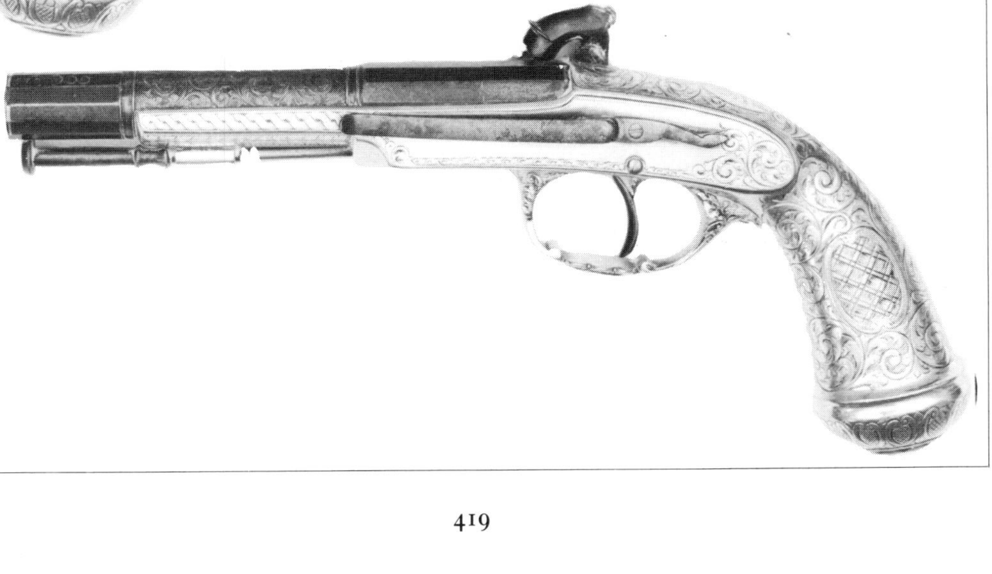

321 Plate from the *Trachtenbuch* by H. W. Formschneider showing a Turkish janissary with matchlock musket and lighted match. German (Nuremberg), 1577. Muzeum Narodowego, Cracow.

322 Detail of miquelet gun, the stock inlaid with mosaic of ivory and brass. Turkish, seventeenth century. Muzeum Narodowego, Cracow.

century. It is rather typical of their period, when Scottish craftsmen were emerging from their anonymity, that so many lockplates and butts carry the name of the maker and his town. Almost all lie near the stretch of Scotland's North Sea coast between Inverness and Dundee. One finds pistols engraved *Elgin*, *Old Meldrum*, *Edzell* and *Brechin*, and the makers of others have been identified in the records of Inverness, Aberdeen and Dundee.

They vary in length from $7\frac{1}{2}$ in to 26 in, but all share the common feature of having their pommels shaped like the popular representation of a human heart. No real case has been made in support of the hypothesis that the design contains an element of symbolism, whether it be religious, political or phallic. When the heart-butt pommel first appeared, gunmakers throughout the rest of Europe had reached the conclusion that a pistol should have a swelling towards the end of its butt to make it lie securely and comfortably in the hand. The heart-shape fulfills this function as well as most. To anticipate the comment that such a typically Scottish shape must have some significance, one can point to the equally unusual slab-sided ram's horn butts that were the heart-butt's contemporaries. They and the earlier flat, flaring butts with scrolled terminals appear to have no symbolism.

No type of Scottish pistol can really be said to be common since the vast majority of firearms made in Scotland were for private individuals. The huge munition orders known to Birmingham and London could never have been met by the Scottish trade, but a large number of heart-butts has survived in Britain, the United States and in museums in Continental Europe. Of these, an astonishingly high proportion were signed by a maker whom we have already met.
318 John Stuart's work was of the highest class and his output considerable but, beyond these facts, we know next to nothing about him. None of his pistols has so far been recorded as having a town or village name, but a pistol signed *And Strachan/Edzell* in the Glasgow Art Gallery and Museum is so close to Stuart's style as to suggest that the two makers were either master and servant or served one master who left a positive influence on both. Where Stuart's pistols are dated the years fall between 1695 and 1705.

Although Stuart seems to have been the outstanding maker of heart-butt pistols, and was the only man who is known to have made one with a wooden stock enriched with silver, he was probably not the first. A brass-stocked pistol by an unknown maker dates from *c.*1680 and closely resembles the only known pictorial representation of a brass heart-butt pistol in John Michael Wright's triple portrait of the actor-playwright John Lacy (d.1681).[17] The decoration of the thin brass sheet from which the pistol stock is made includes an overlapping leaf pattern, rosettes, and a tulip-like flower that has been said, without much evidence, to indicate the Protestant Scots' approval of William of Orange. Although popular with two generations of dagmakers, brass went out of fashion as a stock material around 1650, except for one or two isolated examples, until Thomas Murdoch (1735-*c.*1790) revived it in Leith towards the end of the eighteenth century, for the pistols with rounded lobe-butts which were his speciality.

While most heart-butt pistols are rather long (one in the Perth Art Gallery and Museum measures more than two feet), a group of smaller weapons came into use in the first quarter of the eighteenth century. The best proportioned is signed *David McKenzie* (active 1707-28) and stamped with the Dundee town mark, a pot of lilies, on the narrowest part of the butt before the collar to which the point of the heart, itself made of two halves brazed together, is fixed. The pistol is now in the Albert Institute, Dundee.

A group of even smaller pistols in the same genre are engraved on the lockplate *IA MK*, the pairs of letters flanking a phaeon-like mark that is a stylised version of the arms, *or three piles in point gules*, of Brechin where the gunsmith James MacKenzie is recorded as having worked from 1728 to 1751. This little group which dates from about 1720-30 is the last of a completely Scottish style of pistol whose study is uncomplicated by the presence of foreign copies. Examples are in a number of public and private collections including the National Museum of Antiquities of Scotland and the Metropolitan Museum of Art, New York.

The last decade of the seventeenth century saw the appearance of the fully-developed Scottish pistol, 318-20
the direct descendant of the slab-sided ram's horn butt of the middle of the century. The butt shape was similar but more elegant and the pistol retained the flaring faceted muzzle, the belt-hook, lobed unguarded trigger, pricker and the general lines of its predecessor. It was shorter, with a curved butt, and most of its surfaces were heavily decorated with a combination of engraving and inlaid silver. Its locks were still made in pairs for the right and left hands but the mechanism was fairly new to Scotland, with a combined pan-cover and steel and the improved action described above.[18] Many pistols survive, singly or in pairs, with right- and left-hand locks of this type, from the eighteenth and nineteenth

17 The original was probably the canvas painted *c.*1668-70 for Charles II, now at Hampton Court. Another version was exhibited at the Royal Academy of Arts, London, 1960-1.

18 See p. 416.

centuries. Most lean towards being *armes de luxe*, with free but carefully executed ornament, and many of the vast majority which were stocked in steel were finished most carefully by burnishing to a mirror brightness before being coloured a rich blue which showed the silver ornamental inlays to advantage. To the writer's knowledge no eighteenth century steel pistol has preserved its original colour intact so that the student is teased by tiny areas of perfect brilliant blue under the fretted base of a belt-hook or between the arms of a spring, giving no more than a hint of a finish of the highest quality.

Soon after 1700 a number of pistols were made with a pierced disc comb behind the cock that reminds one of the tailed cocks of the earliest Scottish pistols. It was not always used, even by the same maker, and by the last quarter of the century the disc rarely occurs. On one late pair of pistols the rather handsome disc, with its star-shaped piercing, has degenerated to a poorly-executed fretted heart.

As time passed there was a tendency for the decoration to become stiffer and around 1730 there is a more frequent use of silver escutcheons as an alternative to the inlaid stars and hearts on the flat faces of the butts. Many of the original owners can still be identified by the crests, badges, mottoes, names and other inscriptions engraved on these little oval plaques. For instance, a pistol by one of the several Doune gunmakers called Thomas Caddell, now in the George F. Harding Museum, Chicago, has two such plaques whose inscriptions enable us to date the pistol more closely than is possible with most of the type. On one side of the butt is the owner's name *Capt. James Lockhart* and on the other *of General Colyears's Regt.* James Lockhart was promoted to the rank of Captain on 20 November 1737 and his regiment was renamed Halkett's in 1747. In this case the maker is known to have worked at Doune in Perthshire although the place-name is not on the lockplate. The usual custom was for the place of manufacture to follow the maker's name whether the weapon was one of the poor, late dress weapons or the near-masterpieces which could be had for four to twenty-four guineas from one of the Caddells, Murdochs or Christies of Doune. This little village achieved such fame for the quality of the pistols made there that many dealers and collectors talk of 'Doune' pistols as though the makers of Dundee, Stirling, Perth, and a dozen other places never existed. Perhaps the most interesting Doune maker was John Christie, in whose pistols one finds a variety of styles and materials, and only a very few of the considerable number of recorded examples of his work are other than of the highest quality. One pair in the collection of Her Majesty the Queen at Windsor Castle is incomparable. Where the usual stock is steel the Windsor pair is silver. The inscription *TOTUM HOC OPUS SUA MANU PERFECIT JOANNES CHRISTIE* and *ION CHRISTIE STIRLING* show that this masterpiece was made by Christie after he left Doune in 1751 to work in nearby Stirling. The third material used in the manufacture of stocks in the eighteenth century was brass, and a very good example in this metal is in Warwick Castle. It bears the unknown maker's initials *K.McL.* and the crest, motto and initials of its owner, John Lord Cawdor (d. 1821). The ram's-horn butt terminals are notably stout and tightly curled, and the metal is distinctly thicker than on steel pistols of the period. The Cawdor pistol may date from the granting of the Barony about 1796.

Brass was further revived in a group of pistols which Thomas Murdoch of Leith made towards the end of the eighteenth century. Although some are larger than others, there is such a strong resemblance between them as to suggest that they may have been made for some military formation. Their butts terminate in hemispheres and much of their surfaces are covered with the engraved patterns common to most late pistols. A parallel, but better finished, group by the same maker has steel stocks engraved and inlaid with silver, very like two earlier weapons made by John Christie during his Stirling period (1751-*c.*1760), and now in the National Museum of Antiquities of Scotland, Edinburgh.

Pistols were issued in 1757 to sergeants and other ranks who, under the command of the Colonels Simon Fraser and Archibald Montgomery, comprised the newly-raised Highland Battalions of Foot. The pistols, probably of native manufacture, were bought by the colonels although there does not appear to be any record of their source, but by 1762 the pistols issued to the Highlanders seem to have been the products of Birmingham. Two types have been identified.

The traditional ram's-horn butt terminal was retained in a series of all-steel pistols, weighing a little less than 2 lb, which were engraved on the lockplate with the maker's name *BISSELL*. Isaac Bissell is recorded as having worked at King Street, Birmingham from 1777 to 1783. The pistols are

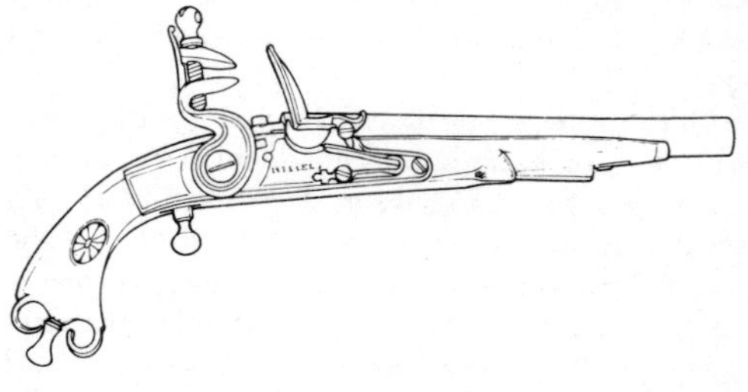

Steel-stocked Highland Scots military flintlock pistol by Bissell of Birmingham, *c.*1775-1800. Tower of London Armouries.

frequently engraved on their eight-inch, 0·560 in calibre barrels with the letters *RHR*, for the Royal Highland Regiment.

The second type, which is mentioned in documents of 1788, is a stylised version of the other; less ornate, slightly lighter, and with a kidney-shaped gun-metal butt. The 7 in barrels are of the same calibre as those mentioned above and are usually

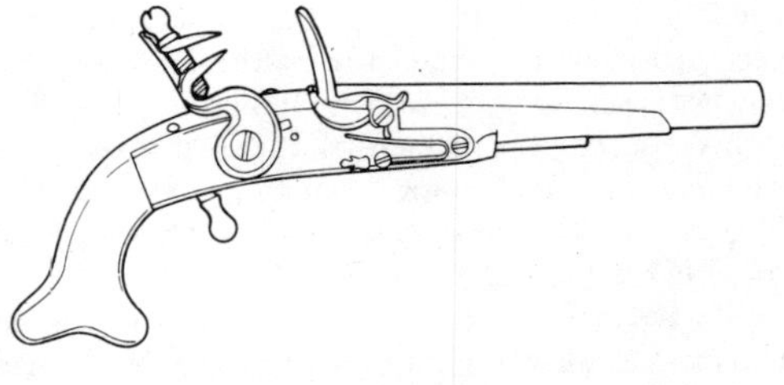

Gunmetal-stocked Highland Scots military flintlock pistol made in Birmingham (probably by J. Waters), *c.*1780. Tower of London Armouries.

stamped with the mark of John Waters, who worked at various Birmingham addresses from 1767 to 1788. It was presumably this type of pistol that the colonels of the 74th and 75th had in mind when they specifically asked if their next supply of pistols could be stocked in wood. Highland troops did not carry pistols after 1795 and it is unlikely that their loss was more than emotional. The weapons, if they could be dignified with that name, were not at all well thought of. The authors of the *Costume of the Clans*[19] described them aptly as 'coarse pop-guns, resembling more the tin toys of a bazaar than the weapons of an army'. There are no records of how inefficient the military pistol was, but some earlier references tell of assaults by men using Scottish pistols being so thwarted by misfires that they ended their business by clubbing their victims.[20] At least one victim lived to recount to a judge and jury his story of how an attack failed when pistols held against his breast misfired.[21] With few exceptions there is a roughness to the finish of locks made before 1750 or so, added to which the absence of a bridle to make the working of the tumbler more regular and the uneven temper of the springs resulted in a lock that was not one of the most efficient in Europe.

The proof of firearms was carried out in Scotland certainly as early as the late seventeenth century when a Mr Balfour was ordered to supervise the proof of guns and pistols for the Company of Scotland Trading to Africa and the Indies, on the afternoon of 21 July 1697.[22] Again, in 1704, under a contract between Daniel Stewart, agent for the Earl of Hyndford's Regiment, and five Edinburgh gunsmiths, 180 muskets and 180 pairs of pistols were to be stamped on the barrels after proof 'by the said Mr. Daniel or such other as he shall appoint . . .'[23]

There is no evidence as to the date of the first proof or of the form of the mark that Stewart was to see stamped on the Edinburgh barrels but a number of eighteenth century pistols bear the mark of a thistle surmounting the letter *P*. It apparently continued in use until about 1775 when it became the usual practice for the Scottish makers to import barrels from London and later from Birmingham.

When the army no longer issued pistols to its Highland soldiers the great days of the traditional Scottish forms were virtually over. A number of fine makers, such as Innes and Wallace in Edinburgh and Alexander Key in St Andrews, continued to make good pistols in the same style as the best of their English contemporaries. This had been going on since early in the eighteenth century from which time weapons in the fashion known to collectors as 'Queen Anne' pistols, stamped with the Scottish proof mark and the initials *AD* have come down to us. Later pistols made in imitation of the products of such masterly craftsmen as the Campbells and the Christies survive in considerable numbers to remind us that they were fit for nothing more than to be accessories to Highland dress or presents to and from men who knew no better; exquisitely made objects, but quite impractical. As early as 1795 a maker as distinguished as Durs Egg of London had mounted the bandwagon and supplied pistols with ram's horn butts to officers in Scottish regiments. The regimental number of the 78th of Foot and its motto are on the pair in the Dineley collection with the name *Malcolm*. Captain, later Major, Alexander Malcolm served in the regiment from 1793 to 1795.

The stocks of the all-metal pistols made in Scotland retained their traditional form with ram's-horn butt terminals until the end but lacked their former freedom. Some butts, even entire stocks, were of gilt

19 John Sobieski Stolberg Stuart and Charles Edward Stuart, *The Costume of the Clans*, Edinburgh, 1846, p. 125.

20 *Register of the Privy Council of Scotland*, Volume V (First series), p. 261, a report of an assault in Edinburgh, dated 28 January 1596.

21 *Register of the Privy Council of Scotland*, Volume XIII (First series), p. 17.

22 From information supplied by the late C. E. Whitelaw to the unpublished *De Cosson Dictionary* of armourers etc, kept in the Tower of London Armouries. The source is given as the *Journal of 'The Company of Scotland Trading to Africa and the Indies'* (the Darien Company) preserved in the Royal Bank of Scotland, Edinburgh.

23 *De Cosson Dictionary* (see n. 22) under 'Proof Mark, Scotland'. The source is given merely as *Register of Deeds. MacKenzie Office*, Vol. 95.

copper decorated with silver and enamel plaques. A blued steel pair, inlaid in gold with floral sprays and with gold and silver prickers, was presented to the Prince of Wales on 13 May 1800 at a time when their makers, Innes and Wallace, made fine guns and pistols which can hardly be told apart from those made in England. A pair of their travelling pistols, cased with accessories which include a carbine stock, is equal to the best that was being made in Britain. The 1800 gift to Prince George was handed over by Sir John Sinclair on behalf of the officers of the Rothesay and the Caithness Fencibles. They have locks in the English style, both fitted to the right side of stocks which are quite noticeably less curved than those of earlier pairs by John Christie and Thomas Caddell which, like them, are in the Royal Collection at Windsor. But these presentation arms alone could not support an entire industry which was in decline when George IV paid his famous visit to Edinburgh in 1822. The presence of the King in Scotland's capital had the result of arousing native and foreign interest in Scotland's traditions, crafts and culture. This led in its turn to a demand for plaid brooches, dirks, *skean-dhus* and pistols such as might not have been seen even before the Disarming Acts that accompanied risings and feared insurrection in the first half of the previous century. A demand that could no longer be satisfied by the Scottish trade was answered from London and Birmingham with trumpery knick-knacks. The end of the story of Scottish pistols is littered with ill-proportioned, plated, percussion lock, oddities which were more at home in a jeweller's showcase than in a gunsmith's shop or at the belt of a soldier. There is no absolute rule of identification but examination of a considerable number suggests that the attachment of barrel to fore-end by a vertical screw indicates English manufacture. The presence of London or Birmingham proof marks does not necessarily point to these cities as the sources of the finished arm, as barrels were imported. The flat, etched decoration, which the sword-makers of England called embossing when they used it on their blades, is another indication that a pistol was made south of the border.

The gunmakers in the main Scottish towns went on making top quality guns and rifles and Scots, like Forsyth, were closely connected with the development of small arms but they were unable to compete with Birmingham's close-knit trade community and the well-advertised, if slightly overblown, reputation of the London houses. In the past century the few remaining makers have been compelled to limit their production to rifles and shotguns made to the special order of a small but discriminating group of patrons who know a good gun and are prepared to pay for the skill and handwork which goes into its manufacture.

CHAPTER FIFTEEN

Oriental and Levantine Firearms

Z. Żygulski

74-77 In comparison with the results of the vigorous
21-34 and successful research into the history of European and American firearms that has been carried out, the information available about firearms in the Levant, Near and Far East is very limited. During the past decades historians engaged in the study of armament have greatly increased our knowledge of weapons produced since the late Middle Ages in the main European countries, but only sporadically extended their research to the Balkans, the basin of the Black Sea, the Arab countries, Persia, Central Asia and the Far East. K. A. C. Cresswell in his *Bibliography of Arms and Armour in Islam*[1] listed very few publications on Oriental firearms. There is no monograph or comprehensive assessment of the problems involved among them and his information is rather on the lines of a catalogue with annotations and extensive notes. The subject was attempted by students of an older generation, writing mostly towards the end of the nineteenth century, such as E. Lenz, Earl Egerton of Tatton, G. F. Laking, O. Potier, J. Szendrei and, among the more recent scholars, H. Stöcklein, G. C. Stone and S. V. Grancsay. The results of the work of these men remain valid to this day.

Large quantities of Oriental arms started flowing into Western collections as early as the eighteenth century. This flow increased, especially in the second half of the nineteenth century, and even led to a certain depreciation in value on the antique market. These firearms were merely labelled 'oriental' and no effort was made to establish a closer definition and date, and in general Oriental arms were valued less highly than those of the West. A serious difficulty in describing and classifying them arose from the fact that the specimens examined had been taken from their original context and the researchers were cut off from written historical sources and oral traditions. It often happened that attempts to decipher inscriptions yielded contradictory results. Even if they were read correctly the information so obtained was not followed by further search as to place and date of origin and maker, which could hardly be obtained anyway from a pious Koranic invocation, or names such as Mahmud, Ali, Hassan, encountered constantly all over the Islamic East. The collections of firearms in Oriental countries, which had been subjected for a long period to exploitation by European and American collectors, became very depleted. Indigenous students avoided the subject for many years or, if they did not, the results of their researches were unknown outside their country.

The difficulties in the classification and dating of surviving pieces are increased by the traditional conservatism of the East on the one hand and the ubiquitous copying of forms and designs on the other. Whilst the great variety of firearms bears witness to the evolution of the gunmaker's art throughout centuries and in various countries, there is proof that some types survived unchanged for decades and even centuries. This particular feature of Oriental arms was summed up by S. V. Grancsay: 'In the West there is always a desire for something new, but in the East changes are few, largely because of Oriental reverence for the past and belief in cyclic occurrence; everything is supposed to come around again.'[2]

Despite these difficulties there are many factors to stimulate research into the history of Oriental armament. Apart from the large quantity of pieces in various museums all over the world and the role which they played in the general development of culture, there is the fascination exerted by the Orient on outsiders and, most of all, the resurgence of Oriental peoples of the Middle and Far East following the political upheavals of our time. Various peoples which used to be described in general terms as 'Oriental' gained their independence after the Second World War; others have carried out far-reaching social and political reforms; everywhere there has been a considerable upsurge of national consciousness, national dignity, of interest taken in history and culture. Naturally, a detailed study of the cultures of these peoples will take time, but much has

1 K. A. C. Cresswell, *Bibliography of Arms and Armour in Islam* (James G. Furlong Fund Vol. XXV), Bristol, 1956.

2 S. V. Grancsay, 'A Loan Collection of Oriental Armor', *Bulletin of the Metropolitan Museum of Art*, XXIII, 1928, p. 127.

already been achieved by historians of various countries, including Turkey, Egypt, Iran, India, China and Japan. Only indigenous scholars are able to define and properly assess their own culture, using their own criteria, which obviously may often differ considerably from those applied by foreign researchers.

The present study does not, therefore, claim to be exhaustive but is rather a summary of observations made to date. It does, however, put forward a number of new ideas and makes an attempt at systematising the problems involved. It is mainly based on material preserved by the leading collections of militaria in Europe; largely, of course, those in the author's own country, that is to say in the Museum of the Polish Army in Warsaw and the National Museum in Krakow. The author is indebted for extensive help received from his English, Russian, German, Dutch, American and Chinese colleagues, and wishes to express his sincere tribute and thanks to them all.

This review of the problems concerning Oriental firearms is mainly confined to small arms and only in a few instances has reference been made to artillery. The subjects are arranged according to national groups and their sequence as well as the space allotted to each was dictated by the author's assessment of their relative importance; to a certain extent this method was governed by the accessibility of available material. Except for the first part, which deals with the earliest discoveries of explosive mixtures in the Far and the Middle East, which led to the creation of firearms, the text deals with their development during four centuries, from the sixteenth to the nineteenth. There is no need to adhere closely to chronology in our attempt at classification, predominantly because of the inherent traditionalism and conservatism prevailing in the civilisations of the East.

The scholar must primarily concentrate on types of firearms which are stylistically pure, i.e. in which all three elements, the barrel, the stock and the lock were made in the same period of time and assembled to make a weapon uniform in form, technique, decoration and function. In addition, firearms composed of heterogeneous parts will be considered as well as importations from the West adapted and ornamented in the East.

Of all types of firearms used throughout the East it was the long-gun that was the most important; it was used in war, for personal defence, for sport and parade. This type of gun eventually evolved into other types of firearms, such as the heavy wall-gun, the musket, the light sporting gun. Some types of pistols even were but miniature replicas of the gun, but generally pistols played only a very minor role in the East.

Beginnings of Firearms in the East: Invention of Gunpowder and the Development of Firearms in Medieval China[3]

Students of the history of firearms often interpret wrongly the evidence for the invention of gunpowder and its first use in warfare in China. Even recent literature on the subject contains statements suggesting that the Chinese had known gunpowder for a long time before the beginning of our era and that its use had been transferred to Europe from China through the intermediary of the Arabs.[4]

The invention of gunpowder in China in the seventh century was due very largely to expanding economic development and a rapid progress in the natural sciences during the Tang period.[5] Just as was to happen later in medieval and renaissance Europe, alchemists in search of the Philosopher's Stone were active in China. Although they did not achieve their ambition, they paved the way for modern chemistry by their examination of various natural substances. In 682 the eminent alchemist Sun-Sy-Miao wrote a treatise entitled *Canon of the Philosopher's Stone* in which he described the processing of sulphur and established in the course of it the explosive properties of a mixture of sulphur, saltpetre and charcoal. This is the oldest, historically confirmed, recipe for gunpowder which, in the early stages, was exclusively used for medicinal purposes and was not adapted for warfare by the Chinese until the beginning of the tenth century. The invention was simple: an arrow carrying, below its barb, a paper or fabric bag filled with gunpowder, with an ignited match, was shot from a bow. This weapon was called *feikho* and

3 This account of the earliest use of firearms in China expresses the opinions of scholars in that country. For reasons given in Chapter 1 (p. 25) they are not generally accepted in the West, though this is not to say that they are necessarily incorrect. *Editor.*

4 F. Lot, *L'Art Militaire et les Armées*, Vol. II, Paris, 1946, p. 439. E. A. Razin, *Istorya Voyennovo Iskusstva* (History of the Art of War) Moscow, 1957, p. 308.

5 T. L. Davis and I. R. Ware, 'Early Chinese Military Pyrotechnics', *Journal of Chemical Education*, Vol. XXIV, 1947, No. 11.
Cheng Tchia Gheny, 'Gunpowder: Its Invention and Spread', *People's China*, 1956.
Wang Ling, 'On the Invention and Use of Gunpowder and Firearms in China', *Isis*, Vol. XXXVII, 1947.
W. B. Wilinbakhov and T. N. Kholmovskaya, 'Ognyvovoye Oruzye Srednyewyekovo go Kitaya' (Firearms in Medieval China), *Is Istorii Nauki i Tyekhniki v Stronakh Vostoka*, Vol. I, Moscow, 1960.
Tchow Way (Materials for the History of Chinese Arms), Peking, 1957.

it is mentioned in a treatise by Siui-Tung, dated 904. The Chinese also used tubes to project incendiary discs and arrows, as well as grenades made of baked clay, filled with gunpowder and ignited by a match through a touch-hole. Another type of grenade, called *khopao*, projected from catapults or thrown by hand, was constructed from several layers of tarred paper fastened together with hemp cord. Recipes have survived for the fabrication of missiles made of bamboo joints filled with powder. The mixture consisted of a correct combination of sulphur, saltpetre, charcoal, colophony, sealing wax, bamboo core, hemp oil, wax, paper, and lead oxide. The ignition of the missile was followed by a whirring noise and the belching of poisonous fumes. At the beginning of the eleventh century the production of gunpowder and incendiary missiles in China was taken over by special state manufacturing plants. In the following century appeared prototypes of weapons exploiting the explosive properties of gunpowder. They were called 'lightning fire-balls' i.e. flame-projectors, similar to the Byzantine projectors of 'Greek Fire'. In China they took the form of bamboo joints filled with powder which were tied to the end of long lances. They were called *khotsian*. It was not until the Sung period that historical annotations for the year 1259 confirm the appearance of the first type of proper bullet-firing weapons, called *tu-khotsian*. Traditionally the barrels of these primitive cannon were made of bamboo, strengthened on the inside with clay and an iron disc; a cord was coiled round the outside and a touch-hole was pierced in the side. Such a barrel was capable of withstanding a pressure of explosive gases of eighty pounds per square inch; the bullets, probably made of stone, were projected to a distance of 150 paces. A further stage in the development of Chinese firearms was the invention of metal barrels made of iron or copper, called *khotun*. According to a thirteenth-century treatise entitled *What It Is Necessary To Know about a War Expedition* the early type of metal barrel was used for flame throwing, chiefly in the defence of towns and fortresses. The attempt was then made to use the *khotun* for projecting arrows powered by the explosive gases and ultimately metal or stone balls were used. The oldest known example of a Chinese copper gun, called 'The Flying Ghost', which was recently discovered in the course of archaeological excavations is dated 1351/2 and is in the National Liberation Army Museum in Peking. Other Chinese museums possess several hundred cannon from the 1368-1449 period. These have rings at intervals so that in shape they resemble lengths of bamboo.

The evolution from the invention of gunpowder through various types of fire-projecting weapons to firearms in the modern sense occurred in China entirely independently. In this respect China exerted some influence on India, the Mongols and to a lesser degree on the Moslim countries of the Middle East, but she made no impact at all on the development of firearms in Europe. In the fourteenth and fifteenth centuries the differences in the construction of firearms in China and Europe were fundamental. In the centuries that followed, China and other Far Eastern countries still made firearms in their own traditional styles, but essentially they were based on models transmitted from Europe.

Byzantium and the Greek Fire

During the early Middle Ages Byzantium, a country that exerted a tremendous influence on the whole Eastern Mediterranean, the Levantine and Arab world and even Europe, played a fundamental part in the development of firearms.[6]

The use of various incendiary mixtures projected from special wooden or clay containers is confirmed in the scientific writings of ancient Greeks, of Thucydides and Aeneas Tacticus. Vegetius, a Roman theoretician of military matters and author of *Epitome Rei Militaris* (*c.* AD 350) noted a recipe for an incendiary mixture containing petroleum. An improved standard of production in the crafts, as compared with classical antiquity, the development of technique and invention, the establishment of production plants for military purposes–all these factors contributed within the Byzantine state to the evolution, as early as the seventh century, of a new weapon of strategic importance, especially decisive in naval battles and known as 'Greek fire'. The nature of this weapon was a bone of contention for a long time in modern historical scholarship. Now it can be taken as proven that the basis of Greek fire was saltpetre. Combined with sulphur and tar it provided an explosive mixture resembling gunpowder but of a different consistency. During the course of centuries the composition of this mixture underwent certain changes. Greek fire already appears to have been in use at the time of the Siege of Constantinople in 673, i.e. it is earlier than the use of gunpowder for warfare in China. In the tenth century Emperor Konstantinos Porphyrogennetos wrote, in *De Administrando Imperio*: 'It should be known that during the reign of Konstantinos, son of Konstantinos also called Pogonatos [who reigned from 648 to 685], a certain Kallinikos, who had fled to Byzantium from Heliopolis, produced a liquid fire projected from siphons; this fire burnt the Saracen fleet at

6 J. R. Partington, *A History of Greek Fire and Gunpowder*, Cambridge, 1960. W. B. Wilinbakhov, 'Bizancjum a Rozwoj Broni Palnej w Europie' (Byzantium and the Development of Firearms in Europe), *Kwartalnik Historii Nauki i Techniki* Vol. 3, Warsaw, 1961.

Kyzikos and the Byzantines won victory.' The use of the new weapon is confirmed by many statements of Byzantine scholars, such as Theophanes or Leo Diakonos, and it is also borne out by Arab chroniclers.

Greek fire was projected from metal, probably bronze, siphons of a peculiar shape. Hand siphons by means of which 'a single man could direct into the enemy's face an unendurable fire' are depicted in the miniatures of Byzantine codices, especially that of Apollodoros of Damascus.[7] A hand siphon was a short tube, narrowing towards the front end, about 45 cm long, width at base about 20 cm, at muzzle about 15 cm; with a handle and a touch-hole in the side. The soldier held the siphon in his left hand, by the vertical part of the handle, and with his right hand ignited it by means of a match. The Byzantine flame-thrower was the earliest of hand firearms, and the prototype of all later weapons of its type. There is also evidence for the existence of large siphons for flame projection, of a special kind known as *khelandria*, installed on warships. Unfortunately no ship siphon, or even a drawing, has survived. One can only surmise that they had suitably long barrels, possibly analogous to cannon barrels of a later age, and that they were probably loaded from the rear. It is possible that hand siphons were used as loading charges for the large ship siphons. In the earliest phase, between the seventh and eighth centuries, these weapons were chiefly manufactured in Constantinople; later production plants were also established in other large towns of the Byzantine Empire, for example in Corinth, where, in the tenth century, a mould was invented for casting the essential part of the flame-projector. Owing to large-scale production and the general use in warfare of Greek fire, the secret of its formula could not be maintained for long. The Bulgars got to know it and it was used by the Polovskian Khans, e.g. Kontshak, in the twelfth century. Western Europe knew about Greek fire from the tenth century onwards and the Crusaders used it in Asia Minor. The oldest formulae for powder mixtures are known to us through the thirteenth century writings of Roger Bacon and Albert the Great and they are practically a repetition of the recipe for Greek fire noted in the famous *Liber Ignium ad Comburendos Hostes* of Marcus Graecus. Byzantine siphons were also imitated in Europe–as shown in the miniature in the early thirteenth-century German manuscript *Der Eneide Heinrichs von Veldeke* in the Stadtbibliothek, Berlin.

Firearms Taken over by the Arabs

The seventh century witnessed the rise and expansion of Arab states in the Middle East, along the Mediterranean Coast and, shortly afterwards, in the immense territories from India as far as Spain. They were, at least in the early stages, of a military character. In their engagement with the Byzantines the Arabs experienced, and suffered from, the efficacy of Greek fire and they soon succeeded in securing the secret of its production. In their expansion into the Far East, and holding as they did the key positions on the great trade routes, the Arabs developed extensive commercial relations. During the tenth and eleventh centuries large fleets of Chinese merchant vessels called at African ports. It is probable that this provided yet another channel through which the Arabs obtained information about the new inventions in military pyrotechnics. They themselves were carrying out intensive research into alchemy and mechanics. In his treatise *The Art of Conducting War in Allah's Name* the thirteenth-century Arab author Hassan Al Ramnah described 'the Chinese arrow' which acted on a rocket principle. It was a spherical container filled with an explosive mixture and provided with a cotton fuse. The same work mentions a weapon resembling the Chinese 'lances of violent fire' the missiles of which were filled with a mixture of saltpetre, sulphur charcoal and iron filings. Another Arab treatise allegedly dating from the fourteenth century, but known only from a fifteenth-century copy in the Institute of Asian Peoples, Leningrad, describes an Arab weapon called *midfa* which was used more for projecting incendiary missiles than for firing.[8]

To sum up, however, it must be admitted that neither the Chinese nor the Byzantines or Arabs succeeded in evolving, on their own, from their early flame- and missile-projecting weapons, a firearm of the gun or pistol type. It was Western Europe that, from the fourteenth century onwards, took the lead in this field of technical progress. The development of European firearms was rapid. The East became the recipient of the new developments and only modified models that arrived from the West.

Turkey

There are many reasons for starting a detailed review 277
of Oriental firearms with Turkey. Since the four- 321-
teenth century, and especially after the capture of Constantinople in 1453, Ottoman Turkey had created on the ruins of Byzantium an empire of her own and had united within her frontiers lands of three continents: Asia, Europe and Africa. After conquering the Balkan countries, a part of Hungary,

7 Vatican Codex No. 1605.

8 Ms. C686 P. Sixl, 'Entwickelung und Gebrauch der Handfeuerwaffen', *Zeitschrift für historische Waffenkunde*, Vol. I, Dresden, 1897–9, p. 109ff. M. K. Lindsay, 'Gunpowder', *Armi Antiche*, 1966, p. 157.

Moldavia and Walachia, Turkey threatened Italy, the Habsburg Empire and Poland. She also extended her domination eastwards by subjugating the Crimean Tartars, Mesopotamia, Syria, Egypt and Tunis and seized from the Arabs the leadership of militant Islam. The strength of the Ottoman Empire was based on a military regime involving a large standing army equipped with modern weapons. It was natural, therefore, that Turkey should develop a large-scale manufacture of arms chiefly for military purposes and in this she availed herself of all known inventions and the help of foreign experts, most of whom were Christians. The Turks were interested in Western developments in firearms as early as the fourteenth century and they soon appreciated the importance of the new weapons. Despite various restrictions imposed by the West on the arms trade, the jealously guarded secrets of production of the new weapons soon penetrated from the West.

Artillery was introduced into the Turkish army at the beginning of the fifteenth century. The manufacture of the equipment was assisted by Italian gunsmiths in the service of the Sultan. The conquest of the Balkans and the capture of Constantinople was mainly due to the efficiency of the Turkish artillery. Muhammad II succeeded in concentrating cannon of exceptionally large calibres which breached the wall of Constantinople and enabled the Turks to penetrate into the city.[9] Shortly afterwards a large cannon foundry was established in Istanbul, known as Top-hane. To this day cannon of unusually large calibres dating from the fifteenth and sixteenth centuries have survived in the yard of the ancient Istanbul Arsenal (near the former Byzantine Church of St Irene). A cannon dating from the reign of Muhammad II (dated 868 H, i.e. AD 1464) was presented in the second half of the nineteenth century by Sultan Abdul Aziz to the British government and mounted in the Rotunda Museum in Woolwich,[10] being later moved to the Tower of London where it now is.

Although we lack sufficient documentary evidence and surviving pieces to be certain, it may be reasonably assumed that hand firearms made their appearance in Turkey as early as the end of the fifteenth century. Iconographic sources of the first half of the sixteenth century prove the existence by then of a characteristic heavy musket used by the janissary infantry that formed the basic battle formation of the Turkish Empire. The matchlock musket, which was a local adaptation of Western European forms, especially the Italian, replaced the bow and arrow formerly used by the janissaries. One of the miniatures of the famous *Hünernameh* MS. in the Topkapi Sarayi Museum, Istanbul, giving the history of the Sultans and dealing with the reign of Suleyman the Great (1520-66), shows janissaries with pointed caps on their heads and carrying on their shoulders heavy guns with barrels thickening towards the muzzle and with inlaid stocks. The existence of the Turkish janissary musket is also confirmed by European sources, for example, the *Trachtenbuch* by Hans Weigel Forschneider, published in 1577 in Nuremberg, portrays *Miles Praetorianus sive Ianizarus* carrying on his right shoulder a matchlock musket with a butt end of polygonal section and holding a lighted match in his left hand, as well as in various 321
miniatures of the *Codex Vindobonensis* 8626 in the Österreichischen Nationalbibliothek, Vienna, dated between 1588-92.

Janissary units were formed of soldiers of Moslem origin and Christians forced into service, and they were the backbone of Turkey's armed forces; a large proportion of them were quartered in Istanbul. Their training was excellent and they usually attacked in deep columns, firing consecutive salvoes, but they were also trained to fight in scattered formation, in which they greatly excelled their Christian enemy. Up to the seventeenth century the number of janissaries exceeded 50,000. The barrel-foundries and arms workshops of the Sultan had to produce large quantities of muskets, as these weapons were quickly worn out in the constant wars of the period: they were, however, frequently modernised, old barrels being used again with new stocks and locks. This is why only a few muskets used by janissaries have survived in their original condition in museums, collections and historical armouries such as the Oruznaya Palace in the Moscow Kremlin and the National Museum, Budapest.

A Turkish matchlock gun, dating from the beginning of the seventeenth century now preserved in the Hermitage Museum in Leningrad, was described by E. Lenz in *Die Waffensammlung des Grafen S.D. Scheremetev in St Petersburg*.[11] The smooth round twist barrel, which is damascened in gold at both ends, thickens towards the muzzle where it is spirally fluted. The back-sight with one peep-hole is on the breech. The lock is placed inside the stock with the cock emerging through a slot: the latter is bent at a right-angle and forked at the top but has no jaw screw. The cock is held in an upright position by means of a spring and is lowered into the

9 H. G. Ferner, 'Turkish Artillery at the Fall of Constantinople', *Glasgow University Oriental Society*, VI, 1934, pp. 9-14.

10 J. H. Lefroy, 'An account of the Great Cannon of Muhammad II recently presented to the British Government by the Sultan with notices of other great Oriental cannon', *Minutes of Proceedings of the Royal Artillery Institution*, VI, Woolwich, 1870, pp. 203-27.

11 Leipzig, 1897, Inv. No. 857, Fig. 2.

pan against the action of this spring when the blade-shaped trigger is pressed. The pan is fixed in the stock under the touch-hole by means of screws and has a hand-operated cover. The part of the stock from the back-sight to the small of the butt is overlaid with silver sheet. Under the pan is a silver tube for the pricker for clearing the touch-hole, which is attached by a chain. The butt, heptagonal in section, slopes down slightly and is inlaid with bone and tortoise shell. A wooden, iron-tipped ramrod is fitted in the stock.

Two other Turkish matchlock muskets in Hungarian collections were described by J. Szendrei in the catalogue of *Kriegsgeschichtliche Denkmäler in der Millenium-Landes-Austellung*.[12] One of them,[13] bears a Hungarian inscription stating that this weapon was captured from a janissary soldier. Its cock is made of brass, the wooden stock is inlaid with bone and the wooden ramrod is iron-tipped. The musket is 161·5 cm long, bore 15 mm, total weight 4·57 kg. The other musket,[14] from the same collection, has a polygonal barrel, thickening at the muzzle and inlaid with brass wire. It bears a gunsmith's mark in the shape of the Zhul Fikar sword. According to Moslem traditions this double-bladed sword was captured by Muhammad in the Battle of Bard and came into the possession of Ali; eventually it became the symbol of Islam and was often represented on flags and seals. The musket under discussion has a very plain stock of unpolished brown wood, it is 150 cm long, and a calibre of 17 mm. Szendrei dated it to the sixteenth century.

The most valuable source for the study of the history of Turkish firearms is the report of Comte de Marsigli on the *Stato Militare dell' Imperio Ottomano* published at The Hague in 1732.[15] Marsigli spent eleven months in Istanbul between 1679-80 in the suite of the Venetian ambassador, Ciurani. He set himself the task of investigating the state of the Turkish army and–what might appear quite improbable–the Turks put no obstacles in his way: on the contrary, they gave him access to a great deal of information, provided him with an interpreter and even gave him a copy of the Turkish manual of army regulations, known as *kanonnameh*, for inspection. On his return to Europe, Marsigli entered the service of the Emperor. During the 1683 campaign he was captured by the Turks. Ransomed, he continued fighting in the imperial army until the Peace of Karlovice in 1699. His book is critical and, on the whole, reliable.

It would appear from his comments that, as late as the seventeenth century, the Turks were still using certain traditional firearms which had probably originated in the dim past in China and which they may have known in their pre-migration habitat in Central Asia. Marsigli describes and reproduces drawings of arrows provided with gunpowder charges (Chinese *feikho*) and various types of incendiary bombs, grenades and mines. In his chapter on artillery he illustrates specimens of heavy-calibre cannon which had handles for ropes tying them to the stock. The barrels were cylindrical and strengthened by hoops and they reminded him of the barrels of Western European fifteenth-century bombards. Turkish cannon of a lighter calibre made of bronze, with barrels narrowing towards the muzzle, were similar in shape to the contemporary European cannon, but much less ornamented. Marsigli also describes various types of Turkish mortars and an original piece of artillery, the camel gun, consisting of two light cannon mounted on a camel. Similar camel artillery was in use at the same period in Persia and India. Marsigli devoted a separate chapter to Turkish hand firearms. He differentiated the matchlock musket (of the type which has survived in the Sheremetev and the Hungarian collections mentioned above) as well as a rifle and a pistol with an oriental type snaplock.

During the sixteenth century, as mentioned in Chapter 2, Western Europe had made tremendous strides in the development of locks for firearms, one of the most important being the wheel-lock. That the Turks must have come across wheel-lock firearms at an early date is shown by documentary evidence. In his description of the capture by the Turks of the Hungarian city of Székesféhervár (Alba Regia) in 1543, Bishop Jovius of Como noted: 'Nothing was taken from our men other than the firelocks which the German cavalry carried on their saddlebow . . . the Turks were greatly delighted with them because they were a novelty and most remarkable.'[16] Nevertheless the Turks did not introduce the wheel-lock into their firearms nor was it used anywhere else in the East. On the other hand the form of snap-lock now known as the miquelet (in Turkish *tchomak*) was highly esteemed. As we have seen in previous chapters, the popularity of this lock in Spain was enormous and it penetrated North Africa, most likely through the intermediary of the Moriscos who settled there after their expulsion from Spain in 1609. It was then taken into favour by

12 J. Szendrei, *Ungarische Kriegsgeschichtliche Denkmäler in der Millenium-Landes-Austellung*, Budapest, 1896.

13 No. 3213 from Forschtenstein Castle, Austria.

14 No. 3211.

15 F. Conte di Marsigli, *Stato Militare dell'Imperio Ottomanno, Incremento e Decremento del Medesimo*, Gose & Neulme, La Haye, Uytwerf, Amsterdam, 1732.

16 J. F. Hayward, *The Art of the Gunmaker*, Vol. I, London, 1962, p. 71.

the Arabs and, through them, found its way into the Turkish dominions. The Turks adopted it at once. The direct change-over from the matchlock to the miquelet was revolutionary. The Oriental version of the miquelet lock very soon became dominant all over the Mediterranean area and passed further East, to the Caucasus and Kurdistan. The advantages of this mechanism were very great: the wide jaws permitted the flint to be fastened securely, the jaw-screws were provided with a ring or were T-shaped for screwing down with the fingers. The powerful spring, placed outside the lockplate, caused the flint to strike against the steel which was wide and grooved for better friction. The lower part of the steel covered the pan. The main elements of the mechanism being placed on the outside allowed any damage to be quickly located and repaired. The principle of the miquelet lock was simple but there are numerous Oriental variations, manufactured in the workshops of many countries, sometimes very distant from one another. Turkey used imported locks to begin with, but very soon founded her own manufacturing plants. During the seventeenth and eighteenth centuries a number of variants of the miquelet lock evolved in Turkey alone. In view of the present state of research it is impossible as yet to establish where and when each variant was manufactured, but the differences are evident. The lock mechanism was used throughout the whole of the Turkish Empire and was basically identical to the Spanish form described on pp. 70-71. When the cock was raised its curved toe engaged first with one of two horizontal sears working through the plate for half cock, then with the other sear for full cock; when the trigger was pressed the sear arms were withdrawn through the plate so allowing the cock to fall. The mainspring acted on the upper long arm against the heel of the cock. The differences in the Turkish variants are seen in the construction of the cock and steel. All are solid and strong but, according to their purpose, their proportions vary as does the size of the entire lock. Some cocks have elongated jaws with parallel edges, others are short with concave edges. One variant has a cock with a crescent profile. The jaw-screws have rings or are T-shaped at the top. The steel is adapted to the jaws of the cock, it is wide or narrow and tall, but always grooved vertically. The lockplates often bear deeply-stamped gunsmiths' marks, usually circular, with short inscriptions as for example *ameli Ali*, *ameli Hassan* (the work of Ali, Hassan, etc.). Some Turkish locks are in plain iron, without any ornamentation, but the majority are wholly or partly overlaid with chased silver sheet; sometimes they are encrusted with gold arabesques and even set with corals.

During the eighteenth century the miquelet lock was ousted in Turkey by the true flintlock which was mass imported from the West and mounted on Turkish hand firearms of all types.

The characteristic Turkish type of gun-barrel was evolved as early as the sixteenth century in Istanbul. These barrels were also highly prized in the West. It was from a gun with a Turkish barrel, with a wheel-lock dated 1604, mounted on a Western-type stock, signed by Hieronymus Borstorffer (working in Munich between 1596 and 1637) that H. Stöcklein, in his study 'Orientalische Waffen aus der Residenz-Büchsenkammer . . . München'[17] was able to differentiate, as early as 1914, a whole group of Turkish sixteenth-century barrels. These, made of twist Damascus, were very heavy and of a very large calibre, of polygonal (mostly octagonal) or rounded section. Sometimes both sections were used and the division was marked by a band of ornament. The muzzles of older, good-quality barrels were belled out to a pear or cup shape or were fashioned in the likeness of a dragon, some other monster, or a dolphin. The eyes and teeth of the monsters were set with precious stones or inlaid with gold and silver. The walls of the barrels varied in thickness and the calibre was between 12 mm and 27 mm. At first the barrels had a smooth, later a rifled bore, with grooves and lands of equal width, the number of grooves being seven, nine, or thirteen of depth about 1 mm, with a right-hand turn. Barrels which were polygonal in section were an exception. The touch-hole was lined with brass or precious metal to make it more resistant to the action of gunpowder and its bore was either cylindrical or conical with the wider end towards the pan. Older barrels were plugged from the rear with a riveted plug, later a screwed breech-plug was used. At first there was no sighting device on the barrels, but later various types came into use. At the end of the sixteenth century Turkish gunmakers introduced a very characteristic form comprising fairly thick triangular leaf with rounded corners, set at right-angles and pierced with a row of conical holes narrowing towards the fore-end and fixed on the barrel near the breech. There were also grooved back-sights of angular or semi-circular section and notches cut out in the tang of the barrel. Later, under European influence, back-sights in the shape of a pierced leaf that could be raised or lowered were adopted. Fore-sights were made of iron, brass or, more rarely, silver and were ball-shaped or took the form of little longitudinal bars.

On the barrels one encounters inscriptions, a verse from the Koran, sometimes the owner's name, quite often gunsmiths' marks. These last were quite different from those used in Western Europe being, as a rule, in the form of a rectangle standing on its

17 *Münchner Jahrbuch der Bildenden Kunst*, 1914/15, pp. 106-44.

shorter side, with a triangle on top of it, the apex pointing towards the muzzle. The name of the maker and sometimes the place and date of manufacture were stamped in the recessed, brass- or gold-lined ground of the design.[18] At times elaborate symbolic emblems were interlaced with the lettering, such as, for example, the Islamic knot which will be discussed below. In addition to gunsmiths' marks official control stamps, known as *imtihan*, were also applied. When Turkish barrels were used in the West, great care was often taken to obliterate any inscription or emblem for fear these might contain anti-Christian spells, but the ornament itself was left. The tops of Turkish barrels were chiselled in bas-relief and decorated with true or counterfeit damascening in gold, silver or brass, and also encrusted with precious stones and corals. The use of precious stones, such as ruby, almandine or turquoise for the ornamentation of firearms was not only in keeping with the Turkish taste for coloured decoration but was also talismanic.

The analysis of ornament on Turkish barrels helps in their classification and dating. Although there existed a repertory of ornamental forms proper to the whole of the Orient, there was a considerable divergence in the selection, arrangement and interpretation of the motifs, sometimes because of regional and national fashions, by which one may identify stylistic areas and periods. The ornamental motif most frequently found on Turkish gun-barrels is a sharp arc surmounted by a trefoil, usually accompanied by arabesques and more or less stylised floral scrolls. Other decorative motifs such as palmettes, wavy parallel lines, wave pattern, rosettes, etc. were derived from Classical antiquities inherited from Byzantium by the Turks. Favourite ornamental forms for the muzzle were fluted spiral grooves or a dragon's head. The top of the barrel above the chamber was regarded as a place of honour and was reserved for the intricate Islamic knot, a symbolic motif usually inlaid in silver. H. Stöcklein has traced the origins of this symbol (*Chang knot*)[19] to India and China. The knot with loose ends was meant to symbolise immortality and infinite happiness, and possibly, in accordance with Hindoo beliefs, the infinite transmigration of souls. The knot symbol is found on innumerable articles, textiles, ceramics, coins, etc. It was known as early as the thirteenth century in Persia, Syria and Egypt and reached Moslem Spain in the fourteenth, and Turkey in the fifteenth century, whence it travelled to Italy and Germany. The motif itself had evolved from a single knot (thirteenth to seventeenth centuries) to a complicated double or treble coil (eighteenth century). At the end of the eighteenth century the form degenerated into two layers of quadrilateral lines, rounded at the corners and superimposed on each other. By the end of the eighteenth century and in the nineteenth a general coarsening of ornamental motifs had become general in Turkey.

The adoption of the miquelet lock led, during the seventeenth century, to the transformation of the original gun into a standard type that was used in Turkey for almost 250 years. Old barrels were still used and the basic shape of stock was a continuation of the traditional one which was massive and heavy. The butt continued to be angular with a hexa- or heptagonal section, flat on the underside, with a sharp step immediately behind the breech, sloping down from the line of the barrel. Maple, pear or walnut was used most frequently. The butt was usually constructed in two parts, the fore and rear, joined together by means of wooden screws or dowels. The line of the join was outlined with an ornamental border. On the underside of the butt there was sometimes a small trap for spare flints or bullets. In old guns the barrel was attached in the West European manner by means of pins passing through loops welded to its underside and also through the stock. Later the general Oriental fashion was introduced of fastening the barrel and stock by means of capucines (barrel-bands), which could easily be slipped into position. At first their number was three to five, later it was greatly increased, reaching up to twenty and more in costly pieces. The capucines were elaborately pierced; they were rarely welded but their ends were hammered together and they were decorated in various styles. Wooden ramrods, iron- or bone-tipped, were fitted in the stocks; air holes facilitated their removal. A pricker for clearing the touch-hole was kept in a special metal tube near the lock. A metal ring on the stock served to fasten the gun to a belt. As a rule guns were equipped with a ball trigger without a trigger-guard.

Gunstocks were decorated in the full splendour of the Ottoman-Turkish style. Its basis was a stock of wood overlaid with various precious materials, such as silver, bronze, mother-of-pearl, ivory, brass, bone, staghorn, rare woods, tortoiseshell, coral, and precious and semi-precious stones. In keeping with the Sunnite character of Turkish art, human and animal figures were avoided and decoration consisted mainly of purely geometrical design or highly stylised plant scrollwork. Attempts were made at first to treat each piece individually but ultimately designs were reduced to certain formal schemes. Marquetry, for instance, followed a pattern of horizontal bands, starting from the buttplate, which was usually formed of a solid piece of ivory or horn.

18 Examples of these marks are reproduced in E. Lenz, *op.cit.*, Pl.XX; also Szendrei, *op.cit.*, Nos. 3211, 3212, 3213.

19 Stöcklein, *op.cit.*, pp. 118-32.

These bands were made up of rosettes, lilies or conventionalised trees resembling cypresses. Large areas of stock and butt were overlaid with ivory plaques or a mosaic of brass and horn rings. Sometimes the six-pointed star formed of two interlaced triangles, known as Solomon's Seal, was placed on the butt among these ornaments. This symbol, derived from the ancient civilisations of Mesopotamia had penetrated into Moslem culture and was particularly popular in Sunnite Turkey.

There is a group of Turkish guns with butts covered with embroidered polychrome textiles, faintly reminiscent of the early European muskets and stocks covered with velvet and ornamented with gilt stars.[20] In the eighteenth century silver- or gold-threaded silk cord was sometimes coiled round the comb of the butt, with three pendant tassels with silver mounts. This, possibly, stems from the Turkish *tug*–the horse-tail standard used as war symbol. In another group of guns elaborately pierced and chiselled panels of sheet silver are nailed direct to the stocks and the ornament thereon indicates the influence of French *Régence* decorative patterns dating from the early decades of the eighteenth century.

A great deal of information for the dating and the classification of various groups of firearms has yet to be obtained from the study of the ornamentation of Turkish guns. It will, however, require further exhaustive research on the verification of hallmarks and the identification of workshops.

Because of their excellence Turkish guns greatly influenced firearms in neighbouring countries, as well as further away, in the Balkans, North Africa, Persia and India. They were the object of legal and illegal export and were used for presentation while, in addition, large numbers fell into enemy hands as war spoils. As early as the beginning of the seventeenth century there is mention of Turkish barrels stocked in the Western manner in Germany.[21] There are reasons to believe that most of the firearms used by the Cossacks of Sicz and their infantry were of Turkish origin. Janissary guns were popular, especially in the seventeenth century, throughout Russia, Muscovy and in Poland. Numerous surviving seventeenth- and eighteenth-century inventories mention Turkish guns in Polish armouries of the kings, magnates and ordinary gentlemen. During subsequent centuries a portion of the original spoils of war passed to museums and has survived until the present day. Sometimes, as in the West, the barrels were dismantled and re-stocked in the local fashion. Examples from the Armoury of the Radziwill family survive in the State Art Collection in the Wawel, Krakow,[22] and those from the Czartoryski Armoury in the National Museum in Krakow.[23]

During the seventeenth century a heavy wall-gun was evolved in Turkey for the defence of fortresses, city gates, houses and also supply columns. The calibre was more than 20 mm, the barrel of twist Damascus, the stock heavy and the butt square. It required a solid base when fired. In shape and decoration it followed closely the standard gun. It had a very large, plate back-sight with a series of peep-holes for different ranges. The weight usually exceeded 10 kg. 324

The Turkish rifle, sometimes referred to as a carbine, also used by cavalry units, was slightly smaller than the standard gun, but equally strong and accurate. These rifles were not longer than 1 metre, in form and decoration following the usual style; their distinguishing feature was a strong octagonal rifled barrel.

As early as the eighteenth century a blunderbuss was evolved in Turkey, probably under Italian influence. Its distinguishing feature is its large bore and a wide bell mouth. Surviving specimens do not exceed 50 cm in length, have twist barrels inlaid with gold, flintlocks, stocks and butts resembling the French type, and are decorated with scrolls of silver wire or inlaid with bone with simple geometric patterns.

Pistols were far less popular in Turkey than in the West. Their shape was modelled on the contempor-

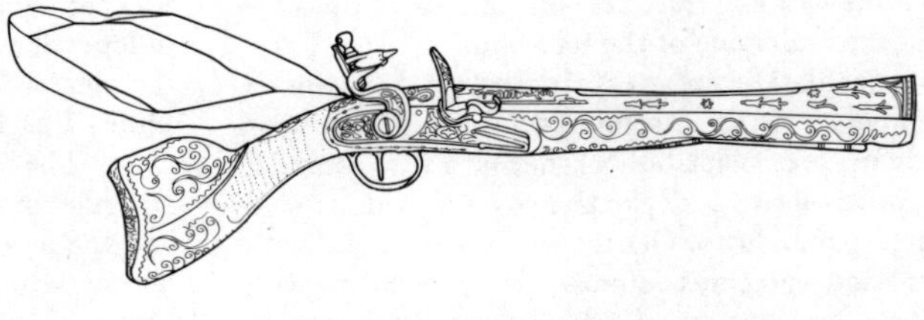

Flintlock blunderbuss, the stock overlaid with silver. Turkish, eighteenth century. Polish Army Museum, Warsaw.

20 See p. 51.

21 See p. 467.

22 Inv. No. 2866.

23 DMNKC 1571.

ary European type. On the basis of an engraved reproduction in Marsigli's book we may assume that the seventeenth-century military pistols had a smooth-bore barrel slightly thickened at the muzzle, an Oriental variant of the miquelet lock, no trigger-guard, a wooden stock with a ball butt and a ramrod fitted in the stock. Pistols were decorated, like the guns, with bone, horn, mother-of-pearl, silver or brass overlay, various techniques and materials being combined. They were mainly used by the janissaries and also cavalry units, who carried them in leather holsters covered with velvet and decorated with ornamental studs or panels of thin *repoussé* silver sheet, or embroidered. The Turks also used imported pistols, as exemplified by a typical Ripoll piece, now in a group of Turkish war spoils in the Dresden Armoury,[24] which were sometimes decorated in the local style. Sometimes barrels were imported, especially from Northern Italy, and stocked in the Turkish manner.

Most of the surviving Turkish pistols date from the eighteenth century and later. They have smooth-bore barrels of circular section, miquelet or flint-locks, pear- or onion-shaped pommels, stocks inlaid or overlaid with silver sheet chased in high relief or inlaid with silver wire and studded with corals. The barrels and stocks are joined together by means of capucines. There was no room for the ramrod, of which the vestigial trace remains in a slight thickening of the underside of the fore-end.

Powder-flasks were an essential part of the shooter's equipment. These were of several types, but were chiefly made of black bullock-horns. There were flat and convex flasks with nozzles covered with a metal spring-operated cap. Ornate pieces were inlaid with silver and precious stones, in particular with nephrite and turquoise which were supposed to bring good luck. There is such a powder flask captured from the Turks at the battle of Vienna in 1683 in a group of war trophies of Hetman Mikolaj Szaniawski in the Czartoryski Collection in Krakow.[25] Other powder flasks made in Turkey were circular, made of leather studded with nails, and with elongated nozzles. In some collections (e.g. the former Charles Buttin Collection) are specimens of Turkish seventeenth- and eighteenth-century rectangular ammunition boxes, made of bronze or sometimes silver, measuring 8 cm to 10 cm in width, worn at the belt.[26] Szendrei in his catalogue of the Budapest exhibition mentioned above[27] lists a very beautiful Turkish ammunition box called *fisheklik* made of calfskin, embroidered and adorned with cords and studs. Soldiers also used metal boxes for lubricants for oiling the lock mechanism. A shooter's accoutrement included a ramrod worn at the belt and called in Turkish *suma*. It was a steel rod, round in section, usually with an elaborate handle, sometimes made of silver and a clasp for attachment to the belt.

The Balkan Countries

The Balkans, inhabited by Greeks, Bulgars, Alban- 326, 32
ians, Serbs, Croats and Slovenes, were subjected to Turkish domination from the fourteenth century onwards but they adhered to Byzantine traditions and were also open to influences from Western Europe. Despite multiple and powerful pressures, and political dependence, these peoples succeeded in retaining their own cultural image and traditions which also found expression in the development of distinctive types of weapons. These–including firearms–have been classified with the rest of the great Oriental group, and must be discussed here.

Arms played an important part in the life of the Balkan nations. During the long centuries of Turkish domination the subjugated peoples never gave up the idea of armed resistance and struggle for their independence. History and legend alike kept alive the memory of the fourteenth-century Serbian state under Tsar Dushan and his defeat at Kosove Pole in 1389. The Albanians cherished memories of their struggle under Skanderberg in the fifteenth century and the heroic resistance of the Montenegrins. The Turks never succeeded in totally subduing the warlike inhabitants of the mountain ranges who continued to wage war on the invaders. These political and geographical conditions led to the survival in the Balkans of a society based on the clan structure, of a high feeling of loyalty and, especially in Albania, of traditions of vendetta. Weapons were indispensable for protecting life, independence and honour and they were also a means of obtaining food.

It appears from medieval documents that in the territories of what is now Yugoslavia, firearms in the shape of European bombards were used in 1351.[28] The new weapons of Western type were supplied by the Republic of Dubrovnik (Ragusa), where numerous cannon foundries had been established under the direct influence of Italy as early as the second half of

24 ill. *Orientalica*, Historisches Museum Dresden (undated) Abb. 10; this item is wrongly described as Turkish manufacture dating from 1670–1700.

25 Inv. No. XIV-346.

26 F. Buttin, *Catalogue de la Collection d'Armes Anciennes Européennes et Orientales de Charles Buttin*, Rumilly, 1933, Nos. 620, 621, 622.

27 No. 3255.

28 K. Jireczek and J. Radonič, *Istoria Srb* (History of Serbia) Vol. II, Beograd, 1952. (Also cf. W. B. Wilinbakhov, *op.cit.*, note 6). D. Petrović, *Dubrovacko oružje*, Beograd, 1976.

the fourteenth century. Allegedly fourteenth-century cannon barrels of Balkan manufacture have been excavated in several localities in Bosnia, in Kupresu and in Klutchu-Gacko.

Later, in the fifteenth and sixteenth centuries, the Balkan peoples, lacking a highly developed industry of their own and anxious to use modern firearms, had to procure them, at least in the early stages, either from the Turks or from Western and North European countries. This process was facilitated by military service. Bosnian and Serb units formed part of the Sultan's army, while groups of Dalmatians, Serbs, Montenegrins and Albanians served as mercenaries in Italian armies, especially those of the Republic of Venice. In the Balkans, therefore, there were firearms stemming directly from Istanbul but in a short time an analogous production was initiated by local workshops, while Western-type firearms were also used. However, neither the heavy Turkish musket nor the Italian variety suited the requirements of the mountain peoples of the Balkans. A combination of Oriental and Western elements yielded a light, long-barrelled gun and, later, a pistol suitable for military and civilian use. This type did not become fully established until the eighteenth century. A large number of these arms has survived and because of certain common stylistic features they have been conventionally grouped under the designation of 'Balkan' arms. The classification of the varieties within this group was largely due to the research of O. Potier and V. Curčič.[29]

Between the seventeenth and the nineteenth centuries the production of *petits maistres* settled in towns and larger villages developed in the Balkans, in particular in Bosnia and Serbia. Such places as Foča, Bihač, Prizren, were famous for the manufacture of firearms. Iron ore was supplied by the mines in Vareš, silver was mined in Srebrenica, Ljubice, and Borovica, gold was washed in the streams of Fojnica and Zeleznica. Gunsmiths stocked firearms and at times they themselves manufactured all the required components. Local goldsmiths collaborated with them in the decoration.

In view of the fairly primitive technical conditions prevalent in the Balkans the production of barrels for long-arms presented the greatest difficulty for the local gunmakers. It may be assumed that this difficulty was never really resolved and that the local output was very small with the result that use was made of Turkish and West European barrels. A. Gaibi[30] has established that Italian workshops – chiefly those active in Lombardy at Val Trompia and in Gardone near Brescia – had developed an extensive manufacture of firearms intended for export to the Balkan market and that, in the eighteenth century especially, their production was greatly increased as also was the assortment of types and parts of firearms which they made. These goods found their way into the hands of Balkan gunsmiths by means of legal, or illegal, trading through Venetian and Dalmatian merchants. Italian gun-barrels, popular in the Balkans, were made of good steel, had an average length of 125 cm to 130 cm, calibre about 15 mm to 18 mm, thin walls 1 cm to 2 cm thick, were usually octagonal at the breech, frequently round in section from half way down to the muzzle. They were always considerably thicker at the breech and slightly flaring at the muzzle. The back-sight was set at a distance of 12 cm to 14 cm from the breech (thus differing from Turkish guns where it was located directly at the breech) and a small ball-shaped fore-sight was placed on the muzzle. Above the chamber the barrel bore marks and inscriptions with the name of the maker, engraved in Latin lettering. Gaibi mentions names of famous seventeenth- and eighteenth-century barrel-smiths from Gardone, such as Lazarino Cominazzo, Venturi, Bertari di Gardone, Maffeo Franzini, Becalossi Franzini. Italian workshops also manufactured gunlocks of several types for the Balkans, generally described as *alla morlacca* or *alla mojacca*, all of them, however, variants of the miquelet lock. They differed from the typical miquelet chiefly in that the upper arm of the mainspring acted on the heel of the cock in a vertical direction (in the Italian type it pressed the toe of the cock downwards). Balkan locks, which must have been copied from Italian models by local gunsmiths were made of smooth unadorned iron; they can also be identified by the fact that the edges of the jaws of the cock are concave when viewed from above.

In addition to Italian barrels and locks, the Balkans also imported semi-manufactured parts from other countries in Western and Northern Europe, especially from France, England and Germany; there was also an extensive import of these goods from Danzig. Imports also included pistol barrels and locks. The fashion for pistols spread widely in the Balkans from the eighteenth century onwards.

The essential distinguishing feature of Balkan firearms is the way they are mounted. In the earlier period, from the mid-seventeenth to the mid-eighteenth century, the most popular firearm in

---

29 O. Baron Potier, 'Die auf der Balkanhaflinsel üblich gewesenen Gewehrformen'. *Beiträge zur Geschichte der Handfeuerwaffen* (*Festschrift M. Thierbach*), Dresden, 1905. V. Curčič, *Starinsko Oruzye* (Ancient Arms), Sarajevo, 1926.

30 A. Gaibi, *Le Armi da Fuoco Portabili Italiane delle Origini al Risorgimento*, Milan, 1962.
'Appunti Sull' origine e Sulla Evoluzione Meccanica . . . della Armi da Fuoco Portatilli', *Armi Antiche*, 1956.
'I Cominazzi; una Famiglia di Artefici Famosi di Gardone Val Trompia', *Armi Antiche, 1960*, Turin, 1960.

the Balkans, especially in Bosnia and Serbia, called *Šišana*, was modelled on the standard Turkish gun. The name is an allusion to the beam-like angular shape of the butt; in Turkish *sis khané* means 'divided into six parts' (hence the name for gunsmith *sis khanedşhi* synonymous with *tufendshi*). A heavy gun probably suited the physique of the Bosnians, who were stocky and strong. Barrels and miquelet locks imported from Turkey were stocked on the spot and decorated in the Turkish manner. *Šišana* was the least original type of Balkan gun, but even so in relation to its Turkish prototype, its proportions were more slender and the decoration less lavish.

The most characteristic Balkan weapon was a light gun with a thin barrel called *tančica* (i.e. thin). These guns were stocked chiefly in Albania, Montenegro and Hercegovina with barrels imported from Italy. The Balkan gunmakers achieved an unusual degree of lightness and slenderness in these weapons, suitable for use in the hilly regions and adapted to the national aesthetic requirements. The Albanian *tančica* has a butt that curves downwards and ends in a triangle, as it were a fish-tail, but with a flat buttplate of almost rectangular section. It is possible that the shape of this butt was distantly reminiscent of the Lombard, French and Dutch butts at the turn of the sixteenth to seventeenth centuries. Both the butt and the very thin hardwood stock of the *tancica* were usually overlaid with iron or brass and, on more costly pieces, with sheet silver panels, chased with a dense tracery of floral scrolls, palmettes, foliage and twigs. Similarly decorated capucines fastened the barrel to the stock. The decorative motifs were largely taken from the repertoire used in Greek and Roman antiquity, as transmitted by the Italian Renaissance, but the arrangement of motifs and their total coverage of available surface was in agreement with the canons of Oriental decorative art. One is reminded of the style of guns produced on the other side of the Italian peninsula, in Sardinia and Corsica.[31] In these islands, especially during the sixteenth century, a distinctive style of long-gun was evolved, so very characteristic that if it is placed with other types, even an inexpert eye can easily pick out a Sardinian gun. The barrels and miquelet lock (*alla morlacca*) for Sardinia were also manufactured in Val Trompia. The guns were slender in proportion, long, with a flattened butt, resembling a fish-tail but broader than in the Balkan type. The most striking feature of the Sardinian gun was the total or partial overlay of the stock with pierced iron or silver sheet chiselled with floral ornament interlaced at times with small grotesque figures. In their technical and artistic execution the Balkan guns were much inferior to those made in Sardinia, but undoubtedly they were created in response to the same stimuli and were the outcome of the crossing of Oriental with Western models.

In addition to the highly popular Albanian gun there evolved in the Balkans other variants of the *tančica*–slender guns with constructional problems resolved in a way which testifies to extensive direct influences exerted on the Balkans by the Orient, excluding Turkey. In the Charles Buttin Catalogue[32] there is a reproduction of a Greek gun with a short octagonal twist barrel and a butt that curves down and then up (i.e. contrary to the outline of the Albanian gun) which is reminiscent of certain types of guns encountered in Persia and India. In the Balkans it was called a *rašak* or *daglinka*. The buttplate is concave, both butt and stock entirely overlaid with metal, usually *repoussé* brass panels with a local mixture of Renaissance, antique, rococo and Oriental motifs. Similar treatment was also given to blunderbusses while guns followed more closely Turkish models. A *tančica* with a buttplate made of horn was known as a *roga*.

During the eighteenth and nineteenth centuries a type of gun, called *dsheferdar*, with French-type stock and flintlock became popular in the Balkans and especially in the Hercegovina region. This foreign model, however, was given Oriental decoration. The butt and stock were richly overlaid with geometrical designs composed of plaques of mother-of-pearl. Even when complete guns were imported from the West, they were additionally ornamented in the local style, a fact that tends to confuse a superficial examiner.

It would appear certain that it was due to Western influence that the fashion for pistols spread in the Balkans to a much greater extent than it did in Turkey proper but here too eclecticism is noticeable. As a rule the pistols had imported Italian, French or German barrels and locks in local, suitably ornamented, stocks. In earlier types the pistols had a ball-butt elongated to a point and the entire stock was overlaid with brass or silver sheet, decorated in high relief. A type of Balkan pistol with stock overlaid with chased brass sheet has an elongated butt only slightly falling away from the line of the barrel and ending in an ovoid pommel stretching into a tail which gave rise to the collectors' name for the type: rat-tailed 'pistol'. In later types the pommel was fashioned on French models with the characteristic pommel mounted in metal, while the greater part of stock and butt was left unadorned. This was therefore subjected to decoration with inlaid silver wire

31 Ch. Buttin, 'Les Fusils de Sardaigne', *Beiträge zur Geschichte der Handfeuerwaffen* (*Festchrift M. Thierbach*), Dresden, 1905.

32 No. 619.

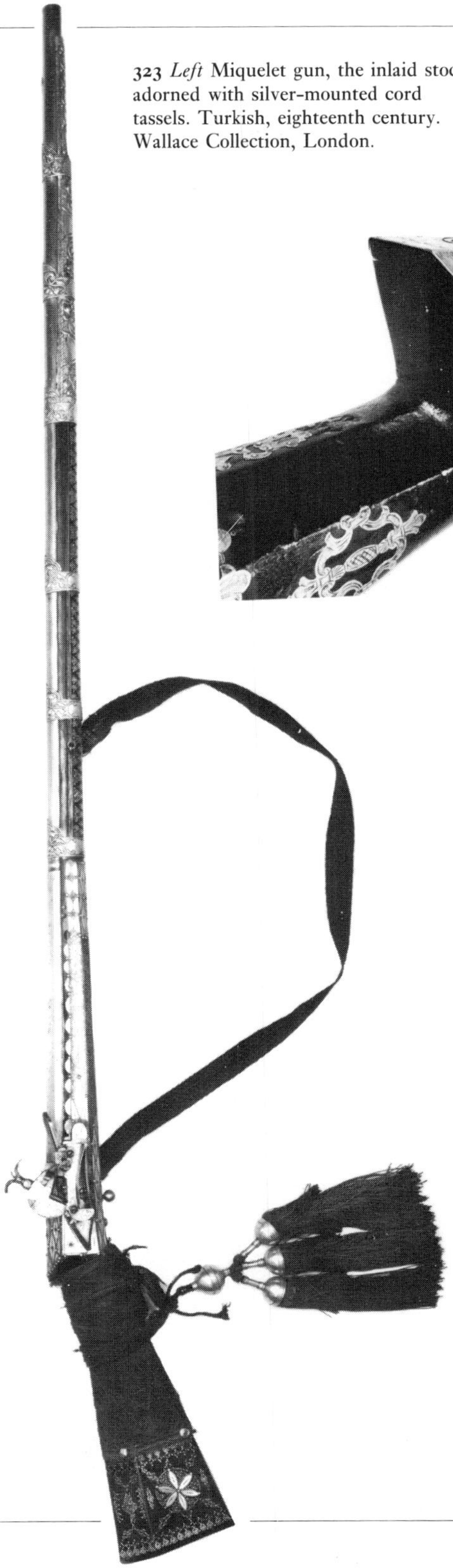

323 *Left* Miquelet gun, the inlaid stock adorned with silver-mounted cord tassels. Turkish, eighteenth century. Wallace Collection, London.

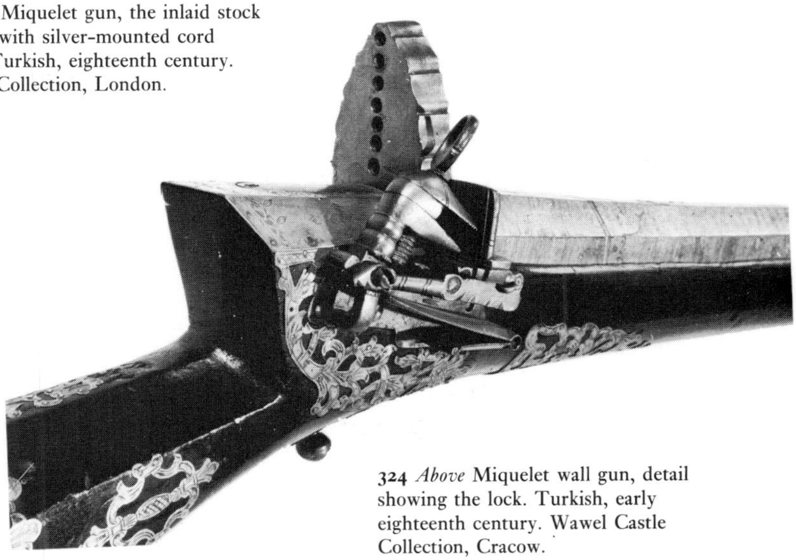

324 *Above* Miquelet wall gun, detail showing the lock. Turkish, early eighteenth century. Wawel Castle Collection, Cracow.

325 *Below* Powder horn mounted in silver set with stones. Turkish, seventeenth century. Muzeum Narodowego, Cracow.

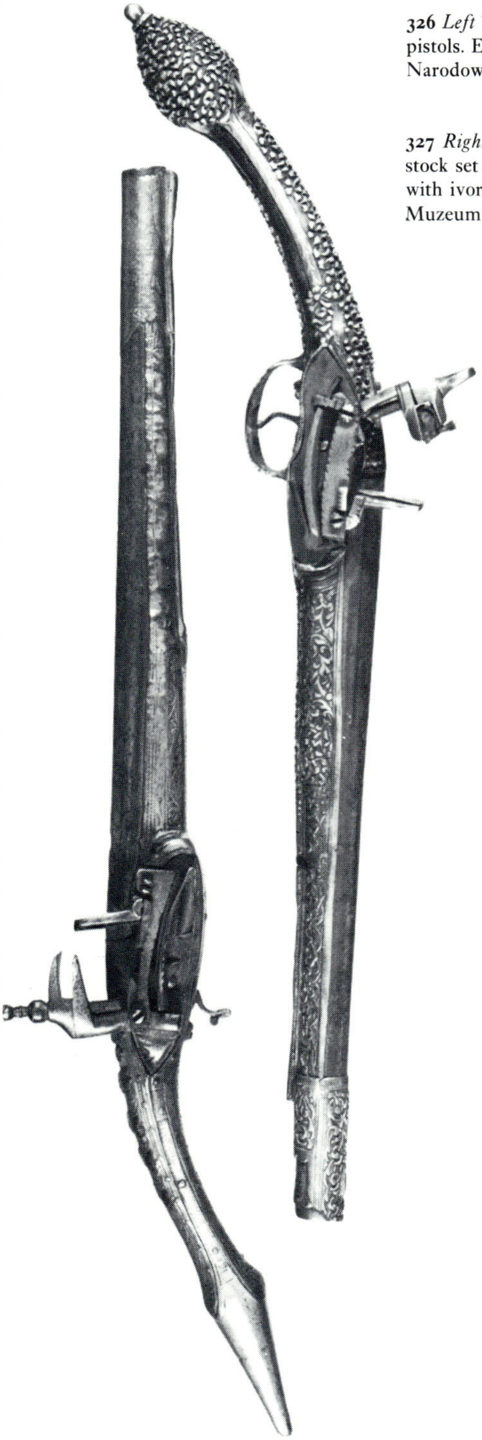

326 *Left* Two Balkan (Turkish) miquelet pistols. Eighteenth century. Muzeum Narodowego, Cracow.

327 *Right* Detail of a miquelet gun, the stock set with brass nails and inlaid with ivory. Arabian, eighteenth century. Muzeum Narodowego, Cracow.

328 Pair of flintlock pistols decorated in the Maghreb. The stocks set with coral. Late eighteenth or early nineteenth century. Wallace Collection, London.

329 *Above* Miniature depicting the gunmaker of Shah Abbas. Persian, *c.*1600. Muzeum Narodowego, Cracow.

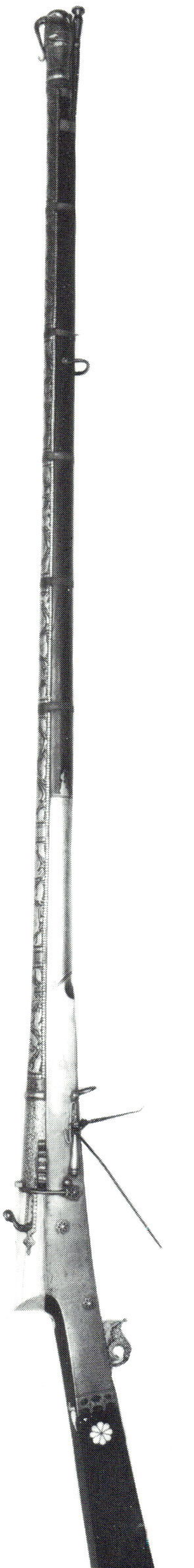

330 *Right* Matchlock gun, the stock sheathed in steel. Indian (Lahore), seventeenth century. Wallace Collection, London.

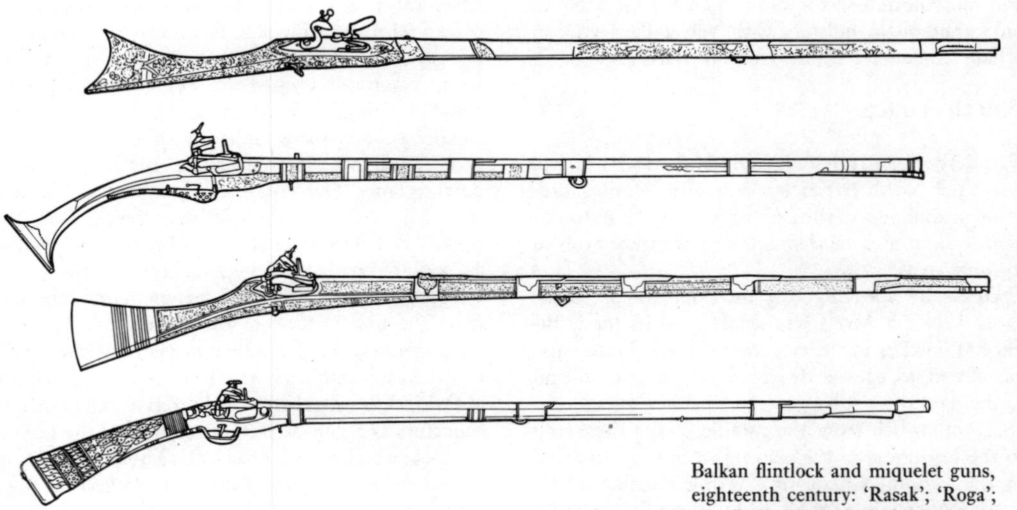

Balkan flintlock and miquelet guns, eighteenth century: 'Rasak'; 'Roga'; 'Tančica'; 'Dscheferdar'. Muzeum Narodowego, Cracow.

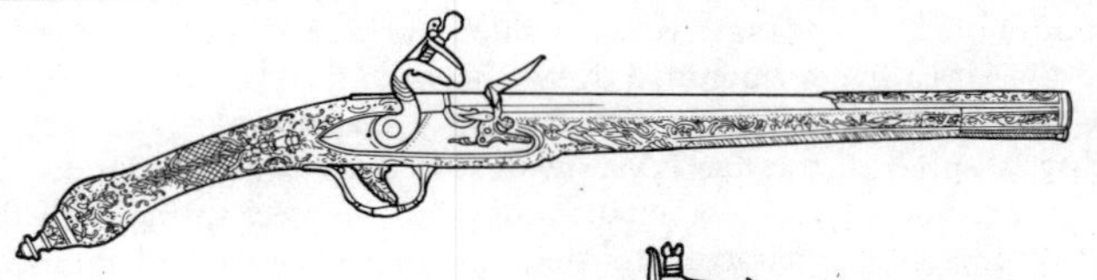

Flintlock pistol with silver stock. Balkan, eighteenth century. Wallace Collection, London.

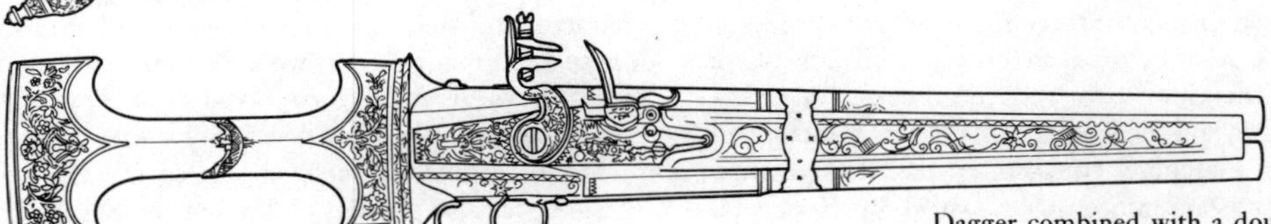

Dagger combined with a double-barrelled flintlock pistol. Balkan, eighteenth century. Muzeum, Narodowego, Cracow.

and encrustations with corals and semi-precious stones. There was no room for the ramrod on the stock of the Balkan pistols and only a vestigial trace of it remains in the somewhat thickened underside of the forestock. The ramrod, as in Turkey, was now worn at the belt. In local parlance the various types of pistols were called from their place of production (e.g. *Lisanka* from Lisa, *Slivanka* from Slivna, *Pečanka* from Peči, etc.), or from their type of decoration: *zlatka* from golden, *merdjankiya* from coral, etc.

It is possible that a small group of combination weapons, consisting of a double-barrelled pistol and dagger[33] is connected with the Balkans. There is a weapon like it in the National Museum in Krakow[34] and another one reproduced in Stone,[35] and there is another in the Hermitage Museum, Leningrad. These weapons have two barrels one above the other and a single flintlock with a double pan. On firing the upper barrel, the upper pan is removed and the lower one disclosed. The butt is formed from the hilt of the dagger, the blade of which is concealed between the two barrels of the pistol. The hilt, mounted in silver and adorned with blue enamel, is reminiscent of the hilts of the daggers called *kindjals* used in the Balkans. Both barrels and the lock of this combination weapon are of foreign origin and it is possible that it was manufactured entirely in the West for export to the Balkans.

Pistol ramrods, horn powder-flasks, metal priming-

33 Charles Buttin Collection, cat. no. 618.

34 XIV-496.

35 G. C. Stone, *A Glossary of . . . Arms and Armor*, Portland, Maine, 1934, Fig. 240/10.

and ammunition-boxes were modelled on Turkish ones, but pistol holsters with velvet flaps and an ornate fringe were copied from Western fashions.

North Africa

327 The Berbers, and other nomadic Arab tribes who had inhabited North Africa for centuries, adopted firearms, as did most of the Levant, during the sixteenth century and in time distinctive types were evolved in these areas.

Generally speaking, the development of small-arms in North Africa was determined by the influence of Turkey in the east and of Italy, France and Spain and, to a lesser degree, England and Holland in the west.

Egypt, which from the middle of the thirteenth to the beginning of the sixteenth century was ruled by the Mamluk sultans of Turko-Circassian origin, was conquered in 1516 by the Ottoman Sultan Selim I. From this time onwards janissary units, formed in Egypt, became an important part of the Turkish army. Their heavy matchlock muskets, decorated with silver and coral were described, as already noted, by Marsigli. Turkish expansion in North Africa extended further west during the reign of Suleyman the Magnificent, when Kair-ed-Din Barbarosa subjugated Tunis in 1525. Ten years later Tunisia suffered an armed intervention by the Emperor Charles V and became an area of constant strife between the Spaniards and the Turks. Surviving descriptions and the iconography of this war confirm the use of matchlock muskets by both belligerents. During subsequent centuries, ruled by Beys who were practically independent, Tunisia became a state with a large corsair fleet; it still continued to maintain lively associations with Turkey and even some commercial relations with a few Christian countries.

Barrels and locks produced in Europe were brought to Tunisia by various routes, often by smugglers. They came chiefly from the region of Brescia in Italy. It is likely, though we have no definite information about it, that local workshops were set up to copy foreign models. In any case, as in Sardinia and the Balkans, a type of firearm was eventually evolved suited to Arab tastes and style. Tunisian guns, known chiefly from surviving eighteenth and nineteenth century pieces, have barrels about 140 cm long, usually of octagonal section, with thin walls (about 1 mm at the muzzle end), and a calibre of approximately 15 mm. The back-sight, usually of brass, with a V-notch, is set at the breech with a small ball-shaped fore-sight on the muzzle. The barrel is fastened to the stock by means of a series of capucines, mostly made of brass sheet with *repoussé* ornament; more elaborate specimens have silver sheet capucines. The capucines were usually placed with the wide side downwards which was a peculiarity of Arab guns; their number varied from six to twenty or even more. Sometimes they were made of coils of wire. Stocks and butts are of wood, usually stained black, inlaid with simple floral or geometrical ornament in brass, coral, mother-of-pearl or bone. The workmanship is coarse. The butt is of fish-tail form, the outline differing from the Balkan and Sardinian shape in being more regular and approximating to an equilateral triangle.

From the Spanish prototype, or more accurately from the first version of the miquelet lock, dated about the end of the sixteenth century, the Arabs evolved their own version. The characteristic feature of this lock is a hand-operated safety-catch known to collectors as a dog-catch, located behind the heel of the cock, which gives half-cock by a hook engaging in a notch cut in the back of the cock. At first the dog-catch had a scroll at the top, later this was replaced by a ring. A strong mainspring acts through the lower arm on the heel of the cock. The cock itself, with a straight arm, has very elongated jaws (about 55 mm) with rounded surfaces. The jaw screw is surmounted by two horns to facilitate the cocking of this lock with its heavy mainspring. The face of the steel is very wide with deep canelures. Under the pan is a small bridge for the steel spring with the characteristic head of an open-mouthed monster. These locks made of iron were decorated with brass sheet inlays or entirely engraved with Arab ornament, floral scrollwork, carnation flowers, etc.

The Arab-made miquelet, modelled on the Spanish version, was also popular in Turkey and Syria.

Algeria, hilly and inaccessible, was inhabited by the Berbers, among whom there were considerable tribal differences. Some tribes, like the Kabyles, settled in the Tell, a rocky and mountainous part of the country; others lived a nomad life in the desert, as did the Tuaregs. There was also a considerable influx of Arabs whom the Europeans called Moors. Like Tunisia, during the sixteenth century Algeria was an area where the interests of Turkey and Spain were ever in conflict. An armed expedition by the Emperor Charles V in 1541 failed to subjugate the country. In the following centuries Algeria was ruled by a local janissary democracy as well as by the Berber corsairs until 1830 when she was conquered by the French. Thus throughout her history she was exposed to a variety of influences emanating from both Turkey and the Christian countries. This led to the introduction of firearms of various types; component parts, barrels and locks, were also imported and assembled locally. The basic type of firearm resembled the Tunisian gun, and the miquelet with dog-catch was the most popular ignition mechanism.

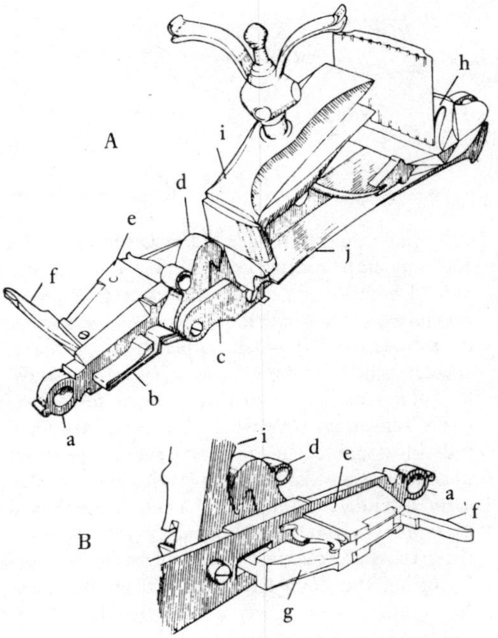

MIQUELET LOCK OF KABYLE TYPE
A shows the lock from outside. B illustrates the operation of the sear-mechanism
a Lockplate
b Spring for back-catch
c Bridle for cock and back-catch
d Back-catch
e Sear-mechanism bracket
f Trigger-lever
g Sear-lever with sear working through plate
h Combined steel and pan-cover
i Cock
J Mainspring
Based on eighteenth- to nineteenth-century N. African lock (No. M. 70-1912) in the Victoria & Albert Museum

The development of firearms in Morocco, the westernmost Moslem country called West Maghreb, also inhabited by Berbers, Kabyles and Moors, followed a somewhat different pattern. These tribes, extremely mobile and warlike, tried to invade Spain on three occasions and subsequently defended their independence against all odds and difficulties. Firearms were introduced during the rule of Ahmad IV ed-Dhahabi, and his successor, Zidan, established friendly relations with Northern European countries, especially England under Queen Elizabeth and the Stuarts (an alliance which was primarily directed against Spain). Trade flourished, merchants and craftsmen were granted protection against corsairs and special privileges were granted to settlers in the coastal towns of Morocco. Firearms of Western and Northern European type flowed into Morocco; imports of semi-manufactured parts were established and these were mounted as well as copied locally with modifications to suit Arab tastes, in such towns as Tangiers, Tetuan, Fez, Mequinez and Marrakesh.

In Western Maghreb the snaphance lock modelled on an early Dutch or English prototype became popular. The characteristic feature of this lock was a mainspring, acting on the inside of the mechanism; a steel made separate from the pan-cover; a circular fence at the end of the pan; and a sear that worked laterally. These locks, still made by Arab gunsmiths late into the nineteenth century, were fairly large and had a solid finish; they were of plain steel or chased or inlaid with silver sheet. The guns in which they were mounted were very long, approximately 175 cm, with barrels of round or octagonal section, engraved and gilded, covered with large Maghreb inscriptions in gold or silver, decorated with niello or enamel. Notched back-sights were used as in Tunisia. The barrels were attached to stocks by numerous capucines made of brass or silver sheet, engraved or pierced, or by coils of wire. Butts were of several forms: one version was similar to those in Eastern Maghreb, but was overlaid with silver sheet, *repoussé* and decoratively cut out along the edge. White or stained bone inlay was also used for ornament. On another Kabyle type of gun the butt, narrowing towards the comb, widened fan-like towards the heel, which was usually made of one piece of bone. These guns had long iron ramrods fitted in the stock and trigger-guards.[36]

Most of the pistols used in West and East Maghreb were imported. French, Italian, Spanish and English pistols, mostly flintlocks, were locally decorated and inscribed in Arab style. Numerous examples have survived in European collections, for example a pair in the Hermitage, Leningrad, presented to the Tzar by the King of Serbia. There is a beautiful pair

36 S. V. Grancsay, 'Firearms of the Mediterranean', *The American Rifleman*, March 1949.

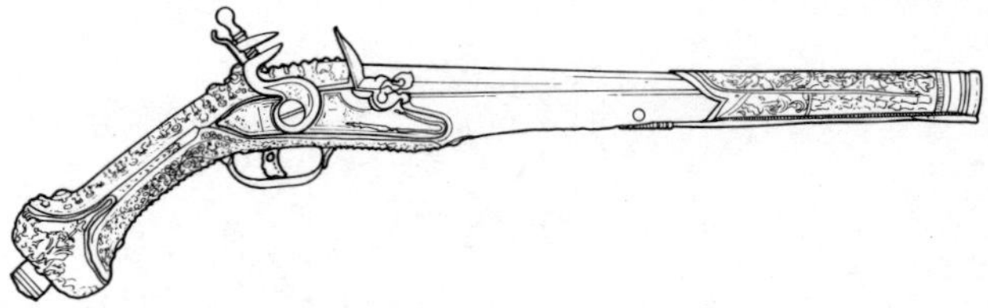

Flintlock pistol with silver-decorated stock. Turkish, eighteenth century.

of pistols richly inlaid with heart-shaped panels of coral and silver in the Wallace Collection in London (probably copied from an eighteenth-century French model) decorated by the Arabs, which in the Laking catalogue is wrongly described as of Armenian manufacture[37] and which closely resembles a piece in the Czartoryski Museum in Krakow[38] which has a pious inscription in Maghreb lettering as well as the name of the maker, Ben Kassem, and date 1127 H (AD 1715). Similar pistols as well as long-guns set all over with coral, presentation pieces from sultans of Morocco for kings of Spain, survive in the Real Armería, Madrid.

There is, however, a group of original pistols entirely made in Morocco. Among these was the piece, formerly in the Charles Noel Daly Collection, with a snaphance lock, inlaid with engraved silver sheet panels with a gold encrusted barrel, a stock inlaid with silver wire and a peculiar mushroom-shaped pommel.[39]

Special mention should be made of Moroccan powder-flasks. They were worn at the belt and were a colourful touch in a warrior's get up. Different forms evolved in various parts of Morocco. Thus in the province of Halen and Shluka they were in the form of cylindrical metal boxes; in Sus that of triangular boxes or flattened pears; in Fez and the whole Riff they were carved in wood or fashioned of hide. There were also powder-flasks made of horn or keeping the traditional horn forms but copied in metal, iron, brass, sometimes in wood covered with embroidered leather, velvet or silk. The most comprehensive and sumptuous collection of Arab powder-flasks is in the De Batha Museum in Fez.[40]

Persia

328, 331 In the article on Persian arms in A. U. Pope's *Survey*
335 *of Persian Art* Hans Stöcklein writes, 'Firearms did not come into general use in Persia until very late in the sixteenth century and they were not highly valued because of the fact that pedestrians were of no consequence in a land where there was so much desert country.' It would appear that the German scholar who has done so much for the study of Oriental arms, failed in this instance to appreciate to the full extent the ability of the Persians to create individual and original products even if the principle of construction was based on foreign models. Persia, a mountainous country in a central position with extensive coastlines, had been since time immemorial the great track followed by the migration of peoples. Lying on the main land routes from the West to India, open to trade, exposed to outside influences, she had herself developed so high a culture that she exerted a tremendous influence on all adjoining countries. Though preferring peace to war, the Persians from the earliest times were great warriors. The bow was then their favourite weapon, later to be replaced by firearms. In Persia artillery was used as early as the fifteenth century. Threatened by Muhammad II, Sultan of Turkey, Uzun Hassan ibn Ali the ruler of Persia, sent a mission to Venice in 1473 to obtain artillery. The Venetians sent him a number of cannon and even a hundred artillerymen under Tommaso di Imola. But neither at this early period nor later – and here we must agree with Stöcklein – was artillery considered of much importance in Persia. To begin with, the Persians never established their own production of artillery. In 1602 the Grand Duke of Muscovy sent Shah Abbas the Great a number of cannon for the siege of Darband. In 1683 a French traveller, N. Sanson, saw numerous Portuguese cannon in Isfahan, which had been captured at the Battle of Ormuz but they were unfit for use. The only type of artillery used by the Persians were light camel guns.

The Persian genius found expression in the adaptation of long-guns, chiefly for sport. As early as the sixteenth century the heavy matchlock musket of Turkish origin (or possibly Portuguese, brought by way of India) was transformed into a light weapon, slim and decorative though not lacking in technical merit. This kind of weapon was suited to the courtly culture of the Persian people and their love of beautiful and delicate objects. The light gun,

37 G. F. Laking, *The Wallace Collection Catalogue: Oriental Arms and Armour*, London 1914 (2nd edn London 1964) Nos. 2041/2.

38 Inv. No. XIV-455.

39 G. C. Stone, *op.cit.* Fig. 649.

40 Buttin, *op.cit.*, No. 1065.

a true masterpiece of art evolved by Persian gunsmiths as early as the sixteenth century, exerted a decisive influence on the design of analogous arms in adjoining countries, especially India, Afghanistan, the Caucasus, the Crimea, and even, to a limited extent, in Turkey. Unfortunately, few pieces have survived and in addition arms produced by Persian craftsmen are often attributed to other countries. For this reason, more than elsewhere, iconography plays a much more important part for the student of firearms; fortunately it is rich, reliable and of high artistic merit. Written sources too are of great importance.

Light matchlock guns are frequently depicted in Persian miniatures of the sixteenth century. An excellent example in a manuscript in the Czartoryski Museum in Krakow[41] represents a gunsmith in
329 the act of damascening the barrel of a long-gun. The gun is shown from the left so that the lock is not visible. The shape of the stock, the outline of the comb, the polygonal butt, show that this gun is different from the Turkish matchlock musket–the proportions are slender and of great elegance. The very representation of the craftsman at work, performing his goldsmith's task with a light hammer, shows the respect given to this new art in Persia. The tools for his work are a masterpiece of functional precision and beauty; there is an original set of such armourers' tools surviving in the Wallace Collection in London.[42] The young man in the miniature who is barefoot but sumptuously dressed is working in the open. Above his foot impressed in black ink is a seal with the inscription: *Bündä-i-sah-i wilajet Abbas 1010 (servant to his holiness Abbas 1010* H–i.e. AD 1601). It may be assumed with reason that the Krakow miniature represents an armourer employed in the royal workshop of Shah Abbas the Great in Isfahan. Of a somewhat later date is a portrait of this ruler holding a gun in his right hand, painted by Višnudaš, an Indian painter who accompanied Shah Jahandir's mission to Persia. The study of this and of other iconographical material suggests that during the sixteenth century firearms in Persia were mainly used for sport and that they had superseded the traditional bow and arrow.

The popularity of firearms in Persia is confirmed by the fact that they were used as ornaments in many branches of artistic manufacture, especially on textiles. Fragments of velvet from a Persian sixteenth-century tent (formerly the property of the Princes Sanguszko in Poland) now in the Boston Museum of Fine Arts are woven with figures of huntsmen with bows and arrows on horseback, chained leopards and shooters using firearms from a kneeling position. It is difficult to make a detailed analysis from pieces of material which of necessity are highly conventionalised by the technique of weaving, but it is possible to see plainly that the guns have the characteristic arched butts and are fired from the shoulder. The same type of gun, popular in Persia as in other Levantine countries, is pictured in a medallion carpet of the sixteenth century now in the Musée du Louvre (formerly in the Church of Notre Dame in Nantes); it also appears in the decoration of a Persian ceramic flagon with blue glaze in the Czartoryski Collection in Krakow.[43]

It is known from documentary evidence that under Shah Abbas the Great (1585-1628) the Persian army used heavy matchlock muskets modelled on Turkish ones. The Shah established an infantry corps 12,000 strong who were intended to oppose janissaries in the event of war with Turkey. Persian infantrymen used wooden forked rests in firing, in the western European manner.

A very informative source of information about Persian firearms is the report written by the French traveller Jean Chardin (1643-1713), who visited Persia and India in the seventeenth century and wrote a book entitled *Voyage en Perse et aux Indes Orientales.*

> The Persians make also very well, Barrels of Fire arms, and damask them as they do the Blades, but they make them very heavy, and cannot avoid it; they bore and scower them with a Wheel, as we do, and forge and bore them so even that they almost never burst. They make them alike strong and thick all along, saying that the Mouth of the Gun being weak, the Report shakes it, and communicates the wavering Motion to the Bullet. That's the Reason that if their Guns be thicker, they therefore carry the Shot further and straighter. They solder the Breech of the Barrel with the Heat of the Fire and reject Screws, saying that a Screw Breech going in without Stress, may be thrust out by the Violence of the Powder, and is not to be rely'd on. They do not understand very well how to make Locks or Springs; those they put to their Fire arms, are very unlike ours, for they have no Steel, the Pan is very fast, being all of a Piece with the Barrel, the which moves along a small rough Iron Branch, that comes out of the Inside of the Gun and moves backward, that is toward the Butt-End, on the Pan, but quite contrary to it; the Pan is usually no bigger than the little Finger Nail, without Snaphaunce; and most Pans are rough within, like a File, that the Prime may stick the better to it. They do not understand how to Mount Fire

41 MS 3456 fol. 5.

42 Cat. No. O1737.

43 Inv. No. XIII-1685.

Arms, and do not observe the Rules of Staticks, but make the Butt End small and light, which is the reason that their guns are light at the Breech, and heavy at the Muzzle.[44]

Chardin's remarks–in spite of his having no specialised knowledge of firearms–reflect his contempt for Persia which to him fell short in technical achievement. Because he found that matchlocks were still used in Persia (and matchlocks at that time
331 were still very widely used everywhere) he failed to appreciate the merit of Persian damascened barrels. We know from other sources, however, that these barrels were much sought after, not only in the neighbouring countries but also in Europe. They were unusually long-lasting so that only stocks and locks needed replacing when the matchlock went out of fashion. Already in the seventeenth century the miquelet lock of an Oriental variety found its way to Persia, to be followed eventually by the flintlock. The Chardin report contains many true comments especially regarding the lack of balance in Persian light guns. Indeed their heavy barrels are not counterbalanced by the butts; and this was even more noticeable by comparison with the perfectly balanced French or Spanish seventeenth-century guns.

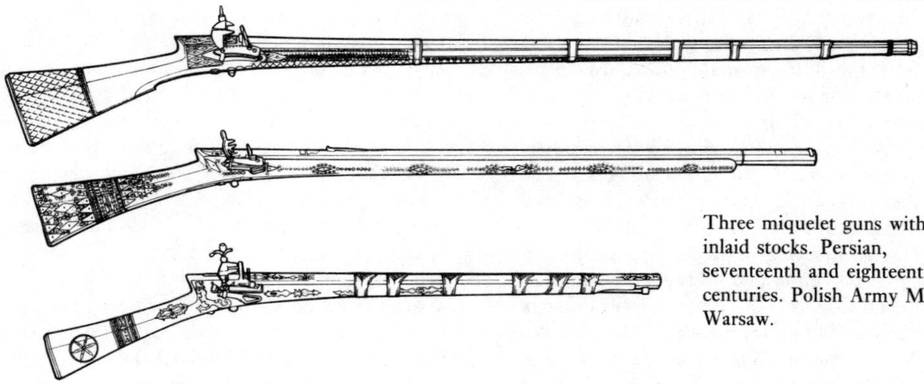

Three miquelet guns with ivory-inlaid stocks. Persian, seventeenth and eighteenth centuries. Polish Army Museum, Warsaw.

Generally speaking, between the sixteenth and seventeenth centuries, a considerable diversity of long firearms was evolved in Persia. In addition to light hunting or parade guns, there were in use Turkish-type matchlock muskets, standard guns, wall guns (called *shir-basha*) and the rifle. The elegance of form peculiar to the Persians is evident in all these versions, so long as they were actually made in Persia. This is expressed chiefly in the barrels, the exquisite but restrained decoration of which emphasises their natural slim outline. In older barrels, dating from the sixteenth century, the motif of a trefoil arc was obtained above the chamber by sinking the ground; the tip of it passed into the central rib running down to the muzzle which terminated in a voluted capital. As a rule only the essential parts of the mechanism were damascened and not until the eighteenth and nineteenth centuries did ornamentation cover the whole upper side of the barrel with arabesques. The decoration of stocks was equally austere. While in Turkey and in the Balkans the tendency was to overlay the entire wooden stock with other materials, the Persians appreciated the beauty of the grain of good wood and left it plain. Moreover they favoured beautiful wood, especially elm root, which, when polished, displayed the golden-brown lines of its grain. In other pieces stocks were ornamented with a mosaic of brass rosettes or a delicate inlay of white or stained bone. Green was a favourite colour as it blended well with white and gold.

Most of the genuine Persian long-arms surviving in museums date from a later period than the above. A large number of older firearms was destroyed in the Afghan invasion of 1722 and during the period of riots and unrest after the death of Nadir Shah in 1747. In eighteenth- and nineteenth-century pieces, richly damascened, round or octagonal barrels are fastened to the stocks by means of capucines; they are distinguished by sights in the form of a leaf with peep-holes; miquelet locks of Oriental type; richly gilt ball triggers; narrow straight butts sloping down slightly from the line of the barrel; iron-tipped ramrods fitted into the stock; and rings for attaching them to a belt or baldric. The decoration is restrained; the stocks are usually inlaid with simple ornament in bone and the buttplates made of a solid cylindrical piece of bone.

Blunderbusses, called *tapancha*, form a separate

44 P. M. Sykes, *Sir John Chardin's Travels*, London, 1927, p. 271.

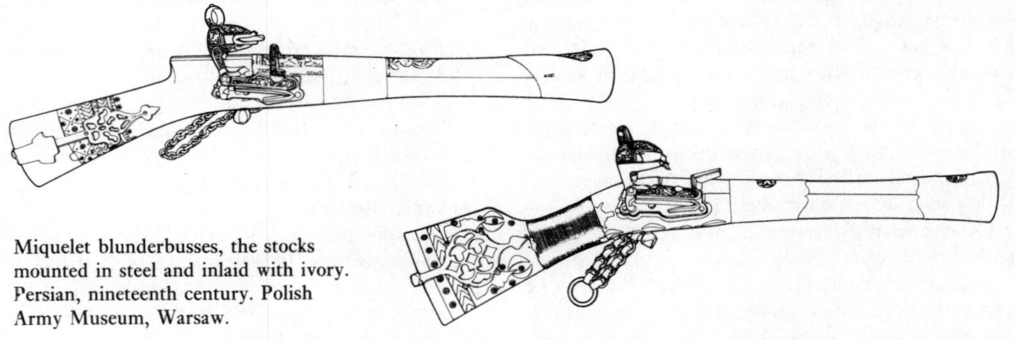

Miquelet blunderbusses, the stocks mounted in steel and inlaid with ivory. Persian, nineteenth century. Polish Army Museum, Warsaw.

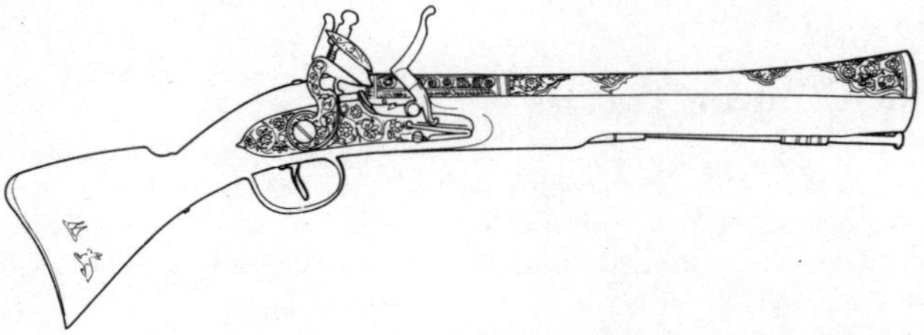

Flintlock blunderbuss, the lock and barrel overlaid with gold. Persian, eighteenth century. Polish Army Museum, Warsaw.

group. As in their Western and Turkish counterparts, the twist barrels bell out widely at the muzzle. Earlier pieces have miquelet locks of Oriental type, later ones flintlocks. Short butts, angular as on guns, are inlaid with bone, silver, and sometimes lacquered.[45]

Very few original Persian pistols have survived. They look like miniature guns. An example in the Museum of the Polish Army in Warsaw[46] has a delicately damascened water-steel barrel of circular section, two ornamental capucines, a miquelet lock, a ball trigger, an elm stock, a butt almost in line with the stock and with its end formed of a solid piece of ivory with a suspension ring.

Persian powder-flasks, called *shahdahane*, achieved an artistic perfection of very high merit. They were shaped like a bull's horn with flattened sides narrowing to a point, or were of zoomorphic (a conventional bird or fish) or phallic form (the Persians used the skin of camels' genitals). The principal materials used for powder-flasks were, however, Damascus steel, horn, ivory, and lizard skin. The stoppers were made of steel tubing on a spring.

European collections often contain a special group of ivory powder-flasks classified as 'Indo-Persian', mostly dating from the seventeenth century. It is probable that their prototypes were made by Persian masters and were then copied in India. Their shape is that of a fish and they consist of two pieces of hollowed ivory carved in relief over the whole surface with interlocked, mutually devouring, animals or birds as well as fantastic

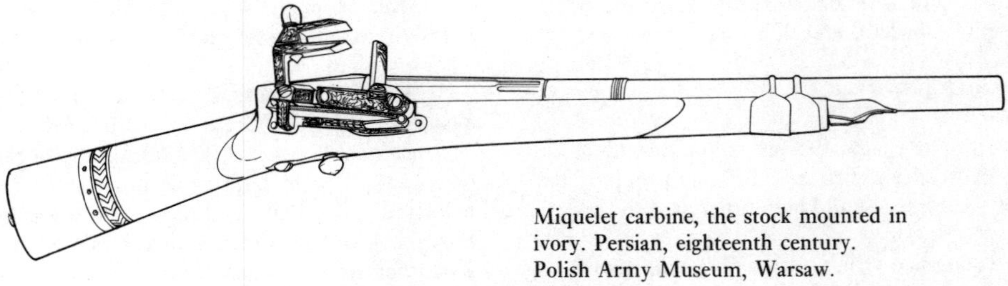

Miquelet carbine, the stock mounted in ivory. Persian, eighteenth century. Polish Army Museum, Warsaw.

45 *Sammlung Henri Moser-Charlottenfels, Orientalische Waffen und Rüstungen*, Leipzig, 1912, Nos. 754, 757, 760, 761.

46 Inv. No. 13171.

monsters; the eyes are made of red stones or amber; sometimes, though rarely, there are human figures in genre scenes. The representation of intertwined animals repeats ancient Asiatic motifs, especially from the Mesopotamian and Scythian cultures. A specimen in the Czartoryski Museum in Krakow still has its original silk fringe with sequins and beads. The Persians carried these powder flasks on elegant wide sashes woven with silver and gold thread.

Other firearms' accessories, primers, measures for powder and round metal boxes for lubricants were equally ornate and exquisitely worked. As in other departments of artistic craftsmanship so in gunmaking the Persians reached the highest perfection among Oriental nations. Their products were sought for and copied and their eminent craftsmen were eagerly invited abroad.

The Crimean Tartars

It appears from historical sources that Tartars of the Crimea did not as a rule use firearms and in rare instances only availed themselves of captured cannon. As they were permanently allied to the Turks, they were fully aware of the efficacy of firearms but found them of little use in their particular way of fighting. The Khans, however, possessed ornamental specimens, received as gifts or war booty, or even specially imported. Pieces have been preserved in the Ethnographical Museum in Munich. A gun barrel[47] bears a gold inscription with the name of Hadji Gerai, Khan of the Crimean Tartars (1683-4); a complete gun[48] bears the name of its owner, Khan Selim Gerai, dated from the middle of the eighteenth century. In the Museum of the Polish Army in Warsaw there are holsters for pistols and a single pistol with a Persian damascened barrel, a western-type stock and a damaged flintlock, formerly the property of Dewlet Gerai, Khan of Crimea (*c.*1775).

The Caucasus

Despite predominant Persian influences the Caucasians evolved a stylistically different group of firearms of great interest and high functional and artistic merit.

The Caucasian tribes, although falling into three large ethnic groups (Circassians and Abkhanians in the West, Chechens and Lesghians in the East and Georgians in the South) all share in common distinct racial and traditional characteristics. Like other hill peoples they have a strong love of freedom, courage, intelligence, patriarchal simplicity and hospitality, but they are at the same time clannish, and sometimes violent, cruel and vindictive. Naturally enough, they have always attached great importance to arms while for centuries they cultivated the art of metal working and decoration. Caucasian master craftsmen took over many techniques from Persia yet they evolved a distinct decorative style of their own, using niello, formed of a metallic amalgam of silver, copper, lead and sulphur.

A detailed history of firearms in the Caucasus has yet to be written. It is unquestionable that Persia exerted a decisive role on the evolution of the typical Caucasian rifle. The traditional Turco-Persian type became even more slender, with the butt almost in line with the barrel. As in Persia, the heavy, usually octagonal, rifled barrel with eight grooves did not have sufficient counterweight in the butt. The barrel was frequently entirely covered with damascened decoration of floral scrolls or typical Persian arabesques. The back-sight was a leaf with several peepholes. Attempts were made to start barrel-production locally, but most barrels were imported from Persia and great value was attached to old ones. Most surviving specimens have locks of miquelet type of Persian or native make; they are small, sometimes minute, richly inlaid with gold, with a gunsmith's mark in Arabic lettering. Original Caucasian locks do not differ from their Turco-Persian prototypes in the mechanism itself, but are characterised by a very low cock with very long jaws. Stocks are mostly made of elm wood, always plain, delicate, discreetly inlaid with bone and silver; buttplates of oval section are made of solid pieces of elephant or walrus tusk. Triggers are ball-shaped and the barrels joined to the stocks by means of silver capucines decorated with niello. Sometimes barrels and stocks are covered entirely with black shagreen with silver *appliqué* ornament. Average length is 140 cm, length of barrels more than one metre and calibre 12 mm to 15 mm.

A beautiful Caucasian rifle dated *c.*1825 was described by S. V. Grancsay in the *Bulletin of the Metropolitan Museum of Art, New York* for September, 1935. The inscription indicates that the rifle belonged to one Bab Muslim Khan and was made in Shamkhal, in Daghestan which is inhabited by the Kubatchi tribe renowned for the production of arms.

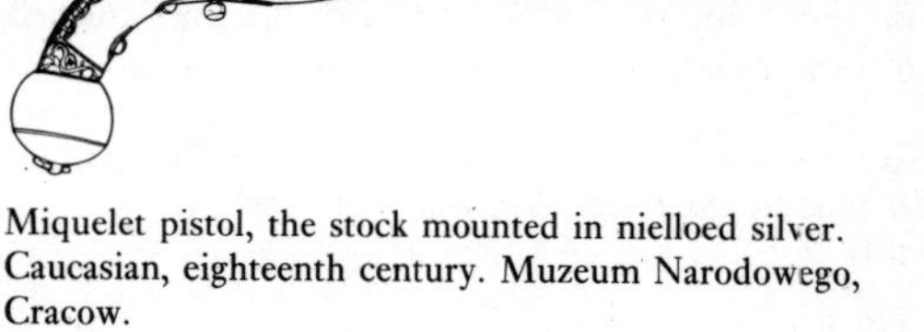

Miquelet pistol, the stock mounted in nielloed silver. Caucasian, eighteenth century. Muzeum Narodowego, Cracow.

47 Inv. No. H 88.

48 Inv. No. H. 168.

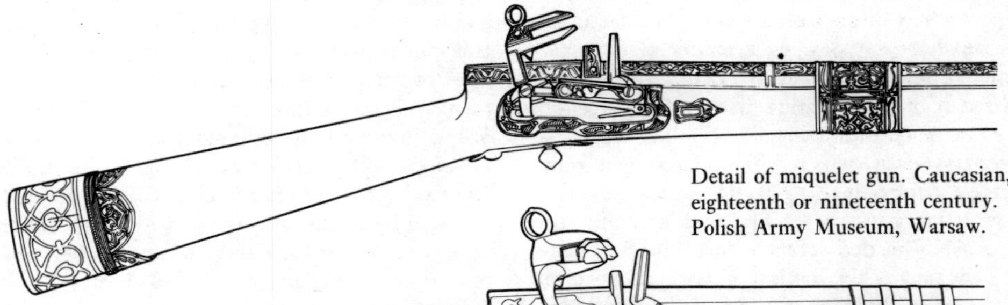

Detail of miquelet gun. Caucasian, eighteenth or nineteenth century. Polish Army Museum, Warsaw.

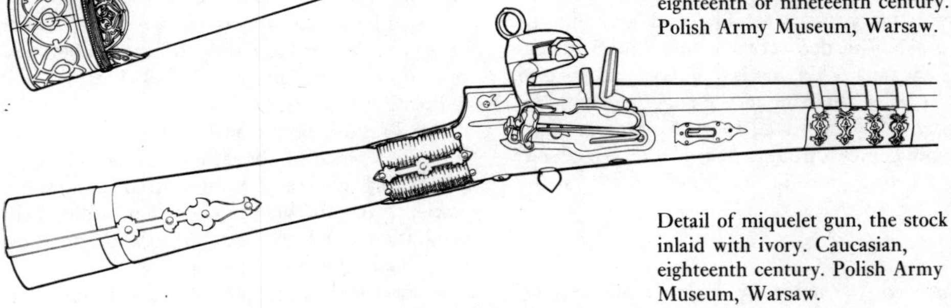

Detail of miquelet gun, the stock inlaid with ivory. Caucasian, eighteenth century. Polish Army Museum, Warsaw.

Like the rifles, Caucasian pistols, surviving mostly from the eighteenth and nineteenth century, are stylistically uniform and easy to distinguish. Of all Oriental pistols those from the Caucasus are best in quality and can easily bear comparison with good-quality European makes. They usually have Persian damascened barrels and miquelet locks of Persian type; some later specimens have flintlocks. The stocks and butts are their most original feature; they are covered with black shagreen, have capucines of nielloed silver, solid globular pommels of walrus ivory, often inlaid with silver, or made entirely of silver and, like Persian pistols, fitted with suspension rings.

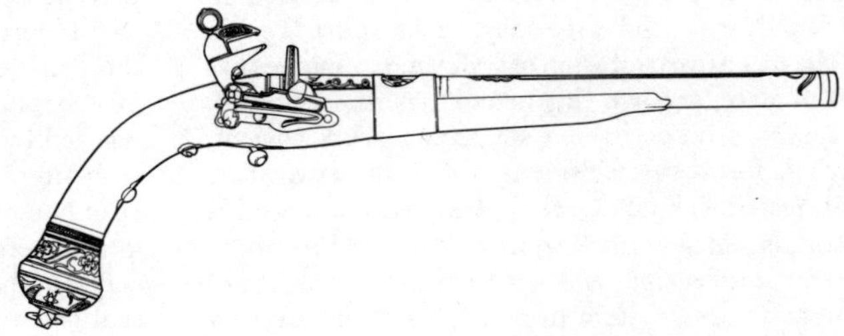

Miquelet pistol, the stock mounted in nielloed silver. Caucasian, eighteenth century. Muzeum Narodowego, Cracow.

An exceptional specimen of a Caucasian blunderbuss in the Buttin Collection[49] was of Persian form with a butt imitating that of a long-gun; it had a snaphance lock which suggests the penetration of Russian influences to the Caucasus. These appear to have been reciprocal, for in the middle of the nineteenth century Russian army officers had a predilection for Caucasian firearms.

Caucasian powder-flasks were similar to those in Persia and were decorated with nielloed silver.

Afghanistan and Kurdistan

Afghanistan, situated on the borders of Persia and India, was open to influence penetrating from both her neighbours, yet an indigenous form of firearm, known as a *jezail*, was ultimately evolved. This was an unusually long gun, reaching up to two metres in length, with an arched narrow butt of oval section, similar to those found on some Persian guns. The butt should not be confused with the conventional 'Afghan' butt which refers to forms mostly encountered in Sind, India. Originally Afghan Jezails were provided with matchlocks with internal mechanism and cocks that operated in a slit in the stock, and were subsequently converted to flintlocks. The length of barrel ensured firing accuracy and long range. They were used with A-shaped rests made of horns or metal, similar to those used elsewhere in Central Asia.

Kurdistan is mentioned in literature on firearms

49 No. 655.

as being the country situated at the greatest distance from Spain where miquelet locks were manufactured from Spanish prototypes. As a matter of fact this distinction probably belongs to Sri Lanka. Locks used in Kurdistan on guns dating from the eighteenth century are a faithful copy of Ripoll locks.[50] A characteristic feature which differentiates them from later perfected forms is a long bridle, joining the cock-screw with the pan-screw. The cock is equipped with a capstan-headed screw with a swivel finger-grip and the tang of the top jaw is short and fits into the solid part of the back of the cock. It should be added that in the perfected form this tang is much longer and comes through behind the jaw-screw. In form Kurdish guns did not differ from Persian.

India

330 More than eighty years ago W. Egerton published an
332-3 outline of arms and armament in India which, despite some shortcomings, still forms the main source of information on the subject.[51]

The political history of this huge sub-continent, the great migrations of peoples, internal wars and invasions from outside, the special veneration for arms and the very high achievement in decorative art and love of beautiful objects – all these factors have contributed to making the history of arms in India a fascinating subject and one in which a great deal more research could usefully be undertaken. Yet the student is faced with the peculiar difficulties, outlined in our foreword, attending on all research on Oriental arms and especially so in India. For in India extensive confusion of styles and influences has taken place largely owing to an innate conservatism, sometimes bordering on stagnation. Very ancient, archaic forms survive side by side with newer ones; antiquated techniques are applied to this day; and in addition, documentary sources, dates and names of makers are lacking, and what original specimens of firearms survive, have been dispersed and are very difficult to trace. Especially after the Sikh wars and the 1857 Mutiny, the British government carried out a general disarmament of the Indian peoples in the course of which a large quantity of ancient arms was destroyed. It should be noted, however, that Indian craftsmen subsequently made copies of old arms for sale. Most of the historical arms of India which have survived to this day do not go back further then the eighteenth century. The best pieces were taken abroad, to England, France and Holland, either as the victors' booty, or as gifts for sovereigns, and for members of the East India Company, or as collector's pieces. Fully aware of these difficulties, Egerton rejected an attempt to present the development of arms in India in a historical chronological order, but used the ethnological approach. In his *Catalogue of Oriental Arms and Armour* at the Wallace Collection in London, G. F. Laking pointed out the need for a minute examination of each firearm in order to discover the subtle differences between the related types of Persian and Indian arms. It often happens that arms, considered to be Indian, are in reality Persian, having been manufactured under the direct influence of the Mogul School. Two pieces which look identical on superficial inspection may disclose, on further examination, differences in decoration which may establish the origin of one as Persian and the other as Indian.

Ancient Indian literary sources mention the use of firearms at a very early historical period. They contain descriptions of incendiary arrows projected from bamboo tubes known as *agny astra* (probably akin to the analogous Chinese weapon).[52] On the other hand neither Marco Polo nor Ibn Battuta mentions the use of firearms in India in the thirteenth century. Modern artillery was introduced in India by the Arabs and Turks as early as the second half of the fifteenth century. In 1482 the Sultan of Gujarat used cannon and hand firearms to repulse attacks of pirates from Bulsar. It is generally accepted that the decisive influence in the spread of firearms in India came from the Portuguese but, according to their own reports, when in 1498 Vasco da Gama was led through the streets of Calcutta, someone in the crowd fired a gun; this proves that firearms must have reached India before the arrival of the Portuguese.[53] In 1510 Alfonso Albuquerque captured Goa; in 1536 Nuno da Cunha built the fort in Diu and came into armed conflict with the Sultanates of Gujarat and Kambay; during the fighting the Portuguese captured a number of cannon of very large calibres. In all probability these cannon had been cast by Turkish experts. Nuno da Cunha sent one of the captured cannon as trophy to Portugal, where it survives in the Castle of St Julian as the 'Gun of Diu'. The Portuguese soon became instructors in the manufacture and use of firearms, the casting of cannon and production of hand firearms.

In Northern India artillery developed chiefly under the impact of Moslem peoples living nearer to Europe. Hence the name *feringiha* for cannon in India probably stems from the term *Francs* (foreigner)

50 W. Keith Neal, *Spanish Guns and Pistols*, London, 1955, p. 9, Pl. 66 and 67.

51 Lord Egerton of Tatton, *An Illustrated Handbook of Indian Arms*, London, 1880 (2nd edn. London 1896).

52 *ibid*, p. 151.

53 S. V. Grancsay, 'An East Indian Gun', *Bulletin of the Metropolitan Museum of Art*, XXVIII, 1933, pp. 196-7.

i.e. guns of European origin although made in India. Many artillery terms are of Turkish origin. Artillery reached its highest development under the Moguls; the founder of that dynasty, Babur, used large numbers of cannon for his conquest of northern India and the forcing of the Ganges. His successor Akbar (1556-1605), who conquered the Deccan, increased the army's war potential, especially as regards artillery, using elephant and camel guns and infantry units armed with muskets.

Numerous Indian cannon, mostly of large calibre and size, dating from the sixteenth to the eighteenth century, have survived in old palace yards, old forts and museums. The most famous cannon, called *Malik i Maidan* (the Lord of the Plain), in Bijapur was cast in 1549 by Muhammad ibn Hussayn Rumi, a Turk from Istanbul. There is the *Jahan Kasha* (the Subduer of the World), weighing seven tons, in Murshidabad, dated 1637; the *Zamzamah*, cast in 1761 by Shah Wali Khan as well as other cannon in Rangpur and Daulatabad Fort.[54]

Some of the large disused cannon were left in public places and worshipped by the population.

Miniatures of the Mogul School from the artistic workshops at the Court of Akbar, which were under the direct influence of Persian art, bring rich material to bear upon our subject. Among other things the artists of this school copied and illustrated the *Book of Babur*, which was the autobiography of the founder of the Mogul dynasty, a copy of which is in the State Museum for Oriental Culture in Moscow. Although the historical events described date from the end of the fifteenth and early decades of the sixteenth centuries, the dresses and arms depicted in the miniatures are those worn in the time of Akbar. Firearms are shown in many miniatures, in battle, court ceremonies, hunting scenes. It is possible to distinguish heavy muskets of matchlock type carried by the Sultan's guard and lighter matchlock guns used for hunting. Barrels are very long, with a straight butt, of flattened polygonal section, very slightly falling away from the axis of the barrel. In a miniature representing the capture of Agra by Babur, cannon barrels are shown abandoned in the palace yard of Sultan Ibrahim. Even cavalrymen carry long-guns. Firing from horseback is also confirmed by other miniatures of the Mogul School. In one, depicting a crocodile hunt, a man is firing from the shoulder with the butt heel pressed fairly low against it. Another miniature shows a gun being loaded. Firearms frequently failed; in a cycle of miniatures showing Shah Jahandir hunting (Mogul School, seventeenth century) the ruler is shown on one occasion lashing at a lion with his sword, having thrown down his gun which lies in the grass at his feet; on another the Shah, mounted on an elephant and attacked by a lioness, is beating the animal's head with the butt of his gun.[55]

The great importance which Akbar attached to firearms, and even his love of them (which may be compared with the similar passion of Louis XIII of France), is also confirmed in the book by Abu-l-Fazl, Grand Vizier to Akbar, called *A'in-i-Akhbari* (Akbar's Mirror). He gives a detailed description of the production of matchlock muskets in the court workshops under the personal supervision of the Sultan,[56] and shows that the Indians had adapted their traditional techniques of metal working to the production of the barrel. There were several methods, the simplest being by hammering an iron rod flat and welding the edges into a tube. The more usual method was to wind the flattened strip of iron on a mandrel, upon which the edges were heated and hammered together. A perfected method, generally used by Persian and Turkish barrel-smiths, was to twist a bundle of iron rods and afterwards to beat them into a solid cylinder; this was bored by a hard steel chisel, the size of which produced the calibre

Indian gun barrels vary in length but are generally much longer than European ones, of polygonal or round section (or a combination of both) with large powder-chambers and thickened muzzles decoratively shaped. As in early Turkish, and some Persian, barrels, the muzzles terminate in monsters' or tigers' heads or fluted capitals. During the forging barrels were tested for endurance; they were partially or wholly filled with gunpowder and fired; accuracy of fire was tested at the same time. If the test was successful, the decoration of the barrel, the form of the stock, lock and ramrod were decided upon and gunsmiths' marks and dates were stamped. Barrels were damascened in gold and silver with floral arabesques and bands of foliated scroll ornament, inscriptions, also animal and figure motifs in low relief, antelopes, tigers, birds, figures of huntsmen, and nautch girls, as well as gods from the Indian pantheon. Stocks were made of hardwoods, such as ebony, teak or palisander and ornament was applied in gold, silver, brass, lacquer or enamel. The barrel was fastened to the stock by means of capucines, sometimes made of coils or wire or even rawhide. Prickers, in tubes, for clearing the touch-hole were near the lock; wooden or metal ramrods were fitted in the stock; the match was coiled into a ball and placed on the upper side of the butt or twisted round the comb of the butt and a leather belt for slinging

54 Creswell, *op.cit.*, pp. 56-61.

55 *Album of Indian and Persian Miniatures of the 16th–18th centuries*, Moscow, 1962, Nos. 61 and 64.

56 Egerton, *op.cit.*, p. 63.

the gun on the shoulder was secured to an attachment on the lower part of the butt.

Obviously this very cursory description of guns made and used during Akbar's reign cannot serve as a basis for their classification. The difficulty lies in that hardly any specimens of the period have survived to this day, and those that have were mostly barrels only. We know the name of Usted Kabir, the most eminent gunsmith at the Court of Akbar but we cannot attribute any particular firearm to him. It is known from other sources that Akbar's arsenal was abundantly equipped, numbering about one thousand firearms, not only of local production but also imported, purchased or received as gifts. One may therefore assume that this number included European firearms fitted with modern wheel-locks and possibly even miquelet locks (which were not permanently adopted in India until much later, as was the true flintlock). The matchlock, even in its most primitive form with the cock issuing through a slot in the stock, and a simple pressure trigger, was always the favourite mechanism.

Most of the surviving Indian guns, dating from the seventeenth and eighteenth centuries, were manufactured in various centres, in Sind and the Punjab, in Rajputana, Bengal, Mysore and Coorg as well as in numerous towns in Madras. The majority are in the possession of English museums and collections (Victoria and Albert Museum, Tower of London Armouries, Windsor Castle, The Wallace Collection); some are the property of Continental museums and just a few are in museums in India. Unfortunately a number of private collections, jealously guarded by their owners, are inaccessible to students. It is therefore not easy to carry out a classification of firearms and here the comments of Egerton, Stone and Laking are of great help, not that their opinions always agree. The classification is primarily based on the shape of the stock, the barrel and the lock being of secondary importance.

Generally speaking the surviving pieces can be divided into two large territorial groups: North and part of Central India, and the South and the other part of Central India.

In the first group the oldest type of gun is known as *toradar*. This probably stems from the standard Turkish musket which had undergone considerable changes when modified by the Persians. It is this firearm which is depicted in Mogul miniatures. Its main features are: a long damascus or twist barrel of round or octagonal section, decorated in the manner described above; ogival plate, Turkish back-sight (which bears out the theory of the Turkish origin of the toradar), though sometimes V-notch back-sights were used instead; very primitive matchlock. Each side of the lock is reinforced with plates of watered steel let into the stock. The pan-cover usually swings on a pin but is sometimes a loose clamp fitting over and under the pan. The lock has a trigger in the form of a recurved lug or a ball and the barrel is fastened to the stock by coils of wire or by rawhide straps, which frequently pass over silver saddles on the barrel. The butts and stocks of toradars are slim and straight, of pentagonal section, practically in line with the barrel. They are frequently painted with polychrome flowers or animals against a green, red or gold ground, more rarely carved and inlaid with gilt metal or enamelled. The stock near the tang of the barrel is usually covered with a fluted ivory plate. A beautiful specimen of a toradar was described by S. V. Grancsay in the *Bulletin of the Metropolitan Museum of Art, New York*.[57] Variants of this form had carved stocks of diamond section, similar to the *jezail*.

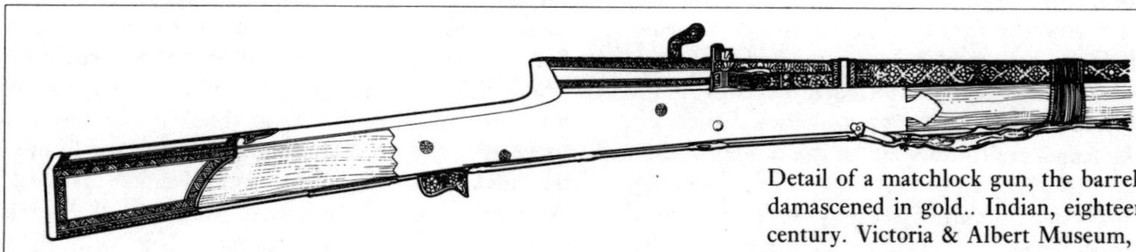

Detail of a matchlock gun, the barrel damascened in gold.. Indian, eighteenth century. Victoria & Albert Museum, London.

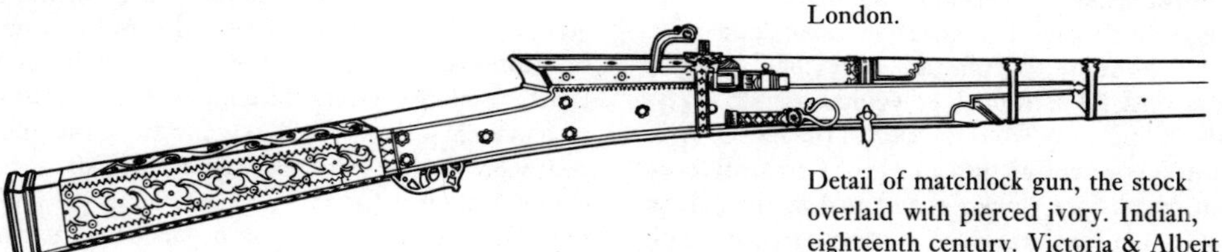

Detail of matchlock gun, the stock overlaid with pierced ivory. Indian, eighteenth century. Victoria & Albert Museum, London.

57 See note 53.

Detail of matchlock gun, the barrel damascened in gold. Indian, eighteenth century. Victoria & Albert Museum, London.

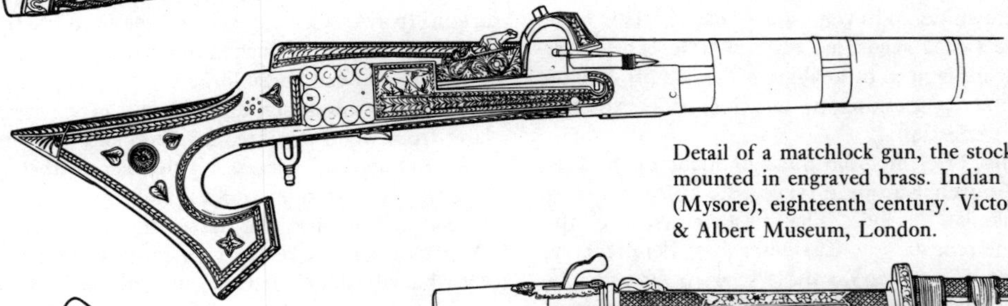

Detail of a matchlock gun, the stock mounted in engraved brass. Indian (Mysore), eighteenth century. Victoria & Albert Museum, London.

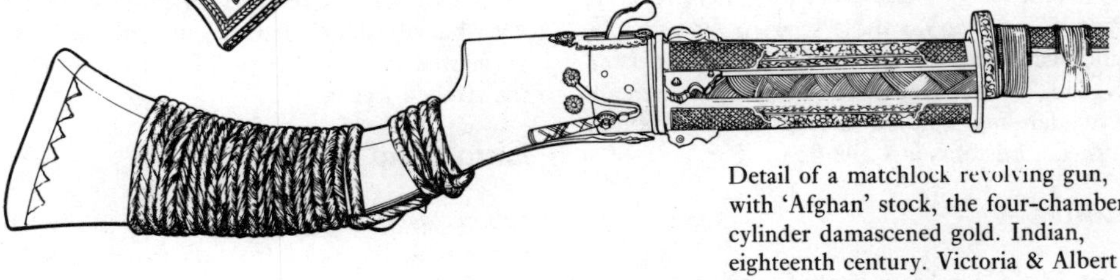

Detail of a matchlock revolving gun, with 'Afghan' stock, the four-chambered cylinder damascened gold. Indian, eighteenth century. Victoria & Albert Museum, London.

The next in popularity to the toradar in Northern India was the gun with the so-called 'Afghan' butt, deep and narrow and curved strongly down, which
333 was used mainly in Sind. It was thus named by the English because Sind at the time of their entry into the country was ruled by Afghans. These guns usually have barrels of finely watered steel inlaid with gold; sometimes they are of twist damascus; and elaborate pieces have enamelled gold mounts.

The South Indian group of guns evolved under distinct Arab influence and it is possible that the name *banduq* ('gun' in Arabic) would fit them best were it not for the fact that this term is ambiguous. Generally it refers to a long matchlock gun of good iron twist. The barrels of these guns are fastened to stocks by means of a large number of silver or brass capucines, beautifully decorated. The stock is overlaid with silver sheet, brass panels or bone ornament with simple geometrical design. There are several variants of butt design, one of which is rather clumsy and rounded in mushroom form (as in a group of Moroccan pistols mentioned before). In the Hyderabad and Coorg regions two other characteristic variants evolved; one with a flat, thin stock with a semi-circular rounded butt, the other with a very peculiar hooked butt which suggests a comparison with the hilt of a typical Arab sword.[58]

The above mentioned guns of the Northern and Southern Indian groups do not exhaust all the types and variants of long firearms that have appeared in India during the course of centuries. There were many local varieties while there was an uninterrupted flow of influence from neighbouring Oriental countries and, above all, from Europe. One of these guns, at least, should be mentioned: in order to increase the rate of fire the Indians copied European models by adopting guns with revolving cylinders, short or long, but always ignited by matchlocks.

The blunderbuss also came to India from Europe, with a barrel flared out at the muzzle and usually a flintlock and a French-type butt. Pistols were never popular in India. Egerton in his catalogue only mentions four. Originally these pistols had matchlocks and were in fact miniature guns. This weapon was used by irregular infantry units during the reign of Sultan Hyder Ali. Later English and French models were copied fairly accurately locally, but were decorated according to local taste. These were provided with flintlocks.

Indian gunmakers showed unusual ingenuity in inventing combined weapons, sometimes of a weird form: a combination of pistol and axe, the barrel

58 Egerton, Fig. 17. Stone, *op.cit.*, Fig. 324.

serving as handle to the axe, or pistols with the talwar type of sword. These weapons, made to special order, were of no military significance.

India also made gun accessories. Sometimes these were combined into sets known as *kamr* consisting of an ornamental belt on which were suspended a powder-flask, priming horns, pouches for bullets, match or spare flints. Indian powder-flasks were made of various materials,[59] metal, horn, bone, shells, rawhide and even papier-maché; their form and size varied according to local style. They were strongly influenced by analogous Persian production but, generally speaking, never achieved its exquisite artistic perfection.

Finally, brief mention must be made of the firearms of purely European type made in India during the colonial period. The best-known are the magazine repeaters by Chalembron of Pondicherry, mentioned on pp. 208-9 and a series of fine-quality guns and pistols made at Lucknow Arsenal under the supervision of General Claude Martin (d.1800). Also, the famous London maker Joseph Manton established a business in Calcutta in 1825.

Sri Lanka

Firearms in Sri Lanka developed quite separately from those of India and achieved a high technical and artistic level. Matchlock muskets were introduced by the Portuguese at the beginning of the sixteenth century and the Sinhalese showed an extraordinary aptitude for copying and perfecting Western inventions, quickly outstripping their Portuguese teachers. Reports of all later European travellers abound in high praise for firearms manufactured in Ceylon, especially for the locally-made barrels.

Probably as early as the seventeenth century the Sinhalese adopted the Arab miquelet. It was produced in Ceylon with very small modifications and as a rule was placed on the left side of the stock. A form of snap-matchlock was also used there.

Sinhalese guns of ornamental type had long octagonal barrels inlaid with silver and a very curious butt shaped into a double scroll. They were elaborately decorated with pierced panels of ivory or tortoise shell edged with silverwork. A beautiful example, seven feet long, is in the Metropolitan Museum of Art in New York.[60] In the museum at Colombo there is a number of Sinhalese undecorated guns, probably used for military purposes, with clumsy stocks with a heavy backward projection from the top that looks as though it was intended to rest on top of the shoulder.

59 Egerton, Fig. 5.

60 Stone, Fig. 325.

Central Asia and Siberia

Long firearms used in the vast areas of Turkistan, Circassia and Siberia in the eighteenth and nineteenth century were produced and developed from models originating in Persia and India and also some influence from the West. Their distinguishing features are technical simplicity and rough execution as well as the assembling of parts of heterogenous origin. It was a Central Asiatic custom to fire from a low A-shaped rest attached to a pivot on the underside of the stock. These forked rests were first made from horn of antelopes, especially the orongo species, later from wood mounted in metal and from metal.

In Siberia and Circassia guns were rather short (3-4 ft) with straight stocks and butts, mounted almost in line with the barrel and with European flintlocks. In Turkistan long-guns were favoured with heavily gilded barrels, matchlocks and stocks of painted wood and curved butts shaped rather like the Afghan jezails.

China and Tibet

Where the development of firearms in China is **274-5**
concerned, the period from the fifteenth to the nine- **334**
teenth century was one of stagnation and passive acceptance of foreign inventions and forms. There is reason to assume, however, that during the sixteenth century the Chinese made independent attempts to evolve a lighter type of hand firearm from the heavy type of cannon. Their solution was simply to produce miniature cannon barrels which were mounted on wooden stocks. Firing took place without a lock mechanism by applying a lighted match to the touch-hole.

Several barrels of primitive weapons of this style have survived in the Historical Museum in Peking, and are reminiscent of those used in fifteenth-
century Europe. A copper barrel with the date 1531, 334
and the name 'Falling Star', and a note that it was produced in an Army Establishment, does not differ from Chinese cannon barrels allegedly of the fourteenth century. It has the same kind of enlarged chamber, a touch-hole on the upper side and angular sights, metal hoops to strengthen the body of the barrel and a belled-out muzzle. It is barely 27·7 cm long, of bore 26 mm, and weighs 1760 g. Another copper barrel called 'Fiery Tube' has the word 'Victory' and the figure 793 stamped on it; its length is 14·7 cm, its bore 17 mm, its weight 740 g. Undoubtedly this weapon was mass-produced in the Imperial workshops for the army.

Specimens of true Chinese seventeenth- and eighteenth-century matchlock guns have also survived in the museum in Peking, but they are among the roughest and poorest made. Their length varies

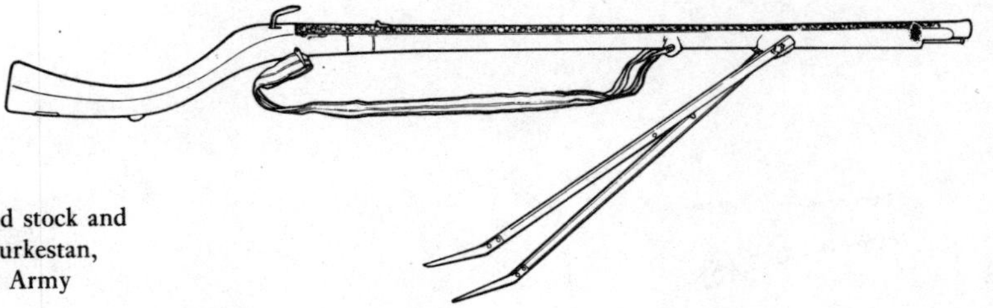

Matchlock gun with carved stock and with fork-rest attached. Turkestan, eighteenth century. Polish Army Museum, Warsaw.

between 110 cm and 160 cm. Most have a matchlock of the Indian type, and on some it is of an even more primitive construction. Here the serpentine is pivoted in front of the pan and a piece of string is fastened to the top of it and to the middle of the trigger; pulling drags the serpentine over and tips the match into the pan. The barrels of these guns, sometimes inlaid with silver or gold wire, have no sights and are attached to the stocks by means of brass capucines. Stocks are plain, roughly made, often painted red, with very characteristic pistol-type butts arching downwards, sometimes with bone buttplates.

These guns were held in the right hand like a pistol while the left hand supported the stock; they could also be fired from the hip. In addition Indian toradars were also used, as were guns with curving butts similar to the Afghan jezail.

In Tibet firearms were more popular than in China. Tibetan guns called *me-da* had metal parts, barrels and matchlocks imported from China or India and straight stocks of the toradar type. The surface of the stock was usually covered with wild asses' skin tightly stretched and sewn on. Spare match was carried in a special pouch near the stock. Firing was done from Central Asiatic A-shaped rests. Surviving examples of Tibetan guns in the Art Museum in Honolulu are three to five feet in length.[61]

In the adjacent countries of Burma and Korea the shape of firearms was modelled on those of India and China; as a rule they were primitive matchlocks, differing, if at all, in local styles of the butt. In other countries on the Pacific seaboard the predominant influence was that of Japanese firearms.

Japan

When the Portuguese landed in Japan in 1543 they brought with them matchlock muskets which were a revelation to the inhabitants of the isolated islands. The Japanese showed great interest in the new weapons, which were of such dominant military significance. Some forms of firearms (bombs and incendiary rockets) had been known in medieval Japan, where they had penetrated from China; they were called *teppo* but were hardly used in warfare. The new Western invention was first adopted and manufactured in the island of Tanegashina near the southern coast of Kyushu. Soon the Japanese had turned to the production of firearms which were known as *tanegashina* from the name of the island. The first Japanese gunsmiths had their workshop on the Kyushu island and soon new production centres were established in Sakai near Osaka in the province of Izumi, in Yokkaichi and Kunitomo in the province of Kai, and also in Negoro in the province of Kii; young apprentices graduating from these production centres in turn opened their own workshops in other, sometimes far distant, localities.[62]

In the sixteenth century two great commanders and statesmen, Nobunaga and Hideyoshi fostered the development of firearms production in Japan. In 1549 Nobunaga placed with the Kunitomo workshops an order for five hundred guns. Several thousand soldiers equipped with guns took part in the battle of Nagashimo in 1575. By the end of the century during a campaign in Korea the Japanese commander Yoshinaga issued orders that every soldier, even a Samurai, must be armed with a gun.

Although based on foreign models, Japanese firearms form a separate group. Once the 'Japanese' form was adapted to the requirements and style of the Japanese squirearchy, it survived with hardly any changes for several centuries, especially when virtually all contacts with the West were broken off after 1640. In the Tokugawa period of peace (1600-1867), firearms were chiefly used for hunting.

Cannon and the art of casting pieces of artillery were known to the Japanese by the second half of the

61 Stone, p. 443.

62 D. Ichikawa, 'Die Einführung der Feuerwaffen in Japan in 1534', *Ostasien*, Vol. IX, No. 99, Berlin, 1906. D. M. Brown, 'The Impact of Firearms on Japanese Warfare, 1534-98', *The Far East Quarterly*, Vol. VII, No. 3, New York, 1948. N. Perrin, *Giving Up the Gun, Japan's Reversion to the Sword, 1543-1874*, Boulder, Colorado, 1980.

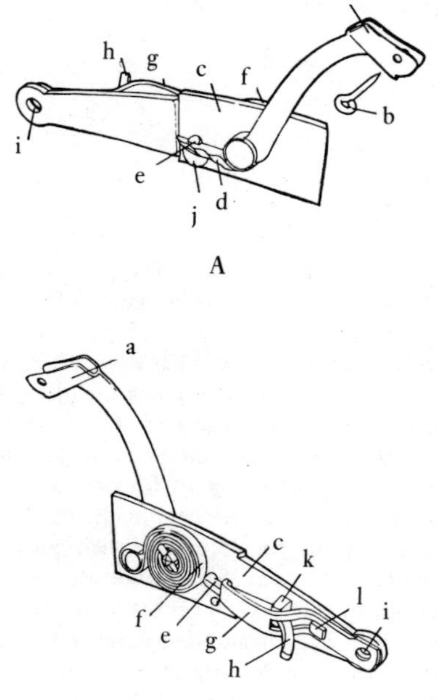

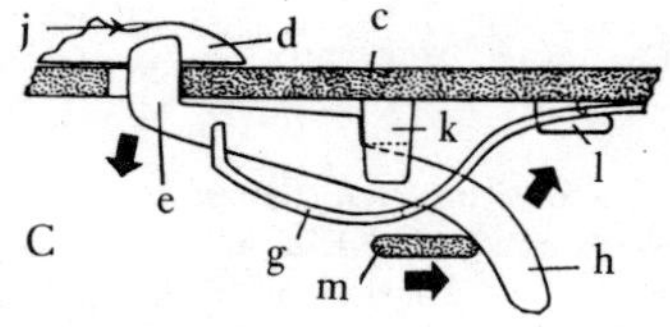

JAPANESE MATCHLOCK

A shows the outside and B the inside of the lock. C shows the sear-mechanism from above.

a Cock (match-holder)
b Pin to secure match
c Lockplate
d Heel of cock
e Sear forming part of combined sear- and trigger-lever
f Mainspring
g Sear- or trigger-spring which also acts as clip retaining the sear-lever
h Trigger-lever
i Hole for retaining-peg passing through the stock (the front of the lock is held by the rear barrel-band)
j Stop on lockplate to prevent the cock from being pulled too far back
k Bracket forming fulcrum for the sear-lever
l Lug retains the trigger-spring
m Trigger, suspended in stock

Based on the lock of a pistol of c. 1800 in the Victoria & Albert Museum (No. M. 367-1923).

sixteenth century. In 1551 Yoshizume received a gift of two light field pieces from the 'King of Rome'. It is also known that Nobunaga had light cannon cast in Kunitomo and that these were subsequently used in the capture of fortresses and breaching of city walls, as for example in the siege of Osaka in 1614. Cannon purchased from the Dutch or the English were frequently valued more highly than those of home-production and the Japanese invited foreign makers to Japan, as, for example, in 1618 the Dutch master Jacques Specx.

Although Japanese iconography provides proof that large-calibre guns were in use, mortars and cannon which have survived to this day are of much smaller size. A cannon in the Polish Army Museum in Warsaw was made, according to an inscription on it, in December 1661, during the reign of the Emperor Kyan Wu. It is cylindrical at the muzzle, with a diameter of 20 cm, with a large front-sight; length 79·5 cm, calibre 8·5 cm, cast in bronze, slightly tapering at the breech, the surface worked to resemble the grain of wood; four handles; on the upper side are inscriptions and a large hollowed cube-shaped back sight with peep-holes and a touch-hole. There is a similar cannon at the Victoria and Albert Museum in London.[63] Other cannon in this museum, probably of later date, follow European models more closely.

The favourite ignition mechanism in Japanese small arms was a snap-matchlock. In this lock the action was cocked by drawing back the cock until an arm of the sear, which passed through the lockplate, engaged with its tail. Instead of its usual position under the cock, the trigger, shaped like a blade or elongated ball, was placed nearer to the butt heel and connected with the other end of the sear. On pressing the trigger the sear released the cock which automatically dipped the match into the pan causing ignition. Except for the iron pan, all parts of the snap-lock including the spring, which was normally spiral, were usually made of brass and the pan had a brass cover. This lock was universally used in Japan in guns and pistols.

The highly developed metallurgical industry in Japan soon solved problems connected with the production of barrels. Made of forged iron they were distinguished by their heavy weight, due to the thickness of the wall (6 mm-7 mm). Surviving examples of ordinary gun barrels are from 50 cm to 100 cm

63 B. W. Robinson, *Arms and Armour of Old Japan*, London 1951, Pl. 25.

331 Group of watered steel barrels. Persian, sixteenth to seventeenth centuries. Staatliches Museum für Völkerkunde, Munich.

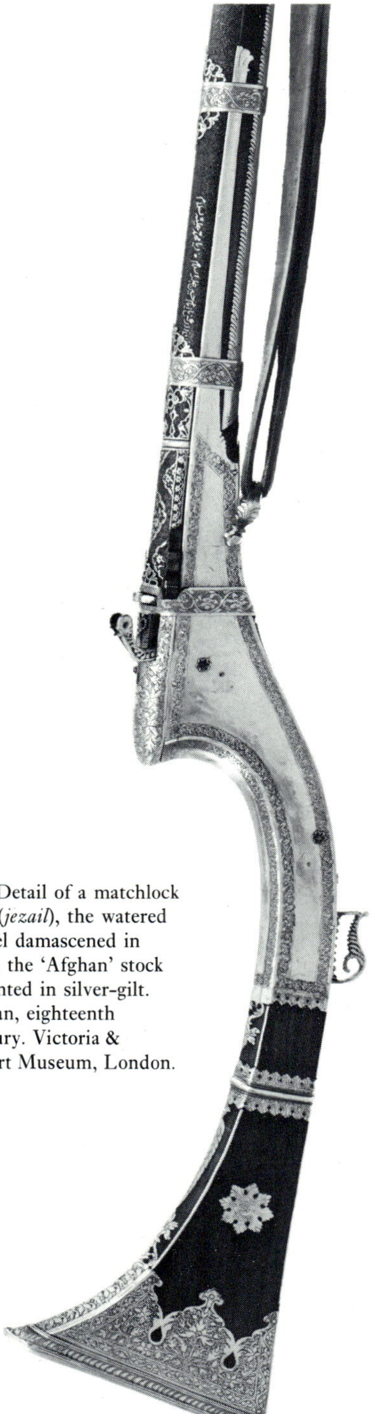

332 Detail of a matchlock gun (*jezail*), the watered barrel damascened in gold, the 'Afghan' stock mounted in silver-gilt. Indian, eighteenth century. Victoria & Albert Museum, London.

333 Flintlock gun (*jezail*), the barrel damascened in gold, with 'Afghan' stock. Indian (Sind), seventeenth or eighteenth century. Wallace Collection, London.

334 Barrel from a gun, cast bronze. Chinese, dated AD 1531. Museum of Chinese History, Peking.

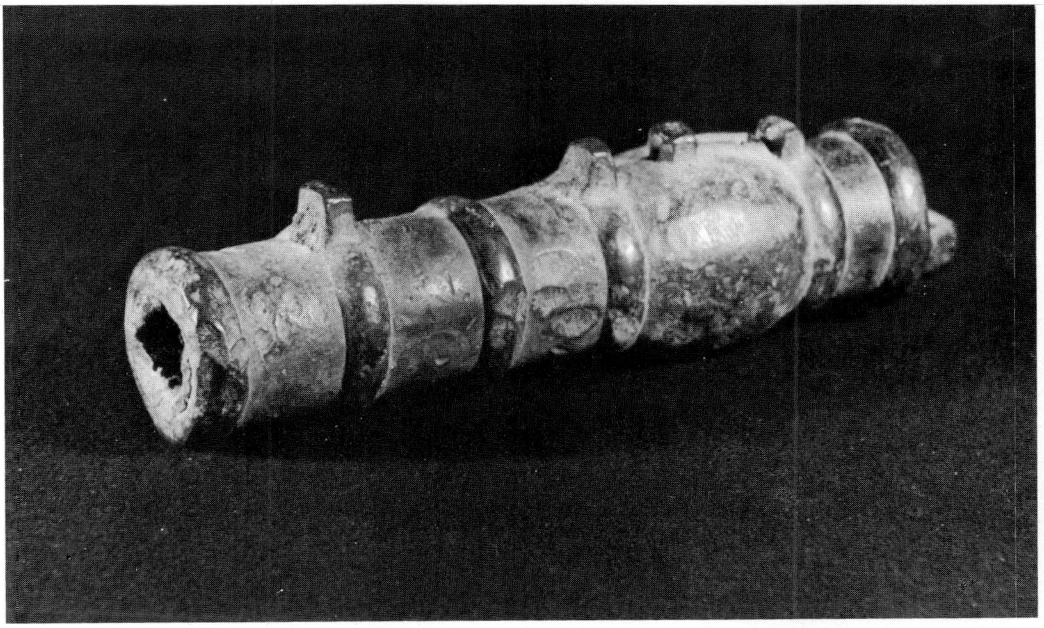

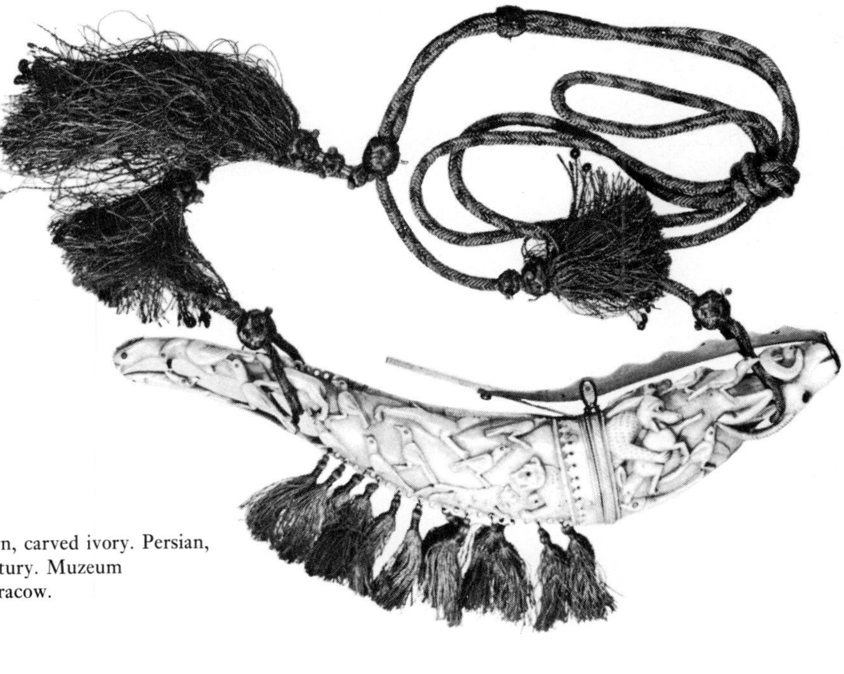

335 Powder-horn, carved ivory. Persian, seventeenth century. Muzeum Narodowego, Cracow.

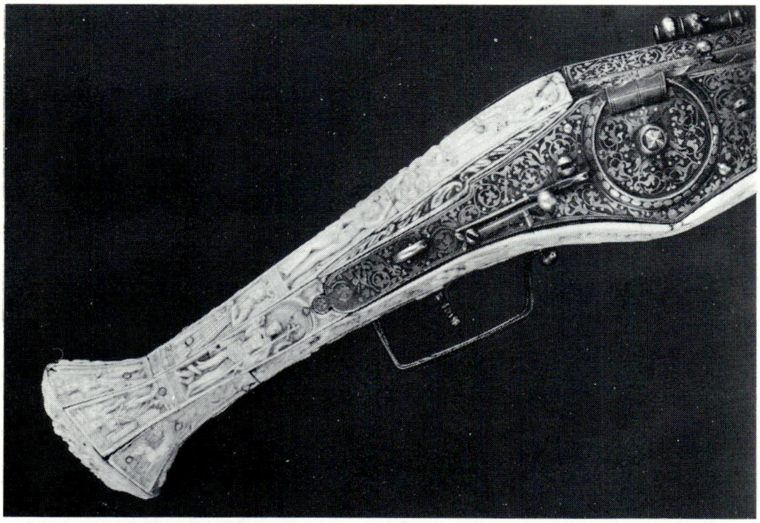

336 *Left* Detail of a wheel-lock pistol, the barrel and lockplate damascened in gold, the stock overlaid with staghorn plaques. German, dated 1557. Historiches Museum, Dresden.

337 *Below* Stock of a double-barrelled wheel-lock pistol. South German, *c.*1580. Muzeum Narodowego, Cracow.

338 *Bottom* Stock of a wheel-lock pistol. German (Nuremberg), *c.*1590. Muzeum Narodowego, Cracow.

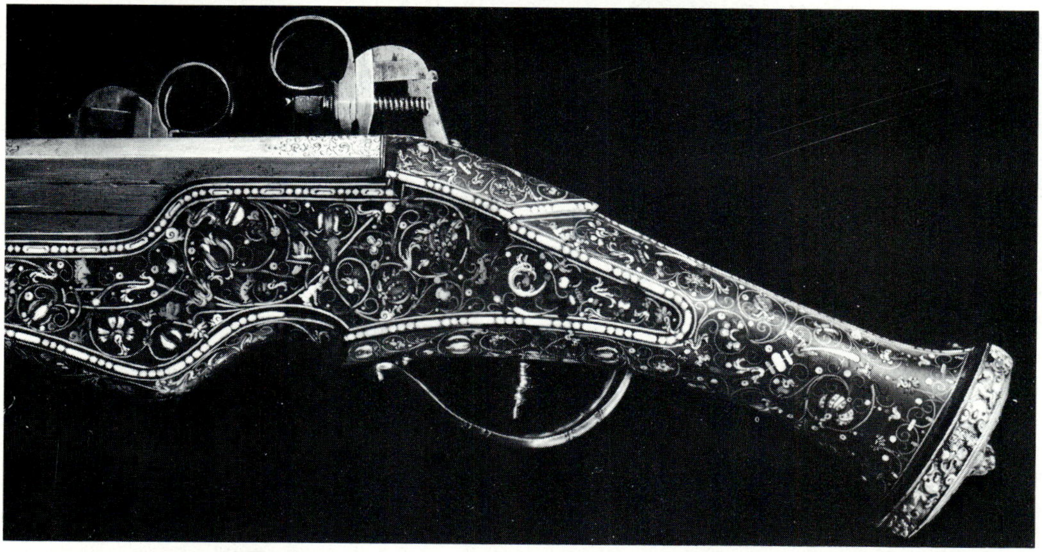

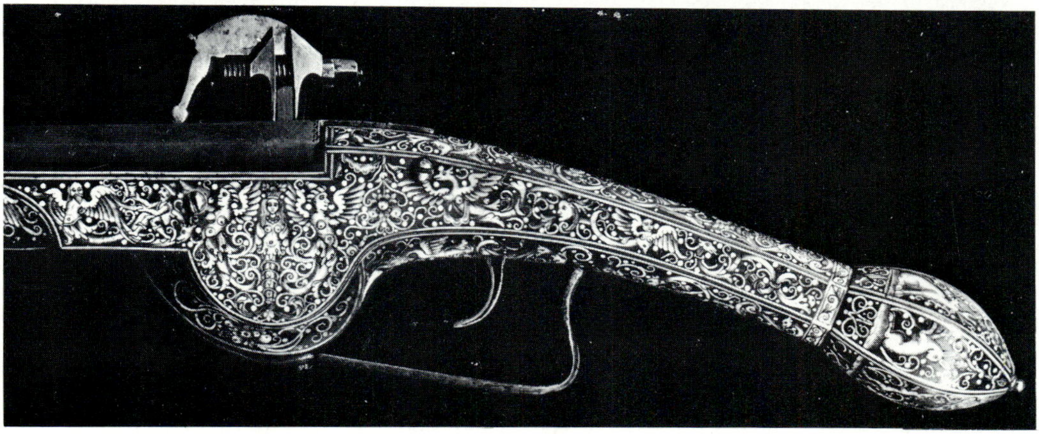

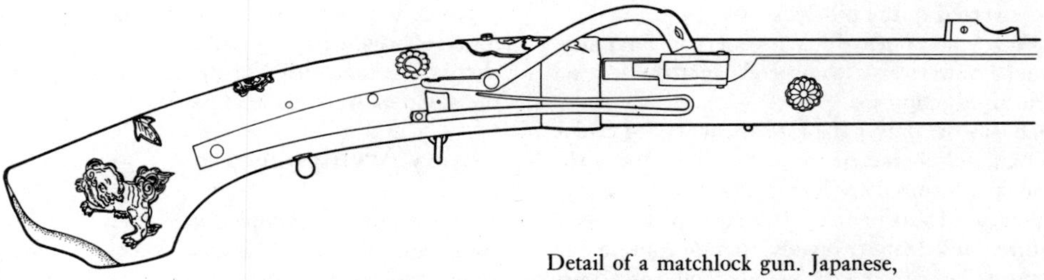

Detail of a matchlock gun. Japanese, eighteenth century.

long, of round or octagonal section, slightly wider at the breech, considerably thickened at the muzzle, sometimes terminating in an onion form of octagonal section, calibre 8 mm-15 mm and smooth-bored, with sighting instruments of iron or brass, massive, and usually in the form of a recumbent parallelogram with peep-holes.

They were decorated in the traditional manner proper to metal, reminiscent of the ornamentation of the mounts of the famous Japanese swords. The technique involved inlaying the iron with precious metals, silver, brass, copper; often several metals were applied in order to obtain a colour effect. Both subject matter and the composition of this ornament are quite original, unlike the decoration used on barrels in other oriental countries or, for that matter, in Europe. The Japanese artist treated the barrel as a surface on which to paint a picture, regardless of its angularities. The space behind the back-sight was reserved for the owner's device or name; otherwise the entire upper part of the barrel was ornamented with plant, animal, landscape, figure and even mythological compositions, arranged on the lines of a *kakemono* painting.

Surviving guns are strikingly uniform and can easily be identified amongst other Oriental firearms. Their construction, weight and massiveness are adapted to the stocky muscular build of the Japanese. A characteristic type of stock was used for mounting guns of all kinds; it was made of dark brown, smoothly polished wood, extending as far as the muzzle, with a place for the ramrod in the underside, and was fastened to the barrel by means of narrow brass capucines; the short butt, falling away in a gentle arc, widened slightly at the heel, with three steps on the underside, but almost oval in horizontal section. In a variant the butt heel is bent downwards almost at a right angle, as in early Catalan guns. The decoration of the stock is very simple, usually consisting of sparsely placed inlaid brass panels, sometimes covered with coloured lacquer. This shape of stock was adapted for firing from the shoulder or from the cheek and not, as claimed by some authors, from the hip.

One type of Japanese gun, large numbers of which have survived to this day, might be called the 'standard Japanese gun'. It has a barrel of round or polygonal section, not exceeding an average length of one metre, a perfected type of matchlock and an undecorated stock. The ornamentation of the barrel is striking as for instance on the piece preserved in the National Museum in Krakow[64] which has a composition, representing the thunder god Kaminari Sama throwing thunderbolts to the earth, inlaid with silver, copper and brass wire. The barrel of the gun in the Museum of the Polish Army in Warsaw[65] has a very rich composition, inlaid with silver, of a hunting scene. Japanese guns are frequently decorated with cloudy landscapes, rocks, waterfalls, animals among trees, and fish playing in water.

Next to the 'standard' gun, revolving guns were popular in Japan. In shape they resembled the former, but were shorter (not exceeding three feet) and had three hand-operated barrels arranged 275
concentrically and a matchlock. An intermediate form between the gun and the cannon was a heavy wall-gun, similar to the Persian and the Indian type but decorated in comformity to Japanese decorative conventions. Stocks and locks were the same as in the standard gun but there was a difference in the shape of the barrels, round or octagonal, with a calibre about 20 mm to 30 mm. In addition, the wall-gun had prominent sights.

A form of pill-lock was introduced into Japan in the second quarter of the nineteenth century, where in a short time a method was invented for converting matchlocks to this particular type of detonator. The old pan-cover was removed and replaced by a cover of spring-steel hinged at the back of the pan. This cover had a projection on the lower side which struck the bottom of the pan where the pill of fulminate was placed. The mainspring was strengthened to make the falling cock powerful enough to force the projection down and fire the gun. During the

64 Inv. No. NI 138791.

65 Inv. No. NI 50815.

nineteenth century many Japanese standard guns were converted to the pill-lock.

In 1853 Japan opened her frontiers to foreigners and shortly afterwards completely modernised her firearms production.

Japan was the only Far Eastern country to evolve a different and characteristic pistol. The idea of the weapon was inspired by Europe, but the style was purely local. In principle, Japanese pistols were miniature guns. Minute pistols, though complete in all respects, were used as *netsuke* and sometimes even large pistols were merely made for show. Another firearm produced was the single-barrel pistol with two movable chambers; revolving pistols, mostly with three barrels, modelled on revolving guns were also made. As with guns, the matchlock on pistols was eventually replaced by the percussion lock. From the second half of the nineteenth century Japan started a modern production of pistols modelled on the latest European and American types.

Japanese powder flasks called *hayago* were chiefly made of wood, papier-maché or lacquer in various shapes, the most usual being that of horn or gourd; the stoppers were made of ivory.

Malay Archipelago

Japanese guns were copied in various neighbouring countries, including Malaya. Malayan guns have similar stocks and matchlocks. The local stylistic difference lies in beautifully worked brass mounts, especially trigger guards.

Another Malayan peculiarity were cannon known as *lantaka*. These were mostly made of brass of varying length, from 20 in to 7 ft, decorated under partly Spanish, partly Chinese, influence. They were used not so much in warfare as for decoration, trade and also for firing festive salvoes.

CHAPTER SIXTEEN

The Manufacture and Proof of Firearms

A.W.F. Taylerson

Little guidance can be offered as to how the first true firearms manufacturers came to their trade. It is logical to assume, however, that manufacture first began in places already devoted (and whether by historical accident, or by the availability of raw materials) to the production of armour, swords, spears, and other hand-weapons; such equipment required skill in metal working, particularly those of the blacksmith, founder and carpenter and the creation of a firearms industry *de novo* seems highly improbable. Indeed, the system of guilds, which was established in Europe from medieval times, makes it unlikely that events took any other course. These guilds were voluntary associations of men, for mutual aid and assistance; the 'guild merchants' held monopolies in the retail trade for particular staples and manufactures, whilst the 'craft guilds' regulated the carrying on of particular crafts, and it was virtually impossible for any man to work or sell within the areas of these monopolies without joining the appropriate guild (or 'company', as it was usually known in Great Britain).

Throughout Europe, separate craft guilds controlled the blacksmiths or armourers, the locksmiths, the joiners or carpenters, and the goldsmiths and silversmiths of particular localities from early times, and J. F. Hayward[1] has clearly demonstrated those ruptures by which, respectively, the barrel makers, gun-lock makers, stockers, and mounters in several European gunmaking cities detached themselves from these older associations, and established guilds of their own. Such separations were often bitterly contested by the parent guild, and Hayward records that in London the gunmakers were not free from the Armourers or the Blacksmiths until 1637, whilst the Locksmiths of Munich and Vienna contained the gunmaker's craft until 1661.

It is therefore suggested that true gunmaking began during the fourteenth century, and was in the hands of conventional craftsmen thereafter, as part of their trade; with a continued growth in demand for firearms, however, certain smiths and armourers specialised in this manufacture to the exclusion of conventional arms. In due course, the better guns and pistols required locking and stocking, which brought into the craft locksmiths, joiners and silversmiths, and particular localities were given over entirely to the craft of gunmaking. The particular point in time at which this specialisation had generally occurred (and dissatisfaction with the disciplines of older craft guilds began to take shape) is difficult to assess, but it was not later than the third quarter of the fifteenth century, and may have been somewhat earlier.

Thereafter, as a broad working hypothesis, it can be said that Northern Italy and Germany were leading centres of European gunmaking in the sixteenth century, but that the former lost something of this prominence, in favour of France, during the seventeenth; the basis of the British industry was laid in this latter period, but the most effective years of London and Birmingham manufacture occurred during the eighteenth century, and the first half of the nineteenth. At various periods, the Austrian (eighteenth), Belgian (eighteenth and nineteenth), Dutch (seventeenth), and Spanish (seventeenth) makers all achieved some degree of success outside their own borders, while sheer weight of output placed Liège in the lead during the period *c.*1850–1914, to face strong competition from the United States, with Brazilian, Finnish, Japanese and Russian activity of equal moment over the past thirty years.

Italy was an important source of European matchlock arms during the first half of the sixteenth century, and important centres for such manufacture existed at Brescia and Milan. In the seventeenth century, the area centring on Brescia was highly regarded both for the magnificently chiselled firearms produced there, and for its barrels, but considerable quantities of coarse service arms were also manufactured there and a substantial contract for musket barrels for the King of Savoy was undertaken by the barrel makers of Gardone in 1698. Bologna, nearby Bargi, Florence and Naples were also remarkable for fine arms.

Of the various countries and cities that may be loosely termed 'German' in the sixteenth century,

1 *The Art of the Gunmaker*, Vol. I, 1500–1600, Barrie and Rockliffe, 1962.

Augsburg, Nuremberg, Dresden, Munich, Suhl and the Rhineland were all of importance as gunmaking centres and exporters by the 1550s; although a gunmakers' guild was not actually formed in the first-named until early in the seventeenth century, the export business was so brisk that city authorities were forced to place a temporary embargo upon it in 1546, to meet their own needs. A sizeable Bohemian industry also flourished at such places as Carlsbad, Eger and Prague, by 1550, and some Austrian activity can be traced two decades earlier. By the seventeenth century such towns as Braunfels, Essen, Mannheim and Kassel were becoming famous for the manufacture of firearms. Ferlach (on the Austrian–Yugoslav border) began gunmaking in the first half of this century also.

As to France, the seventeenth century established Paris as the home of many of the leading gunmakers of Europe. A remarkable provincial industry also evolved in that century, with centres in Alsace (Sedan), Angers (Tours), Brittany (St Brieul, St Malo and Vitré), Burgundy (Autun and Dijon), Champagne (Montmirail), Dauphine (Grenoble), Lorraine (Metz and Nancy), Normandy (Cherbourg and Lisieux), and Picardy (Abbeville).

In England, a gunmaking industry began to form under royal encouragement, during the reign of Henry VIII (1509-47), and by the end of the rule of Elizabeth I (1558-1603) no less than thirty-seven accredited gunsmiths are said to have been repairing firearms in London, at the Minories. Nothing certain is known of their work but the very few decorated English firearms surviving from the late sixteenth and early seventeenth centuries in such places as the Moscow Kremlin and the Real Armería, Madrid, are of very fine quality. Nevertheless many firearms were still imported from abroad at this period.

James I (1603-25) made some magnificent gifts of arms to the rulers of Russia and Spain, but did nothing to foster this native industry. In due course, he was rash enough to bestow a monopoly of gunmaking upon Edmund Nicholson, and by 1607 only five gunmakers remained in London; these unfortunates petitioned Parliament to revoke the monopoly, and eventually (in 1637) the gunmakers of London were granted a charter of incorporation as a City Company in their own right. This charter was fiercely resisted by the equivalent Company of Blacksmiths, but was duly enrolled in 1656, and subsequently the provisions of it were both confirmed and enlarged in 1672.

Thereafter the London Gunmakers' Company controlled British gunmaking for more than a decade, by exercise of the privilege of proof later described, and by their powers of search and confiscation in relation to makers who were not members of the Company. Petitions to Parliament were made in 1680, 1706 and 1710 against the practice of importing firearms, and the last petition revealed the gunmakers of London as creditors of the Crown for no less than £30,000, in respect of arms delivered but not paid for. In 1689, however, the London Company itself encountered competition from another part of the country, which it was unable (despite attempts made over the next century and a half) ever to suppress, and which was in a form that proved extremely difficult to combat by those sanctions available under the charter of 1672.

Birmingham had manufactured nails, cutlery, swords and other ferrous items for centuries, but, although some gunmaking had been carried on at nearby Bromsgrove early in the seventeenth century, no important gunmaking industry was established in the town until 1689. In that year, however, Sir Richard Newdigate (Member of Parliament for Warwickshire) secured a substantial British government contract for the Birmingham manufacturers to supply muskets, and this contract was so successfully executed that (despite bitter opposition from the London Company) further business resulted. A number of manufacturers and smiths then began to concentrate upon gunmaking to the exclusion of any other occupation.

Due to the peculiar circumstances of Birmingham's introduction to the gun trade, no guild or company then existed for the craft, and many of the difficulties and abuses of power experienced by manufacturers in London (or the Continental centres) were never experienced in Birmingham. Naturally enough, a training system was developed in which boys were instructed in their craft, by being apprenticed for seven years to a practising gunmaker, but, his skill once acquired, a man was free to enter the trade (or leave it for another) without difficulties raised by any craft guild or company. Indeed, it was not until 1854 that the equivalent of the old guild-merchant was formed to regulate the activities of the Birmingham gun manufacturers at large.

As a result of this flexibility in Birmingham's labour force, both as to its size and ability to learn the necessary skills required for gunmaking, this town rapidly attracted the attention of merchants and retailers throughout the country. Very large quantities of cheap arms were required for the African trade (which began in the seventeenth century), and many Birmingham gunmakers proved willing to provide anonymous arms for others to sign and retail. When (in the eighteenth century) these activities were allied with the presence of makers able to manufacture arms as fine as any obtainable in Europe, the future of Birmingham's gun trade was established.

In two other parts of the United Kingdom, where the writ of the London Company did not run, gunmaking was also carried on from a comparatively early date. Most provincial towns probably had one or more gunsmiths, some of whom, like the Paris family of Warwick and Derby, achieved more than local fame. Scotland, as already noted in chapter 14, produced many distinguished makers. In Ireland, Dublin was the main centre. A considerable amount of repair work was carried out there on military fire arms but the city also housed a number of makers of fine-quality guns from the late seventeenth century onwards.

As to the remainder of Europe, gunmaking can also be traced at early dates in Spain the Netherlands, Scandinavia, and Switzerland.

German gunsmiths worked in Spain in the second half of the sixteenth century, the most noted being various members of the Marquart (Marcuarte) family of Augsburg who worked in Madrid until the mid-eighteenth century. Other important centres were Barcelona, Eiber, and Ripoll in Catalonia. In the Low Countries, Aachen, Antwerp, and Liège were all established gunmaking towns by the sixteenth century. By the seventeenth century, this area had achieved considerable output, and substantial quantities of arms came from there to Great Britain during the Civil War. At Utrecht, craftsmen like Jan Knoop made arms of the highest quality, whilst Liège (which copied arms, rather than initiating designs) had some 8,000 townsfolk employed in the craft by 1639.

In seventeenth-century Scandinavia, both Denmark and Sweden manufactured firearms in some quantities; the Danes modelled their arms upon German styles, but such makers as P. Kalthoff–who originated in Germany–produced repeating flintlock arms of considerable sophistication, and in surprising quantity, between 1658 and 1675.

In Switzerland, such gunmakers as F. Werder (Zurich) and the Munier family (of Geneva), among others, produced excellent firearms during the seventeenth century.

Although such a late-comer to the gun trade, it would be impossible to close these preliminary remarks without reference to the establishment of an American industry, one curious feature of which for many years was the relative lack of concentration, when compared with established arms-making centres of the old world.

The *Manufactures and Statistics of the US Census of 1810 & c., (US Official Papers to 1843)* showed the US firearms industry as principally located in Worcester, Massachusetts, in 1810, when that town produced 19,095 muskets (valued at $229,085) out of a national total of 65,000 arms. Other factories were then located at Hartford and New Haven (in Connecticut), with 115 establishments in Pennsylvania, ten in Maryland and fourteen in Virginia; this latter state, of course, held the long-famous arsenal at Richmond and produced 20,000 firearms during that censal year. The report also mentioned makers at Providence, Rhode Island; Burlington, New Jersey; with several in Tennessee and North and South Carolina while Kentucky, though apparently containing no arms-makers, boasted not less than fourteen powder mills.

Turning to the year 1823, this same report mentioned an unidentified gun-factory in Connecticut as having used 30 tons of steel in producing 26,000 guns, and it seems reasonable to assume that the reference was to Eli Whitney's establishment at Whitneyville, two miles north of New Haven. Whitney (who died in 1826) had a contract for the US Government Model 1816 flintlock musket, amongst other commitments, but the report noted that this factory was regarded as unprofitable, since 'for the last ten years [it] has not yielded 5 per cent profit on the capital invested'.

The report also took an interesting side-glance at the labour force employed during 1840, with a reference to a Connecticut factory employing forty men to make 2,150 guns, and to another where three men made 150 weapons during the year. Two thousand guns were made by thirty men at Meriden, and 6,340 by seventy-six men in three other factories, whilst one man made twelve at a powder mill in Maine, three men produced 150,000 lb of gun powder, worth $7,500.

A later report on *Manufacturers of the US in 1860*, by J. M. Edmunds, cast light upon the capital employed and values turned out; the author recorded 239 factories in 1862, as having a total capital of $2,512,731, and employing 2,056 hands. These men made $2,342,681 worth of firearms, of which $1,544,090 was the product of twenty-six factories in New England; $625,094 the value produced in the Middle States by ninety-four establishments; $85,834 produced by seventy-two workshops in the West; $72,652 produced by forty-one factories in the South; and $15,011 the produce of six establishments in the Pacific States.

The largest factories were stated by Edmunds to be in Connecticut, where nine plants at Hartford, New Haven and Norwich ('including some of the largest private armouries in the US') produced nearly one half of the total value, or $1,186,500. Seven in Massachusetts (including the Springfield Arsenal) produced arms to the value of $340,000, and the existence of forty-four factories in Pennsylvania, thirty-seven in New York, one in New Jersey, six in Maryland, and twenty-three in Ohio, were also noted by Edmunds.

One important aspect of all the European activity described above has not yet been touched upon, however, and this was the division of individual crafts between both the various workshops in a particular locality and between the various manufacturing centres themselves.

As to the first matter, specialisation of certain workshops in the production of particular components was first noticeable in Germany (during both the sixteenth and seventeenth centuries) and became equally marked in Northern Italy, during the seventeenth century. Thus, a German or Italian 'gunmaker' tended to assemble and finish parts purchased from other workshops, lock-makers being the craftsmen most likely to assemble, finish, and retail a complete firearm. This is not, of course, to say that such men were unable to make more than one of the various components needed. An apprentice to the gunmaker's trade was frequently required by his guild to make a complete firearm (save for the stock) before being permitted to practise his craft unsupervised, whilst other schools of gunmaking (like that of Vienna) followed in any event a system whereby all metal parts were actually made in the individual workshop. By and large, however, it proved more convenient to the German and Italian makers to buy some components from specialist manufacturers, or to hand over a partly completed weapon to an expert, for stocking, decoration, or mounting, and this practice eventually became widespread in Europe.

As to those centres specialising in the manufacture of particular components, four towns (situated near suitable reserves of iron ore) were noted manufacturers and exporters of gun barrels, both rough and finished; Suhl (in Thuringia) was largely destroyed by fire, in 1634, but Eibar and Madrid (in Spain) and Brescia (in Italy) remained active in this one trade until well into the nineteenth century. Other examples of this type of local specialisation may be studied in the export of locks by Augsburg and Nuremberg, during the sixteenth and seventeenth centuries, and by Birmingham and Liège during the eighteenth and nineteenth centuries.

In support of the various gunmaking crafts practised within their limits, many European cities soon required the stamping of an individual mark upon products made by resident workmen, so that they could be identified in case of defect. Some Brescian makers actually signed their arms from the beginning of the seventeenth century, but this practice was not general until the 1700s, and identification of early individual gunmakers, from the marking upon firearms, is thus often extremely difficult. A town mark was also often applied to indicate that the piece met the required standards of quality of the locality. Augsburg used the pine-cone mark in the sixteenth century, Nuremberg a coat-of-arms, and Amsterdam, Maastricht, Madrid, Strasbourg, Suhl and Utrecht followed a similar practice.

Another matter equally difficult to establish, is the actual methods and techniques used in manufacturing the earliest firearms; as will presently appear, something is known of gunmaking practice in the eighteenth and nineteenth centuries, but those crafts in use at the dawn of such manufacture remain obscure.

The earliest gun barrels were the work of founders or blacksmiths – depending on whether they were of brass or of iron – and the wooden stocks of carpenters. Members of these crafts probably started to specialise in this particular field as soon as there was sufficient demand for firearms. It was not, however, until the sixteenth century, when the invention of new lock mechanisms produced an enormous increase in this demand, that a separate craft of gunmaking, involving highly specialised skills, really emerged. As already noted the manufacture of a gun or pistol was usually the work of a number of specialists, the lock, the barrel, the stock, the mounts and the decoration often being produced by separate craftsmen (see also Chapter 17). Until the nineteenth century the work was done by hand with the aid of only the simplest tools, of which the most elaborate would have been the lathe and the barrel-boring bench.

Again, prior to the nineteenth century, craftsmen were no better served in relation to simple drilling. Twist-drills, in universal use today, did not come into general use until the nineteenth century, and were not made by machinery until early in the 1860s; meantime, all holes were drilled with a flat-tipped spear-pointed drill, made by the user himself, as a rule. This type of drill might be mounted in either a brace or a bow drill, but considerable skill was needed to use either of these tools with accuracy.

In barrel manufacture, reaming-out the rough bores of the tubes was commonly accomplished by hand (as was any rifling of them) until well into the nineteenth century, using a rod tipped with a square bit mounted on a special bench. A few early workshops, however, did this heavy work in a water- or horse-powered boring-mill similar to those used for cleaning out the cored hole in cast cannon-barrels, a device recorded in Germany as early as 1373,[2] but such aids to the ordinary European commercial gunmaker were the exception rather than the rule until the late eighteenth century.

The earliest iron barrels were probably made by bending a rectangular strip of metal round an iron rod until the two longer edges could be hammer-welded together. The resultant rough barrel was then bored out, filed into shape and fitted with a breech plug. According to the Madrid gunmaker Isidro Soler, writing in 1798 in his *Compendio Histórico de los Arcubuceros de Madrid*, this method

2 See F. M. Feldhaus, *Die Technik*, Munich, 1965, p. 391.

was the one most commonly used in Europe in his day. He goes on to say that in Spain, the method used for the best barrels was to make a series of short tubes out of plates previously produced from old horse-shoes and to lap weld these together. Each tube was heated and hammered at least thirty-two times in the process so that the metal of the resultant rough barrel, which was then filed and bored in the normal way, was exceedingly homogeneous. The final produce was of superb quality and Spanish barrels were greatly esteemed everywhere in Europe.[3]

Another process that seems to have been used in Europe as early as the seventeenth century involved forging-out ribbons of metal, twisting these into a rough metal tube (round a rod or mandrel), and then welding the joints of the ribbon together by repeated heating and hammering; subsequently, the tube was breeched, and then filed or ground externally to the desired dimensions. This process was used especially for the so-called 'Damascus' or 'stub-twist' barrels, also discussed on pp. 468-9 below, with which nearly all fine-quality firearms were equipped during the period *c.*1780-*c.*1880. They were made by twisting and welding a number of iron and steel rods together to produce a bar consisting of many laminations which was then coiled to form a barrel as described above. The laminations caused the surface of the metal to contain attractive patterns, varying according to the relative proportion of iron and steel used, which were usually intensified after the barrel had been polished by means of a mild corrosive that also gave the surface a pleasant brown colour.

The technique used to produce stub-twist barrels was almost certainly Oriental in origin, for barrels of this kind were being made in Turkey, Persia and Northern India as early as the second half of the sixteenth century. They occur occasionally on European firearms from the beginning of the seventeenth century–for example a German wheel-lock rifle of this period in the Wallace Collection (No. A1084)–but do not start to become common until the end of the century. The reason for this is possibly that the capture of a large number of Turkish firearms with barrels of this type at the Siege of Vienna in 1683 started a fashion for them. Oriental barrels are not infrequently found mounted with European stocks and locks and an example in the Peterborough Museum actually bears a plaque inscribed to the effect that the barrel was captured at the Siege of Vienna. It should be noted, incidentally, that from the early eighteenth century onwards poorer-quality firearms sometimes had barrels of ordinary construction etched to simulate stub-twist ones.

It is proposed now to consider some of the later methods and techniques used to manufacture firearms; save as otherwise indicated, the practice described will be British, but (the American workshops excepted) it is unlikely that normal usages varied to any significant degree in other gunmaking countries.

Many early patents witness the impatience of men more far-seeing than the average master craftsman with the handcraft system of producing firearms. As early as 1628, Arnold Rotispen obtained an English patent for 'a new art, industrie, waye, or meines of makeinge gonnes', and obtained an extension (or a fresh patent) seven years later, covering various types of gun- and bullet-making machinery. This latter patent referred particularly to means 'to draw or to shave barrells for pieces of all sortes, straight, even and smooth', and 'to make anie crooked barrell perfectly straight with greate ease', and 'to rifle, cutt out, or screwe barrells as wyde or as close or as deepe or as shallowe as shall be required, and with greate ease'.

The next English patent of detailed relevance to the guntrade was probably that protecting Samuel Bentham's wood-planer, which could rough-out gunstocks; the original planer, of 1791, was followed by another shaper (in 1793) which used circular saws and cutters for the purpose. A more elaborate machine, invented by an American called Blanchard in the mid-1820s, was introduced in England about 1854. This double lathe turned both stock-blank and a pattern, slowly, in separate frames, with a wheel (or dumb-tracer) resting on the pattern. The slide rest holding the dumb-tracer also carried a rotating cutter-wheel which faithfully followed the movements of the dumb-tracer against the pattern, and so shaped the revolving stock-blank with real exactitude; the finished work-piece had, of course, the marks of cutter-teeth upon it, but a 'maker-off' would obliterate these in the finishing process.

Blanchard's lathes were an importation from America, where they had been in service making shoe-lasts, boot-trees, wheel-spokes and gun-stocks for many years, and were seen in action at the Springfield Armoury by a British Government Commission examining methods for making infantry rifles with fully-interchangeable parts. They were used (with later machines capable of cutting inlets for the lock, trigger-guard, etc.) at the Royal Small Arms Factory, at Enfield, and by the larger of the privately-owned military rifle factories, but British makers of sporting weapons appear to have ignored them.

The United States of America, perpetually starved of skilled manpower until well into the nineteenth century, was the source of other ingenious machines for the fabrication of gun parts to very exact final dimensions, although American manufacturers never

3 The process described by Soler is mentioned as early as 1642 in *Arte de Ballesteria y Monteria* by Alonso Martinez de Espinas, another Madrid gunsmith.

succeeded in producing parts that could not be improved by handfinishing. There always remained the burrs; if quality required the marks of cutting tools were skilfully filed and polished away.

Possibly the best known of all these imported American machines was a 'Universal Milling-machine', designed by Frederick W. Howe in 1852. Eight of these index millers were sold to British purchasing agents, in 1855, at the not inconsiderable price of $850 apiece, along with other gunmaking machinery required after the British decision to adopt service small-arms with interchangeable parts. Howe's 'Universal Miller' was a most flexible machine, capable of making straight cuts like a planer, or spiral cuts at regular distances apart, of slotting or boring holes, and of milling irregular and uneven surfaces. By modern standards it was probably rather dangerous to use, since the work-piece was offered up manually to the revolving cutters by small swinging frames (attached to the work-table as required) in some operations, whilst in others the work-piece was clamped down and the driving shaft moved across to drill or slot the component.

Equally valuable were the imported American drilling and profile-cutting machines. Commercial gunmakers might continue to use the bow-drill, or the brace, for boring holes, but the exactitude required for military arms demanded a multi-spindle drilling machine. Here, the work-piece was contained in a hardened steel box, with suitable holes positioned in the lid, and drills were passed successively through these holes to pierce the work exactly as required. The profile-cutting equipment (or 'edging machines', as some engineers called them) was used to trace out irregular shapes, and was, so to speak, a simplified Blanchard lathe. A dumb-spindle followed the outline of a steel pattern, to guide a cutting-spindle round the work-piece.

A good deal of ingenious machinery of this type came from Chicopee Falls, in Massachusetts. The Chicopee Falls Company built a works there, in 1837, which was taken over by the Ames Manufacturing Company four years later, and became the factory of the Massachusetts Arms Company about 1850. The Company made various types of percussion rifles and revolvers, but also specialised in the manufacture of gunmaking machines, many of which were supplied to the London Armoury Co. Ltd., and to the Birmingham Small Arms Co. Ltd. (via the Ames Mfg. Co.) in 1861. Twenty years later, the firm of Pratt & Whitney (at Hartford, Connecticut) assumed an equal importance as suppliers of advanced gunmaking machinery to government arsenals in America and Europe.

Turning to another aspect of gun manufacture, barrel-making seems to have been a separate trade from very early times and one sufficiently highly regarded for the better-known makers to sign or mark their work in full view, at a period when other craftsmen remained anonymous. Originally, the craft involved only manual forging of a kind previously described, but (after 1813) another method of manufacture also became common in England for making certain types of iron gun-barrel; military and 'common' barrels were thereafter normally rolled, a slab of iron being first passed successively between pairs of grooved-and-ribbed rolls until the edges met, and being then brought to welding heat and rolled through a suitable groove to weld the longitudinal seam. Subsequently, a rod or mandrel was thrust through the heavy 12 in tube thus formed, and the barrel rolled out successively to the required length with the mandrel inside it. This rolling system was invented by a Birmingham manufacturer (named Henry Osborne) during a long strike of barrel-welders, in 1812, and appears to have been part only of a series of such improvements by the same man. The alternative methods of passing the heated skelp through successive swages, or forging it between a grooved anvil and a tilt-hammer with a similarly grooved face, may also have been used to a lesser extent.

However, iron barrels for the better class of British sporting gun continued to be hand-forged upon an anvil, as before. This was one of the few branches of the trade upon which some excellent contemporary books existed, and little space will be devoted here to a subject most expertly and succinctly covered by John Acton (*An Essay on Shooting*, Dublin, 1789) and by W. Greener in his *Gunnery in 1858* (London, 1858).

Metal for these superior barrels was supplied in ribands, which were then heated and wound spirally about a mandrel, in the manner earlier described; as one spiral coil was formed upon the mandrel, another riband was joined to the end of it (by fire and hammer), and so on until a helical coil of desired length had been created. This coil was then jumped up endwise into a rough tube, and the helical seam closed and welded up by further heating and hammering.

As already noted a variety of metals might be used to make these ribands, which gave the resultant barrels such names as 'Damascus', 'stub twist', 'plain twist', and so on, dependent upon the constituents of the bar from which the riband had been originally forged or rolled. 'Damascus' metal, as an example, began as bars forged from alternate thin strips of wrought iron and steel, which had been gripped at one end, and twisted helically; these twisted masses were forged square again, and two (or more) of the resultant bars were forged into one skelp, from which the necessary riband was then created.

When barrels made from such metals were pickled

in a weak acid (which ate away the iron and steel unevenly), a most attractive figure appeared in their metal, being the twisted fibres of the original iron and steel bars, and gave such barrels their 'Damascus' name; completed tubes were sold to the gun trade by barrel-makers under various names, of which 'single Damascus twist', 'Damascus Leclerc', and 'Turkish Damascus' are examples.

One of the better-known British sources for this 'Damascus' metal was a small strip-tilting forge, at Wednesbury Bridge, Staffordshire, worked by Mr Robert Adams. This maker began operating in 1815 on the production of twist iron for the gun trade, and his firm continued in business until nearly the turn of the century. 'Damascus' metal remained popular for many years, despite competition from rolled or Whitworth steel shotgun barrels, but a leading maker of such tubes noted it as a dying trade by 1902.

In France and America, on the other hand, steel barrels were greatly favoured after the 1830s for use in rifles and pistols. For this purpose, a solid bar of best cast steel was forged to correct size (under a tilt hammer) and the bore afterwards drilled out. It is not easy at this distance of time, however, to establish exactly what the makers and writers of those days meant when they termed any metal as 'steel'; a gibe by William & John Rigby of Dublin (in an advertising leaflet published in 1851), that the so-called 'steel barrels' of their day were made of iron decarbonised from the original steel, is a fair example of the differing views of the metal thus described. In those remarks which follow, therefore, the term 'steel' must be accepted as used by contemporary writers, and not as necessarily describing a metal containing the quantity of carbon desired by a metallurgist today.

Deane[4] recorded a celebrated French trial of 1843 between Bernard and Gastinne Renette of Paris, with fourteen gunmakers from the State Arsenal at St Etienne. In this test, a conventional rifle barrel of steel withstood a charge of 8 balls and $2\frac{1}{2}$ oz of powder without failure. Deane was not entirely disinterested in touting the virtue of steel, for 'Laminated Steel Gun-barrels' were greatly favoured by the firm of George & John Deane at London Bridge, and made for them by Robert Adams and John Clive at Birmingham. The American revolver manufacturer, Samuel Colt, also used cast steel for his pistol barrels, the blanks being worked out under a five-hammer Ryder forging-engine (invented by an Englishman) at his London factory.

J. D. Goodman (*The Resources, Products and Industrial History of Birmingham, 1866*) found steel barrels less liable to inner flaws than those of iron, and considerably tougher, but they were not readily adopted in England. He noticed their use in the military arms of America, Austria and Prussia, by 1865, but could report only that 'the subject is under consideration', so far as military rifle manufacture ran in England.

However the barrels were fashioned, the rough tubes had to be shaped internally and externally, and rifled where appropriate. As already noted the boring-out was all too frequently done at a manually-operated boring bench, where (despite the existence of excellent mechanical systems) a series of borers, sometimes as many as twenty-two, were laboriously passed through the tube to bring the interior to a suitable size and finish; similar manually-operated rifling benches were also used, cutting a groove at a time. The interior being completed, the barrel was 'struck-up' on the outside, and, after straightening and breeching, was prepared for proof.

Considerable ingenuity was directed to mechanising these operations, but little was done in England prior to the acceptance of the interchangeable principle for service rifles. As early as 1718[5] the Frenchman Deschamps had proved the ability of his machines to fashion muskets which were interchangeable in all their parts, but little interest was aroused in England. Two Englishmen, Henry James and John Jones, patented an elaborate system of machines for barrel-making (covering forging of the skelp, and turning off the exterior taper), but their patent[6] was ignored in their own country. In Russia, however, their methods were adopted, and the Tula Arsenal became one of the leading State manufactories producing military flintlock arms with machine-made components. A series of illustrations showing certain processes from that arsenal were prepared by a British engineer, Richard Prosser, who was engaged to prepare a historical foreword to a Patent Office publication (unpublished) upon small-arms. Prosser died in 1854, his work uncompleted, but left engravings (taken from an earlier work by von Hamel) with a rough translation of the captions, as prepared by von Bach, a German. The manuscript is in the British Patent Office.[7]

Gun-lock components, as earlier mentioned, were originally forged at the anvil by men whose skill with a hammer must have been something for wonder; the rough parts were then filed to shape and assembled by filers, who passed the lock onto the polishers and hardeners for completion. Exactly when mechanical hammers or stamps began to replace the hand-forger is uncertain, but the first

4 In his *Manual & History etc., of Firearms*, London, 1858.

5 *Receuil des Machines Approuvées par l'Académie Royale des Sciences*, Vol. III, Paris, 1718.

6 No. 3469 of 1811.

7 Ref. PU 20 (15217).

English patent clearly to describe the making of 'plates, hammers, sears, tumblers, bridles and jaws of locks', by means of stamps, dies and presses, was taken out by George Round and Samuel Whitford in 1838. The specification mentioned, with some truth, that the advantage lay in always producing duplicates, 'which may be interchanged at pleasure', and noted that parts were more easily finished.

Experience showed that the impact of the hammer or press upon the die forming the heated metal never produced a perfect facsimile. Distortion and wear on the dies soon led to extrusion of the metal at the sides, and required that the work-piece be filed and fitted as before. However, the advance was real, and the speed with which the rough components could be produced was considerably increased.

Various types of mechanical hammers were used, the Tula Arsenal type being probably the most common, since it was manually-operated and not unduly difficult to construct. The mechanical 'American Drop' was introduced at Colt's London factory, in 1853, and became popular with the larger manufacturers; it was also used at the Royal Small Arms Factory at Enfield Lock. The principle was simple, and depended upon a large vertical screw rotating between four upright support legs, which also acted as guides for the falling weight. The latter could be engaged at will with the turning screw-thread, which wound it up to the top of the guides, and then either released automatically (to fall upon the forming die at the base), or held for manual release by the workman.

Even in the largest arsenals, however, not all of this shaping was done mechanically. The hand hammer played a considerable part in production, aided by suitable jigs and formers, and as late as 1854 the London factory making Adams's revolvers was still cutting out the frame and barrel by hand, in competition with the Colt mechanical stamps and forges.

Inevitably, as the complexity of firearms increased from their first crude origins, the number of tasks to be performed in their manufacture increased also; practice varied considerably in various parts of Europe, but the eighteenth and nineteenth centuries saw the gun trade at its most fragmented, with a wide range of trades involved in making even the cheapest of muskets or shotguns.

In a famous case, tried in the Court of King's Bench, Westminster, in February 1747, this diversification was notably revealed in the London gun trade[8] when the Company of Gunmakers of the City of London (through one Samuel Blanckley) sued John Hirst, for 'using the occupation of gunmaking, contrary to the form of the fifth of Qu. Elisabeth etc., to prevent the unskilful manufacturing of goods, prejudicial to the public'. The defendant, Hirst, proved himself competent by producing a gun made completely by himself, and evidence revealed that the gunmakers' business in London was actually divided into no less than twenty-one different and distinct trades, the 'master-gunmakers' merely assembling the parts thus made. The trades recognised were barrel forger, breech forger, barrel filer, barrel polisher, barrel loop-maker, lock forger, lock filer, lock polisher, lock hardener, trigger and nail-filer, stock maker, side-piece and thumb-piece repairer and polisher, engraver, bluer, stick maker, flint maker, and mounter or screwer together.

Something over a century later, a visiting commission of London and Birmingham gunmakers reported, in 1857, that a similar (but less stratified) system had evolved in Liège. Apparently, however, the 'gunmaker' of Liège dealt only with two men, who stocked, screwed, finished, made off and polished each gun from materials previously supplied to them by the gunmaker; the two men were entirely responsible for their work (replacing defective parts at their own expense), and received no payment until the weapon had passed view at the Proof House. If there rejected, both men lost their payment regardless of the nature of the failure, and might thus be faced with a serious deficit in their expected earnings. When it is appreciated that the men might be handing over a score of weapons, representing six months' work, the probable extent of their debts can be guessed.

When reporting to the British Association in 1865, however, J. D. Goodman[9] revealed that Birmingham still followed a pattern in which (as he wrote) '. . . manufacture of the various parts of the gun, as barrel, lock &c., are distinct trades. These several parts are collected by the manufacturer, known as the gunmaker, and by him are set up.'

As Goodman (then Chairman of the Birmingham Small Arms Company Ltd.) saw the chief branches of the Birmingham gun trade, they dealt with stocks, barrels, locks, furniture (i.e. trigger-guards, side-plates, ramrod pipes, etc.) and odd-work making of pins, screws, barrel bolts, tools and implements; for the military gun trade, he added bayonet, sight, and rammer making. In the classified list of workmen which follows, Goodman's estimates of the numbers employed in each branch of the trade are included as some indication of the labour strength that achieved those extraordinary exports required in the early years of the American Civil War.

Goodman began his breakdown by reference to 'manufacturers' listed in the appropriate Commercial Directory, and under eight branches of the trade:

8 *The Gentleman's Magazine*, Vol. XVIII. See also *Journal of the Arms and Armour Society*, Vol. VI (1968-70), pp. 268-73.

9 *op.cit.*, p. 469 above.

Gunmakers	174
Barrel makers	32
Furniture makers	23
Lock makers	25
Nipple makers	3
Implement makers	61
Case makers	11
Wadding makers	5

Also recognised (but unlisted) were makers of minor gun parts, and such workmen as stockers, finishers and engravers. The latter were labelled as outworkers, that is to say independent contractors working simultaneously for several of the gunmakers (or 'setters up') noticed above.

Goodman then listed the 'Material Makers' and the 'Setters Up', by their crafts:

Material Makers

Stock Makers	100
Barrel Welders	
Borers	
Grinders	
Filers & Breechers	700
Rib Makers	
Breech Forgers & Stampers	
Lock Forgers	
Machiners	1,200
Filers	
Furniture Forgers & Casters	100
Filers	
Rod Forgers	
Grinders & Polishers	100
Finishers	
Bayonet Forgers	
Socket Stampers	
Ring Stampers	
Grinders & Polishers	500
Machiners	
Hardeners	
Filers	
Band Forgers & Stampers	
Machiners	300
Filers	
Pin Makers	
Sight Stampers	
Machiners	300
Jointers	
Filers	
Trigger Boxers	20
Oddwork Makers	100
	3,420

Setters Up

Machiners–*Prepare the front sight and the lump end of the barrel for the nipple*	50
Jiggers–*Lump Filers and Break-off Fitters–Prepare the breech end of the barrel*	200
Stockers–*Let in the barrel and locks, and roughly shape the stock*	1,000
Percussioners–*Finish the nipple-seat, put in the nipple, and adjust the hammer to the nipple*	200
Screwers–*Let in the furniture, and all the remaining pins & screws*	1,000
Strippers–*Prepare the gun for rifling & proof*	20
Barrel Borers	50
Riflers	50
Sighters & Sight Adjusters	50
Smoothers–*Prepare the barrel for browning*	100
Finishers–*Distribute the several parts to browner, polisher, maker-off, and barrel smoother, and when they are returned put the guns together, and finally adjust the several parts*	
Makers-off–*File the stocks to give them their proper finish; glass paper and oil them*	1,000
Polishers–*Lock and Furniture*	50
Engravers *(Lock, &c.)*	50
Browners *(Barrel)*	50
Lock Freers–*Finally adjust the working parts of the lock*	50
	3,920

Summary

Material Makers	3,420
Setters Up	3,920
Total	7,340

It must be emphasised again that this report was made for one centre of the industry alone, and that the period is a late one. Obviously enough, the trades of percussioner or nipple maker post-dated the advent of the percussion-cap, but the breakdown is valuable in revealing those principal crafts practised over the centuries, which were by no means characteristic of Birmingham alone.

Manufacture of firearms by machinery tends to be linked in the mind with the introduction of weapon parts interchangeable with equivalent components from other arms, but at the time when such machinery eventually began to be introduced into Britain, the bait was probably rather different.

The attraction of hand-labour over machines has been mentioned earlier in this Chapter, but as time passed the craftsmen (embittered by experience) became increasingly recalcitrant, and although few British gunmakers were really convinced that machines could make guns on the interchangeable system, without a high proportion of hand-fitting to round-off the job, their interest was at least aroused by the fact that those machines could be operated by almost any labour, if under skilled supervision. Some evidence tendered to the Parliamentary Committee of 1854, examining the interchangeable principle for service small arms, indicated the irritation experienced by manufacturers at the hands of skilled and irreplaceable workmen, viz: 'The delay of sending our supply is caused by the unwillingness of the men to make the locks at the price we understood was to be paid' or 'We have been disappointed by two of our oldest rod-hands, who promised to come to work, but have not.' One maker mentioned 'continued strike of workmen' as the cause for delay, and another grumbled at 'my men, the grinders and filers, turning out for the price'.[10]

In the event, the British Board of Ordnance gave the original lead by opening a lock and barrel manufactory of its own at Lewisham, in 1808, where a fair amount of simple machinery was installed. This factory, which complemented other workshops in Birmingham and at the Tower of London, served as some sort of control over the commercial gun trade, but made no really serious dent in the amount of available business whilst the Napoleonic War lasted. These three official manufactories (with one other at Dublin Castle) faced no less than ten French Government arsenals at Roanne, Culembourg, Liège, Versailles, Turin, St Etienne, Tulle, Maubeuge, Charleville and Mutzig, which deficiency the London and Birmingham manufacturers made good.

The Lewisham irritant worked rather inefficiently, and although no gibes by the trade could close it, the establishment was re-organised at Enfield Lock in 1816. In the years that followed a variety of machines were successively installed, and after 1854 (backed by the report of the Parliamentary Committee above referred to) nearly £70,000 was spent on American gunmaking machinery, which began to produce fully interchangeable Enfield rifles in 1858.

The Birmingham gun trade watched the success of this experiment for a year or two, and then (in 1861) fourteen of the leading manufacturers banded together into the Birmingham Small Arms Company Ltd., with a six acre, fully-mechanised site at Small Heath. Their enterprise was rewarded, two years later, with an order for 20,000 Turkish infantry rifles.

The London Armoury Company Ltd. also re-organised their factory with American equipment, and the two big companies manufactured huge quantities of small arms during the American Civil War. Their example was later followed by the National Arms & Ammunition Co. Ltd. at Birmingham (in 1872), and the military trade can then be regarded as passing from the hands of the small manufacturer. The London Small Arms Co. Ltd. took over the assets of the old London Armoury Co. Ltd., and with the introduction of the Martini-Henry rifle, the three companies split the manufacture of 193,806 weapons between them; Enfield producing 583,798 rifles up to March 1885. The N.A.A. Co. foundered in 1882 (its Sparkbrook arms factory going to the Government), and B.S.A. eventually became the sole survivor (after the First World War) in the private manufacture of service small arms.

In general, the Birmingham gun trade pattern altered little in the sectors devoted to shotguns and firearms for shipping companies, traders and so forth. The big merchant houses which had combined to form the companies mentioned above made little attempt to apply the same processes as those which had galvanised the military trade. The names of Cooper & Goodman, Hollis & Son, Tipping & Lawden and Pryse & Redman continued to stand under the old system, acting as factors, financiers and warehousemen to a host of out-workers and smaller gunmakers, but slowly faded from the scene as markets shrank under the impact of cheap Belgian guns and high American tariffs.

A few makers tried to put their house in order, and the names of The Braendlin Armoury Co. Ltd., The Henry Rifle Barrel & Ordnance Co. Ltd., The Gatling Gun Ltd., Grenfell & Accles Ltd., Abingdon Works Co. Ltd., and Bailey, Noakes & Co. Ltd., rose and fell briefly in attempts to become efficient suppliers to the trade.

The reason for failure in such attempts was not far to seek, and can but be summed up for the listed firms (as for the defunct private makers of military arms) in the words of 'Artifex' and 'Opifex', whose book upon the decay of the Birmingham sporting gun trade remains a classic. 'Short time,' they wrote, 'spells disaster in a machine factory, and even a firm like . . . Smith & Wesson . . . finds it cheaper to close the works for months than to run it two or three days in the week.'[11]

Thus it was also proved in England. The man, the

10 *Report from the Select Committee on Small Arms*, House of Commons, 1854.

11 *The Causes of Decay in a British Industry*, London, 1907.

means and the skills existed; the demand did not.

As to the proving of firearms (by firing them under controlled conditions, and with a charge exceeding that which the barrel is normally called upon to bear), something has been earlier said of the creation of the London Gunmakers Company and it is proposed to deal first with British practice in this matter. The Armourers Company of London had begun proving firearms at least as early as the end of the 16th century. Their official role as controllers of the proof was, however, taken over by the Gunmakers in the seventeenth century.

In 1638 (the year following its Charter of Incorporation), the Gunmakers, Company began to stamp upon the barrels of firearms certain official marks, thus approving the materials and workmanship put into the piece. As a natural extension of that idea, powers were secured under the charter requiring all makers and finishers in London (or within ten miles of it) to stamp their products with an identifying mark known to the Company, and to submit their arms for proof at its official Proof House.

By 1657, the grip of the London Company upon the trade was tightening, and their Proof Master received instructions only to prove guns submitted by members of the Company, which were appropriately marked as to their source. Since the Company had considerable powers of search and seizure, after ordinances effective from 1670, it will be appreciated that makers who displeased the Company, or were unable to pay its dues, could not practise their trade in safety. If they had no mark granted, their barrels would not be accepted for proof, and if unproved were hardly marketable.

English methods of proof have been considerably elaborated over the years since 1670, although the basic ideas obtaining today date only from an Act of 1855. Essentially, however, each barrel was first 'provisionally' proved (by firing a heavy charge whilst it was in a comparatively rough state of manufacture), and then 'definitively' proved when ready for setting up; the provisional test saved the gunmaker from spending time and money on a worthless tube, whilst the second proof saved the ultimate user from harm.

Elaborate tables of powder charges and bullet weights scheduled to the various Proof Acts[12] have been laid down from time to time to ensure the adequacy of the test in each calibre; however, Goodman's examples (in the British Association report of 1866) serve as well now to illustrate the principle evolved in 1670, as they did when published. Goodman chose the then most common 0·577 in rifle and 12 bore shotgun as his examples, and noted:

	Rifle (0·577 in, or about 25 bore)	Double Gun (12 bore)
Ordinary charge of powder for service and sporting	68 grains	82 grains
Provisional proof charge	205 grains	350 grains
Definitive proof charge	137 grains	219 grains
Weight of bullet (conical), provisional proof	715 grains	—
Weight of bullet (conical), definitive proof and service	536 grains	—
Weight of bullet (spherical), provisional and definitive proof	—	535 grains

Despite constant interference with arms coming into London from Birmingham, and other arms-making centres, the London Company was unable to maintain the monopoly that it sought, and eventually the members tried to pass a Bill through Parliament, requiring every manufacturer to mark his guns with a true name and address; such a requirement would, of course, have enabled them to deal more stringently with arms coming into their sphere of control under their various charters. The Birmingham gun trade managed to oppose this Bill, which was dropped early in 1813, and at last took concerted action by requesting a public proof-house in Birmingham (to take over facilities already available at premises erected by makers named Galton and Ketland), with a view to eventual erection of their own proof house.

An Act of Parliament was passed on 10 July 1813, entitled 'An Act to ensure the proper and careful manufacturing of Fire Arms in England, and for making Provision for proving Barrels of such Fire Arms', and in October the foundation stone of the Birmingham Proof House was laid in Banbury Street.

After August 1813, no barrel could be used in the making of any small arm, 'unless it should have been duly proved at the Proof House of the Gunmakers' Company of London, or at the Proof House to be established under this Act, or some Proof House belonging to His Majesty, or other Proof House established as a Proof House by Law'.

Subsequent Acts of 1815 and 1855 instituted uniformity of working by the London and Birmingham authorities in all matters of proof, penalties and so forth. In 1868, the last major administrative Act was passed, which had little effect upon the London Proof House, but radically altered the constitution of that in Birmingham. Thereafter, a permanent

12 See, for example, the *Rules of Proof, 1904*, or the *Rules, Regulations, and Scales Applicable to the Proof of Small Arms, 1925*.

Proof Master was appointed to administer the Act under the authority of a fifteen-man 'Board of Guardians' elected by registered members of the Birmingham Gun Trade.

This Gun Barrel Proof Act of 1868 (with those of 1950 and 1978) now rules the proof of firearms in England, through the medium of 'Rules, Regulations and Scales applicable to the Proof of Small Arms' issued and revised thereunder. The proof marks of the two Houses are well known, the *G.P.* mark being used in London and the *B.P.* in Birmingham, although the marks originally scheduled in the Act have been altered in shape and character by Rules made in 1904, 1925 and 1954. In any event, the number of suitable marks had increased over the years (in recognition of the new smokeless powders and variant firearms) and the old classification of ten classes of small arms has (since 1 February 1955) been now cut down to four.

The simplified marks now relate to a 'service' pressure (which is stamped upon the barrels in witness of their resistance to charges exceeding that pressure by a certain percentage) and no longer requires a stamp setting out the shot charge in shotguns. Further, the almost universal use of smokeless powders has now been recognised by discarding the 'Nitro Proof' stamp in favour of a special marking for arms using ordinary black powder.

The actual methods of proof are little publicised today, but presumably do not differ radically from the systems described by Greener in his various books. Tubes for provisional proof were laid out in batches of a hundred, on suitable horizontal racks, to be fired by a train of powder running along the breeches. No distinction was made for breech-loading barrels, the breeches of which were closed by a temporary plug. The powder train was fired from outside the heavily armoured room, and the unsecured barrels recoiled harmlessly into heaps of sand on discharge. The definitive proof was a more individual affair, since the weapon was virtually completed, and involved the use of slings or rests adapted to the particular weapon. In breech-loading arms it remains today the applicant's task to provide suitable cartridge cases for this definitive proof, and some difficulty can be experienced in re-proving weapons of the less popular calibres.

England has long enjoyed considerable reputation for her excellent proof system, but other countries have not neglected the need for similar establishments, though not all have adopted a compulsory proof.

The Liège Proof House has been justly famous since its establishment in 1672 as one of the earliest of such authorities to make proof compulsory. Their system has always been elaborate, and frequent legislation has made the marks and regulations too difficult for summary. One enactment of 1819 was noticed by Goodman in his report to the British Association, and warrants mention here as a singular example of the nineteenth-century attitude to business. The law required that all arms not marked as proved should be seized, except those intended for the slave trade; the villainous quality of arms for this market was apparently recognised in Clause 9, which forbade their circulation in Belgium and required that they be sent in packages, corded and leaded, to the border town from which they were to be exported. If any feel unduly critical of the Liège manufacturers on this score, they are commended to a study of J. Morfitt's *Sketch of Birmingham*, in which he stated that (in 1802) guns were made at seven shillings and sixpence each, and proved not by powder but by water 'which if they are capable of holding, without permitting it to ooze through their pores, they are sufficiently qualified to discharge their duty'.

The Birmingham trade muskets (or 'park palings', as they were sometimes called) were matched by the Liège makers, and were a source of considerable revenue to those specialising in their manufacture. The business continued for many years, and the proof standards improved, if the quality did not. A retiring chairman, at the 1906 annual meeting of the Birmingham Gun Trade, reported that in the preceding seven years, 775,316 African musket barrels were proved at their Proof House and 45,895 rejected.

Other proof houses existed in America, Austria, France, Germany and Spain, some of which are still active.

In America, the National Arsenal at Springfield had an excellent proof house, but dealt only with service arms. Many of the leading manufacturers have always proved their own products (the Colt Company and the Winchester Repeating Arms Company were notably thorough), but no American proof marks are recognised in England and proof of imported arms, at London or Birmingham, is mandatory.

The Austro-Hungarian Empire had proof houses at Ferlach, Prague, Vienna and Weipert, but although such marks were once acceptable (and scheduled in the Act of 1868, with other countries), they are no longer recognised here.

A French proof house existed at St Etienne from the first quarter of the sixteenth century, and is now the responsibility of the Chamber of Commerce in that town. Another proof house was later established at Paris, and the *E.P.* monogram of that town can be readily distinguished from the *St Etienne* stamps of the other proof house. In their 1952 notes of guidance, the British Proof Masters gave warning that French smooth-bore arms must bear certain markings before they would be regarded as sufficiently proved.

The Brescian and other proof marks of Italy have long been recognised as denoting a sound system of proof. An Agreement relating to the reciprocal recognition of proof marks has run since 24 June 1926, between the British and Italian Governments, but was suspended from May 1940. On the assurance of the Italian Government that their proof standards had been maintained, the agreement was revived as from 2 February 1950.

Germany and Spain have now satisfactory systems of proof, dating effectively from the German Proof Act of 1891 in the former case, and from July 1931 in the latter.

The importance of the foreign proof marks to the ordinary collector cannot be too strongly emphasised. One of the blows which destroyed the small arms industry in Great Britain came from the merchants who imported components (or complete arms) from abroad in savage competition with the native makers. These arms frequently bear proof from the foreign houses, in addition to the retailer's name and the proof of Birmingham or London.

S. B. Allport (reporting as Chairman of the Birmingham Gun Trade, in 1892) gave figures for complete imported arms proved at Birmingham, which may be of interest to collectors of late nineteenth century weapons.

Description	*1889 Number*	*1890 Number*
Martini rifles	608	291
Martini carbines	100	101
Foreign rifles	328	257
Colt's magazine	26	—
Colt's 'Lightning'	300	302
Colt's carbines	195	50
Colt's rifles	188	247
Saloon rifles	421	945
Combination guns	55	35
Sporting shotguns	—	70
Walking-stick guns	573	628
Colt's revolvers	2120	2718
Colt's derringers	352	2262
Foreign revolvers	779	471
Foreign pistols	913	98

An important exception to the British proof requirements, by both the Company of Gun Makers of the City of London and the Guardians of the Birmingham Proof House, has always lain in Military and Service arms. The *Notes on the Proof of Gun Barrels*, published by the two bodies in January 1952, pointed out that such weapons marked with the letter *S* on the barrel near the Ordnance mark were accepted as proved, but that if they bore the letter *O*, or no letter, such barrels had to be submitted for proof. The exception was of long standing.

From 1645, the Office of Ordnance received authority to receive and prove arms ordered for the services from contractors in the trade, an authority extending to edged weapons and armour. By 1682, a suitable proof house had been erected at the Tower, and the royal *C.R.* cipher and crown were adopted for service proof marks. Until about 1702 this mark appeared upon the barrels and locks of firearms, with a rose and crown (viewers) mark also upon the barrel, but thereafter the Ordnance proof mark changed to one showing the crown and crossed sceptres.

It is as well to make clear that neither the royal ciphers (e.g. *G.R.* or *V.R.*) nor the familiar Ordnance broad-arrow stamp were proof marks. They demonstrated that the weapons had been 'viewed' (i.e. examined for obvious defects) and that they were government property. The 'view mark' (*V*) has only disappeared from British commercial proof since February 1955, when it became an integral part of the proof procedure.

The commercial proof houses also had to accept 'Tower proof' on privately-made firearms, if the barrel maker were so inclined. A small fee was charged, and the crown and crossed sceptres were struck twice on the tube, without the royal cipher.

The American War of Independence boosted demand for service arms to a point where Ordnance proof facilities at Birmingham became necessary, and in 1798 their own proof house was opened, off Walmer Lane, 'the explosions of which were very terrific to strangers', as Morfitt remarked in 1802. The whole establishment included view rooms on Bagot Street, where the arms were carefully inspected at various stages of their manufacture. Goodman reported a staff of sixty or seventy in the mid-1860s, a complete gun bearing twenty-two stamps of examination, but the use of the proof room seems to have been dropped during a long closure of the premises between 1818 and 1841.

If Goodman's figures were accurate, the government proof house at Birmingham was operating once more by 1855, and he recorded that 978,249 barrels were proved in it, between 1855 and 1864, for an annual average of 97,824 barrels. This output was split between the setters-up in London and Birmingham, the former producing 382,647 guns to the latter's 595,602.

Of considerable interest also, was the breakdown of these proof figures by description of barrel, it appearing that the designations accepted at the commercial proof house in Birmingham were to 'twisted; plain iron; military twisted; military plain'; and 'pistol'. The 'military twisted' barrels (manufactured in ribands, as earlier described) were an anachronism resurrected by the heavy demands of the American Civil War, which were more than the makers of rolled barrels could supply. Ironically enough, these twisted barrels stood proof rather better than those of plain iron; 1·20 in every hundred failing on proof, against 1·35 for the latter. Costs of production, and difficulties in securing unblemished tubes for rifling, laid this ghost as soon as rolled iron barrels were freely available, and only nine twisted barrels went to proof in 1863.

It says much for the standards required for military barrels, that twisted tubes for sporting guns (admittedly in every quality) failed in a proportion of 5·67 per cent, whilst plain iron barrels for the commercial trade were rejected as 4·57 in every hundred Pistol barrels made a rather better showing (at 2·73 per cent), and the average failure in the five descriptions was 4·15 per cent.

Proof figures give also a sad picture of the slow decline in the Birmingham gun trade after the close of the American Civil War. In his address of 1906 to the Birmingham Gun Trade, the Chairman reported proof exceeding 30,000 completed arms per annum during the preceding ten years. Gun proofs had increased from about 2,400 in 1896 to 5,508 in 1905, whilst revolvers increased from 13,250 in 1896 to 31,664 in 1903. When it is appreciated that these figures probably included proof of foreign arms to a scale similar to that earlier mentioned, the shadow of depression falls clearly. This was a period that embraced the South American, South African and Russo–Japanese Wars and yet yielded no serious lift in proof figures.

One interesting piece of information was given at the same meeting of the Birmingham Gun Trade in relation to the proof of revolvers during the period 1899–1905. 'Artifex' and 'Opifex' later used the figures as an argument against the need for (and expense of) proof, but they serve here as a salute to the firms engaged in this manufacture.

It appeared that there had been 260,791 proofs of English revolvers at Birmingham, and only one pistol rejected as the result of a cracked chamber. The costs of finding this defective weapon (as 'Artifex' and 'Opifex' hastened to point out) was £2,373–16*s* 11½*d* in proof fees. During the same period 114,743 proofs of foreign-made revolvers occurred, of which 35 were rejected.

As the authors saw it, the respective percentages of rejected revolvers was thus 0·000003 English and 0·000302 foreign, requiring one million proofs to trace three English and 302 foreign weapons defective under trial!

Whatever the merit in the arguments of centuries against the 'vexatious proof', there seems no doubt as to the excellence of the arms which must have formed the bulk of English-made revolvers in these figures. The Webley revolver yields nothing to the products of any maker on this showing.

A leading work upon the gunsmith's craft was published by the Americans, J. P. Stelle and Wm B. Harrison,[13] which contained some small reference to American proof practice in the early 1880s.

The service rifle at that time was still the Springfield Rifle, calibre 0·45 in, a robust (if unimaginative) weapon, with an external hammer and a 'trapdoor' breech-block. The service cartridge propelled a 405 grain bullet by 70 grains of musket powder, but the proof load involved the discharge of a 500 grain slug and 280 grains of powder, followed by another proof with the same bullet and 250 grains of powder.

This proof was applied to barrels made by the US Government, or those made for them, and the proof marks applied were a *V* (view) and *P* (proof) stamp with the initials of the inspector who had conducted the proving. This was regarded as a fairly searching test, and it is worth noticing that the equivalent British commercial proof would have required a 714 grain bullet with 205 grains of powder on provisional proof and 137 grains on the second discharge.

Noticed by Stelle & Harrison as particularly severe, was the proof applied to the Peabody-Martini falling-block rifles supplied to the Turkish Government during the 1870s. The weapons were made by the Providence Tool Co. Armory (at Providence, Rhode Island) in 0·45 in calibre and for a service charge of 85 grains of powder and 480 grains of lead; the punishing proof charge was 205 grains of powder and a 715 grain slug.

An important extension of Proof House duties has been provided, since 1912, by the Proof House Laboratory at Birmingham, acting for members of the Gun Trade lacking research facilities of their own. Similar services are available in America, from commercial laboratories or from the ammunition manufacturers, but it would be difficult for the average British maker to secure assistance of this calibre, so reasonably priced, anywhere else.

A list of sixteen services was listed on a descriptive card, dated March 1927, in the writer's possession.

The first five items related to Radial Pressure and Velocity Tests for ammunition, at temperatures from 60°F to 180°F and at various degrees of humidity, for which confidential reports would be given upon 17 different calibres of rifle ammunition, 10 calibres of revolver or automatic pistol cartridges, shotgun ammunition from 10 bore down to 0·410 in, and 'Ball and Shot' cartridges.

In addition, the reports were available upon

Velocity of recoil of 12-bore ammunition

13 *The Gunsmith's Manual*, New York, 1883.

Recoil of 12-bore ammunition
Recoil and velocity of sporting guns and rifles
Cartridge loading
Turnover and cannelure resistance
Ammunition: humidity tests
Gunpowder: density and moisture tests
Shot: hardness and sphericity tests
Barrels: internal and external dimensions, chambers, rimming, etc.
Metal: tensile, tortion, compression and brinell tests.
Guns and rifles: burst, damages, accidents, etc. etc.

It has been this kind of approach to the duties laid down by successive Proof Acts that has enabled a dying British industry to support two Proof Houses through one hundred and fifty years. Were the tests (and marks of success) no more than a symbol of quality in material and workmanship, the falling demand for British firearms might well have extinguished the system established since 1813. The pressure of need that could deliver a hand-made shotgun, through a successively rising wall of tariffs, to compete on their home-ground with machine-made American weapons must have argued the system out of existence. To a man facing the Dingley Tariff of 1897 (25s per gun + 35% *ad val.*), the cost of proof could only appear as the 'trade tax borne wholly by the manufacturer' to which Clive Harris referred[14].

Fortunately, the services of successive Masters and Chairman at the two Proof Houses have been of a quality sufficient to avert success for any such argument, and the British Government has also laid out military contracts to provide the funds shrinking as the demands for private proof fell away.

The Gun Barrel Proof Acts made the establishment and maintenance of public proof houses mandatory, and it is to be hoped that they will never be finally repealed.

---

14 *The History of the Birmingham Gun-Barrel Proof House*, Birmingham, *n.d.*

CHAPTER SEVENTEEN

The Decoration of Firearms

Irena Grabowska

278-80 The decorative treatment of firearms is of consider-
336-51 able importance to the present-day student in helping to establish the date of manufacture and also in connecting them with definite manufacturing centres. An analysis of ornamental motifs often enables us to establish without doubt both the terminus *ab quo* or the terminus *ad quem*, especially with regard to the gunmaking centres which spread fashion in ornament. On firearms destined for the general market decoration of a simple and unsophisticated kind was usually applied in the gunsmith's shop. There survive, however, large numbers of firearms made with such skill that their artistry must be ascribed to craftsmen who were professional decorators.

Signatures of gun decorators have survived on only a very small number of pieces. Most worked anonymously for gunsmiths whose ability to carry out more ambitious decoration must have been limited. Such signatures were sometimes engraved on the lockplate in addition to that of the gunmaker and sometimes placed inconspicuously on the stock.

The decoration of firearms was closely bound up with the development of stylistic forms generally prevalent in the decorative art of the period. All changes in the latter were eagerly noted by the craftsmen who were employed in this field.

Early firearms provided with the unreliable and awkward match mechanism were chiefly manufactured for military purposes and were therefore rarely given elaborate decorative treatment. No important changes took place until the third decade of the sixteenth century with the more general introduction of the wheel-lock. The gun and the pistol then took their place as personal weapons of the nobleman alongside the long-established sword and dagger. The interest taken in firearms by the upper classes caused a major revolution in the history of gunmaking: on the one hand technical development was stimulated and on the other efforts were made to give to the firearm aesthetic values, expressed in the shape of the stock and in decoration suited to the power and social prominence of the owners, to their artistic taste and love of luxury. In addition to their functional use, firearms began to take on a 'status' role which often overshadowed their purpose.

In this chapter we shall adhere to a chronological arrangement with a subdivision into countries wherever national features can be easily identified. For evident reasons this chapter is limited to the most characteristic facts and to the most important representatives in the field of firearms decoration.

The Sixteenth Century

The main features in the history of sixteenth-century 90-95
gunmaking were experiments in the construction of 278-9
the mechanism, the shape of the stock and decoration. All the available techniques were used to increase the attractiveness of firearms. The technique of gilding was often applied to metal parts, as it contributed a great deal to their sumptuous appearance and was relatively easy: the metal surface, which was to be gilt, was covered with an amalgam of gold and mercury and then the latter was driven off by heating. Fire blueing was commonly employed to protect the iron against corrosion by rust and also to provide an effective background for ornament inlaid in gold and silver. The blue colour was achieved by gradual heating and cooling of the metal. Engraved or etched decoration is found on a great number of firearms. In the first technique a decorative design was executed with a steel burin and consisted of incised lines; in the second, patterns were etched with acid while the ground was protected by a coat of wax or paint. Particularly valuable pieces were decorated with chiselled work that often achieved an almost sculptural effect. Stocks were carved or inlaid with ivory, staghorn, mother-of-pearl, various kinds of rare wood or metal plaques engraved with decorative motifs or even decorated with polychrome enamel and precious stones. The ornament usually consisted of floral scrolls, accompanied by grotesques or arabesques executed with considerable fantasy. Historical events, classical mythology, court and military life, heraldic and knightly symbols supplied subject matter to suit the individual purchaser. Many–or perhaps even most–of these motifs were taken from contemporary engravings, especially the pattern-books of ornamental designs, published from the early sixteenth century onwards for the use

of goldsmiths, jewellers and carvers. These pattern-books supplied the currently fashionable motifs which had then to be adapted to the specific shapes of the barrels, the lockplates or the stocks. Designs of this type were engraved by prominent graphic artists, such as Etienne Delaune, Virgil Solis, Jost Amman, Adriaen Collaert and the two de Brys. There were also many anonymous artists (*Kleinmeister*), notably from Nuremberg and Augsburg, who are known only by their initials.

Germany and the Germanic Cultural Area

10-11 Germany was the leading producer of *de luxe* firearms
14, 16 in the sixteenth century, especially its southern
18 21-37 provinces where artistic life flourished. German
89-91 mastery in decoration long governed the appearance
93-95 of firearms and exerted extensive influence on design
336-40 in the neighbouring European countries.

Barrels which at first had been unpretentiously incised with simple ornament, capable of execution in a gunsmith's workshop, now, on the more elaborate firearms, took on the form of fluted columns with the muzzle shaped like a capital or were chiselled or etched with foliate scrolls and strapwork, cherubs' heads, busts of Roman emperors, and the like, derived from contemporary engravings. A novel type of decoration was provided by gold and silver damascening, a technique which came from the East probably through Spain and Italy. Two varieties are found: *true damascening* in which the steel or iron was actually inlaid with precious metal, and *counterfeit damascening*, in which gold or silver foil was applied to a surface that had previously been roughened by cross-hatching. Locks were ornamented in a similar manner to the barrels, and their large flat surfaces provided ample space for elaborate decorative compositions. At first the cock was engraved with simple motifs while its neck imitated architectural forms. Later in the sixteenth century a new form of cock was evolved, shaped in the semblance of a dragon's or a dolphin's head, engraved or chiselled, often with great inventiveness and expression.

As noted in Chapter 2 Germany evolved a characteristic type of stock with a butt designed to be held against the cheek at the moment of firing. On the opposite side of the lock the butt had a broad, approximately rectangular, surface providing additional space for ornament. These stocks were usually of wood, inlaid with staghorn. *De luxe* firearms were inlaid with ivory or mother-of-pearl, and the mass of small and complex motifs testifies to the *horror vacui*, typical of sixteenth century applied art. In many instances the ornament is executed with such precision and care that it is obvious the gunsmith employed professional craftsmen who applied similar ornament to household furniture. The detail of the ornament was emphasised by engraving, and to obtain an effect of relief the lines were filled with black composition. This type of decoration, which was used during the sixteenth century also in France, England, the Netherlands, and, occasionally, in Italy, nowhere achieved such variety as it did in Germany. It was realised that the type of wood used for the stock contributed to the final effect but, fundamentally, throughout the sixteenth century it was of secondary importance, serving chiefly as a background for horn, bone or metal inlay. The inlay looked most effective when set against the almost black colour of ebony, used for the most costly pieces. Apart from ebony, walnut, apple and pear wood were used.

Until *c.*1550 inlaid stock-decoration was generally simple, usually being confined to straight lines that emphasised the outline of the stock, and to a few panels with engraved arabesque or grotesque patterns. By the middle of the century the aesthetic standards of the time demanded a more elaborate treatment; subjects were now drawn commonly from classical mythology or contemporary life, various aspects of which were shown in minute scenes. Although the decoration was often executed in a rather perfunctory manner, sometimes even recalling folk art, there survive some pieces decorated with such refinement, so elaborate in shape that they must be included among the masterpieces of decorative art.

Sometimes the wooden stocks were wholly covered
with an overlay of stag horn and bone, engraved with
figured composition of varied, though by no means
always logically coherent, motifs. An example is the
pistol, dated 1557, in the Historisches Museum
Dresden, signed by the stocker with the initials *ES*. 336
The highly artistic achievement of this piece is shown both in the carving and the decoration of the barrel and lockplate, damascened with delicate foliate arabesques in gold and silver. Although the armorial bearings, placed on the pommel, connect this superlative work of art with Denmark, its decoration is so typically German that it must be regarded as an import from Germany. It is probable that the carving was entrusted to the specialist craftsmen who worked in ivory and bone, making the cups, boxes and figure sculpture so fashionable in the sixteenth century. The manufacture of these objects was mainly concentrated in southern Germany, more particularly in Augsburg and Nuremberg.

Efforts at creating a more solidly constructed fire-
arm that would better balance the weight of the
barrel and the mechanism, led to the introduction of
stocks made wholly of metal. Metal overlays adorned
with etched, engraved or chased patterns were also
used with the same purpose. The finest example of
this style is to be found in three silver-stocked
pistols in the Kunsthistorisches Museum in Vienna: 25-6
uniform in both the technique and subject of their decoration, they may be regarded as products of the

same workshop, active in Leipzig in the middle of the sixteenth century. The unusual splendour of these pieces is explained by the coat-of-arms and initials of Henry V, Burggraf of Meissen on one, and the fact that the pistols became the property of Archduke Ferdinand of Tyrol, one of the most influential magnates of the Holy Roman Empire and founder of the famous collection of arms in the Castle of Ambras near Innsbruck.[1] They illustrate the high standard of the gunmaker's art achieved in Saxony in the course of the sixteenth century. A feature peculiar to many Saxon pieces – though not found on these examples – is ornament of cast gilt-bronze in the shape of cherubs' heads and pierced cartouches. These were used for decorating barrels and lockplates and, occasionally, the stocks as well.

Another attractive creation of the Southern German region was the designing of pistol pommels in the shape of a bird's or animal's head, in which realistic elements were combined with stylised floral patterns.[2]

The overall picture of German gunsmiths' production in the sixteenth century would be incomplete if no mention were made of one of the most outstanding pieces of that era, a matchlock gun, dated 1570, now in the Kunsthistorisches Museum in Vienna which belonged (as is shown by the coat of arms placed on the buttplate) to Archduke Karl of
90 Steiermark. The lockplate and barrel are damascened with floral scrollwork, executed with exceptional care and with a keen sense of artistic form. The barrel is further decorated with medallions and elaborate, though somewhat heavy, strapwork enclosing chiselled classical figures. The match-holder, wrought in an S-shape to resemble the body of a dragon, is covered with minute scales chiselled in the iron. The ornament of the metal parts, the execution and distribution of which reveal the hand of an eminent, possibly Italian chiseller and damascener, is combined with most effective engraved horn inlay on the stock. The initials *HP* on the stock are those of Hans Paumgartner of Graz, who made the stock and possibly engraved the inlays, though the latter are executed with such mastery that one is tempted to ascribe them to a professional graphic artist. Here, too, the subjects are drawn from classical mythology and ancient history: among the most effective scenes is a brilliant composition, showing Marcus Curtius on horseback, charging into the flames belching forth from a cleft in the rocks. The source was undoubtedly a contemporary German engraving, possibly by Jost Amman of Nuremberg, as a collection of his designs, entitled *Neue Biblische Figuren*, published in 1564, contains a similar scene. While it is very difficult to identify the artists who engraved the inlays on stocks, it is easier to establish that their sources were commonly the prints of German and Dutch engravers. Either in single sheets or collected in albums these were circulated in the major cities of Europe and were employed by the workshops producing silverware, textiles and furniture. From them the decorators of firearms evolved ideas for their compositions, transforming and combining them to adapt them to the shape of the barrel, lock and stock. Of particular interest here is a series of water-colour drawings intended to serve as patterns for the decoration of gun-stocks in the Victoria and Albert Museum, London.[3] Although they are in no way original, they did succeed in creating designs that were admirably suited to the awkward shapes that had to be decorated.

In any reference to German engravings giving decorative patterns for firearms, one cannot omit an etched design of which an example is in the Victoria and Albert Museum in London,[4] showing a superb
pair of wheel-lock pistols. There are slight differences 339
in decoration between the two but no more than occurred frequently in high-class pieces forming a pair. The wealth of ornament shown in this etching can hardly be equalled among surviving firearms. It might perhaps be compared with the pistol of Archduke Ferdinand described above. It is worth noticing that its author must have been well versed in the construction of firearms, for the design could be executed without technical modification.

France

Although during the sixteenth century firearms 12, 92
production in France did not equal that of Germany in quantity, yet the sense of form that was characteristic of French art in general can be recognised in the outline of French stocks, which grew lighter, more elegant and convenient to handle than the German variety. As noted in Chapter 2, at the end of the century the stocks of both guns and pistols took on strongly individual shapes.

In the realm of decoration German influences were at first preponderant but floral, arabesque and grotesque motifs, used in France, took on a more delicate form and they were better adapted to the surfaces over which they spread. In decorating guns and pistols, French gunsmiths, while keeping a

1 The pistols are fully discussed by T. Lenk 'To the History of the Pistols of the 16th Century', *Livrustkammaren*, IV, 1946-8, p. 349. The stocks are stamped with the Leipzig mark and an unidentified goldsmith's mark.

2 This pommel is to be found on a pistol dating from *c.* 1590, now in the Historisches Museum, Dresden, No. Ehrenthal F.188.

3 Nos. E. 1990-1993.

4 No. E. 1545.

variety of iconographical motifs, made less use of confused, multi-figural hunting or mythological scenes and strove for greater simplicity and lucidity of design which was increased by a complete mastery of the decorative technique. Their sense of colour effects was manifested by the custom of staining horn or bone green to contrast with sections left *en nature*. Colour effects were heightened by the application of delicate arabesques inlaid in brass, by plaques cut in mother-of-pearl or silver and even by miniature portraits and panels of *verre églomisé*, such as is seen in the magnificent wheel-lock pistol, dated
92 1581, at the Tower of London Armouries.[5]

A particularly high standard was achieved in the technique of damascening blued or polished steel with precious metals. Here French craftsmen equalled their Italian contemporaries. In their hands the graceful arabesques with pliable and light contours and trophies of war, remind one, in the arrangement and precision of motifs, of contemporary French book-bindings. Damascening was applied to barrels, locks and mounts and, when the stock was of metal, the artist entrusted with the decoration would cover it with a minute tracery of ornament, bringing out a striking colour contrast between the gold and silver designs against a blued steel ground. Another type of decoration was chiselled ornament, which was sometimes in very high relief.

Pattern-books compiled by graphic artists and destined for use by craftsmen employed in the manufacture of luxury articles in metal are just as important in relation to French as to German firearms in establishing the origins of decorative style. Sculptors, engravers, chisellers, damasceners and stock makers used pattern-books as a basis for their designs. Amongst the sources were Michel le Blon, a German-born artist working in Amsterdam, whose work was very popular in France and Jacques Androuet Ducerceau (d. 1580). The latter was the author of the designs which were published in the third quarter of the century for use of locksmiths under the title *Modèles de Serrurèrie*; another source was the engraved set of designs with ornaments for wheel-locks ascribed to a follower of Ducerceau.[6] Although the last-named master did not understand the actual functioning of the lock, his designs may well in their time have been used since they could be applied to the lockplate without modification.

5 No. XII-1764.

Italy

It is a suprising fact that Italy, which led the whole 15, 343
world in all the arts during the Renaissance, seems, as regards the art of gunmaking, to have been overshadowed by Germany and France throughout most of the sixteenth century. Too few pieces have survived for us to form a clear idea of Italian gun production as a whole, but there was increased activity towards the end of the century when production, especially of military firearms, was greatly expanded in the area of Brescia.

The Capodimonte Museum near Naples contains numerous examples of guns and pistols, which served either for the personal use of the members of the Farnese family or formed part of the equipment of their bodyguard. Italian long-arms, like their French counterpart, were constructed for firing from the shoulder. The shape of the butt, therefore, was streamlined, and the end widened and slanting. The most characteristic feature of this group of guns is their decoration, consisting of iron inlay of interlacing strapwork and tracery, ranging from the simple to the most elaborate forms. The finest class of Italian firearms is best illustrated by a wheel-lock gun, dated 1596, engraved with the arms and motto of Rainuccio Farnese, Duke of Parma and Piacenza, formerly at Windsor Castle and now in the Museo

6 The designs are illustrated by T. Lenk *The Flintlock, its Origin and Development*, London, 1965, pl. 101, 1-3.

Detail of steel lock chiselled with figures in high relief. Italian (Brescia), *c.*1670. Victoria & Albert Museum, London.

343 Capodimonte, Naples. The lockplate of this gun is deeply engraved with fabulous monsters and cornucopiae amidst profuse foliate and floral scrollwork which spreads all over the plate. The artistic value of this piece is enhanced by the attractive ornamentation of the walnut stock, inlaid with pierced sheet silver tracery, volutes, putti and fantastic human and animal figures. The signature on the plate *Gio.Ba.Vis* is that of a gunsmith who possibly originated from the environs of Brescia.

Other finely decorated Italian firearms of this style include the gun from the Castel San' Angelo in Rome, with a wheel-lock provided with two cocks and another with combination match- and wheel-lock in the Wallace Collection in London.[7] Its restrained decoration, which serves to emphasise the beauty of the line of the stock, consists of charming amorini, so beloved by Italian art, of erotic scenes and beautifully proportioned female figures.

The Netherlands

The main centre of arms decoration was Antwerp. Pieces produced there were struck with the town mark of a severed hand. The chiselling of barrels here reached an exceptionally high standard and there were probably several specialist workshops in the city. The variety of ornamental motifs and the purity of design is enhanced by the technical precision, which is almost on a par with that of the magnificent work of Antwerp goldsmiths. The similarity is the greater, since both chisellers in iron and goldsmiths used identical patterns taken from the engravings of Cornelis Bos and Cornelis Floris, the leading masters of the Netherlandish Mannerist style of the second half of the sixteenth century.

It is possible that certain gun-stocks overlaid with ivory panels carved with mythological or battle scenes in the Flemish Mannerist style come from a workshop active in the middle of the century in the Spanish Netherlands, possibly in Antwerp. An alternative to stocks overlaid with ivory were ebony stocks carved in a similar manner.[8]

In the northern Netherlands, gunmakers were more concerned with the function of firearms produced than with their appearance. Yet, a certain number of *de luxe* arms were made. Dutch musket stocks were characterised by the fish-tail butts the shape of which determined the arrangement of the decorative motifs. The most popular manner of stock decoration made use of mother-of-pearl inlays of small scrolls, dots and plaquettes engraved with animals and mythological subjects.[9] This style of decoration spread to the furthest confines of Europe and this process was fostered by an exchange both of firearms and of craftsmen.

England

Henry VIII's reign witnessed an active development 17
of English gunmaking. The interest which the king 278-9
showed in every kind of weapon must have stimulated the activities of gunmaking shops. The inventory of his possessions made after his death, now in the possession of the Society of Antiquaries of London, lists a considerable number of guns and pistols, and the short descriptions attached suggest that most of them were of great technical and artistic interest; some were doubtless manufactured in England.

German influences penetrated here, too, and are noticeable both in the shape and decoration of the stock of the one sixteenth century English wheel-lock pistol so far identified. The latter is based on the German model, but differs from it in the more restrained use of ornament. A snaphance petronel, dated 1584, in the National Museum in Copenhagen,[10] has its stock decorated with lines emphasising its outline and delicate inlaid foliage in mother-of-pearl and bone. It bears the initials *DI* which are found, accompanied by the initials *RI* (perhaps of a relative),
on a gun dated 1588 at Belchamp Hall, Essex. This 279
proves the existence in England at the end of the sixteenth century of at least one stocker's workshop adapted to the production of *de luxe* firearms.

English luxury firearms of about 1600 were often splendidly damascened in gold and silver. The
barrels, polygonal at the breech, then round, with a 278
slightly belled out muzzle, were, on the richest examples, covered along their entire length with symmetrical ornament damascened in gold and arranged about a central axis. Lockplates were decorated in a similar manner. The absence of signatures or marks prevents us from attributing this superb decoration to a specific workshop.

The Seventeenth Century

In the history of gunmaking the seventeenth century 13
brought not only the perfection of the flintlock 38-69
mechanism but also the introduction of new and 96-111
different fashions in ornament. These changes took 137-39 141-44
place under the predominant influence of France 250,25
which was then at the apex of her political power. 280,34
Under French influences new forms of refined ele- 345-6

7 No. A. 1074.

8 The group is represented by two wheel-lock guns (the Kunsthistorisches Museum, Vienna, No. D 71 and the Metropolitan Museum, New York, No. 29.151.1) and by two wheel-lock pistols (Kunsthistorisches Museum, Vienna, No. A.560 and Real Armería, Madrid, No. K.44).

9 For illustration see T. Lenk, *op.cit.*, pl. 105, 1.

10 H. L. Blackmore, *Guns & Rifles of the World*, London, 1965, Fig. 152.

gance became fashionable all over Europe. The Baroque style with its typical love of movement left its imprint on the vocabulary of ornament and reached its highest expression in the decorative art under the reign of Louis XIV. The universal admiration enjoyed by the work of French gunmakers brought about the introduction in the major European centres of a style based on French models that to a large extent drove out indigenous national traits, which survived chiefly in provincial centres.

France

41-2 The rulers of France, and especially Louis XIII,
46, 48 were keenly interested in firearms and they attached
51 to their court the most eminent gunmakers, granting
60-1 them minor court appointments which exempted
63-4
9, 103 them from the tiresome restrictions imposed by the
8, 280 regulations of the Paris guilds; in addition to a fixed salary the court artists were granted accommodation in the Galeries du Louvre.

The standard of gunmaking outside Paris, which set the official stamp on decorative fashions, remained so high that it is difficult to regard such centres as Lisieux, Abbeville, Sedan, Grenoble and Nancy as merely centres of provincial production. In many of them technical improvements in construction of firearms were accompanied by originality of decoration. An example is provided by the interesting French or Swiss pistol with a waterproof mechanism in the Wallace Collection in London,[11] which is signed
41 on the lockplate *Faict à Morgues par La Fonteyne Inventeur 1645*.[12]

The engraving of the brass barrel and lockplate of this pistol was possibly derived from pattern-books published for craftsmen decorating clock cases. The unusually designed pommel is wrought in silver-gilt in the form of a helmet with visor, which conceals a delicately made compass-dial. In providing his pistol with a metal pommel, La Fonteyne followed the popular, though short-lived, Western European fashion of combining wooden stocks with pommels sculptured in metal with an eagle's or a lion's head. Another variant was a pommel carved in ivory or wood as a helmeted warrior's head, a type that is particularly associated with Maastricht in Holland in the second half of the seventeenth century.

The majority of early specimens of flintlock arms were fairly plain and simple. There were, however, certain exceptions to this rule and already in the fourth decade of the century the tendency was again towards a wealth of formal ornament which at times verged on the extravagant. In a considerable number of firearms surviving from the middle of the seventeenth century the barrels, locks and mounts are chiselled in relief, and some parts are even decorated in full relief. The chiselling was fairly rough but effective and the decorativeness of the pieces was enhanced by the ground, which was usually blued and enriched with silver incrustations. Such pieces belong to a uniform group. Any variations that might occur are due not to a change of technique, but to the introduction of new motifs dictated by the current fashion. Two signatures on pieces decorated in this manner refer to Liège and Sedan which suggests that the whole group was produced in Northern France or in bordering territories.[13]

From the early years of the seventeenth century designs for firearms ornament were provided in pattern-books issued exclusively for this purpose. Many of these pattern-books show a familiarity with firearms construction, suggesting that the authors must at some time have been professionally engaged in their decoration. A collection of designs for wheel- and flintlocks, published between 1634 and 1644 by Philippe Cordier Daubigny was of great practical value, since it provided ornament that was not only in the most fashionable style of the time, but was also designed to fit each particular part of the lock. A feature of this pattern-book is that the designs combine the technique of sculpture in the round with that of chiselling in relief as well as encrusting and etching. This last was a much easier technique and, with experience, it allowed for subtle effects of chiaroscuro, similar to those achieved in graphic art. Demand was such that this pattern-book was re-issued in the 1660s. Daubigny's hunting and mythological scenes are vivid and natural in movement, their composition suited to the available surface although sometimes the space is overcrowded.

Daubigny's compositions were preceded in date by those of Jean Henequin of Metz who was not only a gunmaker but also produced ornamental designs. A set of designs signed by him, dated about 1620, now in the Cabinet des Estampes of the Bibliothèque Nationale in Paris, shows a compromise between two opposite concepts of French decorative art: the spatial style, possibly inspired by Italian influence, and the French northern-inspired predilection for composition in the flat. In Henequin's designs both these tendencies were combined with a great deal of skill and in practice were fulfilled in a gun, dated

11 No. A 1182.

12 See p. 66.

13 There is in the Victoria and Albert Museum, London, a pistol signed with the inscription *Fabri à Liège* (No. M.9-1949) and another in the castle at Schwarzburg signed with the initials *IR* and *Sedan*. The chiselled decoration of the barrels of two fowling pieces at the Tøjhusmuseum, Copenhagen (Nos. B.6601), includes the figure of an Emperor in coronation robes and displays a peculiar combination of Classical and contemporary motifs which was not unusual at that period.

1621, now in the Bayrisches National Museum in Munich.[14] Since Henequin combined the profession of gunmaker with that of a graphic artist (a fact borne out by the designs in the Cabinet des Estampes) it may be assumed that it was he who actually designed and executed the decoration of this gun.

Amongst the most prominent French gunmakers were the three brothers Le Bourgeoys of Lisieux in Normandy. They were represented by Marin (d. 1633), Pierre (d. 1627) and Jean (d. 1625). The most talented of them was Marin, who like many craftsmen of his time had varied interests and abilities: he was a gunsmith and a maker of scientific and mechanical instruments, an engraver and a painter. He worked chiefly for the Court: in 1598 he was appointed *valet de chambre* and in 1608 was one of the first artists to be granted a *brevet de loge-*
46 *ment* in the Galeries du Louvre. The gun by him referred to on p. 73 above differs from the usual contemporary production in its particularly elaborate form of the butt, on the crest of which is placed a female herm cast in bronze, stylistically akin to the herms universally used in the French Mannerist style of architecture.[15] The gun, made before 1627 by Pierre Le Bourgeoys for Louis XIII, formerly in
48-9 the Renwick Collection and now in the Metropolitan Museum, New York, is decorated in similarly individual manner; its butt terminating in a volute is carved with acanthus foliage and adorned with bone and mother-of-pearl inlays cut in the form of graceful scrolls, garlands and arabesques inhabited by parrots and minute animals.[16]

The decorative style of the Le Bourgeoys brothers was made available to a wide circle of master gunmakers by the ornamental designs of Thomas Picquot published in Paris in 1638 under the title *Livre de diverses Ordonances*, and dedicated to Louis XIII. Picquot was a pupil of Marin Le Bourgeoys and his designs were obviously strongly influenced by the ornamental compositions used in the Le Bourgeoys workshop. It must be said to Picquot's credit that he did not slavishly imitate the style of his master but rather continued in his steps and cleverly introduced new motifs derived from other sources. His symmetrically arranged compositions appear to have been inspired by the *Schweifbüchlein* of Gabriel Krammer, published in Cologne in 1611. The latter was a joiner and his designs, intended to be executed in the technique of intarsia, could be expressed without any alteration by the technique of damascening. Picquot's special predilection for floral subjects, so characteristic of the first half of the seventeenth century, may have been connected with the album by Pierre Vallet, dated 1608, and entitled *Jardin du Roy très Chretien Henry IV*. The engraved designs of Michel Le Blon, which represented delicate stems intertwined symmetrically, bunches of fruit suspended from ribbons, animals and birds, especially parrots, may also have been another source of Picquot's style. It would appear almost certain that Picquot also worked as a professional decorator of firearms. Sharing lodgings in the Galeries du Louvre with François Duclos, he may have collaborated with him in making for Louis XIII in 1636 a gun and a pair of pistols which probably formed a garniture. It is noticeable that the butt of the gun is decorated with a carved herm similar to that on the gun signed by Marin Le Bourgeoys.[17] The suggestion that Picquot decorated firearms made by Duclos is confirmed by the similarity between Picquot's designs and the decoration applied to the locks and stocks of firearms signed by Duclos. It should be pointed out, however, that Picquot's designs show a certain ignorance of firearms construction.

Michel Le Blon's and Gabriel Krammer's style was used in the decoration of stocks by Jean Tornier of Massevaux in Alsace, who has been identified as a gunstocker through the presence of a signature, containing the inscription *Monsteur d'harquebisses* on a coffer dating from 1630, now in the Wallace Collec- 103
tion, London. The stocks ascribed to him are ornamented with great care, inlaid in white and stained stag-horn with a somewhat crowded but effective pattern consisting of floral compositions, tiny animals and spiral scrolls of horn and brass wire.

French taste in ornament underwent a change in the middle of the seventeenth century. The Grand Manner, typical of the reign of Louis XIV, introduced new subjects and new formulae into the iconography of ornament. The political absolutism of the era found its expression in art by representing the apotheosis of the *Roi Soleil* and this affected, in particular, weapons made for the personal use of the ruler or for presentation. A typical treatment was to show the King with winged genii above his head, placed on a pedestal flanked by fettered prisoners and trophies of war. Equally frequent are portraits of

14 For illustration see J. F. Hayward, *The Art of the Gunmaker*, I pl. 46 ab. In this exceptionally fine gun the flat decoration of the stock contrasts with the sculptural treatment of the cock, carved in the round in the shape of a naked male figure and a dragon's head. A compromise between these two opposite tendencies is found in the chiselled decoration applied to the barrel in the form of a realistic lion's mask with a drapery-like composition of stylised acanthus leaves.

15 This gun is now in the State Hermitage, Leningrad (No. F.281); ill. T. Lenk, *op. cit.*, pl. 8, 1-3.

16 For illustration see T. Lenk, *op. cit.*, pl. 9.

17 ill. T. Lenk, *op. cit.*, pl. 19.

Louis XIV, in the likeness of a classical hero or deity, and battle scenes with cavalry and pikemen. A typical example of this trend is a pair of flintlock pistols, presented by the city of Lille to Louis XIV and now in the Wallace Collection London;[18] inscriptions damascened in gold on the barrels commemorate the king's victories in The Spanish Netherlands and the decoration also includes fleurs-de-lis and a representation of Hercules who personified the King's bravery. This kind of iconographical programme derives from the baroque practice of glorifying an eminent individual.

It was now possible to give a free rein to the decoration of the lockplates for the steel-spring was some times moved inside in order to leave more space for ornament. From about the middle of the century the sideplate was evolved. At first it had the purely practical function of strengthening the stock where the lock was screwed on; the next stage introduced an S-shaped strip of pierced or engraved metal and the most convenient form proved to be the bodies of serpents coiling round screws. In course of further evolution these forms were replaced by more elaborate chiselled and pierced foliate and figural patterns. Similarly, the evolution of the ornament of the backsight can be traced from the initially simple to a more sophisticated form, ending by the second half of the century in a magnificently chiselled composition of acanthus foliage, lions' masks or grotesque heads which encircled the barrel. On the more important firearms no place was left undecorated; even the triggers and trigger-guards were pierced or chiselled with tiny floral motifs. Gun and pistol barrels were usually blued to a dark shade which provided a striking contrast to the ornament chiselled or damascened in gold or silver. The typical baroque trend towards sculptural effects can be recognised in the pattern-book of François Marcou, published in 1657. His ornament, consisting of picturesque motifs of dolphins, sirens, sea monsters, floral and arabesque patterns was intended for chiselling in unusually high relief. Superbly executed examples of such decoration in relief have survived. Unfortunately, most of those with engraved ornament have suffered from the passage of time and therefore the pattern-books are doubly important to the study of firearms. Equally important are the ink pulls taken direct from chiselled, engraved or etched lockplates. They can be easily identified, because the designs are reversed. Such pulls were made and retained in the gunsmiths' shops as patterns.

The custom of making gifts of firearms to prominent personalities created a large demand for *de luxe* arms, especially as the custom established by the king was imitated by the aristocracy. The leading gunmakers engaged in the production of luxury arms benefited from this situation. A sumptuous gift of this type, consisting in part of guns and pistols, presented to King Charles IX of Sweden by Louis XIV in 1673, included among other pieces a double-barrelled gun, signed by Le Conte. Its decoration was entrusted to Jean Bérain, an artist whose activity in the field of applied art was exceptionally important. The opulence of the ornament and its splendid composition render this gun a unique work of art even among the best works of French gunmaking. The silver inlay of the stock, signed by its maker, belongs to the late, exuberant and highly decorative Baroque style in which, however, the diversity of ornamental motifs is subordinated to the rules of good taste. The superb decoration of the stock is equalled by the very fine ornament running along the barrels in a frieze-like composition representing galloping horsemen, while the sides of the barrels are covered with a delicate tracery of scrolls with minute figures of fauns and woodland animals. The decoration of this gun was undoubtedly made from an original design by Bérain. His style, disseminated by his pattern-book, published in 1659, was imitated by other decorators of firearms who repeated it with greater or lesser modification.

Reference must be made here to the pattern-book issued in 1660 by Claude Jacquinet. In comparison with that in use in the previous decades of the century his ornament is more original though the Classical style is fundamental to it. It consists of fine engraved work and shows the influence of contemporary jewellers' designs; in practice, it was carried out in firearms produced by Thuraine and Le Hollandois. The Classical tendency was even more marked in firearms made by Piraube and Laurent Languedoc. In their later period of activity, they adapted a new style for the shape and decoration of the barrel which was now rounded along its whole length except for a flat sighting rib on the top. The lockplates were usually chiselled with a composition that displayed more repose and restraint and Classical deities appear as though transferred from the frieze in an 108
ancient temple.[19] Such features characterise Piraube's gun in the Tower of London Armouries,[20] where the silver barrel is decorated with finely chiselled trophies of war and a figure of Mars. The attractiveness of this piece is heightened by a

18 Nos. A. 1209-10.

19 Almost the same scheme of decoration is found, amongst others, in Gruché's gun made for Emperor Charles VI, now in the Kunsthistorisches Museum, Vienna (No. A. 1674), and in Le Foullois Le Jeune's gun, made *c.* 1665 for Louis XIV, in the Pauilhac Collection, Musée de l'Armée, Paris. For illustrations see T. Lenk, *op. cit.*, pl. 77,2 and pl. 61,6, respectively.

20 No. XII-1690.

representation of Apollo's chariot adorning the butt. This decoration is probably based on a design especially produced by a graphic artist who collaborated with Piraube on firearms decoration.[21]

In the seventh decade of the century the type of wood used for making gunstocks began to attract more attention. The natural grain of the wood was emphasised by charring it over a flame, thus increasing the contrast between the light and dark fibre. Such stocks were, as a rule, provided with splendidly chiselled barrels and locks.

Among the numerous Paris gunmakers who eagerly exploited the innovations were Gruché and Chasteau. At first Gruché imitated the Bérain style, and the stocks of his firearms showed almost the same vocabulary of motifs cut out of silver sheet and arranged symmetrically along the axis of the butt. These features are marked on the gun made by him for Emperor Charles VI, at present in the Kunsthistorisches Museum, Vienna.[22] His later decorative style is more related to Jacquinet's pattern-book. In a gun in the Tøjhusmuseum in Copenhagen[23] Chasteau introduced into the flowing scrolls, inlaid in silver wire in the butt, the archaic Oriental motif of the fight between the phoenix and the dragon, which was probably introduced into European decorative art from Persian textiles. This motif became fairly popular and is seen on several firearms made during the second half of the seventeenth century.

At the end of the seventeenth century great
341 influence was exerted by the pattern-book published in 1685 by Claude Simonin. A second edition was issued in 1693 jointly with his son Jacques. The elder Simonin was a professional decorator of firearms and worked for Languedoc and other Paris gunmakers. The tang of the Chasteau gun in Copenhagen mentioned above is copied exactly from one of the Simonin sheets and the pierced side-plate with two Classical figures facing each other within rather dryly-rendered foliage–a motif then very fashionable in applied art–is identical with another drawing by the same designer. Simonin's pattern-book created new decorative formulae by introducing grotesque heads with hair, whiskers and moustache fashioned out of acanthus leaves as well as graceful putti, sitting on branches and holding dainty scrolls in their hands. The decorative elements popularised by Simonin broke away from the Grand Manner: they were light, elegant and full of sensuality. The principle of severe symmetry hitherto rigidly adhered to was abandoned in favour of freer and more natural arrangements which anticipated the spirit of the rococo style.

Separate mention must be made of the pistols produced in France, and elsewhere in Northern Europe in the seventeenth century, for the mounted game derived from the tournament known as the carrousel. The stocks of these pistols as well as the accessories were particularly showy. They were often painted or had coloured enamel mounts, sometimes they were even decorated with semi-precious stones or cut rock crystal. Examples are preserved in the Danish Historical Collections at the Rosenborg Castle and in the Tøjhusmuseum in Copenhagen.

Germany

The superb achievements of the French masters in 13
the field of gunmaking and decoration relegate 38–40
German firearms production to a secondary place. 56–7
The fashion for everything French spread also to the 96, 10 104
German provinces and strongly influenced the 106–7
production of workshops making firearms for the use 110
of the courts of the numerous German principalities. 143–4 342
Indigenous German gunmaking did not, however, 345–6
decline; the now archaic wheel-lock mechanism and the old traditional decorative elements, created in the sixteenth century and abandoned in France during the first half of the seventeenth century, were still in production and use.

The quality of German gun production was much more variable than in France, where provincial workshops could often compete with those of Paris. Germany, divided into a number of small principalities, was not in a position to evolve a dominant production centre and this eventually led to the development of considerable differences both in the character and the quality of the firearms produced.

In the middle of the seventeenth century there was a trend towards greater austerity and restraint due, possibly, not so much to a change in prevailing taste as to the general impoverishment following the Thirty Years' War. The painstaking and labour-exacting chiselling of barrels and locks was replaced by engraved or etched ornament which did not necessarily require the collaboration of specialists. Lavish inlays of staghorn, ivory or mother-of-pearl were abandoned by some masters and replaced by engraved iron panels. The wood used for stocking, which had been almost entirely concealed under extravagant ornamentation, began slowly to acquire importance as an aesthetic element.

A high standard in gunmaking was achieved by one school of gunstockers believed to have worked in the Rhineland area or in Lorraine. In the decoration of firearms of this region the staghorn inlays, so popular in lands lying within the radius of German culture, were replaced by inlaid silver wire and silver sheet cut to the shape of birds and flowers in conformity with French fashion. A striking feature of

21 Ill J. F. Hayward, *op. cit.*, II, pl. 7.

22 No. A167A.

23 No. B.960.

these firearms is the vertical arrangement of the ornament where small flower motifs run up the butt like a plant. Amongst the sources used in this region were the engraved drawings of Michel Le Blon.[24] This decoration is to be found on a gun signed by Matteus Nutten of Aachen, now in the National Museum in Copenhagen[25] and on a fowling piece made by Jean Henequin of Metz, whose activities were discussed at length in the section dealing with French decoration. The emergence of identical stocks in various centres distant from each other is not difficult to explain, as highly skilled gunstockers were not numerous and they received orders from gunmakers distributed over a wide area.

Gun production in the south-eastern provinces of Germany followed other lines. The innate conservatism manifested itself in the survival throughout the seventeenth century of the wheel-lock; the decoration of the metal parts and the stocks also repeated old forms.

In the realm of superbly-decorated firearms Munich took pride of place. By the end of the sixteenth century the technique of decorative chiselling had been developed to the highest level in the workshop of the Sadeler brothers, Daniel and Emmanuel, who were in the service of the court of the Wittelsbach. The Sadelers had originally come from Antwerp where the technique of iron chiselling was well established. Both brothers mastered the craft as apprentices to their father who was a cutler. In his workshop, in addition to decorating knife hafts and blades, they were certainly employed on other tasks connected with the decoration of iron or steel. After settling in Munich, the elder Sadeler, Emmanuel, was in the service of Prince Wilhelm V of Bavaria (from 1594 to 1610) and held the post of court *Eisenarbeiter* which ensured him a fixed salary and exemption from the duties exacted by his guild. His functions included the decoration of various articles, such as coffers, caskets, mounts of purses and furniture, candlesticks and also all sorts of arms. Both Sadelers worked exclusively in the chiselling technique, which was difficult and onerous, but produced exceptionally beautiful effects. Their decorative style derived from the Renaissance but showed the effect of the transition to the Mannerist style. The ornamental themes they used, and which continued in use for many decades, were greatly influenced by Étienne Delaune (d. 1583), a gifted French engraver who devoted himself almost exclusively to the production of decorative designs. During his sojourn in Germany he executed a large number of ornamental engravings, designed for craftsmen-decorators. The main elements of his designs were Classical deities, arranged singly or in groups under canopies, surrounded by stylised floral scrollwork and arabesques. The scheme was particularly suited to the decoration of barrels and was adapted by professional decorators in almost all European countries and lasted without major changes until the beginning of the eighteenth century. Delaune's designs were also used by the Sadelers who combined them skilfully with details drawn from the engraved ornament of the Flemish artists Hans Collaert (d. 1622) and Abraham de Bry (d. 1587), whose styles they came to know in their birthplace, Antwerp. Whereas it was previously the custom for the relief ornament to be gilded or silvered, the Sadeler workshop preferred a different plan and weapons decorated by them have the chiselled ornament in its natural fire-blue colour against the fire-gilt background.

Documentary evidence confirms the attribution to Emmanuel Sadeler of a wheel-lock musket, made about 1600, for Wilhelm V and presented fifty years later by Maximilian I as a wedding gift to Prince Charles of Savoy. This musket ranks as one of the most magnificent firearms ever produced. The ornament of the barrel and lock is enhanced by the colour contrast between the blued parts in relief and matt gilt ground. The stock is exceptionally fine and is the work of the Munich stocker Adam Vischer, mentioned in the Court books of payment for 1599–1610. The engraved staghorn inlays are executed with real mastery far surpassing the abilities of an average stocker. In this case, too, the decoration was designed individually. It is possible that both the design and the execution of the interior were carried out by the gifted graphic artist, Johannes Sadeler–a suggestion which is supported by the fact that he had started his career as a gunstocker and later mastered the technique of copper engraving. From the time it was made, this gun and its companion fork were regarded as works of art rather than as articles of practical use. This is borne out by the fact that they were immediately placed in the princely *Kunstkabinett*, where in 1611 they attracted the attention of Philip Hainhofer, the Augsburg scientist.[26]

24 The group of firearms with almost identically decorated stocks is formed by a wheel-lock fowling piece signed by Nicolas Keuck (The Tower of London, No. XIII, 1551); a gun, signed by Mateus Nutten (The National Museum, Copenhagen No. 21.760); a wheel-lock fowling piece by Henequin (The Bayrisches Nationalmuseum, Munich, No. 1733); a pair of flintlock pistols (the Victoria and Albert Museum, London, Nos. M. 175, 175a-1928); and a carbine (the Skokloster, Sweden, No. 188). The decorations of all these pieces show a strong influence of a book of engraved ornament published by Le Blon in 1611 and of engraved designs of Theodore de Bry.

25 No. 21. 760.

26 This is recorded by J. F. Hayward, *op. cit.*, I, p. 177.

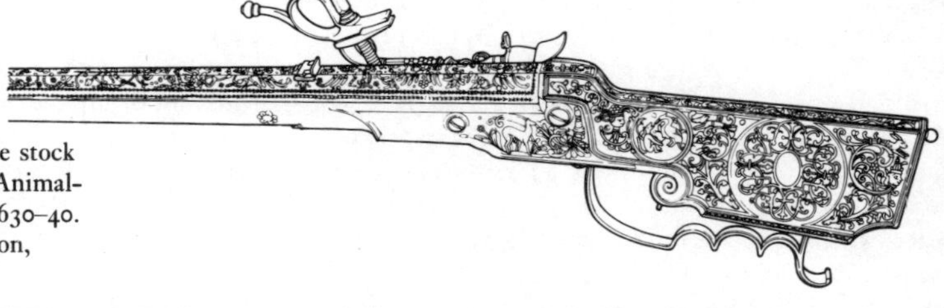

Detail of a wheel-lock gun, the stock carved by the 'Master of the Animal-Headed Scrolls'. Austrian, *c.*1630–40. C. O. von Kienbusch Collection, Philadelphia.

Surviving firearms decorated by Daniel Sadeler are more numerous. Until 1620 he lived in Prague where he was employed as a *Kammervergolder* at the court of Rudolph II. A gun made for the Habsburg Emperor and now in the Kunsthistorisches
96 Museum, Vienna, dates from 1610. The stock of this piece was decorated by the Augsburg goldsmith, David Altenstetter, who covered it entirely with silver panels, ornamented with polychrome translucent enamel *en champlevé*. The ornament consists of festoons, bunches of fruit and flowers, scrolls of foliage with birds and candelabrum motifs (a style rather antiquated in relation to the date of the gun). The same motifs and an analogous technique are seen on a clock-case made about 1600 by David Altenstetter for Rudolph II's *Kunstkabinett*, in which the gun was also probably displayed.

A fairly numerous group of guns and pistols have survived of which the metal parts were chiselled by Daniel Sadeler while the stocks are signed with the linked initials *HB*. These are placed on a staghorn panel below the barrel tang and refer to one of the most gifted German stockmakers, Hieronymus
345 Borstorffer (d. 1637). His work was characterised by great refinement and restraint; he dispensed with complicated figure subjects in favour of delicate arabesque strapwork which recalls the ornament of Virgil Solis. These scrolls, inlaid on an ebony or palisander veneer and made of thin strips of ivory, ebony or bone, form an original and attractive decoration. Another type of decoration is to be seen on a pair of wheel-lock pistols in the Wallace Collection, London[27] with barrels and locks decorated by Sadeler in the early years of his Munich career. The stocks of ebony are inlaid in horn with panels, enclosing small figures in contemporary dress, placed amidst strapwork, floral scrolls and trophies of arms, the design of which bears distinct affinity with the chiselled steel work of Daniel Sadeler.

From 1632 to 1665 the Sadeler workshop was under the control of Caspar Spät, a pupil of and collaborator with the Sadelers. In effect he continued the style and technique employed by both Sadelers, but his work did not compare with theirs in quality, since his ornament was in lower relief and the finish less painstaking. Many of his barrels and locks were mounted by Elias Becker of Augsburg, who signed his stocks with the initials *EB*. These differ from the highly individual forms of Borstorffer and, although attractive, they are more conventional in technique and in the details of decoration.

An individual group of guns has been ascribed to an anonymous stocker, perhaps working in Vienna, who provided the stocks for some of Emperor Ferdinand III's firearms. This stocker is generally known as the *Meister der Tierkopfranken* (Master of the Animal-headed Scrolls) because of the typical scrolls of delicate foliage terminating in animals' or monsters' heads that he introduced. His range of ornamental subjects is conventional but his carving of animals is careful, correct in anatomical details and lively in movement and testifies to his outstanding gift and complete mastery of workshop techniques. The carved decoration is supplemented by brass wire inlays and also, on a large number of pieces, by inset panels of engraved bone or mother-of-pearl. Guns of this group not only have finely-decorated stocks, but also a striking décor on the barrels and locks, in which silver-encrusted foliage or winged cherubs' heads appear against a punched ground. In the group of about forty guns ascribed to this master, two bear the monogram *AS* and one the initials *HN*. Unfortunately these initials do not identify the master and are perhaps those of the owners of the guns. The large number of surviving pieces suggests that the workshop from which they issued must have employed a number of craftsmen, working under a single master who planned the decorative scheme and was also responsible for the final touches.

Another group of firearms with elaborate stocks is the work of Johann Michael Maucher, active in the second half of the seventeenth century, first in his
native Schwäbisch-Gmund, later in Augsburg and 110,3
finally in Würzburg. The stocks either of walnut or pear wood are carved with great imagination and are almost always adorned with panels in relief in ivory or mother-of-pearl. Frequently, one finds that a

27 Nos. A. 1155/60.

scene has been taken literally from an engraving by Goltzius, Stradanus, Jost Amman or Georg Pencz, whose engraved compositions were copied with great skill in relief. The principle of symmetry is closely adhered to, identical designs being repeated on each side of the stock, with the exception of the cheek-piece for which, as a rule, the most elaborate composition was reserved. Maucher often used this space for the subject of the young David with the giant Goliath, picking out both figures from the rest of the scene by making them larger and working them in higher relief.

Some reference should be made to a stocking workshop which was active in the mid-seventeenth century in Augsburg. Wheel-lock firearms produced there had stocks entirely overlaid with translucent tortoise-shell. The effect of this overlay was enhanced by using bright barrels and mounts made of gilt brass. Some of these firearms bear the signature of Martin Kamerer who was working in Augsburg between 1650 and 1667. An example of this group, made for Emperor Ferdinand III, is in the Kretzschmar von Kienbusch Collection, now in the Philadelphia Museum.

In Saxony, where large areas were covered with forests, hunting had since time immemorial been the favourite sport of the upper classes and this led to a heavy demand for firearms. The Electors of Saxony had their own personal armoury which was maintained and replenished with great knowledge and enthusiasm. In addition to strictly functional weapons, it contained firearms which were masterpieces of decorative art, so delicately wrought, so richly adorned, that they are unlikely to have been used. Traditionalism persisted here even more than in other parts of Germany. Until the end of the seventeenth century stocks were decorated with inlaid staghorn or bone panels while the decoration of barrels and locks continued to repeat motifs of gilt cherubs' heads and pierced cartouches of strapwork, *Rollwerk* or auricular scrollwork, placed on a ground of blued steel. At the very end of the century French influences became more marked. The eager propagator of Paris fashion was Andreas Erttel of Dresden, the court gunmaker to Augustus the Strong, King of Poland and Elector of Saxony, for whom he made a magnificent gun which could be compared with the best French achievement in the field of firearms decoration. The iconographical programme, shown in this piece, repeats exactly the ornament applied by Piraube on a gun made for Louis XIV. Unfortunately Erttel's gun was destroyed in a fire of 1934.

The light birding-guns, made in Teschen, known as Tschinkes, are as distinctive in their decoration as they are in their construction. Characteristic of this group is the way its ornamentation assimilates features from both eastern and western European 39
decorative styles. 104 Stocks are inlaid rather coarsely with engraved staghorn and mother-of-pearl and brass wire, creating a dense pattern of tiny scrolls, dots, hunting animals and grotesque masks. Equally original is the decoration of the lock-plates and barrels with applied pierced gilt-brass panels, contrasting with the usually blued steel background.

Italy

The seventeenth century witnessed an impressive 43-45
development of Italian gunmaking. Its universal 47, 53
renown was chiefly due to the superb artistic work- 70-74 102, 105
manship of firearms made in Brescia. The gunsmith 111, 347
here excelled in the chiselling of barrels and lockplates and the ornamentation of stocks with iron or, more rarely, brass sheet, cut and pierced with a precision of design and execution which gives the impression of delicate lace. The main decorative element was an intricate tracery of floral scrolls or arabesques combined with animals, birds and grotesque monsters, which are executed with such fineness that they can only be appreciated fully if viewed through a magnifying glass. These same motifs are to be seen on all the finer pieces made in Brescia and they are also found on the hilts of contemporary rapiers and left-hand daggers, though in the latter their execution is usually more perfunctory. This points to the existence in Brescia and its vicinity of workshops which specialised in this type of decoration. In keeping with the innate conservatism that distinguishes Italian production, the established decorative forms passed from one generation to the next without significant change.

The barrels of Italian guns and pistols were at first decorated with longitudinal grooves and file-cut mouldings at breech and muzzle; in the second half of the century this was modified to correspond to the manner propagated by the Paris pattern-books. The decoration of lockplates and mounts, chiselled in high relief, developed very interesting forms and was lively and imaginative in conception.

The Brescian style of the mid-seventeenth century with its finely chiselled and pierced decoration, is well exemplified by a garniture, in the Livrustkammare, Stockholm, made in 1638–9 for Louis XIII 45
of France. A gift to the King from the Venetian Republic,[28] it now comprises a self-spanning wheel-lock gun and pair of pistols; five craftsmen were involved in its production: G. A. Gavacciolo (locks), L. Cominazzo (barrels), A. & C. Gosi and G. Secardo (pierced and chiselled steel mounts).

28 M. Morin, 'And His Majesty said "All my guns together are not worth one of these!"', R. Held (Ed.), *Art, Arms & Armour*, I, Chiasso, 1979, pp. 252–77.

Another type of decoration, more florid although coarser in execution, is represented by a snaphance lock in the Victoria and Albert Museum in London.[29] The plate is chiselled with mythological subjects which show Hercules overcoming the Nemean lion and Leda and the Swan. The carving of the cock is particularly skilled: it takes the form of a triton and the arm of the steel that of a naked female figure. A certain naivety of form and lack of skill in distribution of ornamental motifs suggest that the decoration may have been designed and executed in the gunsmith's workshop.

veneered with tortoise-shell panels. A fine example of this type is a pair of flintlock pistols, dated 1699, in the Bayrisches Nationalmuseum in Munich.

A different style of decoration was evolved during the second half of the seventeenth century in the Acqua Fresca workshop in Bargi, near Bologna. The metal surfaces here were usually chiselled in low relief with delicate foliage. There is, however, a lock, probably by Sebastiano Acqua Fresca (d. 1692), in the Metropolitan Museum, New York, in which the pierced decoration is executed in a separate plate which then was applied to the main surface and

Right Snaphance lock of chiselled iron. Italian (Brescia), *c.*1670. Victoria & Albert Museum, London.

Below Detached lockplate chiselled with portraits of the Emperor Leopold I and his wife Eleonora whom he married in 1676. Signed by Carlo Bottarelli of Brescia, *c.*1675. Victoria & Albert Museum, London.

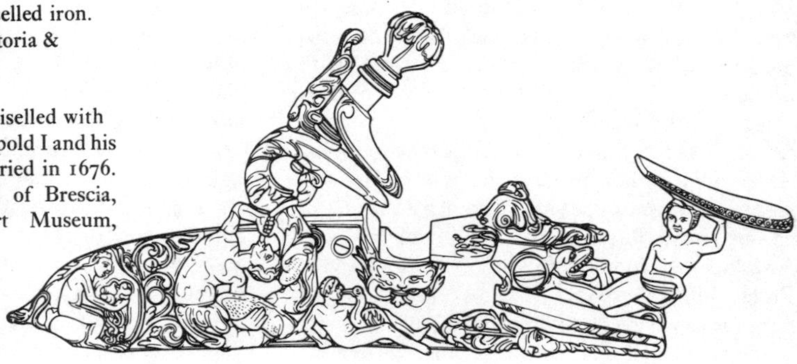

Certain changes in decoration took place in the second half of the seventeenth century. The typical Brescian flat pierced mounts were replaced by another type chiselled in such high relief that they looked almost as though they had been carved in the round. Human and animal figures on a larger scale than hitherto were also preferred. At the same time, in addition to the traditional Italian type of stock, Brescian workshops produced French type stocks decorated with scrolls of inlaid silver wire and ornament cut out of silver sheet, representing flowers and zoomorphic creatures in the manner of the Thuraine and Le Hollandois pattern-book. Metal stocks were also made, chiefly by Stefano Scioli (Sioli or Cioli), but did not differ either in form or in ornament from wooden stocks. Similar stocks were also made in the workshop of Hieronimo Zucolo in Brescia. Some Neapolitan examples of the second half of the century were more original, such as those

backed with gold foil. The most famous member of this family was Matteo Acqua Fresca (d. 1738), both gunsmith and steel chiseller. The genuine artistry of his work places him in the first rank of masters in metal decoration. In addition to firearms he also decorated *objets d'art* such as caskets and snuff-boxes. His decorative style was largely derived from the engraved pattern-books of Theodore de Bry and Jean Berain. He cleverly combined elements drawn from these sources into an individual artistic conception, as may be seen on the lockplate of a pair of snaphance pistols made *c.* 1690–1700, now in the R. T. Gwynn Collection England. He used similar ornament in the lock 111
of a pair of snaphance pistols, now in the Bayrisches Nationalmuseum in Munich.[30] An original feature of these is the overlaying of the blued barrels with a silver sheathing pierced with delicately chased flowers and birds' heads.

29 No. M.362-1923.

30 Nos. 13/10600-61.

Spain

75,256 A most distinctive feature of Spanish firearms decoration introduced towards the end of this period was the decoration of the barrels with gold damascening combining motifs derived from the Spanish *mauresque*. At the same time it became the custom to sign the barrel with the maker's name, damascened in gold, while the maker's marks and counter-marks were stamped at the breech of the barrel and covered with a piece of gold foil. This particular way of signing provided an additional decorative effect. Greater variety of wood was used here for stocking. Apart from the walnut, fruit wood, especially cherry, was frequently used. Sometimes the natural grain of the wood was enriched by artificial colouring, the result of which recalled the effect of tortoise shell overlay. Such stocks were often ornamented with silver sheet cut in simple floral or geometrical designs. Throughout the seventeenth century, locks were rather plain, and not until the end of the century were they given decorative treatment which was composed of fine engraving or chiselling influenced by French fashions.

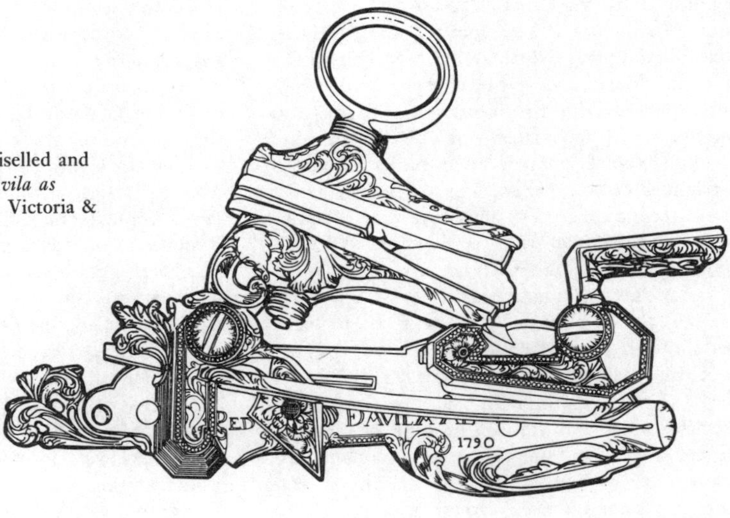

Detail of a miquelet lock, chiselled and engraved. Signed *Pedro de Avila as Malaga 1790*. Spanish, 1790. Victoria & Albert Museum, London.

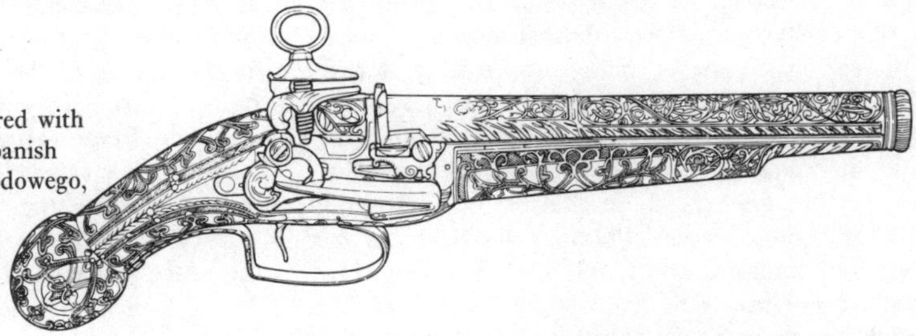

Miquelet pistol, the stock covered with pierced and engraved silver. Spanish (Ripoll), *c.*1740. Muzeum Narodowego, Cracow.

An individual centre of Spanish gunmaking was the town of Ripoll in Catalonia. The entire surface 256
of stocks made here was usually sheathed in delicate iron, brass, or, more rarely, silver tracery, which skilfully combined Renaissance with *mauresque* ornament. Though the repertoire of the motifs was in general reminiscent of the forms used in Brescia, it did not approach the latter and often fell within the category of folk art. This type of stock treatment was maintained in the Ripoll workshops throughout the seventeenth and eighteenth centuries. The design might be more or less elaborate but rarely deviated from the conventional type.

The Netherlands

In the course of the seventeenth century firearms 50
production in Holland achieved a high standard 54–5 66–8
which was parallel to Holland's dominant role in 100

world commerce and finance. The Civil War in England and the Thirty Years' War on the Continent provided the workshops of leading Dutch towns with ample opportunity to capture the European market. Though output was concentrated on military weapons, a certain number of arms *de luxe* was also produced. According to established practice, stocks were inlaid with engraved panels of mother-of-pearl or bone depicting hunting subjects, rustic and military life, often characterised by a sense of vitality and bluff humour.[31] When inlaid stocks went out of fashion French styles were emulated, and in the third quarter of the century the best Dutch work was equal in design and execution to that of Paris. Stocks were adorned sparingly with carved foliate motifs which were placed behind the tang of the barrel and at the trigger-guard. More attention was given to the decoration of barrels and locks. Some with lockplates were chiselled in relief with animal subjects, satyrs, reclining female nudes and trophies of war, while dogs received fanciful forms of coiling dragons or entwined human bodies which were rendered with considerable skill and imagination. Fire-blued barrels were ornamented with cartouches containing figural motifs. An alternative to the sculptural treatment were lockplates and barrels adorned with engraved designs. One of the outstanding masters was Jan Knoop of
50 Utrecht, who was a gunmaker and a stocker. Some of the wheel-lock and flintlock firearms bearing his name are stocked in ebony. Carved ornaments are simple enough to suggest that they may have been executed by Knoop himself. On the other hand, one engraved decoration of locks has a mark in the form of a small stag, which may be that of an unknown professional engraver who collaborated with Knoop. Another very attractive feature of firearms produced by this master is the silver damascened decoration of barrels consisting of dainty arabesque patterns. These are symmetrically arranged and executed with such skill that they can stand a comparison with the damascened decoration of Persian origin. Besides this, they create an effective contrast with the engraved decoration of mounts derived from the designs of Thuraine and Le Hollandois. In general, Dutch decoration reflects the modest character of Dutch people and, like them, avoids extravagance and pretentiousness.

An original group of pistols dating from the second half of the century had stocks made entirely of ivory. They are associated with certain unidentified workshops of Maastricht. The decoration was concentrated on the pommels which were carved from a separate piece of ivory in the form of a helmeted or laurel-wreathed warrior's head or, occasionally, with the turbaned head of a Turk; the carving was usually carried out fluently, though carvers failed to give faces individual character and vivid expression. In some cases the helmets were made of silver giving an attractive colour contrast.[32]

England

It is surprising that so few English firearms of the 52,62
early seventeenth century have survived. Those 100–9
which remain do not, in general, show any original 137-39
decorative conception, adhering to the type evolved 141
during the last decades of the previous century. In the Kremlin Palace in Moscow there are three pairs of decorated English pistols dating from the beginning of the century.[33] They are uniform both in shape and in decoration which, though fine, is a little out of date for this period. The ornament damascened in gold on the belled barrels and locks contains the elements of the candelabrum type which was used on the Continent more than fifty years before. The decoration of the stocks with mother-of-pearl inlays, depicting hunting subjects and floral patterns, is similarly old-fashioned. Yet, the decorativeness of these pieces is exceptional in comparison with the standard production that was usually much simpler, especially during the period of the Civil War, when circumstances forced the gunmakers to switch production to military type firearms. A small number of civil arms was, however, produced in which the Dutch style of decoration was strongly marked. The stocks were for the most part plain and their ornamentation was limited to steel mounts chiselled or engraved with floral compositions similar to those used in Holland. The Restoration of the monarchy in 1660 brought a larger demand for arms *de luxe*. The Dutch influence now became less marked and in its place the English gunmakers gradually adopted contemporary French fashions. A considerable role in disseminating the French style was exerted by numerous refugee gunsmiths, German, Dutch and especially French Huguenots, the last of whom were forced to flee from their country by religious persecution culminating in revocation of the Edict of Nantes in 1685. It was natural that they should introduce to England decorative formulae evolved on the Continent, and inspired by French pattern-books.

Pierre Monlong, a French Huguenot, was prob- 280

31 Ill. by J. F. Hayward, *op. cit.*, I, pl. 38 a,c.

32 Some of these pistols are illustrated by T. Lenk, *op. cit.*, pl. 52. See also A. Hoff, *Dutch Firearms*, London, 1978.

33 These pistols were probably presented to Feodor, the son of Tsar Boris Godunow by the British ambassador, Sir Thomas Smith in 1604; gifts of fitearms were also made to Tsar Michail Fedorovitch by English agents of the Muscovy Company. One of these pieces is illustrated by Dudley Pope, *Guns*, London, 1965, p. 86.

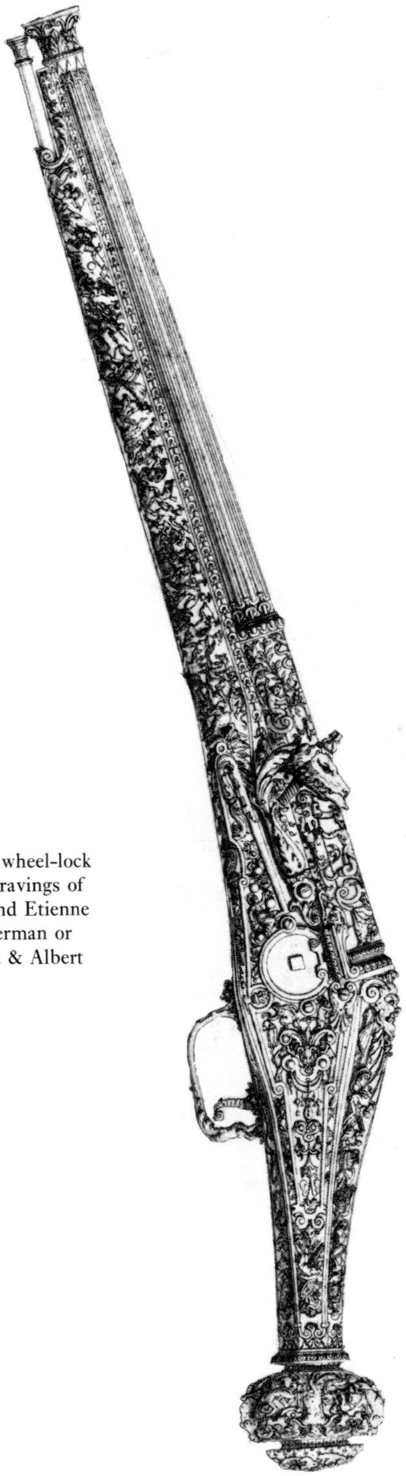

339 Design for a pair of wheel-lock pistols, based on the engravings of Stradanus (1530-1605) and Etienne Delaune (1519-1588). German or Flemish, *c.*1575. Victoria & Albert Museum, London.

340 Wheel-lock gun, the stock of etched iron. German (Nuremberg), *c.*1570. Muzeum Narodowego, Cracow.

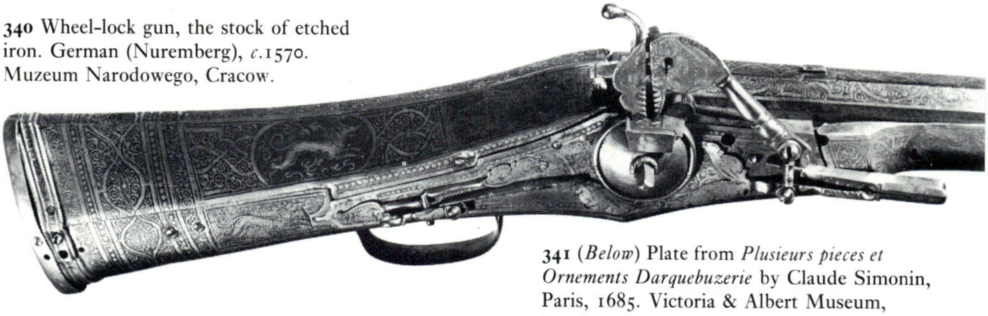

341 (*Below*) Plate from *Plusieurs pieces et Ornements Darquebuzerie* by Claude Simonin, Paris, 1685. Victoria & Albert Museum, London.

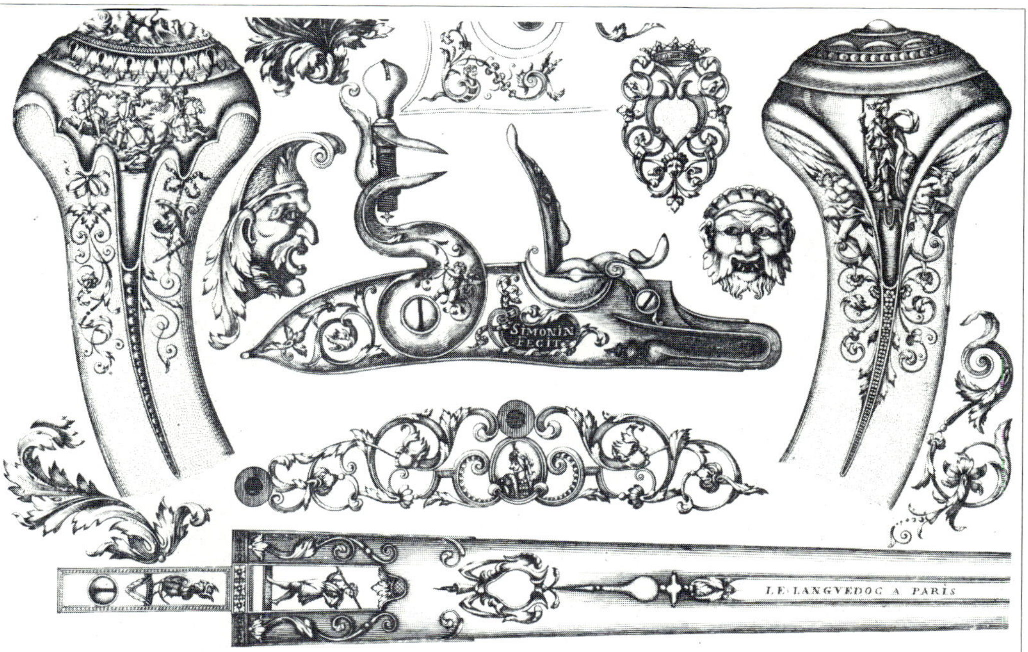

342 Wheel-lock gun. The stock carved in the workshop of J. M. Maucher of Schwäbisch-Gmünd. German, *c.*1670. Landesmuseum, Karlsruhe.

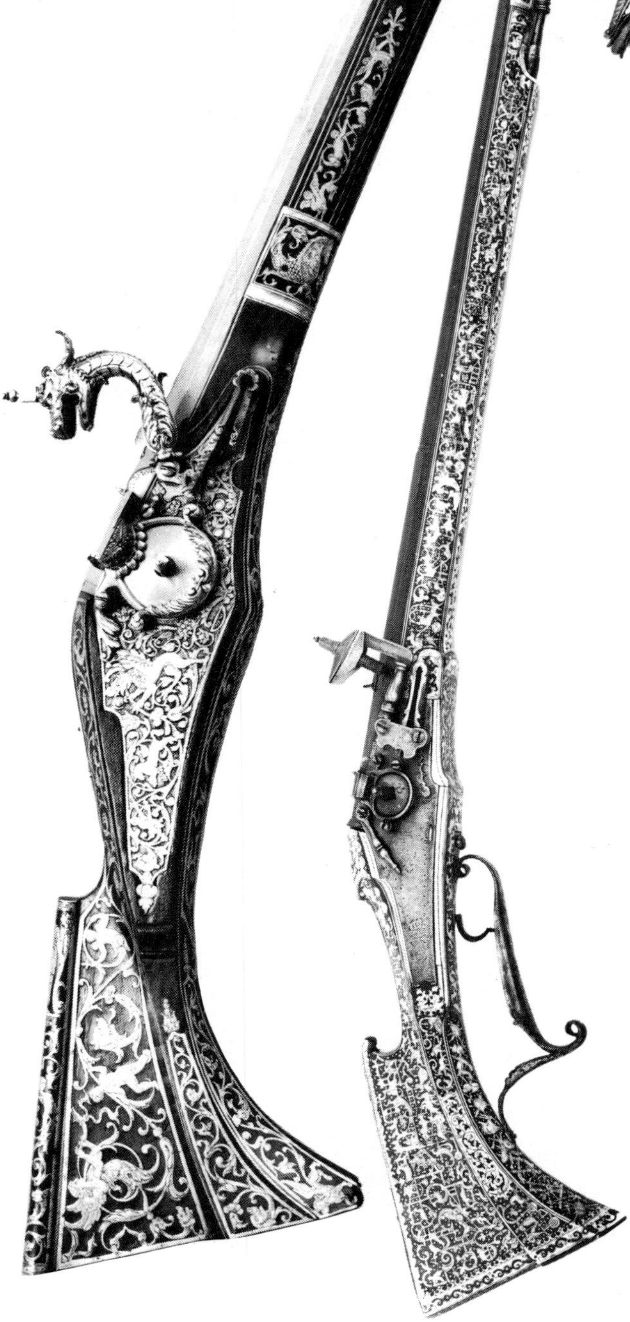

343 Wheel-lock gun of Rainuccio Farnese, Duke of Parma. Walnut stock inlaid in pierced and engraved iron, the lock signed GIO. BAT. VIS. North Italian, dated 1596. Museo di Capodimonte, Naples.

344 *Left* Wheel-lock carbine, the stock inlaid with staghorn, the lock engraved. German, *c.*1580. Formerly collection of Lord Astor of Hever.

345 *Above* Detail of a wheel-lock gun, the lock chiselled by Daniel Sadeler, the stock by Hieronymus Borstorffer. German (Munich), *c.*1620. Wallace Collection, London.

346 *Below* Stock of a wheel-lock gun carved in the workshop of J. M. Maucher. Landesmuseum, Karlsruhe.

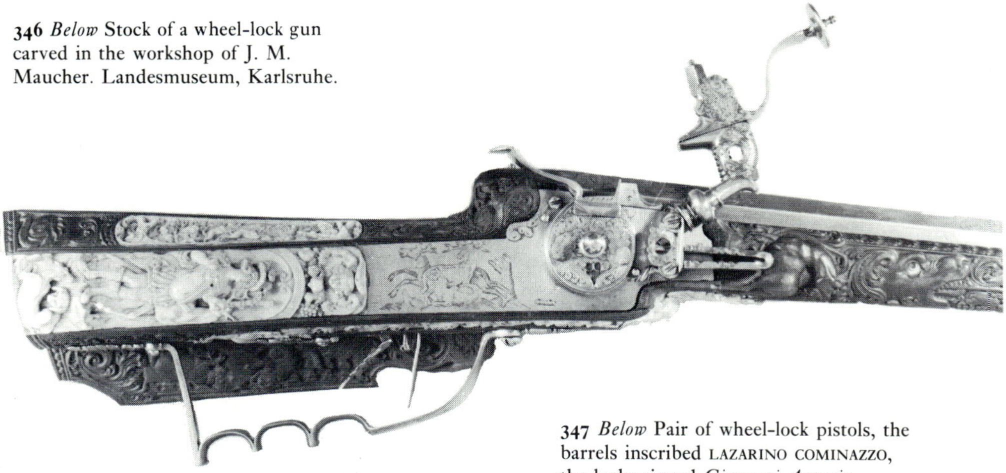

347 *Below* Pair of wheel-lock pistols, the barrels inscribed LAZARINO COMINAZZO, the locks signed *Giovanni Antonio Cavacciolo*. Italian (Brescia), *c*.1640. Livrustkammaren, Stockholm.

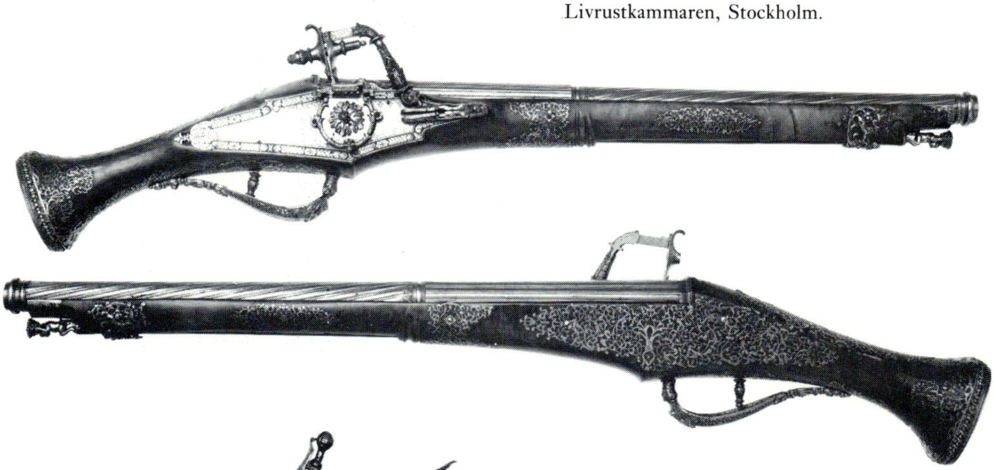

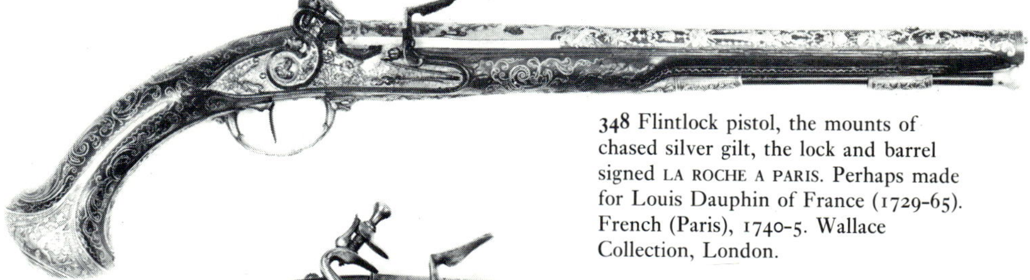

348 Flintlock pistol, the mounts of chased silver gilt, the lock and barrel signed LA ROCHE A PARIS. Perhaps made for Louis Dauphin of France (1729-65). French (Paris), 1740-5. Wallace Collection, London.

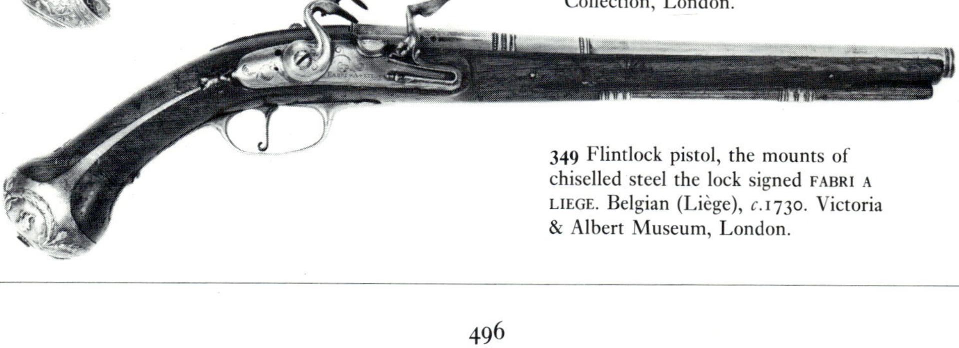

349 Flintlock pistol, the mounts of chiselled steel the lock signed FABRI A LIEGE. Belgian (Liège), *c*.1730. Victoria & Albert Museum, London.

ably the most skilled of these émigrés. He came originally from Angers but he also worked in Paris with Frappier.[34] He brought to England the current Paris fashion based on the Simonin pattern-book. It must be pointed out that Monlong's ornament, far from being a slavish copy, showed a creative interpretation of this pattern-book. His mastery can be proved by a pair of flintlock pistols, now in the Tower of London Armouries, probably made for William III, whose supposed portrait adorns the screws of the cocks. Another foreign gunsmith, probably of Dutch origin, was Andrew Dolep. His firearms, well represented in many collections, are stocked in finely figured wood and, according to the French taste, inlaid with silver wire. The artistic merit of his work is largely due to the handsome cast and engraved silver mounts. More modest was the decoration adapted by Harman Barne, who is also of Dutch origin. A handsome pair of his flintlock pistols in the W. Keith Neal Collection, formerly at Warminster, England, shows a very restrained mood of decoration which is confined to gold damascening on barrels and steel mounts.

Towards the end of the seventeenth century, French decorative schemes were adapted even by provincial English gunsmiths such as Ellis of Doncaster who, in one case at least, in a pair of holster pistols, now in the M. Dinely Collection, England, exactly copied Simonin's pattern.

A certain refinement in decoration can be noticed in the last quarter of the seventeenth century. The engraved or chiselled ornament was not only finer in execution but also treated with increasing freedom and imagination. The conventional floral patterns were enriched with strawberry leaves and more pliant scrolls ending with tiny animal half-figures or serpents' heads. Finely figured burrwood stocks and engraved silver, iron or brass mounts are the characteristic features of English firearms of this period and some of them testify to the high level of contemporary craftsmanship.

Russia

Gunmaking in Russia made great advances from the mid-seventeenth century. While the barrels, locks and mounts were adorned with chiselled decoration that reflected Western, mainly German, fashion, the decoration of the stocks was left entirely to native craftsmen. These developed a scheme of inlaid ornament, composed of small staghorn and mother-of-pearl plaques, geometrical in outline, which are sometimes reminiscent of intricate Oriental designs. Although the general effect of this decoration was attractive, it did not approach in quality the work of contemporary German stockmakers. The most beautiful examples of firearms were made in the Court workshops which had been founded by Tsar Mikhail Fedorovitch in the Oruzeinaya Palata, Moscow. Their characteristic style evolved gradually from the interaction of two opposed aesthetic conceptions, Western and Eastern; the fusion of the two gave rise to strikingly decorative results. Western influences were spread by numerous immigrant craftsmen, recruited from the Baltic countries, Holland, Germany and Poland, while native craftsmen, imbued with Russian decorative traditions, assimilated them but gave them a strong Oriental flavour.

The Oruzeinaya workshops became more active in the 1670s. A large number of Russian gunsmiths and stockers, with Nikita Dawydow at their head, were employed there at the time. Stocks signed by Dawydow were covered with a dense intricate tracery of carved or inlaid ornament, composed of motifs drawn from the art of the Near East, chiefly Turkey; while the ornament chiselled in iron introduced elements of native Russian folk art. Similar stocks were made by the stockers Boltyrew and Kurevlev, who used the two-headed Russian eagle, inlaid in ebony, to decorate the cheek-piece. An original form of chiselled decoration is found on the lock of a gun in the Kremlin Armouries.[35] Here the chiselled ornament and the sculptural shape of the cock correspond to contemporary European fashion, but the figure of a woman, wearing Russian peasant dress, which covers the steel-spring, is an original detail derived from Russian folk art.

The Eighteenth Century and the Beginning of the Nineteenth Century

The type of decoration introduced in the second half 65
of the seventeenth century by French pattern-books 78-81
survived without major change through the first 87 112-14
decades of the eighteenth century. Gunstocks be- 117
came, however, straighter and more slender as a 119-21
result of an elongation of the small of the butt. The 123-4
brittle root or burr walnut wood was replaced by 145 258-68
tougher straight-grained wood. For the same reason 270-71
the fore-end of the stock was now often made of stag- 348-51
horn or metal. This did not imply that the decoration became less exuberant. French fowling pieces now had the cheek-piece padded with velvet or leather, not for decorative reasons but for comfort in use. Barrels were shortened considerably and their

34 Monlong's history is discussed at length by J. F. Hayward 'Pierre Monlong, Bossemager hos to Konger', *Vaabenhistoriske Aarbøger*, VIII, Copenhagen, 1956. In the Duke of Brunswick Collection there is a pair of pistols with the joint signature of Monlong and Frappier.

35 No. 7446.

weight reduced, presumably as a result of an improvement in the gunpowder used. An innovation in the decoration of gunstocks was to concentrate the carving in two places, behind the barrel-tang and on the underside of the barrel between the trigger-guard and the ramrod. The chiselled steel ornament achieved a particular refinement: this may have been due to the brilliant development of the medallist's art. Certain medallists are known to have undertaken the decoration of snuff-boxes, caskets, candlesticks and arms. They usually followed the method, evolved in the course of the seventeenth century by the Sadeler workshop, and placed blued ornament in high relief against a gilded ground.

France

65,79 The heavy and florid forms of the Louis XIV style
112-14 were superseded at the turn of the century by com-
120-24
267,348 positions successively in the Régence and rococo
350-51 styles; the asymmetrical character of the latter
brought new life into decoration.

In addition to the numerous surviving pieces illustrating the change in decorative art, this can also be followed in a number of pattern-books. Claude Gillot, the master of Watteau and a well-known decorative painter, published early in the eighteenth century a collection of plates in which he introduced the strapwork ornament so characteristic of the Régence period. Acanthus leaves in his conception lost their fleshiness and developed a more angular and dry form. These novelties, announcing a new phase in decorative art, were quickly exploited by a number of leading gunsmiths, particularly those working in Liège. Even greater influence was achieved by the pattern-book designed and engraved by Nicolas Guérard and drawn from the work of best Paris gunmakers. Published in Paris about 1720 under the title *Diverses Pieces d'Arquebuserie*; reissued in a pirated edition by Johann Christoph Weigel in Augsburg, these designs were used all over Europe, even as far away as Tula. In his designs Guérard showed such familiarity with the construction of firearms that it may be assumed that, like other masters of engraved
350 ornament, he had actually decorated firearms in a gunmaker's shop. He propagated new forms, light and elegant, evolved in the Régence style which was a transitional phase between that of the Louis XIV period and rococo. His typical subjects were figures in classical costumes, hunters in contemporary court dresses and scrolls of acanthus, arranged with even greater freedom than those in Gillot's designs. Equally influential were the engraved sheets of ornament published by De Lacollombe in 1705 and reissued in 1730 with additional sheets by his pupil Gilles de Marteau, which exploited the now fashionable rococo style.

Designs for gunsmith's ornament were also made by Augustin Dupré from St Etienne, a medallist by profession, who during his sojourn in Paris from time to time decorated barrels and locks. Some of his designs, which date from the latter part of the eighteenth century, are distinctly old-fashioned, but on the other hand he also produced Empire ornament in the taste of the end of the century.

The ideas popularised by the pattern-books of ornament were reflected in the work of gunmakers throughout France. As in the seventeenth, so in the eighteenth century there is no reason to speak of provincial, in distinction to the Parisian, style. Provincial workshops assimilated each innovation both in technique and style of the decoration and produced articles which were fully able to compete with those from Paris.

Towards the middle of the eighteenth century barrels of arms *de luxe* were most lavishly decorated. The polygonal section was usually replaced by a round one and the barrel was divided into two parts, that next the breech being chiselled against a brilliantly blued ground. The cock received a shaped profile and its weakest spot near the swan-neck was reinforced with chiselled minute figures of a dragon, an eagle or, in less elaborate pieces, the curling form of a leaf bud.[36] Chiselled steel mounts were frequently replaced by more easily worked mounts of cast silver, carefully chased, often gilt as well.

Among the many prominent eighteenth-century gunmakers in France mention should be made of Les Laroches, father and son, who followed each other in the same *logement* in the Galeries du
Louvre. The firearms from their workshop were 348
chiefly intended for presentation. The arrangement of their decoration suggests that they were executed after original designs, created separately for each item. The technical perfection of this decoration was so high that its execution should perhaps be credited to a goldsmith's workshop.

A rival worthy of Les Laroches was Puiforcat, Court Gunmaker to Louis XV. His decoration reflects the change of style which occurred in the Classicism prevailing in decorative art during the last phase of the reign of Louis XV. It was expressed in the abandonment of asymmetrical rococo scroll-work in favour of subjects drawn from Classical history and a more static arrangement of the com-

36 This detail is to be found on many fine firearms dating from the Louis XIV period. An exceptionally fine form of the cock reinforcement is shown in a fowling piece made by Arault. The loops of the cock are filled with the minute figures of a dragon and an eagle chiselled in full-relief. The piece is now in the Bayrisches Nationalmuseum, Munich, No. W. 2890.

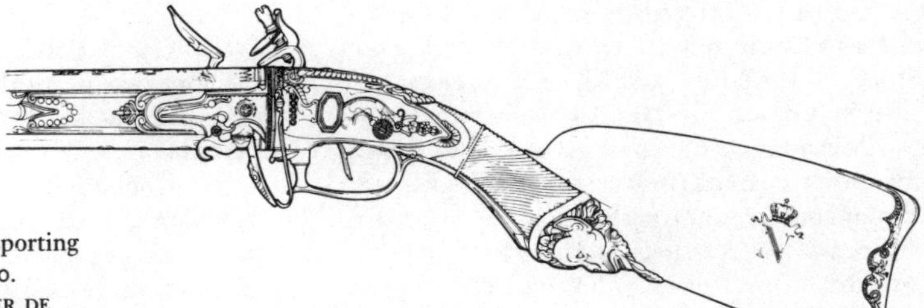

Detail of a double-barrelled sporting gun. French (Paris), *c*.1805–10. Inscribed LE PAGE ARQUEBUSIER DE L'EMPEREUR. Muzeum Narodowego, Cracow.

position. High quality firearms were also produced *c.* 1780 by a Parisian gunmaker, Armand, who had his workshop in Rue du Roule. His double-barrelled fowling piece, now in the National Museum in Krakow (No. V1428), deserves special notice as it is one of the earliest surviving examples with a new method of butt decoration. This took the form of a carved animal head which was placed behind the trigger-guard. This novelty was to become widely used in fowling pieces made in the first decades of the nineteenth century.

Fundamental changes were brought about by the French Revolution and the reign of Napoleon I, when the established conventions were swept away in favour of a new style and an entirely new vocabulary of ornament. These changes were introduced by the factory founded in 1792 at Versailles under the management of Nicolas Noël Boutet (d. 1833). The tremendous demand for luxury firearms during the period of the Directoire, Consulate and especially the First Empire, led to the establishment, within the Versailles factory, of a special workshop, which employed the most gifted French and foreign gun-
267,351 smiths, experienced decorators of firearms and
specialists in every applied technique. The purpose of this special workshop was the exclusive production of *de luxe* firearms, hence no technical improvements of major importance were made. The Empire style affected not only the new vocabulary of subjects, drawn from Roman and Egyptian art, but also the construction of the various parts of firearms. The cock took on a new shape with an acute angle between its lower jaw and the neck; the barrels were mostly octagonal over their entire length and were blued or browned to provide ground for gold-inlaid ornament. The surfaces of gold inlays were often delicately tooled and punched. Pistol stocks were restyled; the butt lowered, sometimes almost to a right angle to the axis of the barrel, the pommel was also cut off at a right angle and the hexagonal or octagonal butt-cap, which was cast of silver or chiselled in steel, was decorated with a classical bust or a grotesque mask. Silver wire inlay was used less in stock decoration. It was replaced by inlaid ornaments of cut and engraved silver – or, in the most expensive examples, of gold sheet.

The mounts were usually stamped with the Paris hallmarks and the maker's mark of Boutet himself. Despite the fact that Boutet produced no pattern-book of Empire ornament, his style spread rapidly all over Europe. This was obviously fostered by the successes of the French armies and establishment of Napoleonic rule in a number of European countries. In the field of fine-quality firearms Boutet found his equal in Le Page, who had been trained in his craft in his father's workshop. The younger Le Page was entrusted with the execution of shoulder arms for the Emperor Napoleon I. They were mainly designed for presentation. Their exquisitely rendered decoration consists of carved animal heads at the bottom of the stock, silver chased mounts, and, in three cases, of a letter N under the imperial crown inlaid in gold on the butt.

England

English decoration followed a different course. The 78,81
profusion of ornamentation, which on the Contin- 87,119 145
ent often bordered on the extravagant, was excep- 260-65
tional in England. The Palladian movement, which 268
rejected the more flamboyant forms of baroque art 270-71
and determined English taste during the first half of the eighteenth century, also made its influence felt in the gunmaking workshops. Revived classical motifs, with their clarity and correctness, were reintroduced and with them the classical sense of proportion. The new style did not lie in novelty of elements of ornament but in the new way of their arrangement. In practice many fine firearms produced during the time of George I and George II mirrored the Palladian ideals and were decorated with classical medallions, Roman emperors' busts, festoons, vases and acanthus leaves, logically arranged, well balanced and often executed with masterful precision. Stocks were rather plain and, as their effect depended chiefly on the natural grain of the wood, the carved ornament was confined to raised borders around the

lock and sideplate and to a little carving behind the tang of the barrel. Silver wire inlay, in the form of delicate scrollwork, supplemented the decoration of the stock. A variety of cast silver butt-caps were supplied by English silversmiths. They were decorated with grotesque human masks or lions' masks and became a characteristic feature of English pistols throughout the eighteenth century. A distinctive type, which deserves a special notice for its popularity, was the turn-off pistol. The stock of this pistol barely reached to the chamber; it was usually undecorated. The barrel was short and solid, narrowing in stepped sections towards the muzzle. The butts, curving gently downwards, had heavy pommels terminating in boldly modelled, cast and chased caps of the type mentioned above. Sideplates, structurally unnecessary in these pistols, were given less attention and were reduced to a silver plaque pierced and chased with simple trophies of arms or conventionalised acanthus foliage.

Rococo ornament first appeared in England in the 1730s. In comparison with the formal creations of the Palladian taste the rococo decoration was freer, although it was on the whole treated in England in a more symmetrical way than in France. Lively scrolls, interlaced with flowers and *rocailles* formed a graceful decoration which never overstepped the borders of rational sobriety. In the middle of the eighteenth century chinoiserie motifs were sometimes introduced into firearms decorations. They were derived from the decoration of Chinese porcelain, lacquer and wallpapers. Oriental birds and fabulous animals, pagoda-like architecture and figures of Chinamen cut out of silver sheet represented a rare but picturesque feature of the decor of some gunstocks.

Among a number of foreign gunmakers who
262-64 worked in England during the eighteenth century, the most prominent was Johann Gottfried Kolbe from Suhl in Thuringia who made, in about 1730, probably for George II, a magnificently decorated air-
262 gun, now in the Victoria and Albert Museum. It is probable that the embossed and chiselled silver mounts for barrel and stock were made by an English craftsman, perhaps a watch-case decorator. Rococo fashion is reflected in the stylised floral scrollwork on the stock and the aysmmetrical form of the cartouche on the top of the butt; the ornament on the barrel and buttplate with the symbols of Courage and Strength is typical of English goldsmith's art at that period.

A great many English-born gunmakers followed the same principles and their work shows the gradual development of the rococo style in England. Among these gunmakers was Henry Hadley whose finest firearms are distinguished both by outstanding quality and by the excellence of their decoration. A pair of flintlock pistols, made about 1770, formerly in the R. T. Gwynn Collection, possesses all the characteristic features of his work. The blued barrels bear Hadley's signature and mark inlaid in gold in the Spanish manner. The silver furniture is cast and chased with emblematic figures, trophies of arms and *rocailles*, while the stocks are carved and inlaid with silver wire in scrolls. All decorative elements are well balanced and have an excellent finish, seldom equalled in English gunmaking.

The decorative style developed in the Versailles factory, which was universally imitated all over Europe, made little impact on English gunmakers. The luxuriant surface ornament which gave to the French firearms the quality of the goldsmiths' art was not often found in English firearms of the end of the eighteenth century, nor did the decorative motifs show such variety as in France. The neo-classical style revived strict symmetry and austerity of design. Silver inlay work was still sometimes used for stocks but the design was plainer and more sober than on the Continent. The silver mounts of this period were nearly all made by a London silversmith, named Moses Brent. His engraved ornament, consisting of military trophies, does not display much artistic ambition and differs completely from the Boutet type of decoration in France.

A special type of presentation firearm produced for the Near East departed from the established English principles in their decoration. Designed to please the exuberant taste of the East, the barrels and lockplates were chiselled in unusually high relief or gilt with trophies of Oriental weapons and turbanned heads. The decoration created a romantic vision of the Oriental world and did not show any knowledge of the ornamental forms evolved in the East. The most sumptuous pieces were furnished with gold mounts and set with diamonds.

Austria

Austrian eighteenth-century gunmaking adhered to tradition. Whereas the major Austrian production centres abandoned the inlaid bone or horn ornamentation of the stock, this style persisted practically unchanged in the provincial centres, especially in the case of firearms provided with wheel-lock mechanism. Simultaneously, flintlock firearms were also produced but these were more French in design. Fine quality firearms made in Austria, and other lands under Habsburg rule, were furnished with silver or gilt-brass mounts. The barrel and the lock were usually decorated with chiselled ornament against a gold ground and the signature on the barrel was inlaid in gold.

Standard production was usually satisfied with simple engraved angular strapwork at the breech and etched scenes on the lockplate.

A certain originality combined with a high degree of technical proficiency was shown in the decoration of guns and pistols made at Ferlach in Carinthia. Very few signed pieces are known: a brace of pistols made by Thomas Hammerlitz deserves a special notice for its individual style of decoration. The barrels, lockplates and mounts are made of heavily gilt bronze, carefully chased. The essential decorative elements here are panels filled with closely set scrolls or conventional leaves, and the same motifs are repeated in the carving of the stock.[37] The Ferlach makers also produced stocks decorated in a more traditional way with mother-of-pearl panels engraved with hunting scenes.

Bohemia

79 During the eighteenth century many skilled gunmakers worked in Prague, amongst them two generations of the Stiffer family. The elder Stifter, employed at the Court of Ferdinand IV, adhered to old-fashioned stocks inlaid with engraved horn panels; his son was more aware of French fashion which, in his case, affected the decoration rather than the stock, still heavy and cumbersome in outline. Some of the finest chiselled ornament found on firearms made by various Prague masters should be attributed to Franz Matzenkopf (d. 1755), who was trained as a gunmaker and worked for a time in Prague. He was also a very gifted medallist but continued to undertake the decoration of luxury firearms at any rate until his appointment as Medallist to the Prince Bishop of Salzburg in 1738.

There was an important firearms production in the provincial town of Eger in the Sudetenland, where the workshop of the Keiner family had been active since the second half of the seventeenth century. They employed with great skill a combined technique of etching and chiselling, achieving an effect of high relief. This technique was widely practised in Eastern Germany and was one of the major contributions of German decorators to the practice of gun ornamentation. It was applied both to lockplates and to barrels. The Keiners did not produce an original style of their own but repeated the currently fashionable motifs of trophies of war, floral scrolls and hunting scenes.

A large-scale production of firearms existed in Carlsbad, which was already then famous as a watering place and which was noted for the manufacture of a wide variety of small steel objects decorated with gold and silver damascening against a blued ground. A characteristic feature of this production was the massive use of gilt brass furniture. A goldsmith must have been responsible for the delicate damascened ornament in the form of running scrolls often found on the barrels of Carlsbad guns and pistols. The colour contrast between walnut stocks, blued and gilt barrel, gilt bronze or brass mounts and bright steel lockplate give them high rank amongst eighteenth-century firearms. The finest Carlsbad guns made by Leopold Becher had, however, steel mounts superbly chiselled with hunting scenes and rococo scrolls against a gold ground.

Germany

In other German-speaking lands sporting rifles were 79
long provided with the wheel-lock mechanism. An innovation was the piercing and chiselling of the cocking spur. This feature had been introduced for practical purposes, but eventually became an element of aesthetic value. The lockplates, of an elongated rectangular shape, were mostly etched; the subjects reflected the passion for the chase or were taken from classical mythology or from the wars against the Turks. As a rule wheel-lock arms were mounted on German-type cheek-stocks, decorated with engraved horn panels and they hardly reflected the changes which had evolved during the previous hundred years.

The evolution of flintlock firearms was strongly influenced by current Paris fashions. In their copying of French fashion the German gunsmiths not only signed their works in the French language, but they also changed their names. Armand Bongarde of Düsseldorf (d. 1727) whose real name was Herman Bongart, alias Bungert, was one of the most ardent propagators of the French style. His chiselled ornament is in the late seventeenth century manner and shows close affinity to the work of Gruché, and like Gruché's his decoration also includes portraits of his wealthy patrons, stylised as heroes of antiquity. Bongart's ornamental compositions not only reflect Paris fashion, but equal the finest products of France. The same applies to Joseph Nies of Mindelheim who was a gunmaker to the Bavarian Court. A pair of flintlock rifles, divided between the Bayrisches Nationalmuseum in Munich and the former Collection of Lord Astor of Hever, made about 1740 for Elector Karl Albrecht, are decorated with exceptional splendour with scenes commemorating incidents in the reign of the Elector.

One of the most important centres of production of high-quality firearms was Suhl in Thuringia. Judging by the number of surviving pieces, the workshops making *de luxe* arms must have been fairly numerous. The Stockmar family, originating from Heidersbach near Suhl, was engaged for thirty

37 The work of Thomas Hamerlitz can be exemplified by a pair of flintlock pistols in the G. Jenkinson Collection: for illustrations see J. F. Hayward, *op. cit.*, II, colour pl. I,

years on the production of magnificently decorated firearms for the personal use of Augustus III, King of Poland and Elector of Saxony. The Stockmars took the designs for their chiselled ornament from the pattern-book of De Marteau. An original style of decoration can be seen on the stocks of a sporting set at the Wallace Collection, London.[38] They are carved with *rocailles* and inset with asymmetrical cartouches of gilded silver, surrounded by small silver stars alternating with stag horn pearls.

Johann Gottfried Kolbe, known for his magnificent air-gun at the Victoria and Albert Museum, London, already mentioned also worked at Suhl. His workshop produced a gun, now in the National Museum in Krakow, signed *Kolbe à Suhl.* Its small size and the Polish and Saxon arms, placed on the escutcheon plate, suggest that this particular piece was made for a lady of the court of Augustus III. The beautifully designed and exquisitely chiselled mounts are probably connected with the Stockmar workshop, since they show the characteristic features of his work.

An anonymous stock carver, probably working in the neighbourhood of Suhl, combined the traditional technique of staghorn intarsia with designs drawn from De Lacollombe's pattern-book. The scrolls, executed elsewhere in silver wire, were in this case formed of thin strips of staghorn–a laborious technique which achieved exceptionally attractive results.[39]

Italy

The interest which Italian firearms aroused during the eighteenth century was to some extent due–as in the preceding century–to the attractiveness of their decoration. During the first three decades of the century Matteo Acqua Fresca (d. 1738) was still working and his style was continued by members of his family after his death.

The work of Michele Lorenzoni (d.1733) of Florence, who started his career as a gunmaker at the end of the seventeenth century,[40] developed along different lines. Like Matteo Acqua Fresca he, too, worked for the Medicis. But, in so far as the main emphasis in firearms produced by Acqua Fresca was laid on decoration, Lorenzoni was more the type of gunsmith-inventor, ever searching for new and more satisfactory technical solutions. The decor of his firearms was therefore plain, yet exquisitely worked, and was entirely based on French pattern-books. From these were derived the elegant profiles of the locks and his harmonious scrollwork composition.

During the eighteenth century Brescia lost her former primacy in firearms production. Even as early as the end of the seventeenth century the stocks were no longer so graceful in shape and the ornament lost something of its appeal by constant repetition of familiar schemes. The old tradition persisted, however, until the French Revolution, when the products of the Versailles factory were largely imitated.

In Tuscany, besides the city of Florence, a number of smaller towns such as Anghiari and Brento developed an individual, though rather retrospective, style. The form of firearms and their chiselled decoration reflected the combined influence of the Acqua Fresca school with French fashion, mainly based on the schemes of Bérain, Jacquinet and Simonin. A detail that survived in Tuscany long after it went out of fashion in France was the elaborately pierced heraldic escutcheon plate. Tuscan firearms usually had stocks made of highly figured walnut wood and were elaborately carved with scrolls and cherubs which were inspired by the Lacollombe pattern-book.[41] A more individual manner of ornamentation with rich variations of theme and technique was devloped by Francesco, Carlo Mario and Carlo Negroni who worked in the second half of the eighteenth century in Brento.

The firearms factory founded in 1757 by Charles III, King of the Two Sicilies, at Torre Annunziata near Naples, developed at first under strong Spanish influence which is shown in the form of the stocks. The peak of development of the factory was reached during the reign of Ferdinand IV. The technique of damascening in gold was also adapted from Spain but it shows more variety than the Spanish prototypes and the damascened designs were sometimes combined with chiselled ornament against a gold ground. An original device was Arabic letters inlaid in gold, showing an unfamiliarity with that alphabet. The barrels were marked with a fleur-de-lis, the cipher *FR* (Fernando Re) over the breech and the incription *FAB:R:DI:NAP* (Fabrica Reale di Napoli) struck on the barrels.

Particularly profuse decoration is found in the work of Michele Battista, who introduced fantastically dressed figures of antique warriors, deities, panoplies of arms and musical instruments into his decorative schemes. The walnut stocks of his pistols were em-

38 No. A. 1119.

39 This kind of decoration is shown on a flintlock gun, dating from the mid eighteenth century and signed on the lock by I. G. Horneffer. The gun is now in the B. Muir Collection, Washington, USA, Ill. J. F. Hayward, *op. cit.*, II, pl. 37 b.

40 The name of Michele Lorenzoni is first mentioned in books of payment of the Saxon Court in 1684 when he was paid by the Elector Johann Georg for a repeating gun.

41 See for illustrations J. F. Hayward, *op. cit.*, II, pl. 45 b, 46, 46.

bellished with inlaid-silver floral scrolls, the details of which were enhanced by delicate engraving. The ornament is of striking richness; the *horror vacui* apparent both in chiselling and silver inlay in stocks is late baroque in style; the rococo style then predominant in both France and Germany had no influence on their design. A remarkable feature of the Neapolitan arms factory was its conservatism as regards decoration. This was only interrupted during the thirteen years of French occupation, which was accompanied by strong French influences, especially of Boutet. French influence was manifested in the use of the French language for signatures and the copying of Empire designs. These latter lasted until the close of the Naples factory and were used until the middle of the nineteenth century without any major modifications.

The stocks of firearms produced in Naples were sometimes overlaid with tortoise shell inlaid with gold. A remarkable example is the fowling piece made for Emperor Charles VI, dated 1722, now in the Kunsthistorisches Museum, Vienna. The stock of this superb specimen is veneered all over with tortoise-shell with an inlaid gold ornament in the Régence style, perfectly adapted to the surface of the stock. An original feature is the use of shell cameos carved with mythological figures, the portrait of the emperor and a view of Naples.

Of lesser importance was the firearms factory established in Turin as early as the seventeenth century by the Kings of Sardinia. This factory was chiefly concerned with the manufacture of military weapons and only a small number of *de luxe* arms were produced there; they are characterised by a symmetrical chiselled ornament applied to a heavily gilt ground, and are evidently derived from de Lacollombe's pattern-book.

Spain

80, 117 In order to understand Spanish eighteenth-century
258 gunmaking it is necessary to remember that in 1701 the Spanish throne passed to the French Bourbons. This opened the way for the introduction of French forms which broke down the decorative conventions indigenous to the Iberian Peninsula. Gun and pistol stocks became lighter and more graceful in outline but the custom persisted of using fruit wood, often with artificially enhanced grain. The decoration of the chiselled steel mounts reached a mastery which survived well into the nineteenth century. On the other hand silver mounts were not, as a rule, so fine, their repertoire consisting of a fairly primitive form of rococo scroll which fell short of the magnificent decoration of this type practised in all the larger manufacturing centres in Europe.

The production of firearms at Ripoll, which had always maintained an individual type, continued in the eighteenth century, but the pierced mounts of the stocks were then more often made of brass or silver sheet. There is a pistol in the National Museum in Krakow, illustrative of this period. The purity of the ornamental design and the stylisation somewhat recall the illuminated initials of romanesque manuscripts. The decoration of other Ripoll pieces did not differ and, as in Brescia, the style lingered on in a mechanical repetition of long-established decorative formulae.

The short episode of Napoleon's rule did not cause Spanish gunmakers to adopt the French style of Boutet. On the contrary, as though in spontaneous reaction against French influence, they returned to the traditional Spanish ornament.

Flanders and Holland

The dynamic expansion of firearms production in Liège is thought to have occured at the beginning of the eighteenth century when Liège came to the forefront of firearms production in Europe. Most of the output was of military weapons, but a considerable quantity of fine quality pieces was also produced. The brass foundries which had been in operation since the Middle Ages were probably responsible for the more frequent use of brass in the production of barrels, lockplates and mounts than was usual elsewhere. In the late seventeenth and eighteenth centuries designs were often taken from Paris pattern books, especially those of De Lacollombe. The Liège firearms were more massive in shape and often rougher in execution, nevertheless the finer
pieces were embellished with steel mounts chiselled 349
against a heavily gilt ground. The steel-chiseller who carried out this type of work in Liège was employed by various gunmakers, such as Daniel Thiermay, Henry Devillers and Claude Niquet. Devillers sometimes mounted his pistols with silver stocks engraved with rococo motifs.[42] The decoration was mostly eclectic and based on the French examples. It should not be forgotten that, owing to increasing factory mass production of arms based on new economic principles, the fine art of individual gunmaking began to decline in the second half of the eighteenth century.

During the eighteenth century Liège produced small pocket-pistols with iron or brass stocks imitating contemporary English products. Better quality specimens were made, amongst others, by Claude Niquet, and are neatly decorated with rococo scrollwork chiselled against a gilt background. Pistols of

42 There is in the Victoria and Albert Museum, London, a pair of flintlock pistols, signed on the locks *Devillers à Liège*. Although the decoration is entirely in the contemporary French fashion, the design of the butt-caps resembles that used in England at that period.

this kind were intended for the English market and in order to sell them more easily, English signatures and proof marks were faked on them.

In the second half of the eighteenth century Liège stockmakers sometimes carved the pommels of pistols in the form of a bird's head, a type which is found also in France and Germany. On the whole these pommels were carved fairly crudely, but a few have details worked with great care, ebony or glass being used for the eyes of birds.

Dutch decorative art, which had reached its peak at the end of the seventeenth century, began to decline, owing to the mechanical copying of French forms and a lowered standard of execution. Mounts of gilt bronze resembled those made in Liège and the Dutch makers may have used mounts made there. Dutch firearms looked particularly attractive owing to the custom of gilding the metal parts, but this was often so thin that only faint traces of it remain on surviving examples. More original features were developed in the second half of the century in the production of firearms destined for the colonial market. These, like their English counterparts, were decorated with semi-Oriental designs such as crescents, trophies of Oriental arms and figures of Turks. These motifs were dictated by fantasy rather than copied from Oriental works of art, which had been long popular in Europe. A snaphance gun and pair of flintlock pistols, executed by Thomson Zoon in 1794 for the Sultan of Morocco and now in Musée de l'Armée, Paris, provide an example of this florid style.

Sweden

Amongst the Scandinavian countries Sweden developed the most active firearms production. Even so she failed to achieve individuality, possibly because she was exposed to the interaction of powerful French and German influences. While the firearms made by provincial gunmakers hardly rose above the level of folk art, the chiselled, damascened or engraved decoration on arms made in Stockholm rises far above this. Their high quality was due to the practice of sending promising young apprentices abroad at the king's expense. Most of them went to Paris where they learned the technique of decoration of firearms. A State School of Design, founded in 1756 in Stockholm, was to have served the same purpose, but was in existence too short a time to exert a real influence.

The qualifications of native gunsmiths do not appear to have been satisfactory, since the Court appointment of Royal gunmaker was usually granted to a foreigner. Among these was Johann Meidinger, a native of Germany, who himself executed the gold inlay designs and inscriptions on his firearms, while the mounts, cast and chased in silver, were made for him by one of Stockholm's silversmiths. Johann Weiss, another foreigner, combined the profession of gunsmith with the ability to execute the decoration.

Russia

The most important centre of firearms production was Tula. Since the end of the sixteenth century this little town was famous for its silver articles, traditionally decorated with niello work. The cannon-foundry, established by Tsar Boris Godunow, was converted in 1705 by Peter the Great into a small-arms factory. Alongside the production of service arms, the factory was required to produce sporting rifles, fowling pieces, small-swords and hunting-swords for the use of the Imperial Court. In the years 1720–50 the Tula industry was developed on a cottage basis. In accordance with the desire of Peter the Great to Europeanise life and art in Russia, the factory engaged foreign craftsmen–mostly from Germany and the Baltic countries–to propagate Western ideas. There were no Frenchmen among them, which is curious, since it was the Parisian fashion that definitely set the tone of the production in Tula. The foreign gunmakers, however, were neither outstanding nor numerous enough to be able to impose an absolutely Western style on the native Russian craftsmen. In many examples produced at Tula the Western ornament took on a different flavour, losing at the hands of local Russian workers its logic and consistency of composition. This is exemplified in a gun, now in the Tøjhusmusèum in Copenhagen, dated 1747, where the decoration of the stock is copied exactly from a page from the pattern-book of Nicolas Guérard depicting a number of unrelated motifs from which it was intended that the carver should make his choice.

Tula barrels often carried a characteristic type of decoration consisting of a symmetrically arranged network of interlacing ribbon and scrollwork. On some specimens the mounts and lockplates are made of gilt bronze. They follow in design and execution the type used in Carlsbad, probably brought to Tula by some immigrant Bohemian craftsman.

Generally speaking the decoration on many firearms produced at Tula, laboriously chiselled on metal parts and inlaid in silver in the stocks, is very
attractive, though it loses a little on closer inspection. **266**
Among the most skilled Tula artists was A. Leontiev, both a gunsmith and a steel chiseller, who decorated firearms, hilts of the court swords and mounts for Court furniture and carriages.[43] During the last years of the century the technique of chiselling in which the decorator needed a feeling for sculptural forms as well as a trained hand, was

43 A flintlock fowling piece, now in the Victoria and Albert Museum; illustrated and described by C. Blair 'Archip Leontiev's Gun', *Connoisseur*, vol. CXLIX, p. 116.

350 *Above* Plate of designs by De Marteau, dated 1749, added to De Lacollombe's *Nouveaux Desseins d'Arquebuseries*, signed *De Marteau Fecit*. Victoria & Albert Museum, London.

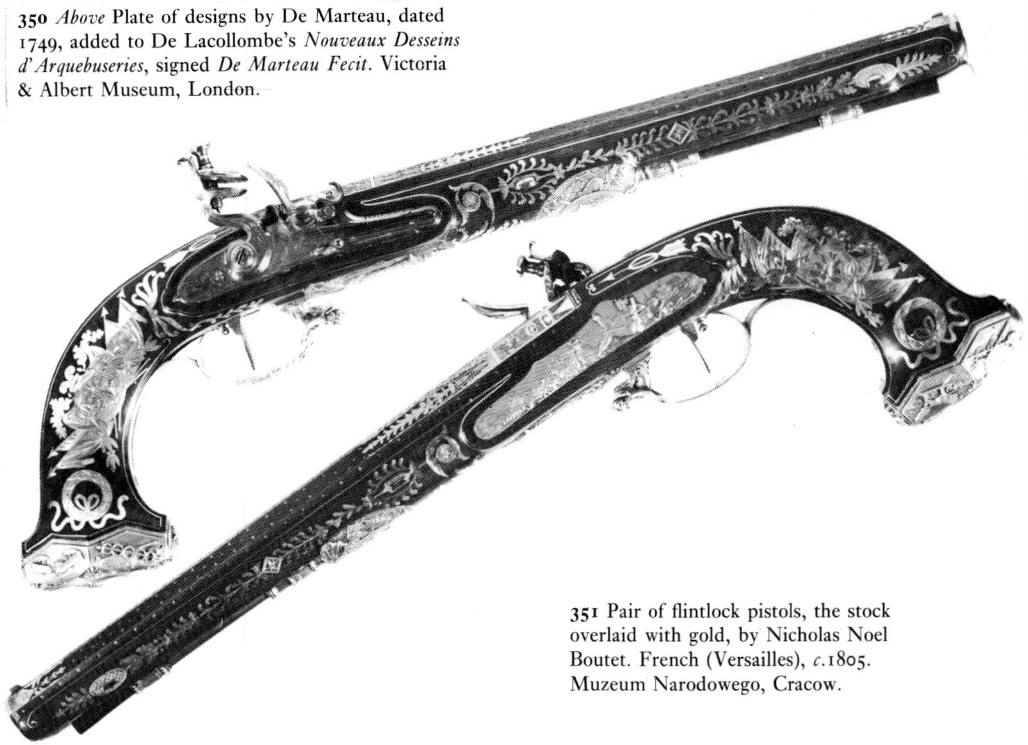

351 Pair of flintlock pistols, the stock overlaid with gold, by Nicholas Noel Boutet. French (Versailles), *c.*1805. Muzeum Narodowego, Cracow.

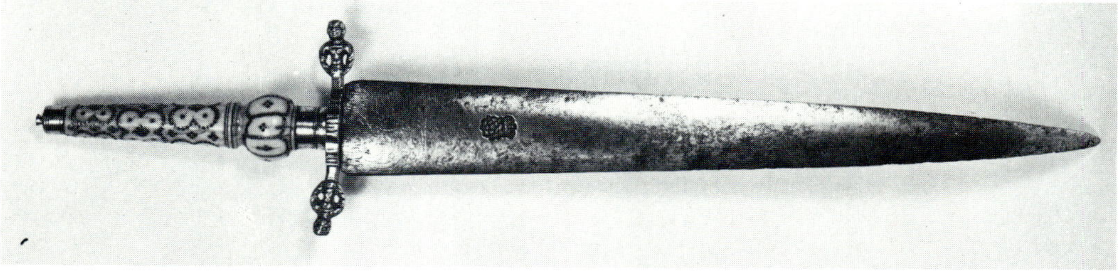

352 *Top* Bandoleer, leather covered with velvet (restored), the mounts of gilt bronze. German, early seventeenth century. Victoria & Albert Museum, London.

353 *Above* Plug bayonet, the handle of ivory decorated with silver piqué. English, late seventeenth century. Victoria & Albert Museum, London.

354 *Far left* Powder flask for a *Tschinke*. Wood inlaid with brass and mother-of-pearl. Polish (Teschen), *c*.1650. Victoria & Albert Museum, London.

355 *Left* Cartridge box, embossed iron. German (Brunswick), *c*.1550. Victoria & Albert Museum, London.

abandoned and replaced by incrustations of coloured metals, tin, silver, copper and vari-coloured gold. This technique not only contributed a great deal to the richness of the decoration but became a dominant feature of Russian firearms of the late eighteenth century.

The end of the eighteenth century witnessed a certain decline in the quality of the productions of the Tula factories, due possibly to a decrease in the number of immigrant craftsmen from the West and a greater demand for military firearms. Exceptional pieces of the highest quality could still be made, such as the double-barrelled flintlock breech-loading gun made for Catherine the Great by Ivan Lialin, stocked in ivory with mounts and barrel damascened in gold with neo-classical motifs and especially designed to the taste of the empress.

St. Petersburg was another centre producing *armes de luxe*. In addition to various anonymous gunsmiths, Johann Adolf Grecke, the son of a Stockholm gunsmith, was working there in the late eighteenth century. While Lialin was a representative of the neo-classical style, Grecke still adhered to the out-of-date rococo designs in the decoration of a blunderbuss for Catherine the Great[44] and a fowling piece for Stanislaw August Poniatowski, the last King of Poland.[45]

North America

From an artistic point of view firearms produced in North America before the nineteenth century are of little interest. In the seventeenth century arms were imported from Europe, chiefly from England. Not till the eighteenth century was the production of Kentucky rifles developed in Pennsylvania on a large scale. These rifles, in their early phase, had a thick, strongly constructed butt with a wooden patch-box cover, a heavy trigger-guard and a barrel of large calibre. The decoration was limited to a little carving on the stock and plain ornament engraved on brass mounts.[46] Owing to the German origin of the great number of gunsmiths, the stock of the Kentucky rifle resembled the contemporary German type.

The years after the War of Independence brought impressive changes. A reduction in calibre and a lengthening of the barrel, the increased use of the German form of double-set triggers, accompanied by the almost exclusive employment of gunlocks imported from Birmingham characterised the Pennsylvania long rifle of the so-called 'Golden Age'. Although the practical performance of firearms remained the chief consideration, the heavy stocks were replaced by more slender forms and were more elegant in outline, being modelled on contemporary English sporting guns. The change also affected the decoration, the stocks were now carved with greater care with rococo compositions which had already been abandoned in Europe, and the pierced silver or brass sheet ornament of the stocks now became more sophisticated.[47] Although in some specimens these ornaments are very neat, they never equal European luxury arms either in artistic inventiveness or refined composition. The poverty of the decoration, applied to the Pennsylvania rifles, was due to different principles of production and the emergence in the New World of a different society from a cultural and economic point of view. While in Europe firearms often served exclusively for presentation purposes and were correspondingly elaborate in design, in America concern with function rendered decoration of secondary importance.

The Nineteenth Century

Although the greater part of nineteenth century firearms production is of exclusively technical interest, and the decoration–if any–is restrained and unimaginative, there are a number of pieces that are worthy of detailed consideration. A pattern-book, published by Lucas in Paris in 1829, did not illustrate any novelties either in the vocabulary of ornament or in composition. The neo-classical decoration was repeated until historic styles came into favour. The revived styles of the nineteenth century were not invariably insipid imitations but often displayed quite interesting stylistic advances. The artists who decorated the firearms of this period achieved an exceptionally high level of craftsmanship and their works often rival in quality the finest works of earlier times. This is exemplified by the firearms made and decorated by Euzebio Zuolaga of Madrid. Connected with the Court of Ferdinand VII, he worked simultaneously as gunsmith and chiseller. His style was formed by his training in the Paris workshop of Le Page and at the factory at St Etienne. In his decoration he introduced the neo-Renaissance motifs which were then coming into fashion. A creative developer of the style of three centuries before rather than an imitator, Zuloaga

136, 269

44 The gun is now in the Wallace Collection, London, Cat. No. A. 1124, ill. pl. 178.

45 The piece is now at the Polish Army Museum, Warsaw. The barrel is signed : *Fait à St. Petersburg l'année 1786 par Jean Adolph Grecke Maître des Armes de la Venerie de S. M. Imperiale.*

46 There is in the Joe Kindig Collection, York, Pennsylvania, an example of an early type of the Kentucky rifle, made *c.* 1770.

47 See for illustration J. F. Hayward, *op. cit.*, II, pl. 85 a, b.

combined purity of design with exceptional excellence of craftsmanship on a scale which was rarely to be found in works of the nineteenth century.

One important source of inspiration was a pattern-book, issued in 1856 by the Belgian publisher, Ch. Claesen. His designs were well suited for the decoration of all kinds of firearms including the then popular saloon-pistols made for indoor practice. Characteristic of these sheets, which were drawn by leading firearms designers of Liège and Brussels, amongst them Boussart, Cloes, Donnay and Falloise, is their romantic, historicising style. Though often neither logical nor consistent in composition the designs are opulent and picturesque. Gothic motifs, such as pinnacles and trefoil-headed arches, were often mixed up with hunting scenes in typical Victorian taste. Such designs circulated widely throughout the main centres of gunmaking in Europe and can be found on firearms produced by Gauvain in Paris, Mangeot in Brussels, Lebeda Frères in Prague, Chaumont and Lemille in Liège. The various international exhibitions of the century gave to the gunmakers, as to every other kind of craftsmen, the opportunity to display firearms of the most complex designs and elaborate finish. These were invariably accompanied by cases made with as much care and skill as the weapons they contained. The cases in turn had embroidered, and even tasseled silk, covers. The pistols were usually rifled duelling-pistols, half-stocked in ebony or finely figured walnut. A typical pair in the Kienbusch Collection, Philadelphia, made by H. Mangeot of Brussels has steel mounts inlaid in gold with subjects taken from popular nursery rhymes. One of the most famous makers of these duelling pistols was Gastinne Renette who worked in Paris until the end of the century.

Although aesthetically the firearms made in the Samuel Colt factory at Hartford and New York offer little of interest, it is essential to refer to their stylistic characteristics. The Colt was, in the first place, a typical mass product and its design was determined exclusively by practical considerations. The barrels were for the most part of octagonal section and the grips were of walnut. A certain amount of simple and unimaginative decoration was applied to the cylinder and its massive frame. This was usually confined to floral patterns or consisted of battle scenes, the composition of which was as unsophisticated as possible. Scenes derived from the history of battles with the Indians and inspired by the adventurous life on the Western frontiers alternated with scenes from a sea-battle of 1843. To eliminate the painstaking technique of engraving, the decoration was applied mechanically by means of rollers. It is obvious that this type of decoration offers very little from the artistic point of view, yet it was of value because it enabled the gunsmith to embellish his products without the help of a professional engraver.

In addition to the standard productions, the Colt workshops produced a limited number of luxury pieces,[48] with engraved decoration in most cases signed by W. L. Ormsby. Small pocket-pistols were very often provided with ivory grips, the colour of which made a pleasant contrast with the polished metal frames. The barrels and frames of more expensive Colts were sometimes encrusted with gold but, except in the very finest examples, the design of this decoration was usually uninspired and only rarely equalled the value of the material used. The general appearance of this type of Colt was effective, and this was the only aim of the producers. There is, however, in the National Army Museum, Sandhurst, an ornate example of the Navy Colt, the decoration of which is damascened in gold with delicate scrolls and flowers on the barrel and frame and with a subtle network of interlacing circles and crosses on the cylinder. Known as *Koft-gari* work, originating in India (and Birmingham) the designers showed a lack of imagination in their repetitive motifs.[49]

During the third quarter of the nineteenth century a considerable number of *de luxe* rifles and pistols were produced in the United States. They were intended for individual purchasers, and many of these firearms were sold to Mexico. The grips of pistols and stocks of rifles were often covered with ivory or mother-of-pearl overlay, and the barrels were enriched with etched or damascened ornament. The stocks were usually carved in bas-relief with the American eagle amidst trophies of arms. Among the American artists responsible for the often fine engraved work on firearms at this time were L. D. Nimschke (1834–1904), Gustav Young, and members of the Ulrich family. Examples of this are a rifle made by B. T. Henry for Maximilian of Mexico and a target rifle made about 1876 by John Meunier of Milwaukee; the stock of the latter piece is carved with finely drawn vine and oak leaves and an eagle on the butt. The decoration in this case is supplemented by silver inlay on the stock and by scrolls damascened in gold on the barrel.[50]

A clientele for luxury guns still exists among the Arabian and Texas oil maganates. Decoration has remained, even in the twentieth century, distinctly conservative, and pattern-books of ornament produced in the mid-nineteenth century are still to be found in the gun decorators' shops.

48 See *Samuel Colt Presents. A Loan Exhibition of Presentation Percussion Colt Firearms*, Wadsworth Atheneum, Hartford, USA, 1962.

49 Ill. by Dudley Pope, *op. cit.*, p. 185.

50 Ill. by L. H. Petersen, *The Treasury of the Gun*, New York, 1962, p. 239.

CHAPTER EIGHTEEN

Firearms Accessories

H.L. Blackmore

88 The implements and accessories necessary to mani-
352-66 pulate and fire the earliest firearms are described in Chapter 1. Basic implements like the ramrod and the powder-flask remained in use until the introduction of the metal cartridge, but with each change of ignition system, and the replacement of the muzzle-loader by the breech-loader, modifications were made and new accessories invented. For the sake of convenience these have been described in alphabetical order.

Ball-drawer (for) Ball Screw Tireball

Described in Garrard's *The Art of Warre* (1591) and Edward Davis's *England's Trainings* (1619) as a 'tyreball' or 'tireball'[1] the ball drawer was a pointed screw used to extract a ball which had become jammed in a gun barrel. It was fastened to the end of the ramrod and screwed directly into the soft lead of the ball, the base of the screw being shaped into a sphere or disc the diameter of the bore to prevent the screw from moving off-centre. This ball-like swelling was often pierced with a hole through which a lever could be inserted to help free the tool from the ramrod after use. The earliest surviving specimens date to the second half of the eighteenth century.

Bandoleer

19,352 The bandoleer was a leather strap or baldric hung diagonally across the body from one shoulder. On the strap were suspended by strings, or thongs, about a dozen cylindrical boxes each containing a charge of gunpowder. Wood was the most popular material used in their construction, although copper, tin, pewter and leather are known to have been used. On the plain military types of bandoleer the chargers or boxes were either painted or covered with leather. In 1646 the bandoleer makers of London received an order for 1500 bandoleers of which the boxes were to be 'Of wood with whole bottomes to bee turned within and not boared, ye heads to be of wood & to be laid in Oyle, (vizt) three times on & to be coloured blew' all at a price of *1s. 8d.* each.[2] For special guards or for the personal equipment of a nobleman, the bandoleer was given a decoration in keeping with the rest of the attire. A bandoleer in the Tower of London[3] is covered with rich velvet and embellished with gilded mounts.

The English word bandoleer, bandalier, etc. is derived from the early French *bandouillere*, which may have originated in the Spanish word *Banda*, a military sash or band. These were worn by the Bandouliers, a bandit tribe in the Pyrenees. George Gascoigne in his *Flowers, Hearbes, Weedes, the Fruites of Warre, etc* of 1587 refers to them 'as Bandolliers for who in mountaines dwelles'. The bandoleer with powder boxes, however, is generally believed to have been developed in the Low Countries during the first half of the sixteenth century and what appears to be the earliest recorded illustration of the device appears in the *Triumph of Maximilian*, first printed in 1526. A woodcut[4] shows a group of handgunners, some of whom are wearing a string of small boxes round their necks and shoulders. It was usually worn in association with the matchlock. To complete the equipment necessary a ball bag and a small powder flask for priming were also suspended from the bandoleer.

Although the boxes were a convenient way of measuring the right amount of powder for a gun, and the weight of powder was well distributed, the bandoleer's collection of dangling objects was a serious impediment to free movement, made an objectionable rattling noise on the march, and was liable to cause an accidental explosion. These inconveniences and the growing popularity of the paper cartridge led to the gradual abandonment of the bandoleer.

Barrel Gauge *see* Calibre Gauge

Bayonet

By tradition the bayonet is said to be named after

---

1 The word was also used to describe the surgeon's instrument for extracting a bullet from a wound (see Cotgrave's *Dictionary*, 1611).

2 H. L. Blackmore, *British Military Firearms*, London 1961, p. 25.

3 No. XIII-91.

4 Pl. 126 in the Dover Publications edition of 1964.

Bayonne, a town in France noted for its cutlery. Des Accords writing in *Les Bigarrures du Seigneur des Accordz* in 1583 spoke of *bayonettes de Bayonne* as one would speak now of Solingen swords of Sheffield scissors. The word may be a diminutive of the old French *bayon* or *baion* 'arrow or shaft or a cross bow', or it may be derived from the Italian *bayonetta* 'Little John'– a possible nickname for a dagger. Exactly when this dagger was first used in conjunction with a firearm is not known. Cotgrave, in his *Dictionary* (1611), refers to the bayonet as 'a kind of small flat pocket-dagger, furnished with knives; or a great knife to hang at the girdle like a dagger'. It is probable that by this date the bayonet was already being carried by sportsmen as a dagger with a cylindrical handle which in an emergency could be jammed in the muzzle of the gun converting it into a spear for personal defence against the attack, say, of a wild boar. This type of bayonet, now known as a
353 plug bayonet, was retained for sporting purposes until the middle of the nineteenth century, especially in Spain. The portrait of Charles IV of Spain by Francisco Goya (*c.* 1800) in the Capodimonte Museum, Naples, shows the monarch holding a sporting gun and wearing a plug bayonet on his waist belt. Many of these later plug bayonets have handles which can be unscrewed and reversed for the convenience of the sportsman, and some are of outstanding decorative quality. A chiselled and gilded steel bayonet in the Victoria and Albert Museum signed *JACOBUS LAVAU INVENIT ET SCULPTIT MADRID* is an example of the latter.

The hunting knife or bayonet does not appear to have been adapted for military use until the second quarter of the seventeenth century. The first reference to it as such is made by Marechal de Puysegur who describes in his *Mémoires* how in 1647 the soldiers under his command in the Netherlands 'did not carry swords but had bayonets with handles a foot in length and blades as long as the handles, the ends of which could be put into the barrels of the muskets in order to defend themselves after they had fired'.

In 1663 a quantity of 'short swords or Bayonetts' which had been brought back from Dunkirk were cleaned and repaired for the British Army by some London cutlers.[5] Later in the year two references to British soldiers in Tangiers[6] drawing their 'short daggers' suggest that the bayonets may have been issued to the garrison there. Military writers like Sir James Turner were now recommending their use. In 1671 the French regiments of fusiliers and grenadiers were officially issued with bayonets and the following year Prince Rupert's Regiment of Dragoons in England were similarly equipped. The new supplementary weapon was rapidly taken into general use, in some cases being of similar structure to a sword, with a long cutting blade and a knuckle-bow.

The plug bayonet, however, had several disadvantages. Once inserted in the barrel it prevented the gun from being fired; if it was thrust in too hard it was difficult to withdraw; if it did not fit tight enough it could be easily dislodged or left in the body of an enemy. In the last quarter of the seventeenth century several improved methods of fixing the bayonet were tried. One method was to attach to the bayonet handle two rings which slipped over the muzzle of the gun. Alternatively the rings could be attached to the side of the barrel and the bayonet thrust in these instead of the muzzle. There are at least two examples of seventeenth-century flintlock muskets which are equipped with folding bayonets, the base of the blade being hinged to the fore-end of the stock so that in one position it lies under the barrel out of the way, and in the other sticks out beyond the muzzle. The folding bayonet was to become popular in the late eighteenth and early nineteenth centuries as an essential adjunct of the blunderbuss and the

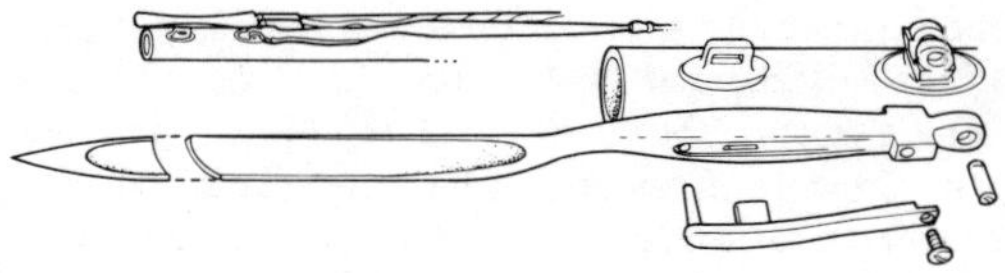

Folding bayonet and attachment.

pocket-pistol. It was patented in France in 1718 by M. Deschamps and in England in 1781 by John Waters.

The most common form of bayonet fitting, which was introduced in the last quarter of the seventeenth century, was the socket handle with a zigzag slot which fitted over the muzzle and locked over a sight-cum-stud. As time went on various improvements

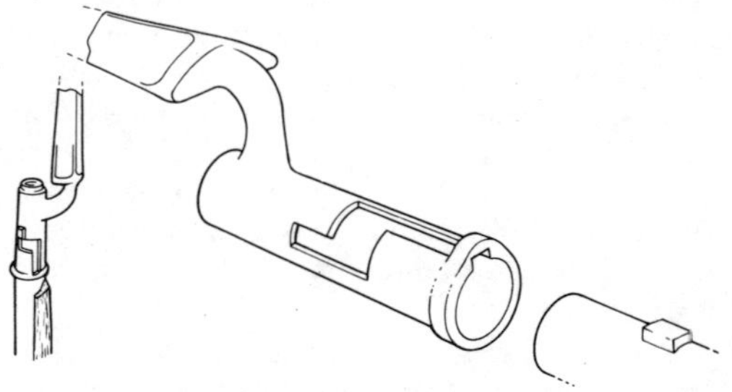

Brown Bess socket bayonet.

5 H. L. Blackmore, *British Military Firearms*, London, 1961, p. 31.

6 British Library. Sloane MSS. 1957-60.

were made to the socket bayonet. The bottom edge of the sleeve of the handle was reinforced against wear and damage and some means of retaining the slot in the correct fixed position was applied. This took the shape of a spring fastener, or in later years a rotating locking collar. The blade of the socket bayonet, a sharp pointed one of triangular section, once established, remained virtually unaltered until its disuse in the late nineteenth century.

In the second half of the eighteenth century the increasing use of firearms of shorter length–carbines and rifles–led to experiments with longer blades. For a short period in the 1780s long spear bayonets were tried on some breech-loading carbines in England and in Austria, but the main result was the introduction of sword bayonets with proper handles (usually made of brass) and long, straight, cutting blades. The usual method of attaching these to the rifle was by a slotted cavity in the handle with a concealed spring catch which clipped on to a bayonet-bar brazed to the side of the barrel muzzle. Once this type of bayonet was brought in– it was used extensively by the German Jäger companies and the British Rifle Corps–different kinds of blade began to appear.

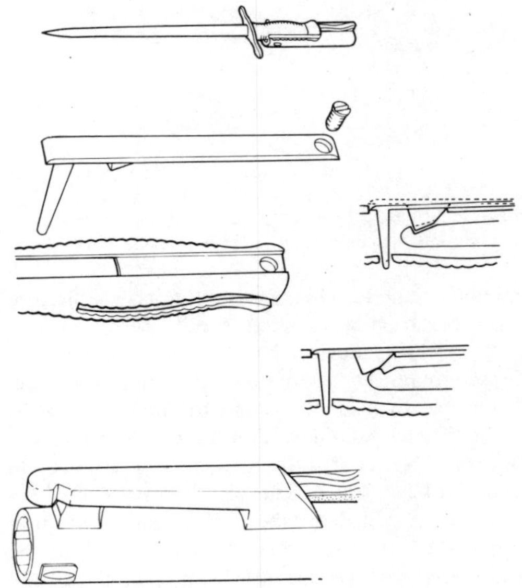

Sword-bayonet with details of spring clip for attachment to Baker rifle.

The saw-back blade of the seventeenth-century hunting sword was re-introduced for the benefit of Engineer and Pioneer units. In the middle of the nineteenth century sword bayonets with long sabre blades were adopted for Norwegian and Russian rifles. In India General Jacob adapted a full-size

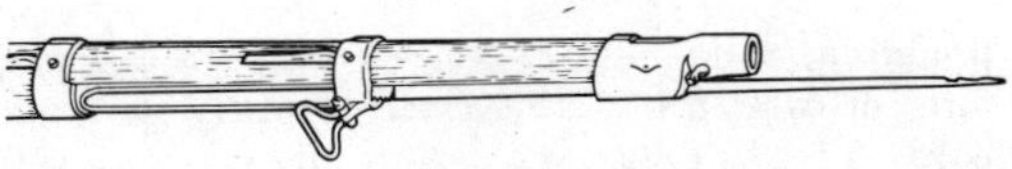

Sliding bayonet (Prussian 1854 Model 54).

sword with a 30 in blade to clip on the double barrels of his rifles. There were freak bayonets like the US models of 1873 (trowel or spade) and 1896 (bolo knife). The Italian army also revived the old sliding bayonet idea. Such a bayonet, contained in a tube under the barrel, against the pressure of a spiral spring, had been patented in France by Deschamps as early as 1718. After the First World War when massed bayonet charges were a feature of trench warfare, the bayonet was shortened and given a purely supporting role. Today it is primarily an all-purpose knife that can be attached to a gun in an emergency.

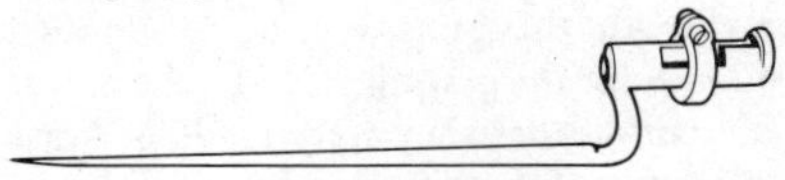

Bayonet with locking ring and socket.

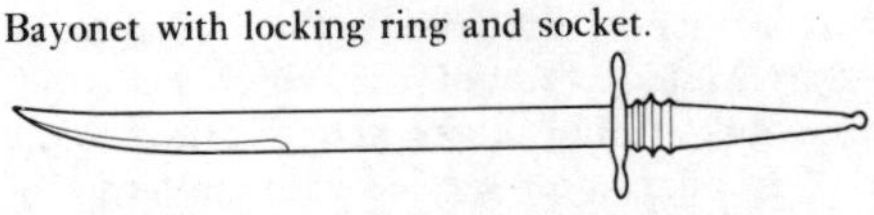

English plug bayonet, late seventeenth century.

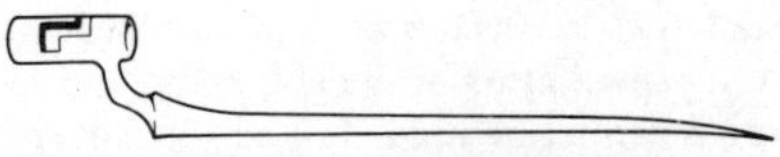

English triangular-section socket bayonet.

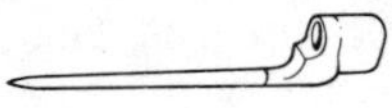

English Mark II spike bayonet for No. 4 rifle.

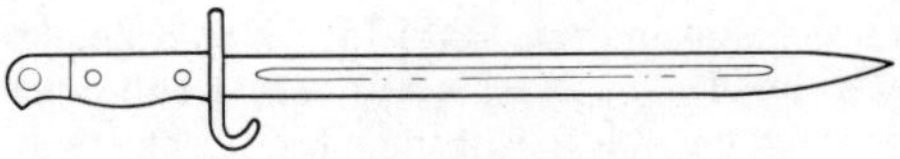

English sword bayonet nineteenth-twentieth centuries.

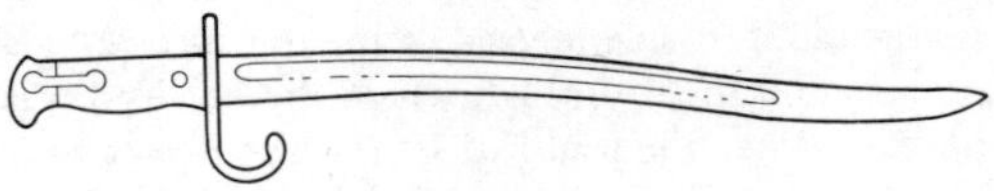

Nineteenth-century French sword bayonet.

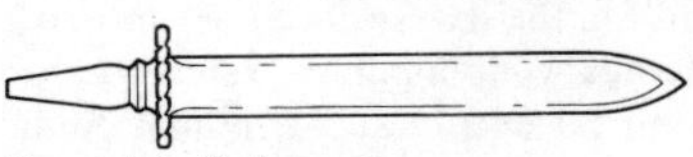

Spanish knife bayonet.

Bullet or Ball Bag

Before the introduction of the cartridge, and afterwards where the use of loose powder and ball was preferred, as in most muzzle-loading rifles, some form of container was necessary to carry the lead balls. The ball bag was nearly always made of leather with a simple draw-string fastening. Illustrations of the seventeenth-century musketeer show the bag attached either to the strap of the bandoleer or to the waist belt. If the *porte tache* (q.v.) was part of the equipment the bullet bag was fastened to it. Sometimes to reduce the number of accessories the ball bag was attached to the side of the priming flask. The difficulties of the matchlock user, with his hands already holding other items, trying to extract a ball from the bag can be imagined. Most military writers of the time advised the soldier to carry a spare ball in his mouth.

Bullet Mould

As early as *c.* 1375 the English Wardrobe Accounts (see Chapter 1) reveal that guns were being supplied with bullet moulds for the casting of lead bullets. But apart from a mention that they were made of brass there is no indication of their design. In 1497 a list of military stores sent to Scotland for the English army included six 'Moldes of stone for castying of pellettes'. When the bulk of these stores were returned to the Tower of London after service with the army of Henry VII, they included four baskets of 'Moldes for pellettes'.[7] These were obviously intended for the casting of shot for the 'hakebusses of iron' which formed the only small arms in the shipment, but in what proportion cannot be judged. The accounts of Henry VIII, however, make it clear that by the beginning of his reign each handgun was accompanied by its own powder flask and mould. Thus, in 1512, the merchant Peter Corsy supplied 420 handguns with 420 'botelles and moldes for the same' at 9 shillings each.[8]

The wreck of Henry VIII's man-of-war, the *Mary Rose*, which sank in 1545, has yielded a few examples of these moulds made of soapstone, a substance easily carved but able to withstand heat. Each mould consists of a square block of soapstone which has been sliced in half. A spherical cavity has been cut inside and this is connected to the top surface by a funnelled channel through which the hot lead was poured. When the lead had set the two halves were pulled apart, the surplus metal being cut off the resultant ball.

From the middle of the sixteenth century onwards there are numerous contemporary references to bullet moulds, but no detailed descriptions. Some other surviving moulds which date to the end of the century are of a curiously complex construction. They are formed by two or three pairs of leaves hinged together, each containing a row of cavities with pouring apertures or a trough on top. Not only were shot of different sizes catered for, but the shape of the shot varies, being round, pear-shaped, conical or cylindrical.[9] A third variety of mould is illustrated in Book VII of Georgius Agricola's *De Re Metallica,* first published in Basel in 1556, but written some years earlier. Agricola describes it as 'a pair of iron tongs about a foot long; its iron claws are so formed that when pressed together they are egg-shaped; each claw contains a hollow cup, and when the claws are closed there extends upwards from the cup a passage . . .'[10] Agricola's mould was designed for the purpose of obtaining lead balls for assaying, but the same pattern was to become the most popular of all bullet moulds.

During the seventeenth century moulds became simpler. The multi-leaved type with its variety of projectile shapes seems to have disappeared and was replaced by a plain two-leaved pattern, still sometimes designed for a number of different sizes. These

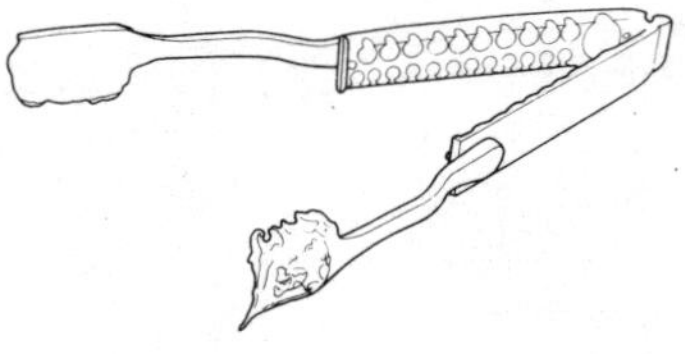

Brass gang mould for casting balls of different sizes. French, late sixteenth century. Private Collection.

moulds, made for ships or army units, are often of heavy construction, their long handles being provided with a locking device. Early in the same century the tong or pincer-type mould became more common. It was usually made to cast one ball only, but a well-made French example, now in the Metropolitan Museum, New York (No. 14.25.1439) is arranged to cast four balls. The handles are also provided with a pair of cutting blades to shear off the lead tail or sprue left on the ball when the mould is opened. From the beginning of the eighteenth century nearly all the pincer-type bullet moulds, even of the smallest size, incorporated a sprue cutter. In the second half of the century, when cased pistols and guns came into vogue, a pincer-type mould was always included in

7 M. Oppenheim (Ed.), *Naval Accounts and Inventories*, London, 1896, p. 122.

8 Letters and Papers of Henry VIII, Vol. I., p. 670, No. 1463.

9 H. L. Blackmore, *Guns and Rifles of the World*, London 1965, No. 844.

10 English edition (ed. H. G. and L. H. Hoover), London, 1912, pp. 239-40.

the accessories. Many of the hinged-leaf moulds of this time had an ingenious movable plate containing the pouring trough and holes which sheared off the sprues automatically when the mould was opened.

During the nineteenth century more attention was paid to the accuracy of the mould, the cavity being carefully machined out with a circular milling head, or cherry bit, from a solid piece of iron. Great care was also taken to ensure that the two pieces of the mould made a perfect join. By the middle of the century the bullet-mould had once more to undertake the casting of some strange shapes ranging from comparatively simple belted balls to cylindro-conoidal, Minié-type bullets with a base cavity, which necessitated the insertion of a separate plug in the mould. At the same time the introduction of mass production methods of gun-barrel manufacture and the standardisation of calibres meant that one mould could serve a number of guns. For military purposes, therefore, the individual bullet mould was soon superseded by the bullet-casting machine, and with the advent of the metal-cased, self-priming cartridge the military bullet mould became obsolete. It has remained in civilian use for those who wish to avoid the expense of factory ammunition by hand-loading, and for the muzzle-loading enthusiast.

Calibre Gauge

In the sixteenth and seventeenth centuries, because of the bewildering diversity of gun sizes and the great variance in weights and measures between one town or country and another, artillerymen were obliged to use calipers, ring-gauges and other instruments to measure shot and bore sizes. The same state of affairs prevailed in small arms, but because the practice had developed for each gun to have its own mould and bullets, there was not the same need for a constant check on measurements. In the eighteenth century, when the bulk casting of military ammunition became customary, armourers and storekeepers found it necessary to employ some form of gauge to verify the calibre of gun-barrels and bullets in their care. One of the earliest dated specimens of gauges of this period is in the Tøjhusmuseum, Copenhagen.[11] It consists of several brass plates pivoted together at one end. One plate is tapered for insertion in the muzzle of a gun barrel and is marked with horizontal lines giving a reading in bullets to the pound. The others are pierced with circular holes corresponding in diameter to bullets of various sizes. The cover plate is marked with the owner's name and the date, *IACOB NELSEN BIRK/ANNO 1740*. A similar set of gauges made for Colonel Albert Borgard of the Royal Artillery in *c.* 1730 engraved *COLL. BORGARD'S GAUGES FOR SMALL ARMES W. DEAN FECIT* is in the Tower of London Armouries (No. XII.138).

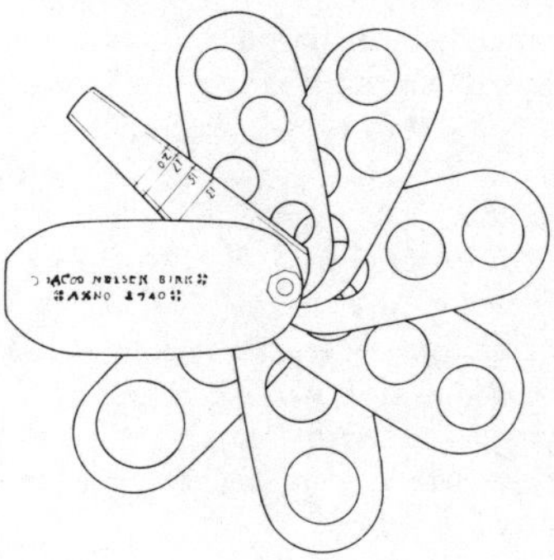

Calibre gauge, signed IACOB NELSEN. BIRK/ANNO 1740. Tøjhusmuseet, Copenhagen.

In the nineteenth century bullet-moulds were generally stamped with the number of their size, and themselves formed a handy gauge to bullet size. The tapered-plate barrel gauge, however, became quite common as a convenient pocket instrument, giving readings in inches, millimetres or bullets to the pound as desired. For workshop or storeroom use more substantial gauges of solid conical form were made. For revolvers, where the small depth of the chamber prevented the insertion of a long tapered instrument, small plugs of different sizes, strung on a chain, were used.

Cap-carrier

Although the percussion-cap became the most popular form of percussion primer, its small size made the act of priming an inconvenient and, in cold or wet weather, a difficult task. Unless a magazine primer was incorporated on the gun some form of container which the ordinary soldier or sportsman could carry and use easily was necessary. Just after the adoption of the percussion-cap system by the British Army, a small brass box with a nozzle opening, invented by Lieutenant Margary, was given a brief trial by cavalry units in 1841. But none of these devices seemed to work with the military, and the majority of soldiers carried their spare caps in leather boxes attached to their equipment. Various kinds of cap-carriers or primers, however, were designed and patented for the use of sportsmen. There were two main kinds. One was a flat rectangular box made of brass whose caps could be ejected from the open pronged end by a platform under pressure by a spring or by manual operation. The other and most popular type was a flat circular box in which the caps were moved round by a spiral spring until ejected from a protuberant nozzle.

11 No. B.1364.

It was the invention of Henry Brownjohn, a wine and spirit merchant of Basingstoke, who appears to have made a patent application in 1830 which was never finalised. Makers' names found stamped on these cappers include Thomas Sykes or Sykes & Sons, Geo. & J. W. Hawksley, all of Sheffield, England; Boche of Paris; Beetz of Vienna; and J. Johnson & Son of Paterson, N.J., USA. A much simpler and cheaper system was patented in England by Antoine Wollowicz in 1853. Straps of leather or rubber were pierced with a number of small holes to hold the caps, which were pushed on to the nipple when required.

Cap Gauge
A rare form of gauge was that issued by some manufacturers of percussion-caps. It consisted of a conveniently-shaped metal plate into which was screwed the various standard size nipples. Over these an unidentified cap could be tested for fit.

Cartridge (*See* Chapters 9 to 12.)

Cartridge Box (Cartouche Box)
355 The first cartridge boxes, the earliest specimens of which date to the middle of the sixteenth century, are of a pattern which remained in use until nearly the end of the seventeenth century. The box consisted of a block of wood drilled with vertical holes for five to seven cartridges. It was semi-circular in section and was held in a metal frame with a hinged lid, closed by a spring catch. When attached to the waist belt, the flat side of the box lay against the body. All these boxes have a wide flat base so that they could be stored upright. Nearly all of them appear to have been made for use with the wheel-lock gun and the ornamentation on decorated examples–usually in the form of engraved horn panels–follows closely the pattern found on the guns. Some boxes were made *en suite* with the gun and the rest of its accessories. Two particularly fine examples are in the Metropolitan Museum of Art, New York, one with staghorn panels engraved with an amusing erotic scene[12] and another with chiselled and engraved mounts bearing the arms of Saxony.[13] When the paper cartridge was adopted by the military a more utilitarian container was constructed. This was a leather oblong box or pouch with a substantial flap-over lid, bearing the regimental crest. It was usually lined with tin. In 1662 the Royal Battle-Axe Guard of Ireland was provided with 'Tyn Cartouch boxes covered with Leather of Calves Skins for Musketts wth Formers, prymeing boxes and neat leather girdles wth white buckles' at 3*s*. 6*d*. each.[14] These military cartridge boxes were worn on a shoulder-strap. In 1686 the London saddler Samuel Baker supplied the Board of Ordnance with 400 'Cartouch Boxes with Pouches fixt to Shoulder Belts of Dromedary Leather and Aprons of Neats Leather to cover ye Pouches', at 10*s*. each. For a further 2*s*. each he supplied 'Brass Badges Chased and fixed to ye said Cartouch Boxes.'[15] Inside the boxes were placed a priming-wire and a wooden former round which to roll the paper when making the cartridge. By the second quarter of the eighteenth century the pattern of the military cartridge box had changed. The leather pouch was filled with a wooden block drilled with holes like that of the old wheel-lock type. The number of holes varied. In 1756 an inventory of stores in the Tower of London[16] showed cartridge boxes for muskets with 9, 12, 18 and 24 holes, and for carbines with 9 and 18 holes.

In the last quarter of the eighteenth century the number of rounds to be carried by each soldier was increased. During the American War of Independence scarcity of proper leather equipment forced the Americans to use plain tin canisters with as many as 36 cartridges laid horizontally. As though in answer to this, in 1784, *Regulations for the Equipment of British Foot Guards and Infantry Regiments*[17] laid down that each man was to carry 56 rounds, 32 in a pouch on his right side and 24 in a cartridge box 'by way of a Magazine upon a new Construction' on his left. The latter was not described but the pouch consisted of 'a Tin Box, with Five Divisions in it, each containing Four cartridges placed upright and another Tin Box underneath, to hold the remaining 12 cartridges placed horizontally with Divisions in it to fit the Length of the Cartridge. The Flap of the Pouch to be plain without any ornament and the Bottom Part of it to be rounded at the Corners.'

During the last part of the flintlock era the American cartridge box was a combination of the old and new designs, with a wooden block on top and a tin compartment underneath holding a reserve supply.[18] By 1850, with the percussion system well established, most countries had adopted sturdy leather boxes with tin inserts of various patterns, with sometimes an additional leather pouch on the

12 No. 14.25.1502.

13 No. 29.158.701.

14 H. L. Blackmore, *British Military Firearms*, London, 1961, p. 30.

15 Public Record Office, London, WO51/32.

16 P.R.O. London, W.O.47/47, pp. 60/64.

17 P.R.O. London, WO 3/26, p. 154.

18 B. R. Lewis, *Small Arms and Ammunition in the U.S. Service*, 1776-1865, Washington, 1960, pp. 72-5, Fig. 10.

356 Oil bottles, engraved steel. (*Left*) Spanish, late eighteenth century. (*Far left*) Inscribed DE EL S^{MO} SENOR YNF^{TE} D^{N} LUIS. Spanish, late eighteenth century. Victoria & Albert Museum, London.

357 *Below* Powder-flask, horn mounted in pierced and engraved brass. German, dated 1603. Victoria & Albert Museum, London.

358 Powder flask, mother-of-pearl mounted in engraved silver. English (?), *c.*1670. Victoria & Albert Museum, London.

359 *Far left* Powder flask in the form of a fish. Engraved brass. French, *c.*1600. Victoria & Albert Museum, London.

360 *Left* Combined priming-flask and spanner (charging spanner), steel engraved with trophies. German, *c.*1650. Victoria & Albert Museum, London.

361 *Below* Powder flask. Horn, mounted in brass engraved with the arms of Fust of Hill Court, Gloucester. English, *c.*1710. Victoria & Albert Museum.

362 *Above* Powder tester, engraved steel, with the arms of Chigi. Italian, dated 1700. Victoria & Albert Museum, London.

363 *Left* Powder tester. English, *c.*1730. Tower of London Armouries.

outside for percussion caps. British regulations for *Equipment of Infantry*, 1865, illustrate boxes of this pattern with 20 rounds for sergeants and 50 or 60 rounds for rank and file.

The introduction of the metallic cartridge with its corresponding increase in weight led to a demand for the burden to be better distributed. The cartridge box became reduced in size and restricted to ceremonial use. Canvas and web equipment in which the cartridges were retained in individual loops or in clip pouches were adopted by most nations. The repeating gun brought new problems. A foretaste of what was to come was seen in the American Blakeslee box of *c.* 1864-5 which was designed to hold six tubular metal magazines for the Spencer repeater. During the Second World War the equipment of both sides included long canvas pouches for carrying machine-gun magazines.

Cartridge- or **Case-extractor**
Introduced in the 1850s, and still in use today, the extractor consists of a double or triple set of metal claws which can be clipped over the partly ejected rim of a jammed cartridge case. The claws, usually on a ring base, can be supplied separately on the end of a lever hook, or combined with a variety of other pocket instruments such as knives, whistles, etc.

Eprouvette *see* **Powder Tester**

False Muzzle
The false muzzle was an accessory invented for use on the muzzle-loading target rifle where any wear on the edge of the muzzle would affect its performance. It consisted of a short removable extension to the barrel with a slightly chamfered or enlarged bore to facilitate the entrance of the patched bullet. A dowel-pin ensured that the rifling in the false muzzle married up with that of the main barrel. It was first patented in the USA by Alvan Clark in 1840. Its efficiency can be judged by the fact that the modern muzzle-loading rifle is often equipped with it.

Gun Cases
Cases designed for the storage and preservation of fine firearms fall into two distinct groups. From the sixteenth century up to the middle of the eighteenth century, guns and pistols of quality were supplied in some form of cloth or leather case, approximating in shape, more or less, to that of the weapon it contained. In 1547 an inventory of King Henry VIII's arms included such entries as

> Itm one guilte chamber pece graven wt a fier Locke wt a white stocke in a case of yellowe velvet.
> Itm one shorte Chamber pece parcell guilte with a Redde stocke wt a fier Locke in a case of purple velvet.[19]

In sixteenth and seventeenth-century records there are references to snaphance pistols being supplied in cases. These were probably made of more substantial cloth like baize, or even of leather. Leather cases, like holsters with lids on them, are illustrated in the *Inventario Illuminado*, the illustrated inventory of the armoury of the Emperor Charles V (reigned 1519-56) in the Real Armería, Madrid. In 1754 and 1773, when sets of miniature military arms were made for the Royal Princes by the Board of Ordnance in London, they were supplied in 'Cases of Fine Scarlet Cloth' costing 10*s*. 6*d*. each.[20]

By the latter date the cased set of pistols had be- **82, 86**
come part of a gentleman's wardrobe. Popularly **112-13**
associated with duelling, they were also taken by **136, 269**
officers on campaigns and by travellers on the Grand **271**
Tour. The case, usually of mahogany strengthened with brass corners and bands, included a powder-flask, bullet mould, screwdriver, spare flints and other accessories. In England few really decorative cases were produced, although some covered with red leather, tooled and gilt, with linings of crimson velvet were made in the Regency period. An interesting and informative feature of nearly all these cases is the gunmaker's trade-label stuck inside the lid[21] With the introduction of the percussion system English cases became very much objects of utility with oak the favourite material. Continental gunmakers and particularly those of France and Belgium, however, indulged in the manufacture of extravagant designs. Cases of ebony and other exotic woods, inlaid and painted, were filled with a host of accessories including mallets, lead-ladles and complicated sets of tools. The shotgun and rifle were also accommodated, the long wooden case being supplied with an outer one of leather for travelling.

Holsters
Holsters may be divided into two general categories, those for wear upon the person and those for attachment to the saddle. The personal holster does not appear until the nineteenth century, but some form of saddle holster can be traced back to the second half of the sixteenth century when the wheel-lock pistol became popular. The woodcuts of Jost Ammon (*c.* 1570) portray the mounted *Reiter* with a couple of pistols stuck through his belt and two

19 H. A. Dillon, 'Arms and Armour at Westminster, The Tower and Greenwich, 1547' *Archaeologia*, 1888, p. 273.

20 P.R.O.; WO 51/258, 51/195.

21 See W. Keith Neal and D. H. L. Back, *British Gunmakers, their Trade Cards, Cases and Equipment*, 1760-1860, Warminster, 1980.

more in leather holsters attached to one side of the saddle. This type of holster is clearly shown in a drawing of a gunmaker's shop by the same artist in *Eygentliche Beschreibung aller Stände auff Erden*, published in Frankfurt in 1568 and a collection of actual examples of the period, apparently unique, survives in the Musée d'Art et d'Histoire, Geneva, together with the wheel-lock puffers belonging to them. With the arrival of the flintlock the holster pistol became part of the standard equipment of cavalry and they were carried in a pair of holsters slung on either side of the saddle. In 1646 the gunmakers of London were given contracts to supply the Commonwealth Army with 'paires of English snaphance pistolls full bore and proofe wth holsters of Calveskinns inside and outside well sewed and liquored att xviii*s* p. paire.'[22]

The shape of the saddle-holster was tubular at the bottom, often ending in a metal ferrule, and enlarged at the mouth to admit the width of the trigger-guard and lock. The mouth was covered by a large flap which was sometimes faced with fur for additional protection against the weather and for the comfort of the rider. If part of a parade equipment, it was embellished with embroidery and gold-wire work. A good example of a pair of decorated holsters is included in the horse garniture of Gustavus II Adolphus now in the Livrustkammare, Stockholm.

Smaller holsters suitable to be worn on the waist belt do not seem to have been introduced in Europe until the percussion lock made it possible for a pistol to be carried in this fashion, though they may have been worn in the Balkans as early as the eighteenth century. English officers in the Colonies with double-barrelled pistols, and American settlers in the West with revolvers, seem to have started the habit in the 1840s. What appears to be the first patent for a belt-holster, designed for the Colt revolver, was granted to Dennet and Pays in England in 1856. As various sizes and shapes of revolvers and automatic pistols came on to the market so did a corresponding number of holsters. To meet the demands of the gangster and the cowboy it was now possible for the pistol to be carried in a holster hung from almost any part of the body, inside or outside the clothing, with an emphasis on the 'quick-draw'. An ingenious wooden holster was made for some models of the Mauser pistol. In normal use this was hung in leather straps and the butt-lid opened to extract the pistol. For long distance shooting, however, the wooden holster itself was detached from its straps and clipped to the butt of the pistol to form a shoulder stock and convert the pistol into a carbine.

Jag

Jag is the modern term for a tool, formerly known as the scourer, which could be screwed on to the end of the ramrod to hold a cloth for cleaning the gun barrel. In the Tøjhusmuseum, Copenhagen, there is a matchlock musket[23] made in Suhl in *c.* 1600 which has a jag in the form of a three-pronged fork. This type of jag, which is illustrated by J. J. von Wallhausen in *Kriegskunst zu Fuss*, 1615, was soon superseded by one in the shape of a tapered, serrated rod ending in ringed plug nearly the size of the bore. This cleaning jag continued in use until the second half of the nineteenth century. It must be added, however, that the worm (*q.v.*) was often used as a cleaning jag and in some military manuals the jag is not mentioned, while the worm is listed as a wiper.

Match-case

The match-case, or -box, was designed to protect the lighted ends of the musketeer's slow match from rain or wind on those occasions when it was not immediately required for service. It was a tube of brass, iron or pewter about a foot long and was worn on the cross-belt in an upright position. It was closed at one end where it was pierced with small holes to provide air for the burning match inside. These match-cases or -holders are often mentioned and sometimes illustrated in military treatises of the early 1600s. Joseph Furtenbach illustrates one of special design, which he invented in 1626, in his *Büchsenmeisterey-Schul*, published in Augsburg in 1643. Few specimens of the match case survive to give any indication of the extent to which they were actually employed. A grenadier's match case is in the Tøjhusmuseum, Copenhagen.[24]

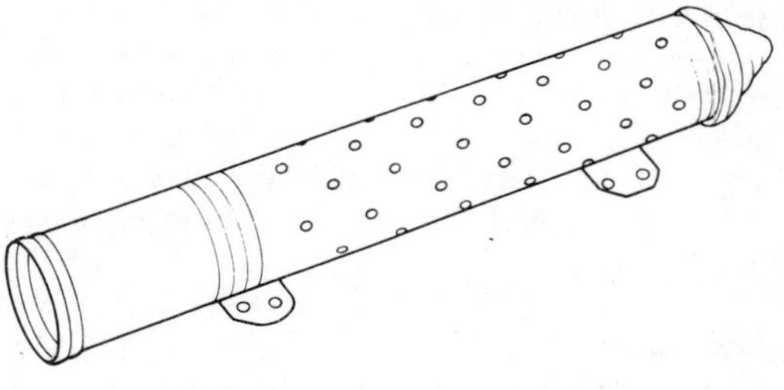

Match case, pierced iron. German, first half of seventeenth century. Tøjhusmuseet, Copenhagen.

Muzzle Brake

In general the muzzle brake was considered only for heavy powerful guns where it was desired to reduce the recoil of the gun by deflecting some of the gases at

22 H. L. Blackmore, *British Military Firearms*, London, 1961, p. 25.

23 No. B3930.

24 No. B.2076.

the muzzle into the opposite direction. A cannon now in the Rotunda, Woolwich, made in England in 1816, has its muzzle pierced with holes bored at an angle pointing to the rear.[25] The intention was that gases entering these holes would tend to thrust the barrel forward. A similar idea, to be applied to the musket, was submitted by M. Deshogues to the Board of Ordnance in London in 1843. The muzzle of his gun was to be bored with two slots pointing forwards but the gases released were caught by two cup-like projections and deflected to the rear, thus achieving the same effect.[26] A device tried on a field gun in the USA in 1901 consisted of a round shield or hood which was attached to the front of the muzzle. This blew back the gases with such effect that the gunners could not endure the blast. Various detachable muzzle-brakes combined with chokes, like the Cutts Compensator, are now marketed in the USA, mainly for use with shotguns.

Nipple Key

When the percussion system was universally adopted the nipple on which the cap was placed was made in a considerable number of different sizes and patterns. With few exceptions all screwed into the barrel, and the base was shaped into a two-sided, square, hexagonal or slotted nut for ease of removal. Each gun or pistol was normally supplied with a nipple key or wrench to fit its particular brand of nipple. The keys were of a fairly standard pattern with an oval handle of ivory, ebony or walnut and a rod-like shank ending in a box spanner of the required shape. Some keys, made entirely of steel were T-shaped, the handle being hollow and acting as a container for spare nipples.

Nipple Primer

The channel of the percussion nipple and that leading into the chamber occasionally became clogged. The easiest way of removing any blockage was to insert a few grains of gunpowder into the nipple and fire off a new cap. The difficulty was to get the powder into the small orifice of the nipple. It could be pricked with a pin and the powder poured in through a small funnel, but the latter was easily lost. The instrument known as the nipple primer was therefore invented. It consisted of a small tubular container of powder with a funnel and pricker attached. H. Mangeot illustrates them in his *Traité du Fusil de Chasse*, Paris, 1851-4, and they were patented in England by E. Paton and C. F. Walsh in 1856. The nipple primer was generally fitted with a swivel ring so that it could be worn on a chain. The nipple-primer was sometimes combined with a cap-carrier or a dog whistle.

Oil Bottle

Most of the early writers on firearms emphasised the 356
necessity for oiling firearms to keep them free from rust and to maintain the smooth movement of the lock, but only Wallhausen describes the lubricant (olive oil) and illustrates a suitable container.[27] By 1772, however, Norwegian ski troops were issued with copper oil bottles with a screw cap and applicator.[28] By this date most cased pistols were also provided with a squat metal bottle with a similar cap. In the nineteenth century the main stem of the percussion nipple keys or combination tools was often made hollow to act as an oil bottle. Many modern military rifles have a receptacle in the stock to take a tubular oil-bottle.

Patch Cutter *see* **Wad Cutter**

Patron

From the German *Patrone*, meaning a cartridge, the word was originally used in that sense in England. Thus Sir James Turner in *Pallas Armata*, 1670, wrote of the advantages of the cartridge to the soldier – 'he hath no more to do but to bite of a little of the Paper of his Patron and put his charge of Powder and Ball in at once'. Some of the Turner's references to Patrons were misunderstood by later writers on firearms, including Sir Samuel Meyrick,[29] who thought he was referring to the cartridge box, and following Meyrick's example (see also *Penny Cyclopaedia*, 1831) the word patron has been widely used since in this mistaken fashion.

Patron Tash

A word used in Scotland in the seventeenth century meaning a cartridge-box, a corruption of the German *Patronentasche* and the Dutch *Patroontasch*.

Porte Tache

This was a piece of leather equipment designed to carry a powder-flask and bullet bag, and, if need be, a wheel-lock key. It was worn hanging down from the waistbelt by horsemen. Illustrations of it appear in J. J. Wallhausen's *Art Militaire au Cheval*, Frankfurt, 1616.

---

25 Dudley Pope, *Guns*, London, 1965, p. 173.

26 H. L. Blackmore, *British Military Firearms*, London, 1961, p. 215.

27 H. L. Peterson, 'Nøgle Bemaerkninger om Tilbekor Til Skydevåber Før 1800', *Vaabenhisoriske Aarbøger* XIIa (1965), pp. 21-45.

28 ibid, p. 32.

29 'Observations upon the History of Fire-arms, etc.' *Archaeologia*, London, 1827, p. 101.

Powder-flask

82,86 Illustrations of the fourteenth and fifteenth cen-
89,107 turies, while contributing much of our knowledge of
112-13 early firearms, reveal little information on the
136,354 subject of powder-flasks or any form of ammunition-
357-61 carrier. After 1500, however, woodcuts and engravings begin to show round and flattened horns, presumably cow-horns, with simple push-in plugs in their nozzles, being carried either on their own or in company with bandoleers. By the end of the sixteenth century several distinct types of powder-flash had evolved, the shape depending initially on the material used. The plain nozzle-plug was replaced by a lid on the end of a spring-controlled lever.

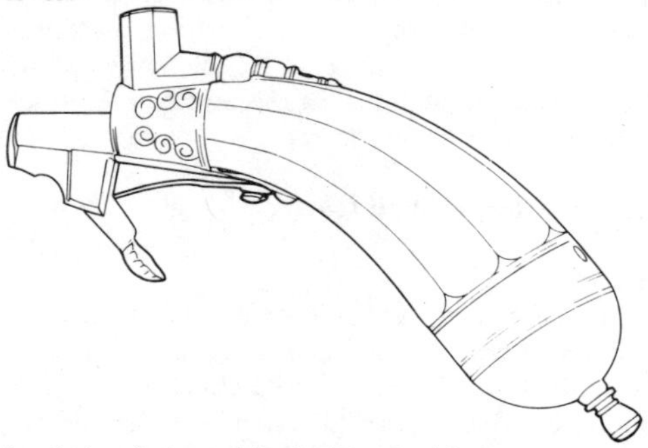

A priming flask combined with wheel-lock spanner (charging spanner). German, mid-seventeenth century. Victoria & Albert Museum, London.

Methods were found of flattening the round cow-horn so that it would hang better against the body. This particular shape of flask with its ends cut off straight, the base blocked with a strip of wood or horn, and a metal nozzle protruding from the top, was not only made of horn but was produced in wood or with a metal frame panelled with wood, horn or ivory. Another popular form of flask, in the shape of an inverted Y, was made from a section of antler hollowed out and capped with metal at its three extremities. One side of the flask was scraped clean and then engraved with some Biblical or mythological scene. On some flasks one of the base prongs was used as a bullet container, the cap having its own opening mechanism. This shape of flask was also copied in other materials. Magnificent specimens in chiselled and embossed gilt bronze are to be found in
89 the Wallace Collection[30] and the Victoria and Albert Museum.[31]

There was also a distinctive rounded form of flask, in section something like the modern rubber tyre, with a space in the centre sometimes filled in with decorative panels. It was usually made of wood decorated with staghorn or brass inlay in the same style as that of the gun it accompanied. One of the finest examples of these round flasks decorated *en suite* with its gun was made by the great gunstock-
maker Hans Schmidt of Ferlach in 1628 for Leopold 101
V, Archduke of Austria. Now in the Kunsthistorisches Museum, Vienna,[32] it is made of black wood profusely inlaid with magnificent silver ornamentation. In the same collection,[33] and of even more arresting beauty, is the round flask of ivory deeply carved with hounds attacking game made by an unknown *Kammerbeinstecher* for the Emperor Leopold I, *c.* 1670. An enamelled cover over the centre hole conceals a small watch. The accompanying rifle bears the signature of Michael Gull of Vienna.

One other class of flask of this period was of
triangular shape with a large flat base. This was the 366
kind worn by the musketeer and was understandably of plain, cheap construction being little more than an iron frame with wood panels. Nevertheless some of the ironwork of these flasks, especially those of Southern Germany and Italy, has been embossed and chiselled with decoration.

During the eighteenth century there was a return to favour of the simple cow-horn flask with a push-in plug in the nozzle, both in Europe and America. Apart from the plain examples used by military and naval personnel for the service of artillery, there were the flasks used by hunters and on these some distinctive national forms of decoration developed. In the Scandinavian countries the horn was deeply carved with rather crude illustrations of Biblical subjects or of heroes of the Charlemagne cycle of romances. In America, during the period of the French and Indian Wars (1755-63) when printed maps of the region were scarce, the custom grew of engraving the powder horn with a map of the territory showing the trade routes and forts connecting New York and Canada. Some of the engraving was the work of professional horn makers and is of fine quality. Much of the decoration, however, was the work of soldiers and settlers and is correspondingly crude in comparison.

Apart from the decoration, the mechanical performance of the powder-flask came under the attention of inventors at an early date. In 1592 Reynold Hoxton was granted a patent in England for some improvements in powder-flasks 'by the help whereof any (be he never so unskillfull) may charge any such peece with a just proportion of powder and bullet at one instant, without removing his hand or

30 No. A 1292.

31 No. 2203-1855.

32 No. D. 93a.

33 No. D. 146.

danger of fireing of himself or any of his fellowes'. Unfortunately, no details of the device are available.

Patents of the seventeenth century were so obscure in their wording that the mechanical innovations concerned cannot now be judged. In 1715 Isaac de la Chaumette took out two patents in France, one for a powder-flask with a swivelling nozzle and another for a flask with one charger for ball and powder. The really outstanding mechanical improvement, which dates back certainly to the late sixteenth century, was the fitting of the spring-pivoted cut-off or gate at the base of the nozzle. The powder in the nozzle, sufficient for the charge, could then be separated from the main store. The two systems of closure, the cap on the end of the nozzle, and the gate at its base were often combined into one lever-operated movement to bring a fixed charge quickly into the barrel.

The final phase of the powder-flask came with the die-stamped metal flasks introduced at the beginning of the nineteenth century. The Sheffield firms of Thomas Sykes, James Dixon & Sons,[34] G. & J. Hawksley and Peter Frith & Sons were foremost in the production of a wide range of copper, brass, zinc, tin and pewter flasks embossed with various floral and hunting motifs.[35] The first-named took out an English patent in 1814 for a powder-flask with a special cut-off with a circular spring, and a nozzle whose capacity could be adjusted to take different charges. It was a mechanism which was widely used until, with the introduction of the self-contained cartridge, the powder flask fell into disuse. The principal French makers were Michel Boche and Gosset, both of whom patented improved flasks and chargers. In America the most prominent makers were The American Flask and Cap Company and John Matthewman.

Powder Measure

The 1542 inventory of the armoury of the Duke of Mantua contains an entry for Bohemian harquebuses whose accessories include 'four powder measures in a wallet'.[36] This is probably the earliest mention of a powder measure, for most references and the earliest specimens date to much later in the century. Until then there was in fact little need for this device. The sportsman or soldier relied on the bandoleer box or the powder-flask nozzle to provide a correct charge of powder. But for wheel-lock rifles, which required careful loading, or for which cartridges were not practical, the powder measure was essential, and many wheel-lock keys incorporate a tubular measuring device. Separate measures usually took the form of a metal tube of the correct dimensions for the required charge, closed at one end and with a loop for carrying. Much rarer are those giving multiple readings. They consist of a long metal tube with a movable bottom attached to a rod which can be pulled out. The further one extends the rod the larger the measure, the size of which can be read off from a series of numbers stamped on the rod. In the late eighteenth and early nineteenth centuries these rather crudely-made iron measures were replaced by brass models, the movement of the platform being effected by turning a knurled knob. Other powder-measures of the nineteenth century, usually supplied with a cased gun, consisted of small adjustable containers like that found on the powder-flask nozzles fitted with wooden handles. The powder-measures used by the modern marksman hand loading his ammunition are, in contrast to all the old pocket models, substantial pieces of bench apparatus giving precision results.

Powder-tester

Before the use of standard cartridges of known muzzle velocities, the powder-tester, or *éprouvette*, was an essential tool for the armourer, storekeeper or sportsman faced with supplies of gunpowder whose strength varied considerably from one batch to another. All powder-testers applied the same basic physical test. A given quantity of powder was placed in a receptacle and fired and the force with which the lid was blown off was measured, the reading on one tester having no relation to that of another. They are mentioned as early as 1587 by William Bourne in his *Inventions and Devices very Necessary for all Generalles and Captains.*

There were three main types. In the first and most popular type, the lid of the powder container was connected to a wheel whose circumference was engraved with divisions and numbers. The force of
the explosion caused the wheel to revolve partially **362**
against the pressure of a spring, a stationary pointer indicating the reading. In the second type a large V-spring provided the necessary resistance, the lid being attached to a metal arc like the modern protractor. Nearly all the first two types were testers which could be held in the hand, being very similar in appearance to a pistol or a tinder lighter. The third type was designed primarily for the bench or table. It had a vertical frame up which the lid rose after the explosion. A weight or the resistance of a spring controlled the climb, and a ratchet arrangement held the lid at its maximum point of travel. The

34 Their 1888 catalogue of flasks and accessories is reproduced in the *Journal of the Arms and Armour Society*, Vol. V, No. 3, Sept. 1965.

35 These have been extensively considered and classified by Ray Riling, *The Powder Flask Book*, New Hope, Pa., 1953.

36 J. G. Mann, 'The Lost Armoury of the Gonzagas', *Royal Archaeological Journal*, Vol. XCV, 1939, p.313.

vertical-ratchet tester is one of the oldest types, a fine sixteenth-century example being in the Kunsthistorisches Museum, Vienna. Examples are also illustrated in Nathaniel Nye's *Art of Gunnery*, London, 1647 and Saint Remy's *Mémoires d' Artillerie*, Paris, 1697.

Most collections have specimens of the wheel type of tester and they range from simple match ignitions to elaborate flintlocks and percussion locks. A German flintlock example in the City Art Museum, St Louis, USA is beautifully decorated with chiselled and engraved steel-work. The majority of the V-spring types are of French or Belgian manufacture and do not appear to have been brought into use before 1800. A number of them are signed by Guillaume Berleur of Liège who may have been responsible for their invention.[37]

Pricker (Proyning Pin)

In 1591 W. Garrard wrote in *The Art of Warre* 'let a Souldier have hangyng ever at the strynges of hys Tutch boxe, or some other ready part of hys garment, a couple of proyning pinnes at the least, that if by fortune the Tutch hole of hys peece be stopped or furred up, hee may therewith both make his pan cleane, and yeeld a ready passage that the fire may have her course.' These instructions were in fact followed by most troops, a priming pin or pricker being carried in the cartridge box with a small brush, or attached to the cross belt or tunic. The T-shaped Spanish and North African combination tool usually had a pricker attached. With the introduction of percussion locks the combination nipple keys and screwdrivers used by military and sportsmen retained this.

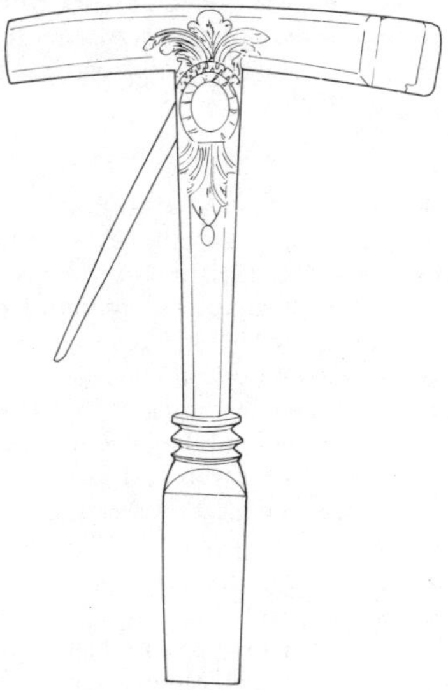

Combination tool for Spanish firearms (*Eslabone*) with pricker, seventeenth and eighteenth centuries. (See TOOLS, SETS OF p. 529.) Victoria & Albert Museum, London.

Ramrod (Rammer)

The first handguns of the fourteenth century were supplied with iron 'drivells' or ramrods (*see* Chapter 1). These were kept separate from the guns but when, in the late fifteenth century, the ramrod was housed in the stock under the barrel the question of weight arose and the ramrod was then produced in wood. Throughout the sixteenth and seventeenth centuries the ramrod, or 'scouring stick' as it was called, was a stout ash or walnut rod with a cap of horn or bone, the latter decorated to match the ornamentation on the gun. On military guns the cap was a flat iron plate. After *c.* 1600 the practice began of fitting the other end of the ramrod with a socket with a female screw into which could be screwed the various cleaning tools. The wooden ramrod continued in use until the beginning of the eighteenth century when, with the largest handgun, the musket, made much lighter and manoeuverable, it was found that the wood ramrod could not stand the strain of the fast and sustained loading movements. The iron ramrod returned to favour in the shape of a long slender rod with a swelling at the end. Where the wooden ramrod was retained, the plain metal plate nailed in the end was replaced by a brass, socketed and slightly recessed cap. A problem raised by the iron ramrod was the difficulty of holding it in the ramrod pipes so that it would not rattle or fall out. This was mainly solved by fitting a spring in one of the pipes or in the groove of the stock. In the 1780s, for ease of handling, some ramrods for cavalry carbines were made with swollen grips near the muzzle with a cannelure or groove which was held by a notch on the noseband. After *c.* 1800 most military carbines and pistols had their ramrods connected to the muzzle by a swivel-link which enabled the ramrod to be pulled out, reversed for loading, and then returned without fear of loss. In 1811 Frederick, Marquis of Dublin invented an automatic swivel ramrod which, on the touch of a button, sprang out from the stock and into the muzzle.[38] An unusual example of a swivel ramrod combined with a spear bayonet is found in the flintlock musket signed *SUSTERBECK 1798* in the Hermitage, Leningrad.[39] (*Susterbeck* was the name of a Russian arms factory).

37 P. J. Wolf, 'Powder Testers', *The American Arms Collector*, Maryland, USA, Vol. II, No. 3, July 1958, pp. 87-93.

38 The only known example is in the Tower of London Armouries. No. XII. 691.

The nineteenth century saw little change in the body of the ramrod but a variety of ends was produced to cope with the different shaped bullets then being tried. There was also the ramrod patented by Thomas Sykes in 1814 with a perforated end to facilitate its downward stroke by allowing the air to pass through. Some inventors sought to combine the ramrod with some accessory. Many of the better quality duelling pistols had one ramrod with a hollow metal end which unscrewed, reversed and became a powder-measure. In 1856 Samuel Colt patented in England a ramrod whose head contained an oiling tube which lubricated the bullet to prevent fouling. The rise of the revolver in the 1840s resulted in a number of patent ramrods applicable to its cylinder of chambers, but the introduction of the metallic cartridge meant that it remained in being only for its use as a cleaning rod.

Rest

The rest was a forked support for a gun which, although known in the fifteenth century, only seems to have come into general use with the musket,[40] a gun with which it is always particularly associated. It was described by Gervase Markham in his *Souldiers Accidence* of 1625 as 'of Ash wood or other tough wood, with iron Pikes in the neather end and halfe hoopes of Iron above to rest the musquet on, and double stringes fastned neare thereunto, to hang about the arme of the Souldier when at any time he shall have occasion to traile the same'. The reference to the pike meant that if need be the rest could be reversed and the pointed spike used as a defensive weapon. Sometimes the rest was in fact armed with a bayonet spike on one prong or with a concealed blade in the hollow haft which could be thrust out by a jerk of the hand–the so-called 'brandistock'. The rest went out of use in the last quarter of the seventeenth century. It was almost entirely a plain military accessory, but mention must be made of the magnificent rest in the Kunsthistorisches Museum, Vienna[41] which was made by Emanuel Sadeler for the garniture of arms presented by the Elector Maximilian I of Bavaria to Duke Carlo Emanuel of Savoy in 1650.

Scouring Stick *see* **Ramrod**

Shot Pouch

Very little is known concerning the making of lead shot (as opposed to lead bullets or balls) until the seventeenth century, and there is little indication that any special form of shot pouch or carrier was devised even then. Richard Blome describes how lead shot was made in the *Gentleman's Recreation* of 1685. Molten lead was poured through a sieve containing hot coals, the drops being solidified in a bowl of water underneath. If you were lucky and the temperature was right you finished up with 'good round Shot without Tails'. The type of shot produced by these methods could be carried in the same sort of pouch as the bullet-bag. In the late eighteenth century the modern shot-tower method of making lead shot was introduced and standard sizes of shot were established, although they varied from country to country. With the introduction of very fine shot the shot pouch and belt were also brought into being.

The pouch, usually made of leather (soft or hardened) looked like a powder-flask but had a different charger or nozzle. In one type the nozzle contained a removable measure which, when filled, was removed and the contents poured down the barrel. In another type a seesaw beam cut-out was used to fill the nozzle with the required amount of shot while the rest of the contents were isolated. The flask itself was then tipped over the muzzle. When filled, the shot-flask was a heavy article to carry in the field and for this reason many sportsmen preferred the shot belt. Resembling a cycle tyre made of soft leather with a metal charger protruding instead of a valve, the belt was carried either round the waist or slung over the shoulder. A much neater means of conveyance was the pocket charger, a small, oval metal box divided into two compartments each sufficient for one charge of shot. These are often found in muzzle-loading shotgun cases.

Sights

The handgun of the fourteenth and early fifteenth centuries was such an inaccurate weapon that any precise method of aiming was superfluous. It was enough to point the barrel in the right direction. In the second half of the fifteenth century, however, with a proper shoulder stock available, the first sights were fitted, consisting of a bead fore-sight and a standing notched rear-sight. In the sixteenth century the tubular rear sight was introduced and it is found on all types of guns from the military musket to the highly decorated sporting-gun. The bead or blade fore-sight was now made of metals other than iron, brass and silver being extensively used, and it was dovetailed into a slot in the barrel so that it could be adjusted for lateral correction. With the increasing use of the rifle, point-blank range was no longer sufficient and a vertical adjustment of the rear sight had to be made. This was done by giving the rear-sight one or more hinged leaves of different lengths which were raised when aiming at greater distances. On the heavy Turkish or Persian rifle barrel the rear-

39 No. 30-586.

40 See p. 54.

41 N.A. 225.

sight was a multiple peep-sight, formed by an upright blade pierced with several holes one above the other. The maximum range of a flintlock rifle rarely exceeded 300 to 400 yards and its accuracy still did not warrant any elaborate form of sighting. Patrick Ferguson, however, when patenting his breech-loading rifle in 1776, considered himself justified in including an elevated rear-sight, a notched blade sliding in a vertical slot cut in the breech.

But it was not until the middle of the nineteenth century, with the introduction of the accurate pillar-breech and Minié-type rifles, that serious attention had to be paid to sights. Most countries adopted a long folding-leaf rear-sight with a sliding notched bar giving ranges up to a 1,000 yards or more. A special type, used on French, Danish and Austrian military rifles, was the arch rear-sight in which a curved leaf with a sighting notch slid in an arched recess on the rear-sight block, being held in the different positions by a screw. Numerous sights were invented during the second half of the nineteenth century and in most cases they indicated ranges far in excess of those of any practical value to the soldier. The height of absurdity was reached in the additional *extreme-range* sights fitted to the left-hand side of the British Lee Metford and Lee Enfield rifles from 1889 on. The aperture rear-sight was stationary; the fore-sight was a bead pointer moving round a dial calibrated up to 2,800 yds.

Telescopic sights are first recorded in Francesco de Lana's *Magister Naturae et Artis* of 1684. A more elaborate lens system was put forward in *Oculus Artificialis Teledioptricus* by Johannes Zahn of Nuremberg in 1702. A flintlock gun made by Georg Keiser of Vienna in 1731 for the Emperor Charles VI, now in the Kunsthistorisches Museum, Vienna,[42] has a sighting lens mounted on the butt.[43] For obvious reasons there are few instances of the use of such sights until the ninteenth century. One of the earliest specimens appears to be on the rifle of advanced design made by Professor Richard Potter of University College, London, in 1864 and now in the Tower of London Armouries. In 1850 Professor Piazzi Smyth read a paper to the British Association 'On the Application of Telescopic Sights to Rifles'. In this he recommended a telescope with internal crosswire sights which had been designed by Capt. D. Davidson of the Bombay Army. Davidson patented his sights in 1862. In the 1860s and 1870s similar sights were fitted to the precision muzzle-loaders of Whitworth and Metford for target shooting. During the American Civil War snipers established a tradition for the advantages of the telescopic sight. Today the greatest use of this sight for sport and target work is made in the USA.

42 No. A 1762.

43 See C. Blair, *European and American Arms*, London, 1962, No. 340.

Silencer

A silencer is a device for reducing the report of a firearm. This is usually done by a tubular instrument which clamps round the muzzle of a gun, traps the gases of the explosion and delays their release. Its effect is considerably reduced if the gun is a revolver where gases can escape through the gap between cylinder and barrel, or if a high-velocity cartridge is fired, when the bullet creates shock waves and a noise of its own. On a semi-automatic firearm, if the breech opens while there is still considerable pressure in the barrel, again the silencer will have little effect.

The first English patent for a silencer was taken out by Stahel in 1893 (No. 7040). He increased the size of the bore near the muzzle to form a chamber for the collection of the gases. This patent was followed by a number of others relating to such devices as trap doors over the muzzle, wads behind the bullet which blocked the muzzle, spring deflectors, etc. In 1899 (No. 6701) J. Börrensen and S. Sigbjörnsen patented a tube containing a series of baffle-plates, which fitted over the end of the barrel. Improved versions were patented by H. Maxim in England in 1908 (Nos 6680 and 25269) and in the USA in 1909 (No. 916885) and 1910 (No. 958934).

The silencer has only a limited use and has never been adopted in any quantity. During the First World War a sniper model of the 1903 Springfield rifle was produced with a Maxim silencer and during the Second World War carbines with silencers were tried on a limited scale by the USA (modified 0·30 in calibre M.1) and Great Britain (De Lisle).

Spanner *see* Wheel-Lock Spanner

Spring Vice

Before a gun lock could be stripped for cleaning or the replacement of a part, the main spring had to be detached. This could be done with the aid of a spring vice or clamp. The spring was first compressed by cocking and the vice adjusted to clamp over its two leaves. When the sear was released the spring could be lifted off without difficulty. The earliest surviving gun vices, of which there are examples in the Dr Thomas J. Hoopes Collection, USA, and in the Tøjhusmuseum, Copenhagen, date back to the late sixteenth century and early seventeenth century, and are something like the modern adjustable grip, the screw being turned either by a large wing-nut or by a handle which would serve as a hammer. In the eighteenth and nineteenth centuries several types of vice were made, the most popular being equipped with one wide movable jaw serrated

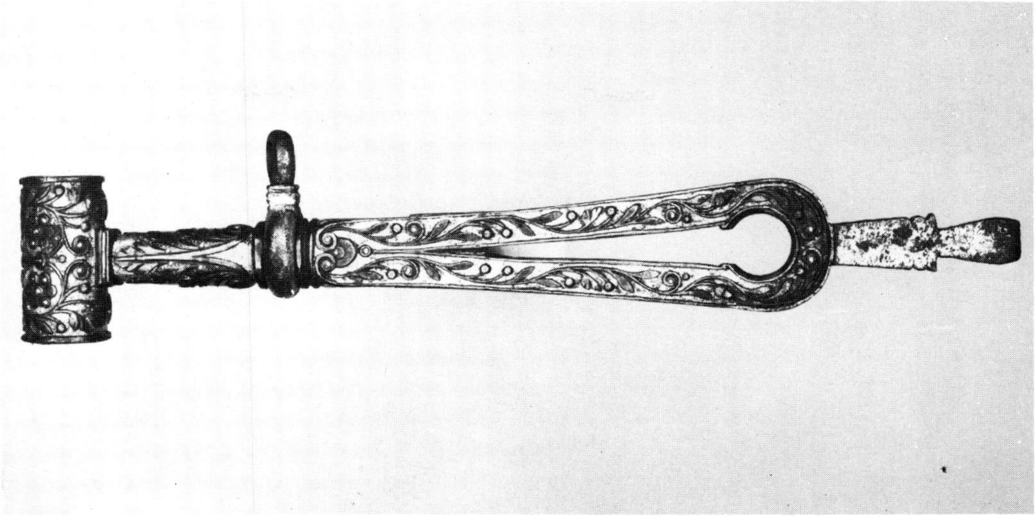

364 *Above* Wheel-lock spanner, gilt and chiselled steel. South German, *c.*1650. Probably made by Caspar Spät of Munich for a signed gun in the Bayerisches Nationalmuseum, Munich. Odescalchi Collection, Rome.

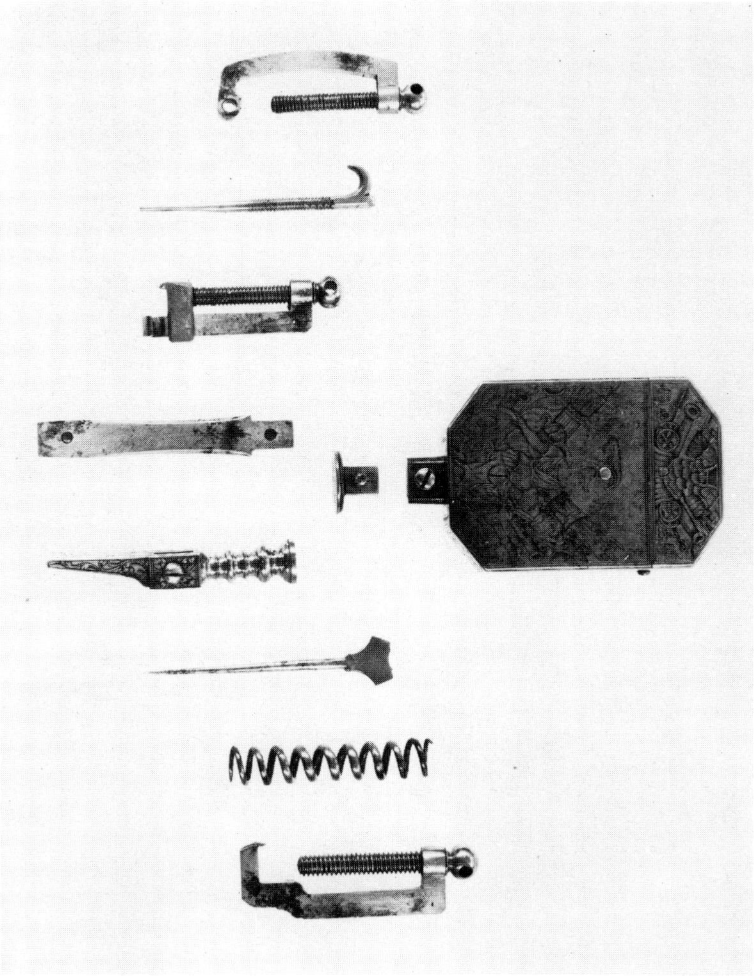

365 *Right* Pocket set of tools, engraved steel, by Andrew Dolep. Made for a set of firearms belonging to the Medici in the Royal Armoury, Turin. English (London), *c.*1685. Tower of London Armouries.

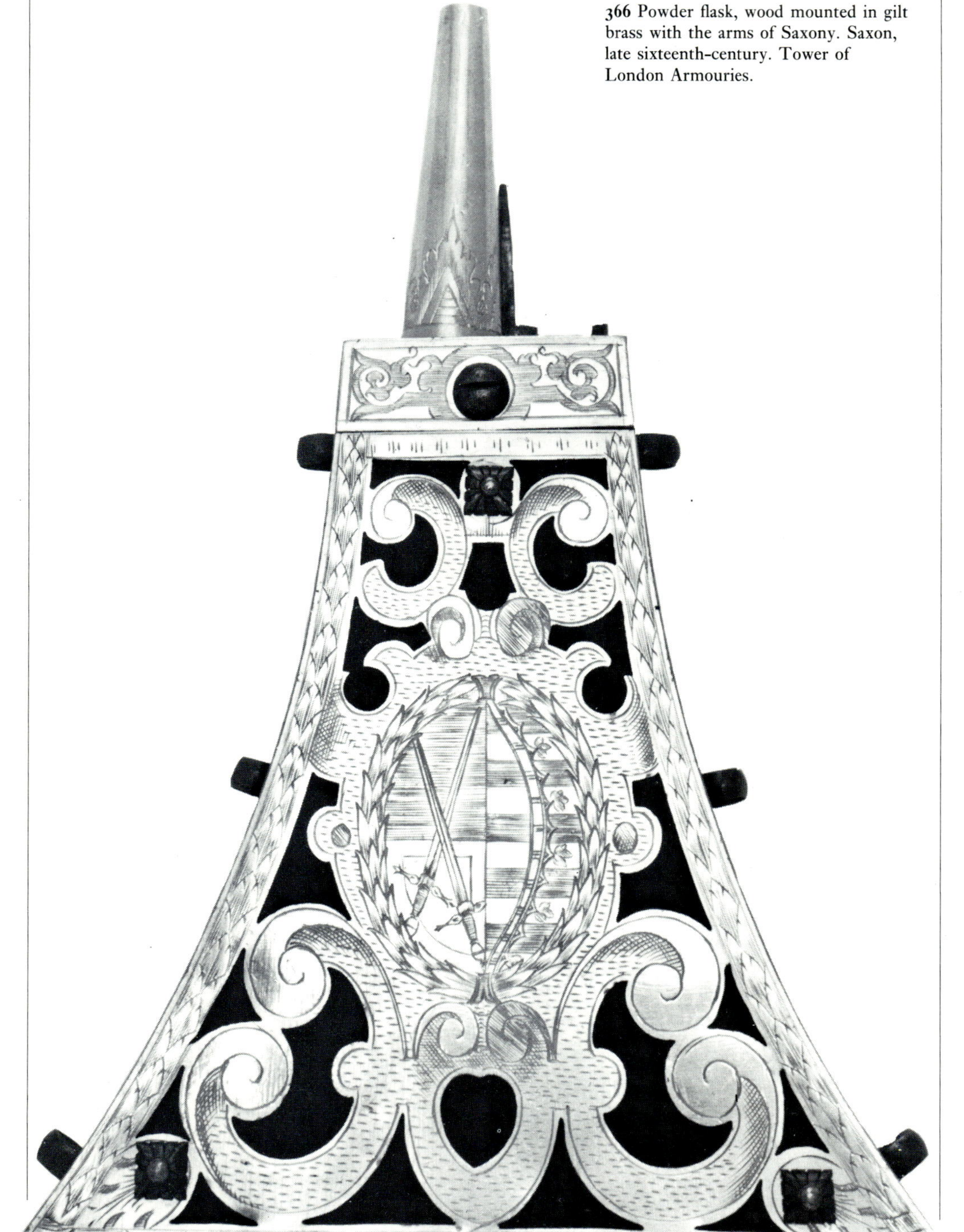

366 Powder flask, wood mounted in gilt brass with the arms of Saxony. Saxon, late sixteenth-century. Tower of London Armouries.

at the extremities and a small fixed jaw which could be swivelled to the angle of the spring. Vices made for the flintlock sometimes consist of fixed arms which envelop the spring, with a winged screw to make contact. Several types were patented in France by Dominique Sisco of Paris in 1828.

Tireball *see* **Ball-drawer**

Tools Sets of

The hunter or soldier of the sixteenth century onwards, being obliged to carry on his person a large number of accessories, often sought to combine some of the smaller articles into one tool or to fit them together in a compact set. The screwdriver and hammer figured prominently in these sets. In the seventeenth century, Spanish gunmakers began making a T-shaped tool, the foot shaped as a screwdriver and the top bar forming a hammer. A pricker was sometimes screwed into the side. These tools, called *eslabones* (See Fig. p. 524), were usually finely made with chiselled decoration, and were sometimes engraved with the name of the maker. There is a good collection of them in the Victoria and Albert Museum. Crude copies were made for the North African guns.

Multiple screwdrivers with three blades were adopted early in the eighteenth century by most military bodies. These became more elaborate as time went on with one blade tapered and threaded to take a worm. When percussion firearms were introduced the British Army issued with them various T- or Y-shaped combination tools including a screwdriver, worm, pricker, nipple key and, in some cases, a mainspring clamp. These developed into an ingenious multiple tool for armourers–a *nécessaire d'armes*–first patented by N. Charoy in Paris in 1837. With extractors and gauges added this became, in British Army parlance, the *Implement Action;* issued with the Lee Metford and Lee Enfield rifles.

The most elaborate sets of tools seem to have been made by French gunmakers. There is a well-known type which consists of a central frame, forming a spring clamp, into which are screwed jag, worm, ball-drawer, scraper, file, hammer, screwdriver, and, in at least one case, a pair of pliers. All these tools could be removed for use and then replaced. In another group, of which there is a fine example in the
365 Tower of London made by Andrew Dolep in *c.* 1685 for Cosimo III de' Medici, all the tools are kept in a small box which, with the aid of an extension arm, forms the handle of the hammer or the screwdriver as desired. Such a set was patented in 1821 by the Parisian gunmaker Joseph Manceaux.

The pocket tool often carried by the hunter was basically a pair of grips or pliers, but a hammer head and flint knapper was attached to the jaws and a whistle and worm were screwed to the handles.

Touch Box *see* **Powder-flask**

Wad Cutter

The wad cutter was a punch with a circular blade for cutting out wads or patches of thin leather, linen, felt or other material in which to wrap the bullet when it was wished to reduce the windage in a smooth bore or grip the grooves in a rifle. In 1644 Alonso Martínez de Espinar in *Arte de Ballesteria y Monteria* recommended for rifles felt wads lubricated with Greek pitch, wax and tallow. During the eighteenth and the first half of the nineteenth centuries the patch- or wad-cutter became standard equipment for rifles and shotguns, and was also supplied to the cased pair of duelling pistols. Decorated specimens are rare but two interesting cutters with unusually shaped blades, made in 1643 by Andreas Neidhart of Elsinore for a wheel-lock gun of unusual bore, are in Tøjhusmuseet, Copenhagen.[44]

Wheel-lock Spanner

The wheel-lock spanner or key was an essential accessory for the wheel-lock gun or rifle, unless the lock was of the rare self-spanning type. It consisted normally of a double-ended box spanner fitted at right angles to a suitable lever which terminated in a screwdriver blade. The spanner portion was sometimes combined with a priming flask when it was
known as a *charging spanner* (See Fig. p. 522). One 360
type is joined to a powder tester and a powder measure, the last forming the handle. Many wheel-lock keys were decorated *en suite* with their guns and are magnificent specimens. Examples are in the Wallace Collection, London[45] the Metropolitan
Museum of Art, New York[46] and the Odescalchi 364
Collection, Rome.

Worm (Ball-drawer)

This tool was screwed on to the end of the ramrod and was used to extract wadding from the barrel. It was similar in appearance to a corkscrew and could have one or two twisted prongs. The single-pronged type, which is found up to the end of the eighteenth century, generally had a long prong of approximately 2½ turns. The double-pronged worm was much shorter and stronger. In the nineteenth century it seems to have become a general-purpose barrel tool used for cleaning instead of a jag, and for extracting not only wadding but the bullet. In the British *Equipment of Infantry* regulations (1865), the worm is called a ball-drawer and vice versa.

44 No. B 163.

45 No. A 1325.

46 No. 14.25.1528.

Glossary

N.B. 1. Consisting of terms not already clearly explained in the text and so not traceable from the index.

2. Words underlined are defined elsewhere in the glossary.

3. 'Automatic' is used throughout to cover both fully- and semi-automatic weapons.

BACK-CATCH. A safety device found on some snap-locks, comprising a small hook pivoted to the lock-plate behind the cock and engaging in a notch in its heel to hold it in the half-cock position. Also sometimes called a dog-catch by collectors.

BALLISTICS. Science of the performance of the projectiles and propellants of firearms.

BARREL. The tube (closed at the rear) that is the essential component of all guns and pistols, in which the propellant charge is exploded and along which the projectile initially travels.

BATTERY. (From the French batterie.) A term used by some modern writers to denote the combined steel and pan-cover on a flintlock.

BENCH-REST SHOOTING. A form of small-bore target-shooting using a rifle clamped into a supporting frame.

BENT. One of the notches in the tumbler of a flint- or percussion-lock into which the nose of the sear engages to give full- or half-cock.

BLOWBACK. The term applied to the operating-system of automatic firearms in which the mechanism is actuated by the explosion of each cartridge blowing back the bolt, which in turn actuates a spring, causing it to eject the spent case, recock the mechanism, and load a new cartridge.

BLOW FORWARD. The term applied to an automatic system like that described under blowback, but in which the explosion of the cartridge causes the mechanism to move forward.

BLUING. Heat or chemically-induced surface colouring on the iron or steel parts of a firearm. Its purpose can be decorative or protective.

BOARD OF ORDNANCE. See Ordnance.

BOLT. The sliding breech-block, containing striker and extractor, in a bolt-action fire-arm. So called because of its resemblance to a common door-locking bolt. The term is also used for the handleless sliding breech-block in some automatic systems.

BORE. The tubular interior of the barrel. Also the measurement of its diameter (calibre) expressed in terms of the number of appropriate bullets that would make up one pound weight.

BREECH. The rear section of a barrel, containing the chamber in which the charge is ignited. A false breech is a block of metal fixed to the stock behind the barrel into which the true breech is hooked.

BREECH-BLOCK. A moveable block of metal fitted into the breech of many breech-loading and repeating firearms. It is opened for the insertion of the charge of cartridge, and closed to seal the breech behind. On some breech-loaders it contains the chamber.

BREECH-PLUG. A screwed plug closing the rear end of the breech. It is found on most post-medieval barrels, which were normally made initially as a tube open at both ends.

BROWNING. A chemically-induced colouring applied to barrels–and occasionally other iron and steel parts–of early firearms. Its purpose was partly decorative, but it also acted as a rust-inhibitor.

BUILT-UP CONSTRUCTION. The barrels of some early cannon and hand-firearms, instead of being made from one piece of metal, are constructed of longitudinal iron bars (sometimes supported on a thin iron tube) held together by iron hoops. This is now commonly called the built-up construction.

BUTT. See Stock.

BUTT-STRAP. A metal reinforcing strip running up the back of the butt of a pistol.

CALIBRE. The diameter of the bore.

CANNELURE. A groove, fluting.

CAP. See Percussion cap.

CHAMBER. The section of the bore normally at the breech designed to contain the explosive charge and projectile, or the cartridge. Also the tubular holes with the same function in revolver cylinders and some moving breech-blocks.

CHARGER. A device for holding a number of cartridges for easy insertion into the magazine of a repeating firearm. The term is also applied to multiple-loading devices made for some multi-barrelled firearms and revolvers.

CHARGER GUIDE BRIDGE. A supporter for the charger across the receiver of a magazine firearm.

CHARGER LOADING. A firearm or magazine which can be loaded by means of a charger.

CHOKE. A slight constriction, towards the muzzle, of the bore of a shotgun barrel which improves the pattern of the shot after it leaves the muzzle.

CLAY-PIGEON SHOOTING. A form of target-shooting with the shotgun. The clay pigeons (American skeet) are clay discs which are projected into the air at varying angles and speeds by a mechanical device.

CLIP. A form of charger for holding a group of cartridges together at their bases for inserting into the magazine of a repeating firearm.

CLIP LOADING. A term used to refer to a repeating mechanism incorporating a magazine that can be loaded with a clip of cartridges.

COCK. The pivoted arm (usually spring-actuated) holding the match, pyrites or flint on an early gunlock. The term was also applied to the hammer on early percussion-locks.

COMB. The keel-shaped top edge of a gun-butt. Also a flat decorative scroll on top of the cocks of some firearms.

DOG-CATCH. See Back-catch.

DOG-HEAD. The jaws of the cock of a wheel- or snaplock firearm, which hold the pyrites or flint.

DOUBLE ACTION. A revolver with a lock that permits use as a self-cocking mechanism, but can also be cocked by the thumb if required.

ESCUTCHEON PLATE. A decorative metal plate–part of the furniture– set in the stock behind the breech on many firearms on which the owner's coat-of-arms, crest or monogram could be engraved.

FENCE. A small metal plate set at right-angles to the edge of the pan on some pre-percussion firearms, serving as flashguard.

FULL-STOCKED. See Stock.

FIRE CHECK. The capacity of a projectile, when travelling along the barrel, to contain the propellant gases behind it by its fit in the barrel.

FOLDING TRIGGER. See Trigger.

FORESTOCK. See Stock.

FRIZZEN. See Frizzle.

FRIZZLE. A colloquial term, as least as old as the 18th century, for the steel. Its rare form frizzen was given widespread popularity amongst modern gun-collectors as a result of its use in Pollard's *History of Firearms.*

FULL-COCK. The position of the cock or hammer of a gunlock when ready for firing. See Half-cock.

FULL-STOCKED. See Stocked.

FURNITURE. The metal mounts attached to the stock of a firearm, excluding only the barrel, lock and trigger.

GATE LOADING. Term applied to a revolver on which the chambers are loaded through a cut-out in the frame filled by a pivoted 'gate'.

HALF-COCK. The intermediate safety position for the cock or hammer of a gunlock. See Full-cock.

HALF-STOCKED. See Stock.

HAMMER. The hammer-like cock (originally called the striker) found on percussion firearms, cartridge revolvers and some other cartridge arms. Before the percussion period the term was the most usual one for the steel or frizzle.

HANGFIRE. When the charge or cartridge fails to ignite.

HEAD SPACE. The small space between the breech-block or head of the bolt, when closed, and the base of the cartridge in a breech-loading firearm.

INERTIA WEDGE BLOCK. A device for temporarily preventing the rearward movement of the bolt of an automatic firearm when it is under maximum pressure from the explosion of the cartridge.

JAW SCREW. The screw operating the jaws of the cock of a pre-percussion firearm, in which the match, pyrites or flint was held.

LANDSKNECHT. A German mercenary soldier (usually an infantryman) of the late fifteenth and sixteenth centuries.

LOCK. The mechanical device for igniting the propellant charge.

LOCKED BREECH. One of the mechanisms used in automatic firearms. When a cartridge is fired the discharge causes the barrel to slide backwards–more rarely forwards–with the bolt locked to it, until a release-mechanism allows the latter to travel on by itself, to opening the breech, ejecting the spent cartridge case, cocking the mechanism, loading a new cartridge ready for the next shot.

LOCKPLATE. The flat metal plate on which the mechanism of the lock is mounted.

MUZZLE. The mouth of the barrel.

MUZZLE-BRAKE. A device fitted to the muzzle designed to reduce recoil.

MUZZLE GAS TRAP. A device for trapping some of the gases propelling a projectile along the barrel and diverting them to operate an automatic loading and firing mechanism.

MUZZLE VELOCITY. The speed at which a projectile leaves the muzzle, usually measured in feet per second in Britain and the United States.

OBTURATION. The sealing of the breech (especially of a breech-loading or repeating firearm) to prevent the backward escape of gases from the exploding charge. Modern cartridge cases themselves expand when fired to seal the breech, and so are termed self-obturating.

OFF-HAND SHOOTING. Target shooting with a rifle, for which the shooter must stand upright on both feet and cannot use any support or rest.

ORDNANCE, BOARD OF. The body governing the Ordnance Office, which controlled the supply of arms and equipment to English (later British) government land forces from the 16th century until 1885, when it was replaced by the War Office.

PAN. A shallow receptacle for the priming placed adjacent to the touch-hole on a match-, wheel- or flintlock firearm.

PERCUSSION CAP. The small copper cap containing detonating powder used to ignite the charge in the developed version of the percussion lock.

PERCUSSION TUBE. See Tube lock.

POMMEL. A shaped knob at the rear end of the butt of a pistol. The term was originally used for the knob-like feature, designed to counter-balance the blade, at the top of a sword-hilt.

POSITIONAL SHOOTING. Target shooting from various positions: standing without a support (off- hand position), kneeling or prone.

PRIMING. The fine gunpowder used to prime the pan of a match-, wheel-, or snaplock firearm for igniting the main propellant charge.

PUMP ACTION. A term applied to repeating firearms activated by a sliding action which is operated by moving a handgrip below the barrel backwards and forwards. Also called trombone action.

RECEIVER. The body of a breech-loading or a repeating mechanism in which the bolt or breech-block works.

RECOIL-STOP. A device–often no more than a fixed lug or block–to prevent the backward recoil of a firearm when fired.

RIFLING. Spiral grooves in the barrel which grip the projectile and impart a rotary motion to it, so equalising its balance in flight and giving improved stability.

SEAR. The catch in the mechanism of a lock which engages in the notches of the tumbler linked to the cock or hammer and holds it at full- or half-cock, and is released by the trigger.

SELF COCKING. A revolver in which the whole firing cycle is accomplished merely by operating the trigger.

SELF-OBTURATING. See Obturating.

SERPENTINE. The match-holder of a matchlock. Also a type of fine gunpowder used for priming and a type of light cannon.

SETTING UP. The expansion of a bullet into the rifling by the explosion of the propellant charge.

SINGLE ACTION. A revolver cocked and the cylinder rotated by the thumb pressing down on the spur of the hammer, and then fired by pulling the trigger.

SKEET SHOOTING. The American term for clay-pigeon shooting.

SKELP. A flat strip of iron or steel which is twisted and welded to form a barrel.

SNAP SHOOTING. Quick shooting at suddenly appearing, and often moving, targets that do not allow for deliberate aim.

SPAN. To wind up a wheel-lock (with a spanner), ready for firing. The term was originally used for the action of bending a crossbow.

STEEL. The pivoted steel plate from which sparks are struck by the flint in a snaphance or flint-lock. Before the advent of the percussion lock it was normally called the hammer. See also frizzle.

STOCK. The shaped wooden–or occasionally metal–support for the barrel and lock. The forward part under the barrel is the 'fore-end' (American 'forestock') and the rear end, which is placed against the shoulder or, on a pistol, held, is the 'butt'.

When the stock extends under the full length of the barrel of a firearm it is called 'full-stocked' and when only part of the way 'half-stocked'.

STRIKER. The device–usually a spring-loaded pin–that strikes and ignites the cap in a cartridge. The term was sometimes applied to the hammer-like cock of a percussion lock when the percussion system was first introduced.

STRIKING UP. The preliminary finishing process on a hand-made barrel, after it has been rough bored. The interior is examined for inequalities of boring, and the exterior struck, with a light hammer to raise any hollows that might have been detected. The term is also used for the process of bringing an old barrel back into true.

SUICIDE SPECIAL. Modern popular American term embracing many different kinds of low-quality pocket-revolvers made for mass sale during the second half of the nineteenth century.

TILLER. The straight wooden stock of an early firearm or of a crossbow.

TOUCH-HOLE. The small hole drilled into the breech of a pre-percussion firearm through which the charge of gunpowder is ignited. Sometimes also called the 'vent'.

TRAJECTORY. The path a projectile takes after leaving the muzzle.

TRAP SHOOTING. Shooting at birds or animals released from special cages ('traps'). The term is now also applied to clay-pigeon shooting.

TRICKER. See Trigger.

TRIGGER. The lever for releasing the discharge-mechanism of a crossbow or firearm, usually set beneath the stock and operated with the fore-finger. On some firearms, notably pocket-pistols, the trigger is pivoted so that it can be folded up against, or into, the stock or body. A 'set-trigger' or 'hair-trigger' is a trigger fitted with a spring mechanism which can be set, usually either by pushing the trigger forward or by pressing a separate trigger. Pressure on the main trigger releases the mechanism, which in turn actuates the lock of the firearm (or cross-bow). The device, by providing purely mechanical release, made possible a lighter but more certain trigger-operation.

TRIGGER LOCK (TRICKER LOCK). The form of conventional matchlock actuated by a trigger of modern form instead of by a lever trigger.

TUBE-LOCK. One of the early forms of percussion lock in which a metal tube containing detonating-compound and inserted into a hole in the breech was used instead of a percussion cap.

TUMBLER. A shaped block attached to the pivot of the cock and bearing on the mainspring which operates on the cock through it. It usually contains the bents.

TURN-OFF. The seventeenth and eighteenth century term for the type of gun or pistol with a barrel that could be unscrewed to enable the charge to be loaded directly into the chamber.

WINDAGE. The space between the bore of a firearm and its projectile; that is, the difference between the diameter of the bullet and the bore.

WRIST. The section of the stock of a long-gun between the butt and the fore-end gripped by the trigger-hand. Also called the small of the butt or hand.

Appendix I
Air, Spring-Air and Gas Guns

Claude Blair

Guns of this type do not come strictly within the province of a work on *fire*-arms but, as they usually resembled these last closely in everything except the propellant they used, some brief account of them must be given here.

Air-Guns[1]

Attempts to use compressed air as a means of expelling a projectile from a tube go back to experiments carried out by Klesibos of Alexandria in the third century BC. According to tradition, however, the invention of the air-gun proper was the work of one Guter of Nuremberg in the fifteenth century, though unfortunately nobody has yet been able to discover evidence to support this or even to establish the existence of Guter himself. Nevertheless, it seems likely that the principle of the air-gun was well known by the early sixteenth century at the latest for a reference to the construction of an air-gun that 'shoots with marvellous force' is contained in one of Leonardo da Vinci's notebooks.[2] The earliest surviving examples, however, date from the late sixteenth century while they do not become common until the eighteenth century. Before going on to describe these it should perhaps be mentioned that all these guns, and the pistols too, were intended to perform the same function as firearms, the idea that an air-gun is little more than a child's toy being a comparatively recent one.

Air-guns fall, according to their mechanisms, into three groups:

1. The Pump-up Air-Gun. This type, which is regarded by many people as the true air-gun, embodies a reservoir of compressed air, filled by means of a pump, and a trigger mechanism that permits the release of sufficient air to propel one shot at a time. The obvious disadvantage of the system is that the power of the gun declines slightly with each shot.

A gun of pump-up type, designed to discharge darts, was devised by the French mechanic Marin le Bourgeoys in the early seventeenth century, but is known only from an illustration in Rivault de Flurance's *Les Eléments de L'Artillerie* of 1607. The earliest surviving pump-up guns appear to be two in the Livrustkammare, Stockholm, which are signed on the barrels *HANS KÖLER VON KITZING ANNO* 1644. Each has an air-reservoir built around the barrel and charged by a pump in the butt; and when the trigger is pressed all the air is expelled. Two guns by Georg Fehr of Dresden, dated respectively 1653 and 1655, in the Tøjhusmuseum, Copenhagen, are of similar design, but have an improved lock-mechanism that releases only sufficient air for one shot. The same maker was also clearly responsible for a pair of air-pistols, the earliest recorded, operating in the same system, also in the Tøjhusmuseum.

The barrel reservoir remained popular during the first half of the eighteenth century, the guns fitted with it often being equipped with a dummy flintlock so that externally they looked exactly like a standard firearm. The finest example of the type is the magnificent silver-mounted air-gun in the Victoria and Albert Museum (No. 494–1894) made in London in
about 1730 by Johann Gottfried Kolbe of Suhl, 262
probably for King George II. Kolbe also invented a repeating air-gun.

At some time, probably round about 1680, an improved reservoir was devised, consisting of a copper ball screwed to a valve either under or, more rarely, at the side of the breech. A number of these reservoirs could be kept ready-charged with air and
substituted in turn for the one attached to the gun or 270
pistol when it became exhausted. This system remained in use until well into the nineteenth century.

It has already been mentioned that air-guns and pistols were regarded as alternatives to firearms until comparatively recently. Nevertheless, only one was ever adopted for military use. This was the repeating air-rifle invented by the Austro-Italian Bartholme Girandoni (or Girardoni) in 1779 in which the reservoir formed a detachable cylindrical metal butt. A tubular, spring-loaded bullet magazine ran alongside the barrel while running through the breech behind this was a transverse metal bar containing what was, in effect, the chamber. Loading was

1 For the best account of this subject see A. Hoff, *Airguns and Other Pneumatic Arms*, London, 1972.

2 E. MacCurdy, *The Notebooks of Leonardo da Vinci*, London, 1930, Vol. II, p. 188.

Pump-up, ball-reservoir airgun by George Wallis of Hull, *c.*1800. Victoria & Albert Museum, London.

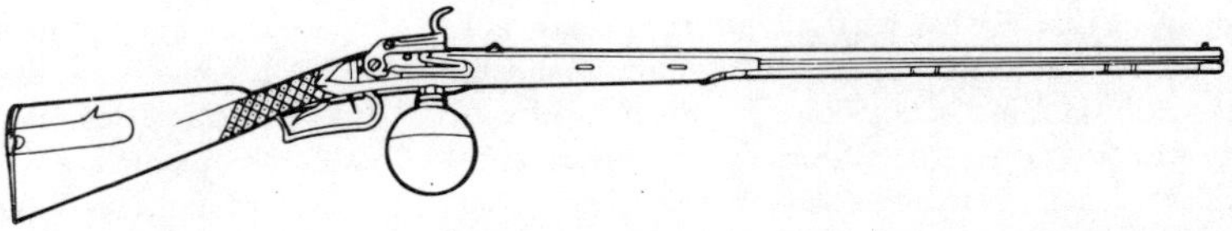

effected by moving the bar laterally by hand until the chamber picked up a ball from the magazine, and then allowing it to return under the action of a spring until the chamber was again in line with the breech.

The rifle was adopted for use by sharpshooters in the Austrian army in 1780 and remained in service until after 1806. Each rifle was accompanied by a hand-pump for recharging the reservoir, but large wheel-operated pumps were issued to each unit for charging the reservoirs centrally. A number of spares were carried by each rifleman so that it was only necessary to use the hand-pump in an emergency.

The success of the Girandoni gun was limited but a number of Viennese makers, notably Frühwirt, produced sporting guns and pistols working on the same system in the early years of the nineteenth century.

2. **Spring Air-Guns.** In this type of air-gun and pistol the bullet or dart was expelled by means of a blast of air produced by a spring-operated piston that had to be recocked between shots.[3] The oldest surviving air-guns operate on this principle, two late sixteenth-century examples being in the Kunsthistorisches Museum, Vienna (No. D159 and D326) and another in the Livrustkammare, Stockholm (No. 1196). Another in the Brahe-Bielke armoury at Skokloster, Sweden, is dated 1637 on the barrel. All appear to be German in origin.

Despite this early appearance in Europe spring air-guns do not seem to have been much used before the mid-nineteenth century. At this period they began to become popular in America for target-shooting. Many types of spring air-gun mechanism were patented on both sides of the Atlantic during the second half of the nineteenth century, but the person most responsible for the development of the guns and pistols that are still in wide use today was Henry Marcus Quackenbush of Herkimer, New York. After taking out US patents for a spring air-pistol in 1871 and a gun in 1876 he started to mass produce these arms with such success that he had within four years forced the more expensive hand-made products of his rivals off the market. He also took over in 1876 Benjamin Haviland and George C. Gunn's US patents of 1871 and 1872, the former of which had covered a pistol cocked by breaking the barrel down. This system is still one of the most popular for weapons of this kind.

Quackenbush's arms were subsequently manufactured under licence in Europe, notably by the German Diana Company founded in 1890. Other companies, both in Europe and America, also produced their own designs, the most important probably being the Daisy Manufacturing Company of Plymouth, Michigan, which in 1888 developed the first of the long series of cheap all-metal air-spring guns designed for the juvenile market.

3. **Bellows Guns.** This type operated in a similar manner to the air spring-gun but the blast of air was produced when a small pair of bellows concealed in the butt was compressed suddenly by means of a powerful spring. They appear to have been chiefly popular in South Germany in the eighteenth and

3 Guns have also been produced, usually for target work only, which employed only a powerful spring to discharge the projectile. In the nineteenth century even india-rubber was used for this purpose, as on a gun patented in London in 1849 by R. E. Hodges. An india-rubber spring was also used in conjunction with a 'condensing syringe' on an air-gun exhibited by J. Shaw of Glossop in the Great Exhibition of 1851.

early nineteenth century, though some may have been produced in America by immigrants. They were used exclusively for target shooting.

Gas Guns

The idea of using gas, with a more powerful rate of expansion, than air to discharge a projectile goes back to the steam-gun described and illustrated in one of Leonardo da Vinci's notebooks,[4] though probably never made. Other steam-guns were devised subsequently, notably the gun demonstrated in London in 1824 by the American Jacob Perkins, but none got beyond the experimental stage.

In 1834 the Danish inventor Peder Rasmussen devised a gun that operated with 'a sort of steam or gas to be generated from a special substance, without the use of fire from the temperature of the atmosphere alone'.[5] The gun appears never to have been produced and nothing is known either of its design or of the nature of the 'special substance', though it is probable that the latter was carbon-dioxide snow (dry-ice).

Other nineteenth-century attempts to use gas as a propellant were no more successful than Rasmussen's, with one exception. This was the gun patented in America in 1873 and, in an improved form, in England and France in 1889 by the distinguished French engineer Paul Giffard. The basic mechanism of this was similar to that of a pump-up air-gun but the propellant-power came from a cylinder of liquid carbon-dioxide, like an enlarged soda-syphon bulb, fitted underneath the barrel from which, it was claimed, as many as 300 shots could be obtained.

Giffard guns and pistols were made for a few years by the Manufacture Française d'Armes et Cycles at St Etienne while an attempt to introduce them in England was made in 1890 by founding the Giffard Gun & Ordnance Company in London. The arms were beautifully made and extremely effective against small game up to about 60 yards and attracted considerable attention at first. Despite this they were not a commercial success and the London company went into voluntary liquidation in 1894. The main reason for Giffard's failure was probably that his arms were not powerful enough to provide an alternative to conventional firearms–though the inventor claimed that they were–and were too complex and costly for use merely to shoot at targets and small game. His invention was, however, the prototype for the many gas guns and pistols, powered by the real soda-syphon bulbs so readily available, that are being manufactured now.

---

4 MacCurdy, *op. cit.*, Vol. II, p. 188.

5 A. Hoff, *The Rasmussen Revolving Guns*, Copenhagen, 1946, p. 25.

Appendix II
Miniature Firearms

Claude Blair

Miniature firearms vary in size from that of a watch-chain charm to that appropriate for actual use by a child. The widely-held belief that they were either salesmen's samples, illustrating in portable form the full-sized products offered for sale, or apprentices' masterpieces cannot be accepted. They were, in fact, made as jewellery, or for the same reasons that induce modern craftsmen to make miniatures now, as toys, like the eighteenth, nineteenth and early twentieth century miniature firearms made for the children of various Tsars now preserved in the Hermitage Museum, Leningrad. The earliest recorded examples date from the sixteenth century, and Michel Mann of Augsburg and Nuremberg (d. *c.* 1630) was particularly famous for making etched and gilt wheel-lock pistols. They are still being made today in a variety of styles. For obvious reasons the criteria used in assessing their full-sized counterparts rarely apply to these miniatures and they are consequently extremely difficult to date accurately. Collectors should not, therefore, be too ready to believe that a miniature gun or pistol is of the period when the type of arm it represents was actually in use.

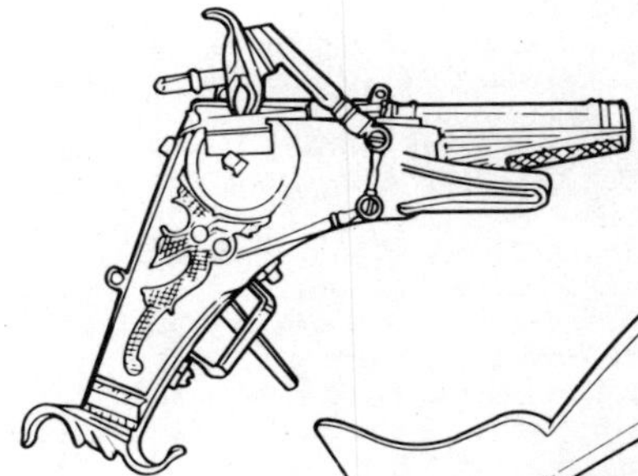

Miniature wheel-lock pistol, of blued steel and gilt engraved brass, by Michel Mann of Nuremberg, *c.*1620. Length approximately 5.5 cm. Victoria & Albert Museum, London.

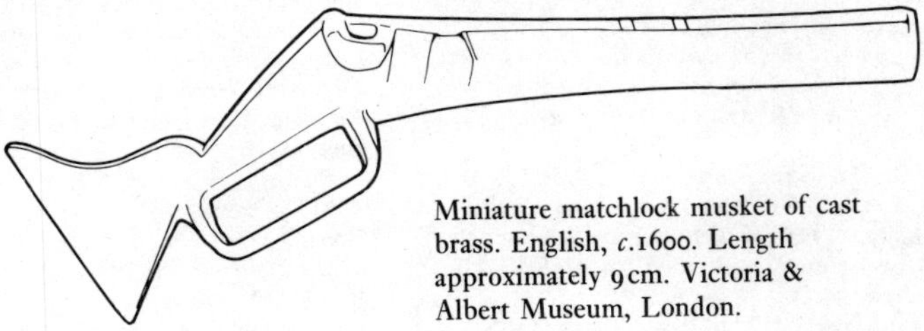

Miniature matchlock musket of cast brass. English, *c.*1600. Length approximately 9 cm. Victoria & Albert Museum, London.

Bibliography

Compiled by A. R. E. North

The select bibliography below is intended solely as a guide to further study and is mainly concerned with separate publications: a few articles of special importance are, however, included. For more extensive bibliographies on the subject of arms and armour in general, the reader is referred to those appended to Sir Guy Laking's *Record of European and American Arms* (5 vols London 1920-22) and to Sir James Mann's *Catalogue of European Arms and Armour in the Wallace Collection*, London 1960. For bibliographies specifically on firearms and related subjects, the reader is referred to: Wirt Gerrare (Oliver Greener), *A Bibliography of Guns and Shooting*, 1894; Maurice J. D. Cockle, *A Bibliography of English Military Books Up to 1642 and of Contemporary Foreign Works*, London, 1900; R. Riling, *Guns and Shooting*, Greenberg, NY 1951; W. Seel, *Bibliographie zur Technik und Geschichte der Handfeuerwaffen und Maschinengewehre*, Schwäbisch Hall, 1978; and also Vol. 3 of Heer's *Neue Stöckel.* In addition the *Journal of the Arms and Armour Society* regularly lists new publications on the subject.

Akehurst, R., *Game Guns and Rifles*, London 1969.
Albaugh, W. A., and Simmons, E. N., *Confederate Arms*, Harrisburg, PA 1957.
Alm, J. *Eldhandvapen*, 2 vols, Stockholm 1933-4.
Alm, J., *Arméns Eldhandvapen Förr och Nu*, Stockholm 1953.
Alm, J., *Flottans Handvapen*, Stockholm 1954.
Angelucci, A., *Documenti inediti para la storia dell'armi da fuoco italiane*, 1850-69. Reprinted Graz 1972.
Arbogast, M., *L'industrie des armes à Saint Etienne*, St Etienne 1937.
Atkinson, J. A., *Duelling Pistols and Some of the Affairs they Settled*, London 1964. New edn: *The British Duelling Pistol*, Bloomfield (Canada) and London 1978.
Ayalon, D., *Gunpowder and Firearms in the Mamluk Kingdom*, London 1956.
Bailey, D. W., 'The Jacob Rifle', *Guns Review*, Pateley Bridge, Oct and Dec 1969, pp. 401-4; 482-7.
Bailey, D. W., 'The Much Maligned Brunswick', *Guns Review*, Pateley Bridge, July and Aug 1970, pp. 265-8; 300-303.
Bailey, D. W., 'The Whitworth Rifle', *Gun Digest*, Chicago 1971, pp. 95-105.
Bailey, D. W., *British Military Longarms 1715-1815*, London 1971.
Bailey, D. W., *British Military Longarms 1815-1865*, London 1971.
Bailey, D. W., 'British Volunteer Rifles 1850-1870', *Gun Digest*, Chicago 1972, pp. 22-36.
Bailey, D. W., 'British Small-Bore Rifles. Part One–The ·451 Muzzleloaders', *Gun Digest*, Chicago 1973, pp. 29-42.
Bailey, D. W., *Percussion Guns and Rifles*, London 1972.
Bailey, D. W., 'The Baker Rifle', *Guns Review*, Pateley Bridge, April, May, June, July 1973, pp. 142-45; 188-91; 226-8; 285-8.
Bailey, D. W., 'Powder Flasks', *The Journal of the Historical Firearms Society of South Africa*, Cape Town, Vol. 7, No. 1, June 1975, pp. 4-24.
Bailey, D. W., and Nie, D. A., *English Gunmakers. The Birmingham and Provincial Gun-Trade in the 18th and 19th Centuries*, London and Melbourne 1978.
Baker, E., *Remarks on Rifle Guns*, 11th edn, London 1835.
Bartocci, A., and Salvatici, L., *Armamento Individuale dell' Esercito Piemontese e Italiano 1814-1914*, Florence 1978.
Baxter, D. R., *Superimposed Load Firearms 1360-1860*, Hong Kong 1966.
Beaufort-Spontin, C., *Harnisch und Waffen Europas. Die militärische Ausrüstung im H. Jahrhundert*, Munich 1982.
Belford, J. N. & Dunlap, J., *The Mauser Self-Loading Pistol*, Alhambra, CA 1969.
Berkovitch, B. M., *The Cape Gunsmith*, Stellenbosch 1976.
Blackmore, H. L. *British Military Firearms, 1650-1850*, London 1961.
Blackmore, H. L., *Guns and Rifles of the World*, London 1965.
Blackmore, H. L., *Hunting Weapons*, London 1971.
Blair, C., *European and American Arms, c.1100-1850*, London 1962.
Blair, C., *Pistols of the World*, London 1968.
Blair, C., and others (eds), *Enciclopedia Ragionata delle Armi*, Milan 1979.
Blanch, H. J., *A Century of Guns*, London 1909.
Boccia, L., *Nove Secoli di Armi da Caccia*, Florence 1967.
Bock, G., and Weigel, W., *Handbuch der Faust-Feuerwaffen*, Neudamm 1964.
Boeheim, W., *Meister der Waffenschmiedekunst, XIV-XVIII Jahrhundert*, Berlin 1897.
Boothroyd, G., *The Handgun*, London 1970.
Bosson, C., 'Histoire et Description de l'Arme à Feu en Suisse, 1817-1957', *Armes Anciennes*, No. 9, pp. 25-61, Geneva 1957.
Bottet, M., *La Manufacture de Versailles, Boutet Directeur Artiste*, Paris 1903.
Bottet, M., *Monographie de l'arme à feu portative des armées françaises de terre et de mer de 1718 à nos jours*, Paris N.D. (*c.*1900). Reprinted Paris 1959.
Boudriot, J., *Armes à feu françaises modèles réglementaires, 1717-1816*, 3 vols, Paris 1961-5. *See also* Lorain, P., and Marquiset, R.
Brooker, R. E., *British Military Pistols 1603-1888.* Coral Gables, FL 1978.
Caldwell, David (ed.), *Scottish Weapons & Fortifications*, Edinburgh 1982.
Calvo, J. L. *Armamento Reglamentario y Auxiliar del Ejercito Español 1717-1922*, 4 vols, Barcelona 1975-7.
Carey, A. M., *English, Irish and Scottish Firearms Makers*, New York 1954. Reprinted London 1955 and 1967.
Carpegna, D. di, 'Notes on Central Italian Firearms of the Eighteenth Century', *Journal of the Arms & Armour Society*, VII (1971-3), pp. 17-48, VIII (1974-6), pp. 1-24.
Carpegna, D. di, *Armi da Fuoco della Collezione Odescalchi.* Rome 1968. English edn: *Firearms in the Prince Odescalchi Collection in Rome*, Rome 1975.
Chamberlain, W. H. J., and Taylerson, A. W. F., *The Adam Revolver*, London 1976.
Chapel, C. E., *The Gun Collector's Handbook of Values*, 4th edn, New York.

Chapel, C. E., *U.S. Martial and Semi-Martial Single-Shot Pistols*, New York 1962.
Cockle, Maurice J. D., *A Bibliography of English Military Books up to 1642 and of Contemporary Foreign Works*, London 1900.
Cooper, C., and Lindsay, M., *Eli Whitney and the Whitney Armoury*, (Eli Whitney Museum) Whitneyville, U.S.A. 1980.
Corcoran, J. E., *The Target Rifle in Australia 1860-1900*, Lane Cove, NSW 1975.
Cripps-Day, F. H., *A Record of Armour Sales, 1881-1924*, London 1925.
Datig, F. A., *Cartridges for Collectors*, 3 vols, Beverley Hills, CA 1958-67.
Deane's *Manual of the History and Science of Firearms*, London 1958. Reprinted Huntingdon, WV 1946.
Demmin, A., *Die Kriegswaffen in ihren geschichtlichen Entwickelungen*, etc., 3rd edn, Leipzig 1891-3, plus two undated supplementary volumes.
Descreux, M., *Notices biographiques stéphanoises*, St Etienne 1868.
Deyrup, F. J., *Arms Making in the Connecticut Valley*, York, PA 1970.
Dillin, J. G., *The Kentucky Rifle*, 4th edn, New York 1959.
Dinklage, *Kurze Geschichte der Ferlacher Büchsenmacherei*, Ferlach 1978.
Dixon, N., *Georgian Pistols. The Art and Craft of the Flintlock Pistol 1715-1840*, London 1971.
Dolleczek, A., *Monographie der k.u.k. österr.-ung Blankenund Handfeuer-Waffen, etc.*, Vienna 1896.
Dowell, W. C., *The Webley Story*, London 1962.
Drummond, J., and Anderson, J., *Ancient Scottish Weapons*, London and Edinburgh 1881.
Dubessy, R., *Historique de la Manufacture d'Armes de guerre de St Etienne*, St Etienne 1900.
Ducharte, P.-L., *Histoire des armes de la chasse*, Paris 1955.
Dunlap, J., *American, British and Continental Pepperbox Firearms*, San Francisco, CA 1964.
Eaves, Ian, 'Some Notes on the Pistol in Early 17th Century England', *Journal of the Arms and Armour Society*, VI (1968-70) pp. 277-344; 'Further Notes on the Pistol in Early 17th Century England', *Ibid.*, VIII (1974-6), pp. 269-329.
Eckardt, W., and Morawietz, O., *Die Handwaffen des brandenburgisch-preussisch-deutschen Heeres 1640-1945*, Hamburg 1947.
Edwards, W. B., *Civil War Guns*, Harrisburg, PA 1962.
Egerton of Tatton, Lord, *A Description of Indian and Oriental Armour*, London 1896. Reprinted London 1968.
Emy, J., and Tinguy, B., de, *Histoire de la pierre à fusil*, Meusnes, Loir-et-Cher 1964.
Engelhardt, A., Baron, 'The Story of European Proof Marks', *The Gun Digest*, 7th edn, Chicago 1953, and succeeding editions.
Essenwein, A., *Quellen zur Geschichte der Feuerwaffen*, Leipzig 1877. Reprinted Graz 1969.
Feldhaus, F. M., *Die Technik*, Leipzig and Berlin 1914. Reprinted Munich 1965.
Fiosconi, C., and Gusero, J., *Espingarda Perfeyta* (or *The Perfect Gun*) [Lisbon 1708]. Ed and trans by Rainer Daehnhardt and W. Keith Neal, London and New York 1974.
Fjodorov, V. G., *The Arms of the Russian Army in the 19th Century*, 1901. In Russian.
Fjodorov, V. G., *Arms Production on the Frontiers of two epochs*, Moscow 1938. In Russian.
Fraiken, J., *L'industrie armurière liègeoise et le Banc d'Epreuves des armes à feu de Liège*, Liège 1940.
Fremantle, T. F., *The Book of the Rifle*, London 1901.
Fuller, C. E., *Springfield Muzzleloading Shoulder Arms*, New York 1930.
Fuller, C. E., and Steuart, R., *Firearms of the Confederacy*, Huntington, WV 1944.
Fuller, C. E., *The Whitney Firearms*, Huntingdon, WV 1946.
Gaibi, A., *Le Arms da Fuoco Portabili Italiane dalle Origini al Risorgimento*, Milan 1962. Rev edn 1978.
Gaibi, A., 'Le Armi da Fuoco', *Storia di Brescia*, Vol. III, pp. 817-84, Brescia 1964.
Gaier, C., *Four Centuries of Liège Gunmaking*, London 1976.
Gardner, R. E., *Small Arms Makers*, New York 1963.
Gay, V., *Glossaire archéologique du Moyen Age et de la Renaissance*, 2 vols, Paris 1887 and 1928.
Gelli, J., *Gli Archiburgiari Milanesi*, Milan 1905.
George, J. N., *English Pistols and Revolvers*, Onslow County, NC 1938.
George, J. N., *English Guns and Rifles*, Harrisburg, PA 1947.
Gill, H. B., *The Gunsmith in Colonial Virginia*, Williamsburg, VA 1974.
Gluckman, A., *United States Martial Pistols and Revolvers*, Buffalo, NY 1944.
Gluckman, Col A., *United States Muskets, Rifles and Carbines*. Buffalo, NY 1948. New edn entitled *Identifying* . . . Harrisburg, PA 1965.
Gooding, J. S., *The Canadian Gunsmiths, 1608-1900*, Ont 1962.
Gooding, J. S., *The Gunsmiths of Canada*, Ottawa, Ont 1974.
Götz, H. D., *Die deutschen Militärgewehre und Maschinenpistolen, 1871-1945*, Stuttgart 1974.
Götz, H. D., *Militärgewehre und Pistolen der deutschen Staaten 1800-1870*, Stuttgart 1978.
Grancsay, S. V., *American Engraved Powder Horns*, New York 1945.
Grancsay, S. V., 'Firearms of the Mediterranean', 2 parts, *The American Rifleman*, Feb 1949, pp. 21-4; 27th March 1949, pp. 30-3.
Grancsay, S. V., 'Miniature Firearms', *The American Rifleman*, July 1949, pp. 28-9.
Grancsay, S. V., *Master French Gunsmith's Designs of the Mid-Seventeenth Century*, New York 1950.
Grancsay, S. V., and Lindsay, M., *Illustrated British Firearms Patents 1714-1853*, New York 1969.
Grant, J. J., *Single-Shot Rifles*, New York 1947.
Grant, J. J., *More Single-Shot Rifles*, New York 1959.
Grant, J. J., *Still More Single-Shot Rifles*, (no other data; recent).
Gras, L.-J., *Historique de l'armurerie Stéphanoise*, St Etienne 1905. A study of the arms industry of St Etienne.
Greener, W., *The Gun*, London 1835.
Greener, W. W., *The Gun and its Development*, 9th edn, London 1910.
Greener, William, *The Science of Gunnery*, London 1841.
Hanson, C. E., *The Northwest Gun*, Lincoln, NE 1955.
Hanson, C. E., *The Plains Rifle*, Harrisburg, PA 1960.
Harris, C. (ed.), *The History of the Birmingham Gun-Barrel Proof House, with notes on the Birmingham Gun Trade*, Birmingham 1946.
Hatch, A., *Remington Arms in American History*, New York and Toronto 1956.
Haven, C. T., and Belden, F. A., *A History of the Colt Revolver*, New york 1940.
Hawkins, *The Price Guide to Antique Guns and Pistols*, London 1973.
Hayward, J. F., *The Art of the Gunmaker*, 2 vols, London, 1962-3, 2nd edn of Vol. I, 1965.
Heer, E., *Geschichte und Entwicklung der Militärhandfeuerwaffen in der Schweiz*, Graz 1971.
Heer, E., *Der Neue Stöckel. Internationales Lexikon der Büchsenmacher, Feuerwaffen-Fabrikanten und Armbrüstmacher von 1400-1900*, 3 vols, Schwäbisch Hall, 1978-82.

Held, R., *The Age of Firearms*, New York 1957.
Held, R., *Art, Arms and Armour–An International Anthology*, Vol. I 1979-80. Chiasso, Switzerland 1980.
Hewitt, J., *Ancient Armour and Weapons in Europe*, Vol. III, London 1860. Reprinted Graz 1967.
Hicks, J. E., *Ordnance Correspondence*, Mount Vernon, VA 1940.
Hicks, J. E., *U.S. Firearms 1776-1956*, Beverly Hills, CA 1957.
Hicks, J. E., *French Military Weapons 1717-1938*, New Milford, CT 1964.
Hillemann, K., *Geschichte der Herzberger Gewehrfabrik nach Urkunden*, privately published by the author, Herzberg/Harz 1959. *See also* Klose, P.
Hoff, A., *Aeldre Dansk Bøssemageri isaer i 1660-tallet*, 2 vols, Copenhagen 1951. Contains an English summary.
Hoff, A., *Feuerwaffen*, 2 vols, Brunswick 1969.
Hoff, A., *Airguns and other Pneumatic Arms*, London 1972.
Hoff, A., *Dutch Firearms*, London 1978.
Hogg, I. V., *Military Pistols and Revolvers*, London 1970.
Hogg, I. V., *Military Small-arms of the 20th Century*, London 1973.
Hogg, I. V., *The Illustrated Encyclopaedia of Firearms*, London 1978.
Hogg, I. V., and Batchelor, J., *Handguns 1870-1978*, London 1978.
Hogg, I. V., and Batchelor, J., *The Machine Gun*, London, 1976.
Jackson, H. J., *European Hand Firearms of the Sixteenth, Seventeenth and Eighteenth Centuries . . . with a treatise on Scottish hand firearms by Charles E. Whitelaw*, London 1923.
Jarlier, P., *Répertoire d'arquebusiers et de fourbisseurs français*, St-Julien-du-Sault 1976. *Suppléments* 1978/1981.
Johnson, M. M., and Haven, C. T., *Automatic Arms*, New York 1941.
Kalmár, J., *Régi magyar fegyverek*, Budapest 1971.
Karr, C. I., and Karr, C. R., *Remington Handguns 1650-1860*, Harrisburg, PA 1951.
Kauffman, H. J., *Early American Gunsmiths 1650-1860*, Harrisburg, PA 1952.
Kauffman, H. J., *The Pennsylvania-Kentucky Rifle*, Harrisburg, PA 1960.
Kempers, R. T. W., *Antieke Vuurwapens*, 3 vols, Haarlem 1977.
Kimborough, R. E., 'Japanese Firearms', *The Gun Collector*, No. 33, pp. 445-65, Madison, WI Sept 1950.
Kindig, Joseph, Jr. *Thoughts on the Kentucky Rifle in its Golden Age.*
Kist, J. B., Puype, J. P., Van Der Mark, W., and Van Der Sloot, R. B. F., *Dutch Muskets and Pistols*, London 1974.
Klose, P., *Beiträge zur Geschichte der Herzberger Gewehrfabrik*, privately published by the author, Herzberg/Harz 1963. *See also* Hillemann, K.
Korn, R. H., *Mauser-Gewehre und Mauser Patente*, Graz 1971.
Lavin, J. D., *A History of Spanish Firearms*, London 1965.
Lenk, T., *Flintlåset, dess uppkomst och utveckling*, Stockholm 1939. English trans: *The Flintlock: its origin and development*; trans. by G. A. Urquhart, ed. by J. F. Hayward, London 1965.
Leutmann, J. G. 'De Sulcis Cochleatis Ad Datam Distantiam Tubis Sclopetorum' and 'Annotationes . . . ad Rem Sclopetariam Pertinentia', *Proceedings of the Imperial Academy of Sciences of St Petersburg*, Vol III (1728), pp. 156-63, and IV (1729), pp. 265-76. Published in German as *Nachricht von gezogenen Büchsen*, etc., Nuremberg, 1735. Annotated English translation by D. W. Bailey in the press.
Lewis, B. R., *Small Arms and Ammunition in the United States Service*, Washington, DC 1956.
Lindsay, M., *One Hundred Great Guns. An Illustrated History of Firearms*, New York 1967.
Lissmark, B., *Svenska Försvarets Pistoler och Revolvrar 1683-1958*, Karlskrona 1974.
Lister, R., *Antique Firearms, their Care, Repair and Restoration*, London 1963.
Logan, H. C., *Cartridges*, Huntington, WV 1948.
Logan, H. C., *Underhammer Guns*, Harrisburg, PA 1960.
Lorain, P., and Marquiset, R., *Armes à feu françaises modèles réglementaires, 1915-1918, chargement culasse*, Paris 1969. *See also* Boudriot, J., and Marquiset, R.
Lugs, J., *Handfeuerwaffen*, 2 vols, Berlin 1956.
Lupi, G., *I primi fucili a ripetizione*, Florence 1979.
McHenry, R., and Roper, W. F., *Smith and Wesson Hand Guns*, Huntington, WV 1945.
Madis, G., *The Winchester Book*, Dallas, TX 1961.
Malatesta, E., *Armi ed Armaioli*, Milan 1939.
Marciano, E., and Morin, M., *Dal carcano al fal*, Florence 1974.
Margerand, J., *Armement et Equipement de l'Infanterie Française du XVIe au XXe Siècle*, Paris 1945.
Marquiset, R., and Boudriot, J., *Armes à Feu Françaises Modèles Réglementaires 1833-1861 chargement bouche et percussion.* Paris 1967. *See also* Boudriot, J., and Lorain, P.
Mattenheimer, A., *Die Rückladungs-Gewehr*, Darmstadt and Leipzig 1876.
May, W. E., and Kennard, A. N., *Naval Swords and Firearms*, London 1962.
Meyerson, Å., *Stockholms Bössmakare*, Stockholm 1936.
Milward, C., 'Some Unusual Japanese Firearms', *The Antique Collector*, Aug 1964, pp. 148-53.
Møller, T., *Gamle Danske Militar Vaben* (Old Danish Military Weapons), Copenhagen 1963.
Mollstadius. A., *Jönköpings Gevärfaktori 1695-1720.* Reprinted from *Meddelanden från Jönköpings Löns Hembygdsförbund, XXXI*, Jönköping 1958.
Morin, M., and Held, R., *Beretta–the World's Oldest Industrial Dynasty*, Chiasso, Switz. 1980.
Müller, H., *Guns, Pistols, Revolvers. Hand-firearms from the 14th to the 19th centuries.* Leipzig 1980.
Müller, R. H., *Geschichte und Technik der europäischen Militärrevolver*, 2 vols, Schwäbisch Hall 1982.
Neal, R. J., and Jinks, R. G., *Smith and Wesson 1857-1945. A Handbook for Collectors*, South Brunswick, NJ and London 1966.
Neal, W. K., *Spanish Guns and Pistols*, London 1955.
Neal, W. K., 'Duelling Pistols', *Antiques International*, Collectors' Guide to Current Trends (ed. by P. Wilson), pp. 256-66, London 1966.
Neal, W. K., and Back, D. H. L., *The Mantons; Gunmakers*, London 1967. *Supplement*, Tisbury 1978.
Neal, W. K., and Back, D. H. L., *Forsyth and Co. Patent Gunmakers 1750-90*, London 1969.
Neal, W. K., and Back, D. H. L., *Great British Gunmakers, 1750-90*, London 1975.
Neal, W. K., and Back, D. H. L., *British Gunmakers, Their Trade-Cards, Cases and Equipment, 1760-1860*, Warminster 1980.
Neumann, G. C., *The History of Weapons of the American Revolution*, New York, Evanston, IL and London 1967.
North, A. R. E., and Hogg, I. V., *The Book of Guns and Gunsmiths*, Glasgow and London 1978.
Nutter, W. E., *Manhattan Firearms*, Harrisburg, PA 1958.
Parsons, J. E., *The Peace-Maker and its Rivals*, New York 1950.

Parsons, J. E., *Henry Deringer's Pocket Pistol*, New York 1952.

Parsons, J. E., *The First Winchester*, New York 1955.

Parsons, J. E., *Smith and Wesson Revolvers. The Pioneer Single Action Models*, New York 1957.

Partington, J. R., *A History of Greek Fire and Gunpowder*, Cambridge 1960.

Patent Office, London, *Abridgements of the Patent Specifications Relating to Firearms and Other Weapons, Ammunition and Accoutrements from 1588-1858*, London 1859. Reprinted London 1960.

Perrin, N., *Giving Up the Gun, Japan's Reversion to the Sword, 1543-1879*. Boulder, CO 1980.

Peterson, H. L., *Arms and Armour in Colonial America*, 1526-1783, Harrisburg, PA 1956.

Peterson, H. L., *The Treasury of the Gun*, New York 1962. English edition: *The Book of the Gun*, London 1963.

Peterson, H. L. (ed), *The Encyclopedia of Firearms*, London and New York 1964.

Peterson, H. L., *Pageant of the Gun*, New York 1967.

Peterson, H. L., and Elman, R., *The Great Guns*, New York 1971.

Polain, A., *Recherches Historiques sur l'Epreuve des Armes à Feu au Pays de Liège*, Liège 1863.

Pollard, H. B. C., *A History of Firearms*, London 1930.

Puraye, J., *La Gravure sur Amres à Feu au Pays de Liège*, Liège 1964.

Rathgen, B., *Das Aufkommen der Pulverwaffe*, Munich 1925.

Rathgen, B., *Das Geschütz im Mittelalter*, Berlin 1928.

Reid, Sir A. J. F., *The Reverend Alexander John Forsyth . . . and His Invention of the Percussion Lock*, Aberdeen 1910. Reprinted 1955.

Reid, W., 'The Heart-butt Pistols of East Scotland', *Scottish Weapons. Scottish Art Review Special Number*, pp. 26-30 and 32, Glasgow 1963.

Rensselaer, S. van, *American Firearms*, Watkins Glen, NY 1947.

Ricketts, H., *Firearms*, London 1962.

Riling, R., *The Powder Flask Book*, New Hope, PA 1953.

Roads, C. H., *The British Soldier's Firearms, 1850-1864*, London 1964.

Rosa, J., *Colonel Colt London*, London 1976.

Russell, C. P., *Guns on the Early Frontiers*, Berkeley and Los Angeles (CA) 1962.

Sawyer, C. W., *Firearms in American History*, 3 vols, Boston, MA 1910-20.

Schedelmann, H., *Die Wiener Büchsenmacher und Büchsenschäfter*, Berlin 1944.

Schedelmann, H., *Die Grossen Büchsenmacher*, Brunswick 1972.

Schmidt, Rudolf, *Die Handfeuerwaffen*, 2 vols, Basel 1875 and 1878. Reprinted Graz 1968.

Schneider, H., *Altschweizerische Waffenproduktion*, Zurich 1964.

Schneider, H., *Schweizer Waffenschmiede vom 15. bis 20. Jahrhundert*, Zürich 1976.

Schreier, K. F., *Remington Rolling Block Firearms*, U.S.A. 1977.

Sell, D. W. E., *Collector's Guide to American Cartridge Handguns*, Harrisburg, PA 1963.

Sellers, F. M., *Sharps Firearms*, North Hollywood, CA 1978.

Sellers, F. M., and Smith, S. E., *American Percussion Revolvers*, Ottawa, Ont 1971.

Serven, J. E., *Colt Firearms 1836-1960*, Santa Ana, CA 1960.

Shannon, R. B., *Colonial Australian Gunsmiths*, Sydney 1967.

Shumway, G., *Rifles of Colonial America*, 2 vols, York, PA 1980.

Skennerton, I. D., *A Treatise on the Snider*, Queensland, Aust 1977.

Skennerton, I. D., *The British Service Lee*, London and Margate (Aust) 1982.

Smith, M. R., *Harpers Ferry Armory and the New Technology*, Ithaca, NY and London 1977.

Smith, W. H. B., *Mauser Rifles and Pistols*, 3rd edn, Harrisburg, PA 1950.

Smith, W. H. B., *Gas, Air and Spring Guns of the World*, Harrisburg, PA 1957.

Smith, W. H. B., *Mannlicher Rifles and Pistols*, Harrisburg, PA 1963.

Smith, W. H. B., and Smith, J. E., *Small Arms of the World*, Harrisburg, PA 1962.

Støckel, J. R., *Haandskydevaabens Bedømmelse*, 2 vols, Copenhagen 1938-43. Reprinted 1964. *See also* Heer, E.

Stöcklein, H., *Meister des Eisenschnittes*, Esslingen a. N., 1922.

Stone, G. C., *A Glossary of the Construction, Decoration and Use of Arms and Armor in all Countries and in all Times*, Portland, ME 1934. Reprinted New York 1961.

Stonehenge (pseud. of J. H. Walsh, *q.v.*), *The Shot-gun and Sporting Rifle*, London 1859.

Sutherland, R. Q., and Wilson, R. L., *The Book of Colt Firearms*. Kansas City, MO 1971.

Tarassuk, L., 'Russian Pistols in the Seventeenth Century', *The Burlington Magazine*, 2 parts, London; Nov 1967, pp. 633-42, Dec 1967, pp. 686-98. Reprinted as a book, London 1968.

Taylerson, A. W. F., *The Revolver, 1865-1888*, London 1966.

Taylerson, A. W. F., *Revolving Arms*, London 1967.

Taylerson, A. W. F., *The Revolver, 1889-1914*, London 1970.

Taylerson, A. W. F., Andrews, R. A. N., and Frith, J., *The Revolver 1818-1865*, London 1968. *See also* Chamberlain.

Terenzi, M., *L'arte di Michele Battista Armaiolo Napoletano*, Rome 1964.

Terenzi, M., *Gli Armaioli Anghiaresi*, Rome 1972.

Thierbach, M., *Die geschichtliche Entwicklung der Handfeuerwaffen*, Dresden 1886-7; Nachträge 1899. Reprinted Graz 1965.

Thomas, B., *Hans Schmidt von und zu Helding. Der 'kunstreiche' Büchsenschäfer von Ferlach*, Klagenfurt 1982.

Thomas, B., Gamber, O., and Schedelmann, H., *Die Schönsten Waffen und Rüstungen*, Munich 1963. English trans: *Arms and Armour*, London 1964.

Thomas, H. H., *The Story of Allen & Wheelock Firearms*, Lexington, KY 1965.

Tout, T. F., 'Firearms in England in the Fourteenth Century'. *English Historical Review*, Vol. XXCI, pp. 666-702, London 1911. Reprinted in *The Collected Papers of Thomas Frederick Tout*, Vol. II, Manchester 1934, pp. 233-75. Reprinted as a separate book with an introduction by Claude Blair, London 1968.

Ullman, K., *Schmuck alter Büchsen und Gewehre, Jagdmotiv in der Büchsenmacherkunst (1650-1850)*, Hamburg and Berlin 1964.

Upper Canadian Historical Arms Society, *The Military Arms of Canada*, Ont 1963.

Viterbo, S., *A Armeria em Portugal*, 2 vols, Lisbon 1907-8.

Wacha, Georg, *Linzer Büchsenmacher*, Linz 1969.

Walsh, J. H., *The Modern Sportsman's Gun and Rifle*, 2 vols, London 1882-4.

Walter, J., *Luger*, London and Stony Creek (Canada) 1977.

Walter, J., *The German Rifle*, London and Stony Creek (Canada), 1979.

Waterhouse, D. B., 'Firearms in Japanese History, with notes on a Japanese Wall Gun', *The British Museum Quarterley*, Vol. XXVII, No. 3-4, Winter 1963-4, pp. 94-9.
Watrous, G. R., *The History of Winchester Firearms*, 3rd edn, New Haven, CT 1966.
Werner, E. T. C., *Chinese Weapons*, Shanghai 1932.
Wesley, L., *Air-Guns and Air-Pistols*, London 1935.
Westropp, M. S. D., 'Irish Gunsmiths and Sword Cutler', *Journal of the Arms and Armour Society*, Vol. II, pp. 13-18, London 1956-8.
Whitelaw, C. E., *See under* Jackson, H. J.
Whitelaw, C. C., *Scottish Arms Makers*, ed. by Sarah Barter, London 1977.
Wilkinson, F., *Small-Arms*, London 1965.
Wilkinson, F., *British and American Flintlocks*, London 1971.
Wilkinson, F., *Flintlock Guns and Rifles*, London 1971.
Willers, J. K. W., *Die Nürnberger Handfeuerwaffe bis zur Mitte des 16, Jahrhunderts*, Nuremberg 1973.
Williamson, H. F., *Pepperbox Firearms*, New York 1952.
Wilson, R. K., *Textbook of Automatic Pistols*, Plantersville, SC 1943.
Wilson, R. K., *Winchester–The Gun that Won the West*, Washington, DC 1952.
Wilson, R. L., *L. D. Nimschke, Firearms Engraver*, Teaneck, NJ 1965.
Wilson, R. L., *Colt Commemorative Firearms*, Wichita, KS 1969.
Winant, L., *Firearms Curiosa*, New York 1955. Reprinted London 1961.
Winant, L., *Early Percussion Firearms*, New York 1959. English ed: London, 1961.
Winant, L., *Pepperbox Firearms*, Los Altos, CA 1964.
Wirtgen, A., *Die Preussischen Handfeuerwaffen, Modelle und Manufakturen 1700 -1806*, Osnabrück 1976.
Żygulski, Z., *Broń w Dawnej Polsce*, Warsaw 1975.
Żygulski, Z., *Old Weapons in Polish Collections*, Warsaw 1982. Main text in Polish.

MUSEUM CATALOGUES, ETC.

ALLENTOWN, Pennsylvania. Art Museum
Grancsay, S. V., *Arms and Armor March 15th-June 14th 1964*. A loan exhibition from the Collection of Stephen V. Grancsay with important contributions from the Metropolitan Museum, New York, and from the John Woodman Higgins Armory, Worcester, MA.
ANGHIARI. Arezzo
Terenzi, M., *Mostra delle Armi da Fuoco dell'Appenino Tosco-Emiliano. Secoli XVII-XVIII, XIX.* Anghiari. Palazzo Taglieschi 1968.
BEDFORD COLLECTION See *Colonial Williamsburg*
BERLIN. Museum für Deutsche Geschichte (formerly Zeughaus)
Müller, H. *Altes Geschütze. Kostbare Stücke aus der Sammlung des Museums*, Berlin 1968.
Post, Paul, *Das Zeughaus, Die Waffensammlung. Erster Teil*, Berlin 1929.
BERN. Historisches Museum
Wegeli, R., *Inventar der Waffensammlung des Bernischen Historischen Museums in Bern*, 4 vols, Bern 1920-48.
Zeller, R., and Rofrer, E. F., *Orientalische Sammlung Henri Moser-Charlottenfels. Beschreibender Katalog der Waffensammlung*, Bern 1955.
BRUNSWICK COLLECTION
See London. Tower of London Armouries
BRUSSELS. Musée Royal d'Armes et d'Armures, Porte de Hal
Prelle de la Nieppe, E., *Catralogue des Armes et Armures du Musée de la Porte de Hal*, Brussels 1902.
BUDAPEST. Milleniums-Landes-Ausstellung.
Szendrei, J., *Ungarische Kriegsgeschichtliche Denkmäler in der Milleniums-Landes-Ausstellung*, Budapest 1968.
CLEVELAND, Ohio. Museum of Art
Gilchrist, H. I., *A Catalogue of the Collection of Arms and Armor presented to the Cleveland Museum of Art by Mr & Mrs John Long Severand 1916-1923.* Cleveland, OH 1924.
COLONIAL WILLIAMSBURG FOUNDATION
Gusler, W. B., and Lavin, J. D., *Decorated Firearms 1540-1870, from the collection of Clay P. Bedford*, Charlottesville, VA 1977.
DRESDEN. Historisches Museum
Ehrenthal, M. V., *Führer durch die Königliche Gewehr-Galerie zu Dresden*, Dresden 1900.
Haenel, E., *Kostbare Waffen aus der Dresdner Rüstkammer, Leipzig, 1923.*
Katalog Sühler Feuerwaffen 17-18.jh, Staatlich Kunstsammlungen, Dresden.
Schall, D., *Katalog Dresdener Buchsenmacher 16-18.jh.*
Schöbel, J., *Pistolen*, Dresden 1962.
EMDEN. Zeughaus
Potier, O., Baron, *Inventar der Rüstkammer der Stadt Emden*, Emden 1903.
FLORENCE. Museo Stibbert
Boccia, L. G., *Il Museo Stibbert a Firenze*, Vol III, Milan 1975.
Lensi, A., *Il Museo Stibbert. Catalogo delle Sale delle Armi Europee*, 2 vols, Florence 1908.
GENEVA. Musée d'Art et d'Histoire
Bosson, C., 'Les Pistolets à Rouet du Musée d'Art et d'Histoire', *Genava N.S. Vol. 1.*, pp. 143-75, Geneva 1953.
Bosson, C., 'Quelques armes du musée d'Art et d'Histoire de Genéve,' *Armes Anciennes*, Vol. 1, pp. 3-23, Geneva 1953-6.
GLASGOW. City Art Gallery and Museum (R. L. Scott Collection)
Joubert, F., *Catalogue of the Collection of European Arms and Armour formed at Greenock by R. L. Scott.* 3 vols, privately printed 1924. 'Arms and Armour from the Scott Collection', *Scottish Art Review Special Number*, Glasgow 1956.
GRAZ. Landes-Zeughaus.
Krenn, P. *Die Steirische Landwehr Erstund Jetzt*, June 3–Sept 4, 1977.
Pichler, F., *Das Landes-Zeughaus in Graz*, Leipzig 1880.
HAGERSTOWN, MD. Washington County Museum of Fine Arts.
Grancsay, S. V., *Loan Exhibition of Mediaeval and Renaissance Arms and Armor from the Metropolitan Museum of Art*, Feb 27–Mar 31, 1955.
HAROLDS CLUB. Reno, NV
Bowman, H. W., *Famous Guns from the Harolds Club Collection*, Greenwich, CT 1967.
HARTFORD, Wadsworth Atheneum
Wilson, R. L., *Samuel Colt Presents. A Loan Exhibition of Presentation Percussion Colt Firearms*, Nov 3, 1961–Jan 14, 1962.
Wilson, R. L., *The Arms Collection of Colonel Colt*, Hartford, CT 1963.
KIENBUSCH COLLECTION, New York (now Philadelphia Museum of Art)
The Kretzschmar von Kienbusch Collection of Armor and Arms, Princetown, NJ 1963.
LENINGRAD, Hermitage Museum
Lenz, E., *Collection d'Armes de l'Hermitage Impérial*, St Petersburg 1908.
Tarassuk, L., *Antique European and American Firearms at the Hermitage Museum*, Leningrad 1971.
Tarassuk, L., 'The Collection of Arms and Armour in the State Hermitage Leningrad', *Journal of the Arms and Armour Society*, Vol. III (1959-61), pp. 1-39; Vol V (1965-8), pp. 205-61.

LIÈGE, Musée d'Armes
Musée d'Armes (Catalogue of the collection), Liège n.d. (*c*.1920).
LONDON, Tower of London Armouries
ffoulkes, C. J., *Inventory and Survey of the Armouries of the Tower of London*, 2 vols, London 1916.
Exhibition of Armour of Kings and Captains From the National Collections of Austria at the Tower of London, May 12–Sept 15, 1949.
Exhibition of Arms, Armour and Militaria. Lent by H.R.H. The Duke of Brunswick at the Tower of London Armouries, April 10-31, 1953.
Norman, A. V. B. and Wilson, G. M., *Treasures from the Tower of London. Arms and Armour*. London, Melbourne and Harrisburg, PA 1982. Sainsbury Centre for Visual Arts 1982.
LONDON, Victoria and Albert Museum
Arms and Armour Society, *The Art of the Armour*, April 19–May 4, 1963.
Hayward, J. F., *European Firearms*, London 1955.
Robinson, B. W., *Arms and Armour of Old Japan*, London 1951. Reprinted 1969.
LONDON, Wallace Collection
Laking, G. F., Wallace Collection Catalogues; *Oriental Arms and Armour*, London 1914. Second edn 1964.
Mann, Sir J., Wallace Collection Catalogues; *European Arms and Armour* 2 vols, London 1962.
LOS ANGELES, County Museum
Grancsay, S. V., *Loan Exhibition of Mediaeval and Renaissance Arms and Armor from the Metropolitan Museum of Art*, Jan 15–March 18, 1953.
MADRID, Instituto de Valencia de Don Juan
Florit y Arizcun, J. M., *Catálogo de las Armas del Instituto de Valencia de Don Juan*, Madrid 1927.
MADRID, Real Armeria
Valencia de Don Juan, Cond. Vdo., de, *Catálogo Histórico-Descriptivo de la Real Armeria de Madrid*, Madrid 1898.
MILWAUKEE MUSEUM
Wolff, E. G., *Air Guns, Milwaukee Museum Publications in History*, No. 1, Milwaukee, WI 1958.
MOSCOW, Kremlin
Donova, K. V., *Gosudarstvennaja oružejrnaja palata Moskovskovo kremlja*.
Gordeev, H. V., and others, *The State Arms Collection of the Moscow Kremlin*. Moscow 1954. In Russian.
MOSCOW, State Historical Museum.
Denisova, M. M., and Portnov, M. E., *Fine Tula Arms of the 18th and 19th Centuries in the Collection of the State Historical Museum*, Moscow 1952. In Russian.
MUNICH, Deutsches Jagdmuseum
Eröffnungs-Katalog, Munich 1966.
NAPLES, Capodimonte
Hayward, J. F., 'Les Collections du palais de Capodimonte, Naples', *Armes Anciennes*, Vol. I, pp. 121-40, Geneva 1953-6.
NEW YORK, Brooklyn Museum
Grancsay, S. V., *Loan Exhibition of European Arms and Armor*, June–August, 1933.
NEW YORK, Metropolitan Museum of Art
Dean, B., and Grancsay, S. V., *The Metropolitan Museum of Art. Handbook of Arms and Armor*, New York 1930.
Grancsay, S. V., *Loan Exhibition of European Arms and Armor, 3rd Aug.–27th Sept. 1931*
Parsons, J. E., *Catalogue of a Loan Exhibition of Colt Revolvers and Conversions 1836-1873*, New York 1942.
See also under Allentown, Hagerstown and Los Angeles.
The Russian Colts. Beinfeld Publishing Inc.
OSLO, Haermuseet, Akershus
Skaar, F. C., and Nielson, O., *Haerens Håndvåpen. Pistoler og revolvers 1814-1940*. Oslo 1951-2.
Skaar, F. C. and Nielsen, O., *Merkekatalog*, Oslo 1960.
OXFORD
ffoulkes, C. J., *European Arms and Armour in the University of Oxford*, Oxford 1912.
PARIS, Musée de l' Armée (formerly *Musée d'Artillerie*)
Robert, L., and Bernardec, F., *Catalogue des Collections Composant le Musée d'Artillerie*, 6 vols, Paris 1889-1902.
Mariaux, Général, *Le Musée de l'Armée; Armes et Armures Anciennes*, Vol. II, Paris 1927.
Reverseau, J.-P., *Musée de l'Armée, Paris, Les armes et la vie*, Paris 1982.
PHILADELPHIA, Museum of Art, See Kienbusch.
ROSENBORG CASTLE, Denmark
Hogg, A., Schepelern, H. D., and Boesen, G., *Royal Arms at Rosenborg*, 2 vols, Copenhagen 1956.
SALM-REIFFERSCHEIDT ARMOURY, Schloss Dyck
Ehrenthal, M., v., *Die Waffensammlung des Fürsten Salm-Reifferscheidt*, Leipzig 1906.
SANDRINGHAM HOUSE, Norfolk
Clarke, C. P., *Arms and Armour at Sandringham*, London 1910.
SCHEREMETEW COLLECTION
Lenz, E., v., *Die Waffensammlung des Grafen S. D. Scheremetew in St Petersburg*, Leipzig 1897. This collection now forms part of the Hermitage Museum, Leningrad.
SCHWARZBURG ARMOURY
Ossbahr, C. A., *Das Fürstliche Zeughaus in Schwarzburg*, Rudolstadt 1895.
SEAFIELD ARMOURY
(Now divided between the Scottish National Museum of Antiquities and the Scottish United Services Museum, Edinburgh)
Reid, W., 'Lady Seafield's Scottish Guns', *The Connoisseur*, May 1961, pp. 258-62
Reid, W., 'Lady Seafield's Scottish Pistols', *The Connoisseur*, pp. 155-7, July 1962.
SEVERANCE COLLECTION
See Cleveland
SOLOTHURN ARSENAL
Wegeli, R., *Katalog der Waffen-Sammlung im Zeughause zu Solothurn*, Solothurn 1905.
SPITZER COLLECTION
Giraud, J. B., and Molinier, E., *La Collection Spitzer*, Vol. VI, Paris 1981.
STAGECOACH MUSEUM, Shakopee, MN
Bowman, H. W., *Antique Guns from the Stagecoach Collection*, Greenwich, CT 1961.
STOCKHOLM, Kungl. Armémuseum.
Katalog, Stockholm, n.d.
STOCKHOLM, Hallwyl House.
Claudelin, B.,*Catalogue of the Collection of Arms and Armour at Hallwyl House. Stockholm*, Stockholm 1928.
STOCKHOLM, Livrustkammaren.
Vägledning for Besökande Livrustkammeren och Därmed Förenade Samlingar, 4th edn, Uppsala 1915; 6th edn, Uppsala 1919.
Cederstrom, R., and Malmborg, G., *Den aldre Livrustkammaren 1654*, Stockholm 1930.
SUTHERLAND, ROBERT Q., COLLECTION
Wilson, R. L., *The Evolution of the Colt. Firearms from the Robert Q. Sutherland Collection*, privately published by Robert Q. Sutherland, U.S.A. 1967.
TURIN, Armeria Reale
Angelucci, A., *Catalogo dell'Armeria Reale*, Turin 1890.
VENICE, Palazzo Ducale
Lucia, G., de, *La Sala d'Armi nel Museo dell'Arsenale di Venezia*, Rome 1908.
Franzoi, U., *Armoury of the Doges' Palace in Venice*, Venice 1966.
VICTORIA, NSW, Museum of Applied Science

Penrose, E. H., *Descriptive Catalogue of the Collection of Firearms in the Museum of Applied Science of Victoria*, Victoria 1949.
VIENNA, Heeresgeschichtliches Museum
Erben, W., *Katalog des K. und K. Heeres-Museums*, Vienna 1895.
Gabriel, E., *Von der Luntenmuskete zum Sturmgewehr. Katalog zur Sonderschau der Entwicklung Der Hand- und Faust feuerwaffen im österreichescen Heer*, Vienna 1967.
VIENNA, Kunsthistorisches Museum
Boeheim, W., *Album Hervorragender Gegenstände aus der Waffensammlung des Allerhöchsten Kaiserhauses*, 2 vols, Vienna 1894-8.
Boeheim W., *Führer durch die Waffen-Sammlung*, Vienna 1889,
Grosz, A., and Thomas, B., *Katalog der Waffensammlung in der Neuen Burg. Schausammlung, Kunsthistorisches Museum*, Vienna 1936.
See also London, Tower of London Armouries.
WADDESDON MANOR
Blair, C., *James A. de Rothschild Collection.*
Arms, Armour and Base-Metalwork, Office du Livre, Fribourg 1974.
WARTBURG, Germany (Collection lost during World War II)
Diener-Schönberg, A., *Die Waffen der Wartburg*, Berlin 1912.
WASHINGTON, DC, Smithsonian Institution
Bowman, H. W., *Famous Guns from the Smithsonian Collection*, New York 1966.
WINCHESTER ARMS COMPANY. New Haven, CT
Bowman, H. W., *Famous Guns from the Winchester Collection*, Greenwich, CT 1958.
WINDSOR CASTLE
Laking, G. F., *The Armoury of Windsor Castle*, London 1904.
Blackmore, H. L., *Royal Sporting Guns at Windsor*, London 1968.
ZURICH, Schweizerisches Landesmuseum
Gessler, E. A., *Führer durch die Waffensammlung*, Zurich 1928.

PERIODICALS

The following are among the most valuable periodicals devoted to the history of arms, armour and militaria. Articles on firearms and related material appear in most of them.

The American Arms Collector, 2 vols, Towson, MD 1957-8. All published.
The American Gun, 3 vols, New York 1961. All published.
The American Rifleman, National Rifle Association of America, Washington, DC. In progress.
Armes Anciennes, 2 vols, Geneva, 1953-9. All published.
Armi Antiche, Bolletino dell'Accademia di S. Marciano, Turin. In progress.
Arms and Armor Annual, 1 vol., Digest Books, Northfield, IL 1973. All published.
Arms Cavalcade, journal of the antique arms collectors of Australia, Sydney, Aust. In progress.
Arsenal, journal of the Polish arms and armour society. One vol, Cracow 1957-8. All published.
Association Suisse pour l'étude des Armes et Armures, Geneva, Switz. In progress.
Black Powder, The official magazine of the Muzzle-Loaders Association of Great Britain, Croydon, Surrey. In progress.
Bulletin of the American Society of Arms Collectors, Dallas, TX. In progress.
Bulletin des Arquebusiers de France, St Maur des Mosses, Sein. In progress.
Bulletin Trimestriel de A.S.B.L., 'Les amis du Musée D'Armes de Liège', Liège, Belgium. In progress.
The Canadian Journal of Arms Collecting, Ottawa. In progress.
Carnet de 'La Rourragère', Brussels. In progress.
De Wapen Verzamelar, Tydeschrift van de Vereniging Nederlandse Wapenverzaelaars S-Gravenhage, Holland. In progress.
Deutsches Waffen-Journal-Schwäbisch Hall. In progress.
Diana Armi, Florence. In progress.
The Gun Collector, Whitewater, WI 1947-57.
Continuation of The Gun Collectors' Letter, Oct 1946–Oct 1947.
The Gun Digest, Chicago, IL. In progress.
The Gun Report, Alledo, IL. In progress.
Guns Review, Pateley Bridge, Harrogate, Yorks. In progress.
The International Cartridge Collector, Tucson, AZ. In progress.
The Irish Sword. The Journal of the Military History Society of Ireland. In progress.
The Journal of the Arms and Armour Society, London. In progress.
The Journal of the Army Society for Historical Research, London. In progress.
The Journal of the South African Muzzle Loaders Association, Cape Town. In progress.
Livrustkammaren. Journal of the Royal Armoury, Stockholm. In progress.
Man at Arms, Providence, RI. In progress.
Military Collector and Historian. Journal of the Company of Military Collectors and Historians, Washington, DC. In progress.
Revue Internationale d'Histoire Militaire, published by the Commission d'Histoire Militaire Comparée du Comité International des Sciences Historiques. In progress.
Studia do dziejów dawnego uzbrojenia i ubioru wojskowego, Publication of the National Museum, Cracow, in conjunction with the Polish Arms and Armour Society, Cracow. In progress.
Svenska Vapenhistoriska Årsskrift. The Yearbooks of the Swedish Arms and Armour Society, Copenhagen. In progress.
Zeitschrift für Historische Waffenkunde. Journal of the Verein für Historische Waffenkunde (from 1923 Waffen-und Kostümunde) 17 vols, Dresden and Berlin, 1897-1944. Continued from 1955-9 as *Mitteilungen der Gesellschaft für Historische Kostüm- und Waffenkunde*, Berlin, and from 1960 to date as *Waffen-und Kostümkunde*, Munich and Berlin.

Many of the larger museums publish bulletins and yearbooks in which articles on firearms and related subjects often appear. Valuable information is also to be found in the publications of local archaeological and historical societies, as well as in the sale-catalogues of principal auction houses.

Index

N.B.
1. Gunmakers are listed by surname, and again under country of origin. Complete page references, including illustrations, are found under surname entry only.
2. Birth and death dates, when known, are indicated thus: (*1651-1718†).
3. Footnotes are referred to by page number thus: 95fn. (or 95 and fn. if there is also a text reference).
4. Colour and black-and-white photographs are referred to by a plate number in **bold**.
5. When there is more than one number the following order is used:
text reference
footnote reference
plate reference in **bold**
line drawing reference in *italic*
e.g. 57, 95fn., **Pl.107**, *74*

Acknowledgements

N.B. Plate numbers (not page numbers) are given.

Colour photographs:
Christ Church College, Oxford 88; City of Birmingham Museum and Art Gallery 106, 259; Hamlyn Group Picture Library 271, 272, 273, 274, 281; Armouries, H.M. Tower of London 92, 103, 108, 257, 258, 265, 266, 270, 280; Kunsthistorisches Museum, Vienna 90, 96, 101, 107; Musée de l'Armée, Paris 100, 267; National Museum of Antiquities, Edinburgh 97, 99; Private Collection–Peter Macdonald Photos 98, 111; Trustees of the Raymond Settled Estates–John Webb Photos 278, 279; Victoria and Albert Museum 89, 91, 93, 94, 95, 102, 104, 105, 109, 110, 256, 260, 261, 262, 263, 264, 268, 269, 275, 276, 277.

Black-and-white photographs:
Armouries, H.M. Tower of London 14, 21, 22, 31, 32, 52, 62, 78, 81, 87, 114, 115, 116, 117, 130, 134, 135, 138, 139, 146, 147, 151, 152, 155, 157, 158, 166, 167, 192, 231, 244, 245, 366; Army Museum, Prague 17; Badisches Landesmuseum, Karlsruhe, Photo Archive 342, 346; Bayerisches Nationalmuseum, Munich 10, 11, 18; Biblioteca Ambrosiana, Milan 7; Birmingham Museum of Science and Industry 150, 198; Castel Sant'Angelo, Rome–Gabinetto Fotografico Nazionale, Rome 15; Christie, Manson and Woods Ltd. 79, 82, 83, 84, 85, 86, 88, 136, 296, 297, 298, 299; City Art Museum of St. Louis, U.S.A. 80; City Library, Bern 6; Glasgow Art Gallery and Museum 162, 319; Heckler and Kock GMBH Oberndorf 313; Hermitage Museum, Leningrad 46; Historisches Museum, Bern 125; Hogg, I. V. 206, 218, 219; Imperial War Museum– A. C. Cooper Ltd. 165, 168, 169, 182, 185, 186, 188, 189, 191, 196, 202, 203, 204, 208, 209, 210, 217, 223, 225, 249, 250, 253, 255, 282, 283, 284, 285, 287, 288, 289, 291, 292, 293, 294, 295, 300, 301, 302, 303, 304, 305, 306, 307, 309, 310, 311; Kunsthistorisches Museum, Vienna 25, 26, 27, 33, 40, 47; Kunstindustrimuseet, Copenhagen 118; Landeszeughaus, Graz 59; Livrustkammaren, Stockholm 45, 51, 53, 54, 63, 347; Metropolitan Museum, New York 20, William H. Riggs Gift 48, 49; Museo di Capodimonte, Laboratorio Fotografico della Soprintendenza alle Gallerie, Naples 343; Museum of Chinese History, Peking 334; Muzeum Narodowego, Cracow 321, 322, 325, 326, 327, 329, 335, 337, 338, 340, 351; Nationalmuseet, Copenhagen 76; National Museum of Antiquities of Scotland, Edinburgh 316, 318; Odescalchi Collection, Rome 23; Österreichische Nationalbibliothek, Vienna 3; Pitt Rivers Museum, Oxford 142; Private Collections 127, 128, 129, 317; Real Armería, Patrimonio Nacional, Madrid 44; Rijksmuseum, Amsterdam 50; Royal Military College of Science, Shrivenham 254, 315; RSAF Enfield Pattern Room– A. C. Cooper Ltd. 149, 154, 170, 171, 172, 174, 175, 176, 177, 178, 179, 184, 193, 194, 200, 201, 205, 207, 211, 212, 213, 214, 215, 216, 224, 233, 234, 235, 236, 237, 238, 239, 240, 241, 242, 243, 246, 251, 252, 286, 290, 312; Skoklosters Slott, Sweden 60; Smithsonian Institution, Washington, D.C.: War Dept. Collection 180, 187, Navy Dept. Collection 183, Roumanian Govt. Collection 181, Winchester Repeating Arms Co. Collection 195, 222, Clark E. Kauffmann Collection 226, Dr. H. Williams Jr. Collection 248, Glen J. Burkhardt Collection 308, 314, Treasury Dept. Collection 131, 132, 140, 159, 160, 163, 164, 221; Sotheby Parke Bernet and Co. 112, 137, 320; Staatliche Kunstsammlungen, Dresden 69, 336; Staatsbibliothek, Berlin 8, 9; Staatsbibliothek, Munich 4, 5; Staatliches Museum für Volkerkunde, Munich 331; Statens Historiska Museum, Stockholm–ATA Photos 1, 2; Tøjhusmuseet, Copenhagen 13, 43, 55, 56, 57, 58, 61, 64, 65, 66, 67, 68, 77, 122, 143, 144; Victoria and Albert Museum, London 2, 3, 12, 16, 19, 24, 28, 29, 30, 34, 35, 36, 37, 38, 39, 42, 75, 119, 120, 121, 141, 145, 278, 279, 319, 332, 333, 339, 341, 342, 344, 349, 350, 352, 353, 354, 355, 356, 357, 358, 359, 360, 361, 362; Wallace Collection, London 41, 70, 72, 73, 74, 123, 124, 323, 328, 330, 333, 345, 348; Wallis and Wallis, Lewes 148, 228, 229, 230, 232; Wawel Castle Collection, Cracow 324; Winchester Gun Museum, Cody, Wyoming 133. Photographs of Hugh Pollard lent by John Brewer.

Illustrations on the following pages are from *European and American Arms*, C. Blair, Batsford, 1962: pp. 34, 49, 50 (bot.), 71, 166, (L., bot. and mid.); *Guns and Rifles of the World*, H. L. Blackmore, Batsford, 1965: p. 241; *Pistols of the World*, C. Blair, Batsford, 1968: pp. 72, 107, 115, 166 (R.), 203, 416, 443, 456.

Giovanni Curatola · Gianroberto Scarcia

THE ART AND ARCHITECTURE OF
PERSIA

Translated by Marguerite Shore

ABBEVILLE PRESS PUBLISHERS

New York London

In memory of H. L. Baharloo

FRONT COVER: Façade of the south *iwan*, flanked by two minarets, at the Congregational Mosque (Masjid-i Jum'a), Esfahān.
BACK COVER, clockwise starting from upper right: capital with bull heads, from the large audience hall of the palace of Artaxerxes at Susa, Musée du Louvre, Paris; bronze statue of an Elymaic sovereign, Shami, first century BC–first century AD, National Museum, Tehran; gold *rhyton* in the form of a winged lion, from Ecbatana, National Museum, Tehran.
FRONTISPIECE: Carpet with animals and medallions, second half of the sixteenth century, Staatliche Museen, Berlin—Preussischer Kulturbesitz, Museum für Islamische Kunst.

FOR THE ENGLISH-LANGUAGE EDITION
EDITORS: Susan Costello and Alaina Davis
COPYEDITOR: Mary Christian
PRODUCTION EDITOR: Erin Dress
PRODUCTION MANAGER: Louise Kurtz
TYPOGRAPHIC AND JACKET DESIGN: Misha Beletsky
TYPESETTING: Julia Sedykh

Visit Abbeville Press online at www.abbeville.com.

The text of this book was set in a custom version of Rilke, a new typeface designed by Jerry Kelly for Nonpareil Type foundry.

Printed and bound in Italy.

ISBN-13: 978-0-7892-0920-7
ISBN-10: 0-7892-0920-9

First edition
10 9 8 7 6 5 4 3 2 1

Curatola, Giovanni.
[Iran. English]
The art and architecture of Persia / by Giovanni Curatola and Gianroberto Scarcia.
p. cm.
Includes bibliographical references and index.
ISBN 978-0-7892-0920-7 (alk. paper)
1. Art, Iranian. 2. Architecture—Iran. I. Scarcia, Gianroberto. II. Title.
N7283.C8713 2007
709.55—dc22
2006035207

For bulk and premium sales and for text adoption procedures, write to Customer Service Manager, Abbeville Press, 137 Varick Street, New York, NY 10013, or call 1-800-ARTBOOK.

The translation of this work has been funded by SEPS
SEGRETARIATO EUROPEO PER LE PUBBLICAZIONI SCIENTIFICHE

Via Val d'Aposa 7, 40123 Bologna, Italy
seps@alma.unibo.it, www.seps.it

"Iranian nation," remained in use by ancient historians and Arab geographers, but the term Iran, as an Iranian ethnic-cultural unit, came into popular use with the poetry of Firdawsī, around AD 1000. The everyday usage of the word *Iran* to mean simply the Iranian state and *Irani* to mean "Iranian" are recent developments, as is the evolution of an Iranian national consciousness in a modern sense, dating back no further than the nineteenth century. The Persians of the classical era had no difficulty in thinking of themselves as *ajam*, that is, barbarians with respect to the Arabs, in the somewhat more substantial sense of *barbare*, or foreign, as it was then used in Rome. An analogous discourse can be made for Afghanistan, which historically was eastern Khorāsān, and, through modern vicissitudes, has become a nation-state, although a rather singular one in terms of its composite and quarrelsome nature. In Europe, the use of the term Iran is extremely recent and barely replaces the traditional western (Greek, Latin, and Arabic) term *Persia*, from *Persae*, applied to the ethnic Iranian group that was in power in the Achaemenid era and derived from the Iranian geographic region of Perside (Pars, Arabic Faris, neo-Persian Fārs), land of the Parsua tribe of Assyrian inscriptions. If the Arabic term *Faris* indicated only Perside, in ancient times *Farisi* or *Farsi* already was understood to be a language disseminated throughout the plateau (without geographic references, moreover, it was also known as *Dari*, which may have meant "courtly"). Beginning in the tenth century this written literary language of many of the Iranian races in a certain sense paradoxically emerged from, or more precisely attested to, Transoxiana (Bukhara). Today the Persian of Afghanistan is artificially called *Dari*, precisely to eliminate western Iranian geographic connotations. The Arabic *furs*, instead, indicates the Iranian population from the pre-Islamic, or in any case "pagan," era, while the other Arabic term *al'Ajam*, means "non-Arabic race" or "foreign" (literally, "of another language," but Iranian par excellence). The multivalence of *Tajik* is analogous. In the past it meant "Arabic" (from *Tayy*, the name of an Arabic tribe close to present-day Iranian populations in the western regions, where *tazi* still signifies "Arabic language"), but later meant "Iranian," as opposed to "Turkish." Tajik is still used as a synonym for Iranian, as opposed to Turkmen and Uzbek, in central Asia and in the eastern regions of the plateau (in Afghanistan, however, the Tajik language, known locally as *Dari*, in contrast with the Iranian language of *Pashto*, is not spoken, and above all is not written, by the Iranian populations). As for the curious term *Afghanistan*, which literally means "place of wailing and troubles," it is probably the result of an intersection and a Persian literary reinterpretation of an ancient local ethnicon, or linguistic slur.

ARCHAEOLOGICAL DATA

Iran's archaeological wealth is enormous, without any one defined prehistoric, protohistoric, or historic periods predominating. For every period, nearly all the principal centers were located along the grand routes that follow the natural east-west passages of the plateau (through Media, from Ecbatana to Rayy to Tus; through lower Mesopotamia, from Susa to Persepolis to Kermān and Seistan) and traverse it from north to south (Rayy, Qom, Kāshān, Esfahān, and from here toward Fārs or toward Yazd and Susa). From Fārs to the Persian Gulf, the ancient caravan route joined Firozabad at the port of Siraf, present-day Bandar-i Tahiri. Apart from the latter, there are, with exceptions, communication routes that are still in use, above all the Persepolis-Susa (now Shīrāz-Ahvaz) route and the Kāshān-Esfahān section of road, although the direct Qom-Esfahān route is now more popular. In the east, the desert lies between Rayy—now Tehran—and Kermān.

The prehistoric era, mentioned briefly in this volume, is characterized in Iran by a multiplicity of ceramic styles, offering proof of the intersection of various cultures.[5] This contrasts to the greater stylistic uniformity of Mesopotamia, with which comparisons are useful to establish a relevant chronology. Studies carried out thus far have made it possible to identify different cultures for every prehistoric era, with each culture known by the name of the locality with which the principal finds are linked. While traces of Paleolithic, Mesolithic, and Neolithic preceramics and ceramics can be traced above all in the north (the Kamarband and Hutu caves in Gorgān and the Tamtama cave in Azerbaijan), and in the cave of Tang-i Pabda in Khūzestān, late Neolithic ceramics are represented by two distinct cultures, Tepe Sialk 1 (the first layer of the famous excavations at Tepe Sialk, near Kāshān) and Gari B, from a site in Fārs.

The Chalcolithic cultures followed, until the early years of the third millennium BC: Sialk II, Sialk III, Tepe Hisar I (the first layer of the excavations of the famous tepe near Damghan), Giyan V (Laristan), Musyan, Susa I (Khūzestān), Mushki, Bakun (Fārs), Anau II (near Iran's border with Turkmenistan to the east), Shah Tepe, and Turang Tepe (Gorgān), Sialk IV, "intermediary Susa," and Kaftari.

The Early Bronze Age is represented by Anau III, Hisar III, Giyan IV, Susa II, Tell-i Qal'e (Fārs), and the culture in the region of Bampur-Khurab (Kermān); the Middle Bronze Age is seen at Giyan III and Tell-i Shugha (Fārs); the Late Bronze Age, until approximately 1200 BC, at Giyan II and Taimuran A (Fārs).

The Iron Age (1200–800 BC) is seen above all in the famous Laristan bronzes from tombs in the valleys of Harsin, Khorramābād, and Alishtar, which first appeared in antiquarian shops in Tehran between 1928 and 1930, and soon made their way into museums and private collections. These were weapons, saddlery, brooches, votive or ritual objects, and tools with naturalistic or stylized decorations, which reveal certain relationships with Hittite items and can be dated between 1200 and 100 BC but no later than the mid-eighth century BC Here we can focus on one example (a highly hypothetical case) that might furnish early evidence of certain aspects of Zurvanism, a problematic Iranian religious form that appeared later. There is an image of a trimorphic divinity, perhaps Time, depicted in the three ages of man.[6] However alongside these beliefs there existed the cultures of Sialk V and VI and the gold- and silverwork of Kalar Dasht, Khurvin, Hasanlu, and Ziviya, all from regions in northern Iran. In any case, these cultures are all represented in many different zones, as well as those mentioned above.

The earliest historical civilization in Iran that has archaeological significance is the Elamite. Closely related to the Mesopotamian civilization, it is often difficult to identify its specific features. This early Iranian culture developed from the third to seventh century BC and, influenced in turn by southern Mesopotamia, Ur, and Assyria, it reached its height between the thirteenth and twelfth centuries BC. The center of this culture's activity was in the southwest region of present-day Iran, but it left traces in other regions. Elamite civilization produced the first stone reliefs (sixteen in all, courtly or religious in inspiration), which would become so significant in the subsequent art of ancient Iran. The principal Elamite centers were the capital at Susa (architectural remains, ceramics, sculptures, jewelry, ivory, glyptic carvings), Chogha Zanbil (with the aforementioned ziggurat, and finds of every genre, as rich as those from Susa), Rishahr, along the coasts of the Persian Gulf, Tell-i Ghazir (architecture and ceramics), and Tulaspid (architecture), in Fārs, as well as sites where stone reliefs have been discovered, including Kurangun and Naqsh-i Rustam (Fārs), Shikaft-i Salman, Kul-e Fara, Kala Tul (Khūzestān), Khurin Shaikh Khan, and Sar-i Pul-i Zuhab (Kurdistan).[7]

The earliest Aryan civilizations, while indebted to Mesopotamia in terms of religion as well, left their traces primarily in northern Iran, succeeding the Urartu civilization (known for the inscriptions of Tash Tepe and Siqindil and for the stele of Kili Sin, all in Azerbaijan). In fact, the stone tombs of Fakhrakah (Azerbaijan), Utaq-i Farhad, Sinna, and Sakavand (in this case a funerary niche) in Kurdistan probably date back to the Medes.

The history of the Medes remains unclear, other than the essential outlines, and the little we know is principally due to Greek sources. In Assyrian sources they made their first appearance on the Near Eastern historical stage around the middle of the eighth century BC. Of the two principal branches present on the Iranian plateau, only the one settled around Ecbatana (present-day Hamadan, as well as the first capital of the Medes) remained independent, while the other branch, located further west, was adjacent to the Assyrian empire. Toward the end of the seventh century, the Medes, under King Cyaxares and in alliance with the Babylonians, destroyed the Assyrian empire (the end of which is traditionally tied to the fall of Nineveh in 612 BC). The Medes then pushed westward as far as Anatolia, although the eastern boundaries of their kingdom have still not been established.[8] Scholars do not agree about the relationships between the Medes and the Persians during this period, and some do not accept the traditional idea that the region of Fārs came under the rule of Ecbatana.[9] Moreover, archaeological investigations have not yet produced substantial results from the ancient site of Ecbatana, in part due to urban development in modern times.[10] Significant archaeological data related to the Mede period comes principally from the two sites of Godin Tepe and Tepe Nush-i Gian.[11]

In any case, as a whole Mede civilization is too ancient for the purpose of this survey, which will principally focus on post-Hellenic culture, in addition to taking advantage of the specific skills of the authors, whose archaeological expertise is somewhat limited. Additionally, the archaeology itself has not always proven to support the Greek myths, particularly regarding Cyaxares and the entire brief initial chapter, which acts as an introduction to Cyrus I and II; Darius I, II, and III; and Xerxes. Even in this case, what fascinates us is the Herodotean image of a capital, Ecbatana, which had concentric circles of walls of different colors, in terrestrial (and political-military) imitation of the heavens: an indication, without rashness, of an astral vocation in the collective psyche of those peoples. Moreover, a continuous tradition links the Medes with Magi (persons endowed with particular powers; the root in Germanic languages remained positive but takes on negative implications). The Magi are a group that floats across clans, castes, and categories, and very often has a problematic and antagonistic connection with political power and with Zoroaster.

Between the fall of the Assyrian empire (612 BC) and the expedition of Alexander the Great (334–323 BC), the eastern portion of the known world was unified by the Persian emperors of the Achaemenid dynasty. And it was then that the discourse became more culturally solid.

ORAL TRADITION, RELIGIOUS TRADITION, AND EPIC POETRY

As we have seen, the cradle of Persian civilization is the region of present-day Iran known as Fārs. We know little about the events preceding the Achaemenid ascent to power. Clearly the Persians were dominated by the Assyrian empire (1366–612 BC) and then perhaps subjugated by the Medes (c. late seventh century–550 BC), before rising up in rebellion.

Leaving aside all the preceding background, the argument of greatest interest to us in our attempt to pursue a path that is not only anthropological, but also based primarily on Iranian

10. Bas-relief of Naqsh-i Rustam, with a depiction of a divinity, perhaps the goddess Anahita

material, we inexorably come up against the unmistakable Iranian national sensibility, dating from before the culture became influenced by the Bedouin world: it is the markedly feverish ideology of the oral tradition, based on the fixations, circumscription, and humiliation of an everyday reality solemnly understood as a living ritual, imprisoned in a written literature, and with a consequent lack of interest in and even hostility toward the dating of events. This accompanies a marked correspondence between the historical memory of those people and the facts with which external evidence, in any case, informs us.

It is striking that neither texts of a conservative religious nature nor Iranian epic poetry pays heed to the certain protagonists of the first significant chapter in Persian history that we study in school. Even the Achaemenids, those figures who are familiar in the West—Darius, Xerxes, and Artaxerxes—are ignored. Indeed during the Islamic era, which was a strongly Hellenized culture, even Persian scholars and sages such as Bīrūnī had to resort to hypothesizing that the Achaemenids were simply the western Iran's lieutenants for the true sovereigns who, according to local tradition, reigned in the East. Do tenacious memories of an east-west emigration of the peoples in question, with eastern origins, present the city of Balkh in present-day Afghanistan as the mother of all cities, and other nearby urban centers as the earliest human settlements? Perhaps, but nostalgia seems to have even more distant and northern roots. First of all there is Chorasmia, in a land of lakes and rivers that wander to the mouth of the Oxus, which might even help explain the Iranians' principal interest in hydraulic engineering, namely *hybris*, from the Hellenic *topos*, whereby those barbarians diverted waters, dug canals, and drained shallow river crossings despite nature and the gods. But in addition to Chorasmia, memory evokes an almost glacial land or era, with a ten-month winter and two-month summer, generating myths of the utopia of an eternal archaic south that would have been inversely shining, the golden village or grassland of an Eden, predating their icy history. This was the era of the fortunate sovereign Giamshid, who, however, at a certain point committed a sin: a sin—naturally, of sex—connected to reproduction, thus metaphorically associated with agriculture and with the history of mankind. The result was winter, and the desperation that follows the autumn equinox, and the alternation of the seasons, and the joy of the explosion of green with the spring equinox, and the expectation of the winter solstice, when the sun and light and warmth of spring are gradually reborn. But this deserved winter would not be seriously eradicated until the end of time.[12] The anguish of darkness, in any case, and the celestial illuminations as soldiers of light in the opposing nocturnal field ("lights with certainty on the black face of doubt," according to a verse by Nāsir-i Khusraw, a poet of the Islamic era), and the reborn and gradually triumphant solar light would dominate Persian poetry to the present. So would the color green-blue, the "sweet color of eastern sapphire" (but the Persians prefer their turquoise, which is also eastern for them, to the sapphire of Dante), seen in Persian ceramics. Light is called Mithra, and this Mithra can never be ousted by any prophet or higher divinity. Likewise the fertile, watery, and roaring Anahita (plate 10) will always prevail. And the green and the water will merge in *pairidaeza*, a Persian word indicating a type of garden from which, indeed, the Christian *paradise* would be derived.

In art, these become the English garden (following nature), the Italian garden (following reason), and the Persian (paradisiac). In Persian religiosity, the monotheistic tendency was tempered in a triad (the supreme Ahura Mazda, Mithra, and Anahita), which also brings to mind an analogous if not imitative trinity seen in Babylonia.

Giamshid was put to death by Dahaka, unique guardian of Eden's intriguing innocence, understood specifically and vehemently as the separation of the sexes.[13] But Dahaka was succeeded by Firaidun, the first king in human history, and Mithra's favorite, who flourished.

Analogous to the erasure from history of Darius and his successors, there was no trace in the scant Achaemenid texts of a figure that should have been the keystone to the religious history of pre-Islamic Iran: the semi-mythical Zoroaster, who was nearly contemporary. He too was popularized and introduced to ancient public opinion from outside traditions. The essential facts can be read in two volumes by Gnoli, the last of which can be compared today with the criticism of Kellens.[14] And so the figure penetrates Iranian epic poetry in a dual fashion: as an extraneous element rejected by heroes faithful to accepted primogenial emblems, and as an abruptly introduced guardian spirit of those wielding power. These are leaders who from the time they officially established their state church broke with tradition. Simply put, the civilizing and savior hero—who crushes enemies, demons, and monsters; an indispensable aid to the kings under the protective wing of the Phoenix, the Rustam type (Rustam, the son of Zal, is a mythical hero of ancient Persia)—dominated the scene during the first part of the history of Iran until the arrival of the Prophet, who cast him out. In the second part of that history, the Rustam-hero type was subjected to a sort of unexpected and completely artificial demonization. The Isfandiyar type, the Zoroastrian king entrusted with a function that the Arabs called the "well-guided caliph," replicated Rustam down to the smallest details of his feats, which were archaic but always perceived as immutably vital, while combating him in the name of a new, absolutely generic faith, which was a sort of interpretation of Islam as a natural religion, as understood by prophetic Mediterranean monotheism. This is why the role of the reformer, evoked in written epic poetry, is completely in line with the canons of the Semitic brand of prophetic history (obviously Arab in particular) and can be easily inserted into an Islamic type of ideology. This goes so far as to paradoxically turn the followers of the religion of the Magi (*magiùs*), those devoted to the oral tradition, part of the People of the Book, namely the precursors of Islam, into a text/memory or testament to be continuously renewed.

The difficulty of the transference is obvious in the efforts to Semiticize the demonic presences that devastate what we have called the first part of Iranian history. Indeed, the protagonist of the world of origins, the guardian of Eden, hostile to history—Dahaka—becomes Hebrew and Arab in that he is rejected by the post-Edenic national historic consciousness. But it is this demeritorious title that, with Islam, will encourage a reinterpretation of origins in a pre-Islamic sense. And in Islamic Iran, Dahaka will preserve both his negativity (he will be an Antichrist) and his participation in the theme of People of the Book.

However epic the euhemerism (whereby mythical figures are believed to be rooted in history), it lead to Zoroastrian reform where—even in terms of banal genealogical and personal data—the Rustam type (Rustam is a *digenìs*) is seen as an inextricable, chromosomally complex interweaving of a good/evil dialectic, that is experienced and suffered daily, and which will mitigate the original dualistic vocation with fatalistic temptations. He will always be ready to regerminate new forms of radicalism, both spiritual (Manicheism) and political-social (Mazdaism). In other words, the Rustam type at this point already represented an early form of compromise between tradition and prophetic innovation, superimposing itself upon the Garshasph type, a more archaic and more violent personification of the naturist savior,[15] sublimated in the official religion for its eschatological value. These archaic types appear inserted in a series of figures simulating a family, or a sort of dynasty, broken up by Zoroastrian reform and reduced to knightly functions with regard to the well-guided sovereigns. The most interesting and significant name is Zal, the historical equivalent of Zurvan, the student/lesser divinity of the Phoenix, precisely like the Hellenistic Aeon/Kronos. This is Zurvan/Time, divided up into cycles, whose body is space, measured by the wind.

The gloomy Zal/Zurvan knows only the fatal alternation of white and black while the prophet is more merciful, offering creatures the possibility of a natural existence that is evidence of and occasion for ethical combat, with a positive outcome of many rewards and final punishment. Linked to this idea of a primordial creator's challenge to creatures is the invention of a soul that translates into poetic form the metaphysical truth of Platonic ideas that are preexistent to the shadowy and corporeal but illusory nature of all things.[16] The soul is the eternal aspect, the creature's subtle and non-dimensional double. It is the yesterday that precedes a today that is the same as an everyday in the centuries, and it will reappear in a tomorrow, equal to a resurrection. This has basic consequences in aesthetics because the visionary reality of the guardian angel is psychic truth of fantasy and the nature of dream, which in inner Hellas distinguished a phenomenon from the abstraction of the numen. It becomes, in this outer Hellas, characteristic of and opposite to the unique absolute that is comprehensible to the human psyche. The oneiric dimension is the heart (albeit fantastic) of our everyday experience.

The divinities of Iran are also angels, symbols, or concepts (virtues) personified and animated (thus the demons are vices). And the supreme Ahura Mazda, the Wise Lord, is instead a Female Wisdom. All this would have fundamental consequences for the *Kunstwollen,* or artistic volition, of late antiquity, where it will clearly re-emerge. This is not to deny that it begins in inner Greece, or rather from a polished Hellenistic syncretism.

As Darius says, with the language of the imperial collector of what is best in this world in the field of beauty:

> At this palace I built at Susa, the ornamentation was brought from afar. Downward the earth was dug, until I reached rock in the earth. When the excavation had been made, then rubble was packed down, some parts 40 cubits in depth, others 20 cubits in depth. On that rubble the palace was constructed. And the earth was dug downward, and the rubble was packed down, and the bricks were molded by the Babylonians, who did this work. The cedar timber was brought from a mountain named Lebanon. The Assyrians brought it from there to Babylon; from Babylon the Carians and the Ionians brought it to Susa. Teak timber was brought from Gandhara and from Carmania. The gold was brought from Sardis and from Bactria and was then worked here. The gems known as lapis lazuli and carnelian, worked here, were brought from Sogdiana. The gem known as turquoise, worked here, was brought from Chorasmia. Silver and ebony were brought from Egypt, from Sind, and from Arachosia. The stone columns, worked here, were brought from a village named Abiradush, in Elam. The stonecutters who worked the stone were Ionians and Sardinians. The goldsmiths who worked the gold were Medes and Egyptians. The men who worked the wood were Sardinians and Egyptians. The men who worked the baked bricks were Babylonians. The men who embellished the walls were Medes and Egyptians. Darius the king says: at Susa an excellent work was ordered, an optimum work was completed. May Ahura Mazda protect me and Hystaspes my father, and my country.[17]

DARIUS
THE CLASSICISM OF THE ACHAEMENIDS

It is quite interesting, and in a certain sense modern, that the recently recognized universality of an aesthetic output intended to celebrate an empire accompanied the Persians' awareness that they belonged to a specific ethnic complex, one that may lead back to the ancient Aryans or Indo-Europeans. Indeed some words from another inscription of Darius I the Great (the Achaemenid sovereign under whom the empire achieved its greatest territorial expansion: from the shores of the Danube to those of the Indus, from the Aral Sea to the Persian Gulf), carved in cuneiform characters on the facade of his monumental tomb in Naqsh-i Rustam, read as follows: [1]

> "I am Darius the great king, king of kings, king of countries containing all tribes, king of this great earth and beyond, son of Hystaspes, an Achaemenid, a Persian, an Aryan, of Aryan lineage."

And to think that some consider Darius a usurper, and for certain scholars—according to a much debated theory—he is not even Persian. In any case it is clear that the term Aryan is used in the sense of both "national" and "universal."

THE HISTORY

Although the Persians date back to their mythical founder, Achaemenid (attested to in ancient Persian, in a form that probably can be translated as "he who possesses a spirit of a disciple"),[2] the initiator of the Achaemenid destiny and the first "great king" was Cyrus II the Great (559–530 BC), son of Cambyses I and a Median princess. He led a revolt against his overlord (his grandfather Astyages, son of Cyaxares) and assumed control over both his kingdom and a much greater territory over the course of only a few years.

In 547 BC he began his conquest of Anatolia, defeating Lydia, the leading power in the region, governed at that time by the enormously wealthy Croesus. The following year Cyrus also succeeded in subjugating the Greek cities along the Ionian coast, which had remained loyal to Lydia thanks to the relative freedom granted them by Croesus; Milatus had long been allied with the great king.[3]

In 539 BC Cyrus conquered the entire neo-Babylonian empire, which extended over Syria, Phoenicia, and Palestine, with the help of both his weaponry and his far-sighted policy that sought to compromise with the ruling priestly class in Babylonia, which was unhappy with the lawful sovereign, Nabonidus. Cyrus, moreover, was successful in gaining the favor of the Jews by allowing them to return to their homeland, from which they had been deported by the neo-Babylonian king Nebuchadrezzar (604–562 BC).

In those distant times the regions of west-central Asia (corresponding roughly to the republics of Turkmenistan, Uzbekistan, Tajikistan, and Afghanistan), inhabited principally by populations characterized by Iranian culture and language, were united under Cyrus's rule but constantly threatened by incursions on the part of nomads. Cyrus was killed while battling one of these restless tribes, the Massagetae, and he was succeeded by his son, Cambyses II (529–522 BC).

Between 527 and 525 BC Cambyses conquered Egypt and may have pushed as far as Nubia to the south and Cyrenaica to the west, although his exploits are still shrouded in an aura of semi-legendary mystery. Cambyses probably even posed a threat to Carthage, but according to tradition, he turned back when his Phoenician admirals refused to participate in the conquest of their African colony.[4] During Cambyses's sojourn in Egypt, the heart of the empire was laid waste by an attempted rebellion, calmed only after the death of the great king, which occurred during his return voyage from Egypt.

11. ABOVE. Detail of the bas-relief of the Tripylon at Persepolis

The greatest extent of Achaemenid territorial expansion was reached during the reign of Darius I (522–486 BC), probably a usurper (although his father, Hystaspes, is the only figure who has a name that accords with that of the sovereign who was converted by Zoroaster, another "usurper"), but extremely able both in his execution of foreign and domestic policy and in his management of the military. In fact, he is credited with unifying weights, measures, and currency according to a completely new system, and he accomplished numerous tax reforms.[5]

After quelling a series of rebellions, the new great king turned his attention once again to his empire's eastern frontiers, taking over Gandhara (present-day southeastern Afghanistan and northern Pakistan) and part of the Indus Valley.[6] Between 516 and 512 BC Darius was not successful in annexing the territory of the Scythians, who had settled in the southern portion of present-day Ukraine,[7] but he did conquer Thrace and Macedonia, thereby assuring his control over access to the Black Sea. Darius reestablished control over another particularly restless province, Ionia, but he was unable to carry out his plan to conquer all of Greece, due to the defeat inflicted on the Persian army by the Athenians and their allies at Marathon in 490 BC.[8]

With the death of Darius, other rebellions took place in the empire, and only after order was reestablished did his successor, Xerxes I (486–465 BC), attempt to invade Greece once again. This undertaking was a failure, due to unexpected resistance by some of the Greek city-states, which were hostile to each other but exceptionally united in opposing the Achaemenid invasion. The Persians were defeated in the naval battle of Salamis and in two battles in the field, at Plataea and Mycale, and they were forced to abandon any claims to continental Greece.[9] Moreover, other rebellions broke out within the Achaemenid territories, although these had no irreparable consequences for the empire's territorial integrity.

During the reigns of Artaxerxes I (464–424 BC, known as the "Long-handed," his right hand being longer than his left); Xerxes II (424 BC); Sogdianus (423 BC); and Darius II (also known as Darius Nothus or Darius the Bastard, 423–405 BC), there were no significant events other than some rebellions, soon quelled, and Persia's indirect participation in the Peloponnesian War

12. OPPOSITE. Head of a prince from Persepolis, in lapis lazuli paste, fifth–fourth century BC, Archaeological Museum, Tehran

between Sparta and Athens.[10] At the time of Artaxerxes II Memnon (404–359 BC) there was an attempted rebellion by some provincial authorities,[11] working in conjunction with another member of the imperial family. Confident of support from Sparta and from some Greek mercenary contingents, Artaxerxes's brother, Cyrus, openly challenged the emperor's authority. Despite Cyrus's defeat, the empire was shaken by a great insurrection in Egypt, which succeeded in establishing its independence for approximately sixty years. Artaxerxes II Ochus (359–338 BC), the same sovereign who stifled a rebellion in Phoenicia, succeeded in reconquering the African province. Upon his death, Egypt again became independent for the entire duration of the reign of Arses (338–336 BC) and was re-annexed in 334 BC by Darius III Codommannus (336–330 BC), a sovereign who ascended the throne after years of interference by the imperial court eunuchs in events related to the imperial succession.

13–14. ABOVE. The monumental Gate of the Nations, and OPPOSITE, detail of the colossal bull figures that flank the principal gates, Persepolis

The new great king lacked the ability to counteract the general weakening of the empire, and his realm easily fell victim to invasion by Alexander of Macedonia (334–323 BC).[12] Alexander originally proclaimed himself the guarantor of the safety of the Hellenic world and the avenger of the past tyrannical actions at the hand of the Persians. In reality he replaced the Achaemenid emperors, conquering much of their original territory, initiating what traditionally has passed for a large-scale fusion of Greek and Iranian elements, an operation that was crucial for the history of the entire Eurasian continent, particularly in terms of art—although we have already seen reasons to question this sort of absolute predominance.

ARCHITECTURE AND SCULPTURE

As usual, one of the greatest problems to be faced with regard to the study of this specific realm of Persian civilization concerns sources. In fact, there are very few direct sources from the Achaemenid era. These are limited to a few inscriptions carved into rock in the form of edicts,

normally in ancient Persian, Elamic, or Babylonian (thus utilizing cuneiform characters, another westernizing feature of the culture in question). Information has also come from clay tablets from Babylonia, again written in cuneiform, or from certain monuments, and above all from papyruses discovered in Egypt, written both in ancient Egyptian and in Aramaic (the language of the imperial Achaemenid administrative offices). Greek historians clearly provide some of the most plausible evidence, although there are frequent inaccuracies due to their presumptuous attitudes toward the "barbarians."[13] This mass of information, already faulty at the source, was then subject to reinterpretation tainted by classicists' well-known prejudices.

15–16. ABOVE AND OPPOSITE. Struggle between a lion and a bull, details of the decoration of the stairway of the palace of Darius at Persepolis

This type of approach explains the persistence of numerous clichés: despotism, blind rage and anger, looseness of morals, the inability of the wild Darius III to deal with the overwhelming civilizing impulse that Alexander brought. In reality—as contemporary scholars such as P. Briant have sought to demonstrate[14]—a phenomenon as complex as the reign of the Achaemenid dynasty must bear in mind a series of historically verifiable facts currently available to us, nearly all of which depend on sources outside Persia itself.

In one celebrated passage, Herodotus (*Histories* 1.131) states:

> The Persians follow these customs: they are not in the habit of erecting statues, temples, and altars, and indeed they consider those who do so to be foolish; this is because, according to me, unlike the Greeks they have never believed the gods

to have the same nature as men. Instead they are accustomed to climbing to the highest mountain summits to make sacrifices to Zeus, which is the name by which they designate the entire heavenly vault, and they sacrifice victims to honor the sun, the moon, the earth, fire, water, and the winds.

17. ABOVE. The tomb of Cyrus the Great at Pasargadae

In only a few sentences, Herodotus seems to have precluded the existence of Persian architecture or religious art; this is a view that in the past has led more than one scholar to erroneous conclusions. On the other hand, one might be led to think that civic structures and monumental arts (particularly sculpture) must have had a real presence.[15]

In reality, the ancient historian was justified in his opinion to some extent. As he states in the same passage, his comments are related to his viewpoint as a Greek faced with the practices and customs evidently known to him, or even directly observed, yet always foreign. In this sense, if one understands that in comparison to a Greek temple or other Hellenic civic or funerary structures, the Persian religious building—of which archaeological traces do remain—seemed trivial.[16] The same might be said of the sculpture favored at the court of the great king (of which we have very few examples in the round, plate 12), compared to the production of the Greek city-states.

The other major problem for the current enthusiast of Persian art is the near total paralysis of pre-Islamic period archaeology in Iran.[17] All things considered, this situation is new, if one takes into account that the principal projects dealing with Iranian art, numerous only before the Islamic Revolution, were carried out with promising results for the time.[18] In this regard, the most productive periods are still the second half of the nineteenth century and the twentieth century until the 1970s, with a concentration of archaeological explorations almost ex-

18. OPPOSITE, LEFT. Achaemenid capital reused and placed atop a column of the mosque, now destroyed, at Istakhr

19. OPPOSITE, RIGHT. Capital from the large audience hall of the palace of Darius at Susa

clusively around the principal centers of Achaemenid power: Pasargadae, Susa, and Persepolis. Minor centers such as Hasanlu, Tureng Tepe, and Tepe Yahya, while extremely important for the study of Achaemenid-era settlements, have not yielded finds that are even vaguely comparable.[19] Other discoveries of some significance are represented by the stone reliefs at Bisutun and the royal stone tombs at Naqsh-i Rustam, although greater interest has been aroused by the inscriptions of Darius I that are on these monuments.

While Susa can boast of a glorious past, as the capital city during the Elamite era, it was only during the reign of Darius I that it recovered from the phase of decline that began with its destruction by the Assyrians, in the mid-seventh century BC. Unlike Pasargadae and Persepolis, where there is evidence of stone construction, architecture in Susa is characterized by brick, a building element inherited from earlier Mesopotamian tradition to which the conquerors adapted. In its turn, Persepolis also experienced a period of splendor dating back to the era of Darius I (plates 11, 13–16), while Pasargadae is linked to the era of Cyrus the Great (plate 17). The city would have been the first Achaemenid capital, and its principal monument is clearly represented by the mausoleum built to contain the mortal remains of the first great king. This is a massive structure built from square stone blocks, in the style of a dwelling (even equipped with a main entrance and a saddle roof), placed on a stepped platform. A similar monumental tomb was built at Takht-i Rustam (and also in Fārs), and is generally attributed to Cambyses. The models for these tombs can be found in funerary monuments from the Lydian era, frequently discovered in various sites in Anatolia.[20] The dissemination of tombs designed like dwellings demonstrates a shared style, widespread in other regions along the coast of the eastern Mediterranean, such as in Phoenicia. Various sarcophagi come from Sidon and are generally dated to the era of Achaemenid domination.[21] Among these, the so-called Alexander

Sarcophagus (c. fourth century BC), now in the Istanbul Archaeological Museum, clearly represents the most important example, not so much because of its uncertain attribution to the Macedonian knight, but because of its relief decoration, executed in pure Hellenistic style, that runs along the outside perimeter, where one can identify scenes of battles between the Greeks and the Persians. One detail worth mentioning is a painting executed on the inside portion of the shield of a Persian warrior. The subject, often portrayed in Hellenistic and Achaemenid art, is an audience before the great king, who is depicted seated on a throne, surrounded by various servants, and consulting with a dignitary, who stands respectfully, slightly bowed, before the sovereign.[22]

20. ABOVE. Capital with griffon heads, Persepolis

At Pasargadae a number of palaces were built on the artificial terrace that made up the citadel. Their function was linked to various aspects of imperial authority exercised by Cyrus.[23] In the palaces of Pasargadae, scholars have also identified consistent influences from the cultures of nearby populations, which were generally subjected to Achaemenid rule. These influences correspond, for the most part, to three phases related to the period of government of the principal Achaemenid sovereigns. The first can be identified in the time span from Cyrus's ascent to power to the early period of Darius's reign; the second phase runs from the later period of Darius's reign to that of Xerxes I; the third runs from the second half of the reign of Xerxes I and the beginning of the reign of Artaxerxes I to the fifth century BC.[24] Other scholars prefer a more precise subdivision;[25] however, the more simplified breakdown better lends itself to tracing the influences that came to bear on Achaemenid art and architecture, which are most evident and detectible particularly in the first two phases. If, in fact, the first phase is rich in elements borrowed from Ionian, late Babylonian, and neo-Assyrian art, the second phase reveals very close ties with Ionia and Egypt, and the last phase corresponds to the attainment of a mature Achaemenid style, imbued with original principles, the seeds of which, however, could be individuated to a slight degree in the earlier phases.[26]

21. OPPOSITE. Capital with bull heads, from the large audience hall of the palace of Artaxerxes at Susa, Musée du Louvre, Paris

22. RIGHT. Ka'ba-i Zardusht and tombs of the Achaemenid kings at Naqsh-i Rustam

23. BELOW. Marble capital discovered at Sultan Uizdag, near Nukus, Uzbekistan, fifth–fourth century BC, Nukus Museum

The Achaemenid emperors had tremendous pride in the vastness of their empire and the numerous peoples under their rule who were called upon to contribute to the celebration of their royal glory, through their experience in various fields of artistic production.

External elements absorbed by Achaemenid art included the use of the completely or partially artificial terraces, upon which vestiges of the royal palaces still stand, and a widespread use of the column, subdivided into various parts, as employed by the Greeks and Egyptians.[27] The development of the Achaemenid capital (plates 18–21), characterized by zoomorphic heads or monstrous composite creatures, can be considered a genuine creation of Persian architecture of this period, one that could be appreciated and exported throughout the empire, or even imitated in remote but highly valued regions, such as Chorasmia. One example is a marble capital discovered in the vicinity of Nukus (Uzbekistan), dated to approximately the fifth to fourth century BC,[28] executed in the local style, based on Achaemenid capitals, particularly those discovered at Persepolis (plate 23).[29]

To go back to Herodotus's statement that the Persians erected neither temples nor sculptures nor altars, we might list certain buildings of worship in the form of towers, such as the Ka'ba-i Zardusht, placed in front of the royal tombs at Naqsh-i Rustam (plate 22), as well as at least two other, much better preserved, examples in Pasargadae and Susa. At the first two sites one can also see structures identified as fire altars.[30] Whether or not a religious interpretation should be attributed to these structures is a secondary problem,[31] since what is more important is the presence at these sites of reliefs that can unquestionably be associated with portrayals of divinities and can be related to stylistic and iconographic conventions that are in abundant evidence in the Near East, Mesopotamia, and Egypt. At Bisutun, the relief that celebrates the victory of Darius I over Gaumata and other rebels is accompanied by—in addition to various inscriptions useful for attributing the entire work—a bust of a bearded man wearing a tall headpiece that emerges from a winged disk, placed in front of the Achaemenid sovereign. While scholars disagree in their interpretation of this symbol, it is evident that it is associated with a divinity, and it makes sense to propose that it is Ahuramazda. The circular element that the figure holds in its right hand would seem, instead, to be a symbol of glory granted by the god to Darius.[32] The Achaemenids indirectly adopted the iconography of the winged disk from Egyptian art. In fact, the addition of the bust, always depicted in profile, with a long beard and an object in the figure's hand, is an Assyrian concept.[33] Composite creatures, normally endowed with wings, or true putti holding a necklace, would persist at length in Iranian art, including outside Persia itself (as in Sogdiana), well beyond the Sasanian era.[34] This plausible depiction of Ahuramazda can be seen in other areas of Achaemenid art, particularly in seals.[35] An Achaemenid seal discovered in southern Russia shows a scene of adoration by a believer wearing a crown, standing before a crowned female deity atop a lion.[36] According to the authoritative opinion of John Boardman,[37] this is the goddess Anahita, depicted in conformity with a much more ancient iconography used throughout the Near East, particularly in the representation of the Hittite divinities, as early as the fourteenth through thirteenth centuries BC.[38]

The figurative language of subjugated peoples was accepted by the Persians and skillfully managed, since it offered iconographic validity that had long been known throughout the eastern Mediterranean region and functioned for the Persians' own propagandistic-celebrative ends. As far as we know with any certainty, the characteristics of Hellenistic art that are most appreciated in the modern era did not enjoy great favor among the Persians. In fact, the so-called

Treasury of Persepolis also yielded statues of Greek origin, where the drapery is rendered in the classical manner but which in no way influenced the predominant style at the Achaemenid court.[39] On the other hand, it is true that certain sculptural portrayals of animals at Persepolis show obvious Greek influence,[40] and represent, along with a few other works, almost all of the Achaemenid sculpture in the round that has survived.

During this period sculptural relief was the most widespread technique chosen by the Persians. This characteristic, along with certain choices of subject matter, mirrors a direct legacy from Assyrian art, which depicted subjugated peoples—a theme also addressed by the Sumerians and the Egyptians.[41] As noted, at Bisutun there are Achaemenid reliefs with depictions of vanquished peoples, but these show a limited number of people, without much emphasis on each individual's physical features or clothing. There, the last figure tied by the hands and neck wears a long pointed hat and a garment typical of the turbulent nomadic populations that were often at war with the central government. This figure can be identified as Shunkha, the rebel king of a Sakas tribe from central Asia.[42] Other depictions of vanquished peoples appear in Egyptian monuments from the Achaemenid era, discovered along the canal built at the behest of Darius I in Egypt, or on the pedestal of a statue, also Egyptian in execution, discovered

at Susa.[43] In these monuments, the various populations are represented by a single figure rendered in summary fashion and only in very few cases recognizable by physical features. The identification of each of these has been possible only through the inscriptions in Egyptian, quoted in a scroll beneath the various figures paying tribute.

The situation is different for the conquered peoples depicted at Persepolis and Naqsh-i Rustam, the burial site of Darius I and other emperors (plates 22, 24–25). Darius is shown at the apex of Achaemenid splendor, seated on a throne supported by thirty representatives from each of the countries that paid him tribute. Here every figure has a characteristic garment, weapon, hairstyle, or headgear, clearly distinguishing him from the others. Scholars do not agree in their identification of the various figures, which is also true of Persepolis, site of the true masterpiece of Achaemenid art that deals with this subject. The identification proposed by Tourovets seems plausible, where he provides a detailed analysis of each group.[44] In-

24–25. Delegations of peoples bearing tribute, on the staircase of the large audience hall at Persepolis. ABOVE: Syrians; OPPOSITE Parthians

deed, unlike other monuments at Persepolis, the figures are not depicted individually but in groups, brought into the presence of the great king, led by a figure who normally does not bear any tribute, whereas the retinue may bring one or more animals typical of their land, or the handicrafts for which each specific group apparently was known in ancient times. Usually the delegations do not bear arms, but in certain cases there are swords, bows, lances, and shields. It is possible that this apparent lack of respect before the great king, in reality, conceals a clear message of relative independence of armed populations. These people are always from the boundaries of the empire, and it is possible that the weaponry alludes also to their role as defenders of Achaemenid realms.[45]

In any case, Persepolis is by far the most representative center of Achaemenid art; this is imperial art, consciously and modernly self-assured in its taste for the varied aesthetic suggestions of the different provinces of the empire, rather than unconsciously open to confused and

hybrid acceptance. In other words, these works are more archaizing than archaic. The impression of a lucid reconciliation and an outright taste for the antiquarian, archaizing as it may be, might be termed neo-Attic, as opposed to authentically Attic, making it possible to speak of Persepolis as a sort of Hadrian's villa. According to myth, Persepolis was the off-season capital (Ecbatana being the summer capital and Susa the winter one), the site of the springtime new year, or *nauruz*. In this regard, some have observed that if the Persian calendar is truly Egyptian in origin, but with the Mesopotamian New Year, the appearance of Persepolis records this, stylistically and in wonderful fashion.[46] In folklore, Persepolis has remained "the throne of Jamshid" (Takht-e Jamshid), the Edenic sovereign who, having built his throne with the help of demons, departed at the New Year for his voyage in the heavens. The myth can be seen to correspond to Imampur,[47] while befuddled local historical memory sees Takht-e Jamshid as a memorial to a "good religion" disrupted by Alexander (a new Dahaka, perhaps for analogous reasons interpreted in another way by Islam), with a resulting flight toward India, among other places, by the artists who had created it: hence the first of the various migrations to India by followers of Mazdaism, a passage that is also a very insistent topos in the Islamic era.

26. ABOVE. Gold *rhyton*. Riza-i Abbasi Museum, Tehran

As for painting, there are no significant discoveries from the Achaemenid era, although a few traces preserved at the principal sites allow us to infer that monumental painting was somewhat widespread. Greek sources from the fourth century BC also mention pictorial decorations in the temples, palaces, and even private houses of the Persians,[48] but as long as it is not possible to carry out extensive excavations in Iran, all information derived from ancient literature is destined to remain unconfirmed. Traces of ornamental painting have been brought to light at both Pasargadae and Persepolis,[49] while the only human figures come from Susa.[50] Judging from the little that remains (head fragments of figures in profile), it seems that these may be images associated with tribute bearers in procession from sculptures of the large audience hall at Persepolis, thus perfectly in keeping with other examples of monumental art from the Achaemenid era.

DECORATIVE ARTS

The study of ceramics from the pre-Islamic era still presents many unknowns compared to the reams of information related to the classical world. This is not true, however, for decorative metalwork, which seems to have been highly prized, even outside Persia itself, as attested to by coins, jewelry, and containers of Achaemenid derivation, found not only at excavation sites in the western part of the empire (above all in Anatolia),[51] but also as far away as southern Siberia, a region never conquered by the great king. It follows that relationships with these regions must have been of a commercial nature and for the most part peaceful.

In the Achaemenid era, one of the most widely disseminated ceramic articles was the *rhyton*, a type of container for liquids in the form of an animal horn, often embellished with the bust of an animal or monster, usually winged (plates 26–27). The origin of the rhyton has been pinpointed as the area of eastern Anatolia and western Iran, and the Persians can be specifically credited with its introduction to Greece.[52] A small number of ceramic objects have been found during excavations at Persepolis and Susa, but without adding up to a truly significant body of work.[53] Some interesting pieces are in various museums and private collections.[54]

However, metalwork objects may be the most compelling decorative art from the Achaemenid period. Plates in precious metals, rhyta, and vases that initially came from unknown sites

27. OPPOSITE. Gold *rhyton* in the form of a winged lion, from Ecbatana, National Museum, Tehran

and, particularly in recent times, from clandestine excavations in Iran, are now in numerous private collections and museums.[55] Principal collections of metal objects recently discovered outside Iran include finds from Scythian tombs in Russia and southern Siberia,[56] or the treasury of Sinope (now northern Turkey).[57] As mentioned earlier, Anatolia was the region outside Iran where Achaemenid influence was strongest, even a long time after the Macedonian invasion.[58] However, Scythian art has numerous elements borrowed from Persia.[59] The famous Oxus Treasure (from southern Tajikistan, plates 28–30), in addition to numerous sculptural figurines and ornamental tablets in embossed gold, known for some time and for the most part housed in the British Museum (those depicting Magi are especially interesting),[60] now brings to mind the acquisition by the Miho Museum (Shigaraki, Japan) of other, similar small three-dimensional statues, generally identified as Zoroastrian priests (or Magi).[61]

Carved gemstones[62] and coins[63] from the Achaemenid era also constitute two groups of objects rather well known to experts. In particular, the study of carved gemstones has revealed both continuity in the use of ornamented and inscribed cylindrical seals, derived from Mesopotamian art, and a certain receptivity to themes popular in the iconography of the Greeks, the Egyptians, and Semitic populations along the Mediterranean coast, primarily the Phoenicians.[64] Achaemenid coinage displays some details borrowed from the Hellenistic world and later transmitted through Greek channels to the Parthians and the Sasanians, such as a dia-

28–30. ABOVE AND OPPOSITE. Three gold objects from the Oxus treasure: a figure carrying a sheaf of branches (*barsom*), a male head, and a pitcher, British Museum, London

dem, the band tied across the forehead of the royal figure portrayed on coins. The diadem initially appeared among the insignia of Achaemenid royal power and was only later adapted by Hellenistic sovereigns.[65]

There are no discoveries of textiles from the Achaemenid era in Iran, and we can only make deductions from a study of the decorations on the garments of statues from the principal archaeological sites. Often these decorations are confirmed by the discovery of objects outside Persia that depict figures wearing Iranian-style dress.[66] Some fragments of textiles decorated with elements clearly borrowed from imperial Achaemenid art come from Scythian tumulus tombs (*kurgen*) excavated in southern Siberia, especially near the site of Pazyryk. Here Soviet archaeologists recovered many objects in organic materials, thanks to the penetration of water into the underground tombs shortly after burial. The water was turned into ice with the first cold spell and never melted, due to the brief Siberian summer, so it was relatively easy for archaeologists to restore the objects with the use of hot water. The textiles discovered at Pazyryk include a carpet that depicts processions of horses accompanied by human figures, very similar to scenes observed at Persepolis, and female figures, perhaps involved with officiating at a ritual in front of an altar.[67] But the most interesting find at Pazyryk is clearly the fragment of fabric showing processions of lions, very similar to those often depicted in official Achaemenid art.[68] Indeed, certain details of the musculature are rendered in Achaemenid style, that is through the use of geometric or drop motifs distributed over the animal's body.[69] The dating recently proposed for these textiles, now commonly accepted, is the third century BC, which shows that the populations active in these regions evidently held Persian motifs in extremely high regard, even after the fall of the Achaemenid empire.[70]

As we have observed frequently in this quick analysis of Achaemenid civilization, many external artistic influences were easily adopted by the Persians. The Achaemenids proved to be receptive above all to the more highly developed cultures located west of Persis, the governmental entity that developed along the shores of the Mediterranean.[71] While at first glance this ease of adoption might lead one to think of an art generated from mixing external elements considered most suitable for expressing regality or self-celebration,[72] in fact the genesis of Achaemenid art is extremely original (as Genito has justly noted)[73] and a phenomenon unto itself, making it worthy of much more than cursory analysis. Moreover, one should not overlook the fact that the exchange or adoption of outside elements was mutual, and there are numerous examples of Iranian influence, or the acceptance of Iranian elements, on the part of nearby peoples. This process affected not only the conquered, and thus those who were more easily influenced, but also populations that were independent from the Achaemenid empire, such as the Greeks. Turning once again to one of the principal categories of Hellenic art—ceramic production—it is clear how certain forms had been accepted in Greece regardless of their barbarian origins, because they were particularly refined or simply beautiful. A similarly open attitude toward the foreign must have prevailed at the central Persian court and also at provincial administrative centers throughout the empire. Indeed, it is quite likely that these latter locations constituted a sort of outpost where exotic influences were felt before being accepted at court, and from which the lifestyle then in fashion spread first to Pasargadae, then to Persepolis.

This makes it absolutely unacceptable to maintain the despotic and tyrannical view of Achaemenid power that has been transmitted by certain types of Greek, anti-Persian propaganda. Even that view, however, is limited to a period quite close to the wars of invasion unleashed by Darius and Xerxes. Instead, the overall image of the imperial structure is one of a state not impervious to external influences, but predominantly focused on maintaining peaceful relations with conquered or neighboring regions. This points to a discrepancy with the traditional view of "antinational" philhellenism that followed—just as the myth that local artists, terrorized by Alexander, fled from Persepolis toward Buddhist India, clearly shows Iranian influence.

ARSACES
THE PARTHIANS AND TIME DENIED

HISTORY

The Parthians' ascent to power in Iran and its neighboring regions and the long duration of their rule constitute an unusual period that was made possible by the specific political conditions in the region about a century after the death of Alexander the Great, thus about 247 BC. The situation was unique because this was not a national dynasty that took control of the plateau and Mesopotamia after the expulsion of the Seleucids, but rather another sort of group—one that had once been subjugated by the Persians.

The peoples of the Arsacid dynasty (247 BC–AD 224)—the only native-born dynasty—were more or less eastern cousins of the Persians, with whom they shared a related language, culture, and lifestyle prior to the Persians' adoption of a settled existence. Yet for more than four hundred years the Arsacids successfully overshadowed the splendors of a not-very-distant past, long relegating to the background the most obvious or natural accumulations of the Achaemenid legacy. They would pay dearly for this expropriation during the subsequent Sasanian period (AD 224–241), when the new national dynasty attempted to blot out all traces of Arsacid history, or at least to cut the duration of their rule in half. The Sasanians' attempt, however, was not successful, and the memory of a "foreign" and yet Iranian dynasty is preserved in classical sources and in those from the Islamic era.[1] But the process of erasure was more successful in the collective unconscious of Europe, and the Arsacids barely made an appearance in Western textbooks—aside from the "Parthian arrow," or the ability of the Parthian riders to shoot from horseback while facing backward, even during a retreat. This has sometimes led to an opportunity for an excursus on a period that Alessandro Bausani, breaking with the usual clichés, considered a sort of lengthening of Iranian history—that is, an interlude of successful open-mindedness that was more fertile than the archaizing contractions that preceded and followed it—that helped to develop a grand Persian culture. We agree with this approach, but without granting much credence to an equally outdated traditional view of the Achaemenids and Sasanians.

The administration of power by the Arsacids still has not been completely clarified. Numismatic study has revealed that vast regions must have enjoyed a certain autonomy, and that the Parthian sovereign seems to have been satisfied with the subjugation—completely

31. Parthia, Iran, Central Asia (revision by M. Compareti from A. Hermann, *An Historical Atlas of China*, Edinburgh 1966).

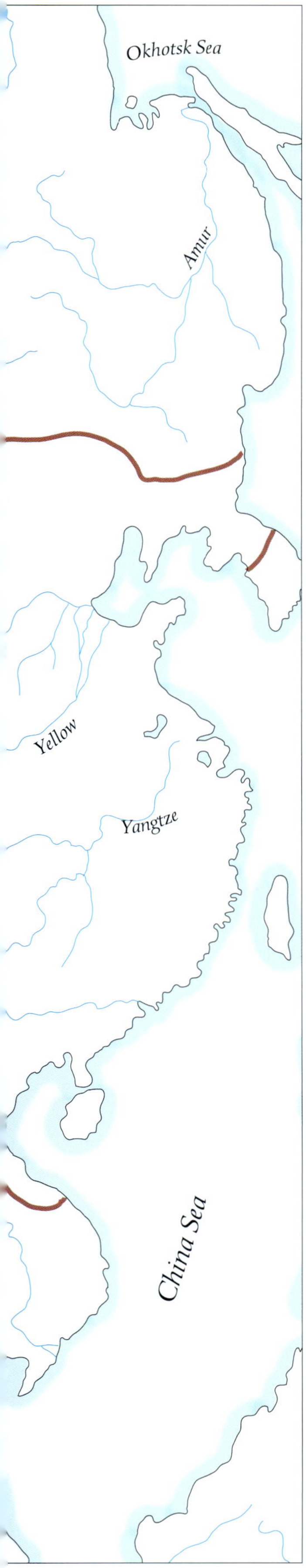

nominal in some cases—of local dynasties and collateral, often rebellious, branches of the Arsacid lineage.[2] Persia itself was one of these semiautonomous realms, forced to recognize its subordinate relationship to foreign Arsacid sovereigns, but, at the same time, custodians of national traditions.[3] The Parthian emperors assumed titles of the Achaemenid type but also defined themselves as pro-Hellenic, having just come into possession of regions that once belonged to the Seleucids, populated by Macedonian and Greek colonies. The principal cities, sites of the official mints, included Seleucia-Ctesiphon, the capital in Mesopotamia, Ecbatana in Media, Rhages near Tehran, Hecatompylos in northeastern Iran, and Nisaea, now located in Turkmen territory.

While agriculture and livestock breeding clearly continued to be an important factor in the economy of the Arsacid empire, commerce was the true source of wealth for the new Persian and Mesopotamian lords. The Parthians raised enormous revenues from tolls levied on merchandise passing along the caravan routes between the countries of the Mediterranean and the East, thanks to the favorable geographic position they occupied. Trade was carried out primarily over land, in part because, as noted earlier, between the first and second centuries AD (but also later in certain cases), the kingdoms in present-day southwestern Iran (Susiana, Elymaïs, and Fārs) were independent in practical terms, and it was in the Parthians' interest to redirect caravans into regions under their direct control.

At this time the Romans had only a vague idea of the realms that lay beyond Parthian territory and India, and they did not know about the techniques for the production of silk, the precious textile so favored by the upper classes in Rome, which was said to come from remote regions. According to a source that can be dated between the first century BC and the first century AD, a work by a Greek, Isidore of Charax (which is in present-day southern Iraq, with a small portion in southwestern Iran), the Parthians had established a series of caravan routes between Syria and the frontiers of India, specifically to allow merchants to move around with greater ease.[4] The Romans certainly were aware of this very important, if incomplete, work on the transport of goods along the easternmost routes, where the Parthians did not exercise direct control. It was not until AD 166–67 that a Roman delegation—probably unofficial, composed of merchants—reached the Chinese court of the Eastern Han kingdom (AD 25–220), traveling by sea, although the frugality of the gifts presented to the emperor aroused suspicion on the part of the authors of Chinese commentaries at the time.[5] A journey of this length by Roman subjects clearly was made possible by the friendly relationships they had with India, and in particular with the Kushana,[6] in the second century AD. In fact, the Parthians did everything possible to thwart a direct encounter between Rome and the Han empire, that is, between the major purchaser of silk and the greatest producer at the time.[7] They issued a series of false and discouraging reports, but it still proved difficult to prevent Chinese envoys from traveling. However, stirring up problems of national security by fomenting hostility between two nearby powers sufficed to stop the Romans.

The Parthians brilliantly succeeded in carrying out this task and for some time contained the advance of the Roman legions, thanks to their military technology, initially completely foreign to the Romans. The latter soon learned not to underestimate the warlike capacity of the Parthians, and above all their arrows, which were soon legendary among ancient authors and often represented in art.[8] The backbone of the Parthian army, however, was formed by their warriors, who were protected by plated armor or by coats of mail, as were their mounts.[9] These cataphract horsemen (*clibanarii* in Latin sources) severely tested the Roman armies stationed along the Mesopotamian frontiers and forced the venerable emperors to adopt similar divisions, specifically to thwart the Parthian cavalry.[10]

Other logistical discoveries that the Romans learned about as a result of their clashes with the Arsacid armies included the use of a particular saddle equipped with high projections on which horsemen could rest during battle, ideal for compensating for the lack of stirrups (plate 32, introduced in Europe only toward the seventh century AD, probably by the Avars),[11] and the use of the camel as a means of transport, especially well suited to the desert regions of Syria and Palestine.[12] In fact, according to commentaries from the Achaemenid era at Persepolis, some delegations from central Asia presented the Persian emperor with a camel as a form of tribute. This was also true of the Bactrian and Aryan representatives, including—according to Herodotus—those who were in the same Achaemenid province as the Parthians (who, in the depictions at Persepolis, are accompanied, instead, by a magnificent horse).[13]

As usual, almost all available source information on the Arsacid dynasty comes from works from the Islamic era or from outside the boundaries of the Parthian empire.[14] Most of what we know about the dynasty is from Greek and Latin authors, and thus is written from a hostile point of view.[15] Useful information can also be found in Armenian documents,[16] but Chinese sources have particularly captured the attention of certain scholars in recent times.[17] In fact, the Chinese may represent the only ancient populace with which the Parthians always maintained friendly relations,[18] and it is not surprising that the first great translator and Buddhist missionary working in the Celestial Empire was, in fact, an Arsacid nobleman known as An Shigao (who died around the late second or early third century AD).[19]

32. Charge of a *clibanarius*, graffiti from Dura Europos. From M. Rostovtzev.

A region in central Asia known as Parthava is mentioned earlier, in inscriptions of the Achaemenid sovereigns beginning in the sixth century BC, and Herodotus (fifth century BC) mentioned it, along with Chorasmia, Sogdiana, and Aria, as one of the countries that made up the sixteenth provincial territory of the Persian Empire. There is very little information regarding the people who inhabited this region, but we can hypothesize that they were a settled civilization, although their language remains completely shrouded in mystery.

Around 238 BC Parthava was invaded by nomadic people from the Dahae confederation, known to ancient authors as the Parni or the Aparni, who subsequently began a process of sedentary settlement in a region east of Irkania, around what would become their first capital, Nisaea (not far from present-day Ashkhabad). According to a commonly accepted hypothesis, the Parni spoke an eastern Iranian language, and it was shortly after they established settled communities that sources began referring to their name, now changed to Parthian.[20]

The region had already undergone a period of bloody struggles, following the death of Alexander in 323 BC, due to the inability of his successors (the Diadochi) to reach a peaceful compromise. Peithon, the governor assigned to Media in 323 BC, initiated hostilities, eliminating the legitimate provincial leader in Parthia and replacing him with his own brother. This did not meet with the approval of Seleucus Nicator (321–280 BC) or the other local provincial authorities, who banded together to drive out Peithon, forcing him to reconcile with Antigonus Cyclops (c. 384–301 BC), whose only response was to execute him.[21] This was probably the same period when Diodotus I of Bactria (c. 356–235 BC) threw off Seleucid control (c. 239 BC), and it was also when the provincial Parthian authority, Andragorus, rebelled against the central power; it was only shortly thereafter, however, that he was attacked by the Parni.[22]

The invasion of the Parni/Parthians—or the Arsacids, from the name of the dynasty founded

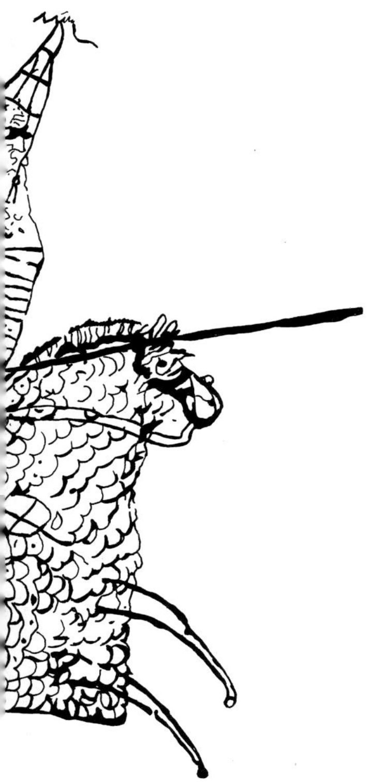

by their leader, Arsaces I (c. 247/238–217 BC)[23]—was made possible by the serious conflict that engaged Seleucus II Callinicus (246–225 BC) both abroad, against Ptolemeic Egypt, and within his own kingdom, due to claims put forth by his brother, Antiochus Hierax. The Arsacids avoided direct conflict with Seleucus II by barricading themselves within the impervious regions of their domain, but upon the withdrawal of the Seleucids, they returned to occupy Parthia and some areas of present-day northeastern Iran, located in Comisene, the region around the site of Shahr-i Qumisj, identified with ancient Hecatompylos, near present-day Damghan.[24] The eastern region of the Seleucid empire thus seemed irremediably lost. In fact, as noted earlier, in 239 BC, Bactria also proclaimed its independence, while around 305 BC, the Indian provinces and part of Arachosia and Gedrosia had already been annexed by Chandragupta (c. 324–300 BC), the founder of the Indian empire of the Maurya (322–182 BC).

The profound crisis of the Seleucids had a temporary respite with the ascension to power by Antiochus III the Great (223–186 BC). He undertook a campaign in Persia and central Asia, with the goal of crushing the numerous rebellions that had broken out in Iranian territory and restoring the kingdom of his ancestors to its ancient splendor. Known in history as the Anabasis of Antioch, this undertaking allowed him to both re-establish control over Persia and Parthia under Arsaces II (c. 217–191 BC) and draw up new treaties with the Greek-Bactrian kingdom and the Maurya. Antiochus III's series of successes was interrupted by the defeat he suffered at the hands of the Romans in Magnesia in 189 BC, after which all Seleucid claims to the east were thwarted.[25] In fact, the Parthians reopened hostilities with Phraates I (176–171 BC), and above all with his younger brother Mithridates I (171–139/138 BC), the first Parthian sovereign who minted coins with a clear reference to his total independence from the Seleucids.[26] The long reign of Mithridates I coincided with the definitive expulsion of the Seleucids from Persia and the weakening of their position in Mesopotamia. The Arsacid sovereign also turned his attention to the eastern frontier of his realm, conquering the Bactrian-Greeks and containing the threat from nomadic Iranian populations known as the Saka.[27] During this period, the territorial structure of all of central Asia was undergoing great upheavals, and a short time later (around 50 BC), the first core of the future Kushan empire would take shape in the territory of Bactria, which had been weakened by nomadic invasions and, finally, abandoned by the Greeks.

The successor to Mithridates I, Phraates II (138–127 BC), was probably the first Arsacid sovereign to permanently occupy Margiana, further consolidating the eastern boundaries of his kingdom.[28] The annexation of Margiana by the Arsacids would play a fundamental role in future developments in the religious history of Asia. In fact, the Chinese monk Zuanzang (AD 602–664), passing through central Asia between 627 and 645, referred in his memoirs to the existence of Buddhist establishments in Persia. This view should be considered with great circumspection, but it is possible that the pilgrim was referring to the eastern frontiers of the Sasanian Empire, namely Margiana, where traces of Buddhism date back to the mid-second century AD, a period corresponding to An Shigao's missionary activity.[29]

With the death of the Seleucid king Antiochus VII Sidetes, who was killed on the battlefield in 129 BC, Mithridates II (124/123–88/87 BC) permanently took over power in Mesopotamia (where the new capital, Seleucia-Ctesiphon, was established on the Tigris) and penetrated as far as Armenia (around 110 BC), as well as Syria, which he sacked in 93 or 92 BC and again in 88 BC. In 96 BC his delegation, led by General Orobazus, met with Sulla, who in the meantime had reached the Euphrates—the new boundary line between the two states[30]—following his first victorious battle against the King of Pontus, Mithridates VI Eupator (121–63 BC). From this point on, the destinies of the two powers were closely linked, which is extraordinarily important for the study of the history of the Parthians, who in large part are known thanks to authors who were Roman subjects.[31] Around 117–115 BC the Parthians received one or more legations from Zhang Qian, envoy of the Chinese empire of the Eastern Han (202 BC–AD 9), who was based in Bactria, where he was looking for allies to join forces against the terrifying confederation of nomadic tribes known as Xiongnu. These missions apparently appeared at the Parthian court, bearing gifts for King Mithridates II, which, it is safe to presume, included a quantity of silk.[32]

The stance of the Arsacids toward Mithridates VI Eupator created something of a breach with Lucullus, who was then in Anatolia, but the result was a treaty suspending hostilities, in 69 BC. An alliance between Phraates III (71/70–58/57 BC) and Pompey in 66 BC completely restored relations, but conflict broke out once again with the expedition of the Roman triumvir, Marcus Licinius Crassus (c. 115–53 BC) against Orodes II (58/57–38 BC). Crassus was stopped in northern Mesopotamia by a well-trained army led by the Parthian general Surenas (a Latinized version of the name of a well-known Parthian clan, the Suren), and he was massacred along with his soldiers, at Carrhae (present-day Haran, in Turkey) in 53 BC.[33] For about thirty years, this battle cast a shadow over the prestige of Rome, and for some time the recently conquered eastern provinces were left undefended.[34] In fact, Syria was first attacked in 51 BC.

According to Western sources, it was at Carrhae that the Romans first saw Chinese silk, since the banners flaunted by the armies of Surenas were made from this precious fabric. It was only six years earlier, in 59 BC, that the Chinese emperor Xuandi (74–49 BC) had succeeded in subduing the desert region of the Tarim Basin (now the Chinese province of Xinjiang), expelling the Xiongnu and turning the area, which was traversed by an important branch of the Silk Route, into a Chinese protectorate. This Chinese presence encouraged the silk trade, which until then had been controlled by nomads but carried out on a very limited scale.[35] In references to relationships with the West during the early centuries of Christianity, extremely informative Chinese sources clearly mention Arsacid attempts to prevent any encounters between the Han ambassadors and Rome. They state that the Roman "kings" wanted to establish contact with China, but were always obstructed by the Parthians, who had no intention of losing their albeit minimal revenue from the silk trade.[36]

Meanwhile, in 47 BC, Caesar had penetrated Anatolia from Syria to restore order in Pontus, where the son and betrayer of Mithridates VI Eupator, Pharnaces II (63–47 BC), sought to reestablish the ancient kingdom of his famous parent, without much success. Despite many victories, Caesar was prevented from achieving his plan to conquer Parthian Iran when he was assassinated by a group of conspirators in 44 BC. The latter fled to Anatolia, where they were hunted down by the new triumvirate, led by Octavian (27 BC–AD 14) and defeated in Macedonia at Philippi (42 BC), but not before attempting to establish an alliance with Orodes II. The Arsacid king organized three powerful armies and pushed into Syria, Phoenicia, and Judea, thereby securing direct access to the Mediterranean. Since the Parthian forces were threatening the stability of all of Anatolia, Marc Antony (c. 83–30 BC)—who still had relatively good relations with Octavian—sent General Publius Ventidius Bassus (c. 85–26 BC) to the east to contain the implacable advance of the Arsacids. The Roman envoy defeated the Parthians twice between 39 and 38 BC and forced them to abandon their western positions.[37] Encouraged by his general's successes, Marc Antony also attempted to subdue the Parthians, without brilliant results. Octavian, instead, having eliminated his domestic adversaries (including, among others, two triumvirs, Marcus Emilius Lepidus and Marc Antony himself) and having assumed absolute power (29 BC), succeeded in imposing a treaty on the Arsacid king Phraates IV (38–3/2 BC) in 20 BC. On that occasion Augustus restored Rome's prestige, regaining possession of the banners that had been lost by Crassus and taking back the prisoners who were still being held by the Parthians. Moreover, some of Phraates's children were even sent to study in Rome. A new treaty was drawn up and new borders were established, although the question of succession to the throne of Armenia, a Caucasic region much sought after by both Rome and the Arsacids,[38] remained unresolved.

Yet the Parthians complied with the requests of Augustus regarding the Mesopotamian front due to their own weakened monarchy and also because of continued pressure from nomadic peoples along the eastern frontiers of their empire. But they still were not ready to renounce their influence in a region that was strategically essential for them, both for defense and for the valuable trade routes that traversed it.

The Arsacids had to be wary of the eastern threat posed by the tough and mysterious Kushan empire (50 BC–c. AD 233). Many points about the latter's history still remain unclear. Their origin is connected to the nomadic Yuezhi people (as they are called in Chinese sources), which comprised one of five principal tribes. Once they settled in the region corresponding to ancient Bactria—exhausted from earlier invasions—and joined with the local, strongly Hellenized population, they soon took over lands that had belonged to the Indo-Parthians (particularly the Gandhara), until the mid-first century AD. They then turned their attention to the fertile regions of northwestern India, taking over the entire Ganges plain.[39] Augustus received some delegations from India, and while we cannot be sure which kingdom sent them, it is likely that these were the Kushana or their allies—which certainly would have alarmed the Arsacids, who were caught in the middle.[40]

Following a period of crisis created by problems of succession and attempted interference by Rome—put into effect with the brief ascent to power by Vonones (AD 8/9), one of the sons of Phraates IV, sent to study in Rome and clearly backed by Augustus himself—Artabanus II (AD 10/11–38) ascended the throne. The Roman counterpart to this Arsacid sovereign was Tiberius (AD 14–37), a notoriously complex personality, but who nonetheless was able to intervene decisively in Armenia and in other areas of Anatolia that were constantly threatened by their proximity to the Parthian frontier. The generals sent by Tiberius had sufficient skills to muster pro-Roman support in the region for some time, but without ever achieving a true annexation of Armenia, which continued to hang in the balance between the two superpowers. The death of Artabanus II was followed by another period of domestic instability that lasted until Vologases I assumed power (AD 51–76/80). His reign was also afflicted by internal rebellions and clashes with Rome, but Vologases proved capable of maintaining control. He was able both to hold his empire together and to press Arsacid claims in Armenia, establishing peace with Nero (AD 54–68) and establishing a collateral branch of the Arsacid dynasty in this Caucasic kingdom.[41]

The successors to Vologases lacked his talents, and they were plagued by invasions from outside, rebellions by subject peoples, troubles within the royal family, and yet another war with Rome, caused by the intervention of Osroes (AD 108/109–127/128) in Armenia. Trajan (AD 98–117), evidently aware of the disastrous situation in which the Arsacids found themselves at that particular moment, wasted no time in intervening and achieving further glory for Rome. The Parthians were not in a position to offer any resistance, and the Roman forces spread into Mesopotamia as far as the Persian Gulf. The Romans conquered Ctesiphon, but did not succeed in subduing Hatra (ancient Al-Hadhr), the principal ally of the Arsacids among the

Semitic peoples in the region and an important commercial center. Subsequently, a series of revolts in the eastern portion of the vast empire forced Trajan to withdraw and abandon part of the conquered territories. On his return journey, in Cilicia, Trajan died, leaving the solution to the Parthian problem to his successor, Hadrian (AD 117–138). An extremely cultured and far-sighted individual, Hadrian restored to the Arsacids the lands that his predecessor had taken and transformed them into the provinces known as Mesopotamia and Adiabene.[42]

Hadrian preferred to concentrate on organizing the province of Armenia, establishing a lasting peace with Osroes in order to have free access to the northeastern frontiers (which were threatened by numerous other enemies), and thwarting rebellions taking place within the empire. The Arsacids found themselves in a similar situation, in that—most likely around this time, according to a Chinese source—they suffered a serious defeat at the hands of the Kushana, who at that time were governed by their most famous emperor, Kanishka, whose precise years of rule still remain unknown, although it was around the mid-second century AD.[43] Hadrian's tactics allowed a relatively long period without war, which also extended to the reign of Vologases III (AD 111/112–147/148), but was interrupted by Vologases IV (147/148–191/192), who took an aggressive approach to foreign policy, in contrast to the caution shown by Antoninus Pius (138–161). In reality, the rule of Vologases IV was ravaged not only by war with the Kushana, but also by an invasion of the Alani, who reached as far as Anatolia and into other territories under Roman authority.[44]

Vologases IV invaded Armenia and, early on, had military victories over the Roman forces stationed in the region, even sacking Syria and Cappadocia. The new Roman emperor, Marcus Aurelius (161–180) responded to the aggression, sending Statius Priscus to the east with the task of recovering Cappadocia and Armenia. He also sent his brother, Lucius Verus (130–169), to Syria, while a large army led by Avidius Cassius prepared a true counteroffensive. In 164–65 this latter Roman general occupied Dura Europos, Edessa, Carres, and Nisibis, and continued as far as Ctesiphon. From there he proceeded through Media, conquering all of Iran. The Parthians did not seem capable of resisting Avidius Cassius's advance, and it took a terrible plague to force the Roman army to withdraw and hurriedly make peace. The providential epidemic allowed Vologases IV to recover much of Mesopotamia, except for Osroene and other adjacent territories, which were reorganized into a Roman province, while Armenia maintained its status as a Roman protectorate.[45]

The disorders tied to succession, long a normal state of affairs among Arsacid pretenders, now afflicted the Roman Empire for some years. Between 193 and 194, four aspiring emperors (supported by their respective armies) clashed in an open civil war, from which Septimius Severus (193–211), who was the commander of the legions stationed in Pannonia, emerged victorious. The Parthians were involved in the conflict when the armies of Vologases V (191/192–207/208) pillaged the province of Roman Mesopotamia, which had been left undefended, and occupied its principal cities. Once he crossed the Euphrates, in 195, Septimius Severus retook possession of the entire region, avoiding, however, direct conflict with the Parthians because of still unquelled disorder within his own frontiers, and perhaps hoping that a rebellion that had broken out in the meantime in western Iran might halt his adversary. Not in the least discouraged, and indeed having put down the rebellion, Vologases attacked Roman Mesopotamia once again, in 198, causing a second Roman intervention that, this time, subsided only in conquered Ctesiphon. Septimius Severus then attempted to lay siege to Hatra on two occasions, but twice had to stand down, due to that city's forceful defense.

33. The Square House of the royal palace at Nisaea, Turkmenistan

Septimius Severus's successor, Caracalla (211–217), attacked the Parthians under a frivolous pretext, as he was well informed about the domestic rebellions then distracting Vologases VI (207/208–221/222 or 227/228). In fact, the Roman emperor met with initial success but was assassinated by his praetorian guards during the operations at Carres, and his successor (also a former praetorian leader), Macrinus (217–218), suffered a harsh defeat. As a result, Parthian armies poured into Roman Mesopotamia, and Macrinus was forced to pay an enormous tribute to Vologases in order to attain a peaceful settlement.[46]

Despite this unexpected success, the Arsacids entered yet another period of crisis from which they were not able to recover. Their Roman enemies, momentarily neutralized, still carried on numerous domestic rebellions, and entire regions proclaimed themselves independent, decreeing the end of the Parthian empire. Ardashīr I (224–241), a figure deeply shrouded in legend, was overlord of Persis (or Fārs, the cradle of Persian civilization and the original site of the Achaemenid dynasty). He rebelled against the Arsacids, represented by Artabanus IV (r. 213–224), and became the founder of the Sasanian dynasty (226–642). In the conflict that followed, the Parthians and their allies were defeated by the new sovereign, who quickly subjugated the entire Iranian plateau and the Kushana empire, reaching as far as central Asia and the frontiers with India. However, not even Ardashīr could prevail over Hatra (a conquest that would be left to his successor, Shāpūr I, r. 241–272), and some pockets of resistance, loyal to the Arsacids, continued to be a thorn in his side, minting their own coins for some time.[47]

ARCHITECTURE

Archaeology has made enormous contributions to our knowledge about the Arsacid empire. The first excavations conducted in Mesopotamia occurred in the late nineteenth century—although in some cases those early excavations damaged layers from the Parthian era, which our predecessors considered less interesting than more ancient finds.[48] The pioneers of this discipline advanced a number of theories that, though partially or entirely dismissed by later discoveries, remain strongly compelling.

There was an early backlash to these studies in the central Asian regions of the Soviet Union. Not far from Ashkhabad—the present-day Turkmen capital as well as the original center of the Parthian empire—explorers and scholars realized that there must have been some misunderstanding in the formulation of the old treatises on Parthian art. This necessitated an overall evaluation based on Mesopotamian discoveries, excavations carried out within Persia itself (unfortunately few in number), and discoveries from central Asia. This approach was broadly adopted by scholars and contemporary archaeologists. The conclusions (drafted with the greatest caution and in utterly provisional fashion) allow us to understand that our knowledge of Parthian history, art, and culture is only in its initial stages, and our understanding is particularly vague for the geographic area corresponding to Iran. As noted above, better documentation exists for the regions of Mesopotamia (present-day eastern Iraq) and historical Parthia, located in what is now southern Turkmenistan.[49]

Going back to our initial observations, while we know little about Parthian artistic production, it still cannot be said that the Parthians' output was comparable to that of other ancient empires. The reason for this must be sought in the great territorial expanse of the Arsacid realm and in the consequent inclusion within those boundaries of a multiethnic and multicultural whole, inherited from the Seleucids, within the framework of tolerance or open-mindedness toward religious matters. Moreover, archaeological excavations concentrated for the most part in the western and northwestern regions of the empire had considerable impact. In Iran itself there are works that can be ascribed to the Parthian period, but these are almost exclusively stone reliefs and, less often, three-dimensional sculptures made according to a tradition well known to their Elamite ancestors.[50] Indeed, Parthian art cannot always be described in terms of defined geographic areas for certain periods of time, for some regions experienced long spells of freedom from the Arsacid yoke, and certain particular forms (above all architectural) existed in a phase of full development when the dynasty died out, thereby generating the illusion that many scientific discoveries could be attributed totally to Sasanian inspiration.[51] Many scholars, however, have taken diametrically opposed positions.[52]

This sort of geographic differentiation also corresponds to a different use of building materials. Throughout central Asia unbaked brick was widely used, while baked bricks or blocks of stone continued to be adopted in large measure in Mesopotamia and in southwestern Iran for the construction of terraces as integral parts of buildings, particularly those used for worship or royal purposes, such as at Masjid-i Sulaiman and at Bard-i Nishanda. The use of terraces is confirmed in the most ancient Mesopotamian architecture, but it was also certainly known in the Achaemenid era, where it found its loftiest manifestation in the so-called temple of Anahita, in Kengāvar in Media, which in a certain sense was a somewhat rough replica of Persepolis. Another architectural element already exploited by the Parthians, subsequently widely used by the Sasanians and also favored after Islamization, is the *iwan*, a building with a square plan, a domed roof, and an arched entrance on one side, opening onto a courtyard or garden. While some scholars have proposed Greek origins for the *iwan,* this form is noticeably different from the dominant taste of the Hellenistic era and late antiquity in the West, but was particularly favored and disseminated in Mesopotamia (at Seleucia-Ctesiphon, Assur, Warqa, Abu Qubur, and Hatra, with regional variations, of course),[53] and in neighboring territories (Armenia and Syria), namely places where the principal artistic influences did not come only from the Greek experience. Although elements of Ionic entablature as well as columns and capitals belonging

34. The southern *iwan* at the temple of Allat, Hatra, with various elements of architectural decoration

mostly to the Ionic order were known in Mesopotamia—including in the monuments listed above—in Khurkha (in central Iran, not far from Qom) there are columns surmounted by interesting capitals that are the result of an encounter between the tradition established after the conquest of Alexander and contributions from the Parthian era.[54]

Dwelling further on this commingling of Iranian and Hellenistic elements, one must mention Nisaea, the ancient Parthian capital in whose artifacts one can see the hand of Greek workers called upon specifically to celebrate the glory resulting from new conquests, or the work of local artists with Hellenistic training.

The original name of the city, discovered on one of the numerous *ostraca* (inscribed terracotta Parthian fragments, in an alphabet derived from Aramaic) was Mithradatkert, the fortress of Mithridates (probably Mithridates I). In the manner of many other central Asian cities, Nisaea was built in large part using unbaked bricks; it consisted of a lower portion surrounded by defensive walls and another portion erected on a nearby rise, which was the citadel, the administrative center. Excavations begun in the Soviet era continue today, thanks to the activity of a joint Italian-Turkmen mission. [55]

There is great indecision as to whether the first appearance of the *iwan* can be ascribed to Mesopotamia or to Nisaea—that is, to Parthia—but it is not yet possible to resolve this issue with certainty. Another matter that immediately struck the archaeologists excavating at Nisaea was the preference of the Arsacid sovereigns for themes prevalent in local and Achaemenid architecture, although modified in original fashion through the use of Hellenistic elements and the *iwan* (the tower), a structure that until recently was unknown at Nisaea but was documented at the nearby site of Mansūr-tepe. The undeniably Hellenistic element at Nisaea appears in sculpture, painting, and luxury items, judging from discoveries at the most important buildings in the city (as well as at the tower and sites known as the Round Hall, the Square Hall, and the Square House, plate 33). These are structures for which it is difficult to establish a specific use, but which, in any case, must have been intended to celebrate the glory of the new dynasty and, by implication, to honor divinities and heroes from the past.

Moving westward at the expense of the Seleucids, the Arsacids established or conquered other cities, which soon were transformed into capitals, thus clarifying the true objective of their conquest: western Iran and the fertile Mesopotamian plains. Excavations at Shahr-i Qumis have not yielded much, in part because of the brief duration of the excavation campaigns (only four between the late 1960s and the early 1970s). It is not possible to add much to the early results, except that the few buildings that have been explored have revealed, in some cases, the use of domed spaces, built entirely from unbaked brick and created according to various techniques that are clearly linked to the Parthian period.

The urban plan of Nisaea fully reflects a tendency that was widespread throughout pre-Islamic central Asia. The Hippodameic-style layout also was known (particularly in the case of the Greek-founded cities that fell into the hands of the Parthians, such as Dura Europos), but there are also examples of circular plans, such as at Takht-i Sulaiman (in Azerbaijan), at Marv (only for the Parthian era; the original layout was, in fact, rectangular), and above all Hatra. This city in northern Mesopotamia was more a principal ally of the Parthian empire than an annexed city. Hatra acted as an ideal buffer state between the Arsacid and Roman realms.[56] Its citizens were Semitic in origin (Arabic and Aramaic), as were their deities and their culture, although the latter was strongly marked by Iranian influence. Hatra's economy was based largely on trade between the Roman and Parthian empires. It is said that the Romans repeatedly sought in vain to take possession of Hatra. In the early third century AD, altered political conditions in Persia pushed the city into a desperate alliance with its old Roman enemies, a futile attempt, since it was then conquered by Shāpūr I, the second king of the Sasanian dynasty.

35. BELOW. Plan of the religious complex of *iwans* at Hatra. The two large *iwans* (A, B) are flanked on the left and right by tripartite access spaces and by two smaller *iwans* to the north (C, D). From the rear side of Iwan A, one enters the temple of Shamash. From M. Sommer, Hatra, 2003

36. OPPOSITE. The facade of the large Iwan B and Iwan C at Hatra

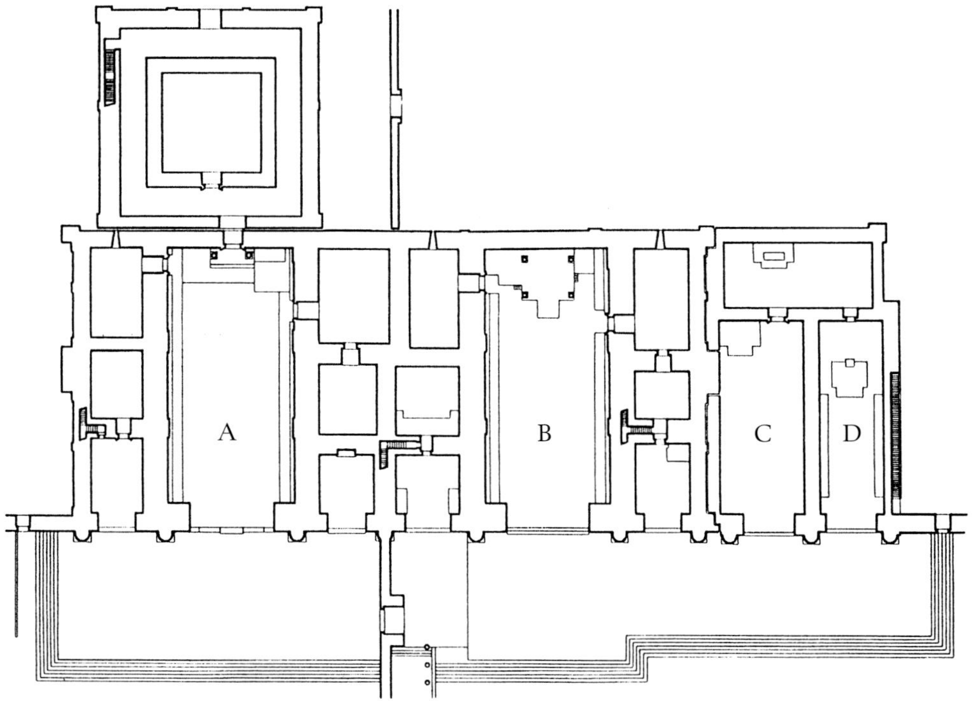

37. Bactrian head and inscriptions, architectural decoration of the pier of the large Iwan A at Hatra

Excavations at Hatra began in the early nineteenth century and were carried out first by German archaeologists, then taken over by their Iraqi colleagues. Since the site of Hatra is located in Iraq, unfortunately, all archaeological exploration is now blocked and seriously compromised, a result of the two recent conflicts that have involved and depleted that Arabic land. After the First Persian Gulf War (1990–91), an Italian mission from the University of Turin promoted a resumption of the excavations at Hatra, begun in the 1980s, in part by displaying a photographic exhibition at Turin in summer 2000 and at Naples in winter 2001–2.[57]

The original center of Hatra consists of the *temenos*, a rectangular enclosure with spaces opening toward the interior and four entrances positioned at the points of the compass, which contained the city's most significant religious structures (plates 34–36), such as the temple of the sun god (Shamash). In ancient times this was a destination for pre-Islamic Arabic pilgrims. Much of the space inside the enclosure has no large structures, since its purpose must have

38. Investiture of the satrap Khwasak at Susa, stele, AD 215, National Museum, Tehran

been simply to accommodate the pilgrims. The western portion of the *temenos,* instead, was occupied by temples in stone and unbaked brick, built on an artificial terrace. The architectural characteristics of the sacred buildings at Hatra are rooted in Mesopotamian, Greek, and Iranian traditions. The *iwan* is widely used within the *temenos,* while the religious structures discovered outside it (fourteen thus far) have features that are typical of Mesopotamian architecture from the Babylonian and Assyrian eras. The temples at Hatra were the principal goal of Iraqi restorations, while the Italian mission was also occupied with the excavation of civil structures, particularly the so-called Building A. It is highly likely that, in addition to serving as a residence for a prominent figure, this structure was used for various functions, and the discovery of religious statues leads us to believe that the inhabitants of Hatra followed domestic religious practices precisely like those of the Romans.

ARCHITECTURAL DECORATION, RELIEFS, SCULPTURES

At Hatra there is also exterior architectural decoration in stone and stucco, derived from classical art (fantastic masks, monstrous creatures, human faces and theriomorphs), although numerous reliefs refer to mythology specific to Semitic peoples (plates 37, 39). But the largest collection of stucco depictions and applications on the walls of the buildings from the Parthian era have been discovered at the fortress of Qal'e-i Yazdigard, in Iranian Kurdistan. Here too, unfortunately, the Canadian team responsible for this important discovery was not able to complete the excavation phase due to the disturbances that broke out in 1979 during the Islamic Revolution in Iran. The function of the buildings at Qal'e-i Yazdigard remains unknown, although there is reason to believe that this was both a fortress and the residence of a local lord, perhaps someone powerful enough to be considered only nominally under the rule of the Arsacid sovereign.[58] The stuccowork includes geometric, phytomorphic, and theriomorphic decorations. There are themes borrowed from the classical world (labyrinths, satyrs, other deities and nude female figures), but also figures dressed according to Parthian fashion and wearing pointed headgear. Another interesting decoration depicts a male bust with a diadem and a typically Parthian hairstyle, portrayed like a framed portrait, a style popular in Roman funerary sculpture. It is easy to understand how exchanges with the Mediterranean world carried over to the field of architectural decoration, where these influences were indeed widespread.[59] A poorly preserved frieze clearly portrays some griffins, larger in scale than the other figures of fantastic animals discovered at Qal'e-i Yazdigard, but only partially discernible because of the fragmentary condition of the stuccowork.[60] In the past, these two animals were thought to be figures of the mythical *senmurv*, a problematic composite Iranian animal that is able to navigate land, water, and air, which might have played a role as a military emblem. However, if the curled wing and coat beneath the lower jaw refer to something that may well be a common prototype, the images at Qal'e-i Yazdigard can be identified as griffins, as seen in, among other features, stucco fragments preserving a beak and a piece of a lion's tail.[61] A final decorative frieze in stucco comes from the same site and reproduces a staggered crenellation with a slit in the shape of an arrow.[62] This is another motif very common in central Asia, particularly in the architectural decoration of fortresses and defensive structures, and it is also found in an incense burner in the form of a building, discovered at Nisaea.[63]

In Parthian culture, sculpture and architecture were initially linked to Hellenistic models, and Iranian deities were depicted using typically Greek iconography, although many details remain indecipherable.[64] The sculptures at Nisaea were created from materials typical of the central Asian tradition, such as clay, and precious materials, such as marble. The marble statues of male and female deities—including Artemis, Aphrodite, and Dionysus—come from the Square House, a building perhaps originally intended for the banquets that were in fashion at Hellenistic courts, but later used to house the royal treasury.[65] According to Antonio Invernizzi, one of the discoverers of the sculptures at Nisaea and one of the greatest experts on these matters, artists must have produced such masterpieces in Parthia; thus, these would have been local sculptors whose training shows a clear dependency on Hellenistic schools, which were certainly present in Iran and central Asia after the invasion of Alexander.[66]

The Hellenistic component of the statues at Nisaea, seen in the gestures, the treatment of drapery, and the rendering of hair and other details, still would seem to disprove observations

39. BELOW. Detail with fish from architectural decoration on a door of the temple of Allat at Hatra

40. RIGHT. Stone head of Heracles, from Masgid-i Sulaiman, first century BC–AD first century, National Museum, Tehran

about the sculpture expressed by early scholars of Parthian art, who focused almost entirely on their frontality.[67] The preference for frontal depictions of royal or divine figures is borne out in Parthian art, but above all in the western territories of the Arsacid empire, where the new rulers reverted to ancient traditions. These solemnly immobile and rigid figures, with their inexpressive faces, communicated their divinity or regal nature to the predominantly Semitic peoples of Mesopotamia. Not even the naturalistic tendency of Hellenistic forms that followed the Macedonian and Greek invaders was able to weaken such a deeply rooted tradition, which the Arsacids—who were tolerant in religious matters—then adapted.[68] The same could be said of neoplatonism and gnosticism, marks of antiquity in their transition to late antiquity.

One example of stone sculpture experts have recognized as a portrayal of Mithridates I (consequently proposing the works's date around 140 BC), with later Elymaic additions, is the relief at Hung-i Nauruzi. Curiously, and despite the reference of many scholars to frontality as

43. OPPOSITE. Bronze statue of an Elymaic sovereign, Shami, first century BC–first century AD, National Museum, Tehran

a principal characteristic of Parthian art, the most ancient part of the monument is an equestrian Mithridates shown in profile—a Hellenistic choice that can be seen in other details, such as the diadem that encircles the sovereign's forehead.[69] Hung-i Nauruzi is located in ancient Elymais-Susiana, a region that was long removed from Parthian domination (c. 45 BC to AD 200). Most of the stone reliefs of Elymais (and those of Tang-i Sarvak) can be attributed to local workers engaged to celebrate the glory of local sovereigns rather than Arsacid overlords.[70]

The other stone reliefs attributed to the Parthians are found at Bisutun and Sar-i Pul-i Zuhab, in western Iran, and they are often accompanied by inscriptions that are difficult to read.[71] Two of the works at Bisutun are badly damaged; in one case there is a procession of dismounted figures with an inscription in Greek in the upper portion, probably dedicated to Mithridates II, accompanied by a Winged Victory of a classical type.[72] The second relief has been interpreted as a scene of a duel between Gotarzes II (c. AD 40–51) and the usurper Meherdates, in the presence of a Winged Victory.[73] Unfortunately, the extremely fragmentary conditions of the two reliefs do not allow us to gain any other information. A massive stone, also in Bisutun, has reliefs with scenes of sacrifice opposite an altar, often interpreted as a pyre, an altar of fire associated with the Zoroastrian faithful.[74] All the human figures are represented frontally, according to a scheme often reproduced in regions influenced by Iranian art, as exemplified in the painting at Dura Europos known as the Sacrifice of Conon.[75] There is great uncertainty about the dating of the relief at Sar-i Pul-i Zuhab, like all the monuments at Bisutun, and its attribution to an Arsacid patron has been debated.[76] It is clearly in a better state of preservation than the other stone sculptures, and it includes what may be an investiture scene accompanied by an inscription, in which a crowned horseman, his body in profile and his head depicted frontally, approaches a dismounted figure with a raised right hand. It is not possible to establish whether the face of the latter was depicted frontally because the entire head has been lost. The identification of this as an investiture scene is supported in that the figure on horseback is clearly the more significant (probably an Arsacid sovereign), while the one who is dismounted might portray a local lord.

One last relief, inscribed on a stele discovered at Susa (plate 38), again shows an investiture scene with a seated, crowned figure and a second, standing figure.[77] The faces are depicted frontally, while the two exchange a disk, which probably was associated, in an Iranian context, with the investiture of a vassal by a sovereign, or that of a sovereign by a god.[78]

41. ABOVE. Frontal detail of a lion, Ecbatana, c. 324 BC

42. BELOW. Statue of Abbu, wife of Sanatruq II, lord of Hatra, statue in situ, third century AD

There are few three-dimensional sculptures from the Parthian era from Mesopotamia and Iran, and these, like the finds at Nisaea, show a certain dependency on Hellenistic models. The preferred materials were stone and, in some cases, marble, although sculptures in metal (particularly bronze) also enjoyed some popularity. Apart from a legendary lion that has always been tied to the folklore of Hamadan (plate 41), fragments of a male head, again from Hamadan (Ecbatana), and a marble head of a queen with a turreted crown and a Greek inscription,[79] the most important discoveries are those in bronze from Shami, a site in Elymais, where a building was uncovered, the function of which remains unclear.[80] There is a noteworthy life-sized statue of a male figure interpreted as a Parthian prince (plate 43), with leggings worn over a pair of puffed-up trousers and a jacket closed in a V shape, cinched at the waist by a belt to which two daggers are attached. The hairstyle is held in place by a diadem of the type used by Hellenistic monarchs (although this is an element that initially was borrowed from the Iranian world, particularly as a distinctive sign of Achaemenid sovereigns);[81] the hair frames an impassive face

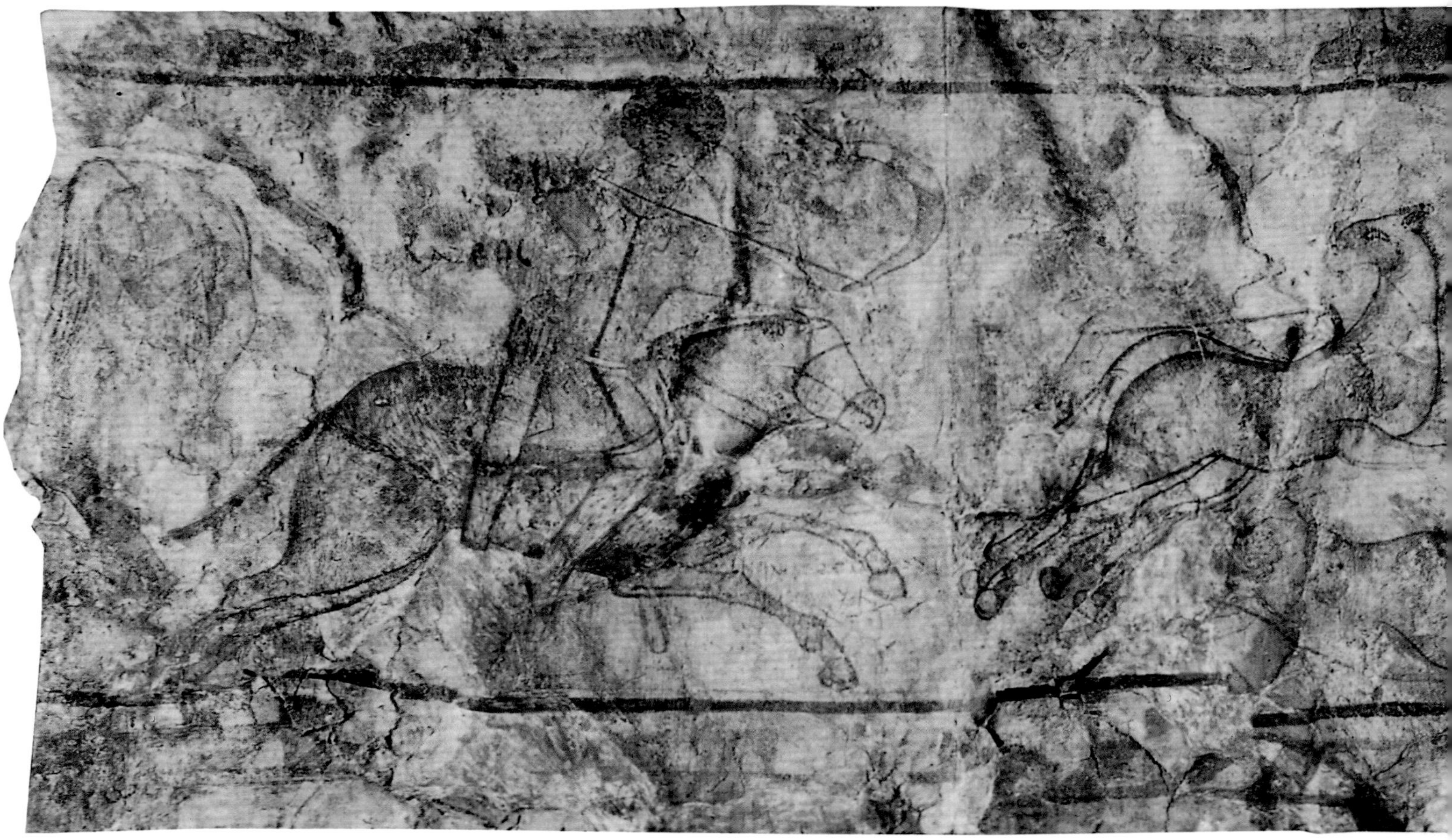

44. Scene of a hunt of wild ass, fresco from Dura Europos, second century AD, Musée du Louvre, Paris (archival photo)

with a moustache and the hint of a beard. Necklaces and earrings are also distinctive features in the royal portrayal of certain Sasanian emperors. Although this is a three-dimensional statue, it is clearly meant to be viewed frontally.

Among the notable works executed in perfect Hellenistic style is a bronze statue of Heracles, discovered at Seleucia by the Italian archaeological team. It bears a Greek inscription carved on the right groin area and a Parthian inscription on the left.[82] The importance of this piece lies in the fact that the iconography of the Greek god recurs frequently in Parthian art and, in particular, in Elymaic stone reliefs;[83] the stone at Bisutun also features a reclining Heracles. In fact, Heracles might be associated with Verethragna (which is explicitly the case at Commagene), a deity for which there probably was no specific figurative rendering in an Iranian context prior to the arrival of the Macedonians and the Greeks. However this figure has been subject to misinterpretations and incautious attributions.[84]

A large number of statues in marble or limestone, characterized by their hieratic and frontal poses, have also been found at Hatra. These are both male and female figures, often accompanied by inscriptions and identified either as kings and other representatives of the local aristocracy (plate 42), or as divinities, recognizable by their fantastic attributes, such as wings or horns. Their clothing is rendered with great fidelity and no accessory seems to have been left out, from fabric decorations to armor and jewelry.[85]

PAINTING

All examples of painting that can be ascribed to the Parthian period at Nisaea and Hatra are recent discoveries, with the exception of some painted pottery from Assur[86] and Mansūr-tepe (at the latter site there are still faint traces of wall paintings).[87] Paintings that are clearly in the Iranian manner have been found at other cities fought over by the Arsacids and the Romans as stations along trade routes. The walls of various buildings, like the hypogeum tombs

45. ABOVE, RIGHT. Two figures in profile near a turreted city, mural painting from Kuh-i Khagia, first–third century AD, National Museum, Tehran

of Palmyra in Syria (ancient Tadmor), have yielded depictions of figures and deities dressed in Parthian fashion, but with elements borrowed from the Greco-Roman world.[88] Likewise, at Dura Europos[89] and Edessa,[90] these two components are quite evident. In Edessa, capital of Osroes's kingdom, mosaics of frontal figures wearing caftans have been discovered. At Dura Europos graffiti have been found that relate back to Parthian or, in some cases, central Asian models (plate 44);[91] numerous buildings in Hatra also have graffiti.[92]

The paintings at Kuh-i Khagia (plate 45), in present-day Sistan, belong to a completely different tradition. We still know very little about antiquity in this region, especially in relation to the Parthian empire. Unlike the paintings discovered at Palmyra, Dura Europos, and Edessa, where there are predominantly frontal depictions of human figures or deities in the Parthian manner, at Kuh-i Khagia (the high ground that Herzfeld identified as the mountain from which the Magi witnessed the appearance of the star of Bethlehem) there is a completely original mix of Iranian and Hellenistic elements, with a preference for the reproduction of human figures in profile or foreshortened view.[93] Moreover, according to more recent studies, there are also traces of Buddhist settlements that can be ascribed to a phase preceding the Hellenistic era.

The oldest Parthian paintings (second century BC) are the very fragmentary ones discovered at Nisaea, in the so-called Tower, a building still undergoing excavation, and they continue to present certain questions.[94] They seem to have been executed in fresco, according to the Russian scholar who carried out the first investigations;[95] this would constitute a significant discovery, since the most widespread pictorial technique previously discovered in Asia was tempera. The painted frieze of the Tower of Nisaea reveals the artist's total dependence on Hellenistic models, where the subject is depicted within the framework of Iranian culture, perhaps still tied to a nomadic lifestyle. In fact, this is a battle scene where the horsemen of two opposing sides fling arrows or seek shelter behind their shields. In the lower portion, one can glimpse the remains of an animal, perhaps a lion, and a wing that belonged to a bird or to some imaginary creature.

The wall paintings at Nisaea clearly can be ascribed to a period that was fortunate for the Arsacids, in a territory they had long ago conquered, and which they thus considered their homeland, despite the population's wandering roots. Hatra has some of the painted scenes that are closest to genuinely Iranian prototypes, widely exploited during the subsequent Sasanian era to express concepts tied to the sovereign's royalty and the infallibity of his divine origins. Briefly put, once again the iconographic formulas specific to the "abominable" Arsacids would be adopted by their principal detractors without substantial modifications, apparently because they were recognized as suitable for expressing concepts that were universally comprehensible during that defined period within that specific culture. It will be worthwhile to keep in mind this observation for the study of not only Parthian art (which is anything but the barbaric output of a dynasty with nomadic origins), but also Sasanian art, which has long and narrow-mindedly been judged the only art worthy of consideration alongside the most ancient artifacts discovered in Iran—classical work from the Achaemenid era.

Paintings at Hatra were uncovered during the Italian excavation in a house referred as Building A and are dated to the third century AD, thus on the eve of the Sasanian invasion. They show equestrian hunting scenes with bows and lances, organized in vertical bands separated by vine branches that also act as a frame. The hunters are all portrayed in profile or in three-quarter view, and they do not wear armor but rather light garments, and the horses, which race at full gallop, also wear no particular protection.[96] One specific case, a boar hunting scene on the east wall of Building A, has drawn the attention of scholars because it provides the first instance of a double depiction of the animal, portrayed while struck by a horseman's lance, and already dead, in the lower portion of the composition.[97] This device alludes to the infallibility of the hunter and later, in the Sasanian era, it would be widely used in the decorations of luxury objects (particularly those in metal) that were associated with the hunting activities of the Persian emperors.[98]

DECORATIVE ARTS

Just as for the Sasanian era, there is scant documentation of ceramics from the Parthian era. Archaeologists have noted some continuity between the two periods, without great ruptures or changes in production.[99] The best-known sites are those in Mesopotamia, in part because they house the most valuable finds. These are often embellished with a green glaze, although unglazed ceramic was widely used.[100] Some recent discoveries from a necropolis near Kermān, in ancient Gedrosia, include objects of everyday use (vases, carafes, bowls, etc.), but also more elaborate forms such as *rhyta*. The *rhyton* with the bust of an animal (almost always horned) is by no means a rare occurrence in Parthian ceramics; one example is the piece from the necropolis at Damavand, not far from Tehran (plate 47).[101] Ceramics from Kermān in some cases have a red surface created by the engobe technique, using a liquid clay slip to apply decorative painting over the entire body of a vase. This find is exceptional but cannot be considered typical of Parthian ceramics, due to the specific geographic position of the region, which was open to exchanges with the principal centers of Arsacid power (Mesopotamia and the Iranian plateau), but also with central Asia and India, as other objects discovered at the same necropolis attest.[102]

Experts consider the so-called pilgrim's flasks to be characteristic of ceramics from Mesopotamia in the Parthian era.[103] These are really water bottles equipped with holes on the sides

46. BELOW. Ceramic jug, from Eshkewar, first–third century AD, National Museum, Tehran

47. OPPOSITE. *Rhyton* in the shape of an ibex protome, Damavand, second–first century BC, National Museum, Tehran

of the neck through which ropes can be slipped, making them easier to carry. Flasks of this type are common among the finds discovered in China, datable to the era of the Tang dynasty (AD 618–906), but they are more likely from Sogdiana, based on their dating.[104]

The Parthians also used glazed ceramic to make sarcophagi, some examples of which have been found at Warka[105] and, very recently, at Shūshtar.[106] The latter have more interesting decoration and are better preserved; in at least one case there is a fragment of a sarcophagus with the remains of a female face.[107] The practice of burying the dead inside sarcophagi, particularly anthropomorphic ones, inevitably relates to Egyptian and Phoenician precedents, although the Jews and the Romans also used stone and marble sarcophagi (certainly not anthropomorphic, except in certain cases in the province of Egypt). Currently not much is known about funerary practices in the Parthian era. Burial practices clearly were carried out, but only future excavations at potentially illuminating sites (first and foremost Nisaea and Hecatompylos, where even royal tombs might be found)[108] will make it possible to flesh out our knowledge of religious customs and religion in general among the Parthians.

The central Asian caravan route known as the Silk Road and its branches were not a one-way street. Silk was clearly the most sought after item in the world outside China, but other products were conveyed in the opposite direction, from the west (Iran and the Mediterranean). Moreover, the central Asian nomads exported to the Han empire products typical of an economy based on livestock breeding. There was Chinese demand for luxurious and exotic articles, including glass and ceramic in particular, although wine, textiles, horses, and arms were also significant imports from western countries.[109]

From the time of the Achaemenid era, Persian metalwork was held in the highest regard and exported to the entire Mediterranean basin. We have no way of knowing what the eastern destinations for this trade were, but we can assume that the Scythian populations of central Asia were interested in acquiring sumptuary products, thus acting as a conduit between Persia and China. True Achaemenid metalwork has never been discovered in China, but some scholars have turned their attention to certain silver vases from the third century BC, discovered in central China and based, with all probability, on Achaemenid models.[110]

Our current state of knowledge does not allow us to advance major hypotheses about the exportation of metal goods in the Parthian era, but it is possible that they were included among diplomatic gifts presented to the Han emperors, and this may be the case for certain Roman silver articles found in Chinese tombs.[111]

Plates and *rhyta* in gilded silver, attributed by experts to Arsacid Persia, are not very numerous and come only from chance discoveries or clandestine excavations. Once again, the link to Hellenistic art is very strong, in terms of both subject matter and forms.[112] Of the few Parthian examples found in an archaeological dig in Georgia, at Mtskheta, the most interesting and best preserved plate has a central medallion with the image of a horse facing a pyre, perhaps datable to the first century AD. All the details of the rendering of the animal relate to Iranian prototypes: the raised front hoof and the serrated mane, the latter a characteristic of the steeds of Eurasian nomadic peoples.[113]

In the Parthian era, the most common decoration for *rhyta* seems to have been that of a feline protome, or head, depicted in a threatening stance, its jaws wide open,[114] although there is at least one case of a horse protome accompanied by vine branches.[115] A *rhyton* now in a private collection in Japan is a variation on the feline theme and depicts a lynx squeezing a rooster

48. Silver plate, second century AD, British Museum, London, no. 134963

between its claws and biting into its flesh.[116] The scene is rendered with extreme vigor, and every detail of the lynx's musculature and the rooster's plumage is conveyed scrupulously.

The most genuinely Parthian plate in this group is one in silver, now in the British Museum, probably from the second century, with an Achaemenid-style embossed decoration on the body and a central medallion containing an engraved festive scene where three figures can be identified (plate 48).[117] The main figure, in the center and reclining on some cushions propped up on a bed, has a beard and hairstyle typical of the Arsacid sovereigns. He holds a bowl, raised in his left hand, and he wears a caftan with a decorative central panel, a belt, and a necklace. His right hand rests on the shoulder of a female figure dressed in a long tunic and seated on the bed. On the opposite side, a servant holds a circular object, perhaps another container, with both hands. Here, too, the Iranian character of the scene is indisputable, and it is a type of portrayal that recurs on Sasanian and post-Sasanian metal objects, in later central Asian paintings, and in decorative metal and ceramics from the Islamic era.

Not much more is known about Parthian metalwork. A limited quantity of silverwork, which can be attributed to Parthian production, has been taken from unmonitored excavations in the ancient region of Gandhara, but these are bowls and plates that can be ascribed entirely to Hellenistic art in their forms and depicted scenes, except for some inscriptions in the *kharoshti* alphabet (used in Gandhara and in other regions of central Asia), relating to the name of the owners and the weight of the object.[118] In Nisaea too, metal objects show a strong dependence on Hellenistic models, with a preference for themes from classical mythology, such as figures of divinities, centaurs, griffins, and sirens.[119]

Among the most well-known finds from the Square House at Nisaea are the famous ivory *rhyta* from the first century BC to the first century AD (plate 49).[120] Once again, the scenes that run along the edges of the *rhyta* reveal glimpses of subjects taken from the Hellenistic tradition, and some also have Greek inscriptions.[121] The end portion of the *rhyta* includes various subjects, such as protomes of human figures and imaginary creatures, clearly Hellenistic in taste, but also monstrous creatures with horns and wings borrowed from Achaemenid art. In contrast, ivory reliefs with Iranian themes have been found in Olbia (now in the Ukraine). In these, the figures wear caftans, but it is above all the hairstyles and poses that bring to mind the Parthian sovereigns depicted in certain sculptures or on various coins.[122]

As noted above, glass production within the Parthian realms must have been well developed, but only a few examples have come to light thus far; a single cup with relief work, now in the Museo Nazionale d'Arte Orientale in Rome, can perhaps be dated between the second century BC and the second century AD (plate 50).[123] Glass vessels almost always have exterior decoration, either applied or in relief. Some bowls, discovered in the imperial storehouse of Shoso-in at Nara, Japan, date to the Sasanian era but share characteristics with Parthian glasswork, since, apparently, the demand from abroad involved a certain continuity in production.[124] Today there are collections of Iranian glass in Japan, and the objects attributed to the pre-Islamic era include, for the most part, bowls, glasses, and other small pieces.[125]

There are not many other examples of luxury goods that can be attributed to the Parthians; there are very few studies devoted to carved gems and seals,[126] and our knowledge of jewelry is primarily deduced from a study of the sculpture.[127] The almost obsessive care taken by Parthian sculptors in the rendering of textile decorations constitutes a great source of information on clothing styles, headgear, and footwear worn by the Arsacids and people in close contact with them (Elymeans, Hatrenes, Palmyrenes, etc.). Generally, the Parthians dressed like most of the sedentary and nomadic Iranian populations, with a preference for caftans made from cloaks closed in front or in a V, leather or cloth belts with worked metal buckles, and rather full trousers that fell over sturdy shoes. This was a style of dress common to people accustomed to moving about on horseback, with the addition of tall headgear (tiaras), different from the usual pointed hats of the Scythian tribes of central Asia or the Phrygian caps (*pilei*) that Rome attributed indiscriminately to all people from the East. This type of dress clearly refers to male fashion; women, instead, wore long garments in the Greek manner (or, also in the Greek manner and as far as we can infer from the sculpture, they were depicted nude).[128] Fragments of textiles discovered in archaeological contexts in Iran and attributed with some certainty to the Parthian era include a fragment of decorated wool from Germi (Iranian Azerbaijan), another from Shahr-i Qumis, with portions in silk but without ornamental elements,[129] and a few others from the coastal region of the Caspian Sea.[130] The textile from Germi has a pattern with checks, swastikas, and curving lines, typical of the Mediterranean region that had contact with the Greeks.[131] The climactic conditions of Iran normally do not allow organic materials to be preserved, and in any case no silk has been found at any excavation site from this period. In Palmyra, in Syria, at least two tombs from the second century AD have yielded fragments of silk decorated with Chinese motifs.[132] Thus, Roman sources can be considered accurate, and the lack of silk finds must be due to the scarcity of Parthian sites that have been explored in Iran.

49. Ivory rhyton discovered in the Square House at Nisaea, second–first century BC

50. RIGHT. Glass cup, Museo Nationale d'Arte Orientale, Rome

Regarding decorations, an examination of the clothing depicted on statues can convey an idea of the motifs most appreciated by the Parthians, although as frequently noted, this entails what, for the most part, was in fashion outside the actual Arsacid realm (plate 51). Plant motifs were certainly widely popular, as were rhomboidal diamond shapes containing a wide variety of subjects.[133] These probably depict embroidery or metal appliqué (so-called *bracteates*, from the name of a type of Byzantine coin that this style apparently recalled), while the frames and diamond shapes are in relief and are formed from small, closely spaced pearls.

More complex subjects have not been discovered in Iran, although some fragments of embroidered wool, datable to the first century BC and decorated with Hellenistic motifs, have been found at Noin Ula (Mongolia).[134] Two of these fragments show a group of horseman in procession and a human head, these too clearly Hellenistic in style.[135] The human head belongs to a male figure with a moustache and a diadem placed to hold down his rather long hair, a type of hairstyle that occurs in some Parthian works, but the rendering of which also recalls portraits of royal Kushana figures. Other wool fragments from Noin Ula depict plant decorations developed in vertical bands;[136] many similar pieces have been discovered at Loulan, in Chinese Turkestan, at Palmyra, and in the Crimea. In these cases too, Parthian production is considered likely.[137] Based on the knowledge we have, it is not easy to establish the origin of these fragments. A Parthian hypothesis clearly cannot be dismissed, precisely because of the Hellenistic character of the ornamentation, which was widely disseminated in the textile decoration of clothing for Arsacid sovereigns. But this does not automatically imply domestic production. In fact, textiles were the most easily transported luxury item, and so we cannot be certain that they were produced by the Parthians.[138]

COINS

It is said that the history of the Parthians is known almost exclusively through outside sources. Numismatics is the only discipline useful for tracing a plausible line of succession of the Arsacid sovereigns.[139] The official mints were located at Seleucia-Ctesiphon in Mesopotamia, Ecbatana in Media, Rhages, Hecatompylos, and Nisaea.

The coins of the Arsacid sovereigns are based on Greek or Hellenistic models in terms of the iconography on the front and back, the weight (absolutely identical to the coin types most common in the Seleucid empire, the drachma and the tetradrachma), and their inscriptions. In fact, as soon as the Parthians took over the Greek cities of Iran and Mesopotamia, they considered themselves philhellenic, and in rare cases—at the time of Phraates IV, when Augustus supported a rebellion to overthrow the legitimate sovereign—even philoroman. From the time of Artabanus II (c. 128–124 BC), the Greek character of the coins was gradually abandoned, and inscriptions in the Aramaic alphabet (the alphabet used by the Parthians with various adaptations) appeared. Two different calendars were referenced; drachmas referred to the date Arsaces I ascended to the throne (c. 247 BC), while tetradrachmas referred to the Seleucid era (312–64 BC).

The front side of coins generally depicts the sovereign's portrait in Hellenistic fashion, in profile, although there are some examples of frontal busts (including those of Artabanus II); there are also portrayals with the corners of the diadem left loose, hair flowing down the shoulders, in keeping with a scheme transmitted to the Sasanians and further developed by them. There is only one instance where a portrait of a woman appears on the front of a coin; this is Musa, wife of Phraates IV (38–32 BC), who overthrew her illustrious consort in an attempted revolt, which was bloodily put down when Artabanus II ascended to power. The backs of coins featured other subjects borrowed from the West: a Hellenistic version of Fortune, standing opposite the seated king and holding out to him an attribute of power; or an enthroned archer busy weighing his bow, a variation on the theme of Apollo trying out his bow and arrow, an image that recurs on Seleucid coins. Bronze coins of lesser value display greater freedom of subject matter and more variety, depending on the region of coinage.

The first move away from strictly Seleucid models occurred at the time of Mithridates I, when inscriptions celebrated the regal quality of the sovereign known as the Great King Arsaces. Other changes in the depiction of clothing were introduced by Artabanus I (128–124/123 BC), Mithridates II (123–88 BC), and Artabanus II, with greater stylization of the subjects on the back of the coin and an increase in inscriptions, although these are rather difficult to interpret. In fact, Parthian coins repeatedly bore the name "Arsaces," or other names that cannot always be associated with a specific king. There are some very detailed systematic studies,[140] but only for certain classes of coins, discovered in great quantity and in an archaeological context, again at the western and eastern edges of the Parthian empire (at Susa and in the historical region of Irkania). Despite the efforts of contemporary numismatists, it is clear that only a resumption of the excavations in Iranian territory will expand our knowledge of this area.

51. Armed male figures dressed in central Asian style, Svat, Pakistan, Royal Ontario Museum, c. first–second century AD

THE DEPICTION OF THE PARTHIANS IN ROMAN MONUMENTS

In Rome contact with the Parthians brought about various changes in military technology beginning in the first century BC, in conjunction, that is, with the first clashes between the two powers, which were initially favorable to the Arsacids. In a historical-artistic context, there is also evidence of changes due to the penetration of iconographic elements that were initially extraneous to the Greco-Roman world. These were particularly significant in the third century, and not only in the eastern provinces, which were obviously more exposed to direct influences.[141]

In reality, the figure of the subjugated Parthian barbarian, kneeling before the Roman emperor or simply depicted in various compositions of an exotic nature (an Eastern exoticism, different from the Western, which was presented for the benefit of China, the other great empire in contact with the Arsacids) first appeared during the time of Augustus. The military exploits of the first Roman emperor, like his diplomatic victories, set in motion a propaganda mechanism that was used to celebrate his glory. The figure of the Parthian kneeling before a podium supporting the enthroned Caesar, or the barbarian, again kneeling, depicted in the act of handing over the Roman insignia, appears on some coins issued under Augustus. The Parthians can be identified by their dress, sometimes by their beards and hairstyles, and above all by the Phrygian cap, which in fact was an attribute of all figures of eastern peoples, real and mythical, including Anatolians, Caucasics, Iranians, and also Dacians, Thracians, and Sarmatians.

One of the first representations of a figure dressed as a Parthian is seen on the breastplate of the statue of Augustus from Prima Porta (Rome), now in the Vatican Museums.[142] On the statue's chest are various figures in relief, including one identified as Romulus, dressed as a centurion, accompanied by a wolf, his arm extended, and another wearing a crown and caftan, with a beard and long hair, holding up an insignia surmounted by an eagle. The latter figure is thought to be Mithridates I (who on some coins is portrayed wearing a crown), since as founder of the Parthian empire, he alone could be considered a true counterpart to the founder of Rome.[143] Three marble statues of kneeling Parthians, one of which is at the Museo Archeologico Nazionale in Naples, also date back to the Augustinian era; they support a pedestal on their backs, which was originally placed on the Palatine to hold a metal tripod.[144]

Finally there are figures of Parthian warriors or prisoners depicted on triumphal monuments from the second and third centuries, created at the behest of emperors to celebrate their glory. The best-preserved examples are on the great altar of Ephesus, from the time of Marcus Aurelius, and on the arch of Septimius Severus in Rome.[145] The characteristics of the clothing are always the same, at this point repeated in almost stereotypical manner, except for the appearance or absence of the beard. The temple at Cyzicus, attributed to the era of Hadrian (specifically the year 138, at the end of his reign), again in Anatolia, has a sculptural frieze that has an interesting portrayal of bearded horsemen dressed in Iranian fashion, shown in the act of fleeing, probably from the Roman legions.[146] The fleeing warriors have been interpreted as Parthians or Scythians because of certain clothing details, such as the necklaces. In fact, a very similar necklace can be seen on a sculpture at Shami, and the headgear of the Cyzicus bearded warriors recalls a sculpted head from Persis, which sports a similar pointed cap.[147] Therefore, the identification of these figures as Parthian horsemen seems plausible, although Hadrian had always sought to maintain peace on the Euphrates frontier, while there were bellicose

incidents along the northeastern borders of the empire during his reign. Once again, the indecisive identification reflects the scarcity of available information.

Reliefs from Gandhara, datable to about the second century, depict processions of figures in Iranian clothing, with a treatment of the hair and beards that is very close to the Greco-Roman rendering of eastern barbarians.[148] Although it is impossible in these reliefs to distinguish between the Kushana and possible representatives of any other Iranian population, it is interesting to note the arrangement of the figures from Buddhist Gandhara in comparison to the sculpted friezes from Palmyra and Dura Europos, which were created far earlier and in a completely pagan context.[149] Moreover, contacts between the Parthian and Kushana worlds must have taken place, as attested to by an ivory disk discovered at Hatra, the style of which recalls objects that are normally made from stone, widely disseminated in Bactria between the first century BC and the second century AD. The use of such objects, often decorated with scenes borrowed from Greek mythology, remains uncertain.[150]

To conclude with other iconographic analogies, the last depictions of a Parthian sovereign are found in two Sasanian reliefs, respectively at Naqsh-i Rustam and Firuzabad.[151] The first depicts the defeat of Artabanus IV by Ardashīr I, who unseats his foe. Likewise in the same monument, the hereditary Sasanian prince, Shāpūr, fells a minister or another aristocrat. Finally, a Persian page assaults one of the Arsacid kings. The stone monument at Firuzabad, instead, depicts the investiture of an equestrian Ardashīr I by Ahura Mazda. The two horsemen symbolically stamp on the stretched out bodies of their respective enemies: Artabanus IV and Ahriman. In the fourth century this practice of depicting the defeated enemy leaders in derisive fashion would serve as a model for those Sasanian monuments, where the humbled and defeated figure beneath the hooves of a horse or at the feet of Shāpūr II (309–379) would be replaced by no less than the body of the emperors Gordianus III and Giuliano,[152] according to a formula that was also fully exploited by Roman propaganda.

However, another and more intriguing Roman-Arsacid iconography would become the norm in depictions of homage, with costumes and ritual gestures that relate back to forms of "Persian" prostration, not to mention images of gifts sometimes presented by veiled hands to a Christian Savior, who seems like a twin of Dionysus in a mosaic at Paphos (plate 52).

52. Presentation of the infant Dionysus, triclinium of the house Aion, Nea Paphos (Cyprus), second quarter of the fourth century AD

Then there is the literature. Parthian origins have been attributed to some later "novels," the most interesting of which is undoubtedly the book of Budasf. In one, more specifically Parthian version, the key figure, which elsewhere is depicted as a prince who chooses the way of asceticism, is a prince tempted by asceticism, who accepts the crown in order to ensure that his people will have a just sovereign. It is a sort of synthesis between the two classical motifs, which remains a curiosity despite its timeless atmosphere.[153]

Archaeological remains on the island of Kharg in the Persian Gulf would attest to an early expansion of Christianity during the Parthian era, with a community professionally dedicated to pearl fishing.[154] This may be the source for the specific economic (though not necessarily Marxist-popular) roots for the famous so-called "Hymn of the Pearl" (a Gnostic document from the Parthian era, which would have great symbolic influence). It is contained in the apocryphal Acts of Thomas, where a young prince descends into the darkness of Lethe to take away the Pearl of the soul held prisoner among the shadows of the physical world:

The Hymn

(The Hymn of Judas Thomas the Apostle in the Country of the Indians)
Translated by G.R.S. Mead

When a quite little child, I was dwelling in the House of my Father's Kingdom,
And in the wealth and the glories of my Up-bringers I was delighting,
From the East, our Home, my Parents forth-sent me with journey-provision.
Indeed from the wealth of our Treasure, they bound up for me a load.
Large was it, yet was it so light that all alone I could bear it.

Gold from the Land of Beth-Ellaya, silver from Gazak the Great,
Chalcedonies of India, iris-hued [Opals?] from Kãshan.
They girt me with Adamant [also] that hath power to cut even iron.
My Glorious Robe they took off me which in their love they had wrought me,
And my Purple Mantle [also] which was woven to match with my stature.

And with me They [then] made a compact; in my heart wrote it, not to forget it:
"If thou goest down into Egypt, and thence thou bring'st the one Pearl—
"[The Pearl] that lies in the Sea, hard by the loud-breathing Serpent—
"[Then] shalt Thou put on thy Robe and thy Mantle that goeth upon it,
"And with thy Brother, Our Second, shalt thou be Heir in our Kingdom."

I left the East and went down with two Couriers [with me];
For the way was hard and dangerous, for I was young to tread it.
I traversed the borders of Maishãn, the mart of the Eastern merchants,
And I reached the Land of Babel, and entered the walls of Sarbãg.
Down further I went into Egypt; and from me parted my escorts.

Straightway I went to the Serpent; near to his lodging I settled,
To take away my Pearl while he should sleep and should slumber.
Lone was I there, yea, all lonely; to my fellow-lodgers a stranger.
However I saw there a noble, from out of the Dawn-land my kinsman,
a young man fair and well favoured, Son of Grandees; he came and he joined me.

I made him my chosen companion, a comrade, for sharing my wares with.
He warned me against the Egyptians, 'gainst mixing with the unclean ones.
For I had clothed me as they were, that they might not guess I had come
From afar to take off the Pearl, and so rouse the Serpent against me....

All this that now was befalling, My Parents perceived and were anxious.
It was then proclaimed in our Kingdom, that all should speed to our Gate—
Kings and Chieftains of Parthia, and of the East all the Princes.
And this is the counsel they came to: I should not be left down in Egypt.
And for me they wrote out a Letter; and to it each Noble his Name set:

"From Us—King of Kings, thy Father, and thy Mother, Queen of the Dawn-land,
"And from Our Second, thy Brother—to thee, Son, down in Egypt, Our Greeting!
"Up an arise from thy sleep, give ear to the words of Our Letter!
"Remember that thou art a King's son; see whom thou hast served in thy slavedom.
Bethink thyself of the Pearl for which thou didst journey to Egypt. . . .

On fabric of silk, in letter of red [?], with shining appearance before me [?],
Encouraging me with its guidance, with its love it was drawing me onward.
I went forth; through Sarbăg I passed; I left Băbel-land on my left hand;
And I reached unto Maishăn the Great, The meeting-place of the merchants,
That lieth hard by the Sea-shore. . . .

The Glorious Robe all-bespangled with sparkling splendour of colours:
With Gold and also with Beryls, Chalcedonies, iris-hued [Opals?],
With Sards of varying colours. to match its grandeur [?], moreover, it had been completed:
With adamantine jewels all of its seams were off-fastened.
[Moreover] the King of Kings' Image was depicted entirely all o'er it;
And as with Sapphires above was it wrought in a motley of colour.

I saw that moreover all o'er it the motions of Gnosis abounding;
I saw it further was making ready as though for to speak.
I heard the sound of its Music which it whispered as it descended [?]:
"Behold him the active in deeds! For whom I was reared with my Father;
"I too have felt in myself how that with his works waxed my stature." . . .

I clothed me therewith, and ascended to the Gate of Greeting and Homage.
I bowed my head and did homage to the Glory of Him who had sent it,
Whose commands I [now] had accomplished, and who had, too, done what He'd promised.
[And there] at the Gate of His House—sons I mingled myself with His Princes;
For He had received me with gladness, and I was with Him in His Kingdom;

To whom the whole of His Servants with sweet-sounding voices sing praises. . . .
He had promised that with him to the Court of the King of Kings I should speed,
And taking with me my Pearl should with him be seen by our King.
The Hymn of Judas Thomas the Apostle, which he spake in prison, is ended.[155]

THE KHOSROW KINGS
CONTINUITY AS REINVENTION

HISTORY

While direct sources about the Sasanian Persian dynasty (224–642) are quite scarce,[1] there are contemporary accounts (although subsequent to the dynasty's fall) from outside Iran. Paradoxically, the greatest stores of information on the Sasanians come from Persia's fiercest enemies: first the Romans, then the Byzantines, through the work of authors who are not always impartial. Historians from the Islamic era have left extremely important but not always illuminating testimony. Finally, Armenian, Syrian, Georgian, and Coptic sources must be approached with caution, for they too display intolerance toward the Persians because of religious differences.[2]

Many ancient authors claimed that the first Sasanian emperor (or *shahanshah*), Ardashīr I (r. 224–241), was motivated by a desire to restore Achaemenid power, but such claims are based on conjecture derived from anti-Persian propaganda set in motion by the Romans (and perhaps the Parthians), and they are not supported by incontrovertible historiographic data.[3] It seems clear that the Sasanians harbored memories of the Macedonian invasion, judging from the negative aura attributed to the figure of Alexander in Zoroastrian literature produced during this period,[4] and consequently they must have been aware of the fracture that ensued in Persia, following the era of Hellenistic domination. Moreover, these stories emerged not only from Fārs, but also from the region of Persepolis, where ancient vestiges of Persian glory were there for all to see.

Beyond hypothetical aspirations, the Sasanians never succeeded in extending their hegemony beyond Mesopotamia and the Caucasus, which would have expanded the territory of the ancient Achaemenid kingdom, except for a brief period during the attempted invasion of the Byzantine Empire by Khosrow Parviz (r. 590–628) in the early eighth century. Nonetheless, the Sasanian domain always included a much vaster territory than present-day Iran. Its western foothills included part of present-day Iraq (where the capital, Seleucia-Ctesiphon, was located) and the coastal areas of today's Arab states that border the Persian Gulf, as far as Oman, Azerbaijan, Armenia, and Georgia. The Caucasus regions, sought after by both the Romans and the Sasanians, were a constant source of conflict between the two powers, and these lands were often divided up in ways that were favorable to one antagonist or the other. To the east the Sasanians managed to maintain almost constant control over some portions of present-day southern Turkmenistan (Irkania and Margiana) and western Afghanistan (Bactria-Tokharistan), and even extended their reach, perhaps nominally more than effectively, to part of present-day Uzbekistan (northern Bactria-Tokharistan) and Pakistan (Gandhara, Sindi). It does not appear that Transoxiana (the lands beyond the Oxus, including Chorasmia, Sogdiana, and Fergana) was ever really occupied by the Sasanians, although Shāpūr I (r. 241–272), in a celebrated inscription, noted it among the regions under his rule.[5] The Sasanians were able to maintain a firm hold on their vast empire (or *Eranshahr*) through the powerful Persian army, which had proved its exceptional talents, defeating, in a brief span of time on various fronts, the Parthians, the Romans, and the Kushans. In any case, in these regions outside Persia proper, artistic production, both religious and laic, reveals a common Iranian matrix, a direct emanation from and irrefutable index of the splendor and prestige of the Ctesiphon court. The Sasanians exercised direct control over the production of luxury articles (particularly metalwork and textiles, which were the items most in demand abroad). Telltale indications of Iranian culture, along with large numbers of coins, make up a significant portion of the archaeological finds in regions quite distant from the cradle of Sasanian civilization, such as Egypt, Russia, and Yemen, and can even be found in China, Korea, and Japan. However, in many cases, these articles can be ascribed not to Persia, but rather to central Asia (Sogdiana and Bactria-Tokharistan primarily), although they are characterized by elements that unquestionably derive from Sasanian art. Their attribution to central Asia can be verified as a result of recent studies and excavations, which have increased our knowledge about many of the regions in the former Soviet Union. Archaeological investigations of pre-Islamic Persia came to a halt in the 1970s, and almost all subsequent (and at times exceptional) finds that can be dated to the Sasanians are the result of chance discoveries.

With the defeat of the last Parthian sovereign, Artabanus V, in 224, Ardashīr I was assured control over the Iranian plateau (plate 53). According to recent studies, in 232–33 he had already invaded Bactria,[6] where he created a buffer state, putting a collateral branch of the imperial family in direct Sasanian control, from about 232–33 to 350.[7] Almost immediately there was conflict with Rome,[8] but the subjugation of Hatra and the eastern coastal band of the Arabian Peninsula was completed around 240, when his son and successor, Shāpūr I, was co-regent.[9]

The period of Shāpūr's rule was also marked by constant warfare with Rome over the control of Syria, Mesopotamia, and the Caucasus regions. But the principal event of his reign was the ministry of Mani (c. 217–275) and the consequent birth of a new faith that took its name, Manicheism, from him.[10] This religious philosophy, initially favored by Shāpūr, spread rapidly beyond the Sasanian realm, even after the martyrdom of its prophet, which occurred during the reign of Bahrām I (273–276). Brought to eastern Asia through the activities of Sogdian missionaries and merchants (but perhaps also nobles),[11] Manicheism even became the state religion of the Uighur Turks (744–840), in present-day Mongolia.[12] Mani's death is attributed to the Mazdean clergy's lack of tolerance for the principal religions practiced in Persia at that time. In particular, under Bahrām II (276–293), the high priest (*mobadan mobad*) Kerdir carried out a series of persecutions against the Manicheans, Jews, Christians, Mandeans, Buddhists, and Hindus, and even several heterodox sects that had arisen within Mazdeism itself.[13]

There is still heated debate regarding whether the Sasanians had what we think of as a state religion. The term Mazdeism is used to designate the religion practiced in Persia during the

53. Relief depicting the victory of Ardashīr I over Artabanus V, Firozabad, third century AD

Sasanian era, and with all likelihood it found favor at the imperial court, at least until the death of Kerdir.[14] As the name itself implies, Mazdeism centered around the figure of the god Ahura Mazda (and in this sense is a more correct term than "Zoroastrianism"), to the detriment of other deities such as Mithra and Anahita. The fact remains that the Iranian pantheon continued to be held in high regard, even by the sovereigns (for example, Narseh, r. 293–302, considered himself to have been invested with authority by Anahita), and Sasanian art also has left obvious traces of worship tied to theoretically secondary deities.[15]

With the ascent to power of Shāpūr II (r. 309–379), fate smiled on the Persians in their rivalry with Rome, but along the eastern frontier, new threats were taking shape. Recent studies of this period have shown that Shāpūr II also assumed control over the southern territories of the Kushan king,[16] although after an interval characterized by the advance of the enigmatic Chionites, he was forced to deal with the invasion of Bactria-Tokharistan by the Kidarites.[17] Thanks to reports by Ammianus Marcellinus, who wrote in Latin but came from Antioch, we know that the Chionites followed their king, Grumbates, and allied themselves with their former Sasanian enemies in the siege (forcing the surrender) of the Roman city of Amida (now Diyarbakir, Turkey) in 360. It is not clear if the Chionites' presence was due to their forced subjugation by the Sasanian army, or if it was a tactical maneuver devised by Shāpūr II.[18] The Kidarites replaced the Chionites, but they in turn were ousted in Bactria by the powerful (and "Iranianized") Ephtalites, beginning in 456. After being restrained by Bahrām V Gor (r. 421–439)—famous, at least in legend and folklore, not only for his skills as a warrior, but also for his hunting exploits—the Ephtalites, as early as 442, began to present a serious threat to Yazdegerd II (r. 439–457) and his successors, until just after the mid-sixth century.[19] In 384 the threat

54. Combat of Hormizd II (302-309), Naqsh-i Rustam, fourth century AD

presented by the turbulent nomadic populations of central Asia had convinced Theodosius I (379–395) to grant regular payments to the Sasanians for control over the mountain passes used by the barbarians for their incursions into both Persian and Roman territories.[20]

Hormizd III (r. 457–459), son of Yazdegerd II, had to cede the throne to his younger brother, Firūz I (r. 459–484), who was backed by the Ephtalites. Relations between Firūz and the Ephtalites, however, soon deteriorated, and during the war that ensued, the Sasanian emperor himself was taken prisoner. The Ephtalites requested a heavy tribute in silver for the emperor's release, and the son of Firūz, Kavadh, was held hostage at the Ephtalite court. Despite these extremely harsh conditions, Firūz once again declared war on the Ephtalites and died in battle. Through shrewd maneuvering on the part of the Ephtalite monarch (probably Akhshunvar, mentioned in Arabic sources),[21] after a brief interregnum by Balash (r. 484–488), Kavadh I (r. 488–497) ascended the throne of Persia. He enjoyed excellent relations with the Ephtalites, having married one of their princesses, and he lived among them for some time during his captivity. Forced into exile by a revolt led by Mazdak, Kavadh once again resorted to Ephtalite support, and he not only recaptured the throne (definitively thwarting rebellions between 528 and 529), but also, with his central Asian allies, lashed out against Byzantium, which at that point paid tribute to Persia, as Rome had done before, at the time of Theodosius.[22] At the height of their power the Ephtalites controlled an enormous territory that stretched from Persia to the Tarim Basin (present-day western China), passing though northwestern India (Gandhara and Kashmir), and they could count on the enormous riches extorted from the Sasanians or accumulated with the help of Sogdian trade routes to the east, which they oversaw.[23]

This interference into the internal affairs of Persia and Sasanian allegiance to the Ephtalites changed completely with the ascent to the throne of Khosrow Anūshīrvan I (r. 531–579), who

55. Equestrian battle scenes, Naqsh-i Rustam

ushered in the golden era of Sasanian rule and became the greatest antagonist of the Byzantine emperor Justinian (r. 527–565). Through a series of political-administrative and military reforms, the first Khosrow king managed to lay the foundation for a cohesive state, further reinforced by incursions into Byzantine territory and by the enormous payments extracted from Justinian. In the meantime Justinian was engaged in taking back the Mediterranean basin from barbarian Europe and was thus eager to end hostilities with the Persians, even in less than honorable fashion.

In 552 a new power, the Turks, appeared on the central Asian stage, once again disrupting the fragile balance of the region. They eliminated the Ephtalites's major eastern allies and thus made the former vulnerable to attack.[24] Quickly taking advantage of the situation, Khosrow forged an alliance with the newcomers, and around 560 the Ephtalite kingdom was completely destroyed and divided up between the two victors. The Persians took Bactria-Tokharistan, with part of the Indian territories, and the Turks took Transoxiana and the eastern domains.[25] Probably because of problems connected to the free movement of Sogdian merchants—now Turkish subjects—within Sasanian territory, the two former allies clashed, and the lands once assigned to the Persians passed to the Turks.[26] Nonetheless, Khosrow managed to maintain firm control over the Sasanian segment of the caravan route, commonly known as the Silk Route, and he established supremacy over trade in the Indian Ocean. This was part of a much larger plan to prevent the Byzantines from acquiring sumptuary products originating in India and China from Turkish-Sogdian merchants.[27] However, the merchants managed in part to get around this obstacle, opening up new trade routes.[28] The Byzantines, forced to pay exorbitant prices for exotic goods, thanks to tolls levied by the Persians, attracted many of the Turkish-Sogdian missions, which reached Constantinople through the Caucasus mountain passes. Moreover,

56. ABOVE, LEFT. The equestrian statue of the large grotto at Taq-i Bustan

they attempted to boycott the sea routes monopolized by Khosrow, pushing the Christian Aksumites (the Abyssinians) to conquer Yemen, an obligatory transit point for traffic moving toward Byzantine Egypt. The reaction was swift, and around 570 a Sasanian expedition—probably naval—seized Yemen from the Aksumites, transforming it into a new province.[29] Sasanian power was at its height, but its territorial expansion continued with the annexations carried out by Khosrow's successors. Toward the end of his reign, Hormizd IV (r. 579–590) succeeded in defeating the Turks in central Asia, with the help of his brilliant general, Bahrām Chūbīn. But a disagreement between the two men led to a military rebellion, followed by a palace revolt, and Bahrām assumed power as Bahrām VI (r. 590–591), forcing the legitimate sovereign, Khosrow Parviz, into exile. The second Khosrow sought refuge from the Byzantine emperor Maurice (582–602), who benevolently agreed, despite the wars that had been conducted against the Sasanians at the time of Hormizd IV. Maurice granted Khosrow Parviz an army, made up in part of Persian prisoners who were pardoned in order to overthrow the usurper, and also (according to an unlikely tradition) gave him one of his daughters as a wife. Having defeated Bahrām (who, however, was portrayed in complimentary fashion in a "novel" with somewhat questionable pedigree, popular in the period spanning the Sasanian and Islamic eras), Khosrow Parviz inaugurated a brief era of exceptionally good relationships with Byzantium,[30] traces of which can also be seen in the artwork produced under the two ancient adversaries.

Subsequent political disturbances—which altered this peaceful state of affairs between the two powers, as well as the entire organization of the Near East in late antiquity—arose within the Byzantine Empire when the rebel general, Phocas (r. 602–610), seized the throne, mas-

57. ABOVE. The bridge of Shahristan at Esfahān, with a Sasanian foundation

sacring Maurice and his family. Khosrow II, perhaps truly indignant about the dreadful end of his benefactor and "adoptive father," intervened to support the Byzantines, who opposed Phocas. However, once the usurper was eliminated, Khosrow refused to recognize Heraclius (r. 610–641) as the legitimate Byzantine emperor, and a vast invasion of the Byzantine Empire ensued. Within a few years the Persian advance led to Khosrow's conquest of Mesopotamia, Syria, Palestine, Egypt, and part of Anatolia, culminating in the siege of Constantinople while working with the Avars and the Slavs.[31] For his part, Heraclius, supported by the Khazars, attacked the Sasanian Empire from the Caucasus front, pillaging and destroying almost as far as the gates of Ctesiphon. Wishing to regain the privileges that their emperor had revoked and backed by generals whose armies were depleted and cowed by Byzantine successes, the Persian nobility supported the removal and assassination of Khosrow II by his son and successor, Kavadh II Shiroe (628). From this point on, the Sasanian Empire entered an extremely confused period, during which a series of rulers (sometimes women) followed one after another within the span of a few years until the Islamic invasion.

There were various reasons for the fall of the Sasanians to Arab forces (including perhaps religious causes, namely the Sasanian relationship to Christianity), but certainly the prolonged and drawn-out war against Byzantium must have been a drain on their resources and those of all of Persia. Moreover, Khosrow II's ill-considered annexation in 602 of the vassal state of Lakhmidi (in present-day southern Iraq) had deprived the Sasanians of a possible buffer zone in case of clashes with Bedouin tribes, even though early signs of this danger, apparently overlooked by Persian strategists, had been sensed when the Sasanians suffered a defeat by the

58. The lake and temple of fire at Takht-i Sulaiman, sixth century and later

Arabs. The last Sasanian emperor, Yazdegerd III (r. 632–651), futilely attempted to free his kingdom from its fate by vigorously resisting the Arab invaders. Once the Sasanian general Rustam was killed at the battle of al-Qadisiya in 636, the Arab armies spread throughout Persia, and in 642 at the battle of Nahavand they defeated Yazdegerd, forcing him to flee into the eastern regions of his territory. There, in the vicinity of Marv, he died, probably assassinated; in keeping with tradition, the Nestorian bishop officiated at his funeral.[32]

This latter, seemingly insignificant detail is in fact revealing and agrees with a series of recent studies regarding the late Sasanians' relationship to the Christians. It would appear that Khosrow II had initiated overtures toward Christianity, at least at the beginning of his reign,[33] and some of his successors openly favored the new religion.[34] Even after the fall of the Sasanian dynasty this attitude continued among its last representatives, who were exiled to the Chinese court, if we are to believe a request Firūz III (r. c. 630–678), son of Yazdegerd III, put to the Tang Emperor: permission to build a Nestorian church in Chang'an.[35]

Firūz III is not the last Sasanian descendent about whom we have information. Chinese and, in some cases, Islamic sources mention bellicose activity in Tokharistan, where losses were suffered by the Omayyad caliphate (661–750) and the descendents of Yazdegerd III received Chinese support or help from local Turkish potentates intolerant of Arab domination.[36] These attempts did not affect Umayyad power in Persia or impede the Islamization of that country, which experienced a period of renewed splendor on the Iranian plateau.

59. *Chahar taq* at Jirra (Fārs)

SASANIAN ARCHITECTURE

Artistic production from the Sasanian era by no means represents a clear break with the previous period (plate 57). As the last two decades of intense research have ascertained, certain iconographic formulas characteristic of Sasanian art, which were once considered an authentic contribution by that culture, in fact date back to older traditions, not only Mesopotamian-Achaemenid, but also Parthian-Arsacid.[37] Unexpected favor in exclusive court circles clearly came from outside elements which are theoretically irreconcilable with a dominant class that was perennially hostile to its neighbors from both west and east. Thus, at Taq-i Bustan there are classicizing mosaics in the palace of Shāpūr I, or figures arranged like sacred images, more in keeping with the apse decoration typical of a Christian church, of people dressed in caftans in central Asian style, again at Taq-i Bustan. Scholars have opposing opinions regarding the appearance of new tendencies in Sasanian decorative metalwork, beginning in the sixth century, which could be attributed to influences from outside Persia.[38] In all these cases, however, the work has an indisputable Iranian character, which is also true of works that are considered the result of the handiwork of prisoners of war from the Roman Empire.

The subject matter of Sasanian art most often comes from the secular sphere, although it deals almost exclusively with themes meant to celebrate the infallibility of the *shahanshah* and the sovereignty granted to the emperor by a god or—less frequently—a goddess (plate 73). Triumphal monuments are well known (particularly carved stone sculpture, although an exquisitely crafted cameo also stands out), depicting Sasanian victories over Iran's enemies (plates 54–56), almost always personified in the figure of a Roman emperor humbled before the *shahanshah* or trampled by his steed.[39]

Genres normally considered "minor" to Western eyes (stucco decoration, textiles, carved gems, etc.) also deserve our attention, and most recent scholarly contributions are the result

60. Building with a quadrangular structure and dome at Kunar Siyah

of explorations in this direction. Decorative metalwork, in any case, requires a separate discussion. While many scholars have focused on themes specific to Sasanian iconography, they have neglected other discoveries (now considerable in quantity), despite their uniqueness and splendor.

It is more than credible that the work of poets and ballad singers active at court and in the service of local governors made a significant contribution to the figurative arts, which is precisely what seems to have occurred in nearby Sogdiana.[40] Scholars have agreed on Sasanian attribution for early versions of literary works in various genres, some of which were intended as pure entertainment for the upper and cultivated classes.[41] For instance, the exploits of Bahrām V Gor and the handmaiden Azada are immortalized in many works from the Islamic era but were certainly already known to the Sasanians, as attested to in metalwork and seals.[42] Unfortunately, unlike Chinese Turkistan, the climate in Persia does not favor the preservation of discoveries of organic origin, making it impossible to recover fragments of such literary works or illuminated texts, which would have been held in extremely high regard by Mani, himself a "painter."

Persian architecture represents a unique case, unlike other regions of the Near East because early explorers focused not on religious buildings, such as the so-called fire temples (plate 58),

61. External manifestation of the four corner pendentives at Degaran. Compare with the building of Kunar Siyah (OPPOSITE)

62. OVERLEAF. Qal'a-yi Dukhtar, palace of Ardashīr I at Firozabad, third century AD

but instead on royal palaces and structures designed to celebrate the ruling class. Many remains of buildings initially considered places of worship are now viewed with some caution by experts, who do not deny the possibility that these structures were destined for other uses. The definition of the fire temple derives from a now discredited romantic view of the nature of Persian religion presented in the principally Islamic sources on the Sasanian era. Unfortunately, the only religious structures analyzed using this criterion are at Turang Tepe (eighth century) and Takht-i Sulaiman (fourth–sixth century). Most of the extant buildings—above all, those of the *chahar taq* type (domed, with a square plan and arched facades on all sides, plate 59), once considered typical of the Zoroastrian "temple"—have proved to be part of much more complicated structures, no longer in existence. The most superb examples known today are undoubtedly those of Kunar Siyah (plate 60), on the ancient caravan route that descended from Firozabad to the Persian Gulf, where a series of niches crown the foundation cube upon which the dome rests: an obvious prototype for the mausoleum of Ismail at Bukhara. Thus, columns must not have been completely unknown for Mazdean religious buildings, although it is true that their presence was limited by the widespread use of the dome and barrel vault. It is clear that certain massive and impressive columns of undoubtedly local style bear proto-Islamic traces (from Damghan to Khiva to Damavand). Byzantium's influence seems to have

been decisive in this sense,[43] although some scholars point to a recently discovered and problematic inscribed capital from the era of Shāpūr I,[44] along with some later ones at Taq-i Bustan, which support a decisive influence in the opposite direction.[45] The few Christian churches known in Iran (island of Karg) and Iraq (Hira, Ctesiphon) attest to the use of columns; they appear in a more classic basilica layout, arranged in two rows that divide the building into three naves. Other discoveries will emerge only with future excavations in Iran and neighboring regions, which thus far have been too few in number. But the Georgian basilica of Bolnisi (plates 96–97) has already yielded eloquent testimony in terms of decorative elements that are structurally functional, rather than occasionally inserted, as in the later cathedral in Ateni.

With the exception of their extensive use of mortar, Sasanian architects, like their Parthian predecessors, employed unbaked brick, baked brick, and stone—all building techniques borrowed in part from the Roman world. They were also familiar with the *iwan*, with its rectangular plan and open front wall, which was also frequently used during the subsequent Islamic period. A typical element of this period was the vault resting on four corner pendentives (plate 61), forming a semiconical shape that allows a passage from a quadrangular structure to a curve, and which is also visible and palpable on the exterior. Its use, while not always present, is seen both in buildings cautiously identified as religious and those destined for secular purposes, such as the palace at Qal'a-i Dukhtar from the era of Ardashīr I (plates 62–64), or the palace at Sarvistan (fifth century). According to a widely but not universally accepted theory, the domed spaces in Christian religious buildings in Europe derive from the Armenian model, which, in turn, comes from Sasanian Persia. This can be attributed to geographic proximity and also to the fact that for long periods Armenia was contained within the Eranshahr.[46] In any case it is curious that a splendid Roman nymphaeum was long designated a "temple of Minerva Media," the Persian Minerva, or Anahita. In any case, the most perfect examples of the "squaring of the circle" in architecture, or perhaps more accurately the "circling of the square" (because it is a question of at least smoothing over the "impossible" passage from a four-directional terrestrial building to the roof that is the image of the celestial vault), are Persian. These have intermediary states of approximation between square and circumference (eight, sixteen, or thirty-two sides), which parallel ideological anxieties about giving plausible and expressible form to the Neoplatonic salvational descent and reascent between unity and multiplicity.

Well-known royal palaces include those in the Mesopotamian part of the Persian Empire, at Kish, and the celebrated Taq-i Kisra palace at Ctesiphon.[47] These are characterized by the use of baked brick and spaces that are vaulted and subdivided into several stories. Blank windows, window slits shaped like arrows, and stepped crenellation comprise some of the decorative elements frequently used in the Near and Middle East.

The Sasanian emperors established numerous cities, and they often used Roman prisoners of war specifically for the construction of public works that included bridges, roads, and canals. While this has not been extensively investigated, city plans could be rectangular (Bishapur, Ivan-i Karkhah)—a layout that was particularly popular in the Hellenistic-Roman world—or, less frequently, circular, according to a scheme employed earlier by the Parthians and later followed by the Arabs (Baghdad). The city of Ardashīr Khurra (Firozabad) represents the circular urban plan par excellence, with a series of streets radiating outward, dividing the rest of the city into twenty principal sectors around the central tower. Following a formula that was customary

63–64. ABOVE, LEFT AND RIGHT. Two images of the interior of Qal'a-i Dukhtar, the palace of Ardashīr, Firozabad, third century

65. PAGE 94, ABOVE. The investiture of Khosrow II (?) on the back of the grotto at Taq-i Bustan, seventh century AD

66–67. PAGE 94, BELOW, AND PAGE 95. One of the half-piers at the entrance to the large grotto and a detail of its decoration, Taq-i Bustan

throughout the ancient world, Sasanian cities were also divided into two parts: the administrative-palatial section and the *shahristan*, or residential portion. An impressive, fortified wall protected cities from possible enemy attacks. Architectural decorations were the same as on the facades of buildings discussed previously (small niches, arrow-shaped window slits, etc.), while long, often vaulted corridors ran inside the walls. It was not unusual for isolated fortifications to be positioned along the areas subject to invasions, and the concept of the defensive *vallum*, or palisade, was not unheard of, as seen in the wall of Darband, in the Caucasus (present-day Azerbaijan). In the late Sasanian era the territories far from the capital city of Ctesiphon had some true forts, probably meant for defensive purposes, but also for the provisioning of ships, as in the case of Ratto Kot (Pakistan). Archaeological exploration of this type of structure is only in the early stages, but it seems legitimate to hypothesize that these were fortified way stations along the coast controlled by the Persians, particularly during the rule of Khosrow I.[48]

The large arched grotto dug out of the stone at Taq-i Bustan is a unique structure in Persian art (plates 65–72). This late work, probably dated to the era of Khosrow II, brings together the characteristics of Sasanian stone sculpture and the Roman-Byzantine triumphal monument, but from a genuinely Iranian viewpoint.[49] In terms of architectural analysis, Taq-i Bustan is a typical *iwan,* embellished in the upper portion by a stepped crenellation made from square stone blocks. Roman-Byzantine influence goes back to the very concept of the triumphal monument, unusual for the Persians (who instead specialized in carved stone art), but elements that are truly imported arise principally in the sculptural decoration of the facade (the two Winged Victories), and inside the large arched grotto.

In addition to the enigma of religious buildings in pre-Islamic Iran, there are also questions regarding tombs. Mazdeism prohibited burial, cremation, or committing remains to water, preferring, instead, to leave the corpse exposed to the elements and to animals, such as dogs and birds, which would convey the spirit to the next world. Only later could the stripped bones be collected and enclosed within special receptacles known as *ostodan.* In Persia itself there were various types of ossuaries: niches carved out of stone or onto slabs of stone in the earth, structures in the form of "fire altars" or columns, and actual pits where the remains of entire cadavers have been found. The latter type of discovery has raised a series of questions, including the impossibility of establishing if the corpse was buried whole in other spacious receptacles.[50] In other areas of central Asia where Iranian culture was present (particularly Chorasmia and Sogdiana, but also in Xinjiang) variously shaped terra-cotta *ostodon* were used, discovered, for the most part, during chance excavations.[51] Roman Ghirshman has identified an unusual stone container without a cover, now in the Archaeological Museum in Tehran, as an *ostodan*; he has

attempted to detect the principal deities in the Iranian pantheon in the partially preserved relief depictions on the four sides.[52] In reality, the object remains emblematic, and this sort of identification is most likely due to the fact that at the time Ghirshman was writing many similar ossuaries, later revealed to be Sogdian in origin, were attributed to Sasanian Persia.

68. ABOVE, LEFT. Left panel of the large grotto at Taq-i Bustan, with a depiction of the royal boar hunt

In the field of funerary architecture mention should be made of the so-called "towers of silence" or *dakhma,* places where bodies were left exposed before the bones were collected in the *ostodan.* The oldest examples are all located in central Asia, specifically in Sogdiana,[53] and they look like actual towers. In Persia (and among the Parsi in India) these seem to date to the Islamic era,[54] except for one at Sar Mashhad[55] and another isolated structure in the vicinity of Bishapur. In the second case, it has been suggested that the structure is an individual tower of silence, erected specifically for a high ranking individual, perhaps a prince,[56] but all attempts at interpretation remain guesswork.

69. Right panel of the large grotto at Taq-i Bustan, with a depiction of the royal deer hunt

ARCHITECTURAL DECORATION

Many palaces from the Sasanian era have architectural decoration on both their exteriors and their interiors, made from square or rectangular tiles.[57] Given the highly perishable nature of the stucco, these tiles must have required nearly continuous restoration, and it is not unlikely that their reorganization also presented an occasion for dismantling the entire damaged decoration and replacing it.

Stuccowork discovered at Bishapur (plate 77) and Hagiabad (plate 74), both in Fārs, provide the only iconographic data related to the early Sasanian period (the third and fourth–fifth centuries AD, respectively). Most of the stucco finds date to the fifth to sixth century and come from sites in Mesopotamia (Kish, Ctesiphon) and northeastern Iran (Damghan, Bandyan). Stuccowork from Chal Tarkhan-Eshkabad (near Tehran) includes decorations that unquestionably relate back to the Sasanian tradition, but all date to the Islamic era.[58]

The stucco tiles generally contain plant (plates 66–67) and animal (plates 68–72, 75) motifs, although human busts or entire figures (plates 74, 76–78), as well as a pair of small outstretched wings accompanied by a monogram or a half-moon, are also common. The latter were popular

70. ABOVE, LEFT. Detail of a horse's saddlecloth, from the relief of Khosrow II (?) at Taq-i Bustan, decorated with *senmurv* (fantastic animal) motifs

71. ABOVE, RIGHT. Fish in a pond, detail of the royal boar hunt at Taq-i Bustan

in official Sasanian iconography and can perhaps be associated with a sovereign's royalty or glory (*khvarnah*); fluttering ribbons and a ram with a necklace are also common motifs in stuccowork,[59] as for example in a paving tile dating from the sixth century found during an undocumented excavation in Iraq.

The animals and, in at least one case, the human figures, are often contained within a circular frame made from a string of pearls with vine branches on the outside. This was a widespread decorative element throughout the ancient Iranian world, but its precise origins and meaning are not known. The only certain information we have, which comes from Sasanian era sites that have been methodically excavated, indicates that the so-called beaded medallion motif is found exclusively in the context of stucco decoration.[60]

In the early 1990s, Iranian archaeologists working at Bandyan made an exceptional and still little-known discovery:[61] a building where the interior has stucco panels created using a technique unlike the row by row arrangement of single-themed tiles. Inscriptions in Median Persian (typical of the Sasanian era) accompany various scenes. The relief panels at Bandyan that have been uncovered thus far constitute only the lower portion, but it is possible to identify the subject through a comparison with similar scenes discovered in their entirety, either at carved stone sites or in Sasanian metalwork. Various scenes delimited by plant motifs or geometric frames have been interpreted by Iranian archaeologists, according to the recognizable details, as a hunt on horseback, a battle against mounted central Asian barbarians, a reception, and various depictions of a religious nature. The horses of the hunters and warriors hurl themselves toward the target in a stylistic solution known as a "flying gallop," frequently employed by Sasanian artists but also widespread in the rest of the Iranian world and beyond; it can even be found in Korea and China, as far back as the Han era (220 BC–AD 224).[62] In the hunt scene the mount of the royal figure is recognizable by its particular harness, which includes a pom-pom shape that hangs over the horse's back, just behind the quiver. This depiction normally char-

72. The sovereign on a boat, and hunting boar detail of the left panel at Taq-i Bustan

acterized the steed of the sovereign or that of Ahura Mazda, portrayed at a larger scale than the secondary figures in the same scene.[63] In these outlying regions of the empire, artists may have broken with official iconography, perhaps to the advantage of local lords. In the battle scene another pom-pom is visible and, beneath the horses lie the bodies of horsemen who have been killed, their mouths wide open, their faces showing moustaches, sparse beards, and elongated eyes. Enemies, thrown from their horses during battle, are rendered in similar fashion in some later Sogdian paintings at Penjikent (western Tajikistan). In religious scenes the anthropomorphic depictions are both male and female, but it is impossible to establish if these are priests or priestesses, deities, or aristocrats. Some seated male figures might be identified as deities, in particular one seated on a spiral-shaped element that has been interpreted as a cushion,[64] which probably refers to the aquatic element. Seated, cross-legged figures rarely appear in Sasanian art,[65] and this is one reason that the Bandyan panels may be local, if not provincial, in production.

Stuccowork has proved fruitful for researchers looking for analogies with late antiquity and the early Middle Ages in the West.[66] Sasanian art is best known through sculpture, since there are not many monuments, and their documentation dates back many centuries. Various voyagers have described Sasanian era stone reliefs, beginning with the Venetian Barbaro, who had visited Persia in 1474.[67] Subsequently, other reliefs were discovered, bringing the total number of such finds in Persia (principally in Fārs) to thirty-eight. There is only a single example of three-dimensional sculpture, at Bishapur, and it is probably a portrait of Shāpūr I. The Sasanians certainly created three-dimensional sculpture in metal, with a preference for the reproduction of royal busts, and a detailed study of the subject is found in publications by Roman Ghirshman and, above all, by the noted Belgian archaeologist Louis Vanden Berghe and his collaborators.[68] Working within the categories proposed by these scholars, Sasanian carved-stone monuments can be catalogued according to the depicted scenes: investiture, homage paid to a sovereign by

73. Stone head of a goddess (?), from Hagiabad, fourth century AD, National Museum, Tehran

74. Stucco bust of Shāpūr II (?), from Hagiabad, fourth century AD, National Museum, Tehran

his entourage, the *shahanshah* and his retinue, triumph over enemies, equestrian combat, the horseman king, and royal hunts. As one can deduce from these categories, there are no truly religious scenes, since the sovereign always appears at the center of the composition, while deities participate as guarantors of the royal position and glory granted to the *shahanshah*.

Inscriptions (including multilingual ones) do not always clarify a monument's purpose. A celebratory function similar to that of Roman reliefs positioned in public spaces would seem refuted by the placement of many Sasanian stone sculptures in places that are practically inaccessible. However, it should be noted that some reliefs were placed next to preexisting and easily visible monuments from the Achaemenid era; more than one scholar has hypothesized that the Sasanian kings were deliberately trying to establish a connection to their illustrious predecessors in the region. At this point we will attempt to examine monumental sculpture, focusing principally on the identification of certain types of representation that characterize Sasanian art, without entering into too detailed an analysis of individual monuments.

In the early sculpted images that portray the investiture of Ardashīr I by Ahura Mazda (depicted in anthropomorphic form), one can already note a disc embellished with ribbons in the right hand of the god, offered to the *shahanshah,* who receives it with his right hand. This disc appears in many reliefs from the ancient Near East (also from the Parthian era) and it has been interpreted in various ways. The most convincing explanation seems to be that this disc image symbolizes the *khvarnah*, or glory, conferred to the *shahanshah* by Ahura Mazda, his divine representative on earth.[69] Scenes of this type, ascribable to Ardashīr's successors, appear in stone sculpture in various parts of Iran, with the figures depicted both standing and on horseback. In only one case—specifically at Taq-i Bustan—the Sasanian emperor identified as Khosrow II simultaneously receives the ribboned disc from two deities, Ahura Mazda and Anahita. All three

75. Stucco plaque with depiction of a ram, Iran (?), Musée du Louvre, Paris

figures appear frontally in a rather unnatural position, sculpted in almost three dimensions. However, Taq-i Bustan represents a case unto itself among Sasanian stone sculptures, and it must be analyzed with extreme caution before drawing any conclusions. But basing his observations on this relief, Vanden Berghe has hypothesized that the symbolism of the disc with ribbons is connected to divine glory and not to coronation, since no king can receive two crowns or two thrones at the same time.[70]

Other characteristics specific to Sasanian art can be deduced from an analysis of carved stone investiture scenes. According to a scheme well known throughout art of the Near East, the dimensions of the *shahanshah* are often (but not always) greater than those of the subordinate figures, but equal to those of the god, who significantly is always depicted without weapons.[71] Only at Taq-i Bustan is Khosrow II slightly taller than the two deities that appear at his side. In the reliefs showing the investiture of Ardashīr I and in a few other cases, the king raises his left hand and extends his index finger toward his mouth, a gesture that has been interpreted as an act of respect toward Ahura Mazda.[72] The other figures shown in this same scene raise their fingers in turn (but on their right hands), or hide their hands inside the sleeves of their garment, perhaps also a sign of respect. This gesture of the hands seems to be specific to Iranian art and is found throughout central Asia, in Gandhara and as far away as Chinese Turkistan.

The king's clothing includes a caftan cinched by a belt on his hips, a sort of sling over his chest known as an *apezac*, and various jewels and weapons.[73] He wears shoes decorated with ribbons, but it is possible that these are boots, mostly hidden beneath his trousers. The crown can be composed of various elements, including the *korymbos* (the spherical shape at the top), outstretched wings, a crescent, or an eight-pointed star (perhaps tied to the goddess Anahita?).[74] The band that runs around the crown's circumference is radial, turreted, or in the form of

76. Investiture of King Narsete by the goddess Anahita, c. AD 300, Naqsh-i Rustam

winged creatures.[75] A more in-depth discussion of the crown as a distinctive feature of each individual monarch is found in the section on coins; for the moment we shall focus on the hanging and fluttering ribbons, attached to the imperial crowns as well as to the saddlery of horses and the necks of various animals. As with many elements of Sasanian art for which there are no clear interpretations, we must await further research. The most reliable hypothesis is that the ribbons refer to *khvarnah*, the divine glory of which the sovereign is a worthy receptacle.[76] The *lemnisci* mentioned by classical authors served the same purpose, namely to confer "great worth to honorary crowns," including in Rome.[77] Some Byzantine sources also describe the emperor's horse, on certain occasions, as harnessed in the Persian manner, namely with ribbons tied to the tail and hooves.[78]

In monuments attributed to Ardashīr I, all figures are depicted in profile. In Sasanian art there is a preference for reproducing the human figure in profile or three-quarter view, with frontality reserved as the sole prerogative of the *shahanshah*, seated on the throne, generally with his hands resting on his sword hilt.[79] The aforementioned investiture scene at Taq-i Bustan, with three figures depicted frontally, is a singular case, for the moment without parallel in Sasanian art. This can be imputed to social transformations, but also, simply, to the influence of Byzantine and central Asian art.[80]

The investiture scene, supposedly of Khosrow II, is not the only relief at Taq-i Bustan (plate 65). On the back wall of the large *iwan* grotto, below this scene, is the image of a horseman with lance and shield, sheathed in armor, as is his steed. Behind the horseman's head is a halo, suggesting that this equestrian sculpture might be a depiction of the *fravashi* of the *shahanshah*, that is, his indestructible soul that existed even prior to his birth, and which is sometimes also

77. Triumph of Shāpūr I over the emperors Gordianus III, Phillip the Arab, and Valerianus, second half of the third century AD, Bishapur

defined as a "guardian angel."[81] To the sides of this work, divided into two registers, are two hunting scenes of boar and deer, respectively (plates 68–69). These were originally colored and were perhaps conceived in imitation of a painting or tapestry.[82] In the boar hunting scene, the larger figure, firing an arrow from a boat, is shown twice, once with and once without a halo. According to the same interpretation, in this case too, the figure with the halo is not the *shahanshah* but rather his *fravashi*. At Taq-i Bustan there are other reliefs outside the *iwan* grotto, and one in particular is important because of the unusual presence of the god Mithra, depicted in three-quarter view to the left of the emperor (in this case Shāpūr II). He holds a sacred bundle of rods (the *barsom*), has a radiating halo, and rests on a lotus flower depicted according to Indian canons.[83] In any case, Taq-i Bustan is an "atypical" high point in Sasanian art, and it still puzzles scholars. In the late 1970s Japanese researchers clarified some of its lesser-known aspects, and they uncovered and photographed some apparently minor details.[84] The identification of the sovereign portrayed inside the *iwan* grotto, however, is still the subject of lively debate.[85] A later date has been suggested, in part because of the presence of a necklace with three pendants, unknown in coins prior to 628, worn by the two winged figures positioned on the facade of the *iwan* and the *shahanshah*.[86] The monument is also significant for the study of pre-Islamic Persian textiles since the garments worn by all the figures have rich decoration that is only associated with the late Sasanian period. At Taq-i Bustan (plates 79–81) there are also some capitals transported from other excavations, decorated with reliefs of frontally portrayed human figures with halos.[87] Various interpretations have been put forth for the identification of the figures on the capitals, and they clearly relate to celestial beings or deified kings seen in earlier works. There is also another capital from Shiraz, inscribed with effigies of Shāpūr I, his father Ardashīr, and

78. Triumph of Shāpūr I over the Romans, Phillip the Arab, and Valerianus, second half of the third century AD, Naqsh-i Rustam

two secondary figures, perhaps ministers.[88] None of these figures have halos, and it has been suggested that the depictions might portray people living at the time the works were created, thus dating the capital to the third century.

Sasanian art frequently features a double depiction of prey shown simultaneously struck by the *shahanshah* and already dead at his feet.[89] In carved stone sculptures this scene appears only once, in a relief at Sar Mashad attributed to the era of Bahrām II,[90] where the sovereign appears standing, positioned between a threatening lion—shown twice, once being killed and then collapsed at the sovereign's feet—and some members of his family.

An iconographic detail worth mentioning is the putto figure wearing a diadem with ribbons, seen in two carved stone reliefs at Bishapur, which depict the scene of Shāpūr I's triumph over Gordianus III (r. 238–244), Phillip the Arab (r. 244–249), and Valerianus (r. 252–268). The placement of winged creatures in front of a figure does not occur often in Sasanian art compared, for example, to Sogdian painting.[91] Their function is to provide supernatural protection for the figure they stand in front of—a clear reference both to the concept of *khvarnah* and to the winged disc containing a human figure, a motif already widely disseminated during the Achaemenid period.[92] At least two carved stone reliefs (significantly datable to the third century, that is, to the early period of the Sasanian dynasty) depict a winged being, demonstrating that certain concepts thought to be characteristic of Iranian art in general were also well known to the Sasanians. In this specific case (but also at Taq-i Bustan), however, a purely Iranian concept is accompanied by an iconographic device specific to Greco-Roman art, such as the Cupid or the Winged Victory,[93] which would support theses maintaining that foreign elements were present from the beginnings of Sasanian art.

79–81. ABOVE AND BELOW. Two reliefs and an image carved on Sasanian capitals, transported (?) to Taq-i Bustan

PAINTING AND MOSAIC

Sasanian painting is the least known form of pre-Islamic Persian art.[94] Once again, we need to look to classical and Islamic sources to find evidence of the existence of monumental painting in the Sasanian era. These works include scenes of battles, hunts, and the triumph of the *shahanshah* over the enemies of Iran.[95] Painting probably occupied a position of some importance, equal to that of carved stone sculpture, but the works that have survived are too few and too fragmentary to allow the advancement of even the slightest theory in this regard.

The technique used by the Sasanians (and in Asia in general) was tempera. It was applied over a layer of plaster, employing colors principally of mineral derivation, diluted with water. There was no use of fresco. There are extremely interesting paintings from the late Parthian era at Hatra (southern Iraq), where one can identify certain characteristics that act as a prelude to truly Sasanian art.[96] The scenes, all of which relate to hunting, are divided into vertical bands delineated by geometric or plant motif frames. Horsemen racing at a full gallop hit their prey with a bow, or, in one case, with a lance. A bearded and turbaned figure, armed with a lance, lashes out against a boar, while a second animal lies in the lower portion of the composition, not because it has been killed earlier, but rather in keeping with a popular formula in Sasanian art (especially in decorative metalwork) whereby the infallibility of the hunter (almost always the *shahanshah*) is implied by the second depiction of the animal, already dead beneath the hooves of the horse.

Sasanian paintings and graffiti have been discovered at Dura-Europos in Syria,[97] but the only finds in Persia itself that are in better-than-fragmentary condition come from Susa and Hagiabad. These can all be dated to the fourth century. The only remaining wall painting at Susa can

82. Male head wearing a crown of laurel, mosaic from the palace of Bishapur, Musée du Louvre, Paris

be identified, with all likelihood, as a hunting scene in which a central figure on horseback, larger in size, appears surrounded by his subordinates and by various animals. The central figure is not recognizable, given the painting's extremely poor condition, but he wears a richly decorated garment with a diamond pattern, clearly indicating his rank. The background is entirely blue. At Hagiabad, however, the fragments recovered by Iranian archaeologists belong to different scenes, although they are scarcely recognizable, with the exception of some human busts depicted in three-quarter or frontal view, mostly reconstructed. Various identifications have been hypothesized, without any definitive resolution, due to our little knowledge of Sasanian painting and its specific characteristics.[98] Normally in Sasanian art, frontal depiction is reserved for the *shahanshah*, deities, or illustrious, mythicized predecessors. The busts in stucco identified as frontal portraits of Shāpūr II (plate 74), which have been used as the basis for dating the site of Hagiabad, and the painted bust, also depicted frontally and cautiously associated with Hormizd II Kushanshah (r. c. 302–309), probably can be linked to such earlier works. They would have been executed after the death of the subject, and it would thus seem appropriate to date them to the fourth–fifth century.[99]

As indicated above, there is some graffiti from Dura-Europos, Hatra,[100] Lakh-Mazar,[101] and especially Persepolis that can be dated to the Sasanian era. The graffiti at Persepolis, commonly dated to the third century,[102] depicts processions of bearded figures in profile, some of which

83. Harp player, mosaic from the palace of Bishapur, Musée du Louvre, Paris

are probably royal, considering attributes such as the disc with fluttering ribbons held by two of them and the usual pom-poms affixed to their horses.

The excavations at Bishapur—the city that Shāpūr I founded around 260, where it appears that he employed Roman craftsmen enslaved after the surrender of Valerianus—have revealed the unexpected as well as emblematic presence of splendid mosaics (plates 82–83).[103] What is problematic, however, is the combination of Iranian and classical elements of a Dionysian stamp,[104] which is difficult to explain since this was not a time of idyllic relations between Persia and Rome. We shall see (particularly in regard to decorative metalwork) that themes popular in Hellenistic-Roman Dionysian iconography met with some success at the court of Ctesiphon, after some adjustments to make them appealing to a Persian audience. This should not be completely surprising. Indeed, Julian the Apostate was not only a follower of Mithra, but also may have been open to other forms of religiosity of an Iranian type.[105]

The most interesting subjects include the heads of various figures, which have been interpreted as having Dionysian origins, and the figure of a harpist. Here, Sasanian qualities are undoubtedly recognizable in the preference for the representation of faces in three-quarter view or profile and the fluttering ribbons tied to the hair of the musician.[106]

Unfortunately, the near total abandonment of archaeological sites from the pre-Islamic

era precludes adding much else to our store of knowledge. There has been news of discoveries of fragmentary traces of mosaics at Susa (with a Greek inscription)[107] and at Ctesiphon,[108] but there is a shortage of literature on these mosaics.

84–87. Iranian decorative metalwork

84. ABOVE, LEFT. Achaemenid plate, Riza-i Abbasi Museum, Tehran

85–86. ABOVE, RIGHT AND OPPOSITE, LEFT. Two post-Sasanian plates from eastern Iran (Marv?), Hermitage Museum, St. Petersburg

87. OPPOSITE, RIGHT. Sasanian plate discovered in the Ural region, not far from Perm' (Russia), Hermitage Museum, St. Petersburg

DECORATIVE METALWORK

While the best-known areas of Sasanian art are carved stone sculpture and architecture, in the last thirty years scholarship has focused on decorative metalwork, admired even by the notoriously particular Cesare Brandi. Thanks above all to research carried out by Russian and American specialists, we now have a more or less methodological system for establishing the authenticity of objects and their attribution to Persia itself rather than to neighboring regions.[109] Other publications have appeared, more modestly, as catalogues of collections that are less well known but extremely significant.[110] On the occasion of an important exhibition,[111] P. O. Harper wrote an introduction to the various collections in museums throughout the world. This American scholar also has proposed a dating system and a detailed categorization of the forms of Sasanian metalwork, in many cases based on models of eastern-Roman derivation. The use of metal articles also coincided with certain Roman and Byzantine examples produced expressly for the exchange of gifts (in a diplomatic context, perhaps), or for propaganda. Sumptuary items, specifically including textiles and metals of an Iranian stamp (in this case from Sogdiana), were probably even commissioned by Chinese emperors exclusively for diplomatic exchanges.[112]

Just as with other luxury genres, such as silk textiles, the production of finely worked precious metals was controlled by the court. Clearly there were peripheral areas of production that ignored "metropolitan" canons regarding the shape and weight of objects, the purity of the

metal, and the iconography. These differences can help in assigning attributions or determining the most likely region of production, at the capital or in other centers.[113] Modern forgeries present a very serious problem for the study of decorative metalwork. Practically all the known metal articles, from both private and public collections, are the result of excavations that were illegal or carried out without following scientific criteria. Many of the finds, including true treasures, have been discovered by chance, outside Persia itself, sometimes in extremely distant regions such as the Urals or China.

Some of the early subjects of Sasanian metalwork are human busts (plate 88), both male and female, generally resting on a vine stock and inscribed within a medallion, sometimes shaped like outstretched wings. Other popular themes, particularly among the lesser nobility, include scenes of hunting (plates 86–87), dancing, music, royal banquets, depictions of the *shahanshah* enthroned (plate 85), and various depictions of animals (plate 84).

Hunting scenes focus around the figure of the emperor, either engaged in shooting an arrow at his prey as he sits upon his steed, traveling at full gallop, or, less frequently, on foot. The hunted animal is generally shown twice: in flight in front of the horse and dead, in a lower portion, according to an iconography mentioned earlier. The halo that in some places appears behind the head of the hunter probably alludes to the Zoroastrian paradise, where the souls of deceased kings reside, and thus does not refer to a figure contemporary with the creation of the work.[114] It has been suggested that the hunt, so often depicted in Sasanian metalwork, is a reference to an esoteric type of Mithraism,[115] and this hypothesis should not be dismissed. Some of the characteristics of Sasanian metalwork include circular elements positioned in correspondence to the joints of both the royal horse and the prey. In one unique instance, the hide of the deer pierced by the lance of the haloed *shahanshah* is rendered through the repetition of polylobate geometric figures scattered over the entire body.

Animals portrayed in Sasanian metalwork often have attributes that make them particularly suitable for the hypostasis of a deity or an abstract concept such as royalty or *khvarnah*.[116] Flying creatures were popular, sometimes depicted with ribbons tied to their necks or a necklace, and they are even endowed with halos. The ram with fluttering ribbons tied to its neck and curved, diverging horns is universally interpreted as an image of *khvarnah*. Other recurring animals are deer, felines such as tigers and lions (plate 89), and boars' heads. One plate has an image of a horse harnessed from head to foot, probably connected to a particular ritual, perhaps involving the immolation of the animal.[117] In many of these cases, however, Sasanian attribution is subject to debate, and it is not unusual for works to be attributed to the Islamic era. The same observation can be made for works decorated with figures of fantastic beings, including Pegasus, griffins, and monstrous composite creatures endowed with wings, horns, and even plant elements that emerge from their bodies.

Two very similar plates, now in the United States and Russia, respectively, have themes that scholars have defined as "Dionysian."[118] There is a procession of mythical figures where the central figure, larger in scale, is normally identified as Dionysus in Hellenistic-Roman contexts, but assumes female connotations in Persia, supporting the possibility that it represents Anahita. Plates decorated with this type of iconography are related to other Sasanian works such as the mosaics at Bishapur, where the composition combines purely Iranian elements and other elements that arrived in Persia by way of Rome and Byzantium. It is interesting that these are pagan and not Christian subjects, as one might expect, considering the dating of the two plates to the fourth–fifth century.

One unique example is a monster with a dog's head, feline paws, wings, and a plumed or reptilian tail commonly defined as a *senmurv*, a mythical creature, part mammal and part bird, associated in Islamic-era Persian literature with other fantastic animals, including the phoenix.[119] This figure seems to make a late appearance in Sasanian art and in only one case (with the exception of the reliefs at Taq-i Bustan) do scholars all agree in an attribution to Sasanian Persia. The object in question is a gilded silver carafe dated to the fifth–sixth century. Most works decorated with *senmurv* (see the image from Ateni, plate 95), particularly those in metal and cloth, seem to be from the Islamic era or from outside Iran. Some experts have hypothesized that the identification is not correct and that this composite creature should be associated once again with a manifestation of *khvarnah*.[120]

Sasanian decorative metalwork was widely disseminated in antiquity, and many Iranian themes were introduced to and accepted by other cultures, which is precisely what happened with other, easily transported articles. In fact, although textiles, metal plates, and pitchers were among the most common funerary objects in tombs in central Asia, Tibet, and China, many silver and gilded silver objects discovered in China proper can definitely be considered Sasanian or Kushan-Sasanian. Articles in precious metals from Persia or neighboring regions where Sasanian metalwork was clearly known (Sogdiana, Bactria-Tokharistan, and Chorasmia) were unearthed during excavations in China,[121] and many of these are now in Japan, in the imperial storehouse at Shoso-in, in Nara.[122] Some hypogeum tombs from the Tang period (618–907), associated with members of the imperial family, have wall paintings depicting women and servants holding vases, carafes, and trays that are typical of the Iranian world.[123] Iranian ornamental motifs would similarly have been widely disseminated in central Asia and the Far East, where they probably would have been highly prized.

88. Bronze bust of Sasanian king, from Lajvard, sixth–seventh century, Musée du Louvre, Paris

TEXTILES

Like painting, Sasanian textile art must have been held in very high regard in the ancient world, judging from descriptions in Latin, Greek, Islamic, and even Chinese sources. Most studies related to Sasanian weaving are based on an analysis of these sources and on the sole carved stone relief at Taq-i Bustan, where textile decorations appear.[124] In reality there is little that can be said in this regard. The only textile finds that can be attributed to a Sasanian site that was excavated in scientific fashion, Shahr-i Qumis,[125] have no particular decorations, and there is no indisputable data about production within Persia.

The commonly held view is that typically Sasanian iconography included figures of animals (isolated and in procession), continuous diamond motifs (Hellenistic in derivation),[126] and the beaded medallion (a circular frame with rows of small white discs along the edge and with various types of subjects on the inside).[127] A comparison with other art forms makes it possible to give Sasanian attribution to the diamond motif, the beaded medallion shown in isolation with a rosette at the center, and the motif of three aligned circlets, which recur above all in the reproduction of royal vestments in metalwork and in the paintings at Hagiabad.

There are no textiles finds that can be attributed unquestionably to Sasanian Persia; studies in this regard have been limited to establishing links with what might have been the iconography of Sasanian textiles, through comparative analyses of fabric fragments found at various sites distributed over a vast area (Europe, Egypt, central Asia, and the Far East). This is clearly the only approach possible, given the near total absence of incontrovertible data, but the vulnerability of this method is apparent in the wake of more recent, illuminating archaeological discoveries and consequent contributions to art history. As a result, most of the textiles that were previously recognized as products of pre-Islamic Persia can, in fact, be associated with Byzantine, Coptic, or Sogdian production, which was influenced by Sasanian art in general.

The only textile that can be attributed with any certainty to Sasanian production is a fragment in linen and wool, at the Benaki Museum in Athens,[128] and that came from an antiquarian market. It depicts a figure on horseback, larger than the other figures, which appear to be servants. The main figure has a quiver at his side and wears a short cloak and a caftan. The garment is decorated along the lower hem, at the wrists, at the waist, and on the chest, with a row of pearls, doubled in two bands on the left shoulder. A series of drop elements appears on the entire remaining portion of the garment. These may depict precious gems, which would have been sewn to the garment. Similar decorations recur on the robe of the *shahanshah*, in the upper portion of the relief at the back of the large arched grotto at Taq-i Bustan, and, in conjunction with the diamond pattern decoration in a silk fragment of uncertain provenance, attributed to Sasanian Persia.[129] Behind this main figure, one of three subordinate figures (all in profile, bearded, with eyes wide open) is depicted in the act of lifting a staff with a rosette with sixteen petals contained in a sort of wheel at its tip. Its base, embellished with two outstretched wings, rests on the rump of the horse. The tips of every ray of the rosette seem to be implanted in a series of discs arranged around the circumference of the wheel. Perhaps this depicts a system that was actually used to support the rosette. This element has been interpreted as an insignia of rank;[130] in fact, in the Sasanian era, the rosette or the eight-pointed star (or multiples of eight) was probably connected to the idea of royalty.[131] The same servant wears a ribbon knotted behind his head and a caftan with heart-shaped motifs, seen earlier on the garments of

89. Lion slaughtering a deer, Sasanian or post-Sasanian silver dish with gilded ground, Hermitage Museum, St. Petersburg

central Asian figures (for example at Gulbayn, Afghanistan, fourth–fifth century),[132] and in a silk fragment discovered in central Asia, now at the Louvre.[133] In the upper portion, two rows of pearls form a frame for the composition, following a formula seen earlier at Hagiabad.[134] In essence, the figure in this textile is markedly Iranian in character, and all the details point to a Sasanian precedent, although its discovery has not been documented. The depicted scene and the technique of execution seem more appropriate for a tapestry than for a fabric used for clothing. Narrative scenes with unquestionably Persian subjects, however, do appear in a silk fragment used as part of a pair of trousers, discovered at Antinoe (Egypt), which can be dated to the sixth century and attributed to Coptic production. The scene seems to be an episode in the war against the Abyssinians (indeed, African warriors are portrayed), in which the *shahanshah* (Khosrow I?) is depicted frontally, enthroned.[135]

The Sasanians' greatest contribution to textile art was the beaded medallion, although, as previously noted, the motif recurs in pre-Islamic Persia principally in architectural decoration in stucco,[136] while its reworking, appreciated in both the west and the east, seems to have been a Sogdian contribution. The beaded medallion motif was used over an extremely vast area, at least until the eleventh century. It is seen nearly everywhere, particularly in early medieval painting in Europe, where it appears on the garments of emperors, bishops, and popes, but also on the clothing of saints, and in some unusual wood crucifixions of the Catalan school, where Christ appears wearing a long tunic decorated in this manner. Entire walls of Christian churches or Buddhist grottos in central Asia reproduce the motif in paint, which was much less costly than the use of so-called *velaria*, actual fabrics, generally ornamented, which were hung on the walls of a religious building or on sacred furnishings.

CERAMICS

The lack of archaeological activity in Iran has resulted in an enormous void in terms of ceramics from pre-Islamic Persia. Nearly all the information in this field comes from chance or undocumented discoveries, and only minimally from excavations carried out in Iran and Iraq, particularly during the 1930s.[137] The few sites where interesting ceramic objects have been discovered include Dailaman (in the region of Mazendaran)[138] and Susa (in southwestern Iran).[139] Some progress has been made, thanks to Italian archaeological expeditions, at the ancient capital, Seleucia-Ctesiphon,[140] and other sites in Iran proper (plates 90–91).[141]

As frequently confirmed in other artistic genres, with ceramics there was continuity rather than a break between the Parthian and Sasanian periods.[142] The type of glazed ceramic that is characteristic of the Sasanian era can easily be distinguished from work from the Islamic era and was disseminated almost exclusively in the Mesopotamian region under Persian control. In any case, in Mesopotamia itself and in other areas of the *Eranshahr*, the prevailing taste was for unglazed ceramic, sometimes decorated through the use of dyes.[143] This technique seems to have been specific to northern Mesopotamia, the site of a ceramic fragment and an entire vase. The two objects were decorated with deer depicted both in isolation, inside a beaded medallion with fluttering ribbons at their necks, and in procession, inside horizontal frames. These animals, endowed with branched horns, appear frequently in Sasanian art, particularly in metalwork. The influence of metalwork seems notably strong in two pitchers with handles from the late Sasanian era, now respectively in Switzerland and Israel.[144] We do not know where they were produced, although we can approximate their location of origin as northern Iran. In both cases the decoration consists of circular frames containing individual goats and deer, motifs that also recur in precious metal vases, objects that were out of reach for the lower social classes who had to settle for imitations in less-expensive materials.

Other ceramic objects are rare; a circular terra-cotta tile depicting tightrope walkers juggling is an example.[145] The tile, which came from an antiquarian market, seems unique to its genre, and it is not improbable that it was made during the Islamic era, considering the decoration on the clothing of the figure to the right, which has never been encountered in earlier art.

90. Amphora in green-glazed ceramic, unknown provenance, fifth–sixth century AD, National Museum, Tehran

GLASS AND JEWELRY

Sasanian society greatly enjoyed luxury and thus could not ignore the use of glass objects.[146] For various reasons there are few finds that can be attributed with certainty to Sasanian Persia. First of all, there is no clear distinction between Persian and Roman glass, resulting in great indecision regarding attributions to one culture or the other.[147] Furthermore, for this art form, too, there have been few discoveries from scientifically conducted archaeological excavations, and these are concentrated principally in Mesopotamia.[148]

In Persia there was generally a preference for transparent glass, blown and then decorated with engraving or with applications and color while the glass mixture was still hot. The most common articles were bowls (plate 92) and containers for liquids, such as carafes, embellished with decorations (often geometric) on both body and handle (plate 93). There are at least two glass fragments from undocumented excavations, and these are decorated, respectively, with gold foil and a relief figure (plate 94). In both cases a *senmurv* is depicted, but it is not possible to establish whether these works can be ascribed to the Islamic era.

Persian glass was probably in great demand abroad. The tomb of a Japanese emperor from the fifth century has yielded a bowl, probably Sasanian in origin, and the Shoso-in treasure also includes some Persian-style glass objects, which may, however, be dated to a later era.[149] Glass pitchers have also been discovered in Korea; their forms immediately bring to mind metal articles, but it is difficult to date them.[150] Some pitchers decorated with circular applications containing a flying creature and executed in a style similar to that of some Sasanian seals can be attributed to the Islamic period.[151] Animals are shown individually, turned to the right or the left, with tails made of long, separated feathers.

Sasanian art abounds with references to precious ornaments worn by kings and queens. Judging from carved stone sculpture and metalwork, the preferred jewelry included necklaces, bracelets, and earrings, worn by both men and women. Other typical objects of ornamentation from this period were rings for holding together part of the beard and finger caps used by archers, all in precious metals. Weapons and harnesses for horses could also be embellished with precious gems and metals.[152] Some Byzantine and Arab sources describe the clothing of the *shahanshah* as being studded with precious gems, and it seems that in earlier eras there was a thin plate of precious metal, pierced with holes, meant to be applied or sewn to the garments of those who could allow themselves such splendor. The Museo d'Arte Orientale in Rome has a silver plaque consisting of a beaded medallion containing a boar's head. It is not clear if this was a decoration for a garment or a harness.[153]

We know of at least three gold medallions, now in a private American collection. They must have originally been applied to a necklace or bracelet. The motifs on these objects are similar to those in other Sasanian art genres: the bust of a king, a ram with fluttering ribbons that rests on a pedestal shaped like outstretched wings, and a wading bird, all in profile view.

The collection at the Bibliothèque Nationale de France includes a cameo that is unique in its genre (plate 94) and is not normally included by scholars in the group of seals. With its engraving, however, it might well be considered a type of jewelry to be worn, after suitable modifications and mounting. This ogival-shaped cameo most likely depicts the victory of Shāpūr I over the Emperor Valerianus, although the plausible date seems to be later.[154]

91. Green-glazed ceramic vase, from Khuzistan, third–fifth century AD, National Museum, Tehran

SEALS AND COINS

The study of small artifacts in the form of semi-precious gems decorated with figures (seals), and impressions made by them on shapeless masses of clay is fundamental for our knowledge of both iconography and inscriptions in the language that was used during the Sasanian era (Median-Iranian or Pahlavi). Given their nature, seals must have been used at all levels of ancient Persian society, perhaps as amulets,[155] but inscribed seals were used above all by the upper and cultivated classes, such as governors, members of the clergy, and aristocrats in general. But their study is also extremely important for understanding the territorial division of the *Eranshahr*, since the provincial authorities in the various provinces had to seal every official document with their personal emblem.[156] The iconography is very rich, given the personal use

to which such objects were put, and this enabled the owner to adopt whatever motif he chose, including those that were neither conceived for nor accepted in works of an official nature.[157] Thus there were animals such as the scorpion (officially held in contempt by the Mazdean religion), or fantastic composite beings (the famous "medieval fancies," also widely disseminated in Romanesque and Gothic art in the West)[158] including sirens and harpies,[159] or deities depicted according to an iconography that was unknown in other artistic genres in Sasanian Persia. These images include, for example, Mithra in a chariot or being born from a stone, themes more consonant with Indian or Hellenistic taste and somewhat frequently encountered in central Asia and even among ancient Tibetans (in certain textiles that may have arrived by way of Sogdiana).[160] The motif of two twins nursed by a she-wolf certainly originated in the Greco-Roman West; this theme was much appreciated among Iranian populations in Persia and also in central Asia, as attested to by Sogdian paintings at Qal'a-i Qahqaha (not far from present-day Khogiand), dating to the fourth century.[161] The cross, another theme widely used for seals, indicates probable Christian patronage; but altars and fire altars also appear.[162]

Seals often feature fantastic animals or beings (Pegasus, first and foremost) depicted according to an extremely ancient iconography that was not often used by Sasanian artists, whose roots probably lay in Mesopotamian art.[163] The most significant group of animals—especially birds, felines, and goats—are portrayed individually. The human figure also occupies a place of prominence, represented in the form of busts, both male and female, and in rare cases understood to be the portrait of the seal's owner.[164] As a rule, only deities and heroes are depicted frontally on seals.[165]

92. OPPOSITE, ABOVE. Bowl "of Khosrow I," solid gold frame, glass paste inlays and a central engraving in rock crystal, sixth century AD, Bibliothèque Nationale, Cabinet des Medailles, Paris

93. OPPOSITE, RIGHT. Glass goblet, provenance unknown, third–fourth century AD, National Museum, Tehran

94. ABOVE. Victory of Shāpūr I over the Roman Emperor Valerianus, third–fourth century AD, Bibliothèque Nationale, Cabinet des Medailles, Paris

The study of engraved gems is perhaps the most recent area of research in Sasanian art. It is hoped that this too will contribute to expanding our knowledge in the field of pre-Islamic Persian iconography.

Numismatics has provided much of the chronology related to the succession to the Persian throne. Sasanian coins could be in various metals, but the use of silver was particularly widespread; gold coins were rare.[166] Coins feature the bust of a sovereign, in some cases accompanied by his consort and heir. Generally the bust of the king appears on one side, in profile view, or, less frequently, frontally with an inscription in Pahlavi.[167] We know of only five sovereigns who are depicted frontally, usually on gold coins; these were distributed throughout the entire duration of the Sasanian dynasty.[168] At the time of Khosrow II, instead, it seems that there was a predilection for the frontal representation of the king on every type of coin. This tendency has been attributed to the influence of Byzantine customs.[169] Various subjects could be depicted on the back, although the most common symbol was certainly the fire altar, sometimes flanked by two armed figures.

It was long believed that each individual *shahanshah* could be identified by his crown, which was different for every monarch. This is true in part, but scholars need to exercise extreme caution, since a single sovereign could wear more than one type of crown.[170] If a king lost his throne but subsequently reconquered it, it is probable that his crown would change, depending on the period of rule to which it referred. This was because it was believed that once a king was dethroned, he lost the glory (or *khvarnah*) granted him by Ahura Bazda, symbolized by the crown. If he returned to lead the *Eranshahr*, he was assigned another crown, evidence of renewed divine acceptance.[171] Another hypothesis regarding the Sasanian crowns principally concerns their reproduction in sculpture. In some cases it is likely that distinctions were based on colors, as certain written sources would seem to attest.[172] Finally, the repetition of crowns could be due to the desire of certain *shahanshah* to be depicted with the specific attributes of kings and heroes from the past. In this way, the *khvarnah* would no longer relate to each individual monarch, but rather to the entire dynasty.[173]

Beginning in the fifth century, silver Sasanian coins were widely circulated, above all in central Asia and China, and their continual use has been confirmed by stratigraphic dating. An explanation for this seems to lie in Sogdiana, where beginning precisely in the fifth century coinage was based on the model of the drachma of Bahrām V Gor. Huge quantities of Sasanian drachmas paid by Firūz to the Ephtalites poured into central Asia, apparently reaching as far as China, by way of Sogdiana.[174] In similar fashion, coins issued by the Persian mint helped not only to furnish a stable model for basing the value of international exchanges, but also to spread the iconography contained on the coins, particularly in central Asia and among the Arabs.

THE FATE OF SASANIAN ART

As readers undoubtedly will have noted, each section of this survey concludes with a discussion of the art form's fate and dissemination in antiquity. In many cases the role played by the Sogdians in this process needs to be specified, since Sogdian art itself is greatly indebted to the Sasanians.[175] At this point it is perhaps best to stress Iranian features in general, both among so-called barbarian peoples and among the most advanced civilizations, such as the Byzantine and the Chinese.

In the past authors such as Roman Ghirshman and André Grabar focused on the dissemination of Sasanian art, primarily looking at the Byzantium and the Western world,[176] but without overlooking Coptic art.[177] Byzantium, in fact, shared an enormous eastern frontier with Persia, and it is obvious that there were artistic exchanges, despite the nearly perennial conflict between the two realms. Syrian Antioch (now southeastern Turkey), often besieged and conquered by the Sasanian kings, is a case in point. The city is the site of some of the most beautiful mosaics of the fifth–sixth century, produced in countries that border the Mediterranean.[178] Iranian elements in the Antioch mosaics were first noted in the 1930s. These are birds with ribbons at their necks, rams' heads on a pedestal shaped like outstretched wings, lions with ribbons at their necks, and plant motifs.[179] True hunting scenes in these mosaics immediately drew the attention of scholars because of similarities between the abduction of a small tiger by a Roman horseman and the exploits of Bahrām V Gor, celebrated in the literature of the Islamic era and illustrated on some silver Sasanian plates. Probably, as Prudence Harper has noted, this is not a scene borrowed from the literary tradition, but rather a general hunting episode, faithfully reproduced in various materials in both Persia and Byzantium.[180] However, it should be noted that very close literary parallels exist between the figure of Bahrām V and the much older Roman figure of Domitian.[181] Also at Antioch, one of the mosaics of the great hunting scene known as the "Megalopsychia" shows a standing figure piercing a leopard with his lance, while

95. *Senmurv*, relief on a fragment reused in the wall of the Georgian church in Ateni, seventh century

a second, identical animal already lies on the ground, perhaps in keeping with a well-known scheme that alluded to the infallibility of the Sasanian hunter.

The *senmurv*, or rather the fantastic animal normally identified as such,[182] is a motif that clearly entered the Christian-Byzantine repertoire through Sasanian channels and was subsequently widely disseminated in Islamic art (plate 95). The *senmurv* was also popular in Byzantine art,[183] in sculpture, painting, and textiles, and in the art of Armenia[184] and Georgia,[185] perhaps because Christians recognized the biblical Leviathan in this figure.[186] Depictions of *senmurv* soon spread throughout barbarian Europe and into the Italian territories that were more or less directly under Byzantine control. One exceptional example appears in the painted decoration that imitates curtains (*velaria*) in the apse of the Basilica of Santa Maria Assunta in Summaga, outside Venice (second half of the thirteenth century).[187]

Recently Boris Marshak has observed that some of the typical solutions seen in Sasanian carved stone sculpture were known to Sogdian painters of the eighth century.[188] It is interesting to note that the Sasanian monuments in question are the third-century reliefs at Firozabad, attributed to the period of Ardashīr I. In fact, the horse on the left of the Sogdian painting recalls the felled steed of the Arsacid sovereign, unseated by the lance of Ardashīr. Excavations of Sogdian sites, now spanning both Uzbekistan and Tajikistan, have yielded other paintings rich in decorative themes of Sasanian origin. At Afrasyab, in pre-Islamic Samarkand, there is a Sasanian-style *senmurv* on the garments of a figure portrayed during the celebration of a ritual that is not clearly identified;[189] some gilded silver plates, also Sogdian, depict the same subject.

In this case, a (late) Sasanian provenance is certain, since a *senmurv* typology that might be considered genuinely Sogdian appears in a painting cycle from the eighth century, discovered at Penjikent (western Tajikistan). These works contain the first depiction of the exploits of the

hero Rustam, who the Persian poet Firdusi described, in the Islamic era, as being protected by the mythical creature called a *senmurv,* which healed his battle wounds; in this instance the creature resembles a winged lion.

96–97. ABOVE AND OPPOSITE. Two details of capitals from the basilica in Bolnisi, Georgia, showing a Sasanian influence

The Sogdians themselves maintained diplomatic-commercial relations with the Byzantines, concerning themselves above all with trade in silk and luxury articles. Specific elements of Sogdian textile art, initially borrowed from the Sasanians but reworked in completely original fashion, appear in the decoration of some of the most ancient silks attributed to Byzantium.[190] The Sogdians' intense mercantile activity acted as an ideal means of dissemination of Sasanian iconography. Moreover, the audience for such sumptuary articles was of a social class that was in a position to support works of certain significance. Items of Iranian derivation made their way to northwestern India, specifically Kashmir, where beaded medallions appear in the decoration of Hindu temples and bronze Buddhist statuettes dating back to the eighth century. During this period the Sasanians no longer existed, and it seems absurd to attribute such elements directly to the Persians when it is universally accepted that the Sogdians were very active along this stretch of the Silk Route.[191]

The last Sasanians had relations with the kingdom of Aksum (present-day Eritrea and Ethiopia), and they occupied Yemen after removing it from the domain of that African entity. There was no direct Persian influence on Aksumite art until after the fall of the Sasanians, which came about through Byzantine or Arab-Islamic channels.[192] In the Arabian Peninsula, instead, recent discoveries attest to a Sasanian presence: a seal depicting a lion, decorative stucco fragments with figures of animals and plants,[193] and especially a sculpted capital and architrave from Yemen, perhaps ascribable to the period of Persian domination.[194] The sculpted decorations

depict hunting scenes, and one in particular shows a lion standing on his hind legs, struck simultaneously by a horseman and a standing lancer. In a scheme that recalls that of other royal hunt scenes, a second lion, already dead, lies beneath the figure of the lancer. However, in the case of the carved Yemenite capital the artist does not seem to have completely understood a concept specific to Sasanian art, lending support to the hypothesis that the two friezes were examples of local production. In terms of architectural decoration, the stepped crenellation that is so widespread in art of the ancient Near East could have been imported into the Arabian Peninsula through Sasanian Yemen. Some of the first examples of the use of this motif in pre-Islamic architecture appear at the temple of Amrit in Yemen.[195]

We have noted how the image of the mythical *senmurv* also appears in Islamic art. In fact, throughout the art of Islam there are elements borrowed from the Sasanians (and others), beginning with the Umayyad era (650–751).[196] With the coming of the Abbasids (751–1258) there was a process of even more intense Iranization of Islamic art, which was felt earlier on a political level with the decision to establish the new capital, Baghdad, in Mesopotamia, not far from the old centers of Sasanian power. In the ninth century the other capital, Samarra, which was later abandoned, had pictorial decorations that directly related to central Asian Iranian art.[197] Such work was enormously popular, at least until the twelfth century, even beyond the Islamic realm, which is particularly apparent in the paintings in the Palatine chapel in Palermo and in the duomo at Cefalù.[198] Animals or fantastic beings connected in some way with the Mazdean religion gradually were abandoned in the Islamic era, while others, such as the boar, were never accepted because of specific Islamic dietary proscriptions.

From an early date, goods from Persia and central Asia were highly valued by the ruling classes in China, Korea, and Japan.[199] Subsequently, elements of Iranian iconography appeared in Chinese art, especially following the introduction of Buddhism. The arrival of Firūz III, son of the last *Shahanshah*, Yazdegerd III, in Chang'an, the capital city, undoubtedly influenced Tang culture. Firūz was accompanied in exile by other Sasanian dignitaries and aristocrats, and many Persians, including Firūz himself, served in the army or at the Chinese court, where they were accorded treatment befitting their social status in their own country.[200] The opening up of Tang China to every type of exoticism had already encouraged numerous Iranian (especially Sogdian) merchants to settle within its borders. Religions such as Mazdeism, Manicheism, and Christianity were widespread in China, although not to the degree of Buddhism. Manicheism in particular was a means for the dissemination of a painting style closely linked to Sasanian Persia, as seen in the discoveries in Xinjiang.[201]

At this point it is legitimate to wonder why Sasanian art was so successful, even outside the boundaries of the Iranian world, and why it was so persistent—a bit like the "Moorish" Mudéjar art, which also prevailed within a "new" religious context—that its influence was still evident centuries after the extinction of the Sasanian dynasty by the Arabs (plates 98–100). Probably the medieval world was able to recycle the celebrative themes in Sasanian art, despite the fact that these could be interpreted—at least initially—in a Christian key in the West and in an Islamic key in the East. In fact, while conditions clearly existed for foreigners to observe the monumental works directly throughout the *Eranshahr*, such travelers were almost exclusively members of the diplomatic corps or occasional groups of viewers who normally would have found it impossible to penetrate an enemy country. As a result, the appreciation of the highest level of refinement achieved by works of Sasanian art and the assimilation of these forms outside Persia occurred above all through the spread of sumptuary objects such as silk, glass, jewelry, and metalwork—articles that would have had an impact on the dominant classes who wished to distinguish themselves from the common people through their access to luxury and their search for the most exotic (and costly) beauty available. As for the exportation of technical developments (for example the architectural vault), this was almost certainly a slower process, though facilitated by geographic proximity.

In any case it is appropriate to mention the development in Persian circles of a late antique sensibility (independent from incessant, particularly Hellenistic, contributions of techniques and iconography from the outside). This is an art that was never conceived as a mimesis of nature, but rather as its "soul," its "angel," or perhaps its psychic reflection. Plotinus understood this, although not necessarily consciously, as a *tertium* produced by an encounter between the intelligible and the perceivable, best expressed by the words of the Islamic Persian poet, Bidel: "the contagion of the imagination into the idea of the cosmos."

And so between the Sasanians and Islam there was no rupture; even the flight into India of the purest of the Zoroastrians is a myth that has been overblown and misdated. Aesthetic language remains the "subtle" dimension of the concrete world, best expressed in the so-called *Ode to the Soul* by Avicenna, a Muslim, but also a native of Chorasmia, an important and archetypal Iranian city.

Avicenna's poem is also a hymn to the pearl, but one that is pared down and shorn of folkloric elements, pointing instead to the purest form of monotheism, or as Bausani has

98. Building with a square plan and pendentives for accommodating the dome, at Fahraj, earliest Islamic period, see also plates 60 and 61

99. A pendentive with *muqarnas* decoration, Esfahān

frequently stated, to that "absolute theism" that clearly borders on, if not atheism, at least a subtle view of religiosity and human experience.

> From the highest of places the glorious Dove, inaccessible saint, has descended upon you.
> Concealed from every eye of Wisdom, yet it reveals itself uncovered, like a young girl unveiled.
> Unwillingly, it reaches you, but defiantly would leave you again, tormented by sorrows.
> It took refuge, disquieted at first, seized by shameful horror at the contact, but now joined with you, it has adapted slowly to the plains of this desolate desert.
> Ah, surely I think it has forgotten the times when it fluttered in celestial gardens, and the sweet dwellings that, earlier, it was not resigned to leave.
> Until, now joined with the D of its fatal Descent, separated from the C of its Center in the supreme lands,
> It hangs on itself its heavy W of Weight, and here it is now amid deserted traces and ruins.
> It weeps at the memory of cool dwellings in the sky, with eyes that know no limits to their tears.
> And, like a cloud, bedewed with tears, traces of ancient dwellings, erased by the four-fold constant breath of the winds

Which entrap it in the densest of snares, and a cage keeps it from the boundless springtime peaks of the sky.
Until, when the day of journey toward its felicitous meadows draws near, and the time of departure for the broad plains approaches,
And it prepares to leave every vestige of the world, and its Earthly Companion, now rejected and deserted,
Dozes off slightly, and the veil is torn away, and reveals even that which sleeping eyes never perceive.
And then it chirps the sweetest songs on the highest branch (which Knowledge purifies and raises up all who are below).
But why did it descend from celestial heights into this profound abyss at the foot of the mountain?
If it were God who wanted to send it down below, with wisdom that the most assiduous and keenest of minds are impotent to ponder,

100. Base of the minaret of a mosque built at Paykand, near Bukhara, Uzbekistan, eighth century (?)

Clearly its descent was a harsh and binding law, *whereby it could listen to what it had never heard before,*
And it returned Home, knowing every secret hidden in the Cosmos, without rending its purest garments.
It is he for whom Time carved a path, until it faded into death, never again to rise to the world.
And it was like a lamp, which shines above the green meadow for an instant, then disperses, *and it is as if nothing had shone.*

101. Overall view of the citadel at Bam, dominated by the fortress, photographed before the citadel and most of the old quarter of Bam was flattened by a severe earthquake in 2003.

ISLAMIC PERSIA

SEVENTH–NINETEENTH CENTURY

Giovanni Curatola

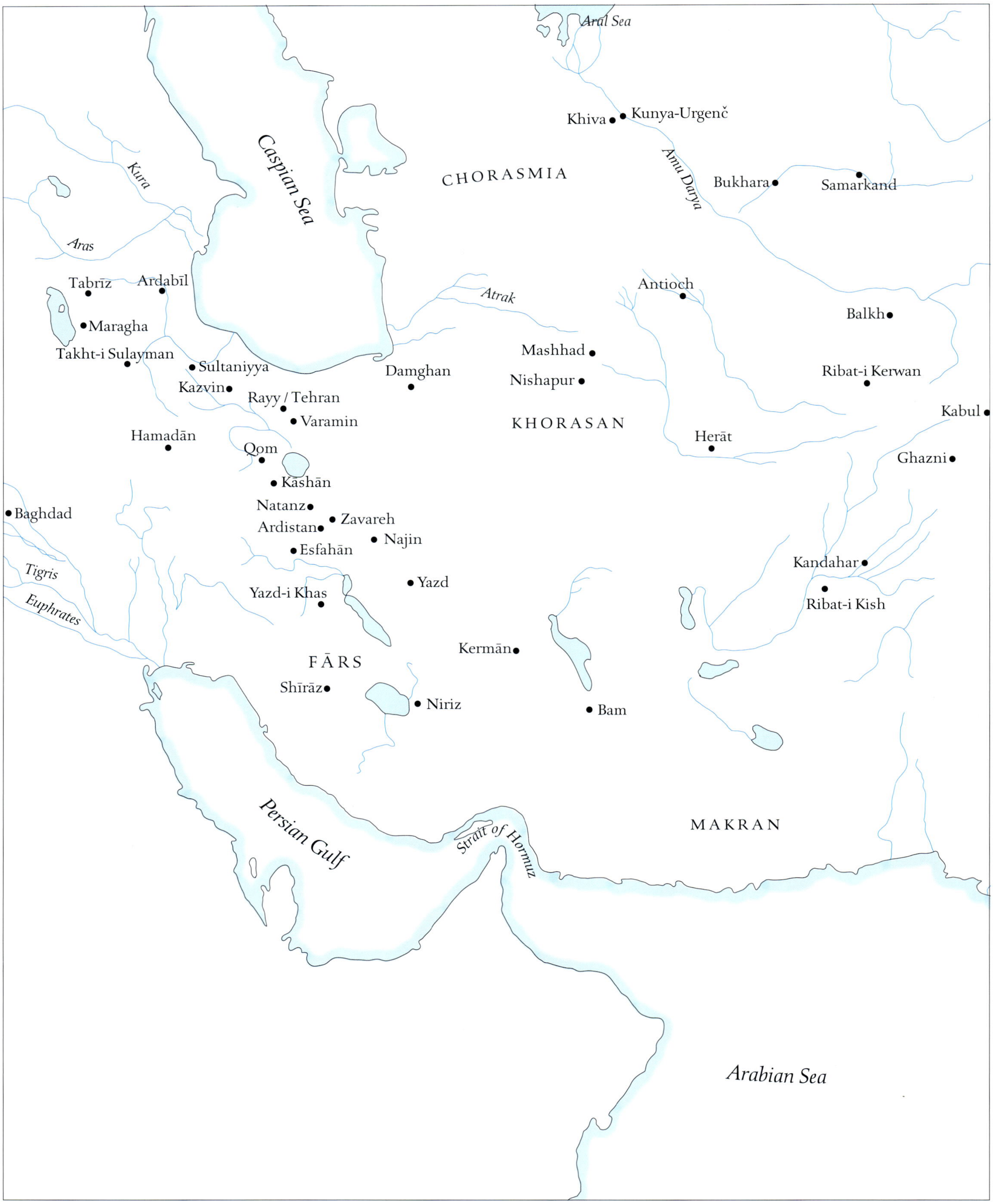
Aral Sea
Khiva
Kunya-Urgenč
Caspian Sea
Kura
CHORASMIA
Amu Darya
Bukhara
Samarkand
Aras
Tabrīz
Ardabīl
Maragha
Takht-i Sulayman
Atrak
Antioch
Balkh
Mashhad
Sultaniyya
Kazvin
Damghan
Nishapur
Ribat-i Kerwan
Rayy / Tehran
Varamin
KHORASAN
Kabul
Hamadān
Qom
Herāt
Ghazni
Kashān
Natanz
Baghdad
Zavareh
Ardistan
Najin
Esfahān
Tigris
Euphrates
Yazd
Kandahar
Yazd-i Khas
Ribat-i Kish
Kermān
FĀRS
Shīrāz
Niriz
Bam
Persian Gulf
Strait of Hormuz
MAKRAN
Arabian Sea

INTRODUCTION

Within the multiform, complex, and variegated universe of Islamic art, contributions from Iran have played a continuous and crucial role—a situation that is so unquestionable and obvious that scholars have often turned their attention elsewhere.[1] At this point even experts feel a certain embarrassment speaking about Islamic art, as they do about Islam in general. While a few generalizations can be made where shared values override historical or minor differences, the West clearly has a blind spot about this culture, which is in fact multifaceted, with important and subtle variations.[2] In other words, Islam must be described in the plural, not the singular. Despite offshoots, there are cultural macro-regions of Islam: Spain and Morocco (with which Sicily should be grouped), Egypt and Syria, the Turkish world (another interesting terrain of syncretic experiences), Iran and central Asia (the latter still relatively unknown, and by no means simply an appendix to Persia), and India, with all its variations. Differences and similarities are anchored in a tenacious substratum over which the unifying mantle of Islam extends, symbolized by its most vital and dynamic precept: the pilgrimage to Mecca, an extraordinary occasion for exchange and a vehicle for acculturation, along with the continuous movement and overflow of energy, goods, and ideas.

Within this theater, Iran—in both the narrow sense of the Iranian nation and in the broader sense of the Iranian world as highlighted in the introduction to this book by Gianroberto Scarcia—holds a position of double centrality: geographic and cultural. And we need to remember that with its immense plateau with deserts, vast plains, and mountains—some of the highest in the world—Iran, even taken in the narrow sense, contains utterly different climates and regions. The Caspian zone, for example, is characterized in some places by intense rainfall. The Steppes and other regions, where cultural "pockets" formed, produced notable works as exemplified by the figurative art pottery created in Nishapur,[3] an ancient and rather important urban settlement in Khorāsān. At the other end of Iran is Fārs, the region from which the traditional name for the entire land of the Persians is derived. This is a rich territory, relatively close to the sea, with the Strait of Hormuz and nearby small islands that point in one direction toward the Arabian Peninsula and in the other toward the Indian subcontinent. Recent archaeological excavations have revealed the importance of the port city of Siraf,[4] a crucial trade center that is thought to have been responsible for the almost mythical expansion toward Africa.[5] In the

102. Islamic Persia (adapted from W. C. Bryce, *An Historical Atlas of Islam*, 1981)

same way, Nishapur became very important in the 1930s as it was one of the few places to be properly investigated. We don't know how many other such sites have yet to be documented. Geographical diversity has always yielded cultural diversity. In ancient times Iran was already a pivotal point between central Asia, India, the Far East, and the Mediterranean basin. Thus it was a place of transit par excellence, but by no means a passive observation post. Indeed, it was a focal point that drew energy from the encounters and clashes with other civilizations that exerted an influence upon it, but which it influenced in turn, in a reciprocal play of mirrors. The Biblical Magi from the East were priests,[6] or in any case representatives or spokespersons, of another religious culture, but that legend is only a parable for the migrations of the great religions from Iran to the Mediterranean, causing us to wonder: who is the final recipient of this

103. The Si-o-Se Pol, the oldest bridge in Esfahān, the foundation of which dates to the Sasanian era; it also served as an ingenious dike to control the waters of the Zayanda Rud during periods of flooding. The bridge was fully restored during subsequent eras.

wisdom? It is clear that with Islam, the spread of ideas experienced a reversal, perfectly summed up in Islamic Iran. In other words, if the great Iranian river of ideas flowed into the Mediterranean, proving Alessandro Bausani's elegant assertion that cultural history is a westward movement, like that of the sun, then this river returned, enriched, to its sources.

Then the Bedouins appeared on the scene, although the term Bedouin is used somewhat inappropriately, in the same way that "barbarian" is used to denote those who invaded Rome of an already "universal" civilization. These were Arabs from the peninsula, only recently united by a shared Muslim faith and organized militarily in a manner that overcame their instinctive tribal identities, which, however, often resurfaced with a passion. They were keenly aware of the perils of becoming bogged down in wars of plunder, and instead felt a sense of duty to firmly

104–5. Bam: the fortress, the residential neighborhoods, and, in the background, the enclosing wall, as it stood before the 2003 earthquake

dominate vast territories. Their impact was enormous. It has often been written, and it is true, that Arab expansion turned westward toward the Byzantine Empire and eastward toward the Sasanian realm more or less simultaneously, but with different outcomes. While the Byzantine Empire was defeated and scaled back, it still remained an important and influential opposing power (as an organizational model, and in part as a model for court ritual and ceremony). The Sasanian world, on the other hand, experienced near total disintegration. Although it was defeated and politically humiliated, Iran did avenge itself, slowly but inexorably, in cultural and artistic spheres. There was resistance, clearly, and there were also important migratory flows, such as that of the Zoroastrians who went to India, where they established the Parsi community (although the period when this migration happened is demythicized, to a certain extent, in an earlier chapter). But the complexity of Iranian culture—profoundly assimilated in a manner that can occur only as a result of a centuries-long process, adapting and changing as needed—powerfully reemerged, no longer *masked* by Islam, as certain nationalistic currents would maintain, but *transformed* into Islam. This shift is essentially similar to what happened, of course with different terms, in Christian Rome, and it was possible not only because the strongly rooted Iranian indigenous tradition became refined over time, but also because Islam is a complex system. Islam is malleable and, once the "modern" dogma of God's absolute uniqueness is affirmed, capable of assimilating the most disparate customs and turning them to its own use. Better put, it is able to *unify* everything. It must be stressed once again: Islam is a pluralistic phenomenon, and one striking example of this is the *Shah-nama,* or Book of Kings, written around

MUD, BRICK, AND TURQUOISE
THE ARCHITECTURE OF PERSIA

THE EARLY CENTURIES

106. OPPOSITE. Facade of the south *iwan*, flanked by two minarets, at the Congregational Mosque (Masjid-i Jum'a), Esfahān

107. BELOW. Būyid column, Congregational Mosque, Esfahān

The first major defeat of the Sasanian Empire at the hands of the invading Arab forces took place under the Sasanian King Yazdegerd III, at the battle of Al-Qadisiyya in 635, after a series of incursions using a highly successful technique typical of the "raid wars" that had taken a tremendous toll among the semi-nomadic Bedouin tribes.

The definitive conquest of Persia would come soon thereafter, in 642, with the battle of Nihawand. However, the transfer of power would be gradual and piecemeal among the various conquered regions. The chronology is significant, since the vast Persian Empire collapsed barely ten years after the death of the Prophet Muhammad. This period was too brief for the newly formed Islamic faith to have established its own unequivocal and clear artistic language, especially if we consider that the two great defeated powers (Byzantine and Sasanian) would contribute toward constructing the artistic and aesthetic foundations for Islam.[1] Thus, Persian Islam would devote its efforts, over a long period of time, to converting preexisting structures at sites that were acceptable for the new prevailing ideology, although from an architectural standpoint this could not have been particularly clear, even to the new rulers.

We know very little about the structures that were created anew, in part because those erected in the most important areas have undergone major alterations, leaving us with a false impression. In any event, we do know of fire temples that were transformed into domed halls to serve as mosques (the tenth-century Yazd-i Khast is an excellent example). We are also aware of isolated *iwans*, as at Niriz.[2] These were elements that were shared by the Sasanians and the Parthians. An *iwan* is a barrel-vaulted structure that has walls on three sides and is open on one side. In later periods, *iwan* ceilings would be highly embellished with *muqarnas*, stalactite-like structures or multiple honeycomb niches, the earliest extant example of which is the mausoleum of Arab Ata (977–78) at Tim in Transoxiana (present-day Uzbekistan). In addition to these, there were, obviously, newly constructed mosques. The custom of erecting a sanctuary or other building adapted to the observance of rituals and religious functions on the foundations of a preexisting structure was so widespread and universal that it hardly needs further mention or explanation.

We have been able to determine that by the end of the year 1000 there were no more than about thirty Islamic sites in Persia. This figure is indeed quite small when we consider that nearly three centuries had passed, and research has not revealed that there was a lull in building activity during this period. The type of mosque generally found features a main prayer hall with hypostyle ceiling, a central courtyard, and *riwaq*, or porticoes, along the other walls, with a portal situated on an axis with the *mihrab* (a rule not always followed), and a single minaret, which was either affixed to the central edifice or freestanding. The hypostyle ceilings, often composed of a series of arches supporting small cupolas, were in part adapted from Sasanian architectural practices. The Sasanians had devised this structure also for climatic reasons: the topography of Iran is characterized by a central plateau at least 3,300 feet (c. 1,000 m) high, where snowfalls can be quite abundant. The weight of the snow, unless evenly distributed, would inevitably lead to the collapse of any extended, flat-roofed structure.

THE CONGREGATIONAL MOSQUE (MASJID) OF ESFAHĀN
CULMINATION OF THE GREAT ERAS OF PERSIAN ARCHITECTURE

One of Persia's pivotal architectural monuments is the Congregational Mosque (Masjid-i Jum'a) of Esfahān (plates 109–110). This masterwork is now quite thoroughly understood, even in its more obscure phases, in large part due to systematic research undertaken by a team of Italian archaeologists.[3] Restoration work directed by Eugenio Galdieri has revealed some of the most minute details of this powerful yet highly intricate architectural complex.[4] This emblematic monument, with its various historical phases of construction, exemplifies the typological varieties found in Persian Islamic architecture, offering a paradigmatic journey through time and history (plate 108). Excavations conducted on the southern part of the mosque (in the great hall with its Seljuq vaulting, which houses the main *mihrab*, and in adjoining sections) have uncovered a massive Sasanian column with decorations in stucco, the only tangible indication of an important preexisting structure. The original building was erected in one of the villages

108. BELOW. Floor plan of the Congregational Mosque, Esfahān: various phases of construction are evident. From U. Scerrato, *Antica Persia. I tesori del Museo Nazionale di Tehran e la ricerca italiana*, 2001.

109. OPPOSITE. Seljuq quincunx, Congregational Mosque, Esfahān

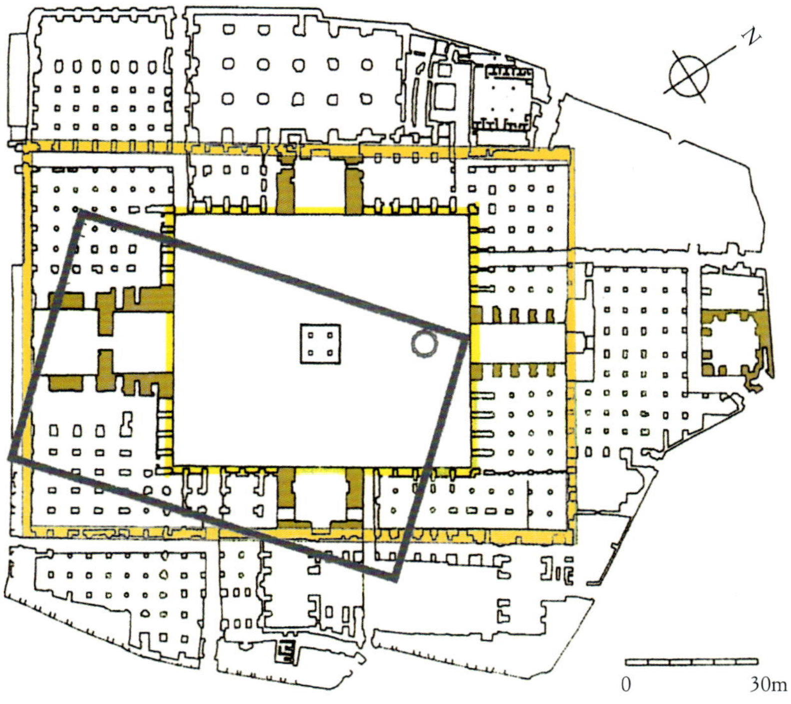

An Il-Khanid intervention is also found in the great dome of Nizam al-Mulk. Perhaps the engineering of the space was deemed risky, for the area between the central piers that support the dome has been reinforced. And the cube below, up to the dome, was covered in a white stucco wash, with noticeable morphological alterations, including at the junctures superimposed triple niches, which do not correspond to the original layout. The architect Eugenio Galdieri is largely responsible for documenting and preserving this alteration, during the works done to restore the original Seljuq floor level. Interventions occurring during the Muzaffarid dynasty (1314–1393; in Esfahān, from 1358 to 1375, under the reign of Sultan Mahmud) were both structural, with the construction of a *madrasah* on the eastern side of the mosque, and decorative,[8] with the insertion of ceramic panels in the southern *iwan*; additionally, the restoration of the *iwan* dome is attributed to Aq Qoyunlu Uzun Hasan in 1475–1476.

More limited, essentially decorative, Timurid alterations to the structure include the lavish onyx tiling which was installed in the southern *iwan* and on the dome of Nizam al-Mulk (removed during excavations and reconstruction work on the historically most recent southwestern section of the mosque), as well as exquisite corner piers, also in onyx, which were added to the courtyard. Another Timurid addition may include the *shabestan* (summer prayer hall), documented in an inscription dated 1447. This structure, located behind the western *iwan*, features superb depressed arches, which are generally attributed to the Safavid period.[9] There are numerous Safavid inscriptions in the ceramic facades of the courtyard, which bear the names of Shah Tahmasp (1531–1532) and Shah 'Abbas II (1642–1667). The two slender minarets that flank the southern dome (plate 106), positioned at the sides of the *iwan* facade, are also Safavid. Numerous changes, more spontaneous than coordinated, occurred in the nineteenth century, well before the more systematic restorations of the 1970s and 1980s.

116. Colonnades, Congregational Mosque, Khiva

FROM THE ABBASID TO THE BŪYID ERA

Having examined such a vast architectural complexity, with its range of styles, materials, and interventions, we can now proceed to a survey of the most important periods of Persian architecture. The Tarik Khana Mosque in Damghan,[10] which dates from the Abbasid period (eighth century)—probably the oldest extant Persian mosque—offers a perfect starting point (plate 117). The structure is quite simple, with its courtyard, porticoes, and three-bayed hypostyle prayer hall in front of the *mihrab* (the central nave being wider and higher than the rest of the complex). The mosque is typically "Arabic" in design, however, expressive of a language heavily infused with Sasanian components: massive piers, circular columns in stucco-faced brick, and pointed arches. All of these elements hint at an expressive continuity that deserves further investigation. As for massive columns, it is impossible to overlook the mosque of Degaran, in the village of Hazara (Transoxiana), which dates to some time around the year 1000. The earliest traditions of hypostyle architecture in central Asia (in Chorasmia, for example) are found in such important monuments as the Congregational Mosque in Khiva (tenth century, although heavily renovated in the eighteenth century), with its characteristic use of wooden colonnades (plate 116).[11] Further to the east (in Kazakhstan, for example) similar linear column arrangements can also be seen, as in the mausoleum of Arestan Bab.[12] Although dating from the thirteenth or fourteenth century, this structure has a decidedly older appearance, the result of extreme conservatism or a tendency toward conscious archaisms, a trend that intermittently occurs at sites that are both geographically and chronologically distant from each other.

117. The imposing piers in the hall of the Semnan Congregational Mosque (Masjid-i Jum'a), in Khorāsān. Recent restorations have revealed a structure quite similar to the mosque in Damghan.

Returning again to Iran, the mosque of Fahraj in the vicinity of Yazd,[13] although less monumental since it served a smaller community, also exhibits great stylistic diversity. The building, which is not as old, is based on a similar floor plan: here, a cylindrical minaret is set to one side of the courtyard arcades. Fahraj provides a rare example—like the paradigmatic mosque of Esfahān—of Islamic design imported into Persia, in this case in the construction of a completely new mosque. An analogous case is the destroyed mosque of Dezful, which was already subjected to profound modifications. It was further to the east, in such places as Khorāsān, Afghanistan, and central Asia, an area that became increasingly important, that we find structures of greater interest. The remains of the Mosque of Hagi Piyade in Balkh[14] (present-day northern Afghanistan, not far from the valleys of Amu Darya, the ancient Oxus) seem simplistic: a square structure, with three closed sides and one open side opposite to the *mihrab*, which rests upon sixteen massive round piers supporting a series of arches and domed ceilings (now absent). The massive columns again reflect a Sasanian construction; however, it is interesting that the closest architectural analogy (also closest chronologically, since the mosque in Balkh dates from the late ninth to early tenth century) should be so distant geographically: the mosque/sanctuary of Bab-i Mardom in Toledo (Iglesia de Cristo de la Luz, 1085).

The vicissitudes of history subjected Iran to a series of invasions from the east. The Būyid dynasty was extremely important in Iran, since it is the first occurrence that a local potentate emerged within a territory otherwise entirely dominated by Arab rule, thus representing something of a national interlude prior to the arrival of the Turkish Seljuqs from central Asia. The Būyids controlled the country from 932 to 1055; however, their influence varied from one region to another, without any overall unifying scheme (Esfahān, for example, was only under Būyid rule from 932 to 1028). There were various rival powers, such as the Sāmānids in Khorāsān

118–119. ABOVE.
The Isma'il Mausoleum in Bukhara, with details of the front facade (OPPOSITE)

and Transoxiana (819–1005), and the Turkish Ghaznavids (977–1186)[15] in Khorāsān, Afghanistan, and India, as well as the Ghūrids (northwestern Afghanistan, 1000–1214). This rather fluid situation was marked by one clear and incontrovertible truth: the importance of the eastern territories within the caliphate.

Among the most celebrated monuments of central Asia, also Iranian in influence, is the mausoleum of the Sāmānid Isma'il in Bukhara (plates 118–119, c. 943, according to a stone engraving mentioning As-Said Nasr II [r. 914–43]),[16] built entirely of fired brick. The structure merits further description, since it is the most renowned mausoleum after the Qubbat As-Sulaibiya in Samarra,[17] the first building known to have been constructed for such a purpose in Islam. The prophet Muhammad condemned sepulchral display (following suggested provisions for his funerary arrangements), although he never issued any specific prohibitions. The Bukhara mausoleum follows a square floor plan, featuring four doors at the center of each of its sides (according to tradition, this was to ensure that the tomb would not be situated in an "open" space) and also a dome. The exterior corners are embellished with engaged columns inserted beneath four small recessed domes; a series of windows runs along the four sides opening onto an interior gallery. The severity of this massive cubic structure is offset by the corner columns and the small windows, and, most strikingly, by the brilliant use of decorative brickwork on the facade, framed by a pierced circle motif, similar to the beaded patterns of Sasanian stuccowork and textiles, but on a much larger scale. The overall visual effect echoes the texture of woven fabric or perhaps the plaiting of wicker or straw. The same repertoire of decorative brickwork is used in the interior, and the corner solution of the passage from the cubic floor plan to the dome is supplied by an elegant tripartite arch. As succinctly described by Robert Hillenbrand, the structure is a "fire temple in Islamic dress;"[18] comparisons to Kunar Siyah immediately come

to mind. The mausoleum is interestingly devoid of stucco, which here would seem superfluous amid the brilliant brickwork.

The Congregational Mosque of Nayin (plate 120),[19] in central Iran, also dates from the Būyid period (tenth century), and those stylistic features are still quite visible in its plan, despite subsequent alterations. The structure of the central courtyard, which includes a stairway leading to the *qanat*[20] (a subterranean channel supplying mountain water through the use of a powerful hydraulic engineering system), indicates that the building underwent expansions along the sides, while still conserving the original "Arabic" floor design. A subsequently modified minaret is perhaps the oldest such structure in Iran. Reinforcement work on the building has "freed up" a series of rounded engaged columns on the courtyard facade, which are embellished with interwoven brickwork, a hallmark of Būyid architecture also found on the Masjid-i Jum'a in Esfahān. But the most striking feature of this mosque is the decorative stucco relief work employed in the *mihrab*, and on the supporting columns (plate 121) and arches of the prayer hall. The motifs are taken from a repertoire of religious inscriptions (in the *mihrab*) and floral elements. Minutely detailed vine leaves grace the lunette above the *qibla* niche. The motifs on the imposing columns, which also feature stylized vine leaves and grapes, as well as bands with geometric patterns and bead motifs reminiscent of woven textiles, form a stylistic link with the persistent Sasanian tradition, even if the Abbasid contributions seem evident, as is clear in a comparison of these styles with the stuccowork at Samarra.[21] The vestiges of the Jurjir Mosque in Esfahān,[22] mainly the entrance, are Būyid in dating (c. 985) and decorative style. The use of dazzling interlaced brickwork serves as a prelude and indispensable introduction to the masterful works of the Seljuqs.

Eastern Persia, in the city now known as Gonbad-e Qabus, contains one of the most extraordinary and idiosyncratic monuments of medieval Islam,[23] the mausoleum of the Ziyarid Sultan Qabus ibn Wushmagir ibn Ziyar (plate 123). The sultan was evidently a man of notori-

120. ABOVE. The tenth-century Congregational Mosque (Masjid-i Jum'a), Nayin

121. OPPOSITE. Detail of decorative stuccowork on a column, demonstrating Sasanian influence, Congegational Mosque, Nayin

ous cruelty, although he was also a poet, calligrapher, and astronomer, and his court served as a refuge for Avicenna and al-Bīrūnī. The perfectly smooth exterior surface of the mausoleum, composed of a cylindrical brick tower (167 feet [51 m] tall) and conical roof, is interrupted by ten inset buttresses formed by triangular sections, with two bands of Kufic inscriptions running above the ceiling and along the base of the structure. This utterly unique building has spawned a wide range of stories and legends. One such legend held that the sharp buttress edges were devised to repel the *jinns* (evil genies referred to in the Koran, in whose language Solomon was alleged to have been versed). Another, which claimed a coffin—originally fashioned from crystal—was suspended midair to catch and reflect the midday sunlight, certainly homage to Qabus' renown as an astronomer. The shape of this mausoleum served as inspiration for two minarets in Ghazni[24] (central Afghanistan), the first built by Mas'ud III (plate 122, 1114–15) and the second by Bahrām Shāh (1118–52), both Ghaznavid rulers. The minarets are all that remain of two rather impressive mosques. The main construction material is fired brick, again displaying intricately intertwined geometric patterns, as well as strikingly beautiful inscriptions. The minaret of Jam, which rises in stark isolation above a riverbank,[25] is also in Afghanistan. This structure, some 210 feet (65 m) in height, rests on an octagonal base and contains a double set of spiral staircases. The minaret is adorned with rather elaborate and sumptuous decoration, reflecting an underlying sense of *horror vacui*. Decorative motifs are essentially geometric[26] or epigraphic, and an inscription refers to the name of the patron, Ghiyath al-Din Muhammad (a Ghūrid sultan who ruled from 1163 to 1203). One of the most significant elements is the insertion of a still-visible inscription executed in turquoise ceramic tiles just below the crown of *muqarnas*, which serves as a transition from the first to the second stages of the shaft. These minarets (the logical antecedents for the Qutb Minar in Delhi, dating from 1199)[27] might have been part of a complex surveillance and sighting system, as has been recently proposed.[28] In this context, the minaret of Kirat (southern Khorāsān, tenth century)[29] is significant, with its high octagonal base and cylindrical shaft, typologically quite similar to the structure at Jam. The Kirat minaret is also adorned with decorative stuccowork. Other important minarets include the Seljuq construction at the Congregational Mosque of Saveh (1110)[30] and the famed minaret of Bukhara,[31] a fired brick structure rising 150 feet (46 m) and dating from 1127.

The importance of the Afghan sites is confirmed by the remains of the palaces of Mas'ud III in Ghazni[32] and at Lashkar-i Bazar,[33] where the palace structures were schematically adapted to include *iwans* arranged on an axis around the courtyard (also used in western Islamic architecture, such as the Ukhaydir Palace in present-day Iraq). The inner walls at Lashkar-i Bazar were also refaced with stucco and decorated with the images of various personages: a profile view of the lower part of a body, a frontal view of a bust, and three-quarter depictions of a face, all of which follow a classical pre-Islamic scheme. This is one of the most important extant examples of figurative mural imagery in Persian art.[34]

THE SELJUQS

The next great culture to emerge in eleventh-century Asia (Tughrïl I rose to power in 1038) would arrive from central Asia, where, as we have seen, considerable advances had been made in architecture and the arts (Firdawsi had dedicated his *Shah-nama*, or "Book of Kings," to the Ghaznavid Sultan Mahmud, and such renowned figures as Avicenna and al-Bīrūnī were denizens of the court at Khorāsān). This group would forcefully extend its control over Iranian territory.

122. ABOVE, LEFT. The minaret of Mas'ud III in Ghazni, central Afghanistan

123. ABOVE, RIGHT. The mausoleum of Qabus ibn Wushmagir ibn Ziyar in Gonbad-i Qabus

Originally nomadic peoples of Turkish origin, evolving from structured clans, the new invaders showed tremendous political and military cohesion. Although we have no Turkish sources, the information from Arab or Persian historical accounts provides a partial, albeit perhaps not too objective, picture. We know that the tribe was organized along male lineage and that territories were governed by an *atabeg*. Theoretically a military chieftain and "tutor" to Seljuq princes, the *atabeg* often became an autonomous governor with an independent fiefdom, passing down his title along hereditary lines. In this way, dynasties were formed, such as the Zanghids, Ildegizids or Salghurids. The Seljuqs exercised an important political role, bringing about significant changes, including those in religious practice. The Būyids were Shiites, as were the Fatimids in Egypt (909–1171). However, the Seljuqs imprinted their own conservative Sunni stamp, showing little tolerance for any heretical forms of the faith. They quickly invaded the Iranian territories, taking Baghdad, the seat of the caliphate, in 1055. In 1071 the Seljuqs defeated the Byzantines farther to the west, at Manzikert (in the vicinity of Lake Van, in eastern Anatolia), opening up access to the Mediterranean. Extremely shrewd rulers, they were able to attract the greatest intellectuals of the time. A powerful monarch, Malik Shāh (r. 1072–92), adopted Arab, Persian, and Turkish regal titles, thus declaring himself the universal sovereign, aided by the expansion of his great empire. Even the selection of *viziers*, as in the aforementioned Nizam al-Mulk, was geared to maintaining a balanced political environment among Turkish and Islamic elements. However, it seems that his successors were not always so wise in their actions, if it is true that the twelve sons of Nizam al-Mulk demanded an almost religious form of veneration. The same political climate that helped Abu Hamid Muhammad al-Ghazali (1059–1111), a theologian, jurist, and philosopher, make the mystic doctrine of the Sufis acceptable to the more intransigent Sunnis, also provoked the Shiites to resistance. One Shiite group, the Nizari

124. OPPOSITE. Caravansary of Ribat-i Sharaf, Khorāsān, 1114–54

125. ABOVE. Central courtyard (*sahn*) and two *iwans*, west and north, at the Congregational Mosque (Masjid-i Jum'a), Ardistan

Ishmaelites, known as "Assassins," barricaded itself at Alamut, in the mountains not far from the Caspian. They resorted to methods we would now define as terrorist until they were finally overcome by the Mongols (1256). Another prominent figure—whose literary importance has been exaggerated among Western critics—was Omar Khayyam, a scientific scholar more than a poet, who was highly appreciated by the greatest Seljuq sultan, Malik Shāh.

The Seljuqs fortunately understood the importance of communications between the various provinces of their empire, and established an efficient system of trade routes with caravansaries, offering protection for people and goods during long periods of travel. In fact, despite the centralization of power, extended territories populated by nomadic Turkish groups remained absolutely indifferent to the official demands for stationary settlements. These groups also had a notorious propensity for raid skirmishes. Nevertheless, it remains clear that despite all these limitations (not the least of which were the exorbitant taxes levied on agricultural produce, one of the reasons that led to the Seljuq's demise), this period was extremely important for its cultural and artistic contributions, which left a considerable legacy of materials, especially when compared to the relative void of preceding centuries.

The caravansary of Ribat-i Sharaf[35] in eastern Khorāsān (plate 124), dating from 1114 (with a restoration in 1154), and located on one of the main caravan routes leading to Bukhara and Samarkand, is an impressively regal edifice. The fired-brick structure features a high wall, which gives the impression of a fortification. The building is distributed around two courtyards: the first, which is smaller, was probably used to house a reasonably well-manned garrison, while the second—organized around an axial scheme of four *iwans* facing a courtyard—also contained domed rooms that could be used for short stays by the sultan. The main portal is flanked by two buttresses in the form of *mihrabs* so that those arriving after the gates had been closed would still be able to use these structures for prayer.

From a decorative standpoint, the building is a triumph of ornamental motifs in brick, ter-

racotta, and stucco, all liberally used and displaying designs and techniques that can be considered an evolution in the stylistic continuity discussed thus far. The caravansary is a pivotal monument in the development of Persian architecture, which significantly employs the axial arrangement of four *iwans* set around a central courtyard.

The fact that this spatial organization of the four *iwans* is applied in civil architecture, perhaps even before its appearance in religious structures, is further evidenced in the caravansary of Dayakhatun (eleventh to twelfth century),[36] located between Bukhara and Khiva. This structure, which is divided into four principal sections, also features an exterior brick wall with semicircular corner towers, typical of military architecture. This military style is also found in the severe and geometrically monumental Ribat-i Malik (1078),[37] located between Bukhara and Samarkand. All that remains of this structure is the impressive gateway, a product of restoration. At Dayakhatun, the four axial *iwans* are linked by a series of porticoes, while the living and storage areas open up along the perimeter walls. The main decorative elements are achieved through the arrangement of flat bricks.

The region surrounding Esfahān, including the previously described Nayin, as well as the Natanz, which will be discussed later in this chapter, features two fascinating congregational mosques, one at Zavareh (1135–1136)[38] and the other at Ardistan (plates 125–126),[39] probably a later construction. These two buildings may have served as models for the great Congregational Mosque of Esfahān. Zavareh is, however, the first four-*iwan* mosque to be built *ex novo* in Iran, and is thus the starting point for a long and magnificent tradition. The mosque is rectangular and somewhat elongated in structure, and the entrance is at the northeast corner; the *mihrab*, at the south end, is adorned with a large dome and anterior *iwan*. The date for this structure is provided by a Kufic inscription in brick and stucco in the courtyard. The three remaining *iwans* are smaller than the *qibla iwan* and are linked by a two-story arcade. On the western

126. ABOVE. Dome with stucco reliefs in the *mihrab*, Congregational Mosque, Ardistan

127. OPPOSITE. Mausoleum of Pir-i 'Alamdar at Damghan

128. OVERLEAF. The twin mausoleums of Kharraqan, 1067 and 1086. Magnificent examples of Seljuq funerary architecture, perhaps inspired by nomad tents, these structures show remarkable craftsmanship and ingenuity, particularly in the geometric interlaced effects achieved by the simple arrangement of bricks.

exterior side of the mosque there is a massive cylindrical minaret, which contains traces of ceramic insets. It is not known whether these are original or the result of later restorations. The *mihrab* is adorned with stucco decorations, and three naves run along the sides of the domed prayer hall, parallel to the *qibla* wall. On the exterior, the simple yet majestic dome reveals the arrangement of the cubic foundation surmounted by an octagonal drum that supports the dome; the interior, however, is a play of niches and pendentives. The mosque at Ardistan is regrettably more a product of various reconstructions. Originally a "kiosk" mosque built on the foundations of a Sasanian fire temple, the structure is now comparable to descriptions of Zavareh. The mosque contains an imposing dome, especially in view of its location in what is even today little more than a large village, rising above a stucco *mihrab* dating from 1158. The anterior *iwan*, constructed two years later (1160), is covered by a barrel-vaulted ceiling with floral and palm stucco reliefs inspired by a plethora of fabric motifs. There is also an interesting painted

129. Remains of a palace in the city of Merv (present-day Turkmenistan)

checkerboard decoration on the intrados of an arch, tentatively dated to the mid-ninth century (940?)[40] and clearly reminiscent of certain woven motifs, particularly those used in kilims.

An entire chapter could be devoted to mausoleums, which, following the example of Bukhara, became a favorite type of architectural structure, in Iran and elsewhere.[41] The mausoleum of Pir-i ʿAlamdar at Damghan (plate 127),[42] with its cylindrical shape (and reconstructed dome), is structurally quite similar to a large minaret. The building also features impressive decorative interlacing in brick. An altogether different structure is found in Yazd, at the mausoleum of Davazdah Imam ("The Twelve Imams"), which dates from 1037.[43] The exterior is visually quite severe, with a massive square foundation. However, there is a constant, precise interplay between the solid volumes of the exterior and interior, where a series of blind lunettes are crowned by arches bearing stunning, original Kufic inscriptions. In Kharraqan (on the plain of Qonqorolong, near Qazvin) a pair of twin mausoleums (plate 128)[44] was recently "discovered"; dating from 1067 and 1086, respectively, these are Seljuq constructions. The design of the two structures is octagonal, with engaged columns at the corners, topped by a domed roof. As Hillenbrand has observed, "many details of the structure and the ornamentation evoke the *yurt*, or tent, of the Turkish nomads."[45] The ability to create complex geometric motifs with simple bricks is brilliantly realized here with a repertoire that, while hardly infinite, often seems so. In the tomb dating from 1086, there are no less than seventy distinct geometric designs. Even the small Seljuq cupolas gracing the Masjid-i Jumʿa in Esfahān are, in number and variety, further evidence of how tremendous skill can transform simple fired brick into an instrument of such singular artistic refinement. It is no accident that this occurred in Iran, where the technique was cultivated over an extremely long period of time. It should be pointed out that the Seljuqs were also responsible for great building projects in Anatolia, where they reigned from 1077 to 1307. There, however, they favored the use of stone, due to a local Christian tradition (Byzantine with Armenian and Georgian variants) that persevered over many centuries. With regard to the mausoleums in Kharraqan, mention should be made of the wall paintings that adorn the interior. These are not merely inscriptions (which, of course, abound) but also representations of mosque lamps (bearing the inscription *baraka li-sahibihi*, "fortune to the owner"), pomegranate trees with birds, and medallions with peacocks, necks entwined, all symbolically alluding to paradise, which was quite suitable to the sepulchral functions of these buildings.[46]

Malik Shāh was the last great Seljuq sovereign to rule within Persian territory, where Esfahān had been established as the capital. His successor, Muʿizz al-Din Sanjar, after governing in Iraq, Fārs, and Khuzistan, left these provinces to his grandsons and moved the capital to Merv, a major crossroads for the caravan routes of Khorāsān in present-day Turkmenistan (plate 129). The city, located in an oasis not far from the Murghab River, was enormous, and its ruins[47] are still impressive, particularly the mausoleum of Sanjar (1157), which predominates, even from a distance. Merv was destroyed by the Mongols, and only the massive looming structure of the mausoleum has been saved from oblivion, although the vicissitudes of time, and several inappropriate restorations, have left their heavy toll. This notable monument, built from fired brick, has a square foundation and mighty walls; the Bukharian concept of an exterior gallery is revived and developed in such a way that the severe mass becomes lightened above, providing a balanced transition to the great dome, which was originally finished in glazed brick. The dome is visible from miles away. The gallery arches are embellished with fragments of decorative stuccowork,[48] a reference to the oblique style of the Samarran Abbasids also found in the stucco motifs in the piers supporting the dome of Nizam al-Mulk in Esfahān.

Another splendidly majestic mausoleum is Mumina Khatun in Nakhchivan (Azerbaijan), which dates from 1186.[49] Here a decorative series of glazed ceramic pieces is inset into the fired brick wall. Seljuq achievements in the arts included the creation of highly refined ceramics, which found numerous applications in both architecture and earthenware. The *mihrab*, coated with a metallic glaze at one point reused at the Masjid-i Meidan in Kāshān, was the work of Al-Hasan ibn al-Arabshah (1226). Inscribed with the names of the twelve Shiite Imams, it is now in Berlin.[50] In terms of earthenware, the most notable technique employed was *mina'i* or *haft rangi* (seven colors). Unfortunately this opulent and refined period, known for its exceptional figurative work,[51] was brief in duration.

THE MONGOL PERIOD: THE IL-KHANIDS

The internal weaknesses of the Seljuq reign and unresolved conflicts between nomadic impulses and permanent settlements continued to undermine political cohesion. This situation was further aggravated by exorbitant property taxes, widespread corruption, and arrogance among the ruling classes, all of which left the Seljuqs ill prepared to confront an ever-growing external threat. By the early thirteenth century, the newly emboldened Mongols, who in Asia had massed around the extraordinary figure of Genghis Khan (1167–1227), began to clash with Islamic forces along the frontier in central Asia. Otrar fell in 1219, and, one year later, Samarkand and Bukhara were besieged, followed by Balkh in 1221. The conquest of Iranian territory was delegated to Hulegu Khan (b. 1217, r. 1256–65) and began with the siege of Alamut and the defeat of the Assassins (the formal beginning of his rule); he entered Baghdad in 1258 (when al-Musta'sim, the last caliph, although in name only, died), and then went on to Aleppo and Damascus (1260); his army was finally defeated by the Mamluks in Egypt.

The destruction was monumental, with massacres (in places such as Merv and Rayy, then a flourishing center for the arts, particularly textiles and ceramics, traditions that would never be revived) that are remembered as some of the most ferocious in the history of mankind. Then came the *pax mongolica*, with its unprecedented ease of contact between west and east, but for more than eighty years, the territory of Iran would be utterly devastated. Construction obviously ground to a halt, although this was clearly not due to lost technologies, since the techniques used for creating fired brick were deeply rooted throughout the Middle East at the time. The Mongol occupation—with its extraordinary Seljuq prelude—was, in fact, an extremely productive period. The new sovereigns were complete strangers to Islamic culture and brought with them their own syncretic amalgam of shamanistic beliefs fused with Hinduism, Buddhism, and Nestorian Christianity. The noblewomen, in particular, tended to be devout Christians, illustrated by the example of the wife of Abaqa Khan, Maria Palaeologina, daughter of Michael VII Palaeologus and sister of Andronicus II (r. 1282–28). After her consort's death, in 1281, she returned to Constantinople, founding the Church of Panagia Mouchliotissa (Our Lady of the Mongols). She later entered this religious order, helping to commission one of the stupendous mosaics adorning the Byzantine basilica of Saint Savior in Chora. People of Jewish faith or origin, such as the enlightened vizier Rashid al-Din, also played key roles. The artistic repertoire underwent radical change with the introduction of elements typical of the Far East: dragons, phoenixes, lotuses and peonies[52] were quickly assimilated and soon became essential

130–131. The mausoleum of Gonbad-i Kabud (Azerbaijan), detail of decorative brickwork (ABOVE, LEFT) and view of overall structure (ABOVE, RIGHT)

fixtures not only in Persian art, but throughout the Islamic world. This can be seen in Syrian-Egyptian Mamluk decoration. East Asian ornamental motifs were already being employed in the lavish palace that Abaqa Khan (r. 1265–81) constructed at Takht-i Sulayman, a site of tremendous scenic and historical significance. The spot was already revered by the Achaemenids, who maintained one of their three sacred fires here (Khosrow II also had the "True Cross" brought here from Jerusalem). The most striking physical feature at Takht-i Sulayman is the cone of an extinct volcano. At its center lies a perennial blue lake of undetermined depth, ringed by Sasanian walls still perfectly preserved in many spots. The Mongol sovereign had his palace built here, on the ruins of a Sasanian citadel.[53]

One of the most significant changes during the Mongol period was the increasing use of decorative inserts made of glazed ceramic, most notably of astonishingly brilliant turquoise, as seen in the city of Marāgheh. The oldest mausoleum (Gonbad-i Sorkh, 1147)[54] was designed following the classic square floor plan and decorated with interlaced brick motifs. This was not unusual, since the same type of structure existed at Kharraqan, even though the main portal here is adorned with ceramic inserts. Gonbad-i Kabud (plates 130–31, 1196),[55] with its octagonal shape and its engaged columns, is a minor masterpiece of its kind. The entire surface of this building features a decorative network of red fired brick. Here, however, the ceiling arches with barely visible *muqarnas* are heavily embellished with ceramics, a decorative approach that seems to approach culmination at Gonbad-i Ghaffariyah (during the period of Abu Said Bahadur Khan, r. 1316–35).[56]

It would be impossible not to mention one of Marāgheh's most outstanding monuments: the observatory used by the great astronomer and philosopher Nasir al-Din Tusi (1201–1274). It is amusing to note that this renowned figure was also a sheer opportunist who followed

132–133. ABOVE. Two details of the decorative work of the Congregational Mosque (Masjid-i Jum'a), Natanz

the faith of his convenience, be it Sunni or Shiite. The observatory was equipped with at least ten high-precision scientific instruments.[57] The hillside on which this structure is located is studded with interesting grottoes, which may have been used either to house scientists or as a Nestorian monastery.

The Il-Khanid Arghun (1284–91) was one of the period's more noteworthy figures. While never converting to Islam, he practiced a form of religious syncretism based on Buddhism. Arghun made powerful inroads into the region of Qonqorolong ("plain of the tawny horses"), an excellent grazing area that must have reminded the Mongols of the steppes of central Asia, where the residence of Sultaniyya[58] was established. The surrounding territory became heavily settled by the Mongols, [59] and by the era of Abaqa Khan, this was the site of Viar. An imposing (and almost Chinese) stone dragon[60] attests to the presence of the sole Buddhist "monastery," which was later Islamicized with the insertion of an incongruous and never completed *mihrab*, interestingly aligned in the wrong direction. Ghazan Khan (r. 1295–1304) converted to Islam and was notorious for his intolerance, even if he allowed the completion of Giovanni Battista's cathedral in Marāgheh and eventually married his father's widow, a practice that might have been common among Altaic Turkish tribes, but certainly existed in stark contrast with Koranic doctrine. Ghazan established his capital at Tabrīz and became a great champion of the arts. Under his vizier, Rashid al-Din, the city was transformed into a dynamic international center, where Ghazan created his own quarter eponymously named Rashidiyya, dying shortly thereafter.[61]

The Congregational Mosque at Natanz (plates 132–34, 1307)[62] rises near a *khanqah*, a traditional religious site, in this case organized around the tomb of a highly venerated figure, which also served as a lodging for pilgrims, generally Sufi mystics. The mosque follows the traditional four-*iwan* design. An earthquake caused portions of the plaster and mortar in the domed prayer

134. OPPOSITE. Old plane tree trunks rise from the gargantuan stump of an ancient tree in front of the *iwan* leading to the massive Natanz complex, 1307. Throughout Iran, centuries-old trees are often found near the tombs of highly venerated religious figures.

hall to fall, revealing fragments of a Kufic inscription composed of skillfully arranged bricks, undoubtedly Seljuq in origin.

Beautiful Mongol Koranic inscriptions adorn the intrados of the *iwan* arches. The gate leading to the *khanqah* is decorated with blue, white, black, and turquoise glazed bricks, interspersed with unglazed terracotta, a work of great originality (plates 132–33). Aside from the inscriptions, which include a particularly elegant square Kufic inscription probably inspired by Chinese seals, there are a series of harmoniously executed intertwined polygonal motifs. By this time, polychrome (although predominantly turquoise) surface decoration was well established, and apparently the techniques tried out at Natanz were later used on one of the most noteworthy buildings in Islam, the mausoleum of Sultaniyya,[63] constructed by Oljeitu (r. 1304–16) and dating from 1313–14 (plate 135). Oljeitu was a remarkable figure: "Originally a Sunni who had then followed Christianity and Buddhism, he reconverted to Sunnism (after being a Shiite sometime around 1310) prior to his death."[64] Oljeitu probably built this impressive monument, with its massive dome rising 175 feet (53 m) high, during his Shiite phase, with the intention of bringing the bodies of Ali and Hussein, the first Shiite martyrs, here to what would be the foundations of a new imperial capital.

Recent archaeological finds indicate that the mausoleum was built on a high platform, a common tradition in the Islamic architecture of Mughal India, but one that is rarely found in Iran. A containment wall with semicircular towers remains. The design is unique, featuring a regular, square foundation with smoothed corners on three sides, while the fourth side is composed of two adjoining sections that create a rectangular space. As in Merv, an octagonal exterior porticoed gallery rises above the massive foundation walls. Above the gallery a series of eight small turrets or minarets literally crown the main ovoid dome, which was once adorned with glazed turquoise tiles. In contrast, the white interior contains rather simple inscriptions.[65] For a long time it was thought that this was a later alteration; however, it is evident from the content and style of the writing that this was a stylistic afterthought, most likely

135. ABOVE. The mausoleum of Oljeitu at Sultaniyya, 1313–14. The structure was built atop a broad platform with semi-cylindrical buttresses. This practice was widespread in the Islamic mausoleums of Mughal India (sixteenth century). Apparently this is one of very few such architectural examples in Iran.

136. OPPOSITE. The monument to Pir-i Bakran in Linjan, interior, 1303–1312.

(materials possibly brought from Venice), while the walls are painted with figures dressed in European fashion, perhaps Dutchmen or Portuguese. Pavilions of this type must have been quite extensively used in Esfahān and elsewhere. In this historic capital city, which was quite proud of its beauty (*Esfahān nisf-i jahan*: "Esfahān is half of the world") contains another noteworthy monument—the Pavilion of Hasht Bihisht ("The Eight Paradises"), dating from the seventeenth to the eighteenth century, which is composed of a central structure and four small exterior *iwans*. The pavilion, which resembles the contemporary architecture of Mughal India, features beautiful ceramic tiles decorating the arch pediments.[125]

Returning once again to the *Maidan*, or Central Square, the fourth great structure facing this open area is the main entrance to the vast and well preserved covered bazaar, which follows along a defined path for over a mile, punctuated by *madrasahs*, mosques, baths, and caravansaries; it is also linked to the Friday Mosque. Due to the modern need for vehicular access, an opening (or disembowelment) was cut next to the mosque about fifty years ago in order to lay down a major thoroughfare, thus interrupting the graceful continuity of the complex.

Since Esfahān lies along a major river, the Zayanda-Rud, bridges were important not only for their functional uses but also as an integral part of Shah 'Abbas's master plan for the city. The oldest of these structures is the Si-o-se Pol (Bridge of the Thirty-three Arcades), which has a Sasanian foundation and which has also been used for regulating water flow. The unusual bridge is the Pol-i Khwaju (plate 156), which was built during the reign of Shah 'Abbas II, in the mid-seventeenth century.[126] This arcaded span is laid out on two levels. The upper level was intended for carriage traffic, but also contains a vaulted passageway for pedestrians. The upper level features a series of small *iwans* facing out onto the river, and a few larger pavilions to accommodate longer visits. The lower section, which is level with the river, was used to control water flow through the use of bulkheads. This level includes a series of small stairways, separated by channels, inserted so that people could enjoy a healthful respite.

The ingenuity of Shah 'Abbas I is also evident in another project, which was built in the rural areas surrounding his capital, where hundreds, if not thousands, of imposing Borj-i Kabutar (literally "pigeon towers") were built.[127] Each of these elegant and complex structures could shelter hundreds of birds. The guano that was collected (pigeons are not considered edible according to Islamic custom) was used as fertilizer, particularly for the cultivation of melons. The Shah had these structures built at public expense, to be paid out over the course of several years. As a result, tax revenues increased markedly. Shah 'Abbas also promoted modifications and expansions to the two "holy cities" of Iran, Qom and Mashhad, with the idea of launching a domestic religious tourism campaign, in opposition to the official tourism in Mecca (and in Karbala and Najaf, for Shiites), then under Ottoman control.[128]

It should be stated in closing that the largest and most important Persian gardens were built during this period,[129] as were the royal buildings at Ashraf and Farahabad.[130] There are few noteworthy examples of civil architecture from this period. Among the most interesting is the Safavid house discovered some years ago at Nayin, which is unusually well preserved and extremely original.[131] This building, structured as a series of many rooms facing a central courtyard, is richly decorated with wall paintings. Particularly significant among these are Chinese-style medallions containing dragons and phoenixes, as well as winged figures, trees, and gardens, the iconography of which is reminiscent of miniatures of the time. Safavid rule, with its magnificent capital city of Esfahān, brought to a close one of the most productive and auspicious periods in the history of Persian art.

TIMELESS FIGURES
PERSIAN MINIATURES

THE MINIATURE FROM THE SASANIANS TO THE SELJUQS

Miniatures constitute one of the most significant chapters in the entire history of Persian Islamic art. As with architecture, there is a regrettable absence of work until the end of the Seljuq era, a void that is all the more significant since it coincides with a complex period of historical transition.

Illustrated books surely must have existed in the Sasanian era, just as there was an extremely ancient and universal practice of embellishing palace walls with pictorial decoration. The widespread diffusion of the Sasanian style can be seen in the influence it had on the Tang[1] dynasty in distant China. In contrast to the large-scale excavations carried out, for example, at Neyshābur,[2] Ghazni,[3] Lashkari Bazar,[4] Takht-i Sulaiman,[5] and Siraf,[6] major projects in Iran have been only sporadic. Additionally, there is an absence of significant finds and, until a few years ago, emphasis was placed on pre-Islamic sites. This situation encouraged scholars to associate Sasanian painting with central Asia, where Soviet excavations of important sites (Afrasiyab, Pandzikant, Varahsha[7]) yielded pictorial cycles of fables and epics that can be linked to two basic texts for miniatures—the *Shah-nama* and the *Khalila wa Dimna.* This international Sasanian style was enormously popular, even though documentation about it was easier to find at the periphery of the empire than at the center, where the Arab invasion resulted in an artistic stasis, if not destruction, leading artists merely to repeat pre-established models.[8]

Another element that should not be underestimated is the use of polychrome stucco to decorate buildings. The change from stone to stucco had already taken place in Sasanian arts—as seen at Kish,[9] Ctesiphon,[10] Dāmghān,[11] and at the Chal Tarkhan palace,[12] a hybrid monument. There is no reason to assume that the use of stucco diminished with the advent of Islam—in fact, the opposite is true.

Excavations at Neyshābur[13] unearthed an enormous and diverse quantity of ceramics, all dating from the tenth to the eleventh century. The most famous, and deservedly so for their quality, are those in cobalt blue and copper green, decorated with inscriptions in Arabic Kufic script written with rose thorns, inspired by the contemporary developments in Samarra. (This work introduced the technological innovation of mixing dyes with liquid clay, a method that resulted in very clear and stable decoration.) There are also examples of three-colored and incised ceramics that have obvious similarities to Tang dynasty works, but these have been attributed to the migration of ceramists from the Far East. (As these were typically funerary ceramics, it would be odd, to say the least, if they were traded.[14]) A different type of pottery is of interest to this discussion, namely the so-called figurative type, characterized by representations of men on horseback or standing figures, with buffware ceramic bodies decorated in black, green, manganese brown, and iron-based yellow. It is interesting to note that unlike epigraphic motifs, which are also found at Afrasiyab and in other sites in central Asia and which are generally produced in the same way, figurative ceramics are nearly exclusively found in the Khorāsān region of Iran. The decorative style is very fresh—almost naive—although it cannot be classified as folkloric (as might the work from Sari,[15] with its ornithomorphic drawings). Perhaps the iconography resembles that of a pre-Islamic past, which had not entirely disappeared, nor had it been forgotten—indeed, it was even embraced. It would not be surprising if such works come to be seen as inspired by Zoroastrian models.

During the Seljuq period representational art took hold (without forgetting the Sogdian precedents)—in ceramics, textiles, and wall paintings—with a human typology and physical characteristics quite different from earlier work. Faces became rounder (the ideal of beauty was moon-like), eyes had a stronger oblique cut (previously they were rounder), mouths were small, noses were aquiline, and eyebrows sometimes grew together as one. Fragments of wall paintings from Rayy and Neyshābur (now at the National Museum in Tehran[16] and at the Metropolitan Museum in New York[17]) clarify this shift in direction. Some typological characteristics remain: figures are viewed frontally with faces in three-quarter view, a style also found at Lashkari Bazar (early eleventh century), although those were more closely linked to Sogdian or Sasanian models, based on the drape of the clothing. There is a paucity of background elements or landscape, and the space is organized into horizontal registers, also found in *mina'i* (enameled) ceramics. This figurative pottery is interesting because it seems to constitute a distinctive iconographic source for painting, given the lack of manuscripts. A large plate (18⅞ in. [47.8 cm] in diameter) painted in this technique, now at the Freer Gallery of Art in Washington, D.C. (inv. N. 43.3),[18] dates from about 1230 and features a scene of a siege, where the figures have "captions" with their names, evoking ancient traditions and popular epic themes. Even though the specific spatial organization is somewhat chaotic, it is noteworthy that the figures are placed in horizontal bands, which is typical of *mina'i* ceramic decoration.[19] Incidentally, a 1310 treatise on ceramic art by master potter Abu l Qasim from Kashan[20] describes how this refined technique[21] was no longer in use, a tangible result of the devastation experienced following the Mongol invasion. Ceramics decorated with luster glaze[22] are stylistically somewhat different, however, and there are examples of these from the Mongol period. These ceramics provide ample evidence of figuration, but in a more monumental pictorial style, indicating that autonomous schools and traditions flourished during the same historical period.

The first manuscript to consider is *Varqa u Gulshah*,[23] a tragic love story of two tormented youths (plate 157, c. 1200). The text is in Persian, and one of the miniatures is signed by the master Shaykh 'Abd al-Mu'min ibn Muhammad with a *nisba* (place of origin) in al-Khuwayyi (known as Khuy, an area in Persian Azerbaijan). The Persian text, the signature, and the style, indicate that this work is Persian, rather than Anatolian, which has been suggested because 'Abd al-Mu'min

appears as a witness to a document in Konya in 1252–53. The space allocated for the illustrations is a long, narrow band, one of several similarities to *mina'i* ceramics; the descriptions are quite lively and the figures have halos around their heads, exactly as in figurative earthenware.

THE VITALITY OF THE IL-KHANID PERIOD

From a documentary and historical point of view, it is interesting that these early Persian miniatures (including those on ceramics) are not very notable artistically—in and of themselves or in comparison to work that was being created at the same time in other places under Muslim rule.[24] In short, nothing during this period hinted of the spectacular developments to come in subsequent centuries. Thus the Seljuq period can be put aside with a certain sense of disappointment (especially when compared to significant developments in architecture). It is quite surprising, on the other hand, to note the incredible vitality that characterizes the Il-Khanid period. There are specific, identifiable reasons for this: the change in the climate at court; the passage from a period when power was being acquired and strengthened (the second half of

157. *Gulshah Kills the Enemy of His Beloved*, from *Varqa u Gulshah*, c. 1200, Topkatpı Saraytı, Istanbul, H. 841 f. 22a

158. ABOVE. *Mare Followed by a Stallion*, from *The Use of Animals* by Ibn Bakhtishu, c. 1290, Pierpont Morgan Library, New York, Ms M500 f. 28r

the thirteenth century, keeping in mind that Baghdad was captured with the formal end of the Abbasid caliphate in 1258); the prevailing cosmopolitanism; and above all, contacts with China and the rest of the world.[25] This is evident in a manuscript, a bestiary now in New York,[26] made in Marāgheh in the late thirteenth century (1291, 1297, or 1299). This work features different styles in two miniatures that depict, respectively, a lioness and lion,[27] and two elephants (plate 159).[28] Considering that this was a meticulously accurate work, the style of the miniatures is tremendously exuberant—the elephants seem to be dancing. The flowers and birds show an analogous attention to detail, which gives context to the main subject. The background of the miniature *Mare Followed by a Stallion* (plate 158)[29] is treated differently; it features a tree, perhaps a willow, with its gnarled trunk painted almost impressionistically, clear and indisputable evidence of Chinese influence. The Far East—not uniquely, as we shall soon see—was a crucial element in the change in style, which would mature within the framework of a profoundly transformed society with many different cultural stimuli. The Mongols were Buddhist,[30] but they were also extremely open-minded.

The vizier Rashid-al-Din was a leading figure and interpreter of this political situation; he served under two Mongol sovereigns—Ghazan (who converted to Islam and was intolerant to the point of persecution) and Oljeitu (who was suspected of having Shiite sympathies). Rashid-al-Din supervised the compilation of a monumental work, *Jami' al-Tawarikh* (History of the World), a historical compendium[31] that celebrated the dominance of the Il-Khanid dynasty, as well as great figures from the past (such as Buddha, Muhammad, Chinese kings, Biblical prophets). The text was in Arabic and Persian, and copies were sent to the main centers of the

159. OPPOSITE. *Two Elephants*, from *The Use of Animals* by Ibn Bakhtishu, c. 1290, Pierpont Morgan Library, New York, Ms M500, f. 13r

160. *Muhammad, Abu Bakr, and a Herd of Goats*, from *History of the World* by Rashid al-Din, 1314–15, Edinburgh University Library, Ms 20 f. 57r

empire. Two examples of these survive, dating from 1307[32] and from 1314–15 (plate 160).[33] Once again, the format is long and narrow, and the colors neatly fill in areas outlined in black. As Fontana has said, they seem like "colored drawings more than paintings."[34] This corresponds precisely to a style of calligraphy from the Far East, except in the treatment of the drapery, which is deduced to have come from the Byzantine West, seen in a page now in London.[35] The relationship to the aforementioned bestiary is clearly established by the image of the *Sacred Tree of Buddha*,[36] a composition without human presence, in which the gnarled tree trunk is similar to the previously cited example. Chinese influence is undeniably very strong, but there is also Western (Byzantine) influence. Indeed, Rashidiyya (a village near Tabrīz, named for the vizier who established it) was home to a group of painters, calligraphers, bookbinders, scientists, and historians—experts whose origins and traditions were heterogeneous, but who all were engaged in the creation of a fundamental work of propaganda for the regime in power. This was a far cry from the Seljuq period, with its forced, fitful output.

This was the context for the creation of the most spectacular manuscript in Islamic art, the "Great Mongol" *Shah-nama*,[37] created around 1335 in Tabrīz. Fifty-eight illuminated pages (out of a presumed total of 190 illustrations for 300 pages of text) have been identified, and they are truly exceptional for their pictorial achievement. This is a veritable leap in quality, made possible by the international nature of Mongol society.

A famous image from this celebrated manuscript, *Mourning over the Coffin of Alexander the Great* (plate 161),[38] is in the Arthur M. Sackler and Freer Gallery of Art in Washington, D.C. The dramatic scene takes place in an interior defined by two symmetrical, crenellated portals, each of which has a hanging lamp. On a platform (in imperial Chinese style) on a carpet-

161. *Mourning over the Coffin of Alexander the Great*, from the "Great Mongol" *Shah-nama*, c.1335, Freer Gallery of Art, Washington, D.C., inv. 38.3. This dramatic composition has elements (the drapery of the clothing and curtains, for example) that indicate a proximity to Western Byzantine models.

covered floor, flanked by four metal candlesticks, rests a cloth-draped coffin beneath a precious mosque-lantern. In the lower foreground a group of women (mourners), seen from behind or in profile, literally pull their hair out in grief. In front of them the mother of the deceased hero kneels, her back to the viewer. On either side are two groups of male figures, their long hair worn loose in a sign of mourning. Their facial expressions are sad and inconsolable, sometimes distorted in grimaces that attest to their sorrow. Two male figures are in the background, behind the coffin; one is Aristotle, the sovereign's tutor and master. The page with *Faridun in Mourning when the Coffin of the Iraj Arrives*[39] is no less dramatic. This scene is set outdoors (symbolized in the Chinese manner by the personification of the sun in a sky filled with Chinese-style clouds). The sovereign, the elderly father of the dead hero, is held up, having fallen from his horse upon suddenly learning the dramatic news of his son's death, at the hands of his brothers. Meanwhile, people have gathered in celebration to welcome home the favorite son, Iraj.

Two other pages are also extraordinarily powerful. *The Battle of Alexander with Kharg*[40] shows the hero in a classical scene of combat with the monster. A crowd of horsemen looks on as the sovereign (in the center of the picture, astride his white steed) prepares to lower a blow with the full force of his unsheathed scimitar. The horse realistically shies away at the sight of the horrible animal. The latter has the body and paws of a lion, the wide-open jaws of a wolf, wings (almost like those of a pheasant), and a single, enormous horn—a perfect hybrid (perhaps a unicorn?).[41] A great deal of space has been given to the very evocative landscape in the background, with rugged mountains of varying heights dotted with pine trees—a Chinese convention not often seen in an Islamic context. The killing of the dragon (which never really takes place in the depiction, as the mythical beast must be fought, but the struggle between good and evil is an eternal one) is a favorite theme in *Shah-nama* painting. In a page at the Cleveland

162. *Bahrām Gur Slaying the Dragon*, from the "Great Mongol" *Shah-nama*, c. 1335, The Cleveland Museum of Art, 1943.658.

Museum of Art (plate 162),[42] Bahrām Gor (identified as the Sasanian King Bahrām V)[43] has dismounted his horse to face a serpentine monster which, already pierced by arrows, now faces the sword. This time the inspiration for the dragon is Chinese,[44] leading one to wonder if the artist had only seen artworks from the Far East. The defeated animal, tied to a gnarled tree, is an interesting beast, and details (such as the claws, the crest along its back, the horn, etc.) indicate the influence of Cathay, also apparent in the mountainous landscape (well-defined peaks and twisted trees) and the pierced rock in the foreground below the horse.[45] However, there was no exposure to Mandarin court painting (familiar to us through works of the Sung period). This is closer to Tang period work, since Islamic artists probably had contact with professional painters, such as those who worked in the grottos of Dun Huang (and also Ajanta in India), rather than the more celebrated, scholarly painters whose work never went beyond an exclusive circle of the elite. The one unfortunate feature in the Cleveland page is the representation of the horse, which is mannered, and despite a raised hoof, extraneous to the unfolding drama.

At this point it is appropriate to touch briefly on the text of the *Shah-nama* by Firdawsi,[46] which was widely disseminated in subsequent centuries, particularly beginning with the Seljuq era. The *Shah-nama* is an epic poem (some fifty-five thousand verses) that assembles and integrates legendary oral traditions. These have continued to circulate, which is very important to keep in mind, especially when an artwork, illuminated or not, breaks away from the familiar story, which is based in part on a *Pahlavi* text, now lost. It begins with the golden age at the dawning of the world under the sovereign Gayomars, moving on to Darius the Achaemenid, Alexander the Great, and the Sasanians (but not the Parthians), including Bahrām Gor and Khosrow II Parvīs (and the beautiful Shirin, which is almost a story within a story), concluding with the Muslim invasion: "The era of Omar had arrived; he brought a new religion and replaced the throne with the pulpit."[47] These words resound bitterly for the bard of Iranian identity. It is precisely the Iranian character of the work, with Iranian heroes such as Zal or Rustam, Isfandyar, the rivals Ardavan and Ardashīr, and Afrasyab, the Turkish enemy par excellence, that prompts the questions: Why were there so many foreign sovereigns? How is it that the Mongols,[48] who were chiefly responsible for the dissemination of illuminated copies, if not the text itself, and also the Timurids gave this volume a place of honor in their libraries? How is it that the Safavids, under the officially Shiite rule of Shah Esma'il, championed, along with Shah Tahmasp, the most acclaimed Persian illuminated manuscript?[49] These are basic and long-standing questions,[50] but we are still a long way from finding answers that aren't purely hypothetical. Certainly, these sovereigns' desire for legitimacy was one factor,[51] as was the quest for acceptance by a culture perceived as superior, though not necessarily in that order. This, however, is contradicted by the fact that the book was a private project, not tied to public display or the need to create an "image," as we might say today. According to the penetrating analysis of Oleg Grabar,[52] the text was a diplomatic gift to other sovereigns and ambassadors, along with the equally popular work of Nezāmī; in any case, it is worth noting that stories tied to the epic exploits of sovereigns, which not only strayed into myth but also became the stuff of myth itself, persisted on a popular level (but also in more rarefied circles). From the Mongol era on, the *Shah-nama* enjoyed extraordinary success and its popularity was rivaled only by the lyrical works of Nezāmī (Abu Muhammad Nezāmī of Ganja [Azerbaijan] 1141–1209), author of the literary classic *Khamsa*.[53]

Although the "Great Mongol" *Shah-nama* is the real starting point for a consistently high-level school of Persian painting, the tradition of painting on a small format in horizontal

bands, exemplified by the *Varqa u Gulshah,* continued in workshops that remained active in various centers after the death of Abu Sa'id (1335), the last Il-Khanid sovereign, and the breakup of the empire. The main cities and courts associated with this period were those linked to the Inju style in Shīrāz and the Jalayirid style, which alternated between Tabrīz and Baghdad. The period has been studied in depth,[54] and despite the vitality of the images, their artistic achievements have not been of the highest order. A series of artworks in several albums in Istanbul (c. 1370), attributed to the Jalayirid school (loose sheets from an unbound and dispersed *Shah-nama*, and perhaps from a similarly dispersed *Mi'raj-nama* [the Book of the Ascension of the Prophet]), in the Topkapı Sarayı library,[55] are linked to the "Great Mongol" *Shah-nama.* The Istanbul album, marked by seal H.2154 (*Hazine*, Treasury) contains a text by Dust Muhammad, who was one of the book's artists (and librarian to the Safavid Prince Bahrām Mirza, son of Shah Esma'il, to whom he dedicated an album in 1544. This contains a text "Painters of Yesterday and Today," an important documentary source,[56] along with a 1606 text by Qadi Ahmad.[57] Among others, the artists Ahmad Musa and his student Shams al-Din are mentioned and credited, perhaps by Dust Muhammad himself, with some paintings now in Istanbul (Ahmad Musa is credited with the celebrated *Offering of a City to the Prophet Muhammad* [plate 163]).[58] The city has been variously interpreted as Constantinople, Medina, and Jerusalem. The miniature depicting *Isfandyar Killing a Wolf,*[59] on the other hand, is attributed to Shams al-Din. Although interesting, these works should be considered with caution because their language is so imaginative and bombastically celebrative[60] in comparison, for example, to Mani, founder of Manicheanism, who, according to legend, was unsurpassed as a painter.

A 1396 manuscript created in Baghdad, consisting of three poems by Khwaju Kirmani,[61] contains nine miniatures, including *The Marriage of Humay and Humayun,*[62] signed by the painter Junayd, to whom the other miniatures are also attributed. In the course of little more than seventy years Persian miniatures achieved a state of near-perfect composition, style, elegance, and balance. Artists were inspired by this ideal and genre until at least the late sixteenth century, that is, well into the Safavid period. There is some point, therefore, in analyzing such works in order to understand the mechanisms established by Junayd and continued by his followers. First of all, it should be emphasized that the miniatures are an integral part of the text, from which they cannot be separated. Illustration, even in the physical act of execution, did not stand alone, but was integrated with and completed the written component, which in some instances was copied by a famous calligrapher. In Islamic art—and Persia is no exception—the copyist is often the true protagonist in the book. The names of many more calligraphers than painters have been handed down through history, underscoring the leading role of this art form. Text and pictures inform each other, alternately clarifying and completing each other in a way that may have no equivalent in western art. Often, if not always, miniatures are traversed by lines of text.

Despite the fact that this work was essentially private in nature, the miniaturist's position was rather delicate[63] given the alleged prohibition against images or iconoclasm. In any case, prudence was required to avoid accusations of deliberate representations of reality that usurped the role of the creator, which belonged to God alone. This reveals a very interesting ideological schism that should merit deeper inquiry. Certain characteristics are quite clear: the absence of shadows keeps figures from appearing lifelike, and the interweaving of perspective planes (as, for example, in the miniature by Junayd), the frontal view of the protagonist, the

163. *The Offering of a City to the Prophet Muhammad,* from a Mi'raj-nama, now dispersed, c. 1370, Topkapı Sarayı, Instanbul, H. 2154 f. 107r. It is interesting to note that artists depicted even the face of the Prophet until the late fourteenth century.

foreshortened architecture, the carpets seen from above, the women of the harem gazing out from a window, and the staircases depicted in perspective work together to create an unnatural, completely unrealistic totality. On the other hand, realistic, even naturalistic, elements abound in the portrayal of clothing, lamps, vase (Chinese celadon, perhaps, and if so, certainly not an invention), curtains, carpets, and almost certainly the tile facades of the architecture. The faces, however, are standardized and immobile, although the young girl modestly covers her mouth while the women examine her sheets for signs of her virginity. There is a remarkable synthesis between movement and stasis. The model is predominantly static, almost ideally Platonic, and the observer—who is alone and engrossed in a personal examination—needs to apply his knowledge of the text, his interpretation, and his imagination in order to add details that may have been omitted, not because they were overlooked, but because they can only be inserted by the admirer. The same is true with other art forms; looking at a stucco *mihrab* (niche) or a wooden *minbar* (raised platform) decorated with geometric motifs or arabesques, the viewer has complete freedom to decide where to look next. This is why it is said that Islamic art has a kaleidoscopic effect, even if artists did not hesitate to suggest their own points of view.

Another miniature from the very same manuscript, *Humayun at the Gate of Humay's Palace*,[64] perfectly highlights the Arcadian ideal that inspired the painter and his relationship with nature. Moreover, if the practice of painting elements (such as a tree, a dome, a rock) beyond the limit of the page frame did not begin at this time, it was now perfected and became indispensable. This was a way to emphasize that nothing is finite, closed, or definitive, that in the end everything continues, everything is a fragment of an infinite reality, of which we can perceive only an instant, since infinity belongs solely to God. A third and final miniature in this exceptional artistic document, *Battle of Humay and Humayun* (plate 164),[65] confirms what has already been said about the relationship to nature and the use of recurrent elements (the circularity of the scene, the stream at the bottom, the rocks that seem like personifications,[66] the processions of birds). Even though this miniature may lack expressive power and characters (which Bihzad, the greatest painter of the time, would have added) and is slightly academic (the clash of the horses replicating that of the heroes looks as though it could have been choreographed by Diaghilev), it is, together with others of the same manuscript, one of the milestones of this art form.

MINIATURES DURING THE TIMURID PERIOD

The art of the miniature made great strides during the Timurid period. This was the result of both relative political stability and also a series of sovereigns and princes who were avid bibliophiles and who left an important mark on Iran's cultural and artistic landscape. A brilliant military leader, Timur (known as Tamerlane in the West, 1336–1405), deserves special mention. Originally from central Asia and head of a clan that professed to be Mongol (Timur, of course, claimed descent from Genghis Khan), he was actually a Turk from the Samarkand region. Timur led innumerable westward invasions and occupied the Iranian plateau for over a fifteen-year period, beginning in 1380. His military campaigns were marked by butchery, such as a massacre in quarrelsome Esfahān, which is said to have taken the lives of seventy thousand people. Timur then pushed farther west with campaigns in the Caucasus (and from there moved on to Moscow), Syria (the sacking of Damascus in 1401), Anatolia (where in 1402 he defeated and captured the Ottoman Sultan Bayazit in a battle near Ankara before traveling to the Mediterranean

164. Junayd, *The Battle Between Humay and Humayun*, from *Three Poems* by Khvaju Kirmani, 1396, British Library, London, Add 18113 f. 31r.

ز هامون برانگیخت هامون نورد
نهان گرد گردون گردان ز گرد

coast at Smyrna), and India (where he took Delhi). Finally, not yet worn out, Timur turned to Samarkand, which he intended to use as his base for launching an attack on China. Timur died at Otrar in 1405, in the midst of this undertaking. Ruy González de Clavijo, an ambassador of Henry III of Castile, spent more than two years in pursuit of Timur, and his account is an extremely interesting source of information about Timur and his court, and a vivid portrayal of the East at the time.[67]

After Timur's death his son, Shahrukh, prevailed in a war of succession.[68] Born in 1377, he ruled from 1409 to 1447 and moved the capital of the empire from Samarkand to Herāt (a move that was immortalized in the game of chess with the term "to castle"). This signaled the start of a relatively long period, nearly the entire fifteenth century, during which the frenzy of conquest that characterized Tamerlane's life gave way to a division of power among a series of sovereigns and princes, in accordance with a traditional hereditary pattern of Mongol command. There was no centralized political power in the empire as occurred in Mongol times, but the separate courts witnessed a flowering of the arts, poetry, and science. Timur's nephews included Ulugh Beg (1394–1449), the great mathematician and astronomer, who ruled Samarkand until 1449, and his brother, Baysunghur (1397–1433), who ruled first in Tabrīz and then in Herāt. He was an extraordinary man of letters who, among other accomplishments, brought out a critical edition of the *Shah-nama* in 1426, which is still the version in use today.

The courts that were significant for the production of miniatures were those of Pir Muhammad (r. 1392–1400), Iskandar (r. 1409–15), and the court of the latter's cousin, Ibrahim Sultan (the son of Shahrukh; r. 1415–35). All these courts were first located in Shīrāz, and then in Herāt during the reigns of Abu Said (1451–1469) and Sultan Husayn Bayqara (1470–1506). Abu Said's realm was challenged by powerful Turkmen rivals,[69] the Qara Qoyunlu (People of the Black Sheep), who occupied Herāt under Jahanshah in 1458) and the Aq Qoyunlu (People of the White Sheep), who gained control of Herāt in 1470 under Uzun Hasan. The latter sovereign was active militarily, politically, and diplomatically. He attempted an anti-Ottoman alliance with Venice—an alliance that endured only on paper, but which received official imprimatur in the form of diplomatic gifts, still in the San Marco Treasury.[70] Under Husayn Bayqara's reign, Mir 'Ali Shir (1441–1501) served as vizier—the prime minister who was in charge of public affairs. Known as Nava'i ("the melodious one"), he was also a poet and bilingual writer in Turkish and Persian. Of Chagatay descent and thus not from the Turkish-Mongol aristocracy, but from the class of *bakhshi* (musicians) and scribes,[71] he became the patron of a painting workshop headed by the artist Hagi Muhammad. The painter Kamal al-Din Bihzad (acknowledged as among the great Islamic miniaturists, if not the greatest) was active in the cosmopolitan capital of Herāt before moving to Tabrīz. From an artistic point of view, this period, more or less the fifteenth century, is notable for the shift of the major schools and workshops involved in book arts from western Persia (from Tabrīz all the way to Baghdad) to the east, in Khorāsān, and central Asia (Samarkand, Herāt, and then the autonomous artistic current known as the "Bukhara school").

165. Muhammad Siyah Qalam, *Nomad Encampment*, early fifteenth century, Topkapı Sarayı, Istanbul, H. 2153 f. 8v. A work from central Asia (with strong Chinese influences) by the most emblematic Muslim artist.

Central Asian society—we don't know whether from Herāt, Samarkand, or another center farther east—produced some exceptional pictures at the beginning of the fifteenth century (1425 at the latest), which are notable both for the quality of the painting and the subject matter. They are found in two of the aforementioned four albums in Istanbul (H.2153; H.2160) and either

bear the signature of or are attributed to Ustad Muhammad Siyah Qalam (Muhammad of the Black Pen),[72] a mysterious individual. The pictures on unbound sheets are clearly influenced by Chinese art (some were even painted on silk scrolls) and are dissimilar in subject matter and feeling. The most interesting, even disturbing, works are a group that seem to depict scenes of nomadic life (plate 165) and groups of shaman (or *jinn?*), sometimes monstrous figures, engaged in bloody combat or ritualistic scenes. No text has yet been identified for which these pictures might be an illustration. Their descriptive power, with no allowance for background and with free images that float in space and time, emerges from a love of detail, from the contrast between the nakedness of the incredibly hairy subjects and the exquisite gold jewelry they wear, and from a much higher than average technical ability. Even some of the works that are clearly Chinese in derivation, such as *Nocturnal Nuptial Procession*,[73] are not easy to interpret in terms of subject matter or the identification of the protagonists. The detail is such that there is no doubt that this depicts an actual event (the nuptial journey of a Chinese or Mongol princess, escorted by Turks), but we do not know precisely which one.

We have documentation of the Shīrāz school from the period of Jalal al-Din Iskander ibn ʿUmar Shakykh ibn Timur, in the form of a sheet from a manuscript of Nezāmī's *Khamsa* (the *Iskandar-Nama*), made in Shīrāz in 1410–11,[74] and which exemplifies the evolution of an art that retains the lessons of Jalayirid Baghdad and Mozaffarid Shīrāz. Along with some thematic conventions (the stream below, the gnarled tree, people or petrified animals hiding behind the abstract rocks),[75] the figures now tend to be elongated, and the compositional quality is livelier

166. *The Prophet Muhammad's Journey to Hell*, from a *Mi'raj-nama* manuscript, c. 1430–1440, Bibliothèque Nationale, Paris, Suppl Turc. 190 f. 67r.

than the somewhat academic coldness of manuscripts dating from the end of the fourteenth century. The elegance of the text on this page should also be noted. It is written on the diagonal within a refined frame that terminates in a point. The continuity of this workshop during the reign of Ibraham Sultan is apparently confirmed by the anthology[76] (now located in Berlin) that was dedicated to his younger brother Bayshunghur. The more interesting text, however, produced under the patronage of this prince is the *Zafar-nama* (Book of Victory), a historical text that celebrates Timor's exploits, what we might call a live broadcast dated from 1436. Unfortunately, it is now dispersed among various collections.[77]

One of the most active *kitabkhana*, or workshops, was in Herāt, the center of power under Shahrukh. When his favorite son, Baysunghur, died prematurely at thirty-seven (1433), power passed to the seventh son, Muhammad Giuki, who died two years before his father (1445). Min-

167. Bihzad, *The Construction of the Khawarnaq Palace*, from a *Khamsa* manuscript by Nezāmī, 1495–95, British Library, London, Or. 6810 F. 154v. This miniature, executed with exceptional technical skill, depicts an episode that draws on themes from everyday life.

iaturists from every corner of the empire converged on Herāt, especially under Baysanghur's reign. (Shahrukh was more interested in history and in fact commissioned the anthology of historical writings by Hafiz-i Abru; he also was probably responsible for bringing to court copies of the Mongol *Jami al-Tawarikh* by Rashid al-Din, which served as a model for the genre.) Baysunghur, the most learned and enlightened of Timurid princes, was also a skilled calligrapher. If accounts are true, his work included Kufic and Thuluth calligraphy for the ceramic mosaics in the mosque built at the behest of his mother Queen Gawhar Shad in Mashhad. Traces of the era of Baysughur's reign in Tabrīz can be seen in the Jalayirid style of painting, and perhaps also in the organization of the workshops. According to a manuscript from 1427 by the workshop superintendent Ja'far al-Baysunqur, the atelier gradually became more specialized, with four calligraphers, six decorators, two decorators/painters, two painters, three bookbinders, one border illustrator, and two designers. A Timurid *Anthology* dated July 27, 1427 was acquired by the noted art historian Bernard Berenson and is now at the villa I Tatti in Settignano.[78] Some scholars have even seen these miniatures as a form of portraiture, but it should be clarified that they are idealized representations.[79] The most striking matter about these works is their formal rigor. With the death of Baysunqur, control of the court workshops passed to his brother, Muhammad Giuki, even though it appears that the actual execution of the work came under the direction of his nephew, Prince 'Ala al-Daula. The latter brought the important painter Ghiyath al-Din from Tabrīz to Herāt. The style imposed by Baysunqur continued long after his death, as seen in the *Mi'raj-nama* manuscript (plate 166, now in Paris),[80] one of the most beautiful ever made, and in a *Shah-nama* now at the Royal Asiatic Society in London.[81] It should be emphasized that, thanks to numerous patrons and perhaps to competition among them, the first half of the fifteenth century saw a flowering of this art form, full of vitality as well as inventive and refined solutions. By this point the artistic canon was established and the artists could express their individual talents. Potential was fully exploited, with the *Shah-nama*, once again, the primary text in use.[82] Indeed, the production of manuscripts seems to have been common, almost frenetic, at this time, yet still characterized by the highest standards.

The extraordinary painter Kamal al-Din Bihzad,[83] a genius whose signature appears on masterpieces of this art form, emerged within this context. Praise of his work verges on the extreme. To cite but one: "The master Kamal al-Din Bihzad has shown us the marvelous form and uniqueness of this art; his technique [of drawing], like the brush of Mani, erases the memory of all other painters in the world . . . . One stroke of his brush, through his mastery, has given life to inanimate forms."[84] With Husayn Bayqara as patron, the workshop (or *kitabhana*, literally: "house of the book"), headed by Mawlana Mirak Naqqash, counted several masters among its artists. The fact that vizier Mir 'Ali Shir Nava'i had his own studio supervised by the painter Hagi Muhammad is interesting. Bihzad was active in Herāt in the last quarter of the fifteenth century and then supervised what would become the Safavid school in Tabrīz. He was a key figure, artistically as well as historically, in the way he bridged the late Timurid and early Safavid eras.[85] In light of the master's fame within his lifetime, it is obvious that not every artwork bearing his signature was created by his own hand. Although a definitive body of work has not yet been established, scholars agree about the unquestionable attribution of certain works, such as the *Bustan* "Garden" of Sa'di manuscript (the great thirteenth-century poet from Shīrāz), created in Herāt in 1488 for Sultan Husayn Bayqara (now in Cairo's National Library).[86]

The composition of the illustration *Court Reception*, spread over two pages, highlights precisely how Bihzad, although continuing in the earlier tradition, makes the entire work freer and less frozen formally, imbuing the figures with naturalness (although they are neither portraits nor realistic pictures), creating an expectation that breaks with accepted precedents. Where previously no more than a glance was needed to perceive the sense of the painting, Bihzad shows details and specific incidents, allowing the viewer to become an active participant in the event, yet with complete respect for the historically established conventions. The left side of the illustration shows two figures engaged in conversation on a carpet beneath a domed tent and another covering that seems like a tapestry or textile. Across from them on a terrace—skillfully rendered in perspective, surrounded by a wall and a hexagonal tower—musicians and servants prepare a feast. A subtle atmosphere of excitement and expectation prevails. On the right page, a large terrace (perhaps a *talar*, although it lacks columns) looks out over the surrounding landscape of trees with tall trunks and a grassy, flowering hill. On the terrace some people are drinking, others are dancing, and servants are bearing food. The entrance on the right is splendid, depicted in careful detail. A servant emerging from the partially closed door threatens to strike an unwanted guest who seeks to barge in on the festivities. It is precisely this well-thought-out blend of classicism and nearly realistic description, with ironic sketches and views from everyday life, which makes Bihzad's work unique. A *Khamsa* by Nezāmī (Herāt, 1494) once belonged to Jahangir, the Mughal sovereign of India (r. 1605–1627), who made marginal notes in his own hand, attributing sixteen miniatures to Bihzad (now at the British Library).[87] It reveals the artist's exceptional ability, in both the more classical representations of interiors (fol. 214r), such as that of *Iskandar and the Seven Sages*, which has complex architecture, an idyllic outdoor landscape, seven individuals with varying physical characteristics and garments, and lastly, some small genre scenes, including one where a watchman sits at the threshold and looks out, bored, at passersby. There are classic outdoor scenes, such as *The Meeting of Sanjar and an Old Woman* (fol. 16), which has perfect balance and a rhythm of composition. Here the old woman is at the center, the sovereign is on horseback followed by three attendants at the right, and on the other side are four horsemen; the barely hinted landscape implies a circular space. There are also more eccentric scenes, such as *The Caliph Ma'mun Bathing* (fol. 27v) or the *Construction of the Khawarnaq Fortress* (plate 167), with stupendous sketches of lively scenes of everyday life. These works form the core of Bihzad's work. A copy of *Sanjar and an Old Woman* in another *Khamsa* by Nezāmī (c. 1490)[88] features a rocky landscape that anticipates the more complex, naturalistic architectural landscapes of the Safavid period. A figure, having dismounted his horse, fills a pitcher from a stream that rushes at the base of the rocks. Slightly above, a baby lamb suckles from its mother under the attentive eye of a shepherd. Great technical skill, an inexhaustible imagination, and studious attention to details (architectural, chromatic, and human) are the hallmarks of this artistic genius.

MINIATURES IN THE SAFAVID PERIOD

Despite all the twists and turns of its history, including during the period of Timurid domination when its political and cultural axis shifted eastward, Tabrīz was always an important artistic center. This quintessential frontier territory never experienced true stability. In the fifteenth century the Turkmen dynasties of the Qara Qoyunlu and the Aq Qoyunlu[89] vied for power and fought against the Timurid empire. Shahrukh defeated the Turkmen of Qara Yusuf and was able to hand over rule of the area to his sons, Iskandar and, especially, Jahanshah, until 1467, when Uzun Hasan (an Aq Qoyunlu) made it his capital and then passed on rule to his son Ya'qub in 1478.

In the early sixteenth century a powerful Turkish-speaking clan of Kurdish origin appeared on the scene; Esma'il I was key to this group's ascendancy. Born in 1487, he was named Shah at the age of fourteen, by which time he had conquered the Aq Qoyunlu, in 1501. He ruled until 1524, during which time he linked the fate of his dynasty to Shaykh Safi od-Din Ardabili (1252–1334), the founder of the Safavid mystic order, of which Esma'il claimed to be a descendent. Under Esma'il I, Persia became officially Shiite (Twelvers or Imamite) and was frequently compelled to face powerful rivals: the Ottomans to the west (who claimed victory in 1514) and the Shaybanid to the east (after 1512 the Safavids took control of Herāt, following a bitter battle at Marv in 1510, which paved the way to the east. The capital of the empire was initially Tabrīz, but it was later moved due to the threat of Ottoman attacks. (The city was occupied by Selim I in 1514, and it was during this period that the Turks first encountered Chinese porcelain. The first significant inventories of such items in the Sultan's possession in Topkapı date from this time.) The capital of the empire moved to Qazvin (under Shah Tahmasp in 1555) and then to the even more central location of Esfahān, at the behest of Shah Abbas I (1597).

From an artistic point of view, Shah Esma'il, like most founders of great empires, left few traces of his reign as he was continuously engaged in military campaigns. Thus, the school of miniaturist art at the court of Tabrīz, which was active throughout the first half of the sixteenth century, is not very distinguishable from the Turkmen work of Ya'qub Beg, which is remembered in association with a *Khamsa* by Nezāmī.[90] Turbans with red plumes (the origin in the Turkish term *Qizil bash*—red head) became a distinctive Safavid trait.[91] According to legend, such figures appeared in a dream to the head of the mystical Safavid fraternity, Shaykh Haydar (1456–1488, father of Shah Esma'il). The headgear in question, unfailingly depicted by painters, is tall and twelve-sided, symbolizing the twelve revered Shiite imams, with what seems to be a red plume at the center. But the first golden age of Safavid miniaturist art is linked to the name Shah Tahmasp I (born in 1514; r. 1524–1576), who arrived in Tabrīz (after having served as the nominal governor of Herāt when he was only two years old) more or less at the same time as Bihzad. The latter, perhaps already old and no longer active as an artist, became superintendent of the Royal Library, to which he brought his own unquestionable prestige, as well as the style and fashions of the late Timurid period in Herāt.

The most important manuscript produced in Iran under the patronage of Tahmasp (even though it may have been commissioned by Shah Esma'il) is a magnificent copy of the *Shah-nama* (760 pages, 18 × 12⅝ in. [47 × 32 cm], with 256 miniatures) known as the "Great *Shah-nama* of Shah Tahmasp."[92] The work entailed the contribution of numerous artists, and it was undertaken in three phases. The first phase was under Sultan Muhammad (the project "coordinator"), the second phase was under Mir Musavvir, and the third was under Aqa Mirak, at least according to Dust Muhammad.[93] In addition to these artists, the names of Mirza 'Ali, Muzaffar 'Ali, Shaykh Muhammad, Mir Sayyid 'Ali, 'Abd al-Samad, and at least five other secondary painters should be added. The work took at least a dozen years to complete (the only recorded date is 1527–28), and it was probably finished in 1535. It goes without saying that the artistic level is uneven.

The most famous miniature in this celebrated manuscript is a work by Sultan Muhammad, *The Court of Gayomars* (plate 168).[94] It covers an entire page and is characterized by pictorial virtuosity and narrative imagination. The sheet is framed and the margins are decorated with sponged gold. The layout is simple and precise, with two pairs of small horizontal blocks for text below and two more above, a double block to the left, and pairs of superimposed lines to the right. This detail is extremely significant, for it determines the rhythm of the composition, which proceeds in orderly fashion, albeit with a consciously disrupted symmetry. Three sides of the frame (with the exception of the fourth side, at the bottom) are characterized by the same decorative "breakthrough," with realistic details, such as rocks and gnarled, twisted trees that clearly emerge. The scene unfolds outdoors in a harsh but idyllic landscape, with Chinese-style clouds against a sky with a gold ground. King Gayomars is at the center of the rocky landscape, sitting with his legs crossed on an outcropping, while along the sides—almost like a Trinity—are two other figures (one standing and one seated) on slightly lower mountain peaks. The bot-

168. Sultan Muhammad, *The Court of Gayomars*, from the *Shah-nama* by Shah Tahmasp, 1525–1535, Collection of the Prince and Princess Sadruddin Agha Khan, f. 20v. The page is painted with such richness of detail and compositional complexity that it is considered one of the true masterpieces of Persian miniatures and Islamic art.

tom half of the miniature brings together a crowd that is divided into two semicircles, on the left and right. The center is dominated by a beautiful verdant landscape with a small waterfall[95] and animals of every species, especially wild beasts that are tamed by the extraordinary peace that reigns in this terrestrial paradise. The colors are soft but clear, extremely varied, and rich in contrast, creating a true symphony of images. The people, once again rather elongated, are soberly elegant, dressed in fur garments.[96]

Sultan Muhammad was a remarkable interpreter who masterfully was able to meld the Tabrīz and Herāt schools, even if here and there one sees a bit of academic mannerism, reminiscent of the coldness seen in the 1396 *Khamsa* by Nezāmī, attributed to Junayd. It is also very interesting to compare a miniature by Sultan Muhammad, *Sanjar with an Old Woman*,[97] with a painting of the same theme by Bihzad. In the former, the scene takes place inside a circular space (a convention already in use, but which then seemed to be particularly popular) below the usual stream (with ducks) and a crescendo of rocks that, running beyond the boundary of the frame, rise upward. Above the rocks, which are painted very abstractly (the space indicates a hill or a mountain), are trees (including a recognizable plane tree and cypress) against a background of Chinese-style clouds and a sun with golden rays in the upper left. The old woman who carries the hem of the sovereign's robe is almost identical in position and composition in both miniatures, but while Bihzad[98] had realistically depicted the sovereign bending forward to pay attention to the woman, the overall effect of this composition, which is technically superb, is much colder and more controlled.

Tahmasp's brother, Abu'l Fath Bahrām Mirza, also should be mentioned in the context of miniatures. He was an expert calligrapher (at least according to a third brother, Sam Mirza) and the sponsor of an album[99] that included the frequently mentioned preface by the Herāt painter Dust Muhammad. It was completed in 1544, when the artist was still director of the Royal Library and its workshop. He should also be credited as the artist of a signed work (c. 1540) contained in the "Great *Shah-nama* of Tahmasp,"[100] *The Story of Haftvad and the Giant Silkworm*. A painting of a rarely represented subject, the work demonstrates that the artist had fully absorbed the lessons of his teacher (Bihzad), but also had his own unique and somewhat contradictory style, expressed in strongly contrasting lines and an alternation between sometimes repetitive and banal motifs and ingenious innovations. Around 1540 artists were not only engaged in large book projects, but also painted individual pages, in a sort of portraiture. These were sometimes idealized, such as a work by Aqa Mirak,[101] but could also correspond to the truth, seen in the sheet with "Sarkhan (?) Beg," now in London.[102] It is said that Tahmasp was a controversial figure, but while not a "despicable coward,"[103] he was a troubled personality who seems to have been stricken by a powerful crisis midway through his long reign, which led him to reconsider his life's priorities. In the 1640s when the Indian Humayun, who was a refugee at the court of Tabrīz, (plate 169) asked to take several popular artists such as Mir Musavvir to his homeland with him (where he returned in 1555), the Shah raised no objections, a sign that he had lost all interest in the arts. In addition to Mir Musavvir, Mir Sayyid 'Ali, and 'Abd al-Samad also followed Humayun back to India. Although uninvited, it appears that Dust Muhammad may have joined them as well, because, it is said, he could not live without wine, which the King had prohibited by this time.[104] In 1548 Shah Tahmasp moved the capital to Qazvin and in 1556 promulgated the famous Edict of Sincere Repentance, which changed the atmosphere at court. Without completely banning artwork, this edict certainly limited the output of artists and dampened their enthusiasm. Yet as we have seen, a constant factor in the history of Persian miniatures is that production was not limited to a single workshop, but was spread among many. Thus the artists who did not follow Humayun to India (and, incidentally, those that did heavily influenced the artistic direction of Mughal miniatures) found refuge elsewhere, most significantly at the court of Ibrahim Mirza (a nephew of Tahmasp), in Mashhad.

The most notable among these artists were Shaykh Muhammad, 'Ali Asghar, and 'Abdallah-i Muzhahib, who worked on a manuscript of *Haft Aurang* (The Seven Thrones) by Jami (1414–1492), a great poet and mystic who lived at the court of Hysayn Bayqara in Herāt. Twenty-eight miniatures, completed for the manuscript over the course of nine years, are now at the Freer Gallery of Art. The miniature *Two Lovers Reach the Isle of Bliss*[105] proclaims the offspring from a

169. Sanwlah, *The Arrival of the Indian Humayun at the Court of Shah Tahmasp*, British Library, London.

great school of painting. Conventional elements dominate, both morphologically and graphically; Chinese-style clouds, which had been a feature for some two centuries, are depicted here almost as spirals, leading Basil Gray to rightly compare them to the even more stylized clouds found in Chinese textiles. The plane tree, still slightly gnarled and twisted, now has an unnatural alternation of yellow and green leaves. Finally, the rocks are much flatter, and after a long process in which this motif grew ever more fanciful, now seem almost realistic.

The transfer of the Safavid capital from Qazvin to Esfahān led to a more or less automatic shift of court workshops as well. The most important work commissioned in Qazvin seems to have been a *Garshasp-nama* (Book of Garshasp), painted by Asadi in the tenth century (now in the British Library, London).[106] Shah 'Abbas I kept the capital in the north for ten years, and followed tradition by commissioning a copy of the *Shah-nama*. Produced between 1587 and 1597, this work (now at the Chester Beatty Library in Dublin[107]) features miniatures signed by the important artist Sadiqi. There is no question that provincial workshops and studios remained active in centers where painting schools had long flourished, such as Shīrāz and Herāt.

A decisive shift occurred at the end of the sixteenth century, when the capital moved to Esfahān. Under Shah 'Abbas, the social, economic, diplomatic, and artistic policies led to a great period in painting (see also the chapters on architecture and carpets), a final flowering before the Safavid decline. The Esfahān school is associated with the name of the painter Riza, who was already active at the end of the sixteenth century and probably in competition (both artistically and from a generational standpoint) with the elderly Sadiqui. After Sadiqui's death in 1609, Riza became the undisputed leader in the world of painting and was accorded the honorific name 'Abbasi. Qadi Ahmad's treatise on painting[108] mentions the artist Aqa Riza (son of the artist 'Ali Asghar from Kāshān), and for some time there was some confusion as to whether this artist and Riza 'Abbasi were in fact the same person, given an uncanny number of coincidences. Riza 'Abbasi founded a school with his son Muhammad Shafi' 'Abbasi, (who derived his name not from his father but from Abbas II [1642–1667]) and other students, such as Mu'in, Muhammad Qasim, Muhammad Yusuf, and Muhammad 'Ali, all of whom, in one way or another, continued their master's style. Riza 'Abbasi did not lend his name to any particular manuscript (moreover, he signed his works most often with the phrase "drawing by the humble Riza 'Abbasi"[109]), but rather to a series of works on individual sheets of the type that had first come into fashion in 1540, with Aqa Mirak. In general, Riza 'Abbasi's painting shows careful attention to detail, with leaning and slightly curved figures[110] against backgrounds that are often painted gold, with plants, and Chinese-style clouds, following the now frequent custom for the decoration of the borders of illuminated manuscripts. Two of Riza Abbasi's well-known paintings provide an opportunity for reflection and comment. *Young Man Dressed in Blue* (plate 170) [111] is a classically idealized portrait of a fashionable youth, executed with painstaking detail. The other painting, in the same museum,[112] *The Archer Nashmi*, is quite different, almost caricature-like. The figure in this painting has a unique physique (nothing at all like the "beauty" in the aforementioned picture): square jaw, pointy nose, large mouth. His clothing does not conceal the prominent belly of a gourmand or heavy drinker. And while this archer does indeed hold a bow in his left hand, in his right hand he holds a pipe (a *qalian*) with a Franciscan monk painted on the glass or ceramic base. Both paintings are classic, as were depictions of pairs of embracing lovers, or young boys and girls stretched out languidly in a meadow. Other works, by later followers, were merely sensual or even erotic. Another important painter was Muhammad

170. OPPOSITE LEFT. Riza 'Abbasi, *Young Man Dressed in Blue*, 1585, Arthur M. Sackler Museum, Harvard University Art Museums, inv. 1936.27.

171. OPPOSITE, RIGHT. Riza 'Abbasi, *The Archer Nashmi*, 1630, Arthur M. Sackler Museum, Harvard University Art Museums, inv. 1960–197. This portrait has such an ironic streak it is almost a caricature. The image of a Franciscan monk in the base of the pipe is probably another playful message.

Zaman, who worked during the last half of the seventeenth century and who was a leading figure during that period. He was under the spell of European art, and his work provides the basis for the study of nineteenth- and twentieth-century Iranian art, which is rooted in this past.

Something should be said about certain recurring themes in Persian painting. In the realm of mural painting,[113] with the exception of the *hammam,* or bathing establishments,[114] decorative writing, geometric motifs,[115] or arabesques long predominated. If, however, we focus on the texts, we can see how narrative epics (especially the *Shah-nama* by Firdawsi and the *Khamsa* by Nezami) surpassed all others, including scientific manuscripts or books with moralizing content (such as the *Khalia wa Dimna*). There were also explicitly religious texts, the most famous being the manuscript of *Mi'raj-nama* (the Ascension or Heavenly Journey of the Prophet). Within the Iranian context, however, it is more interesting to examine books with obviously Shiite content. Oleg Grabar has written, "It is clear, with the single exception of the *Ascension of Muhammad*, Persian painting did not develop what one could call a sacred history in images, such as the Buddhist and Christian worlds did."[116] Miniatures with religious content existed during various periods and in various guises in Arab, Persian, Turkish, and Indian art.[117] But it is in the Safavid period that these themes underwent an interesting development,[118] particularly in relation to the evolution of religious dramas about the martyrdom of Hosayn (*ta'ziya*, literally "funerary sorrows"). A careful and detailed study of the subject, advanced about a decade ago by Maria Vittoria Fontana,[119] seems to clarify that while images (not only in miniatures) pertaining to a Shiite context certainly exist and are important and "curious" iconographically, they are not sufficiently significant to denote a particular school, place, or period.

FLOWERS OF WOOL
PERSIAN CARPETS

FRAGMENTS AND DOCUMENTS UNTIL THE LATE FIFTEENTH CENTURY

Textiles, particularly carpets, have great importance in Persian Islamic art. Even today in the collective imagination, the idea of luxury, splendor, and sumptuousness is associated with carpets, often described with the adjective "Persian." The very word evokes enchanted and distant worlds, extreme exoticism, and a temptation that is difficult to resist. We don't know where the history of Persian carpets begins, and the Iranian plateau could be one of the regions (like the Caucasus or central Asia) where this technique was developed. Both climate and important cultural reasons form the basis for this assumption. The carpet turns an everyday, undefined space into another realm, a space that is reserved, purified, and circumscribed for ritualistic reasons. The carpet can be an altar, and as such it responds to the compelling need to have a place where a priest—quite possibly a shaman,[1] a key figure in religious life in Asia, particularly among those Turkish and Mongol tribes that played such a large role in defining Iranian art—could fulfill his role "secure" from outside influences. This is the same security that each of us claims for our everyday living area, residence, or even tent. The idea of the tent is significant because of its nomadic dimension, and it represents an undeniable historical constant; indeed, it is canonized by the Koran as a tool of pilgrimage. Security and sacredness are specific to the carpet and are transferred to the building (more correctly, to a part of the building: the prayer hall), presenting a place for the community to gather: the mosque. The ground where the mosque is located is never sacred, but it becomes so as soon as floor coverings delimit the profane space—now trod upon by footwear—and set it apart from the area in the building assigned for religious function. Thus, it becomes clear that the entire mosque is not a place of worship, but only the part designated by a floor covering, which can vary, depending on climatic conditions. In Iran, with its harsh winters, covered and heated rooms are used, called *shabestan*, while in the summer an open-air prayer space, known as a *musalla,* is used.

Artistically the carpet looks like a mosaic made from wool. Shāpūr I (241–272), the great Sasanian king, had floor mosaics made by Roman prisoners in the new city he founded.[2] Muslim sovereigns, less inclined to a settled residence, used mosaics woven in wool and silk to embellish their tents and pavilions—an extremely ancient tradition. One of the most famous carpets mentioned in sources was the so-called "Spring of Khosrow,"[3] a work of extraordinarily high quality, used to cover the floor of the *iwan* in Ctesiphon, home to the imperial residence. In fact, judging from descriptions, this was not a true carpet knotted in silk or wool, but rather a sort of woven mat that incorporated precious gems (emeralds, rubies, sapphires, and aquamarines) to simulate brooks, flowers, and plants that would never wither or dry out. This prodigious work was made in pieces, and fragments were taken off as booty by triumphant Arab armies in 642. The concept of the garden carpet, a clear allusion to paradise, is worthy of discussion, although it is not unique to Islamic tradition. Indeed, it reflects beliefs that go back much earlier, to Mesopotamian and Indian cultures, and Koranic descriptions represent a continuation of this earlier tradition.[4] This not only explains, in part, the predilection for floral imagery, but also constitutes a sort of link, an uninterrupted thread between the pre-Islamic past and the Arab conquest, one of those elements and motifs that surface—sometimes unconsciously, sometimes deliberately—throughout Persian Islamic art.

We could easily fill these pages with literary quotes that mention numerous production centers where carpets were knotted in ancient times,[5] but this would not make up for the absence of surviving carpets that can be attributed with certainty to periods prior to the sixteenth century. Among the most notable exceptions is a mat known as a *zilu*,[6] acquired in 1985 by the State Hermitage Museum in St. Petersburg and attributed by A. Ivanov, largely on the basis of inscriptions, to the fourteenth century.[7] Thus, apart from a small number of fragments, whose classification remains debatable, what we do know about carpets—excluding meager literary references—comes from secondary sources, such as miniatures, which provide scant knowledge of the earliest eras. The previous chapter addresses the reliability of miniatures as an iconographic source, and at this point there is an analysis of the principal decorative motifs. The research of A. Briggs on carpets in Timurid miniatures[8] is somewhat dated, although subsequent studies of other manuscripts and miniatures have resulted in significant modifications to her observations. In any case, it becomes clear how the typologies employed belong to a repertoire of geometric-based interlacings, with a broad use of simple figures—circles, squares, hexagons, octagons, stars, and crosses—intersected and superimposed in various ways. More markedly floral ornamentations are derived from and inspired by such geometric figurations. This can be confirmed by a fragment (25⅝ × 12 in. [65 × 30 cm]) now in the Benaki Museum in Athens, for which a fifteenth-century date has been suggested.[9] It is very likely that Persian carpets from the Seleucid to the Timurid period do not differ a great deal from Turkish carpets of that time, examples of which exist in the mosque of Ala ad-Din in Konya.[10] Works of this type have a repeated geometric motif, making even a large-scale carpet's execution rather simple, without requiring the aid of a preparatory drawing.

Italian painting from the thirteenth and fourteenth centuries gives us some idea of the carpets that were popular at that time. Generally the context is a scene involving the Virgin Mary, with the carpet at her feet, reminding us of the sacred nature of the object, even in an utterly different sort of context.[11] Incidentally, despite the tremendous and universal fame of Persian carpets—for example, the Venetian ambassador, Josafat Barbaro, visiting Tabrīz in the second half of the fifteen century, expressed his enthusiasm for them[12]—they do not appear frequently in European painting until the very early seventeenth century (above all in Flemish works, where they often serve as backgrounds for sumptuous tables with still lifes). This coincided with increasing trade and the opening to the west encouraged by the Safavid sovereign Shah 'Abbas I (1587–1629). The geometric decorations on carpets appeared hand in hand

172. Detail of the decoration of the south *iwan* of the Congregational Mosque in Yazd

with contemporaneous architectural ornamentation. Beginning with the Il-Khanid period—actually as early as the late twelfth century, as the mausoleum of M'umina Khatun in Nakhchivan (1186) attests,[13] and more generally in the late thirteenth and early fourteenth centuries—there was an increasing use of enameled ceramics in buildings. This is seen at the mosque in Natanz (1307–8),[14] but also at the mausoleum built by Oljeitu at Sultaniyya (1313/14–16),[15] and the practice evolved during the mid-fourteenth century, with the floral motifs employed at the mosque at Yazd (plate 172, c. 1375).[16] These geometric motifs correspond fairly closely to each other and suggest that if they did not have common models (the most likely candidate would be book arts, to which we will return shortly), at least there was a commonality of spirit. This is corroborated by the interior of the so-called blue mosque in Tabrīz (1465,[17] although the plan of that building is not very Persian), where the wall ornamentation harmonizes closely with the carpets, in this case Turkish.

SAFAVID INNOVATIONS

The Safavid era (1501–1722) brought what K. Erdmann, the most authoritative carpet scholar of the last century, has called a veritable revolution,[18] and fortunately sufficient examples survive to give us an idea of this historic production. The mechanism is quite simple, but ingenious: repeated geometric designs gradually disappear, to be replaced by a scheme with a centralized medallion and quarters of medallions in the corner pieces of the central area. It should be noted that the idea of the infinite possibility of repeated motifs is not abandoned, but rather the scale of the work is vastly expanded. A carpet at the Calouste Gulbenkian Foundation Museum in Lisbon (208⅔ × 87⅖ in. [530 × 222 cm]), formerly in the imperial Hapsburg collections, is a superb example.[19] It is obvious that this is a transitional work, if one notes the size of the central medallion, which is disproportionately large compared to the rest of the field, just as the corner designs seem too small. In any case, the medallion is based on a central octagonal star with a floral background. The rest of the field of the carpet is covered by a lively series of plant shoots that terminate in half-palmette shapes, superimposed upon a geometric grid. The border design, which is often quite difficult to interpret in the absence of a measured preparatory drawing, is discretely resolved, without symmetry or homogeneity, but through the change of direction of the two sides. While the design concept is experimental, the knotting technique is of the highest level, and the color palette is masterfully distributed, making this refined carpet a truly superior and imperial work. It was certainly an extremely rapid transitional phase. The celebrated carpet of the Dukes of Anhalt, now in the Metropolitan Museum of Art (26 ft. 6 in. × 7 ft. 3 in. [8.1 × 4.1 m]; warp in silk, weft in cotton, pile in wool with asymmetrical knotting),[20] is believed to have been part of the booty captured by the Turks during their unfortunate siege of Vienna (1683). Even with its central corner pieces missing, it still strikes a perfect balance between the ornate central medallion and the background. The latter has a vertiginous spiral motif on three different levels, against which vividly colored peacocks stand out; the border motif seems similar to that of the background field in the Lisbon carpet.

Perhaps the most celebrated carpet in the world, the so-called Ardabīl carpet,[21] consists of a pair of identical carpets, not an infrequent phenomenon. One was acquired in 1893, for the then considerable sum of 2,000 pounds sterling by the Victoria and Albert Museum in London, with the money raised through a public financing campaign organized by William Morris. The other, which came to light in 1914, was used in part to restore its matching counterpart and is in the collection of the J. Paul Getty Museum in Los Angeles, California. It is signed and dated to year 946 of the Muslim era (1539–1540) and is quite large (34 ft. 6 in. × 18 ft. 2 in. [10.5 × 5.54 m]) and perfectly conceived and balanced in every part. According to tradition, these carpets came from the sanctuary of Shaykh al-Safi in Ardabīl,[22] although there are some doubts about this, since the impressive dimensions of the two pieces do not match the spaces of the mausoleum. It might be best to relate them to another great religious building, the tomb of Imam Reza in Mashhad. The central medallion has a polylobate shape, surrounded by sixteen ovals, two of which, along the vertical axis, contain two mosque lamps; the corner quarter of medallions are perfectly balanced. The background, which is an intense indigo blue, is studded with myriad floral buds supported by slender curving stalks. The well arranged border has an alternation of elongated scrolls and other polylobate shapes. The inscription reads:

> I have no refuge in the world except Your threshold
> There is no protection for my soul save this portico
> Work of the servant of the Holy Site Maqsud Kashani in the year 946.

The verses are by Hafiz, one of the Shīrāz's greatest poets. Unfortunately, we know nothing about the carpet's creator, but it was most likely only overseen by the Maqsud, who employed a large team of workers for at least three years. It is thought to have been made in Tabrīz, based on stylistic characteristics and because of that city's proximity to Ardabīl (or it might be attributed to a workshop in Kāshān, given the provenance of Maqsud). It was executed, at least in part, in accordance with a preparatory drawing measured off in millimeters. The persistent rolled ribbon motif (*chi-chi*), clearly Chinese in derivation, was seen as early as the Mongol era, but appears throughout the Islamic artistic repertoire of the Safavids until the time of the Ottomans; it is even present in work of the Mamluk era in Syria and Egypt.

Another masterpiece is in Milan, at the Poldi Pezzoli Museum (on loan from the Villa Reale in Monza).[23] This imperial carpet (plate 173), made in Tabrīz and dated (1542–43), featuring a central medallion and hunting scenes, is signed Giyath al-Din Jami (not the same Giyath who signed numerous textiles and worked in Yazd and Esfahān). Technically it is similar

173. Carpet with a hunt scene, from Tabrīz, 1542–43, Poldi Pezzoli Museum, Milan

to the Ardabīl carpet, with a silk warp, three cotton wefts (the example at the Victoria and Albert has a silk weft), and a wool pile, with asymmetrical knotting. Its considerable size (22 ft. 4. in. × 12 ft. [6.80 × 3.65 m]) makes it a serious candidate for the carpet meant to accommodate the sovereign's throne. In fact, each carpet has its own logic and mode of use, which can be understood only by sitting oneself at its center, which allows one to appreciate fully the decorative motifs from the proper distance. The Milan carpet has a sober, eight-lobed central medallion, with a scroll and pendants repeated in the corners and a flowered background against which figures of horsemen are engaged in a hunt. The carpet is symmetrical, along a central axis; the original preparatory drawing was one-quarter the size of the actual carpet and was rotated to achieve the desired effect. It is important to note how, even before Islam, the hunt theme was traditionally associated with royal power (for example, the marshland hunt scene at Taq-i Bustan). Thus, this carpet could be used by the Shah when resting after a long hunt.

Another carpet, which can be dated to the second half of the sixteenth century, also at the Poldi Pezzoli Museum in Milan (16 ft. 7 in. × 4 ft. 1 in. [5.07 × 2.27 m]),[24] belongs to an intermediary typology (plate 177). The warp and weft are in silk, and the pile is wool with silver brocade. At the center is a small polylobate medallion against a blue ground with flowers and birds. Against the red background of the main field, arranged symmetrically with relation to the center, are two vases, angelic figures, animals confronting each other (panthers, or more likely tigers), dragons beneath a tree who threaten a pair of birds, and fighting animals (a realistic lion that attacks a Chinese *chi-lin*)—all amid a riot of flowers and leaves supported by harmonious floral plant volutes (buds and leaves), arranged exuberantly and interspersed with various animals. The inner band between the border and the main field contains a long poetic inscription (until now poorly translated), citing the "Darius of the time," a formula used only for the Shah. This was probably a carpet woven for Tahmasp, but it can also be linked to the so-called Sanguszko carpets, discussed below. There is a carpet in the Khalili Collection in London (97⅝ in. × 78 ⅜ in. [248 × 199 cm]), in wool with silver brocade,[25] with a large central medallion and quarter-medallions, rampant lions, floral motifs against an indigo blue background, and noteworthy for its ten elegantly inscribed bands between the border and the field. At the Berlin museums[26] is another large carpet (plate 174) with medallions and animals, from the second half of the sixteenth century (14 ft. × 88⅝ in. [427 × 225 cm]; warp and pile in wool, weft in cotton). The carpet has a dark blue ground for the medallion and border, an intense red field, and white central corners; the border iconography is unusual, with fish and ducks. The quality is excellent, although it does not reach the heights attained by some of the aforementioned examples. The carpet at the National Gallery of Art in Washington,[27] (14 ft. 4 in. × 11½ in. [437 × 225 cm]; wool pile on silk warp with wool and cotton weft) is more harmonious, and the medallion and animals against a ground with flowers and vines are completely integrated.

The so-called royal Swedish carpet is even more refined than the examples described above. With hunting scenes in silver-brocaded silk (18 ft. 2 in. × 9 ft. 4 in. [5.55 × 2.85 m]; royal collection, Stockholm, inv. N. 447),[28] it can be dated to the late sixteenth century. The ornamentation is simply perfect; the center is marked by an octagonal star-shaped medallion with a scroll and pendants, precisely replicated in the corners. The gorgeous, intense red field has bands of Chinese-style clouds (known as *chi-chi*), interspersed with hunters that stand amid their prey—lions, with other animals scattered about the field; there are also dragons and phoenixes. The border is equally sumptuous, and in this case, too, the only way to describe this carpet, which clearly has an imperial provenance, is as a masterpiece. Another sixteenth-century carpet is notable: the so-called "Chelsea" carpet, named for the London neighborhood where it was purchased from an antiquarian in 1890, by the Victoria and Albert[29] (18 ft. 4 in. × 10 ft. 4 in. [5.41 × 3.15 m]; silk warp and weft, asymmetrically knotted wool pile). The design is not based on a single central medallion, as in the cases discussed previously, but on a multiplicity of these (there are eight: two whole medallions, two half-medallions, and four quarter-medallions), staggered and connected to each other by ovals. The medallions have an intense indigo blue ground, against which the animals seem to move and the flowers blossom. This sort of design, with staggered and repeated diagonal motifs, also appears in a carpet now at the Metropolitan Museum of Art (plate 180; a similar example is in Lyons),[30] in which the grid has alternating colors and the background fields have dragons and phoenixes facing off, an obvious reference to China. This is a classical scheme (formerly seen in Timurid art) perhaps documented by a miniature attributed to the great Bihzad and dated 1487–88.[31]

Kāshān, in central Persia—not far from Esfahān, the third Safavid capital after Tabrīz and Qazvin, famous for earthenware as well as carpets—produced carpets made entirely from silk. The precious nature of the materials employed (with silk one can obtain an extremely high density of knots, resulting in a miniaturist's clarity of detail, and produce colors that are also quite brilliant, particularly the yellow, made from costly saffron) and the quality of the drawing make this work the absolute zenith attained by this art form.

Under the Safavids the conceptual approach to the world of carpets changed, along with the idea of design. While they were once seen as objects of use, more or less the exclusive furnishing for many people, they now became works of art and were conceived and fabricated as

174. Carpet with animals and medallions, second half of the sixteenth century, Staatliche Museen, Berlin—Preussischer Kulturbesitz, Museum für Islamische Kunst, inv. i 7/56

such. The consequences were incalculable. As for every work of art, in every part of the world, there are many different factors that contribute to the birth and development of a movement, and the nature of the client is undoubtedly extremely important. With the sixteenth century Persia experienced the rise of what we might call a national feeling, with a strong religious component.[32] The key figure during this period was probably the long-reigning Shah Tahmasp (r. 1524–1576), an enigmatic personality. After a period of patronage, he underwent a mystical crisis that led him, during the final years of his reign, to become disinterested in the arts, but at this point the seeds had been sown, and the harvest would be reaped regardless. The centuries-long artisan tradition of carpet-making provided a solid foundation for an object that in the sixteenth century was held to be a perfect one, both technically and artistically.

The division of labor was quite important. The selection of wools and their carding preceded what was perhaps the most complex and specialized operation—the dyeing process. Whether wool or silk was used—and there were specific, very different colorants for each material—organic materials were generally employed, from the mineral and plant world, but also some from the animal world (after the discovery of the Americas, red obtained from cochineal insects was also imported to the East); the dyeing profession was handed down from generation to generation. If one compares fifteenth-century miniatures, more classical Turkish carpets (which are very similar to contemporaneous Persian examples), and older nomadic finds (the few surviving examples preceding the introduction of chemical colorants, around the end of the nineteenth century), there is an extraordinary increase in colors and tones during the Safavid era. This factor, often underestimated or even ignored, was decisive for providing the designer of preparatory drawings with a range of choices that was vast and no longer confined to two basic colors, red and blue. The silk carpet from Kāshān with hunting scenes, now in the Angewandte Kunst Museum in Vienna[33] (plate 175, 22 ft. 4 in. × 12 ft. 5⅝ in. [680 × 380 cm]), is striking in its splendor, and it will occur to even the most naive and distracted observer to compare it to a beautiful miniature. Indeed, one of the most illustrious masters of the time—Sultan Muhammad (see "Timeless Figures: Persian Miniatures")—is often credited with the preparatory drawing for this carpet, based on its stylistic features. This may seem logical, but some questions remain. The knotting technique is quite complex, and in a silk carpet with such dense knotting (over 800 knots per square inch), the possibilities for representation increase considerably. The knot does not have the same size horizontally and vertically (it is wider than it is tall, although one can adjust the weft, for example, to achieve more balance), frequently with the result of compression, due to the iron combs used to tighten the knots, and a distortion of the design. In other words, two plus two rarely equals four in carpets (that is, two horizontal knots and two vertical knots do not form a small square), and in order for the most intricate design to be transferred to measured paper (where one point equals one knot), the intervention of an expert is required, someone who functions in an intermediary role, between the designer and the knotter. Thus, the teamwork becomes highly specialized, with all the attendant implications, economically, socially, and artistically.

Two other carpet types should also be assigned to the sixteenth century. Made entirely from silk and more modest in size, they are exemplified by one in the Louvre[34] and another at the Metropolitan Museum of Art. In the Louvre carpet (plate 176, 43 × 48⅞ in. [109 × 124 cm]), the design is directional, that is, the carpet is meant to be viewed from one side. This is the first such instance we know of, and it is a type that would become extremely popular in India, as

175. Carpet with hunting scenes, from Kāshān, MAK—Österreichisches Museum für Angewandte Kunst, Vienna. The preparatory drawing for this carpet, entirely in silk, is attributed to one of the greatest Islamic miniaturists from the Safavid era: Sultan Muhammad.

seen in the floral carpets from the Mughal era.[35] These feature animals, some imaginary and Chinese in origin, such as the mythical *chi-lin*, depicted individually or in combat with each other (the eternal theme of the lion or panther that attacks an ox or a gazelle), against a Chinese background of rocks and flowers. The Metropolitan Museum of Art carpet (96⅜ × 66⅛ in. [245 × 168 cm]; inv. N. 14.40.715) features a central four-lobed medallion against a refined floral ground. Both works have similarities with book arts in general and bindings in particular.[36] It is useful to compare the carpet with animals to lacquered covers such as the one in the Keir Collection in London, signed "Rida" and dated 1612.[37] The same can be said of the Metropolitan Museum of Art carpet, which follows a scheme that was widely used for engraved and gilded leather bindings, a design that would also be revived for book cover plates in the Italian Renaissance.[38]

This leads us to the theory that the development of carpet design was inspired and supervised by court workshops that created illuminated manuscripts, an art form that was held in high esteem by the sovereigns. It is a convincing hypothesis for small-scale carpets, but it seems less convincing in terms of larger scale works, made for an imperial patron or for the court, where we should not underestimate the possible link to architectural decoration (ceramic mosaics, but also painting, although scarce traces of the latter have survived). While the artistic milieu was the same, and the artists would have worked under the supervision of trained workers when they were not employed by the Shah, a degree of autonomy was granted to artists in the *naqqashkhana* (the house of design). Large carpets, conceived for prayer halls in a mosque or a palace (in this case scenes with animals or hunts would be appropriate) probably were intended as an accompaniment to the walls or domes. A carpet that was formerly in the collection of Prince Roman Sanguszko in Paris[39] (21 ft. × 10 ft. 6¾ in. [6.40 × 3.22 m]) fits this description and is only one example of some important artifacts (plates 178–79). It is made from

176. LEFT. Carpet with decoration of animals, from Kāshān, sixteenth century, Musée du Louvre, Paris, inv. n. 6741

177. ABOVE, RIGHT. Carpet, from Kāshān, Poldi Pezzoli Museum, Milan, inv. 424

178–179. PAGE 228. Overall view and detail of a carpet with medallions and animals, from the collection of Prince Roman Sanguszko, Miho Museum, Tokyo, 16th–17th century. The corner motifs in the central section are very similar to ceramics above the arches at the caravansary of Ganj 'Ali Khan in Kermān

wool (executed in Kermān, using the "vase" technique, described below), with a complex decorative layout (symmetrical on a central axis), that seems like a compendium of all the styles in fashion in the sixteenth century: a central medallion and quarter-medallions, with hunting scenes, animals in combat, and a floral ground. The central medallion, which is oval and subtly polylobate, has a central diamond shape with fighting animals and two pairs of elongated ovals with, respectively, pairs of standing angel figures and seated musicians separated by a cypress tree, while the rest of the space is filled with intersecting arched ribbons. The scroll below has two seated lute players, and the pendant shape has figures of angels, also seated. In each of the corner shapes around the center, which are wider than the quarter-medallions, there are three hunters on horseback; at the center of the scroll, there is a half lotus flower with a small fish, and there is a peacock at the center of the pendant shape. The rest of the field is an indigo blue, covered with minute designs of plant vines with flowering buds, individual animals, and pairs of animals (imaginary, Chinese-influenced, and others) in combat. Two pairs of blue gazelles that face each other are not a unique motif, for they also appear on a carpet with animal motifs at Harvard University's Fogg Art Museum.[40] The border is equally magnificent. In the corners there are small medallions with animals in combat, and at the center there is a medallion

180. PAGE 229. Carpet, Musée des Tissus, Lyons, inv. 25423. The decorative grid of this carpet is particularly complex. The clashing dragons and phoenixes are a motif from the Far East, of Mongol derivation, at this point assimilated into the Islamic repertoire.

with two standing figures, one of which is winged; these lie against a red ground where dragons and phoenixes, both Chinese in derivation, face off. This long description is justified by the fact that this is a masterpiece, with no exaggeration or abuse of the term. The carpet was clearly executed in Kermān, as technical analysis confirms. In that city—in the main square, which in a certain sense anticipates the grand royal plaza in Esfahān—there is a monument, a caravansary,[41] dated 1598, that was built by the governor Ganj ʻAli Khan beginning in 1596. He was an intimate friend, follower, and ally of Shah ʻAbbas, and the architectural decorations in ceramic mosaic and tile are perfectly integrated with the carpet. Gang ʻAli Khan had spent a long period of time in eastern Iran (Khorāsān), and there is a persistent tradition, in part supported by archaeological findings, according to which the local blue-and-white ceramic production (inspired by the Far East) was brought to Kermān via the immigration of three hundred Chinese ceramists,[42] which would bring things full circle.

The "vase" technique at Kermān was first identified and described by May Beattie,[43] who observed how in these carpets (floral, where the design may or may not have a vase, from which the name derives), a thread of the warp is raised and almost superimposed upon the contiguous thread, thereby allowing a very dense wool knotting (with a considerable expenditure of

181. Silk carpet, brocaded in silver, sent as a gift to Venice by Shah ʿAbbas I in 1603, Basilica of San Marco, Venice, inv. n. 26

material and therefore resulting in a very solid, heavy, and costly end product), with a compact and velvety pile surface. It is interesting to note how the decorative scheme—based on staggered floral diamond shapes—but not the technique, was used in the seventeenth century in northwestern Persia and in the Caucasus.

Even a concise history of Safavid carpets must mention Shah ʿAbbas I. This brilliant sovereign encouraged the continuity and full evolution of work undertaken by his predecessors, and he elevated carpet-making to the level of industry. The development of the arts and commerce, with international implications, was part of his political and economic program, attested to by the fine carpets that he sent as a diplomatic gift to Venice in the early seventeenth century (1603).[44] These were silk carpets, brocaded in silver (made on looms in Kāshān and Esfahān), and standard in size (137¾ in. × 70⅞ in. [250 × 180 cm]), with delicate floral motifs, although with certain decorative incongruities, typical of an art form that was not yet completely codified (plate 181). These appealed to the imaginations of the recipients.[45] *Kilims* (or *gelims* or *ghilims*), flat textiles without pile (which Europeans undoubtedly thought were eastern tapestries), were

182. Velvet brocade, Civico Correr Museum, Venice, inv. Cl. xxii, n. 37. This is a work with a Christian subject (perhaps a variant of the Virgin and Child), a motif that was not foreign to Safavid Persian culture at the time of Shah 'Abbas I.

respected and treated like works of art, too. One carpet that is particularly noteworthy is made from silver-brocaded silk, with the coat of arms of Sigismund III Vasa, King of Poland, in the center.[46] It was commissioned and imported by an Armenian merchant (the insertion of the coat of arms increased the cost by five crowns) and is now in Munich, at the Residenz Museum (96⅞ × 53⅛ in. [246 × 135 cm]; inv. WC3). Another silk "tapestry" brocaded in silver is at the Metropolitan Museum of Art;[47] the central medallion, which is oval and polylobate (with a scroll and pendants), contains a horseman confronting a mighty dragon, while the background field has individual animals, animals in combat, and flowers. In the corners around the central quarter-medallion is a renowned depiction of Laila and Majnun, from a work by Nezami, which was also a popular theme in textiles from Yazd signed by the master Ghiyath. A well-known artist who is thought to have also been active in Esfahān, Ghiyath was in the service of Shah 'Abbas, teaching him the techniques and secrets of weaving (plate 182).

In 1878 at the Polish Pavilion of the World's Fair in Paris, some carpets belonging to the noble Czartoryski family were exhibited. Although the carpets are Persian in origin, the term "Polish carpet" (or "polonaise") entered carpet literature. Rather small in size (about 80 × 60 in.

[200 × 150 cm]), with silk pile, these carpets have sumptuous floral decorations, some with medallions, and a selection of extremely pleasing color combinations. Many specialists consider these to be among the most beautiful carpets ever produced, although at times they have a hint of self-satisfaction, making them feel a bit affected. A large "Polish carpet" in silk (with a cotton weft; 190 × 86⅝ in. [483 × 215 cm]) is now in the Metropolitan Museum of Art.[48] Much more complex and ornate than the carpet given as a gift to the city of Venice, it has a sort of central diamond shape (with a European noble coat of arms) and a field with lively floral forms; it is dated to the mid-seventeenth century, when workshops were at the height of their carpet-producing activity. A silver-brocaded carpet (90⅞ × 65¾ in. [231 × 167 cm]; inv. VT-1045), formerly in the collection of Baron Stieglitz and now at the State Hermitage Museum in St. Petersburg, can be described as "strange" by virtue of the asymmetry of the field design, which has octagonal (or modified square) medallions with floral backgrounds, connected to rectangular scrolls (these too have four additional points) and small, quadrilobate circular medallions. This carpet, which has a classical floral border, has a fragmentary, repetitive, and decentralized design. Other small format, classic, silk "Polish carpets" (undoubtedly produced in series, using the highest quality techniques) can be found in the Cleveland Museum of Art[49] and the collection of the Dukes of Buccleuch and Queensberry,[50] which, with other examples, document the considerable production capacity for carpets in Persia during the seventeenth century.

Having reached its apogee between the late sixteenth century and the first half of the seventeenth century, Safavid society and art entered a period of decline, which ended in 1722 with another invasion from the east, this time by Afghan tribes. In the mid-eighteenth century an important figure emerged, Nadir Shah,[51] a tribal leader of Khorasanic origin, who promoted military campaigns from India (see the next chapter "Persia from the Baroque to the Neoclassical Eras") to the Caucasus. He brought to Iran the "Peacock Throne," but also many skilled artisans, who were active in several fields of the arts. There was continuous back and forth pillaging and fighting that greatly disrupted the social fabric and also brought about profound changes in the production of carpets (techniques and designs were passed from one part of the country to another, in the wake of more or less forced migrations). From the nineteenth century on, carpet production would also be strongly influenced by European tastes and requirements.[52]

SYMBOLS AND MOTIFS

This chapter, which is only a rapid excursus into a fascinating and complex world, cannot be considered complete without at least mentioning the symbolism of the motifs that appear in carpets, an intricate and nonlinear subject. Floral designs are the easiest motif to trace. Beginning with the more or less mythical "Spring of Khosrow," the idea of the flower and the garden becomes a preponderant and permanent feature of carpets. The importance of green spaces, whether planted or not (easily summarized by the term *bustan*, or garden, which can refer to a meadow, park, garden, orchard, or forest), goes back to the beginning of time and is consciously understood as a reference to paradise (or *paradeisos*) and the mythical garden of Eden.[53]

There have always been flowering gardens, from ancient India to our own time. Islamic culture was no exception, and the Koran has an idealized image of the four-part garden (the Persian *chahar-bagh*), to define the Paradise of the Just, with four rivers (milk, honey, wine, and water), fruit trees, the darkest green, clusters of grapes (misunderstood as the *huri*, the ever-virgin creatures), and finally cushions and carpets, upon which one could rest and contemplate eternity.[54]

This scheme would have tremendous significance for the city planning of Esfahān, but also for the grand mausoleums in India, such as Humayun (conceived by a Persian architect), Akbar, I'timad ad-Dawla, or the Taj Mahal, not to mention the gigantic *baghs*, or gardens, built at the behest of the Mughal sultans in Kabul, but also and above all in Kashmir. The theme of flowers, connected to the idea of paradise, has always been central to the Islamic artistic experience, whether one thinks of the mosaics of the Dome of the Rock in Jerusalem or those of the great mosque in Damascus; and vegetation in its infinite forms has inspired and been reproduced in the arts, from Spain to China. Polychrome flowers and veritable four-part garden carpets, such as those from the nineteenth century (which undoubtedly imitate more ancient examples), are traditionally assigned to the region of Kurdistan in northwestern Iran.[55]

Probably no earlier than the late seventeenth century, the *boteh* motif,[56] an almond shape with the end delicately folded back on itself, became widely disseminated in Persia (principally in carpets, but also in fabrics and then in architectural decoration in enameled brick). This may have been inspired by the cypress, an evergreen that was much loved throughout the east and particularly venerated in Iran (it is associated with Zoroastrianism, but also with the worship of various famous local saints). This motif was extremely popular, not only in Persia and in carpets, but also further east, in India, where it was used in the field or borders of shawls,[57] finally ending its evolution in the west (as *paisley*),[58] where it has been reinterpreted by fashionable designers for foulards and ties.

For long periods the field of carpets was dominated by repeated geometric designs. In addition to practical reasons, tied to facility of execution, these motifs meshed well with Islamic beliefs, which saw in the flow of ornamentation a continuum, proof of infinite divine creation. Once again, the Turkish example is helpful, where these emblems, perhaps totemic schematizations linked to tribal designs, are called *gül* (flower) in Turkish (the flower par excellence being the rose).[59] Safavid carpets are different in that, in addition to a substantial change in layout, they have a different decorative philosophy, linked above all to a presumed Sufi (or mystic) influence[60] in the development of decorative designs. S. van Cammann[61] is mainly responsible for this interpretation. Part of this scholar's analysis is well reasoned and detailed. For example, the Ardabīl carpet is interpreted, in part on the basis of the verses in its inscription, as a means of access to the heavenly spheres, and the hanging lamps in the medallion immediately evoke the celebrated "Sura of the Light" [XXIV] and verse 35. However, van Cammann's analysis seems somewhat distorted by its origins. Before becoming engrossed in eastern carpets, van Cammann was an erudite interpreter of Chinese art (particularly textiles, to which he dedicated at least one masterful essay),[62] and he has adopted the same investigative methods, transferring them to the reality of Islamic mysticism, finding in particular support in Persian poetry. In fact, the latter is strongly symbolic (see the extraordinary interpretation that A. Bausani gave to a celebrated work by Hafiz),[63] and is also connoted by enormous ambiguity. There is a celebration of young boys, even more than young girls, with their curls, beauty spots, coral lips, and perfect pearly teeth, in a passionate love song of the nightingale for its beloved rose (beautiful, but haughty and indifferent), which will pierce the heart with its thorn. There is a constant suspension between sacred and profane love, which is not to negate that a certain symbolism is concealed within the carpet designs, and indeed, in certain circumstances, such influences are clearly present,[64] but these are circumscribed examples that are quite recognizable. We should simply be wary of facile interpretations, the results of a low-level exoticism that carpet merchants have used to market the "mysteries" of the East and to build considerable fortunes for themselves, whereby everything relates to a mystical symbolism with Sufi origins.

The hunt, for example, is a motif that legitimizes power and the laic pleasures of court life (along with dances and banquets), of which we find solid evidence in the pre-Islamic period, in Persia and elsewhere, and which enjoyed formidable historical continuity. Clashes and combat between animals[65] is a simpler and more transparent example, and one that also has a long history, tied to classical symbolism of the male solar principle (the predator animal, above all the lion, but also the eagle, panther, or cheetah, which is in turn defeated by the sovereign, who hunts it down and thus ascends to a higher level). The predator/solar principle overcomes the lunar principle (the prey is almost always an ox or a gazelle with horns, signifying the crescent moon), in this case understood to be negative. A Chinese influence is also obvious on an iconographic level when a dragon attacks a phoenix, which represents a reversal of value, since the dragon in Iran became a creature of the underworld, while the bird, which also has an extremely long and glorious history, acquired solar and positive connotations. But in this case, too, it is often the hero that gains legitimacy by striking the monstrous creature (never really killing it, for there are never images of dragon corpses). In the Far East, there is a face-off, a balance, and an equilibrium, where the *yang* (male) and the *yin* (female) must coexist in perfect harmony.

And so is there no clear symbolism? In reality, there is something more or less constant and verifiable, in the most popular products, such as the *kilims*, but also in many of the carpets that come from looms in towns and villages less touched by the carpet's evolution from object of use to work of art. We have already spoken of the sacred nature of space in carpets. In this sense the borders, as van Cammann has rightly stressed, represent a sort of limit or confine, a "door" that leads to another dimension. All this works as a defense, particularly against the *jinns* ("genies," benign or malign sprites, often mentioned in the Koran), which, for reasons that cannot be analyzed here,[66] are repelled by sharp points or acute angles. Curiously this protection against the *jinns* is the explanation that Gonbad-i Qabus gave to justify the characteristic and unique exterior shape of his celebrated mausoleum. And so in the borders of many carpets we find zigzag or broken lines; indeed one might hypothesize that floral motifs and sinuous lines (often referred to as "in-and-out" design in specialized literature) also respond to this logic, which is rarely understood today.

PERSIA BETWEEN THE BAROQUE AND THE NEOCLASSICAL ERAS

After the Afghan invasion of 1722 the country experienced a period of great turbulence, marked by the rise of a remarkable figure, Nadir Shah Afshar, who was born in 1688 in a small village north of Mashhad and who reigned from 1737 to 1747. A leading commander,[1] he defeated the Indian Muhammad Shah and brought back from Delhi an enormous amount of booty, including the famous Peacock Throne and the *koh-i-nur* ("mountain of light") diamond. Above all, however, he compelled a large number of Indian artisans and artists to migrate to Iran. This was a decisive factor in the subsequent development of Persian art because a phenomenon of great interest had occurred in India. Persian artists, particularly miniaturists, had been attached to the court of Tabrīz with Humayun, as discussed on page 212. Emperors such as Jahangir (r. 1605–27) and Shah Jahan (r. 1628–57) were very aware of European culture, which arrived via splendid English herbariums, popular prints brought in by the Jesuits, and other sources, and which was quickly assimilated.[2] It was this European culture, filtered through the strikingly Eastern taste of India, that influenced Nadir Shah in the construction of his palace at Kalat-i Nadiri (plate 184). Its influence is evident from the palace exterior, which has an octagonal base, a "pumpkin-fluted" drum (which has now lost its roofing), and extremely beautiful reliefs to which we have applied the term "baroque," though certainly not in a derogatory sense.[3] The interior paintings, in contrast, are in line with Safavid output, seen in the pavilion of ʻAli Qapu at Esfahān. This is not to deny that European influence had already reached Persia in the seventeenth century. We wish merely to point out that decorative links can be more complicated than they appear at first glance. This movement would be particularly strong in southern Persia, specifically at Shīrāz, with the Zand dynasty (1750–94), founded by Muhammad Karim Khan, and would be a necessary precursor to the Qajar period (1799–1923).

From an architectural point of view, the Zand and Qajar periods did not contribute significant planimetric innovations. The mosque continued to have four axial *iwans*, with the *qibli* preceding a cupola. The most important monument is the Masgid-i Vakil in Shīrāz (1750–79; the mosque was restored in 1825), the work of Karim Khan.[4] Built of salmon-pink stone, it is specifically reminiscent of India because of its twisted tree-trunk columns supporting acanthus-leaf capitals. The mosque has only two *iwans*, and the walls and arches are decorated with

183. Detail of the decoration of the pavilion of Karim Khan Zand in Shīrāz, eighteenth century

extremely beautiful tiles (plate 183) in an exuberant floral pattern dominated by the color pink. The representation of the flowers is quasi-naturalistic, and it may have served as a source of inspiration for the millefleur pattern in contemporary carpets.

The Nasir al-Molk mosque in Shīrāz, built between 1889 and 1890 by the architect Muhammad Hasan (plate 185), was inspired by the Vakil mosque. The vault, intrados, and small domes contain enameled bricks, recalling Seljuk Turkish ornamentation and the early Il-Khanid period. The Masgid-i Meidan of Kāshān,[5] although established much earlier, has a series of very interesting later additions, including the novelty of a two-level courtyard. The lower portion (which houses a water basin) is ten feet (3 m) below walkway level, which creates a very striking effect. Also noteworthy are the ceramic wall facings, of a type thereafter used only for tiles, with their effective range of colors, where the extensive use of deep yellow and pink is particularly appealing.

The most prolific client for architecture in the Qajar era was Fath 'Ali Shah (b. 1771, r. 1797–1834), who built large mosques in Qazvin, Burejird, Zanjan, and Tehran, the capital of the dynasty. The Qajars were also actively engaged in projects for the "embellishment," expansion, and reconstruction of the mosques, particularly in the "holy" cities of Qom and Mashhad, where the domes of the large sanctuaries were covered with gold-plated brick. Needless to say, large-scale projects, already in existence under the Safavids, for example in the Masgid-i Shah of Esfahān, were not abandoned. One distinctive feature was the accentuation of the bulbous shape of the dome, somewhat reminiscent of Indian work. One characteristic of this phase is the use of polychrome tile roofing, achieved with the *cuerda seca* (fireclay tile) technique,[6] already used by the Timurids (for example, at Herāt in the mausoleum of Gawhar Shad); it was also used by the Safavids in the Hasht Bihisht in Esfahān, and in beautiful and unusual wall facings with depictions of angels in the New Julfa cathedral in Esfahān.[7] This technique enjoyed particular success during the Qajar period.[8]

184. The palace of Kalat-i Nadiri, commissioned by Nadir Shah and built in his native country, eighteenth century

One of the freshest and most original creations (and also the most amusing, because of its incongruous use of Eastern themes reworked in a European key) is the pavilion of Karim Khan Zand in Shīrāz (mid-eighteenth century), with its classic motifs of the royal hunt, a subject that frequently appears in Persian art. But its architecture and landscapes are Western in inspiration, as are the faces (the men almost always have beards and broad moustaches, oval eyes no longer elongated as in the older, central Asian tradition, thick eyebrows, and long hair curled at the nape), which are all purely eighteenth century in appearance.

One of the best preserved buildings in Shīrāz is the Naranjestan ("Orangerie"), the patrician residence of the Qavam family. Built by Mirza Ibrahim Khan between 1870 and 1880, at the height of the Qajar period, it is a good example of civic architecture with related foreign influences (including Russian, a reflection of the political realities of the time). From an entrance pavilion with an interior lining of vivid ceramic tiles, the visitor enters a beautiful garden (customary in all traditional Persian houses, large or small), with orange trees and other fragrant plants, including roses. Of particular interest among the exterior panels are several high-relief stone slabs decorated with neo-Achaemenid molded scenes (plate 187), visibly inspired by examples in nearby Persepolis, a neoclassical mode followed throughout Persia of which very few traces remain today. The two-story gallery of the house provides a large space for reception rooms, but the most evocative area is the entrance portico with its columns and "mirror mosaic" ceiling, inspired by the work of Chihil Sutun, evidence of a taste that had become decidedly more gaudy. Mirrors as a decorative element for architecture, along with stucco, henceforth completely Europeanized in terms of technique and motifs, appear frequently. Shīrāz has the sanctuary (open also to non-Muslims) of Shah Cheragh ("Sovereign of Light"), the principal place of pilgrimage in the south, and the tomb of Sayyid Amir Ahmad, brother of the eighth Shiite Imam, 'Ali al-Rida, who is buried in the complex of the same name in Mashhad. A sanctuary in the traditional architectural style, it has thousands of tiny mirrors that reflect the sunlight with an effect that is far from sober. Mirror decoration of this type is consistently found in the most important sanctuaries of Iran, including those of the Imam Reza in Mashhad and Hazrat-i Ma'sume, sister of the Imam of Qom, who died en route to a visit to the Imam Reza. It also appears in less famous places, for example in the nineteenth-century Imamzada Shahzada Ibrahim in Kāshān. Mirror mosaics appear in civic architecture as well. In the Kharrazi building in Esfahān there are also polychrome glass partitions and stuccoes. The Nasir al-Molk building in Shīrāz (1883) is decorated chiefly with large glass panels and stuccowork, as well as mirrors, combined with paintings of flowers. The combination of the three elements (glass, stucco, and mirrors) also appears in the decoration of the Husainiyya[9] Amini of Qazvin (1873–78),[10] which is divided into three large rooms around a central courtyard.

The nineteenth century witnessed the spread of the *ta'ziya*, the Shiite religious dramas[11] that hinged on the sacrifice of Husain and his family in Karbala. Spaces appropriate for plays of this type were built in the large cities. They include the Takiyya Mo'aven al-Molk in Kermānshah (northwest Iran), which is divided into three parts, each devoted to a phase of the Karbala tragedy. The first, the 'Abbasiyya, was a courtyard with walls faced with polychrome tiles[12] that depict the dramatic events related to Hazrat 'Abbas, younger brother of Husain. The Husainiyya is named for the Imam who was the son of 'Ali (and grandson of Muhammad). It consists of a domed area connected to several rooms referred to as the Zainabiyya (from Zainab, sister of Husain). The courtyard of the Abbasiyaya has interesting wall paintings with figures of dervishes, with their customary long hair and other attributes, such as the *qashqul*, the begging bowl, an object of extremely ancient tradition.[13]

It has been said that one characteristic of Qajar architecture was its polychrome tile wall decorations. In Kermān the *madrasah* of Ibrahim Khan (a cousin and son-in-law of Fath 'Ali Shah) can be dated to 1816–17. It has tile panels done in the *cuerda seca* technique, with vases and blossoms (particularly roses), as well as the angel from the sacrifice of Abraham, executed in warm colors of yellow, green, pink, and white. The polychrome tile decoration of the neighboring *hammam* is also noteworthy; it has an explosion of white and yellow flowers with turquoise leaves against a dark background, in addition to ducklings facing each other and birds depicted back to back. The entrance to the *hammam*, on the large seventeenth-century square (near the bazaar) has interesting pictorial decorations[14] on the outside of the entrance niche.

Shīrāz is also the site of the Bagh-i Iram, a splendid park in the northern part of the city created by Muhammad Qoli Khan Ilkhani, a chieftain of the semi-nomadic group known as the Qashqa'i. He turned it into a large, evocative space with streams and various species of exotic and ordinary plants, including many cypress trees. Some eighty years later the aforementioned architect Muhammad Hasan was commissioned by Nasir al-Molk to build a large tripartite pavilion on several floors, complete with a water piping system that ran through the ground floor and helped to cool the building. The roofs feature fanlights decorated with very vivid tiles, depicting hunting scenes and animals in combat. The colors are combined in a tasteful and striking manner. Another noteworthy object in Shīrāz is the ceramic panel of the Husainiyya Mushir, which portrays a religious subject.[15]

Tehran, the new capital established in 1788 by Agha Muhammad Khan, was obviously at the center of the architectural developments of the new dynasty. The most representative building was the Golestan ("Roseraie") in the citadel, now in the northern district of the city. According to traditional Persian custom, the complex was built in a park with large plantains, cypresses,

185. Detail of the *iwan* of the Nasir al-Molk mosque in Shīrāz, late nineteenth century

186. Figures by Fath 'Ali Shah in the Taq-i Bustan cave, early nineteenth century

and pines. The *talar*, or exterior portico, is supported by two twisted columns made of stone from Shīrāz, as is the large marble throne brought from the palace of Karim Khan Zand, which was used for public audiences and for the principal festivals such as *nouruz*, the Persian New Year in spring. The ceiling is mirrored, and the walls are still decorated with mirrors and oil paintings of the Qajar rulers. Nasir al-Din Shah (r. 1867–92) greatly restored and expanded this royal palace. During this period polychrome tile decoration was extended to a large part of the pavilions,[16] with a variety of subjects, including scenes from everyday military life. More work was done on the Golestan at the beginning of the twentieth century (the period of Muzaffar al-Din Shah, 1896–1907), including a series of two-tone white and black tiles (1899), clearly inspired by photography, with neoclassical subjects, such as portraits of Parthian and Sasanian rulers adopted from antique coins. Another important achievement was the Sultanabad palace. Naturally, the fashion of these neoclassical structures (with one eye on the Persian past and one on certain aspects of European architecture, particularly Russian) was followed in many palaces of courtiers and the nobility.

The typology of the noble house is exemplified by the home of the Burujerdi family of Kāshān.[17] It has a lovely central garden with a large fountain, an entryway, two wings with various rooms (including servants' quarters), and a very beautiful reception room with an ingenious domed roof, reminiscent of the vaults of Amin al-Dawla's Timche in the Kāshān bazaar. The stuccoes depicting Cossack soldiers, hunters, and other representations taken from "the classics" are decidedly individual but not exceptional in comparison to contemporary artistic developments in Tehran. The persistence of these decorative typologies, particularly in stucco, can be seen in a strange early twentieth-century building, the fort of Bandar Tahiri, located

187. Bearers of offerings, detail of the bas-relief decoration in the pavilion of Karim Khan Zand in Shīrāz

in the extreme south of the country, not far from Siraf.[18] At least twenty stucco panels depict episodes from the great age of the *Shah-nama*, including a portrayal of Mahmud of Ghazna (998–1030) enthroned.

We have already alluded to the long reign Fath 'Ali Shah (1797–1834), characterized by particularly intense building activity. He also encouraged and patronized an increasingly visible interest in the European arts, on the one hand, and neoclassical taste, on the other. An impressive example of the latter is the idea of sculpting portraits in stone, seen in the Taq-i Bustan cave, one of the principal sites of Sasanian art. The Shah had his own effigy sculpted on the right wall (plate 186), above a beautiful wild boar hunting scene in the marshes. He is shown enthroned, with attendants and celebratory inscriptions. Fortunately, he was not as presumptuous as a well-known Egyptian, Ramses, who imposed his own features on depictions of many of his illustrious forebears. The fact that this was not an isolated case is confirmed by the sculpture of the same ruler on the rock above the Cheshme-i 'Ali ("Spring of 'Ali"), in the environs of Rayy, today a southern suburb of Tehran. Once a flourishing city, it was destroyed by the Mongol invasions and never truly recovered from the devastation. It is a picturesque site where carpets are washed and then spread out to dry on the surrounding rocks. Fath 'Ali Shah, easily identifiable by his very long beard (although the letters of his name are not clear), is accompanied by an attendant carrying an imperial parasol, like an Achaemenid soldier, except that the hairstyle is typical of the nineteenth century and he has a hunting hawk on his right arm.

There are also several famous oil portraits (on wood or canvas) of Fath 'Ali Shah, such as the portrait by the court artist Mihr 'Ali, now in the Nigaristan Museum in Tehran.[19] The use of a purely Western technique in these portraits is evidence of the new Persian artistic trends between the nineteenth and the twentieth centuries. However, the phenomenon itself is not new and can be fully documented in a brief backward glance. The European fashion had already gained a foothold in the second half of the seventeenth century and took root decisively in Iran, a necessary precondition for the phase we are now examining. The most noteworthy artist in this context is Muhammad Zaman,[20] who has been credited as having spent time in Italy and is believed to have converted to Christianity. He left a major series of works executed using Western techniques and depicting Western subjects, including *Sacrifice of Abraham* (1684–85), *Descent of the Holy Spirit upon Christ, Mary, and Joseph* (1682–83), and *Venus and Cupid* (1676–77),[21] in which a plausible synthesis of West and East is achieved with a sure hand. Mention must also be made of the large pictures of historical subjects, dating from the second half of the seventeenth century, that decorate the palaces of Esfahān. A work entitled *Shah Tahmasp of Persia Receiving Humayun Pasha of India*[22] on the west wall of the audience room is by Chihil Sutun, although it was subsequently retouched. This work is fascinating as it combines European subjects, such as the landscape visible through the window between the two rulers, and Indian typology, in homage to the visitor. Other interesting touches include the large moustaches of the Persian dignitaries and officials (which later would became a permanent feature of such art), as well as the dancers in the foreground, a subject already seen at Samarra, but now treated with a vivacity and a movement that will make it a favorite subject for painters in later centuries.

The European breeze of the seventeenth and eighteenth centuries was to become a steady wind in the nineteenth, a period that produced the striking personality of Abu'l Hasan Ghaffari, a native of Kāshān[23] and perhaps the most talented of the Qajar court painters. Definitely a "painter laureate," with a penchant for still lifes, he was sent by Muhammad Shah (1834–1848) to study in Italy. In addition to numerous large oil paintings and frescoes, such as those of the Nigaristan Palace,[24] two new types of works appeared: paintings on papier-mâché and polychrome enamels on metal. Strictly speaking, the former was not a novelty (painting on a layer of transparent varnish or lacquer had already been practiced in the classical Safavid period), but the technique became widely disseminated. It was applied not only to the covers of manuscripts, but also to mirrors, boxes, penholders, and various objects, in thousands of examples, with subjects ranging from portraits to flowers (which were extremely popular) to classic subjects of miniatures, including episodes from the *Shah-nama*, views of cities, historical events, and even imitation postage stamps.[25]

Cloisonné enamels are more closely linked to Europe (but admittedly also to China, which has a solid tradition in this field); until the nineteenth century these were not as esteemed by Muslims in the East as they were by their cousins in the West.[26] Iconographically these objects, including the *qaliyan* (water-pipe stands), are in complete accordance with lacquerwork and ceramics, heavily relying on the color pink.

NOTES

PERSIA FROM THE ACHAEMENIDS TO THE SASANIANS: 550 BC–AD 650

Introduction

1. Mallory and Adams 1989; Mallory 1997; Wiesehöfer 2003: 9.
2. Gamkrelidze and Ivanov 1984.
3. Scarcia 1985.
4. Brandi 1978: 50.
5. The principal reference is still Vanden Berghe 1959.
6. Ghirshman 1958, see, Duchesne-Guillemin 1978: 153.
7. For a full discussion in this regard, see especially Vanden Berghe 1959 and Ghirshman 1982.
8. Diakonoff 1985.
9. Wiesehöfer 2003: 24.
10. Porada 1962: 142–46; Barnett 1962; Genito 1986; 1995; 2001: 78.
11. Calmeyer 1987a; Stronach 1986; 1987: 288–91.
12. Cristoforetti 2000.
13. Cristoforetti 1999.
14. Gnoli 1980; 2000; Kellens 2001.
15. Molé 1953: 382.
16. See especially Pagliaro-Bausani 1960: 277–80.
17. Kent 1950: 142–44; compare, Goossens 1949: 36–37.

Darius: The Classicism of the Achaemenids

1. Von der Osten 1959: 98.
2. Compare Dandamayev 1985; Schmitt 1985: 414.
3. Sekunda 1991.
4. Cook 1985: 214–16; Eph'al 1988: 156; Dandamaev 1989: 70–102; Briant 1996: 61–72.
5. Briant 1995.
6. Vogelsang 1990.
7. Balcer 1972; Cameron 1975; Gallotta 1980; Fol and Hammond 1988: 235–43.
8. Burn 1962: 236–56; Bengtson 1967: 42–44; Cook 1985: 217–25; Fol 1988: 246–53; Dandamaev 1989: 103–78; Briant 1996: 127–73; Schmitt 2002: 292–94.
9. Burn 1962: 313–567; Bengtson 1967: 45–63; 2002: 294–95.
10. Schmitt 2002: 295–97.
11. Weiskopf 1989.
12. Dandamaev 1989: 234–313; Briant 1996: 586–709; Briant 2002.
13. Bichler and Rollinger 2002.
14. Briant 1995.
15. Huot 1976: 175.
16. Briant 1995: 138.
17. Genito 2001: 77.
18. Sarre 1922; Herzfeld 1941; Godard 1962: 97–140; Ghirshman 1982.
19. Vanden Berghe 1959: 215–22; Stronach 1987.
20. Boardman 2000: 53–60.
21. Boardman 1994: 47–58.
22. Boardman 1994: fig. 2.36.
23. Calmeyer 1987.b: 569–72.
24. Matthiae 1996: 234.
25. Calmeyer 1987.b: 569–78.
26. Matthiae 1996: 234.
27. De Francovich 1966; Francis 1980: 66; Ghirshman 1982: 222–23; Boucharlat 2002: 329–30; Compareti 2002: 49–54.
28. Pugačenkova and Rempel 1982: 42.
29. Huot 1976: figs. 21–26; Ghirshman 1982: 213–21; Boardman 2000: 62–77; Miller 2002: 314.
30. Ghirshman 1982: figs. 183–84, 276–77; Genito 1987; Callieri 1998.
31. Genito 2001: 80–81.
32. Vanden Berghe 1989: 1513–14.
33. Roaf 1983: 133.
34. Azarpay 1975.
35. Boardman 2000: figs. 5.5, 5.8–5.10, 5.13–5.14, 5.17–5.18, 5.20, 5.31–5.32.
36. Boardman 2000: 5.19.
37. A hypothesis also accepted by Briant 1995: 92.
38. Bittel 1983: figs. 239, 247.
39. Boardman 2000: 110–11.
40. Kawami 1986.
41. Walser 1966: 11–19, 55.
42. Briant 1995: 28.
43. Roaf 1974.
44. Tourovets 2001.
45. D'Erme 2002: 180–81.
46. Cristoforetti 2003: 58.
47. Imampur 2003.
48. Marshak 2002: 8.
49. Nunn 1988: plates 108–9.
50. Nunn 1988: plate 110; Calmeyer 1987.b: 577; Boucharlat 1997: 502, fig. 665.
51. Compare Calmeyer 1987.b: 578.
52. Gunter 1987; Miller 1993.
53. Summer 1986: figs. 1–2.
54. Kawami 1992: plates i-iv.
55. Ghirshman 1982: 243–66; Moorey 1986: 856–63; Gunter and Jett 1992: 63–77; Piacentini 2001; Rome 2001: cat. 110–15, 118–20.
56. Milan 2001: 119–23, 127–28, 130, 204–6.
57. Compare Summer 2003.
58. Boardman 2000.
59. Kuzmina 2002.
60. Compare Dalton 1964: 19–26, plates xiv–xv.
61. Compare Pichikian 1997: 313–21, figs. 1–3.
62. Moorey 1986: 864–69.
63. Robinson 1958; Bivar 1986; Boardman 2000: 174–78.
64. Boardman 1970; Boardman 2000: 152–74.
65. Ritter 1965.
66. Shahbazi 1992.
67. Schiltz 1994: 279–84, figs. 214–15.
68. Schiltz 1994: fig. 211.
69. Barkova 2001: 55.
70. Schiltz 1994: 282–84; Compareti, 2004. b: 150.
71. Farkas 1974; Genito 2001: 77; Miller 2002; Boucharlat 2002; Compareti 2004 a.
72. Cool Root 1979.
73. Rome 2001: 77.

Arsaces: The Parthians and Time Denied

1. Curtis 2000: 34; 2001.a: 113.
2. Selwood 1983.a.
3. Wiesehöfer 1998.
4. Schoff 1914.
5. Shiratori 1956: 145, 162–63.
6. Puri 1994.b: 256, 258.
7. Shiratori 1956: 142; Needham 1981: 240–41.
8. Rostovtzeff 1943.
9. Lozinski 1959: 22–25, 33–35; Coulston 1986.
10. Gabba 1966; Kurz 1983: 561–63.
11. Compare Coulston 1986: 61–62; Hermann 1989: 763–71.
12. Debevoise 1938: 86.
13. Compare Tourovets 2001: 229–33, 235–36, 239, 241–44.
14. Widengren 1983: 1261–1269; Leriche 2002: 3.
15. Van Wickevoort Crommelin 1998; Drijvers 1998; Ehrhardt 1998; Rajak 1998.
16. Kettenhofen 1998.
17. Grosso 1966; Posch 1998.
18. Needham 1981: 213, 222–23, 234, 240–41; Watson 1998: 281–87.
19. Compare Forte 1995.
20. Lozinski 1959; Frye 1967: 68–69; Lecoq 1987.
21. Grainger 1993: 40, 44–46, 56.
22. Brodersen 1986; Bernard 1994: 487–89; Lerner 1999: 13–31; Gaslain 2002: 6–7.
23. Compare Wolski 1974; Lozinski 1984.
24. Bernard 1994: 490–97.
25. Musti 1966: 160–77; Errington 1989: 274–89; Sherwin-White and Kuhrt 1993: 188–216; Bernard 1993: 493–97; Koshelenko and Pilipko 1996: 131–33; Lerner 1999: 45–62; Shipley 2000: 286–91.
26. Colledge 1979: 23; Duyrat 2002: 37.
27. Gaslain 2002: 8.
28. Gaïbov and Kochelenko 2002: 50.
29. Daffinà 1985: 163; however, also see Callieri 1996.
30. Gawlikowski 1987.
31. Kurz 1983.
32. Daffinà 1996: 19; Graf and Dreyer 1996: 200.
33. Shahbazi 1992.
34. Bivar 1983: 48–56.
35. Daffinà 1994: 19–21.
36. Shiratori 1956: 142; Needham 1981: 240–41.
37. Bivar 1983: 56–58.
38. Bivar 1983: 66–68; Arnaud 1987.
39. Rosenfield 1967: 41–54, 129–30; Puri 1994.a: 196–99; Boperachchi 1998.
40. Colledge 1979: 154; Puri 1994.b: 256, 258; Daffinà 1995: 17.
41. Lang 1983: 517–20.
42. Bivar 1983: 86–92; Gaslain 2002: 12–13.
43. Rosenfield 1967: 38, 253–58; Colledge 1979: 154; Frye 2002: 17.
44. Colledge 1979: 153.
45. Gaslain 2002: 13; Wiesehöfer 2003: 94.
46. Gaslain 2002: 14.
47. Colledge 1979: 156–60; Bivar 1983: 92–97; Schippmann 1998; Gaslain 2002: 14; Wiesehöfer 2003: 94–95.
48. Compare Ricciardi 2002.a: 19.
49. Schlumberger 1983; Downey 1987.a; Invernizzi 1996.
50. Vanden Berghe 1988.
51. Keall 1987: 327.
52. Lozinski 1995.
53. Compare 1987.b.
54. Colledge 1977; Colledge 1979: 105–31; Keall 1987; Von Gall 1998; Rahbar 1999.a; Gasche 1999; Downey 2002; Ricciardi 2002.b.
55. Invernizzi 1998: 51–53; Invernizzi 2001.a: 114–15; 2001.b; Lippolis 2002.
56. Curtis 2000: 30.
57. Turin 2002.
58. Keall 2002: 70–71.
59. Keall, Leveque, and Willson 1980.
60. Keall, Leveque, and Willson 1980: fig. 17.
61. Keall, Leveque, and Willson 1980: fig. 17.3.
62. Keall, Leveque, and Willson 1980: fig. 19.
63. Koyelenko 1966: 32, 45; Koyelenko 1977: figs. 13–14; Colledge 1979: fig. 43.
64. Invernizzi 2001.b: 138–41.
65. Invernizzi 2002: 39.
66. Invernizzi 2001.b: 136–41.
67. Rostovtzev 1935: 120; Schlumberger 1960: 253–64; 1970: 196–207; Ghirshman 1982: 1, 7–9, 89.
68. Invernizzi 1996.
69. Kawami 1987.a: 209–13; Mathiesen 1992: 17–19.
70. Vanden Berghe and Schippmann 1985; Schippmann 1987: 298–99; Kawami 1987.a: 69–110; Mathiesen 1992, 119–69; Haerinck 1999: 56–57; Boucharlat 2002: 60–63.

71. Vanden Berghe 1984: 41–53.
72. Kawami 1987.a: 35–37; Mathiesen 1992: 19–21, 173–74.
73. Kawami 1987.a: 37–43; Mathiesen 1992: 24–25, 174–75.
74. Kawami 1987.a: 43–45; 1992: 175–76.
75. Ghirshman 1982: fig. 59.
76. Kawami 1987.a: 45–48; 1992: 176–77.
77. Kawami 1987.a; 1992: 168–69.
78. Von Gall 1990.
79. Kawami 1987.a: 51–56; 1992: 22, 177.
80. Kawami 1987.a: 57–68; 1992: 165–68.
81. Compare Invernizzi 2001.a: 114; Invernizzi 2001.b: 134.
82. Invernizzi 1989.
83. Scarcia 1979; Kawami 1987.a: 111–17.
84. Scarcia 1979.
85. Ingholt 1954; Fukai 1960; Homès-Fredericq 1963.
86. Colledge 1979: fig. 20.
87. Compare Koshelenko 1977: fig. 76; Koshelenko, Lapshin and Novikov 1989: figs. 7–10.
88. Colledge 1976: 83–87, 221–34, plates 114–18; Browning 1979: 25, 36–37.
89. Colledge 1979: 148–49; Schlumberger 1970: 104–11; 1982: 47–50, figs. 59, 61, 63c; Downey 1994; Leriche 1996: 589–92.
90. Segal 1970: 9–16, 40, plates 1–3, 16.b, 17.a: 43–44.
91. Goldman 1999.
92. Al-Shams 1981.
93. Herzfeld 1941: plates ci–civ; Kawami 1987.b; Ghanimati 2000: 141.
94. Kawami 1987.b: 25–26.
95. Pilipko 2000: 69–76.
96. Ricciardi 1996.
97. Ricciardi 1996: fig. 7.
98. De Francovich 1984: 96–97.
99. Harper 1978: 160.
100. Debevoise 1934.a; Ettinghausen 1938–39: 646–51; Colledge 1979: fig. 17; Haerinck 1983.
101. Ettinghausen 1938–39: 659–62; Ghirshman 1982: fig. 132.
102. Choubak 1999.
103. Vanden Berghe 1959: plate 4.6; Eiland 1995–96: 113–16.
104. Willetts 1965: 265–74.
105. Ettinghausen 1938–39: 651–54; 1982: fig. 131.
106. Rahbar 1999.b.
107. Rahbar 1999.b: 93.
108. Compare Hermann 1977: 36; Boucharlat 2002: 56.
109. Needham 1981: 223–24.
110. Laing 1995.
111. Baratte 1996.
112. Harper 1987.
113. Maenchen-Helfen 1957; Lucidi 1969.
114. Harper 1987: figs. 97–98.
115. Lukonin 1977: 121.
116. Vienna 1999: cat. 36.
117. Harper 1987: fig. 101.
118. Baratte 2001.
119. Invernizzi 1998: 48; Invernizzi 1999.
120. Masson and Pugačenkova 1982.
121. Bernard 1985; Chuvin 1991; Bernard 1991.
122. Ghirshman 1982: figs. 348, 351–52.
123. Genito 1977: 15.
124. Hayashi 1975: 88–90, 93.
125. Fukai 1977: 21–61.
126. Debevoise 1934.b; Debevoise 1938–39; Ghirshman 1982: fig. 128.
127. Musche 1988: 7–285.
128. Compare Kawami 1987.a: 140–45; Kawami 1992.a; Sarkhosh and Curtis 1998.
129. Kawami 1991: 97; Kawami 1992.b: 14–15.
130. Kawami 1992.b: 14.
131. Pourbahman 1996: 120–21.
132. Pfister 1934–40; Ackerman 1938–39: 688–89; Maenchen-Helfen 1943; Will 1996.
133. Ebert 1982.
134. Schaefer 1943.
135. Ackerman 1938–39: 691; Schaefer 1943: 268; Stawiski 1979: figs. 54–60.
136. Lukonin 1977: 120.
137. Ackerman 1938–39: fig. 237; Ackerman 1946.
138. Ackerman 1946.
139. Sellwood 1980; Sellwood 1983.b; Vardanyan 2001; Duyrat 2002.
140. Duyrat 2002.
141. Bianchi Bandinelli 1966.
142. Ingholt 1969.
143. Ingholt 1969.
144. Schneider 1998: plate 11.
145. Schneider 1998: plates 8.2, 9, 13.3, 16.
146. Barattolo 1995: 104–5, plate 41.
147. Kawami 1987.a: figs. 31–32.
148. Rosenfield 1967: plates 56, 58–59.
149. Ghirshman 1982: 2–4.
150. Fukai 1960: fig. 32.
151. Vanden Berghe 1959: plates 28, 71; Ghirshman 1982: figs. 163, 166–68.
152. Vanden Berghe 1959: plates 71, 77–78, 127; Ghirshman 1982: figs. 197–203, 233–34.
153. Scarcia 1998.
154. Bouman 1974: 217.
155. Festugière 1983: 92–96.

The Khosrow Kings: Continuity As Reinvention

1. Cereti 1995–97.
2. Christensen 1971: 50–83.
3. Frye 1967; Yarshater 1971; Lukonin 1976: 136; Rubin 1998; Huyse 2002; Gignoux 2002: 184–85.
4. Gnoli 1995.
5. Maricq 1958: 307.
6. Sims and Williams 1996: 643.
7. Cribb 1990; Dani and Litvinsky 1996.
8. Kettenhofen 1982: map b v 11; Frye 1986: 124–32.
9. Fiorani-Piacentini 1984: 209; Fiorani-Piacentini 1992: 119–62.
10. Widengren 1964; Widengren 1986.
11. Compare Klimkeit 1982: 20.
12. Widengren 1964: 155–56; Marazzi 1979.
13. Frye 1967: 281–88; Hinz 1971; Hutter 1993; Huyse 1998.
14. Lukonin 1976: 194–96.
15. Shepherd 1980; Callieri 1990; Duchesne-Guillemin 1993.
16. Cribb 1990: 171.
17. Zeimal 1996.
18. Bivar 1998.
19. Cannata 1981: 21–24, 65–67; Litvinsky 1996.
20. Hannestad 1955–57: 436; Angeli Bertinelli 1979: 142–43, 148, 151.
21. Litvinsky 1996: 140.
22. Cannata 1981: 66; Litvinsky 1996: 140.
23. De La Vaissière 2002: 116–18.
24. Cannata 1981: 65.
25. Widengren 1952; Cannata 1981: 67–68.
26. Cannata 1981: 68.
27. Harmatta 2000.
28. De La Vaissière 2002: 222–54.
29. Harmatta 1974; Compareti 2003.a.
30. Stratos 1968: 14–17.
31. Stratos 1968: 103–20; Haldon 1990: 41–45; 2003.a.
32. Christensen 1971: 508.
33. Scarcia 2000.
34. Mango 1985: 105–18.
35. Forte 1984: 188; Pelliot 1996: 288; Forte 1996: 355, 364; Forte 2000: 185.
36. Harmatta 1971; Daffinà 1983; Compareti 2003.
37. Lukonin 1976: 154; Nikitin 1997: 168.
38. Harper 1993; Nikitin 1997: 173.
39. Macdermot 1954.
40. Marshak 2002.a.
41. Klíma 1968: 43–58; Gignoux 1993: 38–40.
42. Fontana 1986; Fontana 2000.
43. Huff 1993: 45.
44. Tavoosi and Frye 1989.
45. Russo 2003.
46. Schippmann 1993: 132.
47. Reuther 1938–39; Watelin 1938–39.
48. Kervran 1992.
49. Christensen 1944: 462–63; Mackintosh 1978.
50. Huff 1987: 334; Huff 1993: 58–61; 1998.
51. Lo Muzio 1993.
52. Ghirshman 1982: 166.
53. Lo Muzio 1993: 126.
54. Huff 1993: 59.
55. Trümpelmann 1984: 317–18.
56. Boucharlat 1999: 89.
57. Baltrušaïtis 1938; Pope 1938; Kröger 1982; Kröger 1993.a; Azarnoush 1994.
58. Thompson 1976.
59. Bromberg 1983: 257–61; Tanabe 1984: 36–39; Vanden Berghe 1989: 1514; Bromberg 1990; Shokoohy 1994.
60. Bromberg 1983: 251–52.
61. Rahbar 1998.
62. Ghirshman 1982: 264–65.
63. Tanabe 1980.
64. Rahbar 1998: 222.
65. Harper and Meyers 1981: 117.
66. Pasquini 2002.
67. Vanden Berghe 1993.a: 13.
68. Ghirshman 1982; Vanden Berghe 1983; Vanden Berghe 1993.b; Haerinck 2001.
69. Tanabe 1984: 36–39; Vanden Berghe 1989; Von Gall 1990; Vanden Berghe 1993.b: 74.
70. Vanden Berghe 1988: 1531; Vanden Berghe 1993.b: 78.
71. Vanden Berghe 1988: 1519; Vanden Berghe 1993.b: 74.
72. Frye 1972; Carter 1987; Choksy 1990; Bromberg 1991; 2002.
73. Goldman 1993.
74. Shokoohy 1994: 70.
75. Frye 1968: fig. 4; Vanden Berghe 1993.b: 74.
76. Bromberg 1983: 257; Bussagli 1986; Bromberg 1990.
77. Favaro 2004.
78. Bromberg 1990: 11.
79. Schlumberger 1960: 290–91; Schlumberger 1966; Harper and Meyers 1981: 99–122.
80. Peck 1969; Mackintosh 1978; Tanabe 1981: 110.
81. Von Gall 1971; Tanabe 1981; Tanabe 1984.a: 39–40.
82. Christensen 1944: 460–61; Vanden Berghe 1993.b: 87; Genito 1999: 382.
83. Kröger 1981: 443–44.
84. Tanabe 1981; Tanabe 1984.b.
85. Tanabe 1984.a: 40–42; Von Gall 1990: 100.
86. Harper and Meyers 1981: 69; Goldman 1989.
87. Tanabe 1981: 42–43; Tanabe 1984.b; Von Gall 1990.
88. Tavoosi, Frye 1989.
89. De Francovich 1984: 89–98.
90. Vanden Berghe 1993.b: 87.
91. Azarpay 1975; Marshak 2002.a: 37.
92. Vanden Berghe 1989: 1514.
93. Vanden Berghe 1993.b: 84.
94. Marshak 2002; forthcoming 2003.c.
95. Arnold 1938: 1811; Morgenstern 1938: 1373; Dimand 1972: 17–18; Gray 1979; Goldman and Little 1980: 292; Grube 1989: 201.
96. Ricciardi 1996.
97. Goldman and Little 1980; Goldman 1999.
98. Azarnoush 1994: 179–82; 2003.c.
99. Kröger 1993.a: 63.
100. Al-Shams 1981.
101. Khorasan and Yamauchi 1996: 143–45.
102. Herzfeld 1941: 308; Calmeyer 1976.
103. Ghirshman 1956; Balty 1993.
104. Ghirshman 1982: 140–46; Von Gall 1971; Keall 1990: 288; Balty 1993.
105. Cristoforetti 2002: 267 n. 245.
106. Ghirshman 1982: 182.
107. Ghirshman 1952: 9–10.
108. Porada 1962: 215; Monneret de Villard 1966: 279; Kröger 1993.b: 447.
109. Harper 1978: 24–100; Harper 1981; Marschak 1986; Trever and Lukonin 1987; Harper 1993.

110. Sasanian Silver 1967; Gunter and Jett 1992.
111. Harper 1993.
112. Compareti 2000.
113. Harper 1993.
114. Tanabe 1984.b: 44.
115. Bivar 1995.
116. Bromberg 1983: 255–61; Tanabe 1984.b: 36–39; Bromberg 1990.
117. Compareti 2003.b: 29.
118. Shepherd 1980: 69–73; Jett 1992: 121–27.
119. Schmidt 1980; Scarcia 2003.
120. Bausani 1978; Belenitsky 1981: 70–73.
121. Xia 1980; Harper 1990; 1993: 104, 106; Qj 1999: 383–97.
122. Harada 1939; Hayashi 1975.
123. Zhang 1995; Qj 1999: 420–27.
124. Ricciardi 1968–69; Bier 1978; Bromberg 1983; Jeroussalimskaja 1993; Scerrato 1994; Otavsky 1998.
125. Hansman and Stronach 1970; Kawami 1991.
126. Jeroussalimskaja 1993: 115.
127. Scerrato 1994: 77.
128. Compareti 2004.
129. Bier 1978: cat. 54.
130. Schuette and Müller-Christensen 1966: fig. 6.
131. Harper and Meyers 1981: 75.
132. Lee and Grenet 1998.
133. Ackerman 1938: 699.
134. Azarnoush 1994: 174–75.
135. Volbach 1966: 59–60.
136. Bromberg 1983.
137. Harden 1934; Schmidt 1934; Ettinghausen 1938.
138. Egami et al. 1966; Sono and Fukai 1968.
139. Rosen-Ayalon 1974.
140. Ricciardi 1967; 1970–71.
141. Wenke 1975–76; Alden 1978; Trinkaus 1986.
142. Harper 1978: 160.
143. Simpson 2000: 65.
144. Simpson 1998.
145. Von der Osten 1959: plate 105.
146. Fukai 1977; Harper 1978; Whitehouse 1993.
147. Harper 1978: 150–51; Whitehouse 1993: 109.
148. Harper 1978: 150.
149. Harada 1939; Scerrato 1961; Hayashi 1975; Harper 1978: 151; Whitehouse 1993: 110–11.
150. Kim 1986: figs. 9–38.
151. Balog 1974; Kröger 1998.
152. Overlaet 1998.
153. Rome 1994: 63 cat. 23.
154. Ghirshman 1982: 152.
155. Gyselen 1993.a: 125.
156. Gyselen 1989.
157. Borisov and Lukonin 1963; Brunner 1978; Gyselen 1993.a.
158. Baltrušaitis 1993: 41–82.
159. Lerner 1975.
160. Compareti 2000.
161. Marshak 2002.a: 142–45.
162. Lerner 1977; Gyselen 1993.a: 125.
163. De Francovich 1984: 83–86.
164. Gyselen 1993.a: 124.
165. Gyselen and Gignoux 2000: 301–2.
166. Göbl 1983.
167. Gyselen 1993.b: 128.
168. Gyselen 1993.b: 128.
169. Gyselen and Gignoux 2000: 301–2.
170. Harper and Meyers 1981: 125; Peck 1993: 413–15.
171. Gyselen 1993.b: 128.
172. Harper and Meyers 1981: 65.
173. Harper and Meyers 1981: 138–39.
174. Thierry 1993: 100, 109, 117; De La Vaissière 2002: 116–18.
175. Azarpay 1976; Silvi Antonini 1989: 119–20; Maršak 1990: 292, 295, 298; Schippmann 1993: 136–37; Marshak 1996.
176. Ghirshman 1982: 282–342; Grabar 1971.
177. Badawy 1987: 18–19.
178. Levi 1947; Lavin 1963.
179. Wilber 1937; Ghirshman 1982: 306–7.
180. Harper and Meyers 1981: 77.
181. Fontana 2000: 17–19.
182. Schmidt 1980.
183. Grabar 1971: 695–96; Romano 1994.
184. Curatola 1978; Compareti 1997–98–99: 91.
185. Curatola 1981.
186. Curatola 1978.
187. Dalla Barba Brusin and Lorenzoni 1968: plate 213.
188. Marshak 2002.a: 67.
189. Silvi Antonini 1989; Marshak 1994.
190. Jerusalimskaja 1972; Compareti.
191. Compareti 2000: 336–39.
192. Compareti 2003.a.
193. Potts 1992: pl. xii.
194. Keall 1995.a; Keall 1995.b; Keall 1998.
195. Compareti 2003.a. Also see Callieri 1998: 34.
196. Rosen-Ayalon 1984.
197. Herzfeld 1926.
198. Gelfer-Jørgensen 1986; Grube 1994.
199. Sun 2002.
200. Compareti 2003.
201. Marshak 2002.b: 12.
202. We will grant him the last word, but not without expressing Heartfelt thanks to Matteo Compareti for his exceptional assistance. He has been a truly tireless "fisher of pearls" in this sea, and without his contribution, I would not have been able to take on this task.

ISLAMIC PERSIA: SEVENTH–NINETEENTH CENTURY

Introduction

1. Even in one of the texts that most perceptively delves into the development and evolution of Islamic art, the Iranian contribution, while not ignored, is perhaps somewhat underestimated; compare with Grabar 1989. Ettinghausen 1972 is extremely up to date in terms of its formal rigor and philological acumen.
2. We are well aware of the ideas in Said (1978) regarding the "colonial" way of looking at the so-called Orient.
3. Wilkinson 1973.
4. Whitehouse 1980, with extensive bibliography.
5. Pope and Ackerman 1938–39.
6. Monneret de Villard 1942; Scarcia 1987: 273–85; Scarcia 2000: 171–227, 175–80.
7. Regarding Viar, see Scarcia 1975: 99–104; for the iconography of this dragon, see Curatola 1982: 45–63.
8. Curatola 1979: 7–11.
9. Rogers 1969: 385–403.
10. Scarcia and Amoretti 1991.
11. Curatola 1987: 77–93.

Mud, Brick, and Turquoise: The Architecture of Persia

1. O. Grabar 1989 is still relevant. Regarding the problem of a Muslim aesthetic, also in terms of figurative work, see the essay in Scarcia 1995.
2. Finster 1994.
3. The archeological mission in Esfahān worked from 1972 to 1978, under the direction of Prof. Umberto Scerrato. See the recent contribution in Scerrato 2001: XXXVII–LIII.
4. Eugenio Galdieri's bibliography on Esfahān (not only on the Congregational Mosque) is vast; see Galdieri 1995: XI–XXII. In terms of this mosque, see the three volumes *Esfahān, Masǧid-i Ǧum'a* 1972, 1973, and 1984. For more on the mosque, also see Grabar 1990.
5. Byron 1993: 239–40.
6. Ventrone 1977: 85–107.
7. Van Berchem 1909: 367–78.
8. It is interesting to note how numerous inscriptions that appear on this monument contain the terms *ta'mir* (to repair or restore) and *ta'zin* (to embellish), which have very different meanings.
9. In the restoration work of the roof structures (including specifically the one corresponding to a *musalla* [open-air oratory] as a *mihrab* documents), white and blue ceramic fragments were discovered from both the Timurid and the Safavid periods. A careful examination of this material might dispel doubts.
10. Adle and Melikian-Chirvani 1972: 229–97.
11. Deniké 1935: 69–83; Voronina 1958.
12. *Corpus of Historical Memories of Southern Kazakhstan* 1994: 133.
13. Zipoli 1977: 41–76.
14. Golombek 1969; Melikian-Chirvani 1969; Pugachenkova 1970.
15. On the significance of Ghaznavidi, compare Bosworth 1968.
16. Rempel 1936.
17. Tomb of the caliph al-Muntasir (built at the behest of his Greek mother), who died in June 862; Creswell 1966: 317–19.
18. Hillenbrand, 1989, p. 83.
19. Fleury 1930: 43–58.
20. Gobolot 1979.
21. For information on the stuccowork in Samarra, see the classic study by Herzfeld 1923.
22. Regarding Jurjir, compare Godard 1938; also see Grabar 1990: 47–48, figs. 44–46.
23. Bartol'd 1921; Bivar and Gunbad-i Kabus 1965, 2:1139.
24. Sourdel-Thomine 1953: 110–21; Pinder-Wilson 1985: 89–102.
25. Maricq and Wiet 1959; Tronsdale 1965: 102–8; Moline 1973–74: 131–48.
26. The decorative analogy with metalwork has been noted in a splendid and very well documented essay: Giuzalijan 1978: 55–83.
27. Regarding this specific issue, see Maricq, "La signification du monument: son rapport avec le Qutb-Minar de Delhi," in Maricq and Wiet 1959: 65–67.
28. Ball 2002: 21–45. Another useful essay in the same publication is by Flood, F. B., "Between Ghazna and Delhi: Lahore and its lost Manara": 102–12. Regarding isolated minarets, see O'Kane 1984; Moline 1978–79: 95–102. Seljuq minarets have been studied in depth in Hutt 1998. Also see Azarpay 1981 and Azarpay 1986. Finally, for bibliography and in-depth analysis of Ghaznavid and Gurid architecture, see the exhaustive Hillenbrand 2000.
29. Burkett 1973; Hutt 1995: 255.
30. Hutt 1995: 256.
31. Crowe 1995: 260.
32. Scerrato 1959; unfortunately there is no definitive publication on this important excavation.
33. Schlumberger 1978.
34. Fontana 2002: 84–86.
35. Kleiss and Kiani 1995: 370–71. Kiani 1981.
36. Pribytkava 1953.
37. Umnyakov 1923.
38. Godard, "Ardistan et Zaware," 1936: 283–309; Ferrante and Galdieri 1968: 475–83.
39. Shirazi 1980: 6–78.
40. Regarding painting in Ardistan, see Fontana 2002: 73, plate 31 and note 131.
41. Robert Hillenbrand's doctoral thesis, which unfortunately has never been published in its entirety, remains the most complete work on the subject, Hillenbrand 1972. Also see Hillenbrand 1994.
42. Regarding this monument, see Pope 1936: 139–41.
43. Holod 1974: 225–88.
44. Stronach et al. 1966: 1–20.
45. Hillenbrand 1999: 107.
46. Oney 1979: 400–8; Daneshvari 1994: 192–200. Also see Fontana 2002: 75–76, figs. 34–35, plates 40–41.
47. Hermann 1999.
48. Kröger 2001: 47–50.

49. Regarding Nakhchivan, see *sub voce*, in *Encyclopaedia of Islam*, ed. C. E. Bosworth.
50. Berlin, Staatliche, Museen zu Berlin. Preussischer Kulturbesitz, Museum für Islamische Kunst.
51. See the chapter on miniatures.
52. Rawson 1984, chapter 5, "Chinese Motifs in Iranian and Turkish Art": 146–98.
53. Naumann 1969: 35–65.
54. Godard 1934; 1936: 125–60.
55. Daneshvari 1982: 287–95.
56. Godard 1934; 1936.
57. Bausani 1977: 161. Regarding Muslim astronomical observatories, see Sayili 1960. Specifically regarding the observatory in Maragha, see Bretanickij and Salamzade 1956: 61–85; Varjavand 1979: 527–36; Bausani 1982: 125–51.
58. Blair, "Mongol Capital," 1986: 139-51.
59. Much has been written on the Mongols and Sultaniyya. The religious situation has been extremely well documented by Scarcia 1981: 159–72. Also see Bausani 1968: 538–49; Zipoli 1979: 15–35. Curatola 1979: 7–11.
60. Curatola 1982: 45–63.
61. Blair 1984: 67–90.
62. For Il-Khanid architecture, a crucial text is: Wilber 1955. Regarding Natanz, see Blair, *Shrine Complex*, 1986. On the Il-Khanid period in general, also see: Komaroff and Carboni 2002.
63. Wilber 1955, n. 47: 139–41, figs. 69–86.
64. Scarcia 1981: 165.
65. Blair 1987: 43–96.
66. Hillenbrand 1989: 94.
67. Regarding Pir-i Bakran, compare Wilber 1955: 121–24; Paone 1995: 265–78.
68. Fontana 2002: 94, pl. 53.
69. Regarding these stuccos, which are truly precious and varied in typology, see the essay by Grube 1981: 85–96.
70. Miles 1978: 89–98.
71. Regarding Arg 'Ali Shah of Tabriz, see Mechkati 1974, n. 170: 6.
72. Krachkovskaja 1931: 25–58.
73. An excellent photographic survey is in Izadpaneh 1993: figs. 131–47.
74. Regarding this technique, see Wulff 1966: 117–25. The problem regarding ceramists is, in reality, quite simple: the colored oxides have substantially different melting points, and placing the colors next to one another runs the risk of undesired superimpositions or dribbles. Resorting to monochrome sheets, which are then suitably cut and reassembled to create the decorative motif, does not entail technical risks other than the labor intensive process. Naturally, over time techniques became more refined, and thus it became possible to produce polychrome tiles. Also see Wilber 1939: 16–47; and more recently Hillenbrand 1979: 545–54. There are also excellent images in Mirfendereski and Zonuzi 1992.
75. Regarding Yazd, a useful publication is Bonine 1975.
76. Golombek and Wilber 1988: 231–32.
77. The most useful and complete survey of Timurid architecture is Golombek and Wilber 1988. For a general view of this period, see the excellent catalogue Lentz and Lowry 1989; also O'Kane 1987.
78. Man'kovskaya 1985: 109–27; Wilber 1988: 284–88; Masson 1999.
79. It is thought that this is the place where Umm Haram, according to some sources a relative of the Prophet Muhammad (and according to others, the Prophet's wet-nurse), fell from a donkey and died.
80. The contents of the inscription on the cauldron are very interesting; verse 19 of Sura IX: "Do ye place the giving drink to the pilgrims, and the visitation of the sacred temple, on the same level with him who believeth in God and the last day, and fighteth on the way of God? They shall not be held equal by God: and God guideth not the unrighteous," and a prophetic *hadith*: "For he who for religious reasons builds a place for drinking, God will build enormous basins in Paradise."
81. Ratiia 1950. Also see Golombek and Wilber 1988: 255–60.
82. Cuneo 1986: 286–89.
83. Le Strange 1928.
84. Wilber 1979: 127–33; Bernardini 1994: 237–48.
85. Golombek and Wilber 1988: 260–63.
86. Monneret de Villard 1921: 315–24; Sanpaolesi 1971: 3–64.
87. Semenov 1949: 49–62.
88. Kouzmina 1985–86; Golombek and Wilber 1988: 271–75.
89. Bulatova 1965. Nemtseva and Shvab 1979; Golombek and Wilber 1988: 233–52.
90. Cuneo 1986: 286–89; Pugachenkova and Rempel 1968; Bier 1926; *Rigistan in Samarcanda* (in Russian), Tashkent 1950; Golombek and Wilber 1988: 263–65.
91. On the astronomical observatories, see note 57. Liebe-Harkort 1968: 160–64; Kennedy 1986: 578–80.
92. On Gawhar Shad in Mashhad, see O'Kane 1987: 119–30; Golombek and Wilber 1988: 328–31.
93. On Gawhar Shad in Herāt, see O'Kane 1987: 167–77; Golombek and Wilber 1988: 305–7.
94. On Ghazur Gah, see Golombek, *Timurid Shrine*, 1969.
95. O'Kane 1976: 79–92.
96. Hillenbrand 1989: 98.
97. The most complete work is Pugachenkova 1959.
98. Compare Curatola 1989: 77 and related bibliography.
99. Crowe 1995: 263.
100. Pugachenkova 1963; Golombek and Wilber 1988: 268–70.
101. For the architecture of Bukhara, see: Shishkin 1936; Dimitriyev 1950. On the Kalan mosque, see Golombek and Wilber 1988: 228–30.
102. On the *madrasah* of 'Abd al-'Aziz Khan, compare Nikiforov 1930.
103. Dibaj 1968; Morton 1974, 1975; Golombek and Wilber 1988: 362–64.
104. Pope 1956.
105. There is a vast body of literature on Persian gardens; see, in any case, the classic essay by Wilber 1962 and the pertinent essays in Petruccioli 1994.
106. Tabataba'i 1968.
107. Scarcia and Amoretti 1979; Membrè 1969.
108. For historical context for the Safavid period, see: Savory 1980.
109. Curatola 1987: 77–93.
110. Bastani 1976: 13–20; Scarcia lviii, 7–8, 1978: 387–91; Scarcia 1980: 57–82.
111. There is a great deal of literature on Esfahān. See Holod 1974.
112. Cuneo 1986: 342–47.
113. Carswell 1968; Karapetian, K. 1974.
114. Galdieri and Orazi 1969; Galdieri 1970: 60–69.
115. Golombek 1972: 5–14.
116. Galdieri 1979.
117. Ferrante 1968: 421–40.
118. Golombek 1972.
119. Galdieri 1979.
120. The extremely beautiful *Planographia Sedis Regiae* by Kaempfer (1712) is quite reliable, according to Galdieri. See the essay by this illustrious scholar: "Esfahan e la *Domus Spectaculi Automatorum*," in *Proceedings of the First European Conference of Iranian Studies*, G. Gnoli, ed., Panaino, Turin, 1987; 2, 1990: 377–88.
121. Grube VII/1 1974: 511–42.
122. See note 83.
123. Galdieri VII/2 1974: 380–405.
124. Ferrante, M., "Chihil, Sutun: études, relevés, restauration," in Ferrante 1968: 293–322.
125. Ferrante, M., "Le pavillion des Hasht Bihisht, ou les Huit Paradis à Ispahan: relevés et problèmes s'y rattachant," in Ferrante 1968: 399–420.
126. Luschey-Schmeisser 1985.
127. Beazley 1966; Beazley 1989.
128. Cuneo 1986: 347–52.
129. Wilber 1962.
130. Alemi 1994: 201–16.
131. Luschey-Schmeisser 1969; Luschey-Schmeisser 1972: 309-14.

Timeless Figures: Persian Miniatures

1. In this regard there are important ideas in Schafer 1963; Rogers 1970: 67–80; Gray 1963: 13–18; the influences, in any case, have never been in just one direction; see Watson 1973.
2. The excavations at Neshabur were carried out in Iran in the 1930s and 1940s by an American mission from the Metropolitan Museum of Art, New York; the finds were divided between New York and the Iran Bastan Museum in Tehran. Wilkinson 1973; Wilkinson 1986; Kröger 1995.
3. An Italian archeological mission worked at Ghazni during the 1950s; Bombaci and Scerrato 1959: 3–55; Scerrato 1962: 263–72; Bombaci 1966; Giunta 2003.
4. Lashkari Bazar, in present-day Afghanistan, has been the subject of French excavations; Schlumberger 1952: 251–70; Schlumberger, "Lashkari Bazar," 1978.
5. Regarding Takht-i Sulaiman, compare Naumann 1969: 35–65.
6. Whitehouse 1980, with extensive bibliography.
7. Regarding Afrasiyab, see Albaum 1975; on Pandzikant, see Belenitskii 1973; on Varahsha, see Shishkin, V. A., *Varahsha*, Moscow, 1963, in addition to numerous articles by B. I. Marshak. The classic text by Bussagli 1963, and Azarpay, ed., 1981, are more accessible.
8. For example, this occurs in metalwork. Certain iconographic incongruities have been noted on some Sasanian type silver plates: "They are, rather, a continuation of Sasanian royal tradition and were, in all likelihood, made in regions free from Umayyad control," Harper and Meyers 1981: 141. Regarding the transition period in Iran, between the Sasanian tradition and the new Islamic model, see Bosworth 1973: 51–62.
9. Harper 1979: 75–79.
10. Kröger 1977.
11. Schmidt 1937.
12. Thompson 1976.
13. See note 2.
14. Watson 1970: 41–47.
15. To our knowledge, there has been no specific study on these ceramics; compare Fehervari 1985: 98.
16. Fontana 2002: 77–83, fig. 37 (from Neshabur, "Vineyard" tepe, 9th century), 88–89, fig. 46 (from Rayy, 12th century).
17. Fontana 2002, figs. 38–42 (Neshabur), fig. 47, and plate 43 (Rayy).
18. Atil 1973, n. 50: 112–15.
19. Argument developed in an essay by Simpson (1981): 15–24.
20. Allan 1973: 111–20.
21. "The height of painted ceramics was achieved in Persia with *mina'i* or *haft rang* ceramics, produced, judging from pieces that have been dated, between 1179 and 1242. . . . The expensive nature entailed with multiple firings . . . makes this a product for the most refined audience"; Curatola and Scarcia 1990: 124.
22. Caiger-Smith 1985; Watson 1985.
23. Istanbul, Topkapı Sarayı, inv. H. 841; Melikian-Chirvani 1970: 1–262.
24. One of the many more or less coeval examples is the title page of the Kitab al-Diryaq (Pseudo

Galeno) at the Bibliothèque Nationale, Paris (Arabic ms. 2964), dated 1199 and executed in Mosul; Grube 1980: fig. 1 in color.

25. Lockhart 1968: 23–31.
26. Manāfi, al Hayawān di Abu Sayyid Ubaydallāh ibn Bakhtishū; Pierpont Morgan Library (ms. M. 500); Gray 1961; Canby 1993; Grabar 2000.
27. Fol. 11r; Gray 1961: figures in color on p. 20.
28. Fol. 13r; Fontana, M. V., *La miniatura islamica*, Rome, 1998: fig. 22 in color. 500, Fol. 28r; 1961: fig. in color on 21; Grabar 2000: fig. 12.
29. Fol. 28r; Gray 1961: fig. in color on 21; Grabar 2000: fig. 12.
30. Scarcia and Grube, "Il mondo islamico al tempo di Marco Polo," in *Marco Polo. Venezia e l'Oriente*, A. Zorzi, ed., Milan, 1981: respectively 159–72 and 101–58.
31. Boyle 1971: 19–26.
32. Private collection, London (formerly at the Royal Asiatic Society of London); Gray 1978.
33. Edinburgh University Library; Rice 1976.
34. Fontana 1998: 65.
35. Fol. 47v; *Abraham, Receiving the Three Strangers and Sarah in the Tent*; Gray 1961; figure in color on p. 25.
36. London, Khalili Coll., fol. 36v; Gray 1961; fig. in color on 24.
37. For a long time this manuscript was known as the Demotte *Shah-nama*; Georges Demotte was a Parisian antiquarian who, when he came into possession on the text (or part of it), he dismantled it, selling the individual illuminated pages to public and private collections. Regarding the manner and time in which acquisitions were made for the collection of Henri Vever (now in Washington, D.C., Arthur M. Sackler Gallery), see Lowry 1988: 31–37. For a study of the text and miniatures, see Grabar and Blair 1980. Robert Hillenbrand is in the process of preparing a book specifically on this manuscript.
38. Inv. n. 38.3; Gray 1961: 32, in color; also see, again in Washington, D.C., the eight sheets formerly in the Vever Collection; Lowry and Nemazee 1988: nos. 7–14.
39. Lowry and Nemazee, 1988: 76–77.
40. Boston, Museum of Fine Arts, inv. n. 30.105; Gray 1961: 28, in color.
41. Regarding this iconography, see Ettinghausen 1950.
42. Inv. n. 43.658; Grube 1980: fig. 6, in color; for a detailed iconographic analysis: Curatola 1989: 74, fig. 66.
43. Fontana 1986.
44. Not copied directly in various materials, which would occur beginning in the Il-Khanid era; Curatola 1989: 66–76, figs. 52–68.
45. A rock analogous to a twisted tree (and Chinese-style mushrooms on the bark) is in the beautiful miniature entitled *Zav Enthroned*, Washington, D.C., Freer Gallery S86.0107; Lowry and Nemazee: 82, figures in color on 83.
46. Abu al-Qasim Firdusi di Tus (Khorasan), c. 935–1025/26; the work is dedicated to the Ghaznavid Turkish sovereign, Mahmud in 1009/10. There is a fine Italian translation, although it is at this point "historical"; Pizzi, I., ed., *Il Libro dei Re. Poema epico recato dal persiano in versi italiani da Italo Pizzi*, 8 vols., Turin 1886–88.
47. Grabar 2000: 100.
48. The Mongols and the *Shah-nama* are the subject of numerous and lengthy studies: Melikian-Chirvani 1984: 249–337; Melikian-Chirvani 1988: 39–46; Melikian-Chirvani 1991: 33–148; Melikian-Chirvani 1996.
49. The so-called Houghton *Shah-nama*; a manuscript that unfortunately was dismantled among various museums and private collections; Welch et al. 1981.
50. Grube and Sims 1989: 220–23.
51. Moreover, something very similar occurs in China, again with the Yuan Mongols; Lee and Ho 1968.
52. Grabar 2000: 99–104.
53. A quintet, made up of five poems in rhyming couplets (*masnavi*): *Makhzano'l Asrar* (the storehouse of secrets); *Khosrow-o-Shirin* (Khosroe and Shirin); *Laila-o-Majnun* (Laila and Majnun); *Haft Peikar* (The Seven Princesses); *Eskandar-nama* (The Book of Alexander); see the introduction by Bausani, A., *Le sette principesse*, Milan, 1982: 5–32. Another excellent edition is Chelkowski 1975. On Haft Peikar, also see Al-awadhi 2001. For the ideology of Nizami, compare Mcdonald 1963: 97–101.
54. Lukens et al. 1994; Simpson 1979; for a summary, also see Fontana 1998: 68–71.
55. On the albums and their contents, see Grube 1981, a monographic issue devoted entirely to this fascinating and mysterious group of works.
56. Chagatai, M., *Hālāt-e, Honarvarān* (Calligraphers and Illuminators), Lahore, 1936.
57. Minorsky, V., *Calligraphers, and Painters*, Washington, D.C., 1959.
58. Istanbul, Topkapı Sarayı, H.2154, fol. 107r; excellent color reproduction in Grube 1980, fig. 9.
59. Istanbul, Topkapı Sarayı, H.2153, fol. 73v; in color in Grube, 1980, fig. 11.
60. Grube and Sims, 1989: 208–9.
61. British Library, inv. Ms. Add. 18113; see Canby, 1993: 44.
62. Fol. 45v; in color in Grabar 2000, fig. 21.
63. The importance of the iconography of miniatures in the more general context of the Islamic arts has been exaggerated by Western critics; rightly, Grabar 2000: 128, reminds us that at the time there were no exhibitions and museums; moreover, while the structure of society, with its extraordinary mobility, may have encouraged comparisons, social organization, which was basically quite rigid, must have favored the acceptance of traditional decorative models and modules.
64. British Library, Ms. Add. 18113, fol. 18v; Canby 1993, fig. 24 in color.
65. British Library, Ms. Add. 18113, fol. 31r; Gray 1961, fig. in color on 47.
66. O'Kane 1991: 219–46.
67. De Clavijo 1928.
68. This period seems to have been rather complicated; an excellent overall and recent study is by Soucek 2000: 123–48.
69. Tapper 1966: 61–84.
70. Curatola, entry no. 26 in Curatola 1993.
71. Soucek 2000: 134.
72. Ipshiroghlu 1976; Karamagarali 1984.
73. Istanbul, Topkapı Sarayı, H.2153, fols. 3v-4r; 2160, fol. 77v; in color in Fontana 1998, fig. 36.
74. British Library, London, Ms. Add. 27261, fol. 230r; Canby 1993, fig. 28.
75. See note 66.
76. Ms. i. 4628; Fontana, 1998: 85.
77. On the *Zafar-nama* see the works of E. Sims, who for many years studied this subject almost exclusively: Sims 1973; Sims 1991: 175–217; Sims 1992: 132–43.
78. See entry no. 221 by Sims in Curatola 1993.
79. See entry no. 221 by Sims in Curatola 1993.
80. Bibliothèque Nationale, Paris, suppl. turc. 190; Robinson 1991: 8, fig. 2 (fol. 67v).
81. Ms. 239; Robinson 1991: 8, fig. 3 (fol. 28v).
82. In this regard, a very interesting work is Davis and Norgren 1969.
83. The most complete study thus far is Bahari 1996.
84. Khwandamir, *Halib al-Siyar*; cited in Grube and Sims 1989: 208, n. 7.
85. The aforementioned work, *Libro degli uomini illustri*, by his contemporary, the historian Khwandamir, who in any case is no Vasari, contains some useful notes.
86. Ms. adab farsi 908; the double title page, in color, in Grabar 2000, figs. 65–66.
87. Ms. Or. 6810; Gray 1961, fig. on 146 (fol. 154v); Canby 1993: 75, fig. 47 (fol. 214r); Grabar 2000: 115–18, figs. 61–62 (fols. 27v, 16). The reproductions mentioned are all in color.
88. British Library, London, Ms. Add. 25900; Grabar 2000: 118, fig. 63 (fol. 18).
89. See note 69.
90. The library in Topkapı Sarayı in Istanbul has 19 miniatures (h. 762), while there are three in the Keir Collection in London; compare, respectively, Stchoukine 1966 and Robinson 1976. The turbulent history of this manuscript is noteworthy, since it explicates the journeys these works sometimes underwent. The manuscript was commissioned by Bābur (son of the famous Baysunghur), but upon his death (1457), it was unfinished, and after the sack of Herāt, it passed into the hands of Pir Budaq (prince Qara Qoyunlu, son of Jahanshah, governor of Shīrāz beginning in 1456; it was then sent to Baghdad in 1460) and then, beginning in 1476, it belonged to Aq Qoyunlu Khalil (son of Uzun Hasan and governor of Shīrāz from 1471 to 1478), to finally come into the hands of the aforementioned Ya'qub Beg, who finally saw to its completion. However Shah Isma'il had eleven miniatures by the young painter Sultan Muhammad added to the compositions of Shaykhu and Darwish Muhammad; Sultan Muhammad would later emerge as one of the leading figures of the Safavid school.
91. Schmitz 1984: 103–12.
92. Unfortunately, this manuscript too, which was given by Shah Tahmasp in 1567 to the Ottoman Sultan Selim II, on the occasion of the latter's ascent to power, and which was formerly owned by a Rothschild baron and then Arthur Houghton, Jr., is presently divided up among numerous museums and private collections. Recently some eighty or so miniatures were acquired by the Museum of Contemporary Art in Tehran, in exchange for a large painting by de Kooning, which had never been exhibited. For more on these miniatures, see the detailed study by Dickson and Welch 1981.
93. See notes 56 and 57.
94. Fol. 20v; collection, prince Sadruddin Aga Khan, Geneva; reproduced in color innumerable times, most recently in Grabar 2000: 137, figs. 72–73.
95. One of the most extraordinary landscapes ever painted (perhaps by Sultan Muhammad himself), in a *Shah-nama* made in Tabriz in 1515 (British Library, OA 1948 12–11.023; Canby 1993, fig. 49), should be compared with "Sleeping Rustam" and a truly astonishing variety of flora and rocks (not unexpected, if one thinks of the Istanbul anthology of 1398, executed in Shīrāz; Gray 1961: 69, fig. on 68 [fol. 26r]), a luxuriant and "exotic" display that brings to mind the work, some centuries later, of Henri Rousseau (1844–1910).
96. Dust Muhammad (compare note 56) mentions Sultan and this painting, where there are "men dressed in leopard skin," a work so overwhelming in its beauty that other artists "bow their heads in shame"; compare Soudavar 1992: 159.
97. Khamsa by Nizami, Tabriz 1539–43; British Library, London, Or. 2265, fol. 18r; Canby 1993: 82, fig. 50.
98. Khamsa, from 1490, Add. 25900, fol. 18; compare note 88.
99. Istanbul, Topkapı Sarayı, H.2154. See note 58.
100. Welch 1979: fol. 521v, private collection.
101. Attributed. Washington, D.C., Arthur M. Sackler Collection, Freer Gallery of Art, inv. s86.0300; Lowry and Nemazee 1988: fig. 65.
102. British Library, London, OA 1930 11–12.02; Canby 1993: 82–83, fig. 52.
103. This surprising opinion—probably tied to the fact that Tahmasp agreed to Ottoman demands, and in exchange for 400,000 pieces of gold, he had Prince

Bayazit, who had been hiding at his court in Iran, executed—has been put forth by Monneret de Villard 1962: 450–652, esp. 547.

104. On this interesting historical period, see the excellent essay by Soudavar 1999: 49–66; particularly regarding Tahmasp's disregard for the arts (but without any explicit prohibition against painting); see pp. 51–52, and regarding the diaspora of Safavid artists, see pp. 52–54.
105. Fol. 147; Gray 1961: 145, fig. on 143.
106. Or. 12985; Canby 1993: 86, fig. 54.
107. Ms. P.277; Fontana 1998: 117.
108. See note 57.
109. Fontana 1998: 121.
110. A characteristic that is also found in other materials; see, for example, the famous Safavid velvet depictions, inspired specifically by the master; one very beautiful example is the silver brocade in Royal Ontario Museum, Toronto, inv. n. 962.60.1; Allgrove McDovell 1989: 166, fig. 25.
111. Dated to 1595; Arthur M. Sackler, Harvard University Museums, Cambridge (Mass.) (inv. 1936.27); compare Grabar 2000, fig. 37.
112. Dated 1630; inv. n. 1960.17; Grabar 2000, fig. 38.
113. There is only one overall study of this subject (and it is excellent), limited to the late fourteenth century; Fontana 2002: 73–97.
114. Specific "boundary" sites par excellence—one arrives impure and leaves pure—where imagery, including human and naturalistic imagery that, as we know, was prohibited in other contexts, was allowed, if not advised; see Arnold, T. W., *Painting in Islam. A Study of the Place of Pictorial Art in Muslim Culture*, Oxford, 1928: 88; for a late example, of these sorts of wall paintings for a bath, see Curatola and Scarcia 1978.
115. In any case, see, in the chapter on architecture, the Seljuq site of Kharragan.
116. Grabar 2000: 95.
117. A useful text is Brosh and Milstein 1991.
118. The brilliant essay by Rogers, " The Genesis of Safavid Religious Paintings," 1970, is still fundamental.
119. Fontana 1994.

Flowers of Wool: Persian Carpets

1. See the classic work: Eliade 1974.
2. Ghirshma 1956, vol. 2.
3. Curatola, *Tappeti*, 1981: 34.
4. Regarding the importance of Paradise in Islamic art, see Piotrovsky 2000: 87–93.
5. The literature on this subject is vast indeed. See Gantzhorn 1991: 13–45.
6. In Iran there was a category of objects woven in two colors (white and blue), known as *zilu*, made using more or less mechanized looms, specifically to cover prayer halls in mosques. They often bear the name of the donor who commissioned the piece, the artisan, the date and place of execution, and the name of the mosque for which they were made. They are an important documentary source, unfortunately little known, and they are gradually disappearing, since they are considered everyday objects, not worthy of preservation and study. For more on *zilus*, see Wulff 1966: 210–12; Gluck and Hiramoto, 1977; Vogelsang-Eastwood 1988; Afshar 1992; Ittig 1992.
7. Ivanov 1990: no. 61: 24–25; it is inscribed with a passage from the Koran (Sura CXII), and the signature of the artisan, Masterro 'Ali Nushabadi. An example of a dated *zilu* (Rabi II d.E. 808 / October 1405), signed by 'Ali Baidak ibn Hajj Maibudi, is found in the Congregational Mosque in Yazd: Ivanov, A., ibid.
8. Briggs 1940; Briggs 1946.
9. Compare Lentz and Lowry 1989: 220–21, cat. no. 119.
10. For more on this renowned group of carpets, see Martin 1908; the carpets in the Eshrefoghlu Mosque in Beyshehir are also noteworthy and are mentioned in Riefstahl 1931.
11. Mills 1975; Mills 1983. Recently we have also published: "Con più color, sommesse e sovrapposte / non fer mai drappi Tartari né Turchi," in *Il Rinascimento in Oriente e Occidente 1250–1490*, E. Carbonell, R. Cassanelli, T. Velmans, eds. 2003: 168–79.
12. Lockhart et al. 1973: 126. Barbaro praises Persian carpets as being superior to Turkish and Egyptian carpets: "and at the bottom of these very beautiful carpets, including those from Cairo and Borsa (unknown to me) there is such great difference, as much as there is between clothing of French wool and the wool clothing of Signor Matheo."
13. Hillenbrand 1999: 108, fig. 80.
14. On Natanz, see Wilber 1955; Blair 1983: 69–94.
15. Wilber, D. N. 1955, n. 47: 139–41, plates 69–86; Blair 1987: 43–96.
16. Hutt 1978: 257–58.
17. Pope and Ackerman 1938–39: 452–56.
18. Erdmann 1960: 32.
19. There is an excellent color image in King and Sylvester 1983: no. 58: 85–86. A carpet in the Textile Museum in Washington, D.C., (inv. R.33.I.2) also has a central medallion with a similar format (46 × 184 cm), where the central corner pieces are omitted, but the medallion is embellished by a scroll and pendants. The background has a design of vines and floral volutes, a bit more complex than the previous example.
20. King 1983, n. 62: 88–89.
21. Stead 1974; Curatola 1981, no. 67.
22. Morton 1974: 31–64 and 1975: 39–58.
23. There are excellent color reproductions of this carpet, one of the most famous in the world, in Balboni Brizza 1993 (Guides for the Poldi Pezzoli Museum in Milan), no. 6: 40–51. Unfortunately the text is not always adequate (Giyath al-Din Jami is considered "probably a miniaturist of the Safavid court" and is confused with the other Giyath).
24. Curatola 1981, n. 70; Balboni Brizza 1993, n. 7: 52–57, with splendid color photographs.
25. Piotrovski 2001, no. 219: 262.
26. Spuhler 1987, no. 78: 80–81; color photos on 229.
27. Torchia 1997: 92.
28. King and Sylvester 1983, no. 65: 91.
29. Housego 1989: 123–24, fig. 6.
30. For the carpet at the Metropolitan Museum of Art, New York, see the color reproduction in Curatola 1981, n. 48 (498 × 340 cm; silk warp and weft, wool pile, and assymetrical knotting with a density of almost ten thousand knots per square decimeter); for the Lyon carpet (inv. n. 25.423; 800 × 400 cm), see King and Sylvester 1983, no. 61: 87.
31. King and Sylvester 1983, no. 61: 87.
32. The development of a Shiite state in Persia is obviously an extremely important event, which in this context cannot be touched upon, and even less dealt with in substantive fashion. Regarding the ideology of Shah Isma'il, see Bausani 1959: 360–65. A brief, concise introduction to Safavid art is in Curatola, "Il periodo Safavide in Persia dal 907/1501 al 1145/1732," in Curatola 1993: 417–23.
33. Curatola 1981, n. 92; the density of the knotting in this carpet is particularly high: 12,700 knots per square decimeter.
34. Color image in Bernus-Taylor 2001. A carpet at the Metropolitan Museum, New York, is very similar; Curatola 1981, no. 93 (238 × 180 cm).
35. Walker 1997: 168–69, nn. 19–20, figs. 88–89. In reality a renowned floral carpet in the Philadelphia Museum of Art (525 × 359 cm; warp and weft in cotton, wool pile) also has a directional design; it can be dated to the seventeenth century and features trees (cypresses, plane trees, cherries, etc.) with springtime and autumnal colors; compare to Curatola 1981, no. 73.
36. Earlier, in the Timurid era, bindings had floral designs that are extremely interesting in this context. See Bernus-Taylor 2001: 173, n. 122 (binding of a *Divan* by Jami made in Herāt in the late fifteenth century (Bibliothèque Nationale, Paris, supp. Pers. 2050). The complex floral design with animals is generally interpreted as the mythical *waq-waq* tree.
37. Bernus-Taylor 2001: 198, n. 137.
38. There are not many fundamental studies on Islamic bindings; see Bosch et al. 1981; Raby and Tanindi 1993. Regarding relationships between Islamic bindings and Italian bindings—an area that has still been studied very little—see the essay by Hobson 1989: 111–23. One of the many examples of binding with a similar scheme as that seen in carpets with a central medallion is in the Arthur Sackler Gallery, Washington, D.C., and published in color in Lowry and Nemazee 1998, n. 74.
39. There is an acceptable color image in Housego 1989: fig. 12: 125–26. A symbolic interpretation of these carpets has been attempted in Van Cammann 1974: 181–208.
40. Harvard University, Fogg Art Museum.
41. Scarcia 1978: 387–91; Scarcia 1980: 57–82.
42. Lockhart 1960: 116. Unfortunately we have not been able to locate the source upon which the scholar bases his assertion.
43. Beattie 1976; Beattie et al. 1977: 455–71.
44. Curatola 1993, entry no. 277. Moreover, Venice was not the only city to be so honored; compare Ferrier 1973: 75–92.
45. Although the accompanying message indicated they were destined for the Treasury of San Marco, whose fame and beauty were known as far as the East and were considered a worthy place of exhibition for these carpets, at least one ended up, instead, in the private chapel, as a prie-dieu for the doge.
46. King and Sylvester 1983: 95–96, n. 73. Color photos in Housego 1989: fig. 21.
47. King and Sylvester 1983: 95, n. 72.
48. King and Sylvester 1983: 93, n. 69.
49. Curatola 1981, n. 101; 206, × 142 cm; silk brocaded in silver.
50. King and Sylvester 1983: 94, n. 70.
51. Curatola 1983: 1–62.
52. Seyf 1992: 99–105.
53. Paradise and gardens are intimately connected. On the art of Islamic gardens (and the architectural, town planning, and artistic implications) see Petruccioli 1994 and the proceedings of a recent conference in Genoa, Matteini and Petruccioli 2001.
54. *Corano* (Italian translation, A. Bausani, ed., Florence, 1978), lv, 76: "and cushions and splendid carpets shall be arranged on the lawns."
55. In some ways, examples of garden carpets, or their antecedents, can be seen at the Philadelphia Museum of Art (see note 35), or in a carpet fragment with a central medallion in Paris, at the Musée des Arts Décoratifs (400 × 345 cm), illustrated in color in Curatola 1991: 136, no. 34 (entry by R. Gilles). One of the most ancient carpets from northwestern Iran is the so-called Wagner carpet, in wool (Glasgow, Burrell Collection, 581 × 432 cm), illustrated in color in Beattie 1976, plate I, cat. 1: 33–34. A more common design is the one seen in a carpet in Kuwait (Jenkins 1983: 143; there is a splendid color reproduction in Denny 1999: 16–19), similar to an example in the Metropolitan Museum, New York (Housego 1989, no. 23). Also see Ellis, C. G., "Garden Carpets and their Relation to Safavid Gardens," in *Hali*, 5, no. 1 1982: 11–17, and our essay, Curatola and Scarcia 1986.
56. On this extremely popular motif, see the chapter dedicated to the subject in Ford 1981: 52–73.
57. Lévi-Strauss 1986.
58. Rossbach 1980.
59. With ambiguous philological and semantic ori-

gins in Europe, sanctioned in inventories of Renaissance archives, where carpets were described as being "*a roda*," we cannot know if the allusion is to rose-window shapes, as in those of Romanesque cathedrals, or to simple wheel shapes, the latter suggestion made plausible by certain "pinwheel" drawings. Compare Rogers 1986: 13–28.

60. On Sufis in a Safavid context, see the wonderful essay by Newman 1999.
61. "God, is the Light of the Heavens and of the Earth. His Light is like a niche in which is a lamp—the lamp encased in glass—the glass, as it were, a glistening star. From a blessed tree is it lighted, the olive neither of the East nor of the West, whose oil would well nigh shine out, even though fire touched it not! It is light upon light. God guideth whom He will to His light, and God setteth forth parables to men, for God knoweth all things."
62. Van Cammann 1951: 1–9; Van Cammann 1952.
63. Bausani 1959: 312–22.
64. Curatola 1996: 229–36, which discusses an iconography, probably of Bektashi Sufi origin, which appears on a door of the sanctuary of the mystic Amir Nuruddin Ni'matullah, in Mahan (in the environs of Kirman).
65. Among the publications, see the brief but essential work by Roux 1981: 5–11.
66. This problem is alluded to in Curatola. "Nota sulla simbologia," 1991: 155–66.

Persia between the Baroque and the Neoclassical Eras

1. On Nadir Shah and his most significant monument, see Curatola 1983: 1–62.
2. Skelton 1982.
3. Curatola, "Le immagini," in *Persia Barocca: In forma di Parole*, xiii, Scarcia and Reggio, curators, 1983: 227–32.
4. Hutt in *Architecture of the Islamic World*, Michell, curator, 1978: 256.
5. Meshkati 1974: 235–39.
6. The term is obviously Spanish. "A ceramic decorative technique that consisted of tracing outlines of ornamental motifs using oil and manganese, mixed in such a way as to separate the different colored glazes used for the ornamented objects. *Cerda seca* was used in Spain and in the Maghreb, or North Africa, beginning in the fourteenth century; its use also spread, although in limited fashion, to other Islamic areas, for example Central Asia during the Timurid era (1369–1500)," "Glossario," Fontana, in Fehervari 1985: 226. Mifrendereski and Zonuzi 1992.
7. Carswell 1968.
8. On the Qajar art of ceramics see above all the writings of J. M. Scarce, in particular: Scarce 1976: 278–88; Scarce 1979: 75–86; Scarce 1989: 270–94, with related bibliography.
9. *Husauniyya* are specific buildings constructed as works of charity; they were used for meetings of confraternities who gathered to hear the stories of martyrs, recounted by *rauza-khvani* (storytellers who would recite, sometimes with the help of paintings on panels or canvas). This should not be confused with the Husayinniyya or Nakhl, which are large pointed structures made from wood, which were carried in processions in remembrance of the martyrdom of Husayin and kept at caravansaries. Some of the most famous of these "devices" are those in Yazd.
10. On this *Husauniyya*, see Mechkati 1974: 223–24, no. 377. A fundamental essay on Shiite iconography is Fontana 1994, particularly, in terms of this discussion: 47–56, as well as the excellent bibliography.
11. Chelkowski 1971.
12. Peterson 1979: 143–51.
13. Melikian-Chirvani, "From the Royal Boat," 1991: 3–111.
14. Curatola, "Notizia," 1978: 143–51.
15. Fontana 1994: 53, fig. 58.
16. Scarce, "Tile Decoration," 1979: 635–41.
17. Scarcia 1962: 83–93.
18. Scarce 2002: 181–93.
19. The portrait is published in Robinson 1989: 224–31, fig. 1. On Qajar painting and the historical period in general, see: Scarcia 1963; Falk 1972; Robinson and Guadalupi 1982; Robinson 1983; Ansari, F. M., *Die Malerei zur Zeit der Qadjaren-Dynastie (1796–1925) im Iran*, Paris, 1986; and finally, the exhibition catalogue Diba and Ekhtiar 1999, with extensive and detailed bibliography.
20. Muhammad Zaman, b. Hajji Yusuf Kuni, worked between 1675 and 1688 at the court of Shah Sulaiman (who reigned from 1666 to 1694). On this artist, see: Martinovich 1925: 106–9; Ivanov 1969: 65–70. On the brother of Muhammad Zaman, who was also a painter, see: Adle 1980.
21. The works mentioned, along with three others, are in the *Muraqqa* ("Album") of the Institute of Orientalist Studies of the Russian Academy of Science, St. Petersburg. See Akimushkin 1994.
22. Sims 1979: 408–18.
23. Scarcia 1961: 198–203.
24. Unfortunately, these are lost. Contemporary sources inform us that this veritable gallery of paintings included "no less than 118 full-length portraits" (Browne, 1926: 105), one of which is in the India Office Library and Records (see: Robinson 1989, fig. 5), and another—with notations in Persian, indicating the figures depicted—is in Bologna. For this latter rare example, see Pudioli 1991: 15–19.
25. The collection of Qajar art in Tbilisi is extremely significant: Scarcia 1962: 203–9. Some lacquer objects of excellent quality are in Florence, at the Federigo Stibbert house-museum.
26. Gonzalez 1994.

BIBLIOGRAPHY

Ackerman, P., "Textiles through the Sāsānian Period," in U. A. Pope and P. Ackerman, ed., *A Survey of Persian Art*, Tehran, London, New York, Tokyo, 1938–39 (reprinted 1967), 2: 681–715.

Ackerman, P., "Note on some Parthian Textile Elements," *Bulletin of the Iranian Institute*; 4, no. 1–4; 7, no. 1 (1946): 19.

Adle, C., Melikian-Chirvani, A. S., "Les monuments du xie siècle du Damqan," in *Studia Iranica* 1 (1972): 229–97.

Adle, C., *L'Ecriture de l'union, reflets du temps des troubles, oeuvre picturale de Haji Muhammad, 1083–1124 to 1673–1712*, Paris, 1980.

Afshar, I., "Zilu," *Iranian Studies* 25, nos. 1–2 (1992): 31–36.

Akimushkin, O. F., *Il Murakkà di San Pietroburgo*, Lugano and Milan, 1994.

Al-awadhi, P., *The Seven Pavillions* (Accademia delle Arti del Disegno, Monographs 7), Florence, 2001.

Albaum, L. I., *Zivopis Afrasiaba*, Tashkent, 1975.

Alden, J. R., "Excavations at Tal-i malyan," Part I. "A Sasanian Kiln," *Iran* 16 1978: 79–86.

Alemi, M., "I giardini reali di Ashraf e Farahabad," in *Il Giardino islamico. Architettura, natura, paesaggio*, A. Petruccioli, ed. 1994: 201–16.

Allan, J. W., "Abu'l Qasim's Treatise on Ceramics," in *Iran* 11 (1973): 111–20.

Al-Shams, M. A., "Arabic Drawings from Hatra," *Sumer* 37, nos. 1–2 (1981): 146–58 (in Arabic with a summary in English).

Amoretti, B. S., *Shah Isma'il I nei "Diarii" di Marin Sanudo*, Venice, 1979.

Amoretti, B. S., ed., "Sguardi sulla cultura sciita nel Deccan. Glances on Shi'ite Deccan Culture," in *Rivista degli Studi Orientali*, 64, no. 1–2 (1990): 1991.

Angeli Bertinelli, M. G., *Roma e l'Oriente*, 1979.

Ansari, F. M., *Die Malerei zur Zeit der Qadjaren-Dynastie (1796–1925) im Iran*, Paris, 1986.

Arnaud, P., "Les guerres des Parthes et d'Arménie dans la première moitié du premier siècle av. n. è.: problèmes de chronologie et d'extension territoriale (95 BC–70 BC)," *Mesopotamia* 12 (1987): 129–45.

Arnold, T. W., *Painting in Islam. A Study of the Place of Pictorial Art in Muslim Culture*, Oxford, 1928.

Arnold, T. W., "Painting and the Art of the Book, Book Painting." a. "The Origins," in *A Survey of Persian Art. Vol. I*, ed. A. U. Pope, P. Ackerman, London and New York, 1938, 1809–19.

Atil, E., *Ceramics from the World of Islam*, Washington, D.C., 1973.

Azarnoush, M., *The Sasanian Manor House at Hagiabad, Iran*, Florence, 1994.

Azarpay, G., "Some Iranian Iconographic Formulae in Sogdian Painting," *Iranica Antiqua* 11 (1975): 168–77.

Azarpay, G., "Sasanian and Sogdian Artistic Patterns: Comparative Study," in *Le Plateau iranien et l'Asie Centrale des origines à la conquête islamique. Leurs relations à la lumière des documents archéologiques*, Paris, 1976: 323–28.

Azarpay, G., "The Islamic Tomb Tower: A Note on its Genesis and Significance," in *Essays in Islamic Art and Architecture in Honor of Katharina Otto-Dorn*, A. Daneshvari, ed., Malibu, 1981: 9–12.

Azarpay, G., ed., *Sogdian Painting*, Berkeley, 1981.

Azarpay, G., *Medieval Tomb Towers of Iran. An Iconographical Study*, 1986.

Badawy, A., "L'art copte: les influences orientales (Perse et Syrie)," *Rivista degli Studi Orientali*, 58, nos. 1–4 (1987): 13–48.

Bahari, E., *Behzad: Master of Persian Painting*, London, 1996.

Balboni Brizza, M. T., *Tappeti*, Milan–Turin, 1993.

Balcer, J. M., "The Date of Herodotus IV," 1: "Darius' Scythian Expedition," *Harvard Studies in Classical Philology*, 76 (1972): 99–132.

Ball, W., "The Towers of Ghur. A Ghurid 'Maginot Line'?," in *Cairo to Kabul. Afghan and Islamic Studies presented to Ralph Pinder-Wilson*, ed. W. Ball and L. Harrow, London, 2002: 21–45.

Balog, P., "Sasanian and Early Islamic Ornamental Glass Vessels-Stamps," in *Near Eastern Numismatics, Iconography, Epigraphy and History. Studies in Honor of G. C. Miles*, ed. D. K. Koumjian, Beirut, 1974: 131–40.

Baltrušaïtis, J., "Stucco. A. Ornamental," in *A Survey of Persian Art. Vol. I*, A. U. Pope and P. Ackerman eds., London, New York, 1938: 601–30.

Baltrušaïtis, J., *Il Medioevo fantastico. Antichità ed esotismi nell'arte gotica*, Milan, 1993.

Balty, J., "La mosaïque," in Brussels 1993: *Splendeur des Sassanides. L'empire perse entre Rome et la Chine [224–642]*, B. Overlaet (curator), Brussels, 1993: 67–69.

Baratte, F., "Dionysos en Chine: remarques à propos de la coupe en argent de Beitan," *Arts Asiatiques* 51 (1996): 142–47.

Baratte, F., "Orient et Occident: le témoignage d'une trouvaille d'argenterie d'époque parthe en Asie centrale, *Journal des Savants*, 2001: 249–319.

Barattolo, A., "The Temple of Hadrian-Zeus at Cyzicus. A New Proposed Reconstruction from a Fresh Architectonic and Ideological Interpretation," *Istambuler Mitteilungen* 45 (1995): 57–108.

Barkova, L., "La cultura nomadica nell'altaj e lo stile animalistico," in *Oro. Il mistero dei Sarmati e degli Sciti*, J. Aruz, A. Farkas, A. Alekseev, E. Korolkova (curators), Milan, 2001: 52–56.

Barnett, R. D., "Median Art," *Iranica Antiqua* 2 (1962): 71–95.

Bartol'd, V. V., "Gunbad-i Qabus, the Earliest Dated Persian Monument" (in Russian), in *Ežegodnik Rossiiskogo Universiteta Istorii Iskusstva I*, 2, Petrograd, 1921.

Bastani Parizi, E., "L'ensemble de Ganj Ali Xan à Kerman," in *VI International Congress of Iranian Art and Archaeology* (Oxford, 1972), Tehran, 1976: 13–20.

Bausani, A., *Persia religiosa*, Milan, 1959.

Bausani, A., "Religion under the Mongols," in *Cambridge History of Iran*, Cambridge, 1968, 5: 538–49.

Bausani, A., *Appunti, di astronomia e astrologia arabo-islamiche*, Venice, 1977.

Bausani, A., "Un auspicio armeno di capodanno in una notizia di Irāanshahrī (Nota ad Ajello)," *Oriente Moderno*, 1978: 317–19.

Bausani, A., "The Observatory of Maraghe," in *Soltaniye III. Quaderni del Seminario di Iranistica ... di Venezia*, Venice, 1982, 9: 125–51.

Beattie, M. H., *Carpets of Central Persia*, Birmingham, 1976.

Beattie, M. H., Housego, J., Morton, A. H., "Vase-technique Carpets and Kirman," in *Oriental Art* 23 (1977): 455–71.

Beazley, E., "The Pigeon Towers of Esfahan," *Iran* 4 (1966): 105–9.

Beazley, E., "Some Vernacular Buildings of the Plateau," in *The Arts of Persia*, R. W. Ferrier, ed., New Haven and London, 1989: 109–17.

Belenitskii, A. M., *Monumentalnoe Iskusstvo Pendjikenta. Zivopis, Skul'ptura*, Leningrad, 1973.

Belenitskii, A. M., Marshak, B. I., "The Paintings of Sogdiana," in G. Azarpay, *Sogdian Painting*, Berkeley, Los Angeles, 1981: 11–77.

Bernard, P., "Les rhytons de Nisa. I. Poétesses grecques," *Journal des Savants*, 1985: 25–118.

Bernard, P., "Les rhytons de Nisa: à quoi, à qui ont-ils servi?," in *Histoire et cultes de l'Asie centrale préislamique*, ed. P. Bernard, F. Grenet, Paris, 1991: 31–38.

Bernard, P., "L'Asie, centrale et l'empire séleucide," *TOπOI*, 4, no. 2 1994: 473–511.

Bernardini, M., "I giardini di Samarcanda e Herat," in *Il Giardino islamico. Architettura, natura, paesaggio*, A. Petruccioli, ed. 1994: 237–48.

Bernus-Taylor, M., *L'Etrange et le Merveilleux en terres d'Islam*, Paris, 2001.

Bianchi Bandinelli, R., "Forma artistica tardo antica e apporti parthici e sassanidi nella scultura e nella pittura," in *La Persia e il mondo greco-romano*, Rome, 1966: 319–33.

Bier, C. M., "Textiles," in P. O. Harper, *The Royal Hunter*, New York, 1978: 119–25.

Bichler, R., Rollinger, R., "Greece Relations with Persian Empire." VI. "The Image of Persia and Persian in Greek Literature," in *Encyclopaedia Iranica*, vol. XI, ed. E. Yarshater, New York, 2002: 326–29.

Bittel, K., *Gli, Ittiti*, Milan, 1983.

Bivar, A.D.H., "The Political History of Iran under the Arsacids," in *The Cambridge History of Iran. Volume 3 (1). The Seleucid, Parthian and Sasanian Periods*, ed. E. Yarshater, Cambridge, 1983: 21–99.

Bivar, A.D.H., "Achaemenid, Coins, Weights and Measures," in *The Cambridge History of Iran. Volume 2. The Median and Achaemenian Periods*, ed. I. Gershevitch, Cambridge, 1985: 610–39.

Bivar, A.D.H., "The Royal Hunter and the God: Esoteric Mithraism under the Sasanians?," in *Au carrefour des religions. Mélanges offerts à Philippe Gignoux*, Res orientales, VII, Bures-sur-Yvette, 1995: 29–38.

Bivar, A.D.H., "The Sasanian Princes at Bamiyan," in *The Art and Archaeology of Ancient Persia. New Light on the Parthian and Sasanian Empires*, ed. V. S. Curtis, R. Hillenbrand and J. M. Rogers, London and New York, 1998: 103–10.

Bivar, A.D.H., Gunbad-i Kabus, S. V., *Encyclopaedia of Islam*, rev. ed., II, Leiden, 1965.

Blair, S., *Epic Images and Contemporary History*, Chicago, 1980.

Blair, S. S., "The Octagonal Pavilion at Natanz: A Reexamination of Early Islamic Architecture in Iran," in *Muqarnas* 1 (1983): 69–94.

Blair, S. S., "Il-Khanid Architecture and Society: an Analysis of the Endowment Deed of the Rab'-i Rashidi," in *Iran* 22 (1984): 67–90.

Blair, S. S., "The Mongol Capital of Sultaniyya, the 'Imperial,'" *Iran* 24 (1986): 139–51.

Blair, S. S., *The Shrine Complex at Natanz, Iran*, Cambridge (Mass.), 1986.

Blair, S. S., "The Epigraphic Program of the Tomb of Uljaitu at Sultaniyya: Meaning in Mongol Architecture," *Islamic Art* 2 (1987): 43–96.

Boardman, J., "Pyramidal Stamp Seals in the Persian Empire," *Iran*, 8 1970: 19–46.

Boardman, J., *The Diffusion of Classical Art in Antiquity*, London, 1994.

Boardman, J., *Persia and the West. An Archaeological Investigation of the Genesis of Achaemenid Art*, London, 2000.

Bombaci, A., Scerrato, U., "Summary Report on the Archaeological Mission in Afghanistan," in *East and West*, 10 (1959): 3–55.

Bombaci, A., "The Kufic Inscription in Persian Verses in the Court of the Royal Palace of Ma'sud III at Ghazni," in *ISMEO Reports and Memoirs*, V, Rome, 1966.

Bonine, E., *Yazd and Its Hinterland. A Central Place System of Dominance in the Central Iranian Plateau*, Austin, 1975.

Boperachchi, O., "Indo-Parthians," in *Das Parthreich und seine Zeugnisse. The Arsacid Empire: Sources and Documentation*, ed. J. Wiesehöfer, Stuttgart, 1998: 388–406.

Borisov, A.J., Lukonin, V. G., *Sasanianskie D'emmy*, Leningrad, 1963.

Bosch, G., Carswell, J., Petherbridge, G., *Islamic Binding & Bookmaking*, Chicago, 1981.

Bosworth, E., "The Development of Persian Culture under the early Ghaznavids," *Iran* 6 (1968): 23–31.

Bosworth, C., "The Heritage of Rulership in Early Islamic Iran and the Search for Dynastic Connections with the Past," in *Iran* 11 (1973): 51–62.

Boucharlat, R., "Susa. Dagli, Achemenidi ai Sasaniani," in *Enciclopedia dell'Arte Antica Classica e Orientale. Secondo Supplemento, 1971–1994*, 5 (1997): 501–3.
Boucharlat, R., "Zoroastrisme et pratiques funéraires," *Dossiers d'archéologie. Empires perses d'Alexandre aux Sassanides*, n. 243, May 1999: 85–89.
Boucharlat, R., "Greece Relations with Persian Empire." VII. "Greek Art and Architecture in Iran," in *Encyclopaedia Iranica*, ed. E. Yarshater, New York, 2002, 11: 329–33.
Boucharlat, R., "Les sites d'époque parthe en Iran," *Les Parthes. Dossier d'Archéologie*, 271, 2002: 54–63.
Bouman, J., "The Sasanian Church in the Khargh Island," *Acta Iranica*, 1974: 217–20.
Boyle, J. A., "Rashid al-Din: The First World Historian," in *Iran* 9 (1971): 19–26.
Brandi, C., *Persia Mirabile*, Turin, 1978.
Bretanickij, L., Salamzade, A., "On the Construction of the Maragha Observatory" (in Russian), in *Iskusstvo Azerbaijdzana* 5 (1956): 61–85.
Briant, P., *I, Persiani e l'impero di Dario*, Milan, 1995.
Briant, P., *Histoire de l'empire perse de Cyrus à Alexandre*, 2 vols., Leiden, 1996.
Briant, P., *From Cyrus to Alexander: A History of the Persian Empire*, Winona Lake, 2002.
Briggs, A., "Timurid Carpets I. Geometric Carpets," *Ars Islamica*, 7 (1940): 20–54.
Briggs, A., "Arabesque and Flower Carpets," *Ars Islamica*, 11–12 (1946): 146–58.
Brodersen, K., "The Date of the Secession of Parthia from the Seleucid Kingdom," *Historia*, 35, 1986: 378–81.
Bromberg, C. A., "Sasanian Stucco Influence: Sorrento and East-West," *Orientalia Lovaniensia Periodica*, 14, 1983: 247–67.
Bromberg, C. A., "Sasanian Royal Emblems in Northern Ccaucasus," in *Proceedings of the First European Conference of Iranian Studies. Part 1. Old and Middle Iranian Studies*, ed. G. Gnoli, A. Panaino, Rome, 1990: 1–17.
Bromberg, C. A., "An Iranian Gesture at Miran," *Bulletin of the Asia Institute*, 5 (1991): 45–58.
Brosh, N., Milstein, R., *Biblical Stories in Islamic Painting*, Jerusalem, 1991.
Browne, E. G., *A Year among the Persians*, 2nd ed., Cambridge, 1926.
Browning, I., *Palmyra*, London, 1979.
Brunner, J., *Sasanian Stamp Seals in the Metropolitan Museum of Art*, New York, 1978.
Bulatova, B., *The History of the Development of Shah-i Zinda in the 15th Century* (in Russian), Tashkent, 1965.
Burkett, M., "The Tower at Karat, Khorassan," *Oriental Art*, n. s. 19 (1973): 43–49.
Burn, R., *Persia and the Greeks. The Defence of the West 546–478 BC*, London, 1962.
Bussagli, M., *La Peinture d'Asie Centrale*, Geneva, 1963.
Bussagli, M., "Il disco 'battriano' del Museo dell'Ermitage. Su un'analogia iconografica con talune figure angeliche posteriori al V secolo," *Rivista degli Studi Orientali*, 60, nos. 1–4 (1986): 13–44.
Byron, R. *La via per l'Oxiana*, Milan, 1993.
Caiger-Smith, A., *Lustre Pottery*, London, 1985; Watson, O., *Persian Lustre Ware*, London, 1985.
Callieri, P., "On the Diffusion of Mithra Images in Sasanian Iran. New Evidence from a Seal in the British Museum," *East and West*, 40, nos. 1–4 (1990): 79–98.
Callieri, P., "Hephtalides in Margiana? New Evidence from the Buddhist Relics in Merv," in *La Persia e l'Asia Centrale da Alessandro al X secolo*, Rome, 1996: 391–400.
Callieri, P., "A proposito di un'iconografia monetale dei dinasti del Fārs post-achemenide," OCNUS, 6, 1998: 25–38.
Calmeyer, P., "Art in Iran." II. "Median Art and Architecture," in *Encyclopaedia Iranica*, vol. II, ed. E. Yarshater, London and New York, 1987.a: 565–69.
Calmeyer, P., "Art in Iran." III. "Achaemenian Art and Architecture," in *Encyclopaedia Iranica*, vol. II, ed. E. Yarshater, London and New York, 1987.b: 569–80.
Cameron, G. G., "Darius the Great and his Scythian (Saka) Campaign. Bisutun and Herodotus," in *Monumentum H. S. Nyberg*, I (*Acta Iranica II.1*), Leiden, 1975: 77–88.
Canby, S. R., *Persian Painting*, London, 1993.
Cannata, P., *Profilo storico dell'Impero turco (metà VI-metà VII secolo)*, Rome, 1981.
Carswell, J., *New Julfa. The Armenian Churches and Other Buildings*, Oxford, 1968.
Carter, L., "A Gandharan Blessing," *Bulletin of the Asia Institute*, vol. 1, 1987: 45–63.
Cereti, C., "Primary Sources for the History of Inner and Outer Iran in the Sasanian Period," *Archivum Eurasiae Medii Aevi*, 9, 1995–97: 17–71.
Chelkowski, P. J., *Mirror of the Invisible World. Tales from the* Khamseh *of Nizami* (with an essay by P. Soucek and introduction by R. Ettinghausen), New York, 1975.
Chelkowski, P. J., ed., *Ta'ziyeh. Ritual, and Drama in Iran*, New York, 1971.
Choksy, J. K., "Gesture in Ancient and Central Asia." II. "Proskynesis and the Bent Forefinger," *Bulletin of the Asia Institute*, 4 (1990): 201–7.
Choksy, J. K., "In Reverence for Deities and Submission to King: a Few in Near Eastern Societies," *Iranica Antiqua*, 37 (2002): 7–29.
Choubak, H., "Une étonnante céramique dans une nécropole parthe dans la région de Kerman," *Empires perses. D'Alexandre aux Sassanides. Dossier d'archéologie*, 243, 1999: 94–95.
Christensen, A., *L'Iran sous les Sassanides*, Copenhague, 1944 (reprinted Osnabrück, 1971).
Chuvin, P., "Fêtes grecques sur les rhytons de Nisa," in *Histoire et cultes de l'Asie centrale préislamique*, ed. P. Bernard, F. Grenet, Paris, 1991: 23–29.
de Clavijo, R., *Embassy to Tamerlane, 1403–1406*, G. Le Strange, ed., New York, 1928.
Colledge, M.A.R., *The Art of Palmyra*, London, 1976.
Colledge, M.A.R., *Parthian Art*, London, 1977.
Colledge, M., *L'impero dei Parti*, Rome, 1979.
Compareti, M., "La décoration des vêtements du roi Gagik Arcruni à At'mar," *The Journal of Islamic Environmental Design Research Centre. Trails to the East. Essays in Memory of Paolo Cuneo*, 1–2, no. 1997–98–99: 1998–99.
Compareti, M., "Iranian Divinities in the Decoration of Some Dulan and Astana Silks," *Annali di Ca' Foscari*, 39, no. 3 (2000): 331–68.
Compareti, M., "Evidence of Mutual Exchange between Byzantine and Sogdian Art," in *La Persia e Bisanzio*, Rome, 2004: 865–922.
Compareti, M., "Presenza Sasaniane in Africa," in *Il falcone di Bistam. Intorno all'iranica fenice/samand: un progetto di sintesi per il volo del Pegaso iranico tra Ponto, Alessandretta e Insulindia*, ed. G. Scarcia, M. Compareti, Venice, 2003.a: 41–49.
Compareti, M., "Note sull'iconografia del pegaso e del cavallo bardato nell'arte iranica," in *Il falcone di Bistam. Intorno all'iranica fenice/samand: un progetto di sintesi per il volo del Pegaso iranico tra Ponto, Alessandretta e Insulindia*, ed. G. Scarcia, M. Compareti, Venice, 2003. b: 27–36.
Compareti, M., "Sasanian Painting," *Annali dell'Istituto Orientale di Napoli*, 2003.c.
Compareti, M., "The Last Sasanians in China," *Eurasian Studies*, 2, no. 1, 2003.
Compareti, M., "La Persia e il Mediterraneo nell'età achemenide," in *Storia del Mediterraneo. L'Antichità*, Milan, 2004.a: 45–55.
Compareti, M., "La Persia e il Mediterraneo da Alessandro Magno alla comparsa dei Parti," in *Storia del Mediterraneo. L'Antichità*, Milan, 2004.b: 140–52.
Compareti, M., "A Possible Sasanian Textile Fragment in the Benaki Museum," in *Scritti in Onore di Giovanni M. D'Erme*, eds. M. Bernardini, N. L. Tornesello, Naples, 2005: 289–302.
Cook, J. M., "The Rise of the Achaemenids and Establishment of Their Empire," in *The Cambridge History of Iran. Volume 2. The Median and Achaemenian Periods*, ed. I. Gershevitch, Cambridge, 1985: 200–91.
Corpus of Historic Memories of Southern Kazakhstan (in Russian), Almat, 1994.
Coulston, J. C., "Roman, Parthian, and Technical Developments," in *The Defence of the Roman and Byzantine East*, ed. P. Freeman, D. Kennedy, Oxford, 1986: 59–75.
Creswell, K.A.C., *L'architettura islamica delle origini*, Milan, 1966.
Cribb, J., "Numismatic, Evidence for Kushano-Sasanian Chronology," *Studia Iranica*, 19, 1990: 151–95.
Cristoforetti, S., *Il Natale della Luce*, Milan, 2002.
Cristoforetti, S., *Izdilāq: miti e problemi calendariali del fisco islamico*, Venice, 2003.
Crowe, Y., "Central Asia and Afghanistan," in *Architecture of the Islamic World*, G. Michell, ed., London, 1995.
Cuneo, P., *Storia dell'urbanistica. Il mondo islamico*, Rome-Bari, 1986.
Cuneo, P., *Architettura armena*, 1988.
Curatola, G., "Il 'vishap' di Aght'amar: nota sulla diffusione occidentale di un motivo iconografico," *Oriente Moderno*, 18, no. 7–8 (1978): 285–302.
Curatola, G., "Notizia di una pittura murale dei primi del secolo a Kirman," *Annali di Cà Foscari*, 17, no. 3 (S. O. 9) (1978): 143–51.
Curatola, G., "Le grotte di Behestan nella Khamse. Descrizione del sito," *Soltaniye II. Quaderni del Seminario di Iranistica ... di Venezia* 5 (1979): 7–11.
Curatola, G., "Iranian Elements in the Decoration of Nikorcminda: The Senmurv Example," *Annali di Ca' Foscari*, 21 (1981): 27–31.
Curatola, G., *Tappeti*, Milan, 1981.
Curatola, G., "The Viar Dragon," in *Soltaniye III. Quaderni del Seminario di Iranistica ... dell'Università di Venezia* 9 (1982): 45–63.
Curatola, G., "Kalat-i Nadiri. Note sul 'barocco' indo-persiano," in *Quaderni del Seminario di Iranistica ... dell'Università di Venezia*, 21, Venice, 1983: 1–62.
Curatola, G., "Le immagini," in *Persia Barocca. In forma di Parole*, XIII, G. Scarcia, ed. Reggio Emilia, 1983: 227–32.
Curatola, G., "Architettura religiosa lignea nella zona di maragha," in *Rivista degli Studi Orientali. Studi in Onore di Ugo Monneret de Villard*, 49, 1–4 [1985] (1987): 77–93.
Curatola, G., *Draghi. La tradizione artistica orientale e i disegni del tesoro del Topkapi*, Venice, 1989: 77–78.
Curatola, G., ed., *Arabeschi. Tappeti classici d'Oriente dal xvi al xix secolo*, Venice, 1991.
Curatola, G., "Nota sulla simbologia dei Kilim," in *Yad-Nama. In Memoria di Alessandro Bausani*, B. Amoretti Scarcia and L. Rostagno, eds., Rome, 1991: 1:155–66.
Curatola, G., ed., *Eredità dell'Islam. Arte Islamica in Italia*, Milan, 1993.
Curatola, G., "Porte lignee a Mahan," in *Ex Libris Franco Coslovi*, D. Bredi and G. Scarcia, eds., *Eurasiatica*, 40, Venice, 1996: 229–36.
Curatola, G., Scarcia, G., "Notizia di una pittura murale dei primi del secolo a Kirman," in *Annali di Cà Foscari*, 17, no.3 (S. O. 9) 1978: 143–51.
Curatola, G., Scarcia, G., "Gardens and Garden Carpets: An Open Problem," in *Environmental Design*, 2 (1986): 90–97.
Curatola, G., Scarcia, G., *Le arti nell'Islam*, Rome, 1990.
Curtis, S. V., "The Parthian Costume and Headdress," in *Das Parthreich und seine Zeugnisse. The Arsacid Empire: Sources and Documentation*, ed. J. Wiesehöfer, Stuttgart, 1998: 61–73.
Curtis, S. V., "Parthian Culture and Costume," in *Mesopotamia and Iran in the Parthian and Sasanian Periods: Rejection and Revival c. 238 BC–AD 642*, ed. J. Curtis, London, 2000: 23–34.
D'Erme, G., "A Rationalist Form of Thought in Ancient and Medieval Iran," in *Iran Questions et connaissances. Vol. I. La période ancienne* (Iranian study cahier 25), ed. P. Huyse, Paris, 2002: 177–205.
Daffinà, P., "La Persia Sasaniane secondo le fonti cinesi," *Rivista degli Studi Orientali*, vol. LVII, 1985: 121–70.
Daffinà, P., "La seta nel mondo antico," in *La seta e la sua via*, M. T. Lucidi (curator), Rome, 1994: 17–24.

Daffinà, P., *Le relazioni tra Roma e l'India alla luce delle più recenti indagini*, Rome, 1995.
Dalla Barba Brusin, D., Lorenzoni G., *L'arte del patriarcato di Aquileia dal secolo IX al secolo XIII*, Padua, 1968.
Dalton, O., *The Treasure of the Oxus*, London, 1964.
Dandamayev, M. A., "Achaemenes," in *Encyclopaedia Iranica*, vol. I, ed. E. Yarshater, London and Boston, Henley, 1985: 414.
Dandamaev, M. A., *A Political History of the Achaemenid Empire*, Leiden, New York, Copenhagen, Cologne, 1989.
Daneshvari, A., "Complementary Notes on the Tomb Towers of Medieval Iran. I: The Gunbad-i Kabud at Maraghe 593/1197," in *Art et sociéte dans le Monde Iranien*, C. Adle, ed., Paris, 1982: 287–95.
Daneshvari, A., "A Preliminary Study of the Iconography of the Peacock in Medieval Islam," in *The Arts of the Saljuks in Iran and Anatolia*, R. Hillenbrand, ed., Costa Mesa, 1994: 192–200.
Dani, A. H., Litvinsky, B., "The Kushano-Sasanian Kingdom," in *History of Civilizations of Central Asia. Volume III: The Crossroads of Civilizations:* AD *250 to 750*, ed. B. Litvinsky, Paris, 1996: 103–18.
Davis, E., Norgren, J., *A Preliminary Index of Shahnameh Illustrations*, Ann Arbor, 1969.
De Francovich, G., "Il concetto della regalità nell'arte Sasaniane e l'interpretazione di due opere d'arte bizantine del periodo della dinastia macedone: la cassetta eburnea di Troyes e la corona di costantino IX Monomaco di Budapest," in *Persia, Siria, Bisanzio e il Medioevo artistico europeo*, ed. V. Pace, Naples, 1984: 78–138.
De La Vaissière, E., *Histoire des marchands sogdiens*, Paris, 2002.
Debevoise, N. C., "The Essential Characteristics of Parthian and Sasanian Glyptic Art," *Berytus*, 1 (1934): 12–24.
Debevoise, N. C., *Parthian Pottery from Seleucia on the Tigris*, Ann Arbor, 1934.a.
Debevoise, N. C. *A Political History of Parthia*, Chicago, 1938.
Debevoise, N. C., "Parthian Seals," in *A Survey of Persian Art*, vol. II, ed. A. U. Pope, P. Ackermann, London and New York, 1938–39 (reprinted, 1967): 471–74.
Deniké, B. P., "Quelques monuments de bois sculpté au Turkestan occidental," in *Ars Islamica*, 2 (1935): 69–83.
Denny, W. B., *Carpets: Reflections of an Ideal World*, Islamic Arts Museum, Malaysia, 1999.
Diakonoff, I. M., "Media," in *The Cambridge History of Iran. Volume 2. The Median and Achaemenian Periods*, ed. I Gershevitch, Cambridge, 1985: 36–148.
Dickson, M. B., Welch, S. C., *The Houghton Shahnameh*, 2 vols., Cambridge (Mass.) 1981.
Diba, L., Ekhtiar, M., *Royal Persian Paintings. The Qajar Epoch, 1785–1925*, New York, 1999.
Dibaj, I., "Historic Monuments from the Safavid Period in the Ardabil Region" (in Persian), in *Barrasiha-yi Tarikhi*, 3 (1968): 147–66.
Dimand, M., *L'arte dell'Islam*, Florence, 1972.
Dimitriyev, U. M., "The Structural Characteristics of the Architecture in Bukhara in the Second Half of the 16th Century" (in Russian), in *Materialy po istorii i teorii architektury Uzbekistana*, I, Moscow, 1950.
Downey, S. B., "Art in Iran," iv. "Parthian," in *Encyclopaedia Iranica*, vol. II, ed. E. Yarshater, London and New York, 1987.a: 580–85.
Downey, S. B., "Regional Variation in Parthian Religious Architecture," *Mesopotamia*, 12 (1987).b: 19–28.
Downey, S. B., "Dura-europos," in *Enciclopedia dell'Arte Antica Classica ed Orientale*, Second supplement, 1971–94 II, Rome, 1994: 401–3.
Downey, S. B., "L'art et l'architecture parthes," *Les Parthes. Dossier d'Archéologie*, 271 (2002): 22–33.
Drijvers, J. W., "Strabo on Parthia and the Parthians," in *Das Parthreich und seine Zeugnisse. The Arsacid Empire: Sources and Documentation*, ed. J. Wiesehöfer, Stuttgart, 1998: 279–93.
Duchesne-Guillemin, J., "Jesus' Trimorphism and the Differentiation of the Magi," in *Opera Minora III*, Tehran, 1978: 147–56.
Duchesne-Guillemin, J., "La chiesa sassanide e il Mazdeismo," in *Le religioni del mondo classico*, ed. H.-C. Puech, Rome and Bari, 1993: 209–39.
Duyrat, F., "Le monnayage parthe," *Les Parthes. Dossier d'Archéologie*, 271 (2002): 34–41.
Ebert, J., "Farb- und Bedeutungswandel eines parthischen Textilornaments," in *Diversarum Artium Studia*, Wiesbaden, 1982: 13–18.
Egami, N., Fukai, S., Masuda, S., *Dailaman II*, Tokyo, 1966.
Ehrhardt, N., "Parther und partische geschichte bei Tacitus," in *Das Parthreich und seine Zeugnisse*, ed. J. Wiesehöfer, Stuttgart, 1998: 295–307.
Eiland, M. L., "Ceramics of the Silk Road: Parthia and China," *Transactions of the Royal Asiatic Society*, 60, 1995–96: 105–20.
Eliade, M., *Shamanism: Archaic Techniques of Ecstasy*, Princeton, 2004.
Ellis, C. G, "Garden Carpets and their Relation to Safavid Gardens," in *Hali* 5, no. 1 (1982): 11–17.
Eph'al, I., "Syria-Palestina under Achaemenid Rule," in *The Cambridge Ancient History. Second Edition. Vol. IV. Persia, Greece and the Western Mediterranean c. 525 to 479* BC, ed. J. Boardman, N.G.L. Hammond, D. M. Lewis, M. Ostwald, Cambridge, 1988: 138–64.
Erdmann, K., *Oriental Carpets. An Account of their History*, London, 1960.
Errington, R. M., "Rome against Philip and Antiochus," in *The Cambridge Ancient History. Second Edition. Vol. VIII. Rome and the Mediterranean to 133* BC, ed. A. Astin, F. W. Walbank, M. W. Frederiksen, R. Ogilvie, 1989: 244–89.
Esfahan, Masǧid-i Ǧum'a—1. Documentazione fotografica e rapporto preliminare. Photographs and Preliminary Report (Restorations I, 1), Rome, 1972; *Esfahan, Masǧid-i Ǧum'a—2. Il periodo al-i Buyide. The Al-i Buyid Period (Restorations I, 2)* 1973; *Esfahan, Masǧid-i Ǧum'a—3. Research and Restoration Activities, 1973–1978; New Observations (Restorations I, 3)*, Rome, 1984.
Ettinghausen, R., *The Unicorn. Studies in Muslim Iconography*, Freer Gallery of Art Occasional Papers, I, 3, Washington, D.C., 1950.
Ettinghausen, R., "Parthian and Sāsānian Pottery," in *A Survey of Persian Art*, vol. II, ed. U. Pope, P. Ackermann, London and New York, 1938–39 (reprinted, 1967): 646–80.
Ettinghausen, R., *From Byzantium to Sasanian Iran and the Islamic World*, Leiden, 1972.
Falk, T. J., *Qajar Paintings. Persian Oil Paintings of the 18th and 19th Centuries*, London, 1972.
Farkas, A., *Achaemenid Sculpture*, Istanbul, 1974.
Favaro, R., "Da Magi a Re Magi ovvero dal pileo alla corona: appunti per una storia iconografica del copricapo dei Magi," *Miscellanea Adriano Alpago Novello* (forthcoming).
Fehervari, G., *La ceramica islamica*, Milan, 1985.
Ferrante, M., Galdieri, E., "Les deux *Masǧid-i Ǧami'* d'Ardistan et de Zawara," in *Travaux de restauration de monuments historiques en Iran*, G. Zander, ed., Rome, 1968: 475–83.
Ferrier, R. W., "The European Diplomacy of Shah 'Abbas I and the First Persian Embassy to England," *Iran*, 11 (1973): 75–92.
Festugière, A.-J., *Les actes apocryphes de Jean et de Thomas. Traduction française et notes critiques*, Geneva, 1983.
Finster, B., "Frühe iranische Moscheen von Beginn des Islam bis zur Zeit salguqischer Herrschaft," in *Archaeologische Mitteilungen aus Iran*, 19, 1994.
Fiorani-Piacentini, V., "La presa di potere Sasaniane sul golfo Persico fra leggenda e realtà," *Clio*, 2, 1984: 173–210 (English trans.: "Ardashir i Papakan and the Wars against the Arabs: Working Hypothesis on the Sasanian Hold of the Gulf," *Proceedings of the Seminar for Arabian Studies* 15 (1985): 57–77).
Fiorani-Piacentini, V., *Merchants-merchandises and Military Power in the Persian Gulf* Atti dell'Accademia Nazionale dei Lincei, series IX, vol. III, issue 2, Rome, 1992.
Fleury, S., "La Mosquée de Nayin," *Syria*, 11 (1930): 43–58.
Fol, A., Hammond, N.G.L., "Persia in Europe apart from Greece," in *The Cambridge Ancient History. Second Edition. Vol. IV. Persia, Greece and the Western Mediterranean c. 525 to 479* BC, ed. J. Boardman, N.G.L. Hammond, D. M. Lewis, M. Ostwald, Cambridge, 1988: 234–53.
Fontana, M. V., *La Leggenda di Bahrām V Gūr e Āzāda. Materiale per la storia di una tipologia figurativa dalle origini al xiv secolo*, Naples, 1986.
Fontana, M. V., *Iconografia dell'*Ahl al-Bayt. *Immagini di arte persiana dal XII al XX secolo*, Naples, 1994.
Fontana, M. V., "Ancora sulla caccia di Bahrām V Gūr e Āzāda," in *Haft Qalam. Cento pagine in onore di Bianca Maria Alfieri da parte dei suoi allievi*, Naples, 2000: 15–37.
Fontana, M. V., *La pittura islamica dalle origini alla fine del Trecento*, Rome, 2002.
Ford, P.R.J., *Il conoscitore di tappeti orientali*, 1981.
Forte, A., "Il Persiano Aluohan (616–710) nella capitale cinese Luoyang, sede del Chakravartin," in *Incontri di religioni tra il III e il X secolo d.C.*, ed. L. Lanciotti, Florence, 1984: 169–98.
Forte, A., *The Hostage An Shigao and His Offspring. An Iranian Family in China*, Kyoto, 1995.
Forte, A., "The Edict of 636 Allowing the Diffusion of Christianity in China," in P. Pelliot, *L'inscription nestorienne de Si-Ngan-Fou*, edited with supplements by A. Forte, Paris, 1996: 349–74.
Forte, A., "Iraniens en Chine. Bouddhisme, mazdéisme, bureaux de commerce," in *La Sérinde terre d'échanges*, Paris, 2000: 181–90.
Francis, E. D., "Greeks and Persians: The Art of Hazard and Triumph," in *Ancient Persia: The Art of the Empire. Invited Lectures on the Middle East at the University of Texas at Austin*, ed. D. Schmandt-Besserat, Malibu (Calif.), 1980: 53–86.
Frye, R. N., *La Persia preislamica*, Milan, 1967.
Frye, N., "La Partia e la Persia Sasaniane," in *L'impero romano e i popoli limitrofi. Il mondo mediterraneo nell'antichità. IV*, ed. F. Millar, Milan, 1968: 270–92.
Frye, N., "The Political History of Iran under the Sasanians," in *The Cambridge History of Iran. Volume 3 (1). The Seleucid, Parthian and Sasanian Periods*, ed. Yarshater, Cambridge, 1986: 116–80.
Frye, R. N., "L'énigme du IIe siècle chez les Parthes," *Les Parthes. Dossier d'Archéologie*, 271 (2002): 16–17.
Fukai, S., "The Artifacts of Hatra and Parthian Art," *East and West*, 11, nos. 2–3 (1960): 135–81.
Fukai, S., *Persian Glass*, New York, Tokyo, Kyoto, 1977.
Gabba, E., "Sulle influenze reciproche degli ordinamenti militari dei Parti e dei romani," in *La Persia e il mondo greco-romano*, Rome, 1966: 51–73.
Gaïbov, V., Kochelenko, G., La Margiane, *Les Parthes. Dossier d'Archéologie*, 271, 2002: 46–53.
Galdieri, E., Orazi, R., *Progetto di sistemazione del Meydan-i Shah di Esfahan*, 1969.
Galdieri, E., "Two Building Phases of the Time of Shah 'Abbas I in the Maydan-i Shah of Esfahan. Preliminary Note," *East and West*, 20 (1970): 60–69.
Galdieri, E., "Les palais d'ispahan," *Iranian Studies. Journal of the Society for Iranian Studies*, 7, no. 2 (1974): 380–405.
Galdieri, E., *Esfahan: 'Ali, Qapu. An Architectural Survey. Restorations V*, Rome, 1979.
Galdieri, P., "Bibliografia degli scritti di (1968–95)," in *L'arco di fango che rubò la luce alle stelle. Studi in onore di Eugenio Galdieri per il suo settantesimo compleanno*, M. Bernardini, F. Cresti, V. Fontana, F. Noci, R. Orazi, eds., Lugano, 1995: XI–XXII.
Gallotta, B., *Dario e l'Occidente pima delle guerre persiane*, Milan, 1980.
Gamkrelidze, T. V., Ivanov, V. V., *Indoevropeijskij Jazyk i Indoevropeicy*, 2 vols., Tblisi, 1984.
Gantzhorn, V., *Il tappeto cristiano orientale*, Cologne, 1991.
Gasche, H., "Abou Qoubour. Une résidence parthe près de Baghdad," *Empires perses. D'Alexandre aux Sassanides. Dossier d'archéologie*, 243, 1999: 47–49.
Gawlikowski, M., "The Roman Frontier on the Euphrates," *Mesopotamia*, 12 (1987): 77–80.
Gelfer-Jørgensen, M., *Medieval Islamic Symbolism and the Painting in the Cefalù Cathedral*, Leiden, 1986.
Genito, B., *Vetri iranici*, Rome, 1977.

Genito, B., "The Medes: A Reassessment of the Archaeological Evidence," *East and West*, 36, 1–3 (1986): 11–83.
Genito, B., "Altari e gradini nell'iran antico," in *Orientalia Josephi Tucci Memoriae Dicata*, II, ed. G. Gnoli, L. Lanciotti, Rome, 1987: 475–86.
Genito, B., "The Material Culture of the Medes: Limits and Perspectives in the Archaeological Research," in *Un ricordo che non si spegne. Scritti di docenti e collaboratori dell'Istituto Universitario Orientale di Napoli in memoria di Alessandro Bausani*, Naples, 1995: 103–18.
Genito, B., "Sasaniani," in *Enciclopedia dell'Arte Medievale*, vol. X, Rome, 1999: 381–86.
Genito, B., "Il periodo achemenide," in *Antica Persia. I tesori del Museo Nazionale di Tehran e la ricerca italiana in Iran*, P. D'Amore, G. Di Flumeri, G. Lombardo, M. Jung, P. Piacentini, P. Torre (curators), Rome, 2001: 77–81.
Germann, G., "Parthian and Sasanian Saddlery. New Light from the Roman West," in *Archaeologia Iranica et Orientalis. Miscellanea in Honorem Louis Vanden Berghe*, vol. II, ed. L. De Meyer, E. Haenrick, Ghent, 1989: 757–809.
Ghanimati, S., "New Perspectives on the Chronological and Functional Horizons of Kuh-e Khwaja in Sistan," *Iran*, vol. XXXVIII 2000: 137–50.
Ghirshman, R., "Cinq campagnes de fouilles à suse (1946–51)," *Revue d'Assyriologie et d'archéologie orientale*, vol. XLVI, n. 1 1952: 1–18.
Ghirshman, R., *Bishapur. Les mosaïques sassanides*, Paris, 1956. 2 vols.
Ghirshman, R., "Le dieu Zurvan sur les bronzes du Luristan," *Artibus Asiae*, vol. XXI, 1958: 37–42.
Ghirshman, R., *Arte persiana. Parti e Sassanidi*, Milan, 1982.
Ghirshman, R., *Arte persiana. Proto-Iranici, Medi e Achemenidi*, Milan, 1982.
Gignoux, P., "L'impero Sasaniane," in *Storia dell'Umanità. Volume 5. Dal VII secolo a.C. al VII d.C. (i)*, J. Hermann, E. Zürcher (curators), Novara, 2002: 184–90.
Giunta, R., *Les inscriptions funéraires de Gazni (IVe–IXe/X^e–XVe siècles)*, Naples, 2003.
Giuzalijan, L. T., "History of a Bucket from Herat" (in Russian), in *Trudy Ermitaža* 19 (1978): 53–83.
Gluck, J., Hiramoto, S., *A Survey of Persian Handicraft*, Tehran, 1977.
Gnoli, G., *Zoroaster's Time and Homeland. A Study on the Origins of Mazdeism and Related Problems*, Naples, 1980.
Gnoli, G., "La demonizzazione di Alessandro nell'Iran Sasaniane (III–VII secolo d.C.) e nella tradizione zoroastriana," in *Alessandro Magno. Storia e mito*, A. Di Vita (curator), Rome, 1995: 175.
Gnoli, G., *Zoroaster in History*, New York, 2000.
Göbl, R., "Sasanian Coins," in *The Cambridge History of Iran. Volume 3 (1). The Seleucid, Parthian and Sasanian Periods*, ed. E. Yarshater, 1986: 322–39.
Gobolot, H., *Les qanats: une technique d'acquisition de l'eau*, Paris and New York, 1979.
Godard, A., *Les Monuments de Maragha*, Tehran, 1934.
Godard, A., "Notes complémentaires sur les tombeaux de Maragha (Adharbaidjan)," *Athar-é Iran*, 1 (1936): 125–60.
Godard, A., "Ardistan et Zaware," in *Athar-è Iran*, 1, no. 2 (1936): 283–309.
Godard, A., "The Jurjir Mosque in Esfahan," *A Survey of Persian Art*, A. U. Pope, P. Ackermann, eds., Oxford, 1938: 3100–3.
Godard, A., *L'art de l'Iran*, Paris, 1962.
Goldman, B., Little A.M., "The Beginning of Sasanian Painting at Dura-Europos," *Iranica Antiqua*, 15 (1980): 283–99.
Goldman, B., "The Imperial Jewel at Taq-i Bustan," in *Archaeologia Iranica et Orientalis in Honorem Louis Vanden Berghe*, vol. II, ed. L. De Meyer, E. Haerinck, Ghent, 1989: 831–46.
Goldman, B., "Later Pre-Islamic Riding Costume," *Iranica Antiqua*, vol. XXVIII, 1993: 201–46.
Goldman, B., "Pictorial Graffiti of Dura-Europos," *Parthica*, 1 (1999): 19–105.
Golombek, L., "Abbasid Mosque at Balkh," *Oriental Art*, 15 (1969): 23–31.
Golombek, L. *The Timurid Shrine at Gazur Gah*, Toronto, 1969.
Golombek, L., "Anatomy of a Mosque. The Masjid-i Shah of Esfahan," in *Iranian Civilization and Culture*, C. J. Adams, ed., 40 (1972): 5–14.
Golombek, L., Wilber, D. N., *The Timurid Architecture of Iran and Turan*, Princeton, 1988.
Gonzalez, V., *Gli smalti dell'Europa Musulmana e del Maghreb*, Milan, 1994.
Goossens, G., "Artistes et artisans étrangers en Perse sous les Achéménides," *La nouvelle Clio*, 1–2 1949: 32–44.
Grabar, A., "Le rayonnement de l'art sassanide dans le monde Chrétien," in *La Persia nel Medioevo*, Rome, 1971: 679–707.
Grabar, O., Blair, S., *Epic Images and Contemporary History*, Chicago, 1980.
Grabar, O., *Arte Islamica. La formazione di una civiltà*, Milan, 1989.
Grabar, O., *The Great Mosque of Esfahan*, London, 1990.
Grabar, O., *Mostly Miniatures. An Introduction to Persian Painting*, Princeton and Oxford, 2000.
Graf, E., Dreyer, L., "The Roman East from the Chinese Perspective," *Les Annales Archéologiques Arabes Syriennes. Special Issue Documenting the Activities of the International Colloquium: Palmyre and the Silk Road*, 42 (1996): 199–216.
Grainger, J. D., *Seleukos Nikator*, Genoa, 1993.
Gray, B., *Persian Painting*, Geneva, 1961.
Gray, B., "Persian Influence on Chinese Art from the Eight to Fifteenth Centuries," in *Iran* 1 (1963): 13–18.
Gray, B., *The World History of Rashid al-Din. A Study of the Royal Asiatic Society Manuscript*, London, 1978.
Gray, B., "The Tradition of the Wall Painting in Iran," in *Highlights of Persian Art*, R. Ettinghausen, E. Yarshater ed., Boulder (Colorado) 1979: 313–29.
Grosso, F., "Roma e i Parti a fine I inizio II secolo d.C. attraverso le fonti cinesi," in *La Persia e il mondo greco-romano*, Rome, 1966: 157–76.
Grube, J., "Wall Paintings in the Seventeenth Century Monuments of Esfahan," in *Iranian Studies. Journal of the Society for Iranian Studies* 7, no. 1 (1974): 511–42.
Grube, J., *La pittura dell'Islam*, Bologna, 1980.
Grube, E. J., "Il Khanid Stucco Decoration: Notes on the Stucco Decoration of Pir-i Bakran," in *Esfahan. Atti del Convegno Internazionale Sultaniya e Esfahan. Venezia, 1977*, Venice, 1981: 85–96.
Grube, E., ed., *Islamic Art* 1 (1981).
Sims, E., "Painting," in *The Arts of Persia*, R. W. Ferrier ed., New Haven, London, 1989: 200–31.
Grube, E. J., "La pittura islamica nella Sicilia normanna del XII secolo," in *La pittura in Italia. L'Altomedioevo*, Milan, 1994: 416–31.
Gunter, A., "Ancient Iranian Drinking Vessels in the Arthur M. Sackler Gallery," *Orientations*, vol. 18, 9, September 1987: 38–45.
Gunter, A. C., Jett, P., *Ancient Iranian Metalwork in the Arthur M. Sackler Gallery and the Freer Gallery of Art*, Washington, D. C., 1992.
Gyselen, R., "La Géographie administrative de l'empire sassanide. Les témoignages sigillographiques," in *Res Orientales*, I, Paris, 1989.
Gyselen, R., "Les monnaies," in *Splendeur des Sassanides. L'empire perse entre Rome et la Chine [224–642]*, Brussels, 1993: 127–30.
Gyselen, R., "La glyptique," in *Catalogo Bruxelles, 1993: Splendeur des Sassanides. L'empire perse entre Rome et la Chine [224–642]*, B. Overlaet (curator), Brussels, 1993.a: 123–26.
Gyselen, R., Gignoux, P., "Un dieu nimbé de flammes d'époque sassanide," *Iranica Antiqua*, 36 (2000): 291–314.
Haerinck, E., *La céramique en Iran pendant la période parthe*, Ghent, 1983.
Haerinck, E., "L'art des bas-reliefs rupestres," *Empires perses. D'Alexandre aux Sassanides. Dossier d'archéologie*, 243, 1999: 54–60.
Haldon, J. F., *Byzantium in the Seventh Century. Transformation of a Culture*, Cambridge, 1990.
Hannestad, K., "Les relations de Byzance avec la Transcaucasie et l'Asie Centrale aux 5e et 6e siècles," *Byzantion*, 25–27, 1955–57: 421–56.
Hansman, J., Stronach, D., "A Sasanain Repository at Shahr-i Qūmis," *Journal of the Royal Asiatic Society. Studies in Memory of Sir Mortimer Wheeler*, 2 (1970): 141–58.
Harada, Y., "The Interchange of Eastern and Western Cultures as Evidenced in the Shôsôin Treasures," *Memoirs of the Research Department of the Toyo Bunko*, vol. XI 1939: 55–78.
Harmatta, J., "The Struggle for the Possession of South Arabia between Aksūm and the Sasanians," in *IV Congresso Internazionale di Studi Etoipici*, Rome, 1974: 95–106.
Harmatta, J., "The Struggle for the 'Silk Route' between Iran, Byzantium and the Türk Empire from 560 to 630 AD," in *Kontakte zwischen Iran, Byzanz und der Steppe in 6.–7. Jr.*, ed. C. Bálint, Budapest, 2000: 249–52.
Harper, P. O., *The Royal Hunter*, New York, 1978.
Harper, P. O., "A Stucco King from Sasanian Kish," in *Bibliotheca Mesopotamica*, 7 (1979): 75–79.
Harper, P. O., Meyers, P., *Silver Vessels of the Sasanian Period*, I, New York, 1981.
Harper, P. O., "Parthian and Sasanian Silverware: Questions of Continuity and Innovation," *Mesopotamia*, 12 (1987): 341–55.
Harper, P. O., "An Iranian Silver Vessel from the Tomb of Feng Hetu," *Bulletin of the Asia Institute*, 4 (1990): 51–59.
Harper, P. O., "La vaisselle en metal," in Brussels 1993: *Splendeur des Sassanides. L'empire perse entre Rome et la Chine [224–642]*, B. Overlaet (curator), Brussels, 1993: 95–108.
Harper, P. O., Meyers, P., *Silver Vessels of the Sasanian Period. Volume One: Royal Imagery*, New York, 1981.
Hayashi, R., *The Silk Road and the Shoso-in*, New York and Tokyo, 1975.
Hermann, G., *The Iranian Revival*, Oxford, 1977.
Hermann, G., *Monuments of Merv I: Traditional Buildings of Karakum*, London, 1999.
Herzfeld, E., *Der Wandschmuck der Bauten von Samarra*, Berlin, 1923.
Herzfeld, E., *Iran in the Ancient East*, London and New York, 1941.
Herzfeld, E., *Iran in the Ancient Near East*, Oxford, 1941.
Hillenbrand, R., "The Tomb Towers of Iran from 1000 to 1550" (unpublished dissertation), Oxford, 1972.
Hillenbrand, R., "The Use of Glazed Tilework in Iranian Architecture," in *Akten des VII. Internationalen Kongresses für iranische Kunst und Archäologie* (Munich, 1976), Berlin, 1979: 545–54.
Hillenbrand, R., "Architecture," in, *The Arts of Persia*, W. Ferrier, ed., New Haven and London, 1989: 81–107.
Hillenbrand, R., *Islamic Architecture, Form, Function and Meaning*, Edinburgh, 1994.
Hillenbrand, R., *Islamic Art and Architecture*, London, 1999.
Hillenbrand, R., "The Architecture of the Ghaznavids and Ghurids," in *The Sultan's Turret. Studies in Honour of Clifford Edmund Bosworth*, vol. 2 (studies in Persian and Turkish culture), C. Hillenbrand, ed., Leiden, 2000: 124–206.
Hinz, W., *Mani and Kardēr, La Persia nel Medioevo*, Rome, 1971: 485–99.
Hobson, A., "Islamic Influence on Venetian Renaissance Bookbinding," in *Arte Veneziana e Arte Islamica*, E. J. Grube, ed., Venice, 1989: 111–23.
Holod, R., "The Monument of Duvāzdah Imām in Yazd and its Inscription of Foundation," in *Near Eastern Numismatics, Iconography, Epigraphy and History. Studies in Honour of George C. Miles*, D. K. Kouymjian, ed., Beirut, 1974: 255–88.
Holod, R., ed., "Studies on Esfahan. Proceedings of the Esfahan Colloquium. Harvard, 1974," in *Iranian Studies. Journal of the Society for Iranian Studies* 7 (1974).
Homès-Fredericq, D., *Hatra et ses sculptures parthes: Études stylistique et iconographique*, Istanbul, 1963.
Housego, J., "Carpets," in *The Arts of Persia*, W. Ferrier, ed., New Haven and London, 1989.

Huff, D., "Architecture. III. Sasanian," in *Encyclopaedia Iranica*, vol. II, ed. Yarshater, London and New York, 1987: 329–34.

Huff, D., "Architecture sassanide," in Brussels 1993: *Splendeur des Sassanides. L'empire perse entre Rome et la Chine [224–642]*, B. Overlaet (curator), Brussels, 1993: 45–61.

Huff, D., "Fire altars' and *Astodans*," in *The Art and Archaeology of Ancient Persia. New Light on the Parthian and Sasanian Empires*, ed. V. S. Curtis, R. Hillenbrand, J. M. Rogers, London and New York, 1998: 74–83.

Huot, J.-L., *Iran I*, Geneva, 1976.

Hutt, M., "The Development of the Minaret in Iran under the Saljuks," London (S. O. A. S.) 1974 (unpublished doctoral thesis).

Hutt, A., "Iran," in *Architecture of the Islamic World*, G. Michell, ed., London, 1978: 257–58.

Hutt, A. M., "Iran," in *Architecture of the Islamic World*, G. Michell, ed., London, 1995.

Hutter, M., "Manichaeism in the Early Sasanian Empire," *Numen*, vol. 40, 1993: 2–15.

Huyse, P., "Kerdīr and the First Sasanians," in *Proceedings of the Third European Conference of Iranian Studies. Part 1. Old and Middle Iranian Studies*, ed. N. Sims-Williams, Wiesbaden, 1998: 109–20.

Huyse, P., "La revendication de territoires achéménides par les Sassanides: Une réalité historique?," in *Iran questions et connaissances. Vol. I. La période ancienne*, ed. P. Huyse, Paris, 2002: 297–311.

Ierusalimskaja, A. A., "K složenju školy chudožestvennogo šelkotkačestva v sogde," *Srednjaja Azija i Iran*, Leningrad, 1972: 5–46.

Imanpur, M. T., "Was Nowrooz celebrated in Persepolis during the Achaemenid Period?" in *V European Conference of Iranian Studies*, Ravenna, October 6–11, 2003.

Ingholt, H., *Parthian Sculptures from Hatra. Orient and Hellas in Art and Religion*, New Haven, 1954.

Ingholt, H., "The Prima Porta Statue of Augustus," Part I: "The Interpretation of the Breastplate," *Archaeology*, 22 no. 3 (1969): 176–87.

Invernizzi, A., "Héracles à Séleucie du Tigre," *Revue d'Archéologie*, 1, 1989: 65–113.

Invernizzi, A., "Partica Arte," in *Enciclopedia dell'Arte Antica Classica e Orientale. Secondo Supplemento, 1971–94*, Rome, 1996, 4: 264–68.

Invernizzi, A., "Parthian Nisa. New Lines of Research," in *Das Parthreich und seine Zeugnisse. The Arsacid Empire: Sources and Documentation*, ed. J. Wiesehöfer, Stuttgart, 1998: 45–59.

Invernizzi, A., "Nisa capitale des parthes au Turkménistan," *Empires perses. D'Alexandre aux Sassanides. Dossier d'archéologie*, 243 (1999): 38–39.

Invernizzi, A., *Sculture di metallo da Nisa. Cultura greca e cultura iranica in Partia*, Louvain, 1999.

Invernizzi, A., "Il periodo portico," in Rome 2001: *Antica Persia. I tesori del Museo Nazionale di Tehran e la ricerca italiana in Iran*, Rome, 2001.a: 112–18.

Invernizzi, A., "Arsacid Dynastic Art," *Parthica*, 3, 2001.b: 133–57.

Ipshiroghlu, M. S., *Siyah, Qalem, Vollständige Faksimile Ausgabe der Blätter des Meisters Siyah Qalam aus dem Besitz des Topkapi Sarayi Muzesi, Istanbul und Freer Gallery, Washington*, Graz, 1976.

Ittig, A., "Notes on a Zilu Fragment dated 963/1556 in the Islamic Museum Cairo," *Iranian Studies*, 25, 1–2 (1992): 37–42.

Ivanov, A. A., "The Life of Muhammad Zaman: A Reconsideration," *Iran*, 17 (1969): 65–70.

Ivanov, A., *Masterpieces, of Islamic Art in the Hermitage Museum* (Dar al-Athar al-Islamiyya), Kuwait City, 1990.

Izadpaneh, B., *Kerman*, Tehran, 1993.

Jenkins, M., *Islamic Art in the Kuwait National Museum*, London, 1983.

Jeroussalimskaja, A., "Soieries sassanides." A. "Historique culturel," in *Catalogo Bruxelles, 1993: Splendeur des Sassanides. L'empire perse entre Rome et la Chine [224–642]*, B. Overlaet (curator), Brussels, 1993: 113–18.

Karamagarali, B., *Muhammed Siyah Kalem'e Atfedilen Minyturler*, Ankara, 1984.

Kawami, T. S., "Greek Art and Persian Taste: Some Animals Sculptures from Persepolis," *American Journal of Archaeology*, vol. 90, n. 3, 1986: 259–67.

Kawami, T. S., *Monumental Art of the Parthian Period in Iran*, Leiden, 1987.a.

Kawami, T. S., Kuh-e Khwaja, Iran, and its Wall Paintings: The Records of Ernst Herzfeldè, *The Metropolitan Museum of Art Journal*, vol. 22 1987.b: 13–52.

Kawami, T. S., "Ancient Textiles from Shahr-i Qumis," *Hali*, 59 1991: 95–99.

Kawami, T. S., *Ancient Iranian Ceramics from the Arthur M. Sackler Collections*, New York, 1992.

Kawami, T. S., "Clothing." IV. "In the Arsacid Period," in *Encyclopaedia Iranica*, vol. V, ed. E. Yarshater, Costa Mesa (California) 1992.a: 737–39.

Kawami, T. S., "Archaeological Evidence for Textiles in Pre-Islamic Iran," *Iranian Studies*, 25, nos. 1–2 (1992). b: 7–18.

Keall, E. J., "Architecture." II. "Parthian," in *Encyclopaedia Iranica*, vol. II, ed. E. Yarshater, London and New York, 1987: 327–29.

Keall, E. J., "Bishapur," in *Encyclopaedia Iranica*, vol. V, ed. E. Yarshater, Costa Mesa (California), 1990: 287–89.

Keall, E. J., "Forerunners of Umayyad Art: Sculptural Stone from the Hadramawt," *Muqarnas*, 12 (1995).a: 11–23.

Keall, E. J., "A Second Attempt to Understand the Historical Context of Husn al-'Urr in the Hadramawt," *Proceedings of the Seminar for Arabian Studies*, 25 (1995).b: 55–62.

Keall, E. J., "Carved Stone from the Hadrawmawt in Yemen: Is it Sasanian?" in *The Art and Archaeology of Ancient Persia. New Light on the Parthian and Sasanian Empires*, ed. V. S. Curtis, R. Hillenbrand, J. M. Rogers, London, New York, 1998: 141–49.

Keall, E. J., "Qal'eh-i Yazdigird," *Les Parthes. Dossier d'Archéologie*, 271 2002: 64–71.

Keall, E. J., Leveque M. A., Willson N., "Qal'eh-i Yazdigird: its Architectural Decoration," *Iran*, 18 (1980): 1–41.

Kellens, J., "Zoroastre dans l'histoire ou dans le mythe? A propos du dernier livre de Gherardo Gnoli," *Journal Asiatique* 289, no. 2 (2001): 171–84.

Kennedy, E. J., "The Exact Sciences in Timurid," in *The Cambridge History of Iran*, 6, Cambridge, 1986: 578–80.

Kervran, M., "The Fortress of Ratto Kot, at the Mouth of the Banbhore River (Indus Delta–Sindh–Pakistan)," *Pakistan Archaeology*, 27 (1992): 143–70.

Kettenhofen, E., *Die römisch-persischen Kriege des 3. Jh. n. Chr. nach der Inschrift Šapuhrs, I. an der Ka'be-ye Zartošt*, Tübinger Atlas des Vorderen Orients (TAVO), Reihe B, m. 55, Wiesbaden, 1982.

Kettenhofen, E., "Die Arsakiden in den armenischen Quellen," in *Das Parthreich und seine Zeugnisse. The Arsacid Empire: Sources and Documentation*, ed. J. Wiesehöfer, 1998: 325–53.

Kiani, M. Y., *Discoveries from Robat-e Sharaf* (in Persian), Tehran, 1981.

Kim, W., *Art and Archaeology of Ancient Korea*, Seoul, 1986.

Kleiss, W., Kiani, M. Y., *Iranian, Caravansarais*, Tehran, 1995.

Klíma, O., "The Middle Persian Era," in *History of Iranian Literature*, ed. J. Rypka, Dordrecht, 1968: 25–65.

Klimkeit, H.-J., "Manichaean Kingship: Gnosis at Home in the World," *Numen*, 29, no. 1 (1982): 17–32.

Komaroff, L., Carboni, A. S., eds., *The Legacy of Gengis Khan. Courtly Art and Culture in Western Asia, 1256–1353*, New York, 2002.

Košelenko, G. A., *Kul'tura Parfii*, Moscow, 1966.

Košelenko, G. A., *Rodina Parfijan*, 1977.

Košelenko, G., Lapshin, A., Novikov, S., "Mansur-deep Excavations," *Bulletin of the Asia Institute*, 3, 1989: 45–52.

Koshelenko, G. A., Pilipko, V. N., "Parthia," in *History of Civilizations of Central Asia. Vol. II: The Development of Sedentary and Nomadic Civilizations: 700 BC to AD 250*, ed. J. Harmattan, Paris, 1994: 131–50.

Kouzmina, N. N., *Aq Saray in Shahr-i Sabz* (in Russian), Tashkent, 1985–86.

Krachkovskaja, V., "Notices sur les inscriptions de la Mosquée Djoum'a à Véramine," in *Revue des Etudes Islamiques*, 5 (1931): 25–58.

Kröger, J., "Sasanianischer Stuckdekor. Ein Beitrag zum Reliefdekor aus Stuck in Sasanianischer und frühislamischer Zeit nach den Ausgrabungen von, 1928/9 und, 1931/2 in der Sasanianischen Metropole Ktesiphon (Iraq) und unter besonderer Berücksichtigung der Stuckfunde vom Taht-i Sulaiman (Iran), aus Nizamabad (Iran) sowie zahlreicher anderer Fundorte" (doctoral thesis), Berlin, 1977.

Kröger, J., "Stucco," in P. O. Harper, *The Royal Hunter*, New York, 1978: 101–4.

Kröger, J., "Iran and India: Questions of Interaction," *South Asian Archaeology, 1979*, ed. H. Härtel, Berlin, 1981: 441–48.

Kröger, J., *Sasanianischer Stuckdekor*, Mainz, 1982.

Kröger, J., "Décor en stuc," in Brussels 1993: *Splendeur des Sassanides. L'empire perse entre Rome et la Chine [224–642]*, B. Overlaet (curator), Brussels, 1993.a: 63–65.

Kröger, J., "Ctesiphon," in *Encyclopaedia Iranica*, E. Yarshater, ed., Costa Mesa (California) 1993.b: 446–48.

Kröger, J., *Neshabur: Glass of the Early Islamic Period*, New York, 1995.

Kröger, J., "Gläser aus spätantiker und islamischer Zeit in der Abegg-Stiftung," in *Entlang der Seidenstraße. Frühmittelalterliche Kunst zwischen Persien und China in der Abegg-Stiftung*, Riggisberger Berichte 6, Riggisberg, 1998: 299–322.

Kröger, J., "The Stucco Programma," in *Iran* 39 (2001): 47–50.

Kurz, O., "Cultural Relations between Parthia and Rome," in *Cambridge History of Iran. Volume 3 (1). The Seleucid, Parthian and Sasanian Periods*, ed. E. Yarshater, Cambridge, 1983: 559–67.

Kuzmina, E., "Acient Iranian and Near Eastern Elements in Scythian Art," in Kuzmina, *Mifologija i iskusstvo Skifov i Baktrijcev (kul'turologičeskie očerki)*, Moscow, 2002: 146–66.

Laing, E. J., "Recent Finds of Western-Related Glassware, Textiles and Metalwork in Central Asia and China," *Bulletin of the Asia Institute*, 9 (1995): 1–18.

Lang, D. M., "Iran, Armenia and Georgia. Political Contacts," in *The Cambridge History of Iran. Volume 3 (1). The Seleucid, Parthian and Sasanian Periods*, ed. E. Yarshater, 1983: 505–36.

Lavin, I., "The Hunting Mosaics of Antioch and Their Sources. A Study of Compositional Principles in the Development of Early Mediaeval Style," *Dumbarton Oaks Papers*, 17 (1963): 179–286.

Lecoq, P., "Aparna," in *Encyclopaedia Iranica*, ed. E. Yarshater, London, New York, 1987, 2: 151.

Lee, J. L., Grenet, F., "New Light on the Sasanian Painting at Ghulbiyan, Faryab Province, Afghanistan," *South Asian Studies*, 14 (1998): 75–85.

Lee, S. E., Ho, W. K., *Chinese Art under the Mongols: The Yuan Dinasty (1279–1368)*, Cleveland, 1968.

Lentz, T. W., Lowry, G. D., *Timur and the Princely Vision. Persian Art and Culture in the Fifteenth Century*, Washington D.C., and Los Angeles, 1989.

Leriche, P., "Dura Europos," in *Encyclopaedia Iranica*, vol. VII, ed. E. Yarshater, Costa Mesa (California) 1996: 589–93.

Leriche, P., "Le mystère parthe," *Les Parthes. Dossier d'Archéologie*, 271 (2002): 2–5.

Lerner, J., "A Note on Sasanian Harpies," *Iran*, 13 (1975): 166–71.

Lerner, J., *Christian Seals of the Sasanian Period*, Istanbul, 1977.

Lerner, J. D., *The Impact of Seleucid Decline on the Eastern Iranian Plateau. The Foundations of Arsacid Parthia and Graeco-Bactria*, Stuttgart, 1999.

Le Strange, G., *Embassy to Tamerlane. 1403–1406*, New York, 1928.

Levi, *Antioch Mosaic Pavements*, Princeton, 1947.

Lévi-Strauss, M., *The Kashmir Shawl*, 1986.

Liebe-Harkort, K., "Das Observatorium Ulugh Begs in Samarkand," in *Mitteilungen der Societas Uralo-Altaica* 1 (1968): 160–64.

Lippolis, C., "L'ancienne Nisa. La forteresse de Mithridate," *Les Parthes. Dossier d'Archéologie*, 271, 2002: 42–45.

Litvinsky, B. A., "The Hephtalite Empire," in *History of Civilizations of Central Asia. Volume III: The Crossroads of Civilizations: AD 250 to 750*, ed. B. A. Litvinsky, Paris, 1996: 135–62.

Lockhart, L., *Persian Cities*, London, 1960.

Lockhart, L., "The Relations between Edward I and II of England and the Mongol Il-Khans of Persia," in *Iran* 6 (1968): 23–31.

Lockhart, della Rocca, R. M., Tiepolo, M. F., *I viaggi in Persia degli ambasciatori veneti Barbaro e Contarini* (il nuovo Ramusio, VII), Rome, 1973.

Lo Muzio, C., "Gli ossuari," in Rome 1993: *Oxus. Tesori dell'Asia Centrale*, P. D'Amore, G. Lombardo (curators), Rome, 1993: 126–29.

Lowry, G. D., Nemazee, S., *A Jeweler's Eye. Islamic Arts of the Book from the Vever Collection*, Washington, Seattle and London, 1988: 31–37.

Lozinski, B. P., *The Original Homeland of the Parthians*, The Hague, 1959.

Lozinski, B., "The Parthian Dynasty," *Iranica Antiqua*, 19 (1984): 119–39.

Lozinski, B. P., "The Phoenix Mosaic from Antioch: A New Interpretation," in *Fifth International Colloquium on Ancient Mosaics*, ed. R. Zing, Ann Arbor (Michigan), 1995: 135–42.

Lucidi, M. T., "Valore e lettura di un motivo culturale caratteristico: la criniera dentellata del cavallo, alla luce di una interpretazione analitica dei reperti artistici," *Rivista degli Studi Orientali*, 44, no. 4 (1969): 295–323.

Lukonin, V., *Iran II*, Geneva, 1976.

Lukonin, V. G., *Iskusstvo drevnego Irana*, Moscow, 1977.

Luschey-Schmeisser, I., "Der Wand-und Deckenschmuck eines Safavidischen Palastes in Nayin," in *Archaeologische Mitteilungen aus Iran*, n.f., 2 (1969): 183–92.

Luschey-Schmeisser, I., "Ein Neuer Raum in Nayin," in *Archaeologische Mitteilungen aus Iran*, n.s., 5 (1972): 309–14.

Luschey-Schmeisser, I., *The Pictorial Tile Cycle of Hasht Behesht in Esfahan and its Iconographic Tradition*, 1978.

Luschey, H., "The Pul-i Khwaju in Esfahan: a Combination of Bridge, Dam and Water Art." *Iran*, 23 (1985): 143–51.

Macdermot, B. C., "Roman Emperors in the Sassanian Reliefs," *The Journal of Roman Studies*, 44 (1954): 76–80.

Mackintosh, M. C., "Taq-i Bustan and Byzantine Art. A Case for Early Byzantine Influence on the Reliefs of Taq-i Bustan," *Iranica Antiqua* 13 (1978): 150–77.

Maenchen-Helfen, O., "From China to Palmira," *The Art Bulletin*, 25, n. 4 (1943): 358–62.

Maenchen-Helfen, O., "Crenelated Mane and Scabbard Slide," *Central Asiatic Journal*, vol. III, 2, 1957: 85–138.

Mallory, J. P., *In Search of the Indo-Europeans*, London, New York, 1989.

Mallory, J. P., Adams, D. Q., *Encyclopaedia of Indo-European Culture*, London and Chicago, 1997.

Mango, C., "Deux études sur Byzance et la Perse sassanide." I. "L'inscription historique de martyropolis," II. "Héraclius, Šahrvaraz et la Vraie Croix," *Travaux et mémoires*, 9 (1985): 91–118.

Man'kovskaya, I., "Towards the Study of Forms in Central Asian Architecture at the End of the Fourteenth Century: The Mausoleum of Khvaja Ahmad Yasavi," *Iran* 23 (1985): 109–27.

Marazzi, U., "Alcuni problemi relativi alla diffusione del manicheismo presso i Turchi nei secoli VIII-IX," *Annali dell'Istituto Orientale di Napoli*, 39 (n.s. 29) (1979): 239–52.

Maricq, A., "Classica et Orientalia." 5. "Res Gestae Divi Saporis," *Syria*, 35 (1958): 295–360.

Maricq, A., Wiet, G., *Le Minaret de Djam. La Découverte de la capitale des sultans Ghorides (XIIe–XIIIe siècles)*, Paris, 1959.

Marschak, B., *Silberschätze des Orients. Metallkunst des 3.–13. Jahrhunderts und ihre Kontinuität*, Leipzig, 1986.

Marschak, B., "Les fouilles de Pendjikent," *Comptes Rendus de l'Académie des Inscriptions et Belles-Lettres*, 1990: 286–313.

Marshak, B. I., "Le programme iconographique des peintures de la 'Salle des ambassadeurs' à Afrasiab (Samarkand)," *Arts Asiatiques*, vol. XLIX, 1994: 5–20.

Marshak, B. I., "New Discoveries in Pendjikent and a Problem of Comparative Study of Sasanian and Sogdian Art," in *La Persia e l'Asia Centrale da Alessandro al X secolo*, 1996: 425–38.

Marshak, B. I., "Pre-Islamic Painting of the Iranian Peoples and its Sources in Sculpture and Decorative Arts," in E. Sims, *Peerless Images. Persian Painting and its Sources*, New Haven and London, 2002: 7–19.

Marshak, B. I., *Legends, Tales, and Fables in the Art of Sogdiana*, New York, 2002.a.

Martin, F. R., *A History of Oriental Carpets before 1800*, Vienna, 1908.

Martinovich, N. N., "The Life of Muhammad Paolo Zaman the Persian Painter of the XVIIth Century," in *Journal of the American Oriental Society* 45, no. 2 (1925): 106–9.

Masson, M. E., *Rigistan and its Madrasahs* (in Russian), Tashkent, 1926.

Masson, M. E., Pugačenkova, G. A., *The Parthian Rhyton of Nisa*, Florence, 1982.

Masson, M. E., *The Mauloleum of Hoja Ahmad Yassavi* (in Russian), Almaty, 1999.

Mathiesen, H. E., *Sculpture in the Parthian Empire*, Aarhus, 1992.

Matteini, M., Petruccioli, A., eds., *Giardini Islamici. Architettura, Ecologia*, the conference in Genoa, November 8–9, 2001.

Matthiae, P., *La storia dell'arte dell'Oriente Antico. I grandi imperi, 1000–330 a.C.*, Milan, 1996.

Mcdonald, V., "The Religious and Social Views of Nizami of Ganjeh," *Iran*, 1 (1963): 97–101.

McDowell, J. A., "Textiles," in *The Arts of Persia*, W. Ferrier, ed., New Haven and London, 1989.

Mechkati, N., *Monuments et sites historiques de l'Iran*, Tehran, 1974.

Melikian-Chirvani, A. S., "La plus ancienne mosquée de Balkh," *Arts Asiatiques*, 20 (1969): 3–20.

Melikian-Chirvani, A. S., "Le Roman de Varque et Golshah. Essai sur les rapports de l'esthétique littéraire et de l'esthétique plastique dans l'Iran pré-mongol, suivi de la traduction du poéme," in *Ars Asiatique*, 22 (1970): 1–262.

Melikian-Chirvani, A. S., "Le 'Shah-Nama,' la gnose soufie et le pouvoir mongol," in *Journal Asiatique*, 272 (1984): 249–337.

Melikian-Chirvani, A. S., "Le livre des Rois miroir du destin," in *Studia Iranica*, 17 (1988): 39–46.

Melikian-Chirvani, A. S., "Le livre de Rois, miroir du destin, III- Takht-e Soleyman et la symbolique du "Shah-Name," in *Studia Iranica* 20 (1991): 33–148.

Melikian-Chirvani, A. S., "From the Royal Boat to the Beggar's Bowl," in *Islamic Art* 4 (1991): 3–111.

Melikian-Chirvani, A. S., "Les frises du shah Name dans l'architecture iranienne sous les Ilkhan," in *Studia Iranica* (Cahier 18), Paris, 1996.

Membrè, M., *Relazione di Persia*, F., Castro, M. Piemontese, eds. introduction by Scarcia, Naples, 1969.

Meshkati, N., *A List of the Historical Sites and Ancient Monuments of Iran*, Tehran, 1974.

Mifrendereski, F. N., Zonuzi, A. F., *Ceramica nell'architettura in Persia*, Florence, 1992.

Milan 2001: *Oro. Il mistero dei Sarmati e degli Sciti*, J. Aruz, A. Farkas, A. Alekseev, E. Korolkova (curators) 2001.

Miles, G. C., "The Inscriptions of the Masjid-i Jami' at Ashtarjan," in *Iran* 16 (1978): 89–98.

Miller, M. C., "Adoption and Adaptation of Achaemenid Metalware Forms in Attic Black-Ware of the Fifth Century," *Archäologische Mitteilungen aus Iran*, 26 (1993): 109–46.

Miller, M. C., "Greece Relations with Persian Empire." II. "Greco-Persian Cultural Relations," in *Encyclopaedia Iranica*, vol. XI, ed. E. Yarshater, New York, 2002: 301–19.

Mills, J., *Carpets in Picture*, London, 1975.

Mills, J., "The Coming of the Carpet to the West," in King, D., Sylvester, D., *The Eastern Carpet in the Western World*, London, 1983: 11–23.

Mirfendereski, F. N., Zonuzi, A. F., *Ceramica nell'architettura in Persia*, Florence, 1992.

Molé, M., "L'épopée iranienne après Firdousi," *La nouvelle Clio*, V, 7–10, 1953: 377–93.

Moline, J., "The Minaret of Ǧam," *Kunst des Orients*, 9 (1973–74): 131–48.

Moline, J., "Salǧuk Minarets In Iran: Structural Developments," in *Kunst des Orients* 12 (1978–79): 95–102.

Monneret de Villard, U., "Sull'origine della doppia cupola persiana," *Architettura e Arti Decorative*, 1 (1921): 315–24.

Monneret de Villard, U., *Le leggende orientali sui Magi evangelici*, Vatican City, 1942.

Monneret de Villard, U., "Arte Cristiana e Musulmana del Vicino Oriente," in *Le Civiltà dell 'Oriente*, 4, Rome, 1962: 450–652.

Monneret de Villard, U., *Introduzione allo studio dell'archeologia islamica*, Venice and Rome, 1966.

Moorey, P.R.S., "Metalwork and Glyptic," in *The Cambridge History of Iran. Volume 2. The Median and Achaemenian Periods*, ed. I. Gershevitch, Cambridge, 1986: 856–69.

Morgenstern, L., "Mural Painting," in *A Survey of Persian Art*. Vol. I, A. U. Pope, P. Ackerman ed., London and New York, 1938: 1365–90.

Morton, A. H., "The Ardabil Shrine in the Reign of Shah Tahmasp I," in *Iran*, 12 (1974): 31–64, and 13 (1975): 39–58.

Musche, B., *Vorderasiatischer Schmuck zur Zeit der Arsakiden und der Sasanianen*, Leiden, New York, Copenhagen and Cologne, 1988.

Musti, D., "Lo stato dei seleucidi. dinastia popoli città da Seleuco I ad Antioco III," *Studi Classici e Orientali*, 15 (1966): 61–201.

Naumann, E. R., "Ein Kiosk im Sommerpalast des Abaqa Chan auf dem Tacht-i Sulaiman und seine Dekoration," in *Forschungen zur Kunst Asiens. In Memoriam Kurt Erdmann*, O. Aslanapa, R. Naumann, eds., Istanbul, 1969: 35–65.

Needham, J., *Scienza e civiltà in Cina. Volume 1. Lineamenti introduttivi*, Turin, 1981.

Nemtseva, N. B., Shvab, Y. Z., *The Complex of the Shah-i Zinda* (in Russian), Tashkent, 1979.

Newman, J., "Sufism and Anti-Sufism in Safavid Iran: The Authorship of the *Hadiqat al-Shi'a* Revisited," in *Iran*, 37 (1999): 95–108.

Nikiforov, B., "The Madrasah of Abd al-Aziz Khan in Bukhara" (in Russian), in *Iskusstvo Srednej Azii*, Moscow, 1930.

Nikitin, A. B., "Sasaniane, Arte," *Enciclopedia dell'Arte Antica Classica e Orientale. Secondo Supplemento, 1971–1994*, vol. V, Rome, 1997: 168–74.

Nunn, A., *Die Wandmalerei und der glasierte Wandschmuck im Alten Orient*, Leiden, New York, Copenhagen, and Cologne, 1988.

O'Kane, B., "The Madrasa Al-Ghiyasiyya at Khargird," in *Iran*, 14 (1976): 79–92.

O'Kane, B., "Salǧuk Minarets: Some New Data," *Annales Islamologiques*, 20 (1984).

O'Kane, B., *Timurid Architecture in Khurasan*, Costa Mesa, (Calif.), 1987.

O'Kane, B., "Rock Faces and Figures in Persian Painting," in *Islamic Art* 4 (1991): 219–46.

Oney, G., "The Interpretation of the Frescoes in the I. Kharragan Mausoleum near Qazvin," in *Akten des vii. Internationalen Kongresses für iranische Kunst und Archäologie* (Munich, 1976), Berlin, 1979: 400–8.

Otavsky, K., "Zur Kunsthistorischen Einordung der Stoffe," *Entlang der Seidenstraße. Frühmittelalterliche Kunst zwischen Persien und China in der Abegg-Stiftung*, Riggisberger Berichte 6, Riggisberg, 1998: 119–214.

Overlaet, B., "Regalia of the Ruling Classes in Late Sasanian Times: The Riggisber Strap Mounting, Swords and Archer's Fingercaps," in *Entlang der Seidenstraße. Frühmittelalterliche Kunst zwischen Persien und China in der Abegg-Stiftung*, Riggisberger Berichte 6, Riggisberg, 1998: 267–97.

Pagliaro, A., Bausani A., *Storia della letteratura persiana*, Milan, 1960.

Paone, R., "Restauro del boq'e di Pir-i Bakran a Lenjan (Esfahan)," in *L'arco di fango che rubò la luce alle stelle. Studi in onore di Eugenio Galdieri per il suo settantesimo compleanno*, M. Bernardini, F. Cresti, V. Fontana, F. Noci, R. Orazi, eds., Lugano, 1995: 265–78.

Pasquini, L., *La decorazione a stucco in Italia fra tardo antico e alto medioevo*, Ravenna, 2002.

Peck, H., "The Representation of Costumes in the Reliefs of Taq-i-Bustan," *Artibus Asiae*, 31 (1969): 101–24.

Peck, E. H., "Crown." II. "From the Seleucids to the Islamic Conquest," in E. Yarshater ed., *Encyclopaedia Iranica* VI, Costa Mesa (Calif.) 1993: 408–18.

Pelliot, P., *L'inscription nestorienne de Si-Ngan-Fou*, edited with supplements by A. Forte, Paris, 1996.

Peterson, S. R., "Painted, Tiles at the Takieh Mu'avin al-Mulk (Kermanshah)," in *Akten des VII. Internationalen Kongresses fur iranische Kunst und Archaologie* (Munich, 1976), Berlin, 1979: 143–51.

Petruccioli, A., ed., *Il Giardino islamico. Architettura, natura, paesaggio*, Milan, 1994.

Pfister, R., *Les textiles de Palmyre*, Paris, 1934–1940.

Piacentini, P., "Elementi di oreficeria achemenide," in Rome 2001: *Antica Persia. I tesori del Museo Nazionale di Tehran e la ricerca italiana in Iran*, P. D'Amore, G. Di Flumeri, G. Lombardo, M. Jung, P. Piacentini, P. Torre (curators), Rome, 2001: 81–83.

Pichikyan, I. R.,"Rebirth of the Oxus Treasure: Second Part of the Oxus Treasure from the Miho Museum Collection," *Ancient Civilizations from Scythia to Siberia*, 4, 4, 1997: 306–83.

Pilipko, V. N., "On the Wall-Paintings from the Tower-Building of Old Nisa," *Parthica*, 2, 2000: 69–86.

Pinder-Wilson, R., "The Minaret of Mas'ud III at Ghazni," in *Studies in Islamic Art*, London, 1985: 89–102.

Piotrovsky, M., "Paradise. The Major Theme of Islamic Art," in *Earthly Art-Heavenly Beauty. Art of Islam*, Piotrovsky, ed., St. Petersburg, 2000: 87–93.

Pope, A. U., "The painted inscription on the interior of Pūr-i 'Alamdār of Dāmghān," in *Bulletin of the American Institute for Persian Art and Archaeology*, 4 (1936): 139–41.

Pope, A. U., "Sasanian Stucco." b. "Figural," in *A Survey of Persian Art*. Vol. I, A. U. Pope, P. Ackerman ed., London and New York, 1938: 631–45.

Pope, A. U., Ackerman, P. (ed.), *A Survey of Persian Art from Prehistoric Times to the Present*, Oxford, 1938–39.

Pope, J. A., *Chinese Porcelain from the Ardebil Shrine*, Washington, D.C., 1956.

Porada, E., *Antica Persia*, Milan, 1962.

Posch, W., "Chinesische Quellen zu den Parthern," in *Das Parthreich und seine Zeugnisse. The Arsacid Empire: Sources and Documentation*, ed. J. Wiesehöfer, 1998: 355–64.

Potts, D. T., *The Arabian Gulf in Antiquity. Volume II. From Alexander the Great to the Coming of Islam*, Oxford, 1992.

Pourbahman, F., *Histoire du costume en Perse antique*, Paris, 1996.

Pribytkava, A., "The Caravansary of Daya Khatun" (in Russian), in *Architekturnoe Nasledstvo*, 3 (1953): 92–106.

Pudioli, M. C., "La memoria degli affreschi perduti: una copia dal Negarestan all'Archiginnasio di Bologna," in *Quaderni. Istituto Culturale della Repubblica Islamica d'Iran in Italia*, II, Rome, 1991: 15–19.

Pugachenkova, G. A., *La moschea di Anau* (in Russian), Ashkabad, 1959.

Pugachenkova, G. A., "Ishrat-Khaneh, and Ak Saray, Two Timurid Mausoleums in Samarkand," in *Ars Orientalis* 5 (1963): 177–89.

Pugachenkova, G. A., "The Noo Gumbad [Nine-Domed] Mosque of Balkh," (in Russian), in *Sovietskaja Archeologija* 3 (1970): 241–50.

Pugachenkova, G. A., Rempel, L. I., *Očerki iskusstva Srednej Azii*, Moscow, 1982.

Puri, B. N., "The Sakas and Indo-Parthians," in *History of Civilizations of Central Asia. Vol. II: The Development of Sedentary and Nomadic Civilizations: 700 BC to AD 250*, ed. J. Harmattan, Paris, 1994.a: 191–207.

Puri, B. N., "The Kushans," in *History of Civilizations of Central Asia. Vol. II: The Development of Sedentary and Nomadic Civilizations: 700 BC to AD 250*, ed. J. Harmattan, Paris, 1994.b: 247–63.

Qi, D., *Research on Tang Gold and Silver*, Beijing, 1999 (in Chinese with a summary in English).

Raby, J., Tanindi, Z., *Turkish Bookbinding in the 15th Century*, London, 1993.

Rahbar, M., "Découverte d'un monument d'époque sassanide à Bandian, Dargaz (Nord Khorassan). Fouilles, 1994 et, 1995," *Studia Iranica*, 27, no. 2 (1998): 213–50.

Rahbar, M., "Shushtar. Les tombeaux d'époque parthe de Gelâk," *Empires perses. D'Alexandre aux Sassanides. Dossier d'Archéologie*, 243, 1999: 90–93.

Rahbar, M., "Khorheh. Une résidence parthe sur le Plateau iranien," *Empires perses. D'Alexandre aux Sassanides. Dossier d'Archéologie*, 243, 1999.a: 44–46.

Rajak, T., "The Parthians in Josephus," in *Das Parthreich und seine Zeugnisse. The Arsacid Empire: Sources and Documentation*, ed. J. Wiesehöfer, Stuttgart, 1998: 309–24.

Ratiia, S. E., *The Mosque of Bibi Khanum* (in Russian), Moscow, 1950.

Rawson, J., *Chinese, Ornament. The Lotus and the Dragon*, London, 1984.

Rempel, L. I., "The Mausoleum of Ismail the Samanid," *Bulletin of the American Institute for Persian Art and Archaeology*, 4 (1936): 198–208.

Reuther, O., "Sasanian Architecture," A. "History," in *A Survey of Persian Art. Vol. I*, A. U. Pope, P. Ackerman ed., London and New York, 1938–39: 493–578.

Ricciardi, R. V., "Wall Paintings from the Building A at Hatra," *Iranica Antiqua*, 31 (1996): 147–65.

Ricciardi, R. V., "Hatra et Aassour," *Les Parthes. Dossier d'Archéologie*, 271, 2002: 72–79.

Ricciardi R. V., "Pottery from Choche," *Mesopotamia*, 2 (1967): 93–104.

Ricciardi R. V., "Note sull'arte tessile Sasaniane," *Mesopotamia*, 3–4, 1968–69: 385–415.

Ricciardi R. V., "Sasanian Pottery from Tell Mahuz (North Mesopotamia)," *Mesopotamia*, 5, no. 6 (1970–71): 427–82.

Ricciardi, R. V., "La découverte des Parthes et l'archéologie d'époque parthe en Mésopotamie et en Iran," *Les Parthes. Dossier d'Archéologie*, 271, 2002.a: 18–21.

Rice, D. T., *The Illustrations of the "World History" of Rashid al-Din*, B. Gray, ed., Edinburgh, 1976.

Riefstahl, R. M., "Primitive Rugs of the 'Konya' Type in the Mosque of Beyshehir," *Art Bulletin*, 13, no. 2 (1931): 177–220.

Ritter, H.-W., "Diadem und Königsherrschaft. Untersuchungen zu Zeremonien und Rechtsgrundlagen des Herrschaftsantritts bei den Persen, bei Alexander dem Grossen und im Hellenismus," in *Vestigia*, 7, Munich-Berlin, 1965.

Roaf, M., "The subject People on the Base of the Statue of Darius," *Cahiers de la Délegation Archéologique Française en Iran*, 4 (1974): 73–160.

Roaf, M., "Sculptures and Sculptors at Persepolis," *Iran*, 21 (1983).

Robinson, B. W., "Part Three: Persian and Pre-Mughal Indian Painting," in B. W. Robinson, E. J. Grube, G. M. Meredith-Owens, R. W. Skelton, *The Keir Collection. Islamic Painting and the Arts of the Book*, London, 1976.

Robinson, B. W., "Persian Royal Portraiture and the Qajars," in *Qajar Iran. Political, Social and Cultural Change 1800–1925*, E. C. Bosworth, C. Hillenbrand, eds., Edinburgh, 1983: 291–310.

Robinson, B. W., "Painting in the Post Safavid Period," in *The Arts of Persia*, R. W. Ferrier, ed., London and New Haven, 1989: 224–31.

Robinson, B. W., *Fifteenth-Century Painting. Problems and Issues*, New York, 1991.

Robinson, B. W., Guadalupi, G., *Qajar. La pittura di corte in Persia*, Milan, 1982.

Robinson, E.S.G., "The Beginning of Achaemenid Coinage," *The Numismatic Chronicle*, 18 (1958): 187–93.

Rogers, J. M., "Evidence for Mamluk-Mongol Relations 1260–1360," in *Colloque International sur l'Histoire du Caire*, Cairo, 1969: 385–403.

Rogers, J. M., "The Genesis of Safavid Religious Painting," *Iran*, 8 (1970): 125–39.

Rogers, J. M., "China and Islam. The Archaeological Evidence in the Mashriq," in *Islam and the Trade of Asia*, D. S. Richards, ed., London, 1970: 67–80.

Rogers, J. M., "Carpets in the Mediterranean Countries 1450–1550. Some Historical Observations," in *Oriental Carpet & Textile Studies II*, R. Pinner, W. B. Denny, eds., London, 1986: 13–28.

Romano, M. C., "Il Senmurv," in Rome 1994: *La seta e la sua via*, M. T. Lucidi (curator), 1994: 135–37.

Rome 1994: *La seta e la sua via*, M. T. Lucidi (curator) 1994.

Rome 2001: *Antica Persia. I tesori del Museo Nazionale di Tehran e la ricerca italiana in Iran*, P. D'Amore, G. Di Flumeri, G. Lombardo, M. Jung, P. Piacentini, P. Torre (curators), Rome, 2001.

Rosen-Ayalon, M., *La potterie islamique*, MDAFA. Mission de Susiane, Paris, 1974.

Rosen-Ayalon, M., "Themes of Sasanian Origin in Islamic Art," *Jerusalem Studies in Arabic and Islam*, 4 (1984): 69–80.

Rosenfield, J., *The Dynastic Art of the Kushans*, Berkeley, 1967.

Rossbach, L., *The Art of Paisley*, New York, 1980.

Roux, J. P., "Le combat d'animaux dans l'art et la mythologie irano-turcs," in *Arts Asiatiques*, 36 (1981): 5–11.

Rostovtzev, M., "Dura and the Problem of Parthian Art," *Yale Classical Studies*, vol. V, New Haven, 1935: 157–304.

Rostovtzeff, M., "The Parthian Shot," *American Journal of Archaeology*, 47, no. 2 (1943): 174–87.

Rubin, Z., "The Roman Empire in the *Res Gestae Divi Saporis*: the Mediterranean World in Sasanian Propaganda," in *Ancient Iran and the Mediterranean World. Proceedings of an International Conference in Honour of Prof. Józef Wolski. Electrum*, vol. 2, ed. E. Dabrowa, Krakow, 1998: 177–85.

Russo, E., "La scultura di S. Polieucto e la presenza della Persia nella cultura artistica di Costantinopoli nel VI secolo," *Conferenza Internazionale sul tema: "La Persia e Bisanzio,"* Rome, October 14–18, 2002.

Said, E. W., *Orientalism*, London, 1978.

Sanpaolesi, P., "Strutture a cupola autoportanti," in *Palladio*, 1971: 3–64.

Sarre, F., *Die Kunst des alten Persien*, Berlin, 1922.

Sayili, A., *The Observatory in Islam*, Ankara, 1960.

Savory, R., *Iran under the Safavids*, Cambridge, 1980.

Sasanian, Silver. Late Antique and Early Medieval Arts of Luxury from Iran, Ann Arbor, 1967.

Scarce, J. M., "'Ali Mohammad Esfahani—Tilemaker of Tehran," *Oriental Art*, n. s., 22, no.3 (1976): 278–88.

Scarce, J. M., "The Tile Decoration of the Gulestan Palace at Tehran. An Introductory Survey," in *Akten des VII. Internationalen Kongresses fur iranische Kunst und Archaologie* (Munich, 1976), Berlin, 1979: 635–41.

Scarce, J. M., "Function and Decoration in Qajar Tilework," in *Islam in the Balkans. Persian Art and Culture of the 18th and 19th Century*, J. M. Scarce, ed., Edinburgh, 1979: 75–86.

Scarce, J. M., "Tilework," in *The Arts of Persia*, R. W. Ferrier, ed., London and New Haven, 1989: 270–94.

Scarce, J. M., "Princes and Heroes of Bandar-i Taheri. A Late Qajar Fort and the *Shahnama*," in *Cairo to Kabul. Afghan and Islamic Studies Presented to Ralph Pinder-Wilson*, W. Ball, L. Harrow, eds., London, 2002: 181–93.

Scarcia, G., "Sulla, famiglia Gaffari di Kashan e sul suo contributo all'evoluzione della pittura persiana degli ultimi 150 anni," in *Annali dell'Istituto Universitario Orientale di Napoli*, n. s., 12 (1961): 198–203.

Scarcia, G., "La casa Borugerdi di Kashan. Materiali figurativi per la storia culturale della Persia Qagar," in *Annali dell'Istituto Universitario Orientale di Napoli*, n. s., 12 (1962): 83–93.
Scarcia, G., "Qagar, Scuola," in *Enciclopedia Universale dell'Arte*, Venice–Rome, 1963, 9: cols. 213–21.
Scarcia, G., "The Vihar of Qonqor-olong. Preliminary Report," *East and West*, 25 (1975): 99–104.
Scarcia, G., "Osservazioni sull'iconografia e la simbologia dei soprarchi con angeli e draghi del caravanserraglio di Ganj 'Alī Khān a Kirmān. II," in *Oriente Moderno*, 58, nos. 7–8 (1978): 387–91.
Scarcia, G., "Ricognizione a Shimbār. Note sull'Eracle iranico," *Oriens Antiquus*, 18 (1979): 255–75.
Scarcia, G., "Sul caravanserraglio di Ganj-'Alī Khān a Kerman," in *Studi e restauri di architettura Italia—Iran* (Istituto italiano per il medio ed estremo Oriente / di cultura di Tehran), Rome, 1980: 57–82.
Scarcia, G., "I Mongoli e l'Iran: la situazione religiosa," in *Marco Polo. Venezia e l'Oriente*, A. Zorzi, ed., Milan, 1981: 159–72.
Scarcia, G., "Bahr-i a hdar, Mu hīt-i islāmī," in *Studi arabo-islamici in onore di R. Rubinácci nel suo settantesimo compleanno*, Naples, 1985: 583–92.
Scarcia, G., "Vent'anni, di ricerche sui magi evangelici," in *Venezia e l'Oriente*, L. Lanciotti, ed., Florence, 1987.
Scarcia, G., *Il, volto di Adamo. Islam: la questione estetica nell'altro Occidente*, Venice, 1995.
Scarcia, G., *Storia di Josaphat senza Barlaam*, Rubbettino editore, Soveria Mannelli, 1998.
Scarcia, G. "Cosroe, Secondo, San Sergio e il sade," *Studi sull'Oriente Cristiano*, 4, no. 2 (2000): 171–227.
Scarcia, G., "Sulla, fenice dei Baluci," in *Il falcone di Bistam. Intorno all'iranica fenice/samand: un progetto di sintesi per il volo del Pegaso iranico tra Ponto, Alessandretta e Insulindia*, ed. G. Scarcia, M. Compareti, Venice, 2003: 7–26.
Scerrato, U., "Summary Report on the Italian Archaeological Mission in Afghanistan II. The Two Excavations Campaigns at Ghazni, 1957–58," in *East and West*, n. s., 10 (1959).
Scerrato, U., "Elementi iranici nell'arte antica del Giappone," *Il Giappone*, 2, 1961: 6–11.
Scerrato, U., "Islamic Glazed Tiles with Moulded Decoration from Ghazni," *East and West*, 13 (1962): 263–72.
Scerrato, U., "Stoffe Sasaniani," in Rome 1994: *La seta e la sua via*, M. T. Lucidi (curator), Rome, 1994: 75–82.
Scerrato, U., "Ricerche, archeologiche nella moschea del venerdì di Esfahan della missione archeologica italiana in iran dell'ISMEO," in *Antica Persia. I tesori del Museo Nazionale di Tehran e la ricerca italiana in Iran*, Rome, 2001.
Schaefer, H., "Hellenistic Textiles in Northern Mongolia," *American Journal of Archaeology*, 47, 3 (1943): 266–77.
Schafer, E. H., *The Golden Peaches of Samarkand. A Study of T'ang Exotics*, Berkeley and Los Angeles, 1963.
Schiltz, V., *Gli Sciti. VIII secolo a.C.-I secolo d.C.*, Milan, 1994.
Schippmann, K., *Grundzüge der partischen Geschichte*, Darmstadt, 1980.
Schippmann, K., "Archaeology." III. "Seleucid and Parthian," in *Encyclopaedia Iranica*, vol. II, ed. E. Yarshater, London and New York, 1987: 297–301.
Schippmann, K., "L'influence de la culture sassanide," in *Splendeur des Sassanides. L'empire perse entre Rome et la Chine [224–642]*, Brussels, 1993: 131–41.
Schlumberger, D., "Les palais ghaznévides de Lashkari Bazar," *Syria*, 29 (1952): 251–70.
Schlumberger, D., "Descendants non-méditerranéens de l'art grec," *Syria*, 37, no. 2 (1960): 253–319.
Schlumberger, D., "La représentation frontale dans l'art des Sassanides," in *La Persia e il mondo greco-romano*, Rome, 1966: 383–93.
Schlumberger, D., *L'Orient hellénisé. L'art grec et ses héritiers dans l'Asie non méditerranéenne*, Paris, 1970.
Schlumberger, D., "Le palais ghaznevide de Lashkari Bazar," in *Syria* 29 (1952): 251–70; *Lashkari Bazar. Une résidence royale ghaznévide et ghoride. 1—L'Architecture*, "Mémoires de la Délégation Archéologique Française en Afghanistan," XVIII, Paris, 1978.
Schlumberger, D., "Lashkari Bazar. Une résidence royale ghaznévide et ghoride. 1 A- L'architecture," in *Mémoires de la Délégation Française en Afghanistan*, XVIII, Paris, 1978.
Schlumberger, D., "Parthian art," in *The Cambridge History of Iran. Volume 3 (2). The Seleucid, Parthian and Sasanian Periods*, ed. E. Yarshater, Cambridge, 1983: 1027–54.
Schmidt, J. H., "L'expédition de Ctésiphon en 1931–32," *Syria*, 15, 1934: 1–23.
Schmidt, H.-P., "The Sēnmurw. Of Birds and Dogs and Bats," *Persica*, vol. IX, 1980: 1–85.
Schmitt, R., "Achaemenid dynasty," in *Encyclopaedia Iranica*, vol. I, ed. E. Yarshater, London, Boston and Henley, 1985: 414–26.
Schmitt, R., "Greece, Relations with Persian Empire," in *Encyclopaedia Iranica*, vol. XI, ed. E. Yarshater, New York, 2002: 292–301.
Schmitz, B., "On, a Special Hat Introduced during the Reign of Abbas the Great," *Iran*, 22 (1984): 103–12.
Schneider, R., "Die Faszination des Feindes. Bilder der Parther und des Orients in Rom," in *Das Parthreich und seine Zeugnisse. The Arsacid Empire: Sources and Documentation*, ed. J. Wiesehöfer, Stuttgart, 1998: 95–127.
Schoff, W. H., *Parthian Stations by Isidor of Charax. An Account of the Overland Trade Route between the Levant and India in the First Century BC*, Philadelphia, 1914.
Schuette, M., Müller-Christensen S., *The Art of Embroidery*, London, 1966.
Schmidt, F., *Excavations, at Tepe Hissar, Damghan*, Philadelphia, 1937.
Segal, J. B., *Edessa, the Blessed City*, Oxford, 1970.
Sekunda, N., "Achaemenid Settlement in Caria, Lycia and Greater Phrygia," in *Achaemenid History VI. Asia Minor and Egypt: Old Cultures in a New Empire*, ed. H. Sancisi-Weerdenburg, A. Kuhrt, Leiden, 1991: 83–143.
Sellwood, D., *An Introduction to the Coinage of Parthia*, London, 1980.
Sellwood, D., "Minor States in Southern Iran," in *The Cambridge History of Iran. Volume 3 (1). The Seleucid, Parthian and Sasanian Periods*, ed. E. Yarshater, Cambridge, 1983.a: 299–321.
Sellwood, D., "Parthian Coins," in *The Cambridge History of Iran. Volume 3 (1). The Seleucid, Parthian and Sasanian Periods*, ed. E. Yarshater, Cambridge, 1983.b: 279–98.
Semenov, A. A., "Inscriptions on the Tombs of Timur and those of His Descendents in Gur-i Amir" (in Russian), in *Epigrafika Vostoka*, 3 (1949): 49–62.
Seyf, A., "The Carpet Trade and the Economy of Iran, 1870–1906," *Iran* 30 (1992): 99–105.
Shahbazi, S., "Carrhae," in *Encyclopaedia Iranica*, vol. V, ed. E. Yarshater, Costa Mesa (Calif.), 1992: 9–13.
Shahbazi, S., "Clothing." II. "In the Median and Achaemenid Periods," in *Encyclopaedia Iranica*, vol. V, ed. E. Yarshater, Costa Mesa (Calif.), 1992: 722–37.
Shepherd, D. G., "The Iconography of Anahita," *Berytus*, 28 (1980): 47–86.
Sherwin-White, S., Kuhrt, A., *From Samarkand to Sardis. A New Approach to the Seleucid Empire*, London, 1993.
Shipley, G., *The Greek World after Alexander 323–30 BC*, London, New York, 2000.
Shiratori, K., "The Geography of Western Studied on the Basis of the Ta-ch'in Accounts," *The Memoirs of the Research Department of the Toyo Bunko*, 15 (1956): 73–163.
Shirazi, B., "Ancient Mosques. Esfahan Region. The Jum'a Mosque in Ardestan" (in Persian), in *Asar*, 1 (1980): 6–78.
Shishkin, V. A., *I monumenti architettonici di Bukhara* (in Russian), Tashkent, 1936.
Shookohi, M., "Sasanian Royal Emblems and Their Reemergence in the Fourteenth-Century Deccan," *Muqarnas*, vol. 11, 1994: 65–78.
Silvi Antonini, C., "The Paintings in the Palace of Afrasiab (Samarkand)," *Rivista degli Studi Orientali*, 43, nos. 1–3 (1989): 109–44.
Simpson, M., *The Illustration of an Epic: The Earliest Shahname Manuscripts*, New York, 1979.
Simpson, M., "The Narrative Structure of a Medieval Iranian Beaker," in *Ars Orientalis*, 12 (1981): 15–24.
Simpson, St. J., *Gilt-Silver and Clay*: A Late Sasanian Skeuomorphic Pitcher from Iran," in *Entlang der Seidenstraße. Frühmittelalterliche Kunst zwischen Persien und China in der Abegg-Stiftung*, Riggisberger Berichte 6, Riggisberg, 1998: 335–42.
Simpson, St. J., "Mesopotamia in the Sasanian Period: Settlement Patterns, Arts and Crafts," in *Mesopotamia and Iran in the Parthian and Sasanian Periods: Rejection and Revival c. 238 BC–AD 642*, ed. J. Curtis, London, 2000: 57–66.
Sims, E., "The Garrett Manuscript of the Zafar-Name: A Study in Fifteenth-Century Timurid Patronage," (doctoral thesis, New York University) New York, 1973.
Sims, E., "Late Safavid Painting: The Chehel Sutun, the Armenian Houses, the Oil Paintings," in *Akten des VII. Internationalen Kongresses fur iranische Kunst und Archaologie* (Munich, 1976), Berlin, 1979: 408–18.
Sims, E., "Ibrahim Sultan's Illustrated Zafar-Nameh of 839/1436," in *Islamic Art*, 4 (1991): 175–217.
Sims, E., "Ibrahim Sultan's Illustrated Zafarnama of 1436 and its Impact in the Muslim East," in *Timurid Art and Culture. Iran and Central Asia in the Fifteenth Century*, L. Golombeck, M. Subtelny, eds., *Muqarnas*, 1992: 132–43.
Sims-Williams, N., "Nouveaux documents sur l'histoire et la langue de la Bactriane," *Comptes Rendus de l'Académie des Inscriptions et Belles-Lettres*, 1996: 633–54.
Skelton, R. S., ed., *The Indian Heritage. Court Life and Arts under Mughal Rule*, London, 1982.
Sono, T., Fukai, S., *Dailaman I II*, Tokyo, 1968.
Soucek, S., *A History of Inner Asia*, Cambridge, 2000.
Soudavar, A., *Art of the Persian Court. Selections from the Art and History Trust Collection*, New York, 1992.
Soudavar, A., "Between the Safavids and the Mughals: Art and Artists in Transition," *Iran*, 37 (1999): 49–66.
Sourdel-Thomine, J., "Deux minarets d'époque Seljoukide en Afghanistan," *Syria*, 30 (1953): 110–21.
Spuhler, F., *Oriental Carpets in the Museum of Islamic Art, Berlin*, Berlin and London, 1987.
Staviski, B., *Mitteilungen. Kunst der Kuschan*, Leipzig, 1979.
Stead, R., *The Ardabil Carpet*, J. P. Getty Museum, Malibu, 1974.
Stratos, A. N., *Byzantium in the Seventh Century. I 602–34*, Amsterdam, 1968.
Stchoukine, I., "Les peintures turcomannes et safavies d'une Khamseh de Nezami, achevée à Tabriz en 886/1481," in *Arts Asiatiques*, 14 (1966): 1–16.
Stronach, D., "Tepe Nush-i Jan: the Median Settlement," in *The Cambridge History of Iran. Volume 2. The Median and Achaemenian Periods*, ed. I. Gershevitch, 1986: 832–37.
Stronach, D., "Archaeology i. Median and Achaemenid," in *Encyclopaedia Iranica*, vol. II, ed. E. Yarshater, London, New York, 1987: 288–96.
Stronach, D., et al., "Three Seljuk Tomb Towers," *Iran*, 4 (1966): 1–20.
Summer, W. M., "Achaemenid Settlement in the Persepolis Plain," *American Journal of Archaeology*, vol. 90, 1, 1986: 3–31.
Summerer, L., "Achämenidische Silberfunde aus der Umgebung von Sinope," *Ancient Civilization from Scythia to Siberia* 9, nos. 1–2 (2003): 17–42.
Sun, J., "The Discovery and Study in China of Ancient Western Objects since the Establishment of the People's Republic," *China Archaeology and Art Digest*, vol. 4, n. 4, (April–May 2002): 179–80.
Swietochowski, M. L., Carboni, S., *Illustrated Poetry and Epic Images. Persian Painting of the 1330s and 1340s*, New York, 1994.
Tabataba'i, J. T., *Decoration and Images in the Blue Mosque at Tabriz* (in Persian), Tabriz, 1968.
Tanabe, K., "An Essay on the 'Tassel' Represented in the Armour-Clad Equestrian Image of the Larger Grotto, Taq-i Bustan," *Orient* 23, no. 1 (1980): 65–82 (in Japanese with a summary in English).
Tanabe, K., "Identification of the Chain-Armoured Equestrian Image at the Larger Grotto, Taq-i Bustan," *Orient*, 17 (1981): 105–18.

Tanabe, K., "Iconographical Description, Investiture of the Upper Part of the Innermost Wall" in S. Fukai, K. Horiuchi, K. Tanabe, M. Domyo, *Taq-i Bustan. IV.* Tokyo, 1984.a: 51–60.

Tanabe, K., "A Study of the Sasanian Disk-Nimbus: Farewell to its *Xvarnah*-Theory," *Bulletin of the Ancient Orient Museum*, 6 (1984).b: 29–50.

Tapper, R., "Black, Sheep, White Sheep and Read-Heads. A Historical Sketch of the Shahsavan of Azarbaijan," *Iran*, 4 (1966): 61–84.

Tavoosi, M., Frye, R. N., "An Inscribed Capital Dating from the Time of Shapur I," *Bulletin of the Iranian Institute*, 3 (1989): 25–38.

Thierry, F., "Sur les monnaies sassanides trouvées en chine," in *Circulation des monnaies, des merchandises et des biens*, Res Orientales, V, Bur-sur-Yvette, 1993: 89–139.

Thompson, D., *Stucco from Chal Tarkhan-Eshqabad*, Warminster, 1976.

Torchia, R. W., "Wiedener's Gift," in *Hali*, 92 (1997): 89–97.

Tourovets, A., "Nouvelles propositions et problèmes relatifs à l'identification des délégations de l'escalier est de l'Apadana (Persépolis)," *Archäologische Mitteilungen aus Iran und Turan*, 33 (2001): 219–56.

Trever, K. V., Lukonin, V. G., *Sasanianskoe Serebro*, Moscow, 1987.

Trinkaus, K. M., "Pottery from the Damghan Plain, Iran: Chronology and Variability from the Parthian to the Early Islamic Periods," *Studia Iranica*, 15, no. 1 (1986): 23–88.

Tronsdale, W., "The Minaret of Jam: a Ghorid Monument in Afghanistan," *Archaeology*, 18 (1965): 102–8.

Trümpelmann, L., "Sasanian Graves and Burial Customs," in *Arabie orientale, Mésopotamie et Iran méridional de l'Age du Fer au début de la période islamique*, ed. R. Boucharlat, J.-F. Salles, Paris, 1984: 317–29.

Turin 2002: *Hatra. Città del Sole*, R. Ricciardi Venco, A. Peruzzetto (curators), Turin, 2002.

Umnyakov, I. I., "Ribat-i, Malik," in *Sbornik v čest' V. V. Bartol'da*, Moscow, 1923: 179–92.

Van Wickevoort Crommelin, B., "Die Parther und die partische Geschichte bei Pompeius Trogus-Justin," in *Das Parthreich und seine Zeugnisse. The Arsacid Empire: Sources and Documentation*, ed. J. Wiesehöfer, Stuttgart, 1998: 11–43.

Van Berchem, M., "Une inscription du sultan mongol Uldjaitu," in *Mélanges Hartwig Derenbourg*, Paris, 1909.

Van Cammann, S. R., "The Symbolism of the Cloud Collar Motif," *Art Bulletin*, 33 (1951): 1–9.

Van Cammann, S. R., *China's Dragon Robe*, New York, 1952.

Van Cammann, S. R., "Cosmic Symbolism on Carpets from the Sanguszko Group," in *Studies in Art and Literature of the Near East. In Honor of Richard Ettinghausen*, P. J. Chelkowski, ed., New York, 1974: 181–208.

Vanden Berghe, L., *Archéologie de l'Irān ancien*, Leiden, 1959.

Vanden Berghe, L., *Reliefs rupestres de l'Irān ancien*, Brussels, 1984.

Vanden Berghe, L., "Les scènes d'investiture sur les reliefs rupestres de l'Irān ancien: évolution et signification," in *Orientalia Iosephi Tucci Memoriae Dicata*, vol. II, ed. G. Gnoli, L. Lanciotti, Rome, 1988: 1511–1531.

Vanden Berghe, L., "Historique de la découverte et de la recherché," in Brussels 1993: *Splendeur des Sassanides. L'empire perse entre Rome et la Chine [224–642]*, B. Overlaet (curator), Brussels, 1993.a: 13–18.

Vanden Berghe, L., "La sculpture," in Brussels 1993: *Splendeur des Sassanides. L'empire perse entre Rome et la Chine [224–642]*, B. Overlaet (curator), Brussels, 1993: 71–88.

Vanden Berghe, L., Schippmann, K., *Les reliefs rupestres d'Elymaïde (Irān) de l'époque parthe*, Ghent, 1985.

Vardanyan, R., "Tendenze culturali e ideologiche nell'impero partico riflesse dalla monetazione," *Parthica*, 3 (2001): 25–132.

Varjavand, P., "La découverte archéologique du complexe scientifique de l'observaitoire de Maraqé," in *Akten des VII. Internationalen Kongresses für iranische Kunst und Archäologie* (Munich, 1976), Berlin, 1979: 527–36.

Ventrone, G., "Nota, preliminare su un pannello con la preghiera per i dodici imam della maseid-i, ĕum'a di Esfahan," in *Studi iranici*, Rome, 1977.

Vienna 1999: *Schätze des Orients. Meisterwerke aus dem Miho Museum*, W. Seipel (curator), Vienna, 1999.

Vogelsang-Eastwood, G. M., "Zilu carpets from Iran," *Studia Iranica*, 17, no. 2 (1988): 225–40.

Vogelsang, W., "The Achaemenids and India," in *Achaemenid History IV. Centre and Periphery*, ed. H. Sancisi-Weerdenburg, A. Kuhrt, Leiden, 1990: 93–110.

Volbach, W. F., *Il tessuto nell'arte antica*, Milan, 1966.

Von der Osten, H., *Il mondo dei Persiani*, Rome, 1959.

Von Gall, H., "Die Mosaiken von Bishapur und ihre Beziehung zu den Triumphreliefs des Shapur I," *Archaeologische Mitteilungen aus Iran*, IV, 1971: 193–205.

Von Gall, H., "Entwicklung und Gestalt des Thrones im vorislamischen iran," *Archäologische Mitteilungen aus Iran*, 1971: 207–35.

Von Gall, H., "The Figural capitals at Taq-e Bostan and the Question of the so-called Investiture in Parthian and Sasanian Art," *Silk Road Art and Archaeology*, 1, 1990: 99–122.

Von Gall, H., "Architektur und Plastik unter den Parthern," in *Das Parthreich und seine Zeugnisse. The Arsacid Empire: Sources and Documentation*, J. Wiesehöfer, ed., Stuttgart, 1998: 75–94.

Voronina, V. L., "The Columns of the Congregational Mosque in Khiva" (in Russian), in *Architekturnoie Nasledstvo*, 11 (1958).

Walker, D., *Flowers Underfoot. Indian Carpets of the Mughal Era*, New York, 1997.

Walser, G., *Die Völkerschaften auf den Reliefs von Persepolis. Historische Studien über den sogenannten Tributzug an der Apadanatreppe*, Berlin, 1966.

Watelin, L. C., "Sasanian Architecture." b. "The Sasanian Buildings near Kish," in *A Survey of Persian Art. Vol. I*, A. U. Pope, P. Ackerman, eds., London and New York, 1938–39: 584–92.

Watson, W., "On T'ang Soft-Glazed Pottery," in *Pottery & Metalwork in T'ang China. Their Chronology & External Relations*, W. Watson, ed., London, 1970: 41–47.

Watson, W., ed., *The Westward Influence of the Chinese Arts*, London, 1973.

Watson, W., "Iran and China," in *Studies in Chinese Archaeology and Art*, vol. II, London, 1998: 271–99.

Weiskopf, M., *The So-Called "Great Satraps' Revolt" 366–60 BC. Concerning Local Instability in the Achaemenid Far West*, Stuttgart, 1989.

Welch, S. C., *Wonders of the Age. Masterpieces of Early Safavid Painting, 1501–1576*, Cambridge (Mass.), 1979.

Welch, S. C., Dickson, B., *The Houghton Shahnameh*, 2 vols., Cambridge (Mass.), 1981.

Wenke, R. J., "Imperial Investments and Agricultural Developments in Parthian and Sasanian Khuzestan: 150 BC to AD 640," *Mesopotamia*, 10–11 (1975–76): 31–221.

Whitehouse, D., *Siraf III. The Congregational Mosque and Other Mosques from the Ninth to the Twelfth Centuries*, London, 1980.

Whitehouse, D., "La verrerie," in Brussels 1993: *Splendeur des Sassanides. L'empire perse entre Rome et la Chine [224–642]*, B. Overlaet (curator), Brussels, 1993: 109–11.

Widengren, G., "Xosrau Anōšurvān, les Hephtalites et les peoples turcs (Études preliminaries des sources)," *Orientalia Suecana*, 1 (1952): 69–94.

Widengren, G., *Il Manicheismo*, Milan, 1964.

Widengren, G., "Sources of Parthian and Sasanian History," in *The Cambridge History of Iran. Volume 3 (2). The Seleucid, Parthian and Sasanian Periods*, E. Yarshater, ed., Cambridge, 1983: 1261–83.

Widengren, G., "Manichaeism and Its Iranian Background," in *The Cambridge History of Iran. Volume 3 (2). The Seleucid, Parthian and Sasanian Periods*, E. Yarshater, ed., 1986: 965–990.

Wiesehöfer, J., "Zeugnisse zur Geschichte und Kultur der Persis unter den Parthern," in *Das Parthreich und seine Zeugnisse. The Arsacid Empire: Sources and Documentation*, J. Wiesehöfer, ed., Stuttgart, 1998: 425–34.

Wiesehöfer, J., *La Persia antica*, Bologna, 2003.

Wilber, D. N., "Iranian Motifs in Syrian Art," *Bulletin of the American Institute for Iranian Art and Archaeology*, 5 (1937): 22–26.

Wilber, D. N., "The Development of Mosaic Faience in Islamic Architecture in Iran," *Ars Islamica*, 6 (1939): 16–47.

Wilber, D. N., *The Architecture of Islamic Iran. The Il Khanid Period*, New York, 1955.

Wilber, D. N., *Persian Gardens and Gardens Pavilions*, Tokyo, 1962.

Wilber, N., "The Timurid Vourt: Life in Gardens and Tents," *Iran*, 17 (1979): 127–33.

Wilkinson, C. K., *Neshabur: Pottery, of the Early Islamic Period*, New York, 1973.

Wilkinson, C. K., *Neshabur. Some Early Islamic Buildings and their Decoration*, New York, 1986.

Will, E., "Palmyre et les routes de la soie," *Les Annales Archéologiques Arabes Syriennes. Special Issue Documenting the Activities of the International Colloquium: Palmyre and the Silk Road*, 42 (1996): 125–28.

Willetts, W., *Origini dell'arte cinese. Dalla ceramica neolitica all'architettura moderna*, Milan, 1965.

Wolski, J., "Arsace 1er, fondateur de l'État parthe," *Acta Iranica*, 3, 1974: 159–99.

Wulff, H., *The Traditional Crafts of Persia* (Mass.) 1966.

Xia, N., "Sassanian Objects Recently Found in China," *Social Sciences in China* 1, n. 2 (1980): 153–61.

Yarshater, E., "Were the Sasanians Heirs to the Achaemenids?," in *La Persia e il Medioevo*, Rome, 1971: 517–31.

Zeimal, E. V., "The Kidarite Kingdom in Ccentral Asia," in *History of Civilizations of Central Asia. Volume III: The Crossroads of Civilizations: AD 250 to 750*, B. Litvinsky, ed., Paris, 1996: 119–33.

Zhang, H., *A Collection of China's Dynasty Frescoes*, Shenzhen, 1995.

Zipoli, R., Alfieri, B., "La Moschea Gāmi' di Fahrag," in *Studi iranici*, Rome, 1977.

Zipoli, R., "Qaidar e Arghun," in *Soltaniye II. Quaderni del Seminario di Iranistica ... di Venezia*, 5 (1979): 15–35.

INDEX

NOTE: *Italic page numbers refer to illustrations and captions.*

PHOTOGRAPHY CREDITS

Archivio Jaca Book: 37, 42; Archivio Scala, Florence: 28-30; Arthur M. Sackler Museum, Harvard University Art Museum, Cambridge, Mass.: 170 (Sarah C. Sears Collection), 171 (Beque
of Abby Rockefeller); Gérard Bertin, Geneva: 89; Bibliothèque Nationale, Paris: 92 & 94 (Cabinet des Médailles), 166; Bildarchiv Preussischer Kulturbesitz (Gerhadr Murze): 174; Britis
Library, London/Scala, Florence: 164, 169; G. Curatola: 9, 10 (Celli), 13–16, 24–25, 26 (Fantini), 54–55, 62, 63 (Cingolani), 64–69, 76–77, 78 (Cingolani), 84 (Fantini), 101, 104–105, 112–115, 119–12
129, 132–138, 140–142, 144, 152–153, 183–184, 186–187; Edinburgh University Library: 160; Gerald Zugman/MAK, Vienna: 175; Kunsthistorisches Museum, Vienna, 2000, 2002: 27, 38, 40, 4
45–47, 73–74, 90–91, 93; Miho Museum, Tokyo: 178–179; L. Mozzati, Milan: 17, 19, 22, 33, 53, 58–59, 103, 106–107, 109–111, 117, 119, 122–128, 130–131, 139, 143, 145–151, 154–156, 172, 185; Musé
des Tissus, Lyon: 180; Museo Nazionale d'Arte Orientale, Rome: 50; Museo Poldi Pezzoli, Milan: 173, 177; M. Ossendrijver da M. Sommer, *Hatra*: 34, 36, 39; Pierpont Morgan Library/A
Resource/Scala, Florence: 159; RMN, Paris: 21 (Lewandowski/Raux), 44 (cliché Louvre), 75 (Lewandowski), 82, 83 (Jean/J. L'hoir), 88 (Chuzeville), 176; G. Scarcia: 1; 3–8, 11, 18, 20, 23, 41, 56–5
60–61, 70–72, 79–80, 95–100; The Art Archive (Picture Desk): 12; The Trustees of the British Museum, London: 48; The Cleveland Museum of Art, Cleveland, Ohio, 2003: 162 (Grac
Rainey Rogers Fund); Topkapi Sarayi Müzesi, Istanbul: 157, 163, 165.